A Blue Water Navy

The Official Operational

History of the Royal

Canadian Navy in the

Second World War,

1943-1945

Volume II, Part 2

A BLUE WATER NAVY

The Official Operational History of the Royal Canadian Navy
in the Second World War, 1943-1945

Volume II, Part 2

W.A.B. Douglas, Roger Sarty, Michael Whitby

Robert H. Caldwell, William Johnston, William G.P. Rawling

Vanwell Publishing Limited
St. Catharines, Ontario

Published by Vanwell Publishing and the Department of National Defence in cooperation with the Department of Public Works and Government Services.

Catalogue Number: D2-132/2002-2-1E (Part 1)
                    D2-132/2002-2-2E (Part 2)

Vanwell Publishing acknowledges the financial support of the Government of Canada through the Book Publishing Industry Development Program for our publishing activities.

Design: Linda Moroz-Irvine
Cover Photograph: Courtesy DND, DHH

Vanwell Publishing Limited
1 Northrup Crescent
P.O. Box 2131
St. Catharines, Ontario L2R 7S2
sales@vanwell.com
phone 800.661.6136
fax 905.937.1760

Printed in Canada

National Library of Canada Cataloguing in Publication Data

Douglas, W.A.B. (William Alexander Binny), 1929-
    A blue water navy : the official operational history of the Royal Canadian Navy in the Second World War, 1943-1945, volume II, part 2 / W.A.B. Douglas, Roger Sarty, Michael Whitby ; with Robert H. Caldwell, William Johnston, William G.P. Rawling. — 1st ed.
ISBN 1-55125-069-1

(The official operational history of the Royal Canadian Navy in the Second World War, 1939-1943 ; v. 2, pt.2) Issued also in French under title: Une marine océanique. Co-published by Department of National Defence. Includes bibliographical references and index.
ISBN 1-55125-067-5

    1. Canada. Royal Canadian Navy—History—World War, 1939-1945. 2. World War, 1939-1945--Naval operations, Canadian. I. Douglas, W.A.B. (William Alexander Binny), 1929- II. Canada. Dept. of National Defence

D779.C2N63 2006   940.54'5971   C2006-906624-8

Contents

Maps and Diagrams vi

Glossary and Abbreviations vii

Acknowledgments xv

SECTION 3: CONSOLIDATION

Chapter 12 New Plans, Familiar Challenges: Fleet Planning, Reorganization and
the Turning Point in the Battle of the Atlantic, April–May 1943 23

Chapter 13 North Atlantic Operations, June–December 1943 67

Chapter 14 Combined Operations in European Waters,
May 1942 to the Eve of Neptune 107

Chapter 15 Towards a Balanced Fleet: Operations in European Waters,
Quadrant, and Fleet Modernization, 1942–1943 149

Chapter 16 Prelude to Neptune: Operations with the Home Fleet and
Coastal Forces, November 1943–May 1944 185

Chapter 17 The Assault on Northwest Europe 231

Chapter 18 Guarding the Seaward Flank, July 1944–September 1945 287

SECTION 4: NEW DIRECTIONS

Chapter 19 The Inshore Antisubmarine Campaign in
European Waters, June 1944–May 1945 349

Chapter 20 The Antisubmarine Campaign in Canadian Waters and
the Northwest Atlantic, 1944–1945 409

Chapter 21 Fleet Operations in European and Arctic Waters, July 1944–May 1945 453

Chapter 22 Outward to the Pacific: The Defence of the West Coast, Pacific Planning, and
Operations with the British Pacific Fleet, April 1943–September 1945 495

APPENDICES

I RCN Senior Appointments, 1939–1945 561

II RCN Warship Losses, 1939–1945 566

III Axis Warship Losses to Canadian Forces, 1939–1945 568

IV Training, Discipline, and Morale in the RCN, 1939–1945 571

V The Women's Royal Canadian Naval Service 594

VI RCN Coastal Forces in the Mediterranean Theatre 607

VII Rank Equivalents 610

Select Bibliography 611

Index 633

Maps and Diagrams

Principal Theatres of Royal Canadian Navy Operations, 1939–1945 . . . . end plate

Royal Canadian Navy Pacific Operations, 1941–1945 . . . . end plate

Theoretical Asdic Patterns 45

U-Boat Operations in Canadian Northwest Atlantic, May-November 1943 66

Convoys to North Russia 1943-1945 187

Sinking of the Scharnhorst, Situation at 0400, 26 December 1943 199

Oropesa Sweep 211

Operation "Tunnel" Tribal Action 26 & 29 April 1944 . . . . 226A

The Assault on Normandy, Operation Neptune 258A

Operation Neptune, Assault & Patrol Areas 6 June 1944 . . . . 258B

Destroyer Night Action, 9 June 1944 . . . . 290A

Anti-Submarine Operations in United Kingdom Waters, September 1944-May 1945 326

Anti-Submarine Operations in the English Channel &
   the Bay of Biscay, June-September 1944 354

Channel and Biscay Area, 1944-1945 373

U-Boat Operations in Canadian Northwest Atlantic, January 1944-May 1945 415

Convoy RA 64, 17-27 February 1945 485

Convoy JW64, 5-13 February 1945 486

Colour Plates

War Art 339-346

Abbreviations, Acronyms and Glossary

AA	anti-aircraft
AASSB	Allied Antisubmarine Survey Board
AB	Able Seaman
ABD	Armament Broadcast System
ABU	Auto Barrage Unit
ACC	Atlantic Convoy Conference held in Washington, DC in March 1943 to resolve command relations in the Battle of the Atlantic
ACHQ	Area Combined Headquarters
ACI	Atlantic Convoy Instructions
ACNS	Assistant Chief of the Naval Staff
Acting	Prefix denoting a higher rank being held temporarily
Admiralty	Royal Navy headquarters in London
ADR	Aircraft Direction Room
AEF	Allied Expeditionary Force
AFHQ	Air Force Headquarters, Ottawa
AIC	Action Information Centre; the operations room in a warship
AID	Action Information Intercom
AIO	Action Information Organization, the means for handling tactical information in a warship
AMC	Armed Merchant Cruiser
ANCXF	Allied Naval Commander, Expeditionary Force
ARL	Admiralty Research Laboratory
AOC	Air Officer Commanding
A/S	Antisubmarine
A/S CO	Asdic Control Officer
Asdic	Underwater sound-ranging apparatus for determining the range and bearing of a submerged submarine, now known as Sonar
ASW	Antisubmarine Warfare
AT	US to UK troop convoys
AUBD	Anti-U-boat Division
AVRC	Armoured Vehicle, Royal Engineers
AWIR	Admiralty Weekly Intelligence Report
BAD	British Admiralty Delegation, Washington, DC
BATM	British Admiralty Technical Mission
B-Dienst	Beobachtungsdienst, the German navy radio monitoring and cryptographic service
BdU	Befehlshaber der Unterseeboote, Commander of the German U-boat service
BHC	British High Commission
BLO	Bombardment Liaison Officer, an artillery officer embarked in a warship to assist and interpret calls for fire support and to keep the CO apprised of the military situation ashore
BPF	British Pacific Fleet
BR	Bomber reconnaissance
BRO	British Routing Officer
BS	Corner Brook to Sydney convoys
BTC	Bristol Channel to Thames convoys
BUCO	Build-up Control Organization for the Normandy invasion and subsequent military operations in Northwest Europe
BW	Sydney to St John's convoys
BX	Boston to Halifax convoys
BYMS	British Yard Minesweeper
CAFO	Confidential Admiralty Fleet Orders
CAM Ship	Catapult Aircraft Merchant ship

CAS	Chief of the Air Staff	CONNAV	US Navy Department's convoy routing authority
CAT	Canadian anti-acoustic torpedo gear	COPC	Commanding Officer Pacific Coast
CCCS	Commodore/Captain Commanding Canadian Ships	COS	Chief(s) of Staff
		CPO	Chief Petty Officer
CCNF	Commodore Commanding Newfoundland Force	CT	UK to Canada troop convoys
CCO	Chief of Combined Operations	CTF	Commander Task Force
CCOS	Combined Chiefs of Staff	CTG	Commander Task Group
CERA	Chief Engine Room Artificer	CVE	Escort aircraft carrier
CF	Coastal Forces	CWC	Cabinet War Committee
CFMU	Coastal Forces Mobile Unit	DAUD	Director, Anti-U-boat Division
CFPR	Coastal Forces Periodic Review	DASW	Director, Antisubmarine Warfare Division
CGS	Chief of the General Staff	D/C	Depth Charge
CHOP	Change of Operational Control, a time or position when command or operational authority changed	DCNS	Deputy Chief of the Naval Staff
		DD	Duplex Drive amphibious tanks
C-in-C	Commander-in-Chief	DDSD(Y)	Deputy Director of the Signals Division, in charge of Y (or interception) services
CINCLANT	C-in-C US Atlantic Fleet		
CJSM	Canadian Joint Staff Mission	Decca	Type of radio navigation aid
CL	St John's-Sydney-Halifax convoys	Deck Log	Record of ship's movements, events, and weather
Cmdre	Commodore		
CNA	Canadian Northwest Atlantic Command	DEMS	Defensively Equipped Merchant Ships, term applied to the ships, weapons, naval or army personnel operating the equipment, and the naval staff coordinating the organization
CNEC	Chief of Naval Engineering and Construction		
CNES	Chief of Naval Equipment and Supply		
CNMO	Canadian Naval Mission Overseas	Degaussing	Measure taken to counter magnetic mines, involves passing a current through an electric cable encircling a ship's hull
CNO	Chief of Naval Operations		
CNS	Chief of Naval Staff		
COAC	Commanding Officer Atlantic Coast	DF	Destroyer Flotilla
COAV	Commanding Officer Auxiliary Vessels	D/F	Direction Finding
COHQ	Combined Operations Headquarters	DMS	Department of Munitions and Supply
Coastal Forces	Light craft used in coastal operations, such as Motor Torpedo Boats and Motor Gun Boats	DNI	Director of Naval Intelligence
		DNP	Director of Naval Personnel
		DNS	Department of the Naval Service
COMINCH	C-in-C United States Navy	DOD	Director of the Operations Division

DOP	Director of Plans
DOR	Director of Operational Research
Drafting	Process of assigning personnel to ships
DSD	Director of the Signals Division
DTD	Director of the Trade Division
DTR	Director of Technical Research
DWT	Director of Warfare and Training
EAC	Eastern Air Command
EBC	Bristol Channel to France convoys
E-Boats	Allied term for German MTBs
Echo Sounding	Means of measuring water depth using the principles of asdic; product is a continuous trace that displays the contour of the sea bottom as well as the shape of objects such as wrecks and submarines lying on the ocean floor
EG	Escort Group (escort groups were also designated C for Canadian, as in C 1, B for British and A for American)
Enigma	German cypher machine adopted by the Kriegsmarine in 1926; the output, when deciphered, was known by the Allies as Ultra
ERA	Engine Room Artificer
ESF	Eastern Sea Frontier
ETC	Thames to France convoys
ETF	Eastern Task Force
FAA	Fleet Air Arm
FAT	*Fader-Apparat Torpedo,* a German pattern-running torpedo
FBC	France to Bristol Channel convoys
FDO	Fighter Direction Officer
FH	Saint John to Halifax convoys
First Lieutenant	Officer in the rank of Lieutenant, serving as second-in-command or executive officer of a warship, also sometimes referred to as Number One or Jimmy-the-One
Flag Rank	Officers of the rank of Admiral of the Fleet, Admiral, Vice-Admiral, and Rear-Admiral
FOB	Forward Obseerver, Bombardment, an artillery officer responsible for calling in and observing fire support
FOBAA	Flag Officer, British Assault Area
Fo'c'sle	Forecastle or foremost weather deck of a ship
FOIC	Flag Officer-in-Charge
FONF	Flag Officer Newfoundland
FOO	Forward Observation Officer, an artillery officer tasked to call in and observe fire support
Foxer	British anti-acoustic torpedo gear
FR	Fishermen's Reserve
Gamma Search	Antisubmarine search, where support groups created an asdic barrier across the estimated mean line of advance of a U-boat. Groups searched in line abreast formation parallel to the submarine's estimated course, patrolling back and forth across a lane 60 miles wide; ships usually zigzagged at 10 knots, and the distance between ships was normally three miles by day and five at night
GMT	Greenwich Mean Time, also referred to as Zulu or Z
Gnat	German Naval Acoustic Torpedo, the Allied designation for the German T5 zaunkönig acoustic homing torpedo
Gooseberries	Artificial breakwaters and piers constructed off the Normandy beachhead
GS	General Service
Gyro Compass	Electrically driven compass pointing to True North and not, like a magnetic compass, to Magnetic North
HA	High Angle, description for naval guns capable of AA defence

HA/LA	High Angle / Low Angle
Hedgehog	Multi-barrelled antisubmarine mortar, firing a large number of contact-fused projectiles
HF	Halifax to Saint John convoys
HF/DF	High Frequency Direction Finding, commonly referred to as "Huff Duff"
HG	Gibraltar to UK convoys
HHX	Halifax section of ships joining HX convoys originating in New York
HJ	Halifax to St John's convoys
HLDF	Halifax Local Defence Force
HMCS	His Majesty's Canadian Ship
HMS	His Majesty's Ship
HO	Hostilities Only
HOMP	Halifax Ocean Meeting Point, location and timing off Halifax where shipping met or detached from HX convoys
HON	Halifax section joining ON convoys destined for New York
HQ	Headquarters
HX	Fast convoys from Halifax and later New York to the UK
HXA	English Channel section of HX convoys
HXF	Halifax to UK fast convoys
IJN	Imperial Japanese Navy
JCS	Joint Chiefs of Staff
JH	St John's to Halifax convoys
Jig	Radar contact
JSC	Joint Services Committee
JW	UK to North Russia convoys from late 1942–45; replaced the PQ designation
KMF	UK to Mediterranean fast convoys
KMS	UK to Mediterranean slow convoys
Kriegsmarine	German naval service
KTB	Kriegstagebuch, or war diary

LCA	Landing Craft Assault, small landing craft launched from LSI, could transport approximately 30 fully equipped troops
LCI(L)	Landing Craft Infantry (Large), landing vessel, could transport approximately 200 fully equipped troops
LCI(S)	Landing Craft Infantry (Small), landing vessel, could transport approximately 96 fully equipped troops
LCM	Landing Craft Mechanized, small landing craft used to transport single tanks or motor vehicles ashore
LCP	Landing Craft Personnel
LCT	Landing Craft Tank, vessel capable of transporting approximately 55 troops and eleven vehicles
LN	St Lawrence to Labrador convoys
LSI	Landing Ship Infantry, large vessels used to carry infantry to assault area, carried LCAs and other small landing craft on davits
LST	Landing Ship Tank, vessel capable of transporting approximately 300 fully equipped troops and 60 tanks
Lower Deck	Term referring to the ratings of a ship
MAC	Merchant Aircraft Carrier
Mess deck	Living accommodations in a warship
METOX	Radar detection equipment issued to U-boats in 1942; German term for the equipment was Funkmess-Beobachtungsgerät, or FuMB
MF/DF	Medium-Frequency Direction Finding
MGB	Motor Gun Boat
MKF	Mediterranean to UK fast convoys
MKS	Mediterranean to UK slow convoys
ML	Motor Launch
MMS	Motor Minesweeper

MOEF — Mid-Ocean Escort Force

MOMP — Mid-Ocean Meeting Point

Monrads — Mobile naval radar stations

MSF — Minesweeping Flotilla

MTB — Motor Torpedo Boat

MT Ships — Mechanized Transport Ships, merchant ships such as Liberty ships capable of transporting approximately 120 vehicles and 480 personnel

Mulberries — Artificial harbours constructed off the Normandy beachhead

MWT — Ministry of War Transport

NA — Canada to UK troop convoys

Nautical Mile — Unit of horizontal measurement 1852 metres in length (about 6076 feet). This is the approximate value of a sea mile, which is the length of one minute of arc of the earth's circumference. During the Second World War a nautical mile referred to a British Standard Nautical Mile, which was standardized at 1853.18 metres (about 6080 feet)

Naval Board — Senior decision-making staff in NSHQ, presided over by the Minister for the Naval Service of Canada, replaced the Naval Council in 1942 and by 1944 consisted of the Deputy Minister, CNS, Chief of Naval Personnel, Chief of Naval Equipment and Supply, Chief of Naval Engineering and Construction, Chief Staff Officer Reserves, and the Secretary to the Naval Board

NBM — Naval Board Minutes

Naval Staff — Naval coordinating staff in NSHQ, responsible for policy, plans and the day-to-day running of the navy; answered to the Naval Council and later the Naval Board

NCETF — Naval Commander, Eastern Task Force

NCSO — Naval Control Service Officer

NCWTF — Naval Commander, Western Task Force

NEF — Newfoundland Escort Force

NID — Naval Intelligence Division

NL — Labrador to St Lawrence convoys

NMCJS — Naval Member Canadian Joint Staff

NOIC — Naval Officer in Charge

NRC — National Research Council of Canada

NSec — Naval Secretary

NSHQ — Naval Service Headquarters

NSM — Naval Staff Minutes

Observant — Antisubmarine search tactic. Escorts used the last estimated position of a submerged U-boat as a datum point from whence they conducted square searches with asdic along the estimated course of the submarine to a distance of one mile; the search could be expanded or concentrated depending on the number of escorts involved

OG — UK to Gibraltar convoys

OIC — Operational Intelligence Centre

OKM — Oberkommando der Kriegsmarine, the German naval high command

ON — UK to North America convoys

ON — Operation Neptune Naval Orders

ONEAST — Operation Neptune Orders for the Eastern Task Force

ONS — UK to North America slow convoys

ORB — Operations Record Book

OS — Ordinary Seaman, the rank of the lowest trained rating before advancement to Able Seaman

PANS — Public Archives of Nova Scotia

Paravane — "Float" portion of minesweeping equipment designed to cut mine cables

PC — Patrol Craft

Phoenix — Concrete caissons sunk as part of

	the Gooseberry breakwaters off Normandy		SC	Sydney, Halifax and New York to UK slow convoys
PHP	Post hostilities planning		SCFO(O)	Senior Canadian Flag Officer (Overseas)
PJBD	Permanent Joint Board of Defence		Schnellboote	German term for E-boats or MTBs, also S-boote
Plot	Record of movement of vessel, made either manually or mechanically to allow a current reckoning of a ship's position		SCNO(L)	Senior Canadian Naval Officer (London)
			SGB	Steam gun boat
PPI	Plan Position Indicator, a type of radar display		SHAEF	Supreme Headquarters, Allied Expeditionary Force
PQ	Original designation for UK–North Russia convoys		SH	Sydney to Halifax convoys
			SHX	Sydney section joining HX convoys
QH	Radio navigation aid based on the RAF's GEE system		SKL	Seekriegsleitung, the German naval staff
QP	Original designation for North Russia-UK convoys		SNO	Senior Naval Officer
QS	Québec to Sydney convoys		SO	Senior Officer
Quiz	Asdic contact		SO (A/S)	Staff Officer, Antisubmarine
RA	North Russia–UK convoys, late 1943–45; replaced the QP designation		SOE	Senior Officer of Escort
			SO(O)	Staff Officer, Operations
RAF	Royal Air Force		Sonar	USN term for Asdic
R-boat	German motor minesweeper		SQ	Sydney to Québec convoys
RCAF	Royal Canadian Air Force		SSC	Feeder convoys from Sydney to SC convoys
RCN	Royal Canadian Navy, the permanent force component of the Canadian Naval Service		Stone Frigate	Naval colloquialism for a naval shore establishment commissioned as an HMC Ship, e.g. HMCS Stadacona
RCNR	Royal Canadian Navy Reserve			
RCNVR	Royal Canadian Navy Volunteer Reserve		Support Group	Escort group used to support convoys under, or threatened by, attack or to conduct searches against U-boats
RDF	Radio Direction Finding, the British/Canadian term for radar			
RN	Royal Navy		TA	UK to USA troop convoys
ROA	Report on Action		TAC	Thames to Ostend convoys
ROP	Report of Proceedings, report describing a ship's activities and any other items of interest not covered by a separate report		TBC	Thames to Bristol Channel convoys
			TBS	Talk Between Ships, an R/T communications system fitted in Allied warships
R/T	Radio Telephony			
Rudeltaktik	Group or Wolf-pack U-boat tactics		TC	Canada to UK troop convoys
SB	Sydney to Corner Brook convoys			

TF	Task Force
TG	Task Group
Triangle Run	Colloquial term for WLEF (later WEF) convoy escort operations after 1942. The "triangle" was usually between Halifax, WESTOMP, and New York City
U-Bootwaffe	German navy's submarine arm
UC	Return UK-Caribbean tanker convoys
Ultra	Allied code word for Enigma decrypts
USAAF	United States Army Air Force
USN	United States Navy
USSR	Union of Soviet Socialist Republics
VCNS	Vice-Chief of the Naval Staff
VHF	Very High Frequency
VLR	Very Long Range, the designation for maritime patrol aircraft with a range of 600 miles and the ability to then remain over a convoy for four hours
V/S	Visual Signalling
WA	Western Approaches Command
WAC	Western Air Command
WACIs	Western Approaches Convoy Instructions
Wardroom	Officers' mess in a warship or naval shore establishment
WATU	Western Approaches Tactical Unit
WEF	Western Escort Force
WESTOMP	Western Ocean Meeting Point, sometimes referred to as WOMP
WIR	Weekly Intelligence Report
WLEF	Western Local Escort Force
Work-up	Training phase to achieve all-around effectiveness, especially after commissioning or a long refit
WRCNS	Women's Royal Canadian Naval Service
WRNS	Women's Royal Naval Service
WS	Wabana, Newfoundland, to Sydney convoys
W/T	Wireless Telegraphy
WTF	Western Task Force
XB	Halifax to Boston convoys
X-craft	Midget submarines
Y	interception of signals including direction finding

Introduction and Acknowledgments

THIS BOOK, THE SECOND PART OF THE OFFICIAL OPERATIONAL HISTORY of the Royal Canadian Navy in the Second World War, serves as a follow-up to *No Higher Purpose* and carries the navy's story from the creation of Canadian Northwest Atlantic Command in April 1943 to the final victory in the Pacific in September 1945. Some crossover could not be avoided, so that the account of the RCN's role in Operation Jubilee, the raid on Dieppe, is included in this volume. Likewise, various appendices that cover subjects such as training, morale and discipline, and the Women's Royal Canadian Naval Service, whose activities and contributions were not limited by our chronological divide, will be found here. Also, like previous Canadian official histories, this work does not cover the hundreds of young Canadians, volunteer and regular, who served in the ships and aircraft of the Royal Navy. That said, the reader should appreciate that wherever British ships operated throughout the Second World War, Canadian sailors served—and many died—and that they are an integral part of Canada's naval heritage.

Many people contributed to the preparation of *A Blue Water Navy*. First and foremost, the Directorate of History and Heritage acknowledges the support that successive ministers, Chiefs of the Defence Staff, deputy ministers, admirals commanding Maritime Command, Chiefs of the Maritime Staff, and other leaders of the department and the armed forces have given the project. Within the directorate itself, Dr Serge Bernier, Director, History and Heritage, has consistently given full support, including the assignment of precious resources at critical times. Dr Norman Hillmer, past senior historian at the Directorate of History, and Dr Steve Harris, current chief historian, Directorate of History and Heritage, supervised the organization of the team and set the scholarly standards that have guided the project throughout.

The great bulk of the research was conducted by the members of the naval history team. They have served for varying periods of time and under varying terms of employment, but all devoted an extraordinary effort to the project; a list of the narratives that they produced, which will become an invaluable source for future research, is included in the bibliography of the present volume. As well as the authors, members of the core team included Colonel (ret'd) Catherine E. Allan (signals intelligence), Dr Shawn Cafferky (operations in the Mediterranean, naval aviation, policy), Mr William Constable (cartographer), Commodore (ret'd) Jan Drent (U-boat operations and policy), Mr Robert C. Fisher (Battle of the Atlantic and Caribbean, 1942), Dr William R. Glover (training), Mr Donald E. Graves (combined operations, naval aviation, coastal forces, policy), Lieutenant (N) Richard Mayne (policy), Ms Gabrielle Nishiguchi (illustrations), Ms Donna

Portre (WRCNS), and Professor Jane Samson (policy). Dr Isabel Campbell, Mr Owen A. Cooke, Ms Donna Porter, and Mr Warren Sinclair, archivists at the Directorate of History and its successor, the Directorate of History and Heritage, efficiently organized the large quantities of documentation acquired for the project, while librarians Mr Réal Laurin, Mr Jean Durocher and Ms Madeleine Lafleur-Lemire left no stone unturned in their search for secondary sources. Mr David Wiens and Commodore (ret'd) Jan Drent researched German sources and translated and analyzed German-language material used in this history.

We were also fortunate to have research reports or other contributions from Captain G.G. Armstrong, RCN (ret'd), Lieutenant-Commander John Bell, Ms Pamela Brunt, Mr Alain Chouinard, Dr Lisa Dillon, Dr Richard Gimblett, Mr Tony Griffin, Mr Bob Gurney, Ms Marilyn Gurney, Professor Michael Hennessy, Professor Keith Jeffrey, Captain(N) Norm Jolin and the ship's company of HMCS *Montréal*, Major Mat Joost, Sergeant Carl Kletke, Lieutenant Matt Kletke, Mr Doug Knight, Major Paul Lansey, Warrant Officer Mike Lever, Dr Wilf Lund, Lieutenant-Colonel Dan MacKay, Lieutenant J.C. Marston, RCNR (ret'd), Ms Ann Martin, Dr Ken Mackenzie, Mr Fred McEvoy, Commander Fraser McKee, Major Mike McNorgan, Mr David O'Keefe, Mr David Perkins, Mr Jody Perrun, Dr Bernard Ransom, Mr Vincent Rigby, Ms Andrea Schlect, Mr Sean Stack, Lieutenant-Commander Gordon Stead, RCNVR (ret'd), Mr Dan Tiffin, Dr Nicholas Tracy, Lieutenant-Colonel Gabriel Tremblay, Ms Sylvie Tremblay and Commander Michael Young, (ret'd). Lieutenant-Commander Malcolm Llewellyn-Jones, RN (ret'd), Lieutenant-Commander Doug McLean, and Professors Michael L. Hadley, Robert Love, Marc Milner, Theodore Wilson, and David Zimmerman graciously shared their considerable expertise with the team. Dr Jean Martin has overseen the production of an acceptable French-language edition. These volumes are a co-production with Vanwell Publishing Limited, and we would wish to thank Mr David Fortin and Ms Christine Leduc of Canada Communication for their assistance in facilitating the co-publishing agreement. Lastly, Canadian naval veterans, too many to name, gave steadfast encouragement to this project and also contributed by giving interviews, responding to questions or by coming forth with papers and photographs. The Naval Officers Association of Canada has also provided strong support.

The bulk of the navy's archives are held by Library and Archives Canada (formerly the National Archives of Canada). For swift, enthusiastic and imaginative help in finding materials among very large collections that were only partially organized, we are grateful to Mr Tim Dubé, Mr Paul Marsden, Ms Barbara Wilson, and Dr Glenn Wright. Ms Laura Brandon and Ms Margot Weiss of the Canadian War Museum made available the war art featured in both volumes. Captain Chris Page, RN (ret'd) and the late Mr David Brown, heads of the Naval Historical Branch, Ministry of Defence, in London, as well as their staff, and, at the Naval Historical Center in Washington, the former directors Dr Dean Allard, and Dr William S. Dudley and their staff gave exceptional help in the discussion of historical issues and in the location of documents. The efficiency of the staff at the Public Record Office in Kew (now the U.K. National Archives), the National Archives and Records Administration in Washington, and the National Security Agency at Fort Meade enabled team members to examine a very broad range of British, American and German naval records that illuminate and provide context for the Canadian story. In Germany, Dr Jürgen Rohwer collaborated in research of German sources.

In acknowledging the assistance of so many people, and the constant encouragement by their colleagues at the old Directorate of History and the current Directorate of History and Heritage, the authors also wish to emphasize that they alone are responsible for any errors or omissions. Moreover, they wish to make it clear that they have been given full access to relevant official documents in possession of the Department of National Defence, but that the inferences drawn and opinions expressed are theirs, and the department is in no way responsible for their reading or presentation of the facts as stated.

SECTION 3

Consolidation

New Plans, Familiar Challenges:
Fleet Planning, Reorganization, and
the Turning Point in the North Atlantic
April – May 1943

REAR-ADMIRAL L.W. MURRAY'S ELEVATION to the status of Commander-in-Chief, Canadian Northwest Atlantic Command in April 1943 recognized the Royal Canadian Navy as one of the foremost escort forces in the Atlantic war. By the end of the year it had become a commonplace—some might have said a canard—that the RCN had "the acknowledged role as guardian of the convoys."[1] That provided the Naval Staff in Ottawa with a stepping stone towards the balanced fleet it envisaged when, in the summer of 1943, along with the other two services and the Department of External Affairs, the RCN turned its attention not only to the end of the war in Europe and the requirements for the war in the Pacific, but, with increasing earnestness, to post-war problems.[2]

"Canadian and Allied opinion," observed Lieutenant-Commander G.F. Todd, RCNVR, head of strategic planning at Naval Service Headquarters, in November 1943, "has admired the work of the Canadian Navy in the Battle of the Atlantic, but there is little doubt the work would have kindled even greater interest had the public not invariably thought of the RCN in terms of small ships." Acquisition of cruisers and aircraft carriers around which to form task forces, on a smaller scale but on equal terms with the Royal Navy and United States Navy, "would offer the RCN an opportunity to win battle honours with them and so greatly enhance the chances of their acceptance by public opinion as part of the postwar Canadian Navy."[3] By the late fall of 1943, thanks to improvements in the technology and training of the fleet and the organization of headquarters and bases in Canada, C groups would be making a much better impression on senior British naval officers in Western Approaches Command and the Admiralty than they had in 1942. Furthermore, the RCN was participating—effectively—in fleet and combined operations with the Royal Navy.

---

1. Narrative "B", 1, 1944, DHH, 84/230

2. W.A.B. Douglas, "Conflict and Innovation in the RCN, 1939-1945," in G. Jordan (ed), *Naval Warfare in the Twentieth Century*. (London 1977); D. Munton and D. Page, "Planning in the East Block: The Post-Hostilities Problems Committee in Canada," *International Journal* 32/4 (1977), 687-726; J. Hilliker, *Canada's Department of External Affairs* I: *The Early Years, 1909-1946* (Montreal and Kingston 1990), 301

3. LCdr G.F. Todd, RCNVR, writing for the Post War Problems Committee, "Canada's Post-war Navy," 17 Nov 1943, LAC, RG 24, 3844, NS 1017-10-34

The improvements in the performance of the Atlantic escort fleet during the course of 1943 were hard-won. The challenges proved considerably greater than members of the Naval Staff had begun to grasp, with mounting concern, early in the year, even while they were building the case for the creation of the Canadian Northwest Atlantic theatre. Although the success of this bid signalled their recognition of Canadian capabilities, the Allies had been cautious in sanctioning the new organization. Full RN and USN acceptance of the Canadian service as an equal in operational effectiveness demanded unremitting effort in bringing the escort fleet up to standard in antisubmarine warfare; so too did the growing impatience of the officers of the escort fleet with the handicaps under which they laboured as compared with their British and American comrades.

Overcoming technological shortfalls was crucial, not only to improved performance, but as the foundation for a balanced fleet. The clearest link between the Atlantic antisubmarine battle, in which the primary need was for highly specialized escort vessels that would inevitably and rightly be sold off at war's end, and the aspirations of the Naval Staff to recreate the Royal Canadian Navy for the postwar era through the acquisition in wartime of large, general purpose warships, lay in the question of naval aviation. The Naval Staff's postwar planning in 1939–40 for the acquisition of larger destroyers and cruisers had made no mention of an air arm for the RCN, but subsequent events in the war at sea made it abundantly clear that there had been a revolution in naval affairs. No national fleet could claim balanced, general purpose capabilities without carrier-borne aviation.[4] That had become evident in the successful British carrier air attacks on the Italian fleet in Taranto in November 1940, the decisive role of British carrier aircraft in hunting down the *Bismarck* in May 1941, the near-crippling damage to the US Pacific battle fleet by Japanese carrier air strikes on Pearl Harbor in December 1941, and the ability of the USN to contain Japanese expansion with the victory by American carriers in the Battle of Midway in June 1942.

The RCN's dependence on Royal Canadian Air Force shore-based aviation to counter the U-boat offensive into North American waters that began in January 1942 underscored the importance of aircraft in antisubmarine warfare, even as the limited resources of the RCAF, and the difficulties of naval–air force cooperation, inevitably raised the need for the RCN to have its own air branch. The successful operations of the first specialized escort aircraft carriers on the Gibraltar run and with the Russian convoys in northern waters suggested that the RCN needed this capability as well as improved surface escorts. Captain H.N. Lay, Director of Operations Division at NSHQ, began promoting the idea of a Canadian naval air arm in the summer of 1942, when Lieutenant-Commander J.S. Stead, a Canadian who had served in the RN and the Fleet Air Arm (FAA) before the war, had been called out of retirement to serve as Staff Officer (Air) in Lay's division.[5]

In September 1942 Commander C.E. Thompson, RN, commanding officer of HMS *Witherington*, one of the RN escorts in the Mid-Ocean Escort Force, submitted a paper that was tabled in the meetings of NSHQ and AFHQ staff officers in November 1942 which sought to coordinate air and sea

---

4. For the impact of naval aviation on different navies see: C. Reynolds, *The Fast Carriers: The Forging of an Air Navy* (Huntington 1968); A. Marder, *Old Friends, New Enemies: The Royal Navy and the Imperial Japanese Navy*, 2 vols (Oxford 1981, 1990); T.C. Hone, N. Friedman, and M.D. Mandeles, *American and British Aircraft Carrier Development, 1919-1941* (Annapolis 1999); and M.P. Peattie, *Sunburst: The Rise of Japanese Naval Air Power, 1909-1941* (Annapolis 2001).

5. *Canadian Navy List*, May and Sep 1942

antisubmarine warfare more closely. This consideration resulted in the modest recommendation that a naval officer be attached to regional RCAF headquarters and an air force officer be attached to regional RCN headquarters. Thompson's initiative received a mixed reception in the Admiralty—who thought his argument would damage efforts to create a unified RCN–RCAF antisubmarine command and was likely to harm relations with the RAF.[6] Nevertheless, in December 1942 it was to Thompson that the Admiralty turned to for advice before offering to take more RCNVR personnel for training in the FAA.[7] In Ottawa, Lay had Stead, in cooperation with Thompson, prepare a study on naval aviation. Lay incorporated their findings in a memorandum dated 11 January 1943 and entitled "Formation of a Canadian Fleet Air Arm." The memorandum went to Angus L. Macdonald minister of National Defence for Naval Services, to Rear-Admiral Percy W. Nelles, the Chief of the Naval Staff, and to Rear-Admiral G.C. Jones, Vice-Chief of the Naval Staff. Accordingly, on 29 January Jones advised Nelles to send Lay to England to find out all he could about the running of a fleet air arm, and to accept the Admiralty's offer.[8]

At the end of February Lay and the Director of Plans, Captain H.G. DeWolf, reinforced this recommendation when they drew Nelles's attention to the disastrous experience of the sixty-three–ship, British escorted convoy SC 118, which had lost eleven ships just one week earlier because of a lack of air support. "If the RCN is to become an efficient Naval Force," DeWolf pointed out, "the development of our air requirements can no longer be neglected." The RCAF could provide important air support, but not ship-borne aircraft: that, DeWolf emphasized, was a problem "of the highest priority." Advice like this by two such experienced operational officers could not be ignored. Jones recommended, and Nelles approved, both acceptance of the Admiralty's offer to train RCNVR personnel for the FAA and the creation of a committee to examine and report what practical steps the RCN could take in the field of naval aviation.[9] In his message to the Admiralty, Nelles specified that RCNVR personnel would have to be returned to the RCN "should Canada form its own air service."[10]

At the beginning of April 1943, Stead visited the United States to consult with FAA officers on the staff of the British Admiralty Delegation (BAD), and to inspect HMS *Tracker*, an escort carrier working up in Norfolk, Virginia. He reported the prevalent view in both the British and American navies "that escort carriers may well take the place of VLR (Very Long Range) aircraft, although medium and long range aircraft will still have a big part to play in coastal zones."[11] Reflecting pro-

---

6.   "The paper by the CO of Witherington on Naval pilots and observers for the RCAF is both sweeping and contentious. It was largely responsible for the Ottawa Committee turning down a unified command for A/S work. It has been seen by the Senior Officers at Coastal Command but not by Air Ministry, and Commander Martineau [the RN liaison officer with Coastal Command who had been on an inspection tour in North America in the fall of 1942] is trying to prevent further circulation in RAF circles: in its present form it can do nothing but harm," PRO, ADM 1/11750

7.   Adm to CNS, 23 Dec 1942, LAC, RG 24 (Acc 83-84/167), 175, NS 1700-913(1)—hereafter NS 1700-913 (1)

8.   Cdr C.E. Thompson, RN, "Formation of a RCN Air Service" (nd but c. 23 Dec 1942-11 Jan 1943) and minute by SO(A) J.S. Stead, (ibid); DOD to MND, CNS, VCNS, 11 Jan 1943; J.S. Stead "Canadian Naval Air Service (nd but with H.N. Lay's signature and date stamp 14 Jan 1943); minute VCNS to CNS, 29 Jan 1943, NS 1700-913 (1)

9.   DCOS Plans to CNP, VCNS, CNS, 21 Feb 1943; DCOS Plans to CNS, 22 Feb 1943, Ibid

10. CNS to Adm, 2 Mar 1943, ibid

11. Report of visit of SO (Air) to Washington, Norfolk and in HMS *Tracker*, 1-7 Apr 1943, ibid. For the significance of VLR aircraft see W.A.B. Douglas, *The Creation of a National Air Force* (Toronto 1986), 537-9, and W.A.B. Douglas and David Syrett, "Die Wende in der Schlacht im Atlantik: Die Schliessung des Grönland-Luftlochs, 1942-1943," *Marine Rundschau*, 83/1-3 (1986)

fessional opinion of the day, Lay and DeWolf forecast that air would probably be the decisive factor in the Battle of the Atlantic, and they informed the Naval Board that, since convoy defence was the most important RCN contribution to the war, it was "desirable that the RCN should give full and immediate consideration to the question of forming a Canadian Naval Air Service."[12] They recommended that a Naval Air Division be formed, and that a senior officer be despatched to study air operations in the United States and the United Kingdom. They also encouraged VCNS Jones to take the long view. Aware that policy was constantly evolving to meet the changing circumstances of war, making obvious "the impracticability of attempting to develop in wartime a navy which will fulfil peacetime requirements," Lay and DeWolf insisted nevertheless that no modern navy was going to be complete without an air service. Even if only the nucleus of a naval air service were established in wartime, plans should be made for expanding it in peacetime. The outcome of all these efforts was that on 12 April 1943 the Naval Board accepted the recommendation to form a naval air staff in Ottawa and on 29 April the minister agreed to send Lay on a fact-finding mission to determine the requirements for a naval air service.[13]

It seems that these decisions did not sit well with Vice-Admiral Nelles, who suspected—correctly as it turned out—that Captain Lay was going behind his back to the minister.[14] For his part, Macdonald decided to put the matter before the Cabinet War Committee, even though the Naval Board had merely recommended keeping the possibility of a naval air service under review. On 4 May Macdonald forewarned C.G. Power, Minister of National Defence for Air Services, that the RCN was considering a Canadian Fleet Air Arm "with the object of manning and operating aircraft carriers and carrier borne aircraft." There was no intention of recruiting for such a service—personnel would be found from within the navy—but there might be a need for training by the RCAF. Apparently disarmed by this diplomatic approach, Power replied the next day, saying that although the RCAF probably could provide personnel to operate from carriers under RCN command it could also, if the navy preferred, undertake the limited training of naval personnel. He suggested that in that case the staffs of the two services would be the best people to work out such training arrangements.[15]

Thus reassured, on 13 May Macdonald took the proposal to the Cabinet War Committee. Opposition came from Minister of National Defence J.L. Ralston, Minister of Finance J.L. Ilsley, and Air Vice Marshal G.M. Croil, Inspector General of the RCAF. The CWC was as usual inviting senior officers of the armed forces to attend meetings where their presence might prove beneficial. All three men said the proposed air service would constitute needless and costly duplication. Ilsley

12. DOD and DOP to VCNS, 6 Apr 1943, NS 1700-913 (1). In view of the supporting documents, it appears that this memorandum took into account what Stead was reporting from the United States.

13. NB min, 12 Apr 1943, LAC, DHH; mem, Macdonald to DOD, 29 Apr 1943, cited in Report of Visit A/Capt H.N. Lay RCN to the UK, 11 July 1943, NS 1700-913 (1)

14. A nephew by marriage to the Prime Minister, Lay told Mackenzie King, who recorded it in his diary, that "Nelles resents some of the suggestions and criticisms he [Lay] has made with respect to the need for air protection over convoys, aircraft carriers with convoys, and some other things ... Has had long talks with the Minister and has given him quite frankly his views on the suggestions," King Diary, 5 Apr 1943, LAC, MG 26, J13, 231—hereafter King Diary. See also entry for 29 Mar 1943; this contradicts Lay's denial, in H.N. Lay, *Memoirs of a Mariner* (Ottawa 1982), 148

15. Stead anticipated RCAF opposition and was anxious to avoid its interference and control in "equipment and training ... for Naval Air Warfare and the type of aircraft necessary for the very highly specialised operations from carriers." Power made the observation that "no great difficulty is foreseen ... in making available at as early a date as you desire personnel trained to a stage fit to undergo specialized naval air training." Stead, "Formation of a Canadian Naval Air Service," 3 May 1943; Macdonald to Power, 4 May 1943; Power to Macdonald, 5 May 1943. NS 1700-913 (1)

Second from the right is Angus L. Macdonald, Minister of the Naval Service; the photograph was taken in Sydney, Nova Scotia, on board an unnamed warship. His executive assistant, John Connolly, who later played a key role in having Vice-Admiral Percy W. Nelles removed as Chief of the Naval Staff, is at right. (DND PMR-98-48)

Vice-Admiral Percy W. Nelles after his removal as Chief of the Naval Staff. Here, in his new position, after being exiled to the United Kingdom as Senior Canadian Flag Officer Overseas, he is visiting Plymouth. (LAC PA 206491)

also argued, with some justification—and without realizing it, in echo of the Admiralty's opinion—that the best means of convoy protection would be better cooperation between the RCAF and the RCN. Power undercut the cost argument with the contention that the only duplication of service would be in one or two manning and training depots. Meanwhile Prime Minister Mackenzie King, who had been converted to the view that cooperation with air forces was more difficult at sea than it was on land, ensured that the formation of a Canadian naval air service would not be rejected out of hand by his Cabinet. After this meeting he confided to his diary that he "had a feeling ... that some of the Ministers were aware of the fact that Nelson Lay and ... others had been strongly pressing for a fleet air arm and that ... my reaction was due to some knowledge of this."[16]

At a time when the RCN was hard pressed to acquire, equip, and man small escort vessels, the bid to get into naval aviation demands explanation. Was this a case of Canada's navy running before it could walk? The RCN could, in 1943, get air support from American and British carriers for convoy defence—but precisely there lay the rub, for dependence on the USN and RN had to a large extent made the RCN a "client navy." Abundant evidence attests that in 1943 Canadian needs were low on the priority list of the Great Powers, and the British Admiralty's assistance in modernization was clearly wanting. It is important to bear in mind that in Ottawa national self-sufficiency was a highly desirable objective.[17] Thus, although within the naval service, between the RCN and RCAF, and within the Cabinet War Committee, bureaucratic politics was certainly much in evidence, the Naval Staff had plenty of justification and it showed commendable vision in electing to press for a naval air arm. Moreover, even as the government of Canada considered the question, escort carriers on their first sustained operations on the North Atlantic routes achieved dramatic results that amply supported the advice received from British and American officers.

In April and May 1943, within weeks of the Atlantic Convoy Conference in Washington, Allied air and naval forces gained the upper hand in the North Atlantic. This dramatic turn of events, just when the Allies reorganized their effort on the basis of the decisions reached at the conference, was unexpectedly swift—but no coincidence. The essential driving force behind the convoy conference (as seen in the previous volume in this series), was the Admiralty's push to have additional sea and air escort forces concentrated in the "air gap" south of Greenland and to extend Admiralty control to that area. It was in this air gap that convoy defences were weakest, while the strengthened U-boat force was enjoying its greatest success, even as Britain's imports crisis, the demands of operations in North Africa, and the buildup for the eventual Allied invasion of northwest Europe made essential the despatch of larger and more frequent convoys from North America.

The transfer of RCN mid-ocean escort groups, or C groups, from American to British control on a temporary basis early in 1943 was the Admiralty's initial attempt to strengthen protection for British convoys while in the middle of the Atlantic. The original plan was to have the C groups operate on the Gibraltar run, thereby relieving more capable British groups for transatlantic serv-

---

16. CWC min, 13 May 1943, DHH; King Diary, 13 May 1943

17. In 1942, Group Capt V. Heakes, RCAF, Director of Plans on the Air Staff, observed with some bitterness, in reference to the acquisition of Liberators and other up-to-date aircraft for the Home War Establishment, that Canada was "a beggar at a rich man's table." Douglas, *Creation of a National Air Force*, 363; cf C.P. Stacey, *Arms, Men and Governments: The War Policies of Canada, 1939-1945* (Ottawa 1970)

ice. However, this plan had to be altered in March when some of the best British groups, as well as the experienced and cohesive mixed Canadian–American group A 3, suffered losses on the scale of the disasters that befell the Canadian-escorted SC 107 and ONS 154 in late 1942. The need was not only for quality escorts, but also for their sheer numbers. This somewhat vindicated the Canadians. In response to Allied criticisms of the C groups, the RCN had explained that being constantly pressed to provide escorts in quantity it had never had the margin to focus on quality. After some brief refresher training and partial re-equipment of the ships at British establishments, the good performance of the C groups on the Gibraltar run further suggested that the C groups were more effective than they had earlier been reputed to be.

The Canadian groups (as noted in Chapter 11 of Part 1) were also strengthened by the assignment, in response to the RCN's long-standing request, of more dependable British ships to compensate for Canada's shortage of destroyers. In particular, the new frigates HMS *Itchen* (C 1), *Lagan* (C 2), and *Jed* (C 3), together with the old but recently refitted Town class destroyers HMS *Broadway* (C 2), *Burnham* (C 3), and *Churchill* (C 4), sailed on nearly every convoy mission that their respective groups undertook during the first half of 1943. The commanding officers of these ships brought much-needed experience to the leadership of the Canadian groups. Indeed, British officers served as Senior Officer Escort (SOE) of all four C groups. Lieutenant-Commander C.E. Bridgman, RNR, formerly commanding officer of the corvette HMS *Dianthus*, a long-time member of the C groups, had taken command of *Itchen* shortly before this and became senior officer of C 1. Lieutenant-Commander E.H. Chavasse, RN, as commanding officer of *Broadway* had often led Canadian groups in 1942, and after the destroyer's refit he became senior officer of C 2. Commander R.C. Medley, RN, and Commander A.M. Mackillop, RN, had both seen wide-ranging service in command of destroyers before they took over *Burnham* and *Churchill* and became senior officers of C 3 and C 4 respectively. The commanding officer of HMS *Lagan* was Lieutenant-Commander A. Ayre, RNR; he had previously commanded the corvette HMS *Primrose* and was another British veteran of the C groups.[18]

Far from resenting the close British supervision that accompanied the return of the RCN groups to Western Approaches control, NSHQ asked that experienced British group commanders be lent to the RCN to command two of four de-classed fleet destroyers that Canada was due to take over from the RN in the spring of 1943.[19] The RCN had a large pool of talent among the officers of the RCNVR, as well as the (far fewer) young officers of the permanent force, but the most experienced among them had only recently become qualified for their first ship commands. Senior, experienced leadership from the tiny cadre of qualified permanent force and RCNR officers was thinly stretched. The first two of the British destroyers commissioned in the RCN as HMCS *Ottawa* (2nd) and HMCS *Kootenay* in March–April 1943. Respectively, their captains were Commander H.F. Pullen, RCN, who had gone ashore for staff duties after his command of *St Francis* in 1940–41, and twenty-seven-

---

18. Marc Milner, *North Atlantic Run* (Toronto 1985), 219-20, 285-90; A. Hague, *Destroyers for Great Britain: A History of the 50 Town Class Ships Tranferred from the United States to Great Britain in 1940* (Annapolis 1990), 29, 31, 43. Bridgman took command of *Itchen* on 27 Jan 1943, Medley took over *Burnham* on 6 Mar 1943, and McKillop took command of *Churchill* on 28 Mar 1943. [Br] *Navy List*, June 1943

19. NSHQ to Adm, 2249z, 25 Mar 1943, DHH, 81/520/8440-60, "Mid-Ocean Escort Force." De-classed fleets were fleet destroyers converted to antisubmarine escorts, which involved, among other things, removing turrets and gunnery control equipment and upgrading antisubmarine weaponry and sensors, as well as increasing depth charge stowage.

year-old Acting Lieutenant-Commander K.L. Dyer, RCN, who was fresh from his first command, *Skeena*, in 1942. In response to the Canadian request, the Admiralty lent Commander Medley to take over the third additional "River," HMCS *Saskatchewan*, in May 1943, and Commander P.W. Burnett, RN, for *Gatineau* in June.[20]

By the time the C groups came back to the North Atlantic in late March and early April, the Admiralty was able to further close the sailing cycles—to six days for the HX-ON series, and eight days for the SC-ONS series—without diverting to close escort duties the five support groups that had been organized in Western Approaches command in March and April. This was critical. Heavy convoy losses from January to March 1943 had confirmed that even the best of the close escort groups could not counter the massed attacks that the U-boats could now muster. The only hope was to deploy reinforcing groups in areas where intelligence indicated enemy patrol lines were located, ready to rush to the assistance of the convoys where they were most likely to come under attack. As we have seen, British—and Canadian—authorities recognized the potential of support groups as early as 1941. They had endeavoured to establish such groups in 1942, but could not sustain them because of the shortage of ships for the close escorts that were the convoys' primary defence and, indeed, the basis of the whole convoy system. The Western Support Force experiment in the winter of 1942 did drive home the point that the old British destroyers available in the western Atlantic were inadequate and that command arrangements needed to be revised (as was done at the conference in Washington). The five new support groups included some of the best-equipped and successful antisubmarine warships of Western Approaches. Numbers were so lacking, however, that following the heavy Atlantic convoy losses in March the British government cancelled the sailing of convoys to North Russia to enable the Home Fleet destroyers that normally screened those convoys to form new support groups. Further reinforcement came from the assignment of two of the Royal Navy's escort aircraft carriers, HMS *Archer* and *Biter*, to the North Atlantic convoys, together with the USN escort carrier USS *Bogue* and its escorting destroyers. The American ships had been allocated to the North Atlantic as part of the agreement reached at the Washington conference, and they functioned as a sixth support group.[21] The escort aircraft carriers were an especially welcome addition to Western Approaches command. Senior Allied authorities were making arrangements to assign large numbers of additional bombers that had been converted to very long range (VLR) capability to the British, American, and Canadian Atlantic air commands. But in the spring of 1943 there were still only about thirty such aircraft operating, all of them part of the Royal Air Force's Coastal Command.[22]

The *U-Bootewaffe*'s success in March was partly the result of delays experienced by Bletchley Park in penetrating the Enigma code, in contrast to the impressive signals intelligence that Grossadmiral Karl Dönitz was receiving from the *Beobachtungsdienst (B-Dienst)*. One account recently went so far as to call March 1943 "the most unpleasant period" in cryptographic and oper-

20. K. Macpherson and R. Barrie, *Ships of Canada's Naval Forces, 1910-2002* (St. Catharines 2002) 47-53; [Br] *Navy List*, Oct 1940, 947; June 1941, 1267; Feb 1943, 1733

21. S.W. Roskill, *The War at Sea* (London 1954-61), II, 366-7, 401. A third British carrier, HMS *Dasher*, had been assigned but was destroyed by an aviation gas explosion on 27 March 1943, which led the Admiralty to improve extensively the very basic aviation fuel-handling facilities in these US-built vessels.

22. "The RAF in Maritime War, IV: The Atlantic and Home Waters. The Offensive Phase, Feb 1943 to May 1944," DHH 79/599, 27, 59

ational terms, comparable to the Ultra blackout between February and October 1942.[23] On the German side, in April 1943, in a series of well placed lines between forty and sixty U-boats were operating against convoys, but by then restored Enigma intelligence was giving Allied routing authorities a major advantage. Support groups, several of them with escort carriers, and the increased presence of VLR Liberators, put U-boats at a further, severe disadvantage.[24]

In the early hours of 10 April about 400 miles northeast of Newfoundland, Group *Adler*—consisting of fifteen U-boats in a patrol line 300 miles long—was sweeping southeast for an eastbound convoy when *U 404* sighted the westbound convoy ON 176 (B 4). Nine boats from *Adler* engaged the convoy and before breaking off the action late on 12 April sank the Town class destroyer HMS *Beverley* and a merchant ship. *U 571* of group *Adler* also intercepted ONS 2 and sank one of its merchant ships. At this same time group *Lerche*, consisting of ten boats that had earlier been involved in the attack on HX 231, attacked HX 232 (of B 3, which was reinforced by the four RN destroyers of EG 4) and in spite of strong air cover sank three of its merchant ships. Between 15 and 18 April HX 233, escorted by A 3 (led by Commander P.R. Heineman, USN, in USCGC *Spencer*, and which included HMCS *Skeena* and the corvettes HMCS *Wetaskiwin* and *Arvida*, reinforced by four destroyers of EG 3), came under attack by the twenty-three boats of group *Meise*. HX 233 lost one merchant ship in exchange for the destruction of *U 175* by USCG *Spencer* and *Duane*.[25]

The sinking of *U 175* was a fitting climax to the last voyage by A 3, which was then dissolved upon the withdrawal of its US warships, as agreed at the Atlantic Convoy Conference. A 3's RCN corvettes were transferred to C 5, the new Canadian group. *Ottawa*, the first of the additional British escort destroyers transferred to the RCN, and later *Kootenay*, took the place of the American ships. C 5 began operations almost immediately, and with Commander H.F. Pullen, RCN, in *Ottawa* as senior officer, it was the only one of the C groups that was led by a Canadian rather than a British officer at this time.[26]

Convoy routing north and south of the U-boat packs, made possible by the rapid decryption of Enigma signals, took the commander of the German U-boat service, or *Befehlshaber der Unterseeboote* (BdU) by surprise and led to the formation of a fourth patrol line, group *Specht*. On 21 April ONS 3 (EG 40, a British support group) ran into some of the *Meise* boats, and in a brief encounter suffered the loss of two merchant ships.[27] Other boats from *Meise* attacked HX 234 (B 4) and ON 178 (B 1), sinking three merchant ships from the former. In response a VLR Liberator from 120 Squadron RAF sank *U 189* on 23 April. Between 23 and 29 April ONS 4 (B 2, under Commander D. Macintyre, RN, supported by the British group EG 5 with the escort carrier HMS *Biter* and reinforced by the five RN destroyers of EG 1), fought its way through *Meise* without the loss of a single merchant ship, while sinking two submarines. Routing authorities then steered

23. W.J.R. Gardner, *Decoding History: The Battle of the Atlantic and ULTRA* (Annapolis 1999), 137

24. British and American participants in the Washington convoy conference were sceptical of C-in-C CNA's ability to control support groups. F.H. Hinsley, *British Intelligence in the Second World War* (London 1979-90), 567; D. Syrett, *The Defeat of the German U-boats: The Battle of the Atlantic* (Columbia 1994), 26-7; Milner, *The U-boat Hunters*, 40-1

25. Milner, ibid, 25-43

26. CO *Ottawa*, "Report of Proceedings 5th Canadian Escort Group with Convoy ON 182," nd, PRO, ADM 199/358. "The Escort Group was formed as such twenty-four hours before sailing" with ON 182 on 7 May 1943.

27. J. Rohwer, *Axis Submarine Successes* (Annapolis 1983), 163, mistakenly places these two ships in ON 178.

ONS 4 safely around *Specht*. Seven more convoys had steamed safely across the Atlantic without being attacked, their routes also informed by Enigma decrypts.[28]

German anxiety about the presence of aircraft in the mid-Atlantic now became evident. The weekly situation reports from the British Operational Intelligence Centre (OIC) described the "incipient decline in U-boat morale" and a lack of boldness that had spread to most U-boat commanders.[29] Furthermore, a respectable exchange rate of four submarines sunk (three by escorts and one by a VLR Liberator) for the loss of one escort and twelve merchant ships in convoy, between 11 and 29 April, was an encouraging improvement over previous months.

On 25 April the next westbound convoy, ONS 5 (B 7, under Commander P. Gretton, RN, in HMS *Duncan*) left Liverpool. Group *Stern*, which comprised sixteen boats disposed roughly on a north-south line, lay in wait between Iceland and Greenland on 28 April. A temporary Enigma blackout hampered convoy routing, but shore-based HF/DF bearings had located *Stern*.[30] ONS 5 skirted the extreme northern end of the line. But five German boats sighted the convoy, and *U 258* sank SS *McKeesport* amid the heavy gales, snow, and rain showers hampering visibility on 29 April. Northeast of Newfoundland two more groups, *Specht* and *Amsel,* awaited instruction. The *B-Dienst* decrypted a position signal from SC 128, which enabled BdU to anticipate that convoy's rerouting signal. *Specht* and *Amsel* were ordered to form a long line of twenty-eight U-boats to cover all approaches to the north and east of Newfoundland.[31]

Fortunately for SC 128, one of the *Specht* boats sighted an EG 3 destroyer, on its way to reinforce ONS 5, and mistook it for the expected eastbound convoy, which therefore avoided detection. On 4 May ONS 5, scattered by storms, had a main group of thirty ships in ten columns, escorted by three destroyers (all with HF/DF and type 271 radar), a frigate, two corvettes (all with type 271 radar) and one trawler. A separate group of four ships was escorted by the corvette HMS *Pink*; ONS 5 also had eight stragglers. Unable to refuel in the heavy seas, four escorting destroyers, among them the SO, Commander P.W. Gretton's *Duncan*, had left to replenish fuel supplies in harbour. Meanwhile the trawler *Northern Gem*, full of survivors from *McKeesport*, was on its way to St John's. The remaining ships of ONS 5 steamed into a terrible concentration of U-boats made up of a patrol line of thirty submarines in group *Fink*—a combination of the former *Stern* and *Specht*—and beyond that a second line of eleven in groups *Amsel I* and *Amsel II*.[32]

ONS 5 had one important advantage: It was now within range of RCAF Canso amphibians and USAAF B-17s flying from Newfoundland. Extensive patrols from 1 to 3 May resulted in several U-

28. Merchant ships lost were: from HX 232, *Ulysses, Fresno City, Pacific Grove,* and *Edward B. Dudley*; from HX 233, *Fort Rampart;* from HX 234, *Amerika* (a straggler) and *Robert Gray*; from ONS 176, *Lancastrian Prince* and HMS *Beverley;* from ONS 178, *Scebeli*; from ONS 2, *Ingerfire*; from ONS 3, *Ashantian* and *Wanstead*. PRO, ADM 199/356, ONS, ON and HX Convoy Reports; ADM 199/575, Atlantic Convoy Reports, HX Convoys, HX 222-235; ADM 199/583, Atlantic Convoy Reports, ON Convoys, ON 122-203; LAC, RG 24, 11090, 48-2-2; LAC, RG 24, 11320, 8280, ON 178, ON 179, ON 186; LAC, RG 24, 11329, 8280, ONS 3, ONS 4; DHH, 81/520/8280 Box 7 ONS 2; DHH, 89/34 vol 9 and vol 23. Rohwer, *Axis Submarine Successes,* has placed some of these ships in the wrong convoys; MOD, *U-Boat War in the Atlantic,* and Syrett, *Defeat of the German U-boats,* have missed *U 571's* attack on ONS 2.

29. Hinsley, *British Intelligence in the Second World War* II, 567-9; MOD, *U-Boat War in the Atlantic* III, 99-103

30. W.A.B. Douglas and J. Rohwer, "The 'Most Thankless Task' Revisited: Convoys, Escorts and Radio Intelligence in the Western Atlantic, 1941-43," in J.A. Boutilier (ed), *The RCN in Retrospect* (Vancouver 1982), 228

31. Ibid.

32. Ibid, 228-31; Syrett, *Defeat of the German U-boats,* 77; MOD, *U-Boat War in the Atlantic,* Diagram 21

boat sightings by B-17s in the vicinity of the two sections of *Amsel*, but BdU ordered these two groups to split into four and tried to confuse Allied forces using radio deception techniques. They may have succeeded. Search patterns ordered for B-17s on 4 May failed to cover the areas actually occupied by submarines.[33] That same day, however, Cansos from 5 (BR) Squadron, RCAF, sighted four U-boats from group *Fink* and attacked three of them, sinking *U 630*, thirty miles astern of ONS 5. One of the RCAF Cansos directed to support the convoy crashed on take-off on 5 May, killing all on board. The second Canso failed to find the convoy, while a VLR Liberator that did succeed in reaching ONS 5 more than 2000 miles from its base in Iceland was able to see little through the fog patches. There remained any number of U-boats in the convoy's path—twenty-eight reportedly had made contact over the previous two days—and on the evening of 5 May, after U-boats had sunk a further nine merchant ships, one of the destroyers of EG 3 picked up such heavy German radio traffic that ONS 5 seemed to be "threatened with annihilation." Indeed, three more ships were sunk, but fog set in and the escorts defending the convoy were able to turn the tables on the U-boats, destroying five of them: *U 192*, *U 638*, *U 125*, *U 438,* and *U 531*. Four others— *U 264*, *U 358*, *U 552* and *U 954*—had to break off action to repair damage. Another four—*U 266*, *U 634*, *U 264*, and *U 377*—all reported being severely handled. As one historian of the period has pointed out, U-boats "were not pressing their strength in numbers and most were not taking their shots."[34] Of forty marauders capable of attacking, no more than fifteen did so at any one time; perhaps this was an indication that pack tactics could suffer from diminishing rates of return.[35] There were yet more signs in this period that the German *guerre de course* was faltering. ONS 4, SC 127, and ON 127 managed to avoid contact with U-boats altogether, and ON 180, which trailed ONS 5, was able to outflank German patrol lines.[36] This was the turning point in the Battle of the Atlantic. The Royal Canadian Navy's ships played no role in the specific convoy battles, but the RCAF had made an important contribution during the crucial phase of the battle that took place in the newly established Canadian Northwest Atlantic Command.[37]

Over the next few weeks Dönitz made extraordinary but unsuccessful efforts to regain momentum.[38] Although still well served by *B-Dienst*, the U-boats simply could not cope with the combination of Allied superiority in intelligence, the rapid deployment of support groups to reinforce threatened convoys, the availability of VLR and carrier-borne aircraft to close the air gap, and the

---

33. In fact, the operational authorities in Newfoundland may have been disposed to think the U-boats were stationed as they were pretending to be, in a single more or less stationary line covering all approaches from the northeast, and consequently too much emphasis may have been placed on area searches. The weekly intelligence report from No 1 Group RCAF on 24 May reveals a mistaken belief in the existence of permanent U-boat pickets, and this could have led to the false assumption on 5 May that ONS 5 was past its greatest danger. No 1 Group RCAF, WIR, 24 May 1943, DHH, 181.003 (D308); Review of Antisubmarine Intelligence, DHH, 80/208; Douglas, *Creation of a National Air Force*, 555

34. M. Gannon, *Black May: The Epic Story of the Allies' Defeat of the German U-boats in May 1943* (New York 1998), 226

35. Ibid, 226-7

36. Ibid, 226

37. HMS *Sunflower*, one of Gretton's B 2, was under the command of LCdr J. Plomer, RCNVR. Douglas and Rohwer, "Most Thankless Task," 228-33; Douglas, *Creation of a National Air Force*, 553-4; Syrett, *Defeat of the German U-boats*, 63-95; Hinsley, *British Intelligence in the Second World War* II, 569-70; MOD, *U-Boat War in the Atlantic*, 104-6; BdU, KTB, 3-6 May 1943, DHH 79/446

38. Syrett, *Defeat of the German U-boats*, 96-144, is the best documented account. See also MOD, *U-Boat War in the Atlantic*, 104-13, and Gannon, *Black May*

improved effectiveness of close escort groups equipped with HF/DF and centimetric radar. ONS 6 (B 6) and ON 181 (B 3), the former supported by EG 4 (with the escort carrier HMS *Archer*) and EG 1 (with four frigates) were routed clear of the new groups *Elbe* and *Rhein*, formed from the surviving U-boats of groups *Fink* and *Amsel*. HX 237, escorted by C 2, was also covered by EG 5 with the escort carrier HMS *Biter*. On 9 May HX 237 encountered boats from *Rhein*, and on 12 May from *Drossel* (a group formed at the end of April in the eastern Atlantic to intercept convoys off Cape Finisterre). C 2 consisted of HMS *Broadway* (Lieutenant-Commander E.H. Chavasse RN, SO) the frigate HMS *Lagan*, the corvettes HMS *Primrose*, HMCS *Chambly*, *Morden* and *Drumheller*, HM Tug *Dexterous* and HM Trawler *Vizalma*. The addition of EG 5 and HMS *Biter* made this convoy a tough nut to crack. German signals intelligence had suggested to Dönitz that Allied naval authorities were deliberately diverting convoys around patrol lines, although on this occasion the diversions do not appear to have been based on Enigma decrypts but on educated guesses following the battle for ONS 5, as well as on a need to find good flying weather for the escort carrier.[39] *Biter*, recalled Chavasse in later years, "rose magnificently to the occasion ... In spite of frequently foul weather, she never once refused a request of mine (her very junior senior officer) to fly off aircraft ... Navy List seniority went to the four winds, and everybody was keen to do what I asked."[40] U-boats sank three stragglers, but ships and aircraft defending HX 237 destroyed three submarines in return: *U 89* on 12 May, by *Broadway*; *U 456,* credited to a VLR Liberator from 86 Squadron RAF; and *U 753* on 13 May.

Both Canadian surface and air forces shared in the kill of *U 753*. A large Short Sunderland flying boat of 423 Squadron, RCAF, based in Northern Ireland, was supporting HX 237 when it sighted the submarine and made a depth charge attack that was wide of the mark. The U-boat remained on the surface and engaged the circling flying boat with its antiaircraft armament. The flying boat, soon supported by a Fairey Swordfish from HMS *Biter*, returned fire with its machine guns. HMCS *Drumheller*, commanded by Lieutenant-Commander A.H.G. Storrs, RCNR, noted the unusual manoeuvres of the circling aircraft in the distance and rushed to investigate. On seeing the U-boat *Drumheller* opened fire with its 4-inch gun. *U 753* dived and *Drumheller* dropped depth charges. The asdic returns, which were not good because of the movement of the corvette's hull in the heavy seas, indicated that the submarine had survived.[41] HMS *Lagan* soon joined, and with benefit of *Drumheller*'s asdic contact, made an attack with Hedgehog, an antisubmarine mortar that threw multiple projectiles ahead of the ship. Hedgehog had been widely fitted in British, but not in Canadian, ships. "Two distinct explosions were heard after this attack ... and large quantity of diesel oil and bits of wreckage (wood) were seen." In the words of Chavasse's report, evoking racial stereotypes typical of the popular culture of the time, "another Redskin bit the dust."[42]

---

39. MOD, ibid, 100-1

40. E.H. Chavasse, "Business in Great Waters", DHH, 88/181, 92-3. This was Chavasse's last convoy in *Broadway*. Promoted to commander, he joined the Captain class frigate HMS *Bentinck* in July 1943 as SO of EG 4.

41. Credit for these sinkings goes to HMS *Lagan* and aircraft from HMS *Biter* for *U 89* and *U 753*, HMS *Broadway* sharing in the first and HMCS *Drumheller* in the second, and to Liberator B/86 for *U 456*. The latter was originally credited to *Lagan*, *Drumheller,* and 423 Squadron, RCAF.

42. "Report of Attack on U-boat, HMCS Drumheller," HMS *Broadway*; "Convoy HX 237, Narrative of Events," 17 May 1943, LAC, RG 24, 11312, 8280-HX 237

The battle for HX 237 set the pattern for the rest of that May. U-boats, largely because of time-ly decrypts of the Allied convoy cypher number 3 by *B-Dienst*, were able to contact four convoys. Allied support groups and air power, however, inflicted heavy losses on the submarines before they could reach the merchant ships, and they exacted retribution from the few U-boats that did manage to get within torpedo range. On 24 May Dönitz ordered "a temporary abandonment of the fundamental principles which have so far governed the U-boat campaign" and ceased wolf pack operations on the northern transatlantic routes.[43]

The Germans had sunk nineteen merchant ships in convoy since 29 April and in exchange lost seventeen U-boats. If April showed encouraging signs of improvement for the Allies, May was a spectacular victory. In the last three weeks of that month, 600 ships crossed the Atlantic in fourteen convoys, and only six of their number were lost.[44] Note that the use of escort carriers to provide almost full-time air cover for convoys was in its infancy, while radar had yet to reach a level of technological sophistication that would make it the primary means of detecting surfaced U-boats. In the convoy battles of 1942–3, HF/DF was more important than escort carriers or radar.[45] It should also be noted that Allied cryptographic sources played no direct role in the defence of ONS 5.[46] The May 1943 victory did not result from some technical *deus ex machina*, but followed upon circumstances that had been developing for a long time. As the historian Michael Gannon so aptly observed, the victory of May 1943 came thanks to

> the intensive training of RN and RAF personnel and the long months of hard experience at sea or in the air that gave them their winning edge; the time-consuming calculation of boffins; the development of new tactics; the invention, manufacture, and installation of new weapons and devices; the sharpening of leadership at all ranks; the tenacity of merchant mariners who, except for the U-boat crews, faced the greatest danger, but never flinched; the growing industrial output of American shipyards and factories; the mines sown by RAF aircraft across the Baltic work-up area in 1942 that seriously disrupted the training of many of the U-boat crews that would appear at sea in May; the refusal of Allied warships and crews to grow faint after the setbacks of March; and the resolute spirit of sailors and airmen who fought the U-boats to a draw in April.[47]

But the U-boats would be back: "We have succumbed to a technical problem," said Dönitz, "but we shall find a solution."[48] Mistakenly blaming the *U-Bootwaffe*'s woes on technology alone, Dönitz placed his hopes on increased anti-aircraft armament, new search receivers to detect Allied radar emissions, and acoustic homing torpedoes with which he was about to arm his submarine fleet. Until he did so, however, the convoy routes to Britain and the Mediterranean would be relatively safe.

As the Admiralty had learned time and again since 1939, offensive forces, like the support groups, could not be effective until shipping was protected in convoys with effective close escorts

43. BdU, KTB, 24 May 1943

44. Gannon, *Black May*, 330-1

45. Ibid, 70

46. Ibid, 229

47. Gannon, *Black May*, 393-4

48. BdU, KTB, 24 May 1943; Admiralty Appreciation of U-boat situation, 1 Aug 1943, PRO, ADM 223/16

Hedgehog in its lair. (LAC PA 112918)

Hedgehog being reloaded. (LAC PA 114737)

of adequate strength. The Atlantic Convoy Conference had set the need for mid-ocean close convoy escorts at fourteen groups, and the Royal Canadian Navy provided five of the thirteen groups that were actually in operation in April and May 1943; the C groups escorted thirteen of the thirty-five North Atlantic convoys that sailed from both sides of the ocean during those two months.[49] In 1941 and 1942, the RCN had enabled the Admiralty to complete the convoy system and keep it running. In 1943 the Canadian navy provided the critical margin that allowed the Royal Navy to create the support groups that tilted the Battle of the Atlantic against the enemy. At this stage the RCN did not have to destroy submarines to earn its keep.

———————

The centre of gravity of the war against the U-boats now shifted south, and it remained there until September,1943. USN escort carrier groups in the central Atlantic, and shore-based air patrols over the Bay of Biscay, mostly RAF, maintained the pressure. From information provided by decrypted Enigma traffic, carrier groups could establish search areas, pinpoint targets, and bring massive effort to bear on submarines in transit to patrol areas or attempting to form patrol lines in the vicinity of the Azores. Similar methods marked the Bay of Biscay Offensive.[50] Also at this time *B-Dienst* suffered a serious setback: after months of work, cypher analysis confirmed for the Allies that their most widely used code had been penetrated by German code breakers. On 28 May Captain Kenneth Knowles of Op20G in Washington, the USN counterpart to the Admiralty's Operational Intelligence Centre, seized upon a lapse of security in German procedure—transmitting the text of a decoded Allied message more or less verbatim—and subsequent repetitions of the same mistake to prove conclusively that the *B-Dienst* was reading Naval Cypher No 3. British code breakers at Bletchley Park were reaching the same conclusion. Accordingly the Allies carried out a gradual reduction of traffic in this code, eliminating it entirely by 10 June 1943.[51] For the time being, therefore, convoys were free from attack, especially on the northern routes.

This breathing space, a period when consolidation of Canadian naval forces could take place, was a useful bonus for the RCN. Although C groups and the Western Local Escort Force were shepherding convoys without serious loss, now with air support in the mid-ocean from RCAF VLR Liberators, there was still a simmering discontent in the fleet about the state of training and equipment. Furthermore, although the RCN, served by an excellent intelligence and communications system, had taken back the routing and diversion function that it had handed over to the USN in 1942, there were systemic problems in command and control that desperately needed to be solved.[52]

---

49. J. Rohwer, *Critical Convoy Battles of March 1943: The Battle for HX 229/SC 122* (Annapolis 1977), 39

50. Syrett, *Defeat of the German U-boats*, 145-80; Roskill, *The War at Sea* III, pt 1, 25-6; Hilary St George Saunders, *Royal Air Force 1939-45* III: *The Fight Is Won* (London 1957), 50-7; R. Erskine, "ULTRA and Some U.S. Navy Carrier Operations," *Cryptologia* 19/1 (1995)

51. Syrett, *Defeat of the German U-boats*, 147-9; Hinsley, *British Intelligence in the Second World War* II, 554-5

52. Douglas, *Creation of a National Air Force*, 537-8, 551, 560-1; memo, DDSD(Y) to DSD, NSS 1008-75-19; 17 May 1943, LAC, RG 24, 3806, memo Sec NB to NSHQ and the Commands, "Naval Staff Branch Re-Organization," 1 June 1943, and undated unsigned minute which reads "Effective Monday June 14/1943 (See 121450Z) (from CNS)," LAC, RG 24, 3807, NSS 1008-75-29. D.A.Clarke, Director of Naval Shipbuilding to DG staff meeting 21 Apr 1943. LAC, RG 28A, 56, 1-1-102; D.B. Carswell, Controller of Ship Repairs to C.D. Howe, MMS, 8 May 1943, Howe Papers, LAC, MG 27III, 51, S-14-(2)—hereafter Howe Papers

The Hedgehog attacks. The pattern of dots in the air is similar to the pattern formed when the projectiles hit the water. (LAC PA 204584)

The officers who formed and advised the Naval Staff were not so blind to these unpleasant truths as some of their critics, then or later, have implied. NSHQ, over the winter months, had formulated some solutions. By the nature of things however these would take months to implement, and in the early summer of 1943 time was a luxury that no one could afford. Long-suffering escort captains and the men they commanded found ways of letting their discontent be known at the highest level. Ultimately their complaints led to a crisis of confidence in the navy's leadership. They reached NSHQ just as the Naval Staff was trying to deal with the criticisms of the Allied Anti-Submarine Survey Board, a powerful investigative committee of senior British and American officers.

The Naval Staff's preferred method of upgrading the fleet's equipment was to procure more modern and capable warships. Efforts to expand Canada's capacity to produce these vessels were successful, but efforts to secure delivery in time to meet the fleet's immediate needs were not. A program for sixty-four additional frigates was approved by the government in late 1942, based on the belief held by the Department of Munitions and Supply that more effective management would be enough to overcome bottlenecks in the shipbuilding program. As subsequent events would prove, however, that view was too optimistic. Morton and G.T. Davie of Québec, the two least experienced yards allocated to the frigate program, made slow progress during 1942. That fall the Department of Munitions and Supply arranged for the Anglo-Canadian Paper Company to establish a specialized outfitting yard at Québec City. This yard was to take over a portion of the newly launched hulls from the original two builders for completion, which had proved to be the most difficult and delay-prone part of construction. Moreover, because of the success of the merchant shipbuilding program, Munitions and Supply was able to designate a large and experienced yard, Davie Shipbuilding at Québec City, for the frigate program once its run of merchant vessels was completed in early 1943.[53]

Munitions and Supply was able to place contracts for all sixty-four frigates by February 1943. Unfortunately, the unusually harsh winter of 1942–1943 in eastern Canada slowed work at the St Lawrence yards. That was not all. NSHQ and the British Admiralty Technical Mission (BATM) were faced with an enormous challenge in modifying the Admiralty's diverse drawings so that they could be integrated with North American industrial practices. In addition, at Morton's and G.T. Davie inexperienced management and labour unrest resulted in strikes that ultimately, in June 1943, compelled Munitions and Supply to take over these firms and combine them with the Anglo-Canadian Paper outfitting facility to create a new Crown corporation, Québec Shipyards. This meant that the five frigates built at Vickers, the largest and most capable yard, were the only ones completed before the summer of that year. These particular warships were not destined for the RCN, however, but were part of the group of ships ordered by BATM in early 1942 and paid for by the United States under lend-lease (the Admiralty eventually transferred two of the vessels to the USN, which commissioned them as USS *Asheville* and *Natchez*).[54]

53. Tucker, *Naval Service of Canada* II, 74-6

54. NHS, "1943-4 Shipbuilding Program River and Loch Class Frigates," nd, DHH, NHS 8200 "Construction of Ships 1939-45," pt 2; J. de N. Kennedy, *The History of the Department of Munitions and Supply Canada in the Second World War* I: *Production Branches and Crown Companies* (Ottawa 1950), 404-6. For a detailed examination of the related problems of drawings and the shortage of expert labour and management, see Milne, Technical Adviser to DG Shipbuilding Branch, "Notes Regarding a Central Engineering Office for the Construction of T.S. Corvettes," 17 Dec 1942; Gilmore, Canadian Vickers, to DG Shipbuilding Branch, 13 Feb 1943, with minute by Milne, 1 Nov 1948, saying that "effort at a centralization was a dismal failure," LAC, W.H. Milne Papers, MG 30 B121(1), file 1-27; Milne to Clarke, DG Shipbuilding Branch, 26 Apr 1943, ibid, file 1-3; DMS, "Fourth Year's Operations," 1 Apr-30 June 1943, 68, Canadian War Museum

The River class destroyer HMCS *Gatineau* in dry dock at Bay Bulls, Newfoundland a month or so after contributing to the sinking of *U 744* while escorting convoy HX 280. (LAC E003525095)

The situation concerning delivery of improved corvettes was similar. In 1942 the RCN ordered thirty-eight corvettes and BATM ordered fifty-one (under US lend-lease), from Great Lakes yards that could not build frigates because they were too large to pass through the canals that gave access to the sea and from coastal yards whose slips were too small for frigates. Known as "increased endurance" or "modified" corvettes, these ships were a considerable advance over even the long-forecastle "revised" corvettes ordered in 1941. Larger fuel bunkers gave a range of some 7,400 nautical miles at ten knots, double that of the earlier corvettes. The sheer and flare of the bows were still more pronounced than those of the revised corvettes and made the vessels drier. The bridge was a full deck higher than in earlier corvettes, being larger and built to full naval standards, while the 4-inch gun mount was also higher, enabling a clear field of fire over the spray in heavy seas. All ten of the new corvettes completed before the summer of 1943 were among the group ordered by BATM.[55]

The Admiralty refused the RCN's offer to take over four of these ships, but suggested more far-reaching cooperation. The Royal Navy was short of minesweepers, so why not organize a larger program whereby Algerine minesweepers under construction for the RCN in Canada be exchanged for corvettes under construction in Britain? This would be a rationalization of effort among the Allied nations much desired in principle but hard to arrange in practical terms.[56] In fact, however ,the first ten Algerines under construction for the RCN were being fitted out as escorts, not minesweepers, and work was too far advanced to switch to the minesweeping configuration.[57] This decision was partly the result of difficulties in obtaining minesweeping equipment in the United States, upon which Canada depended for the supply of key components, and partly the result of Canada's pressing need for escorts. The flat-bottomed Algerines were, like the Bangors, suitable for escort work in coastal waters, and the RCN now urgently required coastal escorts larger than the Bangors to replace the worn-out Town class destroyers that the RN had allocated to the RCN's Western Escort Force.[58] The RCN was willing to make a swap arrangement for sixteen other Algerines that were in the earlier stages of construction, but it wanted the Admiralty to assume responsibility for obtaining timely delivery of the necessary minesweeping gear. The RCN also sought assurance that Britain would deliver sixteen corvettes as quickly as the Algerines were completed so that the arrangement did not result in further delays in the provision of more modern ships to the Canadian fleet.[59] These terms caused no major difficulty—Cabinet War Committee

---

55. DMS, "Third Year's Operations" 1 Jan-31 Mar 1943, 78, "Fourth Year's Operations," 68, ibid; P. Elliott, *Allied Escort Ships of World War II: A Complete Survey* (London 1977), 339-42; K. Macpherson and M. Milner, *Corvettes of the Royal Canadian Navy 1939-1945* (St Catharines 1993), 73-4

56. Adm to NSHQ 1959A/10 Mar 1943, discussed at NS mtg 11 Mar 1943; NB min, 22 and 29 Mar 1943. For a general discussion of this question up to 1943 see Milner, *U-boat Hunters*, 269-79

57. At 950 to 990 tons, 212' 6" in length, and with a breadth of 35' 6," the Algerines were about the size of the original Flower class corvette. See Elliot, *Allied Escort Ships*, 307-16

58. Indeed, Stephens recommended that two ships building at Port Arthur, Ontario for the RN should be completed as escorts, not minesweepers, and taken into Canadian service, because the RCN had already made most of the manning and operational arrangements; CNEC to VCNS and CNS, 13 Apr 1943. LAC, RG 24 (Acc83-84/167), 3611, 8020-4 (1)

59. Because the Algerines were substantially more expensive than the corvettes that the RN was likely to replace them with, BATM would assume control over completion of the Algerines in Canada; payment for the sixteen corvettes completing in the UK, like that for the Tribal class destroyers, would go directly from the Canadian government to the Admiralty. MND for Naval Services to CWC, CWC min, 2 Apr 1943, DHH; Adm msg 032312, Apr 1943, ibid; NB min, 12 Apr 1943; CWC min, 20 Apr 1943, DHH

approved the exchange of ships on 20 April 1943—although much work had to be done to make the detailed arrangements. Canada was to receive four improved Flower class vessels completing in November 1943, and twelve new "lengthened" type corvettes (eventually known as the Castle class) in ensuing months. This is in fact what happened, and the delivery dates of the British-built corvettes fairly well matched the deliveries of the Canadian-built Algerines.[60] Since the Castles would have the newest ahead throwing antisubmarine mortar, Squid, which would probably be subject to teething troubles, the Admiralty asked that these ships be allocated only to those RCN groups based in the Western Approaches. The Canadians, who had scant knowledge of the new weapons system, had no objection to this condition.[61]

Helpful as the Admiralty's initiative was for the long term, it did not meet immediate needs for more modern ships. The RCN was still overwhelmingly dependent upon the seventy-four corvettes remaining, after war losses, from the building programs of 1939–1941. Although thirty-four of these ships had been fitted with type 271 radar by the end of 1942, they were otherwise still mostly unimproved, and the technological gap between these vessels and their sisters in the Royal Navy had widened.[62] Only seventeen of the vessels[63] had extended forecastles, and as late as June 1942 the Naval Staff was unwilling to consider reconstruction of the remainder because of the demands that would place on shipyards already overcommitted with new building and repair work. Only one month later that view changed when a delegation from the Admiralty's antisubmarine section visited Ottawa and underscored the importance of the new Hedgehog armament, which was being fitted in all major RN antisubmarine warships.[64]

Hedgehog—the name came from its bristling appearance—fired twenty-four 63-pound projectiles that landed in a 120-foot-wide circular pattern 200 yards in front of the ship from which they were fired. The advantage of Hedgehog over depth charges was that the attacking vessel did not have to pass over the submarine's estimated position and lose asdic contact with the target in the critical last minute or more of approach—it was in that very minute that experienced submariners changed course rapidly. The Hedgehog bombs, moreover, were contact-fused, so there was no explosion unless they found the target; the disturbance of the water by depth-charge detonations, in contrast, prolonged the period in which asdic was deaf, making the reacquisition of contact an even greater challenge. There was no need with Hedgehog for the ship to run towards the target at speed, as was necessary with depth charges to minimize the period of lost contact and prevent damage to the hull of the ship by the depth charge detonations. Hedgehog-fitted escorts could attack deliberately, constantly tracking the target with asdic. In theory Hedgehog had a 20 percent

60. Elliott, *Allied Escort Ships*, 311-12; Macpherson and Burgess, *Ships of Canada's Naval Forces*, 215

61. NS min, 22 Apr 1943 and 31 May 1943, DHH

62. Zimmerman, *The Great Naval Battle of Ottawa*, 84

63. The ten "revised" corvettes of the 1940-41 program, the two that had been reconstructed in UK yards in early 1942, and five of the ten corvettes Canada had built for the Admiralty in 1940 and then manned on behalf of the RN; the Admiralty had arranged to have these modified in US yards during the winter of 1941-2. Macpherson and Milner, *Corvettes of the Royal Canadian Navy*, 52; see also Chapter 5 in Part 1 of this volume.

64. The present account is based primarily on NHS, "Modernization of Armament and Equipment," nd, DHH, 81/520/8060, "Alterations and Additions," and Hennessy, 'The Expansion, Modernization and Maintenance of the RCN's Principal ASW Forces–1943," DHH, 2000/5, esp 16-26; see also the accounts in Milner, *North Atlantic Run*, 123-4, 153, 216-17; Milner, *U-boat Hunters*, 269-79; Macpherson and Milner, *Corvettes of the Royal Canadian Navy*, 52-61; Zimmerman, *Great Naval Battle of Ottawa*, 86-92

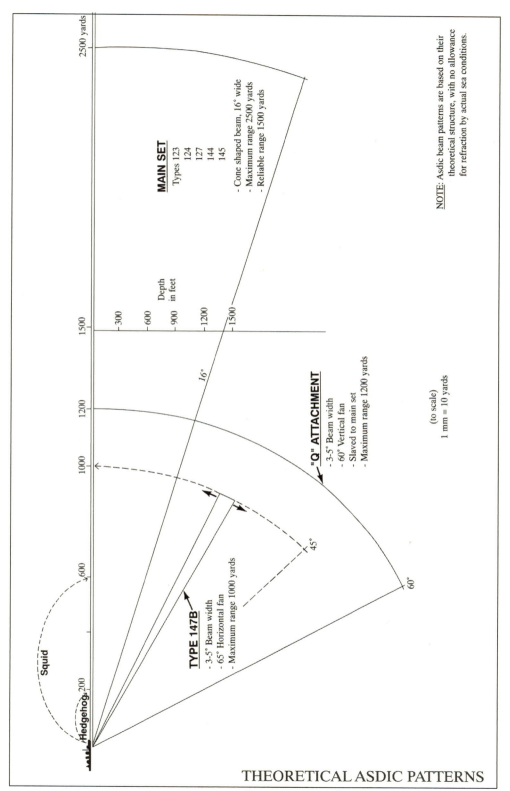

THEORETICAL ASDIC PATTERNS

Source: Marc Milner, *The U-Boat Hunters*, (Toronto 1994)

chance of destroying the submarine, as compared with 10 percent for depth charges; in practice neither weapon system achieved those success rates, although as crews gained experience with Hedgehog during 1943, it did prove to be about twice as effective as depth charges.[65]

The task of fitting Hedgehog was a much greater one for the RCN than for the RN. The large Hedgehog mounting could not be accommodated on the short foredeck of the unimproved Canadian vessels, whereas the British had rebuilt most of their fleet to the "revised" long-forecastle configuration. Fully effective fire control for Hedgehog depended upon new models of asdic that automatically plotted the target. These types of asdic however could only be installed in ships with a gyroscopic compass, which while standard gear in British corvettes still had not replaced the old magnetic compasses in Canadian corvettes. Nor was that all. Since Hedgehog operated on a low-voltage electrical system, its installation also required the time-consuming and difficult task of rewiring the ship. The fitting of Hedgehog in RCN corvettes was thus an enormous undertaking, and this was something that Commander A.R. Pressey, head of the antisubmarine directorate at NSHQ, certainly understood. As he explained in July 1942, unless ships were withdrawn from operations for that specific purpose, the work would have to be done during normal refits, which meant it would take some two years to complete the modernization of Canada's corvette fleet. This estimate, however, only took into account the schedules for the delivery and installation of equipment, and not the structural work required.[66] The true significance of that timetable, which advanced the completion date for the RCN's modernization to July 1944, did not become fully apparent for another sixteen months—at which time Angus L. Macdonald would be charging CNS Nelles and his staff with incompetence for their failure to modernize the fleet (see Chapter 14). Ironically, Vice-Admiral Nelles's successor, George C. Jones, claimed in May 1944 that the RCN's corvette modernization crisis had passed; the minister did not seem to appreciate that the Naval Staff's efforts over the previous year had allowed them to beat their original prediction by some two months.

When the Naval Staff first looked at the modernization issue in 1942, they proceeded cautiously, because such far reaching changes to existing ships posed challenges nearly as great as the construction of entirely new vessels. Moreover, those challenges were precisely the ones that had already caused the greatest difficulty and delay in the Canadian warship program. So it was to prove once again. The original plan of July 1942 was to modernize one corvette as a prototype to define the costs and requirements of the project. HMCS *Edmundston*, the ship ultimately selected for the prototype conversion, did not enter refit at Halifax until 5 January 1943. As Director of the

---

65. Directorate of Operational Research (DOR), "A Resumé of Recent Comparisons of Shipborne A/S Weapons," 5 Feb 1944, DHH, 81/520/1000-973 pt 4. For the development of Hedgehog, see G. Pawle, *The Secret War* (London 1959), ch 11; see also W. Hackmann, *Seek and Strike: Sonar, Anti-submarine Warfare and the Royal Navy, 1914-54* (London 1984), 306-8. Dr Charles Goodeve, an expatriate Canadian scientist who had transferred from the RCNVR to the RNVR before the war, had in 1940 married the skills and resources of a disparate group of British scientists in the so-called Department of Miscellaneous Weapons Development to adapt the army's spigot mortar, "simple in construction, seaworthy and with a dynamically stable shaped charge," itself an adaptation of the German *Granatenwerfer* of 1916, for naval purposes. The prototype was at sea by September 1941, a quite remarkable achievement. PRO Churchill Archive, Goodeve Papers, 3/1; Roskill Papers, 4/14

66. NS min, 15 July 1942. For the information that reached NSHQ early in 1942 concerning Hedgehog and fitting policy in the RN see Bain, Adm, Bath, circular to Mssrs Alexander Hall and Co. Ltd et al; 7 Feb 1942; Director of Anti–Submarine, "Hedgehogs," 15 Apr 1942, LAC, RG 24 (Acc. 83-4/167), 2064, NSS 5301-84 pt 1; see also C.J. Mackenzie Diary, 2 July 1942, LAC, MG 30 B122, C.J. Mackenzie Papers, vol 1, file 1-10

Operations Division at NSHQ, Captain H.N. Lay reacted to the news of slow progress with alarm, which was no surprise coming from a man who was initially bitter at Allied criticisms of the short-comings of the Canadian escort fleet. Yet Lay's rancour would eventually give way to a dawning realization that much more needed to be done. Rapid, subtle, but nevertheless profound developments in the Atlantic war had now made the quality of escorts as important as their numbers, and, as we have seen, the question of refits for the existing fleet was one that deeply worried Lay, even as the Allies agreed to the creation of the Canadian command.[67] Other members of the Naval Board and Staff had come to the same conclusion.

On 15 February the Naval Staff supported Lay in his view that "the proposed conversion of Single Screw Corvettes was a most important and necessary improvement and, even if it means laying up several Corvettes at one time, it should be proceeded with at the earliest opportunity."[68] At that time, seventeen of the Canadian corvettes were serving under Western Approaches command in support of Operation Torch, and the Naval Staff despatched an urgent signal to the Admiralty asking if these ships could be converted in British shipyards. The Admiralty responded that because of the crush of work at those yards, it could only agree to convert six, and those one at a time. The Admiralty also agreed to have the eight surviving corvettes from the ten that had been built for Britain in Canada in 1940 and commissioned in the RCN converted at US shipyards.[69]

This assistance fell far short of the RCN's needs. In effect, the Admiralty threw the problem back onto Canada's overworked repair facilities. The extraordinary demands on the fleet throughout 1942 made it impossible to schedule fourteen of the corvettes for annual refits. Worst yet, pressure on the east coast yards in early 1943 from the hundreds of merchant and naval vessels that had suffered storm damage during that ferocious winter caused refit schedules to slip further. While that alone left the schedule in tatters, it was also discovered that annual refits for warships took far longer than originally estimated, in the case of corvettes an average of ten weeks instead of the planned six-and-a-half.[70]

There was no sign of relief on the horizon. The new ship maintenance facilities that the Department of Munitions and Supply and the RCN had begun to develop at Halifax, Sydney, Saint John, and many outports in 1940–1941 became operational in the spring and summer of 1943, but they could not reach their potential until the following year. In the meantime, demand outstripped available services at an accelerating pace as the large numbers of escorts, especially the Bangors, completed in late 1941 and 1942, became due for full refit, and the Algerines, frigates, and improved corvettes of the new program joined the fleet and increased the burden of demands for the correction of builders' defects and running repairs.

In mid-April 1943 the British government warned Ottawa that the Admiralty and the Ministry of War Transport were "concerned at the increasing evidence that by winter the shortage of repair facilities for warships and merchant vessels on the East Coast of Canada and in Newfoundland will have become acute unless urgent steps are taken now to remedy the deficiencies." Since early 1941

---

67.   NS min, 15 Feb 1943

68.   Ibid

69.   NHS, "Modernization of Armament and Equipment," nd, 16-7, DHH, 81/520/8060, "Alterations and Additions"

70.   Staff officer (refits) to DOD, "Refitting Ships in Maritime Area," 22 Mar 1943, LAC, RG 24, 3996, NSS 1057-1-35 pt 1; "Ship Repair and Salvage Control," report for 1 Jan-31 Mar 1943, DMS, "Third Year of Operations"

the Royal Navy had depended upon Canada to take as much running repair work as possible so as to relieve the pressure on British industry. Now, however, while that pressure remained, the British had become worried that the repair infrastructure on the east coast of Canada was on the verge of collapsing. Accordingly, they wanted to strike a joint committee of Canadian, British, American, and Newfoundland ship repair officials to "examine repair problems for warships and merchant vessels as a whole on the basis that the number of vessels involved will increase considerably."[71] Deputy Minister of National Defence for Naval Services, W.G. Mills, responded to that suggestion, saying that it was "very timely" and that he welcomed the opportunity to discuss Canadian resources with British and American authorities, as well as their advice and assistance in overcoming shortfalls.[72] Rear-Admiral G. L. Stephens, Chief of Naval Engineering and Construction, became chairman of the committee. Its first and only meeting however did not take place until August, largely because of a delayed response from the US State Department, which had to consult the several American agencies concerned with ship repair.[73]

Mills and Stephens responded so positively to the British suggestion because they were already immersed in the emerging ship refit and repair crisis. According to many staff officers, this crisis was one of the toughest challenges that the Royal Canadian Navy faced during the entire course of the Second World War, the more so because the refit problem was largely responsible for the fleet's technical backwardness. Put simply, the installation of modern equipment was a function of the repair yards, but those facilities were much too small to handle even a portion of the RCN's needs. As a result, even if the navy had managed to procure all the required equipment from the British, the Naval Staff knew that it could not be fitted in the RCN's ships unless Canadian industry came to the rescue. As the Allied Anti-Submarine Survey Board soon observed, the problem was that the refit and repair yards were already overwhelmed and themselves in need of rescue. In February 1943 Stephens had raised the navy's difficulties with D.B. Carswell, the Controller of Ship Repairs and Salvage at Munitions and Supply. Carswell controlled most of the available repair facilities and was in a position to negotiate directly with the branches of DMS that administered the building yards.[74] However, such a considerable adjustment of priorities and tasks among the many—often incompletely developed—yards in eastern Canada, and the procurement and delivery of the specialized materials required for the modernization of the corvettes, would take time.[75]

In particular, the shortage of qualified manpower on the east coast posed huge challenges. Long-standing difficulties in attracting suitable workers to the region, not to say retaining them in the face of better prospects in the central provinces, had been exacerbated by the tightening manpower supply throughout Canada as a result of the expansion of the armed forces and because of the war economy. Increased competition for labour within the region and among yards, moreover,

---

71. BHC to USSEA, 12 Apr 1943, LAC, RG 25, 3198, 5206-40c

72. DM, DND (NS) to USSEA, 19 Apr 1943, ibid

73. Canadian minister in the US to SSEA, tg WA-3319, 7 July 1943, ibid

74. Minutes of First Meeting of Naval and Merchant Ship Maintenance Committee on Man Power, held in the Nova Scotian Hotel, Halifax, NS, 29 April1943, LAC, RG 24, 3997, NSS 1057-1-39 pt 1

75. "Ship Repair and Salvage Control," report for 1 Apr-30 Jun 1943, DMS, "Fourth Year of Operations"; CNEC to A/CNS, 9 June 1943, LAC, RG 24, 3997, NSS 1057-1-39 pt 1

had destabilized the workforce that was available. Workers who gained experience with one firm were soon able to win more senior positions with another.[76]

In order to pull together such diverse, competing interests, Carswell, at Mills's urging, established the Naval and Merchant Ship Maintenance Committee on Man Power. Carswell himself took the chair, and there were representatives from the navy, civilian shipyards, and the British Ministry of War Transport's organization in Canada. The committee had its inaugural meeting at Halifax on 29 April 1943.[77] Immediately thereafter it started to work together with the National Selective Service branch of the Department of Labour, Canada's central agency for the regulation of manpower, to ensure that shipyard workers were not called up for compulsory military service, as well as to prohibit those workers from leaving their positions.[78] But these measures were sufficient only to help stabilize the workforce.

The east coast yards needed large numbers of additional personnel. According to a survey by the committee more than 4,800 skilled civilian workers would be needed for the year ending 31 May 1944. This requirement faced two large obstacles at the level of national policy. Fully two-thirds of the additional workers were needed by the naval dockyard and civilian firms in the Halifax-Dartmouth area, which was in the depths of a housing crisis.[79] The government, which had already built nearly 1500 houses for war workers in the twin cities, was extremely reluctant to build more. A detailed survey was undertaken to determine how many "non-essential" workers and their dependents were resident in the cities and whether encouraging them to relocate might resolve the crisis. This, however, promised no early resolution of the problem.[80] At this same time, during the spring and summer of 1943, the Cabinet came to the conclusion that in terms of manpower the war effort had reached the limits of expansion possible without the imposition of controls and compulsion that, for philosophical and political reasons, it was unwilling to consider.[81] New demands, like those for ship repair yards on the east coast, could only be met by reassigning workers made available by corresponding reductions in other programs, and it would be some months before such decisions could be made and implemented.[82]

The early results of efforts to expedite corvette modernization, like the efforts to hasten the production of frigates, were not unimpressive. In terms of operational requirements however, they were glacially slow. By mid June 1943 five ships had been modernized: three in US yards, one in the United Kingdom, and one in Canada, HMCS *Edmundston*, the prototype project for Canadian production. Work was in progress on another eleven ships in Canadian yards, on five in US yards, and on one in a British yard. Worryingly, however, considering that the bulk of the program

---

76. DM, DND (NS) to controller of Ship Repairs and Salvage, 31 Mar 1943 ibid; general manager, Halifax Shipyards to controller of Ship Repairs and Salvage, 13 May 1943, LAC, RG 28, 150, 3-N-5; Minutes of Third Meeting … on Man Power, 16 June 1943, LAC, RG 28, 257, 196-13-8

77. Minutes of First Meeting … Committee on Man Power

78. Minutes of Second Meeting … Committee on Man Power, 1 June 1943, LAC, RG 24, 3997, NSS 1057-1-39 pt 1

79. "Survey of Man Power Requirements for Canadian Ship Repair Industry Total Additional Requirements to May 31st, 1944," LAC, RG 28, 150, 3-N-5

80. J. White, "Conscripted City: Halifax and the Second World War,"doctoral dissertation, McMaster University 1994, 109-14

81. Stacey, *Arms, Men and Governments*, 408-10; M.D. Stevenson, *Canada's Greatest Wartime Muddle: National Selective Service and the Mobilization of Human Resources during World War II* (Montreal 2001), 28-33

82. DM [Department of Labour] to DM, DMS, 7 Sep 1943, LAC, RG 28, 257, 196-13-8

depended upon Canadian yards, the work on *Edmundston* had taken a full six months—double the time required in British and American yards.[83]

The Allied scrutiny that had spurred on the RCN's efforts to accelerate modernization of the escort fleet and to unify Canada's naval and maritime air commands grew in intensity during the spring of 1943. Part 1 of this history explained how in January and February 1943 reform of the Canadian organization had been inspired by probing questions from the subcommittee of the UK-US Combined Chiefs of Staff in Washington that had been struck to investigate methods of more effectively coordinating the antisubmarine war. The combined planners' 170-page report in turn set the agenda for the Training and Material Readiness of Operational Escort Groups subcommittee of the Atlantic Convoy Conference early that March. This group was chaired by Rear-Admiral J.L. Kauffman, USN, whose commands had included the US naval base in Iceland and, most recently, the American Gulf Sea Frontier. The senior British member was the newly promoted Rear-Admiral J.M. Mansfield, who in December 1942 and January 1943 had brought word to Washington and Ottawa of the need to adopt Western Approaches' successful methods. Captain W.B. Creery, then Chief of Staff to Admiral Murray in Halifax, was the senior RCN representative.

Unsurprisingly, especially since Kauffman and Mansfield had participated in the work of the Combined Staff investigation, the Training and Material Readiness subcommittee of the convoy conference strongly endorsed the conclusions of the planners' report. The crews of newly commissioned ships had to receive rigorous collective training, "the group system of operating ASW [antisubmarine warfare] forces" must be "universally adopted and the integrity of groups maintained;" furthermore, it was proposed that all groups must receive regular refresher training, and that air and sea forces must be much more closely integrated in both training and operations. Essentially these were the standards that British forces had developed and that experienced US operational commanders had fully accepted as they struggled with the compartmentalized organization of their service, which, it must be recalled, was in no way prepared for large-scale antisubmarine warfare when the United States had become a belligerent scarcely fifteen months earlier.[84]

On 8 March 1943, before the end of the Atlantic Convoy Conference, Commander-in-Chief of the USN (COMINCH) Admiral E.J. King approved the establishment of the Allied Anti-Submarine Survey Board (AASSB) that he and Admiral of the Fleet Sir Dudley Pound had agreed on at a summit in Casablanca that had met in January 1943. The AASSB's senior members were Kauffmann and Mansfield, together with two maritime aviators, Commander J.P.W. Vest, USN, and Group Captain P.F. Canning, RAF. Canning had played a prominent part in bringing Coastal Command's

---

83.   Note that the figures for the ships completed and undergoing conversion vary from account to account. The present figures are derived from C-in-C WA to Asst Controller, Adm, Bath, 9 July 1943, enclosing list dated 12 June 1943, LAC, RG 24 (Acc 83/84-167), 3727, NSS 8060-331 pt 1, together with additional information from Macpherson and Burgess, *Ships of Canada's Naval Forces*, 68-95. See also, "Ship Repair and Salvage Control," report for 1 Apr-30 Jun 1943, DMS, "Fourth Year of Operations"

84.   Atlantic Convoy Conference min, ACC 4: Training and Material Readiness of Operational Escort Groups, 4 Mar 1943, and app A to ACC 4, 3 Mar 1943, DHH, 181.009 (D268); see also "History of the Joint Chiefs of Staff: The War against Germany," ch VI: "The Battle of the Atlantic (to April 30, 1943)," by Lt Abbot Smith, USNR, 3 June 1948, 114-20, NARA, RG 218, box 6

methods to the Canadian and US air forces during missions to North America in 1942 and Vest had participated in the Combined Staff's investigation.

In April 1943, while the board toured American and British establishments, King rushed ahead with a sweeping reorganization of his headquarters in Washington that resulted in the creation of the Tenth Fleet. This famous "fleet without ships" brought together the operations, trade, intelligence, and research elements of the COMINCH headquarters and Navy Department that were directly involved with antisubmarine warfare. King retained command himself, but in practice delegated all authority to his Assistant Chief of Staff, Rear-Admiral Francis S. Low. The new organization mirrored the centralized model of the British Admiralty that had been successful in the Battle of the Atlantic. Moreover, it was in no small part a response to ongoing criticism from the army and political leaders about heavy shipping losses and the USN's failure to learn more from British experience. In this respect the reorganization served its purpose by bringing the US Army to accept the Tenth Fleet's direction of the army's antisubmarine aviation. Naval control of army resources was a short-lived arrangement, however. Disputes about doctrine made the army abandon maritime aviation; aircraft production was reallocated to allow the USN to take over land-based maritime air operations, a changeover that was completed in the fall of 1943. This was a rather different path from the integrated US antisubmarine organization that had been envisioned in the spring. Nevertheless the scale and speed of the changes in the wake of Admiral King's long-standing resistance and scepticism confirm the intensity of the pressure for reform of command arrangements brought to bear by Allied political leaders—and by renewed German success in the early months of 1943.[85]

In the case of Canada, it was the Allied Anti-Submarine Survey Board that applied pressure for reform. The AASSB's agenda was the product both of concerns raised by King and Pound and the criticisms that Kauffmann and his colleagues had received in their tour of British and American headquarters about the Canadians' performance. The timing of the board's visit to Ottawa, Halifax, St John's, and Gander from 7 to 15 May was significant. Just the week before the visit the RCN had assumed control in the northwest Atlantic, and the RCN's mid-ocean groups had formally passed from American to British operational control.[86] Admiral Nelles asked for "full and frank criticism of existing conditions" and the AASSB did not disappoint. The Allied officers were favourably impressed by the ship training organizations under the Captains (D) at St John's and Halifax, and mainly they urged completion of improvements to the facilities that were already in hand. This can be seen as a tribute to the RCN's training system and in particular, to the efforts of Captain J.D. Prentice and Commander J.C. Hibbard. But in the matters of command organization and ship maintenance the board was scathing. Although the Canadian staff understood the shortcomings in these areas, the AASSB left no doubt that much more needed to be done.

On becoming Vice-Chief of the Naval Staff in the fall of 1942, Rear-Admiral G.C. Jones had taken charge of a far reaching reorganization of the mushrooming headquarters in Ottawa. The princi-

---

85. S.E. Morison, *The Atlantic Battle Won May: 1943-May 1945 (History of United States Naval Operations in World War II,* X) (Boston 1956), 21-31; on the political pressure on King, see Atlantic Fleet typescript history, pts 3-4, 484-90

86. The timing of the AASSB visit to Canada was also indicative of Canada's standing as the junior partner in the North Atlantic alliance. Mansfield told the First Sea Lord that he was concerned that the US might react poorly to British criticisms of their ASW organization and fail to cooperate with the Board. As a result the two agreed that the AASSB should visit Canada first so that the Americans could weigh the criticisms made of them against those raised previously about the RCN. See Mansfield to Pound, nd, PRO, ADM 1/13756.

Captain J.D. Prentice, who made such an important contribution to the training of the RCN and who later commanded EG 11 in European waters. (LAC PA 206681)

Rear-Admiral G.C. Jones, Vice-Chief of the Naval Staff. He later succeeded Vice-Admiral P.W. Nelles as Chief of the Naval Staff. (LAC PA 204268)

pal objective was to relieve senior officers of burgeoning administrative detail so they could more effectively shape the broad development of the RCN. In this respect, the essence of the scheme as it took form in the first months of 1943 was to create a new senior position, Assistant Chief of the Naval Staff, to whom the core Operations, Plans, Signals, Intelligence, and Trade divisions would report. The existing VCNS position, while continuing to deputize for the CNS, would focus on coordination of the Personnel, Equipment and Supply, and Engineering and Construction branches—the logistical and administrative side of the service. Furthermore, while struggling with the challenges of making NSHQ an effective instrument for directing Canada's part in the Battle of the Atlantic, Lay was insistent that there was one additional requirement for a powerful antisubmarine warfare group: there was already an antisubmarine section that Lay himself had recently organized in his own Operations Division at NSHQ, as well as Commander A.R. Pressey's antisubmarine directorate in the Equipment and Supply Division and the Foreign Intelligence Section, under Captain DeMarbois. There was however as yet no organizational link between them. The Allied Anti-Submarine Survey Board seized on this organizational flaw.

> The fact that the Canadian Navy today is primarily employed operationally in Antisubmarine Warfare makes it desirable that the Antisubmarine Warfare Division [which still did not exist] should be the main Operational Division of the Naval Staff, under an A.C.N.S., whose relation to A.O.C., Eastern Air Command should be similar to that between the Admiralty and C-in-C Coastal Command. This ACNS should also be responsible for the co-ordination of all sea and shore training but should otherwise be kept free from all administrative duties. The establishment of an operational research section is also very desirable.[87]

The AASSB was equally unhappy with the state of affairs in Halifax. Rear-Admiral Murray had not yet moved from the naval dockyard, at the north end of the city, to Eastern Air Command headquarters, in the south end, to establish an area combined headquarters (ACHQ) as had been agreed at the Atlantic Convoy Conference. "It is considered that this could and should be achieved in about a fortnight. The Board feel most strongly that full operational efficiency cannot be realized until this is done." By contrast, the AASSB found that the organization at St John's, where the naval and air commanders had been working together in a combined headquarters since 1941, "should prove eminently suitable with minor alterations," but warned that the number of personnel at both Halifax and St John's combined headquarters had to be considerably increased to maintain the operations plot at the high standard required for effective coordination of air and sea operations.

The AASSB was most critical of the poor state of RCN ships as a result of inadequate support from bases in Canada for either modernization of equipment or routine refit. This was at the root of the Canadian fleet's problems. "It is emphasized," the board concluded, "that there can be no question but that escort vessels must be maintained in an efficient condition as the number of these vessels available is very limited. Failing this ships cannot be formed into well trained groups nor can convoys be efficiently protected." Admiral Sir Max Horton of the Royal Navy had personally highlighted the problems with maintenance of the Canadian ships when the AASSB visited Western Approaches Command in April. At both Halifax and St John's Canadian officers had freely

---

87. For this and following paragraphs, Kauffman and Mansfield, AASSB to CNS, Ottawa, "Report on Antisubmarine Warfare, North Western Atlantic Area," 18 May 1943, LAC, RG 24, 8080, NSS 1271-15

unburdened themselves to the board about the overcrowded and inadequately staffed facilities, as well as the frustrations of having to work through the Department of Munitions and Supply.[88] Stephens and Mills, of course, had been working on these matters with DMS for nearly three months, but the committee on manpower in the shipyards which had been established to expedite action on the myriad issues identified by the RCN and DMS had met for the first time hardly a week before the AASSB arrived in Canada. All this was explained to the survey board by Stephens's deputy, as was the progress in organizing the corvette modernization program. Like the subsequent private meeting between Stephens and Mansfield, however the explanation had little impact.[89]

The complexities of merchant ship construction and repair, let alone the organization of Canada's war economy, did not form part of the AASSB's mandate. Board members were impressed most by the bitter complaints they heard from officers responsible for operations.[90] The AASSB, as Mansfield privately informed the First Sea Lord, was "undoubtedly shocked with conditions as they found them on visiting Canada."[91] As a result, the AASSB's report on the maintenance of escorts prioritized the hard decisions that had to be made. Although it failed to acknowledge that Stephens, Mills, and Carswell were already trying to implement those priorities, the report nonetheless confirmed that the Naval Staff was correct to place so much emphasis on rectifying the refit and repair crisis.[92] Nelles had asked the board to be blunt and it had clearly complied: the AASSB's final recommendations made for bleak reading.

The members of the AASSB were not the only people willing to voice sincere opinions about the efficiency of the Canadian fleet. On 1 June 1943, two weeks after the board's visit to Canada, Acting Lieutenant-Commander D.W. Piers, of HMCS *Restigouche*, submitted a seventeen page report entitled "Comments on the Operation and Performance of HMC Ships, Establishments and Personnel in the Battle of the Atlantic" to Captain (D) Newfoundland. Having commanded *Restigouche* since June 1941, Piers was finally appointed to a shore posting. As one of the foremost Canadian veterans of the Atlantic war, immediately upon completing his last ocean crossing, Piers wrote a report in which he passed on the lessons he had learned, stating explicitly that he was speaking not only for himself, as a career member of the permanent force, but also for "experienced Reserve Officers who now command the vast majority of HMC Ships and who are diffident about forwarding their opinions to NSHQ."[93] To his credit, Piers was also speaking for the lower

---

88. AASSB mtg at Liverpool, 11th April 1943, PRO, ADM 1/13756

89. AASSB mtg at Ottawa, 8 May 1943 in Ottawa on "Repair, Maintenance, Material and Equipment," ibid

90. See esp. minutes of AASSB at Halifax, 11 May 1943 on "maintenance and repair," and AASSB mtg at St. John's, Newfoundland, 12 May 1943," [Mansfield] to First Sea Lord, nd, ibid

91. Mansfield, "Extract from Report on A/S Warfare given to First Sea Lord," nd, ibid

92. This may explain an evident lapse in communication between Stephens and Mansfield during their private meeting. Mansfield showed a draft of the report to Stephens who, according to Mansfield, "expressed himself as wholeheartedly in agreement with every word of it." Mansfield to First Sea Lord, nd, ibid. Stephens may well have said this about the analysis in the report, as it was substantially Stephens's own; however, Stephens certainly did not agree with the call for hard and fast decisions. He was at pains to explain to his colleagues that DMS was already cooperating in meeting the navy's needs to the fullest extent practical. See, eg, CNEC to Staff (DOD), 25 May 1943, and CNEC to ACNS, 9 and 12 June 1943, LAC, RG 24, 3997, NSS 1057-1-39 pt 1

93. "Comments on the Operation and Performance of HMC Ships," CO *Restigouche* to Capt (D) Newfoundland, 1 June 1943, ibid, 1057-3-24 pt 1

deck, and he reported complaints from ratings and petty officers about such matters as the lack of recreational facilities at St John's and Londonderry, health concerns resulting from crowded conditions in their ships, and the need for improved life jackets and other safety equipment.

Piers's main points closely echoed the issues that the AASSB had addressed. This was no coincidence. Before coming to Canada, the Kauffman board had visited Western Approaches and its senior officers left no doubt that much still remained to be done to correct the shortcomings of Canadian ships in the Mid-Ocean Escort Force. Piers had previously discussed the problems of the Canadian ships with Admiral Horton and Commodore G.W.G. Simpson, RN, Commodore (D) at Londonderry. These "RN Authorities," Piers reported, shared his view that

> R.C.N. personnel do not get the chance they deserve. Compared to R.N. Ships doing the same job, H.M.C. Ships are almost invariably outdated by 12 to 18 months in the matter of new equipment. Another evil is the constant drafting changes, the end of which is not yet in sight due to our enormous expansion. The formation of permanent Escort Groups is gradually being achieved, but we are already two years late in this most vital requirement. Lastly, the inadequate training and inexperience of Officers and Ratings, and the lack of a sufficient working-up period before becoming operational, have been sad but unavoidable circumstances which no amount of keenness could surmount.[94]

The operational needs of the Mid-Ocean Escort Force, Piers suggested, were not receiving the proper attention at NSHQ. "Since A/S Warfare is the primary function of HMC Ships, it is genuinely felt that this problem should receive the greatest prominence. A glance at the appropriate section of the Canadian Navy List (31st January '43) shows that A/S [is] relegated to section 7 of the Operations Division, on par with Minesweeping and Motor Launches."[95] Similarly the "functions of the Administration of CCCS [Captain Commanding Canadian Ships and Establishments in the United Kingdom] have always been a puzzle to seagoing Commanding Officers ... The RN and USN authorities in Londonderry were no less puzzled as to where their responsibilities ended and those of CCCS began, concerning HMC Ships." At the least, the headquarters had to be "expanded to include the vital necessity of getting allocations of new equipment from the Admiralty for HMC Ships."[96]

The Allied experts and the RCN's own experienced ship commanding officers had essentially joined hands to charge that NSHQ, despite its successful claims for a greatly enhanced role in the Atlantic war, was too far removed from the realities of events at sea to exercise a helpful influence. NSHQ staff were thoroughly familiar with most of the particular issues and in many cases had been seeking solutions for some months. As Captain DeWolf had explained to senior British and American officers in Washington in December 1942, they were also painfully aware that the difficulties in most instances were the result of meagre resources—most notably in qualified personnel—that had been stretched to the breaking point by Allied demands for accelerated expansion of the Canadian effort. Piers had not told the Naval Staff anything they did not already know. Action

---

94.   Ibid, app 1

95.   Ibid

96.   Ibid

was under way to ease both the larger refit crisis as well as the closely related problem of modernization. Based largely on the AASSB's findings, the Naval Staff greatly accelerated a reorganization of NSHQ that had been started in the fall of 1942.

Effective 1 June 1943, Captain W.B. Creery assumed the new position of Assistant Chief of Naval Staff, with a mandate to coordinate the core staff group.[97] Creery had filled senior appointments at Halifax for more than two years, including Chief of Staff to the Commanding Officer Atlantic Coast. Creery had attended the Atlantic Convoy Conference in Washington as Rear-Admiral Murray's representative in March, and in April he had moved to Ottawa to succeed Lay as head of the Operations Directorate at NSHQ. In this capacity he had met with the AASSB during its visit to Ottawa. Thus Creery was well qualified to address the problems of the Atlantic escort fleet. But he was somewhat hamstrung. Creery's terms of reference were broad and laden with administrative duties, as the NSHQ reorganization study had originally recommended. These gave only a nod to the focussed concentration on air and sea antisubmarine warfare that Lay and the AASSB had urged:

> A.C.N.S. is responsible to C.N.S. ... for the unification of all the activities of the "Naval Staff Branch" and is thus responsible for the conduct of antisubmarine warfare.
>
> All matters for consideration by the Naval Staff are referred to A.C.N.S. in the first instance.
>
> He issues all relevant directions and information consequent on the decisions of the Chief of Naval Staff to the appropriate authorities for action...
>
> He maintains close touch with National Defence Headquarters [ie., the Army] and Air Force Headquarters, as may be directed by the C.N.S.[98]

There were nevertheless significant changes within the staff group that promised to provide the ACNS with means to guide and support fleet development and operations. Preparations had been under way since the Atlantic Convoy Conference to build the Foreign Intelligence Section into a full-fledged Operational Intelligence Centre. This change in designation took place in early June 1943, when Captain DeMarbois began to report directly to Creery rather than to the Director Signals Division. At the same time, a new directorate, Warfare and Training, was created within the staff group. Warfare and Training was made responsible for setting standards for the fighting efficiency of HMC warships, monitoring their performance, and providing expert advice on the weapons, tactics, and training required to meet and improve on these standards. These functions, to the extent that they had been systematically addressed at all, had been scattered throughout the Operations Division and the Equipment and Personnel branches. This large enterprise required expertise in analysis, research, and information management. The beginnings of Warfare and Training were modest; the sections of the former Antisubmarine Directorate in NSHQ's Equipment Branch that were not primarily concerned with the production and procurement of equipment were transferred to form the core of the new directorate.

---

97. VCNS to CNS, 27 May 1943, LAC, RG 24 (Acc 83-84/167), 501, 1700-Staff, pt 1

98. Tucker, *Naval Service of Canada* II, 544. See R.H. Caldwell, "Change and Challenge: The Canadian Naval Staff in 1943," 37 n56, DHH, 2000/5. An earlier version of the terms of reference, the one that was distributed, did not include the words "and is therefore responsible for antisubmarine warfare" which strengthens the suggestion that this part of the duties was a last-minute response to the AASSB.

The reorganization at NSHQ was a good step, but the senior staff were aware that it was not enough. More had to be done at the source of the refit crisis, and that was on the east coast. A report submitted by Captain E. Johnstone, RCN, Director of Organization, on 18 June, precisely a month after the AASSB had visited, left no doubt that the Allied officers' message had been received:

> The problem of the present unsatisfactory state of affairs so far as repairs of H.M.C. Ships is concerned, is so urgent and of such vital importance that time does not permit of a full investigation of all the factors contributing to it. It is considered essential that the broad lines on which improvement is to be effected must be established immediately and that steps be taken at once to effect a radical change in the existing conditions.[99]

What precisely that change should be was a difficult question. Operational authorities in Halifax blamed the refit crisis on the Department of Munitions and Supply, complaining that refits took far too long.[100] Beyond that, RCN personnel on the coast also realized that the extraordinary demands of the Battle of the Atlantic had made scheduling a nightmare, the more so once unanticipated new projects such as modernization of the corvettes were thrown into the bargain. Furthermore, the engineering authorities were profoundly aware of the navy's own lack of depth in technical expertise. They found the management of Munitions and Supply reasonable and helpful in the face of technical challenges which the RCN's engineering staff fully appreciated, but officers of the executive branch did not. Thus, Admiral Stephens warned his colleagues at NSHQ against heavy handedness from above that would interfere with progress at the working level.[101]

Johnstone's report accepted Stephens's view and focussed on getting the navy's own house in order. With the great expansion of the Halifax dockyard and of commercial shipyards in the Maritimes to which navy work was contracted, authority had become fragmented. The officers responsible for basic hull work, armament, other equipment, management of civilian personnel in the dockyard, and supervision of contracts in commercial yards reported variously to the C-in-C CNA, or to the Commodore, Halifax, who administered the port on Admiral Murray's behalf, or to NSHQ directly. Johnstone proposed that an Admiral Superintendent, East Coast Repairs, should be appointed at Halifax to command the dockyard and all its departments, and, through dockyard superintendents of the rank of commander or captain, the warship repair facilities under development at other east coast bases as well. In all matters bearing on the operations of the fleet—principally the scheduling of ships for refits and repairs—the Admiral Superintendent would be responsible to the C-in-C CNA; in matters concerning the development and management of the repair facilities, he would report directly to NSHQ.[102]

Murray and, of course, Stephens both supported the creation of the superintendent. The Naval Board, with Minister Macdonald present, gave its approval to this plan. There were, however, some

99. Director of Organization, "Repairs and Refitting, East Coast," 18 June 1943, app A to NB min, 27 July 1943, DHH

100. C-in-C CNA to Sec NB, "Proposed Organization of Atlantic Command," 27 June 1943, para 5, LAC, RG 24, 3997, NSC 1057-1-39 pt 1

101. Mansfield to Noble, nd, and Mansfield to First Sea Lord, nd, PRO, ADM 1/13756. CNEC to Staff (DOD), 25 May 1943; CNEC to ACNS, 9 June 1943; LAC, RG 24, 3997, NSC 1057-1-39 pt 1. NS min, 10 June 1943, DHH

102. Director of Organization, "Repairs and Refitting, East Coast." Much of the detailed analysis in this document echoes Stephens, CNEC to ACNS, 9 June 1943

at NSHQ who wanted to go even further. Captain Creery's staff group believed the refit situation demanded more drastic action. They recommended higher level control through the creation of a powerful Directorate of Dockyards. Creery and his people also wanted a greater degree of high-level interdepartmental cooperation, advising that a ship repair coordinating committee be struck in Ottawa and that it be chaired by no less a personage than Minister of Munitions and Supply C.D. Howe. Given that Howe was one of the more powerful members of the Cabinet, the proposed committee could have gone a long way in rectifying the refit situation. But this idea, like all those proposed by Creery's staff group, was considered "too far reaching" for the time being.[103] Stephens had warned that the RCN's existing engineering establishment was understaffed for want of qualified personnel, and that there was no point in attempting to establish new coordinating bodies.[104] As it happened, the flag-rank superintendent's position at Halifax could only be filled on 15 October 1943, and then at the level of commodore; NSHQ's Chief of Naval Equipment and Supply Captain G.M. Hibbard was promoted for the position.[105]

There were other developments. On 12 August Canadian, British and American officials met in Ottawa to consider ship repair problems. They strongly recommended that the Canadian government address the Halifax housing crisis and channel additional skilled workers to east coast yards.[106] On these fronts there was some action. In September, to save manpower the government cut the program for the construction of additional 10,000-ton merchant ships from eighty-four vessels to forty-two. The Department of Labour informed Munitions and Supply that personnel thus released should logically be transferred to the repair yards, with the warning that it would take some time for this to be arranged.[107] The survey of Halifax housing was finding that there were very few non-essential workers in the city who could be relocated. The RCAF, however, had plans to remove a depot from Halifax, and this promised to open up barracks accommodation for 3000 navy personnel who at the time were occupying civilian housing. The vast majority of foreign officials on the ship-repair committee were extremely impressed with everything NSHQ had done in its attempt to alleviate the repair situation over the summer of 1943 and made a point of saying as much to their Canadian counterparts.[108] The problem of modernizing and refitting the fleet, however, as will be seen in Chapter 15, had become a political issue that would cost the Chief of the Naval Staff his job.

The RCN was able to address more readily the Allied Anti-Submarine Survey Board's criticisms about the inadequate provisions for control of air and sea antisubmarine operations. The transformation in June 1943 of the Foreign Intelligence Section into the Operational Intelligence Centre (OIC), the direct counterpart of those at the Admiralty and in the newly created Tenth Fleet in

103. NB min, 27 July 1943, DHH; ACNS to CNS, 5 July 1943, LAC, RG 24, 3997, NSC 1057-1-39 pt 1

104. CNEC to CNS, 17 July 1943, ibid

105. Tucker, *Naval Service of Canada* II, 143-4

106. Minutes, mtg of Combined Canadian, UK and US Committee to Examine Repair Problem for Warships and Merchant Vessels on the East Coast of Canada and Newfoundland, held in Ottawa 12 Aug 1943, LAC, RG 28, 129, 3-C-21

107. CWC min, 21 and 28 July 1943, 8 Sep 1943; DM [Department of Labour] to DM, DMS, 7 Sep 1943, LAC, RG 28, 257, 196-13-8

108. White, "Conscripted City," 115-18

Washington, provided NSHQ staff with the full and timely information necessary to plan and direct antisubmarine warfare operations. A key element had been completion since the Atlantic Convoy Conference of dedicated, scrambled teleprinter lines that connected NSHQ to the Admiralty and the Tenth Fleet. According to Captain DeMarbois, these new facilities made it possible for the three centres to exchange data on radio direction-finding bearings within ten to twenty minutes of an enemy transmission. The lines also provided the secure means by which the centres in London and Washington could instantly share with Ottawa Ultra intelligence derived from the decryption of enemy signals.[109]

Captain G.A. Worth, Director of the Signals Division, had travelled to the United Kingdom in April 1943, and he modelled the Canadian system on that of the Admiralty. Accordingly the Signals Division was responsible for training personnel, station maintenance, equipment, and transmission of bearings to the OIC. The OIC plotted the bearings, interpreted them in light of other sources of information, and produced estimates of the enemy for action by the Operations Division.[110] This apportionment of responsibility between Signals, the OIC, and Operations, moreover, would allow the RCN to adopt procedures developed in the Royal Navy for effective management of shipborne HF/DF, to ensure its effective use by escort groups, and the integration by the OIC of bearings made by escorts with bearings from shore stations. The Signals Division's responsibility for the acquisition, installation, and maintenance of shipborne HF/DF, moreover, would ensure that this equipment was managed in tandem with other electronic ASW resources.[111] Lieutenant-Commander C.W. Skarstedt, RCNVR, Lieutenant-Commander J.B. McDiarmid, RCNVR, and Lieutenant J.H. Low, RCNVR, key personnel under DeMarbois in the Foreign Intelligence Section, had also returned in late April from a visit to Britain. Skarstedt and Low had spent considerable time at the British intercept operation at Scarborough, and had important contributions to make to the OIC's German "Y" (intercept) and "Z" (classification) sections.[112]

McDiarmid was head of the U-Boat Tracking Room—OIC 5 in the new NSHQ organization—and his trip was far more momentous. Upon arrival at the Admiralty he was told to stand by; unbeknownst to him, the RCMP was conducting a security check on him and his family. After that delay Commander R. Winn, head of the Admiralty U-Boat Tracking Room, indoctrinated McDiarmid on the Ultra secret: this was because NSHQ would be receiving raw, highly classified, decrypt material for the first time.[113] McDiarmid then gained hands-on experience as a watch officer under Winn for about a month. As a description of the Admiralty OIC indicates, the atmosphere took some getting used to. "Newcomers had to contend with the slight claustrophobic effect of dungeons, the urgent running to and fro, the continuous jingling of telephone calls, and the clatter of teleprinters and typewriters, and the apparent 'confusion of all.'"[114] Beyond that, McDiarmid was amazed

109. "Notes on the History of OIC in Canada," DHH 81/520/1440-18, Box 65, file 1, 1943, 8

110. DSD UK Visit Report, May 1943, RG 24, 3805, NSS 1008-33-25, pt 1

111. Ibid

112. "Notes on the History of OIC in Canada." This source credits Winn with ensuring that goodwill prevailed between the two organizations.

113. McDiarmid to Whitby, Jan 1999, DHH 2000/5

114. "NID Notes on Volumes of Papers Collected by Admiral Godfrey," nd, 8, PRO, ADM 223/297. The account was written by Paymaster Cdr N. Denning, RN

at the latitude a junior Canadian reserve officer could have in terms of issuing diversion orders based on Ultra decrypts: when he sought advice from the Director of the Trade Division as to whether or not he should divert a convoy, he was told not to waste time discussing the matter and just get on with it.[115] The experience proved invaluable. "No less important than the details," McDiarmid later recalled, "was the relationship established between the two Tracking Rooms; for effective co-operation depended on the confidence that the Admiralty would supply all the intelligence needed and that NSHQ would safeguard the intelligence and make good use of it."[116]

That proved to be the case. As Lieutenant-Commander P. Beesly of the Admiralty Tracking Room put it: "We passed to [McDiarmid] every scrap of information bearing on his area in exactly the same way that we did with RN commands."[117] In NSHQ's OIC, "the Tracking Room was off the D/F Room and was accessible only through an anteroom that led from the D/F Room. In the Tracking Room all signals containing or referring to Special Intelligence were decoded or encoded. No Special Intelligence ever left the room except to be burned and flushed down the head by an officer of the room ... Admission to the room was severely restricted to those who had a need to know—in effect to a few senior officers and within the OIC to DeMarbois, Macdonald, the deputy head of the OIC, the officers in charge of other sections and the D/F watch officers."[118] Although there is no list extant in the records, evidence suggests that, along with the above officers at NSHQ, Rear-Admiral Murray, his Chief of Staff, and later, perhaps, the Staff Officer (Operations) at the headquarters Canadian Northwest Atlantic Command were also aware of the source of special intelligence.

Mirroring the Royal Navy system where Ultra-indoctrinated staff officers from Admiralty U-Boat Tracking Room, Western Approaches, and Coastal Command discussed the latest U-boat intelligence over a scrambled telephone line each morning, at 0900 in NSHQ the Director of the Operations Division (DOD), the head of the OIC and his deputy, and staff officers from the U-boat tracking room, D/F and "Y" sections gathered to survey the U-boat situation in Canadian waters. "The Staff Officers 'Y' and D/F," McDiarmid recalled, "reported on the night's activity in their sections; and the Staff Officer in the U/B [U-Boat] Room reviewed the current situation and suggested any necessary action needed in routing and diverting." After that meeting, McDiarmid or one of his watch officers "called the Chief of Staff to C-in-C CNA on the scrambled telephone [dubbed the "green line"] and reviewed the U/B situation. Then DOD recommended to the Chief of Staff whatever action in respect to convoys or operations had been agreed upon." At 1730 each day, the DOD chaired a meeting with the Director of the Trade Division, the Staff Officer (Operations), and McDiarmid or one of his staff "to discuss trade and operations that had come up during the day." OIC 5 also distributed a "weekly confidential report on the U/B war" to the CNS, ACNS, and DOD, as well as occasional analyses of individual U-boat patrols to the above officers and the Director of Operational Research. To keep a tight lid on security, just one copy was distributed, and it was returned to OIC 5 for safe-keeping.[119]

115. McDiarmid to Whitby, Jan 1999

116. McDiarmid to Gretton, 23 July 1982, DHH, 2000/5

117. Beesly, "Operational Intelligence and the Battle of the Atlantic," in Boutilier, *RCN in Retrospect*, 185; Hinsley, *British Intelligence in the Second World War*, 551; Beesly, *Very Special Intelligence*, 169

118. McDiarmid to Gretton, 23 July 1982

119. OIC 5, "The History of OIC 5 (U/B Tracking Room)," pts I and II, 12 July 1945, copy in DHH, 2000/5

Like proud parents, officers from the Admiralty OIC were singularly happy with the work of their counterpart at NSHQ. Lieutenant P. Beesly, RNVR, deputy head of the U-Boat Tracking Room, visited OIC 5 in October 1943, and came away impressed. There were problems to be sure: senior officers did not pay enough attention to the organization,[120] liaison needed to be improved with the RCAF on the coast, and the U-boat room needed more space as well as additional telephone lines. These were relatively minor concerns, however, and Beesly concluded that OIC 5 was "an extremely efficient organization which has developed in a remarkable manner in a short period of time."[121] When McDiarmid visited the Admiralty in the spring of 1944, Rear-Admiral J.S Clayton, RN, the Deputy Director for the Intelligence Centre, told him "that he was well satisfied with the co-operation between the U-Boat Rooms and had been impressed by the report of OIC NSHQ made by Lieut. Beesly after his visit to Ottawa last year."[122] As we have seen throughout this history, the Admiralty was not known for pulling its punches when it came to commenting on the performance of the Royal Canadian Navy. That they commented so favourably on OIC 5 is a tribute to its effectiveness, as well as to the bountiful harvest that could be reaped from full cooperation between allies.

During the summer of 1943 the OIC lost little time putting the nuts-and-bolts of its operational system to work. On 18 July 1943 NSHQ promulgated the first Otter signal, a daily Top Secret message sent to C-in-C CNA, Flag Officer Newfoundland Force, Eastern Air Command (EAC), and to No 1 Group RCAF in St John's, Newfoundland. The Otter signals listed the areas where U-boats could be expected to operate on the following day to the west of 40° West, the normal range for the VLR Liberator aircraft that EAC had begun to operate from Newfoundland, and north of 40° North, the southern limit of the Canadian Northwest Atlantic command. The signal was a supplement to daily signals code-named Stipple and Tubular that the Admiralty and Coastal Command respectively had begun to promulgate to Canadian and British commands early that May, when the USN withdrew from convoy control west of Iceland. Stipple indicated, on the basis of the latest U-boat intelligence, which of the transatlantic convoys on passage was immediately threatened ("standing into danger") or might in the "near future" require air protection. Tubular supplied further details concerning the eastern and central Atlantic zones of British control regarding probable U-boat locations and air arrangements made for protection of the threatened convoys by the home air commands. The Otter signals, the counterpart of Tubular, provided detail concerning the enemy in the Canadian area. Probability areas for U-boats appeared with the categories "A", "B" or "C," depending on the reliability of the intelligence. They were designed to give the commands detailed information additional to that in Stipple so that they could more effectively plan their day-to-day operations under the direction of the C-in-C CNA. "A" Category applied

---

120. This was also a complaint of McDiarmid's, but Beesly did not seem to think that the failure of senior officers such as the CNS and ACNS to visit OIC 5 was an operational problem. Rather their interest "is necessary to enable a young organization, however efficient, to establish itself." McDiarmid to Whitby, Jan 1999, 2000/5; Beesly, memo to Officer-in-Charge OIC, NSHQ, Oct 1943, copy in ibid

121. Beesly to the OIC, ibid. Steps to improve liaison with EAC had been taken by the time Beesly submitted his report.

122. OIC 5, "Visit of OIC 5 to Admiralty, April and May, 1944," 1 and 6 June 1944, copy in DHH, 2000/5. Relations with the Americans appear to have been cordial but more distant. McDiarmid made at least two visits to Cdr K. Knowles's tracking room in Washington, but, although invited, Knowles did not come to Ottawa.

to estimates based on fresh intelligence, a sighting, an attack on shipping, accurate D/F fixes, or Enigma decrypts that gave a precise position for the U-boat. Category "B," the most frequently provided, denoted a contact that was some days old or an Enigma decrypt that merely gave the route or destination of a boat. "C" meant that the information depended on stale or vague intelligence and did not require further action. "B" estimates warranted searches of the probability area, normally undertaken by aircraft. In the case of "A" estimates, C-in-C CNA was expected to order a combined air and sea hunt unless the contact was too far distant for warships to reach the scene while the contact remained fresh, or if ships could be found only by stripping the close escort of the convoys in the immediate vicinity of the U-boat.[123]

The Otter signals achieved what the Canadian services had been struggling to set in place since the fall of 1942. This was the instrument, possible only because the senior Allies had dealt Canada into the highest levels of operational intelligence, that gave effect to Canadian command in the northwest Atlantic and that made NSHQ a significant player in Atlantic operations.

The essence of the operational intelligence system developed by the Admiralty and adopted by the USN with the creation of Tenth Fleet was close integration of air and sea forces and their concentration in areas where the enemy was most likely to be present. Given the mobility and elusiveness of submarines, there was never any possibility that Allied defences could be strong in all areas all the time. In 1941, when resources had been insufficient to provide the bare minimum of escort to convoys, the Admiralty had employed the increasingly high quality operational intelligence available to shift a portion of the close escort of unthreatened convoys to reinforce others known to have been located by the enemy. The Admiralty also discovered the great flexibility of air power and used intelligence more and more vigorously to concentrate air patrols in the eastern Atlantic to protect convoys known to have been located by the enemy, as well as to sweep areas where U-boats were known to be patrolling or in transit. Pressed to the wall in the spring of 1943, the British had stretched barely adequate resources and extended this system far out into the central ocean, using high grade operational intelligence to control the deployments of the first support groups and escort aircraft carriers, together with the handful of very-long-range shore-based aircraft then available. These were the "offensive" tactics to which the British had aspired since the outbreak of war.

Perspectives in Canada, and to be sure, the United States, on these important, but rapid and subtle changes, were rather different. Certainly there was no lack of offensive spirit in the RCN. British criticisms of Canadian convoy operations noted the tendency of Canadian escorts to seek out the enemy without making adequate provision for an organized, concerted protection of the merchantmen under their charge. Within the Canadian ocean area, moreover, there was scarcely a hint of the additional resources needed for support groups. To the contrary, even as the RCN struggled to provide minimal defence to coastal shipping in the face of the German thrust into North American waters all through 1942, the senior Allies had drawn off RCN strength to reinforce the Mediterranean, as well as the eastern and central Atlantic. Although Eastern Air Command had adopted offensive tactics in the fall of 1942, the most dramatic successes—the attacks on U-boats patrolling ahead of SC 107 and ONS 5—had been in the traditional role of direct convoy support,

---

123. Sec NB to C-in-C CNA, "Daily Forecast of U-boat Positions," 14 July 1943, LAC, RG 24, 6895, NSS 8910-9; Adm to C-in-C WA, NSHQ et al; 1612B 7 May 1943, DHH 181.002 (D122); Douglas, *Creation of a National Air Force*, 569

and this had suggested that the measures put in place at that time to provide more complete naval intelligence more promptly to the air force were sufficient. In particular, Admiral Murray, who in October and November 1942 had pressed both NSHQ and Commander Task Force (CTF) 24 to make better use of operational intelligence for offensive operations against U-boats, saw the demands arising from the Atlantic Convoy Conference for closer integration of Canadian sea and surface forces as requiring only some fine tuning of the measures taken in the fall of 1942.

It was in this light that Murray understood the conclusion of the Atlantic Convoy Conference that there should be an Area Combined Headquarters in Halifax. Air force liaison personnel were already present in the operational plotting room in Murray's headquarters in the dockyard at the north end of the city, and this he believed met the requirement for a combined headquarters in all the essential functions if not in form. There was no room for the full air force command staff in the dockyard, and therefore the Eastern Air Command headquarters building at the corner of South and Barrington Streets in the south end of Halifax was being expanded and renovated to provide facilities for a large naval complement and the necessary communications so that the air force plot would include the fullest and most current information from naval sources. Murray believed this new facility would support the arrangements for liaison with the air force that he had already made in his own headquarters, and he had no intention of moving to South Street.[124] "It is desired to stress," Murray explained to the CNS,

> the difference in responsibility for the safety of shipping on the high seas as it affects the Navy and Airforce ... Whereas, it is true, the Airforce acts as "guardian angel" over the convoys, when they are at sea and flying conditions permit, the Navy is responsible for every movement of the ships and fills more the role of a "Shepherd with his sheep dogs." The Navy is not only responsible for the safety of the ships at sea but for their every movement and their welfare at sea or in harbour. It is the naval service, not the Airforce, which prepares the ships for inclusion in convoy, routes the convoy, organizes the destination of ships as required by the Ministry of War Transport, prepares the port of arrival for acceptance of such a large body of shipping at one time, and, in case of breakdown or attack, it is the Navy which must arrange rescue tugs, salvage measures, and escort to docking port, and for care of survivors.

It was therefore "essential" that Murray should remain in the dockyard "in closest touch with the operations of the merchant vessels."[125] Nor, Murray argued, would co-location of the naval and air commanders and their operational staffs be in the best interests of Eastern Air Command. "Whereas my sole duty is control of A/S operations, the AOC-in-C is unfortunately saddled with responsibility for fighter protection of the Eastern Seaboard and for the administration and operation of a large number of training stations of the Empire Air Training Scheme."[126]

The Allied Anti-Submarine Survey Board's sharp criticism of Murray in May 1943 for not having already moved in with the air force stung him deeply, not least because such criticism failed to

---

124. COAC to Sec NB, "Commander-in-Chief, North Western Atlantic," 8 Feb 1943, DHH 81/520/8000, "FOAC (1943)"; Sec NB to COAC, "Organization, Canadian North West Atlantic Command,"19 Mar 1943, LAC, RG 24, 11227, 1700-102/1, pt 1; C-in-C CNA to Sec NB, "Report on A/S Warfare and Aircraft," 31 May 1943, LAC, RG 24, 8080, NSS 1271-15

125. COAC to CNS, 30 Nov 1942, DHH 193.009 (D14)

126. C-in-C CNA to Sec NB, "Report on A/S Warfare and Aircraft," 31 May 1943

address the objections he had repeatedly raised. Nevertheless, Murray moved with his staff to EAC headquarters as soon as progress of the renovations allowed, and the new Area Combined Headquarters began to operate on 20 July 1943.[127] The scale of the project was much larger than mentioned in any previous Canadian correspondence, and required, as Murray explained "a complete re-organization of the communications staff of C-in-C, CNA and C[ommodore] Halifax, and the training of 136 new cypher staff, teletype operators, etc."[128] The size of this new communications and communications security organization, and the speed with which Murray completed the new arrangements, suggest that it was not only pressure from the survey board and NSHQ that convinced Murray of the need to move to South Street. Although the available correspondence is silent on the matter, it is possible that Murray was indoctrinated on Ultra at this time, and hence learned of the necessity, given the accuracy and timeliness of the operational intelligence now available, for his command, including especially the air forces, to be prepared to act instantly.

What can be documented is that the AASSB arranged for at least one expert officer, Commander H.M. Wilson, RN, to join Murray's staff to assist in the organization of the ACHQ. Wilson had served in Western Approaches headquarters and was one of the British members of the important "Command Relations" subcommittee of the Atlantic Convoy conference.[129] The survey board also arranged for Commander P.B. Martineau, RN, a staff officer at RAF Coastal Command headquarters, who had already played a key role in advising the RCN and RCAF on improved air-sea cooperation in the fall of 1942, to pay a return visit in the summer of 1943. On 6 August Martineau was able to report to Murray and Johnson that the "general situation has improved out of all recognition ... The co-operation between the RCN and RCAF is excellent." Murray warned, however, that there was still "no [Canadian] naval officer with a thorough understanding of air operations."[130] When, in the coming months, the opportunity arose for offensive action against U-boats that returned to the North American seaboard in small numbers, the lack of air-mindedness in the navy would become even more evident.

127. C-in-C CNA, "War Diary Month Ending 31 July 1943. Part II," LAC, RG 24, 11052, 30-1-10 pt 22; R.H. Caldwell, "Murray and ACHQ," 69-70, DHH 2000/5

128. C-in-C CNA to Sec NB, "Report on A/S Warfare and Aircraft," 31 May 1943

129. Signals, 12-15 May 1943, LAC, RG 24, 11127, MS 0021, discuss Wilson's appointment to Murray's staff. Wilson's signature for Murray on C-in-C CNA to Sec NB, "War Diary, June, 1943," 7 July 1943, LAC, RG 24, 11052, 30-1-10, pt 21, confirms that the arrangement was carried out.

130. Martineau to C-in-C CNA and AOC-in-C EAC, 6 Aug 1943, LAC, RG 24, 3896, file 1034-3 pt 1; Canning to C-in-C Coastal Command, 27 May 1943, 5, PRO, ADM 1/13756

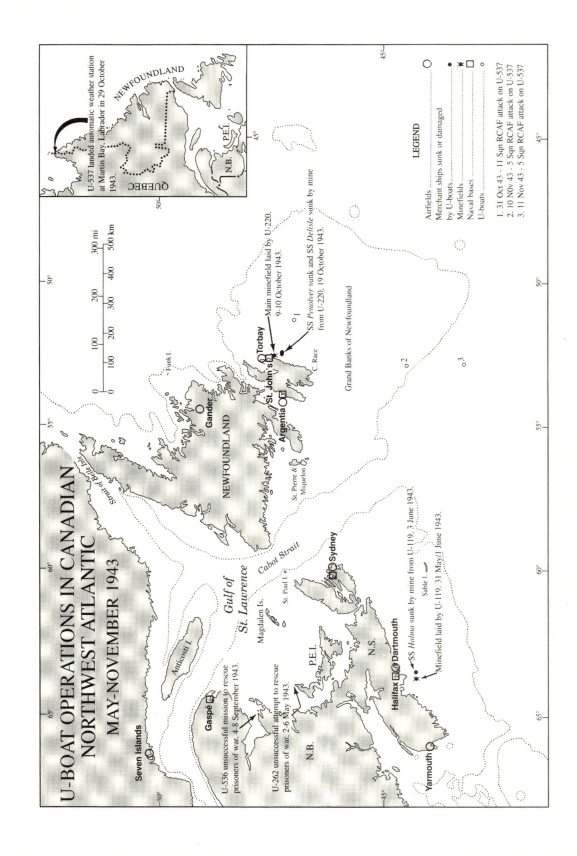

U-BOAT OPERATIONS IN CANADIAN NORTHWEST ATLANTIC MAY-NOVEMBER 1943

NEWFOUNDLAND

U-537 landed automatic weather station at Martin Bay, Labrador in 29 October 1943.

QUEBEC

N.B.

P.E.I.

Seven Islands

Strait of Belle Isle

Gander

NEWFOUNDLAND

Gulf of St. Lawrence

Anticosti I.

Magdalen Is.

Gaspé

U-536 unsuccessful mission to rescue prisoners of war, 4-8 September 1943.

U-262 unsuccessful attempt to rescue prisoners of war, 2-6 May 1943.

N.B.

P.E.I.

Cabot Strait

St. Paul I.

Sable I.

Sydney

N.S.

Halifax

Dartmouth

SS Halma sunk by mine from U-119, 3 June 1943.

Minefield laid by U-119, 31 May/1 June 1943.

Yarmouth

St. Pierre & Miquelon

Argentia

St. John's

Torbay

Funk I.

C. Race

Main minefield laid by U-220, 9-10 October 1943.

SS Penolver sunk and SS Delisle sunk by mine from U-220, 19 October 1943.

Grand Banks of Newfoundland

1

2

3

0   100   200   300 mi

0   100   200   300   400   500 km

50°

45°

55°

60°

65°

45°

50°

55°

60°

65°

45°

50°

LEGEND

○ .... Airfields

● .... Merchant ships sunk or damaged by U-boats

✖ .... Minefields

□ .... Naval bases

○ .... U-boats

1. 31 Oct 43 - 11 Sqn RCAF attack on U-537
2. 10 Nov 43 - 5 Sqn RCAF attack on U-537
3. 11 Nov 43 - 5 Sqn RCAF attack on U-537

CHAPTER THIRTEEN

North Atlantic Operations
June–December 1943

CANADIAN PLANNERS HAD ANTICIPATED a renewed, large-scale U-boat offensive in the north-west Atlantic, and particularly in the St Lawrence, for 1943. Although this did not develop as expected, the continued appearance of U-boats left no doubt about the continuing danger. Indeed, and this was something of a paradox, the much fuller decrypt intelligence available in 1943, compared with the 1942 Enigma blackout, was cause for increased uncertainty and concern. Because the Allies had not been able to read Enigma in the fall of 1942, they had not realized that Canadian defences, whatever the view of Allied authorities, had been strong enough to discourage the enemy. Traffic available in 1943, by contrast, showed that the U-boat force was determined to regain the initiative wherever possible, and the indications were that this could very well be in the northwest Atlantic.

The first of these indications was the arrival of *U 119* off Halifax on a minelaying mission in late May 1943. For such "special tasks," the term used by U-boat command for operations in which a submarine was to approach a specific point on the enemy coast to land agents, pick up escaped prisoners of war, or lay mines, headquarters provided the U-boat commander with sealed written orders before he sailed and avoided any direct reference in radio traffic. These precautions were designed primarily to prevent leaks of information from headquarters or the U-boat bases to enemy agents; investigations of the security of naval radio Enigma had convinced the Germans that it was still impossible for the Allies to decrypt signals on a timely basis. The Germans, although unaware of the full capabilities of the Allied direction finding system, were nevertheless extreme-ly conscious of the threat, and for this reason the U-boat commanders on these special missions observed radio silence for some days before and after landfall.

Thus the Allies, despite the more regular penetration of Enigma and improvements in direction finding, had no warning of *U 119*'s mission. On the moonless night of 31 May/1 June the big type XB minelayer laid sixty-six mines in an arc about thirteen miles seaward of Chebucto Head, the western headland of Halifax harbour, across the main, southern shipping channels, with an east-ern extension that partly covered the approach from the north. The entire cordon was twenty-five miles in length, with a density that varied from two to four mines per mile. Each mine contained 760 pounds of high explosive and was equipped with a magnetic-influence trigger: a ship did not have to hit the mine, only pass in its vicinity. The Germans had developed magnetic mines early in the war as a ground type, usually planted by aircraft or surface ships in shallow waters where they rested on the seabed. Those planted at Halifax were of a moored type, designed to float about fifteen metres below the surface; their long anchoring cables enabled them to be placed at a distance from ports in depths of as much as 350 metres.[1]

"It was nothing short of an amazing piece of good luck" that at least three of the mines, either through improper placement or faulty equipment, bobbed to the surface and were spotted at midday on 1 June—the day after they were sown—by the Town class destroyer HMCS *Hamilton* and the corvettes HMCS *Kamsack* and *Dundas* as they made a preliminary antisubmarine sweep before the sailing of the outbound Halifax to Boston convoy XB 56.[2] Three minesweepers were nearby, just completing their routine morning sweep, and they came to assist. There was a strong possibility that the mines had broken loose from Halifax's own shore-controlled defensive field; Lieutenant George H.C. Rundle, RCNR, the officer responsible for rendering mines safe, came out in another of the port defence vessels to confirm if that was the case. When Rundle reached the scene in the late afternoon, he notified shore authorities that the mines were not from the local defence field, but were German, of the new moored magnetic type and therefore almost certainly part of a large field.[3] The shore staff closed the port. In the fading light it proved impossible to attempt to sweep the mines.

At daybreak on 2 June 1943 eight minesweepers, the whole available strength of the Halifax minesweeping force reinforced by two sweep-equipped trawlers of the Western Local Escort Force (WLEF), cleared a path 2400 yards wide in the main, southern shipping channel, to a distance of about twenty-two miles seaward of Chebucto. Late that afternoon shore authorities opened the port for traffic through the cleared channel, although earlier in the afternoon an outbound convoy had already sailed, escorted through the channel by the sweepers. During the afternoon of 3 June, however, SS *Halma*, a small steamer that had romped ahead of an incoming Boston to Halifax convoy, entered port four miles away from the swept channel, detonated a mine, and sank—fortunately without loss. She was the only victim of the minefield.[4]

Clearance operations for the rest of the minefield continued at high intensity until 27 June. At least thirteen and as many as twenty-five ships carried out these operations each day. Again, fortune played a role: ten wooden minesweepers that had been built in Canada and the United States for the Royal Navy arrived at Halifax with their experienced British crews to do their final fit out for the passage to the United Kingdom, and all these ships joined in. Their wooden hulls were less vulnerable to magnetic mines than even the most carefully degaussed steel ships. In addition, the Canadian Northwest Atlantic command diverted ten Bangors from escort duties. The dockyard had to work under full pressure to prepare the newly commissioned British ships for operations, and

1.   "German 'O' Type Mine," *RCN-RCAF Monthly Operational Review* (Nov 1943), 32-3; "Operations Order St Johns for U 220," 11 May 1943, BdU, KTB, which contains instructions for the same type of mine laid at Halifax; SO (Torpedo), CNA to C-in-C CNA, 23 June 1943, LAC, RG 24, 11019, 6-2-1(B)—hereafter 6-2-1(B)

2.   The following account is based primarily upon Cmdr Halifax to C-in-C CNA, 28 Jun 1943, LAC, RG 24, 3944, NSS 1037-30-2, pt 1—hereafter NSS 1037-30-2(1)—and the more detailed Oi/c Experimental Section, HMCS *Stadacona*, "Report Hx-M/S No. 1: Report on Minesweeping Operations at Halifax, NS June 1st to 27th 1943," 11 July 1943, 6-2-1(B). See also [Admiralty], "Commodore Halifax's Report on Minesweeping Operations Off Halifax—June '43," 28 July 1943, ibid

3.   DWT/Tactics to VCNS and D/DWT, "Mines Laid Off Halifax Approaches," 30 Sep 1943, NSS 1037-30-2(1)

4.   SO (Operations) min, "Mines Laid Off Halifax Approaches," 30 Jun 1943, 6-2-1(B)

The rum ration. Initiated in the early days of the Royal Navy, it was intended to avoid illness through drinking contaminated water. By the Second World War it was more of a morale booster and a means of keeping sailors in touch with naval traditions. (LAC PA 206685)

Washing dishes in HMCS *Trillium*. The cramped conditions in a corvette are evident here. (LAC PA 204267)

to reinstall the heavy minesweeping equipment that had been removed from the Bangors to allow them to carry additional depth charges for escort duties.[5]

All told, fifty-six mines were accounted for. Thirty-seven of them were detonated by the "LL" sweeps—towed electrical cables that created a strong magnetic field to trigger the mines at a distance of about 200 yards from the vessel—that equipped four of the Halifax local defence minesweepers and the ten British ones. Another eleven mines were severed from their moorings by cutting cables towed by all of the minesweepers, and several of them detonated from the shock of impact. Others were seen to scuttle on their own, presumably as a result of equipment failures triggering small destructive charges in the mines. The final ten were never detected and likely scuttled themselves as well. Under Lieutenant Rundle's supervision, three mines were recovered. This was a hair-raising operation in which harbour defence craft towed the mines some fifteen miles to suitable beaches, where Rundle dismantled the deadly devices. Very little was known about this new type of mine, and the successful recoveries provided examples for study by Canadian, British and American naval research laboratories. Rundle received the George Medal and bar for "gallantry, skill and coolness in carrying out hazardous duties" on these three occasions. Leading Seaman John Lancien, who assisted him, received the British Empire Medal.[6]

The Admiralty thought that the clearance operations off Halifax reflected "great credit" on all who participated.[7] The fact that the port was closed only briefly, and that losses were so light, were important accomplishments. Still, the impediments to shipping resulting from the need to route convoys around the danger area and to take special, time-consuming precautions when entering or leaving port, and the scale of effort needed for clearance amply demonstrated the effectiveness of minelaying as a form of attack. The RCN, lucky as it was to have the British wooden minesweepers available to carry a large share of the work, was by no means ill-prepared. The considerable attention that the navy had given to the mine threat from the beginning of the war meant that expert staff was available at Halifax, together with a nucleus of capable ships. There was, moreover, an important reserve in the numerous Bangors. Although they had been converted for escort work, the Bangors had quite readily resumed their original role. This last success foreshadowed the important clearance work that Canadian Bangors would undertake on short notice and under more difficult circumstances for the Normandy invasion in June 1944 (see Chapter 17).

U 119 did not return from its mission in Canadian waters. With the withdrawal of the main U-boat force from the North Atlantic convoy routes, the Admiralty stepped up efforts, hitherto carried out mainly by aircraft, to attack submarines in the approaches to the main U-boat bases at French ports on the Bay of Biscay. On 17 June 1943, the successful Second Support Group, under the legendary U-boat killer, Captain F.J. Walker, RN, sailed from Liverpool to patrol northwest of Spain's Cape Finisterre, the route the U-boats were using to slip south of the hunting forces operating from Britain. On the morning of 24 June, the group made an asdic contact that resulted in the destruction of the returning *U 119*—none of its crew survived.[8]

---

5.   Ibid

6.   F.J. Blatherwick, *1000 Brave Canadians: The Canadian Gallantry Awards 1854-1989* (Toronto 1991), 130-1

7.   Adm, "Cmdr Halifax's Report," 28 July 1943, 6-2-1(B)

8.   Adm, NHB, *The Defeat of the Enemy Attack on Shipping*, 110; A. Burn, *The Fighting Captain: The Story of Frederic Walker, CB, DSO***, RN and The Battle of the Atlantic* (Barnsley, UK 1993), 82-6

Continuation of the offensive by the support groups like Walker's required reorganization of the Commonwealth forces in the North Atlantic along lines somewhat different than had been envisioned at the Atlantic Convoy Conference in Washington that March. Emergency measures adopted by the Admiralty at that time, such as the deployment of Home Fleet destroyers in the support groups, could not be continued indefinitely. Strong covering forces also had to be provided for the Allied landings in Sicily, Operation Husky, scheduled for 10 July 1943. In addition, large escort forces—sixty-eight vessels by July 1943—had now to be established for long-term service in the Mediterranean. Although the Allied victory in North Africa in May had at last opened the Mediterranean Sea for regular through-convoys, these had to be protected against the substantial Axis submarine, surface, and air forces still operating in the area.[9] As so often before, the Canadian escort forces provided the Admiralty with flexibility to meet changing needs, even as the delays in the construction of new ships and in the modernization of existing ones frustrated the Canadian service in its attempts to do more.

The Atlantic Convoy Conference had called for a total of fourteen mid-ocean close escort groups in order to sustain the sailing of fast convoys in each direction every five days, and slow convoys every eight days. By the end of May 1943 the Admiralty had opened the sailings to an alternating cycle of seven and eight days for the fast convoys and eleven days for the slow ones, and had increased the limit on their size from sixty to eighty merchant vessels in order to sustain the flow of shipping despite the less-frequent sailings. These changes trimmed the close escort requirements to nine groups, five of which were the reinforced C groups. This meant that the Royal Canadian Navy was now carrying two-thirds of the burden of close escort between Newfoundland and the United Kingdom so that British warships could be released for other duties.[10]

At the convoy conference the RCN had agreed to create its own support group, and the Admiralty pressed for action.[11] The continuing shortage of destroyers to make up the minimum strength of the close escort groups meant that only corvettes were available to establish the new "Canadian Support Group" early in May 1943.[12] It was based at St John's and it was to take over the role of the Western Support Force.[13] The Flag Officer Newfoundland (FONF) staff, however, was so hard pressed to find running ships for the C groups—many of the additional vessels allocated were undergoing refit—that they recommended the new support group should be discontinued. Captain R.E.S. Bidwell, Rear-Admiral Murray's chief of staff at Halifax, counselled patience:

> All our arrangements and dispositions are being completely wrecked by the refitting situation. Everything possible is being done, and it would take too long to explain here why these delays have occurred. The only possible thing is to make the ships run

9. Roskill, *War at Sea* III, Pt 1, 57-9, 105-11, 118-26, 376-7; Adm, NHB, *Defeat of the Enemy Attack on Shipping*, IA, 299; ibid, IB, plan 55

10. C-in-C, CNA, War Diary "Part II," May 1943, LAC, RG 24, 11052, 30-1-10, pt 20; SO (Plans), "The First Year of Canadian Operational Control in the Northwest Atlantic,"8 Aug 1944, DHH, 81/520/8280, box 1, 8280A pt 1 for this and following paragraph

11. "Report of the Escort and Convoy Sub-Committee," revision of 12 Mar 1943, app A to ACC 2, DHH 181.009(D268)

12. "Summary of Naval War Effort," 1 Apr-30 Jun 1943, 9, DHH 81/520, NSS 1000-5-8, pt 4

13. C-in-C CNA to NSHQ, 2116Z/20 Apr 1943, C-in-C CNA to FONF, 1725Z/10 May 1943, DHH 81/520/8440-140, "Western Support Force"

longer without the refits, and definitely not to send ships in for refit, even if they are due, unless the ships to relieve them have completed except in dire emergency. It is tough on the ships and the personnel but it cannot be avoided. In order to build up your ocean groups I shall have to rob the Western Local Escort Groups.

In a postscript, Bidwell added, "You fellows are the 'Spearhead' so far, and I'm not forgetting it. I would be very loth [sic] to see the first Canadian Support Group die still-born."[14]

Murray's staff, determined to make the best ships available for the offensive role of the new support group, assigned the first corvettes scheduled to complete modernization with Hedgehog, but none of these were yet ready. The group therefore began operations early in June with HMCS *Kitchener*, *Port Arthur*, and *Woodstock*, all recently returned from the Mediterranean, and all 1941 program corvettes that had been built with extended forecastles and improved hulls. Although they were still equipped with the non-gyroscope 123A asdic, they had been fitted with type 271 radar and 20mm anti-aircraft armament for their service with the Royal Navy. In mid-June HMS *Nene* and *Tweed*, recently commissioned British frigates, joined at St John's, and the group received the designation EG 5, or Fifth Support Group—a previous incarnation of EG 5 had been formed by the RN earlier in the spring with Home Fleet destroyers, but had recently been disbanded when those ships returned to fleet duties. During the period from late June through early August, while the group was almost constantly at sea supporting transatlantic convoys, all three Canadian ships were replaced by the first corvettes to complete modernization with Hedgehog; HMCS *Edmundston*, *Calgary*, and *Snowberry*.[15]

The RCN, it turned out, made its first foray into offensive operations at a time of uneasy quiet. "From an operational point of view," observed the Newfoundland war diary for July 1943, "this has been one of the most eventless months ... for over a year. Almost complete avoidance of North Atlantic convoy routes by U-boats has continued."[16] There was a great deal of action elsewhere in the Atlantic, as Allied forces enjoyed enormous success in countering the Germans' effort to keep their campaign alive in southern waters while preparing for a return to the northern convoy routes. In July the Germans lost thirty-eight U-boats, just two short of the slaughter in May. Nearly two-thirds of these losses—twenty-three—were because of Allied shore-based maritime aviation. The focal point of this offensive was the Bay of Biscay, where Allied forces accounted for eleven sub-marines in July, and another four during the first two days of August. This success was largely the result of U-boat headquarters' tactical error in instructing its submarines to remain on the surface to engage their attackers with the improved anti-aircraft armament that was being fitted to them. In the case of the Biscay, BdU substantially corrected this error on 3 August, ordering U-boats once again to run submerged by day, surface to charge their batteries only at night, and to hug the north coast of Spain so that the land mass would interfere with Allied antisubmarine radar.

During July the Admiralty had reinforced the Biscay offensive so that two support groups were always on station. Results had not been encouraging, with only one U-boat destroyed, by EG 2, on

14. Capt R.E.S. Bidwell to Capt F.L. Houghton, 29 May 1943, LAC, RG 24, 11987, NRL 1292, Corr of Capt R.E.S. Bidwell, Private HB-BH—hereafter Bidwell Corr. See also Houghton to Bidwell, 29 May 1943, ibid.

15. SO (Plans), "The First Year"; FONF WD June 1943, DHH 81/520, NSS 1000-5-20, pt 3; *Nene Lives: the Story of HMCS Nene and her Crew* (Ottawa nd), 19, 22; Narrative "A," 191-2

16. FONF WD, July 1943, DHH 81/520, NSS 1000-5-20, pt 3

30 July. The sudden falling off of air contacts after 2 August, however, suggested that a still stronger naval effort was needed to sustain the offensive. British authorities, although they did not receive Ultra intelligence confirming the change in German tactics until later in the month, quickly surmised that the U-boats had reverted to submerged running by day. The Admiralty reassigned EG 5 from the transatlantic routes to join an expanded program of naval sweeps off the northwestern coast of Spain that would begin on 17 August, and asked Western Approaches and Canadian Northwest Atlantic Command to trim the mid-ocean close escort groups to a total of nine vessels apiece—the minimum needed to achieve the required running strength of six—so as to release warships for additional support groups. The nominations from the C groups were the four stack destroyers HMCS *St Croix* and *St Francis*, the frigate HMS *Itchen,* and the corvettes HMCS *Chambly*, *Sackville*, and *Morden*.[17]

Captain F.L. Houghton, Chief of Staff at St John's, was appalled at this selection. "When the Admiralty asked us for some ships, over and above 6 per group, to form a 'Hunting Group,' I think we all felt a bit—well embarrassed to say the least—when they were offered two four stackers and three Corvettes without Hedgehogs ... and all of which have [asdic] 123A. Surely we could have done better than that."[18] In fact, the nomination of any Canadian ships had required some arm-twisting by Murray's staff and NSHQ, who were no less anxious than Houghton to have the RCN play a much more prominent role in offensive operations. The Admiralty's original intention had been to use only British vessels for the additional support groups, and in the case of the C groups to use the occasion to repatriate RN warships that still formed part of their strength. Indeed, the Admiralty suggested that Murray might be willing to release some of the RN four-stackers that had recently been integrated into the Western Escort Force groups. Admiral Horton's staff at Western Approaches supported the Canadian bid, but on condition that the C groups must be able dependably to sail the full minimum complement of six efficient escorts, two of them destroyers or frigates.[19] The C groups were still short of modern destroyers, and the first Canadian built frigates that could fill the gap would not be available until well into the fall. There was thus no hope of assigning one or more of the River class destroyers to offensive operations, which is what the Canadian staffs wanted, not least because this would create the opportunity for a Canadian to serve as senior officer of an offensive group.[20]

While the new group, designated EG 9, formed on 22 August, EG 5 joined the new phase of operations in the approaches to the Bay of Biscay, within some twenty-five miles of the Spanish coast. On 25 August, EG 5 came under German air attack, and was the first Allied force to encounter a new weapon, the radio-controlled jet-powered HS 293 glider bomb. In the words of *Snowberry*'s commanding officer, Lieutenant J.B. O'Brien, RCNVR,

> At 1320 a lone American Liberator appeared overhead going hell bent for leather
> towards Gibraltar, passing with a curt radio-telegraphy signal, "21 enemy planes

17. Adm to C-in-C WA, C-in-C CNA, 0110B 14 Aug 1943, DHH 81/520/8440-60; "Mid-Ocean Escort Force"; SO (Plans), "The First Year"

18. Houghton to Bidwell, 18 Aug 1943, Bidwell Corr

19. Adm to C-in-C CNA, 0925A 15 Aug 1943, C-in-C WA to Adm, 1241Z 15 Aug 1943, DHH 81/520/8440-60; C-in-C CNA to FONF, "COS to COS personal," 2012Z 23 Aug 1943, Bidwell Corr

20. Bidwell to Houghton, 8 Sep 1943, Bidwell Corr

HMCS *Summerside*, a corvette, undergoing work-ups near Pictou, Nova Scotia. (LAC PA 206485)

HMCS *Snowberry* and *Calgary* after sinking *U 536* along with HMS *Nene*. The guns are of HMCS *Prince Robert*, which had been converted into an anti-aircraft cruiser by this time, and had recently fought a two-hour battle with aircraft carrying glider-bombs. (DND HN 907)

heading this way," then ducking into the clouds. At 1342 they appeared ahead at 4,000 feet ... later identified as 14 Dornier 17s and seven JU 88s.

It was evident that this was not an ordinary high-level attack as each bomb appeared to shoot out from under the planes for a distance of 200 feet or so, leaving behind a trail of white vapour. First the bomb ran on a parallel course to the target ship, then it suddenly made a right-angle turn towards the target and followed any evasive actions of the ship.

... *Nene* signalled ... at 1425, "Flag 1," which means take individual avoiding action. At 1430, *Tweed* to *Snowberry*, "What is your best speed?" Answer, "15 knots." *Tweed* to *Snowberry*, "Don't give us that, we are doing 18 and we can't shake you." The chief ERA confessed afterwards to urging 10 more revs out of the old ice cream freezer than he ever had before. He claimed that by the time the news of the enemy planes reached the engine-room, there were at least 50 around, so he figured that we needed all available juice.[21]

On this occasion there were no casualties, but on 27 August the forces that relieved EG 5 suffered heavy losses from a similar attack, including the destruction of the sloop HMS *Egret* of EG 1, and severe damage to HMCS *Athabaskan*, one of two large destroyers providing cover for the antisubmarine vessels guarding against forays by German surface forces (see Chapter 15).

This German success compelled the Admiralty to pull the surface forces watching the approaches to the Biscay further out to sea, thus reducing their chances of interdicting U-boat passages, even as the evasive measures by the submarines and countersweeps by the *Luftwaffe* diminished the effectiveness of the Allied air offensive over the bay. These achievements facilitated the despatch of nineteen U-boats and the U-tanker *U 460*, which sailed with the first group to provide refuelling support, starting on 23 August and continuing until 9 September, to take up waiting positions for renewed mass attacks on the North Atlantic convoys.[22]

U-boat command appreciated that the submarines would need a technological edge to avoid the heavy losses inflicted by the surface escorts on the northern routes in May, and thereafter by Allied maritime air forces. Unaware of the Allies' ability to decrypt Enigma, the German command exaggerated the importance of Allied airborne radar, but rightly pressed more urgently than ever for an entirely new type of submarine with the long underwater endurance and high submerged speed needed to track convoys and attack without exposing itself on the surface. The long-hoped for "Walter" boat, whose main engines were powered by non-oxygen-burning hydrogen peroxide fuel, had proved too radical and trouble-plagued for any chance of early production. The high performance Type XXI and Type XXIII diesel-electric boats, which coupled massively increased batteries with the streamlined Walter boat hull, although given a top priority for rapid construction, had just left the drawing board and were not expected to enter service until at least the spring of 1944.[23] U-boat command, however, rushed new equipment to the Type VIIC boats that sailed from the

---

21. *RC Navy Monthly Review* (Nov 1943), 23, reprinted in Mac Johnston, *Corvettes Canada: Convoy Veterans of WW II Tell Their True Stories* (Whitby 1994), 209

22. Clay Blair, *Hitler's U-boat War* (New York 1996-8), II, 404-5; J.F. White, *U-boat Tankers 1941-45: Submarine Supplies to Atlantic Wolf Packs* (Annapolis 1998) 182-3

23. K. Dönitz, *Memoirs: Ten Years and Twenty Days* (London 1959), 352-7

Biscay ports. This included the improved *Hagenuk Wanze* search receiver, which could detect radar emissions on the 0.75-to 3-metre bands (the Germans were still unaware of the Allied leap to microwave radar technology), *Aphrodite* balloons to give off false radar echoes, the *Gruppen Horch Gerät* (group listening apparatus), which could hear hydrophone effect from individual ships at twenty kilometres and from convoys as far as 100 kilometres, and one quadruple and two twin 20mm automatic cannon mountings to fight off aircraft. Finally, authorities pushed for the development and production of an acoustic torpedo that homed on the cavitation of propellers in the ten to eighteen knot range, the operating speed of most Allied escorts when they were screening a convoy. Called *zaunkönig* by the Germans, it was dubbed GNAT (for German Naval Acoustic Torpedo) by the Allies. Each boat carried fourteen torpedoes, of which four were *zaunkönig* and at least four the improved FAT 3 pattern-running torpedo, which could be set to run a long or short loop, depending upon the range and dispersion of targets.[24]

Because of delays of up to eleven days in the decryption of Enigma signals, the Allies did not know until 6 September that a large number of U-boats had evaded Allied patrols in the Bay of Biscay and broken out into the Atlantic Ocean. By 13 September Commander Winn of the Submarine Tracking Room at the Admiralty was only able to venture that "there are thought to be about 20 U-boats in the general area of the Azores or further north, and it would not be surprising if a marked renewal of activity occurred in the next week or 10 days."[25] Clear texts for signals about refuelling rendezvous by the boats, which gave the best chance for pre-emptive attacks, arrived too late for the hunting forces despatched to make contact with the enemy.[26]

Slow and sparse as precise intelligence was during the first two weeks of September, Winn's conclusions were spot on, and not surprisingly so. On 30 July, ruminating on the nearly complete German withdrawal from the North Atlantic convoy routes, Winn had reflected:

> It is common knowledge both to ourselves and the enemy that the only vital issue in the U-boat war is whether or not we are able to bring to England such supplies of food, oil and raw material and other necessaries, as will enable us, (a) to survive and (b) to mount a military offensive adequate to crush enemy land resistance. Knowing this is so, the enemy must have intended an ultimate return to this area, so soon as he might be able, by conceiving new measures and devising new techniques, to resist the offensive which we might be able to bring to bear upon him there ... but it might be the last dying struggle of a caged tiger for the enemy to send back in September or October into the North Western Approaches his main U-boat forces ... Even if heavy losses of merchant shipping and escort forces on the North Atlantic convoy routes were to be suffered ... no fear need to be felt as to the ultimate outcome.[27]

---

24. BdU, KTB, 15 Sep 1943; E. Rössler, *The U-Boat*, tr H. Erenburg (Annapolis 1981), 144, 188, 335; Syrett, *Defeat of the German U-Boats*, 183 and passim; MOD, *The U-boat War in the Atlantic* III, 23-4; Milner, *The U-Boat Hunters*, 61-3

25. Syrett, *The Battle of the Atlantic and Signals Intelligence*, 238-9, 242

26. Thus, e.g., TG 21.11 with USS *Santee* and TG 21.15 with USS *Card* were within easy range of *U 460*'s replenishment area between 7 and 9 Sep, but they had left it far behind by 13 Sep when the decryption came through, and it was not until 17 Sep that TG 21.12 with USS *Bogue* was close enough to reach the position. By that time the boats had started for their group *Leuthen* stations.

27. Adm Appreciation of the U-boat Situation, 1 Aug 1943, ADM 223/16; W.A.B. Douglas and J. Rohwer, "Canada and the Wolf Packs" in Douglas (ed), *The RCN in Transition, 1910-1985* (Vancouver 1988), 163

Signalling on the bridge of the River class destroyer HMCS *Ottawa* (2nd of name). The open bridge was designed more for open observation than for protection against the elements. A merchant aircraft carrier, or MAC ship, is in the background. (LAC PA 206691)

Action stations in HMCS *Ottawa* (second of name). The bridge was not only open to the elements, it could get rather crowded when the ship was in action. (LAC PA 206686)

This uncanny prescience was the product not only of a brilliant analytical mind, but one that had been nourished by full, regular access to the U-boat force's main radio communications for some eight months. The Allied advantage in intelligence had simply become crushing.

It is not too much to say that the return of the U-boats to North Atlantic convoy routes was what Allied naval authorities had been hoping for. Success, against what was recognized by the Allies—but not by BdU, who remained unaware of the compromise to their codes and cyphers—as a desperate gamble would put the seal on Allied defeat of the German attack on shipping and in turn would open the way to final defeat of the Third Reich. It would also be an important test of the RCN soon after the British and American officers of the Allied Anti-Submarine Survey Board had expressed deep concerns about the equipment and fighting power of Canadian ships. RCN escorts—all but one of them unmodernized veterans of the Battle of the Atlantic—would make up fully a third of the defending Allied naval force.

On 14/15 September, BdU ordered twenty U-boats, seventeen of the Biscay boats and three from Norway (the latter not equipped with *zaunkönig*), to form a north-south patrol line, southwest of Iceland. The boats were to take up their positions by 20 September. They were to space themselves seventeen miles apart, so as to cover on a broad front the northwestern approaches to the United Kingdom. BdU designated the patrol line group *Leuthen*.[28]

The new Canadian support group EG 9 (SO, Lieutenant-Commander A.H. Dobson, RCNR in HMCS *St Croix*) sailed from Plymouth on the 15th to take its turn in the Biscay approaches. The most recent intelligence still only identified a few of the U-boats' refuelling and waiting areas, those north of the Azores. EG 9 proceeded to the west of the normal Biscay operating area, so that it would be closer to the scene of possible action. On 16 September Western Approaches ordered EG 9 into the central ocean to support eastbound HX 256, which appeared to be at greatest risk from the U-boat concentration.

On 18 September cryptographers cracked German signals from three days before ordering the formation of the *Leuthen* patrol line. Deciphering the latter's reference positions caused some difficulties for Allied intelligence. The Allies were able to accurately interpret *Leuthen's* northern and southern limits, but placed it about one hundred miles to the west of its actual position. The decrypts also revealed that the Germans were targeting westbound convoys, estimating the arrival of an ONS convoy on 21 September and a fast ON convoy on about 23 September. Allied communications security analysts commented that the "Germans have accurate knowledge of convoy movements but there is not sufficient evidence to indicate a cipher compromise." That was more correct than the analysts realized: the Germans had estimated that the convoys would reach the patrol line two to four days later than was actually the case, but this was not fully apparent because of the Allied error in estimating the patrol line's location too far to the west.[29]

On 19 and early 20 September intelligence decrypted German messages from the 15th that filled in details of the enemy's plan. "The decimation of the escort must be the first objective. The destruction of a few destroyers will have considerable moral effect upon the enemy and will great-

---

28. BdU, KTB, 14-15 Sep 1943

29. Knowles, "U-boat Intelligence Summary," 20 Sep 1943, NARA, RG 457, SRMN 037; Douglas and Rohwer, "Canada and the Wolf Packs," 167; Syrett, *Defeat of the German U-Boats*, 185-6

ly facilitate the attack on ships of the convoy in addition."[30] This was a near reversal of earlier tactics in which the submarines had sought to evade escorts and close the merchant ships as quickly as possible for fast, multiple point-blank attacks. Other signals suggested that the Germans had a new weapon with which to strike at the escorts, and the intelligence staffs quickly combined this knowledge with statements by captured U-boat personnel to conclude that the weapon was probably an acoustic torpedo.[31] By the time this information was in Allied hands, action had already been joined—some days earlier than either side had anticipated.

The westbound convoys for which the Germans lay in wait were ONS 18, twenty-seven ships in eight columns that had sailed from Liverpool on 13 September, and ON 202, forty-one ships in ten columns that had departed from the same port two days later. The two convoys had plenty of escorts, although not the massive concentration of escort carriers and support groups that had overwhelmed the U-boats in May. B 3, escorting ONS 18, had two destroyers, HMS *Keppel* (Commander M.B. Evans, RN, was the SOE, normally carried in HMS *Towy*, which had been unable to sail with the convoy), and HMS *Escapade*; five corvettes, HMS *Narcissus*, *Orchis*, and the Free French ships *Roselys*, *Lobelia* and *Renoncule*; the HM Trawler *Northern Foam*; and the Merchant Aircraft Carrier (MAC) *Empire MacAlpine*, with three Fairey Swordfish aircraft, slow biplanes that were vulnerable to a U-boat's anti-aircraft armament.[32] ON 202 was screened by C 2, the destroyers HMCS *Gatineau* (SOE, Commander P.W. Burnett, RN) and HMS *Icarus*, the frigate HMS *Lagan*, and the corvettes HMS *Polyanthus*, HMCS *Drumheller* and *Kamloops*, the rescue ship HMS *Rathlin*, the HM Trawler *Lancer*, and the rescue tug HMS *Destiny*. EG 9, which thanks to its recent redeployment was within reinforcing distance of the threatened convoys, had the frigate HMS *Itchen*, the destroyer HMCS *St Croix*, and the corvettes HMCS *Chambly*, *Sackville* and *Morden*. In one respect, the convoys had better support than had been available during the battles in May. There were now sufficient very long range aircraft on both sides of the Atlantic (120 Squadron RAF, based at Reykjavik, Iceland, and 10 (BR) Squadron RCAF, based at Gander) to provide regular air support in daylight hours throughout the passage.[33]

The Admiralty's initial estimate that the eastbound HX 256, to the south of the tracks of the westbound convoys, might be threatened proved to be correct. On 18 September *U 260*, while heading north towards its position in the patrol line, encountered the convoy and in the afternoon made an unsuccessful torpedo attack on the steamer *William Pepperell*. When EG 9 reached HX 256 later that evening, it therefore lent support for a few hours before, early on the 19th, carrying on with new orders to support ONS 18, about 125 miles to the north.[34] By that time the Admiralty knew, from the freshest decrypts of detailed instructions to the U-boat commanders, that the concentration was against the westbound ON and ONS series and that the submariners had been cleared only to make opportunistic attacks on eastbound traffic in the event they found themselves in a good position to strike.

---

30. Cited in Douglas and Rohwer, "Canada and the Wolf Packs," 168

31. Knowles, "U-boat Intelligence Summary," 20 Sep 1943

32. MAC ships were simply large bulk carriers with temporary flight decks, and they had nothing like the capability of Escort Carriers.

33. Analysis of U-Boat Operations: Convoys ONS 18 and ON 202, PRO, ADM 199/2022

34. Pickard, "Christmas Festival," 52, DHH 80/125, file 8

Even as EG 9 parted company with HX 256, shore-based maritime patrol aircraft proved their value and confirmed that the main threat was against the westbound convoys to the north. On the morning of 19 September, Liberator A of 10 (BR) Squadron, while carrying out an area search in support of the convoys during a return run from Reykjavik to Gander, located and sank *U 341* about 160 miles northwest of ONS 18. *U 341's* fate had been sealed by its attempt to stay on the surface and destroy the Liberator with its new anti-aircraft armament.[35] Later that same day, at about 2130Z, HMS *Escapade* of B 3 with ONS 18 attacked two contacts on the starboard beam of the convoy, but suffered a Hedgehog explosion on board and had to return to port.[36] EG 9 was nearing the scene, in accordance with the orders it had received earlier in the day, and shortly before midnight HMCS *Chambly* (Lieutenant A.F. Pickard, RCNR) and HMS *Itchen*, approaching from about forty miles on the port quarter of ONS 18, attacked two radar contacts without success.[37]

The greater menace, however, was to ON 202, which was now about sixty miles to the northeast of ONS 18, on a nearly parallel course. At 0155Z on 20 September, the rescue ship *Rathlin's* HF/DF intercepted the sighting report by *U 270*, commanded by Oberleutnant zur See P. Otto. Burnett delayed about thirty minutes, probably waiting for further reports, before sending the frigate HMS *Lagan* off to investigate. At 0244 *Lagan* obtained a radar contact and *Gatineau* joined the hunt. At 0259 Otto fired a *zaunkönig* torpedo that destroyed *Lagan's* stern at 0303Z. *Gatineau* made an accurate attack that temporarily disabled *U 270*, then screened *Lagan* while the rescue trawler *Lancer* and the tug *Destiny* took the frigate under tow. It was a sobering start to the new German submarine offensive, but it capped a series of events that provided the precise intelligence that the Submarine Tracking Room and BdU both needed. At Western Approaches Admiral Horton was now able to take measures to best meet the impending danger; in Luxembourg Grossadmiral Dönitz heard Otto's report: "Beta/beta: Convoy square 1944 AL, 270 degrees. Otto" and responded with a simple "*An Leuthen 'ran* (Leuthen at 'em)."[38]

U 238, under Kapitänleutnant H. Hepp, was already in firm contact, but *Polyanthus* picked up a radar contact at 0356Z and forced *U 238* off with two depth charge attacks. Hepp got ahead of the convoy and, about fifteen minutes after daybreak, submerged in its path. *Polyanthus* and *Kamloops* steamed over him without getting asdic contact, and at 0732Z, from a range of less than 1000 metres, Hepp fired FAT torpedoes at the 7176-ton *Theodore Dwight Weld*, which sank within twenty-five seconds, and the *Frederick Douglass*, of the same tonnage, which remained afloat with a pronounced list, but was sunk with a *coup de grâce* later that day by *U 645*.[39] Hepp let the convoy pass over him because *U 731* and *U 338* were approaching from the north. Burnett ordered a standard daytime search, a series of ship manoeuvres called Operation Artichoke, and

35. Douglas, *Creation of a National Air Force*, 562

36. Cdr Evans thought *Escapade* would have had a sure "kill" but for a Hedgehog missile that exploded on the foc's'le, killed and wounded several of the destroyer's crew, and forced the ship to return to the Clyde for repairs. Atlantic Convoy Reports, ONS Convoys, ONS 1-18, ON 202, HX 240 and 241, PRO, ADM 199/353—hereafter Atlantic Convoy Reps

37. *Chambly* ROP; Atlantic Convoy Reps, file 561

38. *U 270*, KTB; *Gatineau* deck log, LAC, RG 24, 7347; Atlantic Convoy Reps, files 551, 561, 566-73; PRO, ADM 199/353; Analysis U-Boat Ops; Narrative of U-Boat Attack on Convoy SC 18, f 92, ADM 223/16; ZTPG 17178, 1133/25/9/43, PRO, DEFE 3/343; Douglas, *Creation of a National Air Force*, 562; Rohwer and Douglas, "Canada and the Wolf Packs"

39. Morison, *The Atlantic Battle Won*, 140-3

Polyanthus carried out a series of attacks on *U 238* for two hours, while screening *Rathlin* during rescue operations.[40]

Evans (B 3) and Burnett (C 2), watching the situation develop from their respective bridges, agreed that in view of ON 202's plight and because the remaining escorts provided a rather sparse screen for the convoy, EG 9 should reinforce both ON 202 and ONS 18.[41] Western Approaches preempted this by ordering the two convoys to join up, presenting a much larger and better defended target in the face of a known threat. The principle was a sound one—the fewer the convoys and the stronger the defence the less opportunity there was for submarines to attack—but it was not easy to join two large bodies of merchant ships in mid-ocean.[42] Fortunately, daylight allowed aircraft to provide additional security, especially since broken clouds and visibility of only seven miles at sea level allowed the airmen to remain unseen by U-boat lookouts until they were almost upon them. Thus VLR Liberators from 120 Squadron RAF sighted and attacked *U 386* about twenty miles and *U 731* about fifteen miles north of the convoy. Liberator X of 120 Squadron RAF homed HMS *Icarus* on to *U 731* before assuming its close escort of ON 202, and the destroyer, although failing to destroy the marauder, kept it firmly out of the way during this crucial period.[43]

ONS 18 now steered northeast, almost reversing its course, to join ON 202. Bringing eight columns of merchant ships around in such a radical alteration, and then linking them up with another radical alteration to the larger convoy, ON 202, was terribly complicated. Worse, a corrupt group in the coded message from Western Approaches then led ON 202, instead of maintaining a steady course and speed, to turn to the southwest and thus open rather than close the distance between the two convoys. Both turned directly towards U-boats. Meanwhile, *Itchen* was already hunting a submarine ahead of ON 202, forcing emergency turns almost ninety degrees to port. Liberator X/120 sighted *U 338* and its unidentified consort about six miles on the port beam of ON 202 at 1405Z and a few moments later Liberator F/120 sighted *U 386* about twenty miles on the starboard bow of ONS 18. X/120, which had expended all its depth charges and homing torpedoes on its previous target, attacked with machine-gun fire and homed HMCS *Drumheller* on to the scene. Lieutenant-Commander Storrs sighted and attacked *U 338*. The other submarine, *U 386*, avoiding detection, escaped on the surface. F/120 had also run out of weapons and dropped two markers near the target.[44]

U-boat war diaries leave a distinct impression that their captains were having difficulty orienting themselves to the fluid tactical situation. The possibility that there were two convoys steering almost opposite courses did not occur to them. At 1635Z, as Oberleutnant zur See F. Albrecht in *U 386* was using his periscope to set up his attack against two escorts, HMS *Keppel* appeared sud-

40.   *U 238*, KTB; *Gatineau* deck log, 7357; *Kamloops* deck log, RG 24, 7423; Atlantic Convoy Reps, files 507, 551-4, 565-8

41.   "From all indications of D/F bearings and surface sightings ON 202 ... was the centre of attraction around which the beasts of prey were gathering," *Towy* ROP, Atlantic Convoy Reps, file 507

42.   Horton may have anticipated the confusion that might result–and confusion there was–yet at the same time, as an experienced submariner he could equally have foreseen how confusing the manoeuvre would be both to German Intelligence ashore and to U-boat captains attempting to gain an attacking position, *Towy* ROP; D.W. Waters, "Seamen, Scientists, Historians and Strategy," *British Journal for the History of Science* 13/45 (1980), cited in E.J. Grove (ed), *The Defeat of the Enemy Attack on Shipping, 1939-1945: A Revised Edition of the Naval Staff History* (Aldershot 1997)

43.   Atlantic Convoy Reps, file 507; ORB, 120 Squadron RAF, PRO, AIR 27/911

44.   Atlantic Convoy Reps, files 508, 552; *Drumheller* deck log, LAC, RG 24, 7262; ORB, 120 Squadron RAF

HMCS *St Croix*, lost to *U 87*. Note the four funnels of a First World War-vintage American destroyer.
(DND H 766)

HMCS *Arvida*, part of Escort Group C 5. Corvettes were sometimes described as semi-submersibles, and the reasons why are obvious in this photograph. (LAC PA 167310)

denly 400 metres on his port quarter and turned towards him; just then the U-boat commander felt the shock of four heavy depth charge explosions. "No more likelihood of a shot," Albrecht conceded, and went deep to 160 metres.[45] What had happened was that Commander Evans in *Keppel* had discovered where ON 202 was with the aid of the newly joined Liberator R/120, and he was trying to resolve the problem of linking the convoys up when his asdic detected *U 386* at 1200 yards. "The appearance of a yard and a half of periscope, five yards from the starboard beam [and] attempting to ram her amidships prevented the veriest sceptic from considering [this contact] 'non sub.'"[46] Evans stayed with the contact for three and a half hours. At 2245Z Albrecht made the next entry in his war diary, a survey of damage sustained. *U 386* had survived, but it was now out of the battle.[47] Meanwhile, the surviving sixty-seven merchant ships were still steering the wrong course, and ONS 18 had simply formed up astern. Corrective action would have to be taken after daylight. Fortunately, events conspired to make this a quiet night for the merchantmen, and they drew steadily away from danger as an assortment of escorts from C 2, B 3, and EG 9 assumed their night screening stations.[48]

U 338, trying to intercept the convoy after dark, fell victim to Liberator N/120, flying close escort. Five other boats converged on *U 386*'s position well astern of the convoy.[49] The U-boat captains steered for the guns, assuming they were attacking the convoy screen and intent upon disposing of the escorts. *U 305*, on sighting *Rathlin* and *Polyanthus* with their survivors well astern of the convoy, manoeuvred to get ahead of these vessels, but appears to have been sighted and attacked by another Liberator, possibly R/120. Dobson in *St Croix* left his consorts, who were dealing with *U 386*, while he cooperated with the aircraft. At 1933Z *U 305* came to periscope depth and sighted *St Croix* bows on. When the range closed to 1500 metres, at the limit of reliable asdic detection by the ship and at the ideal inclination for an acoustic torpedo, Kapitänleutnant R. Bahr fired a *zaunkönig*, dove to 160 metres, and heard two loud explosions and a muffled echo. *St Croix*, the second victim of the new acoustic torpedo, immediately took on a heavy port list, and her after mast lurched over at a crazy angle towards the stern. Evans sent *Itchen*, *Polyanthus*, and *Narcissus* to screen the Canadian destroyer, and in another confrontation nearby, Liberator J/120 attempted unsuccessfully to sink *U 952*, which had stayed on the surface to fight it out. At 2040Z Bahr, undetected by any of the screening vessels, finished *St Croix* off with a straight running torpedo. The gallant old four-stacker, which under "Dobbie" Dobson's command had been a respected escort in the Mid Ocean Escort Force (MOEF), broke in two and went down in a pillar of flame with heavy loss of life. Three minutes later another *zaunkönig* from *U 305* exploded harmlessly in *Itchen*'s wake.[50]

---

45. *U 386*, KTB

46. Atlantic Convoy Reps, file 507

47. "I hadn't the heart—nor do I think it would have been right—to order *Keppel* to abandon the hunt immediately to other escorts." Evans turned it over at 2000Z to *Itchen*, *St Croix* and *Narcissus*. Atlantic Convoy Reps, file 507; *U 386*, KTB

48. Evans counted on this: "I did not anticipate a very heavy attack ... [with] the probable disorganization of any planned attack by constant air and surface cover, the unpredictable course of the convoys and the hunting group astern which focused attention away from the danger area," Atlantic Convoy Reps, files 507-8

49. *U 260*, *U 270*, *U 952*, *U 641*, and *U 305*

50. *U 305*, *U 952*, KTB; ORB 120 Squadron RAF; SO EG 9 message 211141Z/9/43, Box 8, DHH, 81/850/8280 ON 202; Analysis U-Boat Ops; Rohwer and Douglas, "Canada and the Wolf Packs"

The scene was one of fire, smoke, starshell, and a melee of escorts searching for their elusive enemy. There was no way to determine who was hunter and who was hunted that night. At 2100Z *U 270* headed for the starshell visible on the starboard bow; about an hour later *U 260*, *U 952*, and *U 641* were attracted by lights and smoke. One of the escorts emerging from the latter sighted *U 260* and at 2154Z Kapitänleutnant H. Purkhold fired at the ship with a *zaunkönig* that failed to find its mark, went deep to 170 metres, and endured a depth charge attack. At 2230Z *U 952*, under attack from *Polyanthus*, fired a *zaunkönig* at the corvette with spectacular results. *Polyanthus* went down in fifteen seconds with the loss of all hands but one. *Itchen* managed to pick up survivors during lulls in the action, eighty-one of them from *St Croix*—including Dobson, whose last signal, "am leaving the office," is one of the classic understatements of Canadian naval lore. Others taken on board included the First Lieutenant and Engineer Officer, and the sole survivor from *Polyanthus*.[51] At 2330Z Kapitänleutnant Rendtel in *U 641* came upon *Itchen* and *Narcissus*, and at 2349Z Otto in *U 270*, convinced that he had found the convoy again, fired at the ships without result, and then stalked them for another three hours. At one point Otto was illuminated by starshell "so well laid that they practically land on my stern, and burn underwater." It was not until 0430Z on the 21st that the U-boats involved in this fierce battle resumed their pursuit of ONS 18/ON 202, now united into one convoy. It had been a rare, perhaps even the only, instance when opposing groups of aircraft and surface warships on one side, and submersibles on the other, engaged in a duel on such remarkably equal terms. The tally, from the time *Keppel* attacked *U 386* until *Itchen* left the scene a little over twelve hours later, was as follows: of five surface ships that took part, two, a destroyer and a corvette, were destroyed by U-boats with heavy loss of life, in exchange for damaging *U 386*, one of the seven submarines involved.[52]

Other boats in group *Leuthen* continued their search. On 21 September *U 377*, hearing a weak hydrophone effect to the southwest at 0015Z, pursued in that direction and caught up with the main body an hour later. Oberleutnant G. Kluth fired at an escort, probably *Roselys*, was put down with depth charges, and surfaced at 0300Z to an empty ocean. *U 378* made a sighting report at 0050Z and HMCS *Sackville* was sent out on a D/F bearing of the transmission about eight miles ahead of the port column. Her captain, Lieutenant-Commander A.H. Rankin, RCNR, attacked with three depth charge patterns and drove the submarine off, unaware that Kapitänleutnant E. Mäder had fired a *zaunkönig* at him. At 0410Z *U 584* fired a *zaunkönig*, possibly at *Morden*, which opened fire on a contact three miles ahead of the starboard wing column at 0455Z. "It was satisfactory," wrote Commander Evans with a touch of bravado after the event, "to find that the Hun had become no more enterprising during his Summer vacation and that the old rule 'A submarine detected is an attack averted' still held good."[53]

Fog, familiar and friendly, enveloped ONS 18 before dawn. When it lifted briefly in the early afternoon of 21 September, Evans discovered that the convoy had moved up to the starboard beam

---

51.   Joseph Schull, *The Far Distant Ships: An Official Account of Canadian Naval Operations in World War II* (Ottawa 1950), 179

52.   *U 641*, *U 270*, *U 260*; SO EG 9 message 22152Z/9/43, Box 8; notes taken on Sunday the 26th and Tuesday the 28th of September re attacks on convoys ONS 18 and ON 202, attached to FONF message 022016/10/43, ibid

53.   Atlantic Convoy Reps, file 508; KTB, *U 377*, *U 378*, *U 584*. According to BdU, KTB, *U 229*, sunk later in the battle, also reported firing at least one, possibly two *zaunkönigs*, on the afternoon or evening of 20 Sep.

of ON 202, more by luck than good management—Commodore E.O. Cochrane, RNR, the Convoy Commodore in ON 202, had no idea this had happened—and although weather prevented the necessary alteration of course by the large and cumbersome formation with its front of nine-and-a-half miles, it was now much easier to defend. HF/DF bearings provided a good indication of a U-boat's disposition. Air cover, both from Iceland and *Empire MacAlpine*, continued in spite of the fog.[54] When aircraft were not present Evans used the remaining ships of EG 9, *Sackville*, *Morden*, and *Chambly*, to sweep astern. As long as the fog persisted the screen kept U-boats at bay. There were several encounters, and in one, *Chambly*, after attacking a U-boat—possibly *U 238*—five miles ahead of the starboard wing column at 0039Z on the 22nd, heard a suspicious hydrophone effect, "a regular swishing noise, quite distinct from the submarine's own HE," went hard a-starboard and dropped two charges, which may have saved the ship from a *zaunkönig*. At 0435Z *Northern Foam* attacked *U 305* astern of the convoy, and at 0620Z on the 22nd *Keppel* steamed down a D/F bearing astern of the convoy and located *U 229*, which she rammed and sank. That same day *Sackville* attacked *U 377* ten miles astern at 1142Z. Several hours later the visibility began to improve, and the situation again began to favour the U-boats.[55]

When the fog lifted on 22 September there were ships as far as the eye could see, spread out over an area of more than thirty square miles, with a four-mile gap between the two convoys. *Keppel* had to serve as a "messenger boy" coordinating the control between the two convoy commodores, and there was much confusion about screening stations and tasks. The air was filled, fortunately, with Canadian VLR Liberators. At 1645Z X/10 attacked *U 377* and strafed the boat with machine-gun fire, seriously wounding the CO and forcing it out of battle. The aircraft then sighted *U 402* and, having expended all main armament, traded gunfire until the boat disappeared in a fog bank. At 1710Z L/10 attacked *U 270* forty miles ahead of both convoys, and in the face of accurate flak damaged the submarine to the extent that it had to return to base. Closer to the convoy at 1934Z *Lobelia* drove *U 758* away from the port quarter with slight damage, and soon after Swordfish aircraft from *Empire MacAlpine* attacked *U 238* ten miles ahead. The Swordfish wisely gave a wide berth to the U-boat's flak—German submariners described the slow, ungainly biplanes as "old crows"[56]—and it was eventually *Itchen* and *Narcissus* that drove Hepp away and forced him to lose sight of the convoy.[57]

In order to sidestep a U-boat that was reported at forty-five miles on a bearing of 250°, Evans had asked Commodore Cochrane to hold the southwesterly course until dark and, in a weak moment, agreed to have ONS 18 then form astern of ON 202 in order to facilitate the turn. It would have been "asking too much to have a convoy of eighteen columns carry out a 50-degree turn in the dark." By evening, therefore, ONS 18 had angled across to its new position, and the combined,

54. "Her aircraft made one of the most amazing landings I have ever heard of getting onto her tiny deck in absolutely dense fog. A laconic signal of 'All aircraft serviceable' was my first intimation that this miracle had been achieved," *Towy* ROP

55. Atlantic Convoy Reps, file 508; *Chambly* deck log, LAC, RG 24, 7185; *Sackville* deck log, RG 24, 7817; *Morden* deck log, RG 24, 7817; KTB, *U 238*, *U 305*, *U 377*; Notes taken on Tuesday 28 Sep 1943, DHH,81/520/8280 ON 202 Box 8

56. *Oberkommando der Kriegsmarine, Section 2, Skl (Seekriegsleitung) BdU—Op—Gkdos 7204, AOp*, 9 Nov 1943, *Geleitoperation Nr. 5: zaunkönig—Geleitzug. Verlauf, Auswertung und Ehrfahrungen* (Convoy Operation No. 5: zaunkönig Convoy: Progress, Evaluation and Experiences), DHH, Steiger Papers (hereafter SGR II 197, Reel 2)

57. Atlantic Convoy Reps, file 511; Analysis of U-Boat Ops; ORB, 10(BR) Squadron, LAC, RG 24, mfm, Reel C-12, 238; KTB, *U 270, U 377, U 402*

somewhat misshapen, and very large formation, was on its new course of 260°. With the arrival of the frigate HMS *Towy* that afternoon, however, Evans had been able to set up a good HF/DF net by placing her on the starboard wing of the screen; thus he obtained firm indication of the threat from ahead and to port, but not from astern. There were in fact ten boats still closing the convoys, and those astern did not give away their positions by transmitting. At 2139Z *Itchen* picked up a radar contact ahead of the convoy and ten minutes later Liberator N/10, joining from ahead, sighted the wake of *U 275*. In the darkness, not being fitted with the Leigh Light that had been so effective for aircraft in the Bay of Biscay offensive, and directed not to drop flares that would have illuminated the ships, the aircraft never found *U 275* itself. But neither did the submarine find the convoy. Just before 2200Z, however, Curio in *U 952* caught up from astern, fired one of his two remaining *zaunkönig* at *Renoncule*, and claimed a kill. Curio was mistaken. *Renoncule* obtained a radar contact at 2006Z and ten minutes later *Northern Foam* sighted the U-boat. The two escorts carried out an effective depth charge attack and *U 952* started taking water at four tons an hour, but still Curio kept up his pursuit. At 2234Z *U 731* fired a *zaunkönig* at the advanced screen without result, dove to 170 metres, and did not surface until the convoy had passed. *Morden* and *Itchen*, in the advanced screen, then both opened fire at a radar target—possibly *U 260*—and fifteen minutes later *Gatineau* also engaged a target ahead of the screen.[58]

At 2359Z *Itchen* opened fire at another U-boat. At almost that very moment *U 666*, the object of the frigate's attention, fired two *zaunkönig*, one at *Morden* and one at *Itchen*. The first exploded in *Morden*'s wake but the second struck *Itchen*; it is no exaggeration to say that the ship blew apart. This tragic event unfolded so quickly that none of the screening vessels realized *Itchen* was missing—*Gatineau* thought the U-boat had exploded—until Evans later took a roll call on radio. By that time the convoy had passed through the debris and the oil-soaked men in the water. The Polish ship *Wahela*, despite the danger, stopped and picked up the only three survivors, two from *Itchen*, and Stoker William Fisher from *St Croix*. The one man who had lived through *Polyanthus*'s earlier disaster failed to survive this one. Nearly four hundred sailors, most of them experienced veterans of the Battle of the Atlantic, had been lost from these three ships.[59] *St Croix*'s Able Seaman Charles Dowler of Windsor, Ontario was one of five brothers serving in the RCN.[60]

Moments after the tragic loss of *Itchen*, *Chambly* got a radar contact, presumably *U 584*. At 0007Z on 23 September *U 584* fired a *zaunkönig* at the corvette. The torpedo failed to find the target. Kapitänleutnant J. Deecke, like the other U-boat captains who had attacked escorts, also failed to get into position for an attack against the convoy itself as *Chambly* kept him down with depth charge attacks. Except for the success enjoyed by *U 238* in the opening moments of the battle, therefore, and in spite of the loss of four escorts to submarine attack,[61] there had still been no penetration of the screen. It must be said that the odds of this record being sustained were long. There

58. Analysis of U-Boat Ops; Atlantic Convoy Reps, files 508-9, 517-20; *RCN Monthly Review* 31 (Aug 1944); KTB, *U 260*, *U 275*, *U 305*, *U 378*, *U 584*, *U 641*, *U 666*, *U 731*, and *U 952*; *Gatineau*, *Morden*, deck logs; Rohwer and Douglas, "Canada and the Wolf Packs"; Milner, *U-boat Hunters*, 70; Syrett, *Defeat of the U-boats*, 199. The Admiralty analysis in ADM 199/2022 is wrong in placing *U 275* sixty miles on the starboard bow of the convoy.

59. Analysis of U-Boat Ops; Atlantic Convoy Reps, files 508-9, 517-20; *RCN Monthly Review* 31; KTB, *U 260*, *U 275*, *U 305*, *U 378*, *U 584*, *U 641*, *U 666*, *U 731*, and *U 952*; *Gatineau*, *Morden*, deck logs

60. *Windsor Daily Star*, 28 Dec 1943

61. Three sunk, one, HMS *Lagan*, was a constructive total loss.

were at least seven submarines still closing, and the escorts had the difficult task of covering the much deeper flanks of the convoys as they were now formed up. U-boats could take advantage of the longer time taken by the merchant ships to pass a given point, time extended by the large gap that then existed between ON 202 and ONS 18.[62]

Not surprisingly, perhaps, it was again Hepp in *U 238* who, as he had done after *Lagan* had been hit, took advantage of the situation upon seeing the huge explosion that marked the loss of *Itchen*. Hepp worked his way over to the starboard side of the convoy, and at 0200Z on 23 September slipped unseen past *Icarus* and *Drumheller* on the starboard wing of ON 202. Even though *Drumheller* obtained a radar contact, went to action stations and fired starshell, Hepp coolly fired three FATs that struck the 5056-ton *Skjelbred*, the 3642-ton *Oregon Express,* and the 7134-ton *Port Jemseg* (all three of which would be lost), then withdrew without being attacked. At almost the same moment *U 260*, on the port beam, fired a *zaunkönig* at *Chambly*. Pickard had already obtained radar and asdic contact when his asdic broke down and "an explosion astern shook the ship considerably"—the number of escapes from the acoustic torpedo by escorts deserves note—but Albrecht did not pursue his advantage. At 0615Z Curio in *U 952* again caught up, this time with ONS 18, which would not have been possible had Commander Evans's preferred formation been maintained. Curio fired at the two leading ships of the port wing column in ONS 18, using both a pattern and straight running torpedo at each. One dud torpedo hit the second ship, the 7167-ton *James Gordon Bennett*, and one of the other three hit the 5098-ton *Steel Voyager*, which eventually had to be abandoned. The U-boats made one more attempt as *U 758* fired at a steamer and a screening vessel, almost certainly *Rathlin*, without result. Aircraft sightings and attacks on the 23rd probably prevented any further approach by submarines, and Dönitz ordered the boats to break off the operation that afternoon if not in attacking position.[63]

Three out of twenty-one escorts were sunk by the new *zaunkönig* torpedo, and two severely damaged, as well as six of sixty-nine merchant ships, and altogether well over four hundred men killed in this battle, compared with three U-boats sunk with more than a hundred men, and two boats damaged, out of twenty-one that took part on the German side. This was an exchange rate that should have comforted neither Allied nor German analysts. Yet, there was great optimism on both sides. Dönitz, drawing his conclusions from an analysis based on a series of incorrect assumptions, thought the *zaunkönig* torpedo and the *Hagenuk Wanze* radar detector had solved the "technical problem" he had blamed for the disasters suffered by U-boats on the northern convoy routes in May.[64] Canadian and British authorities, having expected resumption of the U-boat offensive, were in fact satisfied with the general ability of the escorts, in spite of the acoustic torpedo, to prevent penetration of the screen.[65]

The first mistake in the German analysis was to identify two convoys as one. BdU even chided the two boats that had reported ONS 18 for being fifty miles out in estimating the Allies' position. That may have led to a second mistake, identifying what Commander Evans euphemistically called a "hunting group" on the night of 20 September as a distant screen made up of single destroyers

62. Analysis of U-Boat Ops; KTB, *U 238*

63. KTB, *U 238*

64. SGR II 197, Reel 2

65. Analysis of U-Boat Ops; Atlantic Convoy Reps,; ON 202, DHH 81/520/8280

or destroyers acting in pairs. Belief that this was a new Allied tactic skewed the German analysis. The third mistake was to attribute the loss of surprise entirely to Allied sightings of U-boats as they approached their stations. U-boat Command failed once again to recognize the compromise of their codes and cyphers or the existence of shipborne HF/DF. Fourth, BdU believed the claims of U-boat commanders, that from fifteen *zaunkönig*'s fired on the night of 20 September, seven were definite sinkings and three more were probable, when there were in fact only two sinkings, *St Croix* and *Polyanthus*. That meant that the U-boats thought they were up against at least ten escorts, rather than the five that actually, at various times, engaged in this action. "After the great success against this distant screen of the convoy," stated the report, "one could anticipate the further progress of the operation with well-founded confidence. The preliminary work of doing away with the obnoxious distant screen was completed; now one could expect the convoy to take its turn. The enemy was frightened out of his wits by the losses of so many destroyers; that was clearly confirmed by his radio conversations. And what could the ships now expect with their close screen in this situation? The U-boats could without any difficulty attack the main body of the convoy."[66]

The only thing that could have saved the convoy from destruction, insisted Dönitz, was a miracle, and the miracle that turned up was fog. Nevertheless, after the apparent victory over a distant screen two nights before, when the fog lifted it was surprising to find that there was still such a strong close screen. The attacking boats, Dönitz believed, then sank a further five destroyers, two in a single attack on the advanced screen and three "in close proximity to the convoy" (the only escort actually lost during this period was *Itchen*). The loss of five additional escorts, argued Dönitz, exposed the convoy to attack from the flanks, and to the fifth mistake in the analysis that followed—that only the return of fog saved a demoralised escort force and convoy from the main assault. Because the only U-boat reports received on the final day were of single ship sightings, or ships travelling in pairs, it was believed that the vessels seen had either lost the convoy in fog or deliberately abandoned it following the sinking of so many ships on 23 September. In fact, not only was visibility adequate when the operation was called off but, as already noted, rather than the total of twelve merchant ships that U-boat Command chose to believe had been destroyed in the battle, the actual number was six.[67]

Despite a degree of inaccuracy, some of the German conclusions were nevertheless justified. Although it was hyperbole to say that when one escort was sunk by an acoustic torpedo its consort invariably bolted, it is true that less depth charging was experienced by U-boats than in previous encounters. One reason for this was that some attacks—although not enough, in the opinion of British authorities[68]—were being made with Hedgehog, and those projectiles only exploded if they hit something. It is also clear that the *zaunkönig* gave pause to otherwise intrepid practitioners of antisubmarine warfare. C-in-C Western Approaches issued an instruction on 21 September 1943 warning that the U-boats had adopted an anti-escort policy and that they were working in pairs, one acting as a decoy while the other fired submerged, although that seems to have been a misreading of instructions given to the submarines not to operate on the surface in groups of more than two. Admiral Horton also noted the use of acoustic torpedoes, adding that

---

66. SGR II 197, Reel 2

67. Ibid

68. Atlantic Convoy Reps file 504

active steps were being taken to produce countermeasures and that "For the moment escorts are to adopt less offensive tactics confining the object to immediate defence of the convoy."[69] Western Approaches subsequently cancelled this order, but its existence helps explain why, in spite of over thirty confirmed submarine contacts by escorts in this battle, only *Keppel* managed to sink a submarine, and it did so by ramming rather than using more sophisticated methods.[70]

Circumstances had obviously changed since the spectacular successes of May. Then, there had been a steady buildup of momentum by Allied forces with a deadly combination of escort and support groups enhanced by several escort carriers. In September, however, the momentum of the Bay of Biscay offensive had lost steam, and carrier support groups were too far away to participate in the defence of ONS 18 and ON 202. One must remember too that, in May, not only were aircraft responsible for half of U-boat sinkings, but that five of the kills by escort vessels occurred in a unique tactical situation, when the submarines were on the surface and blinded by fog.[71]

During the post battle wash-up at St John's the British, Canadian, and French escort commanders themselves exhibited none of the alarm Dönitz believed his U-boats had occasioned among them. Captain (D) Argentia observed that the attacks on the convoy "were according to Derby House very little different from what we have been led to expect." Commander Evans's concluding remarks on that occasion reflect, much more vividly than his elegantly written Report of Proceedings, the offensive spirit of the escort captains:

> As regards the acoustic torpedo—it is undoubtedly a menace. The best way of defeating it is to sink the submarine and that is to go for it. I don't think the submarine should be allowed to dictate our tactics to us. [Crossed out in pencil, perhaps because the order had been cancelled: 'I hope my group will not be biased by Admiralty's signal and will go for the submarine.'] We should dictate our tactics to them. The percentage of hits he got with the number of times he fired is obviously very low.[72]

Dealing with the acoustic torpedo had been in the minds of Operations Research groups on both sides of the Atlantic for at least nine months. The "pipe noise-maker," or PNM, developed in Canada to sweep acoustic mines in 1940, had been adopted by the Admiralty and called Foxer. In response to an earlier version of a German homing torpedo, Taffy, which differed from Gnat in having a contact rather than a magnetic pistol, the Admiralty had in April 1943 suggested towing two sets of Foxer gear held a hundred yards apart by paravanes. In Halifax, on 21 September, the day after *St Croix* went down, the RCN began its own experimental work on PNMs as decoys for acoustic torpedoes. It was a remarkable coincidence that J.H.L. Johnstone, the RCN's Director of Operational Research, had reported on possible countermeasures to the Operations Division in Ottawa on 20 September. The next day, sea trials in Halifax led to the recommendation of five-foot-long, $1^3/8$-inch pipes, towed 250 yards astern at speeds between 8.5 and 17.5 knots. Because the $1^3/8$-inch pipe was in short supply, pipe of $1^1/4$ inches was substituted, and the device came into being as Canadian Anti-acoustic Torpedo or CAT gear. That day C-in-C CNA sent a signal to FONF that

---

69.　C-in-C WA message 212333Z Sep 1943, Box 8

70.　Notes taken on Sunday 26 Sep 1943

71.　Syrett, *Defeat of the German U-Boats*, 270-2; Milner, *U-Boat Hunters*, 71

72.　Notes taken on Tuesday 28 Sep 1943

explained how to construct and use the sweeps locally, and production of CAT gear commenced in Halifax. On 24 September fifty sets went to St John's, thirty more went on 25 September, local staff in St John's produced twenty of their own, and production did not stop until 400 sets of CAT gear Mark 1 were available. Commander A.F. Peers, RCN, the staff officer responsible for all this in Halifax, also went to St John's for the wash-up and submitted a useful report on the evidence of acoustic torpedoes in the battle.[73]

As Marc Milner has pointed out, although the Canadian response was superb, the solution to the problem posed by the new weapon was less straightforward than historians have assumed. The staff at Western Approaches had done nothing to prepare a countermeasure. The Admiralty's preference for Foxer, cumbersome though it was, persisted. Towing noisemakers, moreover, was simply one of several options, some complementary, others requiring an entirely different approach. Asdic became very difficult to use while CAT or Foxer was streamed, especially at higher speeds. Remaining at speeds of seven knots or less prevented an escort's propellers from cavitating, and therefore rendered the ship relatively safe from Gnats. Slow speeds, however, were not always sensible. A tactical procedure that greatly reduced the chance of a successful torpedo attack was developed within days by Western Approaches. This "step-aside" procedure literally required escorts to shift themselves about a mile off their initial approach track when they either came within 3500 yards of the U-boat or when the U-boat dove, which often was an indication that a Gnat had been launched, whichever came first. The procedure was relatively straightforward, as the escort altered course by sixty degrees, placing the submarine on the opposite bow from where it had been initially detected. After proceeding for 2000 yards, the escort would then alter back to hunt for the U-boat. The obvious advantage of step-aside was offset by the delay that ensued in approaching the U-boat, which reduced the chance of finding and destroying it. A major question that endured for the rest of the war was whether 2000 yards provided sufficient offset.[74] Finally, some COs, unwilling to brook the delay of a step-aside or the interference of a decoy, simply relied on their asdic operators to hear a Gnat approaching, in which case depth charges set shallow could be dropped astern to set the torpedo off prematurely.

EG 9, after its first major action, ceased to exist for the time being. Western Approaches quickly arranged for the transfer of *Morden* and *Sackville* to C 2, replacing *Lagan* and *Polyanthus*, and for *Chambly* to go to EG 5, part of an augmentation of that group to bring it up to a full complement of nine warships. It is difficult to disagree with these decisions, as both the RN and RCN were particularly hard-pressed in the fall of 1943 to keep ocean escort forces up to strength, precisely when the onset of heavy weather inflicted wear and damage that increased the need for replacements. Canadian and British shipbuilding and US production for Britain under lend-lease, were just beginning to deliver additional destroyer escorts, frigates, and improved corvettes, but it would be some months before these ships were available in significant numbers, worked up and ready for service. Already, however, many of the old Town class destroyers, which still formed an

---

73.   DOR, "Notes on Homing Torpedoes from the Operational Standpoint," 20 Sep 1943, DHH, 81/520/1000-973, and Cdr A.F. Peers RCN to Capt (D) Argentia, "Report on Use of Acoustic Homing Torpedoes (TAFFY) in Attacks on Combined ONS. 202 [sic]; ONS 18 convoys Sep 20 to 24 1943," Box 8; Peers, "Development of Canadian Anti-Acoustic Torpedo Gear (CAT)," 7 Oct 1943, and G.H Henderson, "Present State of CAT Gear," 23 Nov 1943, both LAC, RG 24 (Acc 83-84/167), 2050, S6060-3. Milner, *U-boat Hunters*, 62-3, 72-3

74.   C-in-C WA to C-in-C CNA, 30 Sep 1943, RG 24, (Acc 83/84), 2505, S-6060-3

important part of the British and Canadian escort fleets, had to be withdrawn from transatlantic service because they were worn out beyond economical maintenance. The need for extended repairs to HMCS *St Francis*, which prevented the ship from ever actually joining EG 9, was typical of the reduced effectiveness of the class. The Admiralty concluded that all the Towns would have to be pulled out of North Atlantic service by the end of 1943; there was no reason to hope that they could be kept running through the winter weather, and the crews of the RN-manned ships were urgently needed to man new construction. A further challenge for the RCN came from the accelerated program to modernize the existing corvette fleet; a third or more of the total number were in the shipyards for this extended work during the fall of 1943. Planning soon began to re-establish EG 9 as a Canadian support group, but its ships—three of the first Canadian-built frigates and four modernized or new corvettes—would not be ready for operations until early 1944.[75]

The decision not to rebuild EG 9 immediately reflected in no way on the performance of the Canadian ships. Captain (D) Greenock thought *Chambly* "did extremely well, and it is a pity that none of her attacks resulted in certain destruction of the enemy." *Sackville* also received praise for her attack on 22 September, which was thought to have severely damaged *U 377*. Commodore (D) Londonderry remarked on "the fine offensive spirit maintained by all escorts throughout the attack," which kept losses down and prevented the enemy from seizing the initiative.[76]

While sailing submarines for group *Leuthen* in late August and early September 1943, BdU also despatched new waves of boats to distant theatres, and on 8 September the Submarine Tracking Room at the Admiralty predicted that "an operation of up to half a dozen U-boats in Canadian waters may be imminent."[77] In fact, U-boat Command assigned only two submarines to the Canadian coast at that time, and a third in October. Significantly, the command warned at least one of the boats to "Count on heavy air patrol after being observed," a reflection of the strengthened defences that had driven the submarines back from the coast in the fall of 1942, and *U 262*'s experience of overflights while it lay undetected off Prince Edward Island in May 1943.[78] All three boats, like *U 262* and *U 119* in the spring, were tasked with clandestine operations as their primary mission, pursuit of shipping being a secondary task.[79]

The first submarine of the new wave, Kapitänleutnant R. Schauenburg's *U 536*, arrived off Pointe de Maisonette, in the Baie des Chaleurs, New Brunswick, on 24 September. Its mission, like that of *U 262*, was to rescue escaped prisoners of war to support morale, achieve a propaganda coup and regain the services of some top officers. Arrangements had been made, as in the case of

---

75. Ibid, 76; DHH, NHS 8440, EG 9; C-in-C CNA to Capt (D) Halifax, signals 1658Z, 1729Z, 1742Z 29 Sep 1943, DHH 81/520/8440-60; P. Elliott, *Allied Escort Ships of World War II: A Complete Survey* (London 1977), 197, 218-24, 258-65, 274-5; A. Hague, *Destroyers for Britain*; NSHQ to C-in-C CNA, 1426z 26 Nov 1943, LAC, RG 24, 6797, NSS 8375-354; Bidwell to Houghton, 8 Sep 1943, Bidwell Corr, makes clear that, even before the ONS 18-ON 202 battle, reinforcement of the C groups and EG 5, and the replacement of the Town class in the MOEF and WEF, had priority over the further development of EG 9.

76. Enclosures to C-in-C WA 4256/378/RP of 31 Dec 1943, Atlantic Convoy Reps, files 504, 549

77. Adm, the OIC, "U-boat Trend: Replacing Report Delivered 6 Sep 1943," 8 Sep 1943, cited in Syrett, *Battle of the Atlantic*, 239

78. Knowles, "U-boat Intelligence Summary," 12 Oct 1943

79. IBdU, KTB, Sep 1943

the previous effort, through the efficient, if slow, communications between the prisoners and U-boat Command by the use of pre-arranged codes that appeared as innocuous words and phrases in letters between the prisoners and their families delivered through the Red Cross. U-boat Command also had documents that could assist in an escape meticulously sewn or glued into the bindings of novels and other books that were staples of the comforts sent to prisoners, again through the Red Cross. This time, however, sharp-eyed censors in Canadian naval intelligence discovered the plan, and the RCN coordinated efforts with the army and the Royal Canadian Mounted Police to exploit the escape attempt by setting a trap for the submarine. In the event, the mass escape from Camp 90 at Bowmanville, Ontario, by the famed Kapitänleutnant Otto Kretschmer, in company with a number of other U-boat officers, came to nothing when the RCMP and the army's guards at the camp located the escape tunnel. Another U-boat captain, Kapitänleutnant W. Heyda, nevertheless did break out of the camp on 24 September and, provided with clothes, money, and false papers by the prisoners whose escape attempt had been foiled, made his way to Pointe de Maisonette. There, three days later, he found a welcoming party of army, navy and RCMP personnel, who had been expecting him.[80]

Rear-Admiral Murray, when he received warnings of the operation, had called upon Captain (D) Halifax, Captain W.L. Puxley, RN, Lieutenant-Commander D.W. Piers, who on leaving *Restigouche* had taken up the appointment of training officer under C-in-C CNA, and the British officer who commanded the training submarine at Halifax to prepare a trap for *U 536*. Piers and the British officer visited the Baie des Chaleurs, set up two of the army's mobile radar units and devised an elaborate plan to capture the U-boat with a boarding party. This gave way to what was perhaps a more practical course of action, to seal off the bay with antisubmarine vessels and destroy the submarine. The destroyer HMS *Chelsea*, the corvettes HMCS *Agassiz, Shawinigan, Lethbridge,* and *Rimouski*, the minesweepers HMCS *Mahone, Swift Current, Chedabucto, Ungava,* and *Granby*, as well as a number of Fairmile motor launches, began patrols south of the bay on 25 September, the day after, it turned out, that *U 536* had arrived and lay submerged except for brief periods in the dead of night. *Rimouski* (Lieutenant R.J. Pickford, RCNVR), which had been fitted with diffused lighting to serve as a night-time camouflage, was supposed to detach from the main body and close the U-boat "steaming slowly with navigational lights, and diffused lighting on, pretending to be a small coastal vessel." On the night of 26 September the submarine began to leave the bay, with the intention of surfacing in the safety of the broad waters of the gulf for a long enough period to recharge the depleted batteries of the underwater electric drive system before returning for the rendezvous with the escapees. As *U 536* approached the mouth of the bay, however, Schaunberg and his officers glimpsed warships hovering in the distance. The submarine immediately plunged to the bottom, in shallow waters where the warships were unlikely to hunt, and rested there motionless until the next night, 27–28 September, creeping out into the gulf while still submerged. Once completely clear of the Canadian coast, on 5 October, he made the signal "*Kiebitz verpfiffen* (Magpie Blown)."[81]

80. M.L. Hadley, *U-Boats against Canada: German Submarines in Canadian Waters* (Montreal 1985)

81. J.P.M. Showell, *U-Boats at War: Landings on Hostile Shores* (Shepperton UK 2000), 39–43; Hadley, *U-Boats against Canada*

If aid to escapees occasionally offered moments of comic relief, mining operations were deadly serious. When *U 220* laid sixty-six moored, magnetic mines off St John's on the night of 9–10 October 1943, Allied intelligence had no prior warning.[82] After one of the port minesweepers sighted and destroyed a drifting mine on 11 October, the shore authorities declared a danger area off St John's, restricted traffic to the swept channel into the port, and requested assistance from Halifax. In contrast to the thin cordon *U 119* had laid across the wide approach to the Nova Scotia port, *U 220* laid the mines in clusters between about five and thirteen miles all around the narrow entrance to St John's. This was in accordance with the instructions BdU had given, and the early clearance sweeps established the extent of the scattered field with reasonable accuracy. On 19 October, however, the small Wabana to Sydney convoy WB 65, seven steamers under the escort of the RCN Bangors *Caraquet* and *Miscou*, encountered mines twelve miles off Bullhead, well south of the declared danger area, and the only devices discovered outside the immediate approaches to St John's.[83] Once again, the ill-fated ore ships, which had endured such heavy losses in 1942, suffered misfortune. One of the lead vessels, the British steamship *Penolver*, suddenly suffered a large explosion in the after part of the ship, and, heavily laden with iron ore, plunged beneath the surface within seconds. The next ship in the column, the American *Delisle*, stopped to pick up survivors in the midst of the drifting wreckage, when minutes later an explosion blew open a hold to the sea, and she began to settle. *Miscou* recovered the whole of *Delisle*'s crew, but only fourteen of the forty-one people in *Penolver*. There were, however, no other losses to *U 220*'s field.[84]

As at Halifax, mine clearance required enormous effort, and one that was frequently hindered by stormy weather. Up to a dozen ships operated each day. Nine Canadian Bangors participated, but by chance, as at Halifax, much of the work was done by versatile wooden minesweepers of the Royal Navy. Fortunately, nine of these vessels had put into St John's before making the transatlantic passage from their builders in the United States. Clearance operations continued until 16 December, two weeks after the last mine was located, which accounted for a total of only thirty-four of the sixty-six carried by the submarine. Presumably the rest scuttled themselves in rough seas. Lieutenant Rundle came from Halifax to assist, and succeeded in recovering two of the mines. Although there had been tragedy in October, in subsequent weeks and months the mines did not hinder shipping operations. In December, their impact could be said to have been summed up in FONF's War Diary, which reported "No local activity of note."[85] The third U-boat assigned to the Canadian area in the fall of 1943, *U 537*, under Kapitänleutnant P. Schrewe, erected an automatic weather station in Martin Bay, on the coast of the far northern tip of Labrador, about 15 miles south of Cape Chidley, on 22–23 October.[86] This was not only the first

82. White, *U-boat Tankers*, 184. Knowles, "U-boat Intelligence Summary," 12 Oct 1943, the first mention, evidently based on a decrypt of *U 220*'s signal of success on 11 Oct, which refers only to a "'special task' somewhere off the Canadian coast."

83. This account is based primarily upon Capt (D) Newfoundland to FONF, 20 Feb 1945, with enclosures, LAC, RG 24, 11018, 6-2-1(C). See also "Operations Order St John's for *U 220*," 11 May 1943, BdU, KTB; RCN Press Release, 13 June 1945, Maritime Command Museum; Hadley, *U-boats Against Canada*, 189-91

84. *Caraquet*, "Report of Proceedings: Escorting WB 65 Convoy," 22 Oct 1943, LAC, RG 24, 11330, 8280-WB 65; FONF to Adm, 1849Z, 20 Oct 1943, LAC, RG 24, 6893, NSS 8871-2695

85. FONF War Diary, Dec 1943, LAC, RG 24, 11,505, 1445-102/3, pt 1

86. Showell, *U-Boats at War*, 43-9

automatic weather station in North America, but the only armed landing of German forces on the continent during the Second World War. The station itself went undiscovered. Within a few weeks decrypts of German signals revealed that the U-boat had dropped off a "weather apparatus," but Allied intelligence assumed it was an "automatic weather buoy" that might be floating anywhere "in the Labrador-Newfoundland area."[87] The Canadian Chiefs of Staff, on 29 June 1943, had discounted any threat in the region—they "were of the opinion that the establishment of a [Northeast Arctic Information Centre] could not be justified on Service Grounds"—and on 30 September 1943, the Air Officer Commanding in Chief, Eastern Air Command, arrived at a similar conclusion. The northern reaches of Labrador were, in other words, *terra incognita* to Canadian military authorities.[88]

The Allies had been unaware of *U 537*'s passage to Martin Bay because U-boat headquarters had avoided any radio communication, as was standard procedure for such special missions. On 23 October, however, U-boat headquarters instructed the submarine to pull offshore once its "task" was completed, report, and then begin anti-shipping operations. By 25 October Allied cryptologists had broken the signal and surmised that the super-encrypted reference to the area where the boat was to hunt was off Labrador, most likely the southern part, in the approaches to the Strait of Belle Isle, which the Germans knew to be a focal point of shipping. Direction-finding bearings on a brief signal from Schrewe that placed the boat in the general vicinity of Labrador helped the analysts reach this conclusion.[89] This information caused concern in Ottawa. There had been, as we have seen, indications from Ultra intelligence that the Germans, in their efforts to sustain distant operations, intended to make another concerted push into Canadian coastal waters. News that a submarine was lurking within reach of the Strait of Belle Isle recalled events in the late summer and fall of 1942, when *U 165*, *U 513*, *U 517* and *U 518* had patrolled that focal area in preparation for their destructive assaults southward into the Gulf of St Lawrence and in the St John's–Wabana area. Shipping in the gulf was particularly at risk. The incapacity of the Canadian rail system to move bulk cargoes of timber and grain from the St Lawrence corridor out to the Atlantic ports had resulted in British demands that Canada suspend convoy in the gulf in order to allow the faster movement of more ships, and the Canadian authorities had complied with this in mid September. The first Canadian response to the word of

87. Knowles, "U-boat Intelligence Summary," 14 Nov 1943

88. AVM G.O. Johnson wrote to USAAF Eastern Defence Command at Mitchell Field to say that "while occasional enemy air reconnaissance of Greenland occurs, it is not considered as a serious threat." Canadian Naval Intelligence knew that Schrewe was in Kiel on 22 Aug 1943, "for first cruise of U 537, carried SSR equipment for experiments," but the meaning of "SSR equipment" is not clear. Exactly one week before *U 537* anchored in the bay, and lay there for more than 24 hours with all hatches open, a Canso of 162 Squadron RCAF stationed at Goose Bay had flown an unusual patrol, the reasons for which were not explained—the pilot of this aircraft, when interviewed in 1981, did not recall receiving any warning of a possible U-boat in the area, along the Labrador coast. Douglas, "The Nazi Weather Station in Labrador," *Canadian Geographic* 101(1981), 42-6; *idem* "Beachhead Labrador," *Military History Quarterly*, 8/2 (1996); 162 Squadron Intelligence Report for period Oct 15th to 21st inclusive, EAC file 6-21-7, LAC, RG 24, 5322; W.A.B. Douglas to Grp Capt C.G.W. Chapman, 13 Aug 1981, DHH 2000/5; Canadian Naval Intelligence Records, DHH, 81/520/1480; Chiefs of Staff cte mtg 120, 29 June 1943, DHH 181.003 (D189)

89. Adm to COMINCH, 2236/25 Oct 1943, 0940/28 Oct 1943, SRH 236 pt 5, NARA, RG 457 National Security Agency Records; R. Sarty, *Maritime Defence of Canada* (Toronto 1996), 177

U 537's presence on the northern doorstep to the gulf was quickly to reintroduce convoys between Sydney and Québec City.[90]

German intentions became clearer on 28 October when the Allies decrypted instructions sent by U-boat Command the previous day for *U 537* to hunt off a "harbour," whose identity was revealed by another signal that gave the position of the minefield recently laid by *U 220* off St John's. Evidently the new U-boat was going to attempt to repeat the successes of *U 513* and *U 518* of the year before. The Operational Intelligence Centre in Ottawa promptly issued an "A" category Otter signal for an area of approximately 100 nautical miles by 100 nautical miles off the entrance to St John's.[91] This was an area that could be well covered by an aircraft in a normal patrol of six to twelve hours. Air Force Headquarters in Ottawa recognized the first opportunity to attempt a "hunt to exhaustion" and directed Eastern Air Command to undertake the operation, code-named Salmon. If an aircraft sighted *U 537*, or made an attack, it was to continue to patrol in the vicinity until supporting aircraft could reach the area, and it was to continue to circle the gradually expanding probability area wherein the slowly moving submerged boat might be located. The idea was to keep the U-boat submerged and, therefore, limited in mobility, until warships could reach the scene and conduct an asdic search, while aircraft continued to saturate the area around the warships to make sure the submarine did not attempt to surface and escape at speed. In theory, if the aircraft and warships could maintain a coordinated search for, say, thirty-six hours, the limit of a U-boat's underwater endurance, the enemy, if not already located, would be forced to surface into the jaws of strong air and sea forces.[92]

During the morning of 31 October one of three Lockheed Hudsons from 11 Squadron RCAF that were sweeping the Otter area sighted the surfaced submarine about sixty miles southeast of St John's and made an attack that was wide of the mark. A scratch group of ships from St John's—the Town class destroyer HMS *Lincoln* and three Canadian Bangors—reached the scene that evening, just as stiffening weather forced the aircraft to return to base. The warships searched without air support through that night, until gale force winds brought an end to the operation the next day; such conditions made any chance of contact with the U-boat highly unlikely. The trail then grew cold until dusk on 10 November, when a Canso from 5 Squadron RCAF carrying out sweeps in support of convoy HX 265 sighted *U 576* about 140 miles south of Cape Race and attacked. The aerial depth charges did no damage to the violently manoeuvring U-boat, which put up a brisk fire from its 20mm anti-aircraft gun. The aircraft departed before its relief could reach the position, and the corvette HMCS *Shawinigan*, despatched from the escort of HX 265, returned to the convoy when it became clear that the attacking aircraft had reported its position inaccurately. After sunrise on 11 November, however, a relief Canso from 5 Squadron sighted the submarine, about eighty miles south of the previous evening's action, and, despite anti-aircraft fire that blew a hole in the leading edge of its wing, placed depth charges close enough to damage *U 576's* forward torpedo tubes. This time, the aircraft remained over the position where the submarine dived until relief aircraft arrived, and began Salmon, the expanding hunt to exhaustion. That afternoon, the British Town class

90.   B. Tennyson and R. Sarty, *Guardian of the Gulf: Sydney, Cape Breton, and the Atlantic Wars* (Toronto 2000), 313-14

91.   Adm to COMINCH, signal 0940, 28 Oct 1943; Sarty, *Maritime Defence of Canada*, 177

92.   Operation Salmon: Air Cover during the Escape Interval, DHH 81/50/1650; Douglas, *Creation of a National Air Force*, 570-1

destroyer *Montgomery* and the Canadian Bangor *Kenora*, which FONF had sent to the position of the attack on the day before, reached the new position. Within two hours however a heavy Grand Banks fog rolled in, forcing the aircraft back to base. Some eleven escorts, pulled in from St John's and from Western Escort Force groups escorting convoys safely removed from the threatened area, took part in the expanding search over the next three days, but the fog prevented any air support except for a few hours on one day.[93]

Although poor weather, and the inexperience of air crews and escort crews in hunts to exhaustion, defeated Canadian efforts to mount a properly organized Salmon, Eastern Air Command and the grab-bag of Western Escort Force ships had succeeded in entirely neutralizing *U 537* and driving it out to sea, away from the focal area of local and transatlantic convoys south of Cape Race. The initial surprise air attack off St John's on 31 October had immediately dissuaded Schrewe from continuing the hunt in that area. "For me this part of the coast has been made unhealthy." He had then intended to pull into the approaches to Cabot Strait, the southern entrance to the Gulf of St Lawrence, but instantly abandoned that plan with the attack on 10 November. At the time of the attack on the following day, he was withdrawing back out into the Atlantic. When Schrewe's position was revealed by the attack on 10 November he had radioed news of the action to U-boat Command and announced his intention of retreating; the Allies soon decrypted this message, and Canadian authorities were able immediately to cancel the recently reimposed requirement for convoy of shipping in the St Lawrence, thereby minimizing the disruption in the passage of bulk-goods to Britain.[94] The contrast to events in 1942, when U-boats had been able freely to penetrate Conception Bay and the Gulf of St Lawrence, sink significant numbers of ships, and hinder ocean trade, could not have been more vivid.

While the limited forces available in the Canadian area countered German efforts to reassert a presence there, the main Allied forces that operated to the east of Newfoundland pounded the enemy unmercifully. Allied confidence that the battle for ONS 18 and ON 202 had demonstrated the soundness of the organization and fighting power of the MOEF even in the face of a surprise like the *zaunkönig* proved to be well founded. Meanwhile, U-boat Command sought immediately to capitalize on the success, as it had seemed, of operations against ONS 18-ON 202. A new patrol line formed west of Iceland starting on 24 September, and successive patrol lines, reinforced by fresh boats, took position in a westward sweep, ultimately within four hundred miles of Newfoundland by the end of October. Such was the Allied advantage in intelligence that the Admiralty was able to route the largest and most weakly escorted convoys clear; for others it could arrange timely reinforcement by support groups and shore-based aircraft, which could now reach right across the Atlantic. Unable now to organize multiple patrol lines in different parts of the ocean, as had been possible early in 1943, BdU was no longer in a position to force contact on its own terms. On the few occasions that U-boats succeeded in contacting convoys, they were scarcely able to penetrate the extended screens of aircraft and support groups. Allied losses included two merchant ships, one of which was a straggler and therefore beyond the reach of the convoy defences, and one escort, the Polish destroyer *Orkan*, which went down with heavy loss of life. By

---

93. Douglas, *Creation of a National Air Force*, 572-3

94. Knowles, "U-boat Intelligence Summary," 14 Nov 1943; *U 537*, KTB, 31 Oct 1943, 10-11 Nov 1943; Tennyson and Sarty, *Guardian of the Gulf*, 314

Top: Fairmile exercises with the 77th Flotilla off Gaspé. Memories of the 1942 U-boat campaign in the St Lawrence were still fresh. (LAC PA 140669)

Bottom: A German glider bomb explodes near a freighter 21 November 1943. The photograph was taken from HMCS *Prince Robert* escorting the convoy. (DND HN909)

HMCS *Lindsay* heads out on a sweep while escorting a convoy. (DND Z-68-69-70-71)

contrast the Allies destroyed fifteen U-boats, nine by air attack—including one by the RCAF—and six by support groups.[95]

On 7 November 1943 the German command admitted defeat on the northern convoy routes and moved the U-boats to the eastern Atlantic, to work the Gibraltar–United Kingdom route.[96] This was claimed to be a temporary measure, until air reconnaissance was available for the more distant North Atlantic convoys. The 20mm anti-aircraft weapons, it was admitted, were inadequate to counter air attack, but U-boats would succeed, so the vain belief persisted, with the heavier calibre 37mm weapons being made ready. Under the circumstances, only night operations were to be undertaken. Aircraft were now supposed to home U-boats onto convoys just after darkness fell. With the undue optimism that had marked the return to the northern routes in September, this strategy was based on the assumption that convoys on the Gibraltar–United Kingdom route would be weakly defended, having "been free from operations for a long time," but the Allied ability to react quickly, especially with air cover, was acknowledged. Thus the *Luftwaffe* had to play its part, not only taking over the search function and homing boats onto the target, but combatting the aircraft that were defending the convoys. Without such support, it was emphasized, far ranging wolf packs could not fight effectively.[97]

These assessments were based on the experiences of group *Schill*, that began operating on the Gibraltar–United Kingdom route on 26 October. On 11 November BdU reinforced *Schill*; decryption of the order reached the Submarine Tracking Room on the 14th. Two days later, after a German aircraft sighted SL 139/MKS 30, the U-boats received instructions to intercept the convoy. The group now consisted of twenty-six boats in three patrol lines, the disposition of which was revealed to Allied routing authorities by decryptions of 16 and 18 November. At the same time German aircraft reconnaissance, as well as HF/DF and interception of radio transmissions from the convoy, gave U-boat Command precise knowledge of its position, course, speed and size. It was a very large and heavily defended convoy with EG 40 (two destroyers, two frigates, two sloops, two corvettes, an armed merchant cruiser, and the Canadian auxiliary anti-aircraft cruiser *Prince Robert*) reinforced during passage by the RCN's support group EG 5 (the British frigates *Tweed* and *Nene*, and the modernized corvettes HMCS *Lunenburg*, *Edmundston*, *Calgary,* and *Snowberry*) and EG 7 (three frigates and three sloops). On 21 November the five frigates of EG 4 also joined the screen. Coastal Command provided constant air cover during daylight. In a seventy-eight-hour battle only three U-boats, of thirty-one that eventually took part, were able to carry out attacks. *U 515* blew the stern off the sloop HMS *Chanticleer* with a *zaunkönig* on 18 November, *U 238* fired one at a frigate the next night but missed, and *U 618* shot down a Sunderland flying boat that was attempting to attack on 20 November. In exchange, the defending forces destroyed three U-boats—one of these was the first victory for a Canadian support group.[98]

95. Syrett, *Defeat of the U-boats*, 203-24; Blair, *Hitler's U-boat War* II, 426-41; MOD, *U-boat War in the Atlantic* III, 28-32. For a full digest of the very complete intelligence available to the Allies, see NARA, RG 457, SRMN 037, Knowles, "U-Boat Intelligence Summary," 4 Oct-14 Nov 1943

96. Syrett, *Defeat of the U-boats*, 227; Analysis, EG B7, Second Support Group, U-boat Attack on Convoy SL 138/MKS 28, PRO, ADM 199/2024

97. SGR II 197, Reel 2

98. A Leigh Light Wellington of 179 Squadron RAF sank *U 211*, and HMS *Foley* and HMS *Crane* of EG 7 sank *U 538*. In addition, HMS *Exe* of EG 40 severely damaged *U 333*. Syrett, *Defeat of the U-boats*, 236-46; A. Niestlé, *German U-boat Losses during World War II: Details of Destruction* (Annapolis 1998)

It was a striking coincidence that the target of the successful attack was *U 536*. The boat had joined the convoy action while on the homeward leg of its long mission to North America after escaping the trap laid by the RCN in the Baie des Chaleurs. The submarine had the misfortune to get caught in the pursuit of another U-boat by *Nene* (Commander J.K. Birch, RNR), *Snowberry* (Lieutenant J.A. Dunn, RCNVR), and *Calgary* (Lieutenant-Commander H.K. Hill, RCNVR), which were in the van of the convoy, on the night of 19–20 November. *U 536*, according to one survivor, was suddenly illuminated, possibly by the Canadian attack on the other submarine, and it dived deep. The other marauder had also dived, and the Canadian ships made asdic contact, but lost it after a Hedgehog and depth charge attack. After the ships had searched the area for over an hour, *Snowberry* gained a fresh asdic contact and dropped ten depth charges set to detonate at 350 and 550 feet, then regained contact and fired a pattern set to 150 and 300 feet. One of these was probably the devastating attack recalled by a survivor of *U 536*:

> the men ... suddenly [heard] the hair-raising ping! ping! [of asdic] beating against their bulkheads. A series of depth charges followed right after without giving them time to brace themselves ...
>
> The results ... coming suddenly and without warning out of a clear sky, were catastrophic for the submerged boat. The attack had caused a serious leak in the stern section and ... the boat was literally knocked topsy-turvy, or rather, the other way around, perpendicularly with its bow upward and stern downward. It hung bolt upright, still submerged, between the surface and the bottomless depths.

With heroic efforts by the crew, *U 536* gradually righted itself. *Snowberry* had lost contact. *Nene* and *Calgary* joined, however, and the frigate gained a contact on which it delivered another depth charge pattern. Almost immediately, the conning tower broke surface near *Snowberry*, which quickly made a hit with its 4-inch gun and raked the hull with fire from light weapons; *Nene* and *Calgary* soon joined in the fusillade, which ended when it became clear that the submariners were abandoning ship. *U 536* was still making way, defeating efforts by the Canadian ships to put a boarding party aboard by boat, when it sank by its severely damaged stern. Only seventeen of the fifty-five men aboard survived.[99]

The battle for SL 139/MKS 30 was another dreadful failure for the *Kriegsmarine*, but had the *Luftwaffe* provided adequate cooperation with the U-boats the outcome might have been different. On 21 November, after BdU had ordered the U-boats to break off, a wave of twenty-five Heinkel 177 aircraft, 800 miles from their base, attacked the convoy with glider bombs. *Prince Robert*, which had recently completed conversion into an anti-aircraft cruiser with a formidable armament of five twin-barrelled 4-inch high angle gun mounts, arrived from Plymouth to reinforce the escort just as the action was beginning. Strong anti-aircraft fire from the convoy, particularly by *Prince Robert*, limited the losses inflicted by this strong attack to one merchant ship sunk and one severely damaged, and brought down two enemy machines.[100]

The German analysis of the battle for SL 139/MKS 30 blamed inadequate anti-aircraft defence in U-boats, bad weather, and the proximity to Allied air bases. Dönitz therefore proposed return-

---

99. D.M. McLean, "Escort Group 6," 2-5, DHH 2000/5; Milner, *U-boat Hunters*, 83-4; KTB, *U 536*

100. MOD, *U-boat War in the Atlantic* III, 39; M. MacLeod, "The Prince Ships 1940-1945," CFHQ Report No 5, 31 Oct 1965, DHH 76/98

ing to the northern transatlantic routes as soon as the submarines were fitted with the new 37mm anti-aircraft mounting, a logical but fatally flawed conclusion, because it was based, once again, on a set of inaccurate assumptions.[101]

The defeat of the German attack on shipping administered in the final months of 1943, a convincing demonstration of superior maritime power, was an even more critical blow against Germany than the defeat the U-boats had suffered that May. Tonnage warfare had failed, and Allied naval strategy, despite difficulties of command and control, had triumphed. The North Atlantic lifeline was sufficiently sure to permit the buildup of Allied forces for the invasion of Europe.

C-in-C Canadian Northwest Atlantic and the Trade and Intelligence organizations in Ottawa were functioning efficiently, even if naval and air forces based on the Canadian mainland and Newfoundland were slow in perfecting new tactics against lone U-boats. The Canadian groups of the Mid-Ocean Escort Force and the Western Local Escort Force, in cooperation with four British MOEF groups and various British, Canadian, and American support groups, had safely convoyed millions of tons of materiel necessary for the liberation of occupied Europe. The only losses had occurred with the sinking of six merchant ships and three escorts, one of which was *St Croix*, in the fight for ONS 18 and ON 202. Of twenty-seven U-boats destroyed in the North Atlantic during this period, sixteen were sunk by aircraft, ten by escorts, and one jointly by aircraft and escorts.[102] Two of those successes were achieved by RCAF aircraft and one by Canadian and British escorts from the Canadian support group EG 5. The second Canadian support group, EG 9, had a short life because of its breakup after the battle for ONS 18 and ON 202, but this was no reflection on the effectiveness of its surviving ships. It is noteworthy that the sole U-boat destroyed by an escort from a MOEF group acting as close escort to a convoy was *U 229*, rammed by HMS *Keppel* on 22 September. Virtually all other U-boat kills at this time, if they were not the result of aircraft attack, had been by ships in select support groups, particularly the mid-ocean group B 7 and EG 2, commanded by those exceptionally successful antisubmarine warriors Commander P. Gretton, RN, and Captain F.J. Walker, RN. These groups were responsible for six of the ten U-boats destroyed by surface vessels.

Although offensively minded seamen always made the destruction of U-boats their first priority, and although the exchange rate was a vital factor in Dönitz's acceptance of defeat, the strategic objective was not to sink submarines. Destroying marauders, as had been established by the institution of the convoy system over many centuries, was merely a bonus. The common and great achievement of all Allied ships and aircraft was to ensure the safe and timely arrival of convoys. As we shall see, in Ottawa a crisis in civil-military relations would lead to emphasis on the RCN's shortcomings, and the accomplishment of Canadian escort groups in bringing about the strategic objective would be cast into obscurity. In the end, however, it was that accomplishment, and not the number of U-boats sunk by Canadian ships, that counted. This was what opened the way for a balanced fleet, for the only kind of navy that, in the considered opinion of the Naval Staff, could make a recognizable contribution to the final defeat of enemy naval forces.

---

101. SGR II 197, Reel 2; Syrett, *Defeat of the U-boats*, 247; Analysis, Convoy SL139/MKS30, Ops of the Fourth EG, Convoy SL 140/MKS 31, PRO, ADM 199/2026

102. Syrett, *Defeat of the U-boats*, App 1. This listing omits the sinking of *U 338* by a VLR Liberator of 120 Squadron RAF, on 20 Sep 1943.

A flotilla of Royal Navy R-boats off Dieppe, France during the disastrous raid by 2nd Canadian Infantry Division, 19 August 1942. (LAC PA183770)

Combined Operations in European Waters
May 1942 to the Eve of Neptune

THE ROYAL CANADIAN NAVY accepted its commitment for combined operations, almost by accident, on 10 October 1941.[1] The return of Canada's River class destroyers to join the Newfoundland Escort Force that summer had left a drastically reduced Canadian naval presence in England.[2] Since naval staff appreciations, then and later, consistently emphasized the desirability of having a Canadian naval presence in that region, it was not surprising that when Commodore H.E. Reid, Deputy Chief of Naval Staff, visited the United Kingdom, he was receptive to a suggestion by Admiral of the Fleet Sir Roger Keyes, Director of Combined Operations, that Canadian naval personnel be lent to his organization.[3] Naval Minister Angus L. Macdonald visited England himself later in the year, and gave his blessing to the plan. At that time the Canadians had little idea of the huge demands that would be made upon their resources by Britain and the United States in the coming months, whereas Keyes, who was facing intense scepticism about his intentions, must have welcomed the opportunity to build up his establishment, without having to negotiate with the Admiralty and Chiefs of Staff in Whitehall.

The RCN supplied fifty officers and three hundred ratings "to be maintained as a unit if circumstances permit." Trained personnel were scarce, and therefore six RCNVR sub-lieutenants already on loan to British warships went to combined operations, in exchange for RCNVR sub-lieutenants who had completed basic training. The rest of the people, all volunteers for "hazardous duty," went over in six separate drafts during the first three months of 1942.[4] They were paid by the RCN and administered by HMCS *Niobe*, the RCN shore establishment in London. They served under the operational command of the Royal Navy. Canadian naval authorities estimated that the officers and men provided would form six landing craft flotillas, each with a flotilla officer, seven boat officers, twelve coxswains, twenty-four seamen, and a dozen stoker drivers, a total of fifty-six all ranks.[5]

1   NSHQ to Adm, 10 Oct 1941, DHH 81/520/1250(1)

2. See Douglas, *No Higher Purpose,* 195-6. The CCCS together with his small staff, and personnel serving on loan to the RN, were the only Canadian naval personnel left in the UK after withdrawal of the Canadian River class destroyers.

3. Tucker, *Naval Service of Canada* II, 442

4. Sec NB to CCCS, 31 Dec 1941, LAC, RG 24, 11702, 09-1-2

5. SO(CO) to CCCS, 18 Jan 1943, LAC, RG 24, 3948, 1037-34-1

By the time these measures had been taken Captain Lord Louis Mountbatten had supplanted Keyes.[6] In March 1942 Prime Minister Churchill, in the face of disapproval by the Chiefs of Staff, had Mountbatten promoted two levels to Vice-Admiral as Chief of Combined Operations and a full member of the Chiefs of Staff "whenever major issues are in question and, also, as heretofore, when his own Combined Operations, or any special matters in which he is concerned, are under discussion."[7] The Canadian volunteers were joining an exciting and controversial organization.

If the naval staff saw the combined operations volunteers as a means of helping out the RN, Minister of National Defence Colonel J.L. Ralston saw them—symbolically at least—as being something more. "You leave Canada on a great crusade," he informed them by a message that bore similarity to the words used by General Eisenhower about two years later in addressing the Allied forces just before the invasion of Normandy. "Canadians in the last war honoured their country and themselves. Your fellow Canadians have no doubt that you will keep up that fine record. If [you] can better it you are good indeed. Wherever you serve you have the unbounded support and grateful confidence of your fellow citizens of this Dominion. May you have a safe passage and good health, high courage and great success."[8] The men Ralston thus sent on their way would certainly prove to have high courage, and they certainly kept up the fine record of Canadians in the First World War.

Just as Mountbatten was putting his stamp on the organization, the first two Canadian units arrived in England, in January 1942. Accompanying them was Lieutenant-Commander K.S. Maclachlan, a forty-nine-year-old chemical engineer with no previous naval service. Machlachlan had been a Lieutenant-Colonel in the Non-Permanent Active Militia before the war broke out, and after serving for several months without remuneration as the Associate Acting Deputy Minister (Naval and Air) for the Department of National Defence, he had joined the RCNVR in order to make what he believed would be "the greatest individual contribution to the war effort." Maclachlan joined the staff of Captain R.I. Agnew, Commodore Commanding Canadian Ships and Establishments in the United Kingdom (CCCS), as Staff Officer, Combined Operations, and in March, at the request of the Admiralty, received the additional appointment of Staff Officer, Craft, at Combined Operations Headquarters in London. In the meantime the RCN drafts went to HMS *Louisbourg*, the combined operations training base at Hayling Island, near Portsmouth. Lieutenant W.S. Brooke, RCNVR, serving on the staff of the Rear-Admiral, Landing Bases at Inverary Scotland (HMS *Québec),* looked after their interests. Brooke was an insurance executive and yachting enthusiast who had joined the RCNVR in 1940. He had been loaned almost immediately to the RN and had held his appointment since June 1941.

---

6. The troubled origins of the Combined Operations organization, and the rise and fall of Keyes as its director, can be traced in correspondence; Keyes to Churchill, 4 Feb 1941, Churchill to Keyes, 5 Feb 1941, COS (41) 59, 27 Sep 1941, Keyes Memo [10 Sep 1941], Keyes to Churchill and Churchill to Keyes, 4 Oct 1941, Keyes to Ismay, 11 Oct 1941, Churchill to Keyes, 14 Oct 1941, Keyes Papers; Noble to Pound, 3 Mar 1942, Pound to Noble, 8 Mar 1942, Roskill Papers, ROSK 5/36, Churchill College Archive Centre, Cambridge

7. Churchill to Pound, 7 Mar 1942, quoted in M. Gilbert, *Road to Victory: Winston S. Churchill, 1941-1945* (London 1986), 71-2; Churchill to COS, 8 Mar 1942, PRO, PREM 3 330/2. For a full discussion of Mountbatten's promotion, see B. Villa *Unauthorized Action* (Toronto 1989), 169-72

8. SO(CO) to CCCS, nd, LAC, RG 24, 11702, 09-1-1. There is unfortunately no record of how the audience reacted as this unexpected missive was read out to them.

Maclachlan and Brooke became the RCN's chief advocates of amphibious warfare. This was a role they soon found to be somewhat thankless in the face of a subsequent lack of interest among the naval staff in Ottawa. When the Admiralty proposed putting Canadians into flotillas of Landing Craft Tank (LCT), Ottawa declined to send over the necessary additional personnel, so the RCN units formed Canadian flotillas of Landing Craft Assault (LCA) and Landing Craft Mechanized (LCM) instead. To forestall the possibility that the Canadians would be broken up into smaller units, Maclachlan and Brooke submitted a proposal, which was fully supported by Captain Agnew, who had already asked for a seventh draft of personnel, for a Canadian amphibious base in England. The Admiralty and Combined Operations Headquarters were in favour of the base, which Agnew argued would be "a central point for combined training, experiment and development for the three Canadian services here." Maclachlan, taking advantage of his former position in the Ottawa bureaucracy, wrote personally to Chief of Naval Staff Rear-Admiral Percy W. Nelles to say that in the rapidly changing techniques of combined operations the training given Canadians needed constant updating. "Some benefit can be had through the experience of the personnel in the six assault craft flotillas now trained or in training," he wrote, "but that experience will be lost when the personnel are discharged ... and scattered across Canada. A greater range of experience can be obtained if we actually handle an assault base and gain practical experience in all the different phases of such an activity."[9]

Lieutenant-General A.G.L. McNaughton and Air Commodore H. Edwards, the senior Canadian army and air force officers in England, readily accepted Maclachlan's argument that the RCN must "gain the initiative in the developing of Combined Operations, as compared with the Canadian Army and the RCAF." McNaughton added his weight to the recommendations coming from London during his visit to Canada in March 1942, by suggesting that Canada "build and man approximately 1000 power lighters for the purpose of transporting the Canadian army overseas, in the event of offensive operations being taken on the continent."[10] To be constructed of wood, since steel was in short supply, the lighters would, in the view of the Naval Board, have added undesirable expense and increased the navy's already overwhelming manning problems. The estimate of cost was about $10 million for 1000 craft, which would have required 7000 men for their crews. The commitment, once entered into, was expected to become even more demanding. In April the board referred the matter to the naval minister and CNS for further discussion at the ministerial level.[11] The considerations affecting such discussion—at a time when the German submarine offensive in the western Atlantic was in full swing, and the manning and maintenance of escorts had to be the navy's first priority—made the outcome inevitable. An expansion of the kind proposed by McNaughton to build up a Canadian amphibious operations capability spearheaded by the navy might have demanded up to 20,000 personnel, and it was simply not on the agenda of Nelles and his staff.[12]

9.   Maclachlan to Nelles, 30 May 1942, DHH 81/520/1250 (1), 33-1-6

10. Tucker, *Naval Service of Canada* II, 86. For other references to McNaughton's visit, and his advice to Cabinet in 1942, see Stacey, *Arms, Men and Governments*, 134, and Douglas, *Creation of a National Air Force*, 355

11. NB min, 20 Apr 1942

12. If there was to be further diversification of the naval effort the RCN was bound to turn its attention first to the commissioning and manning of Tribal class destroyers. It bears mentioning at this point that the long-term considerations of a postwar navy, evident in some staff papers, had not yet risen to the surface in Ottawa. Cmdre Reid, DCNS, observed in May 1942 that "I find it very difficult to see how we can plan for a post-war navy now. Its construction will be governed by so many factors which cannot take form until after the war." VCNS to DOP, 12 May 1942, LAC, RG 24, 3844, NS 1017-10-34

The matter was raised again in June. By that time the army had decided to proceed with the construction of one hundred Landing Craft, Mechanized (Wood)—or LCM(W)—for use in amphibious warfare training in Canada. When the Chief of General Staff, Lieutenant-General Ken Stuart, asked the Royal Canadian Navy to man and service the landing craft the Naval Board would consent only to giving naval ratings already under training on the west coast one week of training in the operation and maintenance of the landing craft. The board also offered to assist in training army personnel to man these vessels. The scheme had little bearing on European operations. It did, however, make sense a few weeks later, after the Japanese invasion of Kiska and Attu in the Aleutian Islands. At the request of Captain E.R. Mainguy, Chief of Naval Personnel, the board approved recruiting Fishermen's Reserve crews for this purpose. In July 1942 a landing craft training base for Fishermen's Reserve crews was established at William Head near Esquimalt. It suffered from a shortage of craft and instructors however, and proved of limited value.[13]

McNaughton's proposals could not be dismissed out of hand, and the Naval Board eventually agreed to assist "in the training of Army personnel set aside for the manning of landing craft providing that this training is not conducted at naval bases." To emphasize the navy's desire to avoid becoming involved in the manning of landing craft, the board also stated that this decision governed the request to establish a combined operations base in the United Kingdom. Macdonald approved, and a signal sent to CCCS on 11 June stated that Naval Service Headquarters was "unable to accept commitment for establishment and operation of new ... base for combined operations [as] ... naval training facilities [were] entirely inadequate at present to permit consideration of manning landing craft."[14]

Following this rebuff, Maclachlan arranged a transfer from Mountbatten's headquarters to Inverary as Staff Officer (Combined Operations). His appointment coincided with the completion of training for four Canadian flotillas, which had suffered from a shortage of landing craft at Hayling Island. Some officers expressed reservations about the operational readiness of these flotillas. A good many of the volunteers had failed to meet the stringent medical requirements for combined operations, and this was cause for concern because there were not sufficient volunteers in England to replace all of those who had been rejected. To help solve this problem Captain H. Kingsley, commanding officer of *Niobe*, decided to keep a roster of volunteers.[15] In the meantime, the Canadians who had met the requirements made an excellent impression on their instructors and reached a high state of morale.[16] It is true, however, that without a specific operation to prepare for, and when there was little for the flotilla crews to do beyond mundane camp duties, that morale fell off noticeably. Maclachlan was not privy to the plans then in full swing for carrying out a raid on Dieppe. Thus, he attempted to resolve the morale problem by arranging with the Royal Navy to concentrate the Canadian units at one base where they could work on army commitments with Canadian for-

---

13.   NB min, 4 and 22 June 1942; NS min, 1 July 1942, DHH. See Douglas, *No Higher Purpose*, 363-367

14.   NB min, 28 May 4 and 11 June 1942; NSHQ to CCCS, 11 June 1942, DHH 81/520/1250 (1), 33-1-6

15.   CO *Niobe* to CCCS, 11 July 1942, LAC, RG 24, 11702, 09-1-1

16.   The Canadians, observed a British LCdr, did not live up to their reputation for ill discipline: "he had received reports from Northney and Inver[a]ry to the effect that he might expect to have a lot of trouble with the Canadians, but that he and everyone at Roseneath are very agreeably surprised and are anxious to keep the Canadians there." SO(CO), memo, 28 July 1942, DHH 81/520/1250 (1), Organization

mations up to the brigade level. This of course would require Canadian army units to be committed to raiding operations, which neither Maclachlan nor his RN contact realized was in fact being done. As they were discussing the matter, landing craft flotillas were actually embarking men of the 2nd Canadian Infantry Division for Operation Jubilee. [17]

As the CCCS reported soon after Jubilee, "Dieppe was the first time Canadian flotillas of the Royal Navy's Combined Operations forces were in action against the enemy. The conduct of the personnel was favourably commented upon by senior officers." More specifically, members of the 1st and 2nd Canadian Landing Craft Flotillas were distributed among RN Landing Craft Personnel (Large) or LCP(L) units, themselves carried in a Landing Ship Infantry (LSI). Two officers served in two other LSIs as boat officers, while a sub-lieutenant performed "special duties" in one of the supporting destroyers; stokers, whose exact number was not determined, were also assigned to various vessels. [18]

They were not only participants, but also witnesses to a disaster that saw the deaths of more than nine hundred Canadian members of the assaulting force, with a further 2000 taken prisoner; total casualties amounted to some 65 percent of the 5000 troops taking part in the landings. Since then, scores of analysts have come forward to dissect the faulty planning that preceded Jubilee, but for Canadian combined operations personnel the events of 19 August 1942 were more a kaleidoscope of confusion than a source for study. Sub-Lieutenant D. Ramsay, for example, provided little in the way of context or logical framework in a letter to his father, instead relating "some sights I saw," including "My Ordinary Seaman Owen of Hamilton, blasting hell out of a Ju 88 with a .303 rifle; and Able Seaman Spencer of Toronto, our Cox'n, sweating blood in every pore inside his little box ... and Lewis Gunner Smart, also from Hamilton, muttering 'My bloody oath' at every Jerry plane he saw (which was pretty often) then letting them have a whole pan of ammo ... Stoker Birkenes, from deep in the heart of Alberta, who is in the Black Hole of Calcutta (Engine Room), hearing and seeing nothing. That boy deserves a medal! A squadron of Hurribombers is lacing the front of the town with cannon. I never saw anything as beautiful as a Spitfire." [19]

Ramsay's second series of impressions was of

> a German armed trawler blown clear out of the water by one of our destroyers; a 5-inch shell right through from one side to the other on the boat next to me without exploding; the boat officer, Skipper Jones, RNR (ex Trawlerman as you can guess) screaming invectives at the Jerry and coming out once in a while with the famous Jonesian saying, "get stuffed"; a large houseful of Jerry machine gunners pasting hell out of anybody who dared come near the beach; a Ju 88 whose wing was cut in half by AB Mitchinson of Ontario in the boat astern; a plane swooping down low behind a destroyer and letting go a 2000 lb bomb, which ricocheted over the mast and burst about 10 yards on the starboard bow; peeking over the cox'ns box and looking into the smoking cannon of an Me 109. I'm here to state that that was close. The concussion of the near misses knocked the floorboards up and hit me on the chin. Biggest

17. SO(CO) to CCCS, 11 June 1942, CCCS to RALB, 17 June 1942, misc file, Maclachlan memo, 28 July 1942, CS 33-9, SO(CO) to CCCS, 14 Aug 1942, Programme for Canadians in Combined Operations, DHH 81/520/1250 (1) 33-1-6

18. CCCS, to Sec NB, 11 Sep 1942, DHH 81/520/1650-146/15

19. Clayton Marker and David Lewis, eds, "Combined Operations," nd, 63, DHH 94/171

thrill of the day—picking up a Norwegian pilot who bailed out of his Spitfire ... I never thought I'd be glad to see England but those chalk cliffs were really something![20]

From left to right were five main areas where landings were to take place. British commandos went in on the far left. The Royal Regiment of Canada attacked at Puys, the Essex Scottish Regiment and Royal Hamilton Light Infantry (with the Fusiliers Mont-Royal arriving later) assaulted the town of Dieppe proper, and the South Saskatchewan Regiment and the Queen's Own Cameron Highlanders of Canada landed at Pourville. More British commandos were tasked to take out artillery batteries on the far right. Given their distribution, Canadian combined operations personnel participated in most of these operations. On the far left, for example, off Yellow Beach, Sub-Lieutenant D.J. Lewis was in LCP(L) 15 of the 24th Flotilla. As Lewis related soon after the terrible events of 19 August 1942, as they crossed the English Channel conditions were generally favourable and the various flotillas made good progress, when "at 3.30 a.m. ... starshell went up on the starboard hand and lit the whole fleet in a horrible quivering semi-daylight. Our boat was leading the starboard column. It was immediately enveloped in the hottest tracer fire I have ever seen. The air was filled with the whine of ricochets and the bangs of exploding shells, while after every burst of the streaking balls of fire came the clatter of Oerlikons." Nearby was a British Steam Gun Boat (SGB), but its "thin armour was riddled and the shells exploding inside filled her boiler-room with steam. She lost way. The fleet was stopped. One of the bursts struck LCP(L) 42, and Sub-Lieutenant C.D. Wallace, of Montreal was killed instantly. A shot through the windscreen killed the coxswain. Lieutenant-Commander L. Corke, RNVR, the Flotilla Officer, though himself badly wounded, put a Commando soldier at the wheel and carried on. (He was later killed and the boat sank after successfully landing troops.)"[21]

Before the first commando had been put ashore, Operation Jubilee was already beginning to deteriorate. As Lewis continued, "in my boat men threw off their blankets, fumbled for tin hats and weapons. The flak was flying but a few feet ahead and a few astern. Some was right above us. Where it was coming from was uncertain; then, 'E-boats!' everyone was crying. But it turned out to be a German convoy which had stopped us. They had turned their AA armament on our boats. Our boat put on full speed and went under the stern of the disabled SGB. Orders were to land the troops at all costs or the operation would be a bloody failure." This was no exaggeration, since the commandos were tasked with destroying an artillery battery which could annihilate attempts to land on beaches further to the right. As for the flotilla, wrote Lewis, "at full speed we tore away from the lashing beams of flak ... Astern we could see starshells, flak converging, and a big flash which died down and then blew up and lit the sky. I never found out what this was. Possibly the flashes were E-boats which blew up under the broadside of one of the 4-inch flak ships which accompanied us."[22] The 24th Flotilla succeeded in getting its troops ashore, and although they were unable to destroy the battery, they succeeded in reducing its effectiveness by keeping it under small-arms fire for a time.

---

20. Ibid, 63-4

21. CCCS, to Sec NB, 11 Sep 1942

22. Ibid

Men of the Cameron Highlanders of Canada board a landing craft assault on the morning of 19 August 1942 in preparation for their landing on Green Beach at Pourville, France, on the western flank of the raid on Dieppe. (LAC PA113245)

Plastic armour of a landing craft tank damaged by enemy shell fire at Dieppe, France on 19 August 1942. (LAC PA204692)

One of the beaches the commandos were attempting to protect was in front of the village of Puys. The Royal Regiment of Canada was supposed to land there and occupy the headlands overlooking Dieppe to prevent the enemy from using them to interfere with the attack on the town. The operation was a complete failure, with Canadian troops suffering upwards of 90 percent casualties, although it had started out reasonably well. The landing craft left the Landing Ship Infantry at 0334, with one of them equipped with a 3-inch mortar providing fire support. It managed to land the weapon and its ammunition before being disabled by an enemy shell. Landings began at 0540, all troops disembarking. Then, "the craft were withdrawing from the beach when the Flotilla Officer was seriously wounded by rifle fire from the cliffs and Lieutenant [J.E.] Koyl [RCNVR] assumed command." Koyl was from Saskatoon, and will reappear later in this chapter. After taking command, Koyl moved the flotilla out of the range of shore batteries, "which were maintaining a steady fire." Another threat loomed at 1100, when for about forty minutes "the flotilla was subjected to constant bombing and machine-gunning from the air as well as heavy fire from the shore." The flotilla was ordered to Blue Beach to remove survivors of the Royal Regiment of Canada, but that instruction was then countermanded, and the landing craft headed for England. "All craft of the flotilla had to be towed part way across the Channel owing to the lack of fuel although an extra 30 gallons of petrol had been carried by all craft." Among the naval personnel, the flotilla officer was the only casualty from the landing at Puys, but the Royal Regiment of Canada lost 522 of the 554 men who had embarked in England.[23]

In the centre of the operation, at the town of Dieppe, the Essex Scottish Regiment and the Royal Hamilton Light Infantry fared little better than did their comrades at Puys. Sadly, faulty radio communications led divisional headquarters, afloat in a destroyer, to believe the initial landings had gone well and to send in the reserve battalion, the Fusiliers Mont-Royal. One witness to what followed was Lieutenant R.F. McRae, RCNVR, in a flotilla of River class boats carrying the infantry. As McRae related, "we were off the French coast which was invisible behind a heavy smoke screen and from which there came the awful noises of war. About 0730 the Flotilla orders [us] to go in and land the troops. We quickly formed up in line abreast, went through the smoke screen and saw that we were headed toward a beach under high cliffs with the heads of the enemy looking down over the top and pouring machine-gun fire into our boats. Campbell, who was at the wheel, took a line of bullets across his thighs. (Later, as a POW, he lost his legs in successive amputations and died before Christmas from gangrene.) Cavanagh, who was standing next to him, got it in the chest and died an hour later when his lungs had filled up. Brown, though hit in the stomach, took over the wheel from Campbell. I was the lucky one and received only a piece of shrapnel in the ankle."[24]

"In the meantime," McRae continued, "the engine had been blown up and was on fire and the plywood hull of the boat was well perforated, but we had enough weigh on to make it to the beach. The troops scrambled ashore except for their Captain who had been standing up forward with us and was badly wounded, and I believe, dying. Some of the troops never made it across the beach which was strewn with their bodies, and those who did were easy targets for grenades lobbed down from above. There was no life in the boats on either side of us, and it was, I think, because

23   Ibid

24.   Marker and Lewis, eds, "Combined Operations"

they could see that I was busy with the wounded and that we were unarmed so that the Germans on the top of the cliffs gave up trying to finish us off." McRae surrendered a few hours later, and years spent in prisoner-of-war camps did not ease the bitterness he felt at the sacrifices of that day. "The loss of Campbell and Cavanagh and later Brown, as you can see, was a complete waste and unnecessary," he insisted decades later.[25]

Among the Canadian infantry battalions, the lightest casualties were at Green Beach, in front of Pourville a few kilometres to the right of Dieppe. One who participated in the landings was A.G. Kirby, in an R-boat. Approaching at 0515, there was no enemy activity; then, during the final run-in,

> just as I was climbing up onto the stern to ignite the smoke generator, all hell seemed to break loose, the water ahead of us began to erupt like a massive sea volcano as a rain of mortar fire descended [sic] upon the water in front of us. Smoke billowed from our generator and piled up behind us in great clouds that obscured everything in that direction. Plowing through the wall of mortar fire the noise was deafening, but more than that the concussion of each burst pressed on our ears as though we were being smitten with giant pillows. I looked down the line of landing craft and so far no one seemed to have been hit yet. The Germans seemed to have our range now as the explosions were gushing water all around us. How they could be landing so close without hitting us was almost unbelievable. I am half soaked from the water cascading down on me as I crouch down behind the smoke generator. Looking over the top of the canvas cover, I see the Cameron Platoon Commander pointing off to his right. Looking in that direction, I am amazed at the sight of a piper standing up on the focs'le of the second boat over, playing away as though he was alone in a field of heather in the rolling hills by Loch Lomond. Shortly before touching the beach the din is joined by the staccato chorus of a number of automatic weapons from the cliffs that spring from either side of the stony beach in front of us. The roar, the crash, the rattle and smash have reached such a crescendo that it fairly blocks out my ability to appreciate what is taking place around me. Just as I feel the grinding of the hull on the beach, I step forward and undo the lashings on the bicycle on the canvas cover. As the last of the infantry is jumping down to a dry landing on the stones, I shout to the closest man to take the bike. He looks at me for an instant in disbelief as I attempt to hand it to him, then, ignoring me, he turns and runs for the sea wall, scrambling for all he is worth, stumbling over the bodies of his dead and wounded comrades. I drop the bike in the stones, turn and run back toward the rear of the boat.[26]

Kirby's boat returned to a marshalling area near a destroyer. Damage was deemed to be minimal, so when the time came at 1000 to pick up the Camerons for the return to England, he was called for. Again, all went well until the final run-in, when "the sea erupted just as before, with a great barrage of mortar fire. Immediately, I saw the boat on our left go up in a deafening blast and a fountain of water deluged our boat. A small tidal wave hit the side of our boat and tossed us to starboard like a match stick. As we continued on, R-84, on my right, seemed to be taking a blast of fire from the left hand cliffs, probably heavy calibre machine guns, as bits seemed to be flying from the front of her."

25.   Ibid, 28

26.   Ibid, 53-4

Receiving the order to turn 180 degrees to port, "the landing craft swung around hard and headed out to sea and we left the mortar fire behind us but the automatic weapons continued to hound us for nearly a mile." Four boats seemed to be missing. Kirby and his comrades received word that another attempt to rescue the Camerons would have to wait until fire was put down on the enemy. "Just then, the entire world seemed to explode. A great orange flash over my head, accompanied by the loudest blast I have ever heard, knocked me right out of my seat onto the deck. At first, I thought that our destroyer had been hit with a blockbuster, but as my senses slowly returned to me, I realized that she had just fired a broadside with all six guns, and sitting here, under her muzzles, we had just received the full force of the concussion. We were not long getting out of there." Although it made another attempt to get troops off at about noon, Kirby's flotilla gave up in the face of enemy fire and headed for England.[27] Many Camerons had, however, already managed to get off.

Another who had his baptism of fire in combined operations off Green Beach was Sub-Lieutenant J.E. Boak, RCNVR, who served as a boat officer. After landing the Camerons, Boak was one of a group that was supposed to enter Dieppe harbour to conduct or support sabotage operations. The mission was never carried out, but the flotilla was ordered to help evacuate Yellow Beach on the far left of the landings. "Smoke was heavy as the craft moved towards the beach and it was difficult to determine locations. They moved inshore, found they were in the wrong spot and moved out again. Returning towards the shore through the smoke at what they believed to be Yellow Beach they found a group of Canadian soldiers, thought to be part of the Royal Regiment of Canada, standing on a 'raft.' (This 'raft' was a capsized landing craft.) Apparently in an attempt to keep down fire from the shore these men were waving various white garments. The soldiers motioned the vessels to keep away, warning them of the danger. Nevertheless the craft closed in, coming under terrific fire, including that of heavy guns, mortars and machine-guns. Two craft came alongside the raft, and sailors shouted to the men to jump. Four soldiers managed to grab ropes hanging down from Sub-Lieutenant Boak's craft. Two were immediately hauled aboard, the third was dragged for a considerable distance before it was possible to get him aboard, and the fourth dropped off." There were others, who "were picked up by the other LCP(L). While this was being done two of the crew were killed and the Commanding Officer wounded. One of the ratings killed was a Canadian AB named McKenna. He was firing at the cliffs with a Tommy-gun when he was shot through the chest. He said 'I am afraid I am hit, sir,' spun around and fell dead." Army casualties were transferred to an LCT. The flotilla endured an air attack and then was ordered to pick up survivors off the beaches in front of Dieppe. Fire was too heavy to do so, however. Like so many vessels involved in the operation they returned to England with far fewer troops than when they had left.[28]

Of the fifteen Canadian officers and fifty-five ratings—though figures are not precise—who participated in Operation Jubilee, one officer and one rating were immediately reported killed, while one officer and three ratings were posted as missing, six lost out of seventy naval personnel. The known dead were Sub-Lieutenant C.D. Wallace and Able Seaman J.A. McKenna. The missing were Lieutenant R.F. McRae, Leading Stoker R.W. Brown, Able Seaman L.G. Campbell, and Ordinary Seaman R.A. Cavanagh.[29] McRae and Brown were in fact prisoners of war, while the others died

27. Ibid, 54-5

28. CCCS to Sec NB, 11 Sep 1942

29. Ibid

either that day or later of their wounds.[30] For the remainder, some at least developed a certain camaraderie from the experiences shared at Dieppe. Lieutenant-Commander Maclachlan reported that Koyl had taken thirty-four officers and ratings into the LSI (H) and that "a very strong esprit de corps subsequently developed in this group." After moving north to a combined operations base, Koyl began a lobbying campaign "with the object of keeping this group together in a six-craft LCA flotilla. I learned of this after plans had been agreed … that the 1st flotilla would man LCM (Mark 1)s. Practically all of the officers and ratings prefer LCAs."[31] War, however, and especially the policymakers who attempt to administer it, rarely take into account the wishes and desires of those who fight it. The little group was obliged to serve, as individuals, wherever higher authority saw fit to place them.

Regardless of where and with what units Koyl's men were posted, if their contribution was to be publicized it would have to be through RCN efforts and not those of their British comrades. Lieutenant E.H. Bartlett, RCNVR, who reported to the RCN's Naval Information Officer, was well placed to describe British attitudes on the subject. Submitting fifteen lines of text on the Canadian naval experience at Dieppe, Bartlett had to admit that it was a "meagre story." Noting that he had contacted the Admiralty's Chief of Naval Personnel (CNP) and Naval Personnel Records for further information, he reported that they had been unable to provide any. "Apparently the only means of getting detailed information is to apply directly to London," he related, somewhat dejectedly.[32] Accordingly in the weeks following Operation Jubilee, Maclachlan compiled a useful series of survivors' accounts. At about the same time CCCS Agnew was advising COHQ of the situation. He noted that the Canadian officers and ratings would probably "be employed from time to time on exercises or operations where it will be impossible for my Staff Officer (Combined Operations) to maintain contact with them … While the numbers involved are small, the fact that Canadian Naval personnel are participating in this form of warfare is of importance from the Canadian standpoint. It is desirable that records and photographs of their activities be kept, and copies be forwarded to this office for official War records of the Royal Canadian Navy … It will also be advantageous to have some appropriate comments and photographs made available for current journalistic purposes."[33]

Canadians serving in combined operations, although governed by the same general disciplinary code, presented some unique administrative problems for their counterparts in the Royal Navy. The British commanding officer of HMS *Québec* had a query. "It is requested that a supply of Canadian Naval Regulations and Naval Monthly Orders may be made to HMS *Québec* for distribution to the Flotilla and Divisional Officers of the six Canadian Flotillas now in operation... These Flotillas will very frequently be engaged on detached duties and it would considerably facilitate the accountant

---

30.   Forbes McRae File, LAC, Personnel Records Unit; Robert Wm Brown

31.   SO(CO) to CCCS, 19 Sep 1942, DHH 81/520/1250(1), Organization

32.   CCCS to C(CO) at COHQ, 24 Sep 1942, LAC, RG 24, 11702, 09-1-1

33.   Maclachlan had to rely on the army historical section in London for most of his information. He found this unacceptable and recommended that NSHQ appoint an "official recorder" in the UK to document future RCN operations. The naval historian in Ottawa, Dr Gilbert Tucker, agreed but insisted that personnel assigned to this task have the proper academic training and provide wider functions than just gathering "illustrative material." As a result, two RCN officers with university degrees in history, Lieutenants J. George and F. Tovell, were appointed to London in 1943 to gather historical information on RCN operations in European waters. Maclachlan to CCCS, 1 Sep 1942, DHH 81/520/1700-100, 78A; Maclachlan to CCCS, 18 Jan 1943, misc file, DHH, 81/520/1250(1); Tovell interview, May 1988, Tovell biog file, DHH

work of Divisional Officers and *Québec* if these regulations were available to the Flotillas when dealing with requestmen and disciplinary offences... It is considered that this would be to the advantage of the men and the Service since a considerable amount of extra work is caused in *Québec* in checking requests which could be dealt with at the source."[34]

Discipline therefore required no little liaison work, as Lieutenant-Commander Maclachlan learned in late September 1942. Lieutenant Brooke at Inverary reported "that they were having trouble with one of the stokers, who was expressing and spreading dissatisfaction in one of the flotillas; the story being that ratings who were discharged from *Québec* to *Niobe* as unsatisfactory were sent to Halifax, where they received satisfactory appointments on harbour craft." In effect, the stoker was advising his comrades that washing out of combined operations was beneficial to one's career, which could be detrimental to morale. Therefore, "the Staff at Inverary had contemplated disciplining the stoker, taking him out of the flotilla and using him for three or four months on base maintenance work, in order to eliminate the spreading of dissatisfaction. They asked Lieutenant Brooke for his advice." Maclachlan saw no reason to hesitate and reported, "I advised Brooke that we would have no objection whatever to such a procedure being followed."[35]

Meanwhile, the personnel and organizational structure underpinning the Canadian contribution to combined operations continued to evolve. As of 19 September 1942, precisely a month after Operation Jubilee, the Royal Canadian Navy had provided 344 all ranks, thirty having become casualties or having been transferred for one reason or another. The remainder were organized into six flotillas, numbered 1 through 6, of LCA, LCM (Mark 1), and LCM (Mark 3). One officer had been released for home leave in Canada, subsequently reverting to general service "based on his eight months experience on Trawlers working from Western Approaches to Iceland." In another case, "he has made a good conscientious effort to discharge his responsibilities," however, "there is some doubt in the minds of the Combined Operations officers responsible for appointments as to whether he is now competent to lead his flotilla in a complicated exercise, or in action. Under these circumstances, I indicated that we would have no objection to the appointment of an RNVR officer in his place and that ... we would be glad to take him back into general service in the RCN."[36]

Generally, "experience to date confirms the wisdom of accepting flotilla officers selected by roster at Combined Operations Headquarters, and postponing until later the ambition to have the flotillas manned exclusively by Canadians." As for ratings, "there were 129 Canadians available for allocation to the six flotillas, against a requirement of 232. It was proposed that the deficiency be made up by the allocation of RN seamen to the Canadian flotillas." Regarding stokers, the situation was different, where "we had a surplus of ten stokers. It is planned to allocate these stokers to the flotilla maintenance parties which travel with the flotillas. The requirement of each maintenance party is for three stokers. As all our stokers are trained as drivers they will not only do the maintenance work but will be available as reinforcements." Training was a learning experience for instructors and candidates alike, where "the Canadian ratings had developed beyond all expectations and were considered first-class, but requiring firm control. The officers, on the other

34.   CO HMS *Québec* to CCCS, 1 Oct 1942, LAC, RG 24, 11702, 09-1-1

35.   SO(CO) to CCCS, 28 Sep 1942, DHH 81/520/1250(1), Correspondence (SO Combined Ops)

36.   SO(CO) to CCCS, 19 Sep 1942

hand, had not developed as well as the young Englishmen do under similar circumstances. The Canadians tend to need their instruction in far too much detail, and have not developed the sense of responsibility, or shown the initiative and ingenuity required." It was felt in some circles "that this will come, but that further supervision with this objective in mind is needed."[37] On a more mundane note, at the end of October 1942 the Canadian flotillas, which had at first been numbered from one to six, became the 80th, 81st, 55th, 61st, 88th, and 92nd respectively.[38]

After months of training and the experience of Dieppe, it was with this organization that Canadians participated in Operation Torch, the landings in North Africa of November 1942.[39] Torch was a compromise in Allied grand strategy: the British and American high commands had what one historian has described as "a fundamental and unavoidable difference of opinion over the very basis of strategy."[40] Both British and American planners agreed that the Allies must in the end invade the European continent, but the British War Cabinet and the American Joint Chiefs of Staff disagreed on the timing, with the British insisting on a full buildup of strength in Britain before attempting a cross-Channel invasion. President Roosevelt finally ordered his military commanders, Fleet Admiral Ernest King and General George Marshall, who had suggested diverting forces to the Pacific, to proceed unconditionally with an invasion of northwest Africa in 1942 in order to rally support for "Europe First." This had the important result that planning for the operation, and for all subsequent amphibious operations by the Royal Navy, came directly under the control of the Admiralty. Admiral Sir Bertram Ramsay planned the amphibious operations for Torch, Husky (the Sicily landings in July 1943), and Neptune (the assault landings in Normandy in June 1944). Ramsay later made the blunt observation that "amphibious operations were, one might almost say, in private hands for quite a while ... It was not until they were removed and placed under service ministries and planned and carried out under their direction that sanity prevailed."[41]

Some of the formations detailed for Torch would leave from the United Kingdom. Hence the Canadians were involved, and in keeping with policy already discussed, "on this occasion they were organized as Canadian Flotillas but had a high percentage of RNVR ratings added." Generally, "the opposition was almost negligible compared to that encountered at Dieppe. The Canadian Flotillas carried out the tasks assigned to them in a creditable manner."[42] Koyl was slightly more colourful in his evaluation, reporting that "this operation, as compared with Dieppe, was a complete holiday as the opposition in most quarters was negligible."[43]

The six Canadian flotillas involved in Torch concentrated their efforts on putting British and American troops ashore at Algiers and Oran. At Algiers, landings began on the morning of 8

37.   Ibid

38.   SO(CO) to Navy Office of Canada, London, 30 Oct 1942, DHH 81/520/1250(1), Organization

39.   For the service of RCN corvettes in Operation Torch see Douglas, *No Higher Purpose*, ch11

40.   B. Farrell, *The Basis and Making of British Grand Strategy: Was There a Plan?* (Lewiston 1998), 311-26. See also, G. Weinberg, *A World at Arms: A Global History of World War II* (Cambridge 1994) 359.

41.   Draft letter from Ramsay to Cyril Falls, military correspondent of The *Times of London*, in 1944. Ramsay Papers, Churchill College Archive Centre, Cambridge, RMS 30. See also W.S.J.R. Gardner, "Admiral Sir Bertram Ramsay," in S. Howarth, (ed), *Men of War: Great Naval Leaders of World War II* (New York 1993), 349-62

42.   SO(CO) to CCCS, 18 Jan 1943

43.   Marker and Lewis, "Combined Operations"

November along twelve beaches east or west of the town.[44] Oran was no more difficult, and in the week that followed "the men worked stripped almost to the buff" as they ferried reinforcements and supplies. Shifting sandbars near Oran added some modicum of challenge, but according to Joseph Schull, in *The Far Distant Ships*, "one of the flotilla officers reported that it had actually been difficult to get his men out of their craft to be relieved."[45]

A detailed account of his experiences during the Torch landings was left by Sub-Lieutenant I.A. Barclay, RCNVR, although his story begins some considerable time before the Allied decision to land in North Africa. In the early half of 1942 Barclay was in training on Canada's west coast, where he had "made it known that I thought I was 'the most qualified person there to join combined ops.' I kept plugging the fact that I had been in the Army. Either they agreed with me, or were sick of the sight of me, because in May I was sent over to join the RN for 'combined ops.'" No doubt Barclay was chosen simply because of his willingness to volunteer for hazardous duties, given the turnover in personnel described earlier in this chapter. Regardless, his description of his training is an excellent synopsis of what such an officer was expected to do: "It is very difficult to tell where the Navy leaves off and the Army takes on ... On approaching an opposed beach, the Navy and Army officers together have to decide whether it is advisable to land or not, and each thinks of the other's problems before coming to a decision. Our work entails not only landing commando and assault troops, but also tanks, guns, heavy lorries, jeeps, ammunition, gas—petrol, as they call it here—water, and many supplies. So we deal with every branch of the Army," including not just the combat arms, but administration and logistics as well.[46]

As for North Africa, Barclay reported that "we landed at Arzew which is about twenty miles east of Oran. On our first attempt we had a mechanical breakdown in the craft, and while repairing it were caught in machine gun fire. One of the guns was situated in a factory about three hundred yards away, and being unable to leave the beach, we hit for the sand dunes where we offered a small target. With my 'wide Army summer camp training'—i.e. amongst the poison ivy at Mount St Bruno—we picked out the biggest sand dune and dug in. Fortunately the Yanks soon got control and were entering a house about twenty yards ahead of us, when a shot was fired from it and hit one of them. This sniper had spotted us and had crept into the house and but for the timely arrival of the Army would have had a crack at us. On many occasions during the next few days, Naval ratings and Army men combined to hunt out snipers who treated both alike."[47] Negligible resistance could still pose its hazards.

On another occasion, "the Navy had to dig in and become soldiers. On one of the beaches, orders had been sent to hold the beach at all costs: there were no Army men left as they had gone up ahead. Suddenly the signal was sent that enemy tanks had broken through and might be

---

44. At Algiers, three junior RCNVR engineer officers on service with the RN were borne in the destroyer HMS *Broke*, which crashed the gate into the harbour at the outset of the operation. Their job was to board merchant ships anchored in the harbour to prevent them from being scuttled and blocking the seaway. In the event, there was no sign that the French crews would sink their ships, so the services of the RCNVR officers were not required.

45. Schull, *The Far Distant Ships*, 149-51; For a detailed account of Torch, see C. Barnett, *Engage the Enemy More Closely* (London 1991) 564

46. Experiences of SLt Ian Barclay, RCNVR, in army cooperation in the North Africa landings, nd, DHH 81/520/1250(4), Combined Operations Naval Basic Training

47. Ibid

expected immediately. One of the Naval officers there, who had also had a little taste of Canadian Army life, remembered what he had been told two years ago by a man who had returned from Dunkirk—though shaking at the knees, he calmly told those around him that by digging a little hole and lying flat, a tank didn't have a chance. Greatly heartened by this, everyone dug furiously, but they did not have a chance to prove this correct." Perhaps it was all for the best, but still, in Barclay's opinion, "those of us who do know some of the ways of the Army find it a lot easier—for not only do we understand them better, but we also know a lot of the problems they're up against. In our flotilla alone there are two other Montrealers who at one time or another held sway for brief periods in the McGill Army. It is also surprising the number of ratings that have been in the reserve Army. In my crews 40 percent had been in the Canadian Army reserve."[48]

Whatever their background, if Barclay can be considered a reliable witness the Canadians had cause to be satisfied with their conduct. "Canadian sailors did very well there, as they did at Dieppe, and are trying to uphold the good name given Canadians by the Army in the last war ... The Canadian stokers—you'd call them mechanics—are very adapted to this sort of work and have received much praise from all those who come in contact with them. Our greatest difficulty is trying to keep them with us as several senior officers of the Royal Navy think that they should have some of them." As for officers, at least one was prepared to use his initiative, as on one beach, "a Naval officer for over five days directed all the troops and made rendezvous for all the armoured vehicles and Jeeps. As the road in front of him never seemed to become congested he figured that everything must have been going alright, and so continued to send them on."[49]

Barclay at least found the experience worthwhile, no doubt because of the lack of casualties among Canadian participants. The only loss during the operation was a rating killed during landings at Bougie, although ten more died when ships taking them back to the United Kingdom were torpedoed.[50] Canadians were able to express regional pride, as "our craft in Africa were proudly supporting such names as 'Pride of Montreal,' 'Peaches,' 'Pat,' and 'Miss Galt,' to mention a few. In mine, which had two large red maple leaves, I had some fine lads—like L/Seaman Sweeting of Gull Lake, Sask, L/Seaman Mair of Victoria, A/Bs John Tomlinson of Galt, Ont, Jerry Mulvey, M.W. Key, and H. Billington, all from Winnipeg, J.R. McTavish of Regina, W.G.R. MacDonald from Abbotsford, BC, and Stoker E.J. Corbett who hails from Fort William, Ont. Of the officers S/Lieuts Harry Trenholme, John Keys and George Hampson all come from Montreal. We're all looking forward to the day when we will see action again, and we hope that soon we'll have all-Canadian combined operations."[51]

The Canadians did not linger in North Africa, and by 18 December all had returned to the United Kingdom, except for the casualties detailed above, as had fourteen all ranks retained for special duties and one man hospitalized in Gibraltar.[52] As for Barclay's wish to see combined operations more Canadianized, since that had been NSHQ policy from the very beginning of the commitment there was some hope that it would actually come to pass. "As a result of discussions held with per-

---

48.   Ibid

49.   Ibid

50.   SO(CO) to CCCS, 18 Jan 1943

51.   Experiences of SLt Ian Barclay, RCNVR

52.   CCCS to NSHQ, 18 Dec 1942, LAC, RG 24, 11702, 09-1-1

sonnel returned from Torch," the Staff Officer (Combined Operations) reported in early 1943, "and particularly with Lt Cdr Chancellor, RNVR, and Lt Cdr Davis, RNVR, who had commanded two of the Canadian Flotillas in that Operation, it was agreed between COHQ and CCCS that Canadian Landing Craft Flotillas should be exclusively Canadian and not mixed." Furthermore, "consideration was also given to the number of trained Canadians available, and it was decided that for the time being the Canadians would be formed into only four Landing Craft Flotillas, namely the 55th and 61st LCA Flotillas, the 80th LCM(3) Flotilla and the 81st LCM(1) Flotilla. Personnel available represent only sufficient to man these flotillas and provide reinforcements for them."[53] Like it had in regards to setting up a combined operations base, the RCN was recognizing its limitations.

Nevertheless, by the end of 1942 Canadian combined operations personnel had participated in operations against Bruneval, St Nazaire, Dieppe, and North Africa, "as well as in a number of small Channel raids which take place from time to time but regarding which it is not usual to make any public report," according to the Staff Officer (Combined Operations), Lieutenant-Commander K.S. Maclachlan. He also reported on his efforts to ensure that people on the home front would be able to follow the experiences of their compatriots serving in landing craft and similar vessels. "Special arrangements ... were made with COHQ that Canadians returning from Operations could be interviewed and journalistic material prepared and released after censorship by COHQ ... Arrangements ... have also been made that when a Canadian Landing Craft Flotilla or Flotillas serving with Combined Operations Command takes part in a Combined Operations Raid arrangements will be made, whenever possible, for a Canadian press representative and a photographer or cameraman to accompany the Force. ... Arrangements ... have also been made that whenever a Canadian Flotilla takes part in a Combined Operations Raid appropriate references to the effect will be made in Combined Operations Headquarters' communiques."[54] It remained to be seen, however, whether such "arrangements" would actually work in practice.

Insofar as they did, credit could well go to the Staff Officer (Combined Operations). Maclachlan, however, left for the Near East on 6 April 1943 to take a position on the staff of the combined operations organization preparing for landings in the Mediterranean and was replaced by Lieutenant W.S. Brooke. Between them, Maclachlan and Brooke maintained contact with First Canadian Army, for matters such as "assembly and test of the wooden LCM(W) designed and produced in Canada ... Development of the Administrative Ramped Cargo Lighter from the LCM(W) ... Establishing contacts between the Staff of the Director of Experiments and Staff Requirements (DXSR), COHQ, and the Staff of the First Canadian Army, regarding the development of special assault craft to meet special Army requirements. This matter has grown into the consideration of two or three different craft and is being dealt with by a Committee on which the Admiralty, COHQ, CCCS, First Canadian Army and the War Office are represented ... Maintenance of contact with the group of Expert Officers of First Canadian Army located at COHQ and known as SD Tech (Staff Duties Technical). Their reports are now being regularly transmitted to NSHQ."[55]

As for the Royal Navy, "no difficulty is experienced in maintaining satisfactory contacts with the Training Organizations. It, however, has been difficult to establish close contacts with the

---

53. SO(CO) to CCCS, 18 Jan 1943

54. Ibid

55. Ibid

Organizations carrying out Exercises and Operations. It can be readily understood that for security reasons intimate contact with these matters by persons not actually carrying operating responsibility is undesirable; on the other hand, if the further development of proficiency by the Canadian
Landing Craft Flotillas is to be followed closely, some procedure by which their progress can be
closely followed is desirable."[56]

The numbers of other Canadians involved in combined operations increased almost monthly, so
that by the end of 1942 there were sufficient Canadian flotilla officers to take charge of Canadian
units and vessels.[57] Maintaining numbers, however, was an ongoing challenge, the medical standards having been kept up in the light of experience gained in a variety of small and large-scale
landing operations. On the last day of 1942, in fact, the Senior Medical Officer for the CCCS suggested that "as the number of Canadian Officers and ratings being discharged medically unfit for
Combined Operations is steadily increasing, it is considered that when future candidates are chosen in Canada the following requirements, from a medical point of view, should receive special
attention." The candidate "should be under the age of 35 ... should be mentally stable and there
should be no family history of mental disease or disorder ... There should be no history of chronic illness, such as, Bronchitis, Asthma, Tuberculosis, Rheumatic Fever, Arthritis, disorder of the
heart, or discharging ear." He should have "standard visual acuity and hearing," and he should be
"free from venereal disease."[58]

As of 18 January 1943, after losses to that date, to all causes, of eighteen officers and seventy-
two ratings, there were sixty-nine officers, two warrant officers, and 410 ratings serving in combined operations.[59] Not all of these men wanted to be there, since according to Brooke, "a number
of cases have occurred where Officers and Ratings claim that they were advised to come to the
United Kingdom in Combined Operations Parties and that transfers to other branches of the
Service—particularly Fleet Air Arm and Submarines—could be easily arranged. Such is not the
case. Recommendations ... have been made that all volunteers for Combined Operations understand clearly that they will be trained for Combined Operations and are expected to continue in that
service." Their enthusiasm must have been difficult to keep stoked, however, since "the maintenance of Landing Craft damaged in training, Exercises and Operations, has been—and still is—a
most serious problem. Many interruptions to training have been experienced, and the time spent
in relative idleness at Training Bases has had a detrimental effect on the personnel." Reorganizing
into four flotillas had helped, but the problem remained.[60] As Commander F.A. Price, RCNVR, Staff
Officer (Personnel) for the CCCS, related in February 1943, "I have been in touch with the
Directorate of Staff Duties and Training at the Admiralty, with Combined Operations Headquarters
and with the Senior Psychologist at the Admiralty. It appears that they have no set lectures for new
entry seamen on morale, discipline, etc. These lectures are given by officers and instructors who

---

56. Ibid

57. CCCS to RALB, 20 Dec 1942, LAC, RG 24, 11702, 09-1-1

58. "It has been found impossible," the medical officer observed, "to continue syphilitic treatment in Combined Operations
     because a Medical Officer is not always available. These cases have been returned, therefore, to *Niobe* for continuance of
     treatment." Sr MO CCCS to CCCS, 31 Dec 1942, LAC, RG 24, 3948, 1037-34-1

59. SO(CO) to CCCS, 18 Jan 1943

60. Ibid

draw on their own knowledge of the service."[61] It might not be an approach the Royal Canadian Navy could emulate, since only one member in forty had any long-term experience to share.

Administrators therefore had to spend no little time dealing with symptoms of unhappiness. In June 1943, for example, the Staff Officer (Combined Operations) office replied to one complainant that "Canadian personnel on loan to the Royal Navy, are entitled only to Royal Navy rations. Although they may consider the food only fair, they can only grin and bear it. No extra concessions are made to Canadians in this respect whatsoever." As for another sailor bemoaning his fate, the same officer warned that "it is improbable, but not impossible, that a Canadian on loan to the Royal Navy might transfer to the Air Force. If you believe the rating has reasonable grounds for such a request, have him submit a request, giving full reasons. As the rating is on loan to the Royal Navy, any such request would have to go through the RN administrative authorities." Clearly, such issues were crossing this officer's desk with some regularity, as he replied to one message with the comment that "any official business should no longer be communicated to me personally. In the near future, I am washing my hands of Combined Operations forever."[62]

The Canadian contribution continued to grow, so that by the end of June 1943 there were twenty-four officers and 376 ratings in the four operational flotillas; three officers and 118 ratings in three reinforcement flotillas, and thirty-four officers and seventy-two ratings holding miscellaneous appointments in RN units.[63] Some years after Canada's commitment to combined operations, however, many officers were being promoted out of Canadian flotillas to fill higher positions within the RN hierarchy. They could, however, be kept in the RCN, "if they are appointed to either major craft flotillas or to Landing Ships, when they are due for promotion from minor craft. Major craft and Landing Ships are all independent commands. In the latter and, to a varying extent, in the former, officers will obtain some 'sea-time'"[64]—but the vessels in question had to be RCN, not RN. The suggestion was part of a larger bid to reorient Canada's contribution to combined operations from smaller LCAs and LCMs to larger vessels.

Another consequence of the passage of time since the first drafts of combined operations personnel had been sent to the United Kingdom was that many would soon be eligible for Foreign Service Leave. As Lieutenant Brooke suggested, such men could cross the Atlantic to Canada in recently acquired escort carriers, which would be on working-up exercises at the time. "The Canadian Flotillas are now experienced veterans and their assistance should be very valuable to the crews" of those ships. Alternatively, "it has been suggested that experiments are to be undertaken on the east coast of Canada during the winter with landing craft now being equipped in the UK to withstand zero temperatures. This is another case where Canadian crews entitled to leave could be employed with advantage."[65] The amount of time actually spent on leave would thus be kept to the minimum required by regulations.

---

61. SO Personnel for CCCS to Dir of Naval Training, 3 Feb 1943, LAC, RG 24, 11702, 09-1-1

62. SLt W. Trimble to Lt W.C. Gardner RCNVR, HMS *Helder*, 29 Jun 1943, DHH 81/520/1250(1), CCCS File, Personnel—Status and Administration

63. SO(CO), 6 July 1943, DHH 81/520/1000-5-35

64. SO (CO) to SCNO(L), 7 July 1943 LAC, RG 24, 3948, 1037-34-1

65. SO(CO) to SCNO(L), 13 July 1943, ibid

If Canada were to add to its commitment to combined operations, as recommended by many of its officers overseas, such personnel issues would obviously increase in complexity. As CCCS Agnew noted in April 1943, "assault forces are being organized on the basis of Squadrons consisting of seven flotillas. If an expansion of the Canadian participation in Combined Operations is contemplated, it is recommended that the present force be built up to an all-Canadian Squadron. This would involve the provision of personnel for an additional three flotillas, and the provision of a steady flow of reinforcements for the Squadron." The three additional units would require a flotilla officer, four boat officers, an engineer officer, eighteen coxswains, seventy-two seamen, and eighteen stoker-drivers. "The coxswains can be developed from personnel now serving in the present four flotillas, but an equal number of seamen would be required as replacements. It is recommended that seamen be sent forward for training in groups of 50, and stokers in groups of 20." Losses to date had amounted to about 20 percent per year, so Agnew recommended the provision of reinforcements at a rate of 25 percent, or a hundred seamen and twenty stokers for four flotillas, or a hundred and fifty seamen and forty stokers for a full squadron.[66] This program was in fact approved by the Naval Board in June 1943.[67]

But expansion was overtaken by events. The four operational RCN flotillas in the United Kingdom commenced an intensive training program following their return from the Torch landings. All four had been assigned to the Overseas Assault Force (OAF) which, with a strength of twenty-eight flotillas, was preparing for further landing operations in the Mediterranean. The 55th and 61st LCA Flotillas trained independently in Scotland while the two LCM flotillas, the 80th and 81st, practised at a combination of Plymouth, Roseneath, the Clyde and Southend. Although all four were under the command of RCNVR lieutenants and were still considered to be Canadian units, about one third of the strength of the LCA flotillas was composed of RN ratings. The two LCM units had a sprinkling of RN personnel attached as spare crews.[68]

In March, 1943, the Canadian flotillas joined Force G, commanded by Rear Admiral T.T. Troubridge, RN, under orders to proceed to Egypt by way of the Cape of Good Hope. They arrived in Suez Bay in early May after a lengthy voyage around the African continent. There they commenced nearly two months of training at the combined training centre at Kabret, Egypt on the Red Sea, conducting both individual boat and flotilla exercises, and culminating with a full-scale night landing near Aqaba at the end of June. The indefatigable Maclachlan, determined to maintain closer contact with the Canadians while they were engaged in actual operations, followed them to the Middle East. He had used his connections to find a position on Troubridge's Force G staff and participated in the planning discussions for the next major amphibious operation in the Mediterranean—Operation Husky, the invasion of Sicily.[69]

---

66. CCCS to Sec NB, 3 Apr 1943, ibid

67. NSHQ to SCNO(L), 22 Jun 1943, ibid

68. Maclachlan, "Preparations for Operation Husky," nd; Lt J. George, "The Sicilian Assault: 10th July 1943, 55th and 61st Canadian LCA Flotillas," nd; "After the Assault: 80th and 81st Canadian LCM Flotillas in Sicily and Italy," nd. DHH 81/520/1650, "Operation Husky"

69. George, "Sicilian Assault" and "After the Assault"; CCCS to FO Force W, 4 Feb 1943, FO Force W to CCCS, 5 Feb 1943, untitled file, DHH 81/520/1250(1)

Husky had its origins at the Casablanca Conference of January 1943. At that meeting the Combined Chiefs of Staff had agreed, after the continuing debate between London and Washington over the American preference for a cross-Channel attack in 1943 and the British determination to force Hitler's junior partner, Mussolini, out of the war, that the Tunisian campaign was to be followed by an attack on the "soft underbelly" of the axis.[70] Planning had begun in February. As the buildup of forces in the Mediterranean began in March, the small naval contribution to the coming amphibious operation appeared to be the only Canadian element of Husky. However, in response to pressure from Ottawa to bring an end to the inactivity of the Canadian army in the United Kingdom, on 25 April the British Chiefs of Staff, at the direction of Winston Churchill and Chief of the Imperial General Staff General Sir Alan Brooke, substituted a Canadian for a British infantry division and armoured brigade. The 1st Canadian Infantry Division and the 1st Canadian Army Tank Brigade immediately began amphibious training. Had Maclachlan known of this development he might have taken steps to ensure that the Canadian flotillas stayed in the United Kingdom to train with and help land the 1st Canadian Division in Sicily. As it was the Canadian troops would be ferried ashore by Royal Navy flotillas, and the two Canadian LCA flotillas would land the assault waves of the British 231st Infantry Brigade. The two LCM flotillas were to ferry vehicles and supplies to the beaches around Syracuse.[71]

In late June Maclachlan reported that "the work of the [55th and 61st LCA] flotillas has been good and compares favourably with the general average ... The training for the [80th and 81st LCM Flotillas] has not been as good ... It has now developed that the use of LCM's is decreasing. The t[r]end is for personnel, aside from the original assault, to be carried in [Landing Craft Infantry (Large)] and for vehicles and stores to be carried in [Landing Craft Tank (Large)] and [Landing Ship Tank]."[72] The LCMs in fact would not serve as flotillas but would be parcelled out to landing ships in groups of two to four, so "it is therefore much more difficult to maintain flotilla formation and 'esprit de corps' than in Assault Craft." One did not have to search too far for a solution. Maclachlan discussed the issue with higher British authority and found that at least one high-ranking officer—left unnamed, unfortunately—"is all in favour of working out something better for the Canadians. Possibly the personnel can be used in LCI(L). No change is contemplated for the time being but future policy should take this situation into account." The RCN would indeed procure LCIs later on, but with the landings scheduled for less than a month later other issues were of more immediate importance. As Maclachlan related, "discipline is good and no comments have been made that discipline in Canadian flotillas is worse than in the others. This comment was made from time to time in the UK." On the other hand, "one or two cases have arisen where ratings have proved to be incorrigible and I have recommended that such cases be discharged from the flotillas and moved to Western Med where they can be put on Canadian ships." How that might make them more "corrigible" Maclachlan did not say.[73]

70.   Farrell, *British Grand Strategy*, 525-35; Weinberg, *World at Arms*, 591-3

71.   G.W.L. Nicholson, *The Canadians in Italy* (Ottawa 1956) 20-6; Maclachlan, "Preparations for Operation Husky"; George, "The Sicilian Assault" and "After the Assault"

72.   SO (CO) to CCCS, 19 June 1943, LAC, RG 24, 3948, 1037-34-1

73.   Ibid

Further down the chain of command for combined operations personnel, an engineer officer with one of the Canadian LCM flotillas focussed on other issues. In March 1943 he and his comrades had learned through the grapevine that great things were afoot:

> It was exactly two weeks after this occurrence that the last of the ships carrying our Flotilla left the rain-soaked, mist enshrouded hills of Scotland for what was to prove the most exciting trip of our Naval experience. There were some ships in convoy Y and others steamed out at a good speed and so did their voyage "solo." How perfectly easy this all sounds now, but well do we all remember the frantic scurrying about in those last days of preparation; picking up stores of one kind here, of another kind in another place miles away and checking to see that all the ratings were properly outfitted for the tropics etc. Any casual reader who is not acquainted with the heterogeneous accounting system of the Navy would think such storing a simple job. Whew, how wrong! Naval stores loom large in the list of night-mare subjects of all officers sooner or later. But I suppose that since articles are often "lost" in spite of this red tape, it is fully justified. But far more difficult still is the task of "desk" officers to compute the quantities of such stores required for operations which are to take place months in the future. To them must go high praise, for though mistakes in kind and quantity were made, yet the bulk of the material was found to be highly essential.[74]

Similarly, the 55th Landing Craft Assault Flotilla left port on 15 March 1943, and according to its commanding officer,

> we had no idea of our ultimate objective—we only knew it was going to be something big and we were all looking forward eagerly to the prospects ahead... The voyage was in the main, uneventful. The weather was fine and enemy interference nil. On board, however, there was plenty to be done. Although the Flotilla had done a certain amount of training prior to leaving the UK, they were far from "operationally fit," and much more training was required before they would function as a smooth-working unit. The craft, too, required a lot of work to be done on them as these had only been received a few days before we sailed; the crews needed practice in handling and getting used to them. Accordingly, the long voyage around the Cape was welcome and we had by the time we reached Suez on the 6th May, accomplished much along those lines. Whilst in Freetown, we were able to carry out an extremely useful exercise in the craft, which gave the crews their first real opportunity of handling their own boats, and served greatly to stimulate their interest. No shore leave was allowed here, but it was a grand experience for all who had not been there before to see this West African port, although all were glad enough to leave after four days of its sultry heat.[75]

The LCA flotilla spent four days in Durban, then made its way to Aden, conducting a "crossing the line" ceremony on the way. "Meanwhile, the crews were being continually trained, and the craft painted, stored and generally made ready for action and, on arrival in Suez Bay, were in first class state." The eight weeks that followed were spent in the vicinity of Suez, where "all the remaining

74. Combined Operations in Sicily and Italy, Reminiscences of a Canadian LCM Flotilla Engineer Officer, nd, DHH 81/520/8000-411/80

75 FO 55th Cdn LC Flotilla to SCNO(L), 7 Aug 1943, DHH 81/520/1650, Husky

craft training necessary was carried out and in the final exercise period with the actual assault troops, both the Canadian Flotillas gained beyond doubt the confidence and respect of the troops they were to carry and proved themselves to all as fit and ready for the job. One enjoyable break in this long training period was a day's leave spent in Cairo for each Flotilla in turn and we did not fail to take in all the sights."[76]

While in Egypt, "a great deal of hard work was done here, for we had brought our boats to a small lake a short distance away from the camp and each day boats' crews and maintenance staff worked from 0700 till noon and often again in the afternoon. If the afternoons were too hot we adopted tropical hours and did some work in the cool of the evening. I say cool, but I suppose that there was no evening when the perspiration wouldn't roll off one's brow even when standing still. But everyone threw their heart and soul into the job for they all knew that great things would be expected of them and their boats. Previous operations had taught the officers and men that boats and boat equipment are essentially the heart of the force and if they are not in perfect condition much of the 'punch' is lacking on D day."[77]

On 5 July they put to sea from Egypt, joining the other naval forces descending on Sicily, some of which had sailed from as far away as the United States and Britain. Lieutenant Beecher, aboard the LSI *Otranto*, recorded in his diary that they "spent all day in the Mediterranean steering a course along the north coast of Africa—sailing through the beautiful blue waters of the Mediterranean Sea. Worked like hell all day getting the landing craft squared away for the landing ...We talked about the operation and whether we were going to be torpedoed and all sorts of cheerful things! All of us are scared as hell and walking on tip toes clutching our life belts."[78] In the event, of the sixty motor transport and thirty-two personnel ships in Force A, only one vessel was sunk after being torpedoed by a U-boat off the Libyan coast. By noon on 9 July the Canadians were able to look out from the decks of *Otranto* and see a horizon that was full of ships as the convoys from Egypt reached their rendezvous point with the other assault and support forces south of Malta. The western Mediterranean was at this moment an Allied *mare nostrum*: sixteen separate escorted convoys bound for Sicily enjoyed the protection of two naval covering forces, making a total of 240 warships, 130 transports, and 840 ocean-going landing craft and similar vessels.

"The weather seemed perfect," wrote Beecher, "light northerly wind and good visibility. This is to be expected in the Malta Channel in July ... During the afternoon, however, the wind backed and freshened and by 2000 it was blowing quite strongly from the NW force 6 and gusty, i.e. the worst conditions to be expected ... CinC Mediterranean considered that conditions were not favourable; but it was fine and visibility was good, so he decided to proceed with the operation. Conditions were expected to be difficult, particularly for the American landings ... This weather persisted until after the assault."[79]

In the 55th Canadian Landing Craft Flotilla, "at last the final embarkation of the troops took place, all was ready—the craft and men were fit and morale was high. A few days wait in Port

76. Ibid

77. Combined Ops Sicily and Italy, Reminiscences

78. D. Lewis, L. Birkenes, and K. Lewis, eds, *St Nazaire to Singapore: The Canadian Amphibious War, 1941-1945* (np 1997), 148

79. SCNO(L) to Sec NB, 27 Jul 1943, LAC, RG 24 (Acc 83-84/167), 76, 1250-1

Said after passing through the Suez Canal and then the force was on its way to its final objective which we now learned was Sicily. We were rather amazed that during the whole of our five days approach to the island no enemy interference of any sort was encountered and the great convoy reached its destination in the night of 9th July, intact." In fact some ships were lost to torpedoes in some of the other convoys, so the 55th Flotilla was indeed fortunate. Despite the weather, which was "as bad as any as we had experienced since leaving the UK," the assault went in. The original plan called for motor launches (MLs), allocated one per flotilla, "coming from Malta to join the convoy and to act as navigational leaders, guiding the craft in to their respective beaches but as the three assault ships for our particular sector (Nan sector, opposite the town of Pachino on the East coast just north of Cape Passero) reached their position seven miles offshore where it was intended they should discharge their craft; it was found that only one ML had been able to keep up with the convoy in the heavy weather and that it intended to guide the 61st Flotilla in."[80]

The 55th Flotilla was supposed to lower craft at 0025 and join up on the left of the 61st Flotilla for the run-in at 0115. Six LCAs, known as Group 2, were to carry two assault landing companies on a rocky beach known as Scramble Red, or along a broken-down breakwater; a Landing Craft Support (LCS) would sail on either flank to provide covering fire. Another LCA, on its own comprising Group 4, was tasked to carry a mine-gapping party into Red Beach as soon as assault troops signalled that it had been captured. The party would then clear mines so follow-on troops and equipment could be unloaded safely. Group 6 consisted of four LCAs carrying a battalion headquarters into Red Beach. Finally, two landing craft carried support mortars and a 3.7-inch howitzer, which they were to land when the battalion commander in Group 6 so ordered. The 61st was to carry out similar operations.[81]

Reality was, however, somewhat more confusing. As the flotilla officer for the 55th reported, he attempted to link up with the group that had gone off with the 61st, since only its guide had been able to make it to the marshalling area, but he failed to find it. His group therefore "struck off on its own for the beaches. After a considerable search up and down the coast, the correct beaches were located and Group 4—the mine-gapping party under Lieutenant H.E. Trenholme, RCNVR—was sent in to Red Beach only to find the beach not yet taken and they retired rapidly on being fired upon. Believing they had gone to the wrong beach, they struck off again, finally returning to this Beach at 0452 when the breakwater, mined by the enemy, was blown up on their approach." Furthermore, "Groups 6 and 8 lay off the beaches until daylight. It was some time before Red Beach was taken by our troops and an attempt was made to land thereon but they withdrew on discovering that our forces had not yet occupied it. They then went in to Amber Beach which was being shelled by mortar and light field batteries located about a mile back on a hill overlooking the beach. The craft did not land but again retired, except for LCP(R) 913 Y which was hit by this shelling and troops disembarked. The remaining LCSs were directed to Scramble Red and LCP(R) 623 landed at Red Beach shortly after." Sub-Lieutenant R.J. Crothers, RCNVR, "in 55-7—the craft which became detached from my group, on bailing out, proceeded independently and after searching for some

---

80.   FO 55th Cdn LC Flotilla to SCNO(L), 7 Aug 1943

81.   Ibid

considerable time for the correct beach eventually located the SO's groups and landed at Scramble Red." The flotilla then began conducting a ferry service from the larger ships to the beaches.[82]

Hours of excitement, confusion, and terror were followed by days of routine, with the exception of the odd air attack. For some, day-to-day living became the main challenge, as landing craft provided very little in the way of amenities. As our LCM flotilla engineer officer recalled, "during the greater part of our stay in Sicily our Flotilla used an old rock quarry for living quarters for men and officers. The cave was very large and though it easily satisfied our requirements for space, yet it was mighty damp and dark. Also it was peopled by a wide variety of 'cave dwellers.' These ranged all the way from rats and mice to lizards, flies, mosquitoes (malaria carrying) and other quadrupeds and insects native to that section of the Island." A gasoline fire set to give warmth provided some excitement as well, burning about twenty-five kit bags. Keeping clean was made all the more challenging when a nearby source of water "was condemned due to malaria larvae." Happily, wine was available from the locals, and "the rural people [were] quite anxious to help us out with fresh vegetables and fruits and eggs when they had them."[83]

The extra rations were no doubt much welcomed, as the LCM flotillas remained in the area for four weeks after the landings. At least Captain E.V. Lees, RN, the Senior Naval Officer for George Sector, had some encouraging words for his Canadian comrades. Lieutenant J.E. Koyl, the 80th's flotilla officer, reported that "he thought the 80th Flotilla had been the best Flotilla in the area, carrying more vehicles and supplies and keeping more boats running than any other Flotilla, and that he was giving us the highest of recommendations in his report. This commendation was earned partially through good seamanship and control and general efficient coxswaining in not allowing craft to be stranded or beaten on the rocks. Also we insisted on watches being kept constantly when the boats were not in use. I believe that Captain Lee's commendation was quite justified as we were the only Flotilla who completed the operation and returned to Malta with all the boats with which we had set out on operation still in first class condition."[84] The flotilla engineer officer for one of the formations had a different perspective, however, noting that by the time the craft arrived in Malta they were "just about ready to fall apart after a gruelling four weeks work."[85]

Similarly, their complements were also showing wear and tear, living in a cave or in similar accommodation for a month having taken a toll. Setting out for Malta on D+28, "the men's condition was in a very low state due to their unhealthy living conditions while working on the beaches, their tinned food and lack of proper medical attention." They made their way to No. 12 Army Camp at Hanrun, which was not much of an improvement. "This camp was very rough and difficult to control due to the tents being spread over a wide area. Initial feeding arrangements were poor, no lights or lamps were supplied for the tents and flies were bad." Koyl was obviously not impressed and complained that "following a month of discomfort, hardship and hard work on the landing beaches, I feel some better arrangements could have been made for these men particularly if they were to be used for another operation. The conditions they were made to live in were certainly not conducive to good morale, nor to good health ... After having no Naval medical atten-

82.   Ibid

83.   Combined Ops in Sicily and Italy, Reminiscences

84   Lt J.E. Koyl, RCNVR, FO 80th LCM Flotilla to SCNO(L), 26 Nov 1943, DHH 81/520/1650, Husky

85.   Combined Ops in Sicily and Italy, Reminiscences

tion for a month and a half the general condition of the men was so run down that we had 30–35 away at Hospital during the period of our stay in Malta. We could obtain no comforts for the men, and local entertainment in the towns was very expensive."[86]

The LCA flotillas had returned to the United Kingdom by the end of July 1943, with reports similar to those made for the LCMs. One note to the 55th, from Lieutenant R.M. Smith, RCNVR, Senior Officer Assault Ships and Craft at Combined Operations Command, congratulated the flotillas "on the exceptionally good status of Landing Craft returned by you which reflects credit on all concerned."[87] But ensuring that such good work was made public back in Canada was an endeavour in itself. The Senior Canadian Naval Officer in London—SCNO(L)—the new designation for the CCCS, had his own publicity relations office, which for the month of July reported, among other things, that "six stories and 66 negatives were received from Lt Cdr Bartlett, processed, cleared through Admiralty and Combined Ops HQ, and forwarded Bomber mail to Ottawa. The current issue of 'Canada's Weekly' carries a full page of pictures of Canadians in Combined Ops," although these were "older pictures." Similarly, "the new issue of 'The Rally' carries a series of Mediterranean articles by Lt Cdr Bartlett." Related more specifically to Operation Husky, "during the third week of July, Lt Cdr Bartlett's material on Sicily came in via UP wire and was used as a basis of broadcast on 'Canadian Calendar.'" As well, a Sub-Lieutenant J.S. Keate interviewed an officer and three ratings on their experiences in assault landing craft, the program being broadcast on Canadian Calendar and the BBC on 26 July, and being picked up for the newsreels the following night. Finally, "several officers and ratings returning from Sicily were interviewed and liaison was arranged whereby Sydney Gruson of Canadian Press wrote feature story on same."[88]

As already noted, if Canada's role in combined operations were to be publicized, it would have to be the Royal Canadian Navy that did it, since the Royal Navy seemed to have little interest in relating what the other services of the Empire were up to. Two days after the landings, SCNO(L) Commander F.A. Price noted that "information has been requested from Naval Service Headquarters, Ottawa, as to whether the 55th and 61st LCA flotillas and the 80th and 81st LCM flotillas, all manned by RCN or reserve personnel, were used in the Husky operations for the Sicily landing." Lieutenant Brooke was asked to furnish such information, but it was not easy to find.[89] "As instructed I returned to COHQ and went to Commodore Ellis' office. As a conference was going on I went to his secretary, Pay Lt Polglase RNR. He had me taken to Commander Robinson RN, the Deputy Chief of Naval Craft and Movements [formerly of the Naval Planning Staff] ... Commander Robinson said they had absolutely no details as to how the Force was made up for the assault as that was a matter for the Mediterranean C-in-C. He sent me to Commander Wade who, he said, would get the first news of landing craft flotillas and their crews. The Personnel side had no information either ... In view of this unsatisfactory situation it is submitted that NSHQ be approached for a better means of keeping in touch with Canadians, who form part of an assault force as an organized group. One way in which the information could be obtained would be for the senior officer of any Canadian ship,

86.   Koyl to SCNO(L), 26 Nov 43

87.   SCNO(L)War Diary for July 1943, nd, DHH 81/520/1000-5-35

88.   SCNO(L), Report on the Month of July 1943, on Activities of Publicity Relations Office, ibid

89.   SCNO(L) to Dep Naval COS COHQ, 12 July 1943, LAC, RG 24, 3948, 1037-34-1

squadron or flotilla to be instructed to send off each day a signal addressed to NSHQ and repeated to SCNO(L) giving position and stating whether they have been in action. If this report is sent off as 'Most Secret' it should not cause any difficulty anywhere."[90] But it was not to be.

Other policy issues also kept commanders, staff officers, and their ilk busy, so much so that in the few brief months between the end of Operation Husky in July and the landings in southern Italy, Operation Baytown, in September, a veritable mountain of paper was produced in a wide variety of offices. Commander Price, temporarily serving as SCNO(L), in a letter to the Naval Board encapsulated many of the triumphs, trials, and tribulations that Canadians in combined operations faced at the time. One heading, "Limitation on Advancement Possibilities for Personnel," made one complaint clear, while discussion of "Service Experience" led to the conclusion that it was too limited. The "Views of Personnel" were unmuddled; they wanted to move from minor to major craft, and "Official Organization" was subtitled "Present Unsatisfactory Position of Canadians." The expansion of the Allied offensive against the Axis had changed the relationship between the Canadian naval authorities and Combined Operation Headquarters. Beginning with Torch, operational control had been exercised, not by COHQ, but by an Army commander-in-chief and a Naval Force Commander. "These officers seldom have any knowledge of arrangements made by Senior Canadian Naval Officer (London) with Combined Operations Command, the primary manning and mounting authority." It was thus difficult to obtain information. One possible solution would be to move personnel from minor to major craft and keep them together as a Canadian unit. Specifically, Price recommended the adoption of Landing Craft Infantry (Large), a suggestion that had been made before.[91]

Such admonitions were not falling on deaf ears, although it is worth reminding the reader that Canadian policymakers envisaged combined operations as a wartime commitment only. When discussing a possible contribution to the war against Japan, NSHQ's Plans Division mentioned cruisers supported by fleet destroyers, and possibly aircraft carriers, but no landing craft or ships.[92] Still, "consolidation," as the Naval Board had called it in the early days of the war—or Canadianization as it was called in other circles—gelled in mid-September 1943, as "the Cabinet War Committee have approved that the Naval Service should contribute three flotillas consisting of 36 major craft and one Beach Commando for service with the Royal Navy in Combined Operations. The Royal Navy has confirmed its previous agreement that the Canadians, including those now serving in Combined Operations will be kept together ... The Admiralty have requested that the major craft manned be Landing Craft Tank, but the Naval Board would prefer that arrangements be made for the major craft to be instead Landing Craft Infantry (Large) and personnel are being selected and sent over on the basis that the Admiralty will accede to our request for Landing Craft Infantry (Large) ... The manning of the 36 major craft and the provision of a Beach Commando is being regarded as a fresh commitment, subject to the use of personnel at present in Combined Operations as they become available."[93] How this worked out on the ground will be discussed later in this

90. SO(CO) to SCNO(L), 12 July 1943, ibid

91. SCNO(L) to Sec NB, 20 July 1943, app 1, ibid

92. Plans Division, "Appreciation of RCN Ship Requirements for the War against Japan and for the Post-War Navy," 29 July 1943, LAC, RG 24, 3844, NS 1017-10-34

93. Sec NB to SCNO(L), 14 Sep 1943, LAC, RG 24, 3948, 1037-34-1

chapter, but what is important to note here is that at the very time that officers and ratings in the Mediterranean saw good reason to complain about their lot, higher authority was attempting to improve their situation.

For some members of the RCN, however, it was already too late. Part of Canada's contribution to combined operations had been in the form of stokers, it having been agreed to send forty of them to the United Kingdom in May 1942. Given losses and transfers that were characteristic of combined operations as a whole, in February 1943 CCCS Agnew requested a further eighty.[94] Many of them found themselves on loan to the RN rather than serving with the Canadian flotillas, and it quickly became apparent that their status and expectations differed from those of their RN counterparts. Captain C.M. Campbell, commanding officer of HMS *Hamilcar*, the landing craft base in Algeria, explained the problem in July 1943: "There are a number of Canadian Stokers (M) serving ashore and on LCI(L) on the Mediterranean Station, and difficulty is being experienced with regard to their advancement, and welfare, owing to the fact that particulars of the regulations concerning them are not held ... The ratings feel that their careers are being retarded because of their inability to qualify for advancement, and several requests have been received to return to the Canadian Navy. These ratings cannot be spared without relief, and it is suggested that, as reliefs become available, their case may be given consideration."[95] Admiral Sir John Cunningham, the C-in-C in the Mediterranean to whom the letter was addressed, saw little that could be done, remarking that "it is impossible to relieve these ratings from station resources, and it is not clear in what way they are at a disadvantage as regards advancement and welfare compared with ratings of the Royal Navy."[96]

At least three of the stokers in question (named Sinclair, Bell and Edwards) failed to sympathize with the RN's difficulties, and sometime before the end of August 1943 each was charged with "did wilfully disobey the lawful command of Albert Vivian Rice, Lieutenant (E) RNVR, his superior officer, when ordered to perform his duties in the engine room." As Commander J. Sutton RN, the commanding officer of *LST 319* reported, "after conducting separate inquiries into all the relative facts, they were each formally asked whether they would obey the lawful comments of the Engineer Officer." One replied, "No—only as a Stoker (M)." Another said, "Not necessarily all orders—only those affecting my rate." The third said, "Only in respect of Stoker (M)'s duties. I'm sorry sir—that is all I have to say." They were given sixty days' detention in Tripoli, but their fate could have been far worse. Sutton reported that "it was only after prolonged consideration that these ratings were not charged with the crime of mutiny, as it was apparent that they, if not actually acting in concert, had mutually discussed their intentions before refusing duty. The offences were further aggravated by the fact that the ship was employed on vitally necessary duties in ferrying troops and transport between North Africa and Sicily after the initial assault landings."[97]

Sutton also saw the need to explain his own situation in more detail, and in the process perhaps provided mitigating factors for the stokers. "No service certificates or official papers affecting these men have been received on board HM Ship under my command," he stated, possibly not real-

---

94.   A/SO(CO) to SCNO(L), 28 Aug 1943, app 1, ibid

95   CO HMS *Hamilcar* to C-in-C Med Station, 26 July 1943, DHH 81/520/1250(1), CCCS File, Personnel—Status and Administration

96.   C-in-C Med to CCCS, 7 Aug 1943, ibid

97.   CO *LST 319* to SCNO(L), 30 Aug 1943, ibid

izing that his was a common complaint. "Since they joined the ship ... repeated efforts have been made to obtain information relating to their status and regulations for advancement. These included letters and telephone and personal calls by ship's officers, both at HMCS *Niobe*, and Canadian Naval Headquarters London. A copy of the Canadian Naval Regulations governing Advancement of Stokers (M), and Motor Mechanics, was not received until the 18th August 1943." There was more. "These ratings had apparently been verbally informed by a naval officer at some period during their initial training in Canada that they would be drafted to a seagoing ship as Acting Leading Stokers (M) and during their service in HM Ship under my command, they have on several occasions requested that some action be taken to advance them to that rate, although it was explained that nothing could be done in the absence of their service certificates and Canadian Regulations." Ironically, producing the latter seemed to be the last straw, since "after the Regulations had been shown to them shortly after they were received on the 18th August 1943, the acts of insubordination took place."[98]

No less a personage than Minister of National Defence for Naval Services Angus L. Macdonald became interested in the cases of Stokers Sinclair, Bell, and Edwards. They had enlisted in June and July 1942, completing a course in Toronto on internal combustion engines on 7 September. "All three stokers said that the Chief Petty Officer in charge of them at the Technical school told them that if they did well on their course, they would become Petty Officers within ten months," confirming the wisdom of their decision to become stokers. They underwent another month of training, and "while at Toronto a Royal Naval officer was calling for volunteers for special service. One hundred and fifty volunteered, and fifty were accepted, consideration being given to their standing in the class and their physical fitness. The British Officer, the stokers said, made no promise as to rating or rank." They may therefore have, unwittingly, given up opportunities for rapid promotion.[99]

If so, there were no immediate indications of it, as they were sent to HMCS *Stadacona*, then to Detroit, then to Chicago, in the latter city for "the same course which turns out Petty Officer Machinists Mates for the United States Navy. British Motor Mechanics were there taking the course also." Their next stop was HMS *Safar*, in New York, then Ashbury Park, New Jersey, where they were issued identification cards that gave their rate as "Stoker Mechanics." Joining *LST 319* in December and January, they discovered that there was no such rate in the Royal Navy, but "the Chief Petty Officer said he would endeavour to obtain a higher rate for them, commensurate with the duties they were about to undertake. With this in view he discussed the matter with Engineer Officer Rice, who endeavoured to get in touch with a British Admiral in Washington, but nothing came of this. They remained Stoker Mechanics." Still, "they were put in charge of a watch in the main engine room, they being the only ones that had the courses already mentioned, outside of Chief Petty Officers. They also did repair work on all the engines in the ship under the direction of the Chief Petty Officer."[100]

The stokers had no cause for complaint so far, and in February 1943 they put in a formal request to their commanding officer for higher rates. What followed was a web of correspondence involving

98. Ibid

99. Macdonald diary, 11 Mar 1944, folder 10, DHH 80/218

100. Ibid

the ship's engineering officer, HMCS *Niobe*, Canada House in London, and various addresses in Canada. Sometime after March 1943 the LST was in Greenock, Scotland, and while there, "three motor mechanics were sent to relieve them, but the Captain would not allow them to stay on board, as the ship was sealed." The reason for the latter decision became obvious when the vessel participated in the first landings under Operation Husky, followed by other operations ferrying troops, construction units, and other personnel and materiel to the fighting. It was sometime during this period that one of the stokers "told the Engineer Officer that on *return to their base* he would no longer carry out the duties of Motor Mechanic, but that he would carry out duties of Stoker Mechanic. He denies that he ever refused to carry out an order. They are all agreed on this."[101]

In their minds, the stokers were standing up for their rights. But incarceration must have made clear to them that in the RN respect for the chain of command was more important than fairness. There was, however, some sympathy for these men within the RCN. Commander Price in London "observ[ed] that while breaches of discipline cannot be condoned in any way, it is most unfortunate that ratings have to commit disciplinary offences to have their unsatisfactory plight brought to official notice." Price found that the message from the C-in-C Mediterranean, quoted above, "indicates the lack of appreciation by RN authorities of the differences attending the advancement of Canadian ratings."[102] For the three stokers in question, the RCN's contribution to combined operations had been far from beneficial.

Although their case was the most dramatic, the stokers were not the only lost RCN souls in the Royal Navy. SCNO(L) Agnew related in July 1943 how one of his staff officers, "during a recent visit to Combined Operations' Drafting Establishment, has ascertained that records for a number of Canadian ratings said to have joined Combined Operations are in a rather unsatisfactory state. It is requested, therefore, that confirmation be given that the names in the first group below," he listed eleven, "are of men now serving in the RCN. If your records show any of these as serving in Combined Operations, steps will be taken to ascertain their whereabouts." There was another list, of seven, "of those for whom Combined Operations' records are also vague. It is requested that any information you may have concerning the whereabouts of these men be communicated to us, so that we may have Combined Operations trace any now serving with them." There was also an Able Seaman undergoing medical treatment, "but the location of the hospital is not known."[103]

At the very time staff officers were attempting to round up stray sheep, the two Canadian LCM flotillas were finishing up work in Sicily before making their way to Malta to prepare for the next operation. As our now familiar flotilla engineer related,

> after rather hectic negotiations and the cluttering up of signal services with dozens of sane and insane signals it was finally decided to refit craft in the Malta dockyard. I was enjoying the doubtful luck of a stay in hospital at this time but I heard from day to day of progress in underwater and engine repair. It was a colossal job in as much as spares were as scarce as hens teeth and the war strategy in the Mediterranean called for super speed. The boats were placed in drydock in batches and work proceed-

---

101 Ibid. Emphasis in original.

102. SCNO(L), to Sec NB, 30 Sep 1943, DHH 81/520/1250(1), CCCS File, Personnel—Status and Administration

103. SCNO(L) to CO HMCS *Niobe*, 31 July 1943, LAC, RG 24, 11702, 09-1-1

ed from daylight until midnight with one shift! In eleven days over one hundred boats were repaired, and though some of the repairs proved defective later, still it was a tremendous effort. Once again the boys came through with the goods when we were in a pinch. This is an outstanding feature of combined ops ratings, they may grumble and grouse when work is slack, but when there is a job to be done, they can be counted on to a man ... One man momentarily passed out from the terrific heat in an engine room one morning—he carried on for the remainder of the day and didn't report sick till late that night![104]

Such superhuman efforts did no more than render the LCMs barely useful.

With equipment pretty much in acceptable condition, the flotillas left Malta on 28 August, making their way to Augusta. Then, "just before dusk on September 2nd, a large convoy of craft, small and large, stole quietly out of Augusta harbour and headed northward. We steamed all night and beached just before dawn broke, clear and hot. This day was spent in loading the correct serials, numbers given to army vehicles, in the right craft and sorting out the craft of the various convoys that were to move off that night." One member of the group "spent the afternoon travelling from beach to beach on our motorcycle—acquired legally? In the Sicilian operation—briefing the various crews. By evening, all was in readiness. We had supper on the boats, a culinary feat which I defy any housewife to accomplish better than our boys do it, and spent an hour resting on the sand with some of the army officers who were to be our passengers." After about an hour's rest, "just after dark that night, September 3rd, we left the beach to join our appointed convoy of LCIs, LCTs and LCAs. This convoy was passing at a certain time close inshore but it was like a game of hide and seek to find them. This done, we proceeded up the coast to Mili Marina, where our particular boat was to pick up a Canadian Brigadier and his HQ staff."[105] The flotilla's quota was complete.

Leaving the last rendezvous point, "just as we turned from the coast to proceed due east to the Italian toe, the barrage opened up. And what a deafening roar! It was magnificent to say the least, and even a quarter of a mile off-shore we could feel the concussion from the guns. By the time we reached mid-channel a fog was settling down and this was turned into a good imitation of London's foggiest weather by the smoke from the exploding shells as we neared the coast. Navigation was difficult," but they managed to keep on the stern of a guide vessel. "With all the racket, plus a general expectation of a heavily opposed landing we expected to hear enemy guns opening up any minute. Nothing happened—we crept in closer—still nothing but the pounding of our own guns, then one of the Brigadier's wireless sets began to pick up messages. 'Red beach unopposed' and later, 'Green beach unopposed!' By this time we were able to dimly see the outlines of the hills through the smoke and fog. Coming closer still, we could see the troops of the initial wave walking along the beach. By this time invasion craft of every description were milling about. What a sight! On the beach, while the troops were unloading, gay banter could be heard from the boats' crews. And so easy was the first permanent invasion of Europe!"[106]

The flotilla commander was Lieutenant J.E. Koyl, who noted that "the regiments doing the assault in our sector were all Canadian—the Royal 22nd Regiment, the West Nova Scotians and

104. Combined Ops Sicily and Italy, Reminiscences

105. Ibid

106. Ibid

the Carlton and Yorks [*sic*] Regiment all under command of Brigadier Fennhill [actually Brigadier M.S. Penhale]." Koyl and his complements were part of the assault flight, and "I might point out that each beach for assault on the Italian side had corresponding beaches on the Sicilian side for loading purposes ... From these personnel loading beaches we proceeded up the Straits to our departure point where we picked up a searchlight transit, a tracer shell transit and smoke shell transit to our proper assault beach on the Italian side." However, "it is impossible to describe the confusion and difficulty of forming up the various groups according to time of leaving, serial numbers, time of landing and formation on landing in the dark. But it all worked out quite smoothly in the end." In part, this was thanks to good fire support such as had not been available at Dieppe, although "due to major war vessels like *Warspite* and *Valiant* passing by carrying out bombardment and creating a heavy wash, only good handling of the boats on the beaches prevented many being 'broached to' on the beach." The fire support was, nonetheless, appreciated, and "it was a distinct thrill going in under a great artillery barrage to the assault. We landed on time with little opposition and set off back to St Teresa di Riva for more loads." The rest of the operation consisted in ferrying troops and equipment, a forty-two-mile round trip,[107] the task lasting until 4 October.[108]

The following month Koyl prepared a report on the lessons learned from Operation Baytown, although it was not as inspiring as his operational narrative quoted above. Among the many problems and difficulties the veteran of Dieppe thought needed to be addressed, one of the most disturbing was that some casualties during Baytown may have been avoidable. "Two men were injured rather seriously. Able Seaman La Pensee ... received a serious hand injury from a kedge winch handle on September 6th at Palo, was treated by a Medical Officer there and was removed to Messina. Ordinary Seaman Henderson L. ... was hit by debris and steel from a demolition explosion near E2 beach at Mili Marina on September 7th. There was no warning given that the charge was to be set off by the Army men doing the job. Henderson was 100 yards away and received an arm injury that will immobilise him for the remainder of this war, and probably provide permanent injury." Other personnel issues included living conditions, a continuing concern, as "the men of the Flotilla are naturally not as keen as they were due to the conditions under which they are forced to work. They are not living like the naval ratings they are, and are not fitted to live like the Army." In fact, "I feel the Flotilla should be taken to a United Kingdom base to be kitted up, rested up and problems of pay and advancements sorted out. They have been away from such a base for over seven months and any Combined Operations Naval Base for two and a half months."[109]

Similarly, their landing craft needed looking to, and in spite of previous heroic efforts, "the engineering work done at Malta was of poor calibre, particularly the underwater work. We have had to slip three craft at Messina on a jerry built Italian slip due to faulty workmanship at Malta. If boats are expected to run constantly on these operations facilities must be provided for hoisting or slipping the boats ... The boats at present are all running, but feel they will constantly require attention and work if continued to run. They are long overdue for a top overhaul, and should now have rings and a general overhaul. The hulls are getting very thin and underwater work is badly need-

107 Koyl to SCNO(L), 26 Nov 1943

108. Combined Ops Sicily and Italy, Reminiscences

109. Koyl to SO LCM Flotillas Messina, 26 Nov 1943, DHH 81/520/1650, Husky

ed ... Boats gear is now well down particularly lines, fenders, stores, etc."[110] Unknown to Koyl, the Royal Canadian Navy had, as we have seen, decided on an important reorganization of its combined operations contribution, including the procurement of LCIs.

In the meantime, however, there was one last task for the LCM flotillas to complete. As Koyl explained, in the days following the assaults of 3 September, "as another landing was planned to land the reserved [sic] Brigade of the 8th Army behind the German lines at Gioia on the morning of the 5th, three of the most experienced LCM Flotillas, including ours, were taken from the ferry service to do Operation Kirkwood to Palo, Cape Faroi (NE tip of Sicily), where we loaded vehicles, material and personnel of the 231st Brigade for this assault." The landings were then postponed, but the extra time was put to good use, as "the following day we exercised the operation in view of doing it that night. It was again called off." The flotilla returned to its ferrying work, celebrated the Italian surrender that was announced on 8 September 1943, and left the theatre in October.[111]

Upon arrival in the United Kingdom, it was found that "in the majority of cases, officers and men were without kit and had not received mail for some time. The kit was missing due to orders issued before the assault on Sicily to store it at HMS *Phoenix* at the eastern end of the Mediterranean and the impossibility, due to chaotic conditions, of arranging for personnel to reclaim it before returning to the UK." Officers and ratings probably felt little need to complain, since they were sent to Canada on leave in November (and hence able to spend Christmas at home), eventually returning to England as the 3rd Landing Craft Infantry (Large) Flotilla.[112]

In effect, Canadian policy was leaning towards solving some of the problems that had crept up in regard to combined operations by simply doing away with the latter as a "special duty." As Captain F.L. Houghton RCN, the SCNO(L) since 30 October 1943, reported in November, "the principle upon which development of Canadian Combined Operations is to be based is the elimination of specialist characteristics wherever possible. In other words, the Canadian Combined Operations Landing Ships Infantry (Medium) and Landing Craft Infantry (Large) are to be treated, for purposes of personnel, the same as other ships of the Royal Canadian Navy."[113] Stokers came in for special mention, as "experience with the 250 Stokers (M) drafted to HM Landing Craft (Large) and HM Landing Ships Tank via HMS *Asbury* during the winter of 1942–43, confirms that Canadian ratings are at a serious disadvantage when serving with the RN if they are not immediately under the command of a Canadian Officer appointed to look after them and who has the assistance of a Canadian Paymaster Officer and Staff."[114] The lessons of past years were clear, and in February 1944 Houghton explained that "the basis on which Canadian (Naval) Combined Operations has been organized is to remove as far as possible the unfairness and handicaps from which Canadians on loan [to the] RN have complained bitterly in the past. Unless there is no possible alternative, officers and men should not have to put up with conditions which are inferior to those which

---

110. Ibid

111. Ibid

112. SCNO(L) War Diary for Oct 1943, nd, DHH 81/520/1000-5-35

113. SCNO(L) to CO *Niobe*, 17 Nov 1943, LAC, RG 24 (Acc 83-84/167), 76, 1250-1

114. LCdr W.S. Brooke and LCdr R.B. Wadsworth, Joint Memorandum on Combined Operations, 23 Nov 1943, LAC, RG 24, 11720, 33-26-2

obtain in other Service activities. On the other hand, it is just as important to see that those serving in Combined Operations (RCN) do not get advantages which are not open to personnel who have been detailed for other duties. In view of this principle, Canadian (Naval) Combined Operations is operated in a General Service manner whenever possible."[115]

One part of the implementation of that policy was the conversion and manning of two LSIs, *Prince David* and *Prince Henry*, which as we saw in Part 1 of this volume had started out the war as armed merchant cruisers. They had become somewhat redundant as German blockade runners had been swept from the seas, at the same time as Allied offensive operations in many parts of the world led to a much greater demand for amphibious vessels than industry could provide. Although not part of any Canadianization policy at the time, it nevertheless still made sense to refit the two vessels for combined operations. The Chief of Naval Engineering and Construction reported in January 1943 that such work would cost $450,000 per ship.[116] The following month it was decided that the refits would be carried out by the Burrard Drydock Company of Vancouver, perhaps to begin in June for completion in November.[117]

The worldwide shortage of landing craft and ships proved nearly insurmountable—at one point an exasperated Winston Churchill complained that "the destinies of two great Empires ... seem to be tied up in some God-damned things called LSTs"[118]—and in December 1943 a staff officer reported that "the completion of the work was of the utmost urgency if the LSI (M)s were to arrive in time for the operations for which so much time and money had been spent in converting them." In fact, "the Admiralty wanted to make sure that the Prince David and Prince Henry would be in the United Kingdom well beforehand. Their Lordships therefore gave repeated assurance that they preferred to guarantee to complete the outstanding items for the ships when they arrived in the United Kingdom ... The Admiralty also gave their blessing to priority for the LSIs over their own CVEs [escort carriers] building at Vancouver, both for labour and material ... NSHQ agreed to sail the ships as soon as they could be sailed and leave outstanding items for completion by Admiralty. They also arranged to embark some items of equipment which had been ordered in Canada but not yet fitted and these were to be carried loose for fitting in the United Kingdom. By this plan Prince Henry carried to the UK several pieces of mechanical equipment for Prince David who had preceded her."[119] *Prince David* had in fact commissioned on 20 December, entering the Panama Canal on 2 January and arriving at New York on the 9th. "When the *Prince David* entered the Clyde she was immediately besieged by various authorities wishing to find out what she required to complete." Combined Operations Command provided two lists, one of "essential" equipment, the other for "desirable" items.[120]

Personnel policy was already well in place, and as of September 1943 the Admiralty had been informed that "in the manning of the two Canadian Landing Ships Infantry (Medium) now being converted in Canada and which are due to commission about the end of November, Naval Service

115. SCNO(L), to Sec NB, 29 Feb 1944, LAC, RG 24 (Acc 83-84/167), 76, 1250-1

116. NBM, 18 Jan 1943

117. Ibid, 4 Feb 1943

118. See W. McAndrew, D. Graves, and M. Whitby, *Normandy 1944: The Canadian Summer* (Montreal 1994), 21

119. Ship's 2nd Commissioning and Clyde Refit, nd, DHH 81/520/8000, Prince David

120. Ibid

Headquarters desires to utilize the experienced Canadian Landing Craft personnel who have been trained in the four operational flotillas, viz 55th, 61st, 80th, and 81st. The officers and men for these ships will be required to join in Canada and to take their Foreign Service Leave before the commissioning date." About half of them in fact would come from just one of the flotillas, the 61st,[121] and sufficient officers and ratings were in Canada in October 1943 to provide most of the LCA and LCM crews expected to be carried in the two ships, while crews for the LCS(M) were being trained in the United Kingdom. All were, "due to unsatisfactory experience heretofore encountered by RCN personnel in Combined Operations," appointed to the ships as members of their complements.[122] *Prince Henry* would be home to the 528th Canadian Flotilla, while *Prince David* would serve the same role for the 529th.[123]

Training for the invasion of Northwest Europe began in earnest in early February 1944, with *Prince David* conducting a close range anti-aircraft and 4-inch gun shoot on the 11th of the month.[124] Later, "early in the second week of March, the Commanding Officers, Executive Officers, and Navigating Officers of HMCS *Prince David* and *Prince Henry* proceeded via London to HMS *Vectis*, the headquarters of the Naval Commander Force J, to witness Combined Operations exercises of two days' duration."[125] On 18 April, *Prince David* joined the force that would land the 3rd Canadian Infantry Division on Juno Beach on D-Day. The ship continued its training and on the 30th "slipped from Berth 43 and moved down to Berth 37 to load troops who will participate in a large scale landing exercise which is scheduled to take place early in May. Among the troops embarked was a detachment of the Regiment Chaudiere."[126] The soldiers would have cause to regret the arrangement, as "Exercise Fabius, a large scale exercise, involving LSI and craft of Force J carrying various Army units, and operating in conjunction with other Assault Forces, was scheduled to take place on the 2nd May. Because of unsuitable weather conditions the exercise was delayed 94 hours. It was not until 2358 on the 3rd May, that HMCS *Prince David* weighed anchor and with the other LSI of GJ2 making up the left Assault Group, proceeded out past the gate to the lowering position."[127] By then the troops had been on board for four days, in conditions that could in no way be described as luxurious.

Three miles off a stretch of English coast called Bracklesham Beach, the ship lowered two LCS(M)s at 0550 and 0620 respectively, both craft proceeding towards their objectives with forward observation officers (FOOs) on board to control supporting fire. The six LCA were lowered at 0639, five of them with the first wave of troops and one to pick up brigade headquarters from HMS *Waveney*, which had communications equipment that could not be fitted into a landing ship, and take it into the beach. Remaining troops were transferred into a Landing Craft Tank between 0758 and 0852. "By 0857 all craft were embarked once more having successfully completed their part

121. SCNO(L) to Adm, 23 Sep 1943, LAC, RG 24, 11702, 12-1-1

122. WSB, RCN—Combined Operations Activities, Progress Rep & Survey of Position as of 19th Jan 1944, nd, LAC, RG 24 (Acc 83-84/167), 76, 1250-1

123. Schull, *Far Distant Ships*, 236

124. *Prince David* ROP, 1 Mar 1944, DHH, 81/520/8000, Prince David

125. Ibid, 6 Apr 1944

126. Ibid, 4 May 44

127. Ibid, 3 June 1944

of the exercise," and training continued in the month that followed.[128] *Prince Henry*'s experiences were similar in this period.

The Prince ships represented one component of Canada's contribution to combined operations in 1943–44. Another was made up of Landing Craft Infantry (Large). The genesis of their incorporation into the RCN, as we have seen, could be traced back to the days before Operation Husky. After the success of the landings of 10 July 1943, SCNO(L) reported that "the attack on Sicily was the first where Major Craft of the type known as Landing Craft Infantry (Large) were used to any extent and results are understood to have been satisfactory." Should Canadians abandon the LCM, there would be sufficient personnel all told not only for the Prince ships, but for thirty-six LCIs as well.[129] Adding his voice to the recommendation was now Lieutenant-Commander W.S. Brooke who advised that "the RCN acquire and commission the 36 LCI(L) and that this Squadron ... maintain its Canadian identity and be regarded as a section of the Royal Canadian Navy on loan to the Royal Navy for use in Combined Operations."[130]

Confronted with such unanimity, and well aware of the problems many Canadians had faced while serving in flotillas of LCMs, policymakers in Ottawa agreed with the recommendations, and the Naval Board offered to acquire and operate thirty-six LCIs. As for the British, a message of 5 November 1943 announced that "Admiralty appreciate Naval Board's offer to man 36 LCI (L). For their part Admiralty will be pleased to make craft available for commissioning as HMC Ships. As craft was acquired under lease lend and change in possession requires formal re-assignment Admiralty urgently request whether Naval Board wishes ... to have vessels formally reassigned to RCN which means purchase from USA, or ... have Admiralty try to reach agreement with US Navy Dept for temporary transfer of craft to RCN for manning only without lease-lend formalities." The Admiralty noted that "Alternative (2) may prevent ships being commissioned as HMC ships though it is observed that squadron and flotillas will be designated Canadian."[131] A few weeks later NSHQ learned that the Admiralty was unable to state the purchase price of the LCIs, nor how much it would cost to maintain them, but at the time this was not a serious issue.[132]

The vessels were in fact acquired with little delay, although some had had "previous owners" instead of coming new from shipbuilders in the United States. The celerity with which they were procured had left little time for their erstwhile complements to prepare them for turnover to the RCN. Reporting on *LCI 266*, Lieutenant J.G. Wenman, RCNVR, its new commanding officer, noted in December 1943 that

> taking things by and large they are not going too badly, although they were pretty grim the first few days. The other crew left the ship in a shocking mess, no proper inventories, everything hastily shoved into one of the troop spaces and all mixed up. The whole ship was generally filthy. However the situation is now pretty well under control and we are getting on with the job of making a ship of her ... We are waiting

128. Ibid, 3 June 1944

129. SCNO(L) to Sec NB, 20 Jul 1943, app 1

130. A/SO(CO) to SCNO(L), 28 Aug 1943

131. SCNO(L) to NSHQ, 5 Nov 1943, LAC, RG 24 (Acc 83-84/167), 76, 1250-1

132. Ibid, 25 Nov 1943

for the engines back but are waiting for parts which should be here any day. We are undocking to-morrow and should be ready for sea in another ten days ... The only fly in the ointment, really, is the fact that we have a third officer, Sub-Lt R. Ritchie, for whom we have no accommodation whatsoever. Some of the craft are actually fitted out for three officers but we are most definitely not; no provision ever having been made for a third. Since his arrival I have had him stay at Pennar Barracks, which are fairly close by, but I am afraid that if he made the trip down with us he would have to sleep below in the troop space. I do suggest, therefore, that he be appointed to another craft that can offer him more suitable accommodation as it will be pretty grim for all concerned if he is going to have to try and live aboard.[133]

"Otherwise things are going very well," Wenman concluded. Many of his fellow officers were reporting in like vein. "The general condition of this craft is good" was how *LCI 266* was characterized, while the completion date for *LCI 166* was estimated to be 2 January.[134] Meanwhile, the arrangements by which Canada would take over the craft from the United States were being formalized, and in keeping with policy by which combined operations was only a wartime function, the Cabinet War Committee accepted that the craft would be borrowed only for the cross-Channel invasion, not even for the duration of the war, that there was no obligation to replace losses, and that Canada would assume responsibility for their maintenance and operation costs.[135] The Americans agreed.[136]

The three flotillas would be numbered 260, 262, and 264 and would be part of Force J, which would land Canadian forces at Juno Beach. Ten vessels, not twelve, were to be acquired for each flotilla. They would not be operating together in a single Canadian squadron, but each unit would be part of a Landing Craft Tank organization, with one LCI flotilla joined with two LCT flotillas to form an LCT squadron. "Ships were built with benches to carry 199 men in troop decks plus 46 on the upper deck. Most of the craft have since been altered to carry about 180 men in troop decks in bunks." As for the refits, in spite of some progress in some vessels, generally, "the position is not at all satisfactory. It would appear that no proper advance provision was made for this essential work. Ships are not being accepted until RCN Engineer Officers certify that condition of machinery and electrical equipment is reasonable." Still, two of the flotillas were expected to be ready by the end of January 1944, with the third by the end of February, although minor details abounded.[137] To give just one example, a message of 14 February noted that "inasmuch as the approved policy of the Admiralty is to turn over ships to the RCN with their full complement of stores and equipment and completely refitted, it is felt that the typewriter should remain aboard *LCI(L) 249* and that any other LCI(L)s taken over should have equipment as originally provided by the builders in the United States."[138]

133. CO LCI(L) 266 to SCNO(L), 9 Dec 1943, LAC, RG 24, 11719, 33-16-1

134. Sqn EO to SO(CO), 23 Dec 1943, ibid

135. NSHQ to Adm, 7 Jan 1944, LAC, RG 24, 3948, 1037-34-1

136. NMC'S Washington to NSHQ, 11 Jan 1944, ibid

137. WSB, RCN—Combined Ops ... as of 19 Jan 1944

138. SCNO(L) to Capt MLC, 14 Feb 1944; LAC, RG 24 (Acc 83-84/167), 76, 1250-1; LCdr G.F. Todd to SCFO(O), 28 Feb 1944, LAC, RG 24, 11719, 33-16-1

There was thus plenty of scope for conflict, as encapsulated in a memorandum by Lieutenant-Commander Maclachlan, Staff Officer (Combined Operations) in May 1944, two weeks before the Normandy invasion. Although it had been hoped that the LCIs would be acquired new from US shipbuilders, the RN "did not expect to obtain sufficient new ships to meet the Canadian proposals and, secondly, there was some doubt as to the new ships arriving in time." In the event, "the ships in question had seen service in the Mediterranean, apparently did not receive adequate maintenance there, and there is also evidence of considerable neglect. Shortly after Canadian crews began joining them, it became evident that the refit which the ships were receiving was, in a number of respects, inadequate, and that the spares situation was extremely critical. It was ascertained that the RN were cannibalizing Canadian LCI (L) for the benefit of RN LCI (L), and this matter was taken up with the Admiralty ... From this there evolved the arrangement, which was represented by the Admiralty as the only possible one, whereby Canadian and British LCI(L)s would be placed on a common basis and treated alike for all maintenance and spare part purposes." Fortunately, "in spite of the above," and many other challenges, "the engine room personnel drafted to the LCI(L)s and the 'floating' flotilla maintenance personnel have done a remarkably fine job in making the LCI(L)s serviceable to the extent that the worn-out equipment and lack of spares would permit. In this work we have benefited tremendously by the six engineer officers supplied from Canada for the job, all of whom were trained at General Motors plants in the United States. In addition to these six engineer officers, Lieutenant (E) Young spent a lot of time and effort in 'coaxing' the RN Dockyard authorities to improve upon the refits being given, and we have had the vigorous support of Commander (E) Simpson in urging at the Admiralty the necessity of providing spares and such other facilities as are available."[139]

Parallel with the refit issue was that of manning and indoctrination. Some vessels had to delay commissioning dates because "Canadian personnel require training." However, if morale had been one of the issues leading to the procurement of the LCIs, the lengths to which the RCN had to go to man them risked damage to morale. Since these men were required "in the United Kingdom at the earliest possible date, officers and men who had been serving in Minor Craft flotillas with the RN in the North African, Sicilian, and, to some extent, Italian assaults were recalled from Foreign Service leave and instructions were issued that they should be back in the United Kingdom as soon as possible."[140] Some were wanted for the hard-earned knowledge they had acquired on the beaches, and "Commanding Officers of the First Flotilla all had previous sea experience in Combined Operations or in General Service. First Lieutenants have had little or no sea experience, but seem keen and capable. Commanding Officers who have had some sea experience have been obtained for Second Flotilla by withdrawing some who were on loan RN, although this necessitated deferring appointments of lieutenants who have had no sea experience. First Lieutenants are for the most part inexperienced. Third Flotilla Commanding Officers will be mainly those who have had operational experience in Minor Craft. They are drawn from those originally detailed for Combined Operations and are regarded as a reasonably competent group. No information is available as to the ability and experience of the additional ones being sent from Canada." As for the ratings, "Seamen for the First and Second

---

139. CNMO to Sec NB, 23 May 1944, LAC, RG 24 (Acc 83-84/167), 76, 1250-1

140. WSB, RCN—Combined Ops ... as of 19 Jan 1944

Flotillas were provided from Canada. Those for the Third Flotilla will be men who had previously served in RN Combined Operations and who were returned to Canada for Foreign Service leave. Stokers from Canada have not in the majority of cases been trained in diesel engines. This has been overcome by using men who had been serving on loan RN for HM LCI(L)s." A three-week course was organized to teach thirty stokers how to handle diesels instead of gasoline engines.[141]

Training, as with any type of vessel, began with work-ups so that officers and ratings could familiarize themselves with those characteristics that made an LCI different from their previous ships. Stoker F.J. McParlan, RCNVR, who joined *LCI 302* of the 264th Flotilla in early 1944 left an account of this process: "We spent the last three weeks of February at Tibury for repairs, engine testing and trying out steering gear, compasses and guns. We went to sea for the first time at the end of the month when ordered to Weymouth on the south coast to join the rest of our Flotilla for work-ups." Arriving at destination on 1 March, "we took 302 out nearly every day or night. We practised beaching her and rolling the two ramps down ... The ramps were extended over a set of rollers after the LCI was touching the beach. This was done with a complicated system of blocks and wires driven by an electric winch. The reverse procedure brought the ramps back inboard and the stern winch hauled against the stern anchor and pulled us off in to deep water again."[142]

Ratings proved a greater challenge than materiel, ironically, especially if they had experience in combined operations. One staff officer reported on "the unsuitability of personnel who had previously served in minor craft. The Flotilla Officers claim that the personnel from minor craft are difficult to handle, that they are comparatively undisciplined, that they still require much training in the ways of major craft but that on account of their experience in Combined Operations they are no longer amenable to training. The Flotilla Officers further pointed out that this was not due to lack of experience or standing on the part of the officers, as most of the officers had had as much, and in a number of cases more, experience in minor craft than the men. Among the recent acts of indiscipline of minor craft ratings were the throwing of sentry boxes into the water and the assault of two officers. The Flotilla Officers asked if authority could be given in particular for ratings who had undergone detention to be returned to *Niobe* and replaced, in view of the very undesirable effect upon morale of having them back on board a small craft."[143]

The issue was not lacking in complexity, as "it will be recalled that one of the principal reasons for manning major craft was to get Canadian Naval personnel out of minor craft and it is felt that the anxieties of the Flotilla Officers regarding minor craft personnel may possibly be exaggerated, through their keenness to have everything running smoothly, and are based upon one or two outstanding examples of lack of discipline, which may tend to disappear as the craft shake down. At the same time, unsuitable personnel can have an unduly adverse effect upon the morale of the rest of the crew in a small ship, such as an LCI(L) which has only some 18 ratings, and it is suggested that it might be desirable for the Personnel Department to consider the advisability of not returning personnel who have undergone detention in their craft." But at least the men were being better fed than in the Royal Navy.[144]

141. Ibid

142. Marker and Lewis, "Combined Operations"

143. G.F. Todd, RCNVR LCdr to SCFO (O), 28 Feb 1944, LAC, RG 24 (Acc 83-84/167), 76, 1250-1

144. Ibid

In addition to the Prince ships and the LCIs, yet a third component of the RCN's planned contribution to combined operations was a Beach Commando, initially called a Beach Party. Compared with the other two unit types, it was a small organization, consisting of eleven officers and seventy ratings, but some of the challenges it faced were similar. As Lieutenant-Commander Brooke explained,

> Beach Commandos are landed early in an assault at all places where Landing Craft are likely to need assistance in disembarking their loads. The beach is the weakest link in an opposed landing, and it is for this reason that the beach organization, consisting of Naval and Army personnel, has been created. The Army is responsible for actual unloading, although at times the Navy have to help them. The Beach Commando is designed to handle boats required to land the Brigade, its attached troops, vehicles and stores. The personnel of the Commando should be well informed on the characteristics of the various Landing Craft and how they are to be handled on the beach. They should be able to pick a spot on the shore where Minor and Major Craft as the case may be can beach safely, and they should be prepared to render any assistance necessary; e.g, help to keep a craft square to the beach while helping to disembark vehicles, or helping to float one that has grounded."[145]

Nor was that all. "The Beach Party is responsible on landing for setting up and maintaining the beach signs which indicate to approaching craft where they should beach. Craft themselves are normally called in by a loud hailer or visual signalling by the Beach Master, and the Beach Party are to ensure rapid and safe turn round of the craft, and speedy removal of those that have discharged their passengers and cargo and have become wrecked or stranded ... After the initial assault, the Beach Party is responsible for assisting the Army in determining the best beaching positions for rapid discharge of vessels and stores required to support the assault flights. Their work will include organizing the beach so that the Party and the gear are properly protected and work carried out as efficiently as possible during air raids, etc ... The Beach Master is, in short, the Chief Controller of Traffic to and from seaward at the time of an assault."[146]

As early as January 1943, in spite of the fact that all Canadian ratings assigned to combined operations were needed in landing craft flotillas, some had volunteered for Beach Parties. The CCCS recommended such a unit be formed, but it was not until the Naval Board's decision late in 1943 to rationalize Canada's contribution to combined operations that it was in fact authorized.[147] In keeping with lessons learned, "the personnel of the Canadian Beach Commandos will remain on the books of HMCS *Niobe* and the Commando as a whole and not the individuals ... loaned to the Royal Navy for Beach Commando duty. It would be appreciated if, when the time comes to attach this Commando to some operational unit, a recommendation contemplating the inclusion of the Canadian Beach Commando in a sector where the Canadian Army will operate could be forwarded."[148]

As with the other two components of the Canadian contribution, events concerning the Beach Commando moved quickly in the latter third of 1943. Ratings for the commando, identified by the

---

145. SO(CO) to SCNO(L), 12 Apr 1944, LAC, RG 24, 11720, 33-17-1

146. Ibid

147. CCCS to NSHQ, 28 Jan 1943, LAC, RG 24, 3948, 1037-34-1

148. SCNO(L) to CO HMS *Armadillo*, 19 Nov 1943, LAC, RG 24, 11702, 12-1-3

letter W, arrived in October and officers in early December.[149] They did not get off to a good start, and the senior officer, Lieutenant-Commander W.M. Macdonald, wrote a lengthy memorandum of complaint on 19 January.[150] Vice-Admiral P.W. Nelles, former Chief of the Naval Staff and at the time serving as Senior Canadian Flag Officer Overseas, personally conducted an enquiry into the matter. In an obvious attempt to pour oil on the waters, Nelles reported:

> It appears that there was a certain amount of misunderstanding on both sides. The Canadian personnel arrived full of keenness and fire expecting instant and equal keenness plus action. This was not forthcoming and I gather that the whole party reacted like a pricked balloon... Several factors added to this sense of let-down. The course of lectures, being designed to meet the needs of RN personnel, contained a certain amount of material which the Canadian officers, being generally older and more senior than their RN colleagues, already knew and regarded as elementary. The Force which the Canadian party was to join on completion of their training could not immediately receive them, and consequently they had to remain at *Armadillo* repeating part of their training. HMS *Armadillo* is an isolated establishment, located on the West shore of Loch Long, which can only be reached by water, and the weather prevailing there at this time of the year is bad. All these factors added a depressing influence."[151]

Symptomatic of the resulting problems were two officers who overstayed their leave and two who "borrowed" a landing craft—for an outing—without permission.[152] It would seem, however, that initial misunderstandings were ironed out, as Brooke reported in April that all had done well in training while at *Armadillo*.[153] The Canadians were not, however, immediately required, and at a 17 April meeting a Lieutenant-Commander W.A. Juniper of the Royal Navy stated frankly that "W Commando was away down on the list of reserve Commandos." Although "it had been attached to Force J because they felt that J will ultimately need a fourth Commando," in the event "J had more or less ignored the Commando and had failed to include it in any of the assault exercises." Worse, "J had in fact proposed discharging the Commando from the Force."[154] The Canadian unit would not be part of the initial assault, but as we shall see in chapter 17, which traces the events of Operation Neptune, it would eventually serve in its intended role.

As the day of reckoning approached, only the Prince ships and the Landing Craft Infantry took part in rehearsals, and these made it clear that participants still had much to learn. Stoker F.J. McParlan, whom we met when he first joined his LCI, reported how "on May 4th, 2000 men of the British 50th Northumbrian Division boarded the Flotilla for Operation Fabius, the dress rehearsal for the invasion of France. We sailed that evening about 60 miles to a landing on Hayling Island in Bracklesham Bay. The rehearsal was so large nearly 1000 ships were involved or about one-fifth of the D-Day force." Reaching Hayling Island, there was a brisk breeze, about Force 5, and a heavy

---

149. WSB, RCN—Combined Ops ... as of 19 Jan 1944

150. LCdr W.M. Macdonald, RCNVR, to SO(CO), 19 Jan 1944, DHH 81/520/1250-1

151. Sr Cdn Flag O Overseas to Minister, 8 Feb 1944, ibid

152. Ibid

153. SO(CO) to SCNO(L), 12 Apr 1944

154. SO(CO), memo for file, 19 Apr 1944, LAC, RG 24, 11720, 33-17-1

surf. "This was the first time we had landed troops and for many of them it was also an initiation. The large waves rolling in under our craft pulled us off the beach when they receded. As a result, the bottom ends of our ramps were either on sand or under five feet of water. Many soldiers, laden with rifles and ammunition, were swept off their feet and pulled out by the undertow. Six carried by our Flotilla were drowned." Clearly, "we had to do something to avoid a worse tragedy on D-Day. We finally decided that we would tie one end of a line to the bottom of the ramp and the other to one of our sailors who would go down the ramp first and as far up the beach as possible. Those following could haul themselves along this line if they got in trouble."[155]

Training continued, and all the elements of the RCN's amphibious contribution to Operation Neptune were thus in place some months before the landings. They were better consolidated than for any previous such endeavour of the war, for although the Landing Craft Infantry units were part of British squadrons, the smaller craft were carried on board the two Prince ships and their complements were integrated with the Princes' crews. Even the Beach Commando was a Canadian unit administered by HMCS *Niobe,* although its operational future was somewhat obscure. Operation Neptune, the assault landings in Normandy, would prove to be the high-water mark of combined operations in the Royal Canadian Navy. Combined Operations would shrink to insignificance in the postwar era—it had never enjoyed high priority and was not part of the Canadian naval service's long-term plan. Yet the RCN never abandoned its practitioners, who so often had reason to feel isolated and far from home. Efforts to refit the Prince ships, procure Landing Craft Infantry, and insist that a prospective Beach Commando be Canadian demonstrated commitment to the men who had volunteered for this dangerous work. Operation Neptune would be a brilliant segment of the RCN's history, in large part—as will be seen in chapter 17—because the Canadian naval hierarchy, in the end, accepted the commitment to combined operations so wholeheartedly.

155. Marker and Lewis, "Combined Operations," 156

Towards a Balanced Fleet: Operations in European Waters, Quadrant, and Fleet Modernization, 1942–1943

ON 30 NOVEMBER 1942, a dank misty day in Newcastle-on-Tyne, the new Tribal class destroyer HMCS *Iroquois* commissioned into the Royal Canadian Navy. The ceremony was held with little fanfare, yet it was an important event for the members of the Canadian professional naval establishment who had pushed so hard for the acquisition of the Tribals earlier in the war. But obtaining large destroyers was only half the battle: naval leaders still had to achieve their goal of ensuring that the warships became the RCN's first substantial contribution to offensive fleet operations. That goal would not be easily attained.[1] When Canada lent seventeen corvettes to the Royal Navy to serve as convoy escorts for Operation Torch, Mackenzie King had been worried about the likelihood of their return to coastal defence duties. The prime minister noted in his diary on 4 June that year: "I think Power and Macdonald have come to realize there will be an attack against both the Navy and the Air Force for letting everything go off their coasts—in doing so little to defend our coasts and looking only to the European scene." At a Cabinet meeting on 16 September 1942, following the sinking of the corvette HMCS *Charlottetown* in the Gulf of St Lawrence on 11 September, the prime minister returned to the theme that the primary responsibility of the Canadian navy was to defend Canada's coastline. The new Tribals, he said, would be needed in Canadian waters, perhaps even on the west coast.[2]

The Naval Board was willing to acknowledge that the main effort of the RCN was and would remain convoy escort, but emphasized that these new destroyers would "constitute the RCN's contribution to offence" and should be stationed in European waters where their speed, manoeuvrability, and firepower could be used to best advantage.[3] A memorandum on the subject, written by Director of Plans Captain H.G. DeWolf on the first anniversary of the Japanese attack on Pearl Harbor, and at a time when Canada was negotiating with the Admiralty for the

---

1. For the acquisition and deployment of the Tribals, see M. Whitby, "Instruments of Security: The RCN's Procurement of the Tribal-Class Destroyers, 1938-1943," *Northern Mariner* 2:3 (1992), 1-15.

2. J.W. Pickersgill, ed, *The Mackenzie King Record* I: *1939-1944* (Toronto 1960), 378-9; CWC min, 16 Sep 1942, LAC, RG 2, 7c (11)

3. NBM, 12 Oct 1942, DHH 81/520/1000-100/2

provision of fourteen escort destroyers for the Mid Ocean Escort Force, was meant to educate members of Cabinet, and it thus serves as a valuable guide to the thinking behind Canadian naval policy.[4]

DeWolf's memorandum contained a minimum of technical detail so that its reasoning could be easily grasped by the politicians. He presented escort destroyers as having "been modified to carry an increased number of depth charges at the expense of gunnery and torpedo equipment. In other words, the escort destroyer has sacrificed some of its striking power in order to carry out extended antisubmarine operations, such as are necessary in ocean escort work." Fleet destroyers, on the other hand, were "employed in protection of the more valuable units of the fleet" and in screening the important convoys that had to fight their way through to Malta or carry aid to the Soviet Union. In view of its fighting characteristics—"the largest and most heavily armed of all fleet destroyers ... especially powerful in surface and anti-aircraft gunnery"—DeWolf argued that "it would be most uneconomical to use a Tribal in North Atlantic convoy escort when its guns are so urgently required elsewhere." He therefore recommended that the destroyers be placed under RN operational control, the Admiralty being best positioned to determine where they were most needed: "Only in this way can they contribute to the general cause."[5]

Mackenzie King, whatever his reservations, accepted this advice. On 5 December, the prime minister had made a formal request for additional escort destroyers, without mention of the Tribals. "Canadian escort groups employed in the protection of trade convoys in the North Atlantic," he cabled to British Prime Minister Winston Churchill, "are seriously handicapped by a shortage of destroyers." Mackenzie King inquired whether the Admiralty "would consider the release of fourteen destroyers from new production in the United Kingdom to be purchased by the Canadian government and manned by the Royal Canadian Navy."[6] Chief of Naval Staff Vice Admiral Percy Nelles then sent a signal to First Sea Lord, Admiral of the Fleet Sir Dudley Pound on 9 December with the suggestion that the "Canadian government might agree to allocation of the four Canadian Tribals at present completing or building to fleet work in Britain provided these would assist you to release the escort destroyers requested by us."[7] Assistant Chief of Naval Staff Captain W.B. Creery followed this up by explaining that the RCN's intention "that the four Tribals now completed or completing in England be manned by Canada but turned over to the Admiralty for operational purposes, and that four new escort destroyers be made available for Canada as soon as possible." Creery added, perhaps as a warning of Canadian Cabinet reservations, that "failing acceptance of this proposal it is possible that the Tribals would have to be withdrawn and used as destroyer escorts."[8]

Creery's message may have smacked of blackmail to its recipients. It prompted the Admiralty's Director of Plans to respond by saying he "would dearly like to see the Canadian Tribals British-manned and thus [be] a very valuable addition to our fleet destroyer forces. He has a feeling that the Canadians would now prefer this too, so that the RCN can play a full part in the Battle of the

---

4.   Capt H.G. DeWolf, "Employment of Tribal Destroyers," 7 Dec 1942, LAC, RG 24, 6797, NSS 8375-355

5.   Ibid

6.   King to Churchill, 5 Dec 1942, PRO, ADM 1/12564

7.   CNS to Pound, 9 Dec 1942, ibid

8.   Creery to VCNS (RN), 8 Jan 1943, ibid

Atlantic nearer home rather than a subsidiary one with the Home Fleet in foreign waters."[9] The Admiralty's Director of Operations Division (Home), however, showed a far clearer understanding of Canadian aspirations, expressing the accurate judgment that "the Canadians are proud of these Tribals and will, it is thought, be against a transfer of these, their largest fighting ships, to RN manning." In any case, no matter how they were manned, there was clear understanding on both sides of the Atlantic that the Tribals belonged with the British Home Fleet and not with escort forces. When Ottawa agreed to accept "declassed fleets"—destroyers of the A to I classes modified for use as escorts[10]—Churchill officially informed Mackenzie King that Britain would accept the Canadian proposal to transfer destroyer escorts to the RCN in exchange for the Canadian Tribals being assigned to the Home Fleet.[11]

The RCN Tribals, when they finally emerged from British shipyards, were designated Improved Tribals as a result of modifications Canada had requested based on war experience, including additional and better positioned anti-aircraft weapons, improved communications systems, "arcticization," and upgraded living spaces. Perhaps because of these modifications, especially because her beam was one foot wider than the original RN design, *Iroquois* had more than her share of the teething troubles experienced by most newly commissioned warships.[12] After completing work-ups in January 1943, *Iroquois* had to spend a month docked at South Shields while her builders, Vickers-Armstrong, corrected hull problems that had become evident from the wartime experience of the RN Tribals and made some minor repairs. Upon completion the destroyer sailed independently for Halifax so that naval officers, government officials and representatives of Halifax Shipyards that were building Tribals in Canada could examine a completed vessel. This passage revealed further problems. Rough seas off Newfoundland caused hull damage that required immediate drydocking on arrival in Halifax. *Iroquois* completed the visit without further incident and made a brief stopover in St John's, arriving in Scapa Flow on 24 March, after a stormy return passage.[13]

The second Canadian Tribal, HMCS *Athabaskan*, was commissioned on 3 February 1943 and had similar problems. Upon completion of work-ups her commanding officer, Commander G.R. Miles, reported that the bridge was "undoubtedly the noisiest, draughtiest, [and] wettest ... I have ever known," and the top speed of only thirty knots attained during her trials, when RN Tribals had reached thirty-four to thirty-seven knots, was "as great a disappointment as the length of time required to complete the ship for service." *Athabaskan* then sustained damage while berthing alongside an oiler at Scapa Flow, on 9 March, and had to spend several more days in port to undergo repairs. The destroyer finally embarked on her first major operation on 29 March when she

9.   DOP(RN) appreciation, 10 Jan 1943, ibid

10. Typically such destroyers had fighting equipment such as fire control instruments and some of the armament required for surface action removed in favour of equipment such as type 271 radar and ASW weapons such as Hedgehog and increased depth charge strength.

11. DOD(H) appreciation, 11 Jan 1943, Churchill to King, 23 Feb.1943, DOP min sheet, 3 Feb 1943, PRO, ADM 1/12564

12. The Royal Australian Navy, which built three Tribals at about the same time, did not modify the original Tribal design to anywhere near the same extent as the RCN.

13. During this passage a large wave washed two men overboard as they tried to help an injured shipmate, *Iroquois* ROP, 4 Feb and 24 Mar 1943, DHH 81/520/8000, HMCS *Iroquois* (1942-3); *Iroquois* deck log, Mar 1943, LAC, RG 24, 7418; CNMO(L) narrative, "Canadian Tribal Class Destroyers Built in the United Kingdom—Early Operations of HMC Ships 'Athabaskan' and 'Iroquois,'" nd, ibid, HMCS *Athabaskan* (I) (1943)

HMCS *Micmac*, the first Canadian-built tribal class destroyer in the final stages of construction at Halifax Shipyards. (LAC E003525096)

sailed in company with the RN cruiser *Bermuda* for the Iceland-Faeroes gap to intercept a reported German blockade runner returning from the Far East. Sea conditions, always bad in that area in the winter, were even worse than usual, and both warships failed to make a planned rendezvous with a British destroyer. Indeed, *Bermuda*'s captain was washed overboard as he led a party trying to secure gear on the forecastle. *Athabaskan*'s hull suffered severe damage, flooding a forward provision room, but she was able to keep station with the cruiser until the two warships returned to Scapa Flow on 31 March.[14]

These incidents of storm damage to both RCN Tribals got them off to a bad start with the Home Fleet. The Rear-Admiral (Destroyers), Rear-Admiral I.G. Glennie, inspected *Athabaskan* and informed the Admiralty that "the weakness revealed causes me anxiety with the ability of these ships to stand any degree of pressing on service. Urgent consideration is requested for stiffening of *Iroquois* and the remaining two ships of this class now under construction." Before that could be done, *Iroquois* had her hull battered again—this time while screening the battleship *Malaya* on 24 April. Once more she had to undergo lengthy repairs. All four RCN Tribals, including the two not yet commissioned, *Huron* and *Haida*, now received additional hull strengthening. These appear to have been avoidable setbacks. RN Tribals had reported similar problems early in their commissions, and their hulls were strengthened following an investigation by the Department of Naval Construction in 1940. Whether from incompetence or from lack of oversight, the same hull strengthening measures were not incorporated into the construction of the Canadian Tribals, even though the modifications they already received had given the ships several hundred tons greater displacement and one foot broader beam than their RN counterparts. Canadian officers suspected that Vickers-Armstrong were "more anxious to complete the ships than to modify the design so as to bring them up to date."[15] The RCN had, before the Tribals, for instance, during the construction of HMCS *Saguenay* and *Skeena* in the early 1930s, relied on Admiralty overseers. "It was not until comparatively inexperienced engineer officers were appointed," recalled a Department of External Affairs officer at Canada House, "that Canada had any technical supervisors to see that the Tribals were built to Canadian requirements." The ships suffered no further structural problems, but Rear-Admiral Glennie's views of Canadian ships seem to have been permanently coloured by his first impression.[16]

These tiresome months of trials, work-ups, and repeated dockings left the morale of ships' companies much lower than their captains were prepared to admit. "To those long-experienced in the way of ships," wrote Joseph Schull in his account of Canadian naval operations, "none of this was more than incidental and routine: a process of settling down and shaking in."[17] Typical of all Canadian ships at this stage of the Second World War, only a small proportion of personnel on

---

14. The cruiser HMS *Glasgow* had sunk the blockade runner *Regensburg* in the Denmark Strait the day before. *Athabaskan* ROPs, 16 Feb and 5 Apr 1943, LAC, RG 24, 11298; "Weather Damage to Athabaskan on Patrol with HMS Bermuda," nd, Athabaskan (I) (1943); CNMO(L) narrative, "Canadian Ships with the Home Fleet 1943-45," nd, 8-9, DHH 87/48; Hinsley, *British Intelligence in the Second World War* II, 544-5; Roskill, *The War at Sea* II: *The Period of Balance* (London 1956), 410

15. CNMO(L) narrative, "Canadian Tribal Class Destroyers Built in the UK"

16. "Notes on Interview with Mr E.O. MacLeod of Canada House," nd, DHH 81/520/8200, Construction-Ships (Gen); Glennie to Adm, 5 Apr 1943, *Iroquois* ROP, 1 May 1943; Adm to NSHQ, 25 May 1943, *Athabaskan* (I) (1943); VAdm H.G. DeWolf, videotape interview, *Seasoned Sailors* (Ottawa 1998), set 3, no 4

17. Schull, *Far Distant Ships*, 189

board were, however, "experienced in the way of ships." The commanding officer of *Iroquois*, Commander W.B.L. Holms, RCN, known throughout the fleet as "Scarface" Holms because of the injuries he had received as a cadet during the Halifax explosion of 1917, exacerbated the situation considerably. He imposed uniform regulations that had generally been discontinued during the war, restricted leave to short runs ashore during the ship's last visit to Halifax, and developed a reputation for harsh and inappropriate disciplinary methods, which included physical abuse. Holms's poor leadership skills were not confined to the Lower Deck and extended to his treatment of the ship's officers. His negative impact on morale was not made easier when *Iroquois* lost two men overboard in the return passage from Halifax. "A lot of animosity," recalled one of his officers many years later, "seemed to build up between the captain and the ship's company."[18]

Athabaskan, meanwhile, completed her hull modifications at Newcastle-on-Tyne in mid-May and received sailing orders to join a relief expedition to the island of Spitzbergen. At the time, more than 10 percent of the ship's company were absent without leave: fifteen had jumped ship over a three-week period in late April and early May, eleven "improperly left" the ship on 17 May, and another fifteen were absent without leave over the next two days. The Flag Officer-in-Charge, Tyne Area, instructed Commander Miles to issue warrants for the arrest of these men on a charge of desertion. The warrants did not have to be executed because the absentees had either returned to *Athabaskan* before she sailed on 19 May or they reported to HMCS *Niobe* in Greenock over the next few days. Still, five leading seamen thought to be ringleaders were disrated, and the remaining defaulters were reduced to "second class for conduct," while two petty officers who had shown "considerable lack of tact and understanding ... in handling the raw material" were relieved. This situation reflected badly on the leadership of the ship's officers as well. They appear not to have been in tune with the basic respect demanded by all young Canadian servicemen in the Second World War. Unfortunately, *Athabaskan*'s AWOL sailors were yet another black mark for the RCN in the eyes of the Rear-Admiral (Destroyers) at Scapa.[19]

For the time being, the Tribals escaped Glennie's jaundiced gaze to join naval forces in Plymouth Command preparatory to Operation Husky, the invasion of Sicily. On 10 July 1943, the day of the landings, they finally began operations. *Iroquois* joined the destroyer HMS *Douglas* and the frigate HMS *Moyola* as escort for the troop convoy Faith, sailing from the United Kingdom with reinforcements for the Mediterranean. The convoy consisted of the large troopships *California, Duchess of York,* and *Port Fairy*.[20] Although Commander Holms was the senior officer present, he left the designated British SOE in command, since the RN escorts would be remaining with the convoy to its final destination. The route to Gibraltar lay well offshore, clear of operations in the Bay

18. At Scapa Flow during work-ups RAdm (D) insisted on standard working rig dungarees rather than blue serge, as demanded by Holms, to conform with other ships in the fleet. Hayes interview, 28 Mar 1982, 42, W.P. Hayes biog file, DHH. For a detailed study of the background to the crew problems in *Iroquois* see M. Whitby, "Matelots, Martinets and Mutineers: The Mutiny in HMCS *Iroquois*, 19 July 1943," *Journal of Military History* 65:1 (2001), 77-103

19. Glennie concluded that the absences were "prearranged" and noted that a majority of the offenders were "young 'hostilities-only' ratings with little or no previous experience of discipline." He found that "discipline in the ship left much to be desired." Miles to CO *Niobe*, 18 May 1943, LAC, RG 24, 11746, CS 384-26-3; Miles ROP, 31 May 1943, LAC, RG 24, 11298, CS 379-2-26; CPO George Lauder interview, 21 Oct 1985, George Lauder biog file, DHH. When DeWolf reported to Glennie in command of *Haida* in Sep 1943, the dour British officer suggested "You won't be having any problems in your ship will you?"

20. *Port Fairy* was the ship that had sunk HMCS *Margaree* in a collision in Oct 1940.

of Biscay, where the Allies were conducting an intensified offensive against U-boats.[21]

On the evening of 11 July, when Faith was three hundred miles off the Portuguese coast, enemy aircraft appeared. *Moyola* saw the first one, a Focke Wulf 200K Kondor (a four-engined reconnaissance aircraft and bomber). *Iroquois* sighted it five minutes later, and the ship's W/T office intercepted homing signals being broadcast by the intruder. For the next half-hour the Kondor circled up-sun of the convoy, only intermittently visible but tracked by the Tribal's type 291 air warning radar. Holms noted in his report of proceedings that "at about 2100 a second F[ocke] W[ulf] was seen to join the first on bearing 315, followed a few minutes later by a third. All three were at about 10,000 feet and kept fairly close together." Eleven minutes after the appearance of the second Kondor, the enemy launched a series of high-level bombing attacks against the troopships and their escorts.[22]

The escorts were in an antisubmarine screening formation, with *Iroquois* 3000 yards ahead and the other two escorts on either flank of the three transports steaming in line abreast. The weather was calm and clear. The SOE had not ordered any change of formation, since the appearance of Kondors often meant they were guiding submarines to their target. Now, however, it was clear that this was an air attack. The German pilots showed tremendous determination and astounding accuracy, in spite of heavy anti-aircraft fire. *Moyola* and *Iroquois* attempted to break up the attacks as they came out of the evening sun, while *Douglas* fired on the attackers as they withdrew to the east after each bombing run. During the first attack the fire of *Moyola* and *Iroquois* from their stations ahead and on the starboard beam of the convoy was "short and under." Two bombs hit and two others straddled the *Duchess of York*, the westernmost troopship, and two bombs hit *California*, in the middle of the formation. In a second attack ten minutes later, with the convoy now in some disarray, two bombs straddled *Port Fairy*. *California* had started to settle by the bow, and by the time of the third attack the *Duchess of York* "was burning furiously and dropping astern." In the fifth and final attack "a F[ocke] W[ulf] was seen levelling out as though for a run, apparently on *Iroquois*, from the starboard quarter, at about six thousand feet. (All previous attacks appeared to be at about 10,000 feet.) My twin 4-inch H[igh] A[ngle turret] and multiple pom-pom put up a heavy barrage and the plane turned sharply away." Holms thought this attack had been intended for *Port Fairy* which, although damaged, reached Casablanca safely. But a few minutes later he had to take violent avoiding action as a Focke Wulf ran in for an attack on the starboard bow of *Iroquois*. Two bombs fell about two hundred yards astern of the destroyer.[23]

The three Kondors, which broke off about an hour and a half after the first sighting, had achieved remarkable success. Coastal Command strike squadrons had found it nearly impossible to hit ships when bombing from heights above 4000 feet and generally had to attack from below 1000 feet to have any chance of success at all. In this attack however the *Luftwaffe* had left two large troopships on fire and sinking. Fortunately, despite the loss of two valuable troopships, the escorts rescued all but fifty-seven of the more than 1000 military personnel and crew on board. As the largest of the escorts, *Iroquois* managed to cram over 600 survivors onto her decks—this "had

21. *Iroquois* ROP, 17 July 1943, PRO, ADM 217/208

22. Ibid

23. Ibid

The sleek bridge and forecastle as seen from the crows nest of HMCS *Iroquois* during speed trials in January 1943. (DND UK-012)

Iroquois' captain, Commander W.B.L. Holms, centre, on the destroyer's bridge during work-ups, January 1943. (DND UK-011)

a perceptibly adverse affect on stability"—and she reached Casablanca safely on 13 July.[24] An RCAF airman who survived the attack on the *Duchess of York* and was rescued by the Canadian destroyer remembered some fifty-five years later that "the *Iroquois* crew were marvellous, efficient, considerate, helpful, even donating their own spare clothing to those in need and miraculously producing a mug of hot, rich navy cocoa to lift the spirits."[25]

In his assessment of the disastrous encounter, Commander-in-Chief Plymouth, Admiral Sir Charles Forbes, criticized Holms—as senior officer present—for not assuming command of the escort: then Holms would have been responsible for deciding whether the immediate threat was submarine or air attack. But this has always been a grey area in which each case has to be judged on its merits. It is doubtful whether Holms would have acted differently under the circumstances. Forbes, for his part, was more critical of the troopships for not taking adequate evasive action.[26]

On the return passage from Casablanca the animosity between the ship's company of *Iroquois* and her commanding officer came to a head over what would otherwise appear to have been a rather trivial incident. On 18 July a German officer and two ratings, survivors of *U-506*'s sinking on 12 July by a US Army Air Force aircraft, were transferred on board from a British destroyer for passage to the United Kingdom. The ship's laundry cleaned their clothing but returned them with a badge missing from the German officer's uniform. According to an officer in *Iroquois*, the ship's first lieutenant, Lieutenant E.T.G. Madgwick, RCN, "made a pipe [announcement made with a boatswain's call] that whoever took the eagle, if they'd leave it in the first lieutenant's cabin, nothing more would be said. This pipe, of course, was heard by the captain and he sent for the first lieutenant and he said there would be no leave until this eagle was returned."[27] When the badge failed to turn up after they reached Plymouth, Holms duly cancelled all leave—and most of the unhappy ship's company decided to defy their captain. The C-in-C Plymouth reported to the Admiralty next day that "when both watches were piped to fall in at [0800 hours] ... almost the entire number of ratings below leading rates [some 190] with the exception of stewards and supply ratings but including communication ratings, proceeded to the mess deck and barricaded themselves in there."[28] This was the largest mutiny in Canadian naval history.

Holms responded by demanding a spokesman from the Lower Deck "within the hour." shortly after this he suffered an apparent heart attack "brought on by the emotional strain." The men, moreover, refused to send anyone because they suspected their grievances "would go no further than their captain." They asked instead to see Captain (D) Plymouth, who they thought would give them a fair hearing. Accordingly, Commander R.A. Morice, RN, came on board during the forenoon

24. Ibid; *Iroquois* deck log, 10-18 July 1943; Schull, *Far Distant Ships*, 191

25. Later that year, the survivors presented the ship with a plaque in recognition of the gallantry and hospitality of the ship's crew, still displayed on board HMCS *Iroquois* II. J. Edwards, "Destruction of Convoy Faith," *Observair*, May 1998, 4-5

26. Atlantic Convoy Instructions thereafter permitted an officer senior to the SOE to assume control "if he had strong reasons for doing so." C-in-C Plymouth to Adm, 24 July 1943, C-in-C WA to C-in-C Plymouth, 17 Oct 1943, PRO, ADM 217/208

27. Hayes interview, 5 Nov 1986, W.P. Hayes biog file

28. Adm C.M. Forbes to Adm, 19 July 1943, quoted in SCNO(L) to NSHQ, 20 July 1943, LAC, RG 24, 11751, CS 42-3. Whitby, "Matelots, Martinets and Mutineers"

and "saw the party on the fore mess deck who unbarricaded when told he was coming."[29] Morice told the men to pass their grievances to the First Lieutenant through two senior hands nominated by himself, received assurance that they would return to duty, and ordered them to fall in at 1100. "Since then," reported Admiral Forbes after Morice had reported to him, "there has been no further trouble ... The ship proceeded to sea at 1800 for an operation in company with HMCS *Athabaskan* and ORP *Orkan* and under the command of the First Lieutenant, Lieutenant Madgwick, who I am satisfied is competent to assume command."[30]

These events coincided with the beginning of the second phase of the intensified Bay of Biscay offensive by the British, the first phase of which had begun in June when U-boat Command had turned its attention to the central and southern Atlantic. After U-boats abandoned the North Atlantic routes, the Admiralty had withdrawn support groups that had been reinforcing threatened convoys in the North Atlantic (see Chapter 13) and either returned them to the Home Fleet or used them to back up the aircraft that had been flying antisubmarine patrols over the bay since 1941. These patrols had expanded to include all aircraft from Coastal Command that could be spared from the escort of convoys. The offensive was a combined sea and air campaign involving the Royal Navy, Coastal Command, the US Army Air Force in the Bay of Biscay, and hunter-killer operations by the USN's Atlantic Fleet with escort carriers in mid-Atlantic. It exploited the technological and intelligence advantages that the Allies had acquired through centimetric radar, long-range patrol aircraft fitted with Leigh Lights, and the ability to read German Enigma traffic. Aided by BdU's decision to have groups of submarines transit the bay on the surface in daylight, in the vain hope that their combined anti-aircraft fire would drive off attacking aircraft, the air forces achieved extraordinary results. Between the beginning of June and the end of August aircraft accounted for eighteen of the twenty-one U-boats sunk in the Bay of Biscay, fourteen of the fifteen sunk in Tenth Fleet operations, and eighteen of the remaining twenty-four sunk in other North Atlantic operations. When German surface units started coming out to support damaged U-boats and escort the large *Milch Kuh* replenishment submarines, cruisers and destroyers from Plymouth Command—including *Iroquois* and *Athabaskan*—sailed with antisubmarine support groups to give them added strength.[31]

Athabaskan, *Iroquois*, and *Orkan* made up Force W, with Commander Miles of *Athabaskan* as senior officer. They spent most of their time on their Bay of Biscay patrol in the Musketry sector northwest of Cape Finisterre, engaged in the unpleasant job of stopping and searching Spanish fishing boats. Since it was impossible for Coastal Command's Leigh Light aircraft to distinguish between a night time radar contact on a U-boat conning tower and a fishing boat, attempts were made to drive the Spanish fishermen, who were neutral, from the patrol areas. The three destroyers sank one fishing boat each and took the crews prisoner before tiring of this thankless task. As Miles wrote in his report, "they were not the primary object of the operation [and] I then decided to sink no more unless they were found in a position likely to prejudice the success of operation

29. CNMO(L) narrative, "Canadian Ships with the Home Fleet 1943-1945"

30. Forbes to Adm, 19 July 1943, quoted in SCNO(L) to NSHQ, 20 July 1943

31. B. Greenhous et al, *The Crucible of War, 1939-1945* (Official History of the Royal Canadian Air Force III; Toronto 1994), 396-9; Eric Grove, ed, *The Defeat of the Enemy Attack on Shipping: A Revised Edition of the Naval Staff History* (Navy Records Society 137; Aldershot 1997), IA: 98-113, 259-262, IB: plan 24; Hessler, *U-boat War in the Atlantic* III, 7-13; Syrett, *Defeat of the German U-Boats*, 145-80, app B

'Musketry.'" Force W's only contact with the real enemy was a fleeting one. On 22 July a lone Kondor suddenly appeared out of the low cloud cover and was promptly and accurately fired upon by *Orkan* before scuttling back into the overcast. Before heading back to Plymouth on the 24th the destroyers were ordered to search for the reported survivors from *U 558*, sunk by a Handley-Page Halifax from 58 Squadron. After picking up five submariners they headed northwest, where another U-boat had just been reported sunk. At 0206 on 25 July Force W sighted two flares and eventually rescued five officers and thirty-six men from *U 459*, as well as the tailgunner of the Vickers Wellington that had been shot down in the process of sinking the submarine. With fuel levels low, the three destroyers returned to Plymouth at 0750 on 26 July.[32]

On return from this patrol, C-in-C Plymouth convened a board of inquiry into the "refusal of duty"—in fact, technically a mutiny—by members of the ship's company of *Iroquois*. The three-member board, which included an RCN officer, Captain H.T.W. Grant, interviewed twenty-two members of the crew, among them Holms, Madgwick, the divisional officers, the coxswain, chief stoker, and those ratings who had submitted written grievances in response to Commander Morice's request. The report of the board identified three "contributory factors" to the incident. The first was Holms's practice of stopping everyone's leave in a mess when one of their number was absent over leave. The second, which the board members largely discounted, was the claim that applications for advancement or examinations were "unjustly held up or refused by reason of the applicant having committed some disciplinary offence." More importantly, the board members found evidence of a decided "feeling among a number of the ship's company that they were being treated unjustly and harshly by the captain, but it is considered that this would in itself, not have been the subject of complaint by a more seasoned ship's company. There is, however, evidence that the commanding officer did, at times and under stress, shew [sic] intolerance and an overbearing attitude towards certain of the ship's company." The board also noted that no grievances had been forwarded by the ratings previously because of a "general feeling of fear that such complaints would not be dealt with sympathetically ... [This] in no way exonerates the dissaffected section of the ship's company for not representing their complaints in accordance with the regulations which had been adequately promulgated and displayed on board." Admiral Forbes deplored Holms's methods, especially his policy of stopping leave, but he could not excuse the men for refusing duty.[33]

Forbes, supported by the Admiralty, recommended paying off *Iroquois* and scattering the ship's company among other Canadian ships. This measure was rejected by Canadian naval authorities. Nelles and his vice-chief, Rear-Admiral G.C. Jones, informed the naval minister that the ship "undoubtedly contained a few bad hats ... however, they demonstrated that if properly handled, there is not much the matter with them."[34] Naval Service Headquarters, well aware of Holms's intolerance and his "overbearing attitude," appointed Commander J.C. Hibbard, RCN, in temporary

---

32. *Athabaskan* ROP, 26 July 1943, PRO, ADM 199/1406; G.R. Miles diary, 24 July 1943, DHH 89/23; Lt J. George, "Participation of HMC Ships in Bay of Biscay Offensive A/S Patrols–July and August 1943," 2 Dec 1943, DHH 81/520/1650-239/12; German NS Ops Div WD, 1 Aug 1943, DHH, SGR II/261; Blair, *Hitler's U-Boar War* II, 345

33. It can be argued that these men were merely following long-established RN practice in bringing their grievances to the attention of higher authority; RAdm Jones faulted the first lieutenant for not nipping the situation in the bud. For further discussion see app IV herein, "Training, Morale and Discipline in the RCN, 1939-1945," in "Board of Inquiry re: Iroquois–July 1943," nd, *Iroquois* (1942-3); Anthony Carew, *The Lower Deck of the Royal Navy, 1900-39: The Invergordon Mutiny in Perspective* (Manchester 1981), 140; Whitby, "Matelots, Martinets and Mutineers"

34. Nelles to Macdonald, "Disturbance on the *Iroquois*: July 19, 1943," 31 Aug. 1943, *Iroquois* (1942-3)

command, transferred Holms to HMCS *Niobe* for disposal, and ensured he would never again hold a command in the Royal Canadian Navy. Upon his arrival in the United Kingdom, Hibbard, with the support of Captains Harold Grant and H.N. Lay, who were also in London, successfully lobbied to have the recommissioning decision deferred. On 28 July the Admiralty signalled NSHQ proposing "that after joining [*Iroquois*], the new CO should take necessary corrective action and should in due course forward report of general conduct of ship together with his recommendations as to whether or not ship should recommission."[35]

Hibbard joined *Iroquois* in Troon, Scotland, on 30 July 1943. He promptly mustered the ship's company by open list, a procedure by which "each member of the ship's company comes and salutes the captain and gives his name and number, so that he is aware that he's under the eagle eye of the captain who now knows his name and [that] he is being watched. It had a profound effect." By now the RCN had a thoroughly bad name for indiscipline in the Home Fleet. Perhaps to obviate the possibility of the Admiralty again recommending that the ship be paid off, Hibbard made it known to Rear-Admiral Glennie in Scapa Flow that he had stopped all leave, while at the same time telling the crew that the mutiny was their fault. Under the command of "Jumping Jimmy" Hibbard—as the nickname implies, he could be excitable on the bridge—*Iroquois* went on to a distinguished operational record. The decision to downplay the mutiny, however, set an unfortunate precedent and similar incidents, although not on the same scale, nor in as large a warship, would continue to plague the navy during and after the war.[36]

On 1 August, after *Iroquois* had been transferred north and *Orkan* had gone into refit, *Athabaskan* put back to sea in company with the new fleet destroyer HMS *Grenville*, charged with covering convoys in the Seaslug patrol area of the outer Bay of Biscay. On 2 August the destroyers received orders to screen the 40th Escort Group in the east of the Musketry patrol area because three German torpedo boats—actually small destroyers—were out, providing escort for two returning U-boats. As they headed for the new station at their best speed, a Vickers Wellington suddenly appeared flying low over the sea, pursued by four German JU 88 aircraft. The harried aircraft sought protection under their guns; *Athabaskan* and *Grenville* immediately obliged by opening fire with their main armament, and the JU 88s were last seen making off towards the French coast.[37] This episode heightened the anticipation of engaging enemy surface forces, even though there were conflicting reports about the composition and location of the enemy destroyers. The two anti-submarine forces in the area, the 2nd Support Group and the 40th Escort Group, ordered to close one another for mutual support, had mistaken the radar echoes of their own forces for those of the enemy. When *Athabaskan* and *Grenville* "came tearing up over the horizon" they discovered that

35. SCNO(L) to NSHQ, 28 July 1943, LAC, RG 24, 11751, CS 42-3

36. Hibbard would later command the cruiser HMCS *Ontario* in 1947 when fifty junior hands locked themselves in their messdeck as a protest against the executive officer. Hibbard cleared lower decks on that occasion and listened to his men. The executive officer was replaced. Whitby, "Matelots, Martinets and Mutineers"; A. German, *The Sea is at Our Gates* (Toronto 1990), 157, 207; DND, *Report on Certain Incidents which Occurred on Board HMC Ships Athabaskan, Crescent and Magnificent, and on Other Matters concerning the Royal Canadian Navy* (Ottawa 1949); L.C. Audette, "The Lower Deck and the Mainguy Report of 1949," in Boutilier, ed, *RCN in Restrospect*, 235-49; R. Gimblett, "What the Mainguy Commission Never Told Us: The Tradition of Mutiny in the RCN before 1949," *Canadian Military Journal* (Summer 2000), 87-94

37. Miles diary, 2 Aug 1943. George, "Participation of HMC Ships in Bay of Biscay Offensive." George incorrectly identified the Allied aircraft seeking help as a B-24 Liberator.

the ships they were training their guns on "were the four old sloops of the other escort group." It was a discouraging anticlimax. Plymouth ordered *Athabaskan* and *Grenville* to abandon their chase and screen the two antisubmarine groups for the rest of the night. Despite his efforts, Miles "got a raspberry for not answering [British Captain F.J.] Walker's signals re: an enemy I had been unable to find. He was cross because he had reported 40 EG as enemy."[38]

That no Allied warships intercepted the enemy destroyers was an indication of poor coordination between air and sea forces, and Plymouth Command. Aircraft first sighted the three torpedo boats at 1545Z on 2 August, and over the next five hours relays of aircraft reported the progress of these vessels. The *Kriegsmarine*'s operations division deduced correctly from radio intelligence that "the enemy had *not* formed a clear picture of our situation." In his account of these events, *Grenville*'s commanding officer, Commander R. Hill, RN, revealed that the destroyers were unaware of some of the sighting reports because they were either made on the wrong frequency or they were not passed on by Plymouth Command. Moreover, the course and positions of the torpedo boats given in the sighting reports varied widely, leaving *Athabaskan* and her consort with a confused tactical picture, moving Miles to complain in his diary that "the situation [became] obscure, several people reporting friends as the enemy." The two destroyers, as experience in the following months would show, might have been able to inflict heavy damage on the German force, and it is clear that a good opportunity had been lost.[39]

After two more uneventful sorties in mid-August, *Athabaskan* and *Grenville* left Falmouth on the 26th to patrol the newly designated Percussion area that abutted the north Spanish coast. Dönitz was now routing his U-boats there in an attempt to use Spain's territorial waters to avoid the Allied offensive. At 0700Z on 27 August the two destroyers rendezvoused with EG 1 off Cape Vilano and commenced an antisubmarine sweep to the south. They were now at risk, not only from U-boats, but from the new German radio-controlled Hs293 bomb, first unleashed four days earlier. The so-called glider bomb, powered by a small rocket engine, with a wingspan of 11 feet and a speed of from 300 to 400 knots, carried an 1100-pound warhead. A Dornier 217 or Heinkel 177 bomber could carry one or two of the bombs under its wing, release them beyond the range of a warship's anti-aircraft fire, and guide them to their target by using a small joystick. This dangerous revolutionary weapon required special defence measures. "In the event of rocket bomb attack," signalled the senior officer of EG 1, "intend following tactics. On 'repel air attack' being ordered ... destroyers are to take up stations ahead of frigates who are to close in until they are approximately two miles apart. [The sloop HMS] *Egret* will drop astern and cover the threatened flank. An officer from each ship is to be detailed to observe and report behaviour of bomb."[40]

They did not have long to wait. At about 1230Z, *Athabaskan* monitored a signal from an Allied aircraft reporting thirteen German aircraft approximately seventy miles to the north. Commander Miles passed this information on to the escort's senior officer as the ship went to action stations. Twenty-five minutes later both *Athabaskan*'s and *Grenville*'s type 291 air warning radar detected a

38. Ibid; R. Hill, *Destroyer Captain* (London 1975), 113-14

39. Miles diary, 2 Aug 1943. German NS Ops Div WD, 2 Aug. 1943; George, "Participation of HMC Ships in Bay of Biscay Offensive"; Hill, *Destroyer Captain*, 114

40. S.W. Roskill, *The War at Sea* III: *The Offensive, Part 1, 1st June 1943–31st May 1944* (London 1960), 30; George, "Participation of HMC Ships in Bay of Biscay Offensive," app A and B

formation of aircraft closing from the northeast. Minutes later nineteen Dornier 217 bombers flew into view on the horizon. The Canadian destroyer opened fire at 1303Z but the Dorniers stayed out of range as they split into smaller groups. Five aircraft then swept down the port side of *Athabaskan*, which engaged with every available weapon. "About 1314," recalled Miles in his report of proceedings, "the three leading aircraft dropped their rocket bombs almost simultaneously; two were failures and the third, never deviating from its course for an instant, came straight for *Athabaskan*'s bridge. It was a magnificent shot and there was no dodging it. Striking the port side at the junction of B gun deck and the wheelhouse, it passed through the chief petty officers' mess and out the starboard side where it exploded when twenty to thirty feet clear of the ship."[41]

Signalman Gordon Chadwick, stationed in the destroyer's radio compartment, recalled hearing a warning "so we knew they were dropping something. We just waited and wondered if they'd hit us. I heard a 'whish' and a 'bang'; then the next thing I remember was a funny, gassy smell from the bomb."[42] It was not just luck that the bomb passed completely through the ship before exploding. The Germans aloft had mistaken the large destroyer for a cruiser—not the last time they would make that error with the Tribals—and had set their fuse accordingly. The damage was serious nonetheless.[43] *Athabaskan* soon lost way, but did not cease fire. Admiring the Canadian destroyer's fighting spirit, the CO of *Grenville* reported: "All we could see of her was a mass of flames and smoke from under her bridge. Through this her gun flashes continued uninterrupted, and this was a very fine sight." *Athabaskan*'s luck held out when another Dornier attacked as she lay dead in the water. Its bomb failed to run and fell harmlessly into the sea. Similarly *Grenville*, attacked by a group of Dorniers, escaped unscathed when their bombs fell in the water some distance from the ship.[44] The sloop *Egret*, however, was hit by a bomb minutes after *Athabaskan* and blew up with a violent explosion. All that remained was "a column of whitish yellow smoke, about two hundred feet high, where *Egret* should have been." As Miles concluded in his report, "had this bomb exploded inside the ship, she probably would have shared *Egret*'s fate."[45]

At about 1330 on 27 August the German bombers withdrew, leaving the rest of the force to rescue *Egret*'s survivors while *Athabaskan* licked her wounds. Canadian fatal casualties were surprisingly few. A rating blown overboard by the explosion was presumed drowned, another was killed instantly, and three others later succumbed to their injuries. Another thirty-six men were wounded, three of them seriously. By 1415Z, *Athabaskan* had steam up and could make twelve knots, but most of her communications equipment was out of commission. *Grenville*'s commanding officer assumed

---

41. *Athabaskan* ROP, 30 Aug 1943, PRO, ADM 199/1406

42. Press release, nd, DHH 81/520/8000, "Athabaskan (I) (1943)"

43. The side plating forward on the starboard side "was penetrated by numerous fragments from a position just below the normal waterline to the forecastle and upper deck edges, and the plating and framing in this area was generally stove in. The starboard side of the forward superstructure and bridge was holed and stove in, one fragment penetrating the crow's nest and several the H[igh] A[ngle] director. The forecastle, upper and lower decks were distorted and set up, most particularly near the boundary with the ship's side, and the lower deck plating was penetrated by bomb fragments." Small fires broke out at "A" and "B" mountings, in the CPO's mess, the engineer's office, and the torpedomen's messdeck, and there was flooding in "B" shell room, two of the oil fuel tanks and No. 1 boiler room. The gunnery control system and all lighting forward of the No. 2 boiler room failed. *Athabaskan*, "Damage Report," nd, Athabaskan (I) (1943)

44. *Grenville* ROP, 1 Sep 1943, PRO, ADM 199/1406

45. *Athabaskan*, ROP, 31 Aug. 1943, PRO, ADM 199/1406

Unhappy-looking officers of HMCS *Iroquois* stand behind one of the destroyer's 4-inch gun turrets during the ship's commissioning at Newcastle-on-Tyne, 30 November 1942. The destroyer's first lieutenant, Lieutenant E.T.G. Madgwick, stands with his back to the camera. (DND PL 4291)

H.M.C.S. ATHABASKAN.

PHOTOGRAPH Nº 1.

GENERAL VIEW OF DAMAGE TAKEN FROM DOCK SIDE CRANE.

SHIP LISTED ABOUT 10° TO PORT.

A view of HMCS *Athabaskan* arriving in Plymouth three days after being hit by a German glider bomb in the Bay of Biscay on 27 August 1943. (PRO ADM 267/8)

the senior officer's duties. He signalled Plymouth that he intended to escort the crippled destroyer back to that port, but the new C-in-C, Admiral Sir Ralph Leatham, reminded him of the importance of continuing operations and ordered the British destroyer simply to escort the Tribal further out to sea before returning to his original mission. At 0030Z on 29 August, therefore, the two destroyers parted company and, after taking aboard *Egret*'s survivors, *Athabaskan* was left to struggle on alone. Leatham gave Miles the choice of either proceeding to the closest British port, Gibraltar, or making the longer, more perilous voyage back to England. Perhaps drawing on his experience in May 1940, when as captain of HMCS *Saguenay*, Miles had brought that badly damaged destroyer back to base after being torpedoed by an Italian submarine in the North Atlantic, he chose to head for Plymouth with its superior repair facilities and ready access to the manning depot HMCS *Niobe*.[46]

It was a tension-filled return journey across the outer bay, and a fine display of seamanship by Miles. The ship's company buried four of their shipmates at sea as the medical staff busily treated the numerous wounded from both *Athabaskan* and *Egret*. By herself, down by the bow with a slight list to starboard, and capable of making only ten to fifteen knots, *Athabaskan* presented an easy target for air attack. Although shadowed by a Kondor for some time on the 28th, she escaped further attack, but on three separate occasions came to a complete stop when her engines lost suction because of contaminated fuel. All this time the crew continued to make temporary repairs. By the 29th the fuel problem had been solved and the list to starboard corrected. Finally, at 1506Z on 30 August, after Miles had ignored a tug sent out to help, *Athabaskan* met three Hunt class destroyers off the Scilly Isles and they escorted her safely into Plymouth. Three days later the warship entered drydock for a lengthy ten-week repair.[47]

By the time *Athabaskan* limped into Plymouth, she and *Iroquois* had been joined by the two remaining Tribals built in British yards, HMCS *Huron* and *Haida*, commissioned at Newcastle-on-Tyne on 19 July and 30 August respectively. With four fleet destroyers available for operations in British waters once *Athabaskan*'s damage had been made good, the RCN had completed the first step towards fulfilling its long-term goals. As Naval Service Headquarters drew up plans for the postwar navy, wartime requirements offered further opportunities to lay the foundations for a balanced postwar fleet.

The possibility that Allied success in the Mediterranean and Pacific theatres would require another high-level conference of military and political leaders during the summer had been foreseen at the Trident Conference at Washington in May 1943. The weakness of Italian resistance in Sicily during July suggested that Italy could be knocked out of the war altogether if its mainland were invaded. Prime Minister Churchill proposed to President Roosevelt that they meet the following month to discuss "the larger issues which the brilliant victories of our forces are thrusting upon us about Italy as a whole." At Roosevelt's suggestion, the meeting was to take place in mid-August at Québec. Churchill proposed that, since the meeting was in Canada, Prime Minister King and the Canadian chiefs of staff should be allowed to attend all plenary sessions of the conference. Roosevelt objected, pointing out

---

46. *Athabaskan* ROP, 30 Aug 1943; *Grenville*, ROP, 1 Sep 1943, PRO; George, "Participation of HMC Ships in the Bay of Biscay Offensive," app D

47. Ibid; Miles diary, 30 Aug 1943; "HMCS Athabaskan Damage Report," nd, PRO, ADM 1/14577

that "it would not be easy to refuse the requests of other allies in the western hemisphere" if Canada were invited.[48] When Churchill communicated this rejection to Mackenzie King, he proposed instead that "the Canadian and British staffs should confer together as may be necessary but that the British alone should be represented at the combined meetings of the two principal Allies." The relegation to a less prestigious role did not overly disappoint the Canadian prime minister who as usual had his eye firmly on domestic politics. "My own feeling," King wrote in his diary, "is that Churchill and Roosevelt being at Québec, and myself acting as host, will be quite sufficient to make clear that all three are in conference together and will not only satisfy but please the Canadian feeling, and really be helpful to me personally."[49] For the Canadian prime minister, even if full consultation did not exist in reality, a photo opportunity that created the impression it did would be just as beneficial.

Gathering at the imposing Chateau Frontenac Hotel overlooking the St Lawrence River, the Combined Chiefs of Staff "approached the conference in a mood of mutual exasperation which, on the American side, verged on outright mistrust. General [George C.] Marshall's planning staff still saw behind the British interest in the Mediterranean subtle motivations of a kind political rather than military, concerned with post-war calculations of the balance of power in Europe rather than the defeat of Germany in the shortest possible time."[50] Indeed, the Americans' fears that the British desire to expand Mediterranean operations further could postpone the invasion of northwest Europe until 1945 were not without foundation. Shipping and landing craft resources were already at a premium, but Churchill was still advocating major landings in Norway, Greece, and Sumatra, operations on the periphery that would do little to defeat either the Germans or the Japanese. As it was, the decision to expand the invasion of Italy into a full-scale campaign would require more than 3,500,000 tons of merchant shipping—equivalent to 900 ships—to support it, which was more than one-third of the total shipping that U-boats sank during the entire war.[51] In the face of British insistence that the Italian campaign go ahead, the best that the Americans could achieve was agreement that Operation Overlord would have priority of resources. When the discussions turned to the war in the Pacific, the American Joint Chiefs of Staff expressed their anxiety at the outline plan prepared by the Combined Staff planners, which did not foresee the eventual defeat of Japan until 1948. Anxious to advance the timetable, the Americans managed to obtain British approval in principle for bringing the war in the Far East to a successful conclusion within one year of the defeat of Germany.[52]

Within this high stakes game of strategic give and take, Canadian naval leaders played their own hand with considerable adroitness.[53] It seemed that the restriction on Canadian participation at Quadrant might reduce opportunities for advancing Canadian interests. The RCN's position was

48. M. Howard, *Grand Strategy IV: August 1942–September 1943* (London 1972), 560

49. King diary, 24 July 1943, LAC, MG 26, J13. See also, Stacey, *Arms, Men and Governments*, 181-2 and Pickersgill, *Mackenzie King Record* I, 528-9.

50. Howard, *Grand Strategy IV*, 561. For the US attitude, see M.A. Stoler, *Allies and Adversaries: The Joint Chiefs of Staff, The Grand Alliance, and US Strategy in World War II* (Chapel Hill 2000)

51. Barnett, *Engage the Enemy More Closely*, 662

52. R.H. Spector, *Eagle Against the Sun* (New York 1985), 276-7

53. For the RCN and Quadrant, see also, R. Sarty, "The Ghosts of Fisher and Jellicoe: The RCN and the Québec Conferences," in D.B. Woolner (ed), *The Second Québec Conference Revisited, Waging War, Formulating Peace: Canada, Great Britain, and the United States in 1944-1945* (New York 1998), 143-70

strong because Canada had resources that the Royal Navy desperately needed. Not privy to the Anglo-American discussions, the RCN was able to further its "big ship" aspirations, particularly when the discussions turned to the Pacific war—and they planned to make the most of the Quadrant opportunity. A study by Lieutenant-Commander Geoffrey Todd, RCNVR, who worked under Captain H.G. DeWolf in the Plans Division at Naval Headquarters, offered the first written analysis of the negative impact that the wartime emphasis on small ship escort operations would have on Canadian naval development.[54]

The unique nature of the U-boat offensive, Todd asserted, had handed Canada an unusual opportunity to gain recognition through the creation of an unbalanced fleet of small, specialized vessels. None of these advantages obtained in the Pacific, where Canadian bases and territory had little strategic bearing on the combat theatre, and, in the absence of a concerted Japanese submarine offensive, an escort role was of tertiary importance. If on the defeat of Germany the RCN merely shifted its escorts to the Pacific, then it would lose its international profile and end the war with a fleet ill-suited as the foundation for further development of the service. Ships larger than escorts and with a greater range of capabilities were needed to carry out training programs, for diplomatic missions, to sustain Canada's position within alliances, and to secure Canadian waters against threats other than submarines that could well emerge in another war, one that Todd predicted might be fomented by the Soviet Union.[55]

The time had come, Todd's paper argued, to push for the acquisition of four cruisers and to multiply the fleet destroyer force from eight Tribals (four in commission and four building in Canada) to a total of twenty-four. Todd based his argument on the need for Canadian operational control of Canadian ships. The former Director of the Operations Division, Captain H.N. Lay, had used this argument six months earlier to influence changes to the command and control arrangements for the Battle of the Atlantic. Now Todd adopted the same line of argument to support the case for a Canadian Pacific force of "a squadron of four cruisers to assist in the battles [in] the southwest Pacific, to operate as a separate force, or with other allied [capital ships] as the allied C-in-C should [direct] ... [This] opportunity to win battle honours with the [cruisers would] greatly enhance the chances of their acceptance by public opinion as part of the post-war Canadian Navy."[56]

The RCN's concentration on antisubmarine warfare, Todd submitted, had created a "lack of balance" which, in the Pacific, would translate into a loss of operational control. Canada's coasts did not rest on the main Pacific theatre, and shipping routes were not concentrated there as in the Atlantic. Thus, there was no hope in the western Pacific for an equivalent of the 1941 Newfoundland Escort Force—let alone a C-in-C, Canadian Northwest Atlantic Command—that could stamp escort operations with a Canadian identity. Owing to the geographical expanse of the Pacific and the length of Allied supply lines, escort groups would be shuttled about in penny packets on housekeeping duties by Allied commanders far junior to a C-in-C. A squadron of four cruisers, on the other hand, with attendant fleet destroyers and other vessels, could be assigned by a C-in-C on quasi-independent tasks. Aircraft carriers were also a "possibility," but Todd was well

---

54. Plans Division, "Appreciation of RCN Ship Requirements for the War against Japan and for the Post-War Navy," 29 July 1943, LAC, RG 24, 3844, NSS 1017-10-34, pt 1

55. Ibid

56. Ibid

aware of the difficulties that already surrounded the question of establishing a Canadian naval aviation service.[57]

Todd's paper contained little that was new, and reiterated views that had echoed through the corridors of naval headquarters for years. The fleet he described, and the arguments about capability, status, and sovereignty, were the same ones that had emerged from the Laurier-Borden naval debates of 1909–14, the Jellicoe mission of 1919, and had been urged by senior Canadian naval officers ever since. What was significant was the timing and strong language of Todd's memorandum——"It is vital for the maintenance of Canadian prestige that the Canadian Navy takes a direct and important part in the war against Japan"—which reflected the sense at NSHQ that the service had again arrived at a crossroads. In contrast to those earlier occasions, however, the Canadian navy now had a precious resource with which to pursue its goals at the Québec Conference: manpower. In May 1943 the British Ministry of Labour had warned that Britain was nearing peak mobilization of the population and that no further substantial commitments could be undertaken without finding the manpower by cutting back another part of the armed forces or war industry. Estimates at that time were that less than half of the 912,000 additional men and women already allocated to the services and industry for the last half of 1943 could actually be found.[58] This put the Admiralty in a particularly tight spot. Because of the length of time it takes to build warships, the navy had been slower to expand than had the other services, but it now was confronted by the need to man a flood of new construction. Many of these vessels were being built for the Royal Navy in the United States under lend-lease, and delays in taking them over would raise doubts in Washington about Britain's ability to back up its claims as the fully equal co-leader of the western alliance.

These pressures reflected the inescapable strategic fact that the major offensive operations being planned were almost all amphibious in nature, and they made particularly heavy demands on the navy for the movement of troops and equipment, security of these military convoys, and the landing craft and fire support required for the actual assault. The British insistence on pursuing the Mediterranean campaign would require substantial shipping and landing craft resources to support it, while strength still had to be built up on a massive scale for the landing in northern France the following year. The U-boats had been forced to abandon the North Atlantic. But the German submarine fleet remained as large as ever. Moreover, several major surface ships, most notably *Tirpitz* and *Scharnhorst*, remained in Norway to menace Britain's convoys to Russia, meaning that there could be few economies for the Royal Navy in the Atlantic. It was thus still not possible to expand the RN's presence in the Far East beyond the small fleet of obsolete battleships in the Indian Ocean, even though it was imperative, for reasons of Britain's international stature, that the Americans should not be left as the sole liberators of the Pacific and South East Asia.[59]

---

57. Ibid

58. J. Ehrman, *Grand Strategy* V: *August 1943–September 1944* (London 1956), 41-4

59. Adm to Br Adm Delegation (Washington), 6 Nov 1943, PRO, ADM 1/13009; A.V. Alexander to Stark, 10 Dec. 1943, enclosing aide memoire on British manpower problems, PRO, ADM 1/17025; D.E. Graves, "'Fourth Service or Problem?' The British Combined Operation Organization and the Royal Navy's Manpower Crisis, 1942-1944," in D. Bittner, ed, *Selected Papers from the 1992 (59th) Meeting of the Society for Military History Hosted by the Command and Staff College of the Marine Corps University* (np 1994), 175-86

There was therefore some excitement at the Admiralty when in the summer of 1943 reports came in from officers on duty in North America that the Canadians had a surplus of naval personnel. Construction in Canada of frigates, the new escort type that was half again bigger than a corvette, had fallen behind the rate of recruitment. Out of a total strength of nearly 70,000 personnel in the RCN, fewer than 22,000 were seagoing, when perhaps half should have been. The Canadian naval staff and the Admiralty quickly recognized the possibility of mutual benefit, which sparked a series of meetings in Québec and Ottawa.[60]

On the evening of 11 August 1943, the day after the British delegation for Quadrant arrived at the Chateau Frontenac, First Sea Lord Admiral of the Fleet Sir Dudley Pound, and Chief of Combined Operations Vice-Admiral Lord Louis Mountbatten, supported by other Admiralty staff, met secretly with Canadian Chief of Naval Staff Vice-Admiral Nelles and his Director of Plans, Captain H.G. DeWolf. Pound did not want the other British services—with which he was competing for manpower—to know what was being discussed, and Nelles did not want word to get out to his government. Pound quickly declared that he could help the Canadians in their quest for cruisers. Nelles frankly stated "that, speaking strictly from the service point of view and not committing the Canadian Cabinet, his problem was to see that the RCN did not finish the war as a small ship navy entirely." His intention was to build towards a postwar navy of five cruisers, two light fleet aircraft carriers, vessels twice as large and much better built than the emergency type escort carriers that had previously been discussed, and three flotillas of fleet destroyers. On the carrier question, Nelles and Pound alluded to the fundamental Anglo-Canadian disagreement.[61] The British were only too willing to have the RCN provide ships' crews for carriers but they insisted that the entire flying organization on those carriers should be RN to avoid wasting resources in attempting the large task of organizing a Canadian naval aviation branch.[62]

Pound and Mountbatten steered the discussion towards their more immediate problem, the need to find personnel for combined operations to meet British commitments to Operation Overlord. As we saw in the previous chapter, as early as 1941 the British combined operations organization and the Canadian naval staff had seen mutual benefit in a Canadian contribution to combined operations. Mountbatten and the Canadians now reached a similar consensus. Enjoying the confidence of Churchill as well as the support, albeit muted, of the British Chiefs of Staff, Mountbatten made the case that manpower was needed for Overlord, and not simply warm bodies. He exploited the line of argument put forward by RCN officers in Britain, most notably Commander F.A. Price and Lieutenant-Commander K.S. Maclachlan, that service in major craft would provide "very valuable sea training" that would be both useful and beneficial to RCN officers. Nelles worried that, although the Royal Canadian Navy had a temporary surplus of manpower and could provide some personnel for Overlord, they would have to be reabsorbed into the RCN at a later date as there would be new frigates and corvettes to man. Mountbatten reassured Nelles, however, in observing that the Royal

---

60. DPS, "Canadian Naval Personnel," 1 Aug 1943, PRO, ADM 205/31; "Summary of Naval War Effort," 1 July–30 Sep. 1943, 2-3, DHH 81/520/1000-5-8, pt 4

61. Min of Mtg held in Conference Room B at the Chateau Frontenac on Wed, 11 Aug 1943, nd, PRO, ADM 205/31. The copy of the minutes given to the Canadians is in LAC, RG 24 (Acc. 83-84/167), 1481, NSS 4300-99.

62. ACNS (A) to First Sea Lord, 3 Aug 1943, DOP to First Sea Lord, "Canada—Naval Aviation," 7 Aug 1943, PRO, ADM 205/31

Navy was going to lose ships during the operation and that meant their manpower requirements would likely be reduced to a point where they could spare the Canadians once Overlord was finished. Pound, on the other hand, cut to the heart of the matter by suggesting that " the only immediate solution to getting [Canadian] naval personnel afloat seemed to be the manning of landing craft." Nelles concurred and agreed to discuss the issue further in Ottawa over the next few days with Captain R.H. Buxton, RN, the Admiralty's Deputy Director of Personnel Services. But as the meeting closed, Nelles reminded the First Sea Lord "that he hoped the Canadian post-war plans, which he had referred to earlier in the meeting would be borne in mind."[63]

In the days following the preliminary 11 August meeting, Buxton met with Nelles, Captain W.B. Creery, the ACNS, and Commander H. McMaster, Deputy Director Naval Personnel in Ottawa about the Canadian manpower surplus. Buxton presumed that after informal agreement had been reached about how to deploy the surplus, Nelles would "make the first move either by asking the Admiralty for certain additional vessels which would accord with his general naval expansion policy, or alternatively, by offering personnel to the Admiralty, subject to certain conditions regarding their employment." Nelles, who knew he would have to coax approval from a reluctant Prime Minister Mackenzie King, had another approach in mind. In this instance, years of dealing with politicians allowed him to predict accurately how the cost-conscious prime minister would react to the deal he was hammering out with the Admiralty. King had consistently resisted the acquisition of anything larger than destroyers. Furthermore, since the latter part of 1942 he had made it clear that Canada was doing enough and that the programs approved at that time for 1943 would represent the country's maximum effort. The prime minister was especially worried about manpower—and, despite the army's reassurances, the possibility that this would require overseas conscription. He also wanted to cut expenditures and give the population tax relief. King's formidable political antennae had detected a war-weariness among the Canadian public that found expression in 1943 with the rising popularity of the socialist Co-operative Commonwealth Federation party—and a Liberal slump in the polls. The RCN, at its moment of great opportunity, was feeling the chill of domestic politics.[64]

To counter the political arguments Nelles resurrected a tactic familiar to the Canadian military establishment. On several occasions during the war, King, after casting a cold eye on advice from his own military advisors, had buried his reservations upon receiving the same request as a personal appeal from Churchill.[65] Nelles went to the well again. Buxton informed Mountbatten that "owing to political difficulties in connection with proposals emanating in Ottawa, Admiral Nelles would prefer that the initial move should come from our side. He suggested that the First Sea Lord might approach the British prime minister with specific suggestions as to how Canada might help us in our present manning difficulty, and that Mr Churchill should then take it up with Mr Mackenzie King. Admiral Nelles considered that this line of approach would produce much quicker results than any proposals emanating from him."[66]

---

63. Min of Mtg held in Conference Room B at the Chateau Frontenac at 1800, 11 Aug 1943, PRO, ADM 1/13044

64. King diary, 26 May and 17 June 1943. On the beginnings of strains on the supply of manpower see Stacey, *Arms, Men and Governments*, 405-12.

65. Douglas, *Creation of a National Air Force* II, 503

66. Buxton memo to Chief of Combined Operations, "Manning—Assistance from RCN," 20 Aug 1943, DHH 81/520/1270, vol 3

Nelles added another twist to the negotiations. "While agreeable to making some direct contribution in the way of crews for landing craft," Buxton informed Mountbatten that Nelles "was evidently more anxious to take over two RN destroyers at the end of this year thereby releasing RN personnel for Overlord requirements." This made perfect sense from an RCN point of view. Rather than assigning surplus personnel to British landing craft flotillas, the acquisition of two destroyers would bolster the postwar force. There was little the Admiralty could protest, as the plan would enable them to reassign the personnel they had slated for the destroyers. Buxton and Nelles also fleshed out a plan whereby the Canadians would infiltrate key personnel into British cruisers for training, thus giving early relief to the Royal Navy in its shortages and assuring that complete and qualified Canadian crews would be ready when ships became available for transfer. With Canadian priorities satisfied, it remained to reach a deal about landing craft, the chief British priority. Nelles agreed to take over three landing craft flotillas of either Landing Craft Tanks (LCTs) or Landing Craft Infantry (Large) or LCI(L)s, including squadron staff, to provide personnel for a Beach Commando unit and to contribute ten CW candidates (ratings recommended for commissioning as officers) per month over a period of twelve months.[67] During the next few days, this deal, including the tactic of a prime minister to prime minister approach, was approved by the First Sea Lord, who was in Québec, and the First Lord at the Admiralty. Before it went to Churchill, Nelles, who had shaped the negotiations, was forwarded a copy for approval.[68]

At a meeting on 31 August of the Canadian Cabinet War Committee in Québec at the conclusion of the Anglo-American conference, the British prime minister and Admiral Pound presented the whole list of projects, including Canadian manning of cruisers, as a cry for help with the British manpower crisis. The initial impact upon the Canadian prime minister was slight. At lunch beforehand, Churchill, who according to the Canadian prime minister had dined well,[69] had confided to King that the Canadian's "leadership had meant everything to the war effort," and they exchanged views on the strategic situation in general as well as the involvement of a Canadian division in the forthcoming invasion of Italy. At the formal meeting that followed, perhaps distracted by Churchill's compliments and the informal consultation on grand strategy, King's only response when presented with the naval proposals was that they should be studied carefully in relation to Canadian manpower requirements before final approval by the Cabinet War Committee at a later date.[70]

King had a stronger reaction when the war committee next met on 8 September, and he chided Nelles about the way in which the whole thing had been sprung on the government. The manner of their presentation had placed the war committee in a difficult position; what had the naval staff known? Nelles admitted that Pound "had at an early stage of the conference, discussed informally with members of the Canadian naval staff various proposals for Canadian assistance to the Royal Navy." That much was true. What followed was not. Nelles then said that "it was not, however, known to the Canadian staff that specific proposals were to be brought forward at the meet-

---

67. Ibid

68. Quadrant to Adm, 21 Aug 1943, Adm to Quadrant, 24 Aug 1943, Brockman to First Sea Lord, 24 Aug 1943, PRO, ADM 1/13049. It is clear this exchange of messages was between the First Sea Lord at Québec and the First Lord and Deputy First Sea Lord at the Admiralty. Brockman was a civilian member of Pound's staff.

69. King diary, 31 Aug 1943

70. Ibid; CWCM, 31 Aug 1943

ing of August 31st." Not sure if he had been misled, but suspecting so, King reminded Nelles, at some length, that the manpower ceiling of 84,000 that had been set for the navy of 1943 was the absolute maximum the service could hope for and "that from now on we would have to contract." The prime minister then hinted darkly that his Liberal government could well be replaced within the next year by one much less favourable to the military. Minister of Defence for Naval Services Angus L. Macdonald interjected by observing that delays with the RCN's new construction program had not only freed up manpower for the British proposal but for the possible acquisition of fleet carriers and a Canadian naval air arm too. That Macdonald had raised the carriers, which were not part of Churchill's request, suggests that he shared Nelles's vision of the postwar RCN. Nonetheless, by doing so he had distracted King just enough that Nelles did not have to provide any further details on the origins of the deal.[71]

It is unlikely that Macdonald knew about the arrangements prior to Quadrant, but he was certainly an enthusiastic supporter of the naval staff's gambit at the 31 August and 8 September meetings. After the first meeting he admitted to being "eager to have the cruiser as our training is now purely on convoy escort and in small ships."[72] After the government agreed on 8 September to begin infiltrating Canadians into British cruiser crews, Macdonald enthused that "this step is very significant. The RCN is stepping out of the small ship class—the Laurier plan is being realized after more than thirty years."[73] He was so pleased that two days later, while at a press conference on the Battle of the Atlantic, Macdonald blurted out the news about the cruiser program. "This," he noted with satisfaction, "received the most attention in the papers."[74]

At the 8 September meeting, the Cabinet also approved the RCN's proposal to man a squadron of LCIs. In the interim, Lieutenant-Commander W.S. Brooke, RCNVR, in his capacity as Staff Officer, Combined Operations at the Canadian naval mission in London, had won over the naval staff with strong arguments in favour of the LCI(L) as opposed to the British-built LCT, which he characterized as having poor crew accommodations, being unhandy at sea, difficult to keep clean, and not designed for ocean passages.[75] Brooke had argued that LCTs "provide hardly any improvement over that which the Canadians now in combined operations are receiving." LCI(L)s, on the other hand, were small ships able to cross the Atlantic and could also be treated as normal ships for drafting purposes with reliefs provided from the general service pool. Because "it is not regarded as unreasonable for Canada to ask for these craft" personnel serving in LCI(L)s would gain useful experience and would be available at the completion of their landing craft time for service throughout the RCN:

> (1) They fit in so admirably with the rest of the RCN; (2) the RN endeavour to use Canadian ... ratings in LCI(L)s as these men are quite at home with US engines and equipment; (3) even if Canada did utilize all its Combined Operations personnel to man Landing Craft Tank the RN would still have to man a large number and the RCN would

---

71.   King diary and CWCM, 8 Sep 1943

72.   Angus L. Macdonald diary, 31 Aug 1943, file 391, Angus L. Macdonald Papers, Public Archives of Nova Scotia (PANS)

73.   Ibid, 8 Sep 1943

74.   Ibid, 10 Sep 1943

75.   "Canadian Naval Participation in Combined Operations," 28 Aug 1943, DHH 81/520/1250(4)

be burdened with unsuitable and specialized craft which could not conveniently be used in Canadian waters or in the Pacific and which would prevent Canadian officers and ratings from becoming truly useful seamen and getting the advancement opportunities to which they, in common with the rest of the personnel of the RCN, are entitled.[76]

On 11 September First Sea Lord Pound advised the Admiralty that the Canadian cabinet had approved the RCN manning proposal of one Canadian unit of three flotillas of LCI(L) as well as the beach units.[77] This message took the Admiralty by surprise. On receipt of Pound's signal, an officer at the Admiralty commented that the "original proposal was for Canadians to man LCT squadrons. This has become LCI(L) apparently by chance."[78] What this officer did not know was that Nelles had stated a preference for LCI(L)s over LCTs at his meeting on the subject with Buxton the previous month.[79] Three days after Pound's signal, NSHQ instructed the Senior Canadian Naval Officer in London to "take the matter [of manning LCI(L)s] up with the Admiralty and endeavour to obtain agreement to the Canadian Naval Service point of view."[80] The SCNO(L) and Brooke, who returned from Canada on 17 September, took it up with a vengeance. The Director of Plans at the Admiralty noted in early October that the "Canadians are adamant in their demand for LCI(L)s. Politically it would appear to be unsound to refuse them and, accordingly, the transfer to them of a squadron ... is being examined."[81]

There was still a major hurdle to be overcome. In his single-minded pursuit of LCI(L)s, Brooke had overlooked that these vessels were built in the United States and that they served in the Royal Navy under the terms of lend-lease; lend-lease ships were off limits to the Canadian government. In March 1941, because Ottawa feared the diversion of British production orders to the United States under the generous terms of the lend-lease policy, the Cabinet War Committee had decided to absorb the entire United Kingdom deficit in Canada on condition that no British orders were diverted south of the border.[82] By 1943 this had evolved into a mutual aid policy available to Britain, or any other Allied country, but it also meant that Canada was ineligible for lend-lease and that RN ships obtained under lend-lease, as would be the case with escort carriers manned by Canadian crews, would have to remain on the Admiralty's charge. The transfer of LCI(L)s to Canada would, therefore, be "a nice problem in international casuistry."[83]

The Admiralty agreed to reassign the LCI(L)s as HMC Ships but pointed out that, as they were acquired under lend-lease agreements that were not applicable to Canada, this reassignment would involve purchase at a cost of approximately $19,800,000 in US funds. In addition, maintenance and operating costs would be charged against the RCN. The British offered NSHQ the choice of

76.   Ibid

77.   First Sea Lord to First Lord and Dep First Sea Lord, 11 Sep 1943, PRO, ADM 1/13044

78.   Minute sheet 3, 27 Sep 1943, ibid

79.   Buxton memo to Chief of Combined Operations (CCO), "Manning—Assistance from Royal Canadian Navy," 20 Aug 1943, DHH 81/520/1270, vol 3

80.   Sec NB to SCNO(L), 14 Sep 1943, LAC, RG 24, 11702

81.   DOP, min sheet no. 3, 9 Oct 1943, PRO, ADM 1/13044

82.   Stacey, *Arms, Men and Governments*, 49

83.   Tucker, *Naval Service of Canada* II, 95-6

either purchasing the craft or making arrangements with the United States for temporary transfer to the RCN for manning purposes only. The Naval Board, probably thankfully, opted for the second alternative, noting that although LCI(L)s could not be commissioned as HMC Ships the flotillas in which they served could still be designated as Canadian flotillas. An approach was then made to US Secretary of the Navy Frank Knox for the loan of the LCI(L)s, and he agreed to provide twenty-four vessels. These craft were to be manned as HMC Ships for the duration of the Overlord operation, and, although the RCN would not be responsible for replacing any losses, they would cover maintenance costs. A further six craft, to make up the thirty required to complete the three Canadian flotillas, were loaned by the Royal Navy under a separate agreement with the same status as the others.[84]

Looking ahead to 1944, as the Québec Conference encouraged the naval planners to do, the prognosis was very good. Formation of a naval air branch was under way. British manpower problems had provided the RCN with an entrée into fleet operations on a wider scale than had previously been possible. At Naval Service Headquarters there was satisfaction about Canadian achievements in the Battle of the Atlantic. At this moment, however, a crisis at the very highest level of the Royal Canadian Navy overshadowed the optimism. Seeds of doubt about the navy's performance on the North Atlantic sown in the spring and summer had taken root, and even to professional sailors who were aware of the realities of war in the Atlantic, the paucity of RCN submarine sinkings in 1943 presented an inconvenient contrast with the successes achieved in the latter part of 1942.[85]

By the fall of 1943 Angus L. Macdonald was anxious for positive results from the RCN in the naval war, results that he could put to good political use. Instead, the minister was presented with further evidence that Canada's antisubmarine fleet was still being asked to fight the North Atlantic battle with inadequate equipment—four years after the outbreak of war. That evidence came from a Volunteer Reserve public affairs officer named Lieutenant-Commander H.E.W. Strange who, after visiting Londonderry, wrote a scathing indictment in which he chronicled how some officers at that base feared that RCN personnel were "determined to take some form of drastic step to secure action in this matter of equipment."[86] Having boarded HMCS *Assiniboine* for his return trip to Canada, Strange decided to show his report to the ship's CO, Commander K.F. Adams, RCN, for his opinion. Adams agreed that when it came to equipment the RCN was woefully behind the Royal Navy. With Strange's help, Adams drafted his own report on the situation which was filed through the chain of command. Strange's memo, however, was heading in an entirely different direction; he circumvented normal channels by passing it to Minister Macdonald's executive assistant, J.J. Connolly. Soon after doing so, Strange received a telephone call from the minister, who wanted him to know that "he had read the memorandum, which caused him deep concern. He asked me to give the most definite assurance of the truth and accuracy of statements."[87]

---

84. NB Min, 11 Nov 1943; Tucker, *Naval Service of Canada* II, 96

85. Stacey, *Arms, Men and Governments*, 316-17; Milner, *North Atlantic Run*, 245-58; Milner, *U-boat Hunters*, 40-53; D. Zimmerman, *The Great Naval Battle of Ottawa* (Toronto 1989), 136

86. Strange to Connolly, 13-15 July 1943, LAC, J.J. Connolly Papers, MG 32 C71, v 3.

87. William Strange, "The Canadian Naval Equipment Crisis—1943: A Personal Memoir," Dec 1968, DHH, EC Russel Papers, 91/298, v 4. R.O. Mayne, "Bypassing the Chain of Command: The Political Origins of the RCN's Equipment Crisis of 1943,'" *Canadian Military History* 9/3 (2000), 14-15

Strange's memo had an immediate impact as Macdonald turned to his Chief of Naval Staff and, without telling him why, demanded a detailed report on antisubmarine equipment in Canadian ships of the Mid-Ocean Escort Force with "particular attention given to comparisons as regards to asdic equipment, RDF, gyro compasses and Hedgehogs."[88] Captain W.B. Creery, who as ACNS prepared the naval staff memorandum on the subject, did not address these points to the minister's satisfaction—nor, apparently, could he have after admitting his lack of knowledge about the equipment fitted in British ships. Macdonald promptly ordered Nelles to arrange passage for his executive assistant to England in order to obtain information directly from British naval authorities. He did not explain the purpose of the visit to the CNS. The minister's enquiries quickly developed into an "equipment crisis" in which long-standing rivalries that had simmered just below the surface of the professional naval staff found focus in the complaints of a well-connected lobby of reserve officers—who were, by this point in the war, largely responsible for actually fighting the antisubmarine campaign. These divisions within the service placed Nelles in an untenable situation.

The professional rivalries that existed in the Royal Canadian Navy were not unusual for a small service and it would be misleading to suggest that they caused any great degree of paralysis in the organization. There is, however, no question that some officers on the naval staff had identifiable sympathies towards certain senior officers, particularly those between the Murray and Jones camps, and that in 1943 this served to undermine the position of the chief of the naval staff. In a postwar interview, the Director of Trade, Captain E.S. Brand, alluded to the machinations swirling beneath the surface: "I think there was undoubtably a movement against him [Nelles], an underground movement. Frankly I think Jones was very much in it. He was a great politician ... Now in my own view, of course, Murray was a far, far better officer than 'Jetty' Jones, who was a politician to his fingertips. [Jones] never did anything without thinking of how it was going to affect him and although I have no real evidence I'm pretty sure that he had quite a hand in the Nelles business. Quite a hand—just quiet remarks you know."[89]

In the fall of 1943 Brand had warned Connolly, the minister's righthand man, that the strained relations between Macdonald and Nelles "were providing Jones & some others with good opportunity to 'get the skids under Percy'—as I had warned him sometime before—but he took no notice."[90] Brand was obviously no great admirer of Jones, but Captain H.N. Lay, the former Director of the Operations Division, was. In March 1943 Nelles had accused Lay of going behind his back to the naval minister to complain about the shortcomings of the training establishment, an accusation Lay denied in his memoirs.[91] Mackenzie King's diary, however, reveals that Lay did in fact discuss the state of the navy and training with the prime minister on 29 March 1943. Moreover, in an interview late in life, Lay confessed that he had worked behind the scenes to undermine the CNS, claiming that he "was used by Jones and Angus Macdonald (and he naively let himself be used he admitted) to gain information to erode Nelles' position."[92]

88. Macdonald to Nelles, 21 Aug 1943, LAC, RG 24, 3995, NSS 1057-1-27; Zimmerman, *Naval Battle of Ottawa*, 136

89. E.C. Russell interview with Capt E.S. Brand, 22 Feb 1967, DHH 81/145, v 7, file 26

90. Brand diary, 84, DHH 81/145, v 15

91. Lay, *Memoirs of a Mariner*, 148

92. King diary, 29 Mar 1943; G. Cummings interview with Lay, Oct 1980, LAC, Records Office, Acquisitions File on H.N. Lay

Nelles's position was also compromised by a number of RCNVR officers who provided information and impetus to the investigation of the equipment situation by Connolly. It is evident that by late 1943 Macdonald and Connolly were distrustful of advice from the navy's senior officers. Connolly had developed a network of reserve officers who were willing to ignore the constraints of the formal chain of command to communicate with the minister directly through his executive assistant. The network, the broad extent of which is evident from Connolly's papers, included a number of close friends and associates with whom he had practised law before the war as well as others who saw him as their influential advocate. There was no shortage of advice from this quarter, and the consensus of opinion throughout 1943 was not only that the escort fleet required immediate improvement but that NSHQ had failed to address the problem.[93] While criticism of headquarters from the "sharp end" is typical in any conflict, the reservists' damaging evidence in this case proved far more influential—and effective—than is usually the case.

In an inspection tour of St John's in October 1942 Connolly had spent considerable time with Lieutenant L. de la C. Audette, RCNVR, commanding officer of the corvette HMCS *Amherst*. Audette was a childhood friend of Connolly's, had practised law with him before the war, and kept up a prodigious correspondence with him. Never shy about offering opinions, Audette played an important role in informing Connolly of equipment problems in the escort force, and it is evident that the executive assistant was solicitous of his friend's advice. In one instance, for example, Connolly cryptically wrote Audette:

> I am very much concerned about your wife's condition. I would be particularly interested to know the result of the operation. I should love to be available for the conference of the surgeons under Simpson, when you get to that point. If you have time and can do so, I wish you would let me know what the surgeons did during the summer and if you feel she is in as fit condition as the other ladies, particularly the English ladies, in the set in which she has heretofore moved. I am, personally, very dissatisfied about the treatment which people like yourself have been given for your wives' condition. I need not tell you that Angus is too.[94]

The letter appears completely innocent, but for the fact that Audette was a lifelong bachelor. In that light, "your wife" refers to Audette's corvette *Amherst*; the "operation" was its major refit; the "surgeons" are the engineers under Commodore G.W.G. Simpson, Commodore (D) at Londonderry, who oversaw the refit; the "English ladies" are RN escorts on the North Atlantic; and, of course, "Angus" is the naval minister. In his reply Audette urged that "anything you can do for girls in her position will be more than ordinary good turn. I shall not fail to pass on to other husbands ... that you are helping. It will buck them up no end when they feel so let down."[95] Audette and Connolly were clearly concerned about the condition of the RCN escort fleet. As early as October 1942 the RCNVR officer had suggested that his friend take a close look into the matter and that he should consider crossing the North Atlantic in a corvette. A year later, equipped with the information in

93. Mayne, "Bypassing the Chain of Command," 10, 18-19

94. Connolly to Audette, 25 Nov 1943, Connolly Papers, v 2, file 2-17

95. Audette to Connolly, 5 Dec 1943, ibid

Strange's report, Connolly took passage in a corvette to investigate conditions at sea and look into the refit situation in Londonderry.

Connolly sailed in the corvette *Orillia*, which was under the command of another close friend in the RCNVR, Lieutenant J.E. Mitchell. Seasick for much of the trip, Connolly was appalled by living conditions on board—"moving table, heavy food. No exercise. Red lights. Crooked cabins. Monotony and fearfulness. Meet the Navy." He admitted, "I wouldn't be much at a job like this—even in command—the monotony would get me down. But I am lost in admiration of these young Canadians—leaving so much at home to do this."[96] Prior to taking passage Connolly's meetings with seagoing officers at St John's initially led him to believe that the equipment situation was not as serious as he thought. Almost immediately, however, further talks at St John's with the Vice-Chief of Naval Staff, Rear-Admiral G.C. Jones, the Flag Officer Newfoundland, Commodore H.E. Reid, and the Captain (D), Captain J.W. Rowland, RN, at Reid's headquarters rekindled Connolly's belief that there was indeed a grave problem.[97] Once safely across the North Atlantic, Connolly travelled to Londonderry, where the rails had been greased in anticipation of his arrival. In September Strange had informed him of a network of Canadian, British, and American officers in Londonderry who would be anxious to throw light on the equipment situation and help the RCN. Strange went so far as to send letters to concerned officers informing them of the exact purpose of Connolly's visit.[98] These letters ensured that Connolly got the ammunition he was seeking. Commodore G.W.G. Simpson, senior engineering staff and other officers convinced Connolly that the RCN's lack of modern equipment prevented its escorts from performing at peak effectiveness and that the fault lay with NSHQ. Their testimony appears to have been coordinated, and none of these officers was aware of the recent steps taken in Canada to relieve the situation. Travelling to London, Connolly spent two hours with the C-in-C Western Approaches, who had just attended the funeral of the former First Sea Lord, Admiral of the Fleet Sir Dudley Pound. Connolly found Admiral Horton to be much more sympathetic with the problems faced by NSHQ; indeed the only criticism Horton offered on the equipment situation was that naval headquarters was not doing enough to get the Admiralty to release its grip on equipment.[99]

Connolly returned to Ottawa early in November 1943. He did not provide transcripts of his interviews with various officers, but conveyed his impression, which his diary confirms, that RN officers deplored the inadequate extent of modernization in the RCN. Although these officers assured him that there had been recent and most encouraging changes in the situation, they still recommended further improvements. Connolly sent Nelles an anonymous letter from an officer in the RN—which is now known to have been written by Commodore (D) Western Approaches—that expressed those concerns. The minister's assistant then made a personal report to the naval staff.[100]

---

96. Connolly diary, 13 Oct 1943 and 26 Aug 1943

97. Connolly to minister, 8 Nov 1943, Connolly Papers, v 3; Connolly diary, 6-9 Oct 1943. That Jones was in St John's on the very eve of Connolly's departure is at the very least suspicious, and there is no evidence that he ever informed VAdm Nelles of his knowledge of and the purpose behind Connolly's activities. See R.O. Mayne, "A Covert Naval Investigation: Overseas Officers. John Joseph Connolly and the Equipment Crisis of 1943," *Northern Mariner* 10:1 (2000), 39-40

98. Ibid

99. Connolly to minister, 8 Nov 1943, LAC, MG32 C71, vol 3

100. NS Min 210, 15 Nov 1943, app A, "Report of Visit to UK"

That the information Connolly brought contained inaccuracies mattered less than the growing conviction by Connolly and Macdonald that the Chief of the Naval Staff had deliberately failed to inform the minister about shortcomings in equipment.[101]

The facts of the matter deserve some attention. It is clear, as seen in Chapter 12, that NSHQ had tackled problems well in advance of the minister's enquiries. The naval staff, accepting in February 1943 that modernization and new construction would be subject to unavoidable delay, acted as fast as circumstances permitted to hasten progress. On 21 June 1943 the Director of Warfare and Training recommended, and the naval staff approved, adoption of the Q attachment, the latest asdic device being fitted in British escorts—Hedgehog, which required the type 144 asdic, had been approved in June 1942—and the type 761 echo sounder, which provided traces of bottomed targets, to be fitted in River class destroyers, corvettes, Algerine minesweepers, and River class frigates.[102] Corvettes, however, needed the type 145 set, which did not require a retractable dome.[103] In September, when it became clear that if the RCN was to acquire the newest ahead throwing weapon, the Squid, it would have to acquire the 147B asdic, the Naval Board approved an order for 150 sets. When Macdonald began his enquiry therefore the board simply gave his concerns "sympathetic consideration."[104] By this time Deputy Director of Warfare and Training Commander A.R. Pressey was arguing against the adoption of Squid because of the likelihood of teething troubles, and he pointed out that Hedgehog would only achieve its desired operational efficiency with much practice and training.[105]

The pace of corvette modernization, meanwhile, continued to worry the naval staff. As of 30 June 1943 there were twelve Mid-Ocean Escort Force corvettes still needing this work, twenty-nine more in the Western Escort Force, at a time when new construction deliveries were behind schedule.[106] NSHQ authorized Admiral Murray to seek Admiralty assistance,[107] but although he got agreement to take HMCS *Brandon* in hand,[108] on 24 August the Admiralty informed NSHQ and C-in-C Canadian Northwest Atlantic Command that no further RCN corvettes could be modernized or refitted in British shipyards.[109] Canadian shipyards were already overtaxed, so within a week of receiving the Admiralty's decision the ACNS had approval from Nelles to approach US authorities about modernizing RCN vessels in their east coast yards.[110] At the same time, Chief of Naval Engineering and Construction Rear-Admiral G.L. Stephens recommended modernizing only those corvettes that

101. Zimmerman, *Naval Battle of Ottawa*, 138-44; Stacey, *Arms, Men and Governments*, 316-17

102. NS Min 26 May and 29 June 1942; 27 May, 9 June, and 21 June 1943

103. D/DWT to ACNS, "Subject: Supply of Asdic Sets Type 144-145 Series to RCN Escort Vessels," 1 Oct 1943, LAC, RG 24 (Acc 83-84/167), 3725, file 8060-300, pt 1

104. NS Min, 1 Nov and 11 Nov 1943

105. Ibid, 9 Nov 1943

106. C-in-C CNA to NSHQ, 30 June 1943, cited in ibid, 30 Aug 1943

107. NSHQ to C-in-C CNA, 22 July 1943, ibid

108. Adm to C-in-C CNA, 28 July 1943, ibid

109. British shipyards were even turning away major capital ships. The Admiralty postponed several approved modifications for major fleet units, and decided not to bother repairing seriously damaged vessels. Adm message, 24 Aug 1943, SCNO(L) memo, 15 July 1943, NSM, 30 Aug 1943, CS 41-1-1

110. Ibid, 197-12

could be taken in hand, either in Canadian ports closed by ice during the winter or in US shipyards. That would leave ice-free Canadian ports available to do the heavy refit and running repairs to be expected in the winter. The next three months in the Battle of the Atlantic would constitute a critical stage of the battle, and it would be essential to have as many effective escort vessels available as possible. Time-consuming alterations and additions would simply have to wait. NSHQ however would continue to arrange for the supply of equipment.[111]

When the USN agreed to take a large number of RCN corvettes for conversion between October and November 1943, and Admiral Stephens gained Naval Board approval to assign three corvettes for fo'c'sle extension to Sydney, Charlottetown, and Pictou while those ports were closed for the winter, the refit situation improved. But it still did not meet the needs of the case.[112] Given the planned growth of the RCN and the planning assumption that vessels came due for refit nine months after commissioning, Canadian maritime shipyards would have to refit fourteen major war vessels a month in 1944, and twenty-two in 1945. That was not a realistic target when they were managing no more than nine ships a month in September 1943. The target for modernization of corvettes had been seventy-four. As of 9 October 1943 seventeen had completed some or all required modifications, and twenty-three more were either in hand or had definite allocations for refit and modernization during 1943.[113] Hedgehog and asdic depended largely on British supply and delays in the arrival of components compounded that problem. British efforts to improve asdic with the sophisticated target-plotting equipment needed to take full advantage of Hedgehog's precision had produced a set known as type 144, in the version with a retractable dome for destroyers, frigates, and Algerines, and type 145 for vessels with fixed domes, such as corvettes. NSHQ had ordered type 144 sets for new construction and type 145 for the corvette fleet in 1942, when the new equipment was still in development. Type 145 sets did not begin to become available in Canada until October 1943, when they were allocated to ships scheduled for their major modernization refits. In the meantime, much work could be done to improve the original corvettes' sets and rewire the ships for ultimate installation of type 145s by upgrading the type 123 asdics to type 127D, primarily by fitting gyro compasses. By 1 October some nineteen modernized corvettes, either completed or in hand, had the 127D set.[114] Modernizing River class destroyers as dedicated

---

111. NS Min 201-6, 16 Sep 1943

112. Lay protested that in Jan 1944 the Mid-Ocean groups would be nine vessels and Western Local groups thirty-nine vessels short. The three corvettes should not be kept unavailable for so many months. The Naval Staff called for a full review of Canadian shipyard facilities with a view to expanding all-year facilities, but Nelles approved the decision to modernize three corvettes during the freeze-up. D/DWT, "Refitting Position of HMC Ships and HM Ships under RCN Authorities in Maritime Area, 1942-1945," 12 Oct 1943, LAC, RG 24, 3996, NSC 1057-1-35; NS Min, 206-3, 18 Oct 1943

113. HMCS *Arrowhead, Hepatica, Kitchener, Mayflower, Sorel, Ville de Québec,* and *Woodstock* had received extended forecastles and improved bridge; *Calgary* (UK), *Dauphin, Edmundston, Eyebright* (USA), *Fennel* (USA) *Lunenburg, Rimouski, Snowberry* (USA), *Trillium* (USA), and *Vancouver* (west coast) were fully modernized with extended forecastle, modernized bridge, and Hedgehog. *Amherst, Baddeck, Bittersweet* (USA), *Brandon* (UK), *Camrose, Chilliwack, Dundas, Fredericton, Halifax, La Malbaie, Napanee, New Westminster, Port Arthur, Prescott, Quesnel, Regina,* and *Summerside* were in hand. *Collingwood* (USA), *Dawson* (west coast), *Drumheller* (USA), *Dunvegan* (USA), *Mayflower* (USA), and *Matapedia* were scheduled for refit. D/DWT, "Refitting Position ... in Maritime Area"

114. W. Hackmann, *Seek and Strike,* 272-4; MND NS to Governor in Council, 1 Oct 1942, LAC, RG 24 (Acc 83-84/167), 2585, NSS 6101-1 pt 1; D/DWT to ACNS, "Subject: Supply of Asdic Sets Type 144-145 Series to RCN Escort Vessels," 1 Oct 1943, LAC, RG 24, Acc 83-84/167, 3725, 8060-300, pt 1

escorts was easier.[115] The naval staff authorized Hedgehog for these ships on 26 July 1943, modernizing their asdic from type 124 to 144 when completing the conversion work. As of 1 October *Kootenay, Ottawa, Gatineau, Assiniboine, Saskatchewan, Restigouche, Skeena* and *St Laurent* had either been fitted or scheduled for fitting with 144 asdic by March 1944.[116]

The naval minister's concern evidently prompted Nelles to insist, on 18 November, that the Director of Naval Ordnance keep on pressing for the timely supply of equipment from Britain or seek a reduction in requirements, and if necessary, take the problem up to the First Lord of the Admiralty.[117] The CNS now found himself subject to a barrage of criticism from his political master. In the brouhaha surrounding the circulation of the anonymous letter produced by his executive assistant, Macdonald apparently required Nelles to make available any critical reports concerning the equipment situation. Fearful of possible stonewalling, Connolly took it upon himself to search headquarters' files. His foray into the records produced at least two critical reports which the minister judged had received too uninterested a response from NSHQ. In particular there was a report on equipment dated 1 May from the Flag Officer Newfoundland, in which the British Captain (D) at St John's, Captain J.M. Rowland, had asked for a clear refitting policy, and there was also Captain R.E.S. Bidwell's memorandum on drafting of personnel to RCN vessels, dated 22 June 1943, and forwarded by the C-in-C, CNA on 30 June.

Brandishing these smoking guns, the minister fired a broadside of four salvoes in a long memorandum to the CNS on 20 November. Macdonald began by citing the newly uncovered material, Connolly's report, and the previously undisclosed report by Lieutenant-Commander Strange. The minister reiterated the various criticisms contained therein. He also provided his own evaluation of NSHQ's failure to draw these important items to his attention and, perhaps worse, the naval staff's failure to address the criticisms promptly when they were raised. "There is fault somewhere in our organization," the minister observed, "because these matters should have engaged my attention before it was necessary for me to call for a report on the basis of information secured from unofficial sources." The reply to his August enquiry had not been satisfactory. He summarized the findings of Connolly, including the anonymous RN criticism of staff procedure and RCN priorities. In particular, Macdonald mentioned the allegation, based on an erroneous reading of a cable from Captain J.D. Prentice, that modifications to RCN ships were not being conducted in Londonderry because NSHQ had failed to signal their authorization. Finally, he told Nelles that he had not pressed the Admiralty hard enough. "There has been here, as in many other instances, too

---

115. This was not without controversy. Fitting of whole Hedgehog made them poor prospects for fleet operations, which were thought likely to dominate the next stage of the naval war. Houghton, before he went to Britain as senior Canadian liaison officer, commented on NSHQ's decision to fit whole Hedgehog rather than split it: "If they want to ensure that these destroyers will always be Escorts and unlikely to be borrowed for Fleet work, they are going the right way about it. Whether or not this is in the best interests of winning the war or not still seems to me to be a fairly open question." Houghton to Bidwell, 18 Aug 1943, LAC, RG 24, 11987, file 1292

116. Pressey to ACNS, 1 Oct 1943, LAC, RG 24 (Acc 83-84/167), 3725, 8060-300, pt 1. Note that Pressey's information regarding actual fittings may be inaccurate. A note written in the margin takes exception to the statement that *Assiniboine* carried 144B, and appears to have been written by Ken Adams. The DOP and ACNS also commented on this report at the time of its promulgation, saying that these allocations appeared the fastest way of getting "modern equipment available into service." See ACNS min, 5 Oct 1943, on Pressey memo.

117. Nelles marginal note to DNO, 18 Nov 1943, memo for CNS, "Modernization of Ships—Supply of Armament," 16 Nov 1943, LAC, RG 24 (Acc 83-84/167), 1864, 5000-300, pt 1

much of a lackadaisical attitude at NSHQ ... It seems to me that some officers at NSHQ are impressed mainly with size. Careful planning and estimating, efficiency of equipment, and high skill of personnel rather than mere numbers of ships or men ought to be our watchword."[118]

Macdonald's contention that if Nelles had been made fully aware of the RCN's problems he could have initiated high-level political intervention by prime minister to prime minister discussions, or threatened to withdraw RCN escorts from the North Atlantic run, was difficult to challenge. His argument that members of the naval staff were too far removed from the fleet to realize what was demanded of them would have found support among many in the seagoing navy, even though discussions and actions documented in the records of the naval staff and Naval Board show that this was at least an exaggeration. It can be argued that running a huge organization like the wartime RCN was beyond the capabilities of men who had never held positions of such immense responsibility before. Certainly, in the rapid growth of Naval Service Headquarters, as in the expansion of the fleet, there were bound to be growing pains.

The minister was not exempt from such criticism himself. At the Naval Council, and later the Naval Board, Macdonald had sat and listened to his senior officers complain that the RCN's modernization was being severely hindered by the Admiralty's inability to send plans and prototypes to Canada for evaluation and production. There were also times when Nelles was still more direct. Certainly, the CNS had left little doubt that there was a problem after reporting on 25 February 1943 that "in view of the expected intensification of U-boat warfare, NSHQ considers it essential to have forecastles extended, bridges improved and all modifications to armament on RCN Corvettes carried out as soon as possible."[119] In fact, it is difficult to escape the conclusion that Macdonald "was not interested in the workings of his department as long as the problems did not run the risk of becoming political ones." In fairness, the minister neither always understood the navy's highly technical jargon nor realized that his advisors considered the modernization issue an integral part of the refit crisis and presented it to him as such. Without making that connection, therefore, Macdonald missed what Nelles was trying to tell him when he argued that "I still cannot tell you why you were not specifically informed of our modernization problem which has been going on all about you for a long time. One of my present worries is what else you don't know." Nelles's exasperation is understandable. Few other topics had been more actively discussed with the minister than the repair and refit situation of the navy.

Now that the CNS had become a political liability—at least in Macdonald's eyes—Nelles was quietly elevated to the specially created position of Senior Canadian Flag Officer (Overseas) in January 1944. It was, as one historian has argued, a denial of ministerial responsibility.[120] To a great degree, it was Connolly's hand that wielded the axe. In a handwritten memorandum to Macdonald dated 30 November 1943, he had explained why and how Nelles should be removed. Connolly's memorandum survives as a masterful example of political rationalization:

> You have discovered a condition in the fleet. More significant and dangerous, you
> have discovered a condition at NSHQ. You have made changes. If you were wrong you

118. "Memo on the state of equipment on RCN ships," minister to CNS, 20 Nov 1943, A.L. Macdonald Papers, 80/218, file F276/3

119. Naval Weekly Reports to the minister, 25 Feb 1943, DHH, NS 1000-5-7 v 2

120. Zimmerman, *Naval Battle of Ottawa*, 145-6

would now have been contradicted. If the reaction was not to run for cover at NSHQ, some well founded far reaching proposal would have been made to you. So far that has not been done.

The remedy, in my mind cannot come from those now in charge. Some sweeping changes must be made—changes so significant to all, that all will be impressed with their (and your) seriousness. Only then will the moss on the machine be cleared out.

Connolly also expressed concern about the political consequences if the equipment crisis came to light and Macdonald was seen not to have acted:

Some day this story will be out, in whole or in part. It will be aired in public (parliament, press, platform). If this happens while you are minister, and it could begin this session, yours will be the burden of explaining and justifying your position. Unless you have strong action to point to your lot will not be easy.

Again, you may not be the minister when the public discussion occurs. It may happen after the war, (and parliamentary committees are bound to look into the services—perhaps before the official histories appear). At that time the party may be out of power. You may not be in public life. In any case, your action now must speak for you. It will be your legacy to those who will come after you as naval minister.

To Connolly, the solution was simple: "The navy knows one rule well—the captain bears the responsibility for his ship. This of course must be applied with a view to the equities of a given situation. In this case, looking at the facts, at the man, at the statute, I am unable to escape the conclusion that you must move the CNS." The executive assistant realized that Nelles "will have a story." Allowing for this eventuality, Connolly wrote,

He will say he is blameless personally. He will say his men let him down. He will think it unfair that he suffers for them. He will say why let Jones, Stephens and Lay and others go free while I take it. He will put it off on the British, the US, M and S [Munitions and Supply], Labour etc. He may enlist outside agencies (as e.g. the Governor General). As to his personal liability, I would agree. I don't think *he* willfully kept *important* things away from you. But if all this is admitted, the point need not be laboured that his capacity for the job of CNS in wartime is not great enough.[121]

As it turned out, Nelles said very little—at least publicly—and his promotion drew little attention. Perhaps this was because his transfer was framed in the requirement for an officer of his stature and seniority to lead the significant Canadian naval presence being mustered overseas for the invasion of Europe. There was but one question in Parliament and the newspapers for the most part just noted the transfer to new responsibilities overseas.[122] Certainly, the RCNVR network that had played an important role in Nelles's downfall was satisfied. Shortly after Nelles was transferred, Lieutenant J.L. Clifford, RCNVR, Commodore Simpson's Special Services officer in Londonderry, wrote to Connolly, saying, "Things have certainly moved quickly since your return to

---

121. Connolly memo, 30 Nov 1943, Connolly Papers, v 3; emphasis in original

122. See R.O. Mayne, "Behind the Scenes at Naval Service Headquarters: Politics and the Dismissal of Vice-Admiral Percy W. Nelles," MA thesis, 1998, 136-41, and "A Political Execution: Expediency and the Firing of Vice-Admiral Percy W Nelles, 1943-44," *American Review of Canadian Studies*, 29:4 (1999), 583

Canada and I must say that it suits all of us here very well."[123] Canada's professional navy was no doubt divided over the fate of its leader but a note from Commodore C.R.H. Taylor viewed the long watch of Vice-Admiral Percy W. Nelles from a broad perspective. "The large number of H.M. Canadian Ships now operating on the seven seas is a fitting testimonial to his devoted service to Canada and the cause of the United Nations. Truly it can be said that no one else produced so much from so little."[124]

The officer who replaced Nelles, Rear-Admiral George C. Jones, had the same goal as his predecessor: a balanced fleet. Like Nelles, Jones knew that the RCN's reputation and prospects for the future would be based, at war's end, on forces in being, and that these had to be more significant than a small-ship escort fleet. Where he differed was in his approach. Although it is difficult to create a portrait of Jones—his personal papers were destroyed at the time of his death in 1946—[125] he appears to have had analytical instincts better applied to policy than to operations and equipment. According to another senior officer, Captain E.S. Brand, Director of the Trade Division at NSHQ, Jones "was a politician to his fingertips."[126] A confidant of the naval minister, Jones was at ease in the corridors of power on Parliament Hill and understood the requirement for political subtlety when dealing with a government that was acutely sensitive to any discussion of widening commitments and postwar expansion. This would stand him in good stead for the policy battles on the horizon.

The arrangements made at the Quadrant Conference were only the beginning of RCN assistance to the Royal Navy for the Operation Overlord landings. As British resources fell further behind requirements, in the fall of 1943 and spring of 1944, the Admiralty continued to call for help. In virtually every case the RCN responded.[127] Ultimately, some 10,000 RCN personnel and over a hundred Canadian ships participated in Overlord. Nor was that all. From early May 1944, RCN escort forces took over full responsibility for North Atlantic convoys in order to release British warships for invasion duties.[128] For Mackenzie King, this huge effort was integral to what he saw as Canada's war: the Atlantic battle, the security of Britain, and the liberation of western Europe. By contrast, the prime minister and several of his Cabinet colleagues viewed the carriers, the cruisers and future offensive operations against Japan with increasing caution. Suspicious of the navy's motives, King was not happy with the manner in which the big ships had apparently been thrust upon his government at the Québec Conference, suspecting, quite rightly, that he had been set up. The navy, and the new man at its helm, would have to face a wary prime minister and Cabinet when the time came to implement plans for further wartime expansion and for the postwar fleet.

123. Clifford to Connolly, Connolly Papers, v 2, file 19

124. Sec NB to Nelles, 12 Jan 1944, Nelles personnel file

125. DHH interview with VAdm D.A. Collins, nd, Collins biog file. Collins was personal assistant to the CNS and was ordered to destroy Jones's files upon his sudden death in 1946.

126. E.C. Russell interview with Brand, 22 Feb 1967, DHH 84/145 v 7, file 26

127. Adm to BAD and NSHQ, 6 Nov 1943, NSHQ to Adm, 10 Nov 1943, Adm to NSHQ, 17 Nov 1943, PRO, ADM 1/13009; "Summary of Naval War Effort, 1st October to 31st December 1943," 2-3, DHH 81/520/1000-5-8, pt 4

128. On the complex redeployments and reorganization of the Atlantic escort forces see LCdr J.S. Hodgson, "The First Year of Canadian Operational Control in the Northwest Atlantic," 18 Aug 1944, DHH 81/520/8280A, box 1, pt 1

Prelude to Neptune:
Operations with the Home Fleet, Coastal Forces, November 1943 to May 1944

IN NOVEMBER 1943, Canadian destroyers began to work the Murmansk run. The six RCN fleet destroyers that endured the brunt of this duty—the frigates of the support groups EG 6 and EG 9 also escorted one convoy apiece—formed part of the escort for more than half of the convoys that went to Russia during the last eighteen months of the Second World War. As jacks-of-all-trades, destroyers, especially modern, well-equipped fleet destroyers, were a precious commodity and they were consistently in short supply. The British Home Fleet, in particular, never seemed to have enough destroyers and often loaned out those they did have to other forces. This often proved a limiting factor in carrying out the wide variety of operations for which the Home Fleet was responsible, including the Russian convoys.[1] The Canadian destroyers therefore constituted a more significant reinforcement than their small numbers might have implied.

The crews of the Canadian destroyers benefited from their experience on the Murmansk run. Essentially fleet operations—with convoys of merchant ships protected by powerful covering forces including battleships, fleet and escort carriers, cruisers and fleet destroyers—the convoys to Russia were different and vastly more complex than convoys crossing the North Atlantic, both in terms of their operational concept and the multidimensional threat to them posed by the enemy. For the RCN, particularly the captains of the destroyers involved, the Russian convoys, as they were called, also harkened back to the operations and training they had carried out during the interwar years.[2] Fleet evolutions called for a superior grasp of tactics and a wide variety of skills, including anti-aircraft defence, surface gunnery, and torpedo attack, not to mention quick reflexes and nerves of steel when engaging enemy forces at high speed, especially in difficult weather conditions and with the constant risk of collision and dangerous crossfire.[3] The experience also served another purpose: operations in company with ships that were trained to high levels of efficiency were useful preparation for Operation Neptune, the naval component of the invasion of Normandy. Participation in

---

1. The constraints caused by the continual demands for destroyers echoes throughout the Home Fleet War Diary; see for example III, 5, 10, DHH 2000/5.

2. See M. Whitby, "In Defence of Home Waters," *Mariner's Mirror* 77/2 (1991), 167-77

3. See, e.g., "The Life and Letters of Gilbert Howland Roberts," extracts in DHH 88/182.

the Russian convoys also gave the RCN an opportunity to take part in the immediate task at hand, the delivery of war supplies to the Soviet Union. This had been a fundamental element of Allied policy since the devastating German invasion of the USSR in June 1941. Delivering supplies was a costly and often thankless business, but the need to work together in spite of mutual suspicion between the USSR and the western Allies persuaded Prime Minister Churchill and President Roosevelt, with full support from Canada, to continue sending materiel both by sea, by land across Iran, and by air across northwestern Canada and Alaska, until the end of the war.[4]

Since the first sailing in August 1941 the convoys to Murmansk were a constant drain on the thinly spread forces of the Royal Navy. In May 1942 First Sea Lord, Admiral of the Fleet Sir Dudley Pound, had complained to his American counterpart Admiral Ernest King that the task was a "regular millstone around our necks ... a most unsound operation with the dice loaded against us in every direction."[5] Flanked by shifting seasonal ice barriers on one side and by an enemy occupied coast on the other, the route was inside air reconnaissance range and vulnerable to U-boat and surface attack over its entire 2000-mile length, and within easy range of strike aircraft for 1400 miles of it.[6] The German forces arrayed against the Russian convoys in the summer of 1942 were particularly strong. The powerful battleship *Tirpitz*—which Pound admitted by itself forced the Royal Navy to keep at least five capital ships in British waters[7]—the pocket battleships *Scheer* and *Lützow*, the heavy cruiser *Hipper*, seven destroyers, seven U-boats and more than 250 strike and reconnaissance aircraft were all based in Norway that summer. As the controversial events surrounding convoy PQ 17 proved, they could inflict dreadful losses: twenty-four ships of that convoy alone. The Admiralty had only allowed the convoys to continue because the Soviets were clamouring for the supplies piling up in British ports.[8]

The PQ 17 disaster led many officers to question the viability of the Russian convoys, but C-in-C Home Fleet Admiral Sir John Tovey, whose job it was to mount the operations, firmly believed that convoys could, if unable to evade the enemy, fight their way through air and submarine attack. Surface attack by capital ships, cruisers and destroyers was a different proposition altogether. Tovey's most powerful counters, battleships and aircraft carriers, were too valuable to risk in the Barents Sea where the convoys were most vulnerable to attack. He therefore formulated the concept of a "fighting destroyer escort" that was to consist of twelve to sixteen modern fleet destroyers. Their antisubmarine capability would enable them to reinforce the close escort—usually composed of escort destroyers, corvettes, or minesweepers from Western Approaches—while

---

4. Churchill broadcast of 22 June 1941, quoted in M. Gilbert, *Finest Hour: Winston S. Churchill 1939-1941* (London 1983), 1121; Mackenzie King diary, 22 June 1941, DHH 83/530, folder 7;. CWCM, 24 June 1941, DHH 83/345, reel 1; Weinberg, *World at Arms*, 283-4. For suspicion from the Soviet side, see memoirs of the naval commander at Murmansk, A Golovko, *With the Fleet* (Moscow1979), 142-55.

5. First Sea Lord to CNO, 18 May 1942, PRO, ADM 205/19

6. Adm NHB, *Naval Staff History, Second World War: Battle Summary No. 22, Arctic Convoys 1941-1945* (London 1954), 3

7. COS Cte min, 2 and 3 Jan 1942, DHH 193.009 (D53); Adm, *Arctic Convoys*, 5-20; Roskill, *War at Sea* II, 119-23

8. PQ 17 sparked a famous controversy. Intelligence suggested *Tirpitz* might attack near North Cape, but the First Sea Lord, who did not seek the advice of intelligence officers or leave the decision to commanders on the spot, ordered the escort to turn back and the convoy to scatter. U-boats and aircraft sank twenty-four of thirty-seven unprotected merchant ships. Hinsley, *British Intelligence in the Second World War* II, 214-23; Roskill, *War At Sea* II, 134-45; P. Kemp, "Admiral of the Fleet Sir Dudley Pound," in S. Howarth, ed, *Men of War: Naval Leaders of the Second World War* (London 1992), 34-6

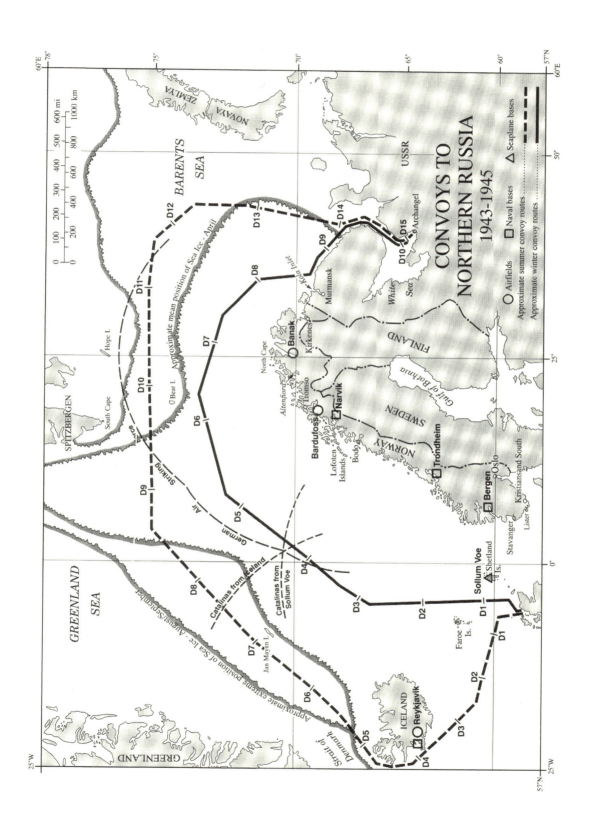

CONVOYS TO
NORTHERN RUSSIA
1943-1945

○ Airfields   □ Naval bases   △ Seaplane bases
Approximate summer convoy routes ⋯⋯⋯⋯
Approximate winter convoy routes ⋯⋯⋯⋯

GREENLAND SEA

BARENTS SEA

NOVAYA ZEMLYA

SPITZBERGEN

South Cape
Hope I.
Bear I.
Approximate mean position of Sea Ice - April

Approximate extreme position of Sea Ice - August/September

Jan Mayen I.

Strait of Denmark

ICELAND
Reykjavik

Faroe Is.

Shetland Is.
Sollum Voe

Catalinas from Iceland
Catalinas from Sollum Voe

German Air Striking Force

North Cape
Altenfjord
Tromso
Bardufoss
Lofoten Islands
Bodø
Narvik

Banak
Kirkenes
Kola Inlet
Murmansk

White Sea
Archangel

USSR

FINLAND

Gulf of Bothnia

SWEDEN

NORWAY
Tröndheim
Bergen
Oslo
Stavanger
Kristiansand South
Lister
Trondheim

Stavanger

0 100 200 300 400 500 600 mi
0 200 400 600 800 1000 km

D1 D2 D3 D4 D5 D6 D7 D8 D9 D10 D11 D12 D13 D14 D15

Lieutenant Commander H.S. Rayner, commanding officer of HMCS *Huron* on the bridge of his destroyer in September 1943. (LAC PA206235)

their anti-aircraft armament would break up air attacks. Against surface units, the fleet destroyers, with their strong torpedo armament, "would seem so formidable to the enemy as to deter him from forcing home an attack on the convoy." If the enemy did persist, Tovey calculated, "the escorts would be strong enough to defeat him."[9]

The tactics for the fighting destroyer escort were formulated by Rear-Admiral R.L. Burnett, Rear-Admiral (D) Home Fleet; they were consistent with those for flotillas that formed the screen of a battle fleet. In normal cruising disposition the sixteen ships (or four divisions) of the fighting destroyer escort would join the other escorts in an elongated screen around the convoy with the tip on either wing. Each destroyer would keep station 2000 to 3000 yards from the convoy. When air attack was imminent eight of the destroyers would close to within 750 yards or less. Should surface attack threaten, upon Burnett giving the order "strike," one division was to form on each bow of the convoy and two on the wings. The division closest to the enemy would lay smoke on the appropriate bearing through which two other divisions would launch torpedo attacks; the remaining division would guard the other wing. When faced with attack from both sides, the closest divisions would lay smoke while the others attacked.[10] These tactics worked with good success when first implemented with PQ 18 in September 1942. As that convoy and the returning QP 14, which sailed at the same time so that the heavy covering force could screen both passages, fought their way through heavy attacks from U-boats and aircraft, seventeen merchant ships and two warships were sunk. These were serious losses, but not unacceptable. The Germans had also suffered heavily, losing forty-one aircraft and three U-boats. Although an aircraft carrier, a light cruiser, and two anti-aircraft cruisers played important roles, Burnett and Tovey both considered the fleet destroyers to have been key to the prevention of more serious losses. Having now proved its worth, the concept of a fighting destroyer escort was implemented on most of the remaining convoys.[11]

Home Fleet commitments to the invasion of North Africa interrupted the convoy cycle until mid-November 1942 when the last of the PQ/QP convoys was able to set out from Archangel. By then the strength of the *Luftwaffe* in Norway had been reduced by the transfer of most of its high level and torpedo bombers to the Mediterranean. QP 15 was the last large convoy to sail the northern route until the strategic situation changed in 1944.[12] Experience had demonstrated that during the long arctic nights, a small convoy stood a better chance than a large one did of evading air and submarine attack, and perhaps even of completing its passage totally undetected. The trouble with large convoys, which in other circumstances were known to have better chances of a good exchange rate with submarines, was that under the challenging arctic conditions they proved unwieldy and were thus prone to dissolve into groups of stragglers that were more vulnerable to detection and attack. Convoys therefore began sailing in two sections of about fifteen ships each. So that the same covering forces could protect both sections, they left the normal assembly port of Loch Ewe in northwest Scotland seven days apart.[13]

9.   Adm, *Arctic Convoys*, 73; Roskill, *War at Sea* II, 280

10.   RAdm (D) Home Fleet, "Operation EV," 29 Sept 1942, app X, PRO, ADM 199/758

11.   C-in-C Home Fleet, "Operation EV," 8 Oct 1942, ibid; Adm, *Arctic Convoys*, 85. For PQ 18, see Roskill, *War At Sea* II, 279-85 and P.C. Smith, *Arctic Victory: The Story of PQ 18* (London 1975).

12.   Adm, *Arctic Convoys*, 86-8; Hinsley, *British Intelligence* II, 527-8

13.   Adm, *Arctic Convoys*, 88

The new system paid immediate dividends. The first convoy that sailed under the new orders was JW 51 (for security reasons the Admiralty had changed the designation to JW/RA, although the Germans continued to refer to them as PQ/QP convoys). JW 51A reached its destination without incident. JW 51B, however, was sighted by a U-boat off Bear Island on 30 December 1942, and attracted the attention of a powerful German surface force. The pocket battleship *Lützow*, the heavy cruiser *Hipper*, and six destroyers put to sea with the intention of using *Hipper* and three destroyers to attack the convoy from the northwest in an attempt to draw off the escorts, while *Lützow* and the other three destroyers approached from JW 51B's unprotected southern flank.[14]

On sighting the German ships during the forenoon of 1 January 1943, the five ships forming the fighting destroyer escort for JW 51B implemented the tactics devised by Burnett for PQ 18. One destroyer laid smoke to shield the merchant ships, while the other four launched a torpedo attack through the dense cover. They came under fire from the 8-inch guns of *Hipper* but—in a masterstroke—the senior officer of the escorts withheld his torpedoes, calculating that his opponents would hesitate to close the convoy until they were certain its torpedoes had been expended. For hours, the British destroyers kept the Germans at a distance from JW 51B by feigning torpedo attacks from out of smoke screens and snow squalls. They suffered heavily for their bravado: one destroyer eventually sank and the others were damaged; the SOE had to be carried from his bridge after being horribly wounded. Yet, despite this stalwart defence, the German tactics should have succeeded. With the British warships fully occupied to the north, *Lützow* and three destroyers closed to within two miles of the convoy on its disengaged southern flank, however, a sudden snow squall had obscured the merchant ships. *Lützow*, perhaps because her captain was under orders to head into the North Atlantic on a commerce raiding sortie after this operation, did not press home the attack. Finally, the two ships of JW 51B's cruiser covering force reached the convoy, and after a sharp engagement, which damaged *Hipper* and sank one German destroyer, the Germans withdrew.[15]

As Admiral Tovey commented, with some understatement, "that an enemy force of at least one pocket battleship, one heavy cruiser and six destroyers, with all the advantages of surprise and concentration, should be held off for four hours by destroyers, and driven from the area by two 6-inch cruisers is most creditable and satisfactory."[16] The victory in the Battle of the Barents Sea cast aside the pall of PQ 17 and left the Home Fleet with a sense of confidence that it retained throughout the rest of the Russian convoys. Outraged at the apparent timidity of the German cruisers, and overlooking the fact that their commander had been forbidden from engaging equal or superior forces or to fight at night, Hitler concluded that this battle proved the uselessness of the big ships of the German fleet. He then ordered Grossadmiral Erich Raeder to scrap all vessels over destroyer size, arguing that their guns could be better used in coastal defence batteries. Raeder could not convince Hitler to change his mind, which left him little choice but to resign in favour of the chief of the U-boat arm, Admiral Karl Dönitz. In fact, Dönitz shared Raeder's views of the necessity of a balanced naval threat but he was held in higher esteem by Hitler and was eventually able to con-

---

14.   Ibid, 90-2

15.   Roskill, *War at Sea* II, 292-8; D. Pope, *73 North* (London 1958)

16.   Quoted in Roskill, *War at Sea* II, 298

vince the dictator to retain the capital ships by promising to use them effectively against the Russian convoys.[17]

During the spring and summer of 1943, the Russian convoy cycle was again interrupted. Home Fleet destroyers were transferred to both the Mediterranean and the Mid-Ocean Escort Force, where they were needed to help overcome the March 1943 crisis on the North Atlantic shipping lanes. Moreover, the Russian convoys were not high on the British naval staff's list of priorities. The new C-in-C Home Fleet, Admiral Sir Bruce Fraser, advised that they should only be resumed if the supply of northern Russia was vital to the prosecution of the war and if they would enable German surface forces to be successfully brought to action.[18] But by September 1943 Allied successes in the Mediterranean had freed up more ships, while the serious setbacks were experienced by German submarines in the North Atlantic, and the attack on the 22nd by midget submarines had put *Tirpitz* out of the war for six months, with *Lützow* gone for refit. Even with the arrival of *Scharnhorst* in March 1943, these factors had materially altered the strategic situation. JW 54A was the first in a new cycle of convoys; its A section departed for northern Russia on 15 November 1943.[19]

To resume the convoys, Fraser required three battleships, a fleet carrier, eight cruisers, one anti-aircraft cruiser, twenty-four fleet destroyers, four Hunt class or other destroyers, and a total of twelve escort destroyers, frigates, or corvettes.[20] As was the case throughout most of the war, fleet destroyers were in short supply and Fraser had to call on five USN destroyers to make up his shortfall. The four Canadian Tribals that joined the Home Fleet in time for the new cycle therefore amounted to a significant contribution to Fraser's forces.[21]

The sailing orders for JW 54 set the pattern for most of the Russian convoys that followed and revealed the complexity of these large-scale fleet operations. The two sections would leave Loch Ewe seven days apart. Each would have a through escort of four or five destroyers, minesweepers, or corvettes and a fighting destroyer escort of eight modern fleet destroyers. Of these, HMCS *Haida*, *Huron,* and *Iroquois* would be with JW 54A. The convoys would receive additional protection from two covering forces: the Cruiser Covering Force, designated Force 1 and comprising HMS *Kent*, *Jamaica* and *Bermuda*, would be deployed to cover the passage through what was called the "danger zone" around Bear Island, where the convoy would be most vulnerable to surface attack. After refuelling at Kola Inlet, Force 1 would cover the homebound RA 54A and the oncoming JW 54B through the danger zone and then protect RA 54B during its homeward passage. The Battleship Covering Force, comprising HMS *Anson*, the cruiser USS *Tuscaloosa,* and four USN destroyers, would give distant cover from southwest of Bear Island when RA 54A and JW 54B moved through the danger zone. In addition, approximately 1000 miles northeast of Iceland, Coastal Command aircraft from 19 Group would carry out antisubmarine patrols to the limit of their endurance while

17. Adm, *Fuehrer Conferences on Naval Affairs, 1943* (London 1947), 1-5; Keith W. Bird, "Erich Raeder," in S. Howarth, ed., *Men of War*, 68-71

18. First Lord to Prime Minister, 4 Jan. 1943, PM to First Lord, 11 Jan. 1943, First Lord to Prime Minister, 12 Jan. 1943, First Sea Lord minute to Prime Minister, 9 Jan. 1943, DOP memo to First Lord, 15 March 1943, PRO, ADM 1/15726, pt II; Home Fleet War Diary, III, 3, DHH 2000/5; Hinsley, *British Intelligence in the Second World War*, II, 531-3

19. Adm, *Arctic Convoys*, 107-8; Roskill, *War at Sea* III pt 1, 65-9; Hinsley, *British Intelligence* III pt 1, 257

20. C-in-C Home Fleet to First Lord, 0002A/26 Sep 1943, PRO, ADM 1/15726 pt 2

21. DOD(H) memo, "North Russian Convoys," 28 Sep 1943, 2, ibid

the Soviets did the same over the approaches to Kola Inlet. Meanwhile, British and Soviet subma-rine pickets stationed off northern Norway would observe German surface activity. All operations in support of the convoys were code-named FT and were led by Vice-Admiral H.R. Moore, second-in-command of the Home Fleet, at sea in HMS *Anson*.[22]

Of the fighting destroyer escort for JW 54A, the O class vessels *Onslow*, *Obedient*, *Orwell*, and *Onslaught* had been operating in northern waters since their commissioning in 1941, and had fig-ured prominently in the defence of JW 51B. They had also played an important role in the defeat of U-boats on the North Atlantic in May 1943 and, having recently completed a rigorous set of work-ups, they were a well-drilled and closely knit team.[23] Another veteran of the Russian convoys was HMS *Impulsive*, a destroyer of the prewar I class. Of the RCN Tribals, *Haida* (Commander H.G. DeWolf, RCN), *Iroquois* (Commander J.C. Hibbard, RCN) and *Huron* (Lieutenant-Commander H.S. Rayner, RCN), only *Iroquois* had any operational experience to speak of. When considered as a whole, the destroyer force for JW 54A substantiated a complaint in the Home Fleet war diary that "the majority [of Home Fleet destroyers] taking part in any one operation generally formed a heterogeneous collec-tion unversed in each others' ways and therefore untrained either to fight collectively or to provide fully efficient A/S protection."[24] That said, they did have the advantage of effective leadership. JW 54's SOE, Captain J.A. McCoy, RN, had been Captain (D) of the 17th Flotilla since March 1943, and prior to that he had commanded a Tribal in the Norwegian campaign and served as Captain (D) Liverpool.[25]

The fighting destroyer escort for JW 54A departed Scapa Flow on 15 November 1943, refuelled at Seydisfjord, and met the eighteen ships of its section 250 miles northeast of Iceland three days later. The seas were getting up as McCoy took position at the head of the convoy and placed Commander DeWolf, who was second in seniority among the escort captains, in charge of the rear of the convoy. Protecting the rear was a difficult task, and at times impossible in the almost con-tinual darkness of the arctic winter, particularly because *Haida* did not have centimetric search radar. Her metric Type 291 "warning air" set could not be used because it could be monitored by the enemy. Luckily, in spite of weather that forced the convoy to reduce speed to eight knots, JW 54A remained undetected through its passage south of Bear Island and across the Barents Sea. On 23 November, eight days after leaving Loch Ewe, one section of JW 54A detached for Archangel with Soviet escorts and the other one entered Kola Inlet.[26]

On 28 November the destroyers rendezvoused with the nine merchant ships of the returning RA 54B outside Kola Inlet. The increased radio traffic between Great Britain and northern Russia had by now persuaded the Germans that an Allied convoy was at sea. Seven U-boats designated as group *Eisenbart* established a patrol line south of Bear Island. At 1810 on the 28th HMS *Inconstant* intercepted a U-boat high frequency transmission and obtained a bearing. But because the U-boat was estimated to be at least thirty miles away, McCoy concluded it could not be a sight-ing report and so held his course. He was right. *Eisenbart* sent no contact reports that day.[27] Two

22.   C-in-C Home Fleet, "Operation FT," 6 Nov 1943, PRO, ADM 199/77

23.   G.G. Connell, *Arctic Flotilla: The 17th Destroyer Flotilla* (London 1982)

24.   Home Fleet WD III, 5

25.   Connell, *Arctic Flotilla*, 136

26.   Capt (D)17, ROP, 12 Dec 1943, PRO, ADM 199/77

27.   Ibid; KTB, *SKL*, 1 Dec 1943, DHH, SGR II 340 (hereafter KTB, *SKL*, with date)

days later, at 2205Z, as RA 54B approached the patrol line, *Haida* and *Inconstant* picked up fresh HF/DF bearings, and at 0449Z on 1 December *Inconstant*, positioned on the convoy's starboard bow detected *U 307* on her radar. Turning towards the target and increasing speed to twenty knots, *Inconstant*'s commanding officer spotted the "distinctive fluffy white exhaust" of a U-boat. The destroyer illuminated the submarine with her powerful 20-inch searchlight at 700 yards, opened fire with her Oerlikons, and claimed hits on *U 307*'s conning tower as it crash-dived 300 yards away. Passing over the swirl *Inconstant* dropped a pattern of ten depth-charges that caused "a vivid red flash" and "heavy detonation." Ordered to join the British destroyer, *Iroquois* reported a brief asdic contact during a lengthy search, after which the destroyers returned to the screen, having dropped one depth-charge pattern each to keep the submarine down.[28]

What had brought about this encounter was *U 307*'s attempt, while searching on a southeasterly course, to find the convoy. Seeing a destroyer closing from port at high speed the U-boat had manoeuvred to a torpedo firing position. However, it was forced to break off the attack when another destroyer—perhaps *Haida*, which lacked the radar to detect the U-boat—appeared 1500 metres to starboard. Sighting yet another destroyer and a "corvette" that started a sweep search with a searchlight, the German concluded that "there were no prospects for getting out of this situation" and crash-dived.[29] Despite *Inconstant*'s claims to the contrary, *U 307* sustained no damage, and evaded further attacks by going deep and launching a decoy. When the sound of propellers faded away to westward, it surfaced to make a sighting report—only to find a destroyer, either *Inconstant* or *Iroquois*, directly astern 400 yards away. The German boat crash-dived again and, although unseen by the destroyers, recorded four more barrages of depth-charges. Three hours passed before *U 307*'s commander could send his report.[30] As it turned out, the convoy had already been reported. When *Inconstant* turned her searchlight on *U 307*, the beam startled *U 636* on the surface three miles away, causing it to crash-dive. It stayed down for three hours before surfacing to make a sighting report. *Gruppe Nord* responded by placing the battle cruiser *Scharnhorst* at three hours readiness and ordered the *Eisenbart* boats to shift their patrol line southwest of Bear Island. The battle group never sailed, primarily because *U 636* failed to maintain contact. Early on 2 December the U-boat again dived after sighting a vessel three miles away. Three hours later hydrophone noises were heard from a vessel moving and stopping every five minutes. It was obviously an escort conducting a search. This kept the boat down for some time longer. The information from *U 636* was therefore stale when transmitted, and by the time the patrol line had completed several shifts in position to intercept the convoy, RA 54B was hundreds of miles to the southwest on its last leg home, while the eastbound JW 54B—which was never detected—lay safely in Kola Inlet.[31]

At the conclusion of this operation both DeWolf and McCoy questioned the suitability of Tribal class destroyers for the escort role. In his report of proceedings, DeWolf noted that the ships had been

28. "Report of Attack on U-boat," 1 Dec 1943, HMS *Inconstant* ROP, 4 Dec 1943; Capt (D)17, ROP, 12 Dec 1943; Adm, Anti-U-boat Division, "Monthly Antisubmarine Report, January 1944," 33, copy at DHH; *Iroquois*, deck log, 1 Dec 1943, LAC, RG 24, 7418

29. KTB, *U 307*, 1 Dec 1943

30. Ibid

31. KTB, *U 636*, 1-2 Dec 1943, DHH, 83/665; KTB, *SKL*, 1-3 Dec 1943

difficult to manoeuvre when forced to match the slow pace of the convoy. Moreover, perhaps made nervous by the close encounter with *U 307*, DeWolf observed that "any speed below 12 knots greatly increases the vulnerability of destroyers to torpedo attack."[32] McCoy, who had commanded the British Tribal HMS *Bedouin* earlier in the war, agreed, adding that "when not fitted with a WS [warning surface radar] set they [Tribals] are a definite menace to their consorts." With the threat of surface attack, argued McCoy, "a gunnery force of Tribal Class destroyers in the immediate vicinity is very desirable," but they should operate further afield from the convoy and not form part of the close escort.[33] In addition, the RCN Tribals proved to be relatively short legged. They were the only destroyers acting as escorts that were unable to make the passage to Kola Inlet without refuelling, which forced McCoy to bring the escort oiler *Norlys* back with RA 54B, contrary to plans to leave her in Russia for future use.[34] Despite these concerns, the Tribals would continue to be used in the escort role, given the shortage of destroyers and the ongoing surface threat to the convoys.

The Canadians found their first experience on the Russian convoys to be challenging, but perhaps less so than the North Atlantic run. The average passage to Murmansk took from six to eight days, and put ships' companies under less strain than the ten to fifteen days it took for a slow convoy to cross the North Atlantic. The severe climatic conditions, however, tested men to their limits. "Usually," suggested *Huron*'s first lieutenant, Lieutenant P.D. Budge, RCN, many years later, "we sailors only remember the good times. The Russian run was an exception." Budge described the experience like this:

> It seemed that gales were forever sweeping over the dark, clouded sea. The dim red ball of the sun barely reaching the horizon as the ship pitched and tossed, the musty smell of damp clothes in which we lived, the bitter cold, the long frequent watches that seemed to last forever. This on a diet of stale bread, powdered eggs and red lead [stewed tomatoes] and bacon. The relief to get below for some sleep into that blessed haven—the comforting embrace of a well-slung hammock. There was no respite on watch for gun, torpedo or depth-charge crews as every fifteen minutes would come the cry "For exercise all guns train and elevate through the full limits"—this to keep them free of ice ... The watch below would be called on deck to clear the ship of ice—the only time the engine room staff were envied. Each trip out and back seemed to last an eternity with nothing to look forward to at either end except that perhaps mail would be awaiting us at Scapa Flow.[35]

U-boats suffered as much or more discomfort in arctic waters as other vessels, and theirs was exacerbated by the severe operational limitations under which they worked. By November 1943 the German submarine fleet in the Arctic had been reduced to its minimum strength of twelve boats, many of them in need of overhaul. The U-boats were further hampered by the weakness of

---

32. *Haida* ROP, 8 Dec 1943, PRO, ADM 199/77

33. Capt (D)17, ROP, 12 Dec 1943; M. Brice, *The Tribals* (London 1971), 89-98

34. The fuel consumption of the Tribals was 46 percent higher than the three O-class destroyers and 54 per cent more than *Impulsive*. The Tribals' poor endurance, which was at odds with the promising figures provided by the RN when they were ordered in 1940, was probably the result of additional top-weight from equipment added to the original design as a result of war experience. Captain (D)17, ROP, 12 Dec 1943

35. Address by P.D. Budge, 19 Sep 1981, 6, DHH 82/92. See also W. McAndrew, W. Rawling and M. Whitby, *Liberation: The Canadians in Northwest Europe* (Montreal 1995), 104-6

the Luftwaffe, which was no longer capable of flying regular reconnaissance patrols over the northern convoy route. While some reinforcement of the arctic U-boat fleet could be expected in the new year—it would grow to twenty-eight boats by March 1944—no aircraft were expected to bolster the air forces in northern Norway. With the few available U-boats having to act as both a search and an attack force, the possibility increased that the enemy would attempt to compensate for its lack of air striking power by substituting the 11-inch guns of the battle cruiser *Scharnhorst*.[36]

The small convoys were extremely difficult to locate in the arctic darkness. As *U 307* could attest, the strength of the escort—about twice that of the average North Atlantic group—made it difficult to penetrate the screen when the U-boats did find a convoy. German naval commanders in the north also lacked Admiral Dönitz's often uncanny ability to guide U-boats onto their target, a problem that the routine lack of cooperation between the *Kriegsmarine* and the *Luftwaffe* only magnified. When the few available patrol aircraft did manage to get aloft in the invariably appalling flying conditions, poor communications between the two services often delayed the flow of information. The disadvantages suffered by Allied surface forces—terrible weather, poor asdic conditions, and atmospheric interference with radio transmissions, as well as frequent radar breakdowns and, in the case of the Tribals, poor endurance—were thus offset by a weakened naval and air effort on the German side.[37] Operation FV, comprising convoys JW 55A/RA 55A and JW 55B/RA 55B, was a case in point.

HMCS *Athabaskan* (Lieutenant-Commander J.H. Stubbs, RCN), formed part of the fighting destroyer escort for JW 55A She was returning to operations after repairing her glider bomb damage (see Chapter 15) and being upgraded with Type 276 search radar—*Athabaskan* was the first RCN Tribal to get centimetric radar. She joined the convoy north of the Faeroe Islands on 15 December 1943. Early on the 18th, after the convoy passed Bear Island, the escorts obtained several HF/DF bearings. At 1605Z *Athabaskan*, while on the port bow of JW 55A, picked up and illuminated a radar contact ahead. The contact faded as *U 354* submerged, but five minutes later the destroyer gained asdic contact with it and dropped a ten-charge pattern before losing the echo. Stubbs's aggressive response prevented the U-boat from shadowing the convoy. Its sighting report, however, led the commander of *Gruppe Nord*, Vizeadmiral Otto Schniewind, to place the *Scharnhorst* at three hours notice, establish a U-boat patrol line, and order aerial reconnaissance of the Barents Sea. As it turned out, the U-boats failed to regain contact and weather grounded the *Luftwaffe*—JW 55A reached its destination without incident.[38]

There had been a strong premonition among many in the Home Fleet that *Scharnhorst* would sortie against the December convoys. In fact, the German naval staff (*Seekriegsleitung* or *SKL*) had decided that heavy surface units in Norway, already "of value in view of our Japanese ally" because they tied down the Home Fleet in British home waters, could now ease the "critical situation on the eastern front and the entire war situation." There had been discussion of withholding

---

36. "Government Code and Cypher School Naval History: The Naval War 1939 to 1945," XVII, 120-1, 132, DHH 2000/5

37. *Haida* ROP, 8 Dec 1943; *Haida* ROP, 10 Jan 1944, LAC, RG 24 (Acc 83-84/167), 695, 1926-DDE-215; Capt (D)17, ROP, 12 Dec 1943; *Starling* ROP, 11 Apr 1944, CS10 memo, "Second Escort Group—Operation FY," 12 May 1944, PRO, ADM 217/189

38. *Athabaskan* ROP, DHH 81/520/8000, *Athabaskan* (I) (1939-44); KTB, *SKL*, 18-20 Dec 1943; Hinsley, *British Intelligence* III pt 1, 263

Scharnhorst until repairs to *Tirpitz* were completed in March 1944, but now it was agreed that Germany could no longer hold back "such a valuable offensive weapon." On 20 December JW 55B departed Loch Ewe. That same day Dönitz informed Hitler that *Scharnhorst* would attack the next Allied convoy "if a successful operation seems assured."[39] As much as the German battlecruiser posed a formidable threat, there can be little doubt that the Home Fleet welcomed an engagement with *Scharnhorst*. The Allies' superior radar gave them a decided advantage in the arctic night, and the opportunity to remove such a valuable asset from the enemy order of battle would enable them to firmly grasp the initiative in the north and redistribute their forces as required. Admiral Fraser, informed by Ultra intelligence of the likelihood of a German sortie, decided to take his flag to sea in HMS *Duke of York* and, for the first time, provide battleship cover right through to Murmansk.[40]

The fighting destroyer escort for JW 55B was nearly identical to that for JW 54A—*Onslow*, *Impulsive*, *Onslaught*, *Orwell*, *Haida*, *Huron*, and *Iroquois,* as well as a newcomer, HMS *Scourge*. The through escort comprised two destroyers, two corvettes and a minesweeper. DeWolf in *Haida*, although still without effective search radar, was again responsible for the rear of the convoy. McCoy's force met the nineteen merchant ships of JW 55B north of the Faeroes Islands on 22 December. Aware that enemy aircraft had sighted them the previous day, McCoy could do little to prevent the enemy from finding the convoy again and shadowing it on 23 December. Concerned that the convoy had only made eight knots during the night, McCoy asked the commodore for an increase to nine knots next day in order to pass south of Bear Island as quickly as possible. [41]

In the forenoon on Christmas Eve, Admiral Fraser, situated about four hundred miles southwest of JW 55B in Force 2 with *Duke of York*, the cruiser *Jamaica*, and four destroyers, received indications from Ultra that *Scharnhorst* might be preparing to leave harbour. Force 1, consisting of the cruisers *Belfast*, *Norfolk*, and *Sheffield* under Vice-Admiral R.L. Burnett, was one day out of Kola Inlet and screening the homeward bound RA 55A. Fraser considered JW 55B, just four hundred miles from *Scharnhorst*'s base at Altenfjord, to be "dangerously exposed" and broke radio silence to order the convoy to reverse course until 1700Z so that Force 2 could close the gap.[42] McCoy, who considered it "a manifest impossibility [to turn] the convoy through 360° and keep it coherent" complied "in spirit if not in letter." He got the commodore to suggest instead a reduction back to eight knots. It was a good decision, even though the *Luftwaffe* had again relocated the convoy, and a patrol line of eight U-boats was established south of Bear Island. RA 55A was leaving the danger area just as JW 55B was entering it. Admiral Fraser therefore ordered the senior officer of the returning convoy's escort to transfer four fleet destroyers to the threatened convoy.[43]

On Christmas morning 1943, *U 601* sighted JW 55B southwest of Bear Island and continued to shadow it all day. German aircraft were also watching the convoy intermittently. As this was happening Dönitz, who was unaware that a Home Fleet covering force was in a position to intervene, ordered Schniewind to deploy *Scharnhorst* and five destroyers on an offensive sortie. It seemed like

---

39. KTB, *SKL*, 20 Nov and 2 Dec 1943; Adm, *Fuehrer Conferences* II, 110; Roskill, *War at Sea* III pt 1, 78-9

40. Interviews with H.G. DeWolf, R. Phillips, and W.H. Howe, biog files, DHH; Hinsley, *British Intelligence* III pt 1, 263-4

41. *Iroquois*, deck log, 23 Dec 1943, LAC, RG 24, 7418; KTB, *SKL*, 23 Dec 1943; Capt (D)17, ROP, 9 Jan. 1944; *Haida* ROP, 31 Dec 1943, PRO, ADM 199/77

42. Hinsley, *British Intelligence* II pt 1, 265; J. Winton, *Death of the Scharnhorst* (New York 1983), 66-7

43. Capt (D)17, ROP, 9 Jan 1944, PRO ADM 199/77; KTB, *SKL*, 25 Dec 1943

a golden opportunity for the "easing of the strained situation on the eastern front," at a time when Dönitz felt bound by his promise to Hitler to deploy the battle group. He directed Schniewind that, if the weather proved too severe for the destroyers, he could detach them and leave the battlecruiser to proceed independently. At 1800 the battle group put to sea from Altenfjord with the crew of *Scharnhorst* reportedly cheering wildly when informed of their mission.[44]

At 0339Z on 26 December, with JW 55B about fifty miles south of Bear Island steering east northeast, Fraser received the signal, "Admiralty appreciates *Scharnhorst* at sea." Four fleet destroyers, *Musketeer*, *Matchless*, *Opportune* and *Virago*, chosen solely on the basis of fuel remaining, had joined McCoy's force. *Athabaskan*, a victim of limited endurance, remained with RA 55A. The three cruisers of Vice-Admiral Burnett's Force 1, approximately 170 miles to the east, steered towards the convoy at eighteen knots, while Force 2 under Admiral Fraser, 370 miles to the southwest, was closing with a speed of twenty-four knots.[45] *Scharnhorst* was flying the flag of Konteradmiral E. Bey and searching northwards with her destroyers, approximately seventy-five miles southwest of Force 1 and eighty miles southeast of JW 55B.

For both sides, the position and location of enemy forces remained uncertain until the moment of contact. Konteradmiral Bey had no knowledge of either Burnett's Force 1 or Fraser's Force 2, and Fraser was not sure of either Bey's or Burnett's position, course, and speed. He therefore ordered JW 55B to turn north away from *Scharnhorst*'s expected position and, again at the risk of betraying his presence, broke radio silence ordering Burnett to report his position. When he found that Burnett was east of the convoy Fraser ordered him to steer northeast so that the cruisers of Force 1 would eventually come between the German battle group and its prey. This turn had scarcely been completed when McCoy learned that HMS *Belfast*, still thirty-six miles southeast of his position, had a radar contact to the northwest: it was *Scharnhorst*—lying between the convoy and Force 1. At 0921Z *Belfast* made a visual sighting, bearing 222°, range 13,000 yards. Bey, who had detached his destroyers to search for the convoy and in accordance with *Kriegsmarine* doctrine was observing radar silence to avoid revealing his position, remained unaware of the cruisers' presence until starshell burst overhead.[46]

This starshell was what made JW 55B's escorts first realize that an engagement with the *Scharnhorst* was imminent. *Iroquois* was in the screening position closest to the action, and the deck log records the sight of starshell to the southeast at 0927Z, an emergency alteration 45 degrees to port at 0938Z, and finally at 0940Z: "Enemy engaged by cruisers bearing 110. Gun flashes." *Haida* was at the rear of the convoy, and DeWolf first thought that the starshell and gun flashes "might be the starboard wing escort in action." In characteristically aggressive fashion he steered to the sound of the guns, pounding into the heavy seas at twenty-four knots until, realizing the action was distant, he returned to his position on the screen with a straggler in tow. Like the rest of the escort, *Haida* could only follow the action on the convoy W/T net.[47]

---

44. P. Padfield, *Dönitz: The Last Führer* (London 1984), 337-42

45. Capt (D)17, ROP, 9 Jan 1944; Hinsley, *British Intelligence* III pt 1, 265; Adm, Battle Summary No. 24, *Sinking of the Scharnhorst* (London 1950), 5; Winton, *Death of the Scharnhorst*, 69-70

46. Adm, *Sinking of the Scharnhorst*, 6-7; Capt (D)17, ROP, 9 Jan 1944

47. Adm, *Sinking of the Scharnhorst*, 6-7; *Iroquois* deck log, 26 Dec 1943, LAC, RG 24, 7418; *Haida* ROP, 31 Dec 1943, LAC, RG 24 (Acc 83-84/167), 695, 1926-DDE-215

In *Belfast*, where some eighty Canadian sailors were gaining cruiser experience, Burnett could not get close enough to achieve hits on his target before *Scharnhorst* turned northeast at thirty knots—the cruisers could only make twenty-four knots in these sea conditions—and disappeared into the arctic darkness. HMS *Norfolk* had found the target with one salvo that put the German ship's *Seetakt* main surface radar out of action. The objective was to protect the convoy, and Burnett therefore decided not to pursue the enemy but to remain between *Scharnhorst* and JW 55B. Calculating that his opponent was attempting to work around to attack the convoy from the north, Burnett headed for a position northeast of the merchant ships. At 0930Z, Fraser ordered JW 55B to head north away from the expected attack. McCoy however took it upon himself to steer northeast to close the cruisers, once he learned they had lost contact with the enemy. When Fraser subsequently signalled permission for McCoy to select a mean course for the convoy at his own discretion, JW 55B came right around to the southeast to place Force 1 between the convoy and the threat, as well as to bring the convoy closer to its destination. Fraser's appreciation and that of Burnett proved sound when at 1205Z *Sheffield* reported a radar contact bearing 075° at 30,500 yards.[48]

In the midst of the first engagement McCoy had determined that Burnett would welcome help from the fighting destroyer escort. Accordingly, he sent the four destroyers that had reinforced him from RA 55A to join the cruisers. Thus, his own group would remain under his command, and the heavy armament of the Tribals would be available to defend the convoy itself. The Canadians were disappointed but cleared away for action in case it became necessary. When gun flashes appeared on the horizon *Huron* and *Iroquois*, on the order "strike port," followed *Haida* out to the port wing of the convoy in preparation for a torpedo attack. This was exactly the type of big-ship engagement for which DeWolf, Hibbard and Rayner had practised endlessly before the war—but it was not to be.[49] In the second action Burnett's ships came under accurate fire from *Scharnhorst*'s 11-inch guns. Y turret in *Norfolk* was put out of action while *Belfast* and *Sheffield* were straddled and penetrated by several fragments. Still, their return fire forced the enemy to break off the action to the southeast. Burnett continued to shadow *Scharnhorst* from about 13,000 yards. JW 55B's destroyers, meanwhile, resumed their positions around the convoy.[50]

The five powerful Narvik class destroyers of the German battle group had lost radar and visual contact with *Scharnhorst* in the forenoon, but they were conforming to the general movements of the flagship as best they could while they searched for the convoy. Had they found JW 55B, the responsibility for dealing with them would have rested largely with the RCN Tribals, which were well suited to engage them. The senior officer of the German flotilla also judged that in the existing sea conditions the "training of guns would have been impossible and use of torpedoes very difficult." After his second encounter with the British cruisers Bey had relayed an old sighting report that placed the convoy south of Bear Island. In fact, JW 55B was no more than ten miles north of the German destroyers. That was as close as the Narviks would get; at 1418Z Bey ordered them to return to base.[51]

---

48. Capt (D)17, ROP, 9 Jan 1944

49. In fact, Canadian warships have never engaged a capital ship.

50. Adm, *Sinking of the Scharnhorst*, 10-11; *Haida* ROP, 31 Dec 1943, in Capt (D), ROP, 9 Jan 1944, app V. H.G. DeWolf to M. Whitby, 23 Sept 1988; Hibbard interview, nd, J.C. Hibbard biog file, DHH; *Iroquois* deck log, 26 Dec 1943

51. KTB, *SKL*, "Report on Operations of the 4th Destroyer Flotilla," 27 Dec 1943; Roskill, *War at Sea* III pt 1, 85

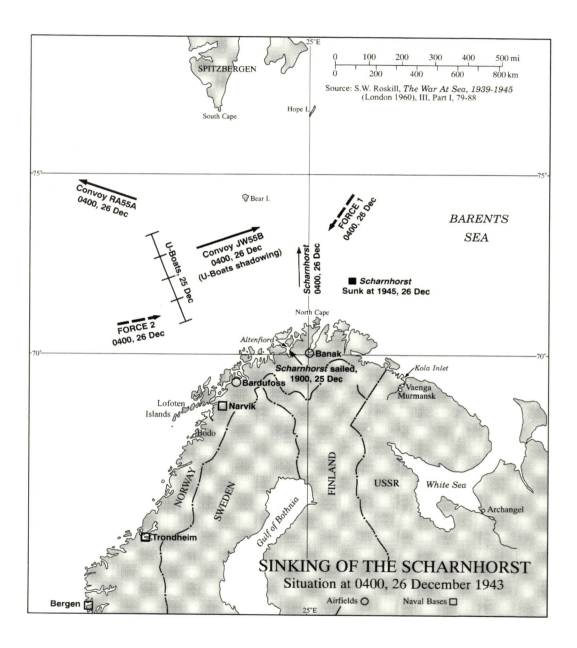

SPITZBERGEN

South Cape

Hope I.

0   100   200   300   400   500 mi
0   200   400   600   800 km

Source: S.W. Roskill, *The War At Sea, 1939-1945*
(London 1960). III, Part I, 79-88

Bear I.

Convoy RA55A
0400, 26 Dec

FORCE 1
0400, 26 Dec

*BARENTS
SEA*

U-Boats, 25 Dec

Convoy JW55B
0400, 26 Dec
(U-Boats shadowing)

Scharnhorst
0400, 26 Dec

■ *Scharnhorst*
Sunk at 1945, 26 Dec

FORCE 2
0400, 26 Dec

North Cape

Altenfiord

Banak

Scharnhorst sailed,
1900, 25 Dec

Bardufoss

Kola Inlet

Vaenga
Murmansk

Lofoten
Islands

Narvik

Bodo

NORWAY

SWEDEN

Gulf of Bothnia

FINLAND

USSR

White Sea

Archangel

Trondheim

SINKING OF THE SCHARNHORST
Situation at 0400, 26 December 1943

Bergen

25°E

Airfields ○   Naval Bases □

Burnett had continued to shadow *Scharnhorst* while homing Fraser's Force 2 onto the target. Once radar contact was made, *Duke of York* and *Jamaica* exchanged fire with *Scharnhorst*, until a shell penetrated the German battlecruiser's engine room, bringing her to a standstill. The destroyers with Force 2 achieved four torpedo hits—even in this sea state, a capital ship was a big target for destroyers—before multiple torpedo hits from *Jamaica*, *Belfast* and the four destroyers from RA 55A that had been sent to reinforce Burnett finally sank *Scharnhorst*. The Battle of North Cape was over, and it would prove to be the last exchange between big-gun ships in the history of the Royal Navy. As one historian has commented, *Scharnhorst* met her end in what "most objective observers must call a useless suicide mission for the ship and the 1900 men who went down with her."[52]

Konteradmiral Bey, it must be acknowledged, had been badly let down by staff at local headquarters in Norway. In the first place, a *Luftwaffe* patrol aircraft shadowing Force 2 at midday on 26 December had sent in two reports based on radar contacts, the latter including mention of a large ship. The recipient of the messages, *Fliegerführer* Lofoten, was slow to forward the information to naval headquarters—there was no direct link between the aircraft and the navy—and when he did, he omitted any reference to the large vessel. When German naval staff officers finally received the report, they apparently thought that the aircraft had sighted their own destroyers returning to base. They did not despatch the report promptly, and by the time Bey received it he could no longer avoid contact with the covering forces. Second, during the morning of the 26th, *Beobachtungsdienst*—the German radio monitoring and cryptographic service—monitored several operational signals that indicated that a naval authority besides the British cruiser and escort commanders was at sea in the vicinity. *Gruppe Nord* suspected this signified the presence of a heavy covering force, but the information was not forwarded to *Scharnhorst*, and because Bey had sailed without his own *B-Dienst* detachment, he remained unaware of this piece of the puzzle. The poor cooperation and communications that so often bedevilled German naval operations in the Second World War thus resulted in Bey not discovering the presence of the cruiser covering force, nor later of the British battle group, until he was surprised by the sudden glare of starshell bursting overhead.[53]

British forces had been much better served by intelligence. Still, there were gaps in the picture, and these had serious implications for Admiral Fraser. Throughout the morning of the 26th, while *Duke of York*, *Jamaica*, and the four destroyers of Force 2 plunged northeast through the heavy seas, Fraser knew that *Scharnhorst* was out, but he had little idea of where she was or what ships were with her. Burnett's first sighting report relieved his mind, until he learned that Force 1 had lost contact. Fraser suspected that the enemy knew where he was—his radar operators had picked up three aircraft shortly after 1000Z, one had remained in contact for four hours, and what could only be sighting reports were monitored by British wireless telegraphy operators. As noon approached the fuel situation of Fraser's destroyers became critical. The C-in-C Home Fleet realized that he would soon have to decide whether to continue through to Kola Inlet or return to Scapa Flow and there was no point in pressing eastward and exposing his ships to air and submarine attack if there was no chance of intercepting *Scharnhorst*. More importantly, Fraser became

52.   E. Grove, "A Service Vindicated. 1939-1946," in J.R. Hill, ed, *The Oxford Illustrated History of the Royal Navy* (Oxford 1995), 372; Weinberg, *World at Arms*, 369

53.   Hinsley, *British Intelligence* III pt 1, 267-8; Winton, *Death of the Scharnhorst*, 93-4, 106; Beesly, *Very Special Intelligence*, 216-17

"increasingly haunted by a possibility which he had previously assessed as remote: that *Scharnhorst*, having being balked of an easy strike at JW.55B, might now break first north, then west, and make a bid for the North Atlantic."[54] There had been no indications through signals intelligence or the movements of support ships such as tankers that the *Kriegsmarine* was considering such a move. Nevertheless, Fraser had to consider the possibility and its potentially catastrophic results to the North Atlantic supply line. At 1150, therefore, after a "ghastly period of worry and indecision,"[55] Fraser turned Force 2 westward towards the Atlantic. The ships had barely settled onto their new course when Burnett's second sighting report came in. Fraser immediately reversed course, and with that the fate of *Scharnhorst* was effectively sealed.[56]

While Forces 1 and 2 closed in on *Scharnhorst*, JW 55B had continued towards its destination. There was no feeling that they were clear of danger, because HF/DF contacts indicated that as many as four U-boats were in contact. Fortunately, the U-boats had difficulty keeping pace in the heavy seas and were unable to launch any attacks. At 1815X on the 26th, when it became apparent to the *Admiral Nordsee* that *Scharnhorst* was trapped, the U-boats were withdrawn to search for survivors. JW 55B completed its passage unmolested.[57] Two stragglers, for which McCoy considered *Haida* responsible, were missing. DeWolf reported, when the weather cleared on the 27th and the senior officer counted his flock, that only seventeen ships had been present since the previous morning. "No report of these stragglers had been made to either me or the Commodore," noted McCoy. "These two ships had presumably lost touch during the alterations of course on the 26th. In view of the proximity of U-boats great concern was felt for the safety of the two stragglers but it was now too late to detach escorts to search for them."[58] DeWolf, in his report of proceedings, pointed out that one of the ships was "a persistent straggler" and that on 26 December *Haida* twice had had to break off rounding up ships because of the two cruiser actions. With no effective warning surface radar, in terrible weather conditions and the enemy in close proximity, it is easy to understand *Haida*'s difficulty. Breaking radio silence to report stragglers would probably, under the circumstances, have done little more than aggravate the situation.[59] As it turned out, both ships made Kola Inlet safely, although one may have had a close call. The German destroyer *Z 33*, returning to port at 1800 on the 26th, had fired four torpedoes at a lone merchant ship—and missed.[60]

As JW 55B approached its destination on 28 December, the three Canadian Tribals, having the least fuel, detached into Kola Inlet. A heavy air raid welcomed them into harbour, and they joined in the anti-aircraft barrage before finally dropping anchor in Vaenga Bay. Despite the bleak Russian surroundings, the Canadians took the opportunity to celebrate Christmas and their recent victory. In *Haida* "the whole mess deck was draped with signal flags; a bottle of beer at each man's plate; the candles throwing a pleasant light; and practically everybody drunk." As was customary in

54. R. Humble, *Fraser of North Cape* (London 1983), 201

55. Winton, *Death of the Scharnhorst*, 96

56. Winton, *Death of the Scharnhorst*, 82-96; Humble, *Fraser*, 200-20. Neither the Naval Staff history nor Roskill's detailed official account in *The War at Sea* III pt 1, 82-5, mention Fraser's turn towards the North Atlantic.

57. KTB, *SKL*, 26 Dec 1943

58. Capt (D)17, ROP, 9 Jan 1944

59. *Haida* ROP, 31 Dec 1943

60. KTB, *SKL*, 27 Dec 1943. Details on the attack are sketchy as *Z 33*'s war diary apparently did not survive the war.

One of the RCN's two V Class destroyers, HMCS *Sioux* in 1944. (LAC PA147119)

Commonwealth navies, the captain visited each mess, and the signal officer and his yeoman of signals came down to wash dishes with the leading hands. In *Iroquois* the wardroom produced a Christmas menu with dishes appropriately named for the occasion: "Hors d'oeuvres Cul de Cheval," "Dindon Rôti Duc de York," "Sauce Sang de Boches," "Crème de Carottes Nordcap Deuxieme," "Pommes de Terre Moulues Scharnhorst," "Parsley Polyarnoe," "Poudingue Nöel aux Prunes en Retard," "Sauce au Rhum Ruse de Guerre," finishing off with "Strike Port."[61]

It was a brief enough celebration, brought to an end by the return passage of RA 55B, a convoy the enemy was particularly determined to intercept. Perhaps in anticipation of the German reaction, Captain McCoy adopted a new screening formation. Instead of positioning *Haida*, *Huron* and *Iroquois* around the convoy, he deployed them in line abreast one mile apart and five miles in advance of the convoy. Their role was to investigate every reliable HF/DF fix, taking station "three to five miles (depending on the weather) beyond the position of the fix along the same bearing" from the commodore's ship. There they were to remain until further HF/ DF bearings indicated that the transmissions were coming from the same U-boat, at which point they were to close the U-boat's estimated position at their best speed.[62] McCoy meant to keep shadowing boats down or, better, trap them between the Tribals and the convoy's destroyer screen. The new formation also helped alleviate problems arising from the lack of centimetric radar in the Canadian warships and their difficulty in manoeuvring at low speed. The disposition paid dividends with a large number of HF/DF contacts, although in the event the German efforts were "half hearted." Only one U-boat sighted any ships, and the escorts quickly drove it off before it was able to locate the convoy. RA 55B entered Loch Ewe unscathed on 7 January 1944, the same day the destroyers anchored in Scapa Flow.[63]

The destruction of *Scharnhorst* and the damage to *Tirpitz* enabled the Admiralty to redistribute its forces. The removal, at least for the time being, of the need to provide battleship cover on the Russian convoys meant that destroyers no longer needed to be assigned to screen the capital units. With the concurrence of the C-in-C Home Fleet, the Admiralty seized upon that opportunity to transfer five destroyers, including the four Canadian Tribals, to Plymouth Command.[64] Fleet destroyers were needed to overcome any threat of German dominance in the English Channel before the invasion of Europe.[65] As compensation, the two newest Canadian destroyers, *Algonquin* and *Sioux*, deployed to Scapa Flow in March, where they became the RCN mainstay with the Home Fleet until the closing months of the war in Europe.

Unlike previous fleet destroyers in the Royal Canadian Navy, the procurement of *Algonquin* and *Sioux* had been almost an afterthought. During discussions associated with the Québec Conference, Vice-Admiral Percy Nelles, playing his manpower card with adroitness, had gained

61. See DHH 81/520/8000, *Iroquois* (Gen); A.D. Butcher, *I Remember Haida* (Hantsport 1985), 36-7

62. Capt (D)17, ROP, 9 Jan 1944

63. Ibid; KTB, *SKL*, 1-4 Jan 1944

64. Home Fleet WD III, 210; C-in-C Home Fleet to Adm, 3 Jan 1944, CS 151-1-1, LAC, RG 24, 11751

65. *Athabaskan*, *Haida*, and *Iroquois* sailed immediately. Much to the disappointment of her ship's company, *Huron* escorted one more convoy to Russia before joining her sisters in Plymouth late in February.

British agreement to transfer two destroyers to the RCN, along with two cruisers (see Chapter 15). This received final Cabinet approval on 3 November 1943, but what type of destroyers would be agreeable to both the RCN and RN was far from clear.[66] The RCN expected destroyers from new construction, but the Royal Navy had in mind to part with something less dear . The list of available destroyers provided by the Admiralty included four prewar-vintage ships, among them two Tribals, and thirteen from new construction, five of which were intended for the Home Fleet and the remainder earmarked for foreign service. "It is probable," wrote Captain J.A.S. Eccles, Director of the Operations Division (Home) at the Admiralty, "that the Canadians would prefer new ships but they already have four RCN Tribals in the Home Fleet and it would be convenient if they manned Tartar and Eskimo of the same class."[67] Convenient indeed. Both Tribals were worn, tired ships that had seen much hard service from the beginning of the war—*Eskimo*, for example, had had its bow blown off at Narvik and been heavily damaged by a bomb in the Mediterranean—and the Canadians would have been doing the RN a great favour if they had accepted them. Eccles's minute, including the hope that the Canadians would man the two Tribals and allow scarce British manpower to be allocated to more valuable new construction, found approval throughout the Admiralty.[68]

The RCN refused to take such rancid bait. At a meeting on 15 November the naval staff, with the fallout of the equipment crisis swirling around them, decided that "it is of particular importance that ships acquired at this time be of the most modern construction with modern weapons and equipment." They recommended that the Admiralty be informed that Canada preferred to take over two Intermediate destroyers completing in January 1944.[69] When this response was forwarded to the Admiralty by the new Senior Canadian Naval Officer in London, Captain F.L. Houghton,[70] it included the proviso that the RCN preferred to take over ships destined for home service. Such ships were earmarked for the Home Fleet instead of foreign service in the Mediterranean or Far East, and were "arcticized," which made them more suitable for Canadian conditions. These stipulations reduced the range of choice that the British could now offer, and after further negotiations, the Canadians accepted HMS *Valentine* and *Vixen*, renamed *Algonquin* and *Sioux* respectively.[71]

As the naval staff had requested, the new destroyers incorporated modern construction and equipment. At 1808 tons standard displacement and 362 feet in length, they were smaller than the Improved Tribals, but their longitudinal construction gave them a stronger hull. First ordered in November 1941, the V class incorporated design improvements that reflected lessons learned from the war. After the heavy losses from air attack in the Norwegian, Dunkirk, and Mediterranean campaigns, the Royal Navy had come to appreciate the need for more powerful and effective high-angle fire. Therefore, the latest generation of British destroyers, including

---

66. SCNO(L) to Sec Adm, 21 Oct 1943, PRO, ADM 1/12564

67. DOD(H) min, 31 Oct 1943, ibid

68. Sec Adm to SCNO(L), 7 Nov 1943, ibid

69. NSM, 15 Nov 1943

70. Houghton succeeded Price as SCNO(L) on 30 Oct 1943.

71. SCNO(L) to Sec Adm, 15 Nov 1943, DOD(H) to NSHQ, 29 Nov. 1943, NSHQ to Adm, 6 Dec 1943, PRO, ADM 1/12564.
     Although evidence is obscure, it seems that the two new destroyers were given Tribal names in an attempt to confuse the enemy. See Tucker, *Naval Service of Canada* II, 93

Algonquin and *Sioux*, were fitted with a main armament of four 4.7-inch guns that elevated to 50 degrees—a significant improvement over the 40 degrees of previous mounts—and a close range anti-aircraft armament consisting of a twin gyro-mounted, radar-controlled 40mm Bofors backed up by four twin power-mounted 20mm Oerlikons. A pair of quadruple 21-inch torpedo tubes and seventy depth-charges that could be launched from two rails and four throwers rounded out the weapons systems. They also enjoyed the benefit of the latest radar and asdic, including Type 293 search radar and the Type 144Q/147B asdic combination, could make thirty-one knots, and had excellent endurance. Their only weakness was that they had been hurriedly built to reduced British wartime standards.[72]

In contrast to the Tribals, the Fleet Vs, as the RCN referred to them officially, were commanded by relatively junior officers, although both had previous experience in command of destroyers. *Algonquin*'s captain, Lieutenant-Commander D.W. Piers, RCN, was a graduate of the Royal Military College in Kingston; he had been at sea almost continually since the outbreak of the war. As CO of HMCS *Restigouche* in 1942, Piers had been the escort commander for convoys ON 137 and SC 107, where he had come to the attention of both American and British naval authorities (see *No Higher Purpose*, Chapter 10), and Piers's report on conditions at sea had been instrumental in improving methods and equipment in the Mid-Ocean Escort Force (also discussed here in Chapter 12). Just twenty-seven years old, and only confirmed in the rank of Lieutenant-Commander on 15 March 1944, Piers ran a "pusser" ship—*Algonquin* was one of the few RCN vessels in which the ship's company always dressed in regulation rig—and his destroyer's performance consistently matched his high standards. *Sioux*'s commanding officer, Acting Lieutenant-Commander E.E.G. Boak, had commanded *Skeena* for nine months and, in contrast to Piers, ran a relaxed ship in which Cowichan sweaters and hockey jerseys were often the dress of choice. *Sioux*'s performance was no less effective for that. It was a noteworthy state of efficiency to have reached, because the ships' companies, like so many others in the RCN, consisted largely of men who had little or no previous seagoing service. A small nucleus of officers, chief petty officers, petty officers, and leading hands, those who had accumulated considerable sea-time, achieved impressive results with their less experienced shipmates.[73]

After commissioning and acceptance trials in the Portsmouth area, the destroyers headed separately to the Home Fleet's base at Scapa Flow for work-ups under the direction of a section dubbed "Scapa Services." At this stage of the war this organization was working up all RN fleet units, and the evolutions they put ships through appear to have been even more rigorous than those of Commodore (Vice-Admiral, ret'd) Gilbert Stephenson's better known work-ups of escorts at Tobermory. Under the direction of Vice-Admiral (D) the ships, with three RN officers embarked, carried out "every possible sort of exercise a destroyer would be called upon to play" during a five week work-up program.[74] The two Canadian destroyers then joined the Home Fleet, just as Operation Tungsten, a Fleet Air Arm attack on *Tirpitz*, was about to take place. They sailed on

---

72. Equipment Card, HMCS *Algonquin*, DHH 81/520; March, *British Destroyers, 1898-1960* (London 1960), 414-18; Whitley, *Destroyers of World War II*, (Annapolis 1988), 133

73. RCN, *Naval List*; Interviews with RAdm D.W. Piers and Cdr L.B. Jenson, biog files, DHH; McAndrew, Rawling and Whitby, *Liberation*, 106, 111

74. Piers interview, nd, 177, D.W. Piers biog file, DHH; R. Baker, *Dry Ginger: The Biography of Admiral of the Fleet Sir Michael LeFanu* (London 1977), 53

Top: RCN Tribal class destroyers *Haida* and *Athabaskan* at speed in the English Channel, 1944. (LAC PA151742)

Bottom: Four future Chiefs of the Naval Staff in Plymouth, 1944. From left, Lieutenant Commander H.S. Rayner, CO of the destroyer *Huron*; Rear Admiral H.E. Reid, head of the RCN mission in Washington, DC; Commander H.G. DeWolf, CO of the destroyer HMCS *Haida*; and Captain H.T.W. Grant, CO of the cruiser HMS *Enterprise*. (LAC PA 191705)

30 March 1944 with Force 1, consisting of the battleships *Anson* and *Duke of York*, the fleet carrier *Victorious*, a cruiser, and six destroyers.[75]

Signals intelligence had revealed that repairs to the damage to *Tirpitz* from the midget submarine attack the previous September would be completed in mid-March. This not only put the Russian convoys at risk but the battleship could also interfere with plans for the seaborne invasion of Europe. *Tirpitz* lay outside the effective range of Bomber Command, and since there was no likelihood of repeating the success of the midget submarine attack, the Admiralty directed the Home Fleet to launch an attack with carrier-borne aircraft while *Tirpitz* lay in its anchorage in Kaa Fjord. Torpedoes would be unable to penetrate the net defences. Therefore, the Fairey Barracuda strike aircraft were to attack with armour-piercing and medium-cased bombs, released from between 1200 and 3000 feet. This would make the lumbering Barracudas vulnerable on the run-in, making surprise and effective flak suppression essential. During March the Fleet Air Arm's air crews sharpened their skills against a life-sized mock-up of *Tirpitz* in Loch Eriboll, and the British Secret Intelligence Service inserted an agent at Kaa Fjord to provide information about the anti-aircraft defences and weather data.[76] Vice-Admiral H.R. Moore, Fraser's second-in-command—who drew up the plan—synchronised Operation Tungsten with the passage of outbound convoy JW 58, so as to draw U-boats into the Barents Sea. The convoy completed its passage safely, covered by Force 1. At the launch point, *Algonquin* and *Sioux* joined Force 2, comprising the venerable fleet carrier *Furious*, four escort carriers, three cruisers, and eight destroyers.

The original intention had been to launch the strike on the morning of 4 April. But when Fraser learned from Ultra that *Tirpitz* would be conducting speed trials on the 3rd, he moved the operation up by twenty-four hours.[77] Thus, 3 April 1944 became "a red letter day" for the Fleet Air Arm. That morning forty-one Barracudas, escorted by Corsair, Hellcat, and Wildcat fighters, attacked *Tirpitz* in two waves, catching the battleship completely by surprise. Several Canadians were among the flight crews. Lieutenant-Commander D.R.B. Cosh, RCNVR, commanded 881 Squadron flying Wildcats off the escort carrier HMS *Pursuer*, and Lieutenant-Commander G.C. Edwards, RCNVR, led HMS *Fencer*'s Wildcats. Three other Canadians flew fighters, and Lieutenant T.G. Darling, RCNVR, led a section of Barracudas. While the fighters strafed flak positions, the Barracudas attacked the battleship. Darling's Barracuda was the seventh in the first wave, dropping its three 500-pound semi-armour-piercing bombs at 2800 feet as it pulled out of a 50-degree dive. As the bomber flew for the protection of the surrounding mountains, Darling's air gunner saw the three bombs hit forward of the battleship's bridge. Analysis after the operation concluded that fourteen hits were scored on *Tirpitz*, putting it out of action for three months at the cost of only three Barracudas, two over the target and one that crashed on take-off.[78]

Algonquin and *Sioux* played their part in the unglamorous but essential role of ensuring the safety of major fleet units. They formed part of the antisubmarine screen and kept a continual asdic watch, all the time maintaining accurate station in various formations designed to deny U-boats a

75.   Adm, Battle Summary No. 27, *Naval Aircraft Attack on the "Tirpitz," 3 April 1944* (London 1945), 3

76.   Ibid, 2-4; Hinsley, *British Intelligence* III pt 1, 271-3; "Government Code and Cypher School,". XVII, 138-9

77.   Hinsley, *British Intelligence* III pt 1, 274

78.   Adm, *Attack on the "Tirpitz,"* app C; CMNO, "The Fleet Air Arm Attack on the Tirpitz at Alten Fiord on 3rd April 1944," nd, DHH 81/520/1650, "Operation Tungsten"

good torpedo-firing solution against an aircraft carrier or battleship. It was both a monotonous and nerve-wracking business in the endless hours of darkness or heavy fog. The formations moved at relatively high speeds, and it was easy for ships to lose track of one another during the frequent course changes; a watchkeeper who was too slow or too quick to make an adjustment could cause a collision with another ship with catastrophic results.[79]

Destroyers from the screen could also be assigned to act as aircraft guards during flying operations. Stationed on the quarter of a carrier at three to four hundred yards, and constantly alert to changes in the carrier's course, they were charged with rescuing pilots who crashed overboard or whose planes were too damaged to risk landing on deck. *Algonquin*, for example, rescued a New Zealander who ditched because his Hellcat's arrester gear had been shot away by flak. Thanks to good boat drill "he was picked up in a matter of minutes, uninjured, and soon recovered from the chilling effect of the cold sea."[80]

When the first news of the mission reached the Admiralty, the new First Sea Lord, Admiral Sir Andrew Cunningham, immediately urged Fraser to launch another strike while the enemy was in disarray, hoping to keep *Tirpitz* out of commission even longer, perhaps permanently. Vice-Admiral Moore considered attacking again the next day but decided against it, citing the success of the first raid and the fatigue of the aircrews, while Fraser preferred to mount antishipping strikes in coordination with Coastal Command against the iron ore trade from Scandinavia. Cunningham continued to press his point after Force 2 returned to Scapa Flow, until Fraser finally agreed "after a considerable exchange of signals with London" to order another strike against *Tirpitz*, "provided that he could find favourable weather and also achieve surprise."[81]

A force similar to that which had carried out Tungsten, including *Algonquin* and *Sioux*, left Scapa Flow on 21 April 1944 and reached the launch point off Altenfjord two days later, only to find the weather "wholly unfavourable." After lingering in the vicinity for three days, Vice-Admiral Moore finally cancelled the operation and headed south to launch antishipping strikes off Bodo. Attacking in less than perfect flying weather, bombers and fighters sank three cargo ships against the loss of four aircraft. After a feint towards Narvik to fuel Germany's fears of Allied invasion, the force returned to Scapa on 28 April.[82]

In the meantime, *Sioux* took part in Operation Pitchbowl off the Norwegian coast. The objective was to interdict German shipping that was transporting iron ore down the Inner Leads from Narvik. Besides stemming the flow of valuable raw material to German factories, these operations augmented Hitler's considerable anxiety about an Allied invasion of Norway, and thus kept Wehrmacht divisions that could have been used elsewhere tied down on garrison duty. Pitchbowl was designed as a joint operation with carrier fighters providing cover for Coastal Command's Bristol Beaufighters as they attacked shipping around Stadtlandet. As often happened in these

---

79. A terrible example of this had occurred on a Russian convoy in May 1942 when the Tribal class destroyer HMS *Punjabi* was literally run over and sunk by the battleship *King George V* in thick fog. Roskill, *War at Sea* II, 130

80. *Algonquin* ROP, 1 May 1944, LAC, RG 24 (Acc 83-84/167), 695, 1926-DDE-224

81. Cunningham and Fraser had apparently clashed in the past and did not enjoy a close relationship. It probably did not help that Churchill had first offered the position of First Sea Lord to Fraser, who had withdrawn in favour of Cunningham. See J. Winton, *Cunningham* (London 1998), 345-6 and M. Stephen, *The Fighting Admirals* (Annapolis 1991), 81.

82. Roskill, *War at Sea* III pt 1, 279; Adm, *The Development of British Naval Aviation* II, app X

waters, continuous fog forced cancellation of the mission.[83] Early in May *Algonquin* and *Sioux* were at sea again for two more antishipping operations, Croquet and Hoops, aimed at shipping in the Inner Leads at Kristiansund North. Air strikes sank two transports and damaged an oil refinery, and fighters destroyed three German aircraft. It was the last such operation off Norway for the next two months, as the two destroyers followed the Tribals to the English Channel to prepare for the now imminent invasion of northern France.

The RCN destroyers were a valuable reinforcement to the surface forces needed to counter the *Kreigsmarine*'s destroyer flotillas in the invasion area. Allied planners also had to provide a minesweeping force that was sufficiently large to clear a path to the invasion beaches. To build up the required contingent of one hundred fleet minesweepers—steel-hulled vessels large and fast enough to operate with a fleet[84]—in addition to an estimated two hundred smaller ones, every flotilla of minesweepers in British waters was expected to be pressed into service, more than half of them of the Bangor class. This still left the invasion forces short of requirements and the Admiralty appealed to the RCN for assistance.[85] In January 1944 the Canadian government approved the loan of twelve Bangors to the RN, for both sweeping and escort duties in the Mediterranean, in order to free up RN vessels for the Channel. At this point, however, the Admiralty realized it would be impossible to form the necessary minesweeping force—ten flotillas of eight sweepers each, as well as additional danlayers (sweepers that had the task of laying danbuoys to mark the swept channels)— without direct Canadian help.[86] The Admiralty wanted at least twelve and as many as sixteen Canadian sweepers to make up the shortfall. Cabinet approved the new request on 21 January 1944. Two flotillas of Bangors, steamdriven rather than diesel because of their longer endurance, were to sail between 18 and 21 February in four divisions of four ships from St John's to Plymouth by way of the Azores. This left little time for preparations, especially because British dockyards were in a state of utter congestion and the Admiralty had therefore specifically requested that all alterations be completed in Canada.[87] This created difficulties; the RCN Bangors had been used as local escorts and their sweeping equipment had been landed in exchange for depth-charges.[88]

In the first two weeks of February the Halifax dockyard took the vessels in hand, gave them additional armament to cope with enemy air attack, and made room for minesweeping gear by reducing their depth-charge capacity.[89] Putting the minesweeping gear back on board—the most

---

83. Ibid

84. P. Elliot, *Allied Escort Vessels of World War II* (London 1977), 553

85. Adm, *Operation Neptune: Landing in Normandy* (London 1947), 36, 49; P. Elliot, *Allied Minesweepers in World War II* (Annapolis 1979), 108-9

86. SCNO(L) to CNS, 6 Jan 1944, CNS to SCNO(L), 10 Jan 1944, LAC, RG 24, 11,740, NSS162-1-2 ; NSM, 17 Jan 1944

87. SCNO(L) to CNS, 12 Jan 1944, Adm to NSHQ, 19 Jan 1944, NSHQ to Adm, 21 Jan 1944, SCNO(L) to NSHQ, 5 Feb 1944, LAC, RG 24, 11740, NSS162-1-2; NSHQ to Adm, 2 Feb 1944, DHH 81/520/8000, Minesweepers Bangor

88. Tucker, *Naval Service of Canada* II, 32-3, 37, 42-7

89. For air defence, 12-pdr HA/LA weapons replaced 4-inch guns, although two of the ships retained their 3-inch guns; single 20mm Oerlikons were fitted on the bridge wings, and a power-driven twin 20mm replaced the original 2-pdr mounted aft. Type 128A or 128B asdic sets remained in place, and no change was made to the SW2C radar. Fighting Equipment Reports, nd, DHH 81/520/8000, Minesweepers Bangor

important alteration—went badly. This was largely because the dockyard staff were unfamiliar with the equipment and its function. During their time in storage, the winches, the key piece of sweeping equipment, had not been properly maintained, and they were not inspected for defects before they were fitted. Instead of installing the specific winches that had been removed from each Bangor, the dockyard staff picked at random from the stockpile taken from both Bangors and corvettes. As a result thirteen of the Bangors destined for Neptune actually received the wrong equipment, getting Mk I heavy sweeping gear instead of the lighter Mk II type. To make matters worse, many had inadequate engines and weak main spars. Thus, the sixteen RCN Bangors proceeded overseas with inadequate and poorly maintained winches—the *bête noire* of the group according to one minesweeper CO—and also most had the wrong sweeping gear.[90]

After event-filled passages across the North Atlantic, the RCN Bangors arrived in Plymouth during the first weeks of March.[91] The Admiralty had expected fully equipped and trained ships, and had tentatively organized them into the 31st and 32nd Minesweeping Flotillas. Commander A.H.G. Storrs RCNR, the Bangors' senior officer, recalled the RN inspecting officers "sucking their teeth wondering if these Canadians are really up to it," after they had taken a good look at the Canadian ships and crews. The officer in charge of their training, Commander J. Temple, RN, recognized that they had virtually no minesweeping experience. He also observed that "the majority of Commanding Officers, Officers and Ship's Companies ... were under the impression that minesweeping was child's play." Temple's assessment may have reflected the belief among the minesweeping fraternity that outsiders never gave the specialty its due. It was undeniable, nevertheless, that only one commanding officer, three other officers, and about a dozen men on the Lower Deck had any minesweeping experience. This, and the defects that constantly showed up in winches and other equipment, forced Temple to scrap the planned training program and start from the beginning.[92]

The skill that the Canadians had to acquire in such a short time required high standards of seamanship and precise navigation. Temple and his staff began by organizing four or five groups of sweepers and rotated them between Plymouth, Torquay and Fowey. The first group, for example, began at Plymouth, went to Fowey for seven days to check calibration and practise the precise formations, turns, and station-keeping demanded in this exacting activity, then went back to Plymouth for training in Channel tide conditions, and at night. During the first part of the invasion the Bangors' principal task was to cut the cables of moored contact mines using a long serrated line or "sweep" streamed singly over one stern quarter or doubly to both sides. The equip-

90. The winches manufactured in Canada by the Letson & Burpee Co., a west coast firm that provided equipment for the logging industry, were said to be the most rugged and gave the least trouble. Interview with K. Whynot, nd, Whynot biog file, DHH; SCFO to Naval Minister, 31 Mar 1944, P. Nelles biog file, folder D 15, DHH; Commander Fleet Minesweeping Office Devonport to Capt M/S Plymouth Command, 22 Apr 1944 (hereafter Temple Report), DHH 81/520/8000-440/31, 31st Minesweeping Flotilla; SCNO(L) to NSHQ, 051515A Feb 1944, LAC, RG 24, 1740, CS 162-1-2

91. They were battered by rough seas and plagued by mechanical breakdowns, one Bangor ran short of fuel, another's Portuguese pilot rammed it into a breakwater at Horta in the Azores, and one accidentally severed the transatlantic cable at the same port when it dragged its anchor. See the reports of proceedings for the various Bangors, DHH 81/520/8000.

92. Temple Report; Interview with Lt R. Morrow, nd, 65-6, Morrow biog file, DHH; Interview with RAdm A.H.G. Storrs, nd, 39, Storrs biog file, DHH; Adm, "Technical Staff Monograph on British Minesweeping, 1939-1945," nd, 36, PRO, ADM 189/130

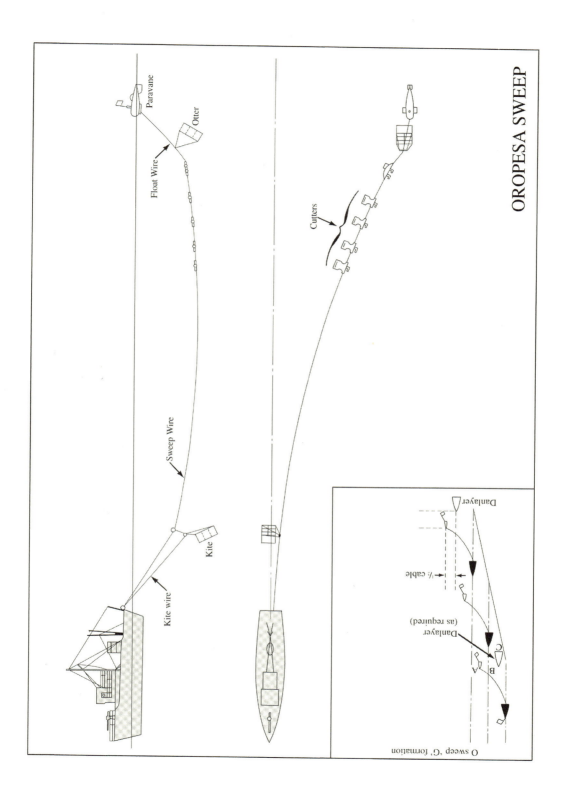

OROPESA SWEEP

Paravane

Otter

Float Wire

Sweep Wire

Kite

Kite wire

Cutters

Danlayer

Danlayer
(as required)

½ cable

A
B
C

O sweep 'G' formation

ment for this was known as the Oropesa sweep. It was marked and supported by a large blimp-shaped "float" or paravane, in turn supported with "kites" and "otters" that kept the sweep below the surface at a designated depth and cutters positioned near the end of the sweep that cut a mine's mooring wire, forcing it to the surface where it could be destroyed by other means, usually small-arms fire. Two powerful steam winches, one port and one starboard, on the Bangors' quarterdeck, or sweep deck, deployed and recovered the sweeps, which could extend 750 fathoms or 1371 metres astern. Smaller wire drums and a pair of davits helped lift the heavy, unwieldy components.[93] When clearing moored contact mines with Oropesa gear the sweepers normally worked in echelon or "G" formation where all vessels deployed single sweeps to the same side or in "H" formation where they steamed in line abreast. On occasion an "A" sweep was streamed between the sterns of two minesweepers steaming in line abreast. Defective winches did not help the exercises of these operations, but despite the frustrating hours spent on repairing them, the training went remarkably well.[94]

At the end of March 1944, nine of the Bangors took part in Gantry, a three-day exercise that involved sweeping a dummy minefield in cold, wet, and windy weather off Torquay. The Canadians did reasonably well. A subsequent exercise, Trousers, called for two flotillas to sweep ahead of a body of landing craft from the Solent to Slapton Sands. Nine RCN Bangors took part from 9 to 13 April and carried out a sweep of 120 miles, including such complicated manoeuvres as altering course 360 degrees while maintaining sweeping formation. By the end of April Temple considered eleven of the sixteen Bangors to be "efficient in minesweeping." This only permitted the formation of one RCN flotilla. The Canadians had impressed Temple as keen and hard working, and it was only defects in equipment that prevented three of the sixteen vessels from completing their work-ups.[95] As the RCN Bangors became operational in early May, they set to work on sweeps that would clear the way across the Channel for the assault forces.

Throughout the Second World War the English Channel was the scene of much bitter fighting between the light forces of the opposing navies, mostly at night, thanks to the strength of air power on both sides. In the war's early months German destroyers had laid hundreds of mines which sank or damaged scores of vessels along Britain's busy east coast convoy lanes and in the

---

93. The best technical description of minesweeping is found in the Adm, "Manual of Minesweeping," 1929, PRO, ADM 186/466. The best published source is Elliott's, *Allied Minesweeping*.

94. Temple recalled one harrowing experience: "At sea for a two day exercise period with the CO sick ashore, the lieutenant in hospital injured by a kite-otter being hove inboard and 30 feet along the deck before the winch could be stopped. The No. 3 a S/Lt RCNVR was in command when M/S winch broke down for third time and rest of the day was spent recovering sweep by hand. Ship detailed as danner [danlayer], developed windlass defect and was unable to weigh dans. Ordered to point, "first dan on each lap." Later a signal, "Have wires around both screws unable to use engines." Exercise completed, training officer left with ship anchored to seven shackles [160 metres] of cable on a lee shore; no engines; no power on deck. Temporary repairs to anchor windlass effected and one propeller cleared during the night. Ship entered harbour and berthed with one engine by breakfast." Minesweeping Diary, Western Task Force, PRO, ADM 199/1555; Temple Report; C-in-C Plymouth to Adm, 4 Apr 1944, LAC, RG 24, 11,740, CS162-1-2

95. Temple Report

Thames estuary.[96] The fall of France in June 1940 had allowed German E-boats to assume the offensive against east coast convoy routes, while German destroyers—usually a flotilla operating out of Brest—laid mines and carried out the occasional antishipping sweeps along Britain's south coast. Few modern British destroyers were available that were not required more urgently elsewhere. The main Allied effort in the Channel had therefore been by Coastal Forces, comprising small, quick, thin-skinned vessels that had difficulty penetrating heavily armed German convoy screens. At first Motor Gun Boats (MGBs) carried out defensive night sorties against the E-boats that were attacking coastal convoys. In 1942 MGBs and Motor Torpedo Boats (MTBs), which had a more balanced armament of light guns and torpedoes, began carrying the offensive to German coastal shipping. MTBs however made a less stable platform than was really needed for the accurate launch of torpedoes, the most effective weapon with which they could expect to sink merchant ships. By 1943, in spite of a "fine offensive spirit," British Coastal Forces had failed to deny Channel waters to the enemy.[97] Possibly because the Royal Navy was so thinly spread, the Admiralty's solution was to expand these antishipping efforts with more coastal forces rather than with heavier units. The worsening manpower situation of the RN led to increased Canadian participation.

In January 1943 Commander K.M. Barnard, an experienced officer in RN coastal forces, had approached Commander F.A. Price, RCNVR, the interim commanding officer at the Canadian headquarters in England, with the proposal that the RCN consider forming coastal craft flotillas, specifically one each of MTBs, MGBs and Motor Launches (MLs). These Canadians would then serve in the RN's Coastal Forces. The Admiralty would provide the craft and be responsible for their maintenance, if the RCN would contribute the personnel.[98] Price forwarded this proposal to NSHQ in May 1943, arguing that the most promising officers in Coastal Forces could later go on to fleet destroyers, "where their previous experience in handling craft at high speeds, keeping station etc. would be of value." Furthermore, the press coverage of Coastal Forces in Britain would "certainly add to the appreciation by the general Canadian public of the widespread participation of the Royal Canadian Navy operating in the English theatre of war." Since the Admiralty proposed using the ML flotillas in Canada as the source for all personnel, while RCNVR officers already serving in RN flotillas could also be transferred to the Canadian MGB and MTB flotillas, manning would present no insurmountable difficulties.[99]

Price hit the right nerve. "Excellent for our ML boys to work for the honour of being 'sent over,' publicity, etc," minuted the Director of Naval Personnel, Captain E.R. Mainguy. The Director of the Operations Division, Commander H.N. Lay, agreed. With the blessing of the RCN's resident expert on Coastal Forces, Captain P.K. Kekewich, RN, Captain (ML) on Rear-Admiral L.W. Murray's staff in Halifax, the minister, Nelles, and Mainguy decided that the RCN would undertake to man one flotilla each of Fairmile D type MTBs and MGBs. D type Fairmiles were the most powerful vessels in

96. It was not until after the war that the Admiralty learned that the mines had been sewn by warships, and not aircraft. See M. Whitley, *German Destroyers of World War II* (Annapolis 1985), 104

97. Roskill, *War at Sea* III pt 1, 101. For the Channel campaign, see also, P. Scott, *The Battle of the Narrow Seas* (London 1945) and P.C. Smith, *Hold the Narrow Sea: Naval Warfare in the English Channel, 1939-45* (Annapolis 1984).

98. Price to Barnard, 6 Jan 1943, LAC, RG 24, 3842, NSS1017-10-23, pt 1; Price to SNB, 29 May 1943, DHH 81/520/8000, MTBs Generally, pt 1

99. CCCS to SNB, 29 May 1943, ibid

Coastal Forces and ones with which the RCN wanted to gain experience; no consideration seems to have been given by the naval staff to a Canadian flotilla of MLs overseas. They agreed that the commanding officers would be selected from RCNVR officers already serving in RN Coastal Forces, who would be replaced by officers in the Fairmile B flotillas in Canada. The remaining officers and all ratings would also come from Canada. These arrangements were gratefully accepted by the Admiralty.[100] Canadian MTB personnel began to arrive in Britain on 8 November 1943. Lieutenant-Commander C.A. Law, RCNVR, who had served in Channel coastal flotillas since 1941, joined SCNO(L) as Staff Officer (Coastal Forces) in late October 1943.[101] A month later, Law was joined by Lieutenant-Commander J.R.H. Kirkpatrick, RCNVR, another officer with considerable experience, which included earning a Distinguished Service Cross in Channel operations.[102] Kirkpatrick was, as his navigator described, an extremely effective leader:

> He was a real professional, and certainly one of the ablest seamen I ever served with because he knew his business thoroughly. The reason he was called "The Brain" was that he had a reputation—deservedly so—for having a fantastic cerebral apparatus. He could always keep track, no matter what time of day or night it was, no matter what stage of the patrol, outgoing, homeward bound, on the patrol lines; he always had a sense of how much fuel there was, how long we could travel, at what speeds, what the state of the engines was, what the state of the crew was, whether they need-ed some relief or they needed some feeding or some hot cocoa. And not just the [MTB] 748; he was "Father" to the whole flotilla, and we younger officers took him as our role model.[103]

Law and Kirkpatrick commanded the two Canadian MTB flotillas for the duration of the war. Fairmile D type MTBs were in short supply, so the first flotilla to commission, the 29th under Lieutenant-Commander Law, received "Short" or "71 and a half foot" MTBs.[104] These boats were the penultimate version of a series of MTBs built by British companies such as British Power Boat, Vosper, and Thorneycroft that were the mainstay of Coastal Forces throughout the war. Their three 1250 hp Packard engines drove them at close to forty knots under optimum conditions, making them the fastest British MTBs in service. They mounted two 18-inch Mk 18 torpedoes, a power mounted 2-pdr pom pom on the bow, twin Vickers .303-inch machine-guns on either side of the bridge, and a twin 20mm Oerlikon on the stern; they were fitted with an armoured bridge and radar. Because of the small size of the Short MTBs, accommodation was minimal; their three offi-cers and twenty-one ratings lived ashore when not on operations. Furthermore, because they were

100. Min on CCCS to SNB, 29 May 1943, SNB to SCNO(L), 30 July 1943, Adm to SCNO(L), 22 Sep 1943, LAC, RG 24, 3842, NSS1017-10-23, pt 1; A/D Sec Staff to DOD and SNB, 9 Oct 1943, DHH 81/520/8000, MTBs Generally, pt 1

101. Tony Law was an artist of considerable talent and Capt Houghton allowed him to use this time to work on official war art. SCNO(L) WD, Oct and Nov 1943, DHH 81/520/1000-5-35(1); SCNO(L) to Law, 1 Oct 1943, LAC, MG 30, E 260 vol 1

102. See, e.g. Scott, *Battle of the Narrow Seas*, 165-7

103. D.B. Wilson ms, nd, 105, Wilson biog file, DHH. Kirkpatrick graduated with honours from RMC in 1938 but then had studied law until the war broke out.

104. Report of SO (CF) in SCNO(L) WD, Dec 1944, DHH 81/520/1000-5-35(1); Law ms, *White Plumes Astern*, LAC, MG 30, E 260 v 4. Law wrote his invaluable war memoirs in 1945 and then edited them for publication in the 1980s as *White Plumes Astern: The Short, Daring Life of Canada's MTB Flotilla* (Halifax 1989).

designed to plane once they reached twenty knots, they pounded unmercifully in anything beyond moderate seas. Breakdowns, impaired performance, and extreme discomfort were the norm. This pounding, Law complained, "was frequently the cause of serious stomach disorders, not to mention the odd broken bone" and led to "a severe nervous strain ... on the system."[105]

The available Fairmile D type MTBs, for which the Canadians had been given priority, went to Kirkpatrick's 65th Flotilla. Known as the "Dog Boat," the D type represented an attempt to match the size and power of German E-boats. With an overall length of 115 feet and a beam of twenty-one feet, they were the largest MTBs in the RN. Their four 1250 hp Packard engines were designed to power them to speeds just over thirty knots, but various modifications increased displacement and reduced their top speed to about twenty-eight knots. The Dog Boats had good manoeuvrability, their wide bow flare made them relatively dry for a coastal craft, accommodation was adequate for the complement of three officers and twenty-seven men, and they could take a heavier armament than the Shorts could. Variations existed across the class, but the 65th's first boats were armed with four 18-inch Mk 15 torpedoes, a 6-pdr Mk VII gun with automatic loading on a power mount forward, four Vickers .5-inch machine-guns in two twin mounts on either side forward of the bridge, four Vickers .303 machine-guns in twin mounts aft of the bridge, and twin 20mm Oerlikons on the stern. D types had longer range and were better seaboats than the Shorts, and their powerful armament made them dangerous opponents for E-boats.[106]

As their boats were commissioned and brought around from the builders' yards in March and April 1944, the 29th and the 65th Flotillas began to work up at HMS *Bee*, the Coastal Forces training establishment at Holyhead, Wales. There, under the watchful eye of Coastal Forces veterans led by Commander R.F. Swinley, RN, they practised torpedo firing, gunnery, signalling, navigation, station-keeping, and manoeuvring. By the end of work-ups, the 29th was so good at high-speed station-keeping that Law later boasted that he could light a cigarette on his bridge and then throw the package over to the bridge of the next boat whose captain would take one and pass it down the flotilla, all the while travelling at 24 knots. A drawback of the time at *Bee* was that the Canadian units arrived piecemeal, making it difficult to conduct flotilla training. Nonetheless, the crews of all boats had about three weeks in work-ups before being sent to their operational stations.

Generally, the RN training staff found the Canadians excellent material. They thought the Canadian officers were "more mature and superior in type to their British counterparts," but criticized their poor navigational skills and slow reaction time. As the training staff pointed out to Vice-Admiral Nelles when he inspected the flotillas in April 1944, "in coastal craft warfare, there were only two classes of personnel—the quick and the dead. The only real teacher of speed was actual battle experience, and through lack of this experience, the tempo of personnel from Canadian Fairmiles was too slow." In Nelles's own estimation, "the Senior Officers are competent and experienced; and all officers and ratings appeared keen and enthusiastic. In fact, I have seen no better representatives of the Canadian Naval service in the U.K. theatre."[107]

105. Law ms, *White Plumes Astern*; "List of Equipment and Weapons of 29th MTB Flotilla," DHH 81/520/8000-469/29

106. J. Lambert and A. Ross, *Allied Coastal Forces of World War II: Fairmile Designs and US Submarine Chasers* (London 1990); J. Lambert, *The Fairmile "D" Type Motor Torpedo Boat* (London 1985), 9-23

107. Law ms, *White Plumes Astern*, 18, 46-7; P.W. Nelles, "Report on the Inspection of Canadian MTB Flotillas," 20 Apr 1944, Nelles biog file, DHH

The tactics that the Canadians practised at *Bee* had evolved throughout the war to meet the unique nature of MTB operations. Coastal Forces actions were not the drawn-out, set-piece affairs typical of most surface engagements but were fast-paced, confused melées usually lasting only a few minutes. The challenge that Coastal Forces personnel on both sides of the Channel faced was to launch an effective attack before the situation was reduced to a highly confused state. Their torpedo tubes were fixed and MTBs had to be aimed at the target, and therefore they tried to fire from ahead or abeam. According to an experienced British Coastal Forces officer, the tactics utilized early in the war were quite straightforward: "one closed the enemy on auxiliary engines to 500 yards, fired unobserved, crash started mains, and pushed off." When stronger convoy defences eventually made these tactics too dangerous, MTBs began to work with MGBs, which would "go racing off and engage from a different sector, rivetting the enemy's attention on themselves while we crept in quietly and dealt the death blow."[108] MGBs had limited striking power and were required for anti-E-boat duties; therefore MTBs often split into two groups, one usually attacking from landward, the other from seaward. If one group was detected, it would act as a decoy while the other tried to achieve a firing position undetected; should both be discovered, at least the defensive fire was split. These tactics proved most effective and were used until the end of the war.

An added complication arose for the 29th Flotilla. Shortly after arriving at their operational base at Ramsgate, its boats lost their torpedo tubes to racks for forty-eight small 100-pound depth-charges. Invasion planners had become alarmed at reports, based upon "a fair amount of evidence" from signals intelligence and prisoners-of-war, of a new German submarine described as "a submersible E-boat." The Walter or "W-boat" was reportedly capable of fantastic speeds of approximately thirty knots submerged. Concerned about the implications of such a revolutionary weapon—the Allies had no antisubmarine vessels that could keep pace—the Admiralty stripped three MTB flotillas of their torpedo tubes and converted them to MGB antisubmarine flotillas. It was considered unlikely that the W-boats could be located with any kind of accuracy, and therefore the intention was to plaster the area in which they were thought to be. MTBs would be directed by asdic-equipped motor launches or frigates, and moving in line abreast or broad quarterline at high speed, lay their depth-charges "across the estimated line of advance of the enemy." These "inaccurate and haphazard" antisubmarine tactics had little chance of success, but it was the best that could be done with the equipment available.[109] The loss of its main offensive weapon devastated the 29th Flotilla. "Mere words," wrote Tony Law in later years, "cannot explain the effect on the Flotilla's morale: the bottom dropped out of everything, and our faces were long as we watched our main armament and striking power being taken away." Law fought hard to get his torpedoes back, but despite lobbying by Nelles and Houghton, the depth-charges remained until mid-June. By then the Admiralty had known for two months that reports of the "submersible E-boat" were false.[110]

The Canadian flotillas went to operational bases on either flank of the forthcoming invasion. The 29th Flotilla at Ramsgate joined the command of the Naval Officer-in-Charge (NOIC) Dover. The

---

108. P. Dickens, *Night Action: MTB Flotilla at War* (London 1974), 57

109. Adm, Directorate of Naval Operation Studies, "E-Boat Attacks on Coastal Convoys: Comparison with Possible Threat From Walter Boat," 19 Apr 1944, PRO, ADM 219/121; SCNO(L) to NSHQ, 22 Apr 1944, DHH 81/520/8000-466/29, 29th MTB Flotilla, Signals 1943-4"; 29th MTB Flotilla—Tactics, May 1944, ibid, 29th MTB Flotilla (Gen)

110. Naval Assistant (Policy and Planning) SCNO(L) to Law, 31 May 1944, ibid; Hinsley, *British Intelligence* III pt 1, 245

65th Flotilla joined Plymouth Command, based at Dartmouth until mid-May, then at Brixham on Lyme Bay. Their main duties were to attack German coastal shipping and to counter increasing E-boat activity in the English Channel. One of the 29th's first missions however was a special operation in support of the upcoming invasion.[111] On the night of 16/17 May, four Shorts covered two British MTBs as they landed engineers attempting to obtain samples of the mines that the Germans were using to defend their beaches. Although it was ultimately successful, the mission demonstrated the confusion that often arose in night operations. The 29th's *MTB 464* was damaged in a collision with one of the British MTBs and had to be towed home stern-first, while *MTB 460* fired on the other British MTB when it failed to respond to five successive challenges; fortunately, the MTB finally identified itself before it sustained any injuries or serious damage. All boats returned to Dover, where "the mine was loaded aboard a truck, and the Army with its new German toy, drove off in triumph to London."[112]

By coincidence, both Canadian flotillas went into action against enemy shipping for the first time on the night of 22/23 May 1944. Four of the 29th's boats joined four RN Shorts on a sweep from Dover in search of a German coastal convoy that was known to be proceeding from Dieppe to Boulogne. Arriving off the French coast shortly after midnight, the eight MTBs began a north-south patrol in extremely poor visibility. At the end of the first southern leg, three of the RN boats lost contact with the rest of the force, and at 0224 engine problems forced the other British MTB to withdraw. Minutes later on the northern leg, as the Canadian boats began to pick up radar contacts on their starboard quarter, the night erupted in starshell and tracer. The remaining British boats had run into German escorts, flashed the challenge and received a hail of intense enemy fire in reply. Seeing the British boats disengage to seaward, the Canadians altered course and attacked the convoy. Law, who brought an artist's eye to the matter at hand, painted a vivid word picture of this action:

> The four boats ... closed the enemy. Radar bearings and ranges poured faster and faster up to the bridge. Through my binoculars I could see four of the low flak barges. The torpedo boats roared through the water, while overhead the sky was full of our red starshells mingling with the enemy's green ones, and spattered with their colourful, dangerous tracer ... Heavy 88-mm [anti-]personnel shells burst above our heads and left angry puffs of black smoke. Others exploded nearby, sending up gigantic needle-shaped columns of water. Green and red tracers, brilliant and terrifying missiles of death, flew through the air in graceful hose-pipe arcs towards our vulnerable wooden vessels. They danced over the waters, then hit with a sharp resounding crackle. By this time, the noise had reached its climax and the smell of cordite was overpowering.[113]

After closing to within three hundred yards—good torpedo range if they had had them—the Canadian MTBs made smoke and disengaged. Despite a sustained radar search they could not relocate the convoy and at 0445 headed back to base, having suffered light damage but no casualties.[114]

111. Adm, the OIC, "The Use of Special Intelligence in Connection with Operation OVERLORD, January 1944-September 1944," nd, PRO, ADM 223/287 Pt II; Adm; *Coastal Forces Periodic Review*, May-June 1944, 5, DHH, 84/7

112. Law ms, *White Plumes Astern*, 31-4

113. Ibid, 42

114. Ibid, 39-46; Law to V-Adm Commanding Dover (VA Dover), 23 May 1944, VA Dover to Adm, 23 May 1944, DHH 81/520/8000-466/29, 29th MTB Flotilla (Signals 1944-5); 29th MTB Flotilla, ROP, 25 May 1944, LAC, RG 24, 11346, CS 164-29-3

The 65th Flotilla's action was equally confused but more destructive. At 0327, four Dog Boats were near the end of their patrol line southwest of the Channel Islands when they gained radar contact with a convoy of three merchant ships and twelve escorts. As the MTBs sought a favourable position from which to fire torpedoes, they were discovered by two of the escorts. Following prearranged tactics, *MTB 735* and *MTB 726* engaged the escorts while the other two boats, *MTB 727* and *MTB 745*, continued the torpedo attack. The two escorts engaged by the Canadians were both forced to a stop when the two MTBs raked them at a hundred yards with their automatic weapons, but the defensive fire thrown up by the Germans made it difficult for *MTB 727* and *MTB 745* to spot their targets; ultimately *MTB 745* fired its torpedoes by radar but without success. Both MTBs then disengaged but were fired upon by the two other Canadian MTBs when they tried to rejoin formation. Tragically, five ratings on *MTB 745* were wounded by friendly fire, one dying before they reached harbour. Two other sailors died when *MTB 726* engaged the escorts and two of the MTBs sustained heavy damage. In return, one German patrol boat suffered serious damage.[115]

Both actions demonstrate the challenges of fast paced Coastal Forces actions and the tactics evolved to overcome them. Above all they show the need for stealth; once surprise was lost it became difficult to bring actions to a successful conclusion. The Germans defended their coastal convoys with numerous escorts. Once their presence was revealed, it became almost impossible for MTBs to penetrate the wall of defensive fire thrown up by minesweepers (*M-boote* to the Germans), motor-minesweepers (*Räumboote* or *R-boote*) and flak barges, which were trawlers that possessed a formidable armament of 88mm guns and automatic weapons. Moreover, the pyrotechnics associated with the defensive fire—gun flashes, tracer, flares and starshell—impaired night vision and made it difficult to see targets let alone make the precise calculations necessary for a decisive torpedo attack. The most effective defence MTBs had was their speed. Even under the most favourable conditions however it was difficult to attain accuracy with automatic weapons or torpedoes when a small, light MTB was bucking about at twenty-five knots or more. Identification of friend and foe was also problematic. Afterwards it was hard to tell exactly what had transpired, let alone calculate the damage that had been inflicted on the enemy. Nonetheless, exposure to the challenges inherent in fighting small attack craft at night was the best training the Canadian flotillas could have for the rigours of the invasion at hand.

Despite these challenges the Allies held one distinct advantage in the Channel: accurate knowledge of German warship and merchant shipping movements derived from special intelligence. In general terms, Ultra could influence operations by providing information that could be immediately applied and by confirming what one former intelligence officer has referred to as their "pattern of behaviour," including their order of battle, dispositions, and standard operating procedures.[116] The official British intelligence history demonstrates how the Operational Intelligence Centre (OIC) at the Admiralty had, over time, formed "a reliable picture of the enemy's routines—showing which swept channels the convoys normally used, where they spent the night, the times at which

---

115. C-in-C Plymouth to Adm, 24 May 1944, DHH 81/520/8000, "65th MTB Flotilla (Signals 1944-45)"; 65th MTB Flotilla, ROP, 2 June 1944, LAC, RG 24, 11,346, CS164-65-3; Adm; the OIC, "Summary of German Naval Situation," 23 May 1944, PRO, ADM 223/10

116. J.P. Campbell, *Dieppe Revisited: A Documentary Investigation* (London 1993), 166-7; Beesly, *Very Special Intelligence*, 15, 23

Captains H.T.W. Grant, RCN and C.P. Clarke, RN, COs of the cruisers HMS *Enterprise* and HMS *Glasgow*, respectively, congratulate each other after their successful engagement of German destroyers in the Bay of Biscay on 28 December 1943. Like many other Canadian officers and men, Grant was gaining experience in RN cruisers before moving to RCN ships of that type. (Grant Papers)

The Tribal class destroyer HMCS *Haida* at Plymouth, England in February 1944. (LAC PA115055)

they made and left harbour, and where and when they met their escorts."[117] When coupled with signals intelligence from the *Heimisch* key, or "Dolphin" as Bletchley Park knew it, which provided precise information about the movements of *Kriegsmarine* surface units in the Channel and the North Sea, the OIC was often able to provide advance warning of German operations.[118] This information was quickly disseminated to senior intelligence officers at the combined headquarters of the naval home commands at Plymouth, Portsmouth and The Nore over secure communications lines—usually via scrambler telephones and teleprinters.[119] As will be seen from the operations of the RCN's Tribal class destroyers in the Channel in the spring and summer of 1944, this intelligence, if received in time, could have a direct bearing on the sailing orders issued to Allied surface forces. That said, there was no guarantee that an interception would take place, and if one did, the action still had to be fought to a successful conclusion amidst the fog of war.

In October 1943, with the goal of gaining control of the English Channel at night by wearing down German destroyer strength and disrupting the movement of enemy supplies, the Commanders-in-Chief, Plymouth and Portsmouth, instituted offensive destroyer sweeps—called "Tunnels"—against shipping off the coast of Brittany. After about a five-hour passage at twenty knots to the other side of the Channel, the ships would steam along the craggy, island-studded coast of Brittany, ten to fifteen miles offshore, and then withdraw before first light so that enemy aircraft could not interfere with their operations. With the advantage of Ultra Intelligence, shore authorities could direct forces to the most advantageous positions for intercepting and attacking the enemy. Moreover, on the rare nights when weather conditions were right, anomalous propagation even allowed the Combined Operations Room at Plymouth to track shipping along the enemy coast using radar. The German *Seetakt* coastal radar was not as effective but it could detect Allied surface forces steering for the German convoys and shepherd ships into safe harbours while directing the escorts on to the attacking ships.

Partly because of *Seetakt*, the first Tunnels failed, sometimes with disastrous results. Not only did German coastal defences and naval units respond effectively, but the forces under Plymouth and Portsmouth commands had little cohesion. The ships, which often had never served together before, had to manoeuvre in the face of the enemy at high speed and in close order during darkness, with an incompatible mix of performance and weapons. Admiral Sir Ralph Leatham, C-in-C Plymouth, had therefore been pressing the Admiralty for a dedicated, homogeneous strike force to combat German destroyers in the western Channel from the time that he first assumed his command in August 1943. In his appreciation of the second Tunnel operation of 22/23 October, when the light cruiser HMS *Charybdis* and the Hunt class destroyer HMS *Limbourne* had been sunk with massive loss of life by German destroyers of the 4th *Torpedobootsflotille*,[120] Leatham, backed by the

---

117. Hinsley, *British Intelligence in the Second World War* III Pt 1, 280

118. Ibid, II, 663-4

119. Campbell, *Dieppe Revisited*, 170-1

120. The warships that the *Kriegsmarine* classified as torpedo boats were actually small destroyers, which the Allies often referred to as "Elbings." The class the RCN Tribals engaged in the spring of 1944 were Type 39 Torpedo Boats with a standard displacement of 1,318 tons, with a main armament of four 4.1-inch guns and six 21-inch torpedo tubes. In terms of speed and size they were roughly equivalent to RCN River class destroyers. See Whitley, *Destroyers of World War II*, 73

C-in-C Portsmouth, stated that future operations of this type should be carried out by an adequately trained division of fleet destroyers. He believed that Tribals, with their powerful gun armament, would be the best choice. There was resistance to the idea at the Admiralty, where certain staff officers expressed a preference for J and K types owing to their lower silhouette and a marginally stronger torpedo armament,[121] but when the five Tribals—including four of the Improved Canadian version, not yet a year old—serving with the Home Fleet came available after the destruction of *Scharnhorst*, they were transferred to Plymouth Command to form Leatham's strike force, which became the 10th Destroyer Flotilla.[122]

At the end of December 1943, in partial compensation for the *Charybdis* fiasco, the British were able to inflict a sizeable defeat on the German destroyer force operating in the Bay of Biscay. On the 28th the Germans were attempting to bring two blockade runners into French ports when the ten destroyers sent to act as escort encountered the cruisers HMS *Glasgow* and *Enterprise*, the latter under the command of Captain H.T.W. Grant, RCN. In a well-fought action, the cruisers cut the destroyers off from their base and sank three of them in a running battle. Actions in the English Channel were, however, more likely to be fought at night. In his report on the *Charybdis* action, Leatham had noted that "the art of night fighting with the added new technique of radar has, up to date in this war, had very little opportunity of practical test, and in the Plymouth Command, at all events, little opportunity of exercise."[123]

As if to emphasize that point to the new flotilla under his command, on the night of 19 January 1944, within days and in some cases hours of the destroyers' arrival at Plymouth, Leatham dispatched the RCN Tribals *Athabaskan*, *Haida*, and *Iroquois*, with their RN sister *Ashanti*, on a Tunnel with three smaller, slower Hunt class destroyers. Predictably, difficulties arose, particularly with communications and direction of the force. In his report on the operation Commander DeWolf "strongly recommended that the Plymouth forces exercise night encounters."[124] Searching for and launching attacks on one another, ideal undertakings for identifying the problems associated with night fighting, was thus the training priority in February and March. The 10th Destroyer Flotilla carried out at least eight of these evolutions, as well as torpedo and gunnery shoots to sharpen its skills.[125]

To increase their night fighting capability the Canadian Tribals finally received centimetric surface warning radar. During an extended period in dry dock to repair her damage from the glider bomb, *Athabaskan* had been fitted with the recently developed Type 276, which could detect destroyer-sized contacts out to a range of about twelve miles. Power-rotation allowed consistent

---

121. When the Js and Ks first commissioned in the late 1930s, they were armed with a pair of quintuple 21-inch torpedo tubes. In the wake of the Norway campaign, however, the after mount was replaced by a 4-inch high-angle gun to strengthentheir anti-aircraft capability. This left them with only a slight advantage in torpedo strength over the Tribals.

122. C-in-C Plymouth, "Action with German Ships on the Night of 22/23 October 1943," pt II, 5, C-in-C Portsmouth to Adm, 27 Nov 1943, CO HMS *Grenville*, "Night Action with Enemy Destroyers," 22 Oct 1943, 2; DOD(H) min, 26 Jan 1944; DTSD min, 27 Nov 1943, PRO, ADM 199/1038; Adm, Battle Summary No. 31, *Cruiser and Destroyer Actions English Channel and Western Approaches 1943-1944* (London 1945), 1-8

123. C-in-C Plymouth, "Action ... Night of 22/23 Oct, 1943," 13 Nov. 1943, pt I, 5, PRO, ADM 199/1038

124. *Haida* ROP, 20 Jan 1944, LAC, RG 24, 11,730, CS151-11-9

125. In February, the training period was interrupted when the destroyers returned to Scapa Flow to screen the forces engaged in Operation Posthorn, a carrier antishipping strike along the Norwegian coast. *Bellona* deck log, Feb and Mar 1944, PRO, ADM 53/118941 and 118942; *Huron* ROP, 1 Mar 1944, LAC, RG 24, 11,426, HU 013; Home Fleet WD III, para 199-200; Meiklem, *Tartar Memoirs* (Glasgow nd), 32.

scanning, and the antenna, mounted high on a lattice foremast, provided optimum ranges and unobstructed search. Echoes were displayed on a Plan Position Indicator (PPI), which displayed contacts on all bearings simultaneously. This was a great improvement on A-scopes, which only allowed operators to see contacts on the bearing of the antenna. When they joined Plymouth Command, *Haida*, *Iroquois*, and *Huron* were fitted with Type 271Q, an older, less effective set. Performance was good—ships of destroyer size could be detected out to nine miles—but the aerial was manually rotated, and even though Type 271Q could utilize a PPI at that stage, the Canadian destroyers appear only to have had A-scopes.

A further serious drawback to the Type 271Q radar was that its aerial had to be located close to the transmitter. Too heavy for the tripod foremasts of the RCN Tribals, the antenna was mounted in the searchlight position forward of the after bridge canopy, only about forty-five feet above the waterline. This not only reduced range but, more importantly, the forward superstructure "wooded" the beam when it swept ahead.[126] For gunnery radar the destroyers had Type 285P, a metric set of early war vintage that was linked with Auto Barrage Units (ABU) to provide accurate shooting under visual conditions and "reasonable" accuracy under blind-fire conditions.[127] For "Warning Combined," or air and surface search, they had Type 291, a well-tried radar that could detect surface contacts out to about nine miles. Power-rotating and utilizing an A-scope display, the 291's great weakness, as demonstrated on the Murmansk run, was that its transmissions could easily be monitored, and for that reason it was normally not switched on until action had been joined.[128]

To assist in navigation off a dangerous coast, the ships received QH-3, the naval version of the air force's GEE radio navigation system, which enabled ships to fix their position with great accuracy. IFF (Identification Friend or Foe) helped them to confirm the identity of ships encountered at night. A so-called Headache receiver, together with a German speaking operator, monitored enemy voice traffic on radio. To enhance their weapon systems, flashless cordite—a development to which Canadian scientists had made an important contribution—both concealed the ships' positions and preserved their crews' night vision. Tracer ammunition for 4-inch and 4.7-inch guns helped to spot the fall of shot.[129]

Even though they came to be well-equipped for night operations, the first Tunnels, during the training period failed miserably. On the night of 25/26 February 1944, *Tartar*, *Athabaskan*, *Haida*, *Huron*, and the cruiser HMS *Bellona* (senior officer, Captain C.F.W. Norris, RN), found that the radar contacts on which they fired were not ships but rocks, and other echoes that puzzled them turned out to be low flying aircraft of Coastal Command near the French coast. They left behind a burn-

---

126. For a comparison of the relative technical strengths of the destroyers in the flotilla and the development of their night fighting tactics see M. Whitby, "Masters of the Channel Night: The 10th Destroyer Flotilla's Victory off Ile De Batz, 9 June 1944," *Canadian Military History* 1/2

127. D. Howse, *Radar at Sea* (Annapolis 1993), 137-8

128. Adm, *Confidential Admiralty Fleet Order* 477/1944; Adm, Signals Division, "RDF Bulletin No. 6," 3 Mar 1944, PRO, ADM 220/204; N. Friedman, *Naval Radar* (Annapolis 1981), 195; A. Mitchell. "The Development of Radar in the Royal Navy (1935-1945), Part II," in *Warship*, no. 14 (April 1980), 123, 129-30

129. For development of tracer and flashless cordite, see Adm, Director of Gunnery Div, *Gunnery Review*, July 1945, 80-2, DHH 89/235, and Adm, DTSD, "Guide Book of Fighting Experience," Dec 1942, 13, DHH 91/79. For the part played by Canadian research and development see J.P. Baxter, *Scientists against Time* (Boston 1946), 246. Whitby "Masters of the Channel Night," 7-8

ing haystack. Five nights later the same group sortied to intercept a westward-bound convoy escorted by four torpedo boats whose intentions were revealed through Ultra.[130] The cruiser was forced to drop out because of a radar malfunction, so the Tribals continued under the flotilla commanding officer, Commander St. J.R.J. Tyrwhitt, RN, CO of *Tartar*.

Just before midnight on 1 March, while the force was about thirty miles off the French coast, *Tartar*'s Type 276 radar detected eight contacts bearing 180° at ten miles range. Tyrwhitt was nonplussed. After plotting the contacts for about half an hour—at that range they might or might not have been large E-boats, "there being no reason to suppose that the enemy had a similar number of large ships in the area"—Tyrwhitt set a course to evade and reach his designated patrol line. Five minutes after beginning the eastward run down the Brittany coast, radar began to detect various small contacts. At 0227Z *Haida*'s Headache operator monitored the signal "Toni Dora." This signal, as Plymouth Command had deduced from analyzing radio traffic from the Tunnels of the previous October, was the 4th *Torpedobootsflotille*'s executive order for firing torpedoes. Tyrwhitt ordered a 90-degree turn away to port. Nine minutes after resuming the eastward course, *Tartar* monitored another "Toni Dora" command. Tyrwhitt again turned away, attempting—without success—to illuminate the bearing where the contacts were believed to lie. He thought the small radar blips were attacking E-boats and, reasoning that "it was obvious that our presence was well known to the enemy," he led his force back to Plymouth.[131]

After this operation Admiral Leatham replaced Tyrwhitt, who had commanded destroyers through the worst of the Mediterranean operations and who was probably badly in need of a rest, with another experienced British destroyer officer, Commander B. Jones. In his analysis of the operation of 25/26 February, Leatham criticized the decision to return to harbour rather than try to locate the enemy and clearly left the flotilla with an appreciation of the need to be aggressive. In future engagements, the Tribals turned into instead of away from torpedoes and became very determined in their efforts to find and destroy the enemy.[132] Commander DeWolf later recalled, "My feeling at the time was that we had failed to go after some ships, some echoes, so from then on in the back of my mind was if we ever get an echo, we're going to go after it. So if we found one we did. That was just natural fear of criticism."[133]

During March and the first part of April the Tribals went to sea almost daily, either for Tunnels or to cover vessels laying offensive minefields off the coast of Brittany. It was not until the third week in April however that they engaged the enemy. At that time, according to Ultra intelligence received by the OIC, three torpedo boats were expected to escort a small convoy from Lezardrieux west to Brest. On the evening of 25 April, after a Tunnel run the night before had come up empty handed—the convoy had delayed its departure—the cruiser HMS *Black Prince* and the Tribals *Ashanti*, *Athabaskan*, *Haida*, and *Huron*, sailed from Plymouth as Force 26. This Tunnel, unlike the earlier and simpler sorties, also included radar search by a Halifax aircraft along the force's patrol

130. Adm, the OIC, "The Use of Special Intelligence in Connection with Operation NEPTUNE," nd, 18, PRO, ADM 223/287, pt 2

131. *Tartar* ROP, 3 Mar 1944, C-in-C Plymouth, "10th Destroyer Flotilla Report on Tunnel, Night 1/2 Mar 1944," 25 Mar 1944, PRO, ADM 199/532

132. Ibid

133. Interview with H.G. DeWolf, 20 Aug 1987, cited in Whitby, "'Foolin' Around the French Coast': RCN Tribal Class Destroyers in Action, April 1944," in *Canadian Defence Quarterly*, 19/3 (1989), 55

line. Three MTBs were positioned at the eastern end of the line to keep the main body informed of enemy activity. Despite these arrangements, Force 26 was fortunate to engage the enemy.

At 0130Z on 26 April the German 4th *Torpedobootsflotille* under Korvettenkapitän F. Kohlauf, who had been so successful against the first Tunnels in October 1943, received warning of the approaching force from coastal radar when the Allied ships were eighteen miles off the coast. Kohlauf chose to hold his westward course on the assumption that the attackers would continue southward to intercept the convoy, which lay to the west of his three destroyers. But at 0201Z he learned, too late, that Force 26 had altered to the east and was just eleven miles ahead of him on a collision course. By that time the German destroyers were showing up on the British and Canadian ships' radar.[134]

Startled by the proximity of the Allied ships, Kohlauf increased speed and reversed his course. This initiated a long chase that provided the first test of new tactics formulated by Plymouth Command and the 10th Destroyer Flotilla. Traditionally, the Royal Navy had relied upon line-ahead as its night fighting formation, because this had proved the most effective at keeping a force intact during high-speed manoeuvring under limited visibility. In the October 1943 actions the formation had proved unwieldy and lead ships had sometimes masked the radar and guns of those behind. For their part, German destroyers reacted to equal or superior forces by turning, firing torpedoes, and retreating at top speed, initiating a stern chase. It was important therefore to keep the pursuing destroyers' arcs of fire open with forward guns bearing and radar unimpeded. On this occasion two sub-divisions of Tribals were stationed 40 degrees on either bow of *Black Prince*, at a distance of one and a half miles, so that the cruiser could use her 6-inch guns for illumination, and the arcs of fire for the Tribals' 4.7-inch guns would be open.[135]

At 0220Z, *Black Prince* began illuminating the torpedo boats at 13,600 yards, and the destroyers fired for effect seven minutes later, aided by the flashes of enemy gunfire—the German ships did not have flashless cordite—and quickly obtained hits. *T 27* was struck four times in fifteen minutes and slowed to 12 knots, forcing Kohlauf to order her to put into nearby Morlaix. *Haida* and *Athabaskan* detected the disengagement but ignored it as they continued after the other two torpedo boats. This allowed the *T 27* to fire all six of her torpedoes at Force 26 as it swept by. They missed, but *Black Prince* took avoiding action to northward and played no further part in the action. The Tribals kept up the chase, enjoying the advantage of speed over *T 29* and *T 24*, and exploiting a fatal weakness in the German ships: the masking of their radar caused by a blind arc of 30 degrees over the stern. The Tribals had difficulty discriminating targets because they were outside starshell range and the Germans were dropping smoke floats and radar decoys to confuse the picture. Nevertheless, the report from *T 24* after the action stated that "the salvoes were tightly spread and straddled continually." At 0320Z, after receiving a full salvo from either *Haida* or *Athabaskan* that damaged her rudder, *T 29* veered out of control and emerged from smoke about 4000 yards off *Haida*'s starboard bow. The two Canadian ships could not miss at that range, and by 0335Z *T 29* was a mass of flames. Meanwhile, *Ashanti* and *Huron* pursued *T 24* eastward, but

---

134. C-in-C Plymouth to SO Force 26, 25 Apr 1944, DHH 81/520/1650-293/13, "Operations; English Channel"; KTB, 3 Defence Div, 26 Apr 1944, DHH, SGR II 340, PG 73989; KTB, 4th *Torpedobootsflotille*, "Evaluations of Actions Fought by 4th Torpedobootsflotille," DHH 81/520/8000, *Athabaskan* (I)(1944); R. Ostertag, "Torpedo Boats in Action with Destroyers," in *Truppenprasas*, Dec 1980, 4-5, DHH, SGR II/239

135. In night actions, the Tribals often used the 4-inch guns in "X" mount astern, for illumination.

after losing contact made their way back to join DeWolf, who in the absence of *Black Prince* was acting as senior officer.

Four Tribals now concentrated their fire on *T 29*. The unexpected appearance of *Ashanti* and *Huron* disrupted *Haida*'s torpedo attack, and subsequent attempts to finish off the enemy with torpedoes—a total of sixteen were fired at the blazing, immobile ship—ended in complete failure as all missed. The Tribals fared better with gunnery, but with an enormous expenditure of ammunition. For more than three-quarters of an hour, the torpedo boat upheld the reputation of German warships in both world wars for being able to withstand punishment. *T 29* maintained a constant return fire of close-range weapons at the Tribals as they circled her, and endured ceaseless close-range shelling which destroyed the bridge, killing Kohlauf—and ignited a torpedo warhead, blowing the entire torpedo mount overboard.[136] Ultimately, *T 29's* crew scuttled their vessel, many of them losing their lives as they abandoned ship or as shells fell among their life rafts. For the victors there had been dangerous crossfire (DeWolf later found shell fragments with British markings embedded in his golf clubs) and *Huron* and *Ashanti* had collided as they reformed after the action. The destruction of *T 29*—the largest enemy warship yet sunk by Canadian naval forces—became the source of considerable satisfaction, both in the ships' companies and among the staff of Commander-in-Chief Plymouth.[137] In his after-action report, the captain of *Black Prince* noted that "there is little doubt that this minor engagement has done much to enhance the already high morale of the ships and men of the ships companies engaged."[138]

Analysis of this action at the Admiralty was less encouraging. Captain St. J. Cronyn, RN, director of the Tactical and Staff Duties Division, criticized *Black Prince* for turning away from rather than towards the enemy, which would have enabled the ship to avoid the torpedo zone and keep in contact with the enemy. This perhaps overlooked the consideration that the captain of the cruiser, which did not have much sea room, did not know he would lose contact by turning away. Cronyn faulted the Tribals for allowing *T 24* to escape when *T 29*, which was stopped and burning, could easily have been dealt with by one or two of them. There was some validity to this criticism, which reflected mostly on *Ashanti*'s decision to rejoin without DeWolf's knowledge. Cronyn reserved his most scathing comments for the procedural breakdowns in each ship which had led to sixteen torpedoes missing *T 29*, and concluded that "the Commanding Officers of destroyers, and to some extent the Senior Officers of the Force, must be held responsible for the bad torpedo training which resulted in a complete failure in this action of the most effective weapon we possess."[139] Officers on the staff of Plymouth Command and in the destroyers of the 10th Destroyer Flotilla did not share the Admiralty's view about the value of torpedoes in actions of the type they were fighting, and this became a point of contention over the summer.

Whether torpedoes were to be used as the weapon of first choice, one that could if used en masse wreak havoc on enemy formations, or whether torpedoes constituted a weapon of opportunity to

---

136. KTB, 3 Defence Division, 26 Apr. 1944, 9

137. DeWolf interview, 20 Aug 1987, in Whitby, "Foolin' Around the French Coast,"55; Sclater, *Haida* (Markham 1980), 115

138. *Black Prince* ROP, 2 May 1944, 8, PRO, ADM 199/263. For this action, see also KTB, "Evaluation of Action Fought by 4th Torpedobootsflotille"; Adm, *Cruiser and Destroyer Actions English Channel and Western Approaches 1943-1944*, 9-11. The after-action reports of the four Allied destroyers are in LAC, RG 24 (Acc 83-84/167), 695.

139. DTSD min, 27 June 1944, PRO, ADM 199/263

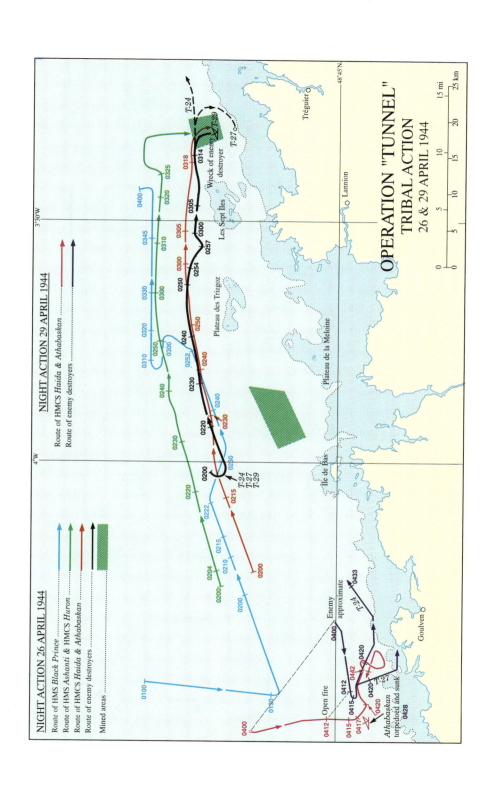

NIGHT ACTION 26 APRIL 1944

Route of HMS *Black Prince* ....
Route of HMS *Ashanti* & HMCS *Huron* ......
Route of HMCS *Haida* & *Athabaskan* ....
Route of enemy destroyers ....

Mined areas

NIGHT ACTION 29 APRIL 1944

Route of HMCS *Haida* & *Athabaskan* ....
Route of enemy destroyers ....

OPERATION "TUNNEL"
TRIBAL ACTION
26 & 29 APRIL 1944

Tréguier

48°45'N

Lannion

Wreck of enemy
destroyer

Les Sept Îles

Plateau des Triagoz

Plateau de la Meloine

Île de Bas

Goulven

Enemy
approximate

Athabaskan
torpedoed and sunk

Open fire

0   5   10   15   20   25 km
0   5   10   15 mi

supplement the ship's main gunnery armament, was disputable. The latter school of thought, to which Admiral Leatham—a torpedo specialist—and Captain Jones subscribed, can be seen as a response to German tactics and technology of the day, especially in the English Channel. In both world wars, when met by equal or superior forces, German destroyers had reacted by turning away, firing a spread of torpedoes, and running for the nearest port. Faced with this situation, Leatham and Jones thought it better that tactics be devised to ensure that their strength—radar-controlled gunnery—was brought to bear in the most effective way as quickly as possible; torpedoes would be used when opportunities presented themselves. This in no way excuses the poor torpedo performance against *T 29*, but it does explain the low priority given to torpedo training.[140]

Huron and *Ashanti* required drydocking to repair their collision damage and *Tartar* was in refit. *Haida* and *Athabaskan* then temporarily took on the full load of 10th Flotilla operations, popularly known on the Lower Deck as "FAFC" or, in polite language, "Foolin' Around on the French Coast."[141] Their next assignment came on the night of 28/29 April. The large invasion exercise Tiger was into its second night. Its screen had been successfully penetrated by E-boats, which had torpedoed two LSTs, killing over seven hundred American soldiers the night before, leading to the requirement for increased vigilance. Plymouth Command helped to provide the close escort for the invasion exercise, and Admiral Leatham stretched his resources to send two steam gunboats, three O class destroyers and three MTBs on patrol lines south of the Channel coast. At the same time he despatched eight MLs to lay mines off Morlaix, as part of Operation Maple, the strategic minelaying plan in support of Operation Neptune, and positioned *Haida* and *Athabaskan* midway across the Channel to provide support for both the exercise and the minelaying operation.[142] At 1940Z, five minutes before the minelaying force passed through the gate and about three hours before the Tribals were due to sail, the OIC informed Leatham that Ultra had revealed that *T 24* and *T 27* had been ordered to proceed from St Malo to Brest to make good repairs from the action three nights earlier.[143] It is uncertain when Leatham received this news, but he clearly thought it too late—or unnecessary—to alter his dispositions. The two Tribals sailed as scheduled, apparently unaware that the nature of their work was to change.

It was a night when anomalous propagation allowed the Combined Operations Room in Plymouth to track by radar the movement of ships across the entire English Channel, including the Elbings as they steamed along the Brittany coast. At 0307Z on 29 April *Haida* and *Athabaskan* were vectored to intercept the German vessels. At 0359Z *Athabaskan* made radar contact in what the Admiralty would later call the ideal position for developing a torpedo attack, but which DeWolf used to launch an attack with his preferred method of radar controlled surface gunnery. This ensured immediate interception and avoided a drawn-out pursuit such as the one two nights before, an important consideration with daylight approaching and ports of refuge close by. DeWolf achieved complete surprise. He straddled the target with the first salvo and met with the usual

140. For further discussion of the torpedo controversy, see Whitby, "The Other Navy at War: RCN Tribal Class Destroyers, 1939-1944," MA thesis, Carleton University 1988.

141. Stuart Kettles, "A Wartime Log: A Personal Account of Life in HMCS *Athabaskan* and as a Prisoner of War," nd, 27, DHH 74/458

142. C-in-C Plymouth to C-in-C Portsmouth (copied to ships involved), 1350B, 28 Apr 1944, DHH 81/520/8000, *Athabaskan* (I)(1944)

143. Adm, "Use of Special Intelligence ... with Operation Neptune"

response—*T 27* and *T 24* turned away and fired torpedoes. DeWolf altered his ships towards the enemy to comb the torpedo tracks, but he limited the turn to 30 degrees so that their after 4-inch guns could continue illuminating with starshell and the forward 4.7s could fire for effect. This also prevented *Haida*'s type 271Q from being "wooded."[144] The enemy torpedo drill was almost as poor as the 10th Flotilla's had been on the 26th—all six of *T 27*'s torpedoes and three of *T 24*'s were fired to the wrong side—but three of *T 24*'s torpedoes were on target. At 0417Z, before the Tribals had completed their turn, *Athabaskan* suffered a torpedo hit that exploded on her port side in the gearing room, located in the hull abaft the engine room. DeWolf laid a smoke screen to cover the stricken ship and continued to chase the Elbings.

In the brief action that ensued *Haida*'s gunnery team exhibited the same proficiency they had shown three nights earlier. *T 27*, the nearest German ship, took two hits along the waterline, and then its fighting power was "severely reduced by hits in quick succession striking the port and starboard quadruple gun mountings as well as the gun plotting station."[145] The torpedo boat sheered out of formation and emerged from a smokescreen into full view of *Haida*. Pulverized by more hits, on fire forward and its steering damaged, *T 27* staggered towards the coast until her captain finally decided to put his ship on the rocks. *Haida* kept firing for another five minutes until 0435Z when it was realized that the target was aground. At 0427Z a powerful explosion had erupted where *Athabaskan* had last been seen. Since contact with the other German destroyer had been lost at 0433Z at 14,000 yards, after a brief search, DeWolf decided to break off the action.[146]

Lieutenant-Commander Stubbs had told DeWolf on radio telephone that the situation in *Athabaskan* looked bleak: "It looks quite serious. Am steering aft." At this stage the main fuel bunkers just abaft the gearing room had erupted into a giant fire, with flames shooting forty to fifty feet in the air, engulfing the entire after part of the ship, including the 4-inch magazine for X turret, and causing pom-pom ammunition to explode in all directions. Stubbs had ordered the ship's company to stand by their abandon ship stations on the upper deck, when a second huge explosion killed almost every man aft of the forward superstructure on the port side, badly burning or hurling overboard those on the starboard side.[147] Burning oil rained over the entire upper deck, inflicting serious burns on sailors who remained on the bridge and forecastle. Survivors believed the ship had been hit by a second torpedo, but the subsequent Board of Inquiry concluded, since no other vessel was known to be in the vicinity, that the explosion was caused by the 4-inch magazine blowing up.[148]

---

144. Whitby, "Masters of the Channel Night," 7

145. Ostertag, "Torpedo Boats," 16

146. DeWolf, "Report of Action," 29 Apr 1944, DHH 81/520/8000, Haida (Prior 1950); KTB, "Evaluation of Action Fought by 4th Torpedobootsflotille"; Adm, *Cruiser and Destroyer Actions*, 12-14

147. The second explosion has been the cause of recent controversy. One historian contends that *Athabaskan* was mistakenly torpedoed by a British MTB, but subsequent research verifies that no RN MTB was in the vicinity and that the second explosion was the result of an internal explosion. See P. Dixon, "'I Will Never Forget the Sound of Those Engines Going Away': A Reexamination into the Sinking of HMCS *Athabaskan*, 29 April 1944," *Canadian Military History* 5/1(1996), 16-25; and M. Whitby, "The Case of the Phantom MTB and the Loss of HMCS *Athabaskan*," *Canadian Military History* 11/3 (2002), 5-14

148. "Summary of Board of Inquiry into the Loss of HMCS *Athabaskan*," 3 May 1944, PRO, ADM 199/263; Whitby, "Foolin' Around the French Coast," 60; J. Watkins, "Actions Against Elbings, April 1944," *Mariner's Mirror* 81/2 (1995), 195-206

All of *Athabaskan*'s boats and carley floats were destroyed, and the survivors who managed to get over the side found themselves in cold and oil-drenched water. Their captain was with them, leading choruses of popular songs like "Wavy Navy Roll Along." Half an hour after the second explosion, *Haida* returned. She stopped engines and waited for eighteen minutes with the way off the ship to allow her sailors to pluck forty-two men from the water. It was a calculated risk of infinite delicacy, so close to the enemy coast and with dawn approaching—the 10th Flotilla was under strict orders to be clear of the coast by daybreak to avoid the threat of air attack—and one that reportedly prompted John Stubbs, from his watery vantage point, to yell out "Get away *Haida*! Get clear!" This selfless gesture has become one of the few heroic traditions that the Canadian navy, noted more for understatement than bravado, has preserved. DeWolf did not in fact hear Stubbs, but by 0515 he needed no prompting. After dropping all of *Haida*'s boats and floats, he shaped course for Plymouth.[149] When he had first learned of *Athabaskan*'s fate, Admiral Leatham had despatched two MTBs to help in the rescue, but he recalled them since dawn was near.[150] Six survivors climbed into *Haida*'s motor cutter, together with three men from *Haida*, and in a demonstration of extraordinary luck and determination crossed the English Channel to safety. Eighty-five men rescued by the Germans became prisoners of war. One hundred and twenty-eight died in this action, among them John Stubbs.[151] On returning to harbour DeWolf, whose ship was now responsible for the destruction of two enemy destroyers within a week, was informed by C-in-C Plymouth that he had been awarded the Distinguished Service Order.

Admiralty reaction to these events was somewhat acerbic: "an unfortunate action in which, quite unnecessarily, we swapped a Tribal for an Elbing." The dispute over tactics again came into question. Captain Cronyn's return to the theme of torpedo training in Plymouth Command received support from the Assistant Chief of Naval Staff (Warfare), who personally brought up the subject with Admiral Leatham. In view of tactical doctrine adopted with notable success by the 10th Flotilla later in the year, it is clear that Leatham and Jones refused to alter their tactics. There was certainly no criticism of *Athabaskan*'s performance under fire, which the Board of Inquiry found to be "in the best traditions of the service." The board did criticize the confidential books officer, who had not followed standing orders to land certain secret publications before the ship sailed. That was a well placed comment because, in fact, some of these publications fell into German hands. When added to statements made by a survivor during interrogation, they provided the enemy with "information of great importance concerning Allied cryptographic procedures."[152]

Tragic as it was, the Allies could afford the loss of one destroyer—the Germans could not. Since their successes against the first Tunnels in October 1943, they had lost five of that type—three to the cruisers *Glasgow* and *Enterprise* in the Biscay action in December 1943 and now two to the

---

149. On reflection, fifty years after the event, Adm DeWolf admitted that his greatest fear, of drifting onto a moored mine, was baseless in the fast-running tides in that part of the English Channel, and that the threat from the air feared by shore authorities was negligible, but at the time the possibility of losing a second Tribal overshadowed such considerations. Videotaped interview by Capt F.C. Frewer, *Seasoned Sailors: Canadian Naval Heritage Videos* (Ottawa 1994).

150. C-in-C, Plymouth to 52nd MTB Flotilla, 29 Apr 1944, DHH 81/520/8000, Athabaskan (I) (1944)

151. Some of them found graves on French soil, and they are still remembered by French people of the region. For a poignant memoir of *Athabaskan* and those who sailed in her, see L. Burrow and E. Beaudoin, *Unlucky Lady: The Life and Death of HMCS* Athabaskan (Toronto 1987).

152. "German War Diary Concerning Documents Captured From HMCS *Athabaskan*," nd, DHH, SGR II/259

10th Destroyer Flotilla. Only *T 24* and four other German destroyers remained in the western Channel and Bay of Biscay, while four older torpedo boats were based at Le Havre. Performance and morale in these forces had declined noticeably after they lost some of their best officers, such as Kolhauf, while a shortage of fuel together with attacks by Allied aircraft and warships seemingly whenever they left harbour had curtailed training. Worse for the Germans, they were vastly outnumbered. By May 1944 reinforcements boosted the strength of the 10th Flotilla to eight destroyers, and dozens of other American, British, Canadian, and other Allied destroyers were being transferred to Plymouth or Portsmouth for invasion duties. The reduction in German destroyer strength meant that the enemy would have fewer warships available with which to mount an effective surface challenge to the coming Allied invasion.[153]

---

153. KTB, Naval Group West, Apr and May 1944, DHH SGR II 340, PG 37579; KTB, "Evaluation of Actions Fought by 4th Torpedobootsflotille"; KTB, 3 Defence Div, Apr 1944, DHH SGR II/340 PG 73989; Whitley, *German Destroyers* , 166

CHAPTER SEVENTEEN

The Assault on Northwest Europe

OPERATION NEPTUNE, the naval component of the Allied invasion of Europe in June 1944, was huge and complex. The armada that crossed the English Channel comprised over 6,900 vessels, including some 1,600 auxiliary and merchant ships required for the build-up phase, 1,213 naval vessels, ranging in size from battleships to midget submarines, and more than 4,100 landing ships or landing craft of one type or another. The RCN supplied only a fraction of the entire force, but among the 444 major warships—from battleships to minesweepers—316 were from the RN, fifty-four from the USN and sixty-three from the RCN. Present at the invasion was the RCN's historical officer, who later characterized the Canadian naval participation in the assault on Normandy as "the culmination of the wartime growth of Canada's navy ... representing the cream of the RCN."[1]

Canadian naval forces in place by mid-May include the following: HMCS *Haida* and *Huron* (*Iroquois*, the third surviving Canadian Tribal, was refitting in Canada), nine River class destroyers, and eleven frigates forming support groups to counter U-boat operations, twenty corvettes responsible for general escort duties, and the 65th Motor Torpedo Boat Flotilla. These forces, depending on their disposition, remained under the direct control of the commanders-in-chief at Plymouth, Portsmouth or Western Approaches. The assault forces proper were under the operational control of Admiral Sir Bertram Ramsay, RN, Allied Commander-in-Chief, Naval Expeditionary Force. The RCN contribution included sixteen Bangor minesweepers, the destroyers *Algonquin* and *Sioux*, the 29th MTB Flotilla, two Landing Ships Infantry (Medium), HMCS *Prince David* and *Prince Henry* (each complete with a Landing Craft Assault flotilla), and three Landing Craft Infantry (Large) flotillas.[2] As seen in Chapter 14, Canada also contributed the personnel for a Beach Commando.[3]

The Tribals, the two Fleet V class destroyers and the MTB flotillas had served their apprenticeship in the months leading up to Neptune. Thanks to hard lessons in the Battle of the Atlantic, the RCN was also in a position to offer combat-tested forces for antisubmarine warfare. This was seen as a vital contribution. Some experts, including operational research scientists

---

1. Lt J. George makes the observation in CNMO Narrative, "The Royal Canadian Navy's Part in the Invasion of France," 9 Jan 1945, DHH 84/230. George was careful to point out that the RCN's contribution was greater than the combined strength provided by the other smaller Allied navies.

2. The thirty LCI(L)s and sixteen LCAs were on loan from the Americans and British but were manned by Canadians (see Chapter 13). DHH, NBM, 11 Nov 1943; Tucker, *Naval Service of Canada* II, 11, 95-6

3. D.G. Chandler and J.L. Collins (eds), *The D-Day Encyclopedia* (New York 1994), 382; S.W. Roskill, *War At Sea, 1939-1945* III, pt 2, *The Offensive, 1st June 1944–114th August 1945* (London 1961), 18-9; E.G. Finlay, *RCN Beach Commando "W"* (Ottawa 1994)

and the head of the Admiralty's Anti-U-boat Division, were predicting merchant ship losses on the scale of twenty to twenty-five a day.[4] That of course would have been unacceptable, and the planners assembled a force of over two hundred antisubmarine vessels, including ten support groups, four of which were Canadian, to counter that threat. North Atlantic convoys adjusted to the situation. The slow convoys of the SC-ONS series were cancelled, while fast convoys, the HX-ON series, were expanded. The only escort groups left in the Mid Ocean Escort Force for the defence of trade convoys were Canadian "C" groups, each with one frigate and four or five corvettes. The frigates in the existing Canadian support groups EG 6 and EG 9, and the destroyers in the newly formed EG 11 and EG 12, formed the principal Canadian antisubmarine contribution to Neptune.[5]

The senior officers of the Canadian support groups were experienced antisubmarine warriors, and as was usual by that time all but one of these were seconded from the Royal Navy. The exception was Commander J.D. Prentice, RCN, of EG 11, who had orchestrated the destruction of *U 501* in September 1941, and had played a foremost part in developing training methods and tactics for escorts in Canadian waters. Both the frigates and destroyers of these support groups were well equipped for ASW, with type 144 asdic if not better, Hedgehog, and in most cases, 10-centimetre radar. The Canadian corvettes assigned to Neptune were, by contrast, indifferently equipped. Most had type 271 radar, but three corvettes had the less effective Canadian-built RXC and SW2C, not a successful combination, and two had not yet undergone modernization to extend the foc's'le and be fitted with Hedgehog and gyro compasses. Like their predecessors in the Mediterranean late in 1942, the corvettes each received six Oerlikon 20mm anti-aircraft mounts to deal with aircraft and E-boats. Most of the ships had been through the work-up period at Somers Isles, Bermuda (see Chapter 20), but the ships' companies generally had far less experience than their counterparts in the support groups.[6]

Advanced training made up to some extent for inexperience. All the ASW vessels—corvettes, frigates, and destroyers—were fresh from work-ups at Western Approaches. These included three or four days of harbour exercises, an anti-E-boat course for captains and navigating officers at the tactical school in Liverpool, and short specialist courses for other personnel. The ships then went to sea for three days of gunnery exercises, culminating in a three-day battle course at Larne, Scotland. Each group also did two day and two night exercises, during which the work-up team subjected them to continual surprise problems. As one corvette officer described it, "the corvettes would have to organize starshell and H.E. fire at towed targets. While carrying out a mock hedgehog attack on a submarine with Mills bombs, a corvette might suddenly be attacked by aircraft splashing live ammunition around the ship at the same time the training officer attached to the ship might let off one of his thunder fire crackers."[7] Rigorous and thorough, these exercises prepared them for all expected forms of attack. Nevertheless, as those who participated in the opera-

---

4.   Adm, D Operational Research (DOR) memo, "The Case for Increasing the Number of A/S Escorts Involved in Overlord," Apr 1944, PRO, ADM 219/120; Hinsley, *British Intelligence in the Second World War* III pt 2, 95-7

5.   "The First Year of Canadian Operational Control in the Northwest Atlantic," nd, 6-10, DHH, 81/520/8280, box 1, v 1

6.   Ships Equipment Charts, DHH, NHS 8000. Deputy Director of Warfare and Training (DWT) memo, "Fitting of Additional Oerlikons in Corvettes," 28 Apr 1944, LAC, RG 24 (Acc 83-84/167), 2137, S 15400-331, pt 1

7.   *Woodstock* ROP, 1 June 1944. LAC, CS161-89-3, RG 24, 11739. CNMO, Narrative B, 61. See also "Information on Proficiency of Corvettes from Work-up Programmes," State of Efficiency and Readiness files, in LAC, RG 24, 6909-6911.

tion would discover, it was impossible to replicate the English Channel's peculiar and difficult asdic conditions, especially in shallow water.

The Canadian minesweepers were a particularly important addition to the force being assembled for Neptune. Minesweepers were indispensable to amphibious landings—fifty-nine of them were involved in the Sicily landings and forty-seven at Salerno—to clear a passage to the landing area, clear the actual approach for the assault, and to maintain a clear area off the beaches. Unopposed, as they had been at Sicily and Salerno, this was a demanding enough task. Much more resistance was expected off Normandy, and minefields were central to the enemy's defence plan. From the beginning of 1944 naval intelligence had monitored signal traffic generated about German minelaying sorties, and since the quality of this intelligence was uneven, planners made the assumption that a continuous mine barrier ran across the Baie de la Seine, seven to ten miles off the coast. It would be necessary to sweep ten corridors through this barrier for safe passage of the assault forces. Minesweepers would therefore be among the first to reach the vicinity of the landing beaches in the face of expectedly strong resistance.[8] Admiral Ramsay expressed great concern over the minesweeping problem. "There is no doubt," he wrote in his diary, "that the mine is our greatest obstacle to success, and if we manage to reach the enemy coast without becoming disorganised & suffering serious losses we shall be fortunate."[9]

When the Canadian minesweeping force became operational at the beginning of May, *Caraquet*, *Cowichan*, *Malpeque*, *Fort William*, *Minas*, *Blairmore*, *Milltown*, *Wasaga*, *Bayfield* and *Mulgrave* (the latter two acting as danlayers) formed the 31st Canadian Minesweeping Flotilla with the CO of *Caraquet*, Commander A.H.G. Storrs, RCNR, in command. The rest of the Canadian Bangors joined British flotillas: *Vegreville*, *Kenora*, *Guysborough* and *Georgian* went to the 14th; *Canso* to the 16th, and *Thunder* to the 4th. For Storrs, being assigned to the Western Task Force, which would lead American rather than Canadian assault groups into the beaches, was a "tremendous disappointment." Nevertheless, the RCN Bangors, some of them newly equipped with the latest electronic navigation aid later known as Decca, were prepared to do their part in clearing a path across the Channel for the assault forces.[10]

RCN forces committed to the actual assault included the Landing Ships Infantry, landing craft, and the Beach Commando. They had been preparing for Neptune for some time but did not come together until the eve of the operation. In fact, the last Canadian Combined Operations unit to be ready for action was Beach Commando W. Personnel first arrived in the UK on 30 October 1943, directly from basic amphibious training in British Columbia, and commenced training in early November at the beach commando training school at Ardentinny, Scotland. The commandos had to learn the elements of their job: how to organize assault beaches and how to ensure the safe and

---

8. German intent was to lay a mine belt along the entire coast of northwestern France and Belgium but differing priorities in the German command structure prevented its completion. See F. Ruge, *Sea Warfare, 1939-1945* (London 1957), 285; Adm; NID, *German Mine Warfare, 1939-1945* (London 1947), 96-9; Adm, the OIC, "The Use of Special Intelligence in Connection with Operation Neptune, Jan1944–Sept 1944," 71-3, PRO, ADM 223/287 pt 2; Hinsley, *British Intelligence* III pt 2, 91-4; Adm, *Operation Neptune: Landing in Normandy* (London 1947), 49

9. Ramsay, PD, 24 Mar 1944, Churchill Archives Center (CAC), Cambridge University, RMSY 8/26. This valuable document has been published in R.W. Love and J. Major, *The Year of D-Day: The 1944 Diary of Admiral Sir Bertram Ramsay* (Hull, UK 1994).

10. Storrs interview, nd, 43, A.H.G. Storrs biog file, DHH

orderly movement of troops, vehicles and stores over the beaches, as well as the clearance of mines, booby traps and other beach obstacles. In April 1944, however, the commander of Force J, Commodore G.N. Oliver, RN, decided that the RCN Beach Commando would not participate in the assault on Normandy because there were sufficient RN units and because W had no signals unit. This was the cause of some bitterness. The Canadians, not informed of the decision, kept on with their training and fully expected to be involved in the early stages of the invasion if not the actual assault itself.[11]

Admiral Ramsay had assumed his command on 25 October 1943 and, along with the army and air force commanders-in-chief, General Sir Bernard Montgomery and Air Chief Marshal Sir Trafford Leigh-Mallory, reported directly to the Supreme Commander, General Dwight D. Eisenhower. Ramsay's responsibility lay in exercising "general command and control over all naval forces other than those providing distant cover" as well as "direct command within an 'assault area' off the French coast." This meant working not only with the British commanders-in-chief of the naval home commands, who would "continue to exercise their normal functions and control, except within the assault area,"[12] but with the American commanders of naval forces involved in the landings. There was a good deal of personal and interservice rivalry among the triumvirate of commanders-in-chief. Ramsay had differences both with his counterparts and other naval commanders, but he never allowed this to interfere with the focus of his preparations. Because he had planned Operation Torch in 1942—Admiral Sir Andrew Cunningham deplored Lord Louis Mountbatten's claim to have made those plans—and Husky in 1943, an operation in which he had also served as the naval commander, Ramsay enjoyed the benefit of being by far the most experienced and capable practitioner in amphibious warfare involved with Operation Neptune.[13]

The navy's role in the invasion of northwest Europe was to ensure "the safe and timely arrival of the assault forces at their beaches, the cover of their landings, and subsequently the support and maintenance and the rapid build-up of our forces ashore." The Eastern Task Force, commanded by Rear-Admiral Sir Philip Vian, RN, supported the British and Canadian landings and the Western Task Force, under Rear-Admiral A.G. Kirk, USN, supported the American landings. Command of the escorts and coastal forces remained with the naval authorities of the British ports at which they were based although some were lent directly to the two task force commanders for the assault phase of the operation. Among the land forces three airborne divisions, to be dropped on the outer flanks of the invasion area across the Vire and Orne Rivers, were to make the initial assault. Subsequently, landings were to take place on five separate beaches: from east to west, the 3rd British Division on Sword Beach at Ouistreham; the 3rd Canadian Division on Juno Beach at Courseulles; the 50th British Division on Gold Beach at Asnelles; the 1st US Division (with a regimental combat team from the 29th US Division attached) on Omaha Beach at St Laurent; and the 4th US Division on Utah Beach at Varrevilles. There were five naval assault forces—S, J, G, O,

---

11. Brooke, "Royal Canadian Navy—Combined Operations Activities," 19 Jan 1944, LAC, RG 24, 1250, 1037-34-7, pt 2; memo, 12 Apr 1944, memo for file of SCNO(L), 19 Apr 1944, CO Beach Commando W to CNMO, 19 June 1944, LAC, RG 24, 11720, CS 33-17-1; A.C. Hampshire, *The Beachhead Commandos* (London 1983), 56-7; Finlay, *RCN Beach Command "W,"* 33-4, 37-9

12. Ramsay, "ON," 10 Apr 1944, ON 1, 1-2, DHH 81/520/1650, Operation Neptune

13. Cunningham to Ramsay, 21 Nov 1942, CAC, RMSY 8/21. For an overview of Ramsay's experience in running amphibious operations, see Love and Major, *Year of D-Day*, xxx-xxxv.

and U—corresponding to each of the five invasion beaches. Assault forces B and L would carry the 7th British Armoured Division and the remainder of the 29th US Infantry Division, respectively, to begin the build-up immediately after the initial assault forces had moved inland.[14]

The massive operation orders for Neptune dealt with twenty-one separate activities, from minelaying and deception to loading schedules and underwater pipelines. The ten flotillas of fleet minesweepers, each with two minesweeping motor launches and three or four danlayers attached, would lead the entire force across the English Channel and into the assault beaches. Fifteen other minesweeping flotillas, primarily made up of smaller yard and motor minesweepers, were available to the task force commanders "to cope with the enemy mining situation in their areas."[15] While moving along the British coast, Neptune shipping would use the swept channels routinely maintained for domestic convoys. From the coastal shipping lanes, four marked channels led down to a swept area Z, five miles in radius, with its centre located some eight miles southeast of the Isle of Wight. From area Z—which was quickly dubbed Piccadilly Circus—eight marked channels, collectively known as the "Spout," led south to the German mine barrier that extended south of latitude 50° North across the mouth of the Baie de la Seine. Beginning at the northern edge of the barrier each of the ten fleet minesweeping flotillas would cut a channel, 400 to 1200 yards wide, while the danlayers marked the boundaries with lighted buoys at one-mile intervals. Once through the mine barrier, the minesweeping flotillas would continue their channels to the lowering positions, some seven to ten miles offshore in the enemy's coastal channel. The minesweepers would then begin their second task: establishing cleared lanes for the bombardment forces and anchorages for the assault ships. Sweeping the fire support lanes would take the flotillas inshore to the limit of deep water, within a mile-and-a-half of the French coast.

After H-Hour (the time at which the landing was to take place) the sweepers would begin the third phase of the plan, progressively widening the ten approach channels until two broad passages had been cleared into the respective task force sectors. Lateral channels would also have to be swept north of the beaches for the larger landing and supply ships. Upon completion of this massive clearance operation the minesweeping forces would have to deal with any mines the enemy laid after the assault. In all, the orders provided for seventy-six separate minesweeping "serials," each of which had to be completed before the next one could be ordered by the respective task force commander. Above all, contact with the enemy was not to be allowed to interfere with the primary task. "The object of each flotilla is to establish a swept channel for the force following it," the orders emphasized. "This force will be committed to a narrow passage through heavily mined waters and must rely solely upon the minesweepers for safety. It is therefore, essential that each flotilla maintains sweeping formation even if heavily engaged."[16]

There was no doubt in anybody's mind that this exposed the minesweepers to the utmost peril. The flotillas were scheduled to enter the German mine belt during the early evening hours of D-1, the day before the landing, when they would be in full view of enemy coastal batteries. Remaining in formation, keeping to rigidly prescribed courses and speeds, they had every expectation of heavy casualties from E-boats and shore batteries. Consequently, one in every three vessels would follow

14.   Ramsay, "ON," ON 1, 2

15.   Ibid, ON 6, 2

16.   Ibid, ON 6, 7

astern to replace losses, leaving six sweepers in each flotilla to clear a passage through the mine-fields and attached danlayers to mark the swept lanes.

Naval gunfire support was to follow up the minesweeping effort. To accompany the assault forces Ramsay had at his disposal seven battleships, two monitors—specialized, shallow-drafted, coastal bombardment vessels mounting twin 15-inch guns in a single turret—twenty-four cruisers and seventy-four destroyers. Half of the 108 warships providing naval gunfire support were from the British Home Fleet, including the Canadian destroyers *Algonquin* and *Sioux*, forty ships were USN, with the remainder being Norwegian, Polish, Free French, and Dutch.[17] *Algonquin* and *Sioux* went to Fire Support Force E, in company with the cruisers HMS *Belfast* (Senior Officer) and *Diadem*, five British fleet destroyers, three Norwegian destroyers and a Free French Hunt class destroyer. In support of Task Force J, taking the 3rd Canadian Infantry Division and the Royal Marines to Juno Beach, their first responsibility was to protect the assault force from enemy surface vessels as it crossed the English Channel. In the event of attack, the transports and landing craft "were to press on and leave an engagement with hostile forces to the escorts." Mines were seen as the main hazard. Ships were to remain within the swept channels, avoid the wake of the ship ahead, and keep a good lookout for swept mines on the surface. Drifting mines were not to be exploded "until it is certain that the enemy is aware of the assault." Similarly, ships were to maintain radar silence throughout the passage, with the exception of intermittent surface warning radar transmissions by the escorts.[18]

Once at their destination, bombarding warships were to neutralize "coast defence and inland batteries capable of bringing fire to bear on the assault beaches or sea approaches until each battery is captured or destroyed," and to engage the beach defences themselves "during the final approach and assault." Thereafter, the bombarding forces would continue to support the army "by the engagement of mobile batteries, counter-attacking formations, defended areas, etc., particularly during that period when the army artillery is not fully deployed."[19] Some historians have been critical of the effectiveness of bombardment but it is important to understand that invasion planners understood that naval forces would not be able to destroy the formidable coastal fortifications under construction in Normandy. In October 1943, the Inter-Service Committee, a combined planning group analyzing the requirements for Operation Neptune, reported, "The best therefore that naval fire can attempt is to put a sufficient density of explosive, spread over the target area, to make the enemy take cover and to demoralize them to such a degree that they will be incapable of recovery in the interval between cessation of fire and the arrival of the assault troops." The report continued, "Passive defences such as obstructions and concrete walls are unlikely to be destroyed by the preliminary bombardment but may be damaged."[20] This would be especially true of the 4.7- and 4-inch guns of destroyers. As it was, Juno received less naval gunfire support than any other sector: for example, both British beaches had five cruisers and thirteen destroyers each, with a

17. Roskill, *War at Sea* III pt 2, 32

18. Cmdre G.N. Oliver, "Operation 'Neptune' Force J Naval Operation Orders" (hereafter ONEAST/J), 1-11, DHH 81/520/1650, Operation Neptune

19. Ramsay, "ON,"ON 8, 1

20. Inter-Service Committee Report, 25 October 1943, App VI, 2. PRO, DEFE 2/1025. The authors thank Mr. Dan Malone for bringing this to their attention. See Daniel P Malone, "Breaking Down the Wall: Bombarding Force E and Naval Fire Support on JUNO BEACH", (MA thesis, University of New Brunswick, 2005).

Commander A.H.G. Storrs, RCNR, whose skill and resolve was in
large part responsible for the 31st Minesweeping Flotilla's success
in Operation Neptune. (DND PMR 93-396)

Minesweeping gear was a complicated apparatus whose operation was strenuous, to say the least. Here sailors are lowering the multi-plane "Kite" overboard; the paravane is already in the water. Note the depth charges, as minesweepers were an integral part of the war against the U-boat. (DND NP 1415)

Two MTBs of the RCN's 29th Motor Torpedo Boat flotilla in the summer of 1944. Note that while *MTB 466* (top) has had her torpedo tubes returned, the other boat still carries the depth charge racks, which, much to the flotilla's chagrin, were fitted to counter fast German midget submarines that never proved a reality. (DND JT 309)

Men of The Highland Light Infantry of Canada of the 3rd Canadian Infantry Division's reserve 9th Brigade board Landing Craft Infantry (Large) of the RCN's 262nd Flotilla for the invasion of Normandy. (LAC PA206494)

further two battleships and one monitor in position on Sword's eastern flank to engage targets east of the Dives River. In contrast, the Juno beaches defences were expected to require the least attention, but the inherent mobility of warships meant that naval gunfire could be redirected from one beach to another in an emergency.[21]

To observe the fall of shot from the air, fifty-two pairs of specially trained flights of Mustang, Spitfire, and Seafire fighters operated above the beaches with one aircraft observing and the other serving as escort. On the ground, thirty-nine Forward Observers Bombardment—typically an artillery officer with a naval communications rating in tow—were to land with the Anglo-Canadian forces to report the army's priorities to the warships. Since the detailed fire plan only applied to the initial stages of the assault, primarily beach defences that were easily identified from off shore, close cooperation was only required to engage targets of opportunity once the troops moved inland. When fire support was required, the forward observers would contact the army Bombardment Liaison Officer aboard the individual warship or headquarters ship. He would then explain the military situation ashore to the gunnery team and help them interpret coordinates. The warship would reply with either direct fire if the target was in sight, or more often, with indirect fire, in which case the FOB would supply the necessary grid coordinates, observe the fall of shot, and pass corrections as required.[22]

The task of both the minesweeping and bombarding forces was of course to clear a path for the actual assault landing on the far shores. The first assault wave would be led into the beaches by amphibious duplex drive (DD) tanks that had been launched from Landing Craft Tank (LCTs) some 5000 to 6000 yards off shore. Touching down five minutes before H-Hour, the DD tanks were to be followed as closely as possible by an assortment of landing craft carrying special equipment, including armoured vehicles Royal Engineer (AVREs), as well as "funnies"—tanks variously fitted with such items as flails to detonate mines, bulldozer blades, or fascines to overcome obstacles. The assaulting infantry would touch down at H-Hour itself, disembarking from the Landing Craft Assault that had carried them from the Landing Ships Infantry anchored some seven miles from the beaches. LCTs fitted with banks of rockets, or carrying self-propelled artillery that could fire on the beach defences during the run-in, would provide added support.[23]

The LSI(M)s HMCS *Prince Henry* and *Prince David* carried elements of the reserve battalions of the 3rd Canadian Infantry Division's assault formations, the 7th and 8th Canadian Infantry Brigades; their LCA flotillas were not scheduled to land until some forty-five minutes after H-Hour. The Landing Craft Infantry, meanwhile, transported follow-up units. Although four of the 260th Flotilla's eleven LCIs were to remain anchored at Southampton as a reserve, the remaining vessels would be among the first LCIs in the Eastern Task Force to touch down, landing engineer and pioneer companies attached to the 7th Brigade at H+1 hour. The twelve LCIs of the 262nd Flotilla carried the troops of the 3rd Division's reserve brigade, the 9th, and would not be landing until the

---

21. Roskill, *War at Sea* III, pt 2, 31-2

22. "Standardized Bombardment Procedure," nd, PRO, ADM 1/16040; Adm, "Gunnery Review: Normandy Bombardment Experience," Feb 1945, 51, DHH 81/285; Amphibious Warfare Headquarters, *History of the Combined Operations Organization 1940-1945* (London 1956), 125-31; Chief of Combined Operations Staff, *The Manual of Combined Operations* (London 1950), 68-9; Roskill, *War at Sea* III, pt 2, 32-3

23. Roskill, ibid, 19, 36-7

two assaulting brigades had moved inland some two to three hours after H-Hour. The seven LCIs of the RCN's third flotilla, the 264th, had a similar job but were attached to Force G in the Gold sector and would be landing troops of the 50th British Infantry Division's reserve brigade, the 56th, several hours after the initial assault.[24]

Some enemy opposition could still be expected on the beaches by the time the RCN's landing craft came ashore, particularly for the LCAs and the 260th Flotilla's LCIs. However, the greatest apparent danger facing the sailors was beach obstacles. "The types of obstacles which will be encountered are," according to Force J's operation orders:

> (a) "Element C," a steel obstacle in "gates" about eight feet in height and ten feet in width strongly buttressed on the landward side;
>
> (b) "Hedgehog," made of lengths of six inch angle-iron joined in the centre and forming a tripod obstacle approximately six feet high;
>
> (c) "Tetrahedra," a pyramid obstacle made of steel bars, about three feet high;
>
> (d) Stakes of wood eight to ten feet long and about ten inches in diameter driven into the beach to a depth of three to four feet.
>
> It is known that Teller mines and [artillery] shells adapted to explode on contact are attached to the tops of many of these obstacles.
>
> The order in which these obstacles are likely to be sited is from seaward "Element C"; Stakes; "Hedgehogs" and "Tetrahedra" in rows from 200 yards out to the high water mark. The Stakes may be sited either to seaward of the "Tetrahedra" or with them.[25]

On Juno Beach, the initial assault waves of LCA were scheduled to "touchdown in front of these obstacles, on Mike Sector about 450 yards and on Nan Sector about 350 yards from the high water mark."[26] Royal Canadian Engineers driving bulldozers would also be landing with the assaulting Group 312 "to clear on Mike Sector, at the junction of the beaches, a minimum gap of 600 yards and on Nan Green in the centre, a minimum gap of 200 yards from seaward through the obstacles. Their responsibility is solely the clearance of obstructions above the tide level." Recent photographic reconnaissance had revealed that the obstacles were more widely spaced than previously known, and therefore the operation orders allowed "for craft to touch down in emergency between the obstacles." Nonetheless, Group 312 was supposed to beach to seaward of the obstacles and prepare gaps for following groups. "Obstacles can and should be rammed at full speed in emergency, however; but only as a last resort since some of them are mined."[27] Unfortunately, this part of the operation would demonstrate the truth of the military axiom that plans seldom survive contact with the enemy.

The vast invasion armada presented a fat target for the *Luftwaffe*, and every fighter aircraft in Britain had a role to play covering the various forces taking part in Neptune and Overlord. But by now, as a result of a well-planned air offensive, the German air force in the west was practically

24.   CNMO, "The RCN's Part in the Invasion," 93

25.   ONEAST/J

26.   Ibid

27.   Ibid

spent, and on D-Day its presence over the invasion beaches proved to be negligible.[28] German naval forces were another matter altogether, but the Neptune planners were able to assess this threat with some precision, thanks to special intelligence. When in March 1944 they were drawing up the disposition of forces required to prevent enemy attack on the flanks, the *Kriegsmarine* had available four large Narvik class (2600 tons) and one smaller (1600 tons) ex-Dutch destroyers in Biscay ports, and four Elbing (1300 tons) and five *Möwe* class (920 tons) torpedo boats at Le Havre and Cherbourg. The German motor torpedo boat forces—judged to be the most serious surface threat to Neptune shipping—were estimated to consist of seventeen E-boats at Cherbourg and a further thirty based in ports from Den Helder to Dieppe. The remaining *Kriegsmarine* units, some 200 M class minesweepers, R-boats (motor minesweepers), and *Sperrbrechers* (merchant vessels heavily armed as flak ships), did not represent a serious threat to the success of Operation Overlord.[29]

The threat had diminished materially by the beginning of June. By that time two of the four large Narvik destroyers were undergoing refit or repair in the Gironde, and two *Möwe* class torpedo boats had been sunk or put out of action; *Greif* was sunk by an RCAF Albacore of 415 Squadron and *Kondor* was badly damaged by a mine in the Baie de la Seine on 24 May while steaming from Cherbourg to Le Havre.[30] As will be recalled (Chapter 16), the 10th Destroyer Flotilla had also inflicted further damage by sinking *T 27* and *T 29* in April. German destroyer strength now amounted to the following: three operational ships of the 8th *Zerstörerflotille* in the Gironde, *Z 32*, *Z 24*, and the ex-Dutch *ZH 1*; the Elbing *T 24* at Brest; and the four ships of the 5th *Torpedobooteflotille*, *Falke, Jaguar, Möwe,* and *T 28* at Le Havre. Two E-boat flotillas, the 5th and 9th *Schnellbooteflotille* with fourteen operational boats and seven non-operational, were at Cherbourg, the 4th flotilla with eight operational boats was at Boulogne, and the 2nd flotilla at Ostend had five operational boats and two on passage from Ijmuiden. Twelve additional boats remained at Ijmuiden. E-boats had attacked Allied forces training off Slapton Sands on 27 April, sinking two Landing Ships (Tank) and damaging another, at the cost of more than seven hundred lives. Nevertheless, the effectiveness of the *Kriegsmarine* in the Channel was severely limited. Admiral Dönitz was to recall in his memoirs that "the losses and damage we sustained were so severe that even the maintenance of a permanent patrol line, let alone any reconnaissance sortie into enemy coastal waters, was out of the question, if we wished to avoid expending such meagre forces as we had before ever the enemy attempted to invade."[31]

U-boats were something of an unknown quantity. Nine *Schnorkel* and twenty-seven conventional boats lay in Biscay ports, and a further twenty-two not yet fitted with the *Schnorkel* were based in southern Norway. Five more *Schnorkel* and seven more conventional boats were on passage from Norway to the Atlantic.[32] Cassandra-like warnings about the submarine menace aside—recall that some operational analysts warned that U-boats might sink twenty to twenty-five ships a day—the strong antisubmarine forces assembled by June proved equal to the task of meeting that threat.

28. See Greenhous, *The Crucible of War*.

29. Ramsay, "ON," ON 1, app VII, 9

30. Greenhous, *Crucible of War*, 463; M.J. Whitley, *Destroyer!*, 206; Hinsley, *British Intelligence* III, pt 2, 161

31. Dönitz, *Memoirs*, 395

32. Hinsley, *British Intelligence* III, pt 2, 156; Roskill, *War at Sea* III, pt 2, 56

German naval forces in northwest Europe were under Vizeadmiral Theodor Krancke, naval commander of *Marinegruppe West*, whose headquarters were in Paris. Krancke appreciated that "the area between Cherbourg and Le Havre was exposed more particularly to invasion than other stretches of the European coast line for three main reasons," which he identified as:

1. The two principal harbours of Le Havre and Cherbourg could be outflanked by a landing in the Seine Bay.

2. The Cotentin Peninsula provided shelter against the prevailing westerly winds.

3. The outlying rocks did not form any real obstruction to landings as not only were there long stretches of beach clear of rocks but many of the offshore rocky ledges were submerged at high water sufficiently to allow shallow draught vessels to pass over them.[33]

After analyzing Allied shipping movements, tidal data, and other intelligence, Krancke actually predicted in his war diary for April 1944 that the expected invasion would take place in Normandy in the early part of June.[34] Krancke backed away from that assessment over the next five weeks, perhaps because the *Wehrmacht* considered the Baie de la Seine to be unsuitable for invasion in view of the rock formations off the beaches, and thought that the Somme-Boulogne area or the north coast of Brittany were more likely areas for the assault. This assessment prevailed, and the coastal defences in the Baie de la Seine area were accorded less attention than the other sites. Krancke attempted to rectify this weakness by an extensive coastal mining campaign in the Baie de la Seine, but his efforts were consistently frustrated by Allied air activity, which hampered both the transport of mines to naval bases and actual mining operations themselves.[35]

Knowing the disposition of Krancke's forces, senior Allied naval commanders realized that the initial passage of the invasion armada was unlikely to be contested by the *Kriegsmarine*. Despite that, and their preponderance of strength, they took nothing for granted. Fifteen MTB flotillas flanked the invasion force to defend against E-Boats and the phantom "W-boats" (see Chapter 16), which planners were assuming would be the greatest threat to the vast numbers of vessels lying off the beaches. Allied air forces could maintain control of the flanks of the beachhead during the day, but at night the job would fall to destroyers and MTBs. The RCN's 29th Flotilla of Shorts, MTBs equipped with depth-charges instead of torpedoes, was to patrol area Tunny, northeast of the British Assault Area.[36] The 65th Flotilla's Dogboats based in Plymouth Command, would be one of the groups of destroyers and MTBs helping to counter possible E-boat sorties against the vulnerable convoys that would be moving supplies to the beachhead. The Dogboats were to carry out nightly patrols along the east and south coast convoy routes. Later, taking advantage of Ultra intelligence, it was anticipated that these forces could commence offensive operations against the enemy's Cherbourg–St Malo–Channel Islands coastal traffic.[37]

---

33. Adm Historical Branch (AHB), "The RAF in Maritime War," volume V, "The Atlantic and Home Waters, The Victorious Phase," 5, DHH, 79/599

34. KTB, *Marinegruppe West*, April 1944

35. AHB, "RAF in Maritime War" V, 5-6

36. Adm, *Operation "Neptune"* I, 108-9

37. Ramsay, "ON," ON 5; Adm, *Operation Neptune*, I, 43-5

On the eastern flank the coastal forces were also bolstered by four fleet destroyers assigned to Dover Command to carry out individual patrols in mid-Channel between Dungeness and Worthing. In Plymouth Command, the 10th Flotilla was now quite a formidable force. Following the loss of *Athabaskan*, which temporarily left *Haida* as the only fully operational ship in the group, *Tartar*, *Ashanti* and *Huron* had returned from refit and repair in May. Two British and two Polish destroyers (a fifth Tribal, HMS *Eskimo*, the J class destroyer HMS *Javelin*, the Polish N class destroyer *Piorun*, and the large prewar Polish destroyer *Blyskawica*) then joined the four flotilla veterans. When they arrived, the flotilla formed two divisions: the four original Tribals in the 19th and the newcomers in the 20th. In order to intercept any German surface vessels heading for the invasion beaches from their Biscay bases, Admiral Sir Ralph Leatham, C-in-C Plymouth Command, assigned the 19th Division to patrol north of the Channel Islands on the Hurd Deep patrol. The less experienced 20th Division would patrol some fifty miles north-northwest of Ushant. Four USN destroyers, meanwhile, would patrol south of the Force U convoy route.[38]

Of the ten support groups assembled for antisubmarine operations in the western Channel and its approaches, the River class destroyers in EGs 11 and 12 were among the four groups assigned to Plymouth Command, and the frigates of EGs 6 and 9 were among the remaining six groups, controlled by C-in-C Western Approaches. Both the antisubmarine and surface vessel screens on Neptune's flanks were integrated with the air forces being provided by the RAF's Coastal Command. No. 19 Group, covering the southwestern approaches, would have twenty-one squadrons available for antisubmarine operations, including three from the RCAF. These aircraft were to be employed in a series of flexible "box" patrols that could be shifted, either individually or as a whole, up-Channel towards the invasion area—much as a cork might be pushed into a bottle. Referred to as "Cork" patrols, those nearest the French coast were deemed most important since "the enemy will almost certainly move his U/Boats under the cover of his fighters and shore defences."[39] To counter the surface threat, Coastal Command also deployed five Beaufighter strike squadrons and a mixed Albacore/Swordfish squadron on the eastern flank—the latter to fly anti-E-boat patrols—and two Beaufighter strike squadrons, including the RCAF's No. 404, on the western flank. Although the strike squadrons began training in the technique of night attacks, they remained most effective when there was sufficient daylight to mount a coordinated assault. As a result, the destroyers of the 10th Flotilla would be charged with the responsibility for intercepting any of the German destroyers based on the Bay of Biscay that might attempt to break into the Channel at night.[40]

The precise date and timing of the assault, meanwhile, would be determined by potentially contradictory factors: airborne divisions wanted some moonlight, air forces a period free of fog, while the navy needed darkness to approach and daylight to provide observed supporting fire. Landing at low tide gave assaulting troops wider beaches to cross but also exposed the mined beach obstacles that, if not destroyed, could tear landing craft apart. The compromise was to approach in darkness and assault in daylight during the early stages of a rising tide. In June 1944 there were two

38.   Adm, ibid, I, 45-6

39.   "Directive on the Role of Coastal Command in Overlord,"18 Apr 1944, PRO, AIR 15/293

40.   Ibid; Greenhous, *Crucible of War* III, 407, 464-5

periods of favourable conditions for crossing the Channel when the moon was not full and there would be a low tide soon after dawn: from the 2nd to the 6th and from the 17th to the 21st.[41] The initial plan was to land early on the morning of 5 June. Given the size of the invasion fleet and its dispersion in ports around Great Britain, the Neptune armada had to be put in motion hours and in some cases even days before the assault. Amongst the first forces to sail, on 31 May from Oban, Scotland, was the corvette HMCS *Trentonian*, leading the first section of twenty-four "Corncobs"— block ships that would be sunk to provide shelter while the Mulberry Harbours were being prepared—bound for the eastern area.[42]

Late on 3 June, in an attempt to effect the landings on 5 June, Eisenhower gave the orders for the invasion force to sail. Ramsay recorded in his diary that "the weather chart was unpromising ... [but] Ike was over impressed with the frightful results of postponement [since the disseminated Neptune plan would have to spend two weeks on shore when the troops and sailors were disembarked] & it was desired *not* to postpone till the last moment." Meeting with his senior subordinates at Supreme Headquarters Allied Expeditionary Force (SHAEF) the next morning at 0415, when the weather forecast proved to be just as bad as had been feared, Eisenhower directed that D-Day be delayed for twenty-four hours. The 6th, as already noted, would be the last available day until 17 June.[43]

The order recalling the Neptune fleet went out an hour later, and only one 133-ship convoy of Force U missed the signal. Group U2A was still steaming for the Normandy beaches at 0900 hours on 4 June when two destroyers were despatched at top speed to turn the wayward convoy around. It did not regain its anchorage in Weymouth Bay until the early morning hours of 5 June, just in time, as it happened, to put back to sea.[44] Eisenhower and his commanders-in-chief had decided late the previous night to continue to proceed with the operation, in spite of the risks. At 0415 on 5 June orders went out again to put the invasion fleet in motion towards the Normandy coast. This time "the prophets came in smiling, conditions having shown a considerable improvement," wrote Ramsay in his diary, and:

> The wind was still fresh & it is clear that Forces will have an uncomfortable initial journey, improving as the day proceeds. Thus has been made the vital & crucial decision to stage & start this great enterprise which will, I hope, be the immediate means of bringing about the downfall of Germany's fighting power & Nazi oppression & an early cessation of hostilities. I am under no delusions as to the risks involved in this most difficult of all operations & the critical period around H Hour when, if initial flights [of landing craft] are held up, success will be in the balance. We must trust in our invisible assets [such as Ultra decrypts] to tip the balance in our favour & to allow the landings to proceed without interruption.[45]

---

41. B. McAndrew, D. Graves, and M. Whitby, *Normandy 1944: The Canadian Summer* (Montreal 1994), 18

42. HMC Ships *Mayflower* and *Drumheller* took a section of sixteen block ships to the western area, while *Rimouski* and *Louisbourg* took the remaining twenty ships that were split up between the two assault areas. *Camrose, Baddeck, Prescott, Alberni, Mimico, Lunenburg,* and *Calgary* would provide additional escort to various tows from the south coast of England on 6, 7 and 8 of June.

43. Ramsay, *Year of D-Day*, 81-2; Barnett, *Engage the Enemy More Closely*, 806-7

44. Barnett, ibid, 808

45. Ramsay, *Year of D-Day*, 83

As will be seen, General Eisenhower's decision proved not only courageous, but fortunate. A far more powerful gale that hit the English Channel during the fall-back period for the assault on 19 to 21 June, would either have caused grievous losses or yet another postponement, either of which might have thrown the success of the invasion into doubt.

As it was, the postponement caused the four RCN Bangors with the 14th Minesweeping Flotilla (MSF), *Georgian*, *Guysborough*, *Kenora*, and *Vegreville*, to endure an extra twenty-four hours at sea. Having spent all of 4 June sweeping an approach channel for the Force U convoys that would be using assault channels 1 and 2, Sub-Lieutenant W.G. Morrow, RCNVR, gunnery officer aboard *Georgian*, recalled that when the "rough sea and dull weather caused us to be called back, we sailed for Portland Bill ... in the dark and, by now, in the rain. On reaching our designated position off Portland Bill, however, the fateful orders came again, we were to turn about, and it was on again, just a day late."[46] HMCS *Canso*, attached to the 16th MSF, was more fortunate, having also spent the early hours of 4 June sweeping the Force U approach channel to the mine barrier but, when no mines were encountered, it was immediately able to turn back to Plymouth when the flotilla received the recall message at 0840.[47]

When the message to resume Operation Neptune went out early on 5 June, the ten RCN minesweepers of the 31st MSF in Portland Harbour weighed anchor at 0230 and once again headed through heavy seas for Area Z south of the Isle of Wight, led by *Caraquet*.[48] The flotilla spent most of 5 June "backing and filling" in Area Z, keeping ahead and to seaward of convoys approaching from the west. The RCN Bangors with the 14th and 16th flotillas again swept the area in which they had encountered mines the previous day, executing two additional passes northwards to widen the searched channel for Force U, but did not cut any more mines.[49] The 4th MSF, to which HMCS *Thunder* was attached, was assigned to sweep assault channel 4. Made up primarily of coal-burning "Smokey Joes," of First World War vintage, the 4th MSF had weighed anchor at 0200 hours. All four flotillas of the Western Task Force were in position to head south from Area Z and begin the approach sweep to the assault channels by 1730.[50]

Having the greatest distance to travel to the assault beaches, Force U was the first to get under way on 5 June. The Force U commander, Rear-Admiral G.P. Moon, USN, left Portland in the attack transport USS *Bayfield* at 0930 hours and set course directly for the entrance to assault channels 1 and 2, being joined on passage by the convoys of landing craft and bombarding warships that were headed for Utah Beach. Even the weary Group U2A, whose late recall forced many of the commanding officers to remain continuously on their bridges for seventy hours prior to H-Hour,

---

46. W.G. Morrow manuscript, nd, 86, DHH 86/167

47. "Report of the Allied Naval Commander-in-Chief, Expeditionary Force, on Operation on Neptune," I, Oct 1944, 143-4, DHH 83/105 (hereafter Ramsay Report on Neptune)

48. While getting under way, *Wasaga* accidentally went astern into *Bayfield*, caused a break in the latter's stem plate, and holed her below the waterline in two places. Since *Bayfield* carried seventy dans and all of the flotilla's starboard lights, needed to mark the swept channel, it was fortunate that her engine room personnel were able to keep the ship seaworthy by shoring up No 1 bulkhead, and rigging a collision mat over her holes. *Caraquet* ROP, June 1944, LAC, RG 24, 11740, CS 162-15-3; Collision report of HMCS *Bayfield*, nd, LAC, RG 24, 11554, D02-12-0; Collision report of HMCS *Wasaga*, nd, LAC, RG 24, 11558, D025-5-31

49. "Minesweeping Diary of the WTF," nd, 5, PRO, Adm 179/474

50. *Thunder* ROP, June 1944, LAC, RG 24, 11742, CS 162-34-3; CNMO, "RCN's Part in the Invasion," 79-80

managed to get all but seven of its 128 LCTs to the beach on time.[51] With a much shorter distance to travel to the assault channels, the convoys in the Eastern Task Force sailed later. Scheduled to land their collection of engineers, pioneers, medical and assorted other beach personnel on Juno Beach only ninety minutes after H-Hour, the seven LCIs of the 260th Flotilla were the first RCN assault craft to sail, leaving Southampton at 1200 hours and making their way south through the thousand-odd ships and craft crowding the Solent. Despite the congestion, the only incident occurred when an LST bumped *LCI 117*, punching a one-foot gash in the starboard side at deck level. They were followed two hours later by the twelve LCIs of the 262nd Flotilla and their 2,106 passengers from the reserve 9th Canadian Infantry Brigade. The seven LCIs of the 264th Flotilla, carrying 1227 soldiers of the 56th British Infantry Brigade, did not sail until 1925. Being part of Force G, the 264th was routed to the west of the Isle of Wight and reached the open sea at 2300.[52]

By virtue of their greater speed the Canadian LSIs were able to delay their departure until after 2100 even though their troops would be landing ahead of those in the LCIs. *Prince Henry* with 529 soldiers on board, primarily from the reserve battalion of the assaulting 8th Canadian Infantry Brigade—Le Régiment de la Chaudière—weighed anchor off Cowes at 2110 and was followed, thirty minutes later, by *Prince David* and its 528 embarkees from the 7th Canadian Infantry Brigade, which included the reserve company of the Canadian Scottish Regiment. The first bombardment destroyer of Force J to sail was HMCS *Algonquin* at 1815. Her sister ship *Sioux* followed through Spithead Gate four-and-a-half hours later.

At 1735 the Bangors of the RCN's 31st Flotilla, which had been marking time south of Area Z for most of the afternoon, altered course for the Normandy beaches. Ten minutes later, advancing at the prescribed speed of 7.5 knots, they streamed port sweeps and took up G formation as they made their way to the "start of sweep" position at the entrance to assault channel 3. Although a search sweep of these waters was not required by the operation orders, they did so to ensure that their gear was working properly. G formation put each ship 800 yards astern and about 200 yards to port of the ship ahead and has been compared to the positioning of snowplows clearing an airport runway. At the head of the flotilla was the minesweeping motor launch *ML 454* towing a single sweep to protect *Caraquet* against shallow mines.[53]

Caraquet, *Fort William*, *Wasaga*, *Cowichan*, *Minas*, and *Malpeque* constituted the actual sweeping formation, with each ship sailing just inside the outer sweep limit of the ship ahead. The starboard danlayer, HM Trawler *Gunner*, was astern of *Fort William*, with *Bayfield*, acting as centreline danlayer, following behind *Cowichan*, and the port danlayer, HMT *Green Howard*, trailing *Malpeque*. Following the formation in the centre of the swept channel were the spare Bangors *Milltown*, *Blairmore*, and *Mulgrave* (the latter serving as a general utility vessel), and two spare motor launches. In this formation the flotilla would cut a swath 1200 yards wide, with the outside dans being laid 150 yards inside the swept area, giving a navigable lane of 900 yards for assault channel number 3.[54]

---

51. Adm, *Operation "Neptune,"* I, 83

52. CNMO, "RCN's Part in the Invasion," 84-5

53. M. Whitby, "There Must Be No Holes in Our Sweeping: The 31st Canadian Minesweeping Flotilla on D-Day," *Canadian Military History* 3 (Spring 1994), 64; Storrs, "Remarks on Minesweeping Sections of the RCN's Part in the Invasion," 30 Nov 1945, DHH 84/230

54. CNMO, "RCN's Part in the Invasion," 72-4

Electronic navigation aids allowed a remarkable degree of precision. The sweepers had laid ten underwater sonic buoys on the night of 31 May/1 June, at a depth of about thirty fathoms, to provide accurate reference points at the head of each assault channel. QH, the naval version of GEE already in use by the Tribals in the 10th Flotilla, measured the differences in time for radio pulses from three or four shore-based transmitters to reach the ship. This gave an accurate measurement of the distance from each transmitter and allowed a cross-bearing to be plotted on a grid or lattice chart. QM, later known as Decca, measured differences in phase, rather than time, of radio signals from three transmitters. Only nineteen preproduction sets were available for minesweeping leaders and other key ships but they provided Lieutenant-Commander Storrs with "positions of far greater accuracy than QH [which was jammed, possibly by the flotilla's own radio countermeasures], and operated satisfactorily throughout the first 36 hours of the invasion."[55]

At 1834 on 5 June, five miles from the mine barrier and about forty miles south of Area Z, the 31st Flotilla checked its position at the beginning of the assault channel and dropped a green flashing dan. Less than half an hour later the minesweepers entered the mine barrier and altered course slightly to the south-southeast to pass through its eight-mile width. The swept channel followed a series of gentle doglegs that required periodic minor course adjustments. They were in clear sight of Point Barfleur on the Cherbourg Peninsula and within radar range of the assault beaches while there were still three hours of daylight remaining on D-1. The 14th Minesweeping Flotilla, clearing channel 2, "was in sight of the French coast from 1957B on 5th June and before dark could distinguish individual houses ashore." Much to everyone's surprise, the approaching minesweepers were "completely disregarded by the enemy."[56] Sub-Lieutenant Morrow felt that the lack of German reaction "was almost unbelievable but I credit it with the enemy assuming it was just a feint, another one of the routine sweeps that they had become accustomed to."[57] As the flotilla swept through the minefield, the danlayers went to work. At one-mile intervals, as indicated by taut-wire measuring gear, or approximately every seven-and-a-half minutes, a dan buoy with seventy-five fathoms of wire shackled to it and weighted with two 175-pound and one or two 60-pound blocks had to be heaved over the side. These dans flew a small flag and displayed a light—red on the channel's starboard edge and white to port—thus giving "a fairyland look to the whole area of sea between the Isle of Wight and the beaches."[58] At turning points in the channel, they positioned special dans fitted with "a white flashing and red occulting light so arranged that no two adjacent channels had lights of the same characteristic."[59] After the eighth dan was laid at the end of the mine barrier at 2010, the 31st Flotilla altered course to the south-southwest and began to sweep the eighteen miles to the terminal point of the assault channel, about nine miles from the beach.[60]

55. Storrs, "Remarks on Minesweeping"; "Navigational Aspects of the Passage and Assault," Sep 1944, "Extracts from Reports on Navigational Aids used in Operation Neptune," 31 July 1944, "Compilation of Verbal and Written Reports on the Accuracy of QH, QM and Type 970 during Operation Neptune," nd, "Analysis and Compilation of Reports on the Value and Accuracy of QH, QM, and Type 970 in Operation Neptune," nd, PRO, ADM 1/16664; Ramsay Report on Neptune, 10, 114

56. "Summary of Naval Reports on Operation Neptune,"nd, 166, DHH 83/185

57. Morrow ms, 87

58. P. Elliott, *Allied Minesweeping in World War 2* (Annapolis 1979), 111

59. Storrs, "Remarks on Minesweeping"

60. *Caraquet* ROP; CNMO, "RCN's Part in the Invasion," 74; "An Investigation into a Time Discrepancy Concerning the 31st Minesweeping Flotilla and Operation "Neptune," 5-6 June 1944," nd, DHH 81/520/8000, Malpeque

At 2110, in anticipation of the expected reversal of the tidal current which, until the high water mark was reached at 2200, had been running from west to east, the flotilla prepared to recover their sweeps and redeploy from G to port to G to starboard. Aided only by very dim station-keeping lights, each of the sweeping Bangors recovered their port sweeps in succession from the rear and formed a single line ahead behind *Caraquet*'s sweep. Turning 180 degrees, the flotilla re-entered the channel and headed north for an hour before reversing course once again to the south and streaming their sweeps to starboard. Upon reaching the last danbuoy in the channel at 2245 hours, they resumed G formation and continued cutting the assault channel from where they had left off. With the exception of one danbuoy that was inadvertently cut while re-entering the channel, the manoeuvre was completed without incident, a mark of marvellous ship handling. The time it consumed was allowed for in the operation orders and allowed the slower landing craft flotillas to close the distance between themselves and the minesweepers so that the invasion fleet would arrive off the Normandy coast in the proper formation at dawn.[61]

The lack of enemy reaction, and mines, was ascribed by Admiral Dönitz to the aggressive Allied naval activities in the months before D-Day. Indeed, the only mines cut during the assault phase were swept by the 18th and 9th Flotillas in assault channels 6 and 7 in the Eastern Task Force, although HMS *Seaham* in the 14th Flotilla did discover a mine in her sweeps while clearing the transport area off Utah Beach. Storrs still took the planned precautions, ordering ships to switch on radio counter-measures equipment while manoeuvring to change sweeps and to ensure that all watertight doors were locked and that none of the ships' companies went below decks unless their duties so required. Sailors not on watch huddled around the funnel for warmth.[62]

Twenty minutes after midnight on 6 June, the 31st Flotilla reached the terminal point of their assault channel and altered course to 119° to sweep the four-and-a-half mile length of the south-western lap of Transport Area 34 off Omaha Beach—the 4th Flotilla would sweep the centre and northeastern laps—a run that brought them within nine miles of the enemy's coastal defences. Reaching the terminal point of the transport area fifty-five minutes later, the flotilla continued on for a further twenty minutes to get well up-tide before turning through 270 degrees to port to head south-southwest down the fire support channel directly towards the beach. This manoeuvre took just under an hour, and it was not until 0200 that the flotilla resumed G formation to starboard and proceeded down the channel. As they did so, the first of the bombardment ships and assault groups could be seen entering the transport area to the northwest. Despite advancing down the fire support channel to within a mile-and-a-half of the coast, the defences of Adolf Hitler's vaunted "Atlantic Wall" remained quiet except when the night sky was "enlivened by displays of coloured flares in the vicinity of Colleville" at the eastern end of Omaha Beach. As the ships altered course to port to sweep back up the starboard side of the channel, the full moon emerged completely from the scattered clouds and fully illuminated the flotilla for a tense, thirty-second period. Their nearness to shore undoubtedly heightened the sailors' apprehension since Storrs later reported that "even when the moon was covered it still provided ample illumination."[63]

---

61. *Caraquet* ROP

62. Dönitz, *Memoirs*, 395; Morrow ms, 85; "Minesweeping Diary of the WTF"; CNMO, "RCN's Part in the Invasion," 79; Adm, *Operation Neptune*, I, 84; Whitby, "There Must Be No Holes," 64

63. *Caraquet* ROP

While embarking on HMCS *Prince David*, soldiers of the Régiment de la Chaudière file under one of the small, fragile LCAs that will take them ashore in Normandy. It is doubtful if any of the sailors looking on would want to change places with them. (DND A-646)

The view over the bridge of HMCS *Algonquin* as she joins the invasion armada on the evening of 5 June 1944. (DND A-796)

The corvette HMCS *Baddeck* passes astern of *Algonquin* off Normandy on 6 June 1944. (LAC PA206710)

The destroyer gun line off Normandy as seen from HMCS *Algonquin*. (DND A-809)

As they completed the starboard side of the fire support channel the Canadian flotilla encountered the USN destroyers *Doyle* and *Emmons*, the battleship USS *Arkansas*, and the French cruisers *Montcalm* and *Georges Legues* steaming to their bombarding positions. "Some of the rear ships [in the flotilla] had difficulty wriggling through them and one ship's float [*Fort William*'s] passed under the *Montcalm* but bobbed up on the other side with the light still miraculously burning."[64] *Minas* in fact had to go hard to starboard to avoid being cut in two by *Georges Legues*. Re-entering the transport area, the flotilla swept west across its southern limits before commencing their next assignment at 0415 hours, a line abreast H formation sweep, south from the transport area to Omaha Beach to open up a clear path for the landing craft. As the flotilla reached its turning point 4000 yards from the beach, the sweepers encountered the first wave of American assault craft. "In order to avoid the LCT's launching their very cranky DD tanks, *Caraquet* and *Fort William* were obliged to go farther in than had been intended and fouled and lost their sweeps on a wreck and a buoy left by the previous occupants" at the mouth of the harbour of Port en Bessin. When the remaining Bangors turned clear and recovered their sweeps, they finally came under fire from a shore battery near St Laurent. They were in an exposed position close to the shoreline but the enemy's fire, poorly directed, was quickly silenced by *Arkansas* and the two French cruisers. In the meantime "a very polite landing craft approached *Mulgrave* and asked the captain if he would be so good as to direct him to Easy Red Beach. To which the captain replied that he was a stranger in those parts himself but believed it lay practically due south."[65] Threading their way through the host of landing craft, the Bangors eventually rendezvoused at the eastern end of the transport area to watch the invasion unfold in front of them as they awaited further orders.[66]

The experience of the other three minesweeping flotillas was, if anything, even less eventful. After clearing the transport areas and fire support channels, the 4th and 14th flotillas rendezvoused at the end of assault channels 3 and 4 and commenced a joint sweep of the area between the channels at 0620 hours to form channel 34. Similarly the 16th Flotilla, after sweeping between the transport area and Utah Beach, helped clear channel 12 before departing for Plymouth at noon on D-Day.[67] These hard-working little ships, so modest in appearance, had made an astonishing contribution to the success of the Normandy landings. Just as the 31st Flotilla formed part of the spearhead for the Western Task Force, similar formations led the way in for the assault forces of the Eastern Task Force.

The assault forces of the Eastern Task Force made the crossing with remarkable ease, although the sea state, in a brisk south-westerly wind setting across the tide, was particularly uncomfortable for landing craft. LCIs, recalled a naval officer who drove one that night, "were very shallow-draft and fairly fast, [and] had a sort of galloping corkscrew motion as they went through the heavy seas." He continued:

> Depending on how close we wanted to pack them, each of our ten landing craft could accommodate a hundred and sixty to two hundred infantrymen. Ours all carried collapsible bicycles, their rifle and their kits, of course. The craft's "Troop space," a

---

64. Ibid

65. Ibid; *Malpeque* ROP, June 1944, DHH 81/520/8000, Malpeque; *Blairmore* ROP, June 1944, DHH 81/520/8000, Blairmore

66. CNMO, "RCN's Part in the Invasion," 76

67. Ibid, 129; Ramsay Report on Neptune, 144

A wounded soldier is hoisted aboard HMCS *Prince David* on 6 June 1944. (LAC PA 203531)

euphemism for a lousy steel hold, had headroom of about seven or eight feet ...
Landing craft certainly weren't built to carry any appreciable number of troops for
more than twelve hours or so ... The poor soldiers! I felt sorry for them ... I have been
seasick myself and there's nothing worse.[68]

It was an accomplishment, when the wind kept forcing the craft off course by as much as 20
degrees, that they kept within the swept channels. Station-keeping was difficult, even in calm conditions, and coxswains had to make continual corrections of course and speed to maintain even a
ragged formation. The situation was aggravated by the slowness of the LCTs, which carried all the
assault group's vehicles, lumbering along at six knots ahead of the LCIs. The infantry had to suffer sixteen hours of acute discomfort.[69]

The seven LCIs of the 260th Flotilla were divided between two assault groups proceeding
abreast of each other down channels 7 and 8. Following behind in channel 7, the twelve LCIs of
the 262nd Flotilla were part of a large convoy of thirty-nine landing craft carrying the reserve 9th
Canadian Infantry Brigade. The seven craft of the 264th Flotilla, meanwhile, being part of the
reserve group for Force G, passed down channel 6 on their way to Gold Beach.[70]

The faster LSIs steamed majestically in line ahead, passing the landing craft groups to reach the
lowering positions ahead of them. In *Prince Henry*, leading her assault group, the night passed
uneventfully, although "spasmodic gun-fire was heard during the night and flares were sighted on
an ahead bearing soon after leaving Spithead Gate." *Prince David*, leading another line immediately
to the east in channel 8, experienced difficulty with some ships in the group that could not maintain
the speed of the formation. For the LSIs as a whole, however, it was a relatively comfortable crossing: "The sky was overcast, with the moon shining through the clouds at infrequent intervals. A wind
of about force 5 was blowing from the west. Occasionally, on the southwest horizon, flashes could
be seen. At 0005, star shells were sighted away to the southwest several miles distance. By 0430,
flashes could be seen along the whole southern horizon." *Prince Henry* received the signal to deploy
to starboard as she entered the transport area at 0540 and anchored in position twenty-five minutes
later. *Prince David* anchored in her lowering position, only a few minutes behind schedule at 0617,
in a freshening wind, as daylight fully revealed the extent of the armada to the enemy ashore.[71]

Sioux and *Algonquin*, escorting five-knot convoys of landing craft down the assault channels,
had an equally quiet night. Lieutenant-Commanders Boak and Piers both heard mines detonating
or saw them drifting in the channel, but it was not until 0400 that signs of combat—bomb bursts
and gun flashes—became visible on the shore ahead. "It seemed as if tactical surprise had been
lost," Boak described in his report. As daylight came, at about 0500, the group was fifteen miles
off the beaches. "Now all seemed quiet again inshore and there was no opposition from heavy batteries. The invasion armada slowly moved in to a position 7 miles off. The cruisers opened fire at
0530. The assault had now commenced."[72]

---

68. J.M. Ruttan, "Race to the Shore," *Salty Dips* (Ottawa 1985), 194-5

69. CNMO, "RCN's Part in the Invasion," 88

70. Ibid, 86-7

71. *Prince David* ROP, 15 June 1944, DHH 81/520/8000, Prince David; *Prince Henry* ROP, 14 June 1944, DHH 81/520/8000
     Prince Henry

72. *Algonquin*,ROP, 1 July 1944, 1, 1926-DDE-224, pt 18; *Sioux* ROP, 21 June 1944, 1, LAC, RG 24 (Acc 83-84/167), 697,
     1926-DDE-225, pt 1

The two Fleet Vs took up their assigned bombardment positions on the east flank of Juno Beach, and the assault craft prepared for their run in from the lowering positions seven miles off the coast. There was "slight opposition from shore batteries, but so little that it seemed as if the enemy were holding their fire until the landing craft touched down on the beaches."[73] *Sioux* reached her position 10,000 yards off the hamlet of Petit Enfer at 0618. *Algonquin* lay one mile to the west, five miles north of the church spire at Langrune-sur-Mer.[74] There they waited for their turn to join the battleships and cruisers of the Eastern and Western Task Forces that had begun bombarding the French coast since soon after 0530. The fire plan assigned both *Algonquin* and *Sioux* to the task of engaging the 75mm artillery batteries located on the eastern flank of the Juno beaches. To ensure that follow-up support could be provided after the preliminary bombardment, warships were instructed to expend no more than 50 percent of their ammunition before H-Hour which, because of delays among some of the Juno assault groups, had been deferred ten minutes to 0745 for the 7th Brigade and to 0755 for the 8th.[75]

Sioux engaged her target—a battery of two 75mm artillery pieces at Enfer—at 0705, starting at a range of 10,600 yards and closing to within 7000 yards over the next forty minutes. Although fire could only be kept up intermittently as the target was often obscured by smoke, *Sioux*'s gunnery appeared to be accurate: Boak later reported that "three or four hits were observed and the battery did not open fire on our troops." At 0748, when the first landing craft were observed to touch down, *Sioux* checked fire. *Algonquin* had opened fire from within three miles of her target—"pretty close," noted Piers, "in terms of modern gunnery"—a 75mm battery 1200 yards east of the church spire at St Aubin-sur-Mer. After forty rounds had been expended the battery was judged to be "almost completely destroyed" and firing ceased at 0740. Encouraged by operation orders to shift to targets of opportunity once the assigned ones were dealt with, *Algonquin* then "set about demolishing any houses along the waterfront which looked likely places for snipers nests" until the first landing craft touched down shortly after H-Hour.[76]

The effectiveness of the preliminary air and sea bombardment, investigated by two British army teams in the days following the assault, was much less than the planners—or the assaulting infantry—had hoped. The army teams found that "in general the buildings along the sea front were 90 per cent destroyed ... the destruction was such that the buildings were rendered untenable for snipers during the bombardment though they would have found suitable cover subsequently." The batteries, by contrast, seem to have survived their punishment. The North Shore RegimentNew Brunswick, landing on Nan Red Beach in front of St Aubin, reported that the strong point there "appeared not to have been touched" by the preliminary bombardment, and the soldiers had to deal with it themselves, supported by tanks and AVREs. It was not until the North Shores had been on the beach for about four hours that St Aubin was reported cleared, and sniping from the buildings

---

73. *Algonquin* ROP, ibid

74. *Sioux* ROP, 21 June 1944; *Algonquin* deck log, 6 June 1944, LAC, RG 24, 7016

75. ONEAST/J app G, ann II; C.P. Stacey, *The Victory Campaign: The Operations in Northwest Europe, 1944-1945* (Ottawa 1960), 100

76. Piers, "HMCS *Algonquin* and the Invasion," *RCN Monthly Rev*, no. 34 (Nov 1944), 41; *Algonquin* deck log, 6 June 1944; *Algonquin* ROP, 1 July 1944; ONEAST/J, app G

was still being reported as late as at 1800.[77] Admiralty intelligence later reported that the bombardment's greatest impact on the enemy resulted from the moral effect of the "rapidly and precisely firing naval guns." Even where it was not reinforced by air-bombing, this drumfire inspired in the
defenders a feeling of utter helplessness; "inexperienced recruits fainted, it appears, and in many
cases were completely paralysed. All offensive spirit was knocked out of them."[78]

Many of the assaulting infantry would have disagreed. The 3rd Canadian Division's 961 casualties on 6 June were for the most part suffered while assaulting the beach defences. Even though
naval planners expected to achieve only neutralization and not destruction of the emplacements,[79]
the bombardment effort was hampered by the fact that Allied intelligence failed to realize that most
of the German coastal guns were sited to enfilade the beaches rather than fire directly at an invasion fleet offshore.[80] If the bombarding ships had fired at an angle to the beach rather than directly at it, they might have had more success in scoring hits on the embrasures of the casemates.
Moreover, the fact that the defenders would not open fire until the men actually hit the beaches
caused the false impression that the Allies had achieved tactical as well as strategic surprise.

With the touch-down of the first landing craft on Juno Beach, not quite believing they had survived "without a scratch," the crews of the Canadian destroyers looked on with awe and fascination:

> The scene around us was incredible ... Landing craft were now swarming ashore on all
> the beaches. Mighty bulldozers were ploughing up the masses of shore obstacles, rac-
> ing against the incoming tide. Sappers were disposing of land mines. The German pill
> boxes and strong points which had withstood the bombardment were subjecting the
> shoreline to incessant fire. Buildings were ablaze, and also a few landing craft.
> Overhead the Spitfires and Thunderbolts roared defiance to the Luftwaffe. But the chal-
> lenge was not accepted, and we enjoyed immunity from air attack. Things were going
> well.[81]

In the meantime the LSI convoys carrying the assaulting infantry assembled at their lowering
positions seven miles off shore, and as the bombardment commenced they began getting the troops
into the LCAs before lowering them into the water. *Prince Henry*, whose 528th Flotilla was transporting part of the 7th Brigade's reserve battalion, the Canadian Scottish Regiment, to Mike Beach
on the Canadian division's right, had lowered all eight of its LCAs by 0645. One of these, *LCA 1372*,
was detailed to act as general duty boat for its assault group, ferrying ashore whomever the deputy
senior officer assigned. The remainder of the 528th Flotilla then formed astern of the motor launch
that would lead them, together with the other two flotillas of LCAs transporting the Canadian
Scottish, on the ninety-minute trip to the beach.[82]

---

77. "Report of Special Observer Party Investigating the Effect of Fire Preparation—Operation Neptune, 1944," nd, DHH,
    571.014 (D1)

78. Adm, Weekly Intelligence Report, 26 Jan 1945, DHH 81/520/1650, Operation Neptune; L.F. Ellis, *Victory in the West* I: *The
    Battle of Normandy* (London 1962), 167; C.P. Stacey, *The Canadian Army, 1939–1945* (Ottawa 1948), 108, 177; Hinsley,
    British Intelligence III, pt 2, 130

79. Inter-Service Committee Report, 25 October 1943, App VI, 2. PRO, DEFE 2/1025.

80. Hinsley, *British Intelligence* III, pt 2, 130

81. Piers, "HMCS *Algonquin* and the Invasion," 42

82. 528th Flotilla ROP, 15 June 1944, DHH 81/520/8000, Prince Henry, pt 2; *Prince Henry* ROP, 14 June 1944

Prince David, immediately upon anchoring, had begun lowering her first assault craft, *LCS(M) 101*, which was to provide small arms covering fire for other LCAs as they approached the beach. In the boisterous sea conditions this proved tricky, but despite having both bows stove in when the forward fall failed to release, it was able to get to the beach and do its job. A second boat, *LCA 985*, carried beach demolition and clearance personnel and proceeded independently after being lowered at 0642. With *LCA 1375* detailed as general duty boat, the remaining five LCAs of the 529th Flotilla joined the other two flotillas in the flight transporting the 8th Brigade's reserve battalion, le Régiment de la Chaudière, and formed up astern of their motor launch shortly before 0700.[83]

The ten minute delay in H-Hour had serious implications for these flotillas. The tide was rising six feet—which meant the water's edge was moving a hundred yards up the beach—every hour. By the time the obstacle clearance parties began work, ten minutes later than planned, the water had risen a foot and had advanced fifty feet up the beach. The offshore rocks were covered, craft beached among the obstacles rather than short of them, and clearance of the outer obstacles had to wait until the tide had fallen some twelve hours later.[84] After some confusion caused by one flight getting among the LCTs trying to beach ahead of them, the 528th Flotilla from *Prince Henry*, landing at Mike Beach, deployed from line ahead to line abreast and beached on Mike Red at 0830. They found that the "fire was moderately heavy in places and beach obstacles with Teller mines and a type of bottle mine attached proved much more difficult and closer together than had been anticipated. The water was just over some of the stakes and at the top of the tetrahedra. Several craft were holed and one blown up by a mine. Lifelines were rigged from all craft to enable the troops to get ashore."[85] Only *LCA 1021*, which hit a mine while backing away from the beach—several seamen suffered shrapnel wounds and one stoker was badly wounded, but none was killed—was too badly damaged to return to *Prince Henry*. *LCA 856* had to be towed back to the LSI after being badly holed by a beach obstacle. In *LCA 1033* a beach clearance unit of British engineers were slow to leave the vessel, which kept it in a vulnerable position on the beach for twenty-five minutes, but by 1230 all craft except *LCA 1021* had been hoisted back on board *Prince Henry*.[86]

The five LCAs of the 529th Flotilla under Lieutenant R.G. Buckingham, RCNVR, heading for Nan White, were not so fortunate. As Buckingham later reported, "the beach was clearly visible and I was able to make out the distinguishing land marks." Describing the action, he wrote:

> The tide was considerably higher than had been anticipated and the beach obstructions were partly covered with water. There were six rows of obstructions but we were able to weave our way through them. At 0840 all craft of the 529th Flotilla were beached. There was quite a heavy swell and a strong current on our starboard quarter but due to the weaving approach it was impossible to use kedges. On the beaches there was considerable enemy fire, mostly from mortars.
>
> About three quarters of the troops had been disembarked from LCA 1150 when an explosion caused either by a mine or by a mortar bomb blew in the port side. One sol-

---

83.   529th Flotilla ROP, 15 June 1944, DHH 81/520/8000, Prince David; *Prince David*, ROP, 15 June 1944

84.   Stacey, *Victory Campaign*, 100-1; CNMO, "RCN's Part in the Invasion," 92

85.   528th Flotilla ROP, 9 June 1944, DHH 81/520/8000, Prince Henry

86.   Sub-Lt J.A. Flynn to CO HMCS *Prince Henry*, 7 June 1944, ibid

dier was wounded. The port side of LCA 1059 was blown in by the explosion of one of the mined obstructions after about one-third of the troops had been disembarked. Casualties in this craft were two soldiers killed.

Another explosion holed LCA 1137 aft and stove in the starboard bow. All troops were cleared from this craft without casualties. All troops had been disembarked from LCA 1138 and the craft was about to leave the beach when a wave lifted it on to an obstruction. The explosion which followed ripped the bottom out of the craft. Lieutenant J.C. Beveridge, RCNVR, the boat officer in the craft, suffered several shrapnel wounds in his legs, a fracture of the right fibula and slight head injuries.

All troops were disembarked from LCA 1151 without loss. Having regard to the extent of the minefield, the quantity of wreckage of sunken landing craft and the rough sea, I held this craft on the beach until 0950, at which time I ordered the crews from the sunken craft to embark for return passage to the ship. By this time, there was a cleared channel through the obstructions, which had been made by an LCT beaching, but as we were leaving, an approaching LCT forced us to alter course. An obstruction ripped the bottom out of LCA 1151. The crews then transferred to an LCT and were eventually brought back to the ship.[87]

Prince David's remaining three landing craft fared little better. *LCS(M) 101* had two of her sailors wounded by snipers in landing on Nan White before striking a mine and sinking while pulling away from the beach. *LCA 985*, with the obstacle clearance party, also sank before any of its specialized equipment could be unloaded. The fate of her crew was unknown on board *Prince David* for over a week, until they managed to make their way back to England. Only *LCA 1375*, among the eight landing craft, eventually returned to the ship, having spent several days ferrying personnel to and from the beaches. The LSIs themselves spent the morning of D-Day embarking their remaining troops into various landing craft for transport to the beaches and caring for the numerous wounded being brought on board. *Prince Henry*'s group of LSIs weighed anchor and left the assault anchorage for the Solent at 1500. *Prince David*'s group sailed thirty-five minutes later. *Prince David*, with a particularly large number of serious casualties, received permission to proceed independently to Southampton, where she docked at 2245 to transfer her dead and wounded to the waiting ambulances.[88]

German resistance in the Juno sector was greatest in the beach defences themselves, and there was little demand for *Sioux* and *Algonquin* to provide fire support once the assault troops had moved inland. *Sioux* made contact with her Forward Observer Bombardment at Langrune-sur-Mer at 0913 but was not called upon for fire support that day. *Algonquin*, which established contact with her FOB at 1009, received her only call for fire support at 1051 when the Royal Artillery's Captain M. Kroyer requested a shoot against two self-propelled assault guns south of Bernières-sur-Mer. *Algonquin* responded within one minute, hitting the target with her third salvo. Twelve four-gun salvoes quickly followed until Kroyer pronounced the target destroyed. In recognition of this feat, the FOB "had 'HMCS Algonquin' painted across the front of his jeep, which was later seen over most of northern France, Belgium and Holland."[89]

---

87. 529th Flotilla ROP, 15 June 1944

88. *Prince David* ROP, 15 June 1944; *Prince Henry* ROP, 14 June 1944; CNMO, "RCN's Part in the Invasion," 97

89. Quoted in Piers, "Comments on the 'Operation Overlord' First Narrative," 14 June 1944, DHH 82/48; *Sioux* ROP, 21 June 1944

Most Canadian LCIs spent the morning of D-Day circling about a mile off their designated beaches, waiting for the order to land their troops, but the four landing craft of the 260th Flotilla were among the earliest of the entire Eastern Task Force to go in. Scheduled to land at Nan Beach, LCIs *121* and *298* made the first run in to Nan Red, just west of St Aubin-sur-Mer, shortly before 0900:

> Each ship could plainly see the rows of obstacles, many of them mined, yet each commanding officer picked a spot on the beach and headed for that at full speed, 16 knots. Had the craft tried to pick their way slowly through the lines of obstacles it is very doubtful that they could have avoided the mines and quite certain that they could not have got far enough up the beach, which had a very flat gradient of about one in a hundred, to give their troops a dry landing. The only course under the circumstances, as had been impressed on all commanding officers in the briefing for the operation, was to think only of landing their troops safely and disregard the safety of their craft. Like the LCAs, the LCIs were expendable.[90]

LCI 298 managed to avoid damage on the run in and landed her troops safely, but *LCI 121*, after losing her first lieutenant overboard in the rough seas, came to an abrupt stop when she struck a mined obstacle that blew a ten by five foot hole in her forward troop space, killing or wounding nine soldiers. The remainder quickly disembarked over the port ramp into four feet of water. To the west, LCIs *301* and *249* beached on Nan White, not far from *Prince David*'s wrecked LCAs. *LCI 249* struck a mine and was badly holed but managed to escape without any casualties. Her 192 soldiers, mainly engineers, had to disembark in deeper water and struggled to get their demolition equipment ashore. *LCI 301* escaped damage on her run in, but had to wait twenty-five minutes on the beach while the mainly British pioneers and engineers unloaded their gear. It was not a comfortable wait. One of her officers later recalled that the commanding officer, Lieutenant R. Smith, "was making a log of what went on. This was his entry at 0930: 'Shells to starboard. Getting closer.' That was some understatement! They seemed to come right up to the side of the ship, and Bob and I absent-mindedly patted each other on the back while we watched them come closer, and told each other so long and good luck. We thought they might be trying to range us with salvoes, but apparently they were just working a beat, up and down the beach. Just when they got close they started back."[91] After repairing the damaged craft as best they could, the four LCIs headed back to England in the early afternoon, with *LCI 298* taking *249* in tow.

Of the 260th Flotilla's second group of three landing craft circling off Mike Beach to the west, only *LCI 117* was scheduled to land in the early morning. Despite damaging her starboard ramp in a collision with another landing craft during the run in, she beached successfully at 0930 on Mike Green near its junction with Red. Delays in clearing the beach exits kept the other two LCIs circling off Mike Green until 1330 when *LCI 177* was ordered in, followed thirty minutes later by *LCI 285*. By that time, shortly after high tide, the water had risen sufficiently to cover the offshore obstacles completely and allow a hazard-free run to the beach. It also meant that the two landing craft were caught on the falling tide and spent the afternoon beached awaiting the evening tide.

---

90. CNMO, "RCN's Part in the Invasion," 99

91. "Experience of Lt Robert Smith RCNVR and crew of LCI(L) #301 in Operation 'Neptune' 1944," 21 July 1944, DHH 81/520/8000, LCI(General); CNMO, "RCN's Part in the Invasion," 100; Schull, *Far Distant Ships*, 278-9

The only incident of note occurred at 1700 hours when a lone Focke-Wulfe 190 fighter made an unsuccessful dive-bombing attack on *LCI 285*. All three craft eventually headed safely back to England that afternoon; the two stranded LCIs followed the next day.[92]

Delays in clearing exits and the general congestion on the beaches also affected the landing of the 262nd Flotilla, carrying the Canadian reserve brigade, the 9th, to Juno Beach. Scheduled to land on Nan Red at 1015, the LCIs circled off the beach until 1129 when they were ordered in to Nan White. Despite higher water that left obstacles partially covered, the same hazards that had claimed all five of *Prince David*'s LCAs on this beach three hours earlier now took a heavy toll. "Numerous teller mines and beach obstacles resulted in all craft but two being holed below the water line," reported the flotilla officer. "LCI(L) 115, 299 and 270 did not unbeach owing to serious nature of hull damage. LCI(L) 135 and 263 after unbeaching were forced to return to the beach to avoid sinking."[93]

In spite of these difficulties only five sailors were slightly wounded by shrapnel, thanks in part to the foresight of the commanding officer of *LCI 270*, Lieutenant A.C. Clark, RCNVR, who had wisely brought his troops on deck before the approach after judging that the threat from mines was greater than that from defensive fire. His craft struck a mine on the run in that blasted a large hole through the evacuated forward troop space. After spending some twenty to thirty minutes on the beach—the reserve brigade's troops having more equipment to land than did those making the actual assault—seven of the 262nd Flotilla's craft managed to get off, despite damage to five of their number, with the aid of LCIs *306* and *276* "who brought their craft off the beach undamaged and returned to tow off less fortunate members of the party. Engine room crew of all damaged craft carried out efficient damage control and in some instances were able to pump out engine rooms and restart generators after they had been flooded with salt water," thus allowing the seven least damaged craft to return to the Solent by 0310 on 7 June. Of the five landing craft stranded on Nan White, *LCI 135* quickly patched her damaged hull and was pushed off the beach by a bulldozer at 1650 and reached England the following afternoon. The remaining four "were able to effect emergency repairs while dried out," unbeached at 2300 on 8 June, sailed for England the following afternoon, and were back in the Solent about thirty-six hours later.[94]

The seven LCIs of the 264th Flotilla, transporting 1,227 soldiers of the 56th British Infantry Brigade, the reserve brigade for the 50th Division landing in Gold sector, arrived off Jig Green, two miles east of Arromanches, at 0940 hours. More than two hours later six of the seven Canadian LCIs, together with three attached American LCIs, finally received word to head for Jig Red. The other Canadian craft, *LCI 255*, which carried the brigade commander and his staff, was instructed to ferry these passengers ashore by LCM. The nine landing craft literally raced for the shore. The commander of *LCI 302*, Lieutenant J.M. Ruttan, RCNVR, described their experience:

> In our own flotilla of ten craft, each CO had put a pound in a pool; the CO of the first
> ship to touch the beach collected the ten pounds from the pool. As we steamed up and
> down parallel to the beach, all of a sudden we got the order "OK, in we go!" Everybody
> made a ninety-degree turn to port and jammed her full-ahead to win the ten pounds

92.   CNMO, "RCN's Part in the Invasion," 102

93.   262nd Flotilla ROP, 1 July 1944, DHH 81/520/8000-411/262, 262nd LCI Flotilla

94.   Ibid

... A friend of mine, Lloyd Williams from Vancouver, the CO of the craft [*LCI 310*] on my starboard side, beat me by about [five feet]. We both hit the beach at such a rate of knots—and went so far up—that we couldn't get off. The tide had started to recede and we were hung up ... for about another six hours until the tide came back in high enough for us to get off. I did win one thing that day. We were all great cribbage players, so we spent a lot of this time playing cribbage. I won the "Arromanches and District Cribbage Championship" ... I never spent a more peaceful day in the war than I did on June the Sixth. We could see firing in the distance but, in our own particular sector, we had no problems.[95]

Because high tide covered most of the obstacles, only LCIs *288* and *295* suffered any damage on underwater obstructions on their inward sprint. The latter also damaged its propellers in riding over a sunken LCM. The three heavier American LCIs, and the first and second place "finishers" found themselves high and dry, but despite a rapidly falling tide, four of the Canadian LCIs managed to back off the beach. Three proceeded to the ferry craft anchorage to spend the next two weeks on the ferry service where they were joined, after the evening tide, by Ruttan's landing craft. LCIs *305* and *255* sailed for England that afternoon, and *LCI 310*, which unbeached too late to join the last convoys back to the Solent that night, followed next morning.[96]

By the evening of 6 June "everything," wrote Admiral Ramsay in his diary, "[was] remarkably good and better than we could have expected but we have still to establish ourselves on land. The Navy has done its part well. News continued satisfactory throughout the day from ETF and good progress was made. Very little news was received from WTF & anxiety exists as to the position on shore. Their comm[unicatio]ns are really bad & their system of command not to be compared with ours. Still on the whole we have very much to thank God for this day."[97]

It was indeed a great achievement. Although the Allies did not gain the tactical surprise that appearances had led many observers to believe, the movement of a massive assault force across about a hundred miles of open sea had taken place without serious enemy interference. Neptune planners had assumed that the Germans would know the invasion fleet had sailed by H-12 hours and would be certain of its destination by H-4 hours, but weather conditions had evidently put the enemy off his guard. The *Luftwaffe*, as we have seen, had already been marginalized, and the *Kriegsmarine* cancelled its normal patrols and minelaying operations in the Channel on the night of 5/6 June. Several senior army commanders felt secure enough to leave their headquarters, including the commander of Army Group B, Field Marshal Erwin Rommel, who left France on 5 June for several days' leave in Germany. It was the airborne landings on the flanks of the invasion area, shortly after midnight on 6 June, that first brought the enemy to the realization that an operation was in progress. But even when they put their forces at the highest state of readiness at 0215, the authorities "still believed they were faced only with a diversionary operation preceding an invasion in the Pas de Calais." Another hour passed before *Marinegruppe West* concluded "that a major operation was in progress" and took measures to contest an assault landing. Radar echoes of shipping off Contentin and Port-en-Bessin led, at 0320, to an order for U-boats in Biscay ports

---

95. Ruttan, "Race to the Shore," 193-4

96. CNMO, "RCN's Part in the Invasion," 107-8

97. Ramsay, *Year of D-Day*, 84

to come to immediate readiness, for the 8th *Zerstörerflotille* to move from Royan to Brest, the 5th *Torpedobooteflotille* from Le Havre to carry out reconnaissance in the area off Port-en-Bessin and Grandcamp, and the 5th and 9th *Schnellbooteflotille* from Cherbourg to patrol off Cape de la Hague and Barfleur.[98]

The E-boats ordered out from Cherbourg headed out into the choppy seas at 0445 but failed to make contact with the patrolling MTBs waiting to intercept them off Pointe de Barfleur, including three Canadian boats from the 29th Flotilla, and then had to turn back before daylight exposed them to air attack. The four operational ships of the 5th *Torpedobooteflotille*, the small destroyers *Falke, Möwe, Jaguar,* and *T 28*, had greater success when they were ordered out from Le Havre at 0348. Aided by a smoke screen laid by Allied aircraft to shield the bombarding warships on the eastern flank from heavy batteries at Le Havre, the torpedo boats fired fifteen torpedoes before making good their escape. Two torpedoes passed between the British battleships *Warspite* and *Ramilles,* while a third sank the Norwegian destroyer *Svenner*—the only success the 5th *Torpedobooteflotille* was to achieve with their most deadly weapon. In view of the *Kriegsmarine*'s decision to station either its larger destroyers or its U-boats in the Channel prior to an invasion—a reflection both of Allied naval dominance in the Channel and the overwhelming air superiority that proved essential to victory on both land and sea—there were no other forces available to disrupt the assault vessels before they hit the beaches.[99]

That being said, Ramsay's concern about the situation ashore by the end of the day was more than justified. Apart from elements of the 21st *Panzer* Division, which arrived north of Caen in the early afternoon, blocking 3rd British Infantry Division's path to the city, the only serious resistance encountered had been in the beach defences, and these were overcome, albeit after some stiff fighting. But an army mind-set that was more geared to consolidating the day's gains and preparing defensive positions for the night than to exploiting an off-balance enemy meant that none of the assault formations reached their planned objectives—a setback fraught with consequences for the Allied plan of campaign. In the Eastern Assault Area, the 3rd Canadian Infantry Division did penetrate some eleven kilometres inland; these were the greatest gains of the day.[100]

In the Western Task Force, the Americans experienced both the easiest and toughest fights to get ashore. On Utah Beach, the 4th US Infantry Division seized the beachhead against minimal opposition, suffering only 197 casualties in the process, but it failed to link up with the 82nd US Airborne Division to the north and west. Omaha Beach—7000 yards wide lying between 100-foot high cliffs and backed by 100- to 150-foot high scrub-covered bluffs—was the only landing site between Arromanches and the mouth of the Vire River that offered a level beach. The Germans were able to concentrate their defences along that stretch of coast at the entrances to the five draws leading through the bluffs. The assaulting elements of the 1st and 29th US Infantry Divisions also had to contend with the presence of the bulk of the German 352nd Infantry Division, a higher-quality formation than the two static divisions manning the defences of the other beaches. As the

98. Hinsley, *British Intelligence* III, pt 2, 126, 128

99. KTB, 5 *Torpedobooteflotille*, 6 June 1944, DHH, SGR II 340, v 24, PG 70321; CNMO, "RCN's Part in the Invasion," 219; Adm, *Operation Neptune* I, 87-8; Hinsley, *British Intelligence* III pt 2, 129; Whitley, *Destroyer!*, 206

100. R. Weigley, *Eisenhower's Lieutenants: The Campaign in France and Germany, 1944-1945* (Bloomington, Ind. 1981), 94; C. D'Este, *Decision in Normandy: The Unwritten Story of Montgomery and the Allied Campaign* (London 1983), 136-50

attack remained stalled near the waterline throughout the morning, the 1st US Army's command-er, Lieutenant-General Omar Bradley, considered evacuation. Through the bravery and initiative of small groups of soldiers infiltrating the German defences in the bluffs, and helped by destroyers that moved dangerously close inshore to provide fire support, the Americans managed to carve out a narrow toe-hold barely a mile in depth by early evening. They had suffered 1953 casualties.[101]

Thus the Allies had broken through the crust of Hitler's Atlantic Wall, landing more than 132,000 men across the beaches and a further 23,000 by air drop. They paid a heavy price—some 9000 killed, wounded, and missing, of which 1074 were from the Canadian Army—but neither the *Kriegsmarine* nor the *Luftwaffe* had been able to offer effective opposition. The RCN, for example, had only seven wounded. The heaviest losses among naval vessels occurred among the various landing craft, 258 of which were sunk or damaged in the Eastern Task Force alone.[102]

As darkness approached on the night of 6 June, attention turned to the seaward defence of the assault area. This, like every other aspect of Operation Neptune, was taken seriously by Ramsay's planners: if German surface units penetrated the defences to get among the scores of thin-skinned transports and landing craft they could disrupt the build up of men and materiel required in Normandy.[103] In the Eastern Assault Area where Canadian naval forces chiefly operated, the close proximity of Le Havre—just fifteen nautical miles from Sword, the easternmost assault beach—meant that naval commanders could not utilize defence-in-depth to the same extent as off other beaches. They partly solved this problem by laying a mine barrier off the port but also realized that the Germans would be able to clear channels through, as indeed they did. The onus therefore fell on air and sea patrols to stop German sorties, with naval forces bearing the brunt of the responsi-bility at night. Rear-Admiral P.L. Vian, RN, the commander of the Eastern Task Force, devised a two-layered scheme for the defence of the anchorage. In earlier landings, close-in protection of the seaward flank was undertaken by "endless chain" patrols—warships steaming back and forth along predetermined lines—but in the English Channel, where strong tidal currents made accurate navigation difficult, Vian thought that this would be "a very chancy business" and instead devised a static system.[104] Each night, smaller vessels, usually minesweepers, anchored stem-to-stern 1,000 yards apart six miles offshore along the entire length of the British Assault Area, a line extending from Cap Barfleur to Cap d'Antifer. From the eastern end of this line to the shore, heav-ily armed Landing Craft Guns (LCG) and Landing Craft Flak (LCF) anchored 200 yards apart on the so-called Trout line. The task of these vessels was to prevent enemy forces from entering the assault area and to illuminate the outer patrol areas.[105]

101. Weigley, *Eisenhower's Lieutenants*, 87-93; Stacey, *Victory Campaign*, 651-2; John Keegan, *The Second World War* (New York 1990), 387

102. Stacey, *Victory Campaign*, 650-2; Ellis, *Victory in the West* I, 223; CNMO, "RCN's Part in the Invasion," 109; Roskill, *War At Sea* III pt 2, 53

103. See also M. Whitby, "The Seaward Defence of the British Assault Area, 6-14 June 1944," *Mariner's Mirror* 80/2 (1994), 191-207

104. P.L. Vian, *Action This Day* (London 1960), 130-1

105. "Report by the Naval Commander ETF," pt II, 16-17

Vian deployed forward patrols to seaward of the static lines. The patrol area was divided into Pike, which extended north from Gold and Juno beaches to the northern boundary of the British Assault Area, and Tunny North and Tunny South, which covered the waters between Sword and Scallops, the mined area off Le Havre, to the east, and between the beachhead and the boundary of the assault area to the north. Each night two or three divisions of MTBs were deployed in Tunny South—the most likely area of German surface activity. These were usually supported by destroyer patrols in Tunny North and Pike, while two or three duty destroyers remained at readiness inside the defence line.[106]

Control of these forward patrols was one of the innumerable special problems that had to be sorted out for Neptune. With the distance across the Channel ruling out reliable land-based radar coverage from England, a system had to be devised using shipborne radar to control forces until three mobile naval radar stations (Monrads) could be established ashore in France. As it was, shipborne control proved so effective that it remained the primary method of control throughout Neptune. The concept was not new. In 1940 the destroyer HMS *Wolsey* had been briefly designated an MTB leader, and the following year two of the early type 271 centimetric radars had been fitted in trawlers for use against E-boats attacking the east coast convoy routes. Both experiments met with mixed results, with the lack of adequate communications and plotting facilities being the major shortfalls.[107] By 1944 better equipment was available—the Plan Position Indicator (PPI), which displayed a plan-view on a radar screen, was a key advance—and the vessels designated as control ships were well fitted out for the role. Vian's flagship, the Dido class cruiser HMS *Scylla*, which had been converted to an Escort Carrier Flagship, had the effective type 276 surface warning radar as well as the plotting and communications systems and staff to take full advantage of it. A number of Captain class frigates equipped with the excellent American type SL search radar were also converted to control ships with the required communications equipment and personnel.[108]

The control procedures in *Scylla* and the frigates varied slightly. The latter operated outside the assault area along the flanks of the "Spout" under the control of the C-in-C Portsmouth or the Admiral Commanding, Dover. Generally they patrolled a six-mile line with the MTBs under their control stopped with engines idling at either end of the beat. *Scylla*, which acted as control ship for MTBs in the Eastern Task Force area, worked from a static position. Each night the cruiser anchored just inside the northeast corner of the defence line, while two or three divisions of MTBs were deployed in Tunny South. As accurate plotting was critical to success, *Scylla*'s operations room staff marked routine PPI echoes every five minutes and suspicious ones every thirty seconds. They observed radio silence until a suspicious echo materialized, then a Surface Force Direction Officer in the cruiser's operations room—an experienced Coastal Forces officer—vectored one or all of the MTB formations in Tunny South onto the target. As the plot advanced, course corrections were transmitted to the MTBs over high frequency R/T.[109]

---

106. Ibid

107. C-in-C Portsmouth, "Report on Operation Overlord (Coastal Forces)," 12 Sep 1944, app I, sect 20, PRO, ADM 179/509; Howse, *Radar at Sea*, 87-8

108. C-in-C Portsmouth, ibid, pt 1, sect 41; A. Raven and J. Roberts, *British Cruisers of World War II* (Annapolis 1980), 294. Eight RN frigates were ultimately converted to control ships.

109. Adm, "Summary of Naval Reports on Operation Neptune," nd, 109-110, 178-9, PRO, DEFE 2/426, pts 1 and 2; *Coastal Forces Periodic Review (CFPR)* (May-June 1944), 34, DHH 84/7

Landing craft assault from HMCS *Prince Henry* pass a sunken merchant ship while ferrying troops into the invasion beaches. (DND PH-273)

A Canadian sailor from the RCN's Beach Commando W guides a British tank landing craft into its billet on a Norman beach. (DND A-874)

The German destroyer *Z 32* hard aground on Ile de Batz after being driven ashore by the 10th Destroyer Flotilla on the night of 8/9 June 1944 (DND CN 6870)

Mines posed a grave threat off the beachhead throughout the summer of 1944. This image shows the dramatic demise of the destroyer HMS *Swift*, which was mined when she berthed ahead of HMCS *Algonquin* on 24 June 1944. (DND PMR 92-484)

Despite all the careful preparation, predictably, friction arose when the defence scheme was first put into effect late on D-Day. Captain A.L. Pugsley, RN, the designated Captain (Patrols) in the control frigate HMS *Lawford*, did not receive the night deployment signal from *Scylla*—presumably because the heavy communications traffic swamped the available channels—so he had to get it visually and pass it on to the forces under his control the same way. Not all got the message. When Pugsley inspected the defence line he discovered that one minesweeping flotilla had not turned up, leaving a large gap. He anchored *Lawford* in the vacant sector, but two nights passed before the errant flotilla materialized. When Lieutenant-Commander Law reached the assault area on the afternoon of 6 June with four MTBs from the 29th Flotilla, loaded with sufficient fuel and provisions for a two-day stay off the beaches, he had trouble finding *Scylla* in the crowded assault area. When Law finally located the flagship, the high swell prevented him from going onboard, so his night orders to patrol an area thirteen miles southwest of Le Havre in Tunny South had to be shouted to him against a background cacophony of wind, sea, engines and the ongoing shore bombardment.[110]

After spending most of the night being "tossed restlessly from side to side" in the dark—interrupted at intervals by "a dazzling display" of anti-aircraft fire from the thousands of ships in the anchorage—the Canadians received a report of enemy activity from *Scylla* at 0400 and, turning to investigate, observed four British MTBs in action to the south. Law led his force towards the engagement at eight knots until firm radar contact was made, then increased speed to twenty-five knots and closed the enemy, six R-boats of the 4th *Raumbooteflotille* on a mining operation. Illuminating with starshell, the Canadians made a fast run in, opening fire at 700 yards and breaking off when they had closed to 150 yards, as they saw mines exploding near their targets. As they turned away gradually to port, making smoke, it seemed as though they had achieved hits on all the R boats and sunk one of them. The Allied MTBs broke off the action when the enemy withdrew into Scallops, the mined area off Le Havre. German records indicate that one R boat was heavily damaged. The Canadian MTBs had all sustained minor hull damage in the brief encounter, and four men were wounded.[111]

With only a first aid kit on board, Law's MTBs returned to *Scylla* for medical attention, only to find that the cruiser's sick-bay, and that of a nearby hospital ship, was already filled. "Hungry and tired," Law later recalled, "we set off in search of the LST which the mercy ship had suggested." They found that

> There were hundreds of LSTs, all looking alike under the gray, sullen sky, and after a desperate search we finally came alongside a British destroyer. The destroyer's doctor came aboard to see what could be done for our wounded, but with no operating equipment his aid was limited. On the doctor's request, one of the destroyer's signalmen agreed to locate the elusive LST-turned-hospital-ship. It took a whole hour for our one hope to be found, after which we thanked the destroyer, set out for the LST, and secured with great difficulty on her port side.[112]

---

110. Capt A.F. Pugsley, "ROP of Captain of Patrols from 1800 Tuesday 6th to 0500 Thursday 8th June," 16 June 1944, 1, PRO, ADM 179/502; CNMO, "RCN's Part in the Invasion," 219; Law, *White Plumes Astern*, 58-9, 73-4; P. Scott, *The Battle of the Narrow Seas* (London 1945), 194

111. Law, Action Report [ROP], nd, DHH 81/520/8000-466/29, 29th MTB Flotilla; Law, *White Plumes Astern*, 74; Report on Coastal Force Activity in ETF Area on Night of 6th and 7th June 1944, nd, DHH 81/520/1650-239/13, "Ops English Channel," pt 1; Rohwer and Hummelchen, *Chronology of the War at Sea*, 282

112 Law, *White Plumes Astern*, 76-8

The Shorts' dependence on support from better equipped ships and establishments had never been more acute. In the miserable weather that now prevailed the only refuge they found from the constant pounding of the sea was a berth in the lee of "a nice, fat merchant ship" or "a nice soft spot behind a [stationary] battleship."[113] That they had lost their torpedoes for depth-charges in May added to their frustrations (see Chapter 16). On the night of 7 June, for example, assigned once again to Tunny South, they were powerless to act effectively when they confronted the German destroyers *T 28*, *Möwe*, and *Jaguar* of the 5th *Torpedobooteflotille*. The four MTBs had been "meandering along, till starshells, which seemed to come from the direction of our destroyer patrol, suddenly broke over us." Picking up a radar contact at 6000 yards, the Canadians switched on their fighting lights and fired off recognition flares, all to no avail. When the range had closed to 4000 yards, "the sky was cluttered with starshells while other shells from heavy-calibre guns crashed about us, sending up tall towers of spray."

> Since the 29th had done everything possible to identify itself, we had to conclude that we were facing enemy destroyers. Increasing speed to 25 knots, our four midget-sized boats burst into action. We opened fire with the pom-poms, forgetful of the fact that some of the guns were loaded with 14 pom-pom starshells, which roared out and landed on the decks of the German destroyers, lighting them up like Christmas trees.[114]

After this initial exchange of fire, the Canadians kept their distance from the enemy destroyers—no doubt cursing the loss of such a splendid opportunity—and shadowed the enemy until four MTBS from the RN 55th Flotilla, which had torpedoes, attacked. Although the British claimed one hit, the German destroyers evaded their torpedoes and returned to Le Havre suffering only light damage and casualties.[115]

The next night, Canadian MTBs achieved a success despite their lack of torpedoes. Three boats under Lieutenant C.A. Burk had relieved Law and on their first sortie in Tunny South encountered two German destroyers on a minelaying sortie. Under accurate defensive fire and with no torpedoes, Burk had no real choice but to withdraw under the cover of smoke. But the Germans, not knowing that the MTBs were without torpedoes, assumed the worst. They reported that several had been fired at them—one destroyer even claimed to have heard them with "active sonar"—and took evasive action. With his radar revealing that his operational area was "full of enemy formations," and with any engagement "an extremely unpleasant prospect because of my load of mines," the German commander abandoned his mission.[116]

As intelligence reports revealed at the time, the Germans were using these forays by their small destroyers "to divert enemy MTB's and gunboats" so that smaller units could attempt to penetrate the defensive screen and lay mines or make torpedo attacks. The inability to respond adequately undoubtedly frustrated Law, especially when a British group of MTBs had been able to carry out a

---

113. Ibid, 78-9

114. Ibid

115. 113 Law, ROA 7/8 June, nd, D.G. Bradford, ROA 7/8 June 1944, nd, PRO, ADM 179/502; KTB, 5 *Torpedobooteflotille*, 8 June 1944, PG 74796

116. KTB, 5 *Torpedobooteflotille*, 8 June 1944; KTB, *T-28*, 9 June 1944, PG 70321; Law, MTB ROA, 8/9 June 1944, nd, PRO, ADM 179/502

torpedo attack on the enemy. The only enemy successes during the first three nights, however, came on the western flank where fourteen E-boats from Cherbourg, in the face of strong MTB patrols, sank an LCT on the night of 6/7 June. The following night, eleven Cherbourg-based E-boats penetrated the Spout but could sink only two LCTs and damage another. Evading Allied forces again on 8/9 June, the E-boats sank two LSTs in attacks on two convoys. Unfortunate as these losses were, they had negligible impact on Allied operations.[117]

Allied naval and air forces had successfully contained German naval units based on Channel ports. The *Kriegsmarine*'s larger vessels, however, still posed a threat. German naval units in the Baltic Sea, too distant to have interfered with the Normandy convoys during the first critical days, were still out of the picture; constant signals intelligence and photo-reconnaissance provided up-to-date intelligence to confirm that fact. The fleet destroyers of the 8th *Zerstörerflotille* based in the Bay of Biscay were, however, better situated to attack. This was borne out when the Operational Intelligence Centre received a decrypted Enigma signal at 0730 on 6 June, ordering the three operational destroyers from the Gironde—the Narviks *Z 32* and *Z 24*, and the ex-Dutch destroyer *ZH 1*—north to Brest. A second signal, indicating that enemy destroyers would be departing Royon at 1230, followed ninety minutes later.[118] A Coastal Command strike force, consisting of thirty-one Bristol Beaufighters, including fourteen rocket-armed Beaufighters from the RCAF's 404 Squadron, with eight de Havilland Mosquitoes providing fighter cover, sortied to intercept the three north-bound destroyers before they entered Brest. They found the three warships steaming northwest, forty miles southwest of St Nazaire, at 2027. Attacking out of the evening sun, the Beaufighters concentrated on the two Narviks in the lead, but failed to inflict serious damage on either vessel, despite scoring rocket hits on both. *Z 24* had to reduce speed after her port oil bunkers were holed and several large fires quickly engulfed the ship in thick black smoke. In *Z 32*, a 25-pound solid-shot warhead passed completely through the forward magazine, but she escaped with a few holes punched in her hull above the waterline. It was dark when several Beaufighters carried out a follow-up strike, and they had no success.[119]

Once reaching Brest the two Narviks required a thirty-six-hour layover to repair damage, land casualties, and hastily add more anti-aircraft armament. Enigma decrypts on 8 June, meanwhile, disclosed that *Z 32* would be available "at reduced war readiness" from 1200 and that the three destroyers, accompanied by the torpedo boat *T 24*, would depart Brest at 1830 that night (later delayed until 2015) to arrive at Cherbourg at 0500 on 9 June.[120]

Weather grounded the Beaufighters that evening, which meant that the 10th Flotilla would be the only force available to deal with the enemy destroyers. Commander B. Jones, CO of *Tartar*, who had missed the April actions while his ship was undergoing refit, had resumed command of

117. Hinsley, *British Intelligence*, III pt 2, 163-4n, app 16

118. Ibid, 161

119. Greenhous, *Crucible of War* III, 465; Hinsley, *British Intelligence* III pt 2, 161-2; R.C. Nesbit, *The Strike Wings: Special Anti-Shipping Squadrons, 1942-45* (London 1984), 120-5

120. the OIC Section 8K, "Extract from Channel Log Book, 6 June 1944 (D day) to 9 June 1944 (D day + 3)," 8 June 1944, PRO, ADM 223/287; Hinsley, *British Intelligence* III pt 2, 162-3

the flotilla. He concluded, having examined the reports of previous actions, that since "the Tribals had only four torpedoes to the enemy's eight, and with their lesser speed, the turn away to fire might well mitigate against eventual close action." The proper tactics to adopt therefore were "to press on into the enemy during his own turn away, to bring about a decisive result, using the comparatively few torpedoes rather as a weapon of opportunity for later use."[121] With seven of his eight destroyers mounting four 4.7-inch guns forward—*Blyskawica* had 4-inch guns—Jones could now, in theory, engage the enemy with thirty-two guns, although a proportion of them might be required to fire starshell to illuminate their targets. The two Narvik destroyers carried a heavier punch, mounting five 5.9-inch guns, of which two fired forward, but their large 45-kilogram shells were difficult to manhandle on a pitching deck and their rate of fire was consequently low. *ZH 1* and *T 24* added only another three forecastle guns, two 4.7-inch in the former and one 4.1-inch in the latter, thus providing the 10th Flotilla with a comfortable thirty-two to seven edge in any head-on encounter.

Added to firepower, and the inestimable advantage of Ultra intelligence, Allied shipborne radar was a generation ahead of anything mounted in German destroyers. The priority given to the *Luftwaffe* in equipment and research meant that the destroyers of the 8th *Zerstörerflotille* were still fitted with the 1940-vintage FuMO25 or FuMO28 metric radar of limited range and accuracy. Having only an A-type scope for display, their radar indicated targets on a rough bearing but provided little information regarding a contact's range. That German naval radar sets "were to the Allied sets as a pocket flashlight is to a car headlight" is the most apt comparison that has been drawn between the German and Allied equipment.[122] Perhaps the single greatest asset of the large Narviks was their thirty-eight-knot speed, but it was an advantage that would largely be negated by the need to conform to *T 24*'s slower speed of twenty-eight knots.[123]

The German flotilla was also at a disadvantage in terms of training, both as individual crews and as a unit. The priority given to the submarine war had seen a constant drain of experienced destroyer personnel to the U-boat arm. This made training that much more important. But training often went by the board owing to the increasing shortage of fuel and the warships' vulnerability to Allied air attack whenever they put to sea by day and the expectation of naval attack by night. German destroyers had been handled roughly, it will be recalled, when they encountered HMS *Glasgow* and *Enterprise* in December 1943. The German vessels had not been able to train as a unit prior to being committed to the Channel operation, a problem made more acute by the disparity in performance between the four warships. Their outlook was gloomy. In commenting on the April 1944 encounters with the 10th Flotilla, the war diary of the 4th *Torpedobooteflotille* had noted "the oppressive general situation existing at the coast of northern Brittany, a situation which had never failed to make [the crews] clearly aware of their inferiority."[124] As they left Brest on

---

121. B. Jones, "A Matter of Length and Breadth," *Naval Review* 38 (May 1950), 139; B. Jones, *And So to Battle: A Sailor's Story* (Battle 1976), 82-3

122. A. Hezlet, *The Electron and Seapower* (London 1975), 264

123. For the relative strengths and weaknesses of the destroyer forces involved in the June action, see M. Whitby, "Masters of the Channel Night, 5-21

124. "Evaluation of Actions Fought by the 4 Torpedo-boat Flotilla on 25 and 26 Apr 44 and on 28 and 29 Apr 44," nd, DHH 81/520/8000, Haida (prior to1950)

8 June, the commander of the 8th *Zerstörerflotille*, Kapitän zur See F. von Bechtolsheim, wrote in his war diary "that he could hardly imagine the British allowing him to reach Cherbourg unmolested; he expected an encounter with British destroyers en route, though he had some hope that rain or poor visibility might enable him to slip by undetected."[125]

Forewarned by Enigma decrypts of the planned departure from Brest, Admiral Leatham, C-in-C Plymouth Command, cancelled the return of *Ashanti* and *Tartar* to Plymouth to refuel on the afternoon of 8 June, and after receiving more detailed information about the enemy's course and speed, he cleared several antisubmarine support groups out of the western Channel and shifted the 10th Flotilla's east-west patrol line to a position roughly fifteen miles north of Ile de Batz. The experienced 19th Division was leading—in line ahead, *Tartar* followed by *Ashanti*, *Haida*, and *Huron*. The less-experienced 20th Division—in order, *Blyskawica*, *Eskimo*, *Javelin*, and *Piorun*—were positioned two miles north and astern to act, in Commander Jones' words, "as a kind of backstop." An officer on board *Ashanti* recalled that "there was a full moon and heavy cloud, a combination that gives rather good visibility at night. The wind was light and the sea calm. We were steering 255 at 20 knots, and zigzagging."[126]

At 0114 on 9 June *Tartar*'s type 276 radar obtained a contact bearing 241° at ten miles range. The flotilla's electronic advantage was apparent during the next eight minutes as the Allied destroyers maintained radar contact and closed the range undetected by the enemy. The Canadian Tribals' type 271 radar established contact at 0117 at 20,000 yards, although Commander DeWolf, in *Haida*, reserved judgment on it: "earlier rain squalls had given good plots."[127] When Jones ordered his eight ships to alter course from line ahead to line abreast at 0122, "thereby exposing their port sides, fully illuminated by the moon," the German warships belatedly became aware of the threat.[128] The 20th Division, two miles to the northeast, remained undetected.[129]

There was an immediate and predictable turn to port by the Germans as they fired torpedoes. Only the first three vessels, *Z 32*, *ZH 1*, and *Z 24*, were able to pick out targets. The slower *T 24* was still too far astern to sight the Allied destroyers. Forewarned by their Headache operators at 0127 to "stand by for torpedoes 40 degrees," the four Tribals easily combed the tracks as they were themselves opening fire.[130] At 0127 *Haida* illuminated the target with starshell:

> Nearest target bearing 255 degrees at 4000 yards. Two destroyers were sighted and the right hand one [*Z 24*] was engaged. HURON was seen to engage the other [*T 24*] while ASHANTI and TARTAR engaged targets farther to the right [*Z 32* and *ZH 1*]. The two left hand ships turned away to the Northward and to the Westward making

125. Von Bechtolsheim, *Gefecht 8 Zerstörerflotille Am 9.6.44*, DHH SGR II 340, v 51; J. Watkins, "Destroyer Action, Ile de Batz, 9 June 1944," *Mariner's Mirror* 78 (Aug 1992), 320

126. Watkins, ibid, 314-5; Jones, *And So To Battle*, 83; Hinsley, *British Intelligence,* III pt 2, 162

127. Cdr H.G. DeWolf, ROA, 9 June 1944, DHH 81/520/8000, Haida (prior 1950)

128. Capt. R.A. Morice, Action Fought with Four Enemy Destroyers by the 10th Destroyer Flotilla off the Ile De Bas on the 9th June, 1944, 13 July 1944, PRO, ADM 1/15784

129. Whitby, "Masters of the Channel Night," 13

130. L-Cdr H.S. Rayner, ROA, 9 June 1944, DHH 81/520/ 8000, Huron (prior to 1950); Jones, "A Matter of Length and Breadth," 140

smoke. The left hand ship appeared to continue her turn to the Southward and presented a better target than mine which was stern on and disappearing behind smoke.[131]

DeWolf reported firing ten to fifteen salvoes at *Z 24*—several possible hits were scored—then shifted fire to *T 24*. *Tartar* and *Ashanti*, at much closer range, turned their attention from *Z 32* to *Z 24* before pounding the smaller and already seriously damaged *ZH 1* into submission. The ex-Dutch destroyer had already absorbed numerous hits including a shell that "penetrated the turbine room, destroying the main steam line and filling the room with scalding steam."[132]

Z 24, seriously damaged by hits to the forward turret, bridge, and engine room, and the unscathed *T 24* retreated westward towards Brest under cover of smoke, with *Haida* and *Huron* in hot pursuit. The only remaining German ship capable of offensive action still in the fight was *Z 32*, and with the flotilla commander on board, she continued northward until she encountered the four warships of the 20th Division. Outnumbered four-to-one, the Narvik received an estimated sixteen to twenty hits but managed to straddle *Blyskawica* before launching four torpedoes and turning away behind a smoke screen. Rattled by the enemy fire and a Headache report that the German was firing torpedoes, *Blyskawica* turned 180 degrees to starboard and also began laying smoke. Having earlier failed to deploy from line ahead to line abreast when the 19th Division had initially made contact with the enemy, the junior division's inexperience continued to show as, in the words of Captain (D), Plymouth, "*Eskimo* and *Javelin*, assuming the Division were turning to fire torpedoes, following round and firing three and four torpedoes respectively, eventually forming up astern of *Blyskawica*, and losing contact due to the smoke screen put up by *Blyskawica* and the enemy destroyer." *Piorun* lost visual contact and reduced speed to twenty knots, allowing the target to get away. *Blyskawica*, meanwhile, confused by the situation and followed by the three other destroyers in the 20th Division, continued away from the main action for fifteen minutes on her course to the eastward before realizing what had happened. Turning back, and knowing that *Piorun*, *Tartar*, and *Ashanti* were somewhere in the vicinity, she then proceeded cautiously to regain contact.[133]

Z 32 in the meantime had run squarely into *Tartar*. In her third gun battle in less than ten minutes, the Narvik was again hit several times but managed to score three hits on the Allied destroyer's bridge superstructure. One officer and two ratings were killed and several others wounded; fires broke out on the forward superstructure, temporarily knocking out all radar and radio equipment, leaving a wounded Commander Jones unable to control his forces. *Z 32*'s luck continued to hold as *Ashanti* bore down on the scene only to have the German destroyer shielded by the thick smoke pouring from *Tartar* when she attempted to engage. When *Ashanti* emerged from behind *Tartar*'s smoke seeking to re-engage *Z 32*, she came across the heavily damaged *ZH 1* stopped dead in the water, proceeded to circle the stricken vessel while pumping shells into her, until she finally blew off the enemy's bows with a torpedo. Abandoned and scuttled, at 0237 *ZH 1* blew up in a massive explosion that echoed across the western Channel.[134]

131. DeWolf, ROA

132. Whitley, *Destroyer!*, 208

133. Capt (D) Plymouth, "Action Fought with Four Enemy Destroyers," 13 July 1944, PRO, ADM 1/15784

134. DeWolf, ROA; Watkins, "Destroyer Action," 316; Whitby, "Masters of the Channel Night," 14-15; Whitley, *Destroyer!*, 209

To the southwest, *Haida* and *Huron* had fallen behind in their chase of *Z 24* and *T 24* after the German destroyers had unwittingly steamed through an Allied minefield, one that the Canadian Tribals were under orders to avoid. By the time the chase was resumed, *Haida* and *Huron* had fallen some nine miles astern. They lost radar contact soon after. As "the position with regard to own forces and remainder of the enemy was obscure," DeWolf decided to turn back towards the rest of the 10th Flotilla. Shortly after doing so they sighted *Z 32* but, suspecting the vessel might be *Tartar*, were unable to make a clear identification. Kapitän zur See von Bechtolsheim, equally unsure, answered *Haida*'s challenge with unintelligible signals. "The fact that, despite German recognition signal interrogation, these shadows do not fire," the German commander later reported, "causes me to make the decision not to use my weapons."[135] Starshell from the Tribals finally removed all doubt about *Z 32*'s identity and they began to engage her at 6,900 yards. According to DeWolf, "the enemy fought back with accurate fire, HE shell bursting overhead and in the water, often very close to the ship." Once again the German ship opened the range by steaming through the minefield, and the Tribals checked fire after an engagement of just under half an hour.[136]

Headache intercepts of *Z 32*'s attempts to contact the rest of the flotilla—intermittent transmissions of "Report if understood," and "Why doesn't someone report, dammit again?" and then simply "Report, report"—give an indication of von Bechtolsheim's frustration with the situation as he swung around from a westerly course to the south searching for the rest of his flotilla.[137] No doubt sensing that he was now facing a large number of Allied warships alone, but uncertain of the location of his remaining three vessels, the flotilla commander had turned east through the minefield (after being fired on by *Haida*) to continue with the planned breakthrough to the invasion area. He decided to make for St Malo, since Cherbourg could not be reached before dawn, where he hoped he would pick up the rest of his flotilla.[138] That hope was shattered when he finally heard from *T 24* and *Z 24* at 0420, requesting permission, which he granted, for them to return to Brest. Ten minutes later *Z 32* altered to westward, deciding it was better to keep the 8th *Zerstörerflotille* concentrated at Brest. "With a heavy heart," he reported, "I must therefore decide to break off the mission ordered. In this situation I cannot force a breakthrough to the east with *Z 32* alone. Will still have to wait and see whether the breakthrough to the west will be successful."[139] Had he known that eight Allied destroyers lurked to westward, two in hot pursuit, it is unlikely that von Bechtolsheim would have turned back to where they could easily intercept him.

Frustrated by having to skirt the troublesome minefield for a second time that night, the Canadian destroyers were nevertheless able to maintain radar contact with their quarry. They passed around the minefield's northern extremity, where they "heard whistles and passed through a large number of survivors, some on rafts and floats" from the sunken *ZH 1*, before resuming the chase. The enemy was ten miles to the southeast when they cleared the minefield at 0342, and the 20th Division was six miles to the north. After losing radar contact with *Z 32*, von Bechtolsheim's decision to return to Brest allowed the Canadians to regain contact on their target at nine miles,

135. Von Bechtolsheim, *Gefecht 8 Zerstörerflotille*

136. DeWolf, ROA

137. Watkins, "Destroyer Action," 321

138. Von Bechtolsheim, *Gefecht 8 Zerstörerflotille*

139. Ibid; Watkins, "Destroyer Action," 322; Whitby, "Masters of the Channel Night," 18; Whitley, *Destroyer!*, 211

directly to the east. As the range slowly closed, *Haida* and *Huron* turned to parallel the enemy's course. Plotting movements by radar, the Canadian destroyers altered course "to the south and southwest to close the enemy who first appeared to be making toward Morlaix and then attempting to return to the westward."

At 0445 they opened fire at 7000 yards, and a few minutes later *Blyskawica* joined in the engagement from well astern. *Z 32* returned fire—accurately but not rapidly. Pummelled by accurate radar-controlled fire from the two Canadian destroyers von Bechtolsheim took his ship through another minefield during a running battle, ran out of sea room, and at 0517 deliberately ran his ship onto the ledges north of Ile de Batz. *Haida* and *Huron* continued firing until 0525. "He was observed to be heavily hit a few minutes before this and again after being stopped and was finally left burning and considered fixed at 0526. As *Haida* and *Huron* returned northward the fire appeared to increase in intensity. The enemy commenced firing distress signals, white and red flares, as soon as he grounded." DeWolf noted the similarity to signals that had been used by the Elbing driven ashore near Ile de Vierge on 29 April.[140]

The 10th Flotilla had fulfilled its task. Two German destroyers were sunk or aground. The other two, including *T 24* which had now survived her third engagement with Canadian destroyers, and which would survive yet another, were making for the Bay of Biscay, where they would be sunk by a Coastal Command air strike six weeks later. "The results of this action," Captain (D), Plymouth wrote the following month, "are likely to prove decisive from an operational point of view. The engagement resulted in a serious defeat of the only remaining enemy surface force which was likely to interfere successfully with our landings in Normandy, and other connected operations in the Channel."[141] For his part, Admiral Ramsay expressed disappointment: "I wanted all to be sunk."[142]

The action reflected well on the Canadians, particularly on "Hard-Over-Harry" DeWolf who had now destroyed, or shared in the destruction of three German destroyers in the space of six weeks. When the RCN had pushed to have the Tribals deployed overseas "in the fight theatres of war," they had not only done so because that was where the powerful destroyers were needed most, but in the hopes of garnering positive publicity for the navy.[143] To help pursue that objective a public relations officer, Lieutenant W. Sclater, RCNVR, was appointed to *Haida* in the spring of 1944. With plenty of good material to work from, Sclater wrote many stirring accounts of the Tribals' actions—including the *Athabaskan* tragedy—that appeared in newspapers across Canada, and immediately after the war he published a book-length account of *Haida*'s operations which became a bestseller.[144] This gave the RCN the type of publicity it sought and raised the navy's profile among Canadians. It also made heroes of *Haida* and her commanding officer, to the point that the atten-

---

140. DeWolf, ROA

141. Capt (D) Plymouth, "Action Fought"

142. Love and Major, *Year of D-Day*, 85

143. DOP, "Deployment of Tribal Destroyers," 7 Dec 1942, LAC, RG 24, 6797, NSS 8375-355; CCCS to Sec NB,13 May 1942, LAC, RG 24, 3840, NS 1017-10-23. See also Douglas, *No Higher Purpose*, 582.

144. W. Sclater, *Haida: A Story of the Hard Fighting Tribal Class Destroyers of the Royal Canadian Navy on the Murmansk Convoy, The English Channel and the Bay of Biscay* (Toronto 1946). In the final sentence of his book Sclater describes the Tribals' return to Halifax in May 1945 and quotes a fictitious dockyard matey saying this of *Haida*: "This is a great ship which sailed into this old Nova Scotia Harbour today, a ship which has earned a great name, a name which will endure forever in our annals of the sea."

The Tribal class destroyer HMS *Eskimo* stands by as a boat from HMCS *Haida* moves in to pull survivors of *U 971* from the water on 24 June 1944. (PA 113918)

Survivors of *U 971* onboard *Haida*. (LAC PMR 94-318)

A view of the damage sustained by the frigate HMCS *Teme* after it was almost cut in half in a collision with the escort carrier HMS *Tracker* in the English Channel on 10 June 1944. The scar left by *Tracker*'s bow when she impaled the frigate is clearly visible. (DND GM-2288)

tion paid to *Huron* and *Iroquois* paled by comparison, a source of some continuing bitterness. Recognizing this, the ever-modest DeWolf had tried to divert attention to his flotilla mates, writing in a personnel evaluation of Sclater; "My only criticism is that he allowed himself to become more interested in the ship in which he was borne (*Haida*) than in the other Tribals, and this was sometimes reflected in his press despatches."[145] DeWolf's attempts to spread the glory notwithstanding, as a result of *Haida*'s tremendous achievements—which would continue throughout the summer of 1944, including the destruction of a U-boat—and no doubt helped by the spotlight shone on them by Sclater, *Haida* has endured as Canada's most famous fighting ship and Harry DeWolf the country's most respected fighting sailor.

———————————

U-boats had no more success than German surface forces in the early days of the invasion of Europe. BdU only ordered its U-boats to sea in the early morning of D-Day, giving them no opportunity whatsoever to counter the invasion directly. Five *Schnorkel* boats available in Biscay ports were ordered into the English Channel, along with nine conventional boats, which were ordered to run at full speed on the surface at night. Still baffled by Operation Fortitude, the Allied deception plan to cover Neptune, BdU deployed its remaining boats along the Biscay coast to defend against an expected assault there, while boats based in Norway were initially held in readiness in case of a landing on that coast.[146]

Allied air patrols wreaked havoc on the U-boats attempting to penetrate the Channel. They destroyed two on the night of 6/7 June, and six more, including a *Schnorkel* boat, were forced to turn back as a result of battle damage. Faced with such heavy casualties, U-boat Command signalled the conventional boats to abandon high-speed surface runs during darkness; nonetheless, the next night Allied maritime patrol aircraft destroyed two more submarines on the surface and damaged two others. On 10 June, all but *Schnorkel* boats were withdrawn from the Channel. Although the 'snort'-equipped boats were more successful in evading Allied antisubmarine patrols, only one of those boats managed to reach its patrol position in the Channel by mid-June.[147]

We will see in Chapter 19 the difficulties that Allied antisubmarine forces encountered in detecting and destroying U-boats in the shallow waters surrounding the United Kingdom. Early clues about the challenges associated with inshore antisubmarine warfare emerged in the patrol of the RCN support group EG 12, which formed part of the ASW barrier at the western entrance of the Channel. Lieutenant-Commander A.H. Easton, RCNR, commanding officer of HMCS *Saskatchewan*, recalled in his memoir *50 North* that the evening of 7 June 1944 was like a "summer excursion" as the four River class destroyers of EG 12 patrolled in line abreast northeast of Ushant with CAT gear deployed against acoustic torpedoes. In the late evening, however, "a low rumble was heard, the unmistakable sound of an underwater explosion." Presuming it to be a torpedo hitting the bottom or exploding prematurely, EG 12 searched for the U-boat but found nothing. An hour later a violent blast shook *Saskatchewan*, and sixty yards off her port quarter "a solid column of water

145. DeWolf report on LCdr W. Sclater, 1 Dec 1944, Ottawa (NPRC), O-65420

146. MOD, *U-Boat War in the Atlantic* III, 67-70; Barnett, *Engage the Enemy More Closely*, 831

147. Barnett, ibid

shot a hundred feet in the air" when an acoustic torpedo exploded in her CAT gear. By the grace of "a miracle," in Easton's words, "this fast-moving, fish-like machine had self-triggered when only four seconds short of wreak[ing] havoc in the bowels of its target."[148] As the destroyers hunted for the U-boat throughout the night and the following morning, two more torpedoes exploded near *Saskatchewan*, while another narrowly missed *Skeena*.[149] When the incident was over, Easton could only signal C-in-C Plymouth, "U-boats suspected but not known."[150] Years later, Easton recalled his frustration: "Where was the enemy who was so persistently endeavouring to sink us? Where were the other U-boats? We had not the slightest idea except that we knew the one who attacked us was probably within a mile or so. The asdic could pick up nothing except useless echoes. It was extremely aggravating. Here was a submarine almost below us and here were we, a modern antisubmarine vessel, quite unable to find it."[151]

EG 12's inability to find its stalkers was the result of the abysmal antisubmarine conditions in inshore waters. Strong tidal currents and sharp temperature gradients often blinded asdic. U-boats, moreover, learned to lie on the bottom among the thousands of wrecks that littered the floor of the shallow waters surrounding the British Isles. As will be seen, antisubmarine forces with experience on the North Atlantic had to get used to a completely new type of warfare.

Positioned in more familiar territory in the deeper water of the southwest approaches, the RCN frigate groups EG 6 and 9 also found the first days of Operation Neptune to be a trying experience. They were at sea as part of Operation CA, mounted by Western Approaches Command to guard against yet another eventuality. "It is appreciated," Admiral Horton's operation order explained, "that with the onset of the invasion, the enemy will be nervous lest his U-boats are mined in their ports, and will therefore wish to get them to sea into a strategic area seaward of the 100 fathom line. From this area they can be sent into the English Channel or into the Atlantic as the situation developed." To counter this eventuality, and to thus provide the outer layer of the cork plugging the western Channel against U-boats, five support groups and maritime patrol aircraft from 19 Group Coastal Command were to patrol a large rectangular area extending about 300 miles southwest from Land's End. Two RN escort carriers accompanied the support groups in case the *Luftwaffe* or the German destroyers based on the Bay of Biscay attempted to attack the vulnerable escort vessels.[152]

Operation CA began on 5 June, and although *Luftwaffe* patrol aircraft occasionally snooped around the various forces involved, the support groups had no contact with enemy submarines in the first days of the invasion. Intelligence later revealed that in the early stages of Neptune U-boats had attempted to enter the Channel by hugging the Brittany coast, and it was only in mid-June when U-boats from Norwegian bases approached the Channel from the northeast that CA forces encountered the enemy—on 24 June *Haida* had the only RCN success when she and HMS *Eskimo*

---

148. A.H. Easton, *50 North: An Atlantic Battleground* (Toronto 1980), 251-3

149. The initial torpedoes that narrowly missed *Saskatchewan* were fired by *U 984*, while the ones later that night came from *U 953*. Rohwer, *Axis U-boat Successes*, 181

150. CO *Saskatchewan* to C-in-C Plymouth, 0935B/16 June 1944, LAC, RG 24, 11730, CS 150-17-8

151. Easton, *50 North*, 255

152. C-in-C WA, "Operation Orders for Anti-U-Boat Operation in South Western Approaches and Bay of Biscay (Operation CA), 28 May 1944, PRO, ADM 199/472. A third aircraft carrier earmarked for Operation CA could not take part due to mechanical defects.

destroyed *U 971* in the CA operating area.[153] Of course, the absence of U-boats was not understood at the time, and the support groups spent a lot of their time chasing down numerous non-sub marine contacts—an "epidemic" according to the SO EG 9—as well as bogus submarine sightings from aircraft.[154] Air-sea cooperation did not work smoothly. The senior officer of the RN's EG 1, which worked closely with EG 6 throughout the early days of CA, noted that cooperation with the Fleet Air Arm aircraft from the escort carriers worked well; "On the other hand," Commander C. Gwinner noted with evident sarcasm, "some of the [Coastal Command] aircraft engaged in Operation 'Cork' appear unaware of the very keen interest that is taken in their actions and move-ments by escort vessels patrolling in their vicinity, and not to realise what an enormous help they can be with full cooperation. One word of R/T from them can clarify a situation which will require two hours' steaming to solve."[155] As a result of this confusion and the numerous false contacts, the escort forces engaged in CA spent a lot of time on fruitless "to-ing and fro-ing." But they still had to be on their toes. Manoeuvring in close quarters with large warships like escort carriers posed considerable challenges for screening forces especially when operating at night—one has but to remember the terrible fate of HMCS *Fraser* when she collided with the cruiser HMS *Calcutta* in June 1940. As the experience of the frigate HMCS *Teme* attests, the danger increased exponentially when the threat of attack is added to the mix.

On the night of 9/10 June EG 6 was sweeping on a forty-mile line, forty-five miles southwest of the Scilly Isles, with the six frigates steaming in fan-shaped formation ahead of the carrier. At 0149 when the force was heading on course 260° with *Teme* furthest to starboard, about 5000 yards off HMS *Tracker*'s bow, the frigate detected an asdic contact at 700 yards, thirty degrees on her port bow. Considering the contact to be an immediate threat to the carrier, the frigate immediately swung to port and at 0156 fired an emergency depth-charge pattern. *Teme*'s commanding officer, Lieutenant-Commander D.G. Jeffrey, RCNR, arrived on the bridge from his sea cabin just as the attack was being carried out. Told by his asdic control officer that they still held contact, "speed was then increased to Full, helm put Hard Astarboard to run out for another attack. Although the carri-er was visible," Jeffrey reported afterwards, "light conditions may however have been unfavourable to accurate estimation of distance and inclination—I seemed to have plenty of room."

> TRACKER appeared to be practically ahead and crossing from Starboard to Port. When I saw TRACKER'S bow wave at approximately 0159B I realized that we were closer than was safe. I switched on Navigation Lights. (To which TRACKER replied with two short blasts), rang engines full ahead and a little latter [sic] put my helm hard Aport in a last effort to try and swing my stern clear. At 2000B TRACKER struck TEME on the Port side just abaft the bridge about midway between frames 45 and 62.[156]

For the next few minutes the carrier's bow chewed into the frigate, propelled by the ocean swell. After *Tracker* had eaten up twenty-four of *Teme*'s thirty-six-foot beam, the carrier finally pulled

153. For the sinking of *U 971* see McAndrew, Graves and Whitby, *Normandy*, 94-6; B.M. Gough and J.A. Wood, "'One More for Luck': The Destruction of *U-971* by HMCS *Haida* and HMS *Eskimo*, 24 June 1944," *Canadian Military History*, 10/3 (2001), 7-22

154. SO EG 9 ROP 14 June 1944, DHH 81/520/8440, EG 9, v 2

155. SO EG 1 ROP 17 June 1944, 2. PRO, ADM 199/472

156. CO *Teme*, "Collision between HMS TRACKER and HMCS TEME," nd, 1-2, DHH 81/520/8000, Teme

free. Amazingly, although her back was broken and her hull was nearly cut in two, *Teme* was towed safely to harbour by her sister HMCS *Outremont*. Casualties were fortunately light: two of the frigate's crew were killed in the collision and two more declared missing.[157]

The subsequent Board of Inquiry learned that *Tracker* had received no contact report from *Teme* and had turned to port on a new leg of her zig-zag just as the frigate was turning to starboard after her depth-charge attack. The carrier then went hard to port moments later in an attempt to avoid the collision, but despite avoiding action from *Teme*, it was too late. There were other contributing factors. Neither *Teme*'s nor *Tracker*'s radar was operating, and the carrier had no talk-between-ships (TBS), which would have facilitated the timely communication of manoeuvring orders.[158] Moreover, *Tracker* received no warning of *Teme*'s attack.[159] Jeffrey was later court-martialled for negligent performance and for hazarding his ship, but was acquitted. The accident was just one of those unfortunate occurrences that are a grim, ever-present feature of war at sea.[160]

Operation Neptune would not officially end until 3 July 1944. Within days of the assault, however, Allied naval forces had met their first two objectives: "the safe and timely arrival of the assault forces at their beaches" and "the cover of their landings." It was a resounding triumph, marked by professionalism and skill, thanks in large part to the meticulous planning of Admiral Ramsay and his staff. A good beginning had also been made on the third of Neptune's objectives: "the support and maintenance and the rapid build-up of our forces ashore." The task of covering the army's ever-expanding coastal flank lay ahead—a responsibility that would only end with the final surrender of Germany eleven months later.

---

157. Ibid, 2; CNMO, "RCN's Part in the Invasion," 187-8

158. *Tracker*'s radar was not switched on, presumably to avoid monitoring by the enemy, while *Teme*'s was under repair. CO *Teme*, "Additional Remarks on Collision Between HMS TRACKER and HMCS TEME," 6 July 1944, DHH, 81/520/8000, Teme. When the ships had taken up their steaming formation on the evening of 9th June, *Tracker*'s CO had directed the frigates that "a good lookout must be kept and individual avoiding action taken observing that we have no TBS." CO *Tracker* to Ships in Company, 1959/9 June 1944, ibid

159. Jeffrey later reported that when he arrived on the bridge he had been told that *Tracker* had been warned of *Teme*'s intentions, but the signal in DHH records indicate only that the visual signal "Have a contact on my port side" was sent to *Waskesieu* and *Grou*. *Teme* to *Waskesieu* and *Grou*, 10 June 1944, CO *Teme*, "Additional Remarks"

160. C-in-C WA to CNMO, 1809B/6 Sep 1944, DHH 81/520/8000, Teme

CHAPTER EIGHTEEN

Guarding the Seaward Flank
July 1944–September 1945

AFTER D-DAY the naval anchorage off the Normandy beaches was a scene of enormous activity. Approaching from seaward, the Motor Torpedo Boat Flotilla commander and war artist Lieutenant-Commander C.A. Law, RCNVR, "could see the other ships lying peacefully at anchor, as if they were back in the quiet Solent. Balloons hovered like a swarm of flies over the mass of shipping, and far beyond them lay the crisp outline of the Normandy coast. The whole crew had come up from below to glimpse the phenomenon, and everyone stared with wide eyes. One of my gunners remarked, 'This sure doesn't look warlike.'"[1] The appearance was, of course, deceiving. There was constant movement of landing craft and barges, and unremitting efforts to get men, vehicles and supplies ashore onto crowded and confused stretches of beach, which in the Eastern Assault Area were exposed to enemy shell fire. Nights in the English Channel after D-Day brought frequent alarms and the occasional contact with German destroyers and E-boats, as well as with the *Luftwaffe*, while submarines, small battle units, and mines remained a constant threat. Thanks to the sea and air supremacy built up over the previous year the enemy was incapable of defeating Allied forces in the Channel and its approaches, but he could have caused some disruption to shipping and rein-forcement operations had the Neptune fleet not done its job so well.

Perhaps the most active Canadian participants, in the first few weeks of Operation Overlord, were the coastal forces. Seven MTBs of the 29th Flotilla, one of the four flotillas guarding the east-ern flank, worked under control of their mother ship, the anti-aircraft cruiser HMS *Scylla*.[2] Rear-Admiral Sir Philip Vian, who commanded the Eastern Task Force and wore his flag in that ship, evidently conveyed his well-known fighting spirit to the sailors in his sector.[3] Both Law and his second-in-command, Lieutenant C.A. Burk, RCNVR, were willing instruments of that spirit, although they had little to work with in the first few days. As will be recalled, on the nights of 6/7 and 7/8 June the Canadian MTBs, encumbered as they were with depth-charges instead of torpe-does, met and engaged enemy surface forces, including destroyers, with their 2-pdr pom-poms, but they could do little more than harass or shadow the enemy.

---

1. Law, *White Plumes Astern*, 71-2

2. See Whitby, "The Seaward Defence of the British Assault Area, 6-14 June 1944," *Mariner's Mirror*, 8/2 (1994), 191-207

3. Vian was not one of Adm Ramsay's favourites: "He is d— d temperamental & at times a great annoyance & trial to me as I feel he is always apt to work against rather than with me." Diary entry for 15 June 1944, Ramsay Papers, Churchill Archive Centre, Cambridge, RMSY 8/26; see also Love and Major, *Year of D-Day*, 89.

Shortly before midnight on 8 June, Burk's three-boat division ran across two very small craft that suddenly appeared out of the night, one of them firing as it sped by. The MTBs crash-started and set off in pursuit but were quickly outdistanced.[4] Three hours later a sudden explosion of starshell close by the MTBs illuminated two enemy torpedo boats. The Canadian boats shadowed the small destroyers until they were finally spotted and fired upon. As Law's had done the night before, Burk's boats returned the enemy's accurate fire with their pom-poms and Oerlikons and escaped under cover of smoke. There was one man killed and another wounded in *MTB 464*, and slight damage was sustained by all three boats—witness to the vulnerability of MTB crews to gunfire and the sort of light but continual casualties that made coastal force operations among the most dangerous in the navy.[5]

For the next several days the fleet as a whole conducted routine patrols, antisubmarine sweeps and minesweeping tasks, and provided gunfire support, mostly from cruisers, monitors, and battleships but it had little contact with the enemy. On 11 June *Algonquin*, which had detached for Portsmouth on 10 June in order to replenish supplies and ammunition, embarked Vice-Admiral P.W. Nelles so that he could spend a day with the Canadian ships off Normandy. During the afternoon of 12 June, as Nelles returned to Portsmouth on board Law's MTB, *Sioux* and a British destroyer spent an uncomfortable three hours under fire from a coastal battery while screening a flotilla of minesweepers as they cleared a bombardment channel off Le Havre. On the 15th *Sioux* returned to Portsmouth for replenishment.[6] Although the Short MTBs of the 29th Flotilla were also given a respite in the form of several quiet nights on routine patrols east of the anchorage, maintenance was already becoming a problem. Motor torpedo boats were notoriously fragile and the constant pounding to which they were subjected was not helped by the large amount of flotsam off the invasion beaches which routinely damaged propellers. The operational cycle—forty-eight hours off the beaches followed by forty-eight hours at Portsmouth—should have allowed sufficient time to complete most repairs, but since the 29th Flotilla's maintenance unit had not been issued with a complete set of standard spare parts, the two divisions were seldom at full strength when they set out for France.[7]

The flotilla received some good news when they learned that torpedo tubes were to be refitted to restore their offensive punch. Only four boats had been re-equipped by the 12th—three in Law's division and one in Burk's—but this allowed the Canadians to confront the enemy with greater confidence when the Le Havre destroyers made another sortie against the anchorage on the night of 12/13 June. Unfortunately, frustration came from another source. As the three boats of Burk's division moved to intercept *T 28* and *Möwe*, directed by the control ship HMS *Scylla*, *MTB 464*— Burk's one boat with torpedoes—was manoeuvring to attack when *Scylla* suddenly recalled the

---

4.   Probably *Linse*, one-man boats loaded with 300 kg of explosives, piloted to within striking distance of a target, where a control boat that picked up the crew was supposed to, but never did, guide the boat by radio-control on to the target. "Coastal Forces Activity—Night of 8th/9th June 1944," nd, DHH 81/520/1650-239/13, Ops English Channel, pt 1; Hinsley, *British Intelligence* III pt 2, 457; Roskill, *War At Sea* III pt 2, 455

5.   Law, *White Plumes Astern*, 72-87; CNMO Narrative, "The Royal Canadian Navy's Part in the Invasion of France," 9 Jan 1945, 221, DHH 84/230; "Coastal Forces Activity ...8th/9th June"

6.   *Sioux* ROP, 21 June 1944, 1926-DDE-225, pt 1; *Algonquin* ROP, 1 July 1944, LAC, RG 24 (Acc 83-84/167), 697, 1926-DDE-224 pt 1; R. Hill, *Destroyer Captain: Memoirs of the War at Sea, 1942-45* (London 1986), 270-3. Hill was CO of HMS *Jervis*.

7.   CNMO narrative, "The Royal Canadian Navy's Role in the Invasion," 9 Jan. 1945, 222, DHH 84/230

entire division so that Allied destroyers could engage.[8] An exasperated Burk, who once again had a German destroyer slip away from him, thought a combined destroyer and MTB attack would have served the purpose better. As it was, such questions became academic on the evening of 14 June when a force of 221 Lancasters from Bomber Command, RAF, mounted a devastating attack on Le Havre. Informed by Enigma decrypts that three E-boat flotillas, the 5th and 9th from Cherbourg and the 4th from Boulogne, had relocated their bases to Le Havre, Bomber Command destroyed the torpedo boats *Möwe*, *Falke* and *Jaguar*; fourteen E-boats; twenty other minesweepers, patrol vessels, and escorts; and a large number of other smaller naval craft and harbour vessels. In the words of the C-in-C, *Marinegruppe West*, Vizeadmiral T. Krancke, the raid was a "catastrophe" and effectively eliminated Le Havre as a threat for the time being. The next night Bomber Command attempted to eliminate the 2nd Flotilla in an attack on Boulogne, but the E-boats were safely within their concrete bunkers and escaped damage. A depot ship, seven R-boats, and a further nineteen smaller vessels were destroyed in the raid. As a result of these attacks and the steady attrition at the hands of Allied maritime defensive forces around the beachhead, by 16 June just ten E-boats—primarily with the 2nd Flotilla—remained operational in the invasion area, and with the exception of sporadic *Luftwaffe* activity and an increasing number of mines being laid in and around the anchorage, the patrol areas on the eastern flank returned to a state of relative calm.[9]

On the western flank, after conducting defensive patrols in the first days of Neptune, the seven Fairmile Ds, or Dogboats, of the 65th MTB Flotilla began offensive operations on the night of 11/12 June with a sweep against German coastal shipping among the Channel Islands, waters that one commanding officer remembered as being "hell because of the tides and rocks and shoals that were there; and during the war, of course, because of the shore batteries that engaged you regularly."[10] On the night of 17/18 June, four MTBs under Lieutenant-Commander J.R.H. Kirkpatrick, RCNVR, the 65th's commander, made radar contact with an enemy convoy of two merchantmen and several escorts, including two minesweepers, east of the island of Sark. The Canadians sped in, fired torpedoes when they had closed to 450 yards, and rapidly withdrew to avoid heavy fire from both escorts and shore batteries. Hampered by difficult radar conditions, they tried in vain to regain contact before returning to base. Kirkpatrick claimed no torpedo hits, but the flotilla had in fact crippled the minesweeper *M 133*, which had to be towed to harbour, and inflicted casualties on board *M 4625*, at a cost of two boats slightly damaged and one man wounded.[11]

As Admiral Ramsay, naval commander for Operation Overlord, had forecast, and signals intelligence had confirmed, mines presented the greatest danger to Allied shipping, and those that presented the greatest difficulties were ground mines, most of them dropped from aircraft.[12] All types of mines were present, but two versions of a new Oyster pressure mine that had been developed

8. Ibid, 223

9. Tarrant, *Last Year of the Kriegsmarine*, 69-70. For a detailed study of the Le Havre raid see T.F. Tent, *E-Boat Alert: Defending the Normandy Invasion Fleet* (Annapolis 1996), 146-82.

10. Lt M.C. Knox, RCNVR, interview, 3 July 1987, 20, Knox biog file, DHH

11. KTB, German Naval Staff (*SKL*), Ops Division, 18 June 1944, DHH SGR/II/261; Plymouth Command to Adm, 18 June 1944, DHH 81/520/8000, 65th MTB Flotilla (Signals)—hereafter KTB, *SKL*; CNMO, "The RCN's Role in the Invasion"

12. Love and Major, *Year of D-Day*, 47-8; "Report of the Allied Naval Commander-in-Chief, Expeditionary Force on Operation 'Neptune,'" Oct 1944, app 14, DHH 83/105—hereafter Ramsay Report on Neptune; Hinsley, *British Intelligence* III pt 2, 62

operational routine, detaching two ships at a time to Plymouth for boiler cleaning. The Canadians swept, in sequence, Channel 14 from the Solent to the assault area, Channel L from the assault area to Cherbourg, and Channel H from Cherbourg back to the Solent. It took an average of five days to complete the cycle, and encounters with mines in the regularly swept channels were rare. During the last week of July, the flotilla had the additional task of replacing American patrol boats along the static defence line eight miles offshore whenever they anchored for the night in the Baie de la Seine. The experiences of the other RCN Bangors were similarly uneventful as the fighting moved inland, quickly settling into "what we ... called the milk run." The only exception came during the final assault on Cherbourg towards the end of June, when *Kenora* and *Thunder* came under fire from shore batteries.[18]

The RCN corvettes assigned to escort the build-up and blockship convoys also had little contact with the enemy. One of several exceptions came in the early hours of 9 June off Portland Bill while *Lindsay* was escorting convoy EBC 3. At 0230 hours two E-boats were illuminated by one of the RN escorts and immediately retired under cover of smoke. Aware that the marauders often returned to attack from the opposite flank, *Lindsay*'s hydrophone operator detected approaching E-boats in time for the corvette to illuminate the appropriate bearing. The enemy was sighted fine on the port bow but once again retired under cover of smoke. At 0315 the corvette was itself illuminated by the enemy, and two minutes later her hydrophone operator reported a torpedo approaching from 040. When *Lindsay* turned hard to port, a torpedo was spotted passing down her starboard side.[19]

Most contacts occurred in the anchorage area off the invasion beaches themselves, where the *Luftwaffe* concentrated its bombing efforts and where most of their air-laid mines were located. It was not always the enemy that posed the greatest danger, however. Assigned to escort the cable ship *Monarch* in laying a much-needed telephone line across the English Channel, HMCS *Trentonian* was approaching the invasion area with her charge in the early morning hours of 13 June when the crew observed a brief engagement between E-boats and destroyers off to the north. At 0235, while still some ten miles offshore, the two ships were suddenly illuminated by starshell as the same destroyers opened fire. "Firing commenced," reported *Trentonian*'s captain, "on a bearing of approximately 160 degrees." At first,

> No gun flashes were seen. Shells were heard, apparently close, afterwards passing between the two ships, then coming directly towards *Trentonian*. All shots fired at or near *Trentonian* were high, except two or three which struck the water ahead and one which passed between the funnel and pom-pom platform. As soon as the projectiles were heard, night display recognition lights were switched on and off continuously. Course was altered to 070 degrees to show silhouette and speed reduced to six knots to eliminate any possible bow wave. Fire then appeared to have been re-directed towards *Monarch*, and clouds of smoke or dust appeared over her. Her barrage balloon was seen to come down and her steam whistle was heard to blow continuously. *Trentonian*'s recognition lights were, at this time, switched on permanently. No challenge was seen at any time.[20]

18. *Caraquet* ROP, July 1944, LAC, RG 24, 11740, CS 162-15-3; CNMO, "The RCN's Part in the Invasion," 126-32; W.G. Morrow manuscript, nd, 96, DHH 86/167; "Minesweeping Summary No. 245, 21-28 June 1944"

19. Lt G.A.V. Thompson, "ROP—Convoy EBC-3," 10 June 1944, LAC, RG 24, 11737, CS 161-56-3

20. A/LCdr W.E. Harrison, "Engagement of HMTS *Monarch* by USS *Plunkett*," 30 Jan 1945, LAC, RG 24, 11739, CS 161-86-1

When the shellfire finally ceased ten minutes later, the Canadian corvette had to avoid an oncoming destroyer before she could close the damaged cable ship and tend to her wounded. Shortly afterwards, an officer from the American destroyer *Plunkett* boarded *Trentonian* to report that his ship had mistaken *Monarch* for an E-boat and opened fire when her challenge had not been answered. Four of the cable ship's crew, including her master, eventually died of their wounds. *Monarch* herself had had her steering gear wrecked and had to be towed back to the United Kingdom, and in a stroke of supreme irony "the cable over which so much time, trouble, and finally blood, had been spent, was shot from the *Monarch*'s bow and had been lost–all within sight of the far shore where it was so urgently needed."[21]

After the initial D-Day bombardment, the destroyers *Algonquin* and *Sioux* were only occasionally called upon to provide fire support for units ashore. Their most notable action came on the 23rd June when German shellfire from the east bank near the mouth of the Orne River was disrupting unloading operations on Sword beach. As part of the Allied response, *Sioux* carried out a number of direct and indirect shoots on a variety of German positions in the woods two miles inland from the village of Dives-sur-Mer. That afternoon and evening, she also fired on German batteries located on the beach west of the village of Franceville-Plage, beyond the 2nd British Army's left flank. Both Canadian destroyers returned to bombard positions beyond the Dives River on the 24th and found the action a little hotter there as German shore batteries ranged in on them. *Algonquin* carried out the final shore bombardment by the Canadian warships the next afternoon when she fired five salvoes at each of four targets behind Franceville-Plage. On 27 June both destroyers departed for Portsmouth to return to Scapa Flow and service with the Home Fleet.[22]

Despite the problems on Sword's open flank, landing ships and craft were busy transporting personnel, stores, and provisions to the other beaches with a marked degree of success. Casualties on D-Day had been lighter than expected, although getting stores and vehicles ashore at first proved more difficult than planners had envisioned. The RCN LCIs, no longer employed as flotillas, made on average two or three trips each during the next three weeks—*LCI 305* recorded five trips, the most of any craft of this type in the Allied naval task forces—and the Canadian LCIs, after landing 4617 troops on 6 June, transported an additional 7871 soldiers through the rest of the month. The six Canadian craft that participated in the ferry service, transporting personnel from ships in the anchorage to shore, carried a further 11,147 troops.[23]

The man-made hazards faced during the buildup—uncleared beach obstacles, submerged wreckage, mines and the nightly air raids—resulted in damaged propellers, anchors, and hulls. Weather, however, presented a different kind of obstacle. On 19 June, after two weeks of favourable conditions—and, ironically, the fall-back date for relaunch of Operation Overlord had General Eisenhower not ordered the landings to go ahead on the 6th—the wind blew up into a strong northeast gale that placed the entire reinforcement and resupply operation at risk. Admiral

21. CNMO, "RCN's Part in the Invasion," 150-1

22. *Sioux* ROP, 4 July 1944; *Algonquin* ROP, 1 July 1944. Although counter-bombardments such as those carried out by *Sioux* and *Algonquin* had a neutralizing effect, they could not stop the persistent German shelling of Sword from the eastern flank of the assault area, and that beach was eventually closed on 1 July. Adm, *Operation Neptune: Landings in Normandy* (London 1947), 144

23. *LCI 270* lost her kedge anchor to an enemy bomb, and *LCI 135* had her port engine damaged by a mine. CNMO, "RCN's Part in the Invasion," 110, 113-15; J. Schull, *Far Distant Ships*, 317-19

Ramsay's diary entry for that day underlines the seriousness of that situation, as well as some other challenges associated with alliance warfare:

> A day of fresh or strong Northerly winds which played havoc with work off and on the beaches in the Assault Area. The Gooseberries much in request and of course the Mulberries. Some Phoenix [breakwater] units starting to break up. Shuttle service LCTs and LSTs stopped. Pilotless aircraft continuing their attacks on London and Home Counties. One over Portsmouth area came down somewhere near Southampton. Received peremptory instructions from CNO Washington to surrender all U.S. warships taking part under me. A perfectly stupid unilateral action made without consultation with me or with Admiralty. I shall fight this and so shall the Admiralty. A typical U.S. action. Went over to Southampton PM to witness loading and assess the situation there. I found it improved but delays are still due to slowness of arrival of U.S. troops. A busy and somehow unsatisfactory day giving a feeling of frustration. Frustration due to inability to get on with the land battle; to cope satisfactorily with the mine menace and to the impending withdrawal of the majority of my naval forces: also due to the increasing number of casualties to craft.[24]

Lieutenant-Commander Law's description gives a sense of the storm's severity at the sharp end.

> The seas were smothered by angry spume, and ships tugged resentfully at their anchors. The cocky tugs which had been towing the breakwater sections lost their complacent attitude and began to look frightened when their tow-lines broke and the usual complications ensued. We MTBs were comparatively safe and snug, riding comfortably in the cosy harbour of Gooseberry ... As the storm raged on we became aware of a large repair ship drifting down toward the sunken ships which formed our breakwater. Her engines had broken down, her two anchors were dragging on the sandy bottom, and when one of the tiny tugs tried to take her in tow, the line became wrapped around the helpless ship's propellor ... In the midst of the excitement *Scylla* sent us a signal ... telling us that all operations were cancelled due to the heavy gales and ordering us to remain in our shelter. The tide continued to rise, and the sea, now blanketed by white caps, tossed tumultuously. The shrieking wind caught the spray in its angry fist and in a frenzy threw it down again, while the powerful waves crashed against the sunken line of ships, knocking them together stem to bow. The American tugs were busy towing in little boats that had fallen helpless in the face of the storm, Then the waves came crashing over the merchant ships to which we were secured, and the spray thundered down on the decks of the MTBs, which seemed to have grown smaller during the furious onslaught.[25]

As Law observed: "what a mess." Landing craft felt the brunt of the storm. *LCI 305*, for example, had to weigh anchor just after midnight when one of the breakwaters started drifting down on the vessel. She put out a kedge anchor, whose cable parted, then tried but failed to get a line across to an American LCI, and when the bow anchor line parted several hours later would have

---

24. Love and Major, *Year of D-Day*, 91-2; see also Ramsay, personal diary, 22 June 1944, Churchill Archives Centre, Cambridge University, RMSY 8/26.

25. Law, *White Plumes Astern*, 91

gone aground had she not drifted down on a fuelling trawler. A spare anchor fared no better than the others, and after finding that it was too rough outside the anchorage to ride out the storm the CO persuaded a tug to take a line, in the process of which the LCI was holed in the bow and suffered underwater damage. When the tug started dragging on the afternoon of 20 June the LCI had to cast off. The fourth and last anchor, when it was dropped, lost both flukes, so *LCI 305* put to sea and rode out the storm all night. On 21 June, when the gale had moderated slightly, the vessel put into Port-en-Bessin, but at high water three of her wires parted. Only at noon on 22 June did the seas relent enough to allow *LCI 305* to sail to Calshot, near Southampton.[26]

Damaged landing craft went to Portsmouth or Southampton for major repairs, but all other work remained the responsibility of three RCN maintenance parties, fifty officers and men altogether, who worked ceaselessly to keep the LCIs operational. Admiral Ramsay wanted the landing craft in good condition for possible further landings. The Canadian LCIs, for instance, were withdrawn from the cross-Channel shuttle service at the end of the third week of June and concentrated in anticipation of an assault on the Channel Islands. The two Prince ships, although available to make a second trip by the evening of 7 June, only made three additional crossings to Normandy that month, *Prince Henry* on 10 and 27 June and *Prince David* on 18 June, carrying a total of 1770 additional troops to France.[27] The shuttle service continued in July and August on a reduced scale. In the 262nd Flotilla only seven of eleven craft made the Channel crossing during July, making a total of twenty-one return trips. By mid-July, the Canadian Naval Mission Overseas had asked the Admiralty for information "regarding plans for future employment of the three Canadian LCI(L) flotillas, as it is understood that while some twenty of the craft are in operational condition, they are no longer being employed. As will be recalled, these craft were provided for one operation only.... As soon as they are no longer required for operational duties in the main or supporting operations, it is intended to pay off the craft and withdraw the personnel." When larger vessels began to take over most of the transportation the following month, the CNMO informed the Admiralty that the RCN would disband three Canadian flotillas as of 31 August.[28]

After 22 June, although the possibility of German interference on the eastern flank continued to occupy attention, more emphasis began to be placed on taking the offensive to the enemy. Lieutenant-Commander Kirkpatrick in the 65th MTB Flotilla, for example, was at sea on the night of 22/23 June as soon as the gale had subsided. Southwest of Jersey on the Cherbourg-St. Malo shipping lane he led his four boats in an attack on a convoy sighted and reported by a British flotilla. Illuminated by starshell and taken under fire as they approached, the Canadians closed to within 500 yards, turned, and ran along the length of the convoy. *MTB 745* had to withdraw when hit in the engine room soon after commencing the high-speed run, with three of four engines knocked out and her steering gear damaged. "*MTB 748* turned off to lay a smoke screen between *745* and the enemy," Kirkpatrick later reported, "and the enemy were within 400 yards of *745* and apparently plotted her to be a friendly escort." The other three boats raked the enemy minesweepers with 6-pounders and Oerlikons, then disengaged—*MTB 745* having managed to repair one of her

---

26.   CNMO, "RCN's Part in the Invasion," 122

27.   Ibid, 110-12, 118

28.   CNMO to Adm, 13 July and 29 Aug 1944, DHH 81/520/8000-411/264, 264th LCI Flotilla; 262 Flotilla ROP, 31 July 1944, ibid, 411/262, 262nd LCI Flotilla

engines—as daylight approached. They had sunk the minesweeper *M 4624*, damaged *M 4613*, and left the supply ship *Hydra* burning so furiously she had to be scuttled.[29]

Following the fall of Cherbourg on 25 June, Plymouth Command decided to tighten the blockade of coastal shipping by sending its MTBs and destroyers right into enemy harbour approaches. Ever aggressive, Kirkpatrick welcomed the opportunity. On the night of 3/4 July off St Malo, in pursuit of a radar contact, he encountered three merchantmen and their escorts. Manoeuvring his MTBs so as to gain an inshore firing position where they would have the shadow of the coast to cover their approach, Kirkpatrick reduced the boats' speed from ten to seven knots to cut down the bow wave, and approached in line abreast from about 3000 yards off the port bow of the convoy. Despite a full moon that extended visibility to three miles the MTBs closed to within 800 yards before they were detected, fired full salvoes of torpedoes at the merchantmen, and disengaged under heavy fire. Because *MTB 748* and *MTB 743* suffered damage and casualties Kirkpatrick decided that he had better withdraw to the west before heading back to base at dawn, but he had done well enough. The flotilla sank the patrol boats *V 208* and *V 210* and damaged the supply steamer *Minotoure*. Gunfire had also damaged another patrol boat and a minesweeper.[30] To his regret, this turned out to be Kirkpatrick's last action for the next two months, enemy coastal traffic having fallen off dramatically after the capture of Cherbourg. Frustrated, he asked Plymouth Command if the 65th could be transferred to "work in the assault area which, from all accounts, provides more opportunity of hitting the enemy" than their current area of operations where there were "few prospects of contacting enemy shipping, which has either ceased to exist, or sails only when the weather is unsuitable for coastal force craft."[31] The request was denied. Three RN flotillas were transferred but not the 65th.[32]

The 29th Flotilla's experience in the eastern assault area during late June and July proved Kirkpatrick's point that the area was more of a hot spot. The introduction of the Oyster mines had an immediate impact when the headquarters ship *Scylla* was seriously damaged by one of the devices on 23 June and had to be towed to Spithead. Lieutenant-Commander Law lamented that the MTBs no longer had "a mother to run to for food and maintenance," but she was quickly replaced by HMS *Hillary* as headquarters ship for the Eastern Task Force.[33] Less threatening, but a strain on nerves nonetheless, were the nightly raids by *Luftwaffe* bombers and the intermittent shelling by shore batteries east of the Dives River.[34]

---

29. CNMO, "RCN's Part in the Invasion," 216; KTB, *SKL*, 23 June 1944; Adm, the OIC, "Summary of German Naval Situation," 23 June 1944, PRO, ADM 223/10—hereafter Adm, the OIC, German Naval Situation

30. "Attack on Convoy off St Malo 3rd/4th July, 1944," CFPR July-August 1944, 13-14, copy in DHH 84/7; Plymouth to Adm, 4 July 1944, DHH 81/520/8000, 65th MTB Flotilla (Signals); KTB, *SKL*, 4 July 1944; Adm, the OIC, German Naval Situation, 5 July 1944; Rohwer and Hummelchen, *Chronology of the War at Sea*, 290

31. 65th Flotilla, ROP, 4 Aug 1944, LAC, RG 24, 11346, CS 164-65-3

32. Although exceedingly aggressive, Kirkpatrick was no glory hound. Press reports exaggerating the flotilla's earlier successes prompted him to complain to CNMO that "there is enough human interest in the individual ratings of the crews or in the daily life and work of the boats without resorting to such bland phrases as 'dare devils,' 'bone crushing,' 'back breaking,' 'finest ever,' 'knocking the stuffing out of,' 'knock 'em down, drag 'em out battle,' and many other phrases which only a newspaper reporter suffering from severe nightmares could construct. If such terms can sell war bonds in Canada, it is requested that the publications be limited to Canadians in Canada." Ibid

33. Law, *White Plumes Astern*, 99

34. Roskill, *War at Sea* III pt 2, 123

After the destruction of so much German naval strength at Le Havre in the 14 June air raid, the *Kriegsmarine* gathered reinforcements from further up the Channel coast and from home waters. By early July the *Führer der Schnellenboot*, or *FdS*, had twenty E-boats in Le Havre, Dieppe, and Boulogne available for operations against the anchorage. Nevertheless, an intelligence appreciation noted that the *FdS* was finding that "operations were more difficult now on account of the heavy defensive action by destroyer and motorboat groups, which prevented a breakthrough from Le Havre to the convoy routes or to the open sea. It was hoped that the introduction of the T5 ("*zaunköenig*") [acoustic torpedo] would improve the position. Success, however, could only be possible after a break through the enemy's flank defences."[35] The *FdS* would find July to be equally frustrating as the Allied MTBs and destroyers continued to block the E-boats' attempts to penetrate the anchorage.

Following a brief, initial skirmish with three E-boats on the night of 23/24 June that caused only slight damage to either side, the 29th Flotilla did not encounter the fast enemy motor boats for another two weeks. On the night of 1/2 July, however, tragedy fell upon the flotilla when *MTB 460* was destroyed. The CO of the accompanying *465*, Lieutenant C.D. Chaffey, witnessed its sudden end and reported:

> There was a very large explosion under *MTB 460* which blew the boat to pieces immediately, followed by a black column of water rising 200 feet into the air. The wreckage, the largest piece of which was about 10 feet long, was spread over a circle of about 100 yards. From the beginning there was no question of salvage and I proceeded to hunt for survivors. Six members of the crew were picked up, almost immediately after the explosion. The remainder must have been killed outright or unable to keep themselves afloat.[36]

In all, the boat's CO, his second-in-command, and eleven ratings perished in the explosion of *MTB 460*, which Chaffey concluded could only have been caused by "a contact mine of large calibre for the explosion appeared to be inside her and she was totally destroyed instantly."[37] Since pressure mines were laid almost exclusively by aircraft within the anchorage while surface boats laid contact mines outside the anchorage, where the unfortunate *MTB 460* was destroyed, Chaffey's assessment was probably correct. Law recalled that "the horrible waste of war was brought home to all the officers and crews of the 29th when they learned the sad news. The next morning there were no smiles. The crews and officers went quietly about their work, outwardly calm, yet inside throbbed a terrible pain, caused not only by the loss of their comrades, but also by the thought of others to whom those comrades were near and dear."[38]

Despite being reinforced the Le Havre E-boats were, in fact, no longer a serious threat to the eastern flank while the British-laid protective minefields immediately east of the anchorage were judged to be safe from German sweeping. As a result, the coastal forces began attacking German

---

35. Adm, "E-boat Operations and Policy, 1939-1945," May 1946, 94, PRO, ADM 223/28; Tarrant, *Last Year of the Kriegsmarine*, 100

36. Chaffey, "Action Report [ROA]," 2 July 1944, 164-29-5, LAC, RG 24, 11/744

37. Ibid; CNMO, "RCN's Part in the Invasion," 291-2

38. Law, *White Plumes Astern*, 102

shipping lanes between Le Havre and Cap d'Antifer. Control shifted from afloat in HMS *Hillary* to a plotting room ashore near Courseulles, where a Coastal Forces officer directed their movements with the aid of two control frigates. The transfer of all but two of the MTB flotillas on the western flank—the 65th being one of those left behind—brought the total on the eastern flank to nine, and on the night of 4/5 July the 29th Flotilla carried out its first offensive patrol. Law led his own and two other boats under the cliffs eight miles southwest of Cap d'Antifer, and in the light of the full moon they "could see anything that might poke its nose around Cap de la Heve [to the south]."[39] Law was soon rewarded with the sight of a "black speck" in the distance. Just before midnight, with the help of radar, the MTBs illuminated the enemy—nine E-boats from the 2nd Flotilla attempting to break out of Le Havre on a torpedo sortie—increased speed to eighteen knots and opened fire at a range of 1200 yards. With one of their number on fire, the E-boats made smoke and turned away to starboard, the RCN boats in pursuit. Since the enemy were headed in the direction of a British MTB flotilla that Law knew was positioned about eight miles to the south, he broke off the chase but was still in position to intercept the E-boats as they retreated northward. This he did, claiming several hits before being required to break off the action after shore batteries ranged in on his boats. The 29th had two more brief brushes with the enemy that night, but in both instances the E-boats retired at high speed after short engagements. The three Canadian boats, their crews exhausted, headed back to Portsmouth next morning.[40]

Losses, and the wear and tear of operations, took their toll. On 6/7 July Burk's division came out with three boats under Lieutenant C.D. Chaffey, since the former's boat was under repair. The next night Chaffey's boat damaged her propellers on flotsam and had to shelter at Courseulles. The CO of *MTB 463*, Lieutenant D.G. Creba, took over, but a mine damaged his boat beyond repair the next morning while he was searching for a midget submarine. The explosion was not as devastating as the one that claimed *MTB 460* but four men were wounded and the boat sank two hours later, leaving *MTB 466*, the last boat in the division, to return to Portsmouth with the survivors of *MTB 463* as passengers.[41]

On the night of 8/9 July, Law's three boats were in position off Cap d'Antifer shortly after midnight when they came under accurate fire from shore batteries. Law sought a new patrol position four times over the next forty minutes, but each time they stopped shells burst nearby. At 0100, as they were avoiding the enemy fire, there were signs of action to the northeast and the Canadians, no doubt happy to leave the area, set off to investigate. They found a melée in progress between two RN boats and the enemy's "night train," a group of ten R-boats that regularly sortied out of Le Havre. The German craft, motor minesweepers armed with two 37mm anti-aircraft guns, proved to be formidable adversaries, having already forced one British MTB to withdraw with heavy damage and incapacitated the second, which was stopped and on fire. The Canadians made two passes down the line of R-boats before laying a smoke screen and rescuing the survivors from the blazing British boat. Law's MTBs had all received damage, two of them with casualties, including one killed. Finding treatment for the wounded continued to pose a problem, and after being turned

39. Ibid, 103-4

40. "Report of Coastal Forces Activity Night of 4th/5th July," nd, DHH 81/520/1650-239/13, Ops English Channel, pt 1; Law, *White Plumes Astern*, 104-5; Scott, *Battle of the Narrow Seas*, 199

41. CNMO, "RCN's Part in the Invasion," 293-4

away by a hospital ship, the Canadians finally found spaces for their wounded in the battleship HMS *Rodney*.[42]

The relentless operational tempo continued unabated. Attacking the "night train" off Cap d'Antifer on the night of 13/14 July, Burk had to withdraw in the face of heavy fire from both escorts and shore batteries after the enemy convoy's alteration of course had put him in a disadvantageous firing position. The next night Law's division forced the enemy to withdraw behind a smoke screen and return to Le Havre, even though one of the Canadian MTBs was holed beneath the waterline. On the night of 15/16 July shore batteries found the range of Law's boat, obtaining a hit in the engine room that killed two men, wounded another, and put a 14-foot hole in the hull. Law managed to salvage the boat, which was eventually returned to England for repair, but the 29th Flotilla was now down to five MTBs. The Germans, however, had been forced to concede that a "breakthrough to [the] beachhead [was] impossible."[43] As was the case in other Allied flotillas, the few remaining Canadian MTBs were long overdue for refits, while the crews were utterly fatigued. "The personnel of the 29th," recalled Law, "were falling victims to horrible, haunting fears, and the boats, whose arduous task of defending the anchorage had almost burnt them out, were badly in need of repair."[44]

A partial solution to the repair problem came through the establishment of a mobile repair base, known as a Coastal Forces Mobile Unit, at Arromanches. Most routine maintenance was carried out there and boats only had to return to England for serious repairs. This allowed the entire 29th Flotilla to remain off Normandy, usually anchoring in the basin at Courseulles, with the five serviceable boats patrolling as a single unit.[45] The new arrangement only lasted two weeks, however. On 9 July Caen had fallen to Canadian and British troops, who were now fighting the arduous battles that would lead to Falaise in August. On 25 July Operation Cobra, the First US Army's breakout attack from the Normandy hedgerows, released Lieutenant-General George Patton's Third US Army to strike westward into Brittany and eastward to the north of Paris. As the Allies advanced inland, the E-boats shifted their objective from the Neptune anchorage to the British east coast convoy system. As a counter to this strategy, during the first two weeks of August the Canadian flotilla moved back to its original base at Ramsgate. It had been a gruelling seven-and-a-half week experience, but the 29th had proved effective in blunting enemy attempts to penetrate and attack the assault area off Normandy.[46]

It was in July that RCN Beach Commando W finally found its way to Normandy. After weeks of uncertainty, and the apparent probability that the unit would not be required as second reserve commando on Force J, it suddenly transpired on 4 July that W Commando was to sail in forty-eight hours.[47] It embarked in one of the Canadian LCI(L)s at Cowes on 6 July and landed on Mike Beach

---

42. KTB, *SKL*, 9 July 1944; Law, *White Plumes Astern*, 108-10; Scott, *Battle of the Narrow Seas*, 202; CNMO, "RCN's Part in the Invasion," 294-5

43. Adm, "E-boat Ops and Policy," 95, KTB, *SKL*, 14 July 1944; CNMO, "RCN's Part in the Invasion," 295-7

44. Scott, *Battle of the Narrow Seas*, 201; Law, *White Plumes Astern*, 113-19

45. Scott, ibid, 201; CNMO, "RCN's Part in the Invasion," 298

46. CNMO, ibid, 371; Roskill, *War at Sea* III pt 2, 123-4

47. Permission had just been received for the men to go on ten days leave, so that only 75 percent of the personnel were able to sail on 6 July. CNMO, ibid, 375

the next morning, just as the fleet began its bombardment of Caen. Only ten miles from the main battle, the beach, which was being used to land motor transport for the British army, remained under enemy fire and was subject to nightly air raids. The unit remained on Mike beach with No. 9 Beach Group for ten days and in that time, despite some difficulty in beaching LSTs in the dark of night, the Canadians increased the landing rate of motor transport by five hundred vehicles a day. On 18 July W Commando transferred to Nan Beach, which was a stores beach and advance headquarters for the NOIC at Courseulles. Here the duties consisted of beaching and drying out seven LCTs and eight to twelve LBVs (Landing Barge, Vehicle) on each tide, and mooring three to six coasters off the beach on each daylight tide. On 29 July the unit returned to Mike Beach. Work gradually decreased, but enemy batteries continued shelling until W Commando left on 23 August. "The unit," according to the report of the Canadian Naval Mission Overseas, "was paid off 31st August when ratings were discharged to leave and ... for disposal. The officers were almost all pleased at the prospect of general service again with its more consistent routine, but the ratings were universally disgruntled at being disbanded. They felt disappointed at not having been through the trial by fire of an assault landing for which they had been trained so arduously for so long."[48]

The Fairmile Ds of the 65th Flotilla continued their somewhat frustrating offensive sweeps along the north Brittany convoy route until the first week of September. When the 6th Armoured Division of the US VIII Corps reached the gates of Brest on 6 August, and placed the port under siege, it was up to the navy to seal it off from the remaining "fortress" ports on the Biscay coast.[49] Destroyers from Plymouth Command, although they had been able to patrol off Brest since mid-July, had too much draft to navigate safely among the shoals lying near the coast while evading fire from the numerous shore batteries. The task of inshore interdiction, therefore, fell to the MTBs. With their current base at Brixham some 130 nautical miles from Brest, in the last weeks of August the 65th Flotilla established an advanced base at L'Avervrac'h, an inlet on the Breton coast, thirty miles northeast of Brest. The inlet provided shelter for the Dogboats as well as a place to transfer fuel and provisions brought over by an RN sloop. The coastal shipping lanes provided little excitement, apart from occasional shelling from shore batteries, but with the Germans holed up in the Brest fortifications, life ashore at L'Avervrac'h provided a welcome vacation for the Canadian sailors until the flotilla moved to Great Yarmouth in September.[50]

Destroyers and cruisers from Plymouth Command, including the Canadian Tribals *Haida*, *Huron*, and later *Iroquois*, were also heavily involved in the antishipping campaign that followed the Normandy invasion. Tactical innovation and flexibility had been key factors in their victories over German destroyers, but an action at the end of June demonstrated that more traditional

---

48. Lt E.G. Finlay RCNVR, seriously wounded while in Normandy, was the only casualty of this group. He has written the only personal reminiscence of its activities, *RCN Beach Commando "W"*; CNMO, ibid, 375-6

49. In keeping with Hitler's policy to hold on to "fortress" ports, enemy units in western Brittany had retreated into the city's formidable landward defences. The garrison finally surrendered on 19 Sept. Weigley, *Eisenhower's Lieutenants*, 184-6

50. 65th MTB Flotilla ROP, 14 Jan 1945, LAC, RG 24, 11/346, CS 164-65-3; CNMO "RCN's Part in the Invasion," 369-70. During their stay at L'Avervrac'h they boarded the wreck of *T 27* driven ashore by *Haida* on 29 April.

tactics had to be used against smaller warships. It also underscored, once again, the critical importance of experience and provided a textbook example of the variables and conditions that could
impose friction on night actions, even if, as in this case, one side had overwhelming superiority.

Huron and HMS *Eskimo* had departed Plymouth late on 27 June with orders to patrol between
St Malo and the Channel Islands to intercept enemy shipping that was attempting to escape following the fall of Cherbourg. To that point *Huron* had always been a junior ship in any operation
she had been involved in but, as her first lieutenant later recalled, "for a change we were senior
ship and therefore in command of the operation."[51] Relying on the tactics used in the actions with
destroyers, *Huron*'s commanding officer, Lieutenant-Commander H.S. Rayner, deployed the two
Tribals in an open line abreast formation and planned to use their speed to advantage.

At 0052 on 28 June, while the ships were heading due east at twenty-four knots, *Eskimo*'s type
276 radar picked up a contact bearing 110° at 11,000 yards. As the range closed the contact grew
into three vessels, and at 0059 Rayner turned towards, increased to twenty-five knots, and at 0100
fired starshell at a range of 8,000 yards. The German force, consisting of a minesweeper and two
patrol boats, had warning of the Tribals' approach so that when their starshell burst overhead only
one vessel was visible, the others being obscured by a smoke screen. *Huron* and *Eskimo* immediately engaged this target and by 0105 the minesweeper *M 4620* was ablaze.[52]

In the midst of this initial skirmish *Eskimo*'s bridge personnel observed "a number of bright
flashes ... from the direction of St Malo." Moments later "six to eight salvoes fell in line with the
Bridge, 40-50 yards short." Under fire from shore batteries, the two Tribals turned away to port,
then turned again to 090° and increased speed to thirty knots to resume their attack on the enemy
ships. According to the subsequent report by *Eskimo*'s CO, Lieutenant-Commander E.N. Sinclair,
RN, starshell revealed "the initial burning ship (Target 'A') and a line of thick white smoke extending for about a mile, to the right of which an enemy ship was observed. She was the smoke layer
(Target 'B')." Then,

> HURON continued to engage the burning ship (Target 'A'); ESKIMO engaged the right
> hand ship (Target 'B'), but shortly HURON shifted her fire to ESKIMO's target ('B').
> HURON was unable to fire more than a few salvoes before the range became foul.
> HURON was slightly abaft ESKIMO's Port beam at this time, distant seven cables
> [1400 yards]. She then, presumably, re-engaged her first target ('A'), while ESKIMO
> pressed on towards the right hand enemy, and passed through the smoke screen close
> to this ship (Target 'B').

The two Tribals had split up, and when the British destroyer emerged from the smoke screen
she found herself under the guns of a third German vessel, the patrol boat *V 213*, which opened
"a rapid and accurate fire on Eskimo using one 3-inch gun, one Bofors and about four Oerlikons.
She obtained hits with Oerlikon on the ship's side and after superstructure almost at once and
before her fire could be returned." This "unpleasantly rapid and accurate fire" had devastating
results. Two 20mm shells damaged pipes in the boiler room and slowed the big destroyer to six

---

51. RAdm P.D. Budge, RCN, "Address to HMCS *Huron* reunion," 19 Sep 1981, 11, DHH, 82/92

52. LCdr H.S. Rayner, ROA, 28 June 1944, 1, LAC, RG 24, 11730, CS 151-12-7; LCdr E.N. Sinclair, ROA, 28 June 1944, 1; PRO, ADM 199/532

knots, while others cut the electrical cabling providing power to the *Eskimo*'s communications, radar and gunnery control system. Finally, the power to the pom-pom failed and a twin Oerlikon jammed, thus as Sinclair ruefully noted, "in effect we were almost outgunned by this determined and gallant trawler." To make matters worse, he could not open up with what guns did work because *Huron* lay somewhere down the same bearing as his assailant.

After beating up *Eskimo*, at 0136 *V 213* escaped eastward under the cover of the clouds of smoke and steam that hung over the area. The British destroyer therefore resumed fire on the only target in sight—the patrol boat that was *Eskimo*'s earlier target B—and a short while later regained enough steam pressure to make twenty knots. Since the target stubbornly refused to go down, Sinclair attempted to sink it through the novel use of MTB tactics, manoeuvring his destroyer to within forty yards of the trawler and firing a depth-charge. This too failed, and *Eskimo* resorted to gunfire.

While *Eskimo* endured her adventure, *Huron* had continued to engage what proved to be *M 4620* to the northwest. At 0137 the minesweeper blew up and sank, and upon learning of *Eskimo*'s damage Rayner ordered Sinclair to disengage to westward. *Huron* took on the task of engaging the patrol boat, quickly setting it on fire. Rayner then searched eastward for *V 213*, but when nothing was found, he returned to finish off the patrol boat. Finally, *Huron* regained contact with *Eskimo*, and the two Tribals returned to Plymouth.

Senior staff in Plymouth Command applauded the results of the action. Admiral Leatham noted that it "was conducted with all the skill and dash to which I am accustomed from the ships of the 10th Destroyer Flotilla, and was brought to a highly successful conclusion." Captain (D) Plymouth claimed that "considerable credit is due to the Commanding Officers and personnel of both ships for their conduct of this enterprising interception, and for the high degree of Gunnery and Operational efficiency revealed in the Reports of this action."[53] The positive reaction can perhaps be expected, given that Leatham and Morice enjoyed close relations with the 10th DF; moreover, their comments were written at a time when the war at sea was going exceedingly well, particularly in Plymouth Command. More sober second thought came from the Admiralty, where officers found the results of the action disturbing. Two powerful destroyers had engaged three light craft under promising circumstances, yet had only managed to sink two, while the third not only managed to escape but had temporarily crippled one of the Tribals. According to them the mistakes were obvious. First, *Huron* and *Eskimo* had lost contact with one another, which Captain St J. Cronyn, the Director of Training and Staff Duties (DTSD)—a persistent critic of the conduct of surface actions fought by Plymouth forces—noted caused the "cohesion" of the force to be lost. Cronyn and other staff officers thought the Tribals should have fought in line ahead "which experience has shown to be the best formation in this type of action." Furthermore, rather than decreasing speed after making contact, Rayner "increased to 30 knots which was quite unnecessary and which must have complicated a true appreciation of the situation and interfered with gunnery."[54]

To his credit, Rayner admitted in his own report that he had made a fundamental tactical error. "I treated the enemy initially as destroyers," he observed, "that is high speed vessels, as from pre-

53.   C-in-C Plymouth, "ROA with Enemy Minesweepers and/or Trawlers," 29 July 1944; Capt (D) Plymouth, "Remarks on ROA between H.M. Ships HURON and ESKIMO on 27th/28th June, 1944," 2 July 1944. PRO, ADM 199/532

54.   DTSD min, 8 Sep 1944. PRO, ADM 199/532

vious destroyer engagements I was obsessed with the idea of not letting the enemy get away."
Thus, the root of the problem lay in the aggressiveness that the 10th DF had demonstrated since
April. As Rayner alluded, that might have been appropriate when countering German destroyer tactics of turning to fire torpedoes and then using their speed to escape, but it was clear that a different method would have to be utilized against enemy light craft, who could usually make only half
the Tribals' speed. *Eskimo*'s ordeal also demonstrated the dangers of getting too close to the enemy
and emphasized the importance of standing off at first contact to take advantage of one's overwhelming gunnery advantage. Plymouth Command absorbed those and other lessons, and subsequent actions against similar opposition often became akin to slaughter.

With the fall or isolation of German bases like Cherbourg and St Malo, Plymouth Command
extended its antishipping sweeps into the Bay of Biscay. The 10th Flotilla's first foray into the bay
on the night of 12/13 July proved uneventful, but two nights later *Tartar*, *Blyskawica*, and *Haida*
intercepted three submarine chasers putting to sea from Lorient, one of which was towing a battle
practice target for a gunnery shoot with a coastal battery. After a thirty-minute gun battle, the
destroyers sank two of the small enemy vessels; the third escaped back to port.[55] This seemingly
minor skirmish had far-reaching consequences. The *Kriegsmarine*'s Commander-in-Chief
Marinegruppe West, Vizeadmiral Krancke, recognized the Allied intention of blockading major ports,
which would make the passage of U-boats into the Atlantic even more difficult. The *Luftwaffe*
accordingly tasked its long range bomber wing, *KG 100*, to attack blockading warships with glider
bombs, and on 20 July, as the Canadian support group EG 9 patrolled off Brest to catch U-boats leaving that port, a glider bomb attack damaged the frigate HMCS *Matane* (see Chapter 20).[56]

When Patton's Third US Army broke into Brittany during the first days of August, the
Kriegsmarine began transferring warships and personnel from outlying ports to the larger
"fortresses," which were expected to hold out indefinitely. Plymouth Command countered with a
series of offensive sweeps known as Operation Kinetic. Antisubmarine groups patrolled offshore
for escaping submarines, supported by destroyers of the 10th DF, accompanied by cruisers from the
10th Cruiser Squadron. By day the destroyers and cruisers screened the support groups and by
night they moved inshore to search for German coastal convoys. Aircraft from Coastal Command
and the escort carrier HMS *Striker* supported both operations.[57]

The first three Kinetic sweeps were uneventful, but on the night of 5/6 August Force 26—the
cruiser HMS *Bellona* and the Tribals *Tartar*, *Ashanti*, *Haida* and *Iroquois*, the latter just returned
from refit in Canada—,intercepted a convoy off Ile d'Yeu. Although German coastal radar detected
these ships an hour before midnight on 5 August, and held contact for nine minutes, the enemy's
coastal traffic does not appear to have been forewarned. Around midnight *Tartar* gained a radar
contact to the northeast at a range of seventeen miles. The contact was soon identified as ships
proceeding on a southerly course, and at 0010 on 6 August *Bellona*, whose CO, Captain C. Norris,
RN, was senior officer of Force 26, altered course towards the enemy and increased speed to twen-

55. KTB, *SKL*, 15 July 1944; 10th DF ROA, 17 July 1944, PRO, ADM 1/15786; *Haida* ROA, 15 July 1944, LAC, RG 24 (acc 83-84/167), 696, 1926-DDE-215, pt 1

56. KTB, *SKL* 14 July 1944, DHH, SGR/II/261

57. CNMO, "RCN's Part in the Invasion," 320-1; Hinsley, *British Intelligence* III pt 2, 247, 464-5; Roskill, *War at Sea* III pt 2, 129-30

LCAs from the Canadian LSI's *Prince David* and *Prince Henry* engaged in a landing exercise on the Italian coast prior to Operation Dragoon, August 1944. (LAC PA206495)

Short motor torpedo boats of the 29th MTB Flotilla. With a crew of three officers and fourteen ratings, the seventy-two-foot-long boats had a top speed of more than thirty knots. (DND JT-307)

ty-five knots in order to circle behind the convoy and cut it off from the coast. As the Allied war-ships closed the enemy formation from the landward side *Bellona*'s search radar broke down, so Norris chose to open the engagement at the relatively long range of 15,000 yards. The four Tribals formed line ahead in front of the cruiser, and she in turn provided illumination with her main for-ward armament. Captain B. Jones, commanding the 10th Flotilla, who enjoyed independent con-trol of the destroyers, directed them to switch on their fighting lights to help reduce the inevitable confusion of a night action[58]

Bellona's starshell burst over an eight-ship convoy transporting some nine hundred soldiers southward from St Nazaire. *Tartar* and *Ashanti* engaged the starboard flank of the convoy, *Haida* and *Iroquois* the port. When *Bellona*'s starshell proved insufficient, Commander H.G. DeWolf requested that *Iroquois* illuminate the target as well allowing his own ship, *Haida*, to open fire on a trawler at a range of 8500 yards. She scored hits with her first salvoes and in four minutes the trawler was ablaze. *Iroquois* and one of the RN destroyers next directed their fire on an M class minesweeper, which also burst into flames. *Iroquois* targeted a second minesweeper and *Haida* a third. Their gunnery was up to its usual high standard, both minesweepers were "soon well alight," and at about 0100 *Haida*'s target blew up. *Bellona* now blocked any possi-bility of escape to the south, so the destroyers circled to the north of the convoy. At 0102 *Haida* and the two RN destroyers engaged a ship "of not less than 3000 tons, with raised fox'le [sic] long fore well deck and bridge deck-house and large funnel aft and had a tower erected right for-ward on the raised fox'le." By 0109 DeWolf considered this ship, the cable layer *Hoher Weg*, to be sinking and directed *Ashanti* to finish it off. At 0117 *Haida* altered to the southwest, and for the next eleven minutes fired on two coasters and a minesweeper, destroying the latter and observing one of the coasters to capsize and sink. Jones ordered *Iroquois* to finish off the ves-sels on the convoy's port side. Commander J.C. Hibbard brought his ship round to a southward course, firing on one burning target and on another that was stopped, turned to the east in the direction of radar contacts and engaged two more stopped ships, then chased a small merchant ship and a trawler trying to get away to the northeast. *Iroquois* sank the merchant ship, set the trawler on fire, then found and engaged two more vessels, one identified as an M class minesweeper.[59]

After concentrating his force, Norris led his warships "on a tour of the battle area with a view to completing the destruction of the enemy ships."[60] *Bellona*, *Haida*, and *Iroquois* began this task by setting a coaster ablaze, but just then a powerful explosion ripped through *Haida*'s Y turret. A high explosive round and charge had exploded in the right gun of *Haida*'s after 4.7-inch mount-ing "just as the tray was being withdrawn and the breech had started to close." Two sailors were killed outright and the gun trainer would likely have perished as well if not for the bravery of Able Seaman M.R. Kerwin who "although blinded and dazed by the explosion and wounded by splin-ters went into the blazing gunshield, at great risk to his own life and succeeded in dragging the injured trainer to safety. Both were seriously injured." The fire was quickly extinguished and

58. *Bellona* ROA, 30 Aug 1944, PRO, ADM 116/4960; *Haida* ROA, 6 Aug 1944, 695, 1926-DDE-215, pt 1; *Iroquois* ROA, 12 Aug 1944, DHH 71/206

59. *Iroquois* ROA, 12 Aug 1944; *Haida* ROA, 6 Aug 1944; Jones, *And So To Battle*, 96

60. Norris ROA, 30 Aug 1944, PRO, ADM 116/4960

Haida, minus Y turret, resumed her role in the action.[61] Force 26 moved through the battle area for another twenty minutes laying down fire on any German vessel that looked as though it might survive. After concluding that no further damage could be inflicted, Norris headed northwest to search for further shipping. Force 26 had sunk six ships: two minesweepers, one patrol boat, one cable layer, and two coastal auxiliary sailing vessels.[62]

After Force 26 had been steaming on their new course for about an hour, *Tartar* made radar contact with another four or five vessels eight miles to the north. At Jones's recommendation Norris briefly withdrew southward to allow the convoy to advance farther out to sea, but after holding this course for six minutes, and fearful of losing contact, Norris could "stand this course for no longer," altered back to 000 degrees and put on twenty knots to close the enemy. At 0335 *Bellona* illuminated a four-ship convoy, three minesweepers and an aircraft tender, at 8600 yards. The destroyers opened up two minutes later but there was a light mist over the sea making targets difficult to discern. Moreover, *Haida* had another round explode prematurely, this time in A turret, so that with DeWolf using X mounting to fire starshell for the remainder of the action he had less than half of his main armament, the two 4.7s of B turret. *Haida* appeared to score a hit, but the heavily outgunned German ships gave a good account of themselves "and put up some well-controlled starshell and HE which burst close above *Haida*."[63]

The friction that typically affected night surface actions now increased significantly. By 0342 both *Bellona* and *Tartar* had lost sight of the enemy in the mist. Finding the situation "most obscure" and feeling "very cramped for room," Norris ordered his forces to withdraw westward "whilst the matter was sorted out." At the same time he learned that *Bellona* had expended almost all her starshell and was then informed by his Headache operator, falsely as it turned out, that E-boats were in the area. Unable to provide illumination, admittedly confused about the tactical situation, and concerned about the lack of sea room for his cruiser, Norris concluded that he "no longer was in a position to control the Force as a whole," and signalled to Jones to "manoeuvre destroyers. I will conform." This did not stop the confusion: when Jones ordered the force to alter to 150° to close the enemy, the signallers in *Tartar* miscommunicated the instructions so that they read 250°—or away from the enemy. Concluding that Jones was breaking off the action and that "no further results could be obtained," Norris intervened to order Force 26 to withdraw westwards, thus allowing the German ships to escape after suffering only light damage. Jones later maintained that at this point he should have suggested to Norris that the destroyers make another run, but in the heat of the moment chose not to do so. The failure to destroy the four enemy vessels, despite overwhelming superiority, overshadowed the earlier success of that night.[64]

With *Haida* out of action for repairs to her turrets and *Huron* on passage to Canada for refit, the only Canadian destroyer left in the 10th Flotilla was *Iroquois*. Less experienced than her sis-

---

61. The mishap was later attributed to a loose or missing protective cap on the cordite charge. DWT (RCN) memo, 28 Sep 1944, LAC, RG 24 (Acc 83-84/167), 695, 1926-DDE-215, pt 1; Adm, Honours and Awards Cte min, 24 Oct 1944, PRO, ADM 116/4960

62. *Bellona* ROA, 30 Aug 1944; KTB, *SKL*, 6 Aug 1944

63. *Haida* ROA, 6 Aug 1944; *Bellona* ROA, 30 Aug 1944

64. Ibid

ters because she had missed the destroyer actions in April and June, *Iroquois* was nevertheless, as a result of a major refit and upgrade, superior in both armament and sensors. The number of her close-range weapons had been increased by fitting six twin 20mm Oerlikon mountings in lieu of single mountings and a power mounting for the quadruple 2-pounder pom-pom. The addition of type 128CV asdic improved her antisubmarine capability. New radar fitted on her return to the UK, moreover, brought *Iroquois* up to the standard of the most modern RN destroyers. Type 285P gunnery radar replaced the old type 285M and, more importantly, type 293 surface warning radar, installed at the head of the new lattice foremast replaced the original type 271Q.[65]

As much as they greatly enhanced a warship's ability to detect, track, and engage the enemy, new and more powerful sensors such as those fitted in *Iroquois*, as well as other related equipment, also created challenges in the dissemination of information. Under the systems that existed in the first years of the Second World War, officers received tactical or "action" information directly from its source. Radar reports, for example, flowed from the radar office, while antisubmarine contact information came from the asdic hut, and signals originated in the wireless office or from TBS on the bridge. As a 1942 report from a destroyer captain working British coastal convoys emphasized, this system had become overburdened. "The introduction of new instruments in ships such as RDF, Headache, VHF, R/T and Asdics, and the rapidly extending use of RDF on shore and in aircraft," commented Commander G.B. Sayer, "have produced the means of providing HM ships at sea, and particularly those employed in narrow waters, with a large amount of information which, if properly used, can be of greatest value in successfully bringing the enemy to action." But,

> Unfortunately, up to date, adequate provision for co-ordinating and handling such information in destroyers has been lacking. As each new instrument has been installed some form of communication with the bridge has admittedly been fitted, but generally without regard to other lines of communication, and with the result that a state has now been reached where complication and confusion is liable to occur and the maximum value cannot be obtained from the many available sources of information.[66]

These and similar comments from other operational commanders caused the Admiralty to form an Action Information Organization (AIO) committee which was charged with formulating staff requirements for such systems in both future and existing ships.[67]

The committee identified arrangement of equipment and effective communications networking as the essential components for AIO. In terms of equipment the main features were to be operational and weapons plots upon which the information from various sources could be displayed. So that this information could then be provided to operational commanders, be they task group commanders or watchkeepers, "the organization in all ships will include a well balanced system of internal communications including radar displays in order to co-ordinate the information received from all sources, plot and filter it as necessary and pass out to the authorities and control centres

---

65.   Ships Equipment Card, 27 Nov 1944, DHH 81/520/8000, Iroquois

66.   Cdr G.B. Sayer, RN, to C-in-C Plymouth, 26 Dec 1942, PRO, ADM 1/13326. Sayer was CO of the Hunt class destroyer HMS *Cleveland*. Similar comments came from the C-in-C Eastern Fleet and the commanders of two destroyer flotillas.

67.   AIO committee's terms of reference are in Adm B.B. Schofield, *Navigation and Direction: The Story of HMS Dryad* (London 1977), 74

who require to take action on it."[68] The committee set out specific requirements for each type of ship, but priority went to Fleet Destroyers, presumably because two new designs, the Battle and Weapons classes, were just being laid down, while another program, the CAs, CRs, and CHs, was in the early stages of construction.

The physical spaces included under the AIO were designated the Action Information Centre or AIC, which would include an operations room, Target Information Room, Asdic Office and Headache room. The operations room, as described by the AIO committee, was the "kernel" of this organization and should contain the equipment necessary to fight and navigate that particular ship or a force under its control, including a strategic and navigational hand plot, a tactical plot based on an ARL (Admiralty Research Laboratory) table, an air plot, a warning combined (WC) radar display with PPI (plan position indicator), asdic range and bearing indicators, echo sounding recorder, gyro repeater, clock, speed indicator and/or distance register, navigational radar, and a box containing the current recognition signals sheet. The operations room was to be situated on the signals deck immediately below the bridge so that officers on the bridge could see the main plot through a view plot. The other compartments in the AIC would be directly connected to the operations room by either doorways or hatches. Sharing of information among these systems and spaces was to include arrangements for both "the supply of incoming information from all sources within the ship" as well as "outgoing information to the Command, Armament Control Positions and external communication positions," and therefore linked the AIC, the W/T, and target indication rooms, all D/F and radar operators, lookouts as well as the CO and gunnery and torpedo control officers. Communications within this system—eventually known as the Action Information Intercom (AID)—were by sound-powered telephones and intercoms. Similarly, the gunnery control officer relayed his fire distribution orders over an Armament Broadcast System (ABD).[69]

The concept formulated by the AIO committee became the basis for action information organization in all new construction destroyers, including the four Tribals being built in Halifax Shipyards Ltd. It was another matter, however, to fit these systems in destroyers already in service; shipyard space was too scarce, and the numbers of modern fleet destroyers too inadequate to consider the modification of existing bridge spaces to comply with the design for new construction ships. The Admiralty therefore concentrated on an interim design that upgraded internal communications systems. The signal and plotting office, located at the front of the signal deck immediately below the bridge in Tribal and subsequent fleet destroyers, was to serve as the AIC, while the fitting of an Action Information Intercom similar to that developed for new construction, would link the various elements that composed the AIO. Commanding officers were directed to insert the latter item as a high priority in their list of alterations and additions but no timetable was given as to when this work was to be done except that the first step, wiring the action intercom and armament broadcast systems, was to be carried out "whenever an opportunity occurs." With dockyard space tight and the operational tempo high that was difficult to accomplish, and by late 1944 many fleet destroyers still had not been fitted with AIO. These included most of the RCN ships, as NSHQ chose to fit the necessary systems when the ships came home to Canada for major refits. As

---

68.   Adm, "Action Information in HM Ships: Outline and Policy," CAFO 1455/43, 15 July 1943

69.   Adm, "Action Information in HM Destroyers," 26 Aug 1943

a result of this policy, although the process was delayed, RCN destroyers received the more comprehensive system rather than the interim AIO package.

The Canadian naval staff first became aware of the new AIO arrangements at its 23 November 1943 meeting when the Deputy Director of Warfare and Training (DWT), Captain H. McMaster, RN, tabled the Admiralty's staff requirements for fleet destroyers. McMaster noted that the requirements only applied to future designs and that the Admiralty still had requirements for existing ships under consideration. In the ensuing discussion the Director of Naval Construction, Captain A.N. Harrison, RN, expressed concern about fitting the system in the first two Tribals being built in Halifax; and the naval staff decided to take no further action until the Admiralty provided additional information.[70] That came in January 1944, when the DWT, Captain K.F. Adams, was able to report to the staff that the Admiralty considered AIO "essential for efficient operation of modern armament," and that ships already in service should be fitted with the interim communications systems—the Action Information Intercom and the Armament Broadcast System. The naval staff accepted Adams's recommendation that the interim AID and ABD be fitted in *Micmac* and *Nootka*, the Tribals furthest along in Halifax. No mention was made of fitting even the interim system in the four Tribals already in commission, an oversight made more surprising by the fact that *Iroquois* was scheduled to arrive in Halifax for a major refit that February.[71]

The Admiralty caught this omission, and on 1 March signalled NSHQ that they "strongly recommended" that AIO be fitted in *Iroquois* during her upcoming refit. The issue had been examined in detail by RN constructors, who informed NSHQ that the work entailed was "not prohibitive during normal course of refit." The Admiralty further reported that the CO of *Iroquois* had been provided with general arrangement drawings before the ship left Great Britain, and that other details would be forwarded through SCNO when they became available.[72] One can only speculate about Commander Hibbard's role in this, but he was a proven innovator—he had developed the Night Attack Teacher that had proved invaluable in training escort personnel for the rigours of the Battle of the Atlantic—and as the aftermath to the *Iroquois* mutiny demonstrated he was willing to go directly to higher authorities to achieve his ends. HMS *Tartar*, *Iroquois'* flotilla mate in Plymouth, had been fitted with an interim AIO organization, and Hibbard may well have understood the opportunity presented by his ship's upcoming refit and recommended that the Admiralty spur NSHQ into action.

The signal obviously caught the Canadian naval staff off guard. In a minute to Adams, Harrison admitted "this is a little beyond me." On one hand, the fitting of AIO was "a must for RCN Tribals if they are to be kept up to date," yet in spite of the Admiralty's opinion, there was "a large amount of work to be done," and *Iroquois'* refit was scheduled to be completed by 28 May 1944. Moreover, the naval staff had yet to approve the scheme, there was no idea of the costs involved, and they did not have a complete set of drawings so that it was unclear

---

70. NSM, 23 Nov 1943. The first two Tribals under construction at Halifax, *Micmac* and *Nootka*, were laid down in May and June 1942 and launched in September 1943 and April 1944 respectively but were not fitted out in time for wartime service. The second batch, *Cayuga* and *Athabaskan II*, were laid down in May and Oct 1943, and were launched in July 1945 and May 1946 respectively.

71. DWT memo, 5 Jan 1945. LAC, RG 24 (Acc 83-84/167), 3617, NSS 8040-300, pt 1; NSM, 10 Jan 1944

72. Adm to NSHQ, 1 Mar 1944, LAC, ibid

precily what work was involved. To expedite matters NSHQ despatched the Deputy Director of the Signals Division and a representative from Harrison's department to review arrangements.[73]

From this point on the RCN's actions with regard to AIO demonstrated the lessons they had learned about embracing new technology and getting it into ships at sea. Within a month of receiving the Admiralty's recommendation they acknowledged AIO to be an "essential requirement" in destroyers and launched an investigation about fitting it in all its major ship types from corvettes to escort carriers. Once this was approved by the Naval Board, NSHQ despatched an officer overseas to obtain the latest technical information required to fit AIO in the destroyers building in Halifax, and in London the SCNO requested that the Admiralty keep them apprised of the latest trends in policy for all ships. Meanwhile the naval staff convened its own AIO committee under the DWT to decide future policy. This included the training of personnel, and in March 1945 an AIO training facility was established at the signals school at Ste Hyacinthe, Québec. And although NSHQ decided not to fit full AIOs in the River class destroyers, frigates or corvettes, by the end of 1944 the three surviving Tribals all had comprehensive AIOs fitted, while the two Fleet Vs, *Algonquin* and *Sioux*, received the same treatment when they returned from the United Kingdom in the late winter and spring of 1945 respectively.[74]

Minor differences existed across the five fleet destroyers, and it was the system used in *Iroquois* that provided the template for those that followed. Her conversion also proved the most difficult. Not only was *Iroquois* the first RCN ship to receive AIO but as has been seen, the RCN had little warning or information about what had to be done, and therefore most of the required equipment had to be fitted when she returned to the UK. Despite the short time lines, however, the Dockyard in Halifax managed to complete the structural changes required for an effective AIO layout. The original combined signals and plotting office was expanded athwartships to encompass an existing lobby, which resulted in an operations room that spanned the entire superstructure one deck below the bridge. Work also began on a Headache office and sleeping quarters for AIO personnel. Upon *Iroquois'* return to England, the Headache office was completed, a Target Indicator Room constructed, and the AID, ABD, and PPI for type 293 radar installed. When the work was completed in July 1944, *Iroquois* had an AIO that was nearly identical to that outlined in the Admiralty's staff requirements for "future destroyers." The only apparent differences were that a distinct navigational radar display was not fitted in the operations room, the asdic hut—positioned at the rear of the bridge—was not moved adjacent to the operations room, and voice pipes still had to be relied upon for some of the communications links.

Hibbard ensured that the AIC was manned to best effect. He initially placed *Iroquois'* navigator, Lieutenant C.J. Benoit, RCN, in charge of the operations room, but when the ship became operational in late July, he designated Lieutenant G.W. Stead, RCNVR, as the AIO officer. It was a good choice. One of the RCNVRs the RCN had loaned to the RN early in the war for service in Coastal Forces, Stead had seen plenty of action in command of motor launches in the Mediterranean and

---

73.   DNC min, 6 Mar 1944; DNC memo, "HMCS Iroquois—Action Information Organization," 3 Mar 1944; DWT memo, "Action Information Organization," 8 Mar 1944. LAC, ibid

74.   NSM, 27 Mar and 17 July 1944; NBM, 10 Apr 1944; DWT memo, "Action Information Systems [AIS] for River Class and Tribal Class Destroyers," 17 Mar 1944; NSHQ to SCNO(L) and Adm, 5 Apr 1944; CNMO to Adm, 3 June 1944; DWT memo, 17 July 1944. LAC, ibid

had been awarded the DSC and Bar.[75] *Iroquois'* CO wanted to tap into that experience. Stead recalled that "Hibbard gave me to understand that in action he wanted me at the other end of the voice-pipe to the bridge as, aside from himself and Coughlin [Lieutenant C.R. Coughlin, RCNVR, *Iroquois'* First Lieutenant], I was the only officer who had been in command in action and might better understand his needs up on the bridge in the dark."[76] When *Iroquois* was at action stations, two ratings, supervised by Benoit, kept the navigational plot and monitored the type 293 PPI. Positioned at the ARL table, Stead plotted that and other information, and reported relevant details directly to Hibbard, providing him with a current and accurate picture of the operational setting. None of AIO crew had attended a special training course, and to ensure they kept sharp, Hibbard always kept the operations room manned at sea plotting all air and sea contacts. This "continual practice," and indeed *Iroquois'* entire action information organization, proved their worth in the actions that followed.[77]

In mid-August *Iroquois* joined the cruiser HMS *Mauritius* and the destroyer HMS *Ursa* to form Force 27 for operations in the Bay of Biscay. Force 27's mission, as outlined by C-in-C Plymouth, was quite straightforward: "To destroy enemy shipping, to obtain information of the situation and to show the flag ... off Biscay coast from Chausse de Sein to Gironde."[78] Prior to setting out on their first patrol on 13 August, Force 27's senior officer, Captain W.W. Davis, RN, CO of *Mauritius*, explained to his two subordinates—Commander D.B. Wyburd, RN, in *Ursa* and Hibbard in *Iroquois*—that he planned to deviate from Plymouth Command's standard operating procedure that now had surface forces attempting to provoke the enemy by closing the coast during daylight, by instead standing some twenty-five miles offshore during daylight so as not to disclose their presence and moving inshore under cover of darkness to sweep the most likely shipping lanes. The cruiser was to lead the two destroyers into action unless a lack of sea room prevented *Mauritius* from doing so, in which case the wing destroyer closest to the enemy, "whichever she might be, would have complete freedom to alter course and speed as requisite for leading in to engage the enemy."[79] This disregard of seniority, which gave either Hibbard or Wyburd control of the force if they led it into action, was an expression of teamwork that could only boost their confidence.

Arriving off Belle Ile south of Lorient at 0100 on 14 August, Force 27 made an uneventful sweep south before heading further out to sea as dawn approached. The next night they headed for the mouth of the Gironde River and turned north towards St Nazaire. As Force 27 swept northwards it was held intermittently by coastal radar, which they jammed. At about 0200 on 16 August, southwest of Les Sables d'Olonnes, *Iroquois* obtained a firm radar contact 27,000 yards to the northeast, confirmed by *Ursa* soon after. Davis assessed these as surface vessels steaming south, and he put Force 27 on an intercepting course. Because they were in shoal waters he adopted line

75.   For his experiences in the Mediterranean, see Stead's excellent memoir, *A Leaf Upon the Sea* (Vancouver 1988).

76.   Stead to M. Whitby, 1 Mar 1990. Coughlin, an enormously popular officer, had commanded the corvette HMCS *Chilliwack* prior to being appointed to *Iroquois*.

77.   *Iroquois* ROA, 28 Aug 1944

78.   C-in-C Plymouth to *Mauritius*, *Ursa*, and *Iroquois*, 12 Aug 1944, DHH 71/206

79.   *Mauritius* ROA, 3 Sep 1944; *Ursa* ROA, 19 Aug 1944, PRO, ADM 116/4960

ahead, *Ursa* leading and *Mauritius* at the rear.[80] Just after 0300, starshell from *Ursa* and *Iroquois* illuminated the aircraft tender *Richthofen*, the minesweeper *M 385* and the RCN's old adversary, the destroyer *T 24*, on passage from St Nazaire to Royan. In the ensuing exchange, during which the German destroyer laid down an effective smoke screen and enemy coastal batteries straddled the Allied ships on several occasions, *T 24* burst out of the smoke screen and launched two torpedoes seen to pass ahead of *Iroquois*. The Canadian warship countered with her full outfit of torpedoes, but it was from a poor firing position and they missed the narrow retreating target. *Ursa* and *Iroquois* chased their quarry for another twenty minutes, well inside an Allied minefield, but gave up the pursuit when shore batteries began to find the range. They had forced the minesweeper to beach and inflicted moderate damage on both the *Richthofen* and *T 24*.[81]

After the destroyers had rejoined the cruiser and had steamed northward for about an hour they found and attacked a coastal tanker, which "obstinately refused to catch fire" despite repeated hits, and drove this vessel aground as well. Another hour later they came upon two minesweepers and an auxiliary vessel heading southeast. Davis, who could not take the cruiser into the shallow water, ordered *Iroquois* and *Ursa* to engage. At 0620 the destroyers opened fire from 3000 yards, but they were unable to stop the enemy vessels even though "all three ships were hit fairly hard." Given the heavy return fire from the German ships and shore batteries, *Iroquois* and *Ursa* circled out to sea where *Mauritius* rejoined. As it was almost full daylight, Force 27 was able to engage from a more comfortable distance of 11,000 yards and by 0715 the three enemy ships were seen to be beached and on fire. The Germans claimed to have inflicted heavy damage upon their attackers, believing that a 10.5cm shell had "cut down" the cruiser's mainmast and set it and one of the "four" attacking destroyers afire. In fact, no damage was sustained by any of the Allied warships during the three engagements while they themselves sank one minesweeper and drove a coastal tanker, two minesweepers, and the mine-exploding vessel aground.[82]

It had been a successful night, but Davis was unhappy at the escape of *T 24*—the fourth time the destroyer had slipped the clutches of an RCN Tribal.[83] He attributed this largely to the poor performance of his own ship's gunnery radar and the obsolescence of her search radar and plotting systems, which were "of little use in a close range rough and tumble in shoal waters." Moreover, *Mauritius* did not have flashless cordite for her main armament, and on more than one occasion Davis's vision was so impaired that he had to cease fire from the forward turrets "to prevent running into the next ahead or possible enemy forces." Because his ship was so poorly equipped for night fighting "the movements of the force were in large measure ordered by the excellent information provided by *Iroquois*,"[84] an opinion shared by Wyburd, commanding *Ursa*. He thought that the Canadian destroyer, which was acting most of the time directly under Wyburd's orders, was particularly efficient in passing regular and accurate information and that her gunnery was excellent. "At no time had I to worry about this ship," he reported, "as I knew instinctively (and correct-

80. *Mauritius* ROA, 3 Sep 1944; *Iroquois* ROA, 17 Aug 1944, DHH 71/206

81. *Mauritius* ROA, 3 Sep 1944, *Ursa* ROA, 19 Aug 1944; *Iroquois* ROA, 17 Aug 1944, KTB, 15 Aug 1944; Rohwer and Hummelchen, *Chronology of the War at Sea*, 295-6

82. Ibid

83. The other escapes came on the nights of 25/26 and 28/29 April and 8/9 June 1944.

84. *Mauritius* ROA, 3 Sep 1944

Commander James Hibbard, right, captain of HMCS *Iroquois*, and his first lieutenant, Lieutenant-Commander C.R. Coughlin, on the bridge of their destroyer on the morning of 6 August 1944. Both officers appear well satisfied with the results of the previous night's action south of St. Nazaire where they took part in Force 26's destruction of six enemy vessels. (PA 179886)

A whaler from the Bangor minesweeper HMCS *Thunder* goes alongside a surrendered German trawler in the Bay of Biscay, April 1945. The trawler was typical of many of the small German units operating along the Biscay coast. (LAC PA206281)

ly) that she was doing the right thing. It is submitted that this reflects the greatest credit on her commanding officer."[85]

On 20 August *Mauritius*, *Ursa*, and *Iroquois*, once again designated Force 27, received orders from Plymouth Command to act as one of three task forces in Operation Assault, during which they were to sweep the Biscay coast from the Franco-Spanish border to Belle Ile around the clock in order to tighten the blockade of the coastal "fortresses." They encountered no enemy forces other than coastal batteries in the first twenty-four hours, but C-in-C Plymouth ordered them north to Pointe de Penmarche on the morning of 22 August to intercept vessels attempting to escape southward from Brest. Admiral Leatham enlarged upon this general direction as Force 27 was on passage to the new station, specifically ordering inshore patrols in Baie d'Audierne that night.[86] Since strong tidal streams were to be found in the northern extremities of the bay, Davis calculated that German shipping would most likely pass through the channel at the time of slack water, between 0100 and 0300 hours. He stood off until it was completely dark, then closed to within about six miles of shore, and began a patrol in a roughly east-west direction between the eastern shore of Baie d'Audierne and the Raz de Sein, the northern entrance into the bay. He limited speed of advance to twelve knots in order to reduce the wake and "to reach the eastern end of the beat at about 0145. My chief concern was to prevent the enemy, if detected, doubling back through Raz de Sein and also not to discourage any forces following on behind the leading German vessels from attempting passage across Audierne Bay."[87]

Force 27 passed the lighthouse at Pointe de Penmarche and commenced the first sweep at 2230. The ships adopted their normal cruising formation with a destroyer on each bow of the cruiser. Since *Ursa*'s type 276 search radar was out of action, *Iroquois* assumed the inshore position and was responsible for controlling Force 27's movements during the approach. Anticipating a postwar innovation, Commander Hibbard decided to take advantage of his ship's advanced radar and plotting systems by conning *Iroquois* from the operations room, going up to the bridge only after he had ordered illumination. By taking this unorthodox step—Hibbard had earlier been instructed by the Vice-Admiral (D) Home Fleet to remain on the bridge, and to rely on the view plot—he was able to commence an action "with the tactical situation clearly in mind."[88]

Shortly after 0100 on 23 August *Iroquois* picked up her first contact at a range of about 15,000 yards. Conforming to Davis's plan, "the Force held on in the opposite direction for a tantalising twenty minutes and let the enemy get well into the Bay." Davis then brought the force around and increased speed to close the enemy, no other contacts having appeared. Once again he allowed for shallow water and limited sea room by adopting line ahead, this time with *Iroquois* in the lead.[89] At

85. *Ursa* ROA, 19 Aug. 1944

86. C-in-C Plymouth to *Mauritius*, *Ursa*, and *Iroquois*, 20 Aug 1944, C-in-C Plymouth to SO Force 27, 22 Aug 1944, DHH 71/206; *Mauritius* ROA, 11 Sep 1944, PRO, ibid

87. *Mauritius* ROA, 11 Sep. 1944

88. Hibbard to Lt J. George, 18 Feb 1945, DHH 81/520/1650-239/15 (prior to 1944); *Iroquois* ROA, 28 Aug 1944, DHH 71/206. According to Hibbard, VAdm I.G. Glennie, RN, told Hibbard that "I want my captains on the bridge." Hibbard to Whitby, 28 Nov 1988. As to why Hibbard would not use the view plot, DeWolf has stated that he never looked into the plot because it spoiled his night vision. Hibbard may have held the same opinion. Finally, according to *Huron*'s first lieutenant, Lt P.D. Budge, Rayner sometimes looked into the plot wearing red glasses to protect his night vision.

89. *Mauritius* ROA, 11 Sep 1944

0209 *Iroquois* fired starshell and illuminated one of two ships that had separated from the third, which was evidently steering north towards Audierne—these were the patrol craft *V 702, V 729,* and *V 730.* Force 27 opened fire and less than five minutes later two of the enemy vessels were on fire, while *Mauritius* had driven the third ashore. For another fifteen minutes the force continued to pound the crippled vessels with the result that they were all destroyed or sunk. Force 27 then resumed formation and set off across Audierne Bay in a southwestward direction in search of more shipping.[90]

Iroquois picked up another radar contact shortly before 0300. Hibbard's Headache operator reported picking up an E-boat call sign, and Davis ordered a hasty retreat in case torpedo attack was imminent. When it was confirmed that the report was false they again closed the coast. At 0336 *Iroquois* regained radar contact and was ordered to lead the approach. At 0408 the Canadian destroyer illuminated three small ships less than 5000 yards away to the east. Overwhelming the enemy with their vastly superior firepower, *Ursa* and *Mauritius* quickly sank one vessel. At 0455 Davis ordered the two destroyers to close the range and finish off the other two German ships. *Ursa* now took the lead, despite her unserviceable search radar and depleted supply of starshell, depending on *Iroquois* for a constant stream of situation reports and illumination. *Iroquois* soon made contact with a flak trawler that had survived the previous action, heading for Audierne Bay. At 0525 the two destroyers engaged the target, made several hits, and drove the vessel ashore on La Gamelle. They then found, engaged, and sank another flak trawler. In both cases they used searchlights for illumination.[91] By the time the two destroyers rejoined *Mauritius* at 0545, their forward 4.7-inch guns had been fired so often that the barrels were too hot for immediate use. Waiting offshore until full daylight, Davis ordered *Iroquois* and *Ursa* back into the bay to ensure the destruction of the German vessels. The enemy ships were "well aground and several were smoking or showing small fires." One "modern heavily armed trawler" aground on the shoal seemed to have escaped serious damage so *Iroquois*, on instructions from *Mauritius*, finished her off with a torpedo.[92]

German records indicate that Force 27 had either sunk or driven aground six patrol boats. The sweep through Audierne Bay had been a complete success. In his report on the action, Captain Davis was critical of the Germans' "lack of sea sense," and wrote: "They placed their trust in shore batteries and coast crawling" rather than standing "some way out to seaward" where "some at least would have got through." He admitted to "some lucky guesses and the excellence of *Iroquois'* radar and plotting teams, who throughout the actions kept track of enemy vessels trying to escape and kept me informed." Wyburd also commented upon the Canadian destroyer's "remarkably high degree of efficiency" and C-in-C Plymouth noted that "the efficiency of HMCS *Iroquois'* plotting organization is particularly creditable." Hibbard, for his effective use of radar and the excellence of his gunnery and plotting teams, and his navigator, Lieutenant Benoit, who had overseen the operation of the AIC, were both awarded the DSC.[93] Davis and Wyburd, who was senior to Hibbard, received the DSO.

90. Ibid; *Iroquois* ROA, 28 Aug 1944; the OIC Intelligence Summary, 26 Aug 1944, PRO, ADM 223/11; Rohwer and Hummelchen, *Chronology of the War at Sea,* 296

91. *Ursa* ROA, 28 Aug 1944, PRO, ADM 116/4960; *Iroquois* ROA, 28 Aug 1944

92. *Iroquois*, ibid

93. *Mauritius* ROA, 11 Sep 1944; *Ursa* ROA, 28 Aug 1944; Adm Honours and Awards Cte min, 24 Oct 1944; CNMO, "Canadian Part in August Surface Actions,"14 Oct 1944, DHH 81/520/8000, HMCS Iroquois (1944-5); KTB, 25 Aug 1944

With movement south to Spain cut off on land by General Patton's armies and at sea by the blockade clamped down by Plymouth Command and Coastal Command, German naval authorities had no option other than to scuttle all vessels still remaining in their Biscay ports. From 11 to 26 August the *Kriegsmarine* destroyed thirty merchant ships totalling nearly 150,000 tons, as well as every remaining minesweeper, flak ship and patrol boat.[94] As a result, German naval activity in the Bay of Biscay had all but ceased by the end of August 1944. The destroyers of the 10th Destroyer Flotilla nevertheless continued to patrol the coast until the end of September. Their primary role was to serve as a liaison with French resistance groups operating along the coast, landing supplies, and gathering military information. After repairing her damaged guns, *Haida* made several uneventful sweeps before departing for refit in Halifax on 19 September. Aside from escorting the *Queen Mary* as far as the Azores in early September—with Prime Minister Winston Churchill and the British Chiefs of Staff embarked for the Octagon Conference in Québec City—*Iroquois* had a similarly uneventful final month in the bay.[95]

As early as April 1943 Anglo-American strategists had discussed the possibility of making an amphibious assault on southern France to coincide with the Neptune landings. From the outset, the British were largely opposed to such an operation, primarily because they lacked the military personnel to open a third front against Germany and feared that it would detract from the British-led campaign in Italy. Realizing that a landing in southern France would divide the enemy's defences while opening the valuable port of Marseilles to help supply a drive into Germany, the American Joint Chiefs, with Soviet backing, pressed their reluctant British counterparts to proceed with planning a three-division assault by the US Seventh Army. On 8 July, with the Allied armies making little progress in Normandy, the go-ahead was finally given for Operation Dragoon.[96] By that time, many of the landing craft needed for the amphibious assault were being released from the Normandy beachhead, including the two Canadian LSIs *Prince David* and *Prince Henry*. After making several more runs ferrying reinforcements to the invasion anchorage, the two Princes departed for the Mediterranean on 24 July. Arriving at the Italian port of Naples a week later, the Canadian landing ships took part in a series of landing exercises before being handed their Dragoon assignments on 6 August.[97]

The three main divisional assaults were to be made on the Riviera coast between Toulon and Cannes, and *Prince Henry* and *Prince David* were assigned to carry commandos covering the western flank of the invasion area. *Prince Henry*, with the American commander of the task group and his staff on board, was to transport 279 men and officers of the First Special Service Force (a joint Canadian-American commando unit of "Devil's Brigade" fame) to capture the offshore islands of Port-Cros and Levant, twenty-two miles east of Toulon. *Prince David*, meanwhile, was to land 248 French commandos on the mainland to capture the defences on Cap Nègres, to the north of Levant.

---

94. Rohwer and Hummelchen, *Chronology of the War at Sea*, 296

95. Schull, *Far Distant Ships*, 354-9; "Report of Landing Parties From HMCS Iroquois," nd, DHH 81/520/8000, Iroquois 1944-5

96. Weigley, *Eisenhower's Lieutenants*, 218-26; Stoler, *Allies and Adversaries*, 168-72; J.J. Clarke and R.R. Smith, *Riviera to the Rhine: US Army in World War II: European Theatre Operations* (Washington 1993), 3-22. Dragoon had previously been dubbed Anvil.

97. Schull, *Far Distant Ships*, 361-2

After transporting the commandos to the French island of Corsica on 11 August, the two Canadian warships re-embarked their assigned troops at dawn on the 14th and headed for the Riviera coast. The "Sitka" task group made an unremarkable passage before splitting into its "Romeo," "Able," and "Baker" components as they neared the French coast at 2155 hours. *Prince David* and the two British LSIs of Sitka Romeo reached their transport area, nine miles off Cap Nègres, fifteen minutes later, while *Prince Henry* and four troop-carrying American destroyers proceeded to an area 7000 yards south of Levant Island. "Weather conditions obtaining at the time were perfect for an operation of this type," *Prince David*'s captain later reported. The "sky was bright and clear, sea smooth with a very slight swell. A slight haze was apparent toward land and visibility was of five or six miles. Navigation to the transport area was by surface radar and despite considerable jamming, position 'Charlie' was satisfactorily ascertained."[98]

With a greater distance to cover, the French commandos were the first to disembark, *Prince David*'s craft being away by 2240 hours. To the southwest, *Prince Henry* had lowered its LCAs for embarkation by the Special Service Force some twenty minutes later. Both groups of commandos made as stealthy an approach as they could, with the LCAs pulling rubber rafts and moving at slow speed so as not to attract the enemy's attention. When several hundred yards off shore, the commandos in the rafts cast off from the landing craft and paddled in to make a silent assault. The French commandos were the first to land. They went ashore without being fired upon and soon reported capturing their objectives. Within an hour they had established a road block across the main road from Toulon to the main landing beaches. The Canadian-American commandos who landed on Levant also had a relatively straightforward assignment. The 2nd and 3rd Regiments of the Special Service Force "beached on the east shore, and scaling eighty-foot cliffs, overran the five-mile length of the island, finding the eastern battery merely wooden guns manned by stuffed dummies." Resistance on the smaller island of Port Cros proved more difficult, however, and it was not until 17 August, after receiving fire support from the battleship HMS *Ramilles*, that the Special Service Force was able to capture the last of a cluster of forts that surrounded the port. Canadian Army casualties in capturing the two islands totalled ten killed and thirty-two wounded, and *Prince Henry* re-embarked sixty-five wounded commandos in the course of the afternoon.[99] At 1700 hours the Canadian LSI departed the assault area and, together with *Prince David* and the other LSIs of Sitka Romeo, sailed back to Ajaccio, Corsica.[100]

Over the next five days *Prince David* made two return trips to the assault area and *Prince Henry* one, both transporting French colonial troops to reinforce the beachhead. By 25 August both ships' Dragoon service had come to an end, and the two Canadian LSIs made the short return voyage to Naples.[101] The reinforcement troops the ships carried were part of the French II Corps that had been handed responsibility for capturing the cities of Toulon and Marseilles and their now essential port facilities. Despite the somewhat hasty final arrangements for the operation, the Dragoon landings

98.   Cdr T.D. Kelly, RCNR, "Narrative: Operation 'Dragoon'—Sitka/Romeo Force," 15 Aug 1944, DHH 81/520/8000, Prince David, pt. 2; *Prince Henry* ROP, 21 Aug 1944, ibid, Prince Henry

99.   G.W.L. Nicholson, *The Canadians in Italy, 1943-1945 (Official History of the Canadian Army in the Second World War II* (Ottawa 1956), 669

100. Kelly, "Narrative"; *Prince Henry* ROP, 21 Aug 1944; Clarke and Smith, *Riviera to the Rhine*, 98-9

101. *Prince David* ROP, 5 Sep 1944, DHH 81/520/8000, Prince David, pt. 2; *Prince Henry* ROP, 21 Aug. 1944

were remarkably successful with all three American divisions taking their objectives against often minimal opposition. As the French moved rapidly along the coast, capturing both well-defended ports by 28 August, the American VI Corps drove up the valley of the Rhône to trap as many Germans as possible in southwest and south-central France. Despite exploiting the mobility of their divisions to mount a vigorous pursuit, the US Seventh Army was nevertheless unable to trap the bulk of the retreating German Nineteenth Army before Franco-American forces linked up with Patton's Third Army in mid-September, forty miles from the German border. Even so, the French Mediterranean ports proved to be an invaluable asset in keeping the Allied armies in France supplied, handling over one-third of all materiel reaching the Western Front during the fall of 1944.[102]

For the remainder of the year the two Canadian LSIs continued to be employed on various duties in the Adriatic and Aegean seas. While *Prince Henry* spent most of September ferrying landing craft from Sicily to the Adriatic coast of Italy for possible amphibious operations in Yugoslavia, *Prince David* carried 530 British commandos to the Greek island of Kithera. With the Red Army's advance towards the Balkans threatening to cut off their occupation troops in Greece, the Germans had begun pulling their forces out of the Peloponnesus. The enemy had already abandoned Kithera by the time *Prince David* arrived and in the next weeks it became increasingly obvious that the Germans were preparing to evacuate Athens.[103]

In mid-October the two Canadian LSIs returned to Greece as part of a British force being sent to re-occupy the country and hasten the German retreat. Protected by four escort carriers, four cruisers, and three flotillas of minesweepers, *Prince Henry* and *Prince David*, the latter carrying the exiled Greek prime minister and his government, and five other landing ships, made a triumphal entry into the port of Piræus, which adjoins the Greek capital.[104] Thereafter, the Canadian LSIs continued to ferry men and supplies between Taranto, Italy, and Athens. It was during one of these relief missions, on 10 December 1944, that *Prince David* struck a mine while steaming down a swept channel in the approaches to the Gulf of Athens. Although the ship "was damaged, she was able to proceed, anchoring in Salamis Straits." Two days later a British diver reported finding "a small hole on the starboard side forward, and a large hole some 17 by 12 feet on the port side of the bow together with other hull damage."[105] Transferring her LCAs to *Prince Henry*, the *Prince David* proceeded to Tunisia for temporary repairs before sailing directly to Esquimalt for refit.

Prince Henry had to remain in Greek waters where a civil war between communists and the government in Athens caused no little concern to the Allies. In her last major operation of the war, the Canadian landing ship spent the final week of December 1944 evacuating several thousand Greek refugees from the northwestern port of Preveza. On Christmas Day, *Prince Henry* managed to crowd aboard some 1400 Greek civilians who were escaping the fighting in the hills above the city and transport them to the offshore island of Corfu. Returning again on the 27th and 29th, she rescued a further 3000 Greeks before returning to Taranto on 31 December. *Prince Henry*

102. Weigley, *Eisenhower's Lieutenants*, 226-37

103. *Prince David* ROP, 9 Oct 1944, DHH 81/520/8000, Prince David, pt. 2; *Prince Henry* ROP, 27 Oct 1944, ibid, Prince Henry

104. *Prince David* ROP "Narrative of Events—Operation Manna," 3 Nov 1944, ibid, Prince David, pt. 2; Schull, *Far Distant Ships*, 366-8

105. *Prince David* ROP 4 Jan 1945, ibid

remained in the Mediterranean until March 1945, before proceeding to the United Kingdom where she was paid off and turned over to the Royal Navy for use as an accommodation ship.[106]

By the end of September 1944 the advance of the Allied armies in northwest Europe had been stalled by the *Wehrmacht*'s stubborn defence of the West Wall, and the focus of coastal activity had shifted to the waters off Belgium and Holland. Most remaining MTB flotillas now operated north of the Thames under C-in-C The Nore, Admiral of the Fleet Sir John Tovey, which placed them in a favourable position for both offensive and defensive operations in the North Sea and off the coast of Holland. Fairmile D flotillas, based on the northern ports of Great Yarmouth and Lowestoft, could with their endurance attack convoys and patrol craft as far east as the West Frisian Islands. Shorter-legged MTBs, based mainly at Felixstowe, the port to which the 29th Flotilla would transfer after its three-month interlude at Ramsgate, were for the most part engaged in guarding Britain's east coast shipping lanes. Eventually, all MTBs would move to Ostend, Belgium, where the establishment of a maintenance unit spared the boats the difficult passage across the North Sea. Here they were in a better position yet to carry out both offensive and defensive missions.

The Canadian flotillas, which were not among reductions being carried out by the Admiralty, needed personnel both to replace casualties and to provide crews for an increase in strength to ten boats in the 29th and twelve in the 65th Flotilla. "From action experience with the enemy since D-Day," argued Lieutenant-Commander Law in a submission to the Canadian Naval Mission Overseas asking for more boats, "it has been found that a small force of three MTBs against a large force of E- or R-boats came out the worse for wear."[107] That was borne out by casualty figures, especially in the 29th Flotilla, which had lost three boats and suffered 37 percent casualties. This coincided with CNMO informing Ottawa that the Canadian MTBs were "in urgent need" of a number of specialist ratings "with previous training in MLs ... as ratings with qualifications are not available in the UK. Request volunteers, repeat volunteers, be drafted immediately to replace casualties ... and for new construction boats. Request ratings be fully informed as to type of operation for which they are volunteering."[108] C-in-C Dover and the Admiralty backed up CNMO's submission and NSHQ eventually compromised, approving an increase of strength to nine boats in each flotilla.[109] For the 29th this meant not only a larger complement but a new generation of British Power Boat "Shorts." Instead of 1250 horsepower Packards, they had similar 1500 horsepower engines that could power them to over forty knots, offering a much better chance of catching the Germans' speedy E-boats. In addition, an auto-loaded, power-mounted, 6-pounder in lieu of the previous 2-pounder pom-pom gave the new boats considerably more punch than their predecessors. The first of the new boats—*MTB 486* commanded by Lieutenant-Commander Law and *MTB 485* by Lieutenant D. Creba—joined the flotilla at Ramsgate in early August.[110]

---

106 Schull, *Far Distant Ships*, 369-70; R. Barrie and K. Macpherson, *The Ships of Canada's Naval Forces, 1910-2003* (St Catharines 2002), 42-3

107. Law to CNMO, 7 Aug 1944, LAC, RG 24, 11744, CS 164-29-1

108. CNMO to NSHQ, 31 July 1944, LAC, RG 24, 11703, NB 64-4; Law, *White Plumes Astern*, 119

109. CNMO to NSHQ, 28 Sep 1944, DHH 81/520/8000-466/29 (Signals)

110. "29th Canadian MTB Flotilla: Latest List Dating up to 17th Aug 1944," nd, DHH 81/520/8000-466/29, 29th MTB Flotilla; CNMO, "Operations of the Royal Canadian Navy in United Kingdom Waters after September 20, 1944—Coastal Forces," nd, app: "Description of the Canadian MTBs and the Craft They Opposed," DHH 84/227

Ramsgate was a quiet fishing village where some much needed rest revived the spirits and the health of the MTB crews. "The weather during our stay," wrote Law, "was glorious. In the mornings the men worked hard cleaning the ships, but in the afternoons they would have 'make and mends'. Officers and crews alike took full advantage of the sandy beach beneath the white cliffs, and after the weary, dreary days of Normandy, it was marvellous to relax and soak in the sunshine." The only drawbacks were the limited accommodations ashore, which were reserved for pool ratings and forced crews to live on board their already cramped boats, and the occasional shelling of the area by German batteries near Calais across the English Channel. At last, after months of effort by the flotilla's accountant officer and the CNMO in London, the men of the 29th began to enjoy RCN rations—a great deal better than the RN ones. The Royal Navy had argued that because the Canadians, those of both the 29th and 65th Flotillas, were manning British boats and operating alongside British flotillas, it would be unfair for them to receive anything other than the smaller and less appetizing RN rations. It was a "great victory," and the crews "could eat like kings."[111]

August operations were defensive, dull, and uneventful. Unable to penetrate the Allied defensive cordon around Normandy, E-boats had started attacking British coastal convoys in mid-July, leaving further attacks on the Neptune anchorage to the *Kriegsmarine*'s "small battle units." (Employed during July and August, the conglomeration of radio-controlled motor boats, manned torpedoes, and midget submarines inflicted little damage, most of the *Kleinkämpfverbände* being sunk or destroyed by vigilant Allied air and surface forces before they could get near enough to their targets to make a successful attack.[112]) By the time the 29th Flotilla reached Ramsgate, the enemy had already made his presence known with two successful E-boat operations off Dungeness and Beachy Head. Under the defensive scheme being utilized by Dover Command, the MTBs occupied designated interception points, called "Z-positions," situated on a "Z-line" some ten miles to seaward of the convoy route. Unfortunately, the Royal Navy had not changed their interception points—even when the E-boats consistently evaded them—and continued to use the same Z-positions. Only after the war did they learn that the Germans had captured a chart from the burned-out remnants of an MTB in September 1942 that revealed the locations of all of the points. Coastal Forces officers had been aware that the Germans were successfully slipping past their defence line even after Ultra disclosed the time and place of attack, but they had attributed this to radar monitoring.[113]

Following two more Bomber Command raids on Le Havre on 31 July and 2/3 August, E-boat strength had been reduced to fifteen operational boats along the entire Channel and Dutch coasts. The only Canadian contact on the Z-line came on the night of 17/18 August, when Dover radar operators directed three of the 29th's boats to intercept a group of E-boats off Dungeness. Unfortunately, the Canadian boats were unable to comply immediately because the senior officer, Lieutenant C.A. Burk, was in the midst of transferring to another boat following a radio failure in his own, while two British boats operating in the same area were unable to locate the intruders because of faulty radar and "apparently misdirected illuminants." In the confusion, the E-boats

111. Law, *White Plumes Astern*, 125-6

112. Tarrant, *Last Year of the Kriegsmarine*, 96-100

113. Law, *White Plumes Astern*, 126; Adm, the OIC, "The Use of Special Intelligence in Connection with Operation Neptune, Jan 1944-Sep 1944," nd, 178, PRO, ADM 223/287, v 2; Capt P. Cazelet, RN, "The War against E-Boats, 1945," *CFPR* (Mar-June 1945), 43-4, DHH 84/7; Scott, *Battle of the Narrow Seas*, 112; H. Frank, "E-Boats in Action off the Coast of England, 1943-44," *Marine-Rundschau* 4/87 (July-Aug 1987), 8; Hinsley, *British Intelligence* III pt 2, 454

were able to approach to within approximately 5000 yards of one of the convoys and torpedo the merchant ship *Fort Gloucester*, which was eventually towed into Dungeness. The Canadians only managed to intercept the enemy force as it withdrew. They exchanged just a few shots with the enemy, who had answered the 29th's challenge with the correct response, before they escaped to the southwest.[114]

The breakout of the Allied armies from Normandy at the end of August 1944 forced the Germans to withdraw their shipping up-Channel from Le Havre. This provided the Allied coastal forces with "their best week's harvest of the war." The Canadians however were restricted to tedious anti-E-boat patrols in mid-Channel until the night of 30/31 August. On that occasion, shortly after 0330, Dover Command vectored three boats from the 29th, together with three Dutch MTBs, onto a contact south of Boulogne. After picking up the enemy convoy on his own radar, Law, as senior officer, ordered the Dutch boats to begin the attack from the westward, while he led the Canadians around to attack from the north. Unfortunately, the Dutchmen illuminated the enemy while still well beyond torpedo-firing range. Believing that their actions "gave the game away," Law also fired rocket flares and was greeted by "extremely intensive" fire from shore batteries and the escorting R-boats. The MTBs had to disengage, and the convoy escaped unscathed.[115]

Over the next several days the German naval units abandoning Boulogne, Dieppe, and Fécamp had to run the gauntlet of Allied forces waiting for them to pass through the Straits of Dover. On the night of 1/2 September a group of E-boats and convoys attempted to escape by running under the cliffs of Cap Griz Nez. Forewarned by Ultra, Dover Command organized a force of aircraft, MTBs, and Dover shore batteries to intercept. *MTBs 485* and *486*, the 29th's new boats—the fastest MTBs in Dover Command—took part in this action. The Canadians intercepted the E-boats as planned, but their 6-pounders jammed at the critical moment, and they were unable to inflict serious damage on the Germans before they escaped into Calais. The 29th then joined a group of British MTBs offshore to watch the enemy convoys being attacked by aircraft, MTBs and the Dover batteries. When the Canadians prepared to follow the British boats in to launch their own attack, *MTB 486*'s steering failed, and the crew only managed to repair it in time to join the other MTBs in heading back to base. German records indicate that in the four convoys making the passage that night, even after more air attacks, several vessels sustained damage but only one landing craft had been sunk.[116]

Disappointed by their tedious defensive patrols, Lieutenant-Commander Law, in his report of proceedings for September, asked the Canadian Naval Mission Overseas for help in seeking more active employment. Captain F.L. Houghton did not take kindly to this breach of naval etiquette. "The disposition of coastal force flotillas," he wrote, "is not the concern of the senior officer of flotillas, who cannot possibly possess the requisite knowledge to make recommendations on the subject." Houghton understood and even sympathized with Law's desire for action; however, the

114. Tarrant, *Last Year of the Kriegsmarine*, 103; Burk to Adm Commanding, Dover, 18 Aug 1944, LAC, RG 24, 11744, CS 164-29-6; Adm Commanding, Dover to Adm, 18 Aug 1944, DHH 81/520/8000, 29th MTB Flotilla (Signals); Adm, "E-boat Ops and Policy," 100

115. Law, "Action Report [ROA]," nd, DHH 81/520/1650-239/13, Ops, English Channel; KTB, *SKL*, 31 Aug 1944, DHH SGR/II/261; *CFPR* (Mar-June 1945), 14

116. Law, *White Plumes Astern*, 132-3; KTB, *SKL*, 2 Sep 1944

The crew of MTB *745* of the 65th MTB Flotilla surround the boat's commander, Lieutenant Oliver Mabee (centre right) and his first lieutenant, Lieutenant John Sale. (DND K-988)

A Belgian civilian looks on as a fire rages in the harbour at Ostend, Belgium, 14 February 1945. The RCN's 29th MTB Flotilla, whose negligence was responsible for starting the blaze, was virtually destroyed. (LAC PA 206288)

HMCS *Iroquois'* Action Information Organization plotting staff played a key role in the destroyer's success in the Bay of Biscay in August 1944. (LAC PA 206245)

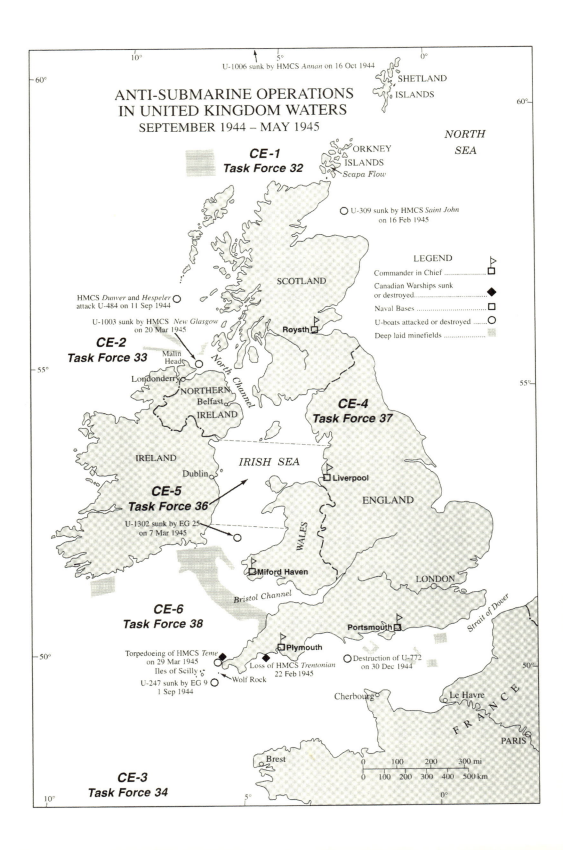

ANTI-SUBMARINE OPERATIONS IN UNITED KINGDOM WATERS
SEPTEMBER 1944 – MAY 1945

U-1006 sunk by HMCS *Annan* on 16 Oct 1944

SHETLAND ISLANDS

ORKNEY ISLANDS
Scapa Flow

NORTH SEA

CE-1
Task Force 32

U-309 sunk by HMCS *Saint John* on 16 Feb 1945

SCOTLAND

LEGEND

Commander in Chief ....
Canadian Warships sunk or destroyed ....
Naval Bases ....
U-boats attacked or destroyed ....
Deep laid minefields ....

HMCS *Dunver* and *Hespeler* attack U-484 on 11 Sep 1944

U-1003 sunk by HMCS *New Glasgow* on 20 Mar 1945

Roysth

CE-2
Task Force 33

Malin Head

North Channel

Londonderry

NORTHERN IRELAND

Belfast

CE-4
Task Force 37

IRELAND

IRISH SEA

Dublin

CE-5
Task Force 36

U-1302 sunk by EG 25 on 7 Mar 1945

Liverpool

ENGLAND

WALES

Miford Haven

LONDON

Bristol Channel

CE-6
Task Force 38

Portsmouth

Strait of Dover

Torpedoeing of HMCS *Teme* on 29 Mar 1945
Iles of Scilly

Plymouth

Loss of HMCS *Trentonian* 22 Feb 1945

Destruction of U-772 on 30 Dec 1944

U-247 sunk by EG 9 1 Sep 1944

Wolf Rock

Cherbourg

Le Havre

FRANCE

0   100   200   300 mi
0 100 200 300 400 500 km

Brest

PARIS

CE-3
Task Force 34

request was "not in accordance with service procedure."[117] The truth was that both German and Allied coastal forces were becoming less relevant in the naval war. The 65th Flotilla's only action came on the night of 30 September when six Dogboats attempted to attack a convoy off Texel Island in the West Frisians, only to be driven off by the heavy fire of the escorts.[118] Bad weather forced the cancellation of many of the defensive patrols during this period, and this restricted E-boat operations as well. The Germans were also hampered by the nightly sweeps by radar-equipped Coastal Command aircraft off the E-boat bases. Together with the normal destroyer, frigate, and MTB patrols, the aircraft made it increasingly difficult for E-boats to penetrate the Allied defences, a frustration that was evident in an *FdS* situation report in mid-September:

> It was my endeavour primarily, to use every opportunity offered by the weather to carry out <u>offensive</u> operations with torpedo and mine, against the British southeast coast convoy traffic. Only once, however, (12-13.9.44) did an opportunity occur, and even then the weather was against us. On this occasion it could be seen that the enemy, having his air force free from ties on the Atlantic and Channel coasts, uses concentrated forces to watch every movement of our ships in the "Hoofden" [Ijmuiden, The Hook of Holland and Den Helder] ports, from the moment they pass the pier head. In practice therefore, the last possibility of a surprise attack by an undetected E-boat advance into the operational area is lost to us, E-boat freedom of movement having been considerably decreased by enemy coastal ship-borne radar, more intensive control of the coastal area, and convoy escort activity; these causes have therefore lessened our chances of success.[119]

With the *Luftwaffe*'s night fighter force fully occupied defending the *Reich*, the odds would remain stacked against the E-boats for the rest of the war. By the beginning of October 1944 E-boat strength along the Dutch coast had been reduced to a mere nine vessels. It was hoped that the use of small battle units would aid the E-boats in their attacks on the convoy routes. They did meet with some initial success during October, but were "roughly handled" by sea and air patrols and never seriously threatened Allied shipping. Canadian flotillas encountered little but inclement weather, and none of these craft. The 65th Flotilla's report of proceedings for October remarked that "other flotillas had the same experience during that period, and it was concluded that the Hun was moving his merchantmen in weather which he would know kept our boats in port."[120]

On 21 October the 29th Flotilla had moved north up the British coast to Felixstowe. The new location did not alter the tedium of the numerous defensive patrols that the Shorts carried out, nor did it lead to any greater contact with the enemy. In fact, from 22 October until the flotilla moved to Ostend on 15 January 1945, it had only one encounter with enemy forces. It occurred on the night of 1/2 November while patrolling off the Hook of Holland during the closing stages of the battle for control of the Scheldt estuary. Although the Belgian city of Antwerp had fallen to the 2nd

117. Law ROP, 1 Oct 1944, CNMO(L) to SO 29th MTB Flotilla, 1 Dec 1944, LAC, RG 24, 11346, CS 164-29-3

118. Lt J.W. Collins (for Kirkpatrick) ROP, 14 Jan 1945, ibid, CS 164-65-3

119. Adm, "E-boat Ops and Policy," 104-5; Sir John Tovey, "Review of Cooperation between Surface Forces and Aircraft in the Nore Command—September 1944 to the End of Hostilities," *CFPR* (Mar-June 1945), 47

120. Tarrant, *Last Year of the Kriegsmarine*, 174; Lt C.E. Edmonds (for Kirkpatrick) ROP, 23 Dec 1944, LAC, RG 24, 11/346, CS 164-65-3; Roskill, *War at Sea* II pt 2, 125-6, 152-4

British Army in early September with its desperately needed port facilities largely undamaged, the British had failed to press on past the city to secure the base of the Beveland Peninsula that guard-ed the approaches to the port along the Scheldt River.[121] By reinforcing their defences along the estuary, the Germans were able to deny the Allies the use of the port until they themselves were cleared from its approaches. Throughout September and October the 1st Canadian Army had main-tained a slow and hard-fought advance along the water-logged lowlands of the Scheldt, clearing the south bank around Breskens and the Beveland Peninsula. By the end of October only the bat-tery-studded Walcheren island remained in enemy hands to block the passage of merchant ship-ping to Antwerp. To capture this final obstacle, Royal Marine and British Army Commandos land-ed at Westkapelle on the morning of 1 November, as the Canadians tackled the narrow causeway at the island's southeastern end.[122]

The navy covered the northern flank of this landing against expected attack from German naval forces. MTBs patrolled off the various ports in northern Holland to prevent E- and R-boats from breaking through to the beachhead. Law's group of four boats was assigned the southernmost position off the Hook of Holland with orders to remain in place from 1900 until 0130, after which the boats were free to attack targets of opportunity. Spotting a small German convoy soon after reaching their patrol position, the four Canadian boats attempted to close the enemy for a surprise attack which was foiled by a group of R-boats approaching from the south. The 29th split into pairs, with *MTBs 485* and *486* distracting the escort while *491* and *464* manoeuvred to attack a merchant ship. *MTB 464* had to break off its attack after a 40mm hit on the waterline started seri-ous flooding, but *MTB 491* fired torpedoes from 800 yards range, claiming one hit. The escorting vessels drove off all attempts to repeat the attack, and the convoy headed back into harbour.[123] Detaching the damaged boat to Felixstowe, the other three MTBs returned to their assigned patrol position only to encounter four flak trawlers of the 14th *Vorpostenbooteflotille*. As Law later recounted, "the coxswain tapped me on the shoulder 'Don't look now, but I think we're being fol-lowed.' Then,

> turning to see who our friends were, I was amazed to find the notorious Four Horsemen, a German patrol of four flak trawlers. Although I hadn't come in contact with these uncouth gentlemen since 1943 when I had been working off the Dutch coast, I knew that these bullies were far from gentle and that no matter what was done they would always get the upper hand, especially on a moonlit night. We spent the remainder of the night playing a game with each other which consisted mainly of bat-ting shells back and forth. No one was getting hurt, but it was a frighteningly danger-ous game. As soon as we had manoeuvred into a possible torpedo position and were ready to pull the lever, what would happen? The Four Horsemen would alter course toward us, and just to keep the game lively they would slam out a few more 88-mms.

121. Adm Ramsay criticized Montgomery about this: "It has at last come home to him [Montgomery] that Antwerp is the first pri-ority of all & he has moved back to Brussels to give it his attention. And high time too." Love and Major, *Year of D-Day*, 161

122. CNMO, "Operations of RCN in UK Waters," 10,13; C.P. Stacey, *The Victory Campaign: The Operations in Northwest Europe 1944-1945* (Ottawa 1960), 301-3, 358-421; W.D. Whitaker and S. Whitaker, *Tug of War: The Canadian Victory that Opened Antwerp* (Toronto 1984)

123. C-in-C, Nore to Adm, 3 Nov 1944, DHH 81/520/8000, 29th MTB Flotilla (Signals); *CFPR* (Nov-Dec 1944), 7, DHH 84/7; CNMO, "Operations of RCN in UK Waters," 21-2

Later on we discovered something which was very embarrassing to both teams: the Four Horsemen and ourselves had been assigned to the same patrol position. The game went on; at the end of the period there was still no score and the flak trawlers and our three boats changed sides. They went to the southern end of the patrol while we took up our position at the northern end, and all the while we eyed each other and dreamed up new defensive plays. This battle reminded me of a hockey match.[124]

After three hours of exchanging fire with the enemy trawlers, the MTBs detected two vessels proceeding south at 0315. Believing the vessels to be E-boats, the three Canadian boats engaged them briefly until they withdrew under cover of smoke. It was later learned that the "enemy" had in fact been two other MTBs. The three Canadian boats returned to Felixstowe at 0500 having suffered only superficial damage but with one rating dead.[125]

On 24 October the Dogboats of the 65th Flotilla departed Great Yarmouth and headed across the North Sea to Ostend where they would be based for the next two months. For much of the winter of 1944-5, their strength was split between Ostend and Great Yarmouth, initially providing flank protection for the Walcheren operation before spending the remainder of November and December engaged in the seemingly endless cycle of defensive patrols—two days on, one off—in the approaches to the Scheldt estuary. With the E-boats operating in this area on only four nights during the six weeks following 1 November these provided "little excitement," even though the flotilla recognized that this defensive work was "perhaps the most important which has been assigned to it since commissioning."[126] The only contact with the enemy came on the night of 15/16 November when Kirkpatrick's boat was vectored on to a group of E-boats laying mines in the Scheldt estuary. After making two high-speed passes that forced the enemy to break off his mining operation, the Canadian boat withdrew to allow two frigates to drive the intruders off. Despite continuing their usual cycle of defensive patrols, they encountered no other German forces.[127]

During this period Kirkpatrick attempted to have the two Canadian flotillas united at one base. After the fall of Walcheren, Coastal Forces planners considered opening a new base at Veere on the northeast shore of the island to enable operations to be extended up the Dutch coast, leading to a more effective blockade of E-boat bases and better opportunities against coastal convoys. Learning of these plans, Kirkpatrick wanted Veere to be the home of both of the Canadian MTB flotillas. Not only would the Dogboats and Shorts complement each other operationally, they would also be better positioned to share spare RCN personnel, something that could not be done when they operated alongside RN flotillas. Higher authorities disagreed, and Kirkpatrick's efforts to form a Canadian MTB base came to nought.[128]

---

124. Law, *White Plumes Astern*, 148. See also CNMO, ibid, 22

125. C-in-C, Nore to Adm, 3 Nov 1944; *CFPR* (Nov-Dec 1944), 7; CNMO, "Ops of RCN in UK Waters," nd, 22

126. Edwards (for Kirkpatrick), ROP, 23 Dec 1944; Adm, "E-boat Ops and Policy," 107-8

127. CNMO, "Operations of RCN in UK Waters," 33-5; *CFPR* (Nov-Dec 1944), 8; Collins (for Kirkpatrick) ROPs, 31 Jan and 2 Feb 1945, LAC, RG 24, 11746, CS 164-65-3

128. CNMO, "Operations of RCN in UK Waters," 17. The citation for this information is missing from the document, but it was most likely LCdr Kirkpatrick. CNMO in London would have been aware of such a request, and they were responsible for producing the cited narrative.

On 15 January 1945 the 29th Flotilla crossed the North Sea for a deployment at Ostend that was to prove as short as it was tragic. After four weeks of uneventful defensive patrols from the Belgian port, an accident within the relative safety of their own base resulted in the destruction of all but two of the flotilla's boats, effectively eliminating the Canadian unit as a fighting force. As determined by a Board of Inquiry, the disaster came about through a series of careless mistakes. *MTB 464* had been carrying out routine gunnery trials on the afternoon of 14 February in preparation for a patrol when water in the fuel system forced the centre engine to shut down. Upon returning to harbour, the boat's motor mechanic, Petty Officer F.A. Walden, discovered that several inches of water remained in the tank. The problem of water-contaminated fuel had recently afflicted several MTBs and it was widely suspected that bad fuel had been unloaded from a tanker into the shore tanks. *MTB 464*'s first lieutenant, Sub-Lieutenant G.M. Hobart, had previously brought the recurring fuel problem to the attention of the base staff, as had Walden, only to be told that he "would have to take the defect in hand himself."

When water was found in the fuel tanks this time, Walden again went ashore and sought the assistance of the base staff. Finding "no responsible person," he decided to solve the problem himself and, without asking permission, took the short cut of pumping out the centre tank with the bilge pump, instructing a stoker to watch over the side and tell him when gasoline and not water started to flow into the harbour. For twenty minutes, from approximately 1515 to 1535, some fifty gallons were pumped over the side. In the midst of this operation Walden informed Sub-Lieutenant Hobart what he was doing, but the officer "made no comment other than 'OK.'" The motor mechanic later told the Board of Inquiry "that he took these steps as he considered it his duty to make the boat operational in time to go to sea at 1730 that day." The board concluded that the fuel was probably discoloured by sludge and would have been difficult to distinguish from the contaminating water, with the result that a large amount of gasoline was likely pumped overboard. The smell of high octane fuel was certainly present in the harbour as several officers and ratings testified that they "all noticed the smell of petrol yet none of them gave any warning to CFMU or other MTBs."[129]

The harbour at Ostend was packed with coastal craft. Sixteen MTBs were berthed in a "crique" approximately 450 feet long and 100 feet wide that lay off the main harbour. Just downstream another thirteen MTBs and three motor launches lay alongside the Coastal Forces Mobile Unit. *MTB 464* lay outboard of three Canadian boats tied together at the head of the creek. In all, thirty-two vessels lay within a constricted area—most of them loaded with high octane fuel, torpedoes, and ammunition. Not far away were several LSTs and minesweepers. At approximately 1602 a fire broke out between two MTBs tied together just downwind from *MTB 464*. Within minutes powerful explosions shook the harbour. Fanned by a strong offshore breeze, the fire spread rapidly throughout the creek area. *MTBs 465* and *462* blew up almost immediately, and the flames quickly engulfed the four MTBs berthed downstream of them. Two of the four went down in a series of explosions, and the other two drifted before burning themselves out. According to the commander of the CFMU,

> heavy explosions were taking place, possibly from torpedo air vessels exploding ...Ammunition, including 6-pounders, were firing in all directions, rockets were exploding and depth-charges were burning, and there was a sheet of flame covering the whole area, covered by a pall of black smoke. LSTs, minesweepers, and MTBs were

---

129. "Board of Inquiry into Explosion at Ostend on 14th Feb 1945—Narrative," 9 Mar 1945, PRO, ADM116/5493

trying to get away and there were numerous men in the water all around the scene of action. At the same time a large number of aircraft were going overhead at 1500 to 2000 feet, who immediately started to fire all their recognition lights, and one man even baled out in his alarm.[130]

It was the quick action of *MTB 485*'s coxswain, Leading Seaman Roland Balmain, that saved the three MTBs tied together at the head of the crique. He started engines and moved the three boats upstream and away from the fire. Two of these, *MTBs 485* and *464*, were the only boats of the 29th Flotilla to survive, although the delinquent *MTB 464* was so badly damaged that she had to be paid off. The MTBs and motor launches alongside the CFMU were all able to survive by moving into the main harbour. Two generator lorries and stores at either end of the mobile unit also caught fire. In all, twelve MTBs were destroyed, while another five were damaged.[131] Sixty-four officers and ratings were killed and scores of others were injured. The 29th Flotilla itself lost twenty-nine killed and twenty wounded. The toll would have been much higher had the boats had not been on a "make and mend," with many of their men ashore in the city. Most of these rushed to the waterfront when they heard the explosions but were forced to take cover from igniting ammunition and flying debris. The 29th's doctor, Surgeon Lieutenant W.L. Leslie, with the aid of two sick berth attendants and the chaplain, was able to save many lives in spite of the heavy explosions nearby. Crews from the MTBs berthed in the main harbour also moved in to rescue over forty men from the burning waters. Given such catastrophic conditions, it was fortunate that the casualties were not higher.[132]

The Board of Inquiry attributed the calamity to shoddy and lax administration within the CFMU and the 29th Flotilla. Standing orders prohibiting the dumping of inflammable substances had been violated, and "other evidence taken ... leads the board to the conclusion that there was considerable disregard of petrol precautions, especially in the 'Short' boats and it is quite possible, therefore, that MTBs other than No 464 added to the quantity of petrol in the creek on this day."[133] Walden received the brunt of the blame for the tragedy, but the maintenance unit commander was censured for not seeing that the written orders were "sufficiently known and implicitly complied with." Relieved of his command, he and two of his staff were also criticized for inadequate fire-fighting measures and training.[134] Canadian officers also received reprimands. The CO of *464*, Lieutenant L.C. Bishop, and Sub-Lieutenant Hobart both received the "severe displeasure" of the Admiralty. Bishop had not been on board his MTB during her gunnery trials, thereby, according to the inquiry, demonstrating little interest in the condition of his craft. Hobart had allowed a dangerous fuelling practice to continue and failed to give warning of the possibility of fuel in the harbour. Both Law, who was at Felixstowe on 14 February, and the acting senior officer, Lieutenant C.D. Chaffey, earned the Admiralty's "displeasure" because they had not issued orders to ensure that there were sufficient duty officers or ratings aboard the MTBs.[135]

---

130. Brind to C-in-C Nore, 16 Feb 1945, PRO, ADM 116/5493

131. "Board of Inquiry," 9 Mar 1945, PRO, ADM 116/5493

132. CNMO, "Operations of RCN in UK Waters," 15

133. "Board of Inquiry," 9 Mar 1945

134. Sir J. Tovey min on Board of Inquiry, nd, PRO, ADM 116/5493

135. "Board of Inquiry," 9 Mar 1945, Adm to CNMO, 24 Sep1945, PRO, ADM 116/1493

The 29th Fotilla was disbanded after the Ostend fiasco. Both Canadian and British officers saw little "useful purpose" in working up new boats and crews when the war against Germany was clearly winding down to its conclusion. Recommendations that the surviving four boats and crews join another unit were similarly dismissed. Instead, the four remaining MTBs were handed over to the Admiralty as replacements for RN flotillas. The 29th's personnel were asked to volunteer for the 65th's spare pool, but when none did, they were scattered among various manning pools across Canada. "It is to the extreme regret of all officers and men of the 29th Canadian MTB Flotilla," Lieutenant-Commander Law sadly concluded in his flotilla's final report of proceedings, "that after many interesting months together, the flotilla must disband in such inauspicious circumstances."[136]

The disbandment of the 29th MTB Flotilla left the 65th Flotilla as the RCN's sole remaining formation in the coastal forces. The Dogboats replaced the 29th at Ostend on 15 February to carry out defensive patrols off the Scheldt estuary. Offensive operations were no longer required since the Germans had stopped sailing convoys along the Dutch coast, but it was necessary to prevent E-boats from mining the shipping lanes off the Scheldt. This was no easy task. Forward air patrols and radar-equipped frigates provided warning of their approach, but the E-boats were elusive and frequently penetrated the shipping lanes. They had, moreover, been heavily reinforced—in early January *FdS* had reported thirty-six operational E-boats in Dutch ports—and were able to employ several flotillas in each operation. On the night of 21/22 February, for example, twenty-two E-boats from six different flotillas had successfully attacked an east coast convoy, sinking two freighters totalling 3,889 tons and a landing craft while damaging a third freighter.[137]

On the night of 24/25 February, when several groups of E-boats attempted to lay mines in the shipping lanes, the Germans planned to engage the covering forces in waves, in the hope that the initial attacks would open up the defences and allow the follow-up groups to penetrate. The strategy worked well, as two out of four groups were able to carry out their mission despite being detected in good time by either forward air patrols or control frigates. Radar picked up the first wave at 0133, but the E-boats managed to lay their mines in between running engagements with the covering MTBs, including the 65th's *726*, *735*, and *736*. Two other Canadian boats, *MTBs 743* and *746*, were on the same patrol line but did not have the opportunity to take part in the first engagements. They had "begun to think they were missing the whole show" when their control frigate vectored them onto four E-boats approaching from the north. At 0255 the Canadians engaged the E-boats on a parallel course from 300 yards. *MTB 746* opened fire with full armament on the first two units while *743* concentrated on the remaining two. The E-boats made smoke and used their superior speed to escape, but as one of the rearmost boats was about to enter the smokescreen the crew of *MTB 743* saw a large explosion. Skirting the edge of the smokescreen, the two Canadian boats found one of the enemy proceeding at reduced speed. The MTBs raked the stricken E-boat from point-blank range for two minutes before the Germans laid scuttling charges and abandoned their boat. *S. 167* sank forty minutes later, and the Canadians plucked twenty-three survivors from the water. The 65th Flotilla had sunk its only E-boat of the war.[138]

---

136. 29th Flotilla ROP, 2 Mar 1945, LAC, RG 24, 11746, CS 164-29-3; CNMO to NSHQ, 19 Feb 1945, ibid, CS 164-29-2

137. Tarrant, *Last Year of the Kriegsmarine*, 212, 216; CNMO, "Operations of RCN in UK Waters," 35,

138. CNMO, ibid, 38-43; *CFPR* (Jan-Feb 1945), 7

A general shortage of MTBs led to increased demands on those boats that remained operational. The 65th Flotilla had three more minor brushes with E-boats in March as the Germans continued their attempts to mine the shipping lanes off the Scheldt, but they only incurred casualties in one of the actions. Nonetheless, the hectic patrol schedule was having its effect on the Canadians. Since moving to the Nore Command in September, Kirkpatrick believed that his flotilla had logged "more sea time per boat than any other MTB flotilla, boat for boat, refits excepted." A medical inspection of the flotilla in April noted that although amenities ashore were good, there was insufficient shore leave:

> For example, the boats are in one night and out two; one watch is given leave at a time, which statistically indicates a rating has shore leave once every nine days. This is supplemented by one rating being away on a forty-eight hour leave in Brussels at a time, which would prove to be forty-eight every ten weeks. This is not considered adequate leave for the type of work and the cramped living conditions that these men endure. The flotilla senior officer and medical officer are fully aware of this and are trying to work out a system whereby more leave may be granted and country accommodation arranged. The medical officer reports that there has been an increase of late in operational fatigue and this can only be anticipated under present conditions.[139]

Germany was on its last legs. By the beginning of April 1945 it had fewer than two dozen operational boats at its Dutch bases, and the general fuel shortage threatened to bring a halt to further sorties. After losing five more E-boats during the first week of that month, *FdS* launched the final raid of the war on the night of 12/13 April. Once again, Coastal Command aircraft detected the E-boats as they left harbour and provided a good plot of their movements. At 0051, the control frigate HMS *Elkins* vectored three MTBs, including the 65th Flotilla's *MTB 797* and *MTB 746*, onto the contact. In the short action that followed, the MTBs engaged the enemy at the point-blank range of twenty yards. Both sides sustained damage and casualties before the E-boats withdrew under the cover of smoke.[140] By mid-April, *FdS* strength in Dutch ports had been reduced to a mere fifteen operational boats, and these were rendered largely immobile by a chronic shortage of fuel. The 65th continued to carry out regular patrols until 2 May and then commenced preparations for paying off soon after VE-Day. They took part in one more operation, the ceremonial surrender of the E-boat command, before finally paying off at month's end.[141]

It was the mine threat that still presented the greatest problem in defending the coastal flank. Of the thirty-one merchant ships sunk by E-boats in 1945, for example, only six were torpedoed while the other twenty-five struck mines. The toll could have been much higher. Unassuming and unglamourous, minesweepers toiled with little respite during the last year of the war—and following its conclusion—to clear the shipping lanes between Britain and the

---

139. D.H. Dixon, "Visit to 65th MTB Flotilla," 5 Apr 1945, LAC, RG 24, 11744, CS164-65-1; CNMO, "Operations of RCN in UK Waters," 19

140. *Elkins* to C-in-C Nore, 13 Apr 1945, DHH 81/520/8000, 65th MTB Flotilla (Signals); Adm, "E-boat Ops and Policy," 114; *CFPR* (Mar-June 1945), 20

141. CNMO, "Operations of RCN in UK Waters," 19; W.S. Blandy interview, nd, 14-16, Blandy biog file DHH; Tarrant, *Last Year of the Kriegsmarine*, 224

European mainland. By mid-October 1944 the 31st Flotilla was clearing swept channels as far east as Dieppe, although much of their time was still spent in the Portsmouth–Cherbourg–Le Havre triangle. That such operations were not without hazard was made abundantly clear to the Canadians during a routine sweep in the approaches to Le Havre. At 0849 on 8 October 1944, while steaming into position with four other Bangors, HMCS *Mulgrave* was rocked by "a violent explosion" eleven miles due west of the French port. A mine had exploded under her starboard quarter and the ship was "enveloped in cascades of water and steam." Her captain surmised that his ship had fallen victim to either an acoustic or Oyster mine but the flotilla's senior officer believed that the explosion (which occurred twenty to thirty feet beneath the stern) was caused by a magnetic mine "as *Fort William* and *Cowichan* had passed over the area before HMCS *Mulgrave*, and had it been an Oyster or contact mine, the presumption is that HMCS *Fort William* would have detonated it."[142] The force of the explosion stopped the main engines immediately, and the ship quickly listed to starboard and began settling by the stern. The after compartments were soon flooded and a damage control party was ordered below to shore up bulkheads and prevent the flooding from spreading forward. The quick reaction of the damage control party undoubtedly saved the ship from sinking, and *Blairmore* took her in tow after transferring the crew. Surprisingly, there were no serious injuries. Taken first to Le Havre and then Portsmouth, *Mulgrave* was beyond repair, and Canadian authorities agreed to pay her off.[143]

Three days after *Mulgrave*'s mishap, *Malpeque* had the distinction of sweeping the flotilla's one hundredth mine.[144] And when *Guysborough* joined the 31st Flotilla at the end of October, it marked the first time that all of the RCN's overseas minesweepers were concentrated into one flotilla. As 1944 drew to a close the ships of the formation, in addition to their sweeping operations, acted increasingly as convoy escorts for both coastal and cross-Channel convoys. The commanding officer of *Fort William* felt that escort duty was "a welcome change from minesweeping" and reported the entire crew to be hungry for a submarine kill.[145] By February 1945 the mine menace was sufficiently in hand that all of the Bangors could return to escort duty, as they had previously done in Canadian waters. They escorted single ships or small convoys between English ports and Cherbourg or Le Havre. Convoy duty in the Channel soon proved as mundane as minesweeping, however, as none of the ships came in contact with the enemy.

The only exception came in mid-March 1945 when the Bangor HMCS *Guysborough* was torpedoed while returning from a refit in Canada. On 17 March the ship was on the last leg of her passage, steaming thirteen knots on a steady course across the Bay of Biscay. Since U-boat activity was reported to be on the rise in the southwestern approaches to Britain, *Guysborough*'s commanding officer, Lieutenant B.T.R. Russell, ordered CAT gear to be streamed 250 yards astern. But with the daily U-boat report indicating that there were no enemy submarines in the immediate vicinity, Russell decided to conserve fuel and take up a zig-zag course only when he drew closer to the English coast. It was his misfortune that *U 868*, returning to Norway after a supply mission

---

142. "Mining of HMCS *Mulgrave*, 8 Oct 1944—Damage Report," 23 Nov 1944, LAC, RG 24, 6790, NSS 8340-443/44; *Fort William* ROP, Oct 1944, LAC, RG 24, 11741, CS 162-19-3

143. CNMO to NSHQ, 16 Nov 1944, LAC, RG 24, 6790, NSS 8340-443/44

144. HMCS *Milltown* and 31st Minesweeping Flotilla ROP, Oct 1944, LAC, RG 24, 11740, CS 162-1-3

145. *Fort William* ROP, Jan 1945, ibid, CS 162-19-3

to St Nazaire, sighted *Guysborough* 220 miles north of Cape Finisterre, and at 1830 fired a *zaunkönig* at the minesweeper.[146] The minesweeper's CAT gear failed to divert the torpedo which struck astern. *Guysborough* immediately began settling by the stern but did not appear to be in imminent danger of sinking. Ordering damage control parties into action, Russell believed that the ship could be saved even though the stern was severely damaged. Bulkheads were shored up, gun crews stood by in case the submarine surfaced, confidential books and papers were disposed of, all hands mustered on the upper deck in warm clothing, and boats and floats were lowered away. An hour after being hit the situation seemed stabilized when a second torpedo hit the minesweeper amidships on the starboard side. The blast opened up the stokers' and seamen's mess and severely injured some of the gun crew. *Guysborough* settled rapidly and Russell gave the order to abandon. Listing to starboard, she stayed afloat until 2010 before slipping beneath the surface midway between Ushant and Corunna.[147]

All but two of the ninety-man crew managed to abandon ship before *Guysborough* sank. Unfortunately, the motor boat was holed and the whaler had overturned, leaving only five Carley floats for the eighty-eight men struggling in the water. The survivors soon drifted into two groups as forty-six of the ship's company clambered onto four of the floats that were secured together, while a second group of forty-two men clung precariously to the fifth float drifting a few miles distant. Designed to carry about ten sailors, most of the forty-two men crowded around the fifth float had to cling to its sides in the frigid, 48° water. Some of them died of wounds suffered during the explosion of the second torpedo; many more either drowned or died of hypothermia in the rough seas of the Bay of Biscay.[148] One who survived, Chief Petty Officer Maurice Benoît, left a poignant account of the awful circumstances that confront sailors forced to take to the sea when their ship is sunk—and the means they take to cope with them:

> I was very lucky through the whole business ... I was just coming from the chartroom on the bridge when the [second] torpedo struck, and was thrown about forty feet away from the ship by the force of the explosion. At the time I think I was alone in the water, and I swam for about half an hour before I came to the Carley Float, which was already supporting forty men. I increased the number to forty-one. A little later we heard someone calling for help and Joseph Norvel Gouthro and I swam out and brought in one of the officers, who was pretty badly wounded. It was a sad disappointment to us both when he died a few minutes later.

Recognizing that "things didn't look very good," the survivors organized themselves. Married men with children were placed next to the float "where they would have the best chance of survival."

> We did pretty well, considering the circumstances until the evening. When it got dark it became a whole lot colder than it had been and it had not been exactly warm at any time. But with the darkness a cold wind came up, and that was what got a number of the boys who had been holding on with all their strength and will until then. It was

---

146. K. Wynn, *U-Boat Operations in the Second World War*, vol 2, *Career Histories, U 511-UIT 25* (Annapolis 1998), 179

147. "Loss of HMCS Guysborough," Jan 1953, "Sinking of HMCS Guysborough," 28 Mar 1945, CNMO to NSHQ, 19 Mar 1945, DHH 81/520/8000, HMCS Guysborough

148. CNMO to NSHQ, 24 Mar 1945, ibid

not long before quite a few started to complain about the cold and to say they didn't think they could hold on much longer. There was nothing that anybody could do about it, you just had to hold on.

The RCN had designed a new pattern lifejacket during the war that was popular with sailors and was credited with saving many lives but, as Benoît recalled, the *Guysborough* ordeal revealed a flaw that proved fatal to some of her survivors:

> The wind was fairly strong as well as cold, and the sea was quite rough. I am afraid that that fact accounted for the loss of quite a few men. If we had better luck with the weather there would have been more survivors ... Twice the Carley Float turned over, and this was one of the worst things that happened in the whole business. Some of the fellows had tied themselves on to the float and when it turned over they couldn't get loose, but were held underneath it and drowned. Eight of them died the first time this happened and five more died the second time.

This tragedy had occurred when sailors secured themselves to the Carley Float by means of a snap hook on their lifejackets. Sadly, when the float flipped over their fingers were too numb to release the snap. To ensure that this would not happen again, a three-metre line was later attached to the snap, which enabled sailors to float free of encumbrances.[149]

> By one o'clock in the morning there were only 20 of us left. Even at that we couldn't all get next to the float, and several of the fellows who had tied themselves on to others who were actually right next to the float. I think the worst part of the whole thing was the roughness of the sea. From time to time the waves would break right over your head, and no matter how much you tried you couldn't avoid swallowing quite a bit of water. We couldn't hold on to each other by this time. Our hands were so cold that they were useless.
>
> We did a lot of singing to pass the time, and to keep ourselves as cheerful as possible in the circumstances. Every now and then the singing would stop and someone would start a prayer, and very soon the rest of us would join in. Coder [John Charles] Gleason was the only one who had a watch that was still working, and every now and then he would sing out the time to the rest of us. That was the only way we could feel really that time was passing. The whole experience seemed to be as if there were no such thing as time, as if it would just go on forever, and as if you might slip from life in[to] death without time having anything to do with it.
>
> We were beginning to feel that way in the early hours of the morning. You couldn't say that the morale was going. Nobody was afraid. Time didn't matter anymore. In fact after a while we told Gleason not to let us know what the time was. It just made it seem as if it was going on longer.
>
> The last time he gave us the hour which was around three o'clock in the morning there were only 11 of us left. Another went sometime between then and dawn.

---

149. This flaw may have been recognized before, as the Board of Inquiry investigating the loss of HMCS *Athabaskan* in April 1944 seemed to probe whether the clasp could be released by sailors who had been in the water for some time. See "Report into the Loss of HMCS *Athabaskan*," 3 May 1944, PRO, ADM 199/263

We didn't really expect to be picked up at all. Daylight is always supposed to make you feel better, but the coming of dawn didn't seem to make any difference. The sea was still there, and the sky, and I guess the wind was still just as cold only we couldn't feel it very much by that time. By noon there were just six of us left. The fellows died without complaints. They just seemed to go asleep from the cold. One minute they would be talking to you and the next they wouldn't be there anymore. It made you realize what a very thin line there is sometimes between life and death.[150]

By the time a British frigate rescued them the next afternoon, there were only six survivors left alive on Benoît's float, including Gleason and Gouthro, and thirty-one of the forty-six on the other four floats. In all, fifty-one of *Guysborough*'s company lost their lives. The ensuing Board of Inquiry concluded that Lieutenant Russell, by failing to carry out a zig-zag course in what were known to be U-boat patrolled waters, had made a serious error of judgment. The board also believed that all COs should be warned of the dangers of streaming CAT gear on a short tow, such as at the 250 yards *Guysborough* was utilizing. Ultimately, however, the board concluded that no one on *Guysborough* was in any way directly responsible for her loss and that nothing could have saved the ship after it had been hit by the second torpedo.[151]

The end of hostilities brought new minesweeping tasks. Several nations, including Germany and Italy, joined in an international effort to clear European waters of mines. The remaining ships of the 31st Flotilla, after assisting French naval forces by sweeping bombardment lanes for their attacks on Bordeaux and L'Ile d'Oleron in April 1945, spent the next five months sweeping the waters of the English Channel. Many of the flotilla's most productive sweeps that summer were in British minefields off the south coast of England.[152] The Canadians completed their final operation on 11 September 1945. HMC Ships *Thunder*, *Kenora*, *Wasaga*, and *Minas* had departed for Halifax earlier in the month. *Blairmore*, *Milltown*, *Fort William*, *Georgian*, *Malpeque,* and *Cowichan* followed on 17 and 21 September. Three other Canadian Bangors, *Caraquet*, *Canso,* and *Bayfield* paid off on 24 September prior to being turned over to the Royal Navy.[153] When the 31st Flotilla had arrived in March 1944 the British had expressed dismay at their lack of experience and the Admiralty had complained about the unsatisfactory state of their equipment. No such doubts remained by September 1945. As the flotilla ended its work in European waters the Admiralty expressed to the officers and men of the 31st its "appreciation of the excellent work of the flotilla in the last eighteen months. Their onerous duties ... have been carried out with outstanding zeal, efficiency, resolution and cheerfulness."[154] It was a well-deserved tribute.

---

150. Transcript of interview with CPO Maurice Benoît, nd, DHH 81/520/8000, Guysborough

151. The board's conclusions are summarized in "Loss of HMCS Guysborough," Jan 1953

152. Various reports of proceedings, June to July 1945, LAC, RG 24, 11740, CS 162-1-3

153. C-in-C Plymouth to SBNO Azores, 3 Sep 1945, C-in-C Plymouth to SBNO Azores, 17 Sep 1945, FOCRF to Adm, 26 Sep 1945, LAC, ibid, CS 162-1-1

154. CNS to 31st MSF, 16 Sep 1945, LAC, ibid

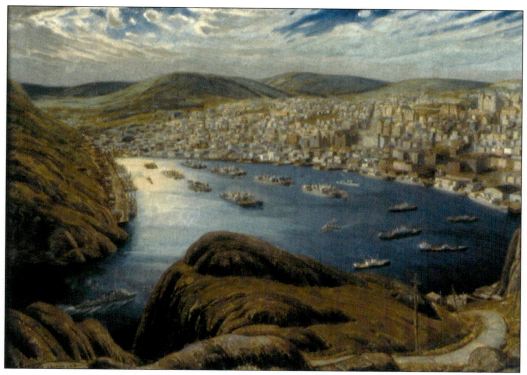

St. John's from Signal Hill, by Harold Beament (CWM 10061)

WRCNS, Naval Headquarters, by P.N. MacLeod (CWM 14198)

Seamen, Tribal Destroyer, by Alfred Leete (CWM 87060)

Destroyer Captain, by Alfred Leete (CWM 87059)

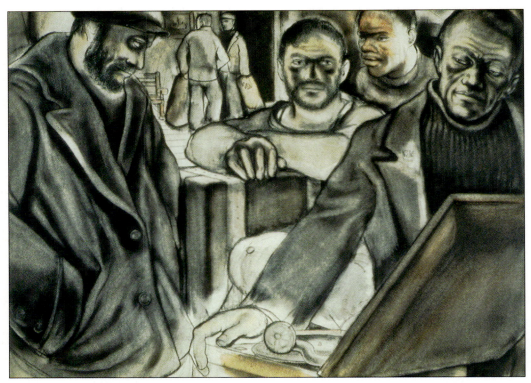

Manning Pool, by Jack Nichols (CWM 10518)

Outfitting a Minesweeper at Night, by C. Atkins (CWM 14055)

HMCS Chaudière, Refit, Portsmouth, by Anthony Law (CWM 10271)

Destroyer Action at Night, by T.C. Wood (CWM 10560)

Fifteen U-boats Surrender, Loch Eriboll, by L. Brooks (CWM 10107)

Embarking Casualties on D-Day, by Harold Beament (CWM 10024)

New Directions

The Inshore Antisubmarine Campaign in European Waters June 1944–May 1945

THE U-BOAT, FOR THE LAST EIGHTEEN MONTHS of the Second World War, was a continuing threat. The introduction of *Schnorkel*—a retractable tube that enabled the U-boat to draw in air, and thus to run on its diesels and charge batteries while submerged—presented a new tactical problem for Allied surface forces. Fortunately for them, the boats initially fitted with *schnorkel* represented an interim and imperfect solution to the German tactical problem. As in other fields of research and development, the German reliance on what had been successful in the past, combined with Allied bombing of U-boat building yards, had seduced the *Kriegsmarine* into retaining things beyond their effective usefulness, in this case type VII and type IX U-boats. What Dönitz really needed to overcome the Allied naval and air dominance, established in May 1943, was an entirely new type of submarine, one that would have many of the advantages of a true submarine rather than a submersible; a boat that was not limited in speed when submerged and that would be far less vulnerable to the latest antisubmarine detection methods and weapons. Not until the serious defeats he suffered in May 1943, however, did Dönitz persuade Hitler to approve mass production of so-called electro boats—the type XXI ocean-going and type XXIII coastal U-boats—with streamlined hulls, greatly improved batteries and *schnorkel*. Their design was a modification of the revolutionary "Walter boat," designed to run on hydrogen peroxide, which was also to continue development.[1]

The limitations of *schnorkel*-fitted boats aside—it took them a long time to reach patrol areas, fuel consumption was high and crews disliked them intensely because of the sudden and constant air pressure changes in the boat[2]—they produced only a very small radar target that was difficult to detect. Furthermore, U-boat captains had learned to use climate and water conditions to advan-

---

1. The Eastern Front dominated German strategic thinking, but Dönitz pressed successfully for manpower and materials for naval building programs. He overcame naval opposition to transfer the building programs in May 1943 to Armaments Minister Albert Speer, and won access to resources in short supply. New assembly techniques produced large numbers of submarines despite Allied bombing, but the first type XXI was not ready for operations until days before the German surrender. M. Salewski, *Die deutsche Seekriegsleitung 1939-45* (Munich 1975), II, 279-93, 507. G. Schultze-Wegener, *Die deutsche Kriegsmarine-Rüstung 1942-45* (Hamburg 1997), 140, 146; MOD, *U-Boat War in the Atlantic* III, para 462

2. It was Dr Walter who developed the *schnorkel* for U-boats. For examples of its shortcomings, see C. Blair, *Hitler's U-boat War,* II: *The Hunted, 1942-1945* (New York,1998), 313-14; MOD, *U-Boat War in the Atlantic* III, para 420.

tage. Improved radar detectors, as well as German signalling techniques, capable of thwarting Allied interception and decryption, further complicated the task of escorts and support groups.[3] New antisubmarine weapons and improved asdic, however, combined with centimetric radar, helped compensate for these German developments. On 5 February 1944 Dr J.H.L. Johnstone, Director of Operational Research at Naval Service Headquarters, produced a comparative study of the ahead-thrown weapons Hedgehog and Squid in order to assess the merit of fitting Squid in Canadian warships. British ships had Hedgehog in 1942, but delays in modernization had kept it from Canadian ships until the latter part of 1943.[4] No RCN ships as yet had Squid, which had its first success on 18 February 1944, with the destruction of *U 406* by HMS *Spey*.[5]

As discussed in Chapter 12, the advantage of an ahead-thrown weapon was that attacking vessels could remain in asdic contact at least until the weapon was fired, thus avoiding the "dead time" of a depth-charge attack, when contact was lost as the ship overran the target to drop its ordnance. Despite Hedgehog's effectiveness, sailors looked askance at the weapon when they first received it. Commander G.H. Oswald, who worked with Dr Charles Goodeve on its development, recalled the commanding officer of an RN Captain class frigate at Argentia in 1943 saying that "the silly asses have given me this idiotic contraption which, if I fire, I will run over the top of the subs and blow myself up" and that it "took two hours education over many drinks to disabuse."[6] The statistical evidence of Hedgehog's success in Canadian ships would become evident by December 1944, when Dr A. McKellar, of the Directorate of Operational Research, reported to a meeting of the Joint RCN-RCAF Antisubmarine Warfare Committee, drawing from results up to 30 September and comparing them to those in the US Navy and also the Royal Navy. McKellar found that about a third of all attacks had been carried out using the weapon, and that "the degree of success achieved by RCN ships was very closely the same as the average for other Allied navies. It is still only from one-third to one-fifth the theoretical value, which has been attained by well drilled ships in trials, so considerable room for improvement exists." Nevertheless, the lethality of Hedgehog in each attack had proven about double that of depth-charges.[7]

Principally as a result of preparations for the invasion of Europe, and of Operation Neptune itself, most Canadian support groups fitted with up-to-date asdic and Hedgehog found themselves in British home waters from May 1944 until the defeat of Germany the following year. The situation they faced presented an unprecedented tactical problem. The *Kriegsmarine*, in an effort to disrupt the flow of Allied reinforcements and supplies for the Allied offensive in northwest Europe, was now sending far more U-boats into the waters surrounding the United Kingdom than to the

---

3.   MOD, ibid, para 419; Hinsley, *British Intelligence in the Second World War* III pt 2, 100-2, 467-89, 627-31. See esp. the OIC Appreciation of 23 Oct 1944, ibid, 479. See also "Note by the First Sea Lord, 6 Jan 1945," PRO, AIR 20/1237/X/P/04895, cited in Douglas, *Creation of a National Air Force*, 606; R. Sarty, "Ultra, Air Power and the Second Battle of the St Lawrence, 1944," in T.J. Runyan and J.M. Copes (eds), *To Die Gallantly: The Battle of the Atlantic* (Boulder 1994), 186-209.

4.   Directorate of Operational Research (DOR) (RCN), Reports, "A Resume of Recent Comparisons of Shipborne A/S Weapons," 5 Feb 1944, LAC, RG 24, 11463

5.   Min 55th Meeting to Consider Trade Protection Measures, 7 Mar 1944, ibid, 8080, NSS 1271-20; E. Grove (ed), *The Defeat of the Enemy Attack on Shipping, 1939-45* (Aldershot 1997), 265

6.   Oswald to S.W. Roskill, 22 Nov 1961, Churchill Archives Centre, Cambridge University, Roskill Papers, 4/14

7.   Joint RCN-RCAF Antisubmarine Warfare Committee (ASWC), Min 37th Meeting, 28 Dec 1944, LAC, RG 24, 8080, NSS 1271-24

western Atlantic. Working mostly in the English Channel and its western approaches, they as always exploited sea and weather conditions. The climate was not so harsh as in the Northwest Atlantic, but variable and generally poor asdic ranges, strong tidal currents in the Channel, less requirement for radio traffic between BdU and boats operating alone, and a wreck-strewn sea floor that created an enormous number of "non-sub" contacts combined with the changing submarine tactics designed for local conditions and objectives to create an entirely new set of operational challenges for the inshore campaign by the British, Canadian, and American antisubmarine forces.[8]

Just as in the Battle of the Atlantic, these forces had as their primary objective the safe movement of shipping. Destruction of U-boats, although a necessary and extremely difficult facet of inshore operations, had to be linked directly with the primary aim. Thus, although there was no dramatic moment as there had been in the spring and autumn of 1943 when antisubmarine forces inflicted incapacitating losses on U-boats in the North Atlantic, U-boats never once disrupted or even seriously threatened the flow of men and materiel to the liberated ports of northwest Europe. This was no mean achievement. It demanded a large numerical superiority over the U-boats, and as a consequence there was a continual need for more support groups, which were the most important weapon in the inshore antisubmarine arsenal. Thus, it was that no fewer than five RCN groups operated from bases in the United Kingdom in the last months of the Second World War, and they proved indispensable to victory in the inshore campaign.

The hunt for one particular U-boat in early July 1944 illustrates well the challenges of inshore antisubmarine warfare. *U 678,* commanded by Korvettenkapitän Guido Hyronimus, had been ordered into the English Channel after leaving Germany on 8 June, and there is evidence that the boat reached the Baie de la Seine late in the month.[9] By that time, however, BdU was reassessing its position. Lack of situation reports from U-boats deployed in the English Channel and intercepts of Allied successes raised fear of "very heavy losses," and on 1 July U-boat Command instructed five boats with orders for the "narrow seas" to divert to Brest; BdU included *U 678* in the order, probably unaware that it had already penetrated up Channel.[10] Whether Hyronimus was withdrawing to Brest is unclear, but on the night of 5/6 July he attacked a convoy in the "Spout" twenty-five miles southwest of Beachy Head, torpedoing the merchant ship SS *Soberg*. The corvette HMS *Statice*, one of the close escorts, quickly gained asdic contact and over the next four hours carried out a series of depth-charge and Hedgehog attacks. *Statice* was frustrated by Hyronimus's skill in disrupting attacks by last-second manoeuvres, by numerous non-sub contacts, and by a number of breakdowns—some caused by the detonation of depth-charges in relatively shallow water—but her commanding officer thought he had inflicted some damage on the submarine. At 0033 6 July, however, the corvette lost contact after a Hedgehog attack and failed to relocate *U 678* among myriad non-sub returns.[11]

It was standard operating procedure to call in support groups in such situations, and after six

---

8. The Admiralty defined inshore waters as "all waters within the 100 fathom line between the Shetlands and 48 North [the northern limit of the Bay of Biscay] and West of the Greenwich meridian," Director of the Anti-U-Boat Division (DAUD), "Review of Results in Inshore Waters," 29 Nov 1944, PRO, ADM 205/36

9. Blair, *Hitler's U-boat War*, 590

10. BdU, KTB, 2 July 1944

11. *Statice* ROP, 9 July 1944, 1, PRO, ADM 217/90

hours of fruitless searching by *Statice*, C-in-C Portsmouth ordered EG 11 to assist in the hunt. The Canadian group was searching for another contact some distance away, and the SO, Commander J.D. Prentice in *Ottawa*, left *St Laurent* on the contact while he took *Kootenay* to help *Statice*. EG 11 had not engaged any U-boats in a busy month patrolling the Channel; nevertheless the hard driving Prentice was reasonably content with their progress. Since D-Day, they had classified about "three dozen wrecks," and although they had not engaged any U-boats, Prentice thought EG 11 was "beginning to work as a Group" and had become "tolerably efficient at hunting A/S contacts as a team in the Channel."[12]

Upon arriving on the scene, *Ottawa* and *Kootenay* augmented *Statice*'s box search. After sweeping two-and-a-half sides of the box, Prentice decided to cut a swath over the datum point where the corvette had lost *U 678*, and at 0938 *Ottawa* obtained a firm contact. As Prentice's report shows, the hunt now proceeded like clockwork:

> At 0950 "KOOTENAY" was ordered to attack with depth-charges. The target was giv-
> ing a bad echo compared with many wrecks that had been previously attacked, but a
> cross tide movement was indicated by plot. At 1018 "OTTAWA" attacked with
> Hedgehog . At 1029 "KOOTENAY" again attacked with a five charge pattern. At 1043
> "OTTAWA" crossed the target by echo sounder obtaining a very distinct trace of a sub-
> marine at 60 feet. At 1059 "OTTAWA" again attacked with Hedgehog obtaining one
> explosion at 100 feet and producing some light oil. The target at this time appeared to
> be stopped but later again moved across the tide. At about 1115 "STATICE" closed and
> obtained contact. Commencing at 1120 "STATICE" carried out an excellent Hedgehog
> attack, which necessitated a large alteration of course in the later stages. An alteration
> which could only have been made successfully by a ship with the manoeuvrability of
> a corvette. The submarine appears to have bottomed after "OTTAWA's" attack and to
> have moved across tide again when he heard "STATICE" approaching. "STATICE's"
> attack produced one definite hit at approximately 60 feet which brought up a consid-
> erable quantity of wood and oil. At 1132 "KOOTENAY" was ordered to attack with
> depth-charges but reported that the echo was too weak due to disturbances in the
> neighbourhood of the contact. "OTTAWA" having held contact continuously whilst
> other ships were attacking. "KOOTENAY" was again ordered to attack and did so at
> 1159. This pattern produced a very large amount of wood, clothing, oil and books.
> "OTTAWA" immediately closed the wreckage, "STATICE" being in firm contact, and my
> 1st Lieutenant recognised the writing in some of the books as German.[13]

It was at this point that some of the unique challenges of inshore antisubmarine warfare became evident. First, Prentice had to ensure that the U-boat was indeed destroyed and not just playing dead on the bottom—something they could not do on the North Atlantic. That meant "opening up" the contact in the hope of raising more evidence, particularly of human remains. On the advice of his staff officer, Lieutenant R.W. Timbrell, RCN, Prentice decided to carry out this grue-

---

12. EG 11 ROP, 5 June–12 July 1944, 16 July 1944, DHH 81/520/8440, EG 11, v 2. Prentice summarized his early experiences in the Channel in "Submarine Warfare in the Channel: 11th Escort Group, June 11 to July 12th," *RCN Monthly Review*, no. 33 (Oct 1944), 67-70

13. EG 11 ROP, 14 July 1944, PRO, ADM 217/90

HMCS *Louisbourg*, showing her armament and crest. Note the loading technique, which could be hazardous in a rough sea. (DND JT 440)

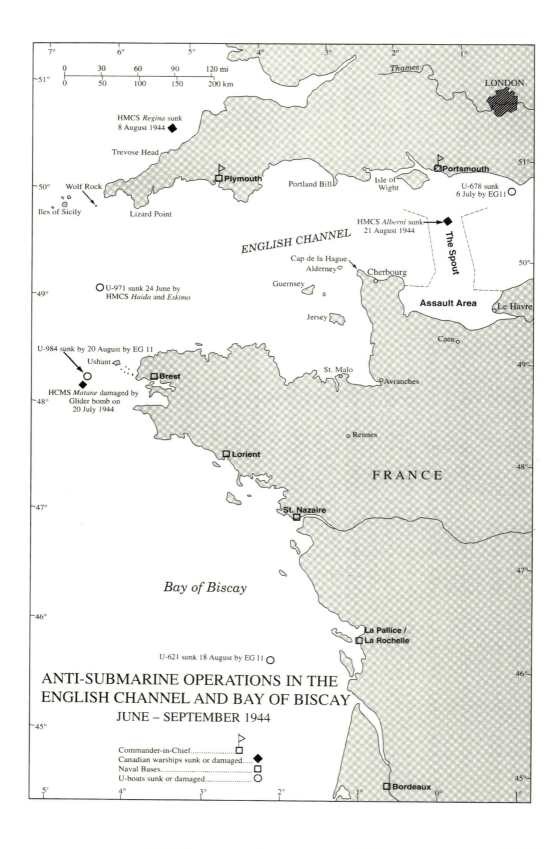

ANTI-SUBMARINE OPERATIONS IN THE
ENGLISH CHANNEL AND BAY OF BISCAY
JUNE – SEPTEMBER 1944

some task by way of a towed charge. A single depth-charge with a grapnel hook attached was dragged over the contact using an echo sounder; when it hooked the target so that the charge lay in lethal range, it was detonated electrically from the surface. The first attempt had little apparent result but pummelling from several towed charges as well as more conventional depth-charge and Hedgehog attacks by *Kootenay* and *Statice* produced more wreckage, including "one tin of German butter, two censor stamps, a tin of white powder and a very worn coat of blue serge with three German buttons attached."[14]

While directing this hammering, *Ottawa* detected another "first class" contact 2000 to 3000 yards from *U 678*. This bunching of contacts was especially frustrating. Hundreds of wrecks littered the seabed surrounding the British Isles, and many bore similar characteristics to a bottomed submarine. U-boat commanders knew this and often lay close by wrecks to throw warships off their scent. As a result antisubmarine vessels had to pick their way through the contacts, classifying each in turn. When this problem first arose in 1940, the Admiralty had promulgated new tactics, whereby ships were issued with updated wreck charts and ordered to mark any unchartered wrecks with a danbuoy. Leaving nothing to chance the Admiralty also directed that "no contact should be classified as a charted non-sub. and left until at least one pattern of depth-charges set to fire on the bottom, has been dropped in the position of the contact."[15] These tactics remained in force when the new campaign opened, but the determined Prentice took them to the extreme. "Chummy had one rule," recalled *Kootenay*'s CO, Commander W.H. Willson, RCN, "attack everything that gives an echo, however bad; keep attacking it as long as you have it; if you lose it don't go away; search and search and search ... [Prentice] would drive everyone nuts because he had not the 'sense' to let go."[16] Following that maxim, Prentice attacked the new contact throughout 7 July and did not leave the scene until relieved by the sloop HMS *Redpole* at 0953.[17] In the final analysis Western Approaches considered the second contact to be a wreck, but there was no doubting the destruction of *U 678*.[18]

Commodore G.W.G. Simpson, Commodore (D) at Londonderry, wondered if it had been necessary "to pulverize the dead hull" of *U 678*. Otherwise the assessment by Western Approaches was favourable. Not only did the hunters keep out of each other's way, but "the tactics of ... carefully investigating and hitting hard any suspected target are considered absolutely correct ... The tactics used by EG 11 to classify asdic contacts are considered very good. Since to classify correctly in the Channel is almost all the battle, it is right that the first ship should go dead slow and bring another ship into contact while other ships distract the U-boat's hydrophone operator by streaming cats on a square search."[19] Simpson was sufficiently impressed that he selected EG 11 to test and perfect the new procedure for classifying contacts using echo sounder traces.[20] From the lower deck of *Kootenay* came another satisfying assessment: "Le sous-marin avait

---

14. Ibid

15. Confidential Adm Fleet Order (CAFO) 753/41. For the buoying of uncharted wrecks, see CAFO 1513/43.

16. W.H. Willson to W.A.B. Douglas, 3 July 1980, Willson biog file DHH

17. EG 11 ROP, 14 July 1944

18. Cmdre (D) WA, "Attacks by Ships of EG 11 Off Beachy Head July 6th–8th, 1944," 16 July 1944, PRO, 217/90

19. Ibid

20. Milner, *U-boat Hunters*, 159

cessé de vivre ... parce que nous lui avions pas donner [*sic*] aucune chance par nos nombreuses et terribles attaques donc tout les gars avaient le sourire aux lèvres, car c'était notre premier sous-marin."[21]

As July continued BdU remained hampered by the lack of information coming from U-boats operating against the invasion. Many boats had been destroyed, and those that survived kept their heads down by maintaining radio silence. A report from *U 984* on 4 July describing "little antisubmarine activity" in the Baie de la Seine area, prompted U-boat Command to send more boats into the Channel, but they received little information as to any success or even their fates; on 10 July, for example, BdU ordered *U 971* back to base, unaware that she had been destroyed by *Haida* and *Eskimo* on 24 June. Perhaps the most valuable information was received from *U 763*, commanded by Korvettenkapitän E. Cordes. On 5 July after attacking convoy ETC 26 in mid-Channel north of the beachhead, *U 763* was subjected to a vicious counterattack—the crew counted no fewer than 550 depth-charge explosions—that lasted some thirty hours.[22] Upon his safe arrival home, Cordes reported "bottoming found very successful when being attacked. To change position, leave bottom silently without using engines and drift in the current." This information was immediately broadcast to other boats.[23]

U 763 had to fight its way into Brest when it returned on 14 July, firing two acoustic torpedoes at antisubmarine vessels, proof of the tight grip of Allied offensive antisubmarine operations on that base. Dubbed Operation Dredger, EG 12 had exerted the first pressure on the night of 5/6 July when it and the RN's EG 14—both comprising older de-classed fleet destroyers—had been ordered into the approaches of Brest to attack U-boats leaving port. Plymouth Command ordered EG 12 to engage the surface escort, while EG 14 hunted the submarines.[24] Although they were novices at night fighting and their main armament accuracy was reduced because their gunnery directors had been removed, EG 12's River class destroyers performed well, sinking a patrol boat and damaging two others in a wild fight that saw the group's SO, Commander A.M. McKillop, RN, badly wounded.[25] Admiral Leatham later commented that the Canadians "carried out the operation in a determined and spirited manner, particularly in view of the age of the ships and their lack of modern night fighting equipment."[26] The two U-boats escaped—McKillop expected to encounter U-boats returning to base but realized too late that they were actually following their escort out of port and was unable to cut off their escape[27]— but the operation forced BdU to divert some U-boats to other bases and to abandon the prac-

---

21. "The submarine had ceased to live ... because by our numerous terrible attacks, which brought a smile to the guys' faces— it was our first submarine—we didn't give it the slightest chance." Journal of Able Seaman Alfred Richard, 6 July 1944, DHH 81/520/8000, HMCS Kootenay

22. Blair, *Hitler's U-boat War* II, 587. *U 763* sank the freighter *Ringen* in the attack.

23. BdU, KTB, 16 July 1944

24. C-in-C Plymouth to All A/S Support Groups at Sea in the Plymouth Command, 1734B/3 July 1944, DHH 81/520/8440, EG 12; C-in-C Plymouth to EG 14, 4 July 1944, Skeena, "Report of Action [ROA] with the Enemy—12 Escort Group," 9 July 1944, PRO, ADM 199/1101

25. Rohwer and Hummelchen, *Chronology of the War at Sea*, 290

26. C-in-C Plymouth Command, "12th Escort Group—ROA with Enemy," 24 July 1944, PRO, ADM 199/1101

27. Cdr A.M. McKillop, RN, "12th Escort Group—Action on Night of 5th/6th July 1944," 13 July 1944, DHH 81/520/8440, EG 12

tice of escorting submarines out of harbour with auxiliary vessels. Later in the month they were forced to close some approach routes into Brest because the threat of attack from Allied surface forces prevented minesweepers from putting to sea.[28]

The *Kriegsmarine*'s situation at Brest worsened towards the end of July 1944 and broke down completely in August. As US forces drove into Brittany following Operation Cobra, it will be recalled (see Chapter 18) that the Allies launched Operation Kinetic to attack enemy vessels trying to flee the embattled French Atlantic ports. Learning through signals intelligence that U-boats were abandoning Brest, Lorient, and St Nazaire for La Pallice and Bordeaux further south, or even for Norway, Plymouth Command deployed support groups into the area.[29] The Allies had the Germans on the run, but patrolling close to the enemy-held coast still proved risky. On 20 July, for example, aircraft had attacked EG 9 off Brest with glider bombs. *Swansea* managed to shoot down one of the weapons, while others missed and fell into the sea, but one hit *Matane* with a glancing blow. According to *Matane*'s damage report, the bomb "came in at a very steep angle from the starboard quarter (estimated at about 70°) hit the edge of the carley float on the roof of Y Gun ammunition hoist, passed through the combing of the gun deck on the port side, through the ladder on to the quarterdeck, through the small bulwark at the break of the upper deck, into the water where it burst alongside." A large hole was punched in the hull, but casualties were surprisingly light: "Two men who were standing in the path of the bomb on the port side of the ammunition supply shelter were never seen again. Everyone in the Engine Room suffered more or less seriously from steam scalding and one man was either killed or trapped and drowned and his body was only recovered on return to harbour. The fact that the bomb burst under water undoubtedly saved the lives of all the after guns crews and supply parties as there was no blast or splinter effect at all. As it was, the Officer of the Quarters at Y Gun was the only casualty, with a severe foot wound."[30] After putting the ship safely alongside in Plymouth after an arduous passage, *Matane*'s CO, Commander A.F.C. Layard, RN, was cheered off the bridge by the ship's company.[31]

EGs 11 and 12 also had to beat off glider bomb attacks in the bay of Biscay, but submarines offered no comparable threat. In the second week of August Allied antisubmarine forces destroyed five U-boats in the Bay of Biscay, and the following week EG 11's skill and determination accounted for two more. EG 11 had been operating in the bay since early in the month with Prentice displaying his usual aggressiveness, searching close inshore for contacts and, despite the danger from shore batteries, even bombarding the village of Concarneau.[32] They had rescued survivors of a U-boat destroyed by a Coastal Command aircraft; however, they had not met with any success of their own. That changed on 18 August when *Kootenay* obtained a contact in poor asdic conditions about sixty miles off La Rochelle. *Ottawa* attacked with Hedgehog and obtained a hit at 210 feet—the bottom was charted at 372 feet—and despite the difficulty of holding the contact, both ships detected movement and a course alteration from the target. After the explosion from the Hedgehog

---

28. BdU, KTB, 4-15 July 1944

29. The OIC, "U-boat Situation, Week Ending 14/8/44" in D. Syrett (ed), *The Battle of the Atlantic and Signals Intelligence: U-boat Situations and Trends, 1941-1945* (Aldershot 1998), 433-6 (hereafter *Battle of the Atlantic* I)

30. CO *Matane*, Damage Report, 23 Aug 1944, LAC, RG 24, 6790, NSS8340-381/30

31. AFC Layard diary, 21 July 1944, DHH 87/214

32. EG 11, "Diary of Events," 28 July–21 Aug 1944, DHH 81/520/8440, EG 11 v 1

an echo sounder trace revealed an object about 100 feet off the ocean floor, giving off oil and air before it bottomed. "The usual difficulties caused by bottomed echoes" were encountered, but in line with Prentice's dogged persistence, over the next eight hours *Ottawa, Kootenay,* and *Chaudière* carried out twelve more attacks.[33] Oil, air bubbles and small amounts of wreckage rose to the surface, but there was no definite proof of a kill when Plymouth Command ordered EG 11 to resume its patrol. Shortly before noon on the 19th, however, Plymouth sent *Chaudière* back to the site of the attacks. Upon her arrival, her CO, Lieutenant-Commander C.P. Nixon, RCN, demonstrated that practical seamanship had its place in modern antisubmarine warfare.

Large amounts of bunker fuel lay on the calm surface but Nixon thought "if oil was no longer rising from the target the oil on the surface might have drifted clear of the contact." *Chaudière's* asdic sifted beneath the patches without success. Finally, a light breeze blew up, which "had the effect of making a series of disconnected oil patches take the form of a large oil slick with what appeared to be a 'leading edge.'" This spot had been searched previously without success, but this time Nixon approached at low speed using echo sounder with the asdic transmitting over narrow arc. At 1550 "a firm metallic contact was obtained." After a successful Hedgehog attack, *Chaudière* "picked up a German letter dated August 11th, 1944, a printed chocolate bar (?) wrapper with Berlin on it, numerous bits of wooden wreckage and three gloves. Dense oil also appeared on the surface."[34] After two more attacks brought up more wreckage and caused a massive explosion *Chaudière* left the scene, certain she had destroyed a U-boat.

Since starting their Biscay patrol on 7 August, EG 11's destroyers had rotated back to Plymouth individually to replenish with fuel, munitions and stores. The sustained operations took a toll on the old destroyers, and on the 19th Plymouth Command ordered the group back to Londonderry for a lay-over. As *Ottawa, Kootenay* and *Chaudière* headed north out of the bay they detected a firm contact about twenty miles off Brest. The three destroyers quickly set about their localization routine, guiding each other in for a series of Hedgehog and depth-charge attacks. *Chaudière* had to detach to Plymouth for fuel, leaving the other two destroyers to their task before they too had to disengage. There were clearly some very effective attacks. Yet, the Admiralty U-boat Assessment Committee concluded, given the lack of debris and the depth of the Hedgehog detonations, that there was "insufficient evidence of the presence of a U-boat," the same conclusion they reached over the attacks off La Rochelle two days earlier. The Canadians felt otherwise. "Regardless of official confirmation at the time," Lieutenant-Commander Nixon later recalled, "my ship's company were wildly elated and promptly painted two swastikas on the funnel to record the victories."[35] Their confidence was well-placed; postwar reassessment confirmed that EG 11 had destroyed *U 621* in the Bay of Biscay and *U 984* off Brest.[36]

EG 11's two kills helped to make August 1944 one of Canada's most successful months in the war at sea. In all, RCN and RCAF antisubmarine and antishipping forces accounted for three U-boats, two destroyers, and a number of smaller surface vessels. But to underscore that the war was far from over the enemy claimed two Canadian warships, both corvettes on convoy duty in British

---

33. SO EG 11, "Attack on U-boat—18 Aug 1944," nd, ibid

34. *Chaudière*, "ROA on U-boat," 23 Aug 1944, ibid. The question mark is in the original.

35. C.P. Nixon, *A River in September* (Ottawa nd)

36. Niestlé, *German U-boat Losses During World War II*, 76, 95

EG 11's HMCS *Chaudière* in between kills. The funnel shows two swastikas, when in fact the ship would be credited with three U-boats destroyed by war's end. (LAC PA 206246)

Lieutenant-Commander C.P. Nixon and Lieutenant T.C. Pullen, Commanding Officer and First Lieutenant of HMCS *Chaudière*, one of the RCN's most successful U-boat killers. (LAC PA 204646)

The asdic hut, showing equipment and seating arrangements. Asdic was of even more limited use in inshore operations than in deep water, and operators had their work cut out for them. (LAC PA 150442)

An asdic team. As with everything else on board Canada's warships, this space was cramped.
(LAC PA 134330)

waters. Escort work for the Neptune corvettes had continued without change as the summer had progressed. The ever-swelling Allied ground forces in northwestern Europe had insatiable demands for materiel and reinforcements, and with U-boats still active along the convoy lanes, the shipping that filled that demand still required escort.[37]

On the morning of 8 August *Regina* set out from Milford Haven with EBC 66, a typical convoy of ten small coasters and the Liberty ship *Ezra Weston*. As the sole escort, *Regina* took up position some 2000 yards ahead of the twin columns of merchant ships. As *EBC 66* passed Trevose Head at 2130, an explosion shook the convoy, and *Ezra Weston* reported that she had been mined. Since U-boats had not operated in the Bristol Channel since the beginning of Neptune, *Regina*'s CO, Lieutenant J.W. Radford, RCNR, accepted this explanation, and after a brief search for mines, closed the stricken Liberty ship. After the Landing Ship Tank *LST 644* took off survivors, Radford suggested that she transfer them to the corvette and stopped engines so she could come alongside. Shortly afterwards *Regina* blew up in a plume of smoke and spray and disappeared beneath the surface in less than thirty seconds.[38]

An officer and twenty-seven sailors, including the entire engine room complement, went down with the corvette. Among the survivors was the ship's doctor, Surgeon Lieutenant G.A. Gould, RCNVR, who wrote:

> The main force of the explosion was expended about the area of the boat station on the port side, aft of the bridge. Trapped between the steel hand rails of the bridge ladder, which had evidently been twisted together in the form of a "V," it was with some difficulty that I managed to extricate myself from this underwater mass of tangled metal. Finally, however, after what seemed an eternity of suffocation, my head broke surface.
>
> When the blinding film of oil cleared from my eyes, there, towering above me, were the last few feet of our funnel. It seemed certain to pin me beneath its massive form, but just as it was about to strike it rolled away, then slithered beneath the surface.
>
> The RCN life jackets functioned admirably for those who had them on. The crew, having followed instructions explicitly, were thus well-equipped. The officers, however, had been in the habit of carrying life-jackets or leaving them within easy reach. The irony of it all was brought home several minutes later when my own life-jacket floated past, well out of reach, identified by the extra red lamp I had previously attached at the shoulder. Thoroughly disgusted with such lack of foresight, I edged through the flotsam, alternately swimming and resting, toward a nearby group of shipmates. Notwithstanding their unpreparedness, all officers on deck at the time of the explosion were rescued—even our non-swimming "Number One," who was clinging hopefully to the barrel of the pom-pom as the corvette went under. But it was impossible to recognize as individuals the oil-smeared blobs who bobbed up here and there, gathering in groups of two or three. It seemed incredible that so many could still be alive![39]

---

37. CNMO Narrative, "The Royal Canadian Navy's Part in the Invasion of France," 138-9, DHH, 84/230

38. "Board of Inquiry into the Loss of US Merchant Ship Ezra Weston and HMCS Regina," 12 Aug 1944, LAC, RG 24, 4107, 1156-331/83

39. Surg Lt G.A. Gould, "The Sinking of the Regina," 2-3, DHH 81/520/8000, Regina

Gould and the others were picked up by *LST 644*. Despite having swallowed bunker fuel and suffering from badly bruised ribs the doctor set up an emergency operating room on the LST's quarter deck. With only flashlights for illumination, Gould and Sick Berth Attendant W. Oneschuk cared for a number of badly wounded sailors, including an amputation. Both were Mentioned in Dispatches for their actions.[40]

The inquiry into *Regina*'s loss could not decide whether the corvette had been mined or torpedoed. Most of her survivors testified that they thought she was mined, but two of *Ezra Weston*'s crew claimed to have seen a periscope.[41] In fact, both ships were victims of *U 667*, one of five U-boats operating in the Channel area in early August, but the only one to enter the Bristol Channel. Although the Admiralty had anticipated activity off the coast of northern Cornwall, analysts at the Operational Intelligence Centre thought that the sinking of a U-boat southwest of the Scilly Isles on 31 July had disposed of the threat. *U 667*'s presence therefore came as a complete surprise. On 14 August the submarine torpedoed two landing craft but was mined while trying to enter La Pallice eleven days later.[42]

U 480, a *schnorkel* boat commanded by Oberleutnant H.J. Förster, penetrated the western Channel at about the same time that *U 667* withdrew from the narrow seas. On 20 August Förster had searched for targets in the Spout, but unable to find any, had shifted position westward. At 1118 the next morning, while *schnorkeling* on a course of 280°, Förster sighted a "frigate" bearing 275°. As the warship approached bows on, Förster estimated its speed at twelve knots, and at 1140 he fired an acoustic torpedo from a depth of thirty metres. A minute and nineteen seconds later the sound of a powerful explosion resonated throughout the U-boat, followed by the noise of a ship breaking up and sinking. After ensuring that there were no other ships close by, *U 480* crept out of the area.[43]

U 480's victim was the corvette HMCS *Alberni*. Antisubmarine patrols had increased in the area of the main shipping lanes to Normandy in response to increased U-boat activity in the Channel, and several corvettes were diverted from convoy escort to these so-called "Spout patrols." On 21 August, fresh from a boiler clean, *Alberni* was on her way to relieve her sister ship *Drumheller* and an RN corvette when *U 480* attacked. Steaming at fourteen knots and maintaining full asdic and radar watches, *Alberni* went down even more quickly than her sister *Regina*. Survivors concluded that the torpedo detonated on the port side towards the aft end of the engine room. The stern was awash up to the funnel within ten seconds of the explosion, and the entire ship was gone ten to fifteen seconds later, taking four officers and fifty-five men with her. Almost all the thirty-one survivors were on the upper deck at the time of the attack. Ironically, *Alberni* had not been modernized with a fo'c'sle extension, and according to one officer "two or three ratings believe they owe their lives to the few seconds thus given to them in extricating themselves from their quarters."[44]

40. E.R. Paquette and C.G. Bainbridge (eds), *Honours and Awards: Canadian Naval Forces World War II* (Vancouver 1986), 210, 416; F. McKee and R. Darlington, *The Canadian Naval Chronicle* (St. Catharines 1996), 170

41. "Report of the Board of Inquiry into the Loss of HMCS Regina," 12 Aug 1944. Upon receiving the final report from the inquiry, C-in-C Plymouth informed NSHQ that Radford had made a "grave error in judgement" by stopping at the scene. NSHQ agreed. C-in-C Plymouth to NSHQ, 29 Aug 1944, DOD min, 12 Dec 1944, LAC, RG 24, 4107, 1156/-331/83

42. The OIC, "U-boat Trend—Period 31 July–9 August," PRO, ADM 223/20; MOD, *U-boat War in the Atlantic* III, 78; Hinsley, *British Intelligence* III pt 2, 462-3: Rohwer, *Axis Submarine Successes*, 184; Niestlé, *German U-boat Losses*, 80

43. *U 480*, KTB, 20-21 Aug 1944

44. CNMO, Report, "HMCS Alberni," 8 Sep 1944, DHH 81/520/8000, Alberni; LCdr I.H. Bell, RCNVR, to Capt (D) Portsmouth, 28 Aug 1944, Navigation Officer HMCS *Alberni* to Capt (D) Portsmouth, "Report of Explosion—HMCS Alberni," 22 Aug 1944, LAC, RG 24, 11735, CS161-9-1; CNMO, "The RCN's Part in the Invasion," 312-14

The Flower class corvette HMCS *Alberni*, sunk in the English Channel by *U 480*. (DND O 6140)

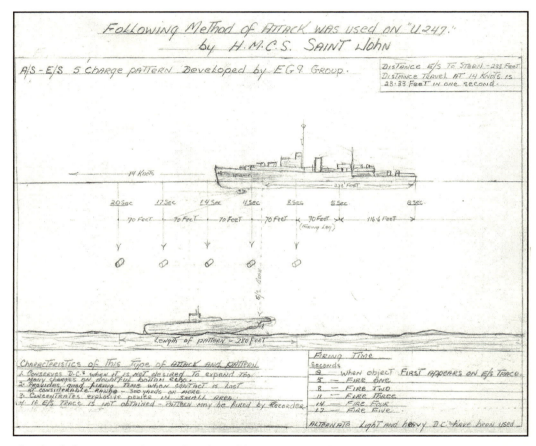

Following Method of Attack was used on "U 247."
by H.M.C.S. Saint John

A/S - E/S 5 Charge pattern Developed by EG9 Group.

Distance E/S to Stern - 233 Feet
Distance Travel at 14 Knots is
23.33 Feet in one second.

14 Knots   233 Feet

20 Sec   17 Sec   14 Sec   11 Sec   8 Sec   5 Sec   0 Sec

70 Feet   70 Feet   70 Feet   70 Feet   70 Feet   116.6 Feet
                              (Firing Log)

Length of pattern - 280 Feet

Characteristics of This Type of Attack and Pattern.
1. Conserves D.C.s when it is not desired to expend too many charges on doubtful bottom echo.
2. Provides good firing time when contact is lost at considerable range - 300 yards or more.
3. Concentrates explosive power in small area.
4. If E/S trace is not obtained - pattern may be fired by Recorder.

Firing Time
Seconds
0   When object First Appears on E/S Trace.
5   Fire One.
8   Fire Two
11   Fire Three
14   Fire Four
17   Fire Five.

Alternate light and heavy D.C.s have been used

This sketch demonstrates the procedure devised by HMCS *Saint John* to attack bottomed U-boats and which proved successful in the destruction of both *U 247* and *U 309*. (PRO ADM 199/1462)

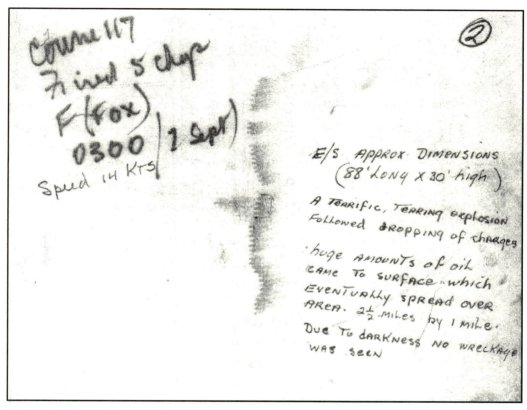

The actual echo sounder trace of *U 247* lying dead on the bottom complete with *Saint John*'s comments and attack data. (PRO ADM 199/1462)

After forty-five minutes in the sea *Alberni*'s survivors were pickedup by two RN MTBs which happened upon them on their way back to Plymouth from the assault area.

As in the case of *Regina*, there was disagreement as to whether *Alberni* was mined or torpedoed, but examination of postwar records revealed her to be a victim of *U 480*.[45] Besides the corvette, Förster also sank the Algerine class minesweeper HMS *Loyalty* and two merchant ships before leaving the Channel in the final week of August. It was one of the most successful patrols of the summer, a fact of which U-boat command seemed completely unaware. On 26 August, the day after Förster achieved his final success, the BdU war diary noted gloomily that "as 5 boats in succession have not returned from the Channel it must be presumed that the enemy has considerably intensified his defences ... For this reason, the boats last reckoned to be in the Channel (*U 92*, *989*, *275*) received orders to return and proceed to Norway." Moreover, the relentless advance by Allied land forces through Brittany, combined with the choke-hold clamped down by antisubmarine forces, caused the cancellation of U-boat operations in the Bay of Biscay, and forced Captain U-boats West to abandon his headquarters at La Rochelle.[46] With the suspension of operations in the Channel the last boats departing from Biscay ports "were detailed to the west coast of England (Bristol and North Channel) in the expectation that these areas would be less heavily defended."[47]

This signal was decrypted by Bletchley Park, and on 28 August the OIC warned Plymouth, Western Approaches, and Coastal commands that the "area in contemplation probably includes St Georges Channel and Bristol Channel and North Channel ... It would not be safe to assume that the south coast of Cornwall is excluded."[48] The latter caution was based on the operational orders issued to *U 247*, which were also broken. *U 247* was one of the last boats to leave Brest on 26 August, and the OIC became aware that "MY," as they designated *U 247*, had orders to patrol an area south of Land's End. Although lacking firm intelligence of the boat's progress after leaving Brest, because it kept radio silence, the OIC made several accurate appreciations of its passage north.[49]

This intelligence placed *U 247* in the clutches of EG 9. The group had been active in both the English Channel and the Bay of Biscay throughout much of August, and had put into Plymouth for a quick three-day layover at the end of the month. At 0900 on 31 August the frigates *Swansea* (SO, Commander A.F.C. Layard, RN),[50] *Saint John*, *Port Colborne*, *Monnow*, *Stormont*, and *Meon* departed with orders to patrol an area fifteen miles south of the Scilly Isles, the precise area thought to be *U 247*'s destination.[51] However, at 1111 Plymouth Command ordered EG 9 to shift its patrol area to the convoy route north of the Cornish coast between Hartland Point and Trevose Head on the basis of a radar contact picked up by a Coastal Command aircraft the previous night,

---

45. As late as 1960 the British official history attributed the loss to mining. Roskill, *War at Sea* III pt 2, 445

46. BdU, KTB, 26 Aug 1944. The advance of US armies had forced Captain U-Boats West to relocate from his headquarters at Angers to La Rochelle in the first week of August. See Tarrant, *Last Year of the Kriegsmarine*, 107-8

47. BdU, KTB, 30 Sep 1944, "Final Summary of Submarine Operations in the Channel"

48. Adm to C-in-C Plymouth, C-in-C WA, AOC-in-C Coastal Command, etc., 281029B/Aug 1944, PRO, ADM 223/203. The authors thank Malcolm Llewellyn-Jones for sharing his research on this subject.

49. A series of reports of MY's probable movements transmitted by the OIC to C-in-C Plymouth, C-in-C WA, AOC-in-C Coastal Command are in PRO, ADM 223/203.

50. Layard was double-hatted as CO *Swansea* and SO EG 9.

51. CNMO, "The RCN's Part in the Invasion," 360

leaving EG 11 to cover the area south of the Scillies.[52] While approaching Land's End on the way to the new area, at 1845 *Saint John* obtained a good asdic contact. Although it was lost almost immediately, *Saint John*'s asdic team considered it promising enough for an organized search, so Layard sent *Monnow*, *Stormont*, and *Meon* onward to EG 9's designated patrol area and continued the hunt with the remaining three frigates. *Swansea* picked up an echo at 2115 and dropped a single depth-charge thinking it was fish. But *Saint John* immediately noticed a slight oil trace. The frigates again lost contact, but at 0210 *Saint John* obtained an echo-sounder trace with the size and characteristics of a bottomed U-boat.[53]

During its service inshore EG 9 had become increasingly frustrated by its inability to make accurate approaches on bottomed contacts, which besides producing indecisive results caused a huge expenditure of depth-charges. Faced with this promising contact, Lieutenant-Commander W.R. Stacey, RCNR, *Saint John*'s CO, and his Antisubmarine Control Officer, Lieutenant J.R. Bradley, RCNVR, implemented tactics designed to concentrate the destructive power of their depth-charges as well as limit the number expended.[54] Their tactics also took full advantage of the precision that could be achieved with effective use of an echo sounder:

1) On getting an echo, on what appears to be a bottomed contact, the target is closed on centre bearing, and passed over with E/S [echo sounder] ...

2) Range is opened to 1000 to 1500 yards and the contact circled at that radius. This enables the operators to examine the contact more closely and by extent of target, etc. to determine the compass bearing on which the supposed submarine is lying.

3) When the above information has been received a run is made over the target at a fine angle to its long axis (20° for example) with E/S switched on. This is done when contact is lost by A/S beam but not later than 100 yards from the target.

4) As soon as the E/S shows that the target is being crossed the order to fire five depth-charges from the rails is given ... Since the length of "ST JOHN" from echo sounder to stern is 233 feet that distance is covered at the attacking speed of 15 knots in 9 seconds. With six seconds lag, therefore, the first charge would drop three seconds or 75 feet short of the target. Since the charges are spaced at 75 feet (3 seconds) the length of the pattern is 300 feet and assures that two or three charges will be within lethal distance of the target.[55]

Saint John's attack at 0300 with these tactics produced "a terrific, tearing explosion," and "huge amounts of oil came to the surface which eventually spread over [an] area 2½ miles by 1 mile."[56] No tell-tale wreckage could be sighted in the dark, nor could the frigates regain firm contact. Shortly after *Saint John*'s attack, however, Layard received a signal from Plymouth Command, likely based on an OIC report that "MY probably within 25 miles of Lands End," ordering him to

52. C-in-C Plymouth to EG 9, 1111B/31 Aug 1944, DHH 81/520/8440, EG 9, v 2

53. SO EG 9 ROP, 17 Aug–18 Sep 1944, 10 Sep 1944, DHH 81/520/8440, ibid

54. *Saint John*, "Following Method of Attack Was Used on 'U 247' by HMCS Saint John," nd, PRO, ADM 199/1462

55. "Description of Method Used by HMCS "Saint John" in Attacking Bottomed Contacts," nd, DHH, 81/520/8000, Saint John. This memorandum was likely prepared by Lt Bradley in Feb 1945.

56. *Saint John*, Notes on Echo Sounder Trace, PRO, ADM 199/1462

remain with the contact.[57] The three frigates kept on it throughout the night, but only "an occasional and very unconvincing echo could be obtained." Even when the oil traces brought up by *Saint John* were investigated at daylight, "nothing but fish echoes could be picked up by the ship's Asdics."[58]

For Layard the operation was becoming all too reminiscent of the many fruitless searches EG 9 had carried out inshore throughout the summer. "But for the fact that we'd been told by the C. in C. to remain," he complained in his diary, "I would certainly have given up and gone on as there was a reported wreck plotted only 2 miles away and I made a signal saying I thought further search waste of time."[59] Finally, at noon on 1 September, when the three frigates again probed the rising oil, *Saint John* obtained a good echo sounder trace, and an attack at 1400 using the tactics described above produced wreckage, letters, photographs, clothing, and part of an engine room register marked *U 247*. After a few more attacks Plymouth Command ordered EG 9 to move on to a new U-boat sighting off Trevose Head. The next day the OIC informed C-in-C Plymouth that it considered "MY sunk 1200Z 1 September," and when *Swansea* and *Saint John* next put into Plymouth they were informed that they had shared in the destruction of *U 247*.[60] Captain C.D. Howard-Johnstone, Director of the Anti-U-boat Division, credited the kill to the "skill and efficiency of the Commanding Officer and A/S team of HMCS St John."[61] Both Stacey and Bradley were awarded the Distinguished Service Cross. *Swansea*'s contribution made her the RCN's leading U-boat killer, with four destroyed.

The destruction of *U 247* coincided with the end of the initial phase of the inshore antisubmarine campaign. In an appreciation written during the last week of August, the OIC concluded that "the U-boat campaign is passing out of one phase into another." Not only were U-boat operations in the Channel suspended but "the essential character of operations must be profoundly affected by the loss of the Biscay bases." Limited to bases in Germany and Norway, U-boats had lost the broad access to the North Atlantic shipping routes they had enjoyed since 1940. "Now that convoys and independents can be spread more freely, pack operations by U-boats will be less certain to find targets, and it will be logical for the enemy appreciating this disadvantage to come closer inshore to operate in focal areas such as the North Channel and the Minches and the Bristol Channel where interceptions would be certain, though, one hopes, hazardous."[62]

Hazardous they would be, but as will be seen, not to the extent that the OIC analysts hoped. However, nor would the interception of shipping by U-boats be certain and it is worth re-empha-

---

57. Adm to C-in-C Plymouth, C-in-C WA, AOC-in-C Coastal Command, etc., 1335B/31 Aug 1944, PRO, ADM 223/203. C-in-C Plymouth to EG 9, 0119 1 Sep 1944, DHH 81/520/8440, EG 9 v 2

58. SO EG 9 ROP, 10 Sep 1944

59. AFC Layard diary, 1 Sep 1944, DHH, 87/214

60. *Port Colborne* made no attacks as her TBS was malfunctioning, which would make it difficult to coordinate attack runs. *Assiniboine* from EG 11 joined the operation after *U 247* had been destroyed.

61. Director, Anti-U-boat Division (DAUD) Memo, "Sinking of U-247 off the Wolfe Rock," 21 Sep 1944, PRO, ADM 199/1462. An analysis of the action based on Layard's ROP was promulgated in the Oct 1944 edition of the Admiralty's *Monthly Antisubmarine Report (MASR)*.

62. The OIC, "U-boat Trend. Period 21/8/44-28/8/44," PRO, ADM 223/20

sizing that although submarines were hard to find and to kill in the inshore environment, it was equally unfriendly to them, and they had extremely limited success in hindering the flow of men and materiel to the American, British and Canadian armies in northwest Europe. An Admiralty Trade Division summary in September reported that merchant ship losses from all causes in Operation Neptune from D-Day up to 28 August "amounted to 18 ocean-going and 8 smaller vessels out of some 10,000 sailings."[63] Between 24 June and 12 September 1.4 million tons of stores, 152,000 vehicles, and 352,570 men were landed in the British Assault Area of Normandy alone.[64] Against that, Allied maritime forces had destroyed twenty-five U-boats. By any measure, that was a triumph of sea power—and one that would be sustained until VE-Day.

As victory fever began to permeate various Allied headquarters in mid-August 1944, the Admiralty increasingly shifted its glance towards the far eastern theatre of operations. This caused tension with Admiral Horton at Western Approaches, who wanted to inflict a knock-out blow on the U-boats moving from Biscay bases to Norway and ensure that his own backyard was in order before sending escorts to the other side of the world. Like the Admiralty, however, Horton had his eye on the escorts beginning to appear on the RCN's order of battle from new construction. In mid-August Horton proposed to the Admiralty that to make "best use" of available Western Approaches and RCN forces, close escort of mid-ocean trans-atlantic convoys be reduced to three B and eight C groups, each with a paper strength of eight ships including, in the case of the B groups, two fast escorts such as frigates or A/S destroyers. "To implement this scheme," Horton continued, "two additional C-groups would be required in late September and mid-October respectively. It is anticipated that Royal Canadian Navy could provide these resources from present resources and new construction." By these measures Horton calculated that one RCN and two or three Western Approaches support groups could be formed in September and early October. Finally, hinting that the Admiralty not get too far ahead of itself by committing forces overseas, Horton recommended that the ships in his command allocated for the Far East be retained in home waters for the present.[65]

When the Admiralty communicated Horton's proposal to NSHQ on 18 August, it expanded the options for the possible uses of Canadian new construction. These included sending River class frigates to the Eastern Fleet, transferring the arcticized Castle class corvettes to the Home Fleet for use on the Russian convoys, and distributing surplus escorts among other overseas commands. The message echoed other information gleaned by the Canadian Naval Mission Overseas earlier in the summer that the Admiralty would prefer that the RCN despatch any surplus River class frigates to the Eastern Fleet, as they were attempting to concentrate their own ships of that type in that theatre, keeping their Loch and Captain class frigates and Castle class corvettes in the Atlantic.[66] Certainly, the Admiralty's message did not share the same sense of urgency about the situation in British home waters as Horton's did, and it included no mention of forming new support groups.[67]

---

63. Adm, Trade Division, Monthly Chronological History and Merchant Ship Casualties, Sep 1944, PRO, ADM 199/2090

64. Roskill, *War at Sea* III pt 2, 136. For a contemporary analysis see Capt R. Winn, "Anti-U-boat Results of Neptune," 28 Aug 1944, Syrett *Battle of the Atlantic*, 303-4

65. C-in-C WA to Adm, 1917B/13 Sep 1944, DHH 81/520/8440, Support Groups (General)

66. See ACNS(H) to CNMO, 25 July 1944, LAC, RG 24, 11752, CS 346-1.

67. Adm to NSHQ, 1846B 18 Aug 1944, ibid

NSHQ's response was lukewarm. New construction "commissioned and working-up" consisted of nineteen River class frigates, nine corvettes, and two Algerines; thus, "other than three Castle class corvettes [it was] unlikely that any more ships will become operational before the end of October." It also cautioned that no allowance had been made for the nineteen corvettes allocated to the Admiralty for Operation Neptune. Nonetheless, by reducing strength in mid-ocean and local escort groups, by accepting "limited" delays in refits, and by temporarily using EG 16—the sole support group in the Canadian Northwest Atlantic Command—for close escort, the RCN could eventually provide enough ships to form the new mid-ocean groups C 7 and C 8. As far as future new construction was concerned, the Castle class corvettes "may be available" for the Russian convoys, and as further frigates became available their deployment to the eastern theatre "will be most desirable." As in the message from the Admiralty, there was no mention of the need for new support groups; indeed, NSHQ was prepared to go without them completely for at least a while.[68]

Strategic appreciations changed drastically at the end of August when a single U-boat sparked a new phase of the inshore battle. On the 30th, *U 482*, under Kapitänleutnant Baron von Matuschka, sank the 10,400-ton tanker *Jacksonville* in the North Channel about twenty miles north of Malin Head. The next day he sank the corvette HMS *Hurst Castle* in the same area. In what one historian considers "the most productive patrol of any Type VII in 1944," *U 482* went on to sink another large tanker and two freighters before leaving the North Channel on 8 September.[69] BdU first learned of this success when von Matuschka reported in two days later and immediately diverted six *schnorkel* boats at sea to the area.[70]

U 482's success made it clear to the Admiralty that the requirement was now to deal with *schnorkel* boats that were attempting offensive operations against shipping in the inshore routes around Great Britain, and came around to Horton's view that more support groups would be required. The key to accomplishing this would be to strip fast escorts (destroyers and frigates) from other responsibilities, and to achieve that the Admiralty proposed measures more drastic than Horton had in mid-August. Citing *U 482*'s success in the North Channel, the Admiralty informed British naval commands, the USN's 10th Fleet in Washington, and the RCN that "a considerable U-boat threat must be expected in UK inshore waters, such as the Northern, North Western and South Western Approaches." More support groups were "urgently required," and to effect that solution the Admiralty planned to withdraw all fast escorts from the B groups, leaving them comprised totally of corvettes, and cut the nominal strength of existing RN support groups to five ships, while reducing the number of escorts for slow convoys moving to and from Gibraltar.[71] Thus, with the North Atlantic transformed into what some dubbed a "milk run" the Admiralty was willing to shift the most effective RN escorts to the inshore campaign. In a follow-up message to NSHQ, the Admiralty asked the RCN to follow course:

---

68. NSHQ to Adm, 2203/24 Aug 1944, ibid

69. Blair, *Hitler's U-boat War* II 630-1. The other ships sunk by *U 482* were the 15,702-ton tanker *Empire Heritage* and the freighters *Fiordheim* and *Pinto*.

70. BdU, KTB, 10-11 Sep 1944. Six more U-boats were sent into the area on 2 Oct.

71. Adm to C-in-C WA etc, 1605B/2 Sep 1944, DHH 81/520/8440, Support Groups (General)

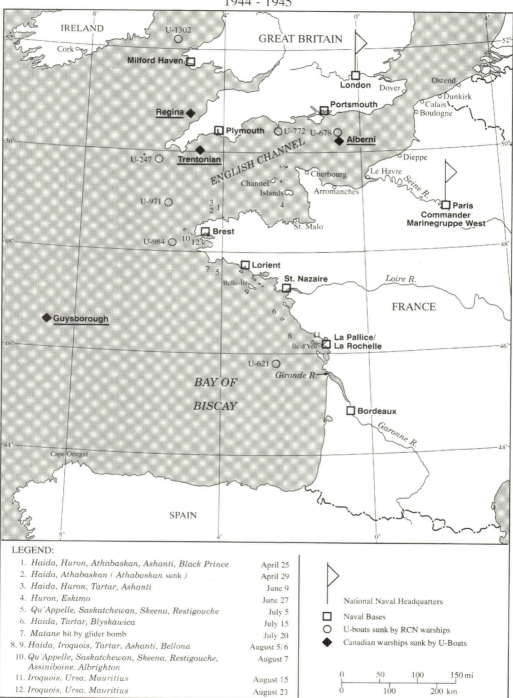

CHANNEL AND BISCAY AREA
1944 - 1945

IRELAND

U-1302

Cork

GREAT BRITAIN

Milford Haven

London

Dover

Ostend

Dunkirk

Calais

Boulogne

Portsmouth

Regina

Plymouth

U-772

U-678

Alberni

Dieppe

U-247

Trentonian

ENGLISH CHANNEL

Cherbourg

Le Havre

Seine R.

Channel
Islands

Arromanches

Paris
Commander
Marinegruppe West

U-971

3 1
2

4

Brest

St. Malo

U-984

10
12

Lorient

7 5

St. Nazaire

Loire R.

Belle-Ile

9

FRANCE

6

Guysborough

8

11

La Pallice/
La Rochelle

Ile d'Yeu

U-621

Gironde R.

BAY OF

BISCAY

Bordeaux

Garonne R.

Cape Ortegal

SPAIN

LEGEND:

1. *Haida, Huron, Athabaskan, Ashanti, Black Prince* — April 25
2. *Haida, Athabaskan (Athabaskan sunk)* — April 29
3. *Haida, Huron, Tartar, Ashanti* — June 9
4. *Huron, Eskimo* — June 27
5. *Qu'Appelle, Saskatchewan, Skeena, Restigouche* — July 5
6. *Haida, Tartar, Blyskawica* — July 15
7. *Matane* hit by glider bomb — July 20
8, 9. *Haida, Iroquois, Tartar, Ashanti, Bellona* — August 5/6
10. *Qu'Appelle, Saskatchewan, Skeena, Restigouche, Assiniboine, Albrighton* — August 7
11. *Iroquois, Ursa, Mauritius* — August 15
12. *Iroquois, Ursa, Mauritius* — August 23

National Naval Headquarters
□ Naval Bases
○ U-boats sunk by RCN warships
◆ Canadian warships sunk by U-Boats

0 50 100 150 mi
0 100 200 km

To meet the urgent need for additional groups, request you will consider conforming as far as C groups and EG 16 are concerned. It is estimated that this should produce 3 additional fast groups in due course, making 7 in all.

It would be appreciated if 2 of these additional RCN groups could be placed under the operational control of C in C WA for use in covering Trans-Atlantic Convoys, thus leaving 2 for operations in Canadian waters.[72]

The RCN was prepared to meet the Admiralty's request, but on its own terms. In doing so its leaders acknowledged that the most serious threat existed in British waters and concurred that this theatre should be reinforced at the expense of others. On 5 September NSHQ "agreed that the formation of support groups is urgent," but its solution indicated how much the RCN had learned during the Battle of the Atlantic. Rather than stripping away all the fast escorts from the C groups as the Admiralty requested or keeping two per group as proposed by Western Approaches, the Canadians replied that they would form eight C groups from the five already in existence, with the new groups each comprising one frigate and five corvettes. "By this means," NSHQ informed the Admiralty, "more suitable Senior Officers ships are retained and the groups will be similarly constituted." Thus the RCN was composing its escort groups the way it wanted to, and by keeping a frigate in each ensured that they maintained a prudent level of effectiveness. That the two sovereign headquarters (the Admiralty and NSHQ) and two national commands (Western Approaches and Canadian Northwest Atlantic) could reach agreeable, yet independent solutions to complex problems indicated that the Royal Navy and Royal Canadian Navy were more true partners in a relationship that had matured to a high state of effectiveness.

These moves allowed the creation of three new RCN frigate support groups. Unless "a serious threat" developed in the Canadian zone, NSHQ agreed that the first two to be formed would be assigned to Western Approaches, with the third retained by C-in-C CNA "as necessary."[73] The group numbers 25 to 29 were allocated to the RCN, thus EGs 25, 26, and 27 came into being.[74] EG 25 was formed in Halifax on 29 September by taking *Thetford Mines* and *Ste Thérèse* from C 6, and *La Hulloise* and *Orkney* (SO) from EG 16. Those four frigates worked up while operating in the Canadian zone throughout October. They were joined in Londonderry by *Joliette* from new construction after going overseas at the end of the month.[75] EG 26 included *Beacon Hill* (SO) from new construction, *Montreal* and *Ribble* from C 4, and *New Glasgow* and *Jonquiere* from C 1 and 2 respectively.[76] Since the majority of the ships allocated to EG 26 were in the vicinity of Londonderry at the end of September, the group assembled there and worked up under the direction of Western Approaches, before carrying out its first operation in late October.[77]

72. Adm to NSHQ, 1713B/2 Sep 1944, ibid

73. NSHQ to Adm, 2013Z/5 Sep 1944, ibid and LAC, RG 24, 11752, CS 389-1. For number and strength of C groups, see RCN Daily States, DHH 81/520/1650-DS

74. C-in-C WA to C-in-C CNA, 1704B/8 Sep 1944, DHH 81/520/8440, Support Groups (General)

75. C-in-C CNA to NSHQ, 1709/25 Sep 1944, ibid, EG 25 v 1; "Notes Concerning Formation of Escort Groups," nd, ibid, Support Groups (General)

76. C-in-C CNA to NSHQ, 2 Oct 1944, ibid, EG 26, v 1

77. C-in-C CNA to C-in-C WA, 1652Z/17 Sep 1944, ibid, EG 25, v 1

The tried veteran HMCS *Assiniboine*—"Bones" to her crew—at speed in the Bay of Biscay in the summer of 1944. (DND PMR 98-30, Courtesy R.P. Welland)

The frigate HMCS *Chebogue* after being torpedoed in mid-Atlantic. Like *Teme* before her, this ship would survive the experience. The ship's captain, Lieutenant-Commander Maurice Oliver, RCNR, is examining what used to be his quarter deck. (DND K-198)

Another view of HMCS *Chebogue* after the torpedoing. It took eight hazardous and difficult days to tow the ship to the safety of harbour. (DND K-211)

The River class frigate HMCS *Dunver*, which contributed to the destruction of *U 484*. (DND GM1166)

HMCS *Skeena*, aground in Iceland. The old war-horse would be the last of six destroyers lost to the RCN in the Second World War. (DND HN 1841)

Squid, the mascot for HMCS *Tillsonburg*, a Castle class corvette. Pets were a way of normalizing life onboard ship—even if they got in the way at times. (LAC PA 204576)

The frigates that comprised EG 25 and 26 were new ships, but the prewar River class destroyers that made up EGs 11 and 12 were showing their age. Not only did the pounding from scores of depth-charge explosions in relatively shallow waters punish their tired hulls, but EG 12's *Skeena* and *Qu'Appelle* had collided during an engagement with enemy trawlers in Audierne Bay on 12 August.[78] Moreover, *Saskatchewan*, another destroyer from EG 12, returned to Canada for scheduled maintenance later that same month, and more refits were on the horizon.[79] As a result, British and Canadian authorities decided to amalgamate the two RCN destroyer support groups into a redesignated EG 11. The group now included *Skeena*, *Ottawa*, *Chaudière*, *Assiniboine*, and *St Laurent*, with Commander J.D. Prentice sailing in *Qu'Appelle* as Senior Officer.[80]

By mid-September this reshuffling of escort forces gave C-in-C Western Approaches nineteen support groups either formed or forming, fourteen RN and five RCN.[81] More reinforcements were on the way, which raised the issue of how best to cope with the new arrivals without overwhelming the infrastructure and resources of Admiral Horton's command. One solution was to form three new RN groups, but Horton was wary of that approach for several reasons, the most important of which were that he did not think he had enough qualified senior officers to lead the new groups, and he feared that more groups would strain the efficient Western Approaches training system. Instead, Horton decided to increase the paper strength of the RN groups to six ships from five. This would ease the personnel and training burden and also provide a buffer against the toll on ships that was bound to arise from intensive operations in the rough winter conditions that were just a few months down the line. Regarding the RCN groups, EGs 6, 9, and 11 already had a paper strength of six frigates, and Horton was prepared to leave EGs 25 and 26 at five ships.[82]

It would take time to implement the arrangements for new support groups. Meanwhile, the Admiralty and Western Approaches still had to deal with the threat at hand. When *U 482* began racking up sinkings in the North Channel in early September, Admiral Horton threw all the antisubmarine forces he could spare—whether support groups or not—to try to snare the intruder. One of the units deployed was the RCN mid-ocean group C 5, now comprising the frigates *Dunver* (SO, Commander G.H. Stephen, RCNR) and *Nene*, the Castle class corvettes *Hespeler* and *Huntsville*, and the Flowers *Long Branch*, *New Westminister*, and *Wetaskiwin*. C 5 departed Moville in two sections on 8 September—the same day that *U 482* left the area—with orders to patrol between Tory Island and Inistrahull, northeast of the entrance to Loch Foyle. The group ran into the usual non-subs and wrecks, but at 2018 on 9 September *Dunver* obtained a radar contact that was immediately classified as a submarine. Half an hour later *Dunver* gained asdic contact. Over the next several hours the frigate attacked with depth-charges and Hedgehog, while *Hespeler* carried out six Squid attacks. Contacts were fleeting and difficult to classify, and in his report Stephens noted that "the

---

78 EG 12 to C-in-C Plymouth, 0532B/12 Aug 1944, ibid, EG 11, v 1

79 *Gatineau* and *Restigouche* returned to Canada for refit in July and Sep respectively. See Barrie and MacPherson, *The Ships of Canada's Naval Forces*, 48-53

80 C-in-C WA to Adm and CNMO, 2304Z/1 Sep 1944, DHH 81/520/8440, EG 11, v 1; CNMO, "RCN's Part in the Invasion" II, 351

81 The RN groups were EGs 1, 2, 3, 5, 10, 14, 15, 17, 18, 19, 20, 21, 30, and 31, and the RCN EGs 6, 9, 11, 25, and 26.

82 C-in-C WA to Adm, NSHQ and C-in-C CNA, 1157A/26 Sep 1944, DHH 81/520/8440, Support Groups (General)

opinion of the ships in contact was that the echo was doubtful, probably non-sub."[83] Analysis by Western Approaches admitted that the contact "might well have been a submarine" but also recognized that "without further evidence from wreckage or definite submarine echo characteristics, it is not possible to say if a U-boat was present or not. The plot indicates a number of scattered echoes and no definite movement of any."[84] Despite the questionable evidence, after the war the Admiralty credited *Dunver* and *Hespeler* with destroying *U 484*. More recent assessments have now credited that U-boat to British ships. It appears therefore that the doubts expressed by C 5 and Western Approaches about the presence of a U-boat were justified.[85] Nevertheless, the sweeps by C 5, which patrolled the area until 14 September, and the efforts of other escort groups did affect U-boat operations. When *U 248* reported in to BdU later in the month it complained that it was "continuously forced off" its attempt to penetrate North Channel by antisubmarine forces on 11 September and that its efforts to *schnorkel* were "consistently interrupted."[86]

The Germans would soon notice a reduction in traffic in the North Channel. In mid-September, as a result of the *U-bootewaffe*'s retreat to Norway, the Admiralty reorganized convoy arrangements, shifting the routing of the majority of transatlantic convoys from the northwest to the southwest approaches through St George's Channel into the Irish Sea or directly into the English Channel.[87] Initially, convoys discharged their cargoes into ports like Liverpool, Milford Haven, and Southampton, but as the war continued and the English Channel became more secure, merchant ships headed right through to the Thames and even to Le Havre and Antwerp. This, of course, extended the distance that U-boats had to steam to reach promising patrol areas. It also took the convoys further south in the North Atlantic. This caused a rare encounter between the close escort of a convoy with a U-boat on the open Atlantic.

In September a new *schnorkel*-fitted type IXC, *U 1227* under Oberleutnant F. Altmeier, departed Norway for the Gibraltar approaches. Late the same month the westbound convoy ONS 33 cleared Liverpool, escorted by C 1, with Commander G.S. Hall, RCNR, riding in the frigate *Chebogue* as senior officer. Lieutenant-Commander M.F. Oliver, RCNR, commanded the frigate. Although the two officers enjoyed a good relationship, the split-command situation whereby Hall controlled the group while Oliver fought the ship had considerable impact on the events that followed.

On 4 October ONS 33 was one-third of the way across the Atlantic when it was detected and reported by *U 1227*.[88] HF/DF operators in *Chebogue* picked up the sighting report and, at 1225, after the frigate turned to run down the bearing, the masthead lookout sighted the U-boat, which was seen to dive at about 10,000 yards.[89] Unable to establish an accurate datum point because of

---

83. C 5 ROP, 14 Sep 1944, DHH 81/520/8440, C 5, v 2

84. Cmdre (D) WA, "Operation C.W.—C.5. Escort Group," 27 Sep 1944, ibid

85. Axel Niestlé has concluded that *U 484* was destroyed on 9 Sep by HMS *Helmsdale* and *Porchester Castle*. Their attack, which brought up wreckage, was originally assumed to have caused the loss of *U 743*, but it is now understood that boat did not enter the area until 11 Sep. See Niestlé, *German U-boat Losses*; Blair, *Hitler's U-boat War* II, 631; and Milner, *U-boat Hunters*, 190

86. BdU, KTB, 24 Sep 1944

87. Adm, *The Defeat of the Enemy Attack on Shipping*; Adm, "Antisubmarine Warfare, 1: Development of the U-boat Campaign," 20-1, PRO, ADM 239/246

88. BdU, KTB, 4 Oct 1944; "U-boat Situation, Week Ending 9/10/44," in Syrett, *Battle of the Atlantic*, 465

89. Unless cited otherwise, this account is based upon "Torpedoing of HMCS 'Chebogue,'" nd, DHH 81/520/8000, Chebogue

the extreme range and distracted by numerous non-sub contacts, the frigate accompanied by other escorts, searched fruitlessly for the submarine throughout the afternoon. Suspecting that the U-boat might attempt to attack after darkness fell, Hall positioned *Chebogue* south of the convoy, dropping scare charges every half-hour. At 2100 *Chebogue*'s type 271Q radar picked up an echo, which Oliver turned towards, firing starshell when he closed to 6,500 yards. A startled *U 1227* found herself bathed in light, but Altmeier recovered quickly. "Remained on the surface," he later reported starkly, "but was firmly driven off. Curve shot at Jervis class destroyer,[90] angle on the bow 0. After firing accurate starshell, dived, torpedo exploded, loud sinking noises heard in multi-unit hydrophones and with the naked ear. Then a dull explosion. Escort kept boat submerged, no depth-charges, contact lost."[91]

Altmeier's "down the throat" shot—the Admiralty's phraseology[92]—with a *zaunkönig* (Gnat) struck *Chebogue* on the port side aft, blowing off thirty feet of her stern. On the bridge, the signals officer, Lieutenant J. Benson, RCNVR, observed that "there was a sudden 'whump'—not as loud as you would expect—and I turned to see bits of steel and other wreckage soaring through the air, higher than the mast. At first I thought it was some kind of heavy depth-charge, but when I saw all that stuff flying I realized what had happened."[93] Heavily damaged, *Chebogue* remained afloat, and despite the fact that they had lost seven of their ship mates, and that a U-boat remained undetected nearby, the entire crew volunteered to remain onboard to help save their ship, although only twenty were required. The next day the corvette *Chambly* began what became an epic tow by a relay of warships and a rescue tug. *Chebogue* eventually reached the United Kingdom; but went aground off the coast of Wales in a gale and was declared a constructive total loss.[94]

In his analysis Commodore (D) in Londonderry concluded that *Chebogue* may have become exposed when a fading asdic signal caused her to reduce speed from 18.5 knots to eleven about a minute-and-a-half before the Gnat hit.[95] That would seem to have been bad luck—the frigate had CAT streamed.[96] Nevertheless, it caused the question to be raised at the Board of Inquiry as to why Oliver did not use the standard "step aside" tactic where the frigate approached the U-boat from no less than 10 degrees on the bow. Neither Oliver nor the officer of the watch was at the inquiry. Hall maintained, however, that he made that recommendation to the CO: "This was not an order,

---

90. Altmeier's mistaken identification is explained by the fact that River class frigates and Jervis class destroyers both had single funnel.

91. BdU, KTB, 7 Oct 1944. See also Dr J. Rohwer to Naval Historian, 16 Sep 1963, DHH ibid. Whether the torpedo was fired from the bow or stern tubes is unclear. *U 1227* subsequently escaped a rigorous hunt by EG 9 and the USN's USS *Card* aircraft carrier hunter-killer group. The boat operated in the Gibraltar approaches for almost a month without achieving further success and returned to Norway after 106 days at sea. See the OIC, "U-boat Situation, Week Ending 23/10/44," in Syrett, *The Battle of the Atlantic* I, 473; BdU, KTB, Dec 1944

92. Directorate of Naval Operational Studies (DNOS), Report no. 4/46, "The History of the Gnat Campaign," (nd, but 1946), 16, PRO, ADM 219/292

93. Quoted in RCN, Press Release, 7 June 1945, 2, DHH 81/520/8000, Chebogue

94. None of the crew were lost because of the grounding thanks to the Mumbles, Glamorganshire, detachment of the Royal Lifesaving Society, which saved a number of sailors from certain death. See "Board of Inquiry into the Events Subsequent to the Torpedoing of HMCS Chebogue," Oct 1944, PRO, ADM 1/16923; LCdr I.A. McPhee, "Autobiography of a Hurricane," *Crowsnest*, July 1955.

95. Cmdre (D) WA, "ONS 33," 30 Nov 1944, 1, Convoy Report ONS 33, DHH 89/34, v 24

96. Hall had some doubts if *Chebogue*'s CAT was working effectively, but Oliver insisted it was, and that seems to be confirmed by Altmeier who reported the "sawing" sound in the water.

but a suggestion. This action was not taken, as Lieutenant-Commander Oliver felt confident that at reduced speed, with CAT streamed, he could make a direct attack."[97] When Oliver later learned of this he was livid. "Extreme caution was again exercised in ensuring that the U-boat was placed not less than ten degrees on the bow. When attack was considered imminent, ie when the U-boat dived at a range of 4600 yards, course was altered 20 (twenty) degrees starboard."[98]

Whether Commodore Simpson ever heard Oliver's side of things remains unclear, but Hall's verbal report to him set off alarm bells:

> This operation, culminating in the serious damage to CHEBOGUE provides an argument against the Senior Officer of a Group not commanding the ship. Hall and Oliver are both efficient Officers and good friends, yet the former explained to me that, under the circumstances ... CHEBOGUE was detached on Hall's decision, returning [to the convoy] by what proved to be the best course for interception on Hall's appreciation. Nevertheless, although Hall agreed very well with the general handling of the ship, incidents occurred in which he found it difficult not to interfere, particularly in the final stages when CHEBOGUE was steering directly towards the U-boat, whereas he would have preferred to keep her broader on the bow. In fact, as Commander Hall remarked to me, he objected to standing on the bridge of a ship commanded by someone else, however efficient they might be, when carrying out the complex operation of hunting and attacking a U-boat which almost certainly carried acoustic torpedoes. His apprehension was certainly justified.[99]

The practice of having SOs and COs on the same ship often caused problems. Commander A.F.C. Layard, SO of EG 9, for example, complained about it when he rode in *Matane* with Lieutenant-Commander A.H. Easton as commanding officer early in 1944. "I had a yarn with Easton," he wrote in his diary, "because I know I'm interfering too much and he resents it, but I just can't help it when I see things not being done as I want them. I must say I wish I was in command."[100] The situation occurred less frequently as most SOs found themselves double-hatted towards the end of the war, and perhaps in the *Chebogue* situation, Hall should have "interfered" more as Layard regretted doing with Easton. As it was, Oliver was not judged to have done anything wrong, but "to prevent the 'down the throat shot' which had caught HMCS CHEBOGUE," the Admiralty amended its anti-Gnat tactics, directing that when ships were attacking U-boats at less then 6,000 yards, the enemy "should be kept not less than 20° on the bow."[101]

In October EG 11 also lost a ship under controversial circumstances, but this time it was the North Atlantic that struck the blow. EG 11 was carrying out an antisubmarine patrol south of Iceland on the night of 24 October in the midst of a steadily worsening gale.[102] At 2020, with the

---

97.   "Board of Inquiry ... Chebogue"

98.   CO *Chebogue* to CNMO, 27 Feb 1945, LAC, ibid

99.   Cmdre (D) WA, "ONS 33," 30 Nov 1944, 1

100. Layard diary, 11 Mar 1944

101. DNOS, Report no. 4/46

102. EG 11's operation was likely in response to the Admiralty's U-boat situation report for the week ending 23 Oct 1944, which reported a U-boat on patrol south of Reykjavik, and others trying to break out to North American waters. See the OIC, "U-boat Trend. Period 9/10/44–18/10/44" and "U-boat Situation, Week Ending 23/10/44," in Syrett, *The Battle of the Atlantic* I, 469, 472

wind at Force 8 with occasional hail squalls, the Admiral Commanding, Iceland, Rear-Admiral B.C. Watson, RN, recalled the group to harbour. Faced with a choice of anchoring in either Hvalfjord or Reykjavik, Commander Prentice ordered his ships to put into the latter location where there would be decent shelter either by Engey Island or in the harbour itself.[103] This order caused consternation on the bridge of the destroyer *Skeena*. Discussing the situation prior to receiving Prentice's instructions, the CO, Lieutenant-Commander P.F.X. Russell, RCN, and his navigator Lieutenant P.G. Chance, RCN, had decided it would be safest to ride the storm out at sea. Years later Chance recalled, "We agreed that the best place for us was to be at sea where our extremely seaworthy vessel could take almost anything."[104] Moreover, they knew from experience that the volcanic silt that covered much of the harbour bottom made for poor holding ground for anchors, and the fact that *Skeena* had only a single centreline capstan made the use of two anchors difficult. When Prentice's order to enter harbour arrived, Chance felt so strongly that the decision was wrong that he asked Russell to relieve him of his duties as navigator.[105] The CO noted his protest but asked him to carry on and *Skeena* anchored in the Reykjavik fairway between Videy and Engey islands.

Russell dropped the port anchor with five shackles of chain down, kept two boilers at immediate notice for steam, and assigned his two most experienced officers—Chance and Lieutenant W.M. Kidd, RCN, the First Lieutenant—to supervise the anchor watch; personnel were to take regular bearings on fixed points ashore to ensure that the ship was not dragging her anchor. After giving them his instructions for the night, Russell retired to his day cabin towards the stern of the ship. When Chance handed over the watch to Kidd at 0050 on 25 October *Skeena* appeared to be holding firm. "After writing up my night orders and satisfying myself that the anchor watch was correctly closed up [on the fo'c'sle]," Kidd recalled,

> I took my station on the Bridge. Anchor bearings were checked every five minutes. During the period [of] approximately one hour, three or four heavy hail flurries had occurred. Just previous to the last one of these, I had checked anchor bearings and found them to be correct. During the last flurry, which lasted between three and four minutes no lights were visible. Just after the flurry had ceased I noticed the arc between buoy F.1 [flashing] ev[ery] 5 seconds and the leading light closed very rapidly. Without checking bearings, I ordered half ahead on both the engines—this being 12 knots. I closed up the cable party, and called the Captain and the Navigator. Seeing the speed not to be enough, I ordered Fifteen knots. It was just then that the proximity to land was clearly visible, and full ahead was rung down. Almost immediately afterwards we touched bottom.
>
> During the period of no more than five minutes in which I estimated it took us to go aground, the ship was not jerked as would normally occur by a dragging anchor, and as the lights were not visible during the flurry, there was no reason to suspect we were dragging.[106]

---

103. Min Board of Inquiry, 9, Testimony of Cdr J.D. Prentice, DHH 81/520/8000, Skeena I, v 1

104. P.G. Chance, *Before It's Too Late: A Sailor's Life* (Sidney, BC 2001), 101. See also Chance to B. Witherspoon, 3 Aug 1989, DHH 90/136

105. Chance, *Before It's Too Late*, 101

106. Lt W.M. Kidd, "Report of Grounding—HMCS Skeena," (nd but probably 25 Oct 1944), 1, DHH 81/520/8000, Skeena I, v 1

Skeena had dragged stern-first onto the reefs off Videy Island. Unable to power the ship off the rocks, Russell requested assistance from a nearby trawler and ordered all hands on deck. Eventually realizing that a tow was impossible, and with *Skeena* appearing to be in imminent danger of breaking up, he ordered the crew to abandon ship. Sadly, fifteen sailors drowned when one float capsized in the heavy seas, and the line to a second parted. Realizing that it was safer on board, Russell waited until the weather moderated in the morning before finally ordering everyone off the ship.[107] After inspection, *Skeena* was judged a constructive total loss.

A Board of Inquiry in Iceland concluded that the incident was caused "by lack of seamanlike precaution" on the part of Russell, and "lack of vigilance" by Kidd. Rear-Admiral Watson recommended that both be court-martialled for negligence in allowing *Skeena* to be "hazarded" and "stranded."[108] The RCN agreed, and separate proceedings held under the authority of Canadian Northwest Atlantic Command in December 1944 found the charges proved. In sentencing Russell and Kidd both received reprimands—-a light sentence that sparked reaction. Captain W.L. Puxley, RN, Captain (D) Halifax and the prosecutor at Russell's court-martial, protested to the C-in-C Northwest Atlantic "that if a Court who have found the accused guilty of hazarding and stranding a valuable ship of His Majesty's Canadian Navy, and an important unit in anti U-boat warfare, cannot see fit to impose a penalty greater than a reprimand, the whole principle of justice and scale of punishments in the Royal Canadian Navy will have to be drastically revised." Puxley argued that he routinely awarded cells or detention to lookouts who had fallen asleep on duty, thus hazarding their ships: "It would appear that the most that can be expected in the case of a rating, who cannot be expected to appreciate the seriousness of the offence to the same extent as a responsible Commanding Officer of a destroyer, would be a caution. This would clearly be farcical, though it is strictly comparable."[109] Rear-Admiral Murray disputed Puxley's comparison, maintaining that cases must be considered individually. Moreover, he stated that he himself was not in a position to offer an official opinion on the verdict and, in any case, could only direct that punishment be lightened, not stiffened.[110]

When informing NSHQ of the outcome of Russell's trial, however, Murray did offer an opinion. "From the extremely light sentence," he suggested to the secretary of the Naval Board, "it would appear that the majority of the Court believed the Commanding Officer to have been badly served by his Officer of the Watch, and that his own negligence had little influence on the final result."[111] That both the light punishment and Murray's explanation did not go over well in Ottawa was evident from a curt letter that Murray received from the Naval Board which informed him that "the Minister considers the sentences in the case of these officers to be completely inadequate, having

107. Lt-Cdr P.F.X. Russell, "Report of Grounding – HMCS SKEENA," (nd, but probably 25 Oct 1944), 1, ibid

108. R-Adm B.C. Watson, "Board of Inquiry—HMCS Skeena," nd, ibid. Three sailors were also placed under open arrest for stealing liquor while the ship was being abandoned.

109. Capt W.L. Puxley to C-in-C CNA, 19 Dec 1944, DHH 90/136. Cdr A.G.S. Griffin, RCNVR (ret), then serving as SO (Operations) at St John's recalls "a sense of cynicism over the Skeena trial" and that there was a sense among the RCNR and RCNVR officers that in such circumstances permanent force officers "got off with comparative leniency." He cites as an example the case of the RCNR captain of the corvette HMCS *Dunvegan* who was "dismissed his ship and severely reprimanded" for going aground in Reykjavik. Griffin to Whitby, Jan 2004, and Griffin, *Footfalls in Memory* (Toronto 1998), 108-9

110. C-in-C CNA to Capt (D) Halifax, 15 Jan 1945, DHH 90/136

111. C-in-C CNA to Sec NB, 15 Jan 1945, ibid

regard to the fact that in both cases the extremely serious charges were found proved with no extenuating circumstances shown." The strong language made this a form of reprimand in its own right, and Murray was directed to make the minister's views known to the members of the two courts.[112] It is likely that Puxley, at least, read his copy with a certain degree of satisfaction.

It is unfortunate that *Skeena*'s end—at the time of her loss she had been in commission longer than any other ship in the RCN save her sister *Saguenay*—was shrouded in tragedy and controversy. As t turned out, EG 11 did not last much longer. Even before *Skeena* went aground, Western Approaches and Captain F.L. Houghton, Senior Canadian Naval Officer London (SCNO(L)), had discussed the possibility of sending its destroyers home in light of their poor condition, as well as unrest among the crews. In November 1944 EG 11 was disbanded, and the old workhorses returned to Canada except *Assiniboine*, which remained in the UK until the end of the war working with RN support groups.[113] Now, all six remaining Canadian support groups were comprised of frigates.

At the time of *Skeena*'s grounding, EG 11 had been attempting to catch U-boats breaking out into the Atlantic between Iceland and the Faeroe Islands. Further to the east, the frigates of EG 6 were part of a similar effort to block the route through the Faeroes-Shetland gap. In September the C-in-C Rosyth, Admiral Sir William Whitworth, RN, had initiated Operation SJ "to destroy U-boats on passage to and from Norwegian ports" with a combined force of Coastal Command aircraft, two support groups and escort carriers.[114] EG 6 was assigned from Western Approaches. Home Fleet destroyers formed EG 18, the second support group.

The first mission under SJ in early October proved frustrating and unproductive. Poor weather limited flying from the escort carriers *Trumpeter* and *Fencer*. Moreover, EG 6's frigates were positioned in pairs only ten miles off the bows of a carrier, which made it difficult to carry out effective antisubmarine searches; working close to the carriers also probably rekindled bad memories of *Teme*'s fate in June.[115] After a few hours Lieutenant-Commander W.E.S. Briggs, RCNR, SO EG 6, gained permission to conduct an independent night search with his group east of the Faeroes. The next day EG 6 and *Trumpeter* were to have rendezvoused early in the morning, but high seas and reduced visibility prevented that until late afternoon. By 6 October the hopelessness of using carriers in this operation appears to have been evident to all, and EG 18 escorted the two aircraft carriers back to Scapa. For the next five days Operation SJ consisted solely of EG 6 patrolling between the Faeroes and Shetlands, gaining only a few non-sub contacts.[116]

The next patrol had a better chance of success. On 2 October U-boat Command had decided to send six *schnorkel* boats dubbed the *Mitte* group into British waters to follow-up *U 482*'s success in the North Channel in early September.[117] The Submarine Tracking Room at the Admiralty

112. Sec NB to C-in-C CNA, 9 Apr 1945, ibid

113. CNMO memo, "Return of Ships of EG 11 to Canada," 7 Nov 1944, LAC, RG 24, 11744, 165-1-5

114. C-in-C Rosyth, "Operation SJ," 26 Sep 1944, PRO, 199/500

115. EG 6 ROP, 10 Oct 1944, ibid

116. Ibid. In his report to the Admiralty, Whitworth recommended that carriers not be used "in a defined U-boat probability area ... The main function of Carrier Force is to maintain continuous A/U patrol, and this can be obtained without entering the danger area." C-in-C Rosyth to Adm, 26 Oct 1944, DHH 81/520/8440, EG 6, v 2

117. BdU, KTB, 2 Oct 1944. The six boats were *U 246, U 483, U 978, U 1003, U 1006,* and *U 1200.*

became aware of this almost immediately, and even though Operation SJ did not originate with this particular deployment in mind, its forces were well positioned to take advantage of the opportunity.[118]

By the time EG 6 put to sea again on 14 October, SJ had settled into a pattern of one or two support groups conducting Gamma patrols across the Faeroes-Shetlands transit gap, supported by air patrols from 18 Group Coastal Command.[119] On 16 October EG 6 was sweeping in line abreast on a northwest-southeast axis on the Faeroes side of the gap, while the British group EG 5 swept closer to the Shetlands. Although Briggs usually spaced his ships at 3,000 yard intervals, on that day he opened out to 4,000 yards in "view of the good asdic conditions." At 1900 while heading 313° at eleven knots, *Annan* gained an asdic contact fine on her starboard bow at 1200 yards, but classified it as doubtful. Nonetheless, Lieutenant-Commander C.P. Balfry, RCNR, circled out to 1400 yards and then moved in to attack with depth-charges. Only a weak, "woolly" echo could be gained afterwards, and even this disappeared—causing Balfry to think that *Annan* had merely dispersed a school of fish.[120]

At 2006, twenty-five minutes after *Annan* classified her contact as non-sub, HMCS *Loch Achanalt* reported a possible "Jig," or radar contact, bearing 094° at three-and-a-half miles. A minute later *Annan* also reported an echo. Guessing they had flushed out a U-boat, Briggs turned the group around in pursuit. After firing rocket flares, *Annan* sighted a submarine on the surface at 2019, and after a short and sharp exchange of gun fire, sank the U-boat with a depth-charge salvo. Eight of *Annan*'s crew were injured in the fight, while six of *U 1006*'s crew of fifty-two went down with their boat.[121]

U 1006 had departed Bergen, Norway, on the afternoon of 9 October on its first operation. Seven days later, steaming submerged at 60 metres, her crew suddenly heard screw noises "immediately overhead," followed quickly by a pattern of depth-charges. The accurate attack put the hydroplanes out of action, damaged the forward torpedo tubes, and flooded the torpedo room. The commanding officer, Oberleutnant zur See H. Voight, surfaced and managed to fire a Gnat at a frigate from the stern tube before sustaining serious damage from a 4-inch shell that opened up the forward casing. When another shell tore into the conning tower, *U 1006*'s crew began to abandon ship, hurried along by *Annan*'s final depth-charges.[122]

Apart from removing a U-boat from the *Kriegsmarine* order of battle, the British sought to gain further advantage. The sinking of *U 1006* presented the Admiralty with the opportunity to deceive the Germans with bogus intelligence. A British official historian calls this "perhaps the most

118. The OIC, "U-boat Situation ending Week of 2 Oct 1944" in Syrett, *The Battle of the Atlantic* I, 461

119. On Gamma searches support groups attempted to create an asdic barrier across the estimated line of advance of a U-boat. According to a report issued by the RCN-RCAF Joint ASWC, "An estimated lane not more than 60 miles in width is established along [the course] a U-boat is expected to pass. A/S vessels are spread in line abreast formation parallel to the U/B's estimated course, and they patrol to and fro across the lane. Distance apart of ships—3 miles by day, 5 miles by night. Ships zigzag together making good at least 10 knots and they transmit on Asdic by day and night." Min RCN-RCAF ASWC, 23 Nov 1944, app II, DHH 181.009 (D 3188). A Gamma search utilizing two support groups could cover a 90-mile wide channel. See, Adm, AUBD, "Asdic Barrier Patrols—Effectiveness," 11 June 1944, PRO, ADM 199/1787

120. SO EG 6 ROP, 21 Oct 1944, PRO, ADM 199/501; Lt C.H. Borsman, RCNVR, "The Sinking of U-1006," 25 Oct 1944, LAC, RG 24, 6909, S 8910-381/107

121. Ibid; "Report on Interrogation of Survivors from *U 1006*," DHH 81/520/1650, U-1006

122. Ibid

important naval deception of the entire war."[123] In September 1940 the counter-intelligence organization MI 5 captured a Danish national of German origin who had been sent to England as an *Abwehr* (German intelligence) agent. The British official history relates that "once broken, Tate, as he was named by MI 5, collaborated wholeheartedly," and for the remainder of the European war he worked as a double agent sending a steady stream of false information to his handlers in Germany.[124] MI 5 had Tate report on 15 November 1944 that *U 1006* had been sunk by mines. The minefields themselves were not a deception, as the RN had begun laying "deep trap" minefields in the St George's Channel, North Channel, and to the north of the Hebrides.[125] Disseminating knowledge about them, however, could deter deployments into inshore waters or at least make U-boat commanders even more wary of operating there. Although the *Abwehr* did have doubts about the veracity of the intelligence that Tate was sending, MI 5's order had the desired effect, and on 18 November U-boats were cautioned about new minefields in British inshore waters.[126] For the next few months Tate embellished information about the minefields even further, evidently with great success, as BdU issued a number of warnings about the dangers they posed. Such activities were, of course, shrouded under the highest security.[127] Even before Tate wired his false information about *U 1006*, the Admiralty instructed NSHQ that "it is of the greatest importance that no hint of the date or method of sinking of *U 1006* should reach Germany for several months to come."[128] As a result, *Annan*'s quick and effective despatch of *U 1006* was not publicized until the following April.[129]

The fate of the five other *Mitte* boats provides a useful snapshot of the inshore campaign in late 1944. *U 1200* made it to the waters south of Ireland before being destroyed by the RN's EG 30 on 11 November. *U 246* aborted its mission on the twentieth day after being damaged in an air attack, and *U 483* had to return to base because of damage sustained from surface forces after it torpedoed the frigate HMS *Whitaker* off Malin Head on 1 November. Only two *Mitte* boats survived unscathed: *U 978* penetrated into the Baie de la Seine, sank an American Liberty ship, and returned safely to Bergen, while *U 1003* made it home though without scoring any successes.[130]

Two Allied ships sunk, against two U-boats lost and two others forced to abandon operations. This was certainly not a promising balance sheet for the *Kriegsmarine*, but it was illustrative of the

---

123. M. Howard, *British Intelligence in the Second World War*, V: *Strategic Deception* (London 1990), 227-8\

124. F.H. Hinsley and C.A.G. Simpkins, *British Intelligence in the Second World War*, IV: *Security and Counter-Intelligence* (London 1990), 322-3

125. Roskill, *War at Sea* III pt 2, 181-2, 288; Adm, *The Defeat of the Enemy Attack on Shipping*, v 1A, 129. Further deep trap fields were laid in the English Channel and the St George's Channel as the campaign wore on. Three U-boats were lost in deep trap minefields in 1945. The Canadian corvettes *Mayflower* and *Snowberry* screened the minelayer HMS *Plover* when deep fields were laid in the Channel in January.

126. Hinsley, *British Intelligence* III pt 2, 470; Tarrant, *Last Year of the Kriegsmarine*, 200-1. Tate sent an amplifying message about the minefields on 24 Nov 1944. Reference to this misinformation appears in the 17 Nov 1944 entry in the BdU war diary. (KTB)

127. Howard, *British Intelligence* V, 227-9

128. NID Adm to NID 3 NSHQ, 14 Nov 1944, DHH 81/520/1650, U-1006

129. The news appears to finally have been released in Canada and the UK on 4 Apr 1945. The transcript of an interview describing the sinking of *U 1006* conducted in Oct or Nov 1944 with *Annan*'s First Lieutenant by Lt J.J. Schull, RCNVR, then an RCN information officer and later author of *The Far Distant Ships*, is marked "Confidential" and minuted "Admiralty Request Publication Be Stopped." See "Radio Interview," DHH 81/520/8000, Annan

trend of the trade war in general. An Admiralty summary for October described U-boat activity as "exceptionally light" and trumpeted that, in terms of merchant ship losses, the month was "the LOWEST on record since the War began."[131] November witnessed a "slight increase" in U-boat activity, but it still had the second least number of merchant ship losses in a month during the war.[132]

German attempts to disrupt shipping were clearly failing, but U-boat Command was determined to increase its efforts, especially in British waters. Because of the dislocation caused by the withdrawal from the Biscay bases to Norway, BdU had only managed to maintain an average of three boats in UK coastal waters in October. In November, however, U-boats such as *Mitte*'s *U 978* returned to the Channel for the first time since August. It was here that U-boat Command would make its greatest concentration of force during the inshore campaign and achieve most of its limited sinkings. As more boats became available, operations were extended to the Irish Sea.

The British were well aware of these intentions. "Though the U-boats have not achieved a great deal up to the present time in their inshore operations," the Director of the Anti-U-boat Division reported in November, "a very large increase in the magnitude and the variety of their efforts is expected."[133] Furthermore, a more aggressive posture from U-boat commanders was expected. "The U-boat arm is rallying," Captain Wynn wrote in an appreciation in the third week of October:

> The German Command may believe and has certainly stated with considerable emphasis in several signals to U-boats that the fitting of snorts [*schnorkels*] has made it possible for U-boats to operate with success and reasonable impunity in narrow channels and inlets where formerly they could not have hoped to survive. Very stringent instructions have been issued to commanding officers to press forward into focal areas where shipping is certain to be found and to steel themselves for the inevitable encounters with A/S forces. Doenitz has expressed the intention of scrutinising all patrol reports and critically examining the measure of tenacity and initiative displayed by individual commanders: the criterion of a boat's value is not the fact that it has survived one or more cruises but its achievements in attacking shipping and outwitting or destroying A/S craft including aircraft which it may encounter.[134]

In preparing for such a resurgence, the Admiralty and Western Approaches had promulgated new tactical procedures tailored to the littoral environment. Western Approaches established a new command arrangement between support groups and convoy close escort groups. In the past support groups sent to strengthen convoys in the open ocean had been placed under the senior officer of the close escort. Support groups generally spent only a few days with a convoy, and it was the close escort senior officer who had the best tactical picture. Now that U-boats had switched from attacking convoys at sea to static operations in focal areas, thorough familiarity with these locations became paramount. Western Approaches Command decided that support groups would

130. See Blair, *Hitler's U-Boat War* II, 631-3; Niestlé, *German U-boat Losses*, 94, 104

131. Adm, Monthly Chronological History, Oct 1944

132. Ibid, Nov 1944

133. DAUD, "Review of U-boat Results in Inshore Waters," 29 Nov 1944, 1, PRO, ADM 205/36

134. The OIC, "U-boat Situation, Week Ending 23/10/44," in Syrett, *Battle of the Atlantic* I, 471-2

now operate in specific geographical areas. They could build up experience of local conditions and the peculiarities of their assigned area, and most importantly, knowledge of local bottom conditions and wrecks. Convoys would still be supported as they passed through an inshore area, but in mid-September the senior officers of support groups were made independent of the close escort while operating in support of a convoy inshore.[135]

The concept of allocating support groups to specific areas was developed further in October when Western Approaches established five patrol areas (a sixth would be added for the Irish Sea in early 1945) that extended from Cape Wrath to St Georges Channel. These were designated CE areas and each was assigned a task force number; for example, the task force for CE 1, the Cape Wrath area, was designated Force 32. Each force consisted of the support groups assigned to that area at any particular time, with command resting with the most senior officer. Task forces were to support any convoys passing through the areas, and when no shipping was present, to conduct Gamma sweeps in search of U-boats. Both convoy protection and antisubmarine sweeps would be supported by aircraft from Coastal Command's 15 Group.[136] Between December 1944 and May 1945 the policy of assigning groups to specific areas but concentrating hunting around convoys would result in twenty-five U-boat kills by ships and aircraft in close support of convoys, compared with eight by surface patrols and seven by air patrols.

Admiral Horton instilled these adjustments in tactics and organization through determined emphasis on training. Even though merchant ship sinkings were few, as Malcolm Llewellyn-Jones has pointed out, Horton "was failing in his cherished aim of sinking large numbers of U-boats."[137] The C-in-C admitted in early October "that from a professional stand point the U-boat war was not at present satisfactory to us," because the *schnorkel* gave U-boats "far too great immunity." The solution was to improve the "fighting standards by training ... particularly against Schnorkel fitted submarines."[138] Horton also prepared support groups for the new fast U-boats on the horizon. The submarine HMS *Seraph*, modified to increase her submerged speed, served as a test bed to analyze the potential threat posed by fast submarines, and then, from November 1944, it was used as a "clockwork mouse" for support groups to hone their skills.[139] EG 26's opportunity came in the first week of December when the group was allocated seven days with *Seraph* at Holyhead, Wales. The weather did not cooperate, and the group only had two evolutions at sea with the fast submarine. The antisubmarine teams, however, got in some time on training simulators, and Commander E.T. Simmons, RCNR, considered that the experience "proved most instructive as to the type of flexible A/S operating procedure and ship handling required when hunting fast sub-

---

135. C-in-C WA to AIG 32, 1903/13 Sep 1944, DHH, 81/520/8440, Support Groups (General); D. McLean, "Confronting Technological and Tactical Change: Allied Antisubmarine Warfare in the Last Year of the Battle of the Atlantic," *Canadian Military History* (Summer 1998), 29

136. C-in-C WA, "Orders for Anti U-Boat Operations in Coastal Waters of the Western Approaches Command (Short Title: 'Operation CE')," 11 Oct 1944, PRO, ADM 199/50. For the expansion into the Irish Sea, see the amendment of 15 Feb 1945.

137. M. Llewellyn-Jones, "British Responses to the U-boats, Winter 1943 to Spring 1945," (Master's thesis, Kings College, London 1997), 18

138. "Min Meeting Held at ACHQ Liverpool on 3rd Oct 1944 to Discuss a Programme of Schnorkel and Other Trials and Practices," 4 Oct 1944, PRO, ADM 1/16121, cited in Llewellyn-Jones, "British Responses to the U-boats," 18

139. In early 1945 the submarines *Satyr* and *Scepter* were also converted. See M. Llewellyn-Jones, "Trials with HM Submarine *Seraph* and British Preparations to Defeat the Type XXI U-boat, Sep–Oct 1944," *Mariner's Mirror* 86/4 (2000), 434-51

merged U-boats."[140] As it turned out, although Western Approaches and the Admiralty had to take the threat seriously, the war ended before types XXI and XXIII got to sea in any numbers. Thus, exercises with *Seraph* proved the closest that RCN support groups would get to fighting fast submarines.

When the anticipated inshore offensive opened, it was not on anything near the scale as at the height of the Battle of the Atlantic earlier in the war. Instead of unleashing dozens of U-boats at a time, over November and December BdU deployed some twenty-eight submarines into the waters surrounding Britain. A change in operational focus is evident from the fact that of those, ten were sent into the English Channel and eight into the Irish Sea. The remaining ten were deployed to waters north of the United Kingdom, but eight of those were part of a particular anti-aircraft carrier campaign designed to disrupt British minelaying operations off Norway.[141] As far as BdU was concerned, with convoys now entering British waters through the southwest approaches, the English Channel and the Irish Sea represented the main focal point for shipping.

Table 19.1 U-boats Deployed into United Kingdom Waters, November to December 1944[142]

U-BOAT	DEPARTURE DATE	OPERATION AREA	FATE RESULTS
U 296	4 NOV 44	NORTH MINCHES	RETURNED 25 DEC 44
U 979	9 NOV 44	IRISH SEA	RETURNED 16 JAN 45
U 680	13 NOV 44	ENGLISH CHANNEL	RETURNED 18 JAN 45
U 322	15 NOV 44	IRISH SEA	SUNK ON 25 NOV 44 WEST OF SHETLAND IS. BY HMS *ASCENSION* AND AIRCRAFT FROM NO 330 RAF
U 400	15 NOV 44	ENGLISH CHANNEL/IRISH SEA	SUNK ON 17 DEC 44 SOUTH OF IRELAND BY FRIGATE HMS *NYASALAND*
U 482	18 NOV 44	NORTH CHANNEL	SUNK (DETAILS UNCONFIRMED BUT POSSIBLY BY MINES IN NORTH CHANNEL) DAMAGED CVE HMS *THANE* AND ONE MV
U 775	18 NOV 44	NORTH MINCHES	RETURNED 22 DEC 44 SANK THE DESTROYER ESCORT HMS *BULLEN*
U 772	19 NOV 44	ENGLISH CHANNEL	SUNK ON 30 DEC 44 IN ENGLISH CHANNEL BY WELLINGTON OF NO 407 RCAF SANK/DESTROYED FOUR MVS AND DAMAGED ANOTHER
U 1209	24 NOV 44	ENGLISH CHANNEL	RAN AGROUND OFF LAND'S END ON 18 DEC 44
U 1020	24 NOV 44	ORKNEYS	SUNK (DETAILS UNCONFIRMED BUT POSSIBLY BY MINES) DAMAGED THE DESTROYER HMS *ZEPHYR*
U 297	26 NOV 44	ORKNEYS	SUNK (DETAILS UNKNOWN)

140. SO EG 26 ROP, 29 Dec 1944, DHH 81/520/8440, EG 26, v 2

141. Tarrant, *The Last Year of the Kriegsmarine*, 165-7; BdU, KTB, Nov-Dec 1944. See Blair, *Hitler's U-boat War*, II, 639-41 for anti-carrier campaign.

142. Based upon a chart in Tarrant, ibid. Amplifying information from BdU, KTB, Nov-Dec 1944; Niestlé, *German U-boat Losses*; Blair, *Hitler's U-boat War* II, 626-53; Rohwer and Hummelchen, *Chronology of the War at Sea*. In instances where uncertainty or discrepancies surround the fate of U-boats, Niestlé's book has been used as the arbiter.

U-BOAT	DEPARTURE DATE	OPERATION AREA	FATE RESULTS
U 486	28 NOV 44	ENGLISH CHANNEL	RETURNED 15 JAN 45 SANK THE DESTROYER ESCORT HMS *CAPEL* AND TWO MVS; DAMAGED ANOTHER DE
U 485	29 NOV 44	ENGLISH CHANNEL	RETURNED 2 FEB 45
U 650	9 DEC 44	ENGLISH CHANNEL	SUNK (DETAILS UNKNOWN)
U 325	11 DEC 44	ENGLISH CHANNEL	RETURNED 14 FEB 45
U 905	11 DEC 44	ENGLISH CHANNEL	RETURNED 1 FEB 45
U 1009	11 DEC 44	NORTH CHANNEL / IRISH SEA	RETURNED 8 FEB 45
U 1055	11 DEC 44	IRISH SEA	RETURNED 8 FEB 45 SANK FOUR MVS
U 312	13 DEC 44	ORKNEYS	RETURNED 3 JAN 45
U 285	20 DEC 44	IRISH SEA	RETURNED 31 JAN 45
U 1172	23 DEC 44	IRISH SEA	SUNK ON 27 JAN 45 IN ST GEORGE'S CHANNEL BY EG 5 SANK TWO MVS
U 313	23 DEC 44	ORKNEYS	RETURNED 15 FEB 45
U 278	24 DEC 44	ORKNEYS	RETURNED 11 FEB 45
U 315	25 DEC 44	ORKNEYS	RETURNED 6 JAN 45
U 764	26 DEC 44	ENGLISH CHANNEL	RETURNED 10 FEB 45
U 825	29 DEC 44	IRISH SEA	RETURNED 18 FEB 45 SANK ONE MV, DAMAGED ANOTHER
U 1051	29 DEC 44	IRISH SEA	SUNK ON 26 JAN 45 IN IRISH SEA BY ESCORTS HMS *AYLMER*, *CALDER*, *BENTINCK*, AND *MANNERS*
U 1017	29 DEC 44	ENGLISH CHANNEL	RETURNED 28 FEB 45 SANK THREE MVS

RCN corvettes escorting coastal convoys in British waters found themselves on the front lines of the offensive. In December four U-boats penetrated the English Channel, of which two met with good success. On 18 December *U 486*, under Oberleutnant zur See G. Meyer, attacked the convoy BTC 10 off Falmouth, sinking the 6,100 ton freighter *Silverlaurel*. HMCS *Algoma*, part of the close escort, failed to locate the assailant. Over the next ten days Meyer caused havoc in the Channel, sinking the frigate HMS *Capel*, two merchant ships, and an LSI, as well as damaging another destroyer. The most devastating success came on 24 December off Cherbourg when he sank the troopship *Leopoldville*, taking the lives of 801 passengers, among them 785 American soldiers.[143] Meyer slipped out of the Channel and made it back to Norway unscathed.

Kapitänleutnant E. Rademacher arrived on the heels of his countryman in *U 772*. After sinking a British vessel off the Isle of Wight on 23 December, Rademacher lay low for six days. Then

---

143. Blair, *Hitler's U-boat War* II, 636

in an incident that demonstrated the vulnerability of coastal convoys, he attacked the westward-bound TBC 21, just four miles south of Portland Bill.

Bound for the Bristol Channel from the Thames, TBC 21 consisted of twenty merchant ships formed in two lines. The corvette HMS *Dahlia* (SO, Lieutenant R. Ward, RNR) steamed at the head of the formation, while HMCS *Calgary* was 2000 yards on the port beam. Both Ward and *Calgary*'s CO, Lieutenant L.D.M. Saunders, RCNVR, later complained about the challenge of escorting such convoys with just two ships. "It will be appreciated," Ward submitted to his superiors, "that two corvettes are inadequate to form an efficient A/S screen to a convoy in two columns which some-times stretches for anything up to 5 miles. Furthermore the seaward side of a convoy cannot be considered to be the only danger side in view of recent events [where U-boats had attacked from coastward positions]."[144] As usual, a shortage of ships prevented local commanders from deploy-ing stronger escorts. Indeed, in January 1945, when the question of bringing some of the RCN corvettes back to Canada for refit arose, CNMO emphasized that the need for such escorts "is still great."[145]

At 1328 on 29 December a torpedo burst against the side of the second-to-last ship in the port column. Officers on *Calgary*'s bridge saw the explosion and after altering course to 195° they ini-tiated an Observant search. About a minute later the corvette gained an echo bearing 160° at 2000 yards, but after carrying out a depth-charge attack the contact was declared "doubtful." At 1335 the last ship in the starboard column was also torpedoed. This time *Calgary* was rewarded with "a good echo" after a twenty-minute search, and as the corvette ran in on a depth-charge run, the asdic department reported hydrophone effect from an approaching torpedo. Saunders altered to starboard to comb the track, and the operators heard it pass harmlessly down the starboard side. The depth-charges brought up an oil slick, which was marked with a buoy. Her asdic damaged in the previous attack, the corvette opened out again before dropping another pattern on the marker. But as three frigates from EG 21 had arrived on the scene, Ward ordered Saunders back to the con-voy.[146] *Conne*, *Deane*, and *Byron* searched throughout the night for the U-boat, but it appears that *U 772* got away. The next night, however, a Leigh Light Wellington aircraft from 407 Squadron RCAF sighted *U 772*'s *schnorkel*, and it destroyed the boat with six accurate depth-charges.[147]

The success achieved by *U 486* and *U 772* in the Channel during the last week of December—seven merchant ships and two frigates sunk or disabled—was cause for concern. The Director of the Anti-U-boat Division, Captain C.D. Howard-Johnston, RN, dubbed it "Black Christmas," while the Trade Division called December "a disappointing close to a successful year."[148] The Admiralty's

---

144. CO HMS *Dahlia*, "Report of Proceedings [ROP] of Convoy TBC 21," 31 Dec 1944, CO HMCS *Calgary*, "ROP of Convoy TBC 21," 2 Jan 1945, PRO, ADM 199/603

145. Naval Assistant (Policy and Plans) Memo, "Necessity of Canadian Overlord Corvettes," 12 Jan 1945, LAC, RG 24, 11752, CS389-1

146. *Calgary*, "Precis of Attack by HMCS Calgary," 29 Dec 1944, PRO, ADM 199/603. This document uses Z time for the time of the hits of the two torpedoes, whereas the ROP in the same file uses B time, or one hour later.

147. There is disagreement about who despatched *U 772*. A recent re-assessment by the Naval Historical Branch of the Admiralty, based on the discovery of a U-boat near the site of *Calgary*'s second attack, has awarded the kill to the Canadian corvette. However, another authority, Axel Niestlé remains convinced that *U 772* was destroyed in the attack by the Wellington. nonetheless, Canadian kill

148. DAUD, "Anti-U-boat Results Inshore in Western Approaches Command for the Period 1st Sep 1944 to 31st Jan 1945," 4 Feb 1945, 1, PRO, ADM 205/44; Adm, Monthly Chronological History, Dec 1944

immediate response was to send two additional support groups into the Channel. Over the longer term the Admiralty planned to reinforce the area with two more escort groups, transfer another two groups home from West Africa, and retain fourteen escorts earmarked for the Far East.[149] But there were doubts that would be enough. The success in the Channel, the blow struck by *U 1232* off Halifax in early January (see Chapter 20) and merchant ship losses in the Irish Sea outdistanced anything the U-boats had achieved throughout the last part of 1944. British officers attributed the result to a more aggressive spirit in the *U-Bootewaffe*. "With their growing experience in the use of Schnorkel and immunity from attack by bottoming tactics," wrote Howard-Johnston,

> the enemy suddenly showed a much more offensive spirit and achieved the successes [in various regions]. This offensive first became evident in the English Channel and later in the Irish Sea and in the approaches to Halifax and the Straits of Gibraltar [where one ship was sunk]. The fact that these efforts were dispersed and spasmodic, indicates that they are largely the results of improved morale in individual Commanding Officers and it is appreciated that as these successes become more widely known by U-boat personnel, the offensive will become more general.[150]

The Trade Division's year-end summary noted that "U-boats have succeeded in gaining, for the time being at least, a great deal of immunity both from air and surface attack ... Up till the end of 1944 the balance was still GREATLY in our favour, since they were not taking advantage of this immunity to sink our shipping. Last half of December was, however, a warning."[151] That final thought caused senior officials to cast a cold, hard look at the antisubmarine war.

The 25 January meeting of the powerful Cabinet Anti-U-boat Warfare Committee in London chaired by Prime Minister Winston Churchill, provided the focus for discussion, and it set the course for the remainder of the antisubmarine campaign in European waters. The First Lord of the Admiralty, A.V. Alexander, told Canadian officials that it was "the most important meeting on U-boat warfare since the beginning."[152] The First Sea Lord set out the context in characteristically blunt manner by stating that, since the third week of December, "our successes compare unfavourably with our losses." Citing the renewed offensive spirit among U-boat commanders, Admiral Cunningham predicted that its continuance would depend upon the state of the land war, the success of the strategic bombing effort against U-boat infrastructure and the rate at which U-boats were destroyed at sea. He warned also that the number of U-boats on patrol could increase from the fifteen or so usually at sea to sixty in February and perhaps even eighty in the spring. Furthermore, Cunningham raised the spectre of fast type XXIIIs operating against the east coast convoy routes in the relatively near future. Beyond the countermeasures implemented in December, the Admiralty had established convoys in the Irish Sea, expanded their defensive mining campaign and initiated inshore patrols with small craft such as motor launches and armed trawlers. Perhaps most importantly, the maintenance of antisubmarine vessels, of which some

---

149. First Sea Lord to PM, 30 Dec 1944. When informed of these measures, Churchill responded: "This is very interesting. You are absolutely right to reinforce strongly." PM to First Sea Lord, 9 Jan 45, PRO, ADM 205/43

150. DAUD, "Review of the Anti U-boat War, from 20th Dec 1944, to 20th Jan 1945," nd (but between 21 and 25 Jan 1945), 1, PRO, ADM 205/44

151. Adm, Monthly Chronological History, Dec 1944

152. J.J. Connelly diary, 26 Jan 1945, "Diary 2nd trip over seas," 11, Connolly Papers, LAC, MG32 C71, v 2

forty percent were under repair, was to be accorded "the highest priority."[153] That said, later in the meeting Cunningham warned that he had "absolutely no spare surface forces" to engage in further antisubmarine operations, such as a barrier offensive that the Chief of the Air Staff had proposed. The C-in-C Western Approaches also complained about a paucity of resources. Horton told the committee that his resources "were stretched to the limit." Indeed, all Western Approaches support groups had been moved into the Irish Sea or the English Channel save one, which was operating under C-in-C Rosyth.

According to one participant, the meeting dissolved into stormy debate, with Churchill browbeating his senior naval advisors. "There was a great row brewing [over the sinking of the *Leopoldville*] for the Cabinet Anti-U-boat committee just then due ... and the great man for anti U-boat operations Sir Max [Horton] was sent for to attend." Howard-Johnston also recalled:

> When the PM started on the First Sea Lord with "what was the meaning of this etc etc" ABC said we have the C-in-C Western Approaches here and the P.M. turned on Max who instead of saying what he knew, which was the Asdic conditions off Le Havre were especially difficult, seemed to become overawed by the PM's repeat of "what is the meaning of this" and said in reply "It's not my area, Sir" which of course added to the PM's fury! It was an astonishing sight to see the bully be bullied. Eventually he got himself off the hook by saying "the Asdic has let us down."
>
> By now the P.M. was really worked-up and flew back to ABC who sent him on to VCNS who passed him on to ACNS U/T, John Edelston. The latter with a twinkle in his eye and his wry smile said "the expert is sitting right behind me."
>
> I had hardly got started with the explanation when Winston tried to silence me with ... "Are you trying to tell me that the sea is any different than it was in 1914" (note the old 1914-18 thoughts). In the end I got it explained that the water conditions for sound waves off Le Havre were impossible at certain states of tide and that anyway there were thirty U-boats east of the Fastnet [off the south coast of Ireland] and up to Dover, all hiding in terror on the bottom due to our effective countermeasures and this was the first ship sunk in over two weeks ... Anyway, he let me go with a smile and kind words ... "Ah, my boy that's a bull point"[154]

There is no mention of the exchange in the dry, sanitized official minutes of the meeting, but it rings true in the context of other heated exchanges between Churchill and his principal military advisors.[155] There is a hint of it at the key moment of the meeting when Horton "agreed that the enemy had so far had little success, but felt sure that this was mainly due to the heavy concentration of antisubmarine forces which he had been able to achieve in the comparatively small area of

---

153. Cabinet Anti-U-boat Committee (CAUB Cte), "Min Meeting held in the Cabinet War Room, on Friday, 26th January, 1945 at 11.30 am," 1, PRO, PREM 3/414/1

154. C.D. Howard to S.W. Roskill, 9 May 1979, Churchill Archives Centre, Cambridge University, Roskill Papers. See also Milner, *U-boat Hunters*, 219-20. Milner suggests that the exchange may have taken place in a meeting on 19 Dec 1944 but other information in the letter makes it clear that it was after the sinking of the *Leopoldville* on 24 Dec, and the next CAUB Cte meeting came on 26 Jan. Howard-Johnston's version rings true, and he mentioned the incident in other correspondence which lies in the Gretton Papers at the National Maritime Museum, Greenwich. Moreover, he and Cunningham exchanged several memos in Jan–Feb 1945, where Howard-Johnston defended the effectiveness of asdic. See, PRO, ADM 205/44

155. See, e.g., A. Danchev and D. Todman (eds), *War Diaries 1939-1945: Field Marshal Lord Alanbrooke* (London 2001), 335-6

present U-boat operations."[156] That indicates that although they were not sinking U-boats, neither were the U-boats particularly dangerous. In other words, the status quo was acceptable. Cunningham seemed to suggest the same when he stated "that the enemy was achieving his present successes entirely with the older type of U-Boat and that there was little doubt that the threatening offensive, with the new type U-Boats, would shortly materialize."[157] Fast U-boats were the critical factor in the antisubmarine campaign. So long as the *Kriegsmarine* deployed old boats into limited operational areas, the Allies could cope with the current levels of sinkings of both U-boats and merchant ships. There could only be trouble if type XXIs and XXIIIs were unleashed into the North Atlantic and British waters in numbers. Although sparring continued over the lack of U-boat kills in inshore waters, Allied naval commanders were essentially thrust into the role of anxious spectators to a great race, hoping that American, British, Canadian, and Soviet armies could overrun U-boat bases and building yards—or even force an overall surrender—before the threat posed by new technology could materialize. Much to their ultimate relief that is precisely what occurred. In mid-March 1945, for example, the Admiralty admitted that the Germans would continue to try to expand their U-boat effort but projected that "the full weight of attack apprehended may never be effectively launched, owing to the general process of attrition and disorganization to which the German forces are being increasingly subjected."[158] At VE-Day just one type XXI and six type XXIIIs were fully operational.[159]

As it happened, in January 1945 Minister of National Defence for Naval Services Angus L. Macdonald was in the United Kingdom on an inspection tour. Macdonald attended the stormy Cabinet Anti-U-boat Warfare Committee,[160] but, from his limited input, and the lack of special preparation evident in British files, it appears that his presence at the meeting was of no real consequence.[161] Certainly, the committee made no attempt to prise any further antisubmarine assets out of him, as they did with the USN representative, Admiral Stark. Instead, there seemed to be satisfaction that Canada was doing its fair share; an attitude the RCN had promoted over the previous weeks. In mid-December, faced with a shortfall of five support groups and noticing unallocated frigates on the RCN Weekly State, the Admiralty had approached the CNMO as to whether the Canadians could form two additional support groups for the Eastern Atlantic from ships working up.[162] As Marc Milner has concluded, the Royal Canadian Navy found itself, once again, "being pulled in several directions."[163]

Frigates and other escorts were indeed emerging from new construction in Canada, but against that the RCN also had to maintain existing support groups at strength, refit ships that had seen

---

156. Ibid, 2

157. Ibid, 1

158. Adm, *Monthly Antisubmarine Report* (Feb 1945), 15 Mar 1945, 3

159. Tarrant, *Last Year of the Kriegsmarine*, 190

160. Macdonald was accompanied by CNS RAdm Jones, his aid, John Connolly, and DPD Capt H.S. Rayner.

161. There is just a brief note from Churchill's secretary saying Macdonald would be in attendance and describing the RCN's role in the war in general terms. See EEB to Churchill, 25 Jan 1945, PRO, PREM 3 414/1.

162. Transcript of telephone conversation between Adm and CNMO, 17 Dec 1944; CNMO to NSHQ, 19 Dec 1944, DHH 81/520/8440, Support Groups (General)

163. Milner, *U-boat Hunters*, 222

hard service, modify those designated for the Pacific theatre (see Chapter 21), and provide additional escorts for the Mid-Ocean Escort Force and the Western Local Escort Force due to a shortening of the convoy cycle. Nevertheless, there was no disputing that ships were available. On 12 January NSHQ offered the Admiralty a reconstituted EG 11 once its destroyers completed refit and EG 28, which was composed of frigates from new construction. But they warned the Admiralty that "it must be realized that available RCN resources will not permit the present and proposed escort commitments to be maintained indefinitely in view of the low nominal strength of the groups now operating and the eventual need to take a large number of new construction ships in hand for refit [in preparation for the Pacific]."[164] In fact, EG 28 proved to be the final RCN support group formed during the war. Rather than going overseas, it joined C-in-C CNA as relief for the experienced EG 16, which joined Western Approaches in March. As for EG 11, although some of its destroyers went overseas, the group itself did not reach operational status before VE-Day.[165]

———————

Even though British, American, and Canadian armies butted against the Rhine River, and the Soviet forces had crossed the German frontier in the east, in the mid-winter of 1945 there was no telling how long the war would continue. When Rear-Admiral G.C. Jones attended a meeting of the British Chiefs of Staff on 19 January 1945, he was told that VE-Day would likely be in September, based "on present information."[166] For Canadian sailors that meant that the war at sea would continue its grim reality. As events in February and March demonstrated, when the RCN destroyed three U-boats but lost two ships to submarine attack, sailors had to remain wary of looking too far ahead.

The first of these events took place during a particularly rigorous patrol by EG 9 in the waters north of the United Kingdom. After three days of training against the fast submarine problem at Loch Alsh in Scotland—Western Approaches had been forced to move its training group there because of U-boat activity in the Irish Sea[167]—EG 9's five frigates were sent to patrol off the north coast of Ireland. They were quickly shifted to the area between the Shetlands and Faeroes under the control of C-in-C Rosyth. After three days of Gamma sweeps, largely marked by non-sub contacts, in the evening of 11 February, HMCS *Nene* gained an echo that was classified as "definite submarine." Unfortunately, the group was unable to corral the contact in a two-and-a-half-hour hunt and the U-boat, probably *U 483*, escaped despite being subjected to a number of Hedgehog attacks.[168] Citing the success of EG 10, which destroyed three U-boats in the same area, the Admiralty criticized the Senior Officer of EG 9, Commander Layard, for relying solely on Hedgehog and not taking advantage of HMCS *Loch Alvie*'s Squid armament.[169] Layard had in fact considered

164. NSHQ to Adm, 2201/12 Jan 1945, LAC, RG 24, 11752, CS 389-1

165. CNA to NSHQ, 17 Feb 1945, DHH 81/520/8440, EG 25, v 1; NSHQ to Adm, 2203/22 Feb 1945; C-in-C CNA, "Monthly Operations Memo, No. 8," 7 Mar 1945, ibid, EG 28, v 1. EG 28 was ultimately formed from EG 25's *Ste Therese* and four frigates from new construction.

166. Connelly diary, 19 Jan 1945

167. Layard diary, 31 Jan 1945

168. SO EG 9 ROP, 3 Mar 1945, DHH 81/520/8440, EG 9, v 2

169. AUBD min, 30 Mar 1945, PRO, ADM 199/198. The attack was assessed "G" or "no damage to a submarine believed to have been present."

using Squid and depth changes but the echo was both deep and weak, and he feared they would lose contact in the resultant explosions. It had probably been worth the chance, however, and afterwards in his diary a frustrated Layard concluded that the failure to destroy the U-boat "is disappointing and depressing beyond measure."[170]

Within days Layard's mood swung completely the other way, when with clinical precision *Saint John* killed a U-boat. Early on the morning of 16 February, EG 9 joined convoy WN 74, bound to the Firth of Forth from the Clyde. As the convoy moved southwards through Moray Firth that afternoon, *Saint John*, stationed ahead of the formation, gained an asdic contact at 900 yards range. Since the target appeared to be on the bottom with no Doppler effect, Layard, who had taken over command of the frigate the previous November,[171] immediately altered course to conduct an echosounder run in an attempt to classify the contact. At the same time its position was fixed and compared against charted wrecks.[172] "As by Q.H. there was no plotted wreck in the vicinity ... I decided to give it a pattern," Layard wrote in his diary,

> and so we dropped 5 which immediately brought quite a bit of oil to the surface so rather unwillingly, as I wanted to get on with the convoy, I returned and attacked again. After the 3rd attack I was just saying "I don't think this is anything, do you?" when on steaming through the oil and explosion cafuffle [*sic*] we saw a lot of splintered wood work and some paper which, on fishing out of the water, proved to be bits of a German signal log!!!!
>
> We lowered a boat and also picked up an aluminium flask and a tube of sorts marked in German "Medical Stores Kiel." All this was most exciting and seemed to indicate that we were on a U-boat. Hoisted the whaler and carried out 2 or 3 more attacks before dark but nothing more came up except a great deal of diesel oil and splintered wood. I recalled *Nene* from the convoy and the two of us held contact all night. The whole thing seems such a complete fluke but at last one of the hundreds of contacts we've obtained and investigated and attacked in coastal waters has proved to be the thing we've been looking for.[173]

Layard's modesty aside, the killing of *U 309* was no fluke at all. *Saint John*'s antisubmarine team had utilized the same tactics they had used to kill *U 247* in September 1944, and the skill with which they were carried out again proved effective against a bottomed contact.[174] Ironically, the quickness with which *Saint John* despatched the U-boat raised doubts as to whether it had been destroyed previously. "There seems little doubt that it was a U-boat," wrote a staff officer in the Admiralty Anti-U-boat Division, "but in view of its lack of movement and general absence of evidence to show that this contact was alive when first sighted [*sic*], it is hard to suggest an assessment. The U-boat was left dead, but who killed it?"[175] OIC thought it may have been the wreck of

---

170. Layard diary, 12 Feb 1945

171. Most sources list LCdr Stacey as CO of *Saint John* well into1945, but Layard was actually double-hatted as SO EG 9 and CO *Saint John* from Nov 1944 to Feb 1945. See Layard diary.

172. SO EG 9 ROP, 3 Mar 1945

173. Layard diary, 16 Feb 1945

174. See "Description ... 'Saint John' in Attacking Bottomed Contacts." *Saint John*'s asdic control officer, Lt J.R. Bradley, received a bar to his DSC for the action.

175. AUBD mine, 30 Mar 1945

a boat that had failed to return from an operation in January.[176] It was later confirmed that *Saint John* had destroyed *U 309*. This was the fifth U-boat sunk by ships from EG 9.

Further to the south, the English Channel had been relatively free of U-boats since their successes at the end of December. Intelligence remained sketchy, mainly because U-boats seldom transmitted reports once they had departed on patrols, but the OIC estimated that at the beginning of the third week of February only one or two boats were in the Channel.[177] The day after that assessment, *U 1004* confirmed her presence in an attack that resulted in the loss of the corvette HMCS *Trentonian* and a merchant ship.[178]

Trentonian was leading BTC 76, bound for the Thames from the Bristol Channel, across Falmouth Bay on the bright, calm early afternoon of 22 February, when an explosion shook the British coaster *Alexander Kennedy*, the second ship in the port column. *Trentonian*'s officer of the watch immediately rang action stations and ordered the helmsman around to port to close the convoy. As this manoeuvre was being executed the asdic operator gained contact in the approximate path of the merchant ships at Green 30. By this time the CO, Lieutenant C.S. Glassco, RCNVR, had arrived on the bridge and, considering that "the bearing and distance from the torpedoed ship ... placed the echo in a highly improbable position for it to be a submarine," steadied on course 250° on the assumption that the attacker, following a favourite U-boat tactic, had fired from an inshore position.[179]

As *Trentonian* approached the convoy at fourteen knots, she let out her CAT gear and prepared to carry out an Observant search. Glassco asked the commodore on which side the *Alexander Kennedy* had been torpedoed, and upon learning it was in fact the starboard side, immediately altered course "to pass under the Commodore's stern and through the convoy to commence an Observant on the starboard side." At 1330, just as the corvette cleared the starboard column, "a heavy explosion was felt on the starboard side aft and the ship slewed to starboard."[180]

The ship's company were fortunate in that *Trentonian* did not go down as fast as *Regina* and *Alberni* the previous August. It appears the torpedo hit in the shaft tunnel and split the aft engine room bulkhead. The engine room flooded immediately and *Trentonian* began to settle by the stern. After receiving damage control reports, Glassco concluded that the ship could not be saved and at 1334 ordered her to be abandoned. Six minutes later she slipped beneath the surface. Two motor launches rescued ninety-five men; one officer and five ratings, all of whose stations were in the stern, perished.[181] The ship that went with them was the last of ten RCN corvettes lost in the war.

A collection of destroyers, minesweepers and MLs converged to try to trap the U-boat. However their search, which lasted throughout the night, proved unsuccessful. According to the colourful

---

176. The OIC, "U-boat Situation. Week Ending 26 Feb 1945," in Syrett, *Battle of the Atlantic* I, 548

177. The OIC, "U-boat Trend. Period 12/2/45-21/2/45," in Syrett, *Battle of the Atlantic* I, 545. For the fuzzy intelligence picture, see Hinsley, *British Intelligence* III pt 2, 627-33.

178. Another U-boat, *U 1018*, was also in the English Channel, but after attacking a convoy and sinking a merchant ship off Lizard Point on 27 Feb it was destroyed by HMS *Loch Fada*. Niestlé, *German U-boat Losses*, 106

179. CO *Trentonian*, "Sinking of HMCS *Trentonian*," 24 Feb 1945, DHH 81/520/8000, Trentonian. See also NOIC Milford Haven, "Fortnightly Report of Events 16-28th Feb 1945," PRO, ADM 199/1443

180. Ibid

181. Ibid. "Board of Inquiry into the Loss of HMCS Trentonian," 27 Feb 1945, LAC, RG 24, 4107, 1156-332/109; CNMO narrative, "RCN Corvettes after 20 September 1944," 9-10, DHH 84/228

language of Lieutenant-Commander D. Jermaine, RN, the conditions in Falmouth Bay frustrated their efforts:

> It appeared that everything possible which could have been done to provide against the U-boat's escape was done on this occasion and an armada of small ships was quickly mobilized to guard the avenues of escape. Some loopholes, however, always arise and no scheme is entirely watertight when 50 per cent of vessels engaged are distracted by "non-sub" contacts. Falmouth Bay is notorious for its "non-subs" which flourish as daisies on a summer golf course and, ever since the summer campaign, this area has proved the despair of hunting groups.[182]

Much like a mole on the same golf links, *U 1004* burrowed successfully out of Falmouth Bay despite being heavily depth-charged, and eventually made it back to Norway.[183]

From the end of February into March, Western Approaches and Coastal Command focussed "considerable" antisubmarine patrols in the southern Irish Sea and off the coast of Cornwall in response to U-boat concentrations in those areas.[184] EG 25 had been one of the support groups so employed. But on 7 March, after the group had seen a brief stint supporting convoys in St George's Channel, Western Approaches ordered EG 25's three frigates—*Strathadam* (SO, Lieutenant-Commander H.L. Quinn, RCNVR), *La Hulloise* and *Thetford Mines*—to shift to the area off Londonderry.[185] Three hours after turning northwards *La Hulloise*, on the port wing of their line abreast formation, picked up a surface contact with her RX/C radar. A quick inspection placed the Jig on the same bearing as a navigational buoy, therefore her commanding officer, Lieutenant-Commander John Brock, RCNVR, ordered the helm back to the original course. Before the bow had swung around, however, the asdic operator report a "Quiz," or asdic contact. Brock brought the frigate around again to classify it with echo sounder but when it reached 1400 yards range he realized that the Jig and the Quiz contacts "coincided." Brock's report provides a sense of the trepidation that exists on the bridge of a ship that is groping through darkness towards an unknown contact:

> The Commanding Officer went out to the bridge [from the plot] to have a look and the A/S C.O. moved into the plot. Nothing could be seen on the bearing but it was very dark and the Commanding Officer thought that the contact was possibly a small boat coaster or fisherman. Radar said it was a good big echo. The engines were stopped at 800 yards and the Officer of the Watch and Commanding Officer vainly looked on the bearing ahead ready to go full astern to avoid collision while the ship coasted in. The A/S reported strong HE at about 800 yards but this was not heard on the bridge where the Commanding Officer was listening to the Radar voice pipe and the Officer of the Watch was peering ahead.
>
> Radar lost contact at 350 yards and a short minute later at 2139, the port 20 inch searchlight illuminated a *schnorkel* and periscope about 200 yards, two degrees on the port bow. The *schnorkel* was on the left very close to the periscope. The submarine

---

182. CNMO, ibid

183. Tarrant, *Last Year of the Kriegsmarine*, 193-4

184. The OIC, "U-Boat Trend. Period 26 Feb 1945/6 Mar 1945," in Syrett, *Battle of the Atlantic* I, 554

185. SO EG 25 ROP, 12 Mar 1945, DHH 81/520/8440, EG 25, v 3

stayed at periscope depth for about ten seconds and then dived. It was decided that it was too close to drop depth-charges but a ram might have been possible so engines were put full ahead. It was instantly realized that a ram was out of the question but engines were left at full ahead to get well clear quickly so that the submarine could not loaf around inside A/S range or inside turning circle.[186]

When informed of the situation, Quinn in *Strathadam* directed *La Hulloise* to make a Hedgehog attack, but having expended all mortar ammunition in an earlier hunt on a non-sub, Brock could only respond on TBS; "Have none left. Go ahead it's all yours."[187] Guided in by *La Hulloise*, *Strathadam* made the most of the opportunity, scoring a hit on its first run. Sailors on the stern of the frigate saw the U-boat break the surface, only to immediately disappear. The three frigates then took turns pulverizing the bottomed submarine with depth-charges over the next hour, and flotsam from *U 1302* soon littered the surface of the Irish Sea.[188]

"Quite the most notable feature of the whole episode," Quinn reported, "which drew my deepest admiration, and furthermore assured success, was the cool and deliberate stand aside by LA HULLOISE ... His steady accurate reports were a masterpiece of direction."[189] Western Approaches and the Admiralty agreed, although the latter noted that *La Hulloise* had missed a "golden opportunity" for a depth-charge attack by eye when she had first sighted *U 1302*.[190] An officer at the Admiralty also observed that it was the first submarine sinking in "several months for which radar was responsible for the initial contact in inshore operations." Although confusion existed about whether *La Hulloise*'s first radar contact was the navigational buoy or *U 1302*, Commodore Simpson came to believe that the frigate had indeed detected the U-boat. At any rate *La Hulloise*'s RX/C had detected something and that had put everything else in train. As such, it would seem to be a victory for the much maligned Canadian set. In fact, research by Marc Milner has revealed that *La Hulloise*'s RX/C had been maintained by a dedicated technician excused from other duties, who had rebuilt the set using British parts.[191]

The grim pattern of a Canadian warship in exchange for the destruction of an enemy submarine continued when the Bangor HMCS *Guysborough* was torpedoed off Ushant on 17 March 1945, while returning from a refit in Canada. *Guysborough* was the last Canadian warship to be lost in European waters during the war. As was seen in Chapter 18, the circumstances of *Guysborough*'s loss were unfortunate, but sadly conventional: a submarine came across a contact, plotted an effective attack position, and fired torpedoes with devastating effect. In stark contrast, the final U-boat sinking by the RCN was anything but commonplace.

In the late hours of 20 March EG 26 was on passage from Londonderry to Loch Alsh for training, steaming in line abreast at fifteen knots. At 2317 the port lookout in the frigate HMCS *New*

---

186. CO *La Hulloise* ROP, 12 Mar 1945, ibid

187. "TBS Messages of HMCS 'La Hulloise' 7th Mar 1945," SO EG 25, ROP, 12 Mar 1945

188. SO EG 25 to C-in-C WA, 1425A/8 Mar 1945, ibid, EG 25, v 1. The wreckage included a prayer book, shattered pieces of an engine room blackboard, clothing, personal photos, a deck log and a massive oil slick.

189. SO EG 25 ROP, 12 Mar 1945

190. AUBD min sheet, Apr 1945, Cmdre (D) WA, ROP—25th Escort Group—Period 19th Feb-9th Mar 1945, 21 Mar 1945, PRO, ADM 199/199

191. Milner, *U-boat Hunters*, 126

Scars on the hull of HMCS *New Glasgow* after her collision with *U 1003*. The RCN's last U-boat kill came from sheer good luck. (DND HN 2347)

HMCS *Teme*, or at least most of her, after being torpedoed. One man was killed and three others wounded in the attack, though the ship survived. (DND HN 2416)

Glasgow suddenly warned, "Low flying aircraft approaching!" which was immediately changed to "Object in the water. Very close!" It turned out that the sailor had been deceived by the whooshing sound made by a *schnorkel*, and bridge personnel sighted it about 50 to 100 yards ahead, closing on a collision bearing. The alarm was given and an emergency pattern of depth-charges ordered to be set but within a matter of seconds the contact ran into *New Glasgow*'s port side, lifting the frigate with the force of the impact. Unfortunately, depth-charges could not be fired as the frigate had run about 200 yards beyond the U-boat by the time the pattern was set. The contact disappeared astern, and despite the subsequent efforts of EGs 26 and 25, and the mid-ocean group C 4, there was no further sign of what had obviously been a submarine.[192]

New Glasgow had collided with *U 1003*. Reports from prisoners of war confirm that the U-boat had been *schnorkeling* when it was suddenly staggered by a violent impact. Although the rating manning the *Tunis* radar warning device had monitored signals close by, he had neglected to warn his captain. The collision caused a 30-degree list and the submarine plunged violently to the bottom, sixty metres below. The "circular saws" of EG 26's CAT gear could plainly be heard above as they searched for the U-boat, and several depth-charges shook the boat, but after about an hour *U 1003* crept out of danger. It was only when the boat surfaced twenty-four hours later that the extent of its damage became apparent: the *schnorkel* and periscope were wrecked, a 20mm gun and antenna had been ripped way and the conning tower was buckled. An approaching contact forced *U 1003* to dive, but the main hatch could not be sealed, and the conning tower flooded. Another twenty hours of being submerged depleted the batteries and shut down the pumps; therefore *U 1003* surfaced, hoping to make repairs or beach on the nearby Irish coast. However, after another contact approached, the captain decided to scuttle the boat. Four hours later HMCS *Thetford Mines*, on passage to Londonderry for repairs, rescued thirty-one survivors.[193]

This bizarre incident underlined the vulnerability of a *schnorkeling* U-boat. With its hydrophones masked by diesel noise, and its search horizon limited to close range by periscope, a U-boat in such a condition was virtually blind, especially during darkness. That said, *New Glasgow* had also been caught unawares and was unable to fire depth-charges as the frigate ran over *U 1003* in the moments after the collision. For that reason the CNMO was informed unofficially that the Admiralty did not intend to transmit a congratulatory message "because they consider NEW GLASGOW ought to have been prepared for action to the extent of having depth-charges ready on the rails."[194] Thus, unaccompanied by accolades, the Royal Canadian Navy had destroyed its final U-boat of the war.

Reviewing the situation in the British coastal zone in the early spring of 1945, the *RCN-RCAF Monthly Operational Review* commented that "U-boat activity in these waters was again heavy in April and several merchant ships were sent to the bottom."[195] This proved to be the *U-Bootwaffe*'s last gasp. At the end of March the combination of mounting losses—fourteen in British waters in

---

192. *New Glasgow* ROP, 26 Mar 1945, DHH 81/520/8440, EG 26, v 2; "Brief History of HMCS New Glasgow," 12, DHH 81/520/8000, New Glasgow; AHB, "The RAF in Maritime War, V: The Atlantic and Home Waters, The Victorious Phase, June 1944-May 1945," 223, DHH 79/599, v 5, pt 1

193. "Report on the Interrogation of Survivors of U-1003," nd, DHH 81/520/8000, New Glasgow

194. CNMO to NSHQ, 1744A 28 Mar 1945, ibid

195. *RCN-RCAF Monthly Operational Rev* 3/2 (Feb-May 1945), 15

that month alone—a muddled intelligence picture, and the realization that the Allies had concentrated their antisubmarine warfare resources inshore, caused U-boat Command to withdraw its boats seaward from the English and North channels, giving commanders the option of lingering in the north or southwest approaches or returning to base.[196] Several of these U-boats achieved success—both inshore and offshore—and in several instances Canadian forces were involved. On 29 March *U 246* torpedoed HMCS *Teme* in the English Channel, blowing sixty feet off her stern with a Gnat. The frigate was eventually paid off and declared a constructive total loss.[197] A week later, on 6 April, *U 1195* sank the large 11,420 ton British freighter *Cuba* off Portsmouth; the boat escaped EG 9, which was distracted by a large number of non-sub returns, but was destroyed an hour later by HMS *Watchman*.[198] The next day *U 1024* attacked HX 346 off Holyhead, Wales, damaging the freighter *James W. Nesmith*. The submarine bottomed to evade the close escort C 5 and the supporting EGs 25, 16, and 5, but was destroyed five days later by EG 8. Sadly, in one attack on a contact, a Hedgehog bomb exploded prematurely over *Strathadam*'s fo'c'sle, killing six sailors.[199] Finally, on 18 April *U 1107* intercepted HX 348 in the southwest approaches, sinking two merchant ships. The boat escaped C 7 only to be destroyed by a USN Catalina at the end of the month.[200]

On 4 May, Dönitz signalled all vessels of the *Kriegsmarine* to cease operations and return to base. Four days later the British Admiralty broadcast a message instructing all U-boats at sea to surface, report their position, fly a large black pendant, and proceed to designated UK ports. Not all U-boats complied—in all 156 U-boats followed the terms set out by the Admiralty, but another 211 chose to scuttle themselves instead.[201] Of those that surrendered, the RCN's EG 9 brought in the largest group.

On 10 May EG 9 had sailed with JW 67 as a cautionary escort for the final Russian convoy of the war. After guiding two U-boats flying black flags clear of the convoy in the first days of the passage, on 16 May EG 9 was ordered to intercept a convoy of fifteen U-boats and five surface ships off Norway and accompany the submarines on the 500-mile passage to Loch Eriboll on the north coast of Scotland. When problems arose with poor station-keeping and mechanical breakdowns, EG 9's senior officer, Commander Layard, warned the U-boats that "these numerous breakdowns are not in keeping with the known efficiency of the German U-boat service. They are all being noted and if on reaching harbour any negligence can be found the CO of the boat and any one else concerned is liable to a long term of punishment instead of returning to Germany."[202] The

196. MOD, *U-boat War in the Atlantic* III, 97. KTB, *SKL* (Operations Division, Naval Staff), 29 Mar 1945. In an attempt to alleviate the pressure inshore, BdU sent a group of boats dubbed *Seewolf* on a westward sweep along the North Atlantic convoy lanes in hope that success against a convoy in mid-ocean would force the Allies to transfer ASW assets out of British waters. Tipped off by Ultra USN hunter-killer groups decimated *Seewolf*, destroying five out of seven boats. See Blair, *Hitler's U-boat War* II, 686-7, and Chapter 20 below.

197. ROP EG 6, 15 Apr 1945, DHH 81/520/8440, EG 6, v 2

198. ROP EG 9, 26 Apr 1945, PRO, ADM 199/232. According to Milner's *U-boat Hunters*, some Canadians think that *Watchman* stole EG 9's kill, but it is evident from various reports that they were prosecuting completely different contacts.

199. DHH 81/520/8280, HX 346; Milner, *U-boat Hunters*, 245-8

200. DHH 81/520/8280, HX 348; Adm, *War at Sea* (Preliminary Narrative) VI, 333-5

201. Roskill, *War at Sea* III pt 2, 302

202. SO EG 9 to Lt Mallett for SO U-boats, 2015/18 May 1945, in Lt J.J. Coates, "Report of Boarding of Armed German Ship 'Grille,'" 17 May 1945, DHH, 81/520/8440, EG 9, v 2. Lt J. Mallett, RCNVR, was the boarding officer in the U-boat of the senior German officer.

threat worked, and there were no further incidents until the strange convoy reached the UK. After arriving at Loch Eriboll EG 9 was ordered to escort four U-boats to Loch Alsh, where the senior British officer found English cigarettes and badges in the possession of German sailors, and levelled charges of fraternization at the Canadian boarding parties. Although frustrated by his sailors' actions, Layard thought their behaviour was understandable. "The evidence of fraternization is much regretted," he reported to the C-in-C Western Approaches, "and shows clearly a great lack of supervision on the part of certain ships. It is submitted, however, that if boats are berthed alongside ships and if it is quite apparent that, by their attitude the German crews are accepting the terms of surrender willingly and without question, it is indeed difficult to prevent English or Canadian personnel from displaying those small acts of kindness and good will which is our National characteristic."[203] It was time to build the peace.

The stealthy and largely submerged operations by determined German submariners in British and Canadian waters posed a new antisubmarine challenge during the final ten months of the war. Operating in areas with difficult asdic conditions, tidal streams, and waters strewn with rocks and other objects that produced false contacts, the U-boats proved elusive targets. Ships proved by far the most lethal submarine killers. Between August 1944 and May 1945 sixty-six U-boats were destroyed around the British Isles; ships sank thirty-eight, aircraft seven, and ships and aircraft together one.[204] It is clear that the littoral campaigns failed to impede even slightly the flow of Allied shipping in both British and Canadian waters.[205] The U-boats, although resourceful in exploiting opportunities to evade detection, were never concentrated in sufficient numbers in shipping focal points to cause more than slight damage. The Allies analyzed encounters with U-boats in the inshore environment, developed new tactics, and adjusted how antisubmarine forces would be deployed. Tactics to deal with the type XXIs were also being worked out. The stated German aim in the inshore campaign was to tie down Allied antisubmarine resources. This was successful, but the costs were high; half of the boats that did inshore patrols were lost. By that stage of the war the Allies had such dominance in materiel that the specialized resources absorbed by antisubmarine forces would not have affected the outcome if available for re-allocation elsewhere.

There is no doubt that permanent groups of antisubmarine ships and aircraft, equipped and trained to razor-sharp operational effectiveness, applying new tactical procedures tailored to the inshore environment, and led by men of unusual experience, determination, and endurance, were required for the hunting down and destruction of U-boats that no longer exposed themselves to the risks of seeking out and attacking convoys but that still posed a serious threat to Allied shipping. The Canadian groups that operated in the eastern Atlantic, the region of greatest submarine

---

203. SO EG 9 ROP, 23 May 1945, ibid

204. Figures derived from Niéstle, *German U-Boat Losses*. Mines accounted for eight U-boats. Twelve are described as being lost to unknown causes.

205. Between Aug 1944 and May 1945 U-boats sank or permanently damaged 354,944 tons (including 37,100 tons by midget submarines) of merchant shipping and warships in the waters around the UK and Iceland. (Derived from Rohwer, *Axis Submarine Successes*.) By contrast, average losses in the North Atlantic during 1942 had been 456,435 tons per month (Roskill, War at Sea III pt 2, 479). Between Dec 1944 and May 1945, 25,000 merchant ships passed through UK littoral waters in convoy. Grove, *Defeat of the Enemy Attack on Shipping*, 228. The sinking of 63 merchant ships (48 by U-boats and 15 by midget submarines) can be seen as having been inconsequential.

density, where training was frequent and rigorous, and the stakes particularly high, had the best results. The defence of shipping still took first priority, and even support groups had more submarine kills while defending shipping than in the hunter-killer role, but their work in that role gave them an edge that was often missing from ships constantly employed in convoy escort. This was especially true when—as was the case in the last sixteen months of the war—Dönitz really gave up on tonnage warfare and shifted the principle submarine effort from the main convoy routes to inshore waters in order to tie down as many Allied naval and air forces as possible. The conduct of this challenging warfare nevertheless brought out and honed the tactical skills, on both sides, of what Admiral Horton called the experts of their profession. The RCN's antisubmarine warriors, despite their many difficulties, could count themselves such experts. Although the "continuing RCN" might have envisaged other roles in the minds of the planners, it was the antisubmarine prowess of the Royal Canadian Navy in 1944-45 that would provide the most lasting foundation on which to build a postwar fleet.

CHAPTER TWENTY

The Antisubmarine Campaign in Canadian Waters and the Northwest Atlantic, 1944–1945

OPERATIONS OFF THE EAST COAST of Canada and Newfoundland, and in the open Atlantic, stood in sharp contrast to the inshore campaign described in the previous chapter. Allied predominance had forced the *Kriegsmarine* to abandon North Atlantic anti-convoy operations early in 1944, just as the RCN was assuming vastly increased responsibility for the escort of North Atlantic convoys. This happened at a time when the acquisition and manning of cruisers, escort carriers, the former armed merchant cruisers in their new roles, and fleet destroyers, had watered down the manpower pool for Canadian antisubmarine forces.[1] Some have questioned whether this emphasis on a balanced fleet was justified when there remained serious training weaknesses in the RCN, and when, despite improvements in technical liaison, Canada continued to lag behind Britain and the United States in the modernization of escort vessels.[2] It is true that in British home waters and on the Russian convoys in 1944–45 Canadian groups performed measurably better, in terms of submarine sinkings—eighteen U-boats in eighteen months—than in the four previous years, but it was to those theatres that the best ASW ships and personnel went. In the western Atlantic, where there were far fewer U-boats, Canadian warships did not sink any submarines in this period. By the same token, U-boats accounted for five RCN escorts in the western Atlantic, compared with the three Canadian ships sunk in British waters in 1944 and 1945. As will be seen, the ships screened by Canadian escort groups almost all arrived safely at their destinations, which was the real measure of success, but is it possible that the manpower and talent diverted to balance the fleet, if allocated to antisubmarine forces, could have ensured fewer warship losses?

Remembering the long-term plans for the "Continuing RCN," it could be argued that the Canadian Naval Board neglected the RCN's first responsibility. Such an accusation would suggest that the naval establishment hoped for a more glamorous role than convoy escort, however useful that role had been, in future naval operations. A few years after the war that may have been the suspicion of then

---

1. The point is made quite forcefully in A. German, *The Sea Is at Our Gates* (Toronto 1990), 96

2. LCdr D.M. McLean, "Muddling Through: Canadian Antisubmarine Doctrine and Practice, 1942-45," in M. Hadley, R.N. Huebert, and F.W. Crickard (eds), *A Nation's Navy: In Quest of Canadian Naval Identity* (Kingston and Montreal 1996); W. Rawling "The Challenge of Modernization: The Royal Canadian Navy and Antisubmarine Weapons, 1944-1945," *Journal of Military History* 63/2 (1999), 355-78

Minister of National Defence, Brooke Claxton, who made the disparaging comment that the navy's senior officers "had all joined in about the year 1914, had been trained largely in the RN, had served together through every rank and every course, had English accents and fixed ideas."[3] The diversification of effort, however, made good strategic sense. The RCN had much to contribute besides the defence of shipping. Operations in support of Neptune and Overlord, and impending contributions to the war in the Pacific, were in response to British requests for assistance: they met Canada's alliance obligations. Naval planners—including reserve officers who did not in any way fit Brooke Claxton's description—undoubtedly believed that this would bring important long-term recognition to both Canada and the RCN, and even if this kindled hopes of the strong peacetime navy that every professional sailor thought necessary, there was ample justification in the needs of the moment.

Both ministers of the Crown and sailors equated submarine kills with efficiency in antisubmarine warfare. Angus L. Macdonald, it will be recalled, had no hesitation in replacing Vice-Admiral Percy Nelles as Chief of the Naval Staff when confirmed submarine kills by the RCN fell off in 1943. Vice-Admiral G.C. Jones, when he became CNS, lost no time in urging emphasis on the destruction of U-boats. Jones was responding to the naval minister's concerns about the modest number of submarines destroyed thus far by the RCN, as well as to the policy laid down by C-in-C Western Approaches, of hunting down every U-boat even after convoys had passed. When he sent Canadian antisubmarine forces to the eastern Atlantic, where they would get more opportunities for U-boat kills,[4] he ensured that those forces had the most experienced personnel, the latest ships, and the most up-to-date equipment.[5] The less experienced Canadian escorts protected ocean convoys. That being said, no matter how many seagoing personnel Canada could assign to antisubmarine warfare, and whether or not they were trained adequately, they could only perform as well as their ships' capabilities and limitations would allow under the prevailing operating conditions. In the northwest Atlantic, and in the coastal waters off Canada's Maritime Provinces and Newfoundland, these conditions were notoriously difficult.[6]

Antisubmarine warfare has been defined as "the art and science of depriving the enemy of the effectiveness of his submarines." The best way of achieving that end in the defence of convoys was to achieve an "exchange rate," the number of ships sunk by submarines in exchange for the number of submarines destroyed, that made it impossible for U-boats to sustain the attack on shipping.[7] That had happened in 1943, and now, as the American naval historian Arthur Marder has observed—he was writing about the First World War, but it applied equally to the Second—sinking submarines was a bonus, not a necessity. "The only necessity in war,"

3.   Cited in James Eayrs, *In Defence of Canada*, Vol 3, *Peacemaking and Deterrence* (Toronto 1972), 56

4.   See Douglas et al, *No Higher Purpose*, Chapter 13; and Milner, *U-Boat Hunters*, 50-2, 98-100

5.   Min 45th mtg U-Boat Warfare Cte, 22 June 1944, citing DAUD, Capt C.D. Howard-Johnston, LAC, RG 24, 11752, CS 638-2; CO HMCS *Forest Hill* to Capt (D) Newfoundland, 24 June 1944, LAC, RG 24, 11022, COAC 7-6-1; SO EG 11 to Cmdre (D) WA, 17 July 1944, LAC, RG 24, 11,022, CS 638

6.   It will be recalled that in the Maritime Provinces and Newfoundland dockyards and shipyards were already overburdened. To maintain operating forces refits were given higher priority than modernization, thus sustaining a vicious circle. The reliability of aging ships and equipment after four hard years of wartime employment was a constant preoccupation in the CNA Command. C-in-C CNA to AIG 409-0-365, 15 Jan 1945, LAC RG 24, 11022, COAC 7-6

7.   See e.g., Grove (ed), *Defeat of the Enemy Attack on Shipping*, 49. This is the updated version of the Naval Staff History by D.W. Waters, originally brought out as CB (Confidential Book) 3304 in 1957, placed in the public domain in 1988.

argued Marder, "is to stop submarines sinking ships ... Indeed, one can safely go a step further: it did not really matter how many U-boats the Germans had, if they were forced to keep out of the way."[8] Canadian escort and support groups in the North Atlantic, supported by the RCAF and RAF Coastal Command, achieved that aim. Whether submarine sinkings were by themselves a valid measure of the navy's overall efficiency and usefulness in the war at sea is therefore an open question. Whatever the answer, Canadian Naval Board policy managed to produce the desired results.

By the last eighteen months of the war, the long-range large type IX U-boats were clearly unsuitable for operating in the eastern Atlantic, because they could not dive as quickly as the smaller type VIIs. Dönitz sent them across the Atlantic as part of a plan to tie down Allied forces and to exploit opportunities. Other tasks included reporting weather conditions, of key importance in planning German land operations on the continent, and gathering intelligence on Allied shipping. Between 1 January 1944 and 8 May 1945, only twenty-six German submarines, all type IXs, entered or patrolled close to the Canadian Northwest Atlantic Command. Their presence was sporadic. Generally two or more U-boats would operate simultaneously, followed by intervals when there were none at all. Other type IXs operated off the United States.[9] The hope of Dönitz that these boats would achieve a measure of surprise was for the most part ill-founded, thanks to Ultra. The immediate availability of Ultra decrypts enabled air and naval forces to mount area searches that largely suppressed the German submarines and seriously hindered their finding targets.[10]

Fortunately for the U-boats, because so much emphasis was being placed on the eastern Atlantic, because submarine detection with asdic was so difficult in the waters off eastern Canada and Newfoundland, and because operational research in the RCN was not as well established as it was in the RN and USN, antisubmarine forces in Canada and Newfoundland still could not exploit Ultra to full advantage. U-boats did operate with some impunity in the region, and the loss of five Canadian escorts in these waters in this period—*Valleyfield* (7 May 1944), *Magog* (damaged beyond repair 14 October 1944), *Shawinigan* (25 November 1944), *Clayoquot* (24 December 1944), and *Esquimalt* (16 April 1945)—was grievous and embarrassing, but the total tonnage of the merchant ships sunk was too little to have any strategic impact.

It is important to remember that the properties of sound in water affected asdic performance, sometimes to such an extent that it defeated all efforts to find the submarine. Different regions gave rise to different conditions, and asdic functioned well in water only when temperature varied quite gradually with depth. When sharp gradients separated layers of water at quite different temperatures, asdic performed badly. Submarines could hide in a layer beneath a distinct temperature

8. Marder, *Dreadnought to Scapa Flow* V, 102-3. For a similar and well documented assessment see Lundeberg, "Undersea Warfare and Allied Strategy in World War I," *Smithsonian Journal of History*, 1/3 (1967), 1-30 and 1/4, 49-72

9. C-in-C CNA reacted to sightings outside as well as in his area. See Milner, *U-Boat Hunters*, 101. For 3 days in Jan, 10 days in Apr, 45 days in July-Aug, 13 days in Jan 1945 and 12 days that March, there were no U-boats in CNA waters. MOD, *U-Boat War in the Atlantic*, Diagrams 24-28 and App III.

10. R. Sarty, "Ultra, Air Power and the Second Battle of the St Lawrence, 1944," in T.J. Runyan and J.M. Copes (ed), *To Die Gallantly: The Battle of the Atlantic* (Boulder 1994), 186

change, which deflected and distorted the asdic beam away from its target.[11] Thermal layering could at this stage of the war be identified by measuring temperatures at successive water depths using a bathythermograph, but it was not until November 1944 that these devices were available to a limited number of Canadian escorts.[12] Layering, often accompanied by salinity changes having similar effects, is more prevalent in coastal and inshore waters than in the deep ocean, where high winds and rough seas tend to prevent the formation of layers, but even in good sea conditions the range of a well-maintained asdic was not usually more than 1300 yards (1200 metres), and asdic maintenance was often imperfect. When poor oceanographic conditions reduced ranges further, detection by asdic became close to impossible.[13] Nor could even 10cm radar such as type 271 be relied on to detect the small target offered by a *schnorkel* mast at any great range, giving *schnorkeling* submarines a good measure of immunity.

In the closing days of 1943, Sub-Lieutenant G.E. Gilbride and Lieutenant G.A. MacLachlan tabled a report on antisubmarine conditions, as they existed from May to November, in the Gulf of St Lawrence area, where U-boats had operated so successfully in 1942.[14] "In view of the importance of thermal gradients in A/S work," the Naval Board advised C-in-C CNA to promulgate this incomplete but valuable report to all Commands under his orders.[15] Rear-Admiral Murray's staff antisubmarine officer agreed, with reservations: "It is about time that we attempted to connect the scientific research at present going on and scientific records at present required with regard to water conditions off the east coast of Canada and in the Gulf with the practical results that can be expected from this research work ... In effect, four years of war have taught us, by experience, what to expect in these waters. If the present research could produce definite areas in which asdic conditions were always good and definite areas in which they were frequently bad during the summer months, it might conceivably be possible to route convoys clear of these areas although this is highly improbable ... Asdic conditions, at any rate from May until August, will almost certainly be bad inside the 100 fathom line, and will occasionally surprise us by being, for no apparent reason, good for short periods."[16] In the English Channel, where water conditions were different and where

---

11. A "Handbook for Commanders of Submarines," issued by the German navy and acquired by NSHQ in Nov 1944 provided advice on how to use temperature gradients to avoid detection, noting that "differences of temperature and salinity in the form of layering ... reduce the conductivity of water. The same thing occurs when the water is rich in air, or in plankton containing air," and that "the efficiency of the enemy's echo-ranging sets is often less in summer than in winter, and it is smaller too in areas of heavy layering ... It is therefore important, when being hunted by echo-ranging set, to take continual measurements of the temperature and the density of the water at various depths, to establish the existence of layering." A/S Research, memo to DWT, 15 Nov 1944, LAC, RG 24, 11580, D023-2-1

12. NSec to C-in-C CNA, Capt (D) Halifax, 15 Nov 1944, LAC, RG 24, 11026, COAC 7-16

13. The laws of physics have not changed, and the range of hull-mounted echo-ranging sonar remains limited even today. Variable-depth (towed) echo-ranging sonar developed after the war, largely by Canadian scientists and engineers, partially redresses the balance by being placed below the layers. In the open ocean, submarine listening sonars can exploit stable deep-water sound paths to obtain much longer ranges against surface ships than the ships can obtain with echo-ranging sonars. Surface ships and submarines can obtain similar ranges with very long towed listening arrays. Detection by a listening sonar relies, however, on the target emitting noise, hence the postwar development of "quiet" ships and submarines.

14. SecNB to C-in-C's Sec's Office, 17 Dec 1943, ibid

15. Ibid

16. Staff A/S O to C-in-C's Sec's Office, 17 Dec 1943, ibid; see Hachey, MacVeigh, and Barber, National Research Laboratories, Division of Physics and Engineering, "Asdic Ranging Conditions in the River and Gulf of St Lawrence in Late Summer," LAC, RG 24, 11463; Sarty, "Ultra, Air Power and the Second Battle of the St Lawrence, 1944," 288

better trained, organized and equipped support groups were at work in 1944, an Admiralty appreciation arrived at a far less negative conclusion. "The outstanding feature of the analysis of surface craft hunts was the difficulty in first detecting the U-boat which adopts anti-asdic tactics when escort vessels are heard approaching. Numerous wrecks, together with difficult water conditions and a high reverberation background which occurs in shallow waters have, in a good many cases, given the U-boat immunity. Once, however, the asdic picks up the U-boat contact and identifies it as such, the chance of success is very much higher than it has been in the past (fifty-three per cent for Neptune as against ten per cent in the first quarter of 1943)."[17]

As always, links between the Admiralty and RN operational commands were much closer than between NSHQ and either Halifax or St John's, largely owing to distance, but also because NSHQ had a far smaller and less experienced core of talent as well as a less developed staff system than did the Admiralty.[18] The scepticism with which the fleet in Atlantic Canada sometimes regarded ukases from headquarters staff was understandable. As shown earlier, and as will be seen in this chapter, the Operational Intelligence Centre at NSHQ was indispensable to C-in-C CNA's antisubmarine operations, but technical and scientific research in the RCN had yet to reach its full potential.[19]

By January 1944 the Directorate of Technical Research (DTR), headed by Lieutenant-Commander A.T.R. Millard, RCNVR, was in place but critically short-handed, with personnel of limited experience and scientific qualifications, and so far down in the naval hierarchy that it had practically no influence on the Naval Staff. This became particularly evident when the directorate's connection with Dr C.J. Mackenzie, head of the National Research Council, was severed by Mackenzie over profound disagreements concerning the RCN's scientific policy.[20] In April 1944, the Director of Warfare and Training (DWT), Captain K.F. Adams, RCN, strongly advised the upgrading of technical research.[21] Not only should DTR report to higher authority—directly to the CNS or the VCNS, were that position to be approved—but it should be staffed with versatile personnel: "They must intermingle and exchange ideas. Their itinerary and available time must be known in order that their services may be utilized in the most effective manner." And rather than being spread out through Headquarters Directorates, they should be "under the direction of one chief who thinks as they do, understands their problems, and who is capable of guiding each in his day-by-day problems. The chief who sees the complete picture is able to give his men new ideas and pool his material and personnel resources to the best advantage."[22] Captain G.A. Worth, Director of the Signals Division, balked at giving up qualified communications and radar personnel to such an organization, so DTR did not get the desired upgrading. Now, however, DTR was to coordinate all research

---

17. Min 53 mtg U-boat Warfare Cte, 9 Nov 1944, LAC, RG 24,11752, CS 638-2; *Ottawa* to Cmdre (D) WA, 17 July 1944, LAC, RG 24, 11750, CS 638

18. Canadian scientists made tremendous contributions to the war effort, as much or more overseas as in Canada. This, and the relatively limited role of scientists in the RCN during the war, is evident in G.R. Lindsey (ed), *No Day Long Enough: Canadian Science in World War II* (Toronto 1998), 163-93 and *passim*

19. DWT to ACNS, 19 Apr 1944, NSS 1700-100/53

20. Zimmerman, *Great Naval Battle of Ottawa*, 36, 156-8

21. Adams, whose report on shortcomings in the fleet had contributed to the replacement of VAdm Nelles as CNS (see Chapter 14), had good reason to take this position.

22. Ibid

and development in NSHQ, and it was to be responsible for the Naval Research Establishment in Halifax. In June, possibly because Adams had reiterated the complaint that Canada was not getting the drawings and technical data needed for the manufacture of new antisubmarine equipment, Millard was also charged with keeping lines of communication open to the Admiralty's Director of Scientific Research.[23]

Parallelling the work of DTR was that of Dr J.H.L. Johnstone, Director of Operational Research. In general terms, DOR's organization followed the British model, as Johnstone explained in December 1944 to P.M.S. Blackett, one of the founders of operational research in Britain. Unlike the Director of Technical Research, who was an observer at Naval Staff meetings, Johnstone was a full member.[24] He reported directly to the Assistant Chief of the Naval Staff (ACNS), who was, in effect, in charge of operations. His organization further differed from Millard's in its personnel, most of them scientific specialists drawn from universities and industry.[25] To keep track of developments in the United States, one of these academics usually attended the monthly meetings of the Antisubmarine Warfare Operational Research Group (ASWORG) in Washington. Unlike Millard, however, Johnstone had no equivalent arrangement with British operational research organizations. Indeed, despite measures to create technical liaison with the Admiralty, information was not getting through to key personnel in Canada.[26]

Responsible for applying scientific research to tactics, and to strategic problems, Dr Johnstone had in September 1943 exerted his influence on the Naval Staff to put the pipe noisemaker, developed in Halifax by the Naval Research Establishment, into service as the CAT (Canadian Anti-acoustic torpedo) gear to deal with the German *zaunkönig* torpedo, much more expeditiously than the RN was able to get its solution, the Foxer, into operation.[27] It was not until July 1944, however, that DOR established a direct link with St John's, when Professor G.H. Henderson from the Halifax office went to see Flag Officer Newfoundland. It was symptomatic of the limitations of operational research in Canada that neither Dr Johnstone nor Professor Henderson knew that Commodore C.R.H. Taylor, who had replaced Rear-Admiral H.E. Reid as Flag Officer Newfoundland on 1 November 1943, was away on leave—the sense of urgency in St John's was not what it had been the year before—and that officers on Taylor's staff "were relatively unfamiliar with the idea and methods of Operational Research."[28]

In January 1944, especially in the western Atlantic, the single most important asset for antisubmarine forces was signals intelligence, the one reliable means of locating and inhibiting the

23. ACNS to distribution, 22 May 1944, DWT, to ACNS, 15 May 1944; NSHQ to CAMO, 7 June 1944, ibid

24. Given the rank of Commander on receiving the appointment, he decided to resign his commission and serve in a civilian capacity. Thus, rank played no part in his relations with the naval staff.

25. These included H.L. Welsh (Professor of Physics at the University of Toronto), A. McKellar, PhD (astro-physicist at the Dominion Observatory in Victoria, BC), LCdr W.R. Christmas (from the mathematics department of Sun Life Insurance of Montreal), SLt E.B. MacNaughton (formerly a physicist at the University of Toronto), Professor G.H. Henderson (Operational Research Staff Officer), and R.M. Petrie, PhD (another astro-physicist at the Dominion Observatory).

26. DOR (RCN), correspondence, J.H.L. Johnstone to P.M.S. Blackett, 26 Dec 1944, and Johnstone to ACNS, 2 Apr 1945, LAC, RG 24,11463. Houghton correspondence with SecAdm, 18-26 Jan 1944, LAC, RG 24, 11750, CS 638; DOR, Reports on Trips, H.L. Welsh to Johnstone, 15 Jan 1945, LAC, RG 24, 11563; ACNS(UT) to Houghton, 23 Jan 1945, LAC, RG 24,11752, CS 638-2; Neale to DWT, 18 May 1944, DHH 81/520

27. Milner, *U-Boat Hunters*, 72

28. Henderson to DOR, 10 Aug 1944, LAC, RG 24, 11464, DOR (RCN), Personnel and Equipment (1943-1945)

U-BOAT OPERATIONS IN CANADIAN NORTHWEST ATLANTIC
JANUARY 1944 - MAY 1945

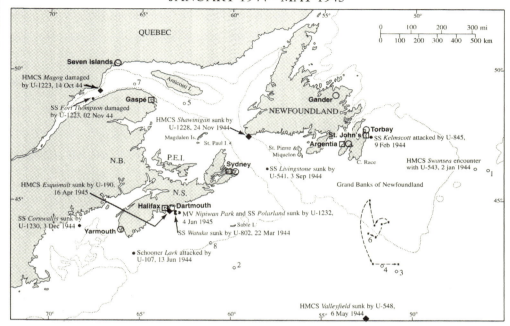

QUEBEC

Seven Islands

HMCS *Magog* damaged
by U-1223, 14 Oct 44

SS *Fort Thompson* damaged
by U-1223, 02 Nov 44

Gaspé

HMCS *Shawinigan* sunk by
U-1228, 24 Nov 1944

Magdalen Is.

St. Paul I.

Gander

NEWFOUNDLAND

St. John's Torbay
SS *Kelmscott* attacked by U-845,
9 Feb 1944

St. Pierre &
Miquelon

Argentia

C. Race

HMCS *Swansea* encounter
with U-543, 2 jan 1944

N.B.

P.E.I.

Sydney

SS *Livingstone* sunk by
U-541, 3 Sep 1944

Grand Banks of Newfoundland

HMCS *Esquimalt* sunk by U-190,
16 Apr 1945

N.S.

Halifax Dartmouth

SS *Cornwallis* sunk by
U-1230, 3 Dec 1944

Yarmouth

MV *Nipiwan Park* and SS *Polarland* sunk by U-1232,
4 Jan 1945

SS *Watuka* sunk by U-802, 22 Mar 1944

Sable I.

Schooner *Lark* attacked by
U-107, 13 Jun 1944

HMCS *Valleyfield* sunk by U-548,
6 May 1944

"APPROACHES TO HALIFAX"

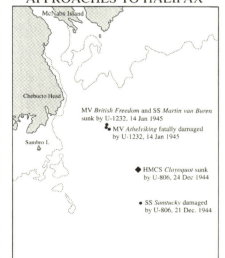

McNabs Island

Chebucto Head

MV *British Freedom* and SS *Martin van Buren*
sunk by U-1232, 14 Jan 1945

MV *Athelviking* fatally damaged
by U-1232, 14 Jan 1945

Sambro I.

HMCS *Clayoquot* sunk
by U-806, 24 Dec 1944

SS *Samtucky* damaged
by U-806, 21 Dec. 1944

LEGEND:

1. 14 Feb 44 – 10 Sqn RCAF attack on U-845
2. 05 Jul 44 – USS *Baker* and *Thomas* sink U-233
3. 19 Aug 44 – USS *Bogue* attack on U-802
4. 20 Aug 44 – USS *Bogue* sinks U-1229
5. 08 Sept 44 – HMCS *Norsyd* vs U-541
6. 08-15 Sep 44 – USS *Bogue* false contacts
7. 14 Sept 44 – RCN group W13 vs U-802
8. USS *Lowe, Menges, Pride* and *Mosely* sink U-866,
   18 March 1945

Airfields...○
Naval Bases..□
Merchant ships sunk or damaged by U-boats.........................●
Warships sunk or damaged by U-boats..................................◆

movements of U-boats.[29] As discussed in Chapter 12, centralized submarine tracking rooms in London, Washington, and Ottawa shared intelligence on U-boat movements the moment they received it. The three tracking rooms then promulgated the daily estimates of submarine locations, and expected future movements, to their respective combined naval and maritime air command headquarters for the conduct of operations. Communications were good enough that any "hot" new information such as an important decrypt, U-boat attack or direction finding bearing could be evaluated in light of the whole picture at the three tracking rooms and revised estimates promulgated within hours.[30] Since July 1943 Naval Service Headquarters in Ottawa had been originating daily Otter signals which predicted the locations of U-boats west of 40° West (500 miles east of Newfoundland) for the following day.[31]

The first signals intelligence acquired was often the message tasking an outbound U-boat for the northwest Atlantic. U-boat Command normally transmitted these tasking signals when the submarine had reached mid-Atlantic, giving the commanding officer considerable latitude and specifying only general operational areas. Detailed signals intelligence on U-boat movements was, however, sketchy. In the final months of the war the Germans passed tasking messages to boats before they sailed, or transmitted the messages using a new high-speed system unreadable to Allied code breakers. U-boats had become very cautious about transmitting radio reports so that D/F fixes by Allied shore stations were sporadic. Planning area searches for U-boats known to be approaching the Canadian area therefore involved large probability areas. As we saw in Chapter 12, when the probability area could be refined, the theatre commander ordered hunts to exhaustion, code-named Salmons. Searches based on signals intelligence took place as each U-boat approached or entered Canadian Northwest Atlantic Command's area of responsibility.

U 543, commanded by Kapitänleutnant H. Hellriegel, had arrived in the theatre on 18 December 1943 and stayed until 20 January 1944. A search based on HF/DF bearings began on 26 December 1943 with the aging four-stackers *Columbia* and *Niagara* from the support group W 10, and an Otter signal on 1 January prompted a Salmon search by HMCS *St Laurent* and the newly commissioned frigates *Swansea, Matane, Stormont,* and *Montreal*, slated to be the core of the new support group EG 9.[32] They had barely completed or were still undergoing work-ups. Short of equipment—*Swansea* even lacked a bearing recorder for her asdic set[33]—and steaming "with, against and

---

29. Sarty, "Ultra, Air Power and the Second Battle of the St. Lawrence"

30. Beesly, *Very Special Intelligence* chs 11-12, esp 174-5, 192-3; B.F. Smith, *The Ultra-Magic Deals and the Most Secret Special Relationship, 1940-1946* (Novato 1993), esp ch 5; Syrett, *Defeat of the German U-Boats*, 21-2; SRH 208 and SRH 236, NAR A, RG 457

31. Sarty, "The Limits of Ultra: The *Schnorkel* Boat Offensive against North America, November 1944–January 1945, *"Journal of Intelligence and National Security,* 12/2 (1997), 49; Sarty, "The RCAF, Naval Intelligence and the Antisubmarine War," in his *Maritime Defence of Canada*, 175

32. *Montreal* never joined EG 9, but instead was part of C 4.

33. Shipyard delays in Canada, influenced by lack of experience, delays in placing orders and drawing up bills of material, delays in production, and the "hand to mouth usage of material, mislaying of material and so forth," the desperate necessity to maintain and repair merchant ships, and the need to get warships to sea in time to prepare for Operation Neptune, imposed bizarre priorities in the modernization of RCN escorts. Capt A.C.M. Davy to NEC, 12 Feb 1944, LAC, RG 24 (acc 83-84/167), 3934, 8440-1; NSM, 15 May 1944, DHH

across the breaking seas ... in the teeth of icy winds,"[34] the frigates gained but not surprisingly were unable to maintain contact. When *U 543* came up to charge batteries on 2 January *Swansea's* radar picked it up, but the boat evaded subsequent detection.[35]

The next boats on the scene were Korvettenkapitän W. Weber's *U 845* and Kapitänleutnant H. Lauterbach-Emden's *U 539*. On 23 January aircraft of Eastern Air Command began investigating Otter reports of their approach. Initially escaping detection, Weber's report on 6 February of an unsuccessful attack north of Flemish Cap provided HF/DF bearings to Canadian intercept stations, and C-in-C CNA launched a Salmon search with an assortment of ships and aircraft available at that moment, including the green frigates intended for EG 9.[36]

The Salmon east of Newfoundland in typical icy winter conditions was unsuccessful. For EG 9's commanding officers, conducting prolonged searches with several consorts was different from convoy escort and the group's senior officer, Commander A.F.C. Layard, RN, noted in his diary: "I suppose one must realise however that this support group work is really much more like destroyer work—manoeuvres, signalling, etc. and although I've been bred and borne [sic] to it these chaps haven't and a lot of training is required."[37] As it turned out, Weber damaged the outbound British freighter *Kelmscott* with torpedoes east of St John's on 9 February. The escorting corvette, HMS *Gentian*, did not detect the attacker.

Suspecting that mines could be responsible, Flag Officer Newfoundland closed St John's for three days while its approaches were swept. Weber moved offshore, evading a prompt air and surface search, but on 14 February a Liberator of 10 Squadron RCAF sighted and attacked *U 845*. Using most of its weapons suite, including machine-guns, depth-charges, and an acoustic torpedo, the aircraft damaged the U-boat slightly, killing a member of its crew and wounding two others.[38] Weber patrolled without further incident, and without any success, until 3 March. The other boat, *U 539*, patrolled from Cape Spear off St John's to Cape Race from 14 to 23 February, often within sight of shore, constantly evading air and sea patrols. Lauterbach-Emden found little shipping. On 1 March, just before beginning his return passage, he sighted the westbound convoy ON 225. It was a standoff: he fired torpedoes that simply detonated at the end of their runs, and in response the escorts searched for him without success.[39]

U 539 started for home on 8 March, two days after *U 845*, and their place was taken by *U 802*, commanded by Kapitänleutnant H. Schmoeckel. Enigma decrypts provided intelligence of the boat's approximate whereabouts during the approach, but the submariners were consciously

34. A. Easton, *50 North: An Atlantic Battleground* (Toronto 1966), 202

35. Douglas, *Creation of a National Air Force*, 573-4; Hadley, *U-Boats against Canada*, 197-8; Milner *U-Boat Hunters,* 101-2; Capt (D) Halifax to C-in-C CNA, 26 Jan 1944, LAC, RG 24, 11023, COAC 7-6-7; TOP *St Laurent*, 10 Jan 1944, ibid; ACNS to CNA and CNS, 21 Mar 1944, LAC, RG 24, 4034, 1070-2-2, pt 1. *U 543* fired a torpedo at *Swansea* but missed.

36. The German submariners found the harsh winter conditions arduous and ice formed outboard of bunks in *U 845*'s forward torpedo room. BdU, KTB, 25 Jan and 5 Feb 1944; "U 845 Interrogation of Survivors," May 1944, DHH 80/582, folder 63; " EAC Weekly Intelligence Report," 27 Jan and 3 Feb 1944, DHH 181.002 (D423); Otter Signals, 20 Jan–9 Feb 1944, LAC, RG 24, 6896, NSS 8910-20 (hereafter Otter Signal with date); Operation Salmon, Signals, 7 Feb–21 Mar 1944, DHH 81/520/1650, Operation Salmon (hereafter DHH Operation Salmon, etc.); Sarty, *Maritime Defence of Canada*, 178-9

37. Layard diary, 12 Feb 1944, DHH. add "Layard was a thirty-year veteran of the RN and had commanded three fleet destroyers in the early 1930s. See Whitby, *Commanding Canadian*

38. BdU, KTB, 14 Feb 1944, Douglas, *Creation of a National Air Force*, 575; Hadley, *U-Boats Against Canada*, 201

39. KTB, *U 539* 14 Feb-1 Mar 1944; Operation Salmon, Signals, 7 Feb-21 Mar 1944, DHH 81/520/1650, Operation Salmon'

reducing their HF transmissions to avoid detection from shore-based D/F stations, and the positions given by decrypts were stale. On 22 March, Schmoeckel announced his presence, much farther west than anticipated, sinking the small Canadian collier *Watuka* off Halifax during an attack on Sydney–Halifax Convoy SH 125.[40] Murray ordered another Salmon; again he had to improvise. From available escorts he formed a fresh group, W 10, with five corvettes, two Bangors, and a new frigate. They were adequately equipped, and joined by Captain J.D. Prentice—who was then Captain (D) Halifax—in the new Algerine HMCS *Wallaceburg*, together with a corvette, later reinforced with yet another improvised group of corvettes led by the assistant training officer at Halifax. This relatively massive response, under the capable direction of an experienced U-boat hunter, together with intense air searches by Eastern Air Command (EAC), simply forced the U-boat to lie low. It did not help that although EAC had published the instructions for Salmon hunts, no one had distributed them to the warships. This was only remedied after HMCS *New Glasgow*, when trying to coordinate a Salmon in response to a possible aircraft contact on *U 802*, received more of the necessary information on air search procedures.[41] The OIC in Ottawa plotted *U 802* with some accuracy from an HF transmission, but Schmoeckel had little difficulty evading detection until, on 8 April as he was leaving the area, RCAF Venturas screening convoy HX 286 forced him to crash dive six times. His subsequent attack on the convoy the next day was a complete failure.[42] By this time, Commodore Taylor in St John's was becoming increasingly dissatisfied. He commented at the end of March that "recent unsuccessful hunts off Halifax and Newfoundland, where a U-boat was known to be present, by motley assortments of ships in various states of efficiency and training, lend emphasis to the fact that none but a highly trained, thoroughly coordinated and ably led team can hope to destroy U-boats at this stage in the campaign."[43]

In the meantime, *U 845* had come to grief in the eastern Atlantic, at the hands of *St Laurent*, *Owen Sound*, *Swansea*, and the destroyer HMS *Forester*. It was during Weber's return passage that he received orders to intercept SC 154. He detected the eastbound convoy and by early on 10 March was shadowing from astern, sending contact reports. As he attempted to close the convoy while submerged, Weber was also drawing down his batteries. SC 154, of thirty merchant ships, had already been diverted to avoid U-boats predicted to be ahead on its old track. Because of the anticipated threat its escort (Group C 1), was also being reinforced by EG 9, now crossing the ocean to join Western Approaches Command after further training in Halifax. Like EG 9, C 1 had a British senior officer, Commander J. Bryan, RNR, in *Assiniboine*. While the U-boat followed in the wake of the convoy two of the escorts were on SC 154's port quarter. Lieutenant-Commander G.H. Stephen, RCNR, CO of *St Laurent*, was a seasoned master mariner with a reputation for fine seamanship and experience in fighting fires at sea. He had been giving aid to the Swedish freighter *San Francisco*, which was on fire and straggling well astern. *Owen Sound* of EG 9 had joined *St Laurent*. Once the fire was under control the two detached escorts started to slowly overhaul the convoy. Then early in the afternoon HF/DF operators in *St Laurent* and two ships screening SC 154, *Assiniboine* and *Swansea*, intercepted U-boat radio transmissions originating between Stephen

40.   CO HMS *Anticosti*, "Report of Proceedings—Convoy SH 125," 24 Mar 1944, DHH (mfm), NSS 8280-SH125

41.   DWT/Tactics to DWT and ACNS, 10 May 1944, DHH Operation Salmon

42.   Douglas, *Creation of a National Air Force*, 577-8; Milner, *U-Boat Hunters*, 127

43.   FONF WD, Mar 1944, DHH 81/520/1926-1102/3

Top: The Castle class corvette HMCS *Humberstone*. Armed with the squid ahead-thrown weapon and modern sensors, she was one of the most advanced anti-submarine vessels in the RCN. (DND Z-1577)

Bottom: HMCS *Border Cities*, an Algerine class minesweeper, which were mainly used for escort work. (DND S-1325)

and the convoy. Stephen shaped a new course to steer through the plotted submarine position thirty miles astern of the convoy with *Owen Sound*. Stephens's plan paid off when *U 845*, batteries depleted after trailing SC 154, unwisely surfaced in daylight to recharge and was promptly sighted by *St Laurent*. A long and intensely exciting hunt—"a macabre dance of death," as Marc Milner calls it in his vivid account of this episode—ensued. As it unfolded, *Owen Sound* was sent to look after the *San Francisco* and HMS *Forester* joined *St Laurent*. First with *Owen Sound* and then with *Forester, St Laurent* carried out a series of creeping attacks, using both depth-charges and Hedgehog. The U-boat, low on battery power, eventually surfaced after being attacked underwater for five and a half hours and tried to make a run for it, displaying an astonishing turn of speed while steering evasive courses. *St Laurent* and *Forester* had been joined by *Swansea* and all three ships opened fire with their guns. The tenacious *U 845* survived a further hour but lay wrecked and sinking just before midnight, her captain and all in the conning tower killed. The scene was captured by Lieutenant-Commander Alan Easton, RCNR, commanding *Matane*, who had listened to the entire radiotelephone (RT) conversation between the attacking escorts (in his ship the RT traffic had been broadcast over their public address systems): "As the destroyer [*St Laurent*] slid past ... the Captain, looking down from the bridge, saw a red glow in the conning tower as though there was a fire burning below inside the boat. As the disc of illumination from her starboard searchlight moved jerkily along the sub's hull the havoc wrought by shell fire was starkly evident. The bridge appeared to be shattered and on the twisted metal lay several bodies. The last of the living crew had gone ... The gun seemed to have been uprooted and was leaning dejectedly towards the water."[44] Forty-five of the fifty-four crewmen survived.[45]

This success reflected the advantages of well-equipped and relatively well-trained antisubmarine forces. Asdic conditions were excellent and the escorts had generally been able to maintain contact, even when, early in the encounter, the U-boat dove an estimated 700 feet. *St Laurent* used her centimetric radar for controlling her devastating gunfire to demolish the U-boat's conning tower, underscoring the advantage of an up-to-date radar. The offensive spirit, tenacity and weapon efficiency of the ships involved were commended in a painstaking post-action analysis by Western Approaches.[46]

Closer inshore, while *U 802* was engaging the attention of Canadian sea and air forces, *U 550* and *U 856* passed through the Canadian Northwest Atlantic on passage to operate off the United States. Both were plotted and tracked, and both were destroyed by American warships off the US east coast.[47]

For nearly three weeks after *U 802* began its homeward passage, there were no U-boats in the Canadian theatre, but on 23 April Enigma decrypts alerted the Operations Intelligence Centre in Ottawa of the approach of *U 548*, commanded by Kapitänleutnant E. Zimmermann. Just relieved from weather-reporting duties, which had exposed him—as he well knew from the fre-

---

44. Easton, *50 North*, 226

45. SecNB to Naval Member C.J.S. Wash, May 1944, LAC, RG 24, 11976, 283-1. There are detailed accounts in Milner, *U-Boat Hunters*, 119-21; Easton, *50 North* 222-6; F. McKee and R. Darlington, *The Canadian Naval Chronicle*, 126-30, and F. McKee, *HMCS Swansea: The Life and Times of a Frigate* (St. Catharines, 1994), 68-77.

46. Remarks by Cmdre (D) WA, 1 Apr 1944, DHH 81/520/8000, U 845 (hereafter DHH U 845, etc.) Milner, *U-Boat Hunters*, 121; McKee, *HMCS Swansea*, 75

47. Douglas, *Creation of a National Air Force*, 578

quent appearance of aircraft—to HF/DF triangulation. He decided to patrol from two to sixteen miles off the coast from Conception Bay to Ferryland Head.[48] Overcast skies prevented astro navigation and ice floes hampered his progress on the surface. On 1 May he established his position with a visual fix on lights "burning in Baccalieu as if it were peacetime" and Cape St Francis. Later, while on the surface to ventilate the boat, he sighted an aircraft in the distance and immediately crash-dived. Zimmermann thought he had evaded detection, but the aircraft, a Liberator returning from a long convoy escort patrol, reported the boat, tracked it with sonobuoys, and triggered another Salmon. This search began with some promise of success, involving over the next several days twenty-one ships from five different groups. When aircraft were not grounded by weather they covered the area quite thoroughly. On 3 May, evidently unaware—despite frequent sightings of Canadian warships, which he identified as "United States destroyer escorts"—that he was the object of such a massive hunt, Zimmermann surfaced to attack HMS *Hargood*, a Captain class frigate just commissioned, with a relatively untrained and inexperienced ship's company.[49]

In view of subsequent developments the events of that day (a comedy of errors) had overtones of tragedy. To Zimmermann the frigate looked like a sitting duck, steaming at a dead slow speed and evidently unaware of his presence, even though it was "bright night conditions" and he was emitting heavy black diesel smoke. His *zaunkönig*, however, which he fired at 0800Z on 3 May, did not find the target, possibly because *Hargood* was moving so quietly and because of the torpedo's long firing range of 2,500 metres. As he prepared to fire a second torpedo, a Liberator taking part in the Salmon search illuminated *Hargood*. Zimmermann could not resist opening fire at the aircraft. The Liberator crew, having identified the target they had illuminated as a destroyer, assumed that the fire came from that source, and flew off in high dudgeon, the pilot complaining that a friendly warship had opened fire on him. *Hargood* sent off a signal to Flag Officer Newfoundland reporting that the Liberator "appeared to have short bursts of Oerlikon fired at it ... Have you any information? Continuing patrol." *U 548* bottomed for two hours, and it appears from the U-boat's war diary that *Hargood* conducted a search, but without gaining any contact, so that Zimmermann was left unimpeded to carry out the one successful attack of his patrol, on 6 May.[50]

It was on the evening of 6 May that the vessels of C 1, the frigate HMCS *Valleyfield* (Lieutenant-Commander D.T. English, RCNR, carrying the senior officer of the group, Commander J. Byron, RNR), and the corvettes *Halifax*, *Frontenac*, *Giffard*, and *Edmundston* entered *U 548*'s patrol area. Relieved from their duties as the escort for convoy ON 234 at the Western Ocean Meeting Point about 200 miles south of Cape Race, they took up a formation of line abreast, 4000 yards apart, bound for St John's. Meanwhile, Flag Officer Newfoundland, apparently following up on *Hargood*'s baffled report had ordered an air and surface search of *U 548*'s area. During the afternoon of 6 May C 1 received reports of a U-boat off the Avalon Peninsula and the position of two

---

48. On 17 April Zimmermann's replacement, *U 342*, fell victim to RCAF Liberators.

49. KTB, *U 548*, 1-3 May 1944; Officer Commanding 10 Sqn to CO RCAF Station Gander, 3 May 1944, EAC A/S Ops Intelligence Summary, 7 May 1944, DHH 181.003 (D1555); Ops Research SO Halifax to COS (O), 6 May 1944, DHH Operation Salmon; Hadley, *U-Boats against Canada*, 209; Douglas, *Creation of a National Air Force*, 577

50. Ibid

corvettes searching the probability area. Since intelligence now placed Zimmermann's boat about 150 miles east or south of Cape Race, he was in position to intercept the homeward-bound warships, but for this mid-ocean group, released as it was from escort duties, the possibility of encountering a single submarine in these waters seemed remote. As night fell, the moon lit up the sea. It was fairly calm. Ice floes and growlers stretched to the horizon. Radar was picking up so many echoes that it lost most of its tactical value. The senior officer and his weary captains turned in, leaving officers of the watch in charge of their ships and, in view of ice conditions, not zigzagging. In *Valleyfield,* as senior ship at the middle of the line abeam, the RX/C radar was living up to its reputation for unreliability, failing even to pick up a large iceberg on a known bearing less than three miles away. Moreover, the radar in *Frontenac*, on the frigate's port beam, had been unserviceable for days. Two of the five ships were thus for practical purposes without radar. At 2100 the starboard wing ships encountered the two corvettes searching for *U 548* and later at 2240 a Canso hunting the U-boat overflew the formation. Around 2230 the group had left most of the ice behind but the zigzag was not resumed. When at 2300 the formation literally stumbled into *U 548* proceeding southwestward on the surface—Zimmermann's first realization that ships were in the vicinity was a fleeting silhouette sighted closing rapidly—the ships were about fifty miles southeast of Cape Race. None of the group's radar operators picked up the boat in the clutter of returns from ice, and the U-boat approached from ahead in the radar gap between *Frontenac* and *Valleyfield*. Zimmermann closed promptly and then because of the bright moonlight dived for a submerged attack with a *zaunkönig* against *Valleyfield*, the ship he had glimpsed. Launched at 2335 from fine on the bow at 1500 metres, an ideal shot for an acoustic torpedo, it found its mark after a run of about three minutes, just long enough for *Valleyfield's* hydrophones to pick up the sound before the *zaunkönig* exploded, probably by its magnetic influence pistol under the frigate's boiler room.[51]

In the ensuing blast, the ship, hit at her most vulnerable point, virtually disintegrated. The bow section, split off from the stern, sank in three minutes. The stern went down in eight. *Giffard*, on *Valleyfield's* starboard beam, had seen the explosion. Receiving no response to a radio call, *Giffard* started closing to investigate but did not report to the rest of the group. For twenty minutes or so the other three ships steamed on, their personnel at first unaware that the explosion they heard was anything more than a single depth-charge.[52] In the icy waters, quickly covered with bunker oil, men who had survived the explosion—some of them clad only in underclothes—had slim chances of survival. When *Giffard* learned from the survivors that their ship had been torpedoed, she radioed her consorts to close and commenced an asdic search, only returning to rescue survivors when *Edmundston,* now the senior ship, took over the search. When all of the remaining men had been pulled from the sea, those who had not succumbed had been in the water from forty to ninety minutes. In the end, just thirty-eight of *Valleyfield's* 168 officers and men survived.[53] In the meantime, *Edmundston* had held contact

---

51. KTB, *U 548*, 6 May 1944; "Recent Events," *Royal Canadian Navy Monthly Review* (May, 1944), 58; Hadley, *U-Boats against Canada*, 210-20

52. DWT/Tactics to DWT, 9 Jun 1944, LAC, RG 24, 4107, 1156-381-65

53. Lts Jake Warren, and Ian Tate, RCNVR, the Navigating Officer and Officer of the Watch, the only officers to survive, have put together valuable first-hand accounts of the ordeal endured by the men of *Valleyfield*. DHH 82/93

briefly, and carried out an unsuccessful Hedgehog attack. *U 548* escaped, as she had three days before, by bottoming.[54]

Valleyfield's agony would later be described by James Lamb, a veteran corvette officer who was preparing for the landings in Normandy when the frigate was sunk:

> Throughout the wartime fleet of the Royal Canadian Navy, the loss of *Valleyfield* was a bombshell, destroying at a stroke the euphoria that had steadily grown as the Allied grip of the Atlantic sea lines tightened, month by month....The realization that the hunted could still destroy the hunter was a salutary shock to the Canadian escort groups, a reminder of the inherent vulnerability of any ship at sea in wartime, warship or merchantman. Adding to the impact of the news was the fact that *Valleyfield* was the first—and, as it was to prove, the last—Canadian frigate to be sunk by U-boat attack.[55]

C-in-C CNA ordered another Salmon on receiving the report of *Valleyfield's* sinking, sending W 2 with HMCS *New Glasgow* and *Agassiz*, joined by the four remaining ships of C 1, to join the hunt for *U 548*. Heavy air coverage kept Zimmermann down, but did not prevent him from escaping to the south, while Flag Officer Newfoundland ordered searches to the east and west of the last known detection. Fog prevented flying after sundown on 6 May, and limited flying to three patrols, two by Cansos and one by a Liberator on 7 May. By that evening the U-boat was hearing the last sounds of the hunt. As it proceeded submerged towards Halifax on the night of 8/9 May, a fast convoy for which there was no appreciable hydrophone warning—possibly UC 2 with its USN escorts—steamed directly over the boat's track.[56] On the afternoon of 9 May, about 200 miles south of Cape Race, Zimmermann broadcast his first signal to BdU since a weather message transmitted on 16 April, reporting his success against a "US destroyer escort" and other activities. Intercept stations ashore and at least two escorts picked up the transmission. They obtained reliable bearings and a USN aircraft providing close escort to UC 21, now about fifty miles away, soon obtained a radar contact. Three destroyers from the convoy screen were detached to conduct a search.[57]

After sunrise on 10 May, the Canadian hunting group joined and took over the search until early next day, and although Liberators from 10 Squadron's detachment at Sydney swept the area con-

---

54. KTB, *U 548*, 6-7 May 1944; Precis of Attack by HMCS *Edmundston*, 7 May 1944, LAC, RG 24, 11026, COAC 7-14-1; "Minutes of Board of Enquiry Convened ... to Investigate the Circumstances Attending the Loss of HMCS Valleyfield, 10 May 1944," LAC, RG 24, 4107, 1156-381-65; Surg-Lt J.F. Simpson and A/Surg-Cdr M. Wellman, "Emotional Reactions in Survivors of HMCS Valleyfield," *Canadian Medical Association Journal* (Oct, 1944). There are detailed accounts of the loss in J.B. Lamb, *On The Triangle Run* (Toronto, 1986), 139-219, and McKee and Darlington, *Canadian Naval Chronicle*, 147-50.

55. Lamb, *On the Triangle Run*, 217-8

56. The UC/CU convoys had been started in early 1943 to transport oil from the Caribbean to the UK. Large new T-2 tankers termed "greyhounds" were being mass produced in the US and the convoy passage speeds were fourteen knots. Fast freighters and liners were also included. These convoys were organized by the US and escorted by American warships. This strategically vital operation has received little attention in general accounts of the Atlantic campaign, partly because it happened largely after the U-boats were no longer a serious threat to ocean convoys, and suffered no losses. D.J. Payton-Smith, *Oil: A Study of War-Time Policy and Administration* (London 1971), 321-3; Hague, *Allied Convoy System*, 183-6; Blair, *Hitler's U-Boat War: The Hunted*, 811-12

57. *Valleyfield*, Signals, 1-17 May 1944, DHH Valleyfield; C-in-C CNA WD, May 1944, LAC, RG 24, 11053, 30-1-10, pt 32; EAC proposed ops and ops signals, 9-12 May 1944, DHH, 181.003 (D3254); ORBs, 5 BR, 10 BR, 10-12 May 1944, DHH; *New Glasgow* ROP, 12 May 1944, LAC, RG 24, 11023, COAC 7-6-6; KTB, *U 548*, 9-17 May 19445

Stowing depth charges on HMCS *Valleyfield*. The three men in the foreground, Leading Seaman D.H. Brown, Leading Seaman S.L. Stilson and Sub-Lieutenant L.J. Sanger, all died when *Valleyfield* was sunk in May 1944. (DND CN-6492)

stantly in daylight until the evening of the 12th, this hunt was also doomed to disappointment. The submarine had not lingered in the area, but continued southwest in search of traffic between Halifax and New York. The OIC lost track of the marauder and stopped issuing probable hunt areas for it on the 14th. *U 548* returned undetected to the Halifax approaches on 17 May. There, the raider lingered for ten days, making contact with two convoys and two independent merchant ships, but without attacking. Sighting aircraft daily, caught by surprise on the surface on three occasions, Zimmermann believed himself to be under bomb or depth-charge attack three times, but there is no mention of such contacts in the Canadian records.[58]

That German submarines were failing to find many targets in the Canadian area can be ascribed to air searches and the convoy system. Air searches were preventing U-boats from readily shifting patrol areas. The concentration of merchant ships in defended groups, successful as it had become in the face of wolf packs, proved itself even more effective against U-boats operating singly in the Canadian Northwest Atlantic area. Convoys were substantially more difficult to locate by boats operating alone, and provided much less statistical chance of sinking tonnage, that is, of achieving an exchange rate favourable to the attacker. Of course, by the same token, finding and destroying U-boats was more difficult when they were not in the vicinity of convoys. The OIC almost invariably gave warning of the presence of a submarine, but the U-boat probability areas to be searched were large. Even though submarine successes were scarce, this inability of the RCN to hunt down the few U-boats coming to the Canadian Northwest Atlantic and adjacent areas was still a concern. Resources were simply not available to flood the probability areas.

Admiral Murray's forces were concentrated on convoy defence. There were seven groups of the Western Escort Force, numbered W 1 through W 7, totalling twenty-four corvettes and five Algerine class minesweepers. These provided the escort for convoys from New York to the Western Ocean meeting point (WESTOMP). The Mid-Ocean Escort Force, which took them over, now consisted of five C groups, comprising eight frigates and twenty-six corvettes. Also available for local duties were five Bangors and a Western Isles trawler in St John's, four Bangors, two Western Isles trawlers, three Fundy minesweepers, a 105-foot minesweeper, a Suderoy minesweeper in Halifax, and a Western Isles trawler in Saint John. For the Gulf of St Lawrence, there were in Sydney four Western Isles trawlers and the Norwegian submarine chaser *King Haakon VII*. Based in the same port was the Patrol Force of nine Bangors which, in addition to sweeping the Cabot Strait and the Gulf shipping routes, escorted convoys to Newfoundland, Halifax, and Saint John, New Brunswick. Forming a striking force were three Fairmile flotillas, two at Gaspé and one at Sydney; after the second week of June three corvettes arrived at Québec to escort Labrador convoys. A Bangor, the depot ship *Preserver*, and a flotilla of Fairmiles that took up station at Red Bay, Labrador, formed the so-called Belle Isle Force.[59]

The trouble was, as Canadian naval authorities were fully aware, that these forces were not really suitable for prolonged hunts to exhaustion. The missing ingredient was a permanent support group, one that was properly trained and equipped for that role, but all available Canadian groups had joined Western Approaches and Plymouth Command for the buildup to the Normandy landings. In March, Commodore Taylor, Flag Officer Newfoundland, had asked that one support

---

58. Ibid

59. "RCN Weekly Report," 2 and 30 May, 20 June 1944, DHH 81/520/1650, DS

group be kept permanently west of WESTOMP, "Preferably frigate in view of their greater endurance and being better sea boats than destroyers." He also noted that air support in the area, from Newfoundland, was only effectively available for ten days in each month. Scientists in the Directorate of Operational Research pressed for an escort carrier as well.[60] Murray would have been happy to oblige had suitable ships been available, but his response reflected the Admiralty's strategic assessment that the best place for such ships was where U-boats were most concentrated. For the moment all he could promise was at least two operational frigates with each MOEF group.[61]

This policy, despite the disappointments that followed, was essentially sound. After Zimmermann had left there was little U-boat activity in the area until early July. *U 1222* and *U 107*, which came to the CNA area in May, carried out successive patrols off Halifax between 14 May and 1 July that were far less aggressive than U-boat Command would have wished.[62] *U 1222* tried to torpedo a British tanker sixty-five miles south of Halifax on 22 May. Aircraft and the corvettes *Agassiz* and *Norsyd* searched the area without success. *U 107* shelled the American fishing vessel *Lark* fifty miles from Cape Roseway on 13 June after two torpedoes had failed.[63] Both were recalled by BdU along with other boats in distant waters five days after the Allies landed in Normandy.[64] *U 1222* fell victim to a Sunderland of Coastal Command in the Bay of Biscay on 11 July. In the meantime, on 24 June an Enigma decrypt alerted the OIC to the approach of *U 233*, a large minelaying boat bent on mining the approaches to Halifax.[65] On 27 June Eastern Air Command mounted a series of air searches based on the Otter signal of 25 June, and the USN carrier support group of USS *Card* and five destroyers joined the search a few days later. *Card*'s aircraft located *U 233* on 5 July south of Sable Island, and two of her destroyers finished off the submarine by depth-charges and ramming.[66]

Although, as will be seen, there were further encounters in coastal waters, convoys sailed without loss to U-boats in the mid-ocean area for the rest of the war.[67] For the people in these convoys, of course, the threat of U-boat attack remained very real, and the need for vigilance was as great as ever. This became tragically evident during the passage westbound of convoy ONM 243. On 4 July the convoy, consisting at that time of eighty-seven ships, met its mid-ocean escort, group C 5 (the frigate HMCS *Dunver* carrying the SOE, the recently promoted Commander George Stephen, and five corvettes), together with the MAC ships SS *Empire MacColl* and *Empire MacCallum*, and arrived without loss at the WESTOMP nine days later. On 8 July, however, a

60. Milner, *U-Boat Hunters*, 128

61. FONF to C-in-C CNA, 9 Mar 1944, and C-in-C CNA to FONF, 10 Mar 1944, DHH 81/520/8440, Support Groups (General)

62. BdU, KTB, memo, "Submarine Situation 1 June 1944 and 17 June 1944,'" DHH 79/446

63. *U 107*'s deck gun jammed. The fishing vessel's crew abandoned *Lark* but subsequently reboarded and returned to Boston. K. Wynn, *U-Boat Operations in the Second World War* (Annapolis 1997) I, 90; Douglas, *Creation of a National Air Force*, 590; C-in-C CNA WD, June 1944, DHH

64. MOD, *U-Boat War in the Atlantic* III, para 457

65. Niestlé, *German U-Boat Losses*, 145; Otter Signal, 25 June 1944. An identical submarine, *U 119*, had lain mines off Halifax in June 1943.

66. *United States Fleet Anti-submarine Bulletin* II (Aug 1944), 22-3; Niestlé, *German U-Boat Losses*, 145

67. All the recorded U-boat attacks against ON and SC convoys in the North Atlantic, between June 1944 and May 1945, took place east of 11° W and west of 63° W. Rohwer, *Axis Submarine Successes*, 182-91

Swordfish aircraft from the *Empire MacCallum* had sighted a surfaced submarine about thirty miles west of the convoy. Stephen, who had been concerned about a U-boat reported to be in his vicinity in both British and American daily situation reports, was heard by the leading signalman then on the bridge to exclaim "Sink the bastard," and five more Swordfish scrambled to attack. About an hour after the original sighting they carried out a well coordinated and successful strike on the submarine.

When the aircraft returned to their ships the crews received the shocking news that, rather than a U-boat, they had sunk the Free French submarine *La Perle*. On the way from refit in New London, Connecticut, to the eastern Atlantic, the boat had only one survivor, a Chief Petty Officer machinist of the French navy.[68] "I remember very clearly," recalled Commander A.G.S. Griffin, RCNVR, Staff Officer Operations at St John's at the time, "giving this submarine her sailing orders, going over carefully with the captain, navigating officer and my own navigating officer the route to be followed by *La Perle*, clear of all convoys and concentrations of U-boats. I also remember drafting the signal, with wide distribution to all concerned at sea and ashore, specifying the route and the 'safe' corridor ... in which ships were not to attack, as they normally would, any surfaced submarine on sighting."[69]

The MAC ships, which depended on the SOs for all information passed on naval broadcasts, should have been informed of this vessel's proximity to the convoy by Stephen or his staff. It was lax communications procedures, both by *Dunver* and the MAC ships, that failed to ensure this happening. In the final instance, Stephen himself might have averted the tragedy, but until the last moment he appears to have been transfixed with the idea that the aircraft had actually sighted a U-boat. When it dawned on him that it could be *La Perle*, he sent a voice message to the MAC ships, asking if the pilots realized that the French submarine might be in the area, but it was too late: the aircraft were already in attacking position. The submarine sent a series of "Ls," the correct identification message for the day, as the first aircraft began its attacking run, but the pilot assumed this was a *ruse de guerre* and took no notice. The Board of Inquiry convened in Halifax on 14 July—composed of an RCN captain (the president), an RN Commander, and one Free French *capitaine de vaisseau*—identified poor signals procedure in *Dunver* and inadequate briefing of pilots in the MAC ships as the principal reasons for this terrible tragedy. They exonerated the pilot, an officer of the Royal Netherlands Navy who, "having many scores to settle with the enemy," perhaps "could not believe that any submarine sighted could possibly be other than a U-boat." Stephen, an experienced and perhaps weary escort commander, a former merchant mariner with extensive and distinguished service in the Arctic, had valiantly saved lives and ships over the past four years. Only four months before this he had played a large part in the sinking of *U 845*. The Board of Inquiry gave him the benefit of the doubt in his lapse of judgment, in view of the ambiguous wording in a signal from US authorities about the submarine's position. However, in addition to the OBE and two DSCs Stephen had previously

---

68. For a detailed account of this episode see W.A.B. Douglas, "'Sink the Bastard!' Friendly Fire in the Battle of the Atlantic," *Canadian Military Journal* 2/3 (2001), 65-73

69. A.G.S. Griffin, *Footfalls in Memory* (Toronto, 1989), 129. The signalman serving at that time in *Dunver*, John Seale, was in hospital at the time of the Board of Inquiry; he has a vivid recollection that Cdr Stephen appeared not to wish to hear the frequent reports he was giving him of the progress of *La Perle*. See correspondence in Griffin biog file, DHH.

earned, he now received the severe displeasure of the Naval Board "for failure to exercise complete control over the escorts under his command."[70]

In their attempt to interdict the Allied landings in Normandy, *schnorkel*-fitted boats had survived intense air and surface opposition and managed to evade detection in the rock-strewn coastal waters. That was ample justification for the policy that U-boat Command had adopted just days before the invasion, that in future only boats equipped with *schnorkels* and radar were to be sailed for operations.[71] As the Allied armies advanced in Normandy, the fitting of new equipment at the U-boat bases in Brittany and on the Biscay coast continued with renewed urgency. Between mid July and the end of August 1944, U-boat Command launched a wave of five upgraded, *schnorkel*-fitted, type IX boats, with the capability of operating largely submerged. Destined for the Canadian area, they initiated a new method of operations. Two were to operate off Nova Scotia, where the unproductive patrols in May and June had confirmed for BdU that Halifax was still the major shipping focal point in the area. The three others were to push deep into the Gulf of St Lawrence, matching the maximum effort of 1942.

Signals intelligence again gave early warning of their approach, and new measures had been taken to exploit this information. Experience earlier in the year had underscored the need for dedicated support groups to search probability areas. New frigates were undergoing work-ups in Bermuda, and six of them—*Charlottetown, Orkney, Springhill, Stettler, Toronto* and the ill-fated *Magog*—were designated as the new support group EG 16, under Lieutenant-Commander W.C. Halliday, RCNR. On 10 July NSHQ informed the Admiralty that the new support group would "operate against U-boats west of longitude 35 degrees west as they approach Canadian coast or on passage to southward."[72] The RCN hoped also to acquire the services of HMS *Nabob*, an escort carrier largely manned by Canadian personnel, to form a carrier support group with EG 16, but the Admiralty, as will be seen (Chapter 21, below), had other plans for *Nabob*. The Admiralty also wanted Ottawa to place EG 16 under the control of C-in-C Western Approaches for service on the Russian convoys. Canadian insistence that the new support group not be released to the eastern Atlantic, and British reliance on USN carrier support groups in the western Atlantic, meant that EG 16 would remain under the control of C-in-C CNA but without an escort carrier.[73]

In the months to come, USN escort carrier groups came into the Canadian area, in an almost informal manner, to cooperate with RCN support groups and RCAF squadrons to mount barrier patrols. In practice that meant that *Nabob*'s absence, although it left Canada entirely dependent on the USN for carrier support, made little difference to the strategic situation. The RCN was still the routing authority for North Atlantic trade convoys from New York out to WESTOMP, but the USN retained overall strategic responsibility for the northwest Atlantic, and maintained its operating

---

70. "Communications HMCS 'Dunver,'" LAC, RG 24, 11128, NS 60-4-112; "Sinking of Submarine 'La Perle,'" CNA 0032; NSec to C-in-C CNA, 28 Sep 1944, RG 24, 11927, NSTS 11150-381/12; Capt D.K. Laidlaw, RCN (Rtd) to W.A.B. Douglas, 1986, Laidlaw biog file

71. MOD, *The U-Boat War in the Atlantic* III, para 425

72. NSHQ to Adm, 1538Z/10 July 1944, DHH 81/520/8440, EG 16 (Signals)

73. Adm to NSHQ, 0606B/22 July 1944, and NSHQ to Adm, 24 July 1944, PRO, ADM 1/16032

base and air stations at Argentia, Newfoundland. These were strengths that, although they left the RCN in the position of a "client navy"—something that planners in Ottawa were hoping they could overcome—compensated for the continued shortcomings of Canadian naval strength in the western Atlantic. Assigning dozens of escorts to support the Normandy landings, simultaneously taking over total responsibility for the close escort of transatlantic convoys from New York to the United Kingdom—thus releasing additional British warships for Operation Neptune—had stretched the RCN to the limit.[74]

The first of a new wave of *schnorkel* boats to sail for Canadian waters was *U 802*, which had already spent two months off Nova Scotia in March and April. By 21 July, four days after the boat's departure from Lorient, Allied cryptologists had intercepted and decrypted its complete tasking instructions. The Americans reacted by tasking the escort carrier USS *Bogue* and her destroyers, already hunting for several boats northwest of the Azores, to search westwards as the U-boat crossed the ocean.[75]

C-in-C CNA, working on the daily U-boat estimate, sent out his only support group on a search. EG 16 was well led, but not so rigorously worked up as its counterparts in the eastern Atlantic, and suffered from inadequate radar and asdic. Only *Orkney* and *Springhill* had type 271 radars. The remainder relied on the flawed Canadian RX/C set for centimetric radar, and none of the ships had the Q attachment to type 144 asdic, nor did they have 147B, which would have increased their chance of penetrating thermal layers.[76] Without a precise datum, this one group's chances of finding *U 802* in the vast ocean spaces east of Newfoundland were slender indeed. On 9 August it took up a Gamma search, used when massive air cover was available. This time the search was perpendicular to the submarine's line of advance rather than along it, moving back towards Newfoundland at the estimated speed of advance of the U-boat. Liberators and Cansos flew at least twenty-two sorties between 9 and 13 August, sweeping an area to seaward of the frigate line. Meanwhile the *Bogue* group had closed to within a hundred miles of Cape Race, and now approached the search area from the northwest.[77]

U 802 had in fact been advancing cautiously and largely submerged. On 12 August its captain, Kapitänleutnant Schmoeckel, reported that he had been detected by an aircraft radar.[78] His position was fixed by D/F, and it was realized that the U-boat was some four days behind and south of its expected position. During the night of 18/19 August one of *Bogue*'s aircraft attacked the submarine on the surface 300 miles south of St John's, but Schmoeckel escaped. Admiral Murray placed EG 16 under *Bogue*'s orders on 19 August, but before they could join, the carrier's aircraft

74. LCdr J.S. Hodgson, RCNVR, "The First Year of Canadian Operational Control in the Northwest Atlantic," 18 Aug 1944, 8280A pt.1, DHH 81/520/8280, box 1

75. Sarty, "Ultra, Air Power and the St. Lawrence," 191; Morison, *Atlantic Battle Won*, 325-6. This account makes no mention of RCN or RCAF participation in the search.

76. DWT/Tactics to DWT and ACNS, 4 Oct 1944, DHH, EG16; Milner *U-Boat Hunters*, 200

77. Morison, *Atlantic Battle Won*, 325.

78. This would have been from a Liberator or Canso. The first USN radar detection was on 13 Aug, and the pilot who reported it failed to return to *Bogue*: he evidently "splashed," perhaps as a result of exhaustion after weeks of demanding operations. Morison, *Atlantic Battle Won*, 326

first surprised another outbound U-boat, *U 1229*, on the surface 250 miles southeast of Cape Race in daylight and destroyed it.[79] When the identity of *U 1229* was established by questioning survivors, it was realized that *U 802* was still at large. Coastal convoys were reinstituted and independent sailings suspended; while EG 16 established another Gamma patrol outside the Cabot Strait, Fairmiles began one inside. Simultaneously, Eastern Air Command carried out extensive sweeps over the Cabot Strait and Gulf. Such intensive air activity—"Pure Bay of Biscay conditions" Schmoeckel later reported—forced him to creep more slowly than expected towards his destination, as little as thirty miles a day and never more than sixty.[80] *U 802* eventually passed through the broad strait into the Gulf of St Lawrence, three days after the main naval forces had begun moving into the area, but only hours after Eastern Air Command had reduced its patrols, and proceeded submerged to the mouth of the St Lawrence, arriving on 6 September.

A third *schnorkel*-equipped type IX, *U 541*, commanded by Kapitänleutnant K. Petersen, by now had also reached the Gulf. Allied intelligence had decrypted signals tasking the boat for the Gulf and the *Bogue* group searched for *U 541* east of Newfoundland. Unlike Schmoeckel in *U 802*, Petersen had made fast surface runs at night, advancing more quickly than expected. Although the OIC learned his precise position from a radio report on the night of 28/29 August, Petersen was able to evade detection because fog grounded aircraft and *U 802* was attracting the attention of all available air and surface forces. When he reached Cape Breton Island on the night of 2 September he was able to run on the surface. Just before dawn on 3 September, Petersen located and sank the independently routed and unescorted small British freighter *Livingston* just south of the Cabot Strait. Petersen was well inside the Gulf and submerged by the time shore authorities got word of the sinking and organized searches.[81]

The intelligence picture was unclear. That there were two submarines in the area did not dawn on the hunters, who were experiencing the vagaries of weather and sonar conditions so prevalent in Newfoundland and Canadian coastal waters.[82] Both boats were unmolested, as *U 541* moved into the Gulf and *U 802* into the mouth of the St Lawrence River. They made good use of thermal layers. Over the next twelve days, unaware of each other's presence because of poor radio propagation, they cruised these waters, and each had the occasion to encounter, attack—and mistakenly claim to have sunk—RCN escorts. During the night of 7/8 September, *U 541* surfaced twenty-eight miles south of Anticosti Island to attack an apparently unescorted merchant ship. Although monitoring high-intensity radar signals Petersen closed in murky visibility. He was alarmed to see the corvette *Norsyd* closing at speed, firing her guns. Petersen crash dived and fired a *zaunkönig*, thinking incorrectly that he heard breaking up noises. *Norsyd* heard the torpedo but was unable to pick up the attacker on asdic. For the corvette the entire encounter from initial detection on radar to the torpedo had lasted four short minutes.[83] *U 541* subsequently became the object of a ten-day

---

79. *U 1229* was tasked to land agents in Maine and then operate off Nova Scotia. Allied intelligence, aware that *U 1229* was at sea, surmised from an absence of radio traffic that she was on a secret mission. Sarty, "Ultra, Air Power and the St Lawrence," 194

80. KTB, *U 802*, 20-31 Aug 1944

81. Ibid; Tennyson and Sarty, *Guardian of the Gulf*, 328-9

82. "Probably the most frustrating time of the war ... for the *Bogue* group," observed Morison in *Atlantic Battle Won*, 328.

83. Hadley, *U-Boats against Canada*, 231

hunt by every available aircraft and escort. However, Petersen was able to proceed to the mouth of the St. Lawrence before turning to leave the Gulf, empty-handed. Meanwhile, Schmoekel in *U 802*, alarmed by the extraordinary search activity, decided to edge back out from the river into the Gulf. On 13 September several frigates from W 13, hastily sent out to participate in the hunt for *U 541*, steamed over his position. He fired a *zaunkönig* that exploded in the wake of *Stettler*, and he incorrectly claimed destruction of a "destroyer" before beginning a slow and extremely cautious departure, even stopping his engines and drifting for twenty-four hours until he was clear of the Gaspé passage. Both *U 541* and *U 802* passed submerged through the Cabot Strait on 22/23 September.[84]

The OIC in Ottawa was now aware of two more boats approaching Canadian waters, *U 1221* and *U 1223*. A routing message ordering Oberleutnant P. Ackermann's *U 1221* to head for a position southeast of Newfoundland was decrypted on 30 August. Two weeks later Allied intelligence fixed *U 1221* by D/F after Ackermann sent weather reports and reported his position southeast of Newfoundland on 15 September. RCAF aircraft and the escort carrier USS *Core*, which had replaced USS *Bogue*, and her destroyers mounted area searches.

Ackermann in *U 1221* had reacted to sea and air searches, betrayed by the distant depth-charge attacks being made on false contacts, and arrived off Halifax on 30 September, four days later than expected. He operated off Nova Scotia for eight weeks, largely well offshore but moving in to the Halifax approaches to attack a convoy without success on 23 October.[85] The second new arrival, Oberleutnant A. Kneip in *U 1223*, revealed his presence through short reports from mid-Atlantic. Allied cryptographers read a routing message instructing Kneip to head for a position southeast of Newfoundland and a subsequent tasking message for the Gulf.[86] Again, area searches over the enormous ocean approaches were unsuccessful. *U 1223* appears to have benefited from a series of false scents followed by searching ships and aircraft, and from weather that grounded aircraft until the second week of October. On the 14th, Kneip was well into the Gulf when an inward-bound convoy of twelve ships, QS 97, with an escort reinforced by EG 16 in view of *U 1223*'s presence, passed close to his position thirty miles below Baie-Comeau in broad daylight. Kneip snapped off two torpedoes, one of which blew sixty feet off the stern of the frigate *Magog*.[87] Using thermal layers, he escaped the subsequent two-day hunt, remained in the St Lawrence, and on 2 November—after the OIC had mistakenly concluded from signals intelligence that all submarines in Canadian waters had begun their homeward voyage and ships had consequently again started to sail independently—torpedoed the unescorted freighter *Fort Thompson* six miles off Matane.[88] Ironically, the merchant ships in QS 97 had crossed the ocean as ONS 33, which had been attacked ten days earlier north of the Azores by *U 1227*, and as was seen in the previous chapter, on that occasion another Canadian frigate, *Chebogue*, had lost her stern.

---

84. Sarty, "Ultra, Air Power and the Gulf," 203

85. Ibid, 206. Ackerman attacked the troop ship *Lady Rodney*, but all three torpedoes missed.

86. Ibid, 202

87. Ibid, 204; Hadley, *U-Boats against Canada*, 237-40. At this stage of the war it was decided not to repair *Magog* and she was later scrapped.

88. Sarty, "Ultra, Air Power and the St Lawrence" 206: Hadley, *U-Boats against Canada*, 240. The British *Fort Thompson* had been built in Vancouver and had a cargo of grain. One hold was damaged and it was originally thought that a mine was responsible. *Fort Thompson* made her own way back upstream and was repaired.

HMCS *Magog* after being torpedoed, by *U-1223*. The frigate survived the encounter, but never went to sea again. (LAC PA 137797)

This was the last successful attack on a merchant ship in the St Lawrence or the Gulf, and *U 1223* was the last of the five *schnorkel*-equipped boats that had each operated for five to six weeks in the area. Kneip cleared the Gulf on 21 November. One submarine sunk in exchange for one merchant ship destroyed, with one freighter and a warship damaged, was a disappointing result for U-boat Command. The *schnorkel*-fitted submarines had largely eluded detection, but their movements had been constrained by air and surface searches. Because the U-boats made virtually no radio transmissions, Allied signals intelligence was limited to intercepting initial tasking messages from BdU, and because they operated largely submerged, the first tangible evidence of a submarine became its attack on a surface vessel. For their part the U-boats lacked intelligence about shipping and attempted to find focal points. Once in coastal areas the German submarines were hampered by their limited ability to scout for targets and restricted submerged speed. Their encounters with targets were therefore sporadic and haphazard, and a large volume of shipping continued to move through the Gulf in convoys. The scale of the German presence in the Gulf and St Lawrence River certainly matched that of 1942, but it never achieved the dramatic impact of the earlier episode.

U-boat Command had decided to maintain a steady presence in the Canadian area. The next wave of long-range *schnorkel* boats left from Norway and started arriving in mid-November. Loss of the Biscay bases had meant that U-boats could no longer reach the Caribbean and Gold Coast of Africa, also considered promising for *schnorkel* operations. The first two boats of the new wave, *U 1228*, commanded by Oberleutnant F. Marienfeld and *U 1231*, under Kapitän zur See H. Lessing, were initially ordered to the Cabot Strait with freedom to advance into the Gulf. Allied intelligence again decrypted the tasking messages, and air and surface searches covered the submarines' estimated tracks. A new frigate Support Group, EG 27, formed at the end of October with the frigates *Meon*, *Ettrick*, *Lévis*, and *La Salle*. *Meon* (Acting Commander R. St Clair Balfour, RCNVR, Senior Officer) and *Ettrick*, transferred from the Royal Navy several months earlier, came from other groups. *Lévis* and *La Salle* had just worked up in Bermuda, and the group would be joined by another newly commissioned frigate, *Coaticook*, in November. As support groups, EG 27 and EG 16, in addition to their hunter-killer operations, were in frequent demand to reinforce convoy screens in the probability areas.[89]

The wave of U-boats that remained in the area until the end of the year achieved scattered successes, which can be attributed to their own enterprise, poor sonar conditions, a good deal of luck, and the weaknesses that still obtained in C-in-C CNA's available resources. These were the factors at work when *U 1228* sank the corvette *Shawinigan* (Lieutenant W.J. Jones, RCNR) with all hands. Expected by the OIC, based on Enigma decrypts, to arrive in the Gulf, Marienfeld had turned back to repair his *schnorkel* mast on the night of 23/24 November. After surfacing five miles off the southern Newfoundland coast for the best part of an hour to lubricate the valve, he submerged and headed back into the Cabot Strait. *Shawinigan* was carrying out an antisubmarine sweep in bright moonlight to seaward of Port-aux-Basques on the evening of the 24th, preparatory to escorting the Newfoundland ferry *Burgeo* to Sydney, Nova Scotia the next morning. *U 1228* first detected the corvette by hydrophone. Marienfeld then sighted *Shawinigan* through his periscope. She zigzagged across the track of the submerged boat, at the limits of asdic range, and Marienfeld fired a single *zaunkönig* from about 2500 metres. His log describes *Shawinigan*'s fate: "Torpedo and screw noises merge. A hit after 4 min 0 secs. High, 50m, large explosion column with heavy shower of sparks, after collapse of explosion column, only 10 m high now, then smoke cloud, destroyer [*sic*] disappeared."[90] There were no survivors, and the corvette went down too quickly to get off an enemy report. Only when the ferry turned up at Sydney on the afternoon of 25 November, without an escort, did shore authorities realize that *Shawinigan* was missing. All available ships and aircraft began to hunt for the submarine, joined by EG 16, already searching for *U 1231* in the southeast ocean approaches to Cape Breton.[91]

Although the trail was cold, the searching forces came close to finding the boat. A Canso flew directly overhead at low altitude while Marienfeld was at periscope depth, and he was lucky to avoid detection. Subsequently he decided that without a reliable *schnorkel* his boat was not fit to operate in the face of such surveillance, and so turned for home.[92]

Lessing in *U 1231* entered the Gulf as Marienfeld attacked *Shawinigan* and heard the torpedo explosion, but pressed on, reaching the mouth of the St Lawrence on 2 December. When the *schnorkel* began icing up, Lessing turned back, reaching Cabot Strait on 7 December. He had fired torpedoes twice against merchant ships and twice against escorts, but without success. Lessing then received permission to work off Halifax.[93]

A third type IX, Kapitänleutnant H. Hilbig's *U 1230*, had been ordered to carry out a "special mission" before operating off Nova Scotia. Allied intelligence surmised correctly that this involved landing agents on the coast of Maine, therefore Hilbig had to make his approach in the face of massive surveillance. From 20 to 24 November EG 16 extended their sweep southeast to cover the approaches of the Bay of Fundy and Gulf of Maine, while USN and RCAF patrol aircraft swept the area when weather permitted.[94] Despite this effort Hilbig succeeded in putting two agents ashore at Frenchman's Bay, Maine, on the night of 29 November.[95] Four days later *U 1230* torpedoed the unescorted Canadian freighter *Cornwallis* ten miles southwest of Mount Desert Rock.[96] The vessel went down quickly, with only five survivors of the crew of forty-nine, but the radio operator managed to transmit a distress signal, which triggered a massive search. Canadian and American aircraft conducted an around-the-clock sweep of the expanding U-boat probability zone and maintained barrier patrols between Yarmouth, Nova Scotia, and Cape Cod, Massachusetts. At sea, in addition to local USN patrol craft, TU 27.1.3, a new hunter-killer destroyer group, joined from Casco Bay, while *Bogue* and her screening destroyer escorts came up from New York. A second carrier support group with USS *Core* sailed from Bermuda to New York, ready if needed to join the

---

90. KTB, *U 1228*, 25 Nov 1944, DHH 85/77; Darlington and McKee, *Canadian Naval Chronicle*, 193-5; Hadley, *U-Boats Against Canada*, 246-8

91. See file NSS 1156-331/93, LAC, RG 24, 4108; NSHQ A/S incident log, 25 Nov 1944, NSS 8910-23, pt 3; Tennyson and Sarty, *Guardian of the Gulf*, 332-4

92. KTB, *U 1228*, 3-7 Dec 1944; the OIC special intelligence summary, week ending 18 Dec 1944, PRO, ADM 223/21

93. KTB, *U 1231*, 22 Nov-7 Dec 1944

94. HMCS *Springhill* movement card, 19-24 Nov 1944, DHH; EAC proposed ops and ops summary signals, 20-24 Nov 1944, DHH

95. The FBI eventually apprehended the agents in New York City. See Morison, *Atlantic Battle Won*, 330 ff

96. *Cornwallis*, operated by Canadian National Steamships, was bound for St John's from Barbados with a cargo of rum and molasses and had been routed independently after reaching New York in convoy. She had previously been torpedoed off Barbados in 1942 by *U 514* and had been repaired. Darlington and McKee, *Canadian Naval Chronicle*, 241

hunt.[97] Hilbig slipped through the net, thanks to *schnorkel*. Nevertheless, the episode revealed a significantly improved ability by Canadian and American forces to coordinate both their intelligence and operational efforts.[98]

The support of American carrier support groups, which operated under the tactical control of C-in-C US Atlantic Fleet (CINCLANT) even when in the Canadian zone, has already been noted. They had become proficient at hunting down U-boats using signals intelligence, but recent operations against weather-reporting submarines had demonstrated, again, that aircraft were significantly less effective against *schnorkel*-fitted boats. The Americans promptly started focussing their efforts on "hunter-killer" groups of destroyer escorts and commenced intensive training at Casco Bay.[99] The USN, keenly aware of the extent to which the RCN had denuded its own coast to support the European theatre, now informed NSHQ that the first three of these destroyer escort hunter-killer groups were not only at the disposal of the RCN if C-in-C CNA needed them, but, if so desired, they would operate under Murray's tactical control. On 27 November CINCLANT sent TU 27.1.2 to Argentia for this purpose. Murray was grateful, and undertook only to exercise this option if offensive sweeps were needed to prosecute fresh submarine data.[100]

At the end of November U-boat Command shifted the focus of its operations from the Gulf of St Lawrence to the area off Halifax. Lacking signals intelligence on convoys and shipping patterns, BdU could only rely on recent operational experience. When *U 1221* reached Norway after operating off Halifax in September, the commanding officer, Ackermann, added to earlier signalled reports about considerable traffic and light defences. Having broadcast these details, U-boat Command ordered *U 1228* and *U 1231* to shift their operations to Halifax. *U 806*, commanded by Korvettenkapitän K. Hornbostel, inbound for Newfoundland and earlier instructed to operate in the Cabot Strait, also received orders for the new area. Allied intelligence had soon broken the new instructions to *U 1228* and *U 1231*, but never intercepted the changed tasking for Hornbostel, possibly because the Germans used a new type of short transmission called *Ursula*.[101] This was "a new type of short signal sent by Control," the OIC in Washington would explain three months later, "which cannot be read as yet but which probably designates operational areas."[102]

Canadian submarine trackers played it safe by allowing for the possibility that one of the boats already in the Gulf might choose to remain there.[103] At the same time, almost certainly reflecting

---

97. Eastern Sea Frontier WD, Nov-Dec 1944, DHH mfm; Douglas, *Creation of a National Air Force*, 603

98. Another example of the close ties between Allied OICs was the correlation in Washington of reports by Canadian escorts in December and Lessing's report of 5 Jan 1945 referring to the two attempts by *U 1231* on 3-4 Dec to torpedo merchant vessels and escorts in the Gulf. CO HMCS *Matapedia* to NOIC Gaspe, 8 Dec 1944, NSS 8280-QS 107, DHH mfm; SRGN 43760, NARA, RG 457

99. D. McLean, "The US Navy and the U-Boat Inshore Offensive" in Cogar, *New Interpretations in Naval History*, 315

100. Knowles, "U-Boat Intelligence Summary," 15 Nov 1944, f 508, SRMN 037, NARA, RG 457. "A/S Killer Groups," 21 Nov and 1 Dec 1944; "TF Composition," 1 Jan to 31 Dec 1944; Washington National Records Center (hereafter WNRC), RG 313 Red, CINCLANT secret files 1944, Box 143. NSHQ to C-in-C CNA, 1431Z/25, Nov 1944, DHH 81/520/8440-130, WEF; Joint RCN-RCAF ASW Cte min, 30 Nov 1944, DHH 181.009 (D3188); C-in-C CNA to CINCLANT signal 1520Z/1 Dec 1944, NSS 8910-166/10; C-in-C CNA to SOs EG 16 and 27, 1745Z/12 Dec 1944, DHH, EG-16 (Signals)

101. There is no mention of *Ursula* signals in Hinsley et al, *British Intelligence in the Second World War*, but its presence is evident from Knowles, "U-Boat Intelligence Summary," 5 Mar 1945, SRH 037, NARA, RG 457

102. Ibid

103. KTB, BdU, 28-30 Nov, 3 Dec 1944; ZTPGU 33754, TOI 1832/30 Nov 1944, NS to ID8G, 2232/1 Dec 1944, PRO, DEFE 3/738. See also, Knowles, "U-Boat Intelligence Summary," 2 Dec 1944, SRH 037, NARA, RG 457

Ultra intelligence of Ackermann's report, C-in-C CNA established a large U-boat probability zone, extending 120 miles from Halifax in all directions.[104] Defensive efforts also reflected the emerging threat. EGs 16 and 27 spent much of their time reinforcing convoy screens in areas off Halifax and Sydney.[105] Meanwhile, with the weather improving, the VLR Liberators at Gander looking for Hornbostel's *U 806* were able to make six sweeps out to maximum range during the first week of December. Aircraft from Sydney continued to make searches, as well as routine convoy protection flights, in the Cabot Strait area where any remaining Gulf boat was estimated to be lurking in view of the winter wind-down of shipping further in the Gulf. At Halifax-Dartmouth, the air force now added a program of search flights to convoy escort missions in order to guard against the U-boat expected to move down from the Cabot Strait.[106]

Further hard information about the location of *U 806* did not become available until the third week of December. On the 10th the OIC estimated, incorrectly, that the boat was in the Cabot Strait. Direction-finding bearings on *U 1228*'s departure signal, broadcast only on 14 December when the boat was already at mid-ocean, brought out three Liberator flights from Gander, but the plot was in fact about five degrees west of the boat's actual position.[107] When Hilbig signalled on 16 and 17 December that *U 1230* was making an early departure from the Gulf of Maine because of equipment problems, he was south of Nova Scotia, about 400 miles due east of Cape Cod— close enough in for a fuller response to the direction-finding fixes. Admiral Murray now called on his new US reserves, TU 27.1.2 from Argentia and TU 27.1.3 from Casco Bay, with support from some twenty RCAF sorties, to conduct a five-day hunt but without result.[108]

In the midst of these intense offshore operations, the inshore waters off Cape Breton and along the Nova Scotia mainland were dead quiet, as they had been for weeks. *U 1228* and *U 1230* were homeward bound, and Allied intelligence concentrated on the constant weather reporting activities of another submarine, *U 1232*, which had sailed from Horten on 11 November.[109] Thus, when on 18 December BdU ordered KapitänzurSee K. Dobratz to resume passage for operations in the whole Newfoundland–Gulf of St Lawrence–Nova Scotia area, intelligence soon had a clear text. On 21 December another directive assigned Dobratz to Halifax, but because it was an *Ursula* transmission, it slipped through the Enigma net.[110] In the message of the 18th, however, BdU had directed the submarine to "approach points where traffic is greatly concentrated according to the situation reports sent by W/T."[111] The next day there was an *Offizier* code message that turned out to be an

---

104. Otter Signals, 5 and 10 Dec 1944; Sarty, "Ultra, Air Power, and the St. Lawrence," 201-2. ZTPGU 3117, 33128, 33223, PRO, DEFE 3/738

105. *Meon* and *Springhill* movement cards, 1-20 Dec 1944, DHH

106. EAC proposed ops and ops summary signals, 2-14 Dec 1944, DHH; 10 and 160 Sqn ORBs, 2-14 Dec 1944, DHH

107. The patrols covered the vicinity of 52°N 43°W, 10 Sqn ORB, 14 Dec 1944, DHH. The boat was actually travelling from the southern part of grid square BD 15 into the northern edge of BD 12, in the general area of 51°N-37°W, *U 1228* log, 14 Dec 1944, DHH 85/77.

108. C-in-C CNA WD, 17 Dec 1944, NSC 1926-102/1, DHH; CTU 27.1.3 WD, 17-22 Dec 1944, USNHC Operational Archives, Flag Reports, box 66; EAC proposed ops and ops summary signals, 17-23 Dec 1944, DHH; 10 Sqn ORB, 17-23 Dec 1944, DHH

109. E.g., ZTPGU 33841, 34049, 34051, 34109, 34163, 34202, 34259, 34263, 34287, 34342, 34406, 34438, 34444, 34451, 34602, covering 3-19 Dec 1944. PRO, DEFE 3/738 and 739

110. *U 1231* and *U 806* KTB, 21 Dec 1944

111. ZTPGU 34497, PRO, DEFE 3/739

HMCS *Clayoquot*, a Bangor class minesweeper, before she was torpedoed by *U 806* near Halifax while escorting convoy XB 139. (DND GM 0367)

Eight members of HMCS *Clayoquot*'s complement died when the minesweeper was torpedoed. Here, some of the survivors are being rescued by the corvette HMCS *Fennel*. (DND GM 3000)

elaboration of Ackermann's report on Halifax, and, also on the 25th, BdU broadcast Kneip's full report on the St. Lawrence in standard Enigma, which was decrypted within twenty-four hours. The signal reporting Ackermann's experience had been specific in its conclusions: "Successes can only be expected directly off Halifax, therefore act accordingly."[112] Before any of this was known to him, because the OIC's daily submarine situation reports had been so accurate, C-in-C CNA dropped his guard a little too easily. The danger was in fact imminent, and when on 21 December Hornbostel in *U 806*, which the OIC imagined was in the Gulf, announced his arrival by torpedoing a ship in convoy off Halifax he caught Allied commanders completely by surprise.

Hornbostel had spent six days carefully scouting the Halifax approaches. When he decided to strike he had the advantage of surprise that Dönitz had hoped all his boats would have in this phase of operations. On the evening of 21 December Hornbostel was ten miles off Chebucto Head, the western headland outside Halifax. He came to periscope depth periodically to sort out ship noises heard on his hydrophones and, late in the afternoon, sighted a small outbound feeder convoy, HHX 327. He attacked and hit the British Liberty ship *Samtucky*. The escorts raced into action without success and were joined by additional warships from the harbour. *Samtucky* reported an internal explosion and it was at first thought that she had struck a mine.[113] Hornbostel escaped to the south in the gathering darkness. On the forenoon of 24 December *U 806* was lurking submerged off the anchored Sambro Light Vessel, even closer to the western headland, and was now in good position to intercept XB 139 as it left Halifax on its way to Boston.[114]

What Hornbostel did not know was that the convoy's designated escorts, the frigate *Kirkland Lake* and two Bangors, *Clayoquot* and *Transcona*, had left harbour earlier to carry out an antisubmarine sweep, a result of the attack on *Samtucky* three days before. On their way back to join the convoy, now outside the harbour, the escorts closed *U 806*'s position. When *Clayoquot* altered course towards the submarine to take up her screening station Hornbostel deduced that he had been detected, fired a *zaunkönig*, then dove to sixty metres. After a run of less than 1000 yards, the torpedo struck. The other escorts began searching for the enemy while *Clayoquot* sank, all but eight men managing to get off alive.[115]

Hornbostel quietly moved to shallower water, which took *U 806* beneath the convoy. He fired another acoustic torpedo at a merchant ship, but it was detonated by *Transcona*'s CAT. Bottoming in sixty-eight metres for ten and a half hours, Hornbostel heard the searchers pass overhead, counting 100 depth-charges exploding at various far distances. He switched off any device capable of producing noise, and kept energy consumption at the barest minimum, off-duty crew breathing through CO_2 exchangers. The cook provided cold meals and Christmas cake to bolster morale. A combined sea and air search ensued, but was hampered by several factors: a delay of two hours before aircraft could take off from the icy runways at Dartmouth; by the absence among RCN and RCAF units in the Halifax area of any joint sea/air tactical doctrine to respond to an attack of the

---

112. ZTPGU 34701 and 34736, ibid

113. *Samtucky* was beached inside Halifax harbour and eventually repaired.

114. D. McLean, "The Loss of HMCS *Clayoquot*," *Canadian Military History* 3/2 (1994), 31-43

115. Ibid. The tactical situation was particularly complex because a second convoy with its own escorts was also outbound. Hornbostel apparently did not sight the outbound transport *Lady Rodney*, which preceded XB 139, but did observe one of her escorts.

kind made by *U 806*; and by the almost complete lack of group organization among the escorts involved. Nevertheless, under the direction of Commander R.M. Aubry, RN, the training commander at Halifax, the escorts prevented any further attacks and then executed an expanding search which was an adaptation of the plan known as Operation Observant. Bottoming to avoid detection was known to be a regular U-boat tactic, and the searches were intended to cover this possibility. A few escorts, normally three, remained in the vicinity of the torpedo attack, and the remainder conducted a square search based on the Sambro Light Vessel, on a perimeter, growing from two to ten miles over the next ten hours, to allow for movement of the submarine. That detection opportunities were missed was probably the result of notoriously poor winter asdic conditions.[116] Just before midnight, the submarine slowly worked its way into deeper waters, remaining just clear of the bottom, not even daring to use its *schnorkel* until twenty-three hours had elapsed.[117]

Hornbostel moved offshore and began his homebound passage. Meanwhile, Lessing in *U 1231* had shifted inshore and on Christmas Day observed that navigation lights just east of Halifax had been extinguished. Lessing heard searching escorts, found no targets, and started homeward.[118] Submarine trackers at the OIC, no doubt influenced by the destruction of *Clayoquot*, plotted Dobratz's *U 1232* also moving towards Halifax, but as luck would have it, this accurate appreciation was contradicted by an RCAF Liberator making a false sighting southeast of Cape Race, about five days' *schnorkeling* away. In the flotsam-filled and fish-rich waters of Newfoundland's Grand Banks the USN's TU 27.1.3 had begun chasing a phantom of its own, northeast of St John's.[119] Thus *U 1232*, like *U 806*, achieved complete surprise, arriving near Halifax on 31 December, a week earlier than expected. The Canadians were taking precautions, notably in holding both support groups in the Halifax area to reinforce convoy escorts, but they did not anticipate early trouble. The submarine trackers still believed it was Lessing in *U 1231* who had achieved recent successes, and knew from the good data on his entry into the Canadian area that he would soon have to leave because of lack of fuel. Their call, on 30 December, was exactly right. *U 806*, on the other hand, which the trackers believed had not yet attacked or otherwise revealed itself, had been the subject of rough guesses based on uncertain contacts at sea, ranging from the south of Nova Scotia to eastern Newfoundland. By late December the intelligence plot placed the boat anywhere to the south and west of Halifax, including the Gulf of Maine, probably the result of a disappearing radar contact by the US TU 27.1.1 near Sable Island that had triggered a hunt on 27/28 December.[120] As the last calender year of the war began, it was Dobratz's *U 1232* which,would have the greatest impact in Canadian waters.

U 1232 arrived off Halifax on New Year's Day 1945 and, lying off one of the two light vessels, Dobratz took some time to study traffic before launching an attack. His first two attempts failed. On 2 January he fired at EG 16, twenty miles off the Sambro Light Vessel, and the next day at the troopship *Nieuw Amsterdam*. EG 16 heard the torpedoes detonate at the end of their runs but, informed

---

116. McLean, "Loss of HMCS *Clayoquot*," 40

117. *U 806* remained submerged for forty-one hours, approaching the limits for operating without fresh external air. KTB, *U 806*, 24-26 Dec 1944

118. Ibid, 269-70

119. Otter Signals, 20-30 Dec 1944; C-in-C CNA WD, 26-27 Dec 1944, DHH; FONF WD, 26-28 Dec 1944, DHH

120. C-in-C CNA WD, Dec 1944, esp 27 Dec and pt 2; Otter Signals, 25-31 Dec 1944; Hadley, "U Boote vor Halifax II," 208

by Admiral Murray's headquarters that an aircraft had dropped depth-charges on a training run at the same time, ignored the explosions. CINCLANT, unaware of what was actually happening and still plotting *U 1232* as inbound, ordered two USN destroyer escort hunter-killer groups, now designated TG's 22.9 and 22.10, to sweep the estimated track further to the east.[121] So, just as had happened two weeks before, the first indication of a U-boat's presence was an unexpected attack.

It was during the afternoon of 4 January, fifteen miles east of Halifax, that Dobratz sighted the Sydney-Halifax convoy SH 194, three ships escorted by a single Bangor, HMCS *Kentville*, and an RCAF Ventura. In the space of ten minutes *U 1232* torpedoed two small vessels, the Canadian tanker *Nipiwan Park*, which later made port, and the Norwegian freighter *Polarland*, which sank within seconds. EG 16, directed to the scene by the Ventura, arrived within two hours, as more aircraft were scrambled and additional escorts rushed out from Halifax. CINCLANT handed over the two USN hunter-killer groups to Murray's control; they joined the hunt on 6 January.[122]

Most of the sorties mounted by Eastern Air Command—the Command provided some forty special search sorties in addition to close escort between 4 and 8 January, even though weather grounded aircraft for two days[123]—took the form of close support for the naval groups, aircraft carrying out very specific patrols ordered by the senior naval officer to broaden the warships' search front. This close sea-air cooperation, unlike previous free-ranging sweeps of large probability areas, indicated the extent to which it had become clear that properly handled *schnorkel* submarines would be neither intimidated nor caught on the surface.[124] The intelligence on which these operations was based was sketchy in nature: it led Canadian and USN authorities to believe that only one boat, possibly *U 1231*, known to have been in the Canadian area for some time, had done all the attacks off Halifax. Good direction-finding bearings on *U 1231*'s departure signal on reaching mid-ocean on 6 January did not initially clear things up.[125] When the message was decrypted the next day, however, the pieces began to fall into place. *U 1231*'s report showed that she had been assigned to the Gulf in November, and had complied with the subsequent advisory to try the Halifax area, but had not sunk anything.[126] The submarine trackers now realized that the unlocated *U 806* had made the attacks off Halifax at the end of December. Extrapolating from the solid data on when the boat had reached Canadian waters they calculated that it was due to depart. Therefore, from 8 January TG 22.9, with RCAF support, searched towards Sable Island, nearly 200 miles from Halifax, to catch the U-boat—but this also was based on faulty intelligence: Hornbostel had in fact left on 4 January because of *schnorkel* problems. Confirmation that he was homeward bound did not come until he signalled from mid-ocean on 17 January.[127]

---

121. CINCLANT to TG 22.9, 1752Z/4 Jan 1945, and C-in-C CNA to EG 16, 1331Z/4 Jan 1945, LAC, RG 24, 6901, NSS 8910-166/10

122. NSHQ log of A/S contacts, 4 Jan 1945, NSS

123. EAC proposed ops and ops summary signals, 4-11 Jan 1945, DHH

124. C-in-C CNA WD, Jan 1945, DHH; NSHQ log of A/S contacts, 4 Jan 1945; 11 Sqn ORB, 4 Jan 1945, DHH

125. NSHQ log of A/S contacts, 6 Jan 1945, NSS; SRGN 43719, NARA, RG 457; Otter Signals, 4-8 Jan 1945

126. SRGN 43760, TOI 2359/6 Jan 1945, clear text 0505/7 Jan 1945, NARA, RG 457

127. Otter Signals, 9-16 Jan 1945; SRGN 44122, Hornbostel's first departure signal, TOO 0548/17 Jan 1945, but not fixed by D/F and clear text not available until 0822/25 Jan 1945; SRGN 44246, Hornbostel's report, TOI 0411Z/20 Jan 1945, clear text 0950/22 Jan 1945, NARA, RG 457; C-in-C CNA WD, Jan 1945, DHH 81/520/1926-102/1

Further precautions to secure shipping in the Halifax approaches and clarification of the over-all intelligence picture did little to interfere with *U 1232*'s operations, for the methodical Dobratz was no ordinary submarine commander. Rather than simply plunging deep after making snap shots, following the attack on 4 January *U 1232* moved up the coast as far as Cape Canso before returning to the Halifax approaches. Here, like Hornbostel three weeks earlier, Dobratz carefully monitored shipping movements and familiarized himself with local currents while remaining submerged.[128] He was waiting for a convoy and patrolled a position between the two entrance approach channels. The point chosen was close to that used by Hornbostel.

During the forenoon of 14 January Dobratz heard the screw noises of what sounded like a convoy and rose to periscope depth. He observed the lead ships of the inbound convoy BX 14, which had started forming a single column to pass up the swept channel into harbour. Three frigates of EG 27, *Meon* (Commander R. St Clair Balfour, RCNVR, SO), *Coaticook*, and *Ettrick*, had joined to reinforce BX 141's ocean escort of two Bangors. The nineteen merchant ships strung out in single file, Balfour realised, would present vulnerable targets. Because a waiting submarine might attack from ahead or either side, he positioned himself at the head of the column, stationed one frigate on the port flank and the third to starboard, and positioned a Bangor at the seaward end. (The second Bangor was astern with a straggler.)

Dobratz, who subsequently noted that his reconnaissance had enabled him to select an "ideal attack position," closed the column from its starboard side, torpedoing the third ship, the tanker *British Freedom,* from only 700 metres. The target broke apart. Next in line—quite literally—was an American Liberty ship, *Martin van Buren*, which increased speed but was hit by an acoustic torpedo that damaged her beyond repair. The column dissolved into disarray, ships overtaking each other. Balfour had ordered the other frigates to join him and implement "scare tactics," dropping random depth-charges. "The torpedoings," recalled Lieutenant-Commander L.C. Audette, commanding officer of *Coaticook*, "ugly and effective as they might be, were not spectacular: the usual puff of smoke from the victim's funnel and the muffled explosion heard only by the near-er ships."[129] Dobratz continued his deliberate attack, taking nine minutes to set up his next shot, and torpedoed the British tanker *Athelviking*, originally seventh in the column, which sank seven hours later.

No torpedo tracks had been sighted, so the escorts could not determine from which direction the attack was coming. Visibility was poor—no flying had been possible since early the previous day—and heavy fog closed in immediately after the attack, followed by sleet and snow. The asdic range was virtually nil. Dobratz heard the depth-charges but continued his attack. Just as two merchant ships came into view, he suddenly glimpsed an approaching "corvette"; Dobratz neverthe-less snapped off another *zaunkönig*, which failed to find a target. Twenty seconds after firing, *U 1232* lurched as she was run over by *Ettrick*. The frigate, passing through the column near the scene of the first attacks, had closed a patch, dropping depth-charges where what looked like a tor-pedo track had been seen minutes earlier. Although the frigate heaved on impact, nobody on board realised she had struck the U-boat. Below the surface there was no such doubt. The collision had caused structural damage to the submarine's conning tower and, more significantly, smashed the

---

128. KTB, *U 1232*, 10 Jan 1945

129. L.C. Audette, "Naval Recollections," 239, DHH

HMCS *Calgary*, which sank *U 536* along with HMCS *Snowberry* and HMS *Nene*. A revised Flower class corvette, her career would last ten years, the ship being paid off in 1951. (DND HN 893)

The River class frigates HMCS *Lasalle* (foreground) and HMCS *Coaticook*. Both were members of EG 27, the RCN support group based on Halifax, which experienced only frustration in attempting to hunt U-boats over the winter of 1944-45. (DND S 2869-12)

attack periscope and damaged the radar antenna.[130] Dobratz therefore broke off further attacks, moving southwest under the convoy at slow speed. Balfour grasped the situation as the attacks ceased and promptly organized an expanding search to the southwest along the submarine's possible escape routes.[131] Additional escorts from Halifax, including EG 16 and later TG 22.9, came out to join the hunt. Flying was not possible until the 18th, but air operations then resumed on a large scale. Despite these measures *U 1232* crept steadily out to sea.[132] The search continued fruitlessly until 23 January, when Dobratz signalled from mid-ocean that he was homebound.[133]

Dobratz's achievement was that of an exceptionally bold commander. Although the fact could not be revealed to the hard-pressed Canadian and American seamen and aviators in the northwest Atlantic, intelligence soon revealed that the Germans had been equally impressed by his success. On receiving Dobratz's signalled report, Dönitz personally replied with the single word "Bravo!" and signed the message with a warm "Your Cominch and Comsubs."[134] A few hours later, Dönitz signalled that he had personally delivered the good news to Hitler, who had immediately conferred the Knight's Cross on Dobratz.[135]

Hornbostel and Dobratz had both achieved surprise and evaded searches. Several factors contributed to their escape. In both cases the searchers used tactics that had been developed from experience with U-boats in British inshore waters. These included saturating the area with sound to keep a submarine immobile and classifying contacts on the bottom with echo sounders. Although this was current tactical doctrine, the effectiveness of the searches suffered from insufficiently rigorous training and the ad hoc nature of the search groups.[136] In stark contrast to RCN groups operating in Western Approaches, who regularly trained against "clockwork mice," EG 27 had never done exercises as a group against a live submarine, although individual frigates had done this type of training during work ups.[137] In the case of *Clayoquot*, a quarter of her crew were replacements drafted on board when she had been sent to sea hurriedly with many of her company on Christmas leave.[138] Fate decreed that this partly worked-up ship would be destroyed before she could be tested against a U-boat, but the situation points up the risks of operating with thin resources. This was the price of sending the RCN's best trained and equipped groups to the east-

---

130. KTB, *U 1232*, 14 Jan 1945

131. A penetrating analysis of the attacks and subsequent searches is in D. McLean, "The Battle of Convoy BX-141," *Northern Mariner* 3/4(1993), 19-35. McLean reconstructed the tracks of EG 27's frigates and *U 1232* and established that "sometime between 1216 and 1300 the search ships and the sub should have passed in close proximity ... that no detection took place was probably the result of poor acoustic conditions"(29). He concluded that poor acoustics and the rocky bottom probably accounted for the lack of detection. *U 1232*'s operations and the subsequent searches are also described in detail in Hadley, *U-Boats Against Canada*, 275-84.

132. KTB, *U 1232*

133. C-in-C CNA WD, Dec 1944, DHH; EAC, proposed ops and ops summary signals, DHH

134. C-in-C CNA WD, Dec 1944; EAC, proposed ops and ops summary signals

135. Douglas, *Creation of a National Air Force*, 610

136. M. Milner, "Inshore ASW: The Canadian Experience," in W.A.B. Douglas (ed), *The RCN in Transition* (Vancouver 1985), 154

137. McLean, "Battle of Convoy BX-141," 22. The contrast with the USN destroyer escort hunter-killer groups worked up that fall at Casco Bay is uncomfortable. EG 27 could not be spared for this type of training because of the pressure of ongoing area searches for U-boats.

138. Hadley, *U-Boats Against Canada,* 258; Darlington and McKee, *Canadian Naval Chronicle*, 157

ern Atlantic. Had Canada acquiesced in the Admiralty's earlier request for EG 16, the situation would have been still more difficult.

Environmental conditions also favoured the attackers. In the approaches to Halifax the rocky slate and granite quartz bottom, which has jagged ridges, produces severe reverberations, masking asdic echoes from a submarine at depth.[139] In winter, sharp temperature gradients bend sound rays back upward so that they have difficulty in penetrating to the bottom. As Marc Milner has recorded, "at one point escorts passing close to the wreck of SS *British Freedom* lying upended with her stern on the bottom and her bows pointing skyward in the crisp winter air, could not even get an asdic contact on the submerged part of the hull."[140] *Ettrick*, actually colliding with the attacking U-boat, failed to gain asdic contact. Although it did not apply in this case, submarines going deep or sitting on the bottom could escape asdic detection. Perversely, even though asdic was largely ineffective, U-boats at periscope depth could hear the screw noises of approaching convoys and patrolling escorts through their hydrophones.[141] In addition to the poor asdic conditions, Halifax itself is particularly vulnerable to hostile submarines because it opens directly onto the open ocean and has deep approaches. The ocean approaches to the great convoy ports in the United States, New York City and Boston, as well as those to the destination ports in the British Isles, such as Liverpool and the Clyde, are more difficult for a submarine to penetrate. A mix of factors thus combined to make Halifax an ideal "choke point" for submarine operations.

After Dobratz's departure U-boat activity in the Canadian Northwest Atlantic became sporadic. *U 1233* had left Norway in late December 1944 and operated in the Gulf of Maine and off southern Nova Scotia from 24 January until 24 February, but without any success, Seven more type IXs sailed at intervals between early February and the first week in March to operate off North America. One of them, *U 866*, was passing through the Canadian area when USN destroyers sank the boat southwest of Sable Island on 18 March. *U 190* arrived off Nova Scotia on 25 March and remained for six weeks, until the German surrender. A final wave of six type IXs left Norway for the eastern seaboard of North America during the second week of March. By early April they were one-third of the way across the Atlantic and were formed into a patrol line subsequently designated group *Seewolf* to sweep westward along the great circle convoy routes. *Seewolf* lost four boats, but the two survivors, *U 548* and *U 805*, reached the Canadian area in the fourth week of April. The final U-boat that sailed for the Canadian area was *U 889*, which left Norway on 5 April, did not arrive until after the German capitulation, and would be sighted on the surface on 10 May south of the Virgin Rocks by an RCAF Liberator.

During the first months of 1945, Allied intelligence, aware of the numbers of the capable new type XXI boats working up, kept predicting the start of a major submarine offensive in the Atlantic, which would unleash these powerful submarines. At the beginning of March it was thought that

---

139. Dr Gordon Fader, a geologist with the Bedford Institute of Oceanography, describes the bottom as "having ridges which extend vertically like book ends and have sheer 5-10m cliffs." Telephone conversation with J. Drent, 12 Mar 2002

140. Milner, "Inshore ASW," 154

141. LCdr M. Tunicliffe, an oceanographer at NDHQ, to J. Drent, 12 Apr 2002. This was because the screws produced low frequency noises that were not blocked by bottom reverberations.

over forty type XXIs were ready for operations and that the offensive was imminent.[142] It was against this dire background that Eastern Air Command maintained its close watch on the Halifax approaches and supported the two RCN frigate groups, EGs 27 and 28, that carried out almost continuous sweeps in the area. On the transit routes east and south of Newfoundland and off Nova Scotia, six USN destroyer groups searched the Otter areas under cover of aircraft from 1 and 3 Groups, RCAF. The OIC knew that *U 866*, one of four boats in the first wave, was bound for the Halifax area.[143]

This submarine would be the object of a search by forces under the operational control of Admiral Murray. EG 27 left Halifax to start searches for *U 866* on 6 March. On the same day a brand-new hunter-killer group of four USN destroyer escorts, designated TG 22.14, sailed from Casco Bay to search for the westbound submarine, and was transferred to the operational control of C-in-C CNA on 10 March.[144] The day before a Canso from 160 Squadron had sighted the enemy south of Virgin Rocks while covering HX 342. When the convoy's escort, C 6, followed up the aircraft's report and made asdic contact, C-in-C CNA ordered a Salmon with EG 16, which was on passage to the United Kingdom, and Task Group 22.14. EG 16 only conducted a cursory search until 10 March because there was no longer a firm datum. Task Group 22.14 then began to sweep back to the west along the U-boat's expected line of advance, while EG 27 concentrated on the area closer to Sable Island. As had happened before, it was the Americans who would reap the rewards of inter-allied cooperation. On 18 March TG 24.14 was on the last leg of its sweep southwest of Sable Island when USS *Lowe* obtained a sonar contact. The target initially appeared to be moving slowly, but subsequently it bottomed. After vigorous Hedgehog and depth-charge attacks the group sank *U 866*.[145]

Dönitz kept up pressure on the North American coast in April, even as Germany was on the verge of capitulation, but his final thrust met a wall of American escorts and naval aircraft off Newfoundland. The six type IXs, designated group *Seewolf*, were thought to be armed with the V-weapons then being used to attack London and Antwerp, so they were especially worrisome to the Americans. The response was Operation Teardrop, the largest undertaking of its kind yet mounted, with two barrier forces each made up of two escort carriers and twenty destroyer escorts. Such was the American superiority in materiel that the USN could, without denuding its Eastern Sea Frontier, maintain hunting groups in the Canadian zone with ships and aircraft whose strength nearly equalled the whole of Rear-Admiral Murray's command. The RCAF, without ceasing to support RCN convoy operations, worked flat out in support of the American offensive patrols. Not only

---

142. Knowles "U-Boat Intelligence Summary," 5 Mar 1945; Hinsley, *British Intelligence* III, pt 2, 627-30. In the event, the OIC learned in March from intercepted messages from the Japanese Naval Mission in Berlin that the type XXIs were experiencing problems and would not be ready for large-scale ops until May or even June.

143. C-in-C CNA WD, Mar 1945, pt 2 and C-in-C CNA to SO EG 27, 9 Mar 1945, DHH 81/520/1926-102/1, 1

144. McLean, "The U-Boat Inshore Offensive," 317. It happened that TG 22.14 had formed only on 5 March and had not undergone group training. The destroyer escorts were manned by US Coast Guard crews.

145. At about the same time, from 11 to 18 March, the OIC plotted three submarines, probably *U 857*, *U 879*, and *U 190*, as they entered the eastern fringes of the Canadian zone, possibly bound for the Halifax approaches or the Gulf of Maine. *U 857* and *U 879* arrived off Cape Hatteras in March, *U 859* then worked its way to Cape Cod about 1 April. C-in-C CNA WD, Mar 1945, pt 2; EAC, proposed ops and ops summary signals, 26-27 Mar 1945, DHH; DHH 81/520/1650, *U 866*; *US Fleet Anti-submarine Bulletin* (Apr 1945), 31-2

did the USN not have to call on the RCN for help, but CINCLANT did not consider it necessary to advise the Canadians of the situation until three U-boats—*U 1235, U 880,* and *U 518*—had been destroyed.[146] *U 546* and *U 881,* which had crossed the Atlantic independently also fell victim to the Teardrop force.[147]

The RCAF's 3 Group and the RCN focussed their attention on the Halifax approaches at this time because the OIC advised that at as many as four U-boats were in the Halifax–Cape Cod area.[148] There was in fact one in the Halifax area, *U 190,* commanded by twenty-five-year-old Oberleutnant H. Reith, which arrived on station about 27 March. Never rising above *schnorkel* depth, Reith made two unsuccessful torpedo attacks against a tanker. At first light on 16 April he believed that the Bangor minesweeper HMCS *Esquimalt* (Lieutenant R.C. Macmillan, RCNVR), on a routine patrol five miles to the east of Chebucto Head, had detected him.[149] Contrary to standing orders, *Esquimalt* was not zigzagging, and made an easy target. An acoustic torpedo ripped a gaping hole in the starboard quarter, and the ship sank in less than four minutes without transmitting a distress signal. Most of the complement got away on Carley floats, but neither an aircraft that flew overhead nor minesweepers that passed about two miles distant saw the survivors, who may have been mistaken for fishermen or some other innocuous grouping of small craft. Shore authorities suspected nothing until *Esquimalt* failed to appear at a planned rendezvous with *Sarnia* (Lieutenant R.P.J. Douty, RCNVR) about four hours after the sinking. C-in-C CNA ordered EG 28, then supporting HX 350 south of Sable Island, to hurry to the scene, and also ordered the merchant ships of outward-bound HJF 45, which had just cleared the Halifax boom, to turn back so its escorts could join the search for *Esquimalt's* survivors. Finally, after they had been in the chilly water for six hours, *Sarnia* arrived on the scene. Only twenty-six of a complement of seventy remained alive. *U 190* went straight to the bottom after the attack, waited for the situation on the surface to stabilize, then got away, starting for home on 29 April without doing any further damage.[150]

The surrender of U-boats in the Canadian Northwest Atlantic when Germany capitulated was the final act in what had been a long struggle. Dönitz ordered all vessels of the *Kriegsmarine* to cease operations on 4 May. When V-E Day came on 8 May there was no longer a functioning German high-power radio transmitter capable of passing messages to U-boats, and the process of communicating to boats in distant areas was laborious.[151] Eventually, *U 805* followed British

---

146. This was precisely the trouble with having to rely entirely on the USN for carrier support. FONF, WD, Apr 1945, DHH; W.T. Y'Blood, *Hunter Killer : US Escort Carriers in the Battle of the Atlantic* (Annapolis 1983), 260-3, 278; P. Lundeberg, "Operation Teardrop," in Runyon and Copes (eds), *To Die Gallantly,* 210-30

147. Douglas, *Creation of a National Air Force,* 607-8; Y'Blood, *Hunter Killer,* 263-72; Morison, *Atlantic Battle Won,* 345-6. *U 881* had originally been sailed along with the six *Seewolf* boats but had to return to Bergen for repairs. This boat probably did not receive the order broadcast on 4 May to cease hostilities and on 5 May was detected by an escort closing the carrier USS *Mission Bay* 320 nm southeast of Newfoundland and was sunk in an urgent depth-charge attack.

148. Douglas, *Creation of a National Air Force,* 608-9; C-in-C CNA WD, Apr 1945, DHH; Adm OIC Special Intelligence Summary, 16 Apr 1945, in Syrett, *Battle of the Atlantic and Signals Intelligence,* 576

149. "Report on an Interrogation ... of the Crew of *U 190,*" 22 May 1945, DHH 81/520/1650, *U 190,* NID 3

150. NSec to Cmdre RCN Barracks Halifax, "Loss of HMC Ship Esquimalt," 8 Nov 1952, DHH Esquimalt; C-in-C CNA WD, Apr 1945; SO EG 28 to Capt (D) Halifax, 20 Apr 1945, DHH, EG 28, v 1; NID 3, "Interrogation," 22 May 1945; Michael Hadley, *U-Boats Against Canada,* 290

151. Syrett, *U-Boat Situations and Trends,* 590

The Naval Board, four days before the end of the war in Europe. Note the maps on the walls.
(LAC PA 206510)

U 190, which had sunk HMCS *Esquimalt*, entering the harbour of St John's, Newfoundland, after surrendering following the end of the conflict. The boat remained with the RCN until it was paid off in 1947. (LAC PA 128268)

instructions and radioed her position south of Cape Race on 9 May, was joined by two destroyer escorts from Argentia, and escorted to Portsmouth Navy Yard in Maine. Reith in *U 190* reported his position to radio stations on Cape Race and in Boston and New York on 11 May. The frigate *Victoriaville* and corvette *Thorlock,* detached from escorting convoy ON 300, found *U 190* the next day, 500 miles east of Cape Race and escorted the boat to Bay Bulls, Newfoundland. *U 889* had already been intercepted by Western Escort Group W 6 on 10 May, and was accompanied to Shelburne. Her commanding officer, Friedrich Braeucker, ended that first day in company with the Canadians on a civil note: he flashed a signal to *Dunvegan,* the senior of the two Canadian escorts: "And so to bed. Have a good night."[152]

Canadian antisubmarine operations in the open Atlantic and in the Canadian Northwest Atlantic during the last eighteen months of the war against Germany demonstrated an economy of effort that was made possible by a remarkable spirit of cooperation between Britain, Canada and the United States. That Canadian ships and aircraft sank no U-boats in the Canadian Northwest Atlantic itself, unlike the Canadian forces operating in European inshore waters, and unlike American antisubmarine forces operating on the North American littoral, does not mean that the RCN and RCAF failed in their tasks. In August 1945, after comparing Canadian antisubmarine performance in Canadian and British coastal areas, R.M. Petrie of the Directorate of Operational Research in Ottawa concluded that "the prospects of success would have increased a great deal if ... one or more additional Support Groups had been made available [to C-in-C CNA] ... and if hunting groups of some A/S experience had been used in place of newly formed groups."[153] Even so, the nine Canadian hunts on which Petrie's study was based should have resulted in one U-boat destroyed, a statistic that was not significantly different from results achieved in European inshore waters. The fact that on various occasions the USN provided badly needed support to reinforce Canadian escort groups, and to fill the gap left by the absence of a Canadian carrier group, points up two important considerations. First, as described in the previous chapter, Canada itself was providing badly needed reinforcement to British naval forces on the other side of the ocean at the expense of the Canadian Northwest Atlantic theatre, and American cooperation was exactly what was needed to compensate for that fact. Second, USN assistance, which by 1944 was far more readily available than it had been before the formation of the Tenth Fleet in 1943, was called upon or offered—or on at least one occasion simply provided without consultation with C-in-C CNA, a fact of life Admiral Murray accepted as a necessity—only when there was a submarine datum to work from.[154] Even when that assistance was more than substantial, and although it did result in the destruction of three U-boats in or near the Canadian zone, the result was more often to keep a submarine from gainful activity rather

---

152. Cited in Hadley, *U-Boats Against Canada*, 297

153. DOR (RCN) Reports, R.M. Petrie, "A Comparison of A/S Hunts in Canadian and British Coastal Areas," 27 Aug 1945, LAC, RG 24, 11,463

154. It will be recalled, from Part 1 of this history, that in 1941 Admiral King told RAdm Percy Nelles that the USN's Atlantic Fleet could undertake no further commitments because it had strained US resources simply to provide escorts for HX convoys. Douglas, *No Higher Purpose*, 270

than to sink it.[155] To reiterate Arthur Marder's observation: "The only necessity in war is to stop submarines sinking ships." Not until submarines began to assume major strategic roles other than attacks on shipping did this comment lose some of its validity.

It bears repetition that U-boats themselves had disappointing results against ocean convoys and inshore shipping defended by the RCN and RCAF. The U-boat campaigns of 1944–45 in North American waters and the open Atlantic, even if they forced the Allies to devote enormous effort and large numbers of ships to antisubmarine operations, were in the end desperate measures in a losing cause. Between 1 January 1944 and the end of the war (more than sixteen months) twenty-six boats operated in the waters off Newfoundland and Nova Scotia. During that period U-boat attacks were responsible for sinking, or damaging beyond repair, eight merchant ships, for a total of 44,747 gross registered tons. Dobratz alone accounted for four of these ships, totalling 15,848 tons, in January 1945. U-boats, as previously noted, did sink four Canadian warships and damaged a fifth beyond repair, but in the harsh currency of war these successes were not significant. U-boats, no longer trying to pursue tonnage warfare, had still less success against North Atlantic convoys in 1944–45. Insofar as the German objective was an attempt to disrupt shipping, it failed. As an attempt to tie down Allied surface forces it was also ultimately ineffective, largely because Canada, rather than squander all its naval strength on a relatively quiet theatre, contributed generously to the Allied efforts against Germany's main strength in European waters. This Canadian generosity, based on the professional advice given to their political masters by the Canadian Naval Staff, had in fact become a familiar pattern. To an ever greater extent, from the despatch of destroyers to reinforce the Royal Navy in 1940, the participation in Mediterranean operations in 1942, the build-up to the Normandy invasion in 1943–44, and finally in support of operations in European waters leading up to the defeat of Germany in May 1945, the Royal Canadian Navy had become a blue water navy.[156]

---

155. *U 233,* 5 July 1944; *U 1229,* 20 Aug 1944; and *U 866,* 18 Mar 1945;, as well as *U 1235,* 15 Apr 1945; *U 880,* 16 Apr 1945; and *U 518,* 22 Apr 1945, the latter three from group *Seewolf,* destroyed before they could enter the area. P. Kemp, *U-Boat Destroyed* (Annapolis 1997); Niestlé, *German U-Boat Losses*

156. W.A.B. Douglas, "How the RCN Became a Blue Water Navy," in Yves Tremblay (ed), *Canadian Military History since the 17th Century: Proceedings of the Canadian Military History Conference, 5-9 May 2000* (Ottawa 2001)

CHAPTER TWENTY-ONE

Fleet Operations in European and Arctic Waters July 1944–May 1945

IN THE SUMMER OF 1944 Prime Minister Winston Churchill and President Franklin Roosevelt again turned their attention to the problem of supplying the Soviet Union by the northern route. On 23 May, Churchill had promised he would "try to resume the convoys at the earliest date after Overlord was launched," a commitment that Stalin had "strongly welcomed." On D-Day Roosevelt sent Churchill a telegram saying he was "in full agreement [as] to the high desirability of re-opening the Northern convoys to Russia at the earliest practicable date" in order that the Western allies "should give to the Soviet attack on Germany all the support and assistance that we can provide." On 7 June, as Allied navies focussed their attention and much of their might on the landings in Normandy, Churchill minuted the First Lord of the Admiralty, A.V. Alexander, "I am expecting you to organize a convoy to Russia in July, and to run them regularly thereafter as long as the Americans will send anything or there is anything due from us."[1]

The Admiralty agreed to resume the JW-RA series of convoys in mid-August. The Home Fleet, command of which had passed to Admiral Sir Henry Moore on 14 June, once again took up as a primary task the safe passage of shipping to and from North Russia. A number of fleet destroyers, including *Algonquin* and *Sioux*, therefore returned to Scapa Flow from Operation Neptune in mid-July. At that time British intelligence indicated the German battleship *Tirpitz* was about to undergo sea trials following repairs to the damage received from Operation Tungsten in April. She was then to sail for the Baltic, where she would have been beyond the reach of the Fleet Air Arm, and in a position to return to full fighting efficiency.[2] Admiral Moore responded to this situation with Operation Mascot, designed once again to carry out an air strike on *Tirpitz* while she lay in Kaafjord. The fleet carriers *Formidable*, *Furious*, and *Indefatigable*, the battleship *Duke of York*, four cruisers, twelve destroyers—including *Sioux* and *Algonquin*—and four frigates, left Scapa at 0800 on 14 July for their fly-off position one hundred miles west of Altenfjord. At 0135 on 17 July, forty-five Fairey Barracudas, all but two of which were armed with single 1600 lb armour-piercing bombs, together with a flak-suppression escort of twelve Fairey Fireflies and twenty Grumman Hellcats, and a top cover escort of eighteen Chance Vought Corsairs, set off for their deployment point ten miles southwest of the *Tirpitz*.[3]

1. Churchill to Field-Marshal Dill, 29 May 1944, and Roosevelt to Churchill, 6 June 1944, Churchill to First Lord, 7 June 1944, PRO, ADM 1/17127

2. D. Brown, *Tirpitz: The Floating Fortress* (London 1977), 34-6; Hinsley, *British Intelligence in the Second World War* III, pt 2, 276

3. Adm, Historical Section narrative, "Home Fleet," IV, para 2-6

The surprise achieved with Tungsten was difficult to repeat on Mascot because the *Kriegsmarine* had improved its radar warning and communication facilities in the area, and increased the smoke generating capacity around the battleship. The strike force was forty-three miles from the target when enemy radar picked up the aircraft, and by the time the formation, slowed by the ponderous Barracudas, reached the anchorage in Kaafjord some twenty minutes later, an effective smoke-screen rose nearly 1000 feet. The airmen bombed blind, using the flashes of anti-aircraft guns as aiming points. They obtained only seven near misses, which did no great damage to the battleship. One destroyer received a direct hit—it was out of action for eight days— and a small flak ship went aground while under attack by fighters.[4] Fortunately for the attackers, flak and smoke were the Germans' only defences: the *Luftwaffe* as usual failed to cooperate with the *Kriegsmarine* in providing fighter cover, so that despite the intense anti-aircraft barrage only two aircraft were lost.[5] It was nevertheless a dangerous and demanding operation for the naval airmen. For the screening destroyers—as had been the case with Tungsten in April—it involved procedures that, demanding as they were, amounted to little more than routine. When fog over Kaafjord forced cancellation of a planned second strike the task force headed back to Scapa.[6]

Moore was of the opinion that further carrier-launched strikes against *Tirpitz* would have little chance of success on account of the efficient smoke screens put up by the Germans. The Admiralty disagreed, thinking that continuous strikes over a forty-eight-hour period would wear down the defences and force the Germans to expend their smoke supply. Moore agreed to launch another attack but synchronized it with the passage of convoy JW 59 to Russia, which he hoped would draw U-boats away from the carriers as they hovered around the launch position and also allow him to cover both operations with *Duke of York*.[7] Among the ships that sailed for Operation Goodwood was HMS *Nabob*, an escort carrier commanded and for the most part manned by Canadians. She had arrived in Northern Scotland in August, ending a journey that had begun nearly a year earlier in the corridors of Naval Service Headquarters in Ottawa.

Nabob's presence in the Home Fleet had considerable bearing on the RCN's development of naval aviation and a balanced fleet. The thrust of the argument for a Canadian naval air branch, it will be recalled, was that it would give Canadian antisubmarine forces their own shipborne air support, and provide a basis for the postwar development of self-contained Canadian task forces. In August 1943, at the Quadrant meetings in Québec, the manning of British escort carriers with Canadian crews was one of the options discussed for relieving the Royal Navy's manpower crisis. Captain H.N. Lay, slated as of October 1943 to command HMS *Nabob* on an exchange basis with the RN, had reinforced his original arguments after a four-month tour of British Fleet Air Arm and

4.   Tarrant, *The Last Year of the Kriegsmarine*, 129-31

5.   The Luftwaffe's fighter operations in Norway were seriously weakened in 1944; in the first half of the year they averaged 497 sorties per month but that number plummeted to just 31 per month in the second half. A.R.A. Claasen, *Hitler's Northern War: The Luftwaffe's Ill-Fated Campaign, 1941-1945* (Lawrence, Kan 2001), 239

6.   German NS, Operations Division (OpsD) WD, 17-18 July 1944, DHH SGR II/261; *Algonquin*, deck log, 14-19 July 1944, LAC, RG 24, 7016; *Sioux*, ROP, 6 Aug 1944, LAC, RG 24 (acc 83-84/167), 695, 1926-DDE-225, pt 1 (hereafter DDE-225 etc.); C-in-C Home Fleet WD, July 1944, PRO, ADM 199/1427; CNMO(L) narrative, "Canadian Ships with the Home Fleet: Operation Mascot," nd, this and all other cited CNMO(L) narratives in this series are in DHH 87/48; Brown, *Tirpitz*, 37; Dönitz, *Memoirs*, 299, 310-11

7.   Adm, "Home Fleet," para 6-7

USN air establishments and ships. That the acquisition of an escort carrier would further NSHQ's drive to procure larger fleet units made the relative advantages of the scheme obvious to sailors on both sides of the Atlantic. As early as August, 1943, an Admiralty staff officer had noted: "Lay intends to recommend such a development [Fleet Air Arm] as no modern navy, however small, can operate without an air element. He considers that a start should be made now, *while political opportunity offers*, if Canada is to achieve a balanced fleet after the war." And, in November, the Acting Director of Plans at NSHQ argued that "the acquisition of such ships [cruisers and aircraft carriers] before the end of the war would offer the RCN an opportunity to win battle honours with them, and so greatly enhance the chances of their acceptance by public opinion as part of the post-war Canadian Navy."[8]

In the event, the Cabinet War Committee in Ottawa had approved the manning of cruisers and landing craft with RCN personnel. In May 1943 Macdonald had already won some key members of the committee over to the idea of a naval air branch, but although the prime minister influenced the Cabinet not to reject that proposal out of hand, in September they still reserved judgment on the manning of escort carriers. Mackenzie King wanted to "see the Navy have this particular [naval air] arm ... [but] they would have to get it at the expense of something else." Manpower and finances could not be ignored. "It was essential," the prime minister explained at the 21 October meeting, "that the Service understand the necessity of avoiding commitments additional to such as were already included in their approved programmes. If new undertakings, such as the present one, involving additional outlays were regarded as imperative, then corresponding reductions must be made in other directions."[9]

The Naval Board and the minister nevertheless continued to pursue the idea of a Canadian naval air service. On 10 November, in accordance with the Cabinet War Committee's request for precise financial and manpower requirements, they requested $39 million to acquire carriers, emphasising their importance to the postwar navy. That reflected the work of the Postwar Planning Committee convened in July 1943 and had perfectly legitimate political as well as strategic under-pinnings, but it was a tactical error. The prime minister scolded Macdonald: the time had come, he pointed out, for reductions to service programs, and only expenses essential to the prosecution of the war were to be brought to Cabinet. Once again the Cabinet War Committee deferred the question for later consideration.[10]

Compromise was in order, and Nelles did not have to go far to find one. He had received, only a few days before, an appeal from the new First Sea Lord, Admiral of the Fleet Sir Andrew Cunningham, for further RCN assistance in solving an even more serious manpower problem than had faced the RN in August 1943. In the absence of sufficient fleet and light fleet aircraft carriers, American-built escort carriers were now "the core of the fleet," and the delay in getting such vessels operational had placed the British carrier program at risk, since the United States was

---

8.   Min by H of M Branch, Adm, 24 Aug 1943 (emphasis in original), PRO, ADM 1 17498; Plans Division, "Appreciation of RCN Ship Requirements for the War against Japan and for the Postwar Navy," 29 July 1943, LAC, RG 24, 3844, NSS 1017-10-34, pt 1

9.   CWC min, 21 Oct 1943, LAC, MG 26, J4, 425

10. Planning paper, 29 July 1943, and "Canada's Post-War Navy," 17 Nov 1943, LAC, RG 24, 3844, NS 1017-10-34; "Canadian Naval War Plan, 1944," 30 Nov 1943, ibid, 3845, NS 1017-10-56; CWC min, 10 Nov 1943

threatening to hold back further supplies under the lend-lease arrangement.[11] Officers at the Admiralty had already tried to discourage the Canadians from trying to create their own Fleet Air Arm, but without Canadian help it would be impossible to find enough personnel to commission the American-built escort carriers now being modified in Vancouver.[12] Cunningham thought Canada could help if the RCN drafted men to bring British ships' companies up to strength, providing engine room artificers for all seven escort carriers, and as many men as possible to combine with RN ratings in other ships being constructed in the United States. Nelles did not take the bait. He replied that "RCN policy is definitely to maintain its own ships company identity," although possibly a "policy of infiltration with the intention of completing the whole RCN crew in time is acceptable." His solution was to provide the ships' companies for two RN escort carriers, and "release RN personnel to man other essential craft." That would surely qualify in the prime minister's eyes as essential to the prosecution of the war. Nelles sent the Assistant Chief of Naval Staff, Captain W.B. Creery, to England, who persuaded the Admiralty to accept the Canadian conditions. "We understand RCN may be able to provide ships company of one CVE now" the Admiralty signalled on 23 November, "and one in six weeks time excluding flying and maintenance personnel."[13]

Cabinet approval still had to be obtained. To that end, Admiral Sir Percy Noble, head of the British Admiralty Delegation in Washington, came up to Ottawa in November in an attempt to impress the prime minister and others with the importance of RCN assistance in manning escort carriers. By accident or design he let it slip to the press that it was the Canadians, not the British, who during the Quadrant meetings had initiated the proposal to man cruisers. What he told King in private conversation, moreover, was "very different from what the Navy Department proposed." The pieces fell into place as the prime minister listened to the British admiral's easy and well-informed chat about the RCN's plans for a "big ship" postwar navy, as exemplified by the cruiser program. This confirmed King in the belief that the naval staff had been manipulating the Cabinet. "I do not think the war ministers have played the game with the rest of the Cabinet in the way they have forced the pace for their services," he noted in his diary. "Certainly none have had consideration for the taxpayer."[14]

If Noble had been trying to make the case for the Admiralty solution, in which the RCN would simply help man Captain class frigates and provide engine room artificers rather than the bulk of the ships' companies for the carriers, he could hardly have done it more effectively. Macdonald put forward the suggestion on 16 December that the RCN obtain two escort carriers on loan from the United States, but he failed to distinguish between this and the original proposal to purchase such

---

11. ACNS (W) to First Sea Lord, 13 Nov 1942, and DFSL to First Sea Lord, 18 Nov 1942, PRO, ADM 205/14. BAD to Adm, 25 and 27 Aug 1943; ACNS (UT) to VCNS, 8 Sep 1943; VCNS to ACNS (UT), 10 Sep 1943; BAD to Adm, 11 Sep 1943. PRO, ADM 1/12857

12. The RN insisted on modifying the US-built CVEs even though congested British shipyards were slow in completing the work. Under pressure from Washington to have the carriers operational as soon as possible or see them reassigned to the USN, the Admiralty appealed to the RCN, and Ottawa agreed to have some of the CVEs modified at Vancouver by the Burrard Drydock and Shipbuilding Co. Ltd. The first carrier to be converted—at Canadian expense—by Burrards was the HMS *Khedive* in August 1943. It was followed in September by the *Nabob*. K. Poolman, *Escort Carriers, 1941-1945* (London 1972), 88-9

13. Adm to NSHQ, 6 Nov 1943, PRO, ADM 116/4915; CNS to Adm, 11 Nov 1943, PRO, ADM 205/31; Nelles to minister, 13 Nov 1943, LAC, RG 24, 11759, 1700-913; Adm to NSHQ, 30 Nov 1943, PRO, ADM 1/16045

14. King diary, 27 Nov 1943, LAC, MG 26, J13

vessels for a Canadian naval air branch. The prime minister, who had gained an admission from Nelles on 21 October that the aviation scheme was really for a postwar navy, accused Macdonald of demanding a commitment "which related directly to the postwar period and future naval policy." Moreover, as Norman Robertson, Under-Secretary of State for External Affairs, pointed out, Canada did not accept lend-lease material. The prime minister, favourably disposed to the RCN's acquisition of carriers in May, seemed by December to have become unequivocally opposed. Because Macdonald had mentioned, however, that Captain Lay, who was the prime minister's nephew, would command *Nabob*, the first escort carrier in question, King pulled back, not feeling "I should be the one to decide the matter." That may have tipped the balance in Cabinet. Even though the Cabinet War Committee once again refused to decide on the question until further details were available, the navy's submission was not rejected.[15]

The Cabinet War Committee next considered the question on 5 January 1944. NSHQ and an increasingly impatient Admiralty had in the meantime gone ahead with preparations for *Nabob*'s commissioning. It was confirmed a month earlier that the two carriers under consideration, *Nabob* and *Puncher*, could not be made available to the RCN on loan, but would have to be commissioned as British ships. Making himself a hostage to fortune Nelles, before receiving Cabinet approval, had gone ahead with the necessary measures to draft officers and men to *Nabob*. On 8 December he so informed Captain Lay, then standing by the ship in Vancouver, and by the end of the month 504 RCN personnel had joined the ship, along with 327 RN and Royal New Zealand Navy officers and men. *Nabob* began work-ups early in January, at about the same time that the Cabinet War Committee, with the prime minister abstaining, voted by the narrowest of margins to give approval in principle to the manning of two RN carriers. Nelles, had shown a rather cavalier disregard for parliamentary authority, but in his defence it must be observed that under the circumstances, with so much riding on the availability of escort carriers to the RN, he would have been open to serious criticism if he had delayed the completion of *Nabob*'s preparation for sea. The naval staff—by no means alone among the services in tending to bypass Cabinet—had, said King in his diary, "kept at the business until they achieved it by one method or another."[16]

Battle honours, it will be recalled, were what the planners hoped for in order to make carriers and cruisers acceptable in the eyes of the general public. For *Nabob*, this was a distant prospect. Administration of the ship suffered from an awkward mixture of Canadian, British, and New Zealand men on the lower deck, receiving differing rates of pay and, although under the same code of discipline—Dominion navies followed the RN's *King's Regulations and Admiralty Instructions*—and used to different types of messing arrangements. It was not long before trouble was brewing between British seamen and their higher paid Canadian shipmates. The Canadians themselves were disgruntled to find themselves in a British ship, putting up with less appetizing and smaller amounts of food than they were used to, when they had been led to expect the ship would be commissioned into the RCN. There was friction, as well, between anglophones and fran-

---

15. CWC Min, 16 Dec 1943.

16. VCNS to Adm, 8 Jan 1943, PRO, ADM 1/13989; NSHQ to Adm (R) *Nabob*, 8 Dec 1943; NSHQ to *Nabob*, 14 Dec 1943, PRO ADM 1/16045. "Brief History of HMS *Nabob*," nd, 5, DHH 81/520/8000, Nabob (hereafter DHH Nabob etc.); CWC min, 5 and 12 Jan 1944; King diary, 12 Jan 1944; "Canada's Post-War Navy," 17 Nov 1943. See also Greenhous, *The Crucible of War* III, 27-43.

cophones. It did not help that the ships' company lacked familiarity with carrier operations, and the competence of some officers was suspect. During trials, the ship ran aground in the Strait of Georgia, for which Lay earned the Admiralty's "severe displeasure" and the merciless attention of the national press, with references to "HMS Sandbob" and "HMS Canada Dry." The ship went through three executive officers before sailing on 7 February for San Francisco. By the time *Nabob* reached Norfolk, Virginia on 14 March there had been a minor refusal to work by some Canadian seamen, and large numbers of the ship's company had "jumped ship." Lay, who was not popular either in the wardroom or on the lower deck, warned NSHQ that conditions were ripe for a mutiny, flew to Ottawa to confront the Cabinet War Committee itself with the situation, and although unsuccessful in his bid to have the ship commissioned into the RCN, obtained agreement to pay the entire ship's company at Canadian rates and to provide Canadian messing arrangements. *Nabob* sailed on 23 March with a less than happy ship's company, but carrying the highest paid, best fed RN ratings afloat.[17]

After the ship arrived in Liverpool, like all RN escort carriers—to the exasperation of American naval opinion—she went into refit for modifications to make her suitable for fleet operations as well as antisubmarine warfare. In mid-June *Nabob* landed on the eleven Grumman Avenger torpedo-bombers and four Wildcat fighters of 852 Squadron before sailing for her work-ups. The logical use for a Canadian escort carrier, especially in view of the arguments put forward by Captains Lay and DeWolf in 1943, would have been with a Canadian antisubmarine support group in the North Atlantic, for which six frigates would be ready at the end of July, preferably under the operational control of C-in-C Canadian Northwest Atlantic. There might have been opportunities to emulate the sensational results achieved by USN escort carrier hunter-killer groups with the aid of Ultra—forty-one U-boats sunk in the past twelve months.[18] Lay had requested an antisubmarine role for *Nabob*, and C-in-C Western Approaches, Admiral Sir Max Horton, recommended it, but the Admiralty never had any intention of complying with the request: U-boat activity on the northern mid-ocean convoy routes was no longer great enough to justify carrier support groups. Instead, the RN desperately needed every available escort carrier for fleet operations to replace the larger fleet carriers that were slated for, or had already gone, to the Far East. The Admiralty suggested taking the proposed RCN group for support of Russian convoys, but, as noted in the the previous chapter, Ottawa declined. *Nabob* thus went to the Home Fleet and the Canadian support group of frigates went to the western Atlantic without a carrier.[19]

The Smiter class, to which *Nabob* belonged, was 492 feet in length and 69 feet in the beam, displaced 15,160 tons and had a top speed of eighteen knots. A high freeboard and single screw made these ships difficult to manoeuvre, especially in high winds. The class was well fitted with superior American radar and gunnery outfits, including SG (warning surface) and SK (warning air) search radars and two 5-inch mountings, eight twin 40mm Bofors, and a sizeable array of 20mm Oerlikons for anti-aircraft defence. *Nabob* could operate as many as twen-

17. Lay to CNP and minister, 15 Mar 1944, DHH Nabob; CWC min, 15 Mar 1944; "Report on RN-RCN Administration in HMS Nabob," 10 Apr 1944, PRO, ADM 1/16045; Adm to SNB, 31 Mar 1944, Nelles biog file, DHH; Lay, *Memoirs of a Mariner*, 157-9; B. Warrilow, *Nabob: The First Canadian-Manned Aircraft Carrier* (Owen Sound 1989), 11, 30-1

18. Y'Blood, *Hunter-Killer*, 282-3

19. Lay to FOCT, 19 June 1944, LAC, RG 24, 11733, CS159-2-1. NSHQ to Adm, 5 July 1944; Adm to NSHQ, 22 July 1944; NSHQ to Adm, 24 July 1944. PRO, ADM 1/16032

The launch of HMCS *Nootka* at Halifax, Nova Scotia May 1944. The second of the Tribal class destroyers to be launched in Canada, she was built by Halifax Shipyards Limited. (LAC PA206683)

The escort carrier HMS *Nabob* aground on a silt bank near the mouth of the Fraser River on 25 January 1944. Although the sand bank was located several miles west of where it was shown on naval charts, Captain H.N. Lay received "The severe displeasure of My Lords of the Admiralty" for driving his ship aground. (DND F2033)

ty aircraft, with two elevators or lifts providing good access to a hangar deck that extended the length of the vessel. Although the small 450 by 80 foot flight deck could make landing a difficult proposition and required great reliance to be placed on the single catapult for the take-offs, the ships could operate modern high-performance naval aircraft, and it does not appear that their accident rate was any higher than on British fleet carriers.[20] The inauspicious circumstances under which *Nabob* had been commissioned, and subsequent administrative problems, however, continued to create difficulties after her arrival in England. She was not, reported Vice-Admiral Nelles, now Senior Canadian Flag Officer Overseas, a happy ship, nor in the opinion of the Royal Navy's Flag Officer Carriers (Training), was she efficient. Experienced petty officers were in short supply, there had been a large turnover of officers, and an unacceptable number of crashes pointed to a poor flying organisation. This led to the replacement of the RN Commander (Air). Nevertheless, the ship completed workups and joined the Home Fleet at Scapa Flow on 1 August.[21]

Nabob arrived in time to participate in Operation Offspring, the first and largest of a series of mining sorties carried out by the Fleet Air Arm off Norway to resume the offensive against enemy coastal convoys.[22] Mining these waters led to the sinking of some ships and, just as importantly, forced traffic out from the shelter of the "Inner Leads" into the open sea, where it was exposed to attack from motor torpedo-boats, submarines, and the aircraft of Coastal Command's strike wings. Mining operations could also be launched at locations where there was only light opposition, whereas direct strikes against the normally heavily defended convoys would be perilous for the relatively slow Barracudas and Avengers that comprised the bulk of the Home Fleet's aerial strike force.[23]

The target for Operation Offspring was the Lepsoyev channel and Harhamsfjord, a section of the Leads north of Stadtlandet. The mission called for the escort carriers *Nabob* and *Trumpeter* to launch two strikes of twelve Grumman Avengers each, protected by Supermarine Seafires, Fairey Fireflies, and Grumman Hellcats from the fleet carrier *Indefatigable*. Seven destroyers, including *Algonquin* and *Sioux*, provided a surface screen while fighters from *Nabob* and *Trumpeter* flew cover over the naval force. Although the fly off was delayed three hours because of bad weather, the first strike achieved complete surprise. The fighters shot up an airfield and several flak positions while the Avengers successfully laid twenty-two of twenty-four mines. All aircraft returned safely to their carriers by 1430. The second strike encountered greater resistance—an Avenger from *Trumpeter* and a Firefly from *Indefatigable* were shot down—but all twenty-four mines were laid in their designated positions. This effectively closed Lepsoyev Channel and Harhamsfjord to ship-

20. N. Friedman, *British Carrier Aviation* (Annapolis 1988),181-8; D. Hobbs, *Royal Navy Escort Carriers* (Lodge Hill, UK 2003); J.D.F. Kealy and E.C. Russell, *A History of Canadian Naval Aviation, 1918-1962* (Ottawa 1965), 138; LCdr J.B. Goad interview, nd, Goad biog file, DHH

21. Nelles, "Report on Visit to HMS *Nabob*," 4 Apr 1944, Nelles biog file; Lay, ROP, 31 July 1944, LAC, RG 24, 11304, CS159-10-22; Lay, *Memoirs*, 148; Goad interview

22. An earlier minelaying mission, Operation Turbine from 2-4 Aug 1944, had to be cancelled due to poor flying conditions over the target. Adm, "Home Fleet," para 76

23. Ibid, para 75; "Enemy Naval Losses during Overlord Operations," 30 Apr 1945, PRO, ADM 223/50; Greenhous, *Crucible of War* III, 444-74

ping from 10 August to 27 September, caused two sinkings, and according to an Admiralty summary, "was an encouragement to continue with the mining policy."[24]

After months of frustration and controversy, it was an encouraging start for *Nabob*. Her maintenance crews kept the entire complement of thirteen Avengers and six Wildcats serviceable, and the aircraft handling party successfully overcame the difficulties common to escort carriers. With low winds, heavy aircraft loads, and a ship that was only capable of eighteen knots, aircraft had to be launched by catapult, a time-consuming business. Recovering the full complement of aircraft was also a lengthy process; the limited space on the flight deck meant that the aircraft had to land in two waves, with the second wave circling the carrier while the first was struck below. It was up to the flight deck crews to complete their tasks quickly and without incident, and the ship's hangar officer reported with evident satisfaction that his men had worked with the precision of a well-drilled football team. *Nabob* returned to Scapa well prepared for the next operation, Goodwood.[25]

The fleet carriers *Indefatigable*, *Formidable* and *Furious*, supported by the battleship *Duke of York* (with Admiral Sir Henry Moore), two cruisers and thirteen destroyers, including *Sioux* and *Algonquin*, designated Force 1, formed the main attack group for the renewed assault on *Tirpitz*. Three squadrons of Fairey Barracuda aircraft from the fleet carriers were to carry out the bombing strike. At the same time, adopting a new tactic, the Avengers from Force 2—the escort carriers *Nabob* and *Trumpeter*, the cruiser *Kent* and five frigates of EG 5—were to mine the waters of Altenfjord. Fighter aircraft from the fleet carriers would attack flak positions and airfields, and provide cover in case of intervention from German fighters. Wildcats from *Nabob* and *Trumpeter* would fly combat air patrol over the fleet itself. The two forces left Scapa Flow on 18 August and reached the launch point, approximately two hundred miles northeast of Altenfjord, two days later.[26]

The operation did not go as planned. As so often happened in northern waters, weather played havoc with flying programs. On 21 August, when the first strike was supposed to cover the passage of convoy JW 59 past Bear Island, bad weather conditions forced a twenty-hour postponement. The next day low cloud over Altenfjord hampered visibility, making it impossible for the Barracudas and Avengers to coordinate their attacks, which in view of *Tirpitz*'s strong anti-aircraft defences was necessary to accurate mining. Mining operations thus did not take place and, with the exception of four Wildcats flying combat air patrol over the task force, none of *Nabob*'s aircraft left the deck, a development that was, in the captain's view, a bitter blow for the ship's company. The fleet carriers launched a strike, but the Barracudas and Corsairs involved were turned back by persistent low cloud, leaving the Fireflies, Hellcats, and Seafires to continue on and make diversionary attacks. They inflicted no damage on *Tirpitz*, although several other vessels were damaged, including *U 965* at Hammerfest, and two seaplanes destroyed. Late on 22 August, Admiral

---

24. Adm,"Home Fleet," para 75; UK, MoD, *British Mining Operations* I (London 1973), 438-9, 458; Nabob, ROP, 11 Aug 1944, LAC, RG 24, 11752, CS369-2; CNMO(L) narrative, "Operation Offspring," nd, 1-2

25. *Nabob* ROP, 11 Aug 1944, LAC, RG 24, 11752, CS369-2; *Nabob* ROP, 2 Sep 1944, ibid, 11304, CS159-10-22; Goad interview

26. *Nabob*, ROP, 27 Aug 1944, PRO, ADM 1/18122; Operation Orders, Operation Goodwood, nd, DHH 81/520/1650-239/14, Operations in NW European Waters; CNMO(L) narrative,"Operation Goodwood," nd

Moore withdrew Force 1, including *Sioux* and *Algonquin*, to the west to cover the passage of JW 59. He intended to launch further strikes against the German battleship on the 24th.[27]

At the end of this unsatisfactory day, just after 1500 on 22 August, *Nabob* recovered her Wildcats and withdrew to the west so that, starting at 1800, she could refuel her destroyer screen. In company with *Kent* and *Trumpeter*, she steered a zigzag pattern, screened by the frigates of EG 5, commanded by Captain D. Macintyre while *Nabob*'s Avengers flew antisubmarine patrols. "There had been no sign of enemy reaction," wrote Macintyre years later. "Our squadron set off with my group disposed ahead and abeam of them as a screen. The sea was calm, a leaden, sullen, quietly heaving mass under a grey sky. Test on surface targets with our asdic sets had been giving results which showed that conditions would be bad for detecting submarines." Remarking that he could not understand the absence of U-boat activity, MacIntyre settled into the wardroom for a game of bridge.[28]

In fact, nine U-boats of group *Trutz* were in the area attempting to intercept JW 59. These boats had sighted carrier aircraft, and on receiving their reports, forwarded by the *Führer der U-boote*, (*FdU*) Norway, the commander of *Marinegruppenkommando Nord* noted that in view of the heavy carrier aircraft activity and the high speed of the convoy, ten knots, it was unlikely the boats would be able to reach their attack positions. However, *U 354*, a veteran of arctic operations under the command of Oberleutnant H.J. Sthamer, had sailed from Narvik the day before to join the group, and late on the afternoon of 22 August intercepted Force 2. His sighting report went undetected at the time, either by German shore authorities or by the HF/DF operators in the force, and aided by the poor asdic conditions he penetrated the screen with ease. At 1716, he fired a FAT pattern-running torpedo that struck *Nabob* on the starboard side. Immediately all electrical power failed, the ventilation fans in the engine room and all auxiliary machinery stopped, and with the increase of temperature in the engine room to about 150°, the main engines were stopped as well. The ship settled rapidly by the stern, and gave every sign of sinking quickly. Lay gave the order to prepare for abandoning ship.

In fact, *Nabob* survived, saved by a strong engine room bulkhead, an additional 1200 to 2000 additional tons of ballast that gave the ship enough stability to survive major hull damage without capsizing, an extra supply of timbers, and above all, the crew's determined efforts at damage control. Lay later reported

> At about 1850, it was reported that the engine room bulkhead was holding and that the engines, shaft and propeller, were apparently undamaged. A diesel generator was running and power was available at the diesel switchboard. This board was quickly cross-connected to the main switchboard to the engine room, so that ventilation fans and auxiliaries could be started. By 1900, the flooding was under control and at 2000 the engine room commenced raising steam. At 2139, the engines were put slow ahead and it was confirmed that the shaft, propellor, and rudder were not seriously damaged.[29]

---

27. *Nabob* ROP, 27 Aug 1944; CNMO(L) narrative,"Operation Goodwood"

28. D. Macintyre, *U-Boat Killer* (Annapolis 1976), 164-5

29. *Nabob* ROP, 27 Aug 1944, 2-3

While engineering and electrical crews restored power, shipwrights began the continual process of shoring bulkheads and decks in the after part of the ship; a task facilitated by the extra supply of timber. At 2214, although well down by the stern, she was under way again.

In the meantime Sthamer in *U 354*, having fired a *zaunkönig* torpedo eight minutes after his first attack, heard two explosions, assumed the carrier was sunk, and would confirm this apparent success later that night when he surfaced to inspect the scene. Sthamer was mistaken. All he could see then was a large oil slick, a lot of flotsam, and a sea of empty yellow carley floats that had been launched when Captain Lay ordered his men to prepare for abandoning ship. In fact, his *zaunkönig* had missed the carrier and blown the stern off the frigate HMS *Bickerton*, as Macintyre was closing *Nabob* to provide what help he could. The frigate remained afloat, but HMS *Vigilant* received orders from Admiral Moore to sink her, just as *Nabob* was getting under way. If the carrier had been unable to steam, she was to have met the same fate.[30]

Nabob faced a long, perilous passage back to Scapa Flow. Even though the shored up bulkheads were likely to hold, *Nabob* remained a large and easy target for a U-boat. The ship had suffered surprisingly few casualties—twenty-one killed (eleven Canadian and ten RN ratings) and forty wounded—but Lay was concerned for the safety of the remaining ship's company. Within hours of the torpedoing he had transferred 214 men to the frigate HMS *Kempthorne*, and on the night of 23 August he shifted another 202 to *Algonquin*, which had returned from escorting *Trumpeter* and *Kent* away from the danger area. *Nabob*'s remaining sailors were kept busy. HF/DF bearings obtained by the carrier and her escorts indicated that they were being shadowed by a U-boat—it was *U 354* attempting to finish off the stricken warship. Despite the slope of the deck—the vessel was trimmed some forty-two feet forward and fifteen feet aft—and uncertainty as to whether the catapult would work, two Avengers were flown off in an impressive piece of flying. Although they were unable to spot the U-boat, their ASV radar transmissions succeeded in keeping it down long enough for *Nabob* to escape. Lay surmised that a final HF/DF bearing received the next morning was the U-boat signalling that it had lost contact. Landing for the Avengers was an extraordinary and extremely tense business. Despite the severely sloping flight deck and zero visibility the first Avenger managed to land successfully. The second failed to catch an arrester wire and crashed through the barrier. The pilot had neglected to set his guns to safe and a few anxious moments ensued as the Avenger's machine-guns sprayed the deck and the flight crews struggled to corral two loose depth-charges that could have sunk the ship had they rolled overboard. Fortunately, all was eventually secured without injury. On 27 August, after a five-day, 1093 mile voyage, in constantly changing weather, *Nabob* entered Scapa Flow.[31]

The senior officer of Force 2, Rear-Admiral R.R. McGrigor, placed on record a tribute to the outstanding seamanship and effective damage control that resulted in *Nabob* arriving safely in Scapa. Vice-Admiral Nelles was similarly impressed, and he tried to bring the feat to public attention by having the Admiralty waive their policy of withholding information about damaged warships. The Admiralty, not surprisingly in view of the security implications, refused.[32] Ironically for Lay, there-

---

30. Adm to C-in-C Home Fleet, 23 Aug 1944, PRO, ADM 223/203; German NS, OpsD WD, 22 Aug 1944, DHH SGR/II/261; *Nabob* ROP, 27 Aug 1944; Blair, *Hitler's U-Boat War* II, 599; Warrilow, *Nabob*, 99

31. Rohwer and Hummelchen, *Chronology of the War at Sea*, II, 445; *Nabob* ROP 27 Aug 1944, App. IV; Warrilow, *Nabob*, 101-2

32. McGrigor to Moore, 16 Sep 1944, LAC, RG 24, 11751, CS159-10-2; VCNS (RN) to Nelles, 6 Oct 1944, ibid, 11733, CS159-10-1

fore, his worst moment, the grounding off Esquimalt, received national attention while his finest, bringing *Nabob* back to Scapa Flow, went publicly unrecognized for months. Moreover, *Nabob*'s return marked the end of her operational career. In early September she sailed to Rosyth, where divers discovered that the torpedo had blasted a hole fifty feet by thirty feet and, as would happen with another escort carrier, HMS *Thane*, torpedoed in January 1945, it was decided to cannibalize her for parts. The repairs would have involved extensive work in already congested British ship-yards, and more American-made escort carriers were coming into service. So the RCN's initial foray into naval aviation came to an abrupt and disappointing end. RCN personnel were granted twenty-eight days' survivors leave in Canada and the last Canadians left the ship when she was paid off on 30 September. *Nabob*'s sailors, after overcoming so much adversity, deserved better.[33]

In the meantime, bad weather continued to plague Home Fleet operations. On 24 August, two days after *Nabob* was torpedoed, another Goodwood strike by fifty-two Hellcats and thirty-three Barracudas met a fate similar to the first. Releasing bombs blindly through the smoke screen, one Hellcat scored a hit on the roof of *Tirpitz*'s B turret with a 500 lb semi-armour piercing bomb, destroying the quadruple 20mm anti-aircraft mount but only denting the 5.1-inch armour plate. One of the Barracudas managed to hit the battleship a few feet to port of the bridge with its 1600 lb bomb. After penetrating five decks before coming to rest in a switchboard room on the platform deck—where the potential for causing considerable structural damage was great—it failed to explode. In dismantling the bomb the Germans not only discovered that the fuse had malfunctioned but also that the bomb itself was less than half filled with explosive. A final strike launched on 29 August achieved even less. Although he had lost only eight strike aircraft in 168 sorties, the failure to inflict any serious damage despite the expenditure of fifty-two tons of bombs persuaded Admiral Moore to abandon Goodwood. *Algonquin* escorted *Indefatigable* back to Scapa, and *Sioux* and five other destroyers screened *Duke of York* and *Formidable* as they covered convoy RA 59A. That convoy was undisturbed by German air or surface forces, and the escort destroyed three U-boats, including *U 354*. By 1 September, both Canadian destroyers were anchored at Scapa Flow.[34]

Goodwood's cancellation marked the end of the Home Fleet's attacks on *Tirpitz*. Since carrier-borne aircraft lacked the necessary punch to sink or cripple the battleship, Moore made the novel suggestion that RAF Mosquito fighter-bombers fly off a fleet carrier, attack *Tirpitz* and then land in bases in Russia.[35] Although apparently accepted in principle the idea fell through, and Lancaster heavy bombers modified to carry the 12,000 lb "Tallboy" bomb, took up the task. Unable to reach *Tirpitz* from northern Scotland, thirty-eight Lancasters of Nos 617 and 9 Squadrons flew to a Russian air base near Archangel on 11 September, and four days later twenty-eight of these aircraft carried out the attack. Although the smoke-screen once again made accurate bombing difficult—bombs landed up to a mile from the ship—one "Tallboy" passed through the *Tirpitz*'s starboard bow before detonating, blowing a hole forty-eight feet long and thirty-two feet high and destroying most of the bow section. Totally unseaworthy, the battleship moved to a shallow berth

---

33. *Nabob* ROP, 14 and 30 Sep 1944, ibid, CS159-10-22; Friedman, *British Carrier Aviation*, 187

34. Adm, Historical Section, *The Development of British Naval Aviation, 1919-1945* II (London 1954), 307; Adm, Director of Naval Construction, *Tirpitz: An Account of the Various Attacks Carried Out by the British Armed Forces and Their Effect upon the German Battleship* I (London 1948), 9-10, 20; Hinsley, *British Intelligence* III, pt 1, 277; Brown, *Tirpitz*, 38-9; *Sioux* ROP, 9 Sep 1944, DDE-225; *Algonquin* ROP, 1 Sep 1944, DDE-224, pt 1

35. Adm, "Home Fleet," para 11

in the Tromso area for use as a static anti-aircraft platform. This put her within range of bombers operating from northern Scotland, and on 12 November thirty-one Lancasters from the same squadrons inflicted at least two direct hits and several near-misses on the beleaguered ship. She capsized.[36]

The destruction of *Tirpitz* removed a large thorn from the side of the Home Fleet. Not only had that fleet been forced to provide heavy cover for Russian convoys but it had undertaken six major carrier strikes against the powerful battleship as well as a bold midget submarine attack that had *Tirpitz* as the objective. Now the only capital ships left to the *Kriegsmarine* were the pocket battleships *Scheer* and *Lützow*, but they were deployed in the Baltic in support of ground forces, and unlikely to attempt a break out. Three serviceable Narvik type destroyers remained in Northern Norway but they were ordered to the Baltic in January 1945. German service strength in Norway therefore fell to its weakest point since the invasion in 1940, and there was no "immediate" surface threat to the Russian convoys.[37] With the "fleet in being" gone, more resources could be devoted to carrier strikes and surface attacks against enemy shipping off Norway, as well as minelaying operations.

Convoys nevertheless remained the principal responsibility of the Home Fleet, and as the men in Canadian Tribals had found in 1943, it was particularly exhausting service. Scapa Flow, moreover, was a dismal haven. Lieutenant-Commander Piers recalls that the remote, storm-tossed anchorage was "very bleak, a rather forbidding place, [with] practically no facilities. It was a rough, tough life. The wind was always blowing like hell."[38] When *Algonquin* and *Sioux* were not at sea they were usually lying in the destroyer anchorage at Gutta Sound or berthed alongside the depot ship HMS *Tyne*. This left them exposed to the climate, and not only allowed the men little opportunity for relaxation but also made it difficult to conduct anything more than routine maintenance. Even in summer, the results were plain to see. Captain Macintyre, arriving in August 1944 with the 5th Escort Group, fresh from operations in the Western Approaches, cast his jaundiced eye on the Home Fleet destroyers, much as he had done on an earlier occasion with Canadian escorts on the mid-ocean run:

> On arrival at Scapa we steamed through the lines of the Home Fleet destroyers swinging at their buoys in Gutta Sound and I was horrified at the state of dirt and dishevelment they displayed. Their sea-time was probably less than that of most Western Approaches ships and there seemed no excuse for this appalling condition. I can only suppose that lack of action and the general dreariness of their employment when at sea, and of their surroundings when in harbour, had led to a general lowering of tone.[39]

---

36. C. Webster and N. Frankland, *The Strategic Air Offensive against Germany*, vol III, *Victory* (London 1961), 191-6; Adm, *Tirpitz* I, 10-11, 23-4

37. Barnett, *Engage the Enemy More Closely*, 747; Whitley, *German Destroyers of World War II*, 172

38. Piers interview, 14 Sep 1992, 183, Piers biog file

39. Macintyre, *U-Boat Killer*, 163-4. Macintyre's criticisms of the RCN escort force in his memory were especially stinging but he appears to have been a particularly "pusser" officer. When he moved to the frigate *Aylmer* after *Bickerton* had been torpedoed, he immediately ordered the bridge crew to their cabins to shave and to change into proper uniform even though the U-boat was still undetected in the area. He also seemed to have something against the RCN. Known to be gruff and short tempered, he apparently mellowed after the war, but a colleague noted that two subjects were still guaranteed to set him off: the RCN and Coastal Command. A.L. Hammond, "Six Months at Sea with a U-Boat Killer," *Warship World*, 7/3 (2001), 22-4

Macintyre's comments would have raised the eyebrows of destroyer crews in the Home Fleet. The ships may have seemed to do little credit to their first lieutenants, and the men who served in them may have had a great deal to "gripe" about, but in no way could this be attributed to any lack of action. The Home Fleet carried out fifty-six operations against the enemy in the eleven months from June 1944 to May 1945, the period under consideration in this section, and Home Fleet destroyers participated in all except MTB raids against the Norwegian coast.[40] Moreover, Scapa Flow was the main work-up base for major warships heading out to the Eastern Fleet, while Home Fleet battleships, aircraft carriers and cruisers routinely carried out training evolutions in the Orkney practice areas. The onset of the inshore U-boat offensive in northern UK waters meant that "full A/S precautions" had to be taken for all training, which usually meant cover from destroyers.[41] With just four flotillas for the C-in-C Home Fleet to draw from, the demands on destroyers were extraordinary; the historical narrative based upon Admiral Moore's dispatches to the Admiralty is full of references to how the chronic shortage of destroyers hampered operations. As a result destroyers logged a lot of sea time, and with only a destroyer tender providing maintenance support, like soldiers who have been in the line too long, the ships were bound to appear haggard and run down.

Until the end of the war Home Fleet destroyers wracked up most of their sea time on the arctic convoys. Beginning in the summer of 1944, and especially after *Tirpitz* was removed from the equation, these convoys—which were really fleet operations—embodied some important new concepts. JW 59, which had set out in mid-August to coincide with Operation Goodwood, sailed with thirty-three merchant ships, one rescue ship, and eleven Soviet submarine chasers, screened by a cruiser, two escort carriers and eighteen other escort vessels. For the first time the escort commander flew his flag in an escort carrier, which enabled him to have a clearer understanding of both the air and surface tactical pictures than was possible from a cruiser. Privy to Ultra, he had available the latest naval decrypts, which provided current and comprehensive intelligence about the composition and movements of U-boat patrol lines. Perhaps most importantly, although safe and timely arrival of the convoys remained the primary objective, the destruction of U-boats became an important "subsidiary objective."[42] With such large escort forces the commander had no hesitation in sending screening vessels ahead to attack U-boats in their known waiting positions, while aircraft from the carriers kept the U-boats down ahead of the convoy.[43] In JW 59 carrier aircraft made some fourteen attacks at distances between fifty and seventy-five miles from the convoy resulting in two kills, including *U 354*, although on 21 August *U 344* sank the frigate HMS *Kite*.[44]

JW 59's merchant ships escaped losses because of the speed of the convoy, the strong escort, and evasive routing. Similarly, JW 60, thirty merchant vessels escorted by a battleship, a cruiser, two escort carriers, and fourteen destroyers and frigates, including *Algonquin* and *Sioux*, managed

---

40. Adm,"Home Fleet," para 123

41. Ibid, para 246-248

42. Ibid, para 39-40

43. Ibid; "Government Code and Cypher School Naval History: The Naval War 1939 to 1945," XVII, 152, DHH 2000/5; Hinsley, *British Intelligence* III, pt 2, 490-1; Adm, Historical Section, *Arctic Convoys, 1941-1945* (London 1954), 117-19; Andrew D. Lambert, "Seizing the Initiative: The Arctic Convoys, 1944-45," in N.A.M. Rodger (ed), *Naval Power in the Twentieth Century* (London 1996), 151-62

44. B. Ruegg and A. Haig, *Convoys to Russia, 1941-1945* (Kendal UK 1992), 66

The view across the listing *Nabob*'s flight deck as HMCS *Algonquin* approaches the stricken carrier to remove non-essential ratings. (DND HN-1472)

HMS *Nabob*, listing to starboard and settling by the stern, after being torpedoed by *U 354* on 22 August 1944. (DND HN-1502)

to avoid both *Luftwaffe* reconnaissance aircraft and a patrol line of seven U-boats. The convoy arrived on 23 September. By the time convoy RA 60 sailed from Murmansk nineteen U-boats were on station, but of these only one, *U 310*, made contact, simply by being overrun. The submarine managed to sink the merchant ships *Samsuva* and *Edward H. Crockett* on 29 September. Over the next two days, aircraft and escorts were occupied carrying out offensive sweeps. *Algonquin* was sent to locate two U-boats forced down by aircraft on the 30th, but was unable to gain asdic contact in the difficult arctic water conditions. Later that afternoon, the destroyer did obtain "a clear but doubtful echo" astern of the convoy on which it dropped a ten charge pattern, "but contact could not be regained and the hunt was abandoned." Thanks to poor asdic conditions, and an apparent lack of aggressiveness by the U-boats, the offensive policy adopted in these convoys, although effective in defending the merchant ships, had the disappointing result of destroying only one U-boat, *U 921*, sunk by a Fairey Swordfish from *Campania*.[45]

Another new feature of the Russian convoys was the addition of Western Approaches support groups, the most effective U-boat hunters in the European theatre. In the past, such groups had occasionally been used to reinforce the antisubmarine defences of the convoys; in the winter of 1944-45, however, they were deployed in an offensive capacity. The concept was first tried with JW-RA 61 when the Captain class frigates of EGs 15 and 21 as well as three escort carriers joined the escort, forming the most powerful antisubmarine force yet to accompany a Russian convoy.[46] It did not produce the expected results, however, because asdic conditions were poor on the northern route. No contacts were made on the outward passage, and as the convoy neared its objective, the two support groups were sent ahead to clear any U-boats that might be lurking off the entrance to Kola Inlet. The convoy arrived unscathed, but even though a number of U-boats were sighted, the bad asdic conditions prevented the support groups from hunting them to destruction. The same situation developed on the return passage when eighteen U-boats were positioned off the entrance to attack the departing convoy. The support groups sent out in advance of the convoy gained a number of contacts but, again, achieved no kills. For their part, the U-boats were unable to penetrate the strong defensive screen to sink any merchant ships but did damage the frigate HMS *Mounsey* of EG 15.[47]

The RCN support group EG 9 was one of two Western Approaches groups lent to the Home Fleet for the next convoy; JW-RA 62. Upon learning of the assignment, the group's SO, Commander A.F.C. Layard, wrote a gruff "Ugh!!" in his diary.[48] EG 9's experience on the convoy validated that emotion, and also demonstrated some of the challenges associated with conducting fleet antisubmarine operations in a harsh northern environment. Although Layard had abundant experience in both fleet and convoy operations, he found the Russian convoys to be vastly different. They were faster than North Atlantic convoys, they operated in almost perpetual darkness under strict radio silence (even the invaluable TBS could not be used), escort carriers operating aircraft from the cen-

---

45. *Algonquin* ROP, 1 Oct 1944, DDE-224, pt 1; *Algonquin* deck log, 14 Sep-1 Oct 1944, LAC, RG 24, 7016; Röhwer and Hummelchen, *Chronology* II, 452; Adm, *Arctic Convoys*, 118; Hinsley, *British Intelligence* III, pt 2, 491

46. Ruegg and Haig, *Convoys to Russia*, 67

47. Adm,"Home Fleet," paras 53-57; Ruegg and Haig, *Convoys to Russia*, 69. *Mounsey* was torpedoed by *U 295*.

48. Layard diary, 21 Nov 1944. See also Michael Whitby (ed), *Commanding Canadians: The Second World War Diaries of A.F.C. Layard* (Vancouver, 2005)

tre of the formation caused numerous speed and course changes, and the convoys were opposed by a more multi-dimensional threat. All of these differences called for different defensive schemes from those used in the North Atlantic. Special North Russian Convoy Instructions outlined how escort captains were to deal with these factors but there was still a lot to learn. Layard immediately discovered that station-keeping posed the greatest problem. During the darkness or poor visibility that accompanied much of the passage, support groups were usually stationed on either bow of the convoy about fifteen miles ahead of the forward destroyer screen. "I found that during the long nights," Layard complained in his diary, "it was far from easy to keep contact with an outer screen, which was itself, faced with the problem of keeping touch with the convoy, and consequently proved a very fluctuating point of contact. The problem became a real headache during alterations of course. Although a very careful plot was kept, there were many times when I was quite uncertain whether I was ahead or on the bow of the convoy."[49] Moreover, information of convoy alterations or speed changes often failed to reach outlying support groups raising the danger of collision or of losing contact.

After they passed Bear Island, EGs 9 and 20 were given some respite when they were ordered to leave the convoy and sweep ahead to Kola Inlet where they were to patrol until JW 62's arrival.[50] A day out from the convoy the groups lost their position—although they were steaming side-by-side, their separate dead reckoning positions placed them thirty-five miles apart—but they eventually reached the approaches to Kola Inlet to find themselves surrounded by a number of good HF/DF cuts from U-boats, none of which they could prosecute in the poor asdic conditions. At 0930 on 6 December they rejoined JW 62 to lead it into port, after which EG 9 was ordered to screen the White Sea section of the convoy out of the danger area. Darkness descended at 1300, and an hour later, as Layard's diary describes, the situation dissolved into confusion:

> From about 1400 life was hell. The convoy was zigging about, there were some false alarm Quizes [asdic contacts] and I had to manoeuvre my party about by light. The T.B.S. traffic from the Admiral was terrific [once contact was joined with the enemy radio silence was no longer required]. At 1630 we were detached with the White Sea portion, who were taken over by a group of Russian destroyers. By this time, in the pitch dark, I was really rather uncertain where we were. We were told no course or speed and no exact time for detaching. I hoped in time the situation would sort itself out and we'd gain radar contact with our 8 ships. At 1930, however, we got some good HF/DF bearings, fixing a U-boat 17 miles to the W. and turned to close. Nothing when we got there and so we turned back to what I hoped was an intercepting course for the White Sea party, but never got a sniff of them. A really v. cold S. wind off the land.
>
> Thursday, 7 December—At Sea
>
> A really bitterly cold day. Came the dawn and no sign of the White Sea portion. I'm pretty sure now they are ahead of us in which case we can't catch them. Turned round at 1430 so as to make our arrival at Kola Inlet by daylight [next day]. Had some dif-

---

49. SO EG 9, ROP, 19 Dec 1944, 1, DHH 81/520/8440, EG 9, v 2

50. Adm, *Monthly Anti-Submarine Report* (*MASR*), Dec 1944, 8

ficulty in spite of D/F fixes in figuring out our position but I'm confident now that convoy is safely past the furthest on position we were told to escort him to. At 1630 we all got HF/DF bearings of a U-boat, which I plotted 20 miles to the W. and so we turned and swept up to the position and went to action stations, but we never found a thing. Between then and 0200 we got 3 more U-boat signals all in a general W'ly direction in which we were heading anyhow, but not a thing sighted or detected. My sea cabin was bitterly cold. Temperature was never below 22° [Fahrenheit] but the strong S'ly wind cut like a knife. This is a truly ghastly part of the world at this time of year.[51]

The return passage promised to be even more challenging. Taking advantage of their *schnorkels*, twelve U-boats were positioned in the narrow approaches of Kola Inlet to attack the convoy when it was at its most vulnerable.[52] Due to a miscalculation of RA 62's departure time, however, the U-boats were temporarily withdrawn to the northeast to escape the expected antisubmarine cleansing operation that preceded sailings. The main body of the convoy was able to slip by before the U-boats could recover, and they managed only to damage the destroyer HMS *Cassandra*.[53] EG 9 picked up a number of HF/DF cuts but they were left astern as the convoy moved away from the Russian coast. Once RA 62 reached open sea, Layard again assumed position ahead of the convoy in line abreast search formation, but this time opened the distance between individual frigates from the normal 1.5 miles to 2.5 miles and allowed his COs to zigzag independently.[54] These moves eased station-keeping and lowered the risk of collision but also stretched asdic ranges in the difficult conditions and thus impaired the group's ability to detect submarines. That proved to be of no consequence, however, as the *schnorkeling* U-boats lacked the mobility to overtake the convoy from their static position off Kola Inlet.

A new threat now emerged. With no surface forces to attack the Russian convoys, Dönitz convinced Hitler to transfer *Luftwaffe* maritime strike forces to northern Norway from the Mediterranean. Ju 88s and JU 188s of KG 26 had proved particularly effective in the battles over PQ 17 and 18 in 1942, and in October 1944 some seventy of these high performance torpedo strike aircraft had arrived in the north.[55] On 12 December they launched their first attack against RA 62. Tipped off by shadowers and Ultra intelligence, Rear-Admiral McGrigor brought the distant escorts into the close anti-aircraft screen in preparation for the attack. Visibility was so poor that only *Saint John* and *Monnow* from EG 9 sighted the torpedo bombers, but the latter's Oerlikons knocked some chunks off one JU 88 that passed low at about 400 yards range. Two hours later *Monnow* sighted distress signals and rescued four German airman from a raft. Interrogation of the survivors made it clear that their aircraft had been knocked down by the frigate. The aircraft commander, who spoke halting English, described how he had lost contact with the rest of his force but had flown towards flak sighted on the horizon: "as he zoomed down through an opening below low-

51. Layard diary, 6-7 Dec 1944

52. The situation off Kola Inlet was not helped by the Soviet failure to take adequate countermeasures with surface and air forces. Adm, "Home Fleet," para 138

53. OIC, "U-Boat Situation Report, Week Ending 11 Dec 1944," in Syrett, *Battle of the Atlantic*, 502-3; Adm, *MASR* Dec 1944, 8-9

54. SO EG 9, ROP, 19 Dec 1944

55. Claasen, *Hitler's Northern War*, 244-7

lying clouds he came into direct range of MONNOW's guns. He added that he never saw the ship until flak started bursting in the plane."[56] *Monnow*'s JU 88 was one of two destroyed that day; RA 62 suffered no torpedo hits, and, despite horrible weather, and a number of HF/DF reports and aircraft sightings, the convoy made it home without any further incident.[57]

Although they suffered few merchant ship losses, the experience of JW-RA 62 and the other Russian convoys run in the fall and early winter of 1944 demonstrated that the "subsidiary object" of destroying submarines would be difficult to achieve. "At first glance," Admiral Moore reported to the Admiralty, "it would appear that these waters provide an ideal hunting ground for U-boats. Considerable experience amassed from a large number of convoys showed, however, that this was not the case. Weather, especially in winter, was not in general suitable for flying and Asdic conditions were so poor that several ships were torpedoed without the U-boat concerned ever being attacked." Despite pressure from the typically aggressive Admiral Horton in Western Approaches, who wanted to use the Russian convoys as a vehicle to destroy U-boats and increase the Allies' initiative in the antisubmarine war, Moore, at least for the time being, held to a more defensive philosophy, using support groups and antisubmarine aircraft from escort carriers to keep U-boats down while the convoy skirted around them.[58]

While EG 9 escaped south to return to inshore operations, *Sioux* and *Algonquin* continued to operate from desolate Scapa Flow. When not escorting convoys the Canadian destroyers screened carriers during anti-shipping and minelaying sorties off Norway. For the first few months, this involved only one report of unidentified vessels, when *Algonquin* was assigned as the air-sea rescue ship during Operation Begonia in September. As she steamed to take up her position twenty miles nearer the coast than the carriers, she sighted two large merchant ships. These turned out to be the Swedish passenger liner *Drottingholm* and the British *Arundel Castle*, both carrying repatriated prisoners of war back to the United Kingdom.[59]

For some time Admiral Moore had considered using cruiser and destroyer groups to attack enemy shipping along the coast of Norway but had been hamstrung by a shortage of destroyers.[60] Finally, in November 1944 he had the necessary resources to launch such a sweep. Operation Counterblast was to be carried out at night by a task force under the command of Rear-Admiral R.R. McGrigor, RN. The cruisers *Kent* and *Bellona*—the latter having the advantage of training and operations with Plymouth Command's 10th Destroyer Flotilla—the destroyers *Myngs*, *Verulum*, *Zambesi*, and *Algonquin*, left Scapa Flow at 2100 on 11 November and arrived off Utsire Light, on the Norwegian coast between Stavenger and Egersund, after darkness on 12 November. The area selected for the sweep, based upon good intelligence of the composition and scheduling of German coastal convoys in this area, was at the southern exit of the Inner Leads passage where shipping

56. CNMO, "Murmansk Convoy," 23 Apr 1945, Monnow; SO EG 9, ROP, 19 Dec 1944

57. Adm,"Home Fleet," para 138; Layard diary, 13-15 Dec 1944

58. Adm, "Home Fleet," para 71-7; Lambert, "Seizing the Initiative"

59. *Algonquin*, ROP, 1 Oct 1944

60. Adm, "Home Fleet," para 97

had to round the southwestern tip of Norway on the open sea without the benefit of either offshore islands to screen their movements or fjords in which to take refuge.[61] McGrigor's plan called for an attack in line ahead with the two cruisers leading and the four destroyers following astern. *Algonquin* was the fourth ship, and second destroyer, in the formation. The admiral stressed that "the objective must at first be to cripple as many enemy ships as possible so as to prevent them escaping, finishing them off at a later stage."[62]

After manoeuvring to avoid contacts located off the approaches to Stavanger, the warships proceeded southeast about ten miles off the coast. They navigated by radar, but also found that the Norwegian lighthouses were "burning for short periods in what appeared regular intervals with maximum brilliancy" in order to guide the coastal convoys that moved at night so as to avoid Coastal Command's strike wings.[63] At 2150 three small contacts appeared close inshore. McGrigor "decided to neglect these, as they did not seem to be a worthwhile target at this stage, and I hoped for bigger game further south." His patience was rewarded five minutes later when *Kent* "obtained a number of radar contacts indicating a northward bound convoy. There appeared to be three or four lines of ships, the furthest and largest group being some 5 miles on the quarter of the nearest line and only about 2 miles off-shore." The problem then facing McGrigor "was how to get at these inshore ships and prevent them from escaping. I decided to pass ahead of the nearer column at 25 knots before reducing speed and opening fire. I realised that the enemy would be sure to see *Kent*'s large silhouette broadside on and her big bow wave and wake, but I thought it more than probable that he would not recognise us as hostile. This old fashioned manoeuvre of crossing the T worked admirably."[64]

The task force achieved complete surprise, and was able to proceed across the face of the convoy unscathed before opening fire. In *Algonquin*, supported by excellent starshell illumination from *Bellona*, Piers engaged an escort vessel 5400 yards distant at 2315 hours, and obtained a hit with his first salvo. Concentrated fire from McGrigor's ships soon left the vessel in flames and *Algonquin* almost immediately shifted fire to a merchant ship at a range of 8000 yards. "Using No. 2 (B) gun for star-shell illumination and the remainder of the main armament firing SAP [semi-armour piercing], this second target was also reduced to flames by the first few salvos."[65] As the line of Allied warships blasted away, the merchant ships attempted to close the shore to come under the protection of coastal batteries. Two of their escorts "in the face of hopeless odds," headed for the three destroyers at the rear of the line. *Algonquin* experienced several near misses, but joined other ships in engaging an escort lying 3000 yards on the starboard beam.[66] This vessel, too, was soon a mass of flames. HMS *Verulum*, the destroyer directly astern of *Algonquin*, then pulled out of the line to

61.   Hinsley, *British Intelligence* III, pt 2, 494

62.   *Algonquin* ROP, 13 Nov 1944, DDE-224, pt 1; CS 1, ROP, 17 Nov 1944, PRO, ADM 199/530

63.   CS 1, ROP, 17 Nov 1944

64.   Ibid, 27 Nov 1944

65.   *Algonquin* ROP, 13 Nov 1944

66.   When action was joined McGrigor ordered his force to switch on their fighting lights. *Algonquin*'s navigator, Lt R.M. Steele, RCNVR, later learned that this caused confusion for German shore batteries as the red/green fighting lights on the Allied ships matched the current enemy emergency recognition colours causing the batteries to lift their fire. See Jenson, *Tin Hats, Oilskins and Seaboots*, 253

Officers of HMCS *Algonquin* in RCN-issued clothing for operations in northern waters, including rose-coloured goggles to accustom the eyes to darkness. The officers are, from left to right, Lieutenants V.M. Knight, W.H. Toller and P. Cock. (DND X-143)

Members of HMS *Puncher*'s flight deck party prepare a Grumman Wildcat fighter of 881 Squadron for take-off. (DND HN-2516)

A Fairey Barracuda torpedo-bomber of 821 Squadron takes off from *Puncher*'s flight deck. The carrier is at anchor and the Barracuda is utilizing a rocket-assisted take-off to get aloft. (DND HN-2048)

Rear-Admiral R.R. McGrigor, RN, inspects ratings during Sunday Divisions on *Puncher*'s flight deck. Directly behind the admiral is Lieutenant (E) G.H. Somers while the ship's commanding officer, Captain R.E.S. Bidwell follows to the right. (DND HN-2508)

carry out a torpedo attack against one of the merchantmen. She launched a full salvo of eight, one of which blew up the target while the remainder ran on until they exploded beneath a battery of 4.1-inch guns on shore.[67]

At the head of the line, *Kent* had run past the convoy and was only two miles from shore, prompting the cruiser to lead around to port "in order to re-engage the rear ships of the convoy and at the same time avoid masking the fire of our own ships astern."[68] Piers noted that as the line circled to port it came under the accurate fire of the shore batteries and "most of our ships were near-missed and straddled on several occasions, but no hits were obtained." By 2337 the line had almost come around full circle. *Algonquin* joined the other ships in firing on a merchant ship that soon blew up before engaging a patrol boat which burst into flames. With no other targets for *Kent* to engage, McGrigor withdrew the cruisers to the west and ordered in the destroyers to finish off the enemy. Piers in his report of proceedings noted that "only three enemy ships remained floating, one of which was aground and burning."

> At 0013 *Algonquin* opened fire on one merchant ship at an initial range of 4000 yards. *Myngs* was also engaging this target, which lasted about 2 minutes before becoming enveloped in flames. The sole remaining merchant ship was engaged at 0017. It took the concentrated fire of all four destroyers for almost five minutes before it finally caught ablaze. It was intended to fire a torpedo at this target, but just as the sights were coming on, the line of fire was fouled by adjacent ship restrictions. Shore batteries opened fire on the destroyers during this second phase of the action, but achieved nothing more than near misses. When the destruction of the enemy ships had been completed, the destroyers withdrew to join the cruisers at 0028.[69]

In all, the German convoy KS 357, of four merchantmen and six escorts, lost the freighters *Greif* of 996 tons and *Cornouailles* of 3324 tons, two minesweepers, and three submarine-chasers. Senior British and Canadian naval officers and the crews involved were understandably pleased with the results, particularly with opportunity to engage in offensive operations after being on the defensive for so long.[70]

It was, of course, a most unequal contest as minesweepers and submarine chasers had virtually no chance against cruisers and fleet destroyers. As Captain St John Cronyn of the Tactical and Staff Duties Division at the Admiralty observed, "had the German escort included some Elbing destroyers the whole operation would have assumed a very different aspect. The approach of the two forces bore some resemblance to the [Tunnel] operation in which *Charybdis* and *Limborne* [*sic*] were lost and a well-aimed zone [of torpedoes] across the British line of advance would have created an interesting situation."[71] But McGrigor knew through intelligence that no such vessels would be present, and his tactics were appropriate to the task and the enemy. From an RCN viewpoint, *Algonquin*'s performance was more than satisfactory. Piers reported with justifiable pride

---

67. Ibid; CS 1, ROP, 27 Nov 1944, and *Verulum* ROP, 15 Nov 1944, PRO, ADM 199/530

68. CS 1, ROP, 17 Nov 1944

69. *Algonquin* ROP, 13 Nov 1944

70. Hinsley, *British Intelligence* III, pt 2, 495; Röhwer and Hummelchen, *Chronology* II, 467-8; Capt D26, ROP, 16 Nov 1944; CS 1, ROP, 17 Nov 1944

71. Cronyn min, 31 Dec 1944, PRO, ADM 199/530

that the performance of both personnel and equipment was of a high standard. He was particularly pleased with his type 276 radar with PPI, which gave "a clear picture of the situation at all
times," and with the accuracy of the gunnery, which he credited to Lieutenant V.M. Knight, RCNVR.
The ship came out of this brief action with neither casualties nor serious damage, and morale was
sky-high; Lieutenant L.B. Jensen, *Algonquin*'s First Lieutenant, recalled "I don't think I have ever
seen a happier or more proud ship's company than we were when we returned home."[72]

The effects of Operation Counterblast added to the results already being achieved by motor tor-
pedo boats, carriers, submarines and Coastal Command's strike wings. During September and
October, for instance, ten ships had been sunk off Norway by submarines, nine by carriers, one by
MTBs, and eighteen by Coastal Command. In the last two months of 1944, MTBs accounted for six
vessels, carriers for six, the warships of Counterblast for seven, and the strike wings for sixteen.
The attacks, moreover, had the added effect of completely disrupting the German convoy schedule.
By year's end, the threat of attack on shipping was such that the Germans decided to reinforce their
fighter squadrons in Norway, despite the fact that fighters were also desperately needed over
Germany. At the same time they moved an ever-increasing portion of their northern-bound troops
and supplies overland through Oslo rather than by sea in order to reduce their exposure to attack.[73]
According to a postwar report, the German naval commander-in-chief in Norway, Admiral O. Ciliax,
believed that "of the measures Great Britain took ... in Norway the most effective were the air
attacks ... The enemy appears to have obtained news ... from agents and a very efficient communications system. The same applied to MTB attacks which, based on a good knowledge of local
conditions, were carried out with great bravery and skill. At one time the situation along the open
stretch of coastline between Kristiansand and Stavanger (after British surface vessels had succeeded in breaking through for the first time) was extremely critical."[74]

Ciliax, of course, could only guess at the extent to which the anti-shipping campaign was provided with valuable, if indirect, aid from Britain's extensive intelligence network. Photo-reconnaissance and espionage by the Secret Intelligence Service and Special Operations Executive provided
constant information about German defences and convoy routes. Even though signals intelligence
about shipping movements was often of dubious direct value in this region, owing to the great distances involved and unpredictable weather, analyses of decrypts over a period of several months
revealed German convoy policy, minefields and other defences, the methods of German convoy
routing, and reactions to various types of Allied attack.[75]

Despite the success of Counterblast, it was not until late December that Moore could scrape
together enough destroyers for a second offensive sweep. On the 22nd of that month a task force
under the command of Vice-Admiral F.H.G. Dalrymple-Hamilton, RN, consisting again of two cruisers and four destroyers, including *Sioux*, approached the coast for a sweep off Stadtlandet. Unlike
the earlier operation, however, Dalrymple-Hamilton's force was detected by German coastal radar

72. *Algonquin* ROP, 13 Nov 1944; Jenson, *Tin Hats*, 251

73. "Government Code and Cypher School," XVII, 168; Greenhous, *Crucible of War* III, 468-72; Hinsley, *British Intelligence* III,
     pt 2, 494; Röhwer and Hummelchen, *Chronology* II, 446, 465, 467-8, 473, 475; R.C. Nesbitt, *The Strike Wings: Special
     Anti-Shipping Squadrons, 1942-45* (London 1984), App. I

74. Quoted in Hinsley, *British Intelligence* III, pt 2, 495

75. Ibid

and no shipping was found. The warships had to satisfy themselves with firing off several hundred star-shells into the night sky in an attempt to disrupt convoy movements. An all-RN sweep several weeks later achieved far better results, badly damaging two freighters and sinking a minesweeper.[76]

An amusing incident following Counterblast reflects the way in which British and Canadian naval personnel retained their national prejudices while fighting side by side. "The Admiral aboard the cruiser *Kent* gave a little party at night, a dinner for the officers involved in this action," Lieutenant-Commander Piers recalled, "and it was a very pleasant affair":

> The Admiral was able to stand up and say what a fine lot we were and we were very pleased of course with our modest success. Following dinner, we had the usual wardroom shenanigans. The young officers vying with each other with various forms of games and sports, and swinging from the chandeliers, or deck head I should say. Jumping and leaping and having a good time all around, and this went on for awhile. I, as captain, had stayed rather aloof from the gymnastics that were going on although I enjoyed something like that. After this had been going on for about half an hour, it seemed that the senior officers were getting rather bored with it all and one of the ship's officers in the *Kent*, who was a Commander by rank, looked at me and at this time we did not have our Canada flashes on and had not been introduced, and I presume since I was standing aloof from all this, and dressed rather formally for an evening dinner and standing close to the Admiral, he came up and murmured over my shoulder, "I say, old boy, how are we going to get rid of these bloody Canadians?" Whereupon I looked at him and said, "I don't think we'll have any trouble sir, I'll just get my officers and we'll be off." It was one of those lovely moments when you can say almost anything you like, and our friend of course was duly embarrassed, and apologized.[77]

In some ways the incident probably says as much about "Debbie" Piers as it does the unfortunate British officer, but such tensions—based largely upon long standing stereotypes—are a constant of alliance warfare. And, of course, the opinions were not one-sided, as some RCN personnel were decidedly, and openly, anglophobic.

As a British career officer leading a Canadian support group operating for the most part under RN operational control from various bases in the United Kingdom, Commander Layard had an almost unique perspective from which to observe the British–Canadian relationship, and he described it fully in his diary. Layard first learned he would be operating with the RCN in the summer of 1943, and expressed no particular reaction to the news of his appointment, beyond being away from home. He soon got an inkling, however, that things might be difficult. When he paid a courtesy call at Western Approaches before heading to Canada, the Chief of Staff, Commodore A.S. Russell, RN greeted him with "What have you done to be sent out there?," which Layard observed,

---

76. *Sioux* ROP, 11 Jan 1945, DDE-225, pt 1; Adm, "Home Fleet," para 189-90, 196-8; Adm, *Development of British Naval Aviation*, 309; Rohwer and Hummelchen, *Chronology* II, 483-519

77. Piers interview, Piers biog file. See also McAndrew, Rawling, and Whitby, *Liberation: The Canadians in Northwest Europe*.

"seems to imply it is a God awful job."[78] The environment Layard found upon arriving in Halifax was in stark contrast to the stability he had grown used to in the RN. All seemed chaotic and disorganized by comparison, sentiments he expressed after going to see the film *Corvette K-225*, a Hollywood propaganda film about the wartime RCN.[79] "Very good," he wrote, "but to my mind it depicted something so entirely different from the RN as to be almost completely unrecognizable. But of course the RCN *is* very different."[80]

At Halifax, Layard initially took over the destroyer HMS *Salisbury* from Commander B.J. de St Croix, RN who he later described as the "great Canadian hater,"[81] and who had dubbed the RCN the "Royal Chaotic Navy."[82] Layard observed that "The attitude in this ship initiated by the Captain is intensely hostile to the RCN. I think it is deplorable and I shall do my best to alter it."[83] That he did, but he was never completely comfortable with Canadians. Consider comments from March 1945, after he had served eighteen months with RCN ships, when he was temporarily riding in the frigate HMCS *Loch Alvie*: "At about 1500 we shoved off [from Scapa Flow]. I've never been so ashamed of a ship's company. There were men in khaki trousers, in filthy duffel coats, sea boots, jerseys, mostly smoking and not one man in No 3s. The RCN [destroyer] *Iroquois* was on the other side of the oiler with every man in rig of the day. Thank God we were only seen by another RCN ship. I felt furious and also despairing because obviously apart from me there wasn't another officer who saw anything wrong with it."[84]

Although Layard complained about his Canadians to the end, he realized he had to adapt to them and altered his leadership style to do so. Normally a distant, hands-off captain, with the RCN he found he had to become more involved in the day-to-day running of his ships. Due to the inexperience of certain officers, and depending upon the effectiveness of individual vessels—he ultimately rode in five different RCN frigates—he sometimes had to fulfill the role of First Lieutenant as well as Captain. Layard also observed that a schism existed between senior RN officers and RCN ships operating under their command, and he attempted to build bridges between them. After EG 9 killed *U 247* in early September 1944, Layard persuaded the Commander-in-Chief, Plymouth's Chief of Staff to come on board the frigate HMCS *Saint John* to say "Well done." "I told him I thought the R.N. treated the R.C.N. unfairly—all criticism and no help and we'd never seen a senior R.N. officer on board."[85] There were also problems in EG 9's usual home port, Londonderry, base to Commodore (D) Western Approaches, Commodore G.W.G. Simpson, RN. As the senior officer responsible for RCN operational effectiveness on the eastern side of the Atlantic, Simpson faced a significant challenge in transforming undertrained, poorly equipped RCN ships into effective escorts. Unhappily, he was sometimes quite scornful of Canadians, and although he reviewed oper-

---

78. Diary, 7 Sep 1943; original emphasis. For more on Layard's career, see Whitby, *Commanding Canadians*.

79. The motion picture *Corvette K-225* (Universal 1943) was produced by Howard Hawkes, directed by Richard Rossen, and featured Randolph Scott, Andy Devine, and Robert Mitchum.

80. Layard diary, 17 Oct 1943

81. Layard diary, 22 Jan 1944

82. Layard ms, 1943, 66, in Layard papers

83. Layard diary, 11 Oct 1943

84. Layard diary, 21 Mar 1945

85. Layard diary, 15 Sep 1944

ations with Canadian COs upon their return to harbour, he rarely visited RCN ships. On one occasion Layard tactfully suggested to Simpson's chief of staff "what a pity it was [the Commodore] didn't try to get to know the Canadian COs better."[86] For his part, Simpson recognized the challenges that the Canadians posed on Layard. In his final assessment on Layard he wrote that he had performed "entirely to my satisfaction. He has led with distinction a difficult team of individualistic Canadian officers."[87]

Evidence that some Canadian officers shared Layard's opinion that senior RN officers did not pay them enough attention was provided in an incident that occurred in Scapa Flow shortly after the encounter in *Kent*'s wardroom described by Piers. When EG 9 was preparing to depart on JW 62, Commodore R.M.J. Hutton, RN—"Tubby" to Layard, a long-time friend—"told me a Canadian officer had left a parcel at his house saying no message and no answer, which when opened proved to contain 2 bottles of whisky. It put Tubby in a very difficult position." Presenting such gifts to senior officers ran against *King's Regulations and Admiralty Instructions*, but Layard soon discovered the motives behind the action: "I heard today that all my C.O.s had conspired together as they were so delighted at being asked by Tubby to lunch one day. The first time any serving R.N. officer had taken any notice of them."[88] The incident demonstrates that no matter what they thought of the RN and its officers, Canadians wanted, and thought they deserved, their respect.

In early January 1945, *Sioux* and *Algonquin* returned to the slog of the Russian convoys, forming part of the escort for convoys JW 63 and RA 63. The passage to Kola Inlet was uneventful, and although the facilities there were hardly an improvement over northern Scotland, the Canadians were better able to find distractions than their British counterparts by challenging their hosts to a hockey game.[89] The return journey had to be made in northerly gale force winds that at times reached force 12. As it became increasingly difficult for the escorts to hold their course in the forty-five foot seas, twelve of them, including *Sioux*, hove to while *Algonquin* and the remainder of the escort stayed with those merchant ships that were able to run before the gale. This convoy escaped enemy attention.[90]

JW 64 and RA 64 in February ran into much more dangerous opposition. The escort, again commanded by Rear-Admiral R.R. McGrigor, consisted of the carriers *Campania* and *Nairana*, the cruiser *Bellona*, eight fleet destroyers, including *Sioux* (*Algonquin* having sailed for Canada for refit the day before the escort joined the convoy) and eight ships from the 7th and 8th Escort Groups. A *Luftwaffe*

---

86.   Layard diary, 28 Dec 1944

87.   Cmdre D WA, Form S-450, 25 June 1945, Layard papers

88.   Layard diary, 28 Nov 1944

89.   "The local skating rink was a tremendous attraction for all the Canadian officers and ratings. *Algonquin* and *Sioux* played a hockey match, to the amusement of all concerned. Skates were available, but ground hockey sticks had to be used, and a tennis ball instead of a puck. *Algonquin* was the winner, 3 to nil. *Algonquin* then took on the local Russian team. The Russian version of ice hockey is played with a ball, and a flat, short stick with a broad, curved head. In this 'international' match the Russian players showed great skill both in skating and stick-handling. Our Canadian team was defeated 3 to 2 in a very sporting game." *Algonquin* ROP, 1 Feb 1945, DDE-224, pt 1

90.   *Algonquin* ROP, 1 Feb 1945; *Sioux* ROP, 4 Feb 1945, DDE-225, pt 1; CS 10, "Operation Greystoke," 24 Jan 1945, PRO, ADM 199/602

reconnaissance aircraft acting on intelligence from *B Dienst* sighted JW 64 near the Faeroe Islands on 6 February, and aircraft continued to shadow the convoy until the day before arrival at Kola Inlet. Given the long hours of darkness and the fact that the two carriers had only "one antique night-fighting [Fairey] Fulmar" between them, shaking enemy reconnaissance would have proven problematic even if the Fulmar had not crashed at the end of its first operational flight. A torpedo attack at dawn on 7 February seemed inevitable, but the German strike force of forty-eight JU 88s received inaccurate sighting reports from a shadower and failed to find the main body of the convoy. They were close enough to be sighted and fired upon by some of the escort vessels, however, and only returned to base after losing six aircraft. As the convoy approached Bear Island three days later, the escorts began to obtain HF/DF contacts from the eight U-boats of the *Rasmus* group deployed south of the island. Despite having the benefit of reports from the convoy's shadowers, the submarines were unable to get into attack positions in the face of the strong escort, and the convoy proceeded unscathed around the northern end of the patrol line. The *Rasmus* boats then withdrew to form a new line in the approaches to Kola Inlet, leaving it to the *Luftwaffe* to make any more immediate attack.[91]

On the morning of 10 February, the torpedo-bombers did make another attempt on the convoy aided by the mistaken identification of an aircraft approaching JW 64 from the south as Russian. As outlined by Lieutenant-Commander Boak, it was left to *Sioux*, steaming in the outer screen on the convoy's starboard wing, to correct the error.

> At 1002 a JU 88 appeared from a bearing of Green 90 (240 true), about 50 feet off the water and 3000 yards away, flying directly towards the ship. At about 1500 yards the plane dropped a torpedo and banked away to starboard, flying up between HMCS *Sioux* and HMS *Lark* who was about 3500 yards away.
>
> Ship went "Full ahead together, hard-a-port," and steadied up on a course of 060. Starboard Oerlikons opened up on the plane just before the torpedo was dropped and followed him out of range, also one round from "B" gun was fired at him but was short. Enemy's port engine was seen to be smoking heavily before he disappeared into a snow flurry.[92]

Boak immediately reported the attack to McGrigor. *Sioux*'s message was, in fact, "the only warning received of the torpedo attack which was on its way. It was fortunate for us as it gave the screens time to start moving into their anti-aircraft positions and brought everyone to the alert."[93] At 1019, thirty-two JU 88s appeared out of the snow flurries and low overcast bearing down on the outer escort. *Sioux* was confronted by "a group of about 12 to 15 aircraft ... bearing 130, steering about 350, about 50 feet off the water and at 5000 yards range. Opened fire with main armament, which in conjunction with *Lark*'s and *Whitehall*'s fire turned them away. One plane which was closer than the others, due to his turn towards, appeared to be continually hit by the Bofors gun and when last seen was about 100 feet off the sea diving towards it. A snow flurry unfortunately obscured any definite result."[94]

91. CS 1, "Operation Hotbed," 28 Feb 1945, PRO, ADM 199/759; *Sioux* ROP, 1 Mar 1945, DDE-225, pt 1; Claasen, *Hitler's Northern War*, 248; Adm, *Arctic Convoys*, 119-20; Roskill, *War at Sea* III, pt 2, 169-72; Rohwer and Hummelchen, *Chronology* II, 491

92. *Sioux*, "Narrative of Air Attack on Convoy JW 64, 10th February, 1945," 12 Feb 1945, DDE-225, pt 1

93. CS 1, "Operation Hotbed," 28 Feb 1945

94. *Sioux*, "Narrative of Air Attack on Convoy JW 64"

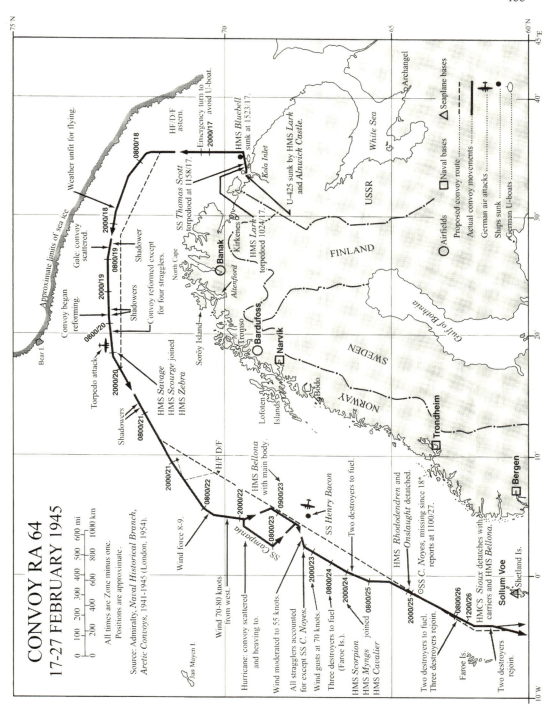

CONVOY RA 64
17-27 FEBRUARY 1945

All times are Zone minus one.
Positions are approximate.

Source: Admiralty, *Naval Historical Branch,
Arctic Convoys, 1941-1945* (London, 1954).

0   100 200 300 400 500 600 mi
0 200 400 600 800 1000 km

Jan Mayen I.

Wind 70-80 knots
from west.

Hurricane: convoy scattered
and heaving to.

Wind moderated to 55 knots.

All stragglers accounted
for except SS *C. Noyes.*

Wind gusts at 70 knots.

Three destroyers to fuel
(Faroe Is.).

HMS *Scorpion*
HMS *Myngs* joined 0800/25
HMS *Cavalier*

Two destroyers to fuel.
Three destroyers rejoin.

Faroe Is.

Two destroyers
rejoin.

Shetland Is.

Sollum Voe

HMCS *Sioux* detaches with
carriers and HMS *Bellona.*

SS *C. Noyes*, missing since 18°,
reports at 1100/27.

HMS *Rhododendron* and
Onslaught detached.

Two destroyers to fuel.

SS *Henry Bacon*

0900/23

SS *Campania*

HMS *Bellona*
with main body.

H/F/D/F

Wind force 8-9.

Shadowers

HMS *Savage*
HMS *Scourge* joined
HMS *Zebra*

Torpedo attack

Convoy began
reforming.

Gale: convoy scattered.

Shadowers

Shadower

Convoy reformed except
for four stragglers.

0800/18

2000/18

0800/19

2000/19

0800/20

2000/20

0800/21

2000/21

0800/22

2000/22

0800/23

2000/23

2000/23

0800/24

2000/24

2000/25

0800/26

1200/26

Bear I.

Approximate limits of sea ice

Weather unfit for flying.

Emergency turn to
avoid U-boat.

2000/17

HMS *Bluebell*
sunk at 1523/17.

SS *Thomas Scott*
torpedoed at 1158/17.

HF/D/F
astern.

North Cape

Banak

Altenford

Kirkenes

Kola Inlet

U-425 sunk by HMS *Lark*
and *Alnwick Castle.*

HMS *Lark*
torpedoed 1024/17

Soröy Island

Tromsö

Bardufoss

Narvik

Bodö

Lofoten
Islands

Trondheim

Bergen

NORWAY

SWEDEN

FINLAND

USSR

White Sea

Archangel

Gulf of Bothnia

Seaplane bases

Naval bases

Airfields □ Naval bases

Proposed convoy route ....

Actual convoy movements ....

German air attacks ....

Ships sunk ....

German U-boats ....

75°N

70

65

60°N

45°E

40

30

20

10

0

10°W

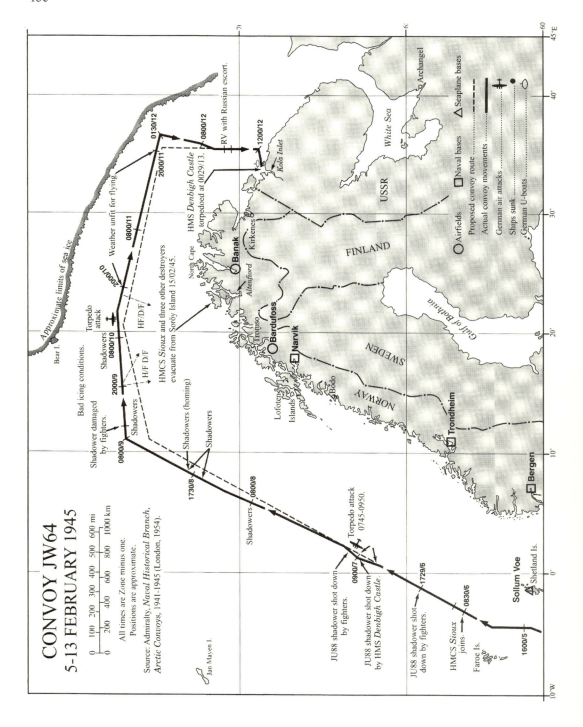

CONVOY JW64
5-13 FEBRUARY 1945

0   100 200 300 400 500 600 mi
0 200 400 600 800 1000 km

All times are Zone minus one.
Positions are approximate.

Source: Admiralty, *Naval Historical Branch, Arctic Convoys, 1941-1945* (London, 1954).

While the starboard wing was breaking up the main attack, Wildcats from the two escort carriers and accurate fire from the inner escorts also contributed to the fragmentation of the enemy formation. Nonetheless, the merchant ships were hard pressed to comb the numerous torpedo tracks that streamed through the convoy when the bombers attacked from several directions simultaneously. None were hit, although several torpedoes exploded in ships' wakes. The anti-aircraft gunners aboard the merchant ships regarded all aircraft as unfriendly and damaged several RN fighters as they made their landing approaches to the escort carriers, earning some scathing comments from McGrigor in the process. They "showed a quite inexcusable lack of ... discipline even taking into account the bad visibility, low cloud and the pace of events. There is little resemblance between a JU 88 and a Wildcat, and none with a Swordfish." After a thirty-minute lull, a second wave of JU 88s failed to achieve any hits as they ran into the convoy's anti-aircraft fire. McGrigor claimed seven JU 88s shot down, four probables and eight damaged; in fact, only five aircraft failed to return to their Bardufoss air base. One Wildcat was shot down—by the Germans—but the pilot was rescued. There were no more air attacks, but the submarines took on the convoy on the 13th, when *U 992* torpedoed the corvette HMS *Denbigh Castle* at the entrance to Kola Inlet, the only enemy success in the battle for JW 64. [95]

If the sailors in *Sioux* expected any respite in their layover at Polyarnoe it was not to be. Informed by the Admiralty that the Norwegian resistance on Soroy Island in the approaches to Altenfjord was under attack by the Germans, McGrigor had planned to detach four destroyers to evacuate the inhabitants as JW 64 passed northern Norway. Enemy attacks on JW 64, however, forced him to wait until the convoy was safely anchored in Kola Inlet to send four destroyers, including *Sioux*, on Operation Open Door. The warships arrived off the island in early afternoon on 15 February and "within three and a half hours, the civilian population had been embarked on the destroyers, and food, small arms, and ammunition had been landed for the small garrison remaining, all by the ships' boats and local small craft." The destroyers were back by the 16th to Kola Inlet where they transferred their 499 Norwegian passengers to the merchant ships for the return journey to the United Kingdom with RA 64. [96]

Frustrated by the U-boats' poor results against the Russian convoys since their resumption in the summer—between August and December 1944 they had sunk just two merchant ships in return for the loss of nine submarines—Dönitz changed tactics. His boats were too slow to conduct "mobile warfare because of their low submerged speed," but wanting to take advantage of the fact that most were now equipped with *schnorkel*, Dönitz decided to deploy U-boats directly across the entrance to Kola Inlet. That way, he thought, the convoy would be unable to avoid them. [97] These barrier tactics had met with no success until three days before RA 64 sailed, when U-boats in that area had sunk three ships on the three days. McGrigor knew from Russian intelligence and HF/DF intercepts that other U-boats were clustered along the first forty miles of RA 64's route. "Russian counter-measures were confined to day flying and a few small craft patrolling the

---

95. CS 1, "Operation Hotbed"; Adm, *Arctic Convoys*, 121; R. Woodman, *The Arctic Convoys, 1941-1945* (London 1994), 423-4

96. CNMO(L) narrative, "Operation Hotbed," nd; *Sioux* ROP, 1 Mar 1945; CS 1, "Operation Hotbed"; Adm, "Home Fleet," para 255-257

97. Adm, *Fuehrer Conferences on Naval Affairs*, 47-8; Tarrant, *The Last Year of the Kriegsmarine*, 149-50; Lambert, "Seizing the Initiative," 156-7

entrance and were quite ineffective. There was no night flying, no hunting groups, and no thought on their part of taking the offensive against the U-boats so handily placed."[98]

There was no alternative to fighting the convoy through this concentration, since neither Ultra nor other signals intelligence could offer any means of evasive routing. Consequently, McGrigor decided to sail five escorts of EG 7 the night before, to carry out an antisubmarine sweep, and have Russian aircraft "flood" the area next morning to keep the submarines down. It was a successful tactic, although not without cost. The sloop *Lark* and the corvette *Alnwick Castle* sank *U 425* shortly after midnight on 17 February, but as the convoy was forming up later in the day *U 968* blew *Lark*'s stern off with an acoustic torpedo at 1024, and then sank the merchantman *Thomas Scott* ninety minutes later. The corvette *Bluebell* blew up and sank with only one survivor after being torpedoed by *U 711* at 1523. That was the last contact the U-boats were able to make, however, and the remainder of the convoy passed safely through the German gauntlet.[99]

It was not until two days later that the convoy, scattered by sixty knot winds and a heavy swell, was again sighted by an enemy reconnaissance aircraft. Getting the ships back into station became a matter of some urgency in order to meet the *Luftwaffe* torpedo attack anticipated for dawn on the 20th, when the ships would be passing south of Bear Island. *Sioux*, stationed 3000 yards astern of the convoy on the starboard wing, was once again in the forefront of the action when "the first aircraft was sighted about green 30 (300°) passing down the starboard side" at 1004 on 20 February. Five minutes later many more appeared through snow squalls, and the destroyer engaged as many as four targets at a time from all directions, hampered by violent rolling and pitching, for at least fifteen furious minutes. In the end, it appeared that one aircraft had been damaged if not destroyed, and none had been able to complete their attacks against the convoy.[100]

The escorts were helped by sea conditions, resulting in a "large number of torpedoes which exploded prematurely, apparently on breaking surface in the trough of the rough seas, as well as on crossing wakes of ships." Nonetheless, several sharp emergency turns were required to frustrate the attack. Six of the forty attacking JU 88s were lost, most being accounted for by the Wildcat fighters of the *Nairana*, which flew off the carrier despite fifty knot winds gusting over the flight deck. The gale force winds also restricted the ability of those U-boats deployed in the vicinity of Bear Island to locate the ships. Although several HF/DF fixes were obtained around the convoy, no submarine made contact, and by 22 February the only remaining obstacle was the unrelenting weather. Headwinds of seventy to eighty knots put ships in real danger and forced many of them to straggle, owing to "engine trouble, defective steering, shifting cargoes and splitting decks." The carrier HMS *Campania* had to heave to after rolling to an angle of 45°. Not until the evening of 23 February could the ships form up in some sort of order. The one remaining straggler, the freighter *Henry Bacon*, fell victim to the *Luftwaffe* about forty-seven miles east of the convoy. She was the only ship to be sunk by torpedo-bombers since their deployment to northern Norway in December 1944, and the last to fall victim to the *Luftwaffe* in the war.[101] As one historian has concluded, the

---

98.   CS 1, "Operation Hotbed"

99.   Ibid; Adm, *Arctic Convoys*, 122-3; Tarrant, *The Last Year*, 152

100. *Sioux*, "Report of Air Attack on Convoy JW [sic] 64, February 20th, 1945," 28 Feb 1945, DDE-225, pt 1

101. CS 1, "Operation Hotbed"; Rohwer and Hummelchen, *Chronology* II, 492; Woodman, *Arctic Convoys*, 428-30; J.R. Smith and A. Kay, *German Aircraft of the Second World War* (London 1972), 417; Tarrant, *The Last Year*, 152-3

Luftwaffe's failed efforts against JW-RA 64 demonstrated that its "days as an effective fighting force were long gone."[102]

Over the next four days, most of the destroyers had to be detached to the Faeroe Islands to refuel. *Sioux*, one of only three destroyers to complete the entire voyage without refuelling, left the convoy at 1830 on 26 February to screen *Campania*, *Nairana* and *Bellona* back to Scapa Flow.[103] The role played by *Sioux* in the successful passage of convoys JW 64 and RA 64 had certainly been one of the most active of any Canadian destroyer that served with the Home Fleet. Often deployed, albeit by chance, on the convoy's most threatened quarter, her prompt reporting of enemy air activity and the tenacity and accuracy of her anti-aircraft gunners had helped to prevent the torpedo-bombers from pressing home their attacks. The operation was undoubtedly *Sioux*'s finest moment and was probably the most effective performance of any Canadian ship on a Russian convoy. Lieutenant-Commander Boak was awarded the Distinguished Service Cross, and the Norwegian government made him a Knight of the Order of St Olaf.[104]

Sioux's final operation with the Home Fleet before returning to Canada, escorting convoys JW 65 and RA 65, "was chiefly remarkable for the almost continuous favourable weather and the fact that the enemy were unable to find the convoy either on the outward or homeward journeys." Once again, however, the Germans concentrated their U-boats at the entrance to Kola Inlet and torpedoed two merchantmen and an escort as they entered harbour. Faced with the now familiar problem of getting the homeward-bound convoy safely beyond the approaches, the escort commander used four fleet destroyers, including *Sioux*, to create a diversion along the usual departure route by dropping depth-charges and firing starshell, while RA 65 stole out of the inlet through a newly swept channel. The tactic succeeded and the remainder of the passage went without incident.[105]

The return to Canada for refit of both *Algonquin* and *Sioux* was offset by the arrival at Scapa of the RCN's three Tribal class destroyers. Each had a new commanding officer: Commander K.F. Adams, RCN, in *Iroquois*; Lieutenant-Commander R.P. Welland, RCN, in *Haida*; and Lieutenant-Commander H.V.W. Groos, RCN, in *Huron*. *Haida* and *Huron* had also undergone the same modernization as *Iroquois* had received the previous year. They joined the second of the Canadian-manned escort carriers, HMS *Puncher*, commanded by Captain R.E.S. Bidwell, RCN, which had begun its operational career with the Home Fleet in early February. Another Smiter class carrier that had commissioned in Seattle before being sent to Burrards in Vancouver for modification, *Puncher* had spent the last half of 1944 ferrying aircraft across the Atlantic. Despite the lack of operational activity, Bidwell reported that "there was a very good spirit in the ship"[106]—a decided contrast to *Nabob*'s morale. *Puncher*'s crew, he later reminisced, "were a motley bunch; I was one of the only two RCN officers, the rest were an assortment of RCNVRs and RCNRs, but we were a happy ship. We soon outgrew our original nickname of 'floating coffin' (which we somewhat

102. Claasen, *Hitler's Northern War*, 248

103. CS 1, "Operation Hotbed"; G.G. Connell, *Arctic Destroyers* (London 1982), 197

104. LCdr E.R. Paquette and Lt C.G. Bainbridge, *Honours and Awards: Canadian Naval Forces, World War II* (Victoria 1986), 5

105. VAdm F. Dalrymple-Hamilton, "Operation Scottish: Passage of Convoys JW 65 and RA 65," 31 Mar 1945, PRO, ADM 199/759; *Sioux* ROP, 4 Apr 1945, DDE-225, pt 1; Ruegg and Haig, *Convoys to Russia*, 75-6; Tarrant, *The Last Year*, 153

106. Bidwell to NB, 27 July 1944, LAC, RG 24, 6744, NS 8000-500/413; CNMO(L) narrative, "Operation Scottish," nd; Kealy and Russell, *History of Canadian Naval Aviation*, 29-30

resembled) and earned a reputation of being a lucky ship." He acknowledged Lay's role in solving "the many complications" involved in running a British ship manned by Canadians, but it is apparent that Bidwell and his officers worked hard to solve problems and gain the respect of the ship's company.[107]

There were still adjustments that had to be made by Canadian seamen unfamiliar with the more rigid discipline of a big ship. Bidwell told NSHQ in May 1944 that "the general training and disposition of the average RCN or RCNVR rating, who has had no experience in larger ships of war, does not make him lend himself readily to the discipline that must be enforced." This situation was the result of "the natural independence of the present day Canadian rating," the fact that the RCN "had always been a 'small ship' navy," and because training establishments spent "an undue amount of time ... fostering athletics, personnel welfare etc., perhaps at the expense of the inculcation of a more rigid sense of discipline." On the other hand, Bidwell believed there were compensating advantages since "the national fair-mindedness inherent in all Canadians has made a very large proportion of the ship's company very glad to be in this ship, and very keen on her. There was quite a lot of competition to get into the 'Flight Deck Party.' This augurs well for the manning of RCN carriers if it is decided to acquire such ships."[108]

That *Puncher*'s air group contained 821 Squadron, the only Fairey Barracuda torpedo-bomber unit remaining with the Home Fleet—the others having departed for the Far East with the fleet carriers—influenced the ship's employment. Since Grumman Avengers were rarely used in the torpedo-bomber role, *Puncher*'s Barracudas were the only torpedo strike force available to guard against an attempted breakout into the Atlantic by the remaining German fleet units.[109] Bidwell observed that the ship "couldn't depart too far from the Home Fleet area, and for this reason we were, thank heavens, never detailed for Russian convoys."[110] Her principal operational employment consisted of a few minelaying sorties along the Norwegian coast. As the war in Europe was drawing to a close, the C-in-C Home Fleet believed this anti-shipping campaign would serve "to tie down forces there which might otherwise have been withdrawn to reinforce Germany's western front" and for "cutting off supplies to the German garrison in Norway and so weakening any will to maintain resistance and to continue U-boat warfare, as from a 'fortress', after the collapse of Germany." Two factors identified by Admiral Moore hampered these operations, however:

> (A) The distances from the bases and the slow speed of the escort carrier. These have made it difficult to forecast the weather to be expected on the date of attack. The slow speed has meant that the forces have not been able to exploit the fleeting improvements in the weather on different stretches of the coast as I was able to do earlier on when operating [the fleet carrier] *Implacable*. The weather has also restricted the motor torpedo boat and submarine chaser operations.

107. Bidwell, "Random Memories," nd, R.E.S. Bidwell biog file, DHH. See also L.M. Outerbridge, *HMS Puncher D-Day–1944 to V.E. and V.J.–1945* (Vancouver nd).

108. Bidwell to NB, 30 May 1944, LAC, RG 24, 6744, NS 8000-500/413

109. O. Thetford, *British Naval Aircraft Since 1912* (London 1971), 210

110. Bidwell, "Random Memories"

(B) Lack of destroyers. Heavy calls have been made on the Home Fleet destroyers for escort duties owing to the shortening of the North Russian convoy cycle and the U-boat threat in inshore waters, leaving few for operations elsewhere.[111]

Puncher satisfied her classification as a general purpose carrier by serving as a fighter carrier on her first operation with the Home Fleet.[112] Operation Selenium was conceived as a combined shipping strike effort. In the first part of the operation Wildcat fighters from *Puncher* and *Premier* would cover Force 1, consisting of two cruisers and three destroyers detailed to carry out an anti-shipping strike in an exposed stretch of the Leads between Bud and Kvitholm. After covering the withdrawal of the strike force, *Puncher*'s fighters—twelve Wildcats from 881 Squadron—would support the second part, a mine lay by *Premier*'s Avengers in the Leads off Skatestrommen.[113] The operation achieved mixed results. Force 1 encountered no shipping on its sweep on the morning of 11 February but the aerial mine lay was conducted with five of seven mines being dropped accurately. 881's fighters faced neither anti-aircraft fire nor fighter opposition over the target, and an otherwise perfect operation from *Puncher*'s point of view was only marred when a Wildcat's machine guns sprayed the flight deck upon a rough landing, wounding five sailors.[114]

Puncher was back at sea within ten days on another combined operation. Under Operation Shred eight RN minesweepers cleared a German minefield that blocked the approaches to the southwest coast of Norway, thus hindering the movements of surface striking forces attempting to attack coastal shipping. The carriers *Premier* and *Puncher* covered that operation, and then under Groundsheet, 821 Squadron's Barracudas were to lay mines in the Leads off Stavanger. It was *Puncher*'s first minelaying strike and things went awry. The Barracudas made an inaccurate landfall and then haze caused them to lose touch with their covering force of sixteen Wildcats, eight from each of the two CVEs, and they lost surprise while searching for their target. Forced to drop their mines unsupported in the face of intense flak, 821 lost two aircraft. According to a later study, the problem was attributed to 821's inexperience and the notoriously unreliable compasses fitted in Barracudas. It is worth noting, however, that upon completion of their workups earlier in 1945, the Flag Officer Carrier Training noted that 821 needed to spend more time on navigation exercises. As it turned out, the two Barracudas that were shot down proved to be the only FAA aircraft lost in the minelaying campaign off Norway in the latter part of the war.[115]

Bad weather and the chronic shortage of destroyers–in this case the result of the demands associated with the running of JW 64 and RA 64[116]—combined to keep escort carriers bottled up in

---

111. The modern Fleet carrier *Implacable* could make about thirty knots while CVEs could only manage eighteen. Moore, "Dispatch of the C-in-C Home Fleet Covering the Period 19 December 1944, to the End of May 1945," 20 Jun 1945, PRO, ADM 199/1440

112. Four Barracudas were retained onboard.

113. Adm, "Home Fleet," para 207-212; Home Fleet Escort Carriers (HFEC) WD, 1 Jan-31 Mar 1945, PRO, ADM 199/1440; Excerpts of Op Orders for Selenium I and II, DHH 81/520/1650-239/14, Operations in NWest Europe waters ; Adm, *Development of British Naval Aviation* II, App XI, 310

114. *Puncher* ROP, 15 Feb 1945, LAC, RG 24, 11306, CS 159-15-22; HFEC WD, Jan-Mar 1945; Adm, "Home Fleet," para 207-12

115. HFEC WD, Jan-Mar 1945; Adm, "Home Fleet," para 213-20; FOCT to Adm, 30 Jan 1945, DHH Puncher; C-in-C Home Fleet, "Dispatch of the C-in-C Home Fleet, Covering the Period 19 December 1944 to the End of May 1945," 20, PRO, ADM 199/1440; Adm, *British Mining Operations* II, 451; CNMO(L) narrative, "Operations Shred and Groundsheet," 1-2

116. Three destroyers had to be sent to make good the losses suffered off Kola Inlet, three more were sent as reinforcements when others required refuelling, and twelve of sixteen participating destroyers required repairs from weather damage following the operation. Adm, "Home Fleet," para 151-53

Scapa Flow until mid-March. But even when *Puncher* was able to embark upon operations towards the end of the month she continued to be dogged by the climate. From 24 to 29 March she was at sea for Operation Muscular, but poor weather forced cancellation of a planned torpedo attack by Barracudas on shipping off Trondheim. On Operation Newmarket *Puncher* was one of four CVEs detailed to attack submarine depot ships at Kilbotn in an attempt to cripple U-boat operations against the Russian convoys. Again the weather was unsuitable for flying and after cruising near the Lofoten Islands for several days waiting for it to clear, the operation was abandoned and the force entered Scapa on 12 April. Eight days later, not realizing their ship's brief operational career was over, *Puncher*'s crew took her south for boiler clean and refit.[117]

The three RCN Tribals serving with the Home Fleet also had little contact with the enemy during the closing two months of the war. During the first week of April a task force of four destroyers, including *Iroquois*, under the command of Captain H.W.S. Browning, RN, undertook an antishipping sweep given the codename Foxchase. Approaching the southwestern tip of the Norwegian coast near Lister Light shortly before midnight on 3 April, the British destroyer *Zealous* reported a contact northeast of the task force at eleven miles distance. After a twenty-minute pursuit, the four destroyers closed on what turned out to be a convoy of four merchant ships and three escorts heading northwest at eight knots. Browning steered to cut the enemy off from shore and at 0027 ordered the convoy illuminated with starshell. *Iroquois* opened fire on a tanker of approximately 6000 tons at 4400 yards range. The salvos were on target—of sixteen broadsides, six were seen to find their mark—and within minutes the tanker was on fire.[118]

The other destroyers were also scoring hits when, after firing a salvo of torpedoes and ordering the other destroyers to follow suit, Browning suddenly turned his force away after receiving a report from *Iroquois* that she had sighted two U-boats on the surface. Browning was also concerned about E-boats, and he led his ships up the coast and away from the action. Although further contacts were made, no targets were sighted and the ships returned to Scapa Flow.[119] Browning's decision to abandon the operation, despite having engaged a vastly out-gunned convoy, was heavily criticized by his superiors. According to the RCN's historical officer, "both Commodore (D) Home Fleet and C-in-C Home Fleet considered that this action was unsatisfactory. It was considered that Captain (D)'s decision to turn away was not justified either by the existing danger to Force Three or by the damage inflicted on the convoy. Later intelligence reports had shown that none of the enemy ships had been sunk and none seriously damaged, and it was considered that danger from E-boats and U-boats had been overestimated."[120]

The poor results of Foxchase, reminiscent of the early Tribal actions in the Channel, accentuated, yet again, the critical importance of training and experience. Two of the four COs had never before participated in a night surface action, Browning led the action from the worst equipped

---

117. *Puncher* ROP, 17 Apr and 9 May 1945, LAC, RG 24, 11306, CS 159-15-22; Adm, "Home Fleet," para 226-31 and 237-39

118. *Iroquois* ROP, nd, DDE-217, pt 1; CNMO(L) narrative, "Operation Foxchase," nd

119. Capt H. Browning (Capt D 17th Destroyer Flotilla) ROP, 12 Apr 1945, PRO, ADM 199/22

120. Ibid. See also Adm to C-in-C Home Fleet, nd; C-in-C Home Fleet to Adm, 2 May 1945, Cmdre (D) to C-in-C Home Fleet, 19 Apr 1945. PRO, ADM 199/22

destroyer in terms of Action Information Organization and radar, and the force did not exhibit the cohesiveness that would have come from long service together.[121] Moreover, Browning was unlikely to have been privy to Ultra, and therefore would not have had the same faith in the intelligence given to him as Rear-Admiral McGrigor had had in Counterblast in November 1944. This probably led him to react with greater alarm to reports of MTBs and submarines than he would have had he been in the Ultra picture. The above factors would likely have given Browning the confidence necessary to bring the engagement to a successful conclusion, but the heavy demands imposed on Home Fleet destroyers prevented the opportunity to conduct the dedicated training that would have instilled that most critical ingredient of successful naval warfare. No matter what the cause, it was a disappointing note upon which to end RCN destroyer operations off the Norwegian coast.

In late April, the three Tribals joined the escort for convoys JW 66 and RA 66. The Germans concentrated their U-boats in the approaches to Kola Inlet but, once again, could not penetrate the defensive screen set up by the numerous escorts, although *U 968* sank the frigate HMS *Goodall*, and *U 427* narrowly missed *Iroquois*. The rest of the passage was completed without incident and the three Tribals came to anchor at Scapa Flow on the day before the German surrender was signed. One month later, the three fleet destroyers entered Halifax harbour to a boisterous welcome and went into dry dock to prepare for the war in the Pacific.[122]

Despite the apparently routine nature of their tasks, the experience of fleet operations acquired by the RCN during its service with the Home Fleet should not be underestimated. First and foremost, perhaps, were the lessons derived from carrying out convoy and antisubmarine operations in the harsh northern climate; an issue that would be raised again during the Cold War. The captains of the two escort carriers also gained practical experience of naval aviation and both eventually held positions at NSHQ in which they could apply their knowledge, Bidwell as Director of the Naval Air Division in 1946 and Lay as Assistant Chief of Naval Staff (Plans and Air) in 1948 and 1949. During the 1950s, Lay and Bidwell, as VCNS and Flag Officer Atlantic Coast (FOAC) respectively, played influential roles in boosting the development of the helicopter carrying destroyer that became the backbone of the RCN.[123] In contrast, unlike regulars such as Lay and Bidwell, the vast majority of the Canadian complement in *Nabob* and *Puncher* were volunteers who left the navy after the war. Only a few permanent force engineering personnel later served in the light fleet carriers acquired after the war, HMCS *Warrior* and *Magnificent*, and although they undoubtedly learned much about big ships, their experience had little to do with aviation. There were, of course, no Canadian personnel in the two escort carriers' squadrons or air maintenance units, and the nucleus of the first RCN naval air squadrons was composed of ex-RCAF airmen and fitters led by Fleet Air Arm officers.

Canadian naval personnel with the Home Fleet in British Home Waters benefited from experience that could only have been acquired by serving as part of a larger navy. Because the Home

---

121. Browning ROP

122. *Iroquois* ROP, 9 May 1945, DDE-217, pt 1; CNMO(L) narrative, "Operation Roundel," nd; Adm, *Arctic Convoys*, 128; Rohwer and Hummelchen, *Chronology* II, 511. *U 427*'s *KTB* indicates that it fired three pattern running torpedoes at a destroyer at the rear of the screen. Whether she was the target or not, one of the torpedoes narrowly missed *Iroquois*. Thanks to Jan Drent and Dr Axel Niestlé for this information.

123. See S. Cafferky, "Unchartered Waters: The Development of the Helicopter Carrying Destroyer in the Postwar Royal Canadian Navy, 1943-1964."

Fleet's operations, especially after June 1944, involved rather limited contact with enemy surface forces, there was less opportunity to draw the Canadian public's attention to the achievements of its fleet destroyers and Canadian-manned escort carriers than the Naval Staff had hoped for. *Nabob*'s brief and checkered career, despite the remarkable conduct of her ship's company in the ship's second and last operation, at the time offered less inspiration than embarrassment. *Puncher* had only a brief taste of action. Possibly for that reason, when Germany was defeated Canadian naval authorities asked the Admiralty not to send *Puncher* to the Pacific as planned, but to sail the ship to Halifax instead in order that she might "show the flag." It was "highly desirable that an opportunity should be afforded for Canadians to see the aircraft carrier which has been manned and whose expense has been borne mainly by the Dominion. It is further considered that such a visit would assist the future development of the air side of the Canadian naval service."[124] With the end of hostilities in Europe, it was apparent that the RCN would have to impress upon the Canadian public the advantages of acquiring a "big ship" navy in the Pacific.

---

124. CNMO(L) to NSHQ, 14 May 1945, LAC, RG 24, 11643; CNMO(L) to Adm, 25 May 1945, DHH Puncher

Outward to the Pacific: The Defence of the West Coast, Pacific Planning, and Operations with the British Pacific Fleet April 1943–September 1945

IN THE FIRST PART OF THIS HISTORY we saw that once war broke out in 1939, naval defence of the west coast of Canada played second fiddle to the Battle of the Atlantic. Although a reasonable defence force was still in place when war erupted in the Pacific in December 1941, it became clear, especially after the American's momentous victory at the Battle of Midway in June 1942, that the Japanese would mount no more than pin-prick raids along the west coast of North America. With the situation on the North Atlantic remaining critical, NSHQ had really no choice but to strip forces away from Pacific Coast Command to reinforce the Atlantic. These are typical of the hard decisions that have to be made in war, but they left just a pittance of forces to defend Canada's Pacific frontier.

The situation changed in the spring and summer of 1943. The decisions at the Washington Convoy Conference had brought a sense of stability to the Atlantic situation, and NSHQ was finally able to give the Pacific more than cursory consideration. Key staff officers from headquarters inspected the west coast, and their findings resulted in a general tightening up of procedures as well as a shakeup in the command structure. These changes set the command on a far better course than had been maintained before, one that was followed with just slight variations until the final cessation of hostilities.

There was evidence that a certain degree of slackness had pervaded Pacific Command before these changes were implemented. One example of this was found in the patrol situation in the Strait of Juan de Fuca. In September 1942 the commanding officer of the Bangor HMCS *Canso*, Lieutenant H.S. MacFarlane, RCNR, complained to the Commanding Officer Auxiliary Vessels (COAV) in Esquimalt that patrol procedures should be standardized. As it was, each time a new senior officer arrived he imposed his own instructions, which resulted in a great deal of signalling and confusion until things were straightened out. Moreover, gaps were created in the patrol system because some vessels interrupted operations to carry out training and exercises.[1] There were

---

1. CO *Canso* to COAV, "Standardization of Routine on Sheringham and Pillar Point Patrols," 3 Sep 1942, NAC, RG 24, 11872, DE16-10, Patrols

also problems with the Fishermen's Reserve (FR), the special force that carried out inshore patrols in converted fishing vessels. The same month MacFarlane voiced his complaints, Lieutenant G.L. Draeski, an officer on the staff of NOIC Esquimalt who had gone out on patrol in the FR vessel *Ripple*, came ashore with a number of concerns. FR vessels were undependable in making contact with adjacent patrols, thus creating gaps in the system. Night patrolling in the fog or rain that often cloaked inshore areas was ineffective, because engine noise on the bridge prevented personnel from hearing anything and if vessels stopped to drift they lost their bearings. Draeski also found that the FR's W/T communication was unreliable.[2]

More troubling was the loss of efficiency through lack of discipline. As one example Draeski cited the poor watch kept by lookouts, which led to sightings going unreported. He thought the root of the problem lay in the fact that the Coxswains who commanded FR vessels were simply unaware of how to set up a proper ship's routine. This was compounded by the realization that these men would have to fish with their crews after the war; they took it easy on then as a result. Exacerbating the situation was Draeski's discovery that "the ship's company as a whole are ashamed of their [lack of] armaments and consequently lose their esprit de corps."[3] Once ashore, Draeski had few recommendations about how these problems might be solved, but despite the unique conditions that existed in the FR, a general tightening of discipline should have been possible.

The most serious evidence of laxity within Pacific Coast Command came from Captain M. Goolden, appointed NOIC Esquimalt in August 1942. Goolden was familiar with the Canadian navy, having served as the RN's senior naval representative in Halifax during the late 1920s and as NOIC Sidney after being called up to the RCN at the outbreak of war. Highly regarded by RCN officers and with experience in running a base in wartime, Goolden, who kept a rather frank diary, seems a reliable witness of conditions in Pacific Coast Command.[4]

Upon his arrival, Goolden found the quiet of Esquimalt to be in complete contrast to the bustle of wartime east coast ports. Early on he noted that his job "is like a peacetime one"; when he remarked upon that to a fellow officer he was told "you should have seen it before Pearl Harbor!"[5] After being in his appointment for a month, Goolden penned a severe critique of what he had experienced at Esquimalt:

> I consider the base to have been a neglected one. Individually the various departments seem to work all right but there is a lack of cooperation and cohesion which indicates lack of something from the top. Personally I have found the various heads of Departments helpful and keen on their jobs, but since I have been here I have received no assistance, or advice and very little courtesy from C.O.P.C., whose place at Esquimalt I presume I shall eventually take when he goes to Vancouver. The base as a whole has not been well administered. I see waste and overlapping and lack of unity and my position here is uncomfortable. Whether Beech (who is strictly speaking jun-

---

2.   Lt G.L. Draeski to COAV, 30 Sep 1942, ibid. Draeski was at sea from 18 to 30 Sep 1942.

3.   Ibid

4.   DHH conversation with VAdm H.G. DeWolf, 8 Jan 1993. Goolden had married a Canadian and retired to a farm on Vancouver Island in the early 1930s.

5.   Goolden diary,1 Sep 1942

ior to me as a Captain) is too shy or resents my being here I cannot tell, but until he moves elsewhere I do not see how matters are to improve.[6]

And, according to Goolden, they did not improve. Over the next months he complained about a growing number of problems, which seemed to worsen after the Commanding Officer Pacific Coast (COPC), Commodore W.J.R. Beech, RCN, moved to a new joint headquarters alongside his army and air force counterparts at Jericho Beach, outside Vancouver. COPC would not discuss service matters with NOIC Esquimalt—his most important subordinate—and generally kept him out of the loop as far as memo and signal distribution was concerned. Moreover, Beech and his Chief of Staff, Commander C.M. Cree, RCN, regularly sent operational signals to Esquimalt ships over the heads of Goolden and his operations staff. Furthermore, Beech showed little interest in the base, and until Goolden made a specific request, he did not bother to inspect the base or its ships during any of his frequent visits to Victoria.

Goolden's criticisms ring true. Some of Beech's actions, such as his uneven handling of the seizure of the Japanese-Canadian fishing fleet and the problems with NSHQ over the deployment of ships to Aleutian operations (see Part 1, chapter 8), were indicative of a lack of grip. But Beech was not incompetent; he was just in over his head. His quiet reserved personality was ill-suited for high command in wartime, and, unlike other RCN officers who found themselves in similar circumstances, he lacked the initiative that would have overcome his lack of experience. That NSHQ devoted most of its attention to the more important North Atlantic theatre and left Beech largely to fend for himself probably did not help.

Beech was also hamstrung by a lack of effective ships. While casting around to find corvettes to contribute to Operation Torch, NSHQ plucked five from the west coast, leaving COPC with just *Dawson* and *Vancouver,* which were supporting operations in the Aleutians.[7] That left eight Bangor class minesweepers as the backbone of the west coast patrol system, but because of maintenance requirements only five of them could be operational at any one time. Beech and his staff devised a new system for the so-called Western Patrol whereby one Bangor would patrol Queen Charlotte Sound and another Millbanke Sound, two others would cover the west coast of Vancouver Island while transiting to and from the aforementioned areas, and the fifth would join the Straits Patrol. Even with these changes, just one vessel now covered the important focal area of Queen Charlotte Sound, whereas two had done the job in the past; the Gordon Head patrol was discontinued; and the force guarding the Strait of Juan de Fuca was weakened to a Bangor, an armed yacht, and three Fairmile motor launches.[8] The situation stabilized for the winter with the return of *Dawson* and *Vancouver* from the Aleutians in November 1942, but the next spring brought more reductions.

When senior Allied naval officers met at the Atlantic Convoy Conference in Washington they agreed, among other things, to increase the flow of trade across the North Atlantic by stepping up the convoy cycle (see Part 1, Chapter 11). This required additional escorts, and Beech was forced to part with five of his valuable Bangors. The departure of these ships on 17 March 1943, while *Dawson* and *Vancouver* were in the midst of their second Aleutian deployment, left Pacific Coast

6.   Ibid, 19 Sep 1942

7.   DOP and DOD to CNS, 7 Sep 1942, DHH 81/520/1650, Operation Torch

8.   COAV memo, "Reorganization of Esquimalt Patrols,"17 Sep 1942, DE16-10

Command with just six modern patrol vessels.[9] The impact of this was felt immediately. The NOIC Prince Rupert was forced to press the decrepit armed yacht HMCS *Cougar* into service as the Chatham Sound patrol, and by May Captain (D) Esquimalt could only scrape up one Bangor for the Western Patrol. The next month, maintenance and training requirements forced that patrol to be suspended altogether.[10] As Pacific Coast Command reached perhaps its lowest ebb, however, the seeds of its revival were being sown.

At the Washington convoy conference, the American Chief of Naval Operations, Admiral E.J. King, had caused the Canadian naval staff to cast their gaze to the Pacific. "It seems to me important," he stated in his opening remarks to senior American, British, and Canadian officers, "to take note at once that we are here concerned with the Atlantic, but that the Pacific has potentialities for submarine difficulties. In my view, not only should you recognize this fact, but remember that the development of that potentiality may well require transfer of antisubmarine means to the Pacific where they are now meagre to the point of emaciation."[11] As much as anything, King was probably reminding his British allies—as he was wont to do—not to forget the Pacific; certainly, the escort situation in that theatre was not nearly as critical as it was in the Atlantic. King had just returned from one of his regular conferences with Admiral Chester Nimitz, the USN's C-in-C Pacific, on the conduct of the war against Japan, and their only stated concern regarding escorts was that "if and when" the Japanese stepped up their submarine operations against American shipping, they might have to "increase their scale of escorting."[12] They agreed that the situation was to be monitored on a monthly basis but, although King "was forever worried that Japanese submarines would attack America's vulnerable shipping in the Pacific," there was no indication that the enemy was going to change their strategy.[13]

No matter what King's motivations, senior Canadian officers took his comments seriously, and looked down the road to future requirements on the west coast.[14] Important considerations such as the number of escorts needed to protect the increase in shipping that was bound to accompany expanded efforts in the Pacific, and the facilities needed to support them required study. An appreciation submitted to the Naval Staff by the Director of Plans, Captain H.G. DeWolf, addressed these concerns and ultimately shaped RCN policy towards Pacific Coast Command for the rest of the war.

DeWolf was not helped in his task by the fact that planning for the Pacific war was still in a state of flux. Considerable disagreement stemming from bitter interservice rivalries existed among the US Joint Chiefs of Staff about how best to fight through to Japan across the vastness of the Pacific. Moreover, as will be seen later in this chapter, the British, let alone the Canadians, were not yet a factor in, nor privy to, these discussions. All DeWolf could do, therefore, was base his appreciation on how he thought the war would unfold from the current situation. At that point, the

9.   Capt (D) Esquimalt ROP, 7 Apr 1943, DHH 81/520/1000-5-10, v 20

10.   SO HMCS *Chatham* ROP, Apr 1943, ibid, v 22; COPC WD, Mar–June 1943, ibid, v 22 and 23

11.   Quoted in DOP memo, "Appreciation of A/S Requirements on the West Coast," 28 May 1943, 1, app A; NSM, 31 May 1943, DHH

12.   "Conference Notes," 22 Feb 1943, 4, DHH 91/431, Fleet Adm E.J. King papers, series IV, roll 8

13.   Buell, *Master of Sea Power*, 298-9

14.   The Director of Plans used King's remarks in the introduction to the appreciation described below. See DOP memo, 28 May 1943, 1, app A; NSM, 31 May 1943, DHH

The dockyard at Esquimalt looking east towards Victoria. The harbour is not a large one, but there is room for two of the escort carriers that worked up in the area, berthed (centre left) at the government graving dock. (LAC E0035250)

Commander Hugh F. Pullen (seated right), the executive officer of HMCS *Uganda*, prepares to join the "Crossing the Equator" brotherhood. (DND M 2066)

The auxiliary anti-aircraft cruiser HMCS *Prince Robert*. The ex-civilian vessel did not look particularly war-like but her 4-inch high-angle guns could be devastating against aircraft. (DND HN-405)

Twin 4-inch anti-aircraft guns in the former armed merchant cruiser HMCS *Prince Robert*. Because of the importance of air power in the Pacific, the ship would be sent there, though not in time to see action. (DND K-81)

American counteroffensive against Japan was proceeding mainly through the southwest Pacific, but there were indications that another prong would be launched across the central Pacific. Shipping in support of these operations mainly flowed from either San Francisco or through the Panama Canal, both well beyond the scope of the RCN's responsibility. DeWolf thought it possible, however, that a supply route might be established through the Aleutians, "the shortest route to Japan itself." Much would depend upon relations between Japan and the Soviet Union, who had maintained a neutrality agreement since 1940, but if the Aleutians did become the "springboard for direct attack upon Japan," the scale of RCN operations on the west coast would see a dramatic increase.

Although there had been almost no Japanese submarine activity along the Pacific coast of North America since *I 25* and *I 26* had patrolled the area in June 1942, DeWolf concluded that "a change in this policy is within the means of the enemy and therefore must be anticipated." That said, he thought the threat, if mounted, would be minor. A heavy increase in shipping traffic could be expected along all Pacific routes following the defeat of Germany, and this would diminish the threat in North American waters because the Japanese would concentrate their submarines closer to home. He estimated that "the number of submarines which could be maintained continuously east of the Aleutians would not exceed four," meaning "the A/S forces required [on the west coast] would not therefore increase in proportion to the increase in shipping." DeWolf thought that a "reasonable degree of protection" against this scale of attack could be effected by air and surface patrols through the important focal points—Strait of Juan de Fuca, Queen Charlotte Sound and Dixon Entrance—and by evasive routing and air patrols beyond those areas. With the expected amount of shipping traffic, he thought for planning purposes that eight destroyers or frigates, eighteen corvettes, and ten Bangors would be required at Esquimalt, and eight corvettes, ten Bangors, and six Fairmiles at Prince Rupert.[15]

In an inspection tour of west coast facilities, DeWolf found that much had to be done to improve the infrastructure to the point that it could support increased naval strength in the theatre. At Esquimalt, DeWolf found that repair and maintenance had "been left out of the picture." Instead development had concentrated on the construction of storing and barracks, which he thought understandable given the few ships based there.[16] To bring the dockyard up to standard various workshops and a 200-ton marine railway would have to be built, but because the site was too congested additional space would have to be found elsewhere. Prince Rupert was in even worse condition with ship repair facilities "almost non-existent," but as at Esquimalt, there was no room for expansion. Conditions were better at Vancouver and Nanaimo, but as with the other sites, maintenance facilities had to be developed. [17]

DeWolf presented his findings to the Naval Staff on 31 May, emphasizing that because of the poor state of ship repair facilities it was "essential to establish a basis for future development." He acknowledged that the RCN's shortage of escorts might preclude the envisioned increase in strength on the west coast but thought the situation would improve in 1944 when the war swung in the Allies' favour. The Naval Staff certainly shared the opinion that resources would be avail-

15.   Ibid

16.   DOP, "Diary of Visit to West Coast May 1st to 20th,1943," 13 May 1943, NSS 1037-3-7, pt 1

17.   DOP to CNS, 1 June 1943, ibid

able. They directed that DeWolf's summary of escort requirements "be accepted as the basis of immediate development of West Coast naval facilities," but added the caveat that the plan "represented bare minimum requirements as seen at this time and should not be considered as in any way limiting future development."[18] They backed up their ambitious vision of a thriving west coast navy with increased spending on infrastructure. At Esquimalt, for example, NSHQ authorized the acquisition of new land, the construction of the haulout and repair shops, as well as the expansion of the armament depot. By 1945 these steps, along with refurbishment of the old graving dock, had according to Gilbert Tucker transformed Esquimalt into a "small but complete base."[19]

The increased effort in the Pacific would also impact upon the control of shipping, and with the situation on the east coast "being well settled," in April 1943, Captain E.S. Brand, Director of the Trade Division at NSHQ, inspected Naval Control Service facilities on the Pacific.[20] Visiting all major ports from San Pedro, California north to Prince Rupert, Brand found mixed results: "while the West Coast of the USA was found to be in good shape, the same could not be said of the Trade Position on the West Coast of Canada."[21] Quite simply, the system established so carefully before the outbreak of war (See Part 1, Chapter 1) had not been improved upon, and in some instances had fallen into serious disrepair. An example of the latter was the plot of merchant ship movements kept at Esquimalt. In February 1943, the Naval Control Service Officer (NCSO) Esquimalt, Mate J. Barr—his rank was perhaps indicative of the low importance COPC attached to the position—complained that:

> All efforts to keep the plot accurate and up-to-date are at present being greatly hindered by a lack of information. If the plot is to adequately serve the purpose for which it is intended, more reports of ship movements are considered essential. Coasting vessels of the CPR [Canadian Pacific Railway] and Union Steamship Co. are particularly difficult to keep track of. To overcome this in some degree, permission has recently been requested to have Customs Officers in certain ports, not now reporting, pass times of arrivals and departures to the Naval Control office.
>
> With regard to deep sea vessels, a much more comprehensive picture of the shipping situation in the whole area could be kept if complete shipping reports were obtained daily from Ketchikan, Kodiak, Dutch Harbor, Seattle, Portland, Astoria and San Francisco.[22]

Although the latter statement indicates that all was not well in the US ports, given such an overall situation, plus the fact that shipping volume was increasing in the Pacific, it is not surprising that a colleague of the Director of Trade recalled of Brand's tour that "Changes followed in his wake."[23]

His first step was to reorganize the reporting situation. Brand appointed Lieutenant G.A.C. Fallis, RCNVR as Staff Officer (Trade) for COPC. Working closely with customs officials Fallis "proceeded vig-

---

18. NSM, 31 May 1943, DHH

19. Tucker, *Naval Service of Canada* II, 227-8

20. Director of Naval Intelligence and Trade (DNIT), "Outline History of the Trade Division," 42, DHH 81/520/1440-127

21. Ibid

22. NCSO Esquimalt, "Monthly Report for January 1943," 1 Feb 1943, COPC WD, Jan 1943, DHH 81/520/1000-5-10, v 16

23. F.B. Watt, *In All Respects Ready: The Merchant Navy and the Battle of the Atlantic, 1940-1945* (Scarborough 1985), 199

orously to organize a reporting system on the West Coast comparable to that which was in force on the East."[24] The system put in place in 1942 was upgraded and expanded with more customs officials pressed into service as reporting officers. By the end of 1943, Brand reported that Esquimalt's "new expanded system was working smoothly."[25] The situation at Prince Rupert was more serious. Not only was shipping departing the busy northern port unrouted, but Brand was concerned that the Americans might install their own port director over the head of the Canadians. Beating them to the punch, he appointed Lieutenant F.N. Eddy, RCNR as NCSO Prince Rupert in June, and routing and reporting systems as well as a local shipping plot were set up immediately. Eddy reported full cooperation from the Americans, who were delighted to get a better appreciation their widely dispersed shipping.[26]

Another important improvement that Brand made was to set up a naval boarding service on the west coast. According to the NCSO Esquimalt this "filled a long-felt need":

> Prior to the inauguration of the Boarding Service, many ships were delayed at the outports by crew troubles, desertions and carousing. Combining firmness with tact and, at times, exercising authority considerably beyond their powers, the Boarding Service effectively put a stop to all unnecessary sailing delays. Outgoing trains and buses were watched for would-be deserters; the inevitable crew troubles were smoothed over and stragglers rounded up and placed on board their ships in time for sailing. The Boarding Officer always placed one or two ratings on gangway duty two or three hours prior to sailing time. The sight of two or three smartly dressed naval ratings in belts and gaiters acted as an effective deterrent to unauthorized last-minute shoregoings and would-be desertions. The authority of the Naval Boarding service to police gangways in this manner was never questioned in this area.

This was challenging duty for naval ratings, but the Boarding Service mitigated their authoritarian aspect by helping to distribute various amenities to merchant seamen and by expediting delivery of mail. Along with the other tightening up by Brand, it put COPC in a better position to deal with the demands of increased activity in the Pacific.

Perhaps the most important shakeup that occurred in Pacific Command was the replacement of Commodore Beech as COPC. Rumours about a change of command had begun to circulate in December 1942,[27] but, as Captain Goolden noted the following April, frustration grew when nothing seemed to be forthcoming. "The withholding of the command changes," he complained in his diary, "is doing intensive harm to the Naval Service on this coast. Morale and with it efficiency is being lowered. I believe it is even worse [at COPC headquarters] at Jericho and it brings out how out of touch NSHQ is with this coast."[28] In fact, NSHQ recognized that both Beech, and his successor, Rear-Admiral V.G. Brodeur, Naval Member of the Canadian Joint Staff in Washington, were overdue for relief but it was hamstrung by a shortage of qualified senior officers.[29] Finally, on 1

---

24. DNIT, "Outline History of the Trade Division", 42

25. DTD, "Annual Report of Director of Trade Division, Ottawa 1943," 5, E.S. Brand papers, v 1, DHH 81/145

26. NCSO Prince Rupert, "History of the Naval Control Service at Prince Rupert, BC," 9 Jan 1946, 2-6, DHH 81/520/1440-127

27. Goolden diary, 11 Dec 1942

28. Ibid, 2 Apr 1943

29. CNS to Naval Minister, 7 June 1943, V.G. Brodeur personnel file. NPRC 0-8970

September, Brodeur relieved Beech, who although originally slated to become Senior Canadian Naval Officer (London), was instead appointed as Chief of Staff (Administration) to C-in-C Canadian Northwest Atlantic.

According to the command war diary, Brodeur's arrival coincided with a turning point in the Pacific war. In August the diary trumpeted the fact that "With the unopposed capture of Kiska by the combined United States–Canadian forces the last foothold of the Japanese on the North American continent has disappeared. There has been a noticeable lessening of tension on the Canadian Pacific Seaboard which has been reflected in the press and it is generally appreciated that our Naval, Air and Military forces must now think more in terms of 'offence' rather than 'defence'."[30] Though no doubt encouraged by the relaxing of tension, Brodeur must have wondered precisely what he was to go on the offensive with; his command had received no additional forces since the five Bangors had gone to the Atlantic in March, the west coast patrol had rarely run since June, and the officers commanding at Esquimalt and Prince Rupert had barely been able to scrape forces together for other commitments. Any talk of an offensive, at least by Canadian naval forces, was therefore decidedly inappropriate.

Brodeur, nonetheless, quickly put his stamp on his new command, changing some key appointments and tightening up procedures. Goolden—no fan of Brodeur's—grudgingly admitted that the new COPC represented "a great change for the better," and month later went so far as to describe him as "the best of the COAC's and COPC's that I have so far come into contact with since 1939."[31] Unfortunately, the honeymoon between COPC and NOIC Esquimalt soon came crashing to an end.

No Japanese naval activity had occurred on the Pacific coast of North America since October 1942, when a float plane from the submarine *I 25* attempted to set Oregon's forests ablaze with incendiary bombs. But there had been some scares, or "flaps." In November 1942 two Japanese aircraft carriers were reported 600 miles off Vancouver Island, and the following March forces were put on alert when it was thought that an enemy task force was approaching the coast.[32] These false alarms had no real repercussions but an incident in December 1943 set off a minor panic, led to the relief of an important officer, and generally caused embarrassment.

On the evening of 18 December 1943 at Ferrer Point—about thirty miles north of where *I 26* bombarded Estevan Point in June 1942—personnel at an RCAF radar station were observing an unidentified ship pass by when they saw about twenty six-foot waterspouts appear about 100 to 200 yards offshore. No doubt recalling what had happened at Estevan Point they assumed they were being shelled and called in the alarm. Response was quick. Western Air Command sent aircraft to search the area, and the Staff Officer (Operations) at Esquimalt despatched two ships to investigate. It was quickly established that no shelling had actually taken place and, operationally at least, things returned to normal. Within the naval hierarchy, however, the affair had severe repercussions. On the 19th, NSHQ sent a rocket to COPC, criticizing Brodeur for being slow to report the incident; they had learned about it from the army and air force three hours before he

---

30. COPC WD, Aug 1943, DHH. For the Aleutians campaign see C.P. Stacey, *Six Years of War: The Army in Canada, Britain and the Pacific* (Ottawa 1955), and G. Perras, *Stepping Stones to Nowhere: The Aleutian Islands, Alaska, and American Military Strategy 1867-1945* (Vancouver 2002).

31. Goolden diary, 25 Sep and 24 Oct 1943

32. HQ Pacific Command (PC) to COPC, 1020Z 18 Nov 1942, LAC, RG 24, 11764; COPC to "All FR Vessels at Sea," 0450Z 31 Mar 1943, AOC WAC to COPC, 0215 31 Mar 1943, ibid, PC05-11-7

informed them. Brodeur replied in his defence that he had not reported it earlier because he thought it was a false alarm—a dubious defence as some three hours and forty-five minutes after the first report of the shelling he had ordered all Fishermen's Reserve vessels to carry out an intensive search.[33] Then,in the days following the incident COPC and NOIC Esquimalt exchanged acrimonious correspondence over each other's actions, which finally resulted in a bitter Goolden asking to be relieved of his command. NSHQ obliged.

In the final episode of the affair, a tri-service board of inquiry sought to discover what had actually occurred off Ferrer Point. At first it was thought that the airmen had seen shell splashes from the steamer *Princess Maquinna*, which had been conducting gunnery exercises near by, but the time and place did not match the reports from Ferrer Point. Finally, an embarrassed board was moved to conclude:

(a) No shots were fired from the sea in the vicinity of Ferrer Point on December 18th 1943.

(b) The splashes, which led to the report of the incident, were caused by whales.[34]

As the Ferrer Point incident played out, an important change was made to the joint defence network along the Pacific seaboard with the establishment of an integrated Canadian–American patrol network in the Strait of Juan de Fuca. Previously, both countries were aware of each other's operations in the straits through joint defence agreements like ABC-22-Pacific and various liaison efforts, but a lack of detailed information had led to near collisions and friendly fire incidents, especially in the days following the attack on Pearl Harbor, when fears were rampant (see Part 1, Chapter 6). Close relations existed among the defence forces in the Pacific, especially between COPC and the 13th Naval District in Seattle, and in December 1942 they had taken the first step towards a more integrated system when a joint communications network was set up for American and Canadian aircraft and vessels patrolling the strait. After helping to negotiate the agreement, Commander C.M. Cree, COPC's chief of staff, noted that "it was a base from which future joint Co-operational effort may develop."[35]

The next step was not long in coming. At the Joint Services Committee–Pacific Coast meeting on 26 March 1943, the Canadian Army representative asked COPC if fast patrol boats could be used to identify contacts detected by the coastal radar station at Triangle Mountain, about ten miles west of Victoria. In responding, Commodore Beech suggested that the entire defence system for Juan de Fuca be reviewed.[36] Following that lead, at its next meeting the JSC recommended that a joint US–Canadian subcommittee be established "with a view to effecting closer co-ordination in the matters of control of shipping, warning installations and dissemination of relevant information to all concerned."[37] Composed of air force, army, and naval representatives from each country, the sub-committee inspected defence facilities and held meetings to devise a new plan. The Extended Defence Officer at Esquimalt, Lieutenant-Commander Roland Bourke, RCNVR, who had

---

33. NSHQ to COPC, 1531Z 19 Dec 1943; COPC to NSHQ, 1854Z 19 Dec 1943; NOIC Esquimalt, memo to COPC, 19 Dec 1943. PC09-21-2

34. Summary of Board of Inquiry, nd, DHH 193.009 (D27)

35. COS, COPC min, 23 Dec 1942, USN, 13th Naval District, "Canadian–US Patrol Communication System," 17 Dec 1942, PC013-13-13, v 1. COPC to NOIC Esquimalt, 14 Dec 1942, LAC, RG 24, 11,872, DE16-10, v 1

36. Joint Services Committee—Pacific Coast (JSC–PC) min, 26 Mar 1943, DHH 193.009 (D18)

37. PC to COSC Sec, 14 July 1943, DHH 193.009 (D25)

earned a Victoria Cross during the raid on Ostend during the First World War, formulated a new patrol system and, with the help of Commander Cree, sold it to the Americans. Applauding the effort in his diary, Captain Goolden noted that "the final scheme will be drawn up by the Joint US and Canadian staffs, but we have at least set a lead and suggested anyhow something to start off with. Very good work on the part of Bourke."[38]

The system arrived at consisted of four layers. A USN vessel at the entrance to the western approaches of the Strait of Juan de Fuca served as Recognition Vessel, contacting all incoming ocean-going ships in order to provide them with current recognition signals. Next came the Strait Entrance Patrol, a USN antisubmarine screen that traversed between Waadah Island (near Neah Bay) on the American side to Own Point on the Canadian shore. Forty miles up the strait, USN and Canadian vessels were moored about four miles off each shore, tasked to direct incoming ships to the examination vessels off either William Head or Port Angeles. Finally, COPC provided a Mid-Straits Patrol, another antisubmarine barrier about seven miles west of the line Tongue Point–Beechy Head. The nerve centre of the system was on the American side at Port Angeles under a USN officer designated the Strait Patrol Officer, who had a RCN liaison officer on his staff and who was connected by teletype to the various headquarters and operational bases. Aerial patrols and harbour defence systems were not integrated directly into the system but could be called upon by the Strait Patrol Officer as required; plans to back up the sea patrols with shore-based search-lights and asdic were deemed unnecessary.[39] When the joint patrol organization was formally implemented on 28 January 1944, COPC deployed the antiquated armed yacht HMCS *Wolf* as its moored control vessel, and rotated four ships—two Bangors and two Fairmiles—on the Mid-Strait Patrol. Although it was never tested by the enemy, the integrated patrol organization proved a success and, with the exception of minor adjustments, remained intact until September 1945.

While working to establish the joint patrol system in the Strait of Juan de Fuca, Brodeur modified other operational aspects of his command. In November 1943, guard ships were withdrawn from RCAF stations at Ucluelet, Coal Harbour, and Alliford Bay; the next month patrol areas were enlarged so that fewer vessels were required to cover them. Later, in the summer of 1944, Brodeur used the three corvettes now under his control to reconstitute the offshore patrols last carried out by the Prince ships in 1941-42. A more drastic move, however, concerned the Fishermen's Reserve, who carried out most of the inshore patrol work. Towards the end of 1943 Brodeur recommended that all but three Fishermen's Reserve vessels be returned to their original owners, a proposal linked to personnel decisions made at NSHQ.[40] With the now limited threat of attack and with new construction on the way in the form of eight Fairmile B motor launches and eight Llewellyn class minesweepers—both of which classes could shoulder some of the inshore patrol burden—the Naval Board, acting on a recommendation of the Chief of Naval Personnel, approved the discharge of large numbers of FR personnel.[41] Officers and ratings were presented the choice of transferring to the

38. Goolden diary, 21 May 1943

39. "ROP of Joint Canadian–US Cte to Study and Investigate the Defences and Warning System of the Strait of Juan de Fuca," 27 May 1943, 1-2, DHH 191.009 (D5); NSM, 16 Aug 1943; Sec, JSC-PC to Sec, COS Cte Sec, 27 Oct 1943, DHH 193.009 (D25)

40. COPC, memos, 12 Nov 1943 and 20 Jan 1944; COPC, "Inshore Patrol, West Coast of Canada," 17 Dec 1943, COPC, "Off-Shore Patrol," 9 Aug 1944. LAC, RG 24, 11879, ES-0016-5

41. For the use of the Fairmiles and Llewellyns see NSM, 16 and 30 Oct 1944 and 3 July 1945.

RCNR or RCNVR, depending on their qualifications, or being discharged outright. By February some transfers—100 volunteered for overseas duty—and discharges had occurred, allowing Brodeur to return eleven vessels to private hands, but the system remained unwieldy.[42] Almost 200 FR personnel were still awaiting release in August, and were showing signs of unrest at the slow pace of discharge. In response, Captain F.G. Hart, RCN, Brodeur's Chief of Staff, recommended that all inshore patrols be cancelled, which would eliminate the need for any FR personnel whatsoever. COPC and the naval staff agreed, not only because it would solve personnel problems but also because the USN had recently suspended many of its inshore patrols along the west coast and off Alaska.

It was unfortunate that the Fishermen's Reserve did not survive until final victory was won. Although they had seen no action, and their existence had in the words of G.N. Tucker "been troubled," they had fulfilled a most necessary function. When fear of Japanese attack was at its highest, the vessels of the Fishermen's Reserve often provided the only reminder to the inhabitants of isolated communities that the navy was there to protect them.[43] This may not have been much and may not have happened often, but it was nonetheless important.

Besides the suspension of inshore patrolling and the disbandment of the Fishermen's Reserve, October 1944 saw the final changes to Pacific Command operations. Brodeur cancelled the offshore patrol that the three corvettes on strength had carried out since the summer, instead rotating them singly on the Queen Charlotte Sound patrol; while on passage to and from that duty they would patrol some ten to twenty-five miles off Vancouver Island while Llwellyn class minesweepers periodically carried out sweeps closer inshore. Esquimalt also provided four Bangors, nine Fairmiles, and two armed yachts to the ongoing Straits patrol. Further north NOIC Prince Rupert's three Bangors patrolled Dixon Entrance while the Llewellyns there occasionally swept Chatham Sound, Hecate Strait, and the western shore of the Queen Charlotte Islands.

This restructuring did not seriously weaken Canada's west coast naval defences. The most sensitive area, the Strait of Juan de Fuca, had not lost any protection, and the other important focal areas, Queen Charlotte Sound and Dixon Entrance, were both still guarded by standing patrols. Moreover, despite its own force reductions in the summer of 1944, Western Air Command still maintained antisubmarine patrol squadrons at Alliford Bay, Coal Harbour and Tofino, as well as fighter and strike squadrons at Patricia Bay, all supported by an effective chain of radar stations.[44] The only real change was the loss of continual inshore patrols, but with American forces moving in on Japan—that month they landed in the Philippines and decimated the Japanese navy in the Battle of Leyte Gulf—the chance of even pin-prick raids seemed remote.

That prediction proved accurate, although the Japanese did attempt a final offensive against North America when they released thousands of small paper or silk balloons in a desperate attempt to set North American forests on fire. This campaign was mounted between November 1944 and March 1945 to take advantage of strong upper air currents that could carry the balloons eastward across the Pacific; this was also, of course, the time of year that rain-soaked or snow-covered forests would be most difficult to ignite. Although about 285 balloons reportedly reached North

42. Naval Board minutes, 30 Aug and 28 Dec 1943, and COPC, "Fishermen's Reserve Vessels," 9 Mar 1944, LAC, RG 24, 11879, ES-0016-5; COPC to Sec NB, 10 July 1944, DHH 81/520/1700-902; Tucker, *Naval Service of Canada* II, 317

43. Tucker, *Naval Service of Canada* II, 317

44. Douglas, *Creation of a National Air Force*, 422

America, no massive fires resulted, and the only casualties were six people killed in Oregon while inspecting a balloon on the ground. The strange weapons also failed to ignite any effective propaganda, because a strict news blackout prevented the Japanese from learning any results of their campaign. Their only success was to force—albeit only to limited degree—the Canadian and American armed services to devote some forces to anti-balloon duties.[45]

The army and air force carried out the brunt of anti-balloon duty, but the RCN also played a small role.[46] In January 1945, Brodeur instituted new patrols whereby two Bangors from Esquimalt—Fairmiles took their place on the Strait patrol—anchored near the RCAF bases at Ucluelet and Winter Harbour, while another from Prince Rupert maintained station in Skidegate Channel. Maintaining constant communications with the bases, the Bangors were to be ready to transport bomb disposal teams to locations along the coast where balloons were observed to touch down. As it was, no balloons were sighted by the patrols. On the few occasions that a suspected balloon did land on the coast it was between Vancouver Island and the mainland or in areas where other RCN vessels were better able to respond. RCAF motor launches also accounted for a number of responses. Often, these leads turned out to be drifting mines or other items of naval ordnance of Allied or Japanese origin.[47] Thus, for the RCN the duty assumed the same uneventful character as most other operations on the west coast.[48]

The west coast naval war wound down quickly. At the end of July 1945, as the Allies tightened their grip on Japan and made preparations for an autumn assault on Kyushu, ships sailing the eastern Pacific received permission to burn dimmed navigation lights. On 10 August, the cruiser HMCS *Uganda* arrived in Esquimalt for refit. As will be seen later in this chapter, she had taken part in the fierce fighting around Okinawa, and her sailors undoubtedly told stories of determined kamikaze and stifling living conditions to those who had volunteered for the war against Japan. But the mood turned to celebration when on 14 August the Japanese announced their acceptance of Allied surrender terms.

With this happy news, COPC moved quickly to dismantle the naval patrol system but their American allies were not persuaded. On 25 August when Brodeur suggested, at NSHQ's behest, that patrols be withdrawn from the Strait of Juan de Fuca, the USN Commandant of the Northwest Sea Frontier replied that he wanted to wait until the surrender was actually signed.[49] Indeed, concerned that a fanatical submarine captain might mount a suicide mission up the strait, the American commander suggested that COPC assign two corvettes to carry out a special patrol at its entrance. The Canadians complied but there was no submarine within thousands of miles and all remained quiet.[50] After the Japanese formalized the surrender on 2 September 1945, Brodeur wait-

---

45. Ibid, 426; C.W. Conley, "The Great Japanese Balloon Offensive," *Air University Review* 19/2 (1968), 68-83; see also Major Mathias Joest, "Western Air Command and the Japanese Balloon Campaign," *Canadian Military Journal* 4:2 (Summer 2005), 59-68

46. Director of Military Operations and Planning (DMOP), "General Summary Japanese Balloons in Canada," 15 Mar 1945, DHH 74/715

47. For the results of the various balloon sightings, see PC daily reports in DHH 322.009 (D660), v 1-6, and WAC Weekly Intelligence Reports in DHH, mfm, roll 16.

48. COPC to NOICs Esquimalt and Prince Rupert, "Disposition of Bangor Minesweepers," 31 Jan 1945, LAC, RG 24, 11879, ES-04-11-1; COPC WD, Feb and Mar 1945, DHH

49. COPC to Commandant, NW Sea Frontier, 1813Z 25 Aug 1945, and COPC to NSHQ, 0002Z 28 Aug 1945, LAC, RG 24, 11872, DE16-10

50. COPC WD, Aug 1945, DHH

ed another four days before ordering all routine patrols to be withdrawn.[51] Six years and seven days after the west coast destroyer division had headed to the Atlantic, and almost four years after the attack on Pearl Harbor, Canada's west coast naval war came to an end.

Although NSHQ generally paid scant attention to the west coast, it had ambitious intentions for naval operations deeper into the Pacific. As the prospect of victory in Europe brightened on the horizon, the RCN initiated plans to take part in offensive operations against Japan, a campaign expected to last into 1946.[52] The rationale of Canada's naval leadership was both straightforward and understandable: Canadian ships attached to British, and possibly American, fleets in the Pacific, equipped and trained to rigorous standards, would be an appropriate reflection of Canada's place among the Allies. In a region where immense distances presented logistical problems unknown in Atlantic or European waters, and where blue water navies had proved instrumental to success, the RCN could take its place alongside the navies of two great powers, not simply providing convoy escort but as part of the principal fighting force. Moreover, the Pacific commitment would provide a useful model of what would come to be called "the continuing RCN" in that the fleet proposed for the Pacific war, defined in the context of post-hostilities planning, would contain elements of a permanent navy capable not only of cooperating with allies against a common enemy, but of assisting in the joint defence of the oceans adjacent to North America.[53]

Prime Minister Mackenzie King often said that what the naval establishment was really after was a strong postwar navy. He was, of course, correct. The navy had no intention of returning to what it considered to be the unsatisfactory prewar status of a few destroyers and auxiliary vessels. The motivation behind the acquisition of the Tribal class destroyers early in the war, the decision to deploy them overseas in European waters and the planning papers of mid-1943 calling for a balanced fleet were all directly related to the shape of the postwar navy. And, as we have seen throughout the war, the RCN had been largely successful in using a variety of means, some of which can be characterized as cavalier, to get what they wanted from the King government. But in the fall of 1943, the prime minister became aware of some of the games the RCN had been playing. On 21 October, Vice-Admiral Nelles admitted to the Cabinet War Committee that the RCN's aviation scheme was really for the postwar navy.[54] Then, in November, Admiral Sir Percy Noble, RN, head of the British Admiralty Delegation (BAD) in Washington, told King in an informal conversation how the RCN had manipulated events at the Quadrant conference to acquire modern cruisers. This last revelation, which King had long suspected, stirred him to complain in his diary that "it

---

51. COPC to NOICs Esquimalt, Prince Rupert, and Vancouver, 2232Z 6 Sep 1945, DE16-10

52. Although plans were tentative, the actual invasion of Japan, Operation Downfall, was divided into two main operations, Olympic, the assault on Kyushu scheduled for the autumn of 1945, and Coronet, the final assault on Honshu planned for March 1946. Spector, *Eagle against the Sun*, 542

53. This section relies on a narrative written by R. Sarty, since published as "The Ghosts of Fisher and Jellicoe: The Royal Canadian Navy and the Québec Conferences," in D.B. Woolner (ed), *The Second Québec Conference Revisited: Waging War, Formulating Peace: Canada, Great Britain, and the United States in 1944-1945* (New York 1998), 143-70. See also W.A.B. Douglas, "Conflict and Innovation in the Royal Canadian Navy, 1939-1945," in G. Jordan (ed), *Naval Warfare in the Twentieth Century* (London 1977), 210-32

54. King diary and CWC min, 21 Oct and 10 Nov 1943

was our department rather than the British that occasioned the cruisers being forced upon us by Churchill and Dudley Pound."[55] The result was a hardened attitude towards the RCN that lasted throughout the Pacific planning process.

When First Lord of the Admiralty A.V. Alexander sent a message confirming that two modern cruisers would be transferred to the RCN as a free gift, Canada's formal reply noted that the cruisers "will become an integral part of the Canadian Navy ... at the sole disposal of the Canadian Government." A private note to Canadian High Commissioner Vincent Massey put it more strongly: "it must be clearly understood, both by the United Kingdom authorities and by the public, that no strings are attached to the transfer of ships," meaning they would not be part of a united Commonwealth navy that could be deployed at the discretion of the Admiralty.[56] When Massey protested at the mean-spirited message, Assistant Under-Secretary of State for External Affairs H.H. Wrong warned that he had already tried to cool Ki[...] it had done no good.[57] The prime minister was on the warpath ag[...] ement to absorb Canada into a scheme for integrated P[...] ering, there had been a sea change in the p[...] htened his grip on the helm.

One way in which [...] Advisory Committee on Post-Hostilities Pla[...] the horizon in terms of Canada's role in the [...] ensure the primacy of civilian control in al[...] and that commitments were not made li[...] the war against Japan—and despite som[...] the contribution should be substantial. T[...] al principle he was enunciating in Parliament, [...] ld not be restricted to the largest, nor extended to [...] ntribution the state has to make."[58] Yet, at the same [...] balance in Pacific diplomacy, something that the m[...] eciate. Maximum national commitment to the war agai[...] nt already made to the war against the European axis pow[...] Canada too thoroughly under the direction of either Great Britain—helping [...] colonies in South East Asia—or the United States. Too little, and Canada would squander the international respect the country had earned through its war effort.[59]

To keep options open, either with regard to the Pacific war or post-hostilities Germany, authority for overseas commitments was centralized through the Advisory Committee on Post-Hostilities

55. King diary, 27 Nov 1943

56. SSEA to BHC, tg 58 and 59, 9 Jan 1944, in J.F. Hilliker (ed), *Documents on Canadian External Relations: 1944-5*, X, pt 1, 316-18, (hereafter *DCER*)

57. BHC to SSEA, tg 116, 12 Jan 1944, and AUSSEA to BHC, 18 Jan 1944, *DCER*, 319-20

58. HofC Debates, 9 July 1943, 4558

59. See e.g. R. Sarty, "'Entirely in the Hands of the Friendly Neighbour': The Canadian Armed Forces and the Defence of the Pacific Coast, 1919-1939," in his *The Maritime Defence of Canada*; G. Perras, "Canada as a Military Partner: Alliance Politics and the Campaign to Recapture the Aleutian Island of Kiska," *Journal of Military History* 56 (July 1992), 423-54; J.W. Holmes, *The Shaping of Peace: Canada and the Search for World Order, 1943-1957* (Toronto 1979), 23

Planning, which served as an adjunct to the Cabinet War Committee. It is beyond the scope of an operational history to outline the complex process through which the PHP committee was established or to discuss, in detail, the reports of the initial working group that shaped the direction of higher policy; the salient points are that the advisory committee became the de facto strategic planning cell of the Cabinet War Committee, that its direction reflected MacKenzie King's international outlook, and that it was firmly under the control of senior officials in the Department of External Affairs and the Privy Council.When the committee first met on 19 January 1944, the influential Under-Secretary of State for External Affairs N.A. Robertson served as chair, where he worked closely with two other powerful civil servants, Assistant Under-Secretary of State for External Affairs H.H. Wrong, and Secretary of the Privy Council Office A.D.P. Heeney. The three military chiefs of staff sat on the committee but, as will be seen, throughout the Pacific planning process their ability to shape policy was limited.

Despite the nationalistic stridency in Ottawa, Canada's naval contribution to the Pacific depended upon how the Royal Navy would act. Detailed planning by the Admiralty did not begin until late in 1943, and the plans that then materialized proved, for the most part, difficult or impossible to realize.[60] Thus, apart from the realization that convoy escort operations in the Pacific would offer little scope for the antisubmarine fleet developed during the war, all that NSHQ planners really had to go on until late in 1944 was Winston Churchill's inspiring rhetoric of June, 1943, in the London Guildhall: "I stand here to tell you today, as I told the Congress of the United States in your name, every man, every ship and every air plane in the King's service that can be moved to the Pacific will be sent and there maintained in action by the people of the British Commonwealth and Empire in priorities for as many years as are needed to make the Japanese in their turn submit or bite the dust."[61]

Churchill, in fact, had placed the Admiralty in an embarrassing position when in September 1943 he offered British naval support for the US effort in the Pacific before the RN was ready to give it.[62] Profound differences between Churchill and his chiefs of staff, and between the British and American high commands, at a time when Overlord and operations in the Mediterranean were matters of immediate and intense concern on both sides of the Atlantic, further complicated the situation. It is not too much to say that, so far as planning for the Pacific was concerned, confusion reigned in Whitehall, and it was not surprising that the guidance that the RCN sought and received from the Admiralty through the Canadian Naval Mission Overseas (CNMO) had been, to say the least, imprecise.[63]

The situation was not helped by a serious disconnect between the CNMO and NSHQ. It will be recalled that Vice-Admiral Nelles had incurred the displeasure of Angus L. Macdonald and in

---

60. Unsigned memo to SCFO (O), "Conversations with Admty Officers," 29 Feb 1944, CNMO Policy and Plans Reports, 14 Jan–7 Sep 1944, DHH 81/520/1650-1, Policy, v 3; H.P. Wilmot, *Grave of a Dozen Schemes: British Naval Planning and the War Against Japan, 1943-1945* (Annapolis 1995), *passim*

61. DOP to ACNS, "Appreciation of RCN Ship Requirements for the War against Japan and for the Post-War Navy," 29 July 1943, NSS 1655-2

62. Wilmot, *Grave of a Dozen Schemes*, 28-30

63. A.J. Marder, M. Jacobsen, and J. Horsfield, *Old Friends, New Enemies: The Royal Navy and the Imperial Japanese Navy: The Pacific War 1942-1945* (Oxford 1990), 334-44; C. Thorne, *Allies of a Kind: The United States, Britain, and the War against Japan, 1941-1945* (New York 1978), 403-4, 455; Wilmot, *Grave*, 102-34; Adm to Br Adm Delegation, Washington, signal 1847A 6 Nov 1943, PRO, ADM 1/13009; A.V. Alexander to Stark, 10 Dec 1943, enclosing "Aide Memoire on British Manpower Problems," PRO, ADM 1/17025; DOP to ACNS, 29 July 1943, NSS 1655-2.

January 1944 had been reassigned to London in the new and nebulously defined appointment of Senior Canadian Flag Officer Overseas (SCOFO(O)). He served as chief of the naval mission on Haymarket Square, created from the staff of the Senior Canadian Naval Officer (London), but it is clear that he remained out of favour in Ottawa. For his part, Nelles' successor as CNS, Rear-Admiral G.C. Jones, had his hands tied by the new policy environment in Canada's capital. Moreover, Jones was a careful bureaucrat and he seems to have left Nelles, who always prized and guarded his personal connections in the Admiralty, to lobby in London for the allocation of big ships to the RCN. Jones, meanwhile, kept himself and the rest of the staff in Ottawa out of the fray. Indeed, among Jones' first actions as CNS was to withhold further action on Pacific fleet recommendations until the King government laid down its policy. Thus, Nelles and his staff in England, who were attempting to advise the Admiralty on Canadian capabilities for supporting naval operations in the Pacific, could neither report exactly what the Admiralty intended for Canadian naval forces, nor receive adequate information from Ottawa about the forces Canada planned to make available.[64]

Working as they did in a kind of policy vacuum, Nelles and his staff improvised—enthusiastically. As 1944 wore on, his ability to open doors was bolstered by the fact that he was also serving as senior member of the newly established Canadian Joint Staff Mission (CJSM) in London, composed of Nelles, Lieutenant-General Kenneth Stuart and Air Vice-Marshal L.S. Breadner. Concerned with Canada's lack of input into high level strategic planning, the King government had established the CJSM, which, after difficult negotiations with Canada's American and British allies, was reluctantly granted formal access to the British Chiefs of Staff in the form of regularly scheduled consultations.[65] The mission's actual activities lie beyond this work, but Nelles used his position as senior member of the CJSM to gain direct access to senior commanders and their policy papers, particularly the First Sea Lord, Admiral of the Fleet Sir Andrew Cunningham, and Admiralty planners. Moreover, Nelles had the foresight to bring the talented Lieutenant-Commander G.F. Todd, RCNVR to London as his chief policy advisor and, later, secretary to the CJSM. Todd developed some useful contacts at his own working level in the Admiralty. He had become aware almost immediately of the planning difficulties in Whitehall, and came to believe that the Admiralty staff simply assumed that Canada would fall in line with its proposals.

On 14 June, 1944, the Admiralty finally gave Nelles an informal estimate of the help they envisioned from the RCN for the Pacific. The estimate, by including the cruisers and escort carriers already allocated or earmarked for the RCN, all of the Canadian fleet destroyers, ninety-one of the RCN's most modern escorts, and the possible transfer of additional modern ships such as a flotilla of fleet destroyers, reflected the British awareness, from their contact with Nelles and Todd, of what the RCN wanted to commit. In a thinly disguised quid pro quo, the Admiralty also urged the Canadians to undertake substantial new commitments among the less glamourous chores, especially the manning of landing craft and other amphibious warfare vessels whose seemingly endless thirst for manpower was the bane of the RN. The British proposals estimated a total of 40,000 personnel including immediate reserves in theatre to replace casualties. This figure was carefully calculated. British forces were planning to remain as fully

---

64.   NSM, 24 Jan 1944, DHH; Douglas, "Conflict and Innovation"; Sarty, "Ghosts of Fisher and Jellicoe"; Stacey, *Arms, Men and Governments*, 60. For parallel discussions about RCAF commitments, see Greenhous, *The Crucible of War*, 113-18.

65.   Stacey, *Arms, Men and Governments*, 187-95

mobilized for the Japanese phase of the war as the deepening manpower shortage would allow, which amounted to 70 percent of their peak wartime strength. Canada, the Admiralty hoped, would follow suit.[66]

Nelles and Todd were excited about the promise of a major RCN presence in the Pacific but the staff in Ottawa was more restrained. Observing that reorganization and partial mobilization after the defeat of Germany would create a manpower "squeeze,"[67] the staff proposed a ceiling of 25,000 for the Pacific, put the demand for landing craft at the bottom of the list, and suggested that planning should be limited to major warships and escorts.[68] Nor was that all. The proposal had to be reviewed by the Naval Board, on which the minister sat as chairman, and it concluded that in the absence of an overall plan for Commonwealth participation in the Pacific nothing could yet be decided; it therefore withheld approval.[69]

There was good reason for caution. In Ottawa, the air and army staffs raised concerns about British secrecy on the one hand and the delay in planning for the offensive against Japan on the other. Both services feared that they might be embarrassed by sudden demands that Canada pour large contributions into Southeast Asia, an area peripheral to Canadian interests and known for meagre gains at the cost of heavy losses to tropical disease and determined Japanese resistance. There was no evidence that the British had taken into account the Canadian preference, expressed in British Commonwealth Air Training Plan negotiations of January 1944, to participate in the main assault against Japan in the central or northern Pacific, even if that meant serving with the Americans.[70] The Canadian prime minister sent off a restatement of this position to Winston Churchill at the end of June, with a copy to the Americans.[71]

In London, Nelles and Todd were concerned with the lukewarm reception that the British proposals for a major RCN contribution to the Pacific had received. Although the British Chiefs of Staff accepted the limit of 25,000 personnel,[72] Canadian hopes of getting additional modern warships, particularly the light fleet carriers and eight fleet destroyers, might be disappointed if the RCN could not guarantee that the vessels would be available to serve under British control in the Pacific.[73] Still, an appeal from Nelles to Jones for a firming up of the Canadian commitment evoked only the evasive response that the government had yet to decide.[74] All that Nelles could give to the First Sea Lord, as the latter departed in early September for the second Québec Conference, code-named Octagon, was a reiteration of the naval staff's 25,000-man proposal of July with an explanation that it had

66. Higham, Military Branch, Adm to Todd, 14 Jun 1944, Todd to Sec NB, 14 Jun 1944, DHH 81/520/1650-1 (Policy and Plans), CNMO file MS 46-1-1, Far Eastern Policy

67. LCdr J.S. Hodgson, RCNVR, to DOP, 21 Jun 1944, NSS 1655-2, pt 1

68. NSM, 3 July 1944

69. Ibid, 12 July 1944

70. "Extract from min of 289th mtg COSC held at 1200 hrs, Wed 7th June 1944," DHH 193.009 (D32); A.D.P. Heeney, "Re: Canadian Participation in the War against Japan: The Position of the Three Services," 14 June 1944, *DCER*, 375-78

71. SecS to DSec, 27 June 1944, *DCER*, 380-1

72. (Br) Joint Planning Staff, "Employment of Canadian Forces after the Defeat of Germany," JP (44) 176 (Final), 24 July 1944, CNMO, NA (PP) 104, "Japan War—Policy"

73. Todd to Sec NB, "Canadian Participation and the General Strategy for the War after the Defeat of Germany," PP1/44, 3 Aug 1944, DHH81/520/1650-1, (Policy), pt 3, file Policy and Plans Reports, 14 Jan–7 Sep 1944

74. NSHQ to CNMO, 28 Aug 1944, "Personal for Head of Mission from CNS," DHH 95/197, pt 2

not received the sanction of either the Naval Board or Cabinet.[75] Unlike at the first Québec Conference, Nelles was in no position to foist any deals on an unsuspecting prime minister.

That King was unwilling to brook any surprises was clear from the stamp he imposed on Pacific policy in the Cabinet War Committee meeting of 31 August. He laid it down as a hard rule that Canadian forces should be committed only north of the equator, and pressed for a reduction of those forces to a bare minimum. He was able to use to good effect intelligence from Washington that the Americans did not want or need substantial British forces in the Pacific. Angus Macdonald was absent from the meeting but King nonetheless grasped the essence of the naval proposals—to send virtually the entire RCN to the Pacific—and braced himself for the "struggle" to cut back that ambitious scheme.[76] Clearly, King was determined to avoid a repetition of Quadrant.

Nothing was left to chance. On 6 September, King pulled out the heavy artillery at a rare meeting of the full Cabinet to demonstrate to the service ministers how weak support was for a major effort in the Pacific. Macdonald was present this time and his account shows the influence of domestic politics on Pacific planning: "Mr. King then said there was one point that had not been mentioned that was very important. The Tories generally were always talking about an Empire force, while the Liberals should stick to the doctrine of national forces. Dispatches from England were constantly talking about Imperial armies and Imperial forces. We must not lose our identity. He felt that our forces should not fight below the Equator. The climate in those areas was very unsuitable for our men. Consequently he was favouring an approach on the north." It dawned on the naval minister that King was turning a "preference" for operations in the central and northern Pacific into a rigid principle: "The Equator theory seems to me fantastic. It is true that our troops are not used to hot weather, but certainly in air and naval operations it is impossible to draw lines arbitrarily and say that you will not go beyond them."[77]

At Québec, on 13 September, the War Committee thrashed out the Pacific question for three and a half hours in preparation for a meeting the next day with Churchill and the British chiefs of staff. According to Macdonald's account:

> Prime Minister then went on to the question of a Canadian election, and said that we must not let it develop into an argument about Imperialism and the use of Canadian forces as part of an Imperialistic Army. We have done a great deal in this war, our taxes are very high. How much more could our people stand? The great financial contributions that we had made should be considered and should be taken to some extent as in lieu of manpower contribution.
>
> We must have a national force and not be swallowed up in an Imperial Army. Otherwise we would lose the support of Québec and the West. If Canadians were killed in Burma, people would say "What were they killed there for?" Even a few casualties there would make a lot of talk. It was all right for Britain to want to recapture lost territory, but is it our job to help in such an effort? [78]

---

75. CNMO, "Aide Memoir for the First Sea Lord on the Employment of Canadian Naval Forces after the Defeat of Germany," PP8/44, 31 Aug 1944, CNMO, MS 46-1-1

76. King diary and CWC Min, 31 Aug 1944

77. Macdonald diary, 6 Sep 1944, file 392, Angus L. Macdonald papers, Public Archives of Nova Scotia (PANS)

78. Ibid, 13 Sep 1944. See also King diary of same day

When the Canadian Chiefs of Staff joined the meeting, Vice-Admiral Jones said he favoured a substantial naval effort, along the lines of the seventy per cent of peak wartime strength that the British were applying. He also argued that the geographical demarcations were meaningless in the naval context, especially because of news from the main conference that the RN would be mounting a Pacific fleet that would be an integral part of the main USN fleet. Macdonald, for his part, took on the prime minister directly, accusing him of distorting agreed policy by converting the "preference" for the north and central Pacific into a demand.[79] Jones and Macdonald's arguments appear to have won an alteration to the draft statement from Cabinet. Previously having read, in part, "should be based on this principle," of participating in the North and Central Pacific, the statement was amended by the addition of the phrase "as a matter of preference." However, the qualifier was short-lived. At some point it was struck, and, when discussed at the joint meeting with Churchill and the British Chiefs of Staff the next day the statement stood word for word in its original form.[80]

To ensure his view held, King had also prepared the ground in personal discussions with Churchill. The British leader was receptive, not least because of earlier decisions that the main British push against the Japanese would be in the Pacific with the Americans, rather than as an independent Commonwealth effort in Southeast Asia. As a result, the main Anglo-American meeting on 14 September was notably different from the similar meeting at Quadrant the year before. Churchill readily agreed that Canadian forces should be engaged north of the equator, and that the recovery of colonies in Southeast Asia was properly a British responsibility. He chided Air Marshal Sir Charles Portal about the huge demands the RAF was placing on the RCAF, and agreed to support the Canadian desire to have its army contingent serve with the Americans. On the naval side, he referred to the struggle he had just had in getting the Americans to accept a British Pacific Fleet (BPF) that would work alongside the USN. He doubted that the RCN could hope for anything other than "sub-participation" as a part of the BPF. King found that acceptable, and agreed that the Philippines, upon which such a force might be based, qualified as a northern theatre in terms of his geographic formula.[81]

It reveals much about the strained relations between NSHQ and Admiral Nelles that the only inkling the London staff got of the developments at Québec was a 14 September report on the Anglo-Canadian meeting from the British Chiefs of Staff. Nelles smelled trouble, and was under considerable pressure because the Admiralty, not fully understanding the hedging from Ottawa, pressed for Canadian action to prepare for the despatch of ships through the Indian Ocean. On 30 September, Nelles asked NSHQ for some guidance in dealing with the Admiralty Plans Division, having learned from that source that, owing to the limited endurance of the Canadian Tribals, the recommendation would be to use them with RN Tribals in South East Asia. *Prince Henry* and *Prince David* were also definitely earmarked for operation Dracula, an amphibious assault at Rangoon, Burma. The answer from Ottawa was that the actual extent of participation was not yet decided, and that the CNMO would be informed when a decision had been reached. Finally, on 5 October, an exasperated Nelles signalled a plea directly to Macdonald, urging that he be allowed

---

79. Ibid

80. CWC min, 13 and 14 Sep 1944, *DCER*, 411-15

81. Macdonald diary, King diary and CWC min, 14 Sep 1944; Greenhous, *Crucible of War*, 113

to return to Ottawa from England to get the full picture: "I now feel that I and my immediate staff are quite out of touch with the views of NSHQ regarding the plans and/or proposals for the war against Japan, and that in effect we are representing Admiralty to NSHQ rather than NSHQ to Admiralty."[82]

For the time being this visit was not approved. Vice-Admiral Jones and Angus Macdonald no doubt wanted to put off any visits from Nelles until they had put the navy's case to the Cabinet War Committee, armed with the results of the meeting of 14 September. This they did on 5 October. It generated a heated discussion. Following the Octagon conference, Macdonald had tried in vain to head off the cuts that he knew King wanted to make in light of Churchill's statements on 14 September. The argument he advanced was that "we were the first to declare war on Japan. We had been summoned to a meeting at eight o'clock on Sunday evening [7 December 1941] and even before the US had declared war, the Government stated that we should declare war. We did not even wait for Parliament, furthermore, we have consistently talked about an all-out effort, about being in the war until the end, about standing side by side with our Allies, and so on. We were quite generous about giving away millions and billions of dollars in Mutual Aid, UNRRA, and so on, but when it came to our own service, we seemed to apply a different rule."[83] This failed to move an intransigent prime minister. He not only made it a specific naval requirement to abide by the "north of the equator" rule, but when Macdonald protested that the whole effort of the British Pacific Fleet would have to be staged through the Indian Ocean before it could fight in the north Pacific the prime minister asked, "why not keep our navy on our own coasts ... and use it when the final thrust was made against Japan." Cabinet was sympathetic to these views; Minister of Justice Louis St Laurent voiced the main concern, "whether our navy was to be appendage of UK navy or not."[84] With these types of suggestions, Macdonald later told Vincent Massey in London that King made "nonsense of naval warfare."[85] Warships simply could not join the main body of a fleet at the last moment, and hope to be capable of effective service. King's views, however, did make perfect sense to those who opposed, failed to understand, or gave little support to the concept of a blue water navy—of those who felt that such a navy would be operating in British, not Canadian, interests. The naval minister was forced to return to Cabinet on 11 October. When he did so, with estimates that had been more or less sliced in half, he had at least preserved the concept, and that would be of prime importance in the shaping of future naval policy. [86]

Nelles learned of these developments from a signal sent on 13 October. The ceiling of 25,000 personnel had been cut to 13,000 personnel afloat. There was to be no involvement whatsoever in operations in the Indian Ocean—if the British needed specialized Canadian ships for that theatre

---

82. CNMO to NSHQ, 1600Z/5 Oct 1944, DHH 75/197, pt 2. See also CNMO to NSHQ, signal 1800A 2 Oct 1944, File 376, Macdonald papers, PANS

83. Macdonald diary, 22 Sep 1944

84. Ibid, 5 Oct 1944

85. This statement might indicate Macdonald's "education" by his naval advisers. It appears in Vincent Massey, *What's Past is Prologue: The Memoirs of the Right Honourable Vincent Massey* (Toronto 1963), 415

86. Memo to CWC, 11 Oct 44, King papers, v 366/3876, ff C-253661. Ironically, shortly after the Cabinet had battled over limiting RCN operations to north of the Equator, the naval centre of gravity shifted north to Japanese waters as a result of the USN's momentous victory in the battle of Leyte Gulf (23-26 Oct 1944). See Marder, Jacobsen, and Horsfield, *Old Friends*, 349, and T.J. Cutler, *The Battle of Leyte Gulf* (New York 1994).

they would be welcome to man them with their own personnel. Plans for the early movement of RCN frigates to Southeast Asia to gain experience in tropical operations were cancelled because of the need to maintain antisubmarine defences on the Canadian Atlantic coast where *schnorkel*-equipped U-boats were sinking ships and successfully evading Allied forces. The First Sea Lord was unhappy that the personnel ceiling had apparently been reduced from 25,000 to 13,000, although later amplification of the Canadian proposal helped calm some of Cunningham's legendary temper when it turned out that there would be 13,412 "seagoing personnel." With about 4000 personnel in reserve, and another 20,000 in shore bases, the total commitment would be more than 37,000. Eventually, the Admiralty accepted the Canadian contribution as offered, but by that time Nelles was gone. He had received permission to return to Ottawa at the end of October 1944, when the naval minister informed him his services were no longer required. Macdonald had Nelles retired with effect from January 1945, when he was only 53. The minister allowed him the one honour of promotion from Vice-Admiral to Admiral, but it took effect after retirement and did not entitle Nelles to a full Admiral's pension. The negotiations that resulted in Admiralty acceptance of the Canadian proposals were conducted by the SCNO(L), Captain F.L. Houghton, assisted by Lieutenant-Commander Todd.[87]

Although the RCN had lost the battle over the size and thrust of its Pacific commitment, Nelles' earlier achievement at the 1943 Quadrant conference in Québec was bearing fruit. On 21 October 1944 HMCS *Uganda* commissioned in Charleston, South Carolina, where she had completed a major refit. As described by the British Ambassador to the United States, Sir Gerald Campbell, it was an occasion of pomp and—especially for the RCN—circumstance:

> When I reached Charleston I found quite a stir, for the Canadian Ambassador had arrived (at the tail end of a hurricane) with his Naval Attache, with Rear Admiral Reid, Captain Grant, Captain Thompson (these last two from Ottawa), and Lt. Commander Pemberton, Canadian Naval Liaison Officer in New York...Angus Mcdonald [sic] had been expected from Ottawa, but was unable to make the trip.
>
> All this shows what importance the Canadians attached to the transfer, and I found them all labouring happily under a feeling of excitement and anticipation caused by the acquisition of what they called in their official leaflet "the first Canadian cruiser." It was as though the Canadian Navy was reaching manhood and that, through its Navy, Canada herself was stepping forward and upward.
>
> ... It would not have been surprising had a note of independence been struck, but just the opposite was the case ... [The Canadian Ambassador] did just the thing that we often hope that Canadians will do, namely, played the part, throughout his remarks, of an interpreter of Great Britain to the United States. He followed the same line the next day during and after the ceremony of transference from the Royal Navy to the Royal Canadian Navy of H.M.S. Uganda, and the Canadian officers who were

---

87. NSHQ to CNMO, 1712Z 13 Oct 1944; CNMO to NSHQ, 1736A 16 Oct 1944; NSHQ to CNMO, 2009Z 20 Oct 1944; Personal for Hd of Mission, "Draft report on Visit to NSHQ," 15 Nov 1944; CNMO "Aide-Memoire for the First Sea Lord," PP21/44, 18 Dec 1944, CNMO CS 46-1-1, War against Japan—Policy

present endorsed his remarks in conversation asserting, amongst other things, that they were British first and Canadian second.[88]

Mackenzie King would have been horrified. Campbell's comments about the RCN representatives' predilection to Britishness may have been overstated; nevertheless, it was probably not by coincidence that the RCN chose 21 October, the anniversary of the Battle of Trafalgar—the greatest victory in the history of the Royal Navy—as the commissioning date for *Uganda*.

The ship had not, in fact, originally been intended for the RCN. Rather, the modified Fiji class cruisers *Minotaur* and *Superb*, still under construction, had been earmarked for delivery upon completion in June and August, 1944. This choice was not universally popular in British circles and left the First Lord, A.V. Alexander, to comment that "It comes as something of a shock to me to find that we propose to hand over to the Canadians two of the last and best of the modified FIJI cruisers ... would it not be possible to choose two vessels not quite so new?"[89] As it was, the completion dates for *Minotaur* and *Superb* had to be set back as a result of a number of problems, including congestion in the shipyards, the reordering of priorities to meet the RN's urgent need for light fleet carriers, and not least, trade union and management practices that were adversely affecting the entire industry in the United Kingdom.[90] In February, the Admiralty had announced that delivery would be delayed until October 1944 for *Minotaur* and March 1945 for *Superb*, the latter, as Houghton learned privately, to devote resources to the light fleet carrier HMS *Vengeance*. Accordingly, the Naval Board had decided to take *Minotaur* as planned and accept *Uganda*, which was offered in place of *Superb*.[91] But *Uganda*'s name created a minor problem. In previous transfers of ships from the RN to the RCN during the war, the name had been changed, but in this case an exception was made. Because the colony of Uganda had adopted the ship, and provided generous gifts of comforts and equipment in her first commission, the Admiralty prevailed upon the Naval Board at least for the time being to retain the original name.[92]

Ordered as part of the prewar rearmament of the RN in December 1937, and designed in accordance with the second London Naval Treaty limiting cruisers to 8,000 tons displacement, *Uganda* was the lead ship of a class of three, the others being *Ceylon* and *Newfoundland*. Inadequate anti-aircraft defences had resulted in serious losses to all types of British warships at the hands of the *Luftwaffe* off Norway and Dunkirk in 1940. In consequence the Uganda class ships, like other light cruisers still under construction, received modifications that included the replacement of one of four triple 6-inch turrets by additional anti-aircraft weaponry and improved high-angle fire control equipment. This gave her an impressive dual-purpose armament of nine 6-inch guns in triple mounts, eight 4-inch high-angle guns in twin mountings (two on each side of the ship) two quadruple 40mm Bofors, three quadruple 2-pounder pom-poms, eight single and four twin 20mm

88. Sir Gerald Campbell to DO, 30 Oct 1944, PRO, ADM 1/18371

89. First Sea Lord min, 16 Nov 1943, ibid

90. Asst Controller min, 7 Feb 1944, Director of Warship Production to Hd, Military Branch, 1 May 1944, ibid

91. NBM, 28 Feb 1944, DHH. Hd, Military Branch min 2 Feb 1944; Asst Comptroller min, 7 Feb 1944; "Private office," unaddressed and unsigned memo, 8 Feb 1944. PRO, ADM 1/18371

92. Adm to CNMO, 30 May 1944, Sec NB to Sec CNMO, 19 June 1944, LAC, RG 24, 11732, CS 153-15-1. In January 1952, she was commissioned as HMCS *Québec*

93. A. Raven and J. Roberts, *British Cruisers of World War Two* (London 1980), 296-315; P.C. Smith and J.R. Dominy, *Cruisers in Action, 1939-1945* (London, 1981), 31

Oerlikons, and six 21-inch torpedo tubes.[93] HMS *Uganda* entered service in January 1943 with the Home Fleet, intercepting blockade runners in the Bay of Biscay, and carrying out similar duties off the west coast of Africa, based on Freetown, before escorting convoys, mostly troop transports, to North Africa. She took part in coastal bombardments to support the landings in Sicily in July 1943, and conducted further similar operations in August.[94]

On 13 September 1943, while operating in the Gulf of Salerno in support of Allied landings on Italy's mainland, an Hs293 glider bomb—like the one that had struck HMCS *Athabaskan* less than a month before in the Bay of Biscay—damaged the ship so severely that she had to be taken in tow, and eventually made her way to Charleston, South Carolina, for a refit that incorporated extensive repairs. The ship was transformed through alterations and additions that included the latest radar, barrage directors, aircraft plotting equipment, fighter direction communications, fire control, damage control arrangements, and an action information centre, all in an attempt to incorporate the latest developments in naval warfare, particularly in anti-aircraft defence. Most of the work was done in Charleston, but a certain amount of improvisation proved necessary. "We knew what equipment we were going to get," recalled the ship's gunnery officer, Lieutenant W.M. Landymore, RCN "but we had nothing about them [sic] except one or two very sketchy handbooks. So, Dick [Lieutenant-Commander R.P. White, Torpedo Officer] and I took these handbooks, showing pictures of [the equipment]. We identified (using my magnifying glasses) what kind of cathode [tube] arrangements they had. We found a cathode arrangement, measured it, and we converted all these things into sizes and then put them on the bulkheads. We laid out the whole Ops room with nothing. All we knew was the correct dimensions of one of the 'idiot boxes'." The ship completed her new action information centre, which was situated in the starboard aircraft hangar, at Newcastle-on-Tyne in the United Kingom before proceeding to the Pacific.[95]

In command was Captain E.R. Mainguy, RCN, a future Chief of Naval Staff, who enjoyed a popular reputation in the wartime navy. With extensive experience before the war, both in cruisers and battleships of the Royal Navy, and in command of two RCN destroyers, he had commanded the destroyer HMCS *Ottawa*, which as we have seen had been the first Canadian warship to take part in the destruction of an enemy submarine, from April 1940 to July 1941. In subsequent appointments he had served as Captain (D) in St John's, where he had made innovative arrangements for the welfare of seagoing personnel, and had been Chief of Naval Personnel in Ottawa. His executive officer was Commander H.F. Pullen, RCN, who also had extensive wartime command experience in the destroyers *St Francis*, *Ottawa*, *St Laurent*, and *Ottawa* II, before taking up his appointment in *Uganda*.

Of great benefit was the fact that *Uganda*'s company consisted to a significant extent of officers and men who had been purposely sent to British cruisers for experience. About eighty Canadians had been serving in HMS *Belfast* during the engagement with *Scharnhorst* in December 1943, and others went to *Sheffield*, *Glasgow*, *Nigeria*, and *Jamaica*.[96] By March 1944 the program was well in place but it soon became apparent that there were not enough 6-inch cruisers in British home waters to take

94. J.M. Thornton, *The Big 'U'* (Unknown,1983), 7-11

95. BAMR Washington to Chief of the Bureau of Ships, Maint Div, USN, 24 Nov 1943, LAC, RG 24 (acc 83-84/167), 3634, 8060-CCL-31 v 1.; Interview with RAdm William Moss Landymore, 55, Landymore biog file; J.C. Littler, *Sea Fever* (Victoria, 1995), 231

96. Adm to C-in-C HF, 2 Feb 1944; Director of Personnel Services min, 2 Feb 1944; DPS to NSHQ; 18 Mar 1944. PRO, ADM 1/18371. Littler, *Sea Fever*, 208-25

on all personnel the Canadians were making available, even after senior officers allowed an extra dozen in each of *Belfast*, *Nigeria*, and *Jamaica*. Possible solutions were not lacking. Canadians could be sent to the Mediterranean, they could be posted into 8-inch cruisers operating with the Home Fleet, or they could gain experience in capital ships, such as the battleships *Nelson* and *Rodney*. The latter choice seemed best, since it offered the opportunity to train on their 6-inch secondary armament, similar to the main battery in Uganda and Fiji class cruisers. Some lower deck personnel therefore found themselves in *Rodney* with the possibility of further teams serving in *Nelson*.[97]

Learning about life and work in a British light cruiser was a culture shock for young Canadian sailors, but one they soon adapted to. In early 1944, Lieutenant W.H. Pugsley, RCNVR, a public relations officer who gained authorization to wear the uniform of a seaman to experience life on the lower deck, accompanied a draft of about 700 who made their way to *Niobe*. "They felt they were forgotten men, a sort of Lost Horde," Pugsley later reported. Other accounts confirm this impression: "There were trains waiting for us in Liverpool, took us to *Niobe* in Greenock, Scotland. We arrived in *Niobe* and they didn't even know we were coming—typical ... They didn't know what to do with us. They sent us all on two weeks leave." It was, of course, a sensible decision. "When we came back we were relatively organized. They had a list of cruisers and everyday they used to muster the draft and they would call out (for instance) '*Jamaica*—we need this and this and this. Okay? I want two STs [Seamen Torpedomen], I want three stokers, I want two signalmen—over there—step out.' So whoever wanted to do it, stepped out and that was the draft off to *Jamaica*, say."[98]

Pugsley accompanied the *Jamaica* group, which immediately ran into accommodation problems, with no slinging billets available for their hammocks: "Eventually some were found, but several of the Canucks who lived and ate in my mess had to sleep miles away in odd corners nearer their guns." For men used to uncomfortable, wet escort vessels this was no particular hardship, but the British sailor's diet reminded Pugsley of the French peasant who gave his horse less and less to eat because it was still working adequately, until the horse died. "If the peasant had known at what point in the process to stop, he would still have had his horse. He didn't know where that point was, but the Royal Navy knows—to a teaspoonful."[99]

Officers also went to cruisers for familiarization and training. Like *Uganda*'s navigator, Lieutenant-Commander J.C. Littler, RCNR, Landymore went to HMS *Belfast*, in his case as "fifth gunnery officer," in the four-turret ship. "*Belfast* was to get me groomed up so I could run a 6-inch cruiser ... And of course, they were identical. Everything—there was more of it that's all, in the *Belfast*. So, by the time they wanted me back in Canada, I had already had a very, very good basic education in 6-inch cruisers." Lieutenant H.E. Makovski, RCNVR, and some others, who unlike Landymore were not trained gunnery specialists, had different preparation. Apart from some time in the anti-aircraft cruiser HMCS *Prince Robert*, his training consisted of a ten-week high-angle control course in the UK, followed by two weeks of aircraft recognition, before joining *Uganda* in Charleston.[100]

---

97. Littler, Ibid

98. W.H. Pugsley, *Saints, Devils and Ordinary Seamen* (Toronto 1945), 152; DHH interview with ABS Andrew A. Lawson, 8 Apr 1987, 13, Lawson biog file

99. Pugsley, *Saints, Devils and Ordinary Seamen*, 152-3

100. SCNO(L) to NSHQ, 30 Dec 1943, LAC, RG 24, 1747, CS 384-45-2; Landymore interview, 54; interview with Cdr Hugh Eric Francis Makovski, 2 Apr 1988, 14-15, Makovski biog file. Makovski's experience was notable because his action station was the after director, where the glider bomb had hit, killing his predecessor.

Notwithstanding these careful preparations, *Uganda*, at least at the beginning of her commission, ran up against the same dislike of big ship routine that had plagued *Nabob*. As Makovski relates, "I heard a lot of grumbling and that sort of thing."[101] According to one of the ratings, A.A. Lawson, "I have to agree that it was a bad start, simply because there were so many men that real-ly didn't want that draft and I can't understand why ... I cannot understand the full reason why the attitude was such in this ship. I think in time, once we got to the Pacific, I think, much of that left."[102] Lawson suggested that the lack of leave prior to being sent down to Charleston may have had something to do with poor morale, but a young officer, Lieutenant E.M. Chadwick, RCN, proposed that "They were all corvette men and if they were half a mind whether they wanted to [join *Uganda*], as soon as they got there they wished they hadn't. For one thing it was bloody hot. The other thing was they never arrived with the proper kit ... And there wasn't much to do in Charleston, either."[103] The fact was, despite the training companies onboard British cruisers, two-thirds of the drafts had just completed service in small ships, and that may have had something to do with poor morale; perhaps "they didn't like big-ship routine."[104]

The cruiser sailed to Halifax for stores, then to the UK to complete its refit, and on New Year's Eve 1944 departed from the Clyde, working up during its passage down the Bay of Biscay and through the Mediterranean to Alexandria. The decision to deploy her with the British Pacific Fleet was an obvious one, given her anti-aircraft capability, and was covered under the Cabinet War Committee's final delineation of Canada's naval commitment to the Pacific war in October 1944. *Uganda* completed her work ups on 12 February 1945 and set out for the world's largest ocean. As often occurs, morale had improved with activity, although the discomforts were considerable. The quality and quantity of food was adequate but, for instance, as the ship's surgeon reported, "Vegetable supplies are variable and precautionary treatment requires much time and effort. The oatmeal purchased in Alexandria was found to be infected by 'Mealy Bugs'. These do not poison or impair the porridge, but they act as an effective barrier to it's consumption. Alterations in the refrigeration department are going to increase work and beef handling but promise more adequate and safe meat thawing." Cockroaches flourished: "It was not out of the ordinary" recollected another sailor, "to be munching on your de-hydrated peas and carrots to feel a sharp 'crunch.' That was another roach being broken up. Flour deteriorated into a life form—a tiny worm with a white body and a little black head. It would be found in the bread which was baked aboard ship. At first we would pick the worms out, but as we were told, and came to realize, they would not hurt us, we just ate them with the bread and called it our meat ration for the day."[105] Besides this, the heat brought on various forms of skin rash and fungal infections, unpleasant but not incapacitating. The prospect of interesting activity seems to have reconciled the men to these nuisances.

As *Uganda* made her way towards the Pacific the RCN's second cruiser, to be commissioned as HMCS *Ontario*, was nearing completion in Belfast. *Ontario* had even more enhanced anti-aircraft

---

101. Makovski interview, 15-16

102. Lawson interview, 25-26

103. Chadwick interview, 17-18

104. Makovski interview, 22

105. A. Murray Rogerson diary, note to 19-21 Feb 1944, Rogerson biog file

capability than *Uganda*. Her armament was similar to *Uganda*'s but *Ontario* was the only wartime cruiser of RN design to be fitted with the advanced type 275 gunnery control radar and the Mark VI high-angle director. Moreover, she was a beneficiary of the "Bubbly" program, which beginning in January 1945 provided ships intended for Pacific service with special kits to upgrade the performance of their radar receivers.[106] These upgrades caused the Admiralty to pay close attention to the officers and men assigned to the ship. The British naval staff vetted RCN appointments of officers, and did not hesitate to offer critical comments. "The Admiralty and the [RN] generally," reported the SCNO(L) from London, "are very interested if J3370 [HMCS *Ontario*] which is said to be at least a year ahead of her sister ship in modern fittings and this signal [is] be[ing] made only with the object of ensuring that the RCN makes the best possible showing in its first acquisition of a cruiser navy by appointing the best and most experienced specialist officers we possess."[107] The ship, it was noted, had sixteen radar sets, and there was concern that the radar officers selected had too little seagoing experience. Similarly, it was suggested that the gunnery officer should be exceptionally competent. The Admiralty recommended appointing Lieutenant-Commander K.L. Dyer, RCN in place of Lieutenant E.T.G. Madgwick, RCN, who had not yet held command, but Dyer was wanted by the RCN for one of the anticipated light fleet carriers.[108]

The commanding officer designate was Captain H.T.W. Grant, RCN. He, like Mainguy, would become a Chief of Naval Staff, and had considerable big ship service on exchange with the RN as well as in the Canadian cruiser HMCS *Aurora*, in commission in the RCN from 1920 to 1922. He had commanded *Skeena* at the outbreak of war, and later became the only Canadian officer to command RN cruisers–*Diomede* and *Enterprise*. He distinguished himself in the latter ship in an engagement with enemy destroyers in the Bay of Biscay in December 1943 and in the bombardment of Cherbourg after D-Day. His executive officer in *Ontario*, Commander E.P. Tisdall, RCN, had previously commanded *Skeena* and *Assiniboine*. As in *Uganda*, the department heads were some of the most senior and experienced specialists in the RCN. The ship's company was in place by mid-March 1945 and the ship commissioned on 26 April. *Ontario* immediately began working up for the Pacific.[109]

In addition to the cruisers, the RCN earmarked its four Tribal class destroyers, including the new Canadian-built *Micmac*, and the two Fleet Vs, *Algonquin* and *Sioux,* for the Pacific. The River class destroyers serving as escorts in the RCN were "considered unsuitable for Pacific operations in view of their age and consequent maintenance requirements, their limited endurance as compared with modern destroyers, and their lack of adequate A/A armament to operate with a fleet against shore-based aircraft."[110] The Admiralty, in spite of an overall shortage of destroyers available to meet Pacific commitments, was shorter still of manpower and offered the RCN eight new Crescent class destroyers, which were accepted. The first torpedo and gunnery officers arrived in Britain for

106. Raven and Roberts, *British Cruisers*, 320; Howse, *Radar at Sea*, 237-42

107. SCNO(L) to NSHQ, 3 June 1944, LAC, RG 24 (Acc 83-84/167), 3610, 8020-CCL

108. Ibid

109. RCN Depot Halifax to NSHQ (R) Niobe and Ontario, nd, LAC, RG 24, 11731, CS 153-10-7; Adm/Supt of Contract Built Ships to Adm Sec, 2 May 1945, ibid, CS 153-10-15; Nominal List of Officers Borne in HMCS *Ontario*, 26 Apr 1945, ibid, CS 153-10-7; John M. MacFarlane, *Canada's Admirals and Commodores* (Victoria 1992), 22, 44

110. CNS to minister, 20 Feb 1945, NSS 1655-9

familiarization in April 1945. It would therefore be some time before these ships were ready for operations.[111] In the event, the war ended before they could see service.

Along with the cruisers and fleet destroyers, the RCN planned to commit a significant number of escorts to the Pacific. Numbers fluctuated as plans evolved but in May 1945 the service was looking to deploy some thirty-six River class frigates and eight Castle class corvettes.[112] But even as they jostled with numbers, planners recognized that the ships involved would have to be modernized not only to suit a tropical climate but also to fight a type of warfare that was vastly different from what they had experienced on the North Atlantic and in European waters.

The first steps in the process began in December 1943 when J.H.L. Johnstone, the RCN's Director of Operational Research, met with the Royal New Zealand Navy's Director of Scientific Research to discuss conditions in the South Pacific. Johnstone reported that "The chief difficulty is with the hot salt water and the driving rain, which soaks and penetrates into everything. It is, therefore, essential that all components of fighting equipment on ships should be tropicalized." Also, given the heavy use of the carrier- and land-based aircraft, "Emphasis was placed on the most modern fire control for long range AA guns. Distances to base are so great that economy in the expenditure of ammunition is a very important consideration," and the importance of fighter direction ships was also stressed.[113] The following month, Johnstone inspected the cruiser HMNZS *Leander*, which was undergoing a major refit at the Boston navy yard. It quickly became clear by comparison that Canadian ships were not prepared for operations in the Pacific, and Johnstone suggested that research be carried out on, among other things, ventilation, refrigeration, the special treatment of electronic equipment, the protection of exposed metal surfaces (including guns), cold drinking water machines, improved facilities for personnel, and the elimination of fire hazards.[114]

Operational research scientists also looked into the actual task of fighting a war in the Far East, and since the RCN had come to focus most of its resources on antisubmarine warfare, studying it was something of a priority. A new theatre, quite clearly, meant different characteristics, and therefore different requirements. For example, whereas radar made the first contact 19 percent of the time in encounters with enemy units in the North Atlantic, the figure for the Pacific was 48 percent, with asdic falling to second place at 26 percent, and visual sighting only responsible for 10 percent of first contacts, an important change in emphasis from the combination of asdic/visual sightings to reliance almost exclusively on electromagnetic means. This was due in part to the USN's superior radar technology.[115] Also different was the very importance of antisubmarine warfare, which "in the Pacific has not been urgent." Only two merchant vessels were sunk in the Pacific Ocean and forty-one in the Indian Ocean in the course of 1944. The Japanese had only about sixty submarines of over 500-tons displacement, as compared with the Germans' 400,

---

111. *Niobe* to FOIC Glasgow, 23 Apr 1945, LAC, RG 24, 11733, 156-1-1. Ultimately, with the sudden end of the Pacific war, only *Crescent* and *Crusader* were commissioned into the RCN.

112. Naval Asst (Policy and Plans) to CNMO, 4 May 1945, DHH, 81/520/8000, Frigates (River Class)

113. DOR to ACNS, "Notes on a Conversation on Dec 20th, 1943 with LCol Marsden, C.B, M.C, Director of Scientific Research for New Zealand," 22 Dec 1943, LAC, RG 24, 11463, DOR—Reports

114. "Report of Visit of J.H.L. Johsntone ... to Washington and Boston, January 12th to January 15th, 1944," 20 Jan 1944, LAC, RG 24, 11,463, DOR—Reports on Trips

115. "Submarine Warfare in the Pacific, No 1, 31 May 45," 31 May 1945, DOR—Official Memoranda

and the former had to use theirs for evacuation and resupply, leaving them very little time (or space for torpedoes) to engage in a *guerre de course*." Furthermore, Japanese boats had weaker hulls, and hence were able to dive less deeply, while being less manoeuvrable. In the Allied experience, therefore, "It has proved impossible to maintain enthusiasm for A/S work on board the ships without artificial stimulation due to the Japanese submarine menace not having proved sufficiently serious."[116]

Aerial warfare represented another extreme. Although Japanese strength in carrier-based air power was largely eliminated in the "Great Marianas Turkey Shoot" at the Battle of the Philippine Sea in June 1944, there was still a potent land-based force that could threaten fleets operating in the seas around the home islands.[117] Moreover, the introduction of unconventional *kamikaze* tactics during the Philippines campaign of October 1944 was sobering, to say the least.

> The planes appear to follow no hard and fast rules in delivering attacks. They may approach at high, medium or low altitude. Frequently they will come in low on the water to take advantage of the inability of ship-borne radars to supply low coverage at moderate distances. Low altitude approaches are particularly common along land-blocked areas where radar coverage against such an approach is practically nil because of land echoes. In many cases, weather conditions seem to be the factor deciding the altitude of approach, with the enemy exploiting every possible advantage to be gained from existing cloud cover. Where high-flying planes used to make level approaches, suicide planes show a tendency to vary altitude continuously. This has made the tracking problem more difficult as present ship-borne radar is unable to give continuous altitude presentation. "Window" has been used extensively by the enemy but this has not yet proved a major problem in tracking, although it has at times affected adversely the fire control sets.[118]

Most worrisome was the statement that "Expert aviation opinion now holds that if a suicide plane has not A/A fire to contend with, it should always be able to hit the target."[119] Added to the problem was that the aircraft had to be completely destroyed and not just damaged, because so long as it could fly at all it remained a potential danger.

Staff officers still had to determine what modifications to the ships were necessary to allow them to operate effectively in the Pacific. Relying heavily on the operational research described above, in February 1944 the Naval Staff discussed the work required. "While it was appreciated that no concrete action can be taken until the plans for the RCN participation in the War against Japan are made known, ACNS, for Naval Staff, recommended to Naval Board that approval in principle be given to commence planning for the many requirements involved; the technical details to be worked out at a later date."[120] Given priorities elsewhere, it was not until September that the Naval Staff discussed the issue in more detail, noting requirements for awnings to keep direct sunlight off portions of the ship, table and bracket fans, measures to guard against vermin, refrigera-

---

116. DOR, "Notes on the A/S Problem in the Pacific," 18 Jun 1945," ibid

117. Peattie, *Sunburst* 189

118. DOR, "Suicide Attacks on Naval Units by Japanese Aircraft," 1 Aug 1945," DOR—Official Memoranda

119. Ibid

120. NSM, 14 Feb 1944, DHH

tors, light camouflage instead of the darker colours used in the North Atlantic, and additional motorboats.[121]

The devil, it is said, is in the details. A ship is certainly no exception, especially given its nature as a compromise between space, technology, comfort, and role. Fresh water, for example, was a crucial element in tropicalization, whether as drinking water or for keeping illness at bay by, for example, laundering clothes to prevent skin complaints. Still, trade-offs were required. In August 1944 it was decided to purchase $170 thousand worth of water coolers for 208 ships, "as this is considered to be a prime necessity under the subject study of Tropicalization,"[122] but in November it became necessary to reduce the number of such coolers in each ship to conserve fresh water and save space.[123] Similarly, the October 1944 minutes of a Naval Staff meeting proclaimed that "it is evident that the spread of tropical diseases amongst Naval personnel is directly affected by the equipment supplied for dish washing and laundering," and that the Chief of Naval Equipment and Supply (CNES), "is of the opinion, after consideration of the various reports available, that the provision of adequate dish washing and laundering equipment is of such importance to the health and welfare of ships' personnel, that, if necessary, reductions in complement and/or armament should be made to accommodate this equipment."[124] By April of the following year, however, NSHQ received the ominous report that "commercial laundering equipment cannot be obtained from US sources within a period of approximately one year and even that date is dependent on schedules given electrical manufacturers by the US Army and Navy Bureau."[125] Even when researchers and staff officers were agreed on the need for certain equipment, therefore, its installation was far from guaranteed.

And if policymakers were not agreed? Such was the case with air conditioning, and here the USN was less helpful than in other areas, with its own experts unable to reach a consensus on the issue. As was reported to the Naval Staff in October 1944, "It has now been determined that there is a strong demand from the Medical Branch of the USN and the US Navy air-conditioning section of the Bureau of Ships for air-conditioning to be fitted. The Operations Branch, however, are not convinced of the absolute necessity for this and whether the improvements which might result would justify the loss of space and added weight occasioned in the fitting."[126] There had, however, already been a fair amount of study conducted by the United States, the United Kingdom, and Canada, so the Naval Policy Committee for the War against Japan could recommend in November that equipment be installed to maintain a corrected temperature of 80° Fahrenheit. The Chief of Naval Engineering and Construction suggested that the words "as practicable" be added to the recommendation, since the target temperature was something of an ideal condition; a visit to the US had determined that certain spaces, such as action information centres, plotting rooms, and flag officers' conference rooms should be air-conditioned, while living spaces should not. He noted that

121. Ibid, 25 Sep 1944. For more on the shortage of motorboats and other logistical challenges faced by the USN in the Pacific, see Worrall R. Carter, *Beans, Bullets and Black Oil*.

122. NSM, 7 Aug 1944

123. Ibid, 27 Nov 1944

124. Ibid, 10 Oct 1944 (CNES, Chief of Naval Equipment and Supply)

125. Ibid, 2 Apr 1945

126. Ibid, 2 Oct 1944

the goal was "not to produce maximum comfort but full efficiency." The meeting, nevertheless, agreed to a more comprehensive approach, the goal: to maintain an 80° temperature in magazines, living spaces, and control stations, a decision the CNS confirmed.[127]

There was more, of course, than comfort and efficiency to consider—the ships' very role could change given the different nature of the Pacific war. As Operational Research reports were making evident, and as we have seen elsewhere in this chapter, in 1944-45 air power proved a much greater threat to Allied operations in that theatre than it did in the Atlantic. In May 1944, in spite of preparations for the landings in Normandy, the Admiralty requested that twenty frigates under construction in Canada be completed as anti-aircraft escorts equipped with twin 4-inch High Angle (HA) main armament, and additional 40mm Bofors close-range weapons, as well as improved radar and gunnery control instruments. The necessary staff requirements were made available the following month, although it was on six rather than twenty ships that work was stopped so that the changes could be implemented. Yet another month went by before the Naval Staff learned that the first dozen sets of armament and controlling gear would not be available until about May 1945—ten months away. It was therefore decided that all frigates then under construction would be completed to their original configuration.[128]

The need for anti-aircraft vessels in the Pacific could not be denied, but required or not, neither British nor Canadian shipbuilders were able to provide them in adequate numbers. In November 1944 the CNMO reported from London that, according to unofficial information, "it is anticipated that there will be an overall shortage of A/A escorts," so that instead of equal numbers of anti-aircraft and antisubmarine vessels, "now proportion of 1 to 2 to 3 will have to be accepted." The air arm of the Imperial Japanese Navy was not what it had once been, however, so that "Requirements for A/A escorts will vary depending on proximity of enemy land based aircraft. As a general indication in a group of 6 escorts 2 should be A/A in a group of 8, 3 should be A/A. It is possible groups in the Pacific may have to be composite groups RN and RCN according to types of ships available." To add bitter herbs to an already foul tasting soup, the CNMO reported that even though planners had suggested that "the RCN might convert 10 or 12 frigates to A/A frigates, experts" had concluded that "River Class Frigates are not suitable for conversion."[129]

One problem was that equipping a ship with a high-angle gun marked only one step towards making it an anti-aircraft vessel: it also needed some form of specialized fire control so it would have a reasonable chance of hitting its aerial target. Therefore, even those ships that had been or were about to be armed with high-angle 4-inch guns could not be considered for anti-aircraft duties. At a December 1944 meeting of the Naval Staff, the Director of Warfare and Training "was of the opinion that Naval Staff must accept the fact that if RCN ships are convoying in waters where air attack is likely, it is probable that RN AA escorts will be included in the groups and Carriers will be in company. It would, therefore, not be essential for RCN ships to be converted for AA or FD [Fighter Direction] purposes at the expense of their A/S equipment,"[130] although they would still need anti-aircraft weapons to increase their survivability. Oerlikons, with their 20mm

127. Ibid, 13 Nov 1944

128. Ibid, 12 and 26 June 1944

129. CNMO to NSHQ, 9 Nov 1944, LAC, RG 24, 8150, 1655-12

130. NSM, 18 Dec 1944

bore, were found to be "of little value against Suiciders," and the BPF had chosen to replace them with 40mm Bofors. Indeed, by March 1945 it had become BPF policy to "Add as many single Bofors as possible wherever space can be found."[131]

Though the record is somewhat sketchy, it seems that the RCN followed suit, a message from NSHQ to the C-in-C BPF Admiral Sir Bruce Fraser, advising that "Boffins"—single Bofors guns on Oerlikon powered mountings—would be installed at the rate of two each in Fleet destroyers, three each in thirty-six frigates, and four in *Uganda*.[132] This still begged the question of effectiveness, especially given the specific roles the C-in-C BPF had determined for the Canadian ships, roles that overturned previous RCN speculation that the RN might take on the anti-aircraft task in toto. "RCN Tribals and Destroyers will be employed with the fleet with main functions A/A and A/S screens. They may be required for bombardment. Opportunities for surface action will probably be rare but cannot be ruled out entirely. The need for A/A efficiency is paramount." As for smaller vessels, "RCN Frigates will be employed mainly as A/A and A/S escorts for fleet train ships in or proceeding to the fleets [sic] area of replenishment at sea."[133] Captain J.D. Prentice, commanding officer of the RCN work-up base in Bermuda, HMCS *Somers Isles*, did not think the frigates would be up to the task. At a meeting held in Halifax on 3 July, he "spoke of his visit to the USA Work-Up Base at Guantanamo showing the great stress that was laid on A/A practices of every kind. He gave figures with regard to the casualties which the US Navy had experienced from suicide bombers and the steps relative to equipment and training which they were taking to reduce these. He said that in his opinion ... it would be equivalent to murder to send our Frigates as at present equipped to the Pacific War, and recommended that C-in-C BPF be asked whether or not he would accept ships in this condition."[134] The meeting agreed that "Every effort should be made to equip and train HMC Ships so that they would be able to meet the enemy on an equal footing,"while admitting that the first ten frigates slotted to sail to the Pacific would not be on such footing, lacking as they were modern radar and action information centres.[135]

Given such complex issues of research, development, doctrine, and policymaking, only a wide-eyed optimist could have expected frigates and corvettes to be prepared for duty in the Pacific according to anything but the most flexible schedule. By November 1944 the Director of Warfare and Training, for one, was suggesting that surveys be made of both coasts for facilities that could refit frigates and Castle class corvettes, that several possible dates for ending the war against Germany be determined for planning purposes, and that various equipment programs (such as for the Bofors and radar) be finalized. There did not, however, seem to be much sense of urgency within the Naval Staff; a meeting of 22 November noted that only one frigate per month was due for refit in February, March, and April, none in May, two in June, and seven in July. The Director of Operations, Captain D.K. Laidlaw, went so far as to suggest that the first detachment to the Pacific consist of new construction ships, untropicalized, with more appropriate vessels replacing them when ready, hence avoiding having to accelerate the refit program.[136] The U-boat war threatened

131. C-in-C BPF to AC11, 28 May 1945, DHH, 81/520/1000-146/21, v 3

132. NSHQ to C-in-C BPF, 19 June 1945, ibid

133. C-in-C BPF to NSHQ, 2 July 1945, LAC, RG 24, 11121, 71-1-1

134. Min mtg at Halifax, 3 July 1945, ibid

135. Ibid

136. NSM, 27 Nov 1944

to continue in one form or another for an indeterminate period, and this relaxed attitude towards Pacific operations continued until February 1945, when the Naval Staff noted that at current refitting rates only two frigates and two Castle class corvettes would be completely modernized by November. "Thus if more than four ships are required for the Pacific before the end of the year, the balance would lack tropicalization and certain other equipment."[137]

The Assistant Chief of the Naval Staff, Captain H.G. DeWolf, may have been attempting to light a fire under his colleagues when he suggested that planning for a Pacific fleet be based on sending half the allocated frigates and Castles (eighteen and four respectively) as an initial allocation, two months after the defeat of Germany being required before any ships could proceed to the new theatre. The minimum state of modernization for the frigates would include water coolers, awnings, ventilation, twin 4-inch guns, twin Bofors, type 144Q and 147B asdic, type SU or 277 radar, updated communications equipment, and power supplies. The Castle class corvettes would be somewhat easier to modify, requiring new radar, insulation, and increased ventilation.[138] The CNS confirmed the decision, but a little over a month later an engineering review concluded that the ACNS's plan could not be carried out until the end of the year. Although *New Glasgow*, the last ship requiring twin 4-inch guns, would be taken in hand in April, delivery of the Bofors guns was indeterminate and certainly not expected before June—leading to Prentice's July charge that it would be murder to send these ships into harm's way.[139]

The German surrender removed the most important distraction to planning for Pacific operations. Only a few days later the Director of Plans, Captain H.S. Rayner, recommended to DeWolf that the first order of priority after the definite end of the U-boat campaign (called X-day) should be implementing the requirements for the war against Japan, followed by coastal patrols in Canadian waters, mine clearing, returning ships to the RN, and disposal of the rest. Rayner felt the need to note that "action regarding the disposal of ships must in no way interfere with the tropicalization or refit of ships earmarked for the Canadian Pacific Fleet, where this can be avoided." In carrying out such priority tasks, "Some degree of interference is perhaps inevitable," but the C-in-C Canadian Northwest Atlantic had the authority to clear shipyards to ensure vessels requiring tropicalization were first in line. The need for such measures was obvious, for although "The Japanese War will be the major operational task of the RCN after X-day," the Director of Plans advised that "no frigates (nor Castles) will have been tropicalized during refit by X-day: therefore tropicalization will be the most urgent requirement." Rayner's plan called for the first four frigates with more than six months out of refit to be released from operations and steamed to west coast yards for refit and tropicalization. Frigates which had become operational in the preceding six months would be taken in hand on the east coast at the rate of eight per month. "When the 'tropicalization only' program on the East Coast is virtually completed, new refits may be begun. Ships longest out of refit should be taken first for refit: in this way the most serviceable ships of these classes (Frigates and Castles) may be kept in operation to meet residual requirements in the Atlantic (including Canadian and UK coastal waters)."[140] The Admiralty, which was coordinating

137. Ibid, 12 Feb 1945

138. Ibid, 12 Feb 1945

139. Ibid, 26 Mar 1945

140. DOP to ACNS, 10 May 1945, LAC, RG 24 (acc 83-84/167), 3923, 8375-300, v 1

alterations and additions for RCN Tribals and fleet destroyers,[141] was kept informed about RCN plans concerning the frigates and Castle class corvettes, including the proviso that each ship refitting on the east coast would require a month's work up and two months' steaming time before arriving in Manus or Sydney.[142]

X-day had clearly come and gone by the end of May, and on 3 July, at the Halifax meeting mentioned earlier in this study, Engineer Captain J.G. Knowlton, representing the Commodore Superintendent Halifax, provided a tropicalization and refit progress report. Of the destroyers, he estimated that *Algonquin* would be ready on 15 August, *Sioux*, *Haida* and possibly *Micmac* on 1 September, and *Huron* and *Iroquois* on the 15th. Ten frigates would be tropicalized by 20 July with ten others, if fitted with action information centres, ready by 1 September, a further twelve by 1 October, and six more as yet unnamed, accepted on 1 August for completion by 1 November. The main problem, then, was no longer getting ships ready, but putting trained sailors into them. The education and indoctrination they had undergone for operations in the North Atlantic was in many ways inadequate for the war then raging in the Pacific. Captain J.C. Hibbard, Captain (D) Halifax, predicted that "he considered that the efficiency of the ships' personnel would be similar to that encountered in 1942." He added "that he considered that the efficiency of the ships (material and personnel) upon arrival at Bermuda would be lower than that encountered in the past, the main reasons for this being lack of maintenance and training during refit as none of the personnel proceeding to the East were at present in the ships and would not be there until just before the ship sailed." Captain Prentice of *Somers Isles* agreed with Hibbard and noted that "we were facing an entirely new problem, and that relatively we were in the same position as we had been in 1941 as regards the submarine war." The meeting agreed that "Improved equipment, facilities, and instructors were required at all points, Cornwallis, Halifax and Somers Isles; it is recommended that officers with Pacific operational experience be temporarily appointed."[143]

By mid-July NSHQ could report to the Admiralty that the first group of about eight frigates would be arriving on station around mid-November, with further groups, totalling twenty-eight ships, arriving in the month and a half that followed (the CNMO had advised NSHQ on 28 May that the Admiralty had decided not to use Castle class corvettes).[144] However, "it is pointed out that no frigates will have warning air radar or main armament directors. 10 will not be fitted with AIO and could not be so fitted without delaying the whole program at least one month." Further, "All 36 frigates above will be fitted with 3 Boffins. To fit twin Bofors in these frigates in place of one Boffin would entail a delay of at least 2 months in the whole program."[145] Given the various delays, shortfalls and uncertainty, war's end must have come as a great relief to those involved in planning such refits.

---

141. Cdr (L) E.G. Cullwick, Dir Elect Eng, to DSR, 22 Nov 1944, LAC, RG 24 (acc 83-84/167), 3655, 8060-DDE/V

142. CNMO to Adm, 23 May 1945, DHH 81/520/1000-146/21, v 3

143. Min mtg at Halifax, 3 July 1945

144. CNMO (NAPP) to NSHQ, 28 May 1945, DHH 81/520/1650-1, Naval Plans and Policies, War against Japan—Escorts

145. NSHQ to Adm, 17 Jul 45, DHH 81/520/1650-1, Naval Plans and Policies, War against Japan—Escorts. The AIO is the Action Information Organization.

As the RCN planned the modification of the ships destined for the Canadian Pacific Fleet, *Uganda* was arriving in the war zone. Her ship's company not only had to face the challenges of the new theatre of war but also the bizarre outcome of Canadian manpower policies that had already brought on two conscription crises during the conflict. Mackenzie King and other members of Cabinet were highly sensitive to the issue of conscription, which had split the country under Sir Robert Borden's government in the First World War, and had been the subject of a referendum in 1942 that received a "No" vote in Québec and in French-Canadian constituencies in Ontario, Manitoba, and New Brunswick, as well as areas with large German and Ukrainian populations in Alberta and Saskatchewan, while receiving a "Yes" vote in English-speaking parts of the country. In 1944 the controversy had been heightened by the bitter disagreement among Cabinet members about the need to impose conscription for service overseas under the terms of the National Resources Mobilization Act. This did not affect directly the navy or the air force, all of whose members were volunteers, but after much agonizing, and after the forced resignation of Minister of National Defence J.L. Ralston, conscription for overseas service in the army was adopted. When it became likely that Canadians would serve overseas in the war against Japan as well as in the war in Europe, King feared that the conscription issue would again split public opinion as it had done in 1918 and 1942. His first and consistent objective was to bring Canada out of the war as a unified country, and he was determined to keep his promise never to impose conscription unnecessarily.[146]

On 22 March 1945, Arnold Heeney, the secretary of the Cabinet War Committee, "reported that the Prime Minister [who was indisposed and absent from the meeting] proposed to make a short statement in Parliament, in the near future, on the government's intentions as to Canadian participation in the war against Japan ... The statement would inform the House that there would be no conscription for service in the Pacific, that Naval and Air Force units to be despatched to that theatre would be constituted on a voluntary basis, and that the Army contingent would be made up of volunteers, plus short service GS personnel; no difficulty was anticipated in obtaining the numbers of personnel required for any of the three Services." In subsequent meetings the ministers agreed that King's proposed statement would require substantial revisions, "particularly in relation to those paragraphs which dealt with the method of selecting personnel for the Pacific contingents; in this respect government policy was not clear."[147] But King's point, one that exemplified his overwhelming concern for the avoidance of domestic strife, placed him at odds with the ambitions of the Canadian military establishment."The mere desire," he confided to his diary, "of having token contribution for prestige purposes was not sufficient reason for raising the conscription issue or indeed needlessly sacrificing lives."[148]

The prime minister announced his policy to the House of Commons on 4 April. Only those specifically volunteering for service in the Pacific would be sent to that theatre, and "All personnel returning from abroad will be granted thirty day's disembarkation leave, in addition to any nor-

---

146. Stacey, *Arms, Men and Governments*, 397-484; J.L. Granatstein, *Canada's War: The Politics of the Mackenzie King Government, 1939-1945* (Toronto 1975), 201-48, 333-81; J.L. Granatstein and J.M. Hitsman, *Broken Promises: A History of Conscription in Canada* (Toronto, 1977) 171 (see also 60-104, 133-244)

147. Min CWC, 22 and 29 Mar 1945, cited in W. Rawling, "Paved with Good Intentions: HMCS *Uganda*, the Pacific War, and the Volunteer Issue," *Canadian Military History* 4/2 (1995), 23-33. This article provides much of the basis for this discussion.

148. Mackenzie King diary, 29 Mar 1945

HMS *Formidable* during a towing exercise with HMCS *Uganda*. The cruiser's *raison d'être* in the British Pacific Fleet was to defend aircraft carriers from air attack. (DND M2110)

Mission accomplished. HMCS *Uganda* after shelling an airstrip on Myako island as part of support operations for the invasion of Okinawa. (DND M 2290)

During the shelling of the Sakishima group of islands, the fleet had to defend itself against enemy aircraft. Note the anti-aircraft explosions dotting the sky. (DND M 2287)

mal leave to which they may become entitled during their period of duty in Canada while the several forces are being reorganized."[149] This prompted a number of questions in the House, particularly about the manner in which this policy would be applied to *Uganda*, since she was already in the Pacific. Angus Macdonald, who was on the verge of resigning his portfolio and leaving federal politics as a result of differences with King over the conscription issue, made a statement that was not only disarming but largely in contradiction of the policy just announced. And, as events would reveal, it was more than somewhat sanguine:

> That ship has been in commission now for six months, and I should think that during the summer or fall, assuming the European war to be over, if some men on board the *Uganda* feel they should return home, we would allow them to do so if we felt that we could replace them. Perhaps I should not make that broad statement, but I should think very sympathetic consideration would be given any man on the *Uganda* who, having put in a year of service on that ship, and the European war being over, wished to return to civilian life. I think such a request would be very carefully and sympathetically dealt with.[150]

In fact, the terms of the new policy meant that those declining to volunteer had to be brought home, and those agreeing to serve in the Pacific would also have to return for thirty days disembarkation leave. Only one MP, the Progressive Conservative John Diefenbaker, seems to have realised that such difficulties would arise, and he conveyed that opinion during subsequent debate.[151]

NSHQ had in fact anticipated that this issue would arise, and as early as November, 1943, had prepared a contingency plan. The Chief of Naval Personnel informed Vice-Admiral Jones that once a clear government policy was in place, about five months lead time would be necessary to identify, and draft to their ships, personnel willing to serve in the Pacific. NSHQ was thus able to issue instructions, adapted to the Prime Minister's statement about volunteering for this service, within two weeks of his announcement. A Naval General signal stated that the RCN planned to send only "modern and effective men of war" to the Pacific, that suitable personnel would be needed to man these ships, and that this would mean a large percentage of men now serving would be wanted for them. The signal then called for volunteers in language that was a faithful echo of government policy: "Commanding officers are to explain the situation, and give all officers and ratings an opportunity to sign the following undertaking: 'I hereby volunteer for service in the war against Japan and agree to serve in the Pacific Theatre and/or any other theatre for the duration of hostilities should my services be so required.'"[152]

Since the navy was an all-volunteer force it may have been thought that this decision would be a relatively easy one for most personnel. In fact, there was widespread resentment at the wording of the undertaking, and the principle behind it. Lieutenant-Commander W.H.Willson, RCN, the commanding officer of HMCS *Kootenay*, in refusing to volunteer but asking to be transferred to the

---

149. HofC *Debates*, 4 Apr 1945, 435

150. Ibid, 439

151. Ibid, 440

152. NSHQ general message 138, 19 Apr 1945, LAC, RG 24, 17706, 1425-1, pt 1

Pacific, voiced the general complaint: "I do not feel that as an officer of the Royal Canadian Navy I should be called upon to sign a contract binding me to do the work which I joined the Service to do ... The demand that Officers of the Royal Canadian Navy sign this statement insinuates that there is some doubt as to whether officers holding His Majesty's Commission can be relied upon to do the duty for which, in years of peace, they are constantly preparing themselves." The Naval Board moved rapidly and firmly to nip that negative reaction in the bud, but it was an unfortunate beginning to their efforts at implementing this particular government policy, which reflected an imperfect understanding of what motivated personnel in the armed forces. Some careful acclimatisation was evidently needed before promulgating the signal; the way in which NSHQ made it known proved inadequate to the task. [153]

When the undertaking to volunteer was presented for signature to each man in HMCS *Ontario*, 512 officers and men—64 percent—stated they were willing to accept its conditions, while 388 turned them down. When offered a choice they had to consider not only the consequences of serving in a dangerous theatre of war, but the possibility of missing benefits available to men who began demobilisation before them. Men with family responsibilities, moreover, would be hard pressed to explain to their wives and dependents why they had willingly delayed their return to civilian life.[154] The dilemma facing *Ontario*'s personnel would repeat itself in *Uganda*, under much more difficult circumstances.

Uganda joined the British Pacific Fleet in April 1945, in the midst of Operation Iceberg, the massive amphibious assault on Okinawa. The BPF had been formed in November 1944 under the command of Admiral Sir Bruce Fraser, who for command and control considerations flew his flag ashore at the main base in Sydney, Australia.[155] Command arrangements at sea were somewhat awkward. Vice-Admiral Sir Bernard Rawlings served as second-in-command of the BPF and exercised command of the fleet at sea, except when air operations were under way; then Rear-Admiral P.L. Vian, commander of the 1st Aircraft Carrier Squadron, assumed tactical control.[156] Rear-Admiral E.D.P. Brind commanded the 4th Cruiser Squadron, Rear-Admiral J.H. Edelsten was Rear-Admiral (D), while Rear-Admiral D.B. Fisher commanded the fleet train. In April 1945, when *Uganda* joined, the BPF's main fighting component comprised some twenty-two ships, including four fleet carriers, two King George V class battleships, five light cruisers—six with the arrival of *Uganda*—and eleven destroyers. Air power was the BPF's main weapon, and at that time consisted of some 153 fighters and sixty-five strike aircraft.[157]

In many ways, the experience of the British Pacific Fleet was analogous to that of the RCN when it had been thrust into the Battle of the Atlantic earlier in the war. Throughout its operations, the BPF had to overcome a number of significant obstacles, some brought on by the relative sudden-

---

153. CNMO to NSHQ, Apr 1945, and CNMO memo, "Volunteering Scheme for Japanese War," 1 May 1945, ibid; CNMO to Sec NB, 23 May 1945, and Dy Sec NB to Willson, 30 May 1945, LAC, RG 24, 11751, 46-8-1

154. *Ontario* to CNMO, 1532B 1 May 1945, LAC, RG 24, 11706, 1425-1

155. Adm, AHB, *War with Japan,* vol VI, *The Advance to Japan* (London, 1959),14

156. Marder, Jacobsen, and Horsfield, *Old Friends*, 405-8; R. Humble, *Fraser of North Cape* (London 1983), 285

157. Adm, *War with Japan* VI, App S, 276

ness with which it had to begin its service, others by the fact that it entered a dramatically unfamiliar operational environment. These included a support infrastructure that could not keep pace
with operational demands and could barely support the fleet at sea; equipment, systems and procedures that compared poorly with those of the ally with whom it was operating; inadequate training and experience for the job at hand; and a prickly working relationship with an ally who at one
level could be cooperative and generous but on another, obstructive and malevolent. All the while,
the BPF had to maintain a high tempo of operations against a determined enemy who was willing
to go to unprecedented lengths to defend their cause.

The major challenge facing the BPF concerned the sheer breadth of its operational setting; in
the Second World War, a British fleet had never fought so far from its bases for so long. During
Iceberg, the BPF's advanced base at Leyte in the Philippines was some 800 miles from its theatre
of operations off Okinawa, while Leyte itself was some 3,500 miles from its forward base in
Australia, and that was 12,000 miles from its rear base in the UK. "The distances involved," Fraser
explained to the Admiralty, "are similar to those of a fleet based in Alexandria, and with advanced
anchorages at Gibraltar and the Azores, attacking the North American coast between Labrador and
Nova Scotia."[158] Such vastness also meant that the ships, which had been designed for and were
experienced in relatively short operations lasting days, were now expected to be at sea for weeks.
This placed a considerable strain on resources, facilities, and personnel, with the result according
to a postwar RN study that "essential support was always a little late and there was always the
constant aggravation of unavoidable troubles of inexperience in the type of operation called for."[159]
One area in particular where this hit home was in refuelling at sea. After each phase of operations
off Okinawa, which lasted two to three days, the fleet would withdraw to a refuelling area to
replenish from the tankers of the fleet train. To meet its operational schedule, this had to be done
expeditiously, but as Rear-Admiral Vian recalled the process did not always go well:

> The British method of fuelling big ships at sea, which was by means of buoyant hoses
> trailed astern of the tanker, was primarily at fault. It was an awkward, unseaman-like
> business compared with the American method, in which the two ships concerned
> steamed along abreast of one another a short space apart ... Furthermore, our tankers
> of the Fleet Train, hastily collected and hastily fitted out, were often inexperienced
> and ill-equipped. The fuelling gear would become entangled, or hoses would burst. On
> such occasions fuelling took up to six hours longer than it should have done; and
> only by steaming at full speed through the night could the flying-off position be
> reached in time for our first day's operations.[160]

Effective logistical support is key to any naval operation, and even more so in the planet's
largest body of water; indeed, the RN liaison officer on Admiral Nimitz's staff informed the
Admiralty that "Logistics is the most important aspect of the war at sea in the Pacific."[161]
Nevertheless, it became apparent that the BPF was truly operating on a shoestring, and it faced a
constant struggle to ensure that its ships and aircraft could meet operational commitments.

---

158. Adm, Historical Section, *Battle Summary No. 47: Naval Operations in the Assault and Capture of Okinawa* (London 1950),
    7; Adm, *War with Japan* VI, 196-7

159. Adm, *War with Japan* VI, 196-7

160. P.L. Vian, *Action This Day* (London, 1960), 175

The naval war in the Pacific was primarily an air war, and here, too, the BPF faced significant handicaps. Quite simply, the RN was unfamiliar with modern carrier warfare. In the words of a recent study, until Operation Iceberg, "British fleet carriers had been employed on operations that involved their use rather than carrier operations per se. Small-scale and fragmented operations, which seldom involved the use of more than one carrier, had been poor preparation for the type of warfare that the British Pacific Fleet was called upon to wage in the Far East in 1944 and 1945."[162] In terms of ships, the BPF's four fleet carriers were not in the same league as their USN counterparts; they were slower, and had shorter endurance and a smaller aircraft complement than the USN's Essex class fast attack carriers. They were, nonetheless, effective ships and their armoured decks and enclosed hangers enabled them to survive damage from bombs and *kamikazes* and continue operations when wooden-decked USN carriers were forced to withdraw for major repairs.[163] Another weakness lay in the Fleet Air Arm's aircraft. As a consequence of a variety of factors, not least of which was RAF control over the Fleet Air Arm for most of the interwar period, aircraft developed for the RN lacked the performance required for modern air operations in terms of ruggedness, range, and striking power. As a solution, the FAA had procured RAF designs adapted for carrier use or USN-developed aircraft, but this still raised problems. For example, the Supermarine Seafire, the naval variant of the magnificent Spitfire, made up about a quarter of the BPF's fighter strength in Iceberg but lacked the range required of a naval offensive fighter in the Pacific. This forced the BPF to operate closer inshore, with its inherent dangers, and largely restricted Seafires to an air defence role over the fleet. Moreover, the machine's undercarriage had not been designed to withstand the rigours of punishing, high-speed deck landings. This weakness, combined with a poor view from the cockpit during the final approach caused by the Seafire's long nose and a lack of wind over the deck, as a result of Vian's decision to limit fleet speed to maximize the endurance of his destroyers, caused a high number of deck crashes, which boosted maintenance demands and cut into the fleet's air strength. American types, such as the Chance Vought F4U Corsair and the Grumman F6F Hellcat fighters, as well as the Grumman TBF/TBM Avenger torpedo-bomber, acquired through lend-lease, had the necessary durability, performance, and striking power, and became the mainstays of the BPF. Unfortunately, the RN had made alterations to "bring them up to British standards"[164] but that prevented the pooling of maintenance and parts with the USN, and exacerbated an already critical shortage of air stores.[165] The BPF also suffered in terms of its shipborne anti-aircraft capability. In his final report on BPF operations, Admiral Fraser evaluated the overall standard of anti-aircraft gunnery as low, a situation that according to postwar RN study stemmed from a lack of training facilities and practice targets available to fleet units

---

161. Cdr H.S. Hopkins, RN, to Adm, cited in C. Reynolds, *The Fast Carriers: The Forging of an Air Navy* (New York 1968), 306. Hopkins was a British naval liaison officer with the USN.

162. Wilmot, *Grave of a Dozen Schemes*, 139-40

163. Adm, *War with Japan* VI, 197; Friedman, *British Carrier Aviation*, 145-54

164. Often these "improvements" had the opposite effect. In the case of the Grumman Wildcat fighter, the RN moved the radio from one side of the cockpit to the other, with the unfortunate effect that when the pilot cranked down the manual, gravity-assist undercarriage prior to landing, the radio cord attached to his helmet sometimes became wrapped around the crank, pulling his head down into the cockpit—not a good state of affairs in the midst of a deck landing. Capt D.H.P. Ryan, RCN, to DHH

165. Adm, *War with Japan* VI, 198; Friedman, *British Carrier Aviation*, 210-16. For an excellent study of the Seafire, see D. Brown, *The Seafire: The Spitfire That Went to Sea* (Annapolis, 1989)

throughout the war. This weakness was magnified by *kamikaze* tactics. No longer was it sufficient to damage an enemy aircraft to the point where a pilot abandoned either his mission or his machine; it was now necessary to break it up before it could fly into its target. This required greater hitting power, particularly in short-ranged weaponry, but the 20mm Oerlikon gun that had heretofore proved to be an effective short-range anti-aircraft weapon did not have the stopping power to knock down determined *kamikazes*. The 40mm Bofors gun was best suited for this role but the BPF had few of them. And there were other problems; a postwar study concluded that in terms of the anti-aircraft systems in service with the BPF in the spring of 1945, "The older and well-established weapons and devices had been overtaken by events, and not all the later developments were found to be effective. A gap existed, too, between mechanical reliability and, due to the unavoidable degree of dilution in the Navy, skill in maintenance."[166] Not a good situation when air attack was the primary threat facing the fleet.

Beyond these shortfalls, which were often made good by the sheer determination of the personnel involved, there was the relationship with a volatile ally. The USN saw the Central Pacific as its war and some of its officers were determined to keep the BPF out. Admiral Ernest King had vehemently protested against a role for the BPF in the Central Pacific at the Octagon conference in Québec the previous autumn, and even after President Roosevelt overruled him, King obfuscated. The RN was supposed to participate "in the main operations against Japan" but after grudgingly accepting that policy King fought hard to keep the BPF in the Indian Ocean or under General MacArthur in the southwest Pacific theatre, both of which he regarded as backwaters. The RN, however, had allies in the USN, particularly Admiral Chester Nimitz, who insisted that the BPF could play an important role in Operation Iceberg.[167] The issue remained in doubt until almost the last moment, with the BPF tugging at its anchors in Manus, the advanced fleet anchorage in the Admiralty Islands, as the operation got under way. Only after considerable pressure from London did United States authorities agree to include the BPF, and then only on the understanding that it could be transferred elsewhere at seven days notice. For *Uganda* the timing was both fortunate and fortuitous as her arrival, just days after US forces launched what was one of their most ambitious undertakings of the war, allowed the RCN to participate in the largest campaign of its kind.[168]

Planning had begun for Operation Iceberg in October, 1944, as the Battle of Leyte Gulf reached its climax. Okinawa was part of the Ryukyus, an archipelago which, with Formosa, flanked the East China Sea, and formed an essential strategic objective, since this was where an airfield and an advanced naval base would have to be set up before an invasion of either the Chinese mainland or Japan could be launched.[169] Before *Uganda* joined much preparatory work for the assault had already been done. USAAF B-29s and USN carrier aircraft had been carrying out strikes to suppress enemy air power, particularly the Japanese capability to launch *kamikaze* attacks. Japanese

---

166. Adm, *War with Japan* VI, 197

167. E.B. Potter, *Nimitz* (Annapolis 1976), 347-9

168. Marder, Jacobsen, and Horsfield, *Old Friends*, 345-8, 413-6; Buell, *Master of Sea Power*, 469-71, and App VI; Morison, *Victory in the Pacific*, 88, 90; Roskill, *War at Sea* III pt 2, 333

169. By the time the orders were ready to be issued (9 Feb), the USN in the Pacific had rotated the command of its main fleet, so that when it was under Admiral R.A. Spruance it was called Fifth Fleet and when under Admiral W.F. Halsey it was called Third Fleet. Seventh Fleet supported General MacArthur's operations in the Philippines at this time. Morison, *Victory in the Pacific*, 79

naval forces had suffered terrible losses and no longer posed a major threat, so bombarding ships had moved into position with no surface opposition eight days before L-Day, set for the 1st of April 1945. Four army and three US Marine divisions of the Tenth Army were to land on a four-division front over five miles of beach. In support of the operation were 1200 ships of the USN, including fast carriers launching strikes against airfields on Kyushu before the landings took place. When finally committed, the BPF's task was to carry out interdiction missions against the Sakishima Gunto, a group of islands between Okinawa and Formosa that represented an object of some concern for Iceberg planners. The Japanese Army had substantial air forces in China, including sixty-five airfields on Formosa, which could use the Sakishima Gunto and its aerodromes as a staging area for conventional fighter-bombers and dive-bombers as well as *kamikaze*. Disrupting the use of these facilities became a task of the British Pacific Fleet, alternating with the American Task Group 51.2.[170]

Uganda's primary role was to help protect the carriers against air attack while BPF aircraft repeatedly beat up Japanese airfields. Her first shots against the Japanese were fired from the anti-aircraft guns, on 13 April, when four enemy machines attacked the fleet. None of the ships suffered damage, but the episode served to demonstrate that the British force still had much to learn about fighting off Japanese air attack. High-flying planes had been detected, and Rear-Admiral Brind ordered a barrage at high altitude, but the result was not the kind of coordinated fire plan he had a right to expect. Some ships, thinking they were supposed to deter enemy attack, fired below cloud, while others, attempting to engage the Japanese before they could begin to dive, fired blindly at estimated range and height. Worse, warning radar, which operated on a wide beam to cover as large an area as possible, was not always able to "hand off" information to gunnery radar, whose narrow beam allowed a ship to engage a precise target. Fire discipline was also a problem, and one that proved annoyingly persistent. On a later occasion, recalled one of *Uganda*'s officers, "the sky was full of puffs—a gunnery officer's delight. Bill Landymore [Lieutenant-Commander W.M. Landymore, the gunnery officer] spent most of his time pressing the *cease* fire button. He couldn't stand the waste of this sort of random stuff." Since cruisers were designed to provide anti-aircraft protection, it is easy to understand why such problems angered senior officers.[171]

There was more satisfaction with the ship's performance in the more traditional role of providing naval gunfire support. On 4 May *Uganda* participated in the bombardment of airfields on Myako Island, part of the continuing campaign to hinder its use as a staging area against American operations in Okinawa. As Vice-Admiral Rawlings reported to the Fifth Fleet Commander, Admiral R.A. Spruance,

> The plan for the opening of operations was ... To make airfields of the SAKISHIMA GUNTO unserviceable by bombing runways and air installations ... To conduct an offensive against flak positions and to assist in cratering runways by ship bombardment ... To maintain an offensive CAP over the islands ... The particular plan for the first day was for the bombarding force to bombard MIYAKO airfields and flak positions

---

170. Ibid, 79-80, 89-90, 94

171. Chadwick interview; Brind to VAdm 2IC BPF, 18 Apr 1945, PRO, ADM 199/595

at about noon, from medium range, with the Carrier Force about 30 miles to the
southward, so that their Radar would not be fouled by land.[172]

The decision to use this form of attack rather than an air strike rested on the fact that naval
gunfire was more accurate than bombing, and that adjustments to the bearing and elevation of
ships' guns could be made immediately. Moreover, airfields were better protected against air attack
than they were against bombardment from the sea, and there was the consideration of morale on
board the bombarding ships to take into account. Sailors are happy when busy, and long periods
at sea without serious naval opposition made for dissatisfaction and discontent. The need to call
upon surface gunnery, and the challenge of carrying out an accurate bombardment with the main
armament, the triple six-inch turrets, was thus of inestimable value in that regard.

The operation began at 1205, when the cruisers *Euryalus* and *Black Prince* fired air bursts over
the anti-aircraft defences of Nobara airfield, and the battleships *King George V* and *Howe* targeted
the runways and associated facilities. When this phase of the operation was complete, *Swiftsure*
and the New Zealand cruiser *Gambia* took over the shelling of Nobara while *Uganda* concentrated on the Sukuma air strip. There was no reply from the Japanese, and Brind was pleased with the
results.

> The organization worked very well which is creditable to all concerned since time at
> Leyte only permitted very short meetings, and it was not easy to arrange exercises at
> sea to ensure complete understanding and precise communication procedure ... The
> task of the pilot from "Formidable" who did all the spotting for Cruisers was difficult,
> particularly as firing time was short and "Swiftsure" and "Gambia" were at the last
> moment ordered to shoot simultaneously instead of separately. He was quick to
> understand requirements and acted promptly, definitely and correctly ... HMCS
> "Uganda" fired at ... Sukuma air strip. It was unfortunately not possible to arrange
> air spotting for her, but she had a better view of her target than had the others.
> "Swiftsure"'s spotter reported that he saw a few of "Uganda"'s salvoes and they were
> well on the target. From this and "Uganda"'s report I think that an accurate shoot was
> carried out.[173]

Rawlings agreed, reporting that "In particular the bombardments by the six inch cruisers were
highly successful, their shoots were admirably controlled by the air spotter, ranging was quickly
carried out and fire for effect was accurate. Both the airfields allocated as targets for the Cruisers
were well plastered."[174]

The bombardment may have been a success in those respects, but while the battleships and
cruisers were off Miyako, the aircraft carriers, stationed some thirty miles away and denuded of
the bulk of the BPF's anti-aircraft protection, were open to air strikes. *Formidable* suffered temporary damage when a *kamikaze* crashed into its flight deck. Vice-Admiral Rawlings estimated that
sixteen to twenty Japanese aircraft were involved in the attack, some acting as decoys for British
fighters, and one *kamikaze* group penetrated to the carriers. "Analysis shows that this group

---

172. Rawlings to CO US Fifth Fleet, App 1, 3 May, PRO, ADM 199/590

173. Brind to 2IC BPF, 13 May 1945, ibid

174. Rawlings to CO US Fifth Fleet, App 1, 25 May 1945, ibid

escaped detection either because, in the absence of the Bombarding Force too many of the reduced number of Radar sets were fully engaged tracking the diversionary planes, and too few acting as warning sets, or else because they made a very low approach followed by a very high climb at about 15 miles range."[175] Vian later admitted he "was not sufficiently alive to the effect on our defensive system which would be caused by the temporary absence of the radar sets and anti-aircraft armament of the battleships. The Japanese were."[176]

In the months that followed, *Uganda* concentrated on her role as a radar picket and anti-aircraft ship. On the day that war in Europe ended, for example, Japanese air strikes on Allied naval forces in the Pacific were particularly intensive. Captain Mainguy recorded in his report to Rear-Admiral Brind that the warning was issued at 1647 on 8 May; eight minutes later a *kamikaze* was seen to hit *Victorious*, followed thirty seconds later by another. Both aircraft were seen to burst into flames on impact and ricochet off the armoured flight deck and into the sea, without causing serious damage. A minute later a *kamikaze* headed for *Howe*, burst into flames, and missed its target. Then, at 1705, *Formidable* was struck by a twin-engined plane, and a third of its flight deck seemed to be ablaze, but the ship reported itself operational at 1730. An hour later the fleet retired from the scene.[177] A diarist on board *Uganda* described the action:

> Radar picks up six enemy aircraft at sixteen miles. First thing we know they are diving in at Fleet and are these suicide bastards. Two passed down our starboard side— opened fire with everything we had. [One] crashed on bow of Victorious destroying aircraft on deck. Another crashed on her stern. A Dinah came in on Howe and Howe blew her to bits when she opened up. At the same time two more attacked Formidable—one of which was shot down and the other crashed on deck among planes with great explosion and upper deck spread with flames. D[amage] control goes into action at once and got it out in about fifteen minutes. Quite a few casualties—eight of enemy shot down during day.[178]

"The disappointing feature of the attack," Brind commented in his report to Rawlings, "as you have already pointed out to the Fleet, was that although we all knew the direction of approach and that the enemy had evaded our fighters at about 25 miles the Fleet did not bring them under intense and effective gunfire before the attack developed ... Much can be done to effect improvement by practices during the fuelling periods and by your direction I have been arranging practices for the Fleet." Rawlings himself suggested that "The difficulty of aircraft recognition when friendly and enemy planes are in vicinity of the Fleet is an ever present problem," which would have to be solved without delay. Fortunately, the armoured decks of the British carriers prevented the fleet from losing half its strike force.[179]

---

175. Ibid, 4 May 1945

176. Vian, *Action This Day*, 185

177. Mainguy to CO 4th Cruiser Sqn, 10 May 1945, PRO ADM 199/590. For the press account of this action see e.g., "Uganda Crew Tell of Japanese Fanaticism," *Halifax Daily Star*, 31 May 1945; LAC, RG 24, 11651, Uganda.

178. Rogerson diary

179. Brind to CO 4th Cruiser Sqn, 13 May 1945, PRO, ADM 199/590; Rawlings to VAdm 2IC BPF, 9 May 1945, PRO, ADM 199/595

As a radar picket positioned anywhere from thirty to 300 miles from the main body, *Uganda* was more exposed to attack than while on the screen of the task force. The USN normally deployed destroyers in that role, and they had suffered heavily from *kamikaze* attacks, especially from 6 to 12 April, "because the stations were too remote from the Combat Air Patrol and the number of vessels in each was too few for protection against multiple attacks." *Kamikaze* aircraft sank four of the original nineteen USN destroyer pickets and damaged eight more seriously and three slightly. They sank one of the fourteen replacement vessels, seriously damaged five others, and slightly damaged two more. One picket hit a mine and sank. Although losses were heavy, the air attacks were in Admiral Spruance's judgement a serious misdirection of effort by the Japanese, who should have concentrated on troop transports. That in no way, of course, lessened the hazards to the radar pickets, which occupied "the premier posts of danger in this Okinawa operation." By 10 April the more exposed stations were manned by no fewer than six craft of various types. [180]

Commonwealth ships were not well endowed with the sophisticated electronic equipment needed for this role. "In the absence of any destroyers fitted with adequate Radar or Communications and in view of the pressing need to identify homing strikes and other aircraft before they close to within 30 miles," explained a report to the Admiralty, "it has been necessary to use a cruiser, which can ill be spared from the AA screen and provides all too good a target to enemy aircraft."[181] Even then there proved to be too few cruisers to carry out normal anti-aircraft duties and serve as long-range observers, and by mid-April enemy aircraft had "on three occasions penetrated the screen and fighter melees have taken place within the gunnery zone, much to the detriment of target indication and AA gunnery."[182] The air warning radar and its associated equipment in *Uganda* was nevertheless effective for its day. Operators of the Aircraft Direction Room (ADR) could rely on three main types: type 281, the principal air search radar for British heavy ships, designed to detect aircraft at long range; type 277 for surface search, which could also be used to pick up low-flying aircraft; and type 293, a centimetric target indicator able to give bearing and, in the case of aircraft, height. Making the various parts of the system work together required skill, however, for type 277 could not interrogate contacts to determine if they were friend or foe, and an operator had to put the type 281 onto the proper bearing to do so. It was perhaps because of the need for such evolutions that "The two Fighter Direction Officers and the ADR Crew were continuously extended throughout the period as Picket Cruiser." Also, communications needed improvement, and after one shift on picket HMS *Swiftsure* reported "occasional fades with *Uganda*."[183]

When on 12 and 13 May the Canadian cruiser and the destroyer HMS *Wessex* took up their positions, Mainguy reported to Brind that "No difficulties were experienced and no enemy sighted." Similar conditions obtained on the next two periods of picket duty that month.[184] *Uganda* was thus spared a repetition of what the USN's official historian, Samuel Eliot Morison, called "The Ordeal of the Radar Pickets," of 6 to 12 April. The fact remained that by 27 May, when the US Fifth Fleet

---

180. Adm, *Naval Operations in the Assault and Capture of Okinawa*, 48; Morison, *Victory in the Pacific*, 178

181. Letter to DDSD, 15 Apr 1945, App B, LAC, RG 24, 11499, NSS 11600-1

182. Ibid

183. Friedman, *Naval Radar*, 193-7; McLaughlin to RAdm Comd 4th Cruiser Sqn, 17 May 1945, PRO, ADM 199/l041

184. Mainguy to RAdm Comd 4th Cruiser Sqn, 17 and 25 May 1945, ibid

became the Third Fleet, the loss of ninety vessels sunk or seriously damaged had made Iceberg the most costly operation of the naval war in the Pacific.[185]

On 25 May the battle to capture Okinawa came to a successful close. Although mopping-up operations would still take considerable time—and no little bloodshed—the British Pacific Fleet was no longer required to mask the Sakishima Gunto. Part of the fleet thus made its way to Sydney, Australia, and the remainder, including *Uganda*, to Manus. Before its arrival at the anchorage, however, the latter group received orders for Operation Inmate, whose mission was to "neutralize air installations in Truk Atoll in order to decrease the threat of air attack on own forces and to provide battle experience for newly reporting units," notably the carrier HMS *Implacable*.[186] Truk was well defended, and in March 1944 it had been decided not to try to take the position by storm, but neutralize it instead—it would be the most important Japanese facility to "wither on the vine" in the Americans' island-hopping strategy. After over a year of periodic air raids and no reinforcements, the garrison at Truk was seriously weakened, cruelly reduced to serving as target practice for elements of the British Pacific Fleet.[187]

After some air warning and engaging exercises, as well as training in bombardment procedure and communications, the little group made its way to the bypassed Japanese base and prepared to shell it.[188] Brind transferred his flag into *Uganda* for the operation, which began on 15 June, met absolutely no opposition, and "was sort of a Sunday picnic."[189] For the ship's company, according to one of the gunnery team, it "was a huge joke. Everybody was in training, at this point, in shore bombardment. We'd had shore bombardment when we were in Egypt on the way out. But this was to be a practice deal for ourselves, *Newfoundland*, and another [*Achilles*]."[190] The view from the air was less complimentary. One of the pilots involved thought that the operation "had been ghastly."

> The shoot had been a complete waste of time, as the ship's r/ts [radio-telephones] had not been working properly. Furthermore, one of the ships reported that her "gunnery table" aiming system was u/s [unserviceable] and she was shooting independently. This she did all over the place, and confused the rest.
>
> However, shore bombardment was important to the Navy for it was the only independent contribution which the non-carrier fleet was capable of making in the Pacific. It therefore figured large in their reports to their Admirals and to the Press, and thus the history books, in spite of its insignificant accomplishments and vast consumption of valuable stores.[191]

Although some bias is probably evident, it is true that in an indirect shoot such as this one signalling procedures had to be nearly perfect, and Mainguy's report on Inmate made clear that the Canadians still had much to learn about bombardment missions. In the brief period allowed for

---

185. S.E. Morison, *The Two-Ocean War* (Boston, 1963), 542, 555

186. Brind to C-in-C BPF, 2 Jul 1945, PRO ADM 199/1510

187. S.E. Morison, *Aleutians, Gilberts and Marshalls, June 1942–April 1944* (Boston, 1951), 315-32

188. Brind to C-in-C BPF, 2 July 1945

189. Ibid

190. Makovski interview

191. R. Crosley, *They Gave Me a Seafire* (Shrewsbury, 1986), 161

training on the way to Truk, *Uganda* had not once successfully completed an exercise with a spotter. During the operation itself communications proved inadequate, so much so that HMNZS *Achilles* had to be called upon to act as a link between the Canadian ship and the aircraft, and even then "three way communication only ensued for short periods." Brind and Mainguy conceded that a direct bombardment could have been carried out with more effect, "but at the late stage this was apparent and since there was no reason to doubt Run 1 had been effective it was not employed."[192] The Admiralty comment was, as usual, hard-nosed and uncompromising. "This is really a tale of communications disasters," wrote the Director of Gunnery and Anti-Aircraft Warfare, "and, apart from technical failures, amounts to another strong recommendation for adequate pre-bombardment exercises *with the aircraft airborne*." The results of the operation were, he judged, "disappointing."[193]

The breakdown in communications will strike a familiar note among sailors of that era—fighter direction facilities then and for some time into the postwar period were hampered by the limitations of the technology of the day.[194] Voice transmissions were more effective and consistent when used with Forward Observers Bombardment, as in the Normandy landings, than with aircraft, and often were not up to the kind of communications load imposed by bombardment operations with air spotters. This was borne out at Truk, where the pilot reported that he had been able to establish contact with *Achilles*, but not *Uganda*. "After a period of ranging with HMNZS 'Achilles,' R/T contact failed, and although both aircraft transmitted long and frequent transmissions to both ships and flew directly over them, no further contact was established ... HMNZS 'Achilles' was heard endeavouring to pass the spotter's initial orders to HMCS 'Uganda' without success."[195]

Inmate was *Uganda*'s last operation of note. Although the ship continued to serve with the BPF until the end of July, it did so as part of the cruiser/destroyer screen, and the main work of attacking Japanese facilities was left to the Fleet Air Arm. Picket duty could be somewhat unnerving, as it placed the cruiser out on its own, (one gunnery officer commenting that he hoped "not to leave anyone with six inch bricks at their feet"[196]), but for the most part the cruise was uneventful. Living conditions in the debilitating heat were increasingly difficult. When movies were shown, "It would be so hot, with so little air, that the rig to wear was mostly a towel and a pair of shoes. At the end of the movie the deck would be wet from the perspiration running off our bodies."[197] Well aware of the situation, Canadian shore staffs tried to mitigate conditions whenever they could. Captain F.L. Houghton of the Canadian Naval Mission Overseas on one occasion requested of NSHQ the number of Canadian personnel expecting to be serving in the Pacific in future "in order to estimate beer requirements."[198]

In mid-July *Uganda* began the return passage to Canada. This had become necessary in order to replace members of the ship's company who had declined to volunteer for service in the war

---

192. Mainguy to Brind, 19 June 1945; enclosure in Brind to C-in-C BPF, 5 Aug 1945, Enclosure 4, PRO, ADM 199/1510

193. Director Gunnery and Anti-Aircraft Warfare min, 13 Oct 1945, ibid

194. Raven and Roberts, *British Cruisers*, 311

195. Brind to C-in-C BPF, 5 Aug 1945, Enclosure 6, "Report on Bombardment Spotting"

196. Rogerson diary, 15 July 1945

197. Ibid, 23 June 1945

198. CNMO (NAPP) to NSHQ, 13 July 1945, LAC, RG 24, 11751, 46-8-1

against Japan. It has already been suggested that the policy created an unusually difficult dilemma for men who were already serving at sea. It was worse when they were actually participating in the war for which they were being asked to volunteer. Some higher-ranking officers were far from sanguine as to the results; for example, Captain Houghton reported from London that "It is the general opinion of Senior Canadian Officers overseas that the percentage of volunteers will be disappointingly low."[199] In *Uganda*, Mainguy was to come face to face with that phenomenon, as he related years later. Having received the message instructing officers and ratings to sign—or not—an undertaking to serve in the Pacific,

> The way this signal and exchange of the signal was received annoyed everybody, every single soul on board. The permanent force were insulted because they'd spent all their lives getting ready for a war and then, when in the middle of the war, we were asked whether we wanted to go on and finish it. All the Reserves and everybody else had volunteered for the duration of hostilities, and if we were fighting against Japan, of course we'd go on. So from one point of view, there were those two main incentives just to be annoyed and say, "Well, if we're not wanted, of course, we don't want to fight the Japs if it's not necessary." Then there were those who thought if they said yes and their wives heard about this, that they'd volunteered to go on fighting Japan when they could have gone home, there would be trouble there. The single men on board all thought a lot of people are going to say no and if we don't go home, we're going to miss out on a lot of civilian jobs, so we'll say no.[200]

Mainguy, like many others, described the events of those days over four decades after they had occurred, and accounts differ as to what followed. Lieutenant E. Chadwick suggests that the captain "decided they would ask anybody who did *not* want to volunteer to hand their names in and next time we refuelled from the fleet train we'd put them on the fleet train and they could go home. The troops actually, seemed to accept that." But officialdom did not, and insisted it wanted a list of those who *did* wish to volunteer; Mainguy's reaction was to announce, in the first days of May, that procedures would be implemented to determine who wished to continue to serve in the war against Japan.

What he said next is a matter of some confusion, for it seems that the captain noted, publicly, that he would have little respect for those who might decide to quit while the ship was on operations, which according to Chadwick, "was a bad thing. That finished it. And the next morning the Commander's office flat was just flooded with non-volunteers."[201] The captain's remarks may well have been a factor in the crew's decision, another witness insisting in his diary that the "Skipper made speeches and turned the men against him more than ever. Called us foreflushers [*sic*] and quitters. Those who were in doubt soon made up their minds at a statement like that."[202] Able Seaman A.A. Lawson agreed, remembering that Mainguy was held in high regard by the crew, but that his speech may have put the men off nonetheless.[203] According to another, when it was

---

199. CNMO to NSHQ, 20 Apr 1945, ibid

200. Edited transcript of interview with VAdmiral E.R. Mainguy, DHH 84/301

201. Chadwick interview

202. Rogerson diary

203. Lawson interview

HMCS *Uganda* arriving in Esquimalt on 10 August 1945. The decision by the majority of the ship's complement not to volunteer for further fighting in the Pacific proved controversial. (LAC PA 206516)

Lieutenant Robert Hampton Gray, RCNVR, who died attacking an enemy escort vessel in his Corsair fighter bomber. He was flying with the Fleet Air Arm at the time, and earned Canada's last-ever Victoria Cross for his courage. (LAC PA 133296)

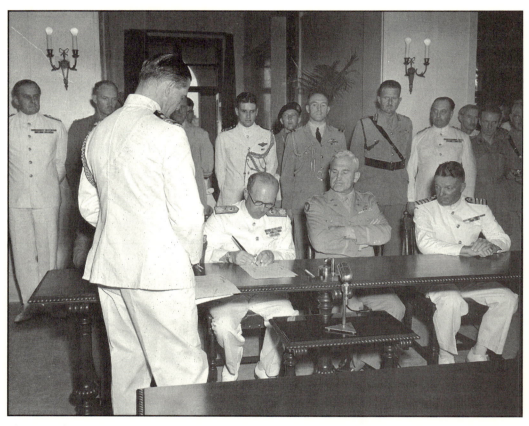

The surrender ceremony in Hong Kong. Captain Wallace B. Creery of HMCS *Prince Robert* is present as a Canadian observer, sitting at the far right. (DND PR-555)

Following the arrival of HMCS *Prince Robert*, food and other items were distributed to prisoners in Shamshuipo prison camp, in Kowloon. About one in five Canadians who were captured at Hong Kong died in such camps. (DND PR-483)

"Demob": a sailor returns issued equipment. (LAC PA 206514)

announced they would have to decide whether to stay or leave, "everybody more or less laughed about it. They couldn't believe it. But the captain made the announcement and explained what had to be done." Before attestation papers were made available, however, the captain "actually made some nasty remarks (which was probably a mistake) about anybody who didn't volunteer to stay there."[204] Ironically, that same officer, Lieutenant Makovski, also claimed that "As a matter of fact we would have had to leave about the time we did anyway, because we had been at sea then just under a year [sic—actually seven months] and we had been travelling a good part of that time at 30 knots. The chief engineer told Mainguy when he was coming home that no matter where we went he'd have to go in for a refit because he couldn't guarantee more than 20 knots when we left there,"[205] although there is no corroborating evidence for this.

Whether or not Mainguy's remarks to the crew affected their decision, he was not the only one to suggest that they still had a duty to perform. As Lieutenant-Commander Landymore recalled,

> Well, I think that at some levels there was some bad feeling. It never occurred to me not to volunteer. As a regular force officer there was no difficulty in the decision... And as far as my own activity was concerned—I called together all my Gunnery Chiefs and POs and I said, "It may occur to you, some of you who aren't regular force people (or permanent force we called them then) may feel it's better to go home and get the leave that's been promised and the big money and all that sort of stuff. But I'm sure that if you do, if you don't volunteer for service in the Pacific and if a sufficient number do that—the ship will have to go home. No matter what you think about it now, you're going to regret it all your life. You're going to be sorry you made that decision. Because it doesn't matter how you rationalize it, there's something in the view that, in the face of the enemy, you're turning your back. And I'm sure that if you reflect on this long enough, you'll decide that this isn't the way to do it."[206]

In the event, 576 ratings and twenty-nine officers—about 80 percent of the ship's complement—opted not to volunteer. One of them, Able Seamen Lawson, echoed the views of W.H. Willson a month before: "Why should we volunteer again. We volunteered once to get here. We were quite happy to stay here. We'll do our job that we're supposed to do and then go home ... I was one of the ones who did *not* volunteer. I was prepared to stay there, but if they were going through this nonsense of volunteering (which was all it was) I wasn't going to volunteer again. They could send me to China, Timbuctu, if they wanted, I belonged to them for the duration of the war."[207]

Fifty years after the fact, historian Stephen Geneja reviewed events with some of his comrades, who offered additional reasons for choosing to return home. First, after entering the tropics, many sailors began suffering from respiratory problems, especially those working in extremely hot engine rooms. "Some of the stokers had served in up to five other naval ships in the Atlantic and Arctic Oceans and had not been bothered with any breathing problems."[208] The strains of operating in the

204. Makovski interview

205. Ibid

206. Landymore interview

207. Lawson interview, 31-2

208. S.C. Geneja, *The Cruiser Uganda* (Corbyville, 1994), 232

Pacific, far from any home port, may have made a bad situation worse; Geneja reported that a combination of "Absence of shore leave, dehydrated food, lack of fresh vegetables, fruit, and meat, a continuous shortage of fresh water, and too 'pusser' [rigorous] a routine when not in action were other reasons given."[209] Not mentioned, but undoubtedly a factor, was the prospect of continuing to fight an enemy who, with *kamikaze* tactics, had extended warfare to a new grim reality.

On 17 May Mainguy reported the results of the process to Brind, who is said to have responded with sympathy, although not for Canada's representative democracy: "One should not blame those who had voted to return, and it was sad that a vote-catching political system should return too soon to peaceful ways, while their navy was still engaging the enemy."[210] Admiral Fraser initially prepared to have replacements join the ship in the theatre of war, but later decided the better solution would be to send the ship home. Canadian naval authorities had in fact drafted about 600 men to *Uganda*, representing some of the 37,000 who had signed the necessary undertaking. They were expected to be completely operational by the end of March, 1946. The Canadian Pacific Fleet was to consist of two light cruisers, two light fleet carriers with Canadian air groups, an anti-aircraft cruiser, eight Crescent class destroyers, eleven other destroyers, and a variety of smaller craft. *Uganda* herself was to work up with her new ship's company in the first weeks of September before returning to the 4th Light Cruiser Squadron. *Ontario* would join at about the same time, bringing that squadron up to seven cruisers. The 4th would be paired with the 2nd Light Cruiser Squadron in the BPF.[211]

When *Uganda* headed home many Canadian navy personnel remained in the Pacific and Far East theatres as part of British units. Their experience ranged from the conventional to the extreme. Amongst the latter was Lieutenant-Commander B.S. Wright, RCNVR, who commanded a special operations detachment in Central Burma called the Sea Reconnaissance Unit. Their job was to swim across the Irrawaddy River at night on "jitter raids" to keep the Japanese off guard. On some occasions they engaged the enemy but on others they would take cover and tap two bamboo sticks together: "they know something is out there but they don't know what."[212] More conventional was the contribution of RCNVR radar officers. As mentioned in Part 1 of this volume, in 1940 some 123 RCNVR officers had transferred to the RN for radar duties and they had gone on to make a valuable contribution to operations in virtually every theatre of the war. The Pacific was no different, and by the summer of 1945 at least eight Canadians were serving as radar officers in BPF ships, five of them in fleet carriers where fighter direction was involved.[213] One of these, Lieutenant C.C. Costain, RCNVR, in HMS *Indomitable*, was awarded the DSC for his role in the air defence of

---

209. Ibid

210. Mainguy to CO 4th Cruiser Sqn, 17 May 1945, PRO, ADM 199/590; Littler, *Sea Fever*, 247

211. DOP to CNS, 25 June 1945, LAC, RG 24, 11721, CS 41-1-1; C-in-C BPF to Adm, 18 July 1945, and RCN Depot to NSHQ, 7 July 1945, LAC, RG 24, 11731, CS 153-10-1. Sec NB to COPC, 9 July 1945, LAC, RG 24 (acc 83-84/167), 4043, 8970-CCL-31

212. Interview with S.M. Sellars in NOAC Ottawa, *Salty Dips*, Vol 5, *Up Sprits*, 82-7. See also A. Phillips, "Operation Irrawaddy," *Argosy* (Canadian ed), Sep 1959, copy in DHH 90/84

213. RN *Navy List*, July 1945

the fleet during a raid on Palembang, Sumatra, in January 1945.[214] Another, Lieutenant F.R. Paxton, RCNVR, was the radar officer in the destroyer HMS *Venus* when she detected the Japanese heavy cruiser *Haguro* at the extreme range of thirty-four miles, and then helped four other destroyers sink her in a classic torpedo attack in the Strait of Malacca on 16 May 1945.[215]

Carrier-borne aircraft formed the vital component of the BPF's striking power, and there was a considerable contingent of Canadian aircrew in the BPF by the summer of 1945—one author claims there were as a many as 200.[216] During Operation Iceberg the fleet's mission, as we have seen, was to neutralize Japanese airfields in the Sakishima Gunto in order to prevent them from being used to launch attacks against the invasion fleet off Okinawa. This proved both challenging and dangerous because the Japanese would repair the runways at night, forcing the operation to be repeated. Attacks were usually pushed in at low level by Corsair and Hellcat fighter-bombers, and at higher level by more vulnerable Avenger bombers. Anti-aircraft fire could be intense around some targets, and the Japanese also created flak traps around decoy aircraft. In the first twenty-six days of Iceberg the BPF lost nineteen aircraft to enemy fire and twenty-eight more to other causes. In return, they destroyed twenty-eight Japanese aircraft in the air and another thirty-four on the ground, although many of the latter were thought to be non-operational aircraft and decoys. In the meantime, as mentioned previously, the Japanese launched *kamikaze* attacks on the British carriers.[217] As one naval aviator described Iceberg "We bombed the hell out of their runways on the islands and they tried to fly down our funnels—it was a lose-lose situation."[218] Following a replenishment and repair period after the Okinawa campaign, in July and August the BPF carried out operations against the Japanese home islands. These included a number of bombardments carried out by battleships and cruisers against factory complexes near the coast, but the main effort was carried by the naval aviators, who flew numerous "Ramrod" strikes against airfields, coastal shipping, and minor naval vessels—the USN kept the destruction of the Japanese Fleet to itself. The final BPF strike against Japan before the surrender was flown on 13 August when Corsairs, Fireflies and Hellcats attacked targets in the Tokyo area.

It is beyond the scope of this work to describe the experiences of the Canadians in the Fleet Air Arm, but some individual accomplishments can be highlighted. Lieutenant-Commander R.E. Jess, RCNVR, qualified as an Observer in 1941 and saw wide-ranging service, which included a tour with Bomber Command and anti-E-boat patrols during Operation Neptune. In April 1945, as a result of casualties to the senior pilots in his unit, Jess found himself in the unusual position of commanding 854 Squadron of Grumman Avengers and planned its operations during the campaign over the Sakishima Gunto. After returning to England Jess was appointed Deputy

214. E.R. Paquette and Bainbridge, *Honours and Awards*, 120. See also interview with C.C. Costain in NOAC Ottawa, *Salty Dips*, Vol. 6 'Ready Aye Ready', 225-41

215. Roskill, *War at Sea* III pt 2, 319; J. Winton, *Sink the Haguro! The Last Destroyer Action of the Second World War* (London, 1978), 115

216. Soward, *Formidable Hero*, 102. Based on research in the *Navy List* this number seems excessive and probably includes aircrew in transit to the Pacific or in squadrons working up in the UK that were expected to join the BPF.

217. Adm, *War with Japan* VI, 200-10

218. R.E. Jess quoted in E.C. Carson (ed), *The Canadian Raleighites: Ordinary Seamen and Officers at War, 1940-1945* (Aylmer 1988), 101

Director of Naval Aviation at NSHQ but shortly after taking up the appointment he was diagnosed with tuberculosis and was invalided out of the RCN.[219] Canadian fighter pilots also achieved distinction in the Pacific. Lieutenant D.J. Sheppard, RCNVR, a Corsair pilot with 1836 Squadron in HMS *Victorious*, and a veteran of the Op Tungsten attacks against *Tirpitz*, was credited with shooting down five Japanese aircraft and thus became the only Corsair ace in the BPF. Lieutenant W.H.I. Atkinson, RCNVR, flying Hellcats in 1844 Squadron was also credited with five kills, three of which were the result of challenging night intercepts.[220] Sheppard and Atkinson, along with other Canadian naval aviators in the BPF or working up with squadrons destined for the Pacific, would go on to lend critical operational flying experience to the postwar RCN.

––––––––––––

In early August 1945, as *Uganda* arrived in Esquimalt and the anti-aircraft ship HMCS *Prince Robert* joined the BPF, the Pacific war was reaching its climax. On 6 August American aircraft dropped the first atomic bomb on Hiroshima, with apocalyptic results. Three days later, the second atomic bomb devastated Nagasaki. That same day, a Canadian pilot with the Fleet Air Arm, Lieutenant Robert Hampton Gray, RCNVR, led a flight of Corsair fighter-bombers from HMS *Formidable* against Japanese warships in Onagawa Bay. Hit by anti-aircraft fire as he went into his attacking run, "with the cold precision of an instructor at a training school," he pressed on to within fifty yards of his target. His bombs struck home, sinking an escort as his plane plunged into the bay. Commended by Vian for "his brilliant fighting spirit and inspired leadership," Gray's heroism won him a posthumous Victoria Cross, the only such award earned by a Canadian sailor in the Second World War.[221] He personified the determination with which the British Pacific Fleet, despite the difficulties that marked its participation in the war against Japan, continued to conduct offensive operations in cooperation with the USN. On 14 August the Japanese announced they were willing to surrender, and on 2 September, on board the battleship USS *Missouri* in Tokyo Bay, the act formalizing that decision took place.

No Canadian ship or naval officer was there to represent the country in this famous ceremony, although HMCS *Prince Robert* had sailed into Hong Kong harbour as part of Task Group 111.2 on 30 August. *Prince Robert* had helped take the ill-fated battalions of the Royal Rifles of Canada and the Winnipeg Grenadiers to help garrison the colony in 1941, and was now returning there to take the survivors home after nearly four dreadful years of incarceration as prisoners of war. Captain W.B. Creery, RCN, in an act of particular significance to Canadians, was present for the Japanese surrender there on 2 September, before bringing the repatriated prisoners of war home to Canada on 20 October, when the ship arrived at Esquimalt.

Canada's naval contribution to the war against Japan had been much smaller than expected. Its impact on events had indeed been almost negligible. That being said, Canadian naval ships

219. Ibid, 95-102; DHH interview with R.E. Jess, 7 Nov 1990, Jess biog file

220. Soward, *Formidable Hero*, 102-3, 123-5; C. Shores and C. Williams, *Aces High: The Fighter Aces of the British Commonwealth Air Forces in World War II* (London, 1966), 87, 263; M. Styling, *Corsair Aces of World War 2* (Oxford, 1995), 69-70; B. Tillman, *Hellcat Aces of World War 2* (Oxford, 1996), 78

221. Schull, *Far Distant Ships*, 414-17. See also Soward, *Formidable Hero*

and personnel had demonstrated the capability for, as well as some of the shortcomings of, undertaking offensive fleet operations alongside the navies of the great powers. In six years of war the RCN had overcome extraordinary difficulties to provide indispensable and unexpected services to the Allied cause. As in the First World War, Canadian naval forces had exerted their most significant influence by undertaking the defence that other navies could not provide for shipping on North Atlantic routes. How that would translate into the long-term requirements of the RCN would depend on postwar developments. The ships now in commission, the foundation on which the RCN would build over the next fifteen years, were what the naval staff considered the most effective combination of numbers and types for alliance warfare. Inevitably, the concepts on which this judgment rested were those that had been handed down by the RN; and it was an important consideration that the USN, powerfully influenced by that great Anglophile Captain Alfred Thayer Mahan, shared the conviction that national interests were best served by blue water navies. All the planning carried out in Naval Service Headquarters since mid-1943 reflected that doctrine, and betrayed the desire to somehow implant the same idea in the minds of all Canadians.

The immense achievement of the so-called "corvette navy" was undeniable, and touched a highly receptive nerve in the public mind. That it was an improvisation, that it was inadequate during many of the most dangerous phases in the enemy attack on shipping, was a fact that planners had to live with, while advocating measures that would prevent a repetition of the problem. The Pacific war offered the opportunity to reveal the new horizons to which the navy could aspire, and provide a model that would help the naval staff demolish myths about the ease of building up an effective national navy in time of conflict. The war ended before the full effectiveness of the "continuing RCN" could be assessed in operations against Japan. The limitations of a single-purpose navy, which in Canada's case tended to be a purely antisubmarine force devoted to the defence of shipping, had nevertheless been pointed out, with examples of the need for diversification, in British Home Waters and the Mediterranean, and an indication of what the navy might be able to accomplish in a full scale naval war in the Pacific. To some degree these arguments had been accepted by government. On 9 October 1945, almost exactly a year after Macdonald's bitter acceptance of a reduced naval commitment in the Pacific, his successor, the Honourable Douglas Abbott, told the House of Commons that the postwar RCN would comprise "two cruisers, probably two light fleet carriers, ten to twelve destroyers, and the necessary ancillary craft, all ... of the latest and most modern type, while in reserve and for training purposes, we will continue to hold a certain number of frigates." His description of this as "a good, workable little fleet" indicates that the country's political establishment, educated by wartime experience, had come to terms with the idea of a blue water navy.[222]

This account has attempted to tell a story of human endeavour, of great sacrifice and occasional triumph, and of the ineradicable establishment of an important national institution. Its trial of fire in the Second World War had commenced only twenty-nine years after HMCS *Niobe* and *Rainbow* had steamed into Halifax and Esquimalt harbours, to mixed receptions and a doubtful future. In the First World War the RCN had performed some essential but largely unappreciated functions, and it is to the credit of the small band of sailors and their few supporters

---

222. HofC *Debates*, 2nd session, 1945, I, 876, and II, 1368, cited in Eayrs, *In Defence of Canada* III, 87

in government that the navy had survived that experience. In the Second World War the Royal Canadian Navy, in tandem with the country as a whole, came of age. The RCN, in giving Canada a measure of autonomy in maritime affairs that the country had never known before, laid the foundations of the naval forces that would serve Canada both in defence of her enormous coastline and as a respectable contribution to postwar collective defence organizations.

Appendices

A P P E N D I X I
RCN Senior Appointments, 1939–1945

NAVAL SERVICE HEADQUARTERS (NSHQ) OTTAWA

Minister of National Defence for Naval Services

Angus L. Macdonald	12 July 1940 – 18 April 1945*
Douglas Charles Abbott	18 April 1945 – 12 December 1946

* Prior to Macdonald's appointment, the Navy was under the direct authority of the Minister of National Defence.

Deputy Minister of National Defence for Naval Services (DM)

W. Gordon Mills

Chief of the Naval Staff (CNS)

Vice-Admiral Percy W. Nelles	1 January 1934 – 15 January 1944
Vice-Admiral George C. Jones	15 January 1944 –

Deputy Chief of the Naval Staff (DCNS)/Vice Chief of the Naval Staff (VCNS)*

Captain Leonard W. Murray	30 August 1939 – 15 October 1940
Commodore Howard E. Reid	15 October 1940 – 9 October 1942
Rear-Admiral George C. Jones	9 October 1942 – 15 January 1944 **

* Title changed from DCNS to VCNS January 1942.
** When Jones assumed the duties of CNS the position of VCNS was left vacant for the duration of the war.

Assistant Chief of the Naval Staff (ACNS)

Captain Wallace B. Creery	1 June 1943 – 1 December 1944
Captain Harry G. DeWolf	1 December 1944 –

Chief of Naval Personnel (CNP)

Captain Cuthbert R.H. Taylor	15 December 1938 – 2 September 1940
Captain Harold T.W. Grant	2 September 1940 – 23 September 1942
Captain E. Rollo Mainguy	15 November 1942 – 15 August 1944
Captain Humphrey McMaster, RN	15 August 1944 – 1 April 1945
Captain Adrian M. Hope	1 April 1945 –

Director Technical Division (DTD)/Chief of Naval Equipment and Supply (CNES)*

Engineer Commander John F. Bell	15 July 1940 – 18 February 1941
Captain Godfrey Hibbard	18 February 1941 – 15 October 1943
Captain Edmund Johnstone	29 December 1943 – 1 November 1944
Captain Geoffrey B. Hope	1 November 1944 –

* Title changed from DTD to CNES during January 1942.

Engineer in Chief (Naval Engineering Branch)/Chief of Naval Engineering and Construction (CNEC)*

Engineer Captain Angus D.M. Curry	1 May 1935 – 10 February 1941
Engineer Rear-Admiral George L. Stephens	10 February 1941 –

* Engineer in Chief was changed to CNEC on 24 October 1942.

Chief Staff Officer Reserves (CSOR) *

Captain Paul Cross, RCNVR	15 January 1944 – 21 May 1945
Captain Paul W. Earl, RCNVR	21 May 1945 –

Naval Secretary

Paymaster Captain M.J.R.O. Cossette	1 May 1934 – 9 February 1942
Paymaster Captain Robert A. Pennington	9 February 1942 – 26 June 1943
Captain Joseph Jeffrey	26 June 1943 –

Director Operations Division (DOD)

Commander Joseph W.R. Roy	20 December 1937 – 10 June 1940
Captain R.E.S. Bidwell	10 June 1940 – 1 June 1941
Captain Horatio N. Lay	30 June 1941 – 24 April 1943
Captain Wallace B. Creery	24 April 1943 – 1 June 1943
Captain George H. Griffiths, RN	1 June 1943 – 9 October 1944
Captain David K. Laidlaw, RN	9 October 1944 – 7 July 1945

Director of Trade Division (DTD)

Captain Eric S. Brand	29 July 1939 –

Director of Naval Intelligence (DNI)*

Captain Eric S. Brand	29 July 1939 – 1 July 1942
Commander Charles H. Little, RCNVR	1 July 1942 – 12 June 1945 **

* Prior to 7 January 1942 Intelligence was incorporated with Trade (Director of Naval Intelligence and Trade) under Brand.
** DTD and DNI were recombined into one directorate on 12 June 1945.

Director of Plans Division (DPD)

Captain Frank L. Houghton*	8 July 1939 – 25 May 1942
Captain Harry G. DeWolf*	25 May 1942 – August 1943**
Lieutenant-Commander George F. Todd, RCNVR	August 1943 – 6 December 1943
Captain George R. Miles	6 December 1943 – 30 September 1944
Captain Herbert S. Rayner	30 September 1944 –

* Also served as Secretary to the Chiefs of Staff Committee
** Although the Navy List indicates that LCdr Todd became Acting DPD on 1 July 1943, Captain DeWolf actually remained in the
 appointment through the first days of the Quadrant Conference in Québec in August 1943.

Director Signals Division (DSD)*

Captain George A. Worth   16 February 1942 –

* Prior to the January 1942 reorganization Signals was incorporated with Plans (Plans and Signals Division) under Houghton.

Director of Warfare and Training (DWT) *

Captain Humphrey McMaster, RN	7 June 1943 – 6 December 1943*
Captain Kenneth F. Adams	6 December 1943 – 1 August 1944
Captain Duncan L. Raymond, RN	1 August 1944 –

* McMaster was actually the Deputy DWT. Although created in June this position was not filled until Adams assumed the post in December 1943.

HALIFAX

Commanding Officer Atlantic Coast (COAC)*
Commander-in-Chief Canadian Northwest Atlantic (C-in-C CNA)*

Commodore Howard H. Reid	1 October 1938 – 28 September 1940
Rear-Admiral George C. Jones	28 September 1940 – 18 September 1942
Rear-Admiral Leonard W. Murray	18 September 1942 – 12 May 1945
Vice Admiral George C. Jones	12 May 1945 –

* C-in-C CNA replaced COAC effective 1 April 1943, but Murray did not relieve Vice-Admiral Brainard, USN until 30 April 1943.

Chief of Staff to COAC/C-in-C CNA

Lieutenant-Commander Horatio N. Lay	27 August 1939 – 1 December 1939
Captain Harold T.W. Grant	2 December 1939 – 26 August 1940
Commander Harry G. DeWolf	1 October 1941 – 28 April 1942
Captain Wallace B. Creery	28 April 1942 – 24 April 1943
Captain Roger E.S. Bidwell	24 April 1943 – 1 April 1944
Captain David K. Laidlaw, RN	1 April 1944 – 20 October 1944
Captain George R. Miles	2 October 1944 –

Commodore/Captain Halifax Force (CCHF)

Commodore G.C. Jones	7 June 1940 – 24 September 1940
Commodore Leonard W. Murray	24 October 1940 – 12 February 1941

Captain (D)

Captain E. Rollo Mainguy	27 August 1941 – 1 November 1941
Captain George R. Miles	1 November 1941 – 7 December 1942
Captain James D. Prentice	7 December 1942 – 15 April 1944
Captain William Puxley, RN	15 April 1944 – 4 May 1945
Captain James C. Hibbard	4 May 1945 –

ST JOHN'S

Commodore Commanding Newfoundland Force (CCNF) / Flag Officer Newfoundland Force (FONF) *

Commodore Leonard W. Murray	10 June 1941 – 28 August 1942
Captain E. Rollo Mainguy	28 August 1942 – 24 October 1942
Commodore Howard E. Reid	24 October 1942 – 1 November 1943
Commodore Cuthbert R.H. Taylor	1 November 1943 –

* The title of CCNF was replaced by FONF in September 1941.

Chief of Staff

Captain Roger E.S. Bidwell	3 July 1941 – 22 March 1943
Captain Frank L. Houghton	22 March 1943 – 15 September 1943
Captain George A.M.V. Harrison, RN	15 September 1943 – 16 October 1944
Captain George Griffiths	16 October 1944 –

Captain (D)

Captain E.B.K. Stevens, RN	June 1941 – 8 November 1941
Captain E. Rollo Mainguy	8 November 1941 – 23 September 1942
Captain Harold T.W. Grant	23 September 1942 – 10 March 1943
Captain James Rowland, RN	10 March 1943 – 26 June 1944
Captain Edward Gibbs, RN	26 June 1944 –

ESQUIMALT / VANCOUVER

Commanding Officer Pacific Coast (COPC)

Captain Victor G. Brodeur	14 October 1938 – 4 September 1940
Commodore William J.R. Beech	4 September 1940 – 1 September 1943
Rear-Admiral Victor G. Brodeur	1 September 1943 –

LONDON

Senior Canadian Flag Officer Overseas [SCFO (O)]

Vice-Admiral Percy W. Nelles	15 January 1944 – 6 January 1945

Head of the Canadian Naval Mission Overseas (CNMO)

Captain Frank L. Houghton	6 January 1944 –

Commodore / Captain Commanding Canadian Ships (CCCS)

Captain Cuthbert R.H. Taylor	January 1941 – 12 February 1941
Commodore L.W. Murray	12 February 1941 – 1 June 1941
Captain Cuthbert R. H. Taylor	1 June 1941 – 1 February 1942
Captain Ronald I. Agnew	1 February 1942 – 20 April 1943

Senior Canadian Naval Officer (London)

Commander Fred Price, RCNVR	20 April 1943 – 23 October 1943
Captain Frank L. Houghton	23 October 1943 – 6 January 1945

WASHINGTON

Naval Member of the Canadian Joint Staff Washington

Rear-Admiral Victor G. Brodeur	1 July 1942 – 1 September 1943
Captain Valentine S. Godfrey	1 September 1943 – 1 December 1943
Rear-Admiral Howard E. Reid	1 December 1943 –

Canadian Naval Attaché*

Commodore Victor G. Brodeur	4 September 1940 – 4 August 1942
Commander Hilary G. Nares	4 August 1942 – 1 February 1943
Captain Edson C. Sherwood	1 February 1943 – 11 June 1945
Commander Francis J.D. Pemberton	11 June 1945 –

* Position remained but was subordinate to NMCJS after its creation in July 1942

A P P E N D I X   I I
RCN Warship Losses, 1939-1945

DATE	HMCS	CAUSE	TASK	POSITION	AREA
1940					
25 JUNE	*FRASER* (DESTROYER)	COLLISION WITH HMS *CALCUTTA*	EVACUATION	45°44N 01°31W	BAY OF BISCAY
19 OCT	*BRAS D'OR* (AUXILIARY)	UNKNOWN	PATROL	UNKNOWN	GULF OF ST LAWRENCE
22 OCT	*MARGAREE* (DESTROYER)	COLLISION WITH SS *PORT FAIRY*	ESCORT OL 8	53°24N 22°50W	NORTH ATLANTIC
1941					
26 MAR	*OTTER* (ARMED YACHT)	EXPLOSION AND FIRE	PATROL	44°23N 63°26W	OFF HALIFAX
19 SEP	*LEVIS* (CORVETTE)	TORPEDOED BY *U 74*	ESCORT SC 44	60°07N 38°37W	NORTH ATLANTIC
7 DEC	*WINDFLOWER* (CORVETTE)	COLLISION WITH SS *ZYPENBERG*	ESCORT SC 58	46°19N 49°30W	OFF GRAND BANKS
1942					
10 FEB	*SPIKENARD* (CORVETTE)	TORPEDOED BY *U 136*	ESCORT SC 67	56°10N 21°07W	NORTH ATLANTIC
7 SEP	*RACCOON* (ARMED YACHT)	TORPEDOED BY *U 165*	ESCORT QS 33	49°01N 67°17W	ST LAWRENCE RIVER
11 SEP	*CHARLOTTETOWN* (CORVETTE)	TORPEDOED BY *U 517*	ESCORT SQ 30	49°12N 66°48W	ST LAWRENCE RIVER
14 SEP	*OTTAWA* (DESTROYER)	TORPEDOED BY *U 91*	ESCORT ON 127	47°55N 43°27W	NORTH ATLANTIC
1943					
6 FEB	*LOUISBURG* (CORVETTE)	TORPEDOED BY GERMAN AIRCRAFT	ESCORT KMS 8	36°15N 00°15E	MEDITERRANEAN SEA
22 FEB	*WEYBURN* (CORVETTE)	MINED	ESCORT MKS 8	35°46N 06°02W	OFF GIBRALTAR
20 SEP	*ST CROIX* (DESTROYER)	TORPEDOED BY *U 305*	ESCORT ON 202	57°30N 31°10W	NORTH ATLANTIC
21 OCT	*CHEDABUCTO* (MINESWEEPER)	COLLISION WITH SS *LORD KELVIN*	PATROL	48°14N 69°16W	ST LAWRENCE RIVER
1944					
29 APR	*ATHABASKAN* (DESTROYER)	TORPEDOED BY *T 24*	PATROL	48°32N 04°32W	ENGLISH CHANNEL
7 MAY	*VALLEYFIELD* (FRIGATE)	TORPEDOED BY *U 548*	ESCORT ONM 234	46°03N 52°24W	OFF CAPE RACE
2 JUL	*MTB 460* (MTB)	MINED	PATROL	OFF LE HAVRE	ENGLISH CHANNEL
8 JUL	*MTB 463* (MTB)	MINED	PATROL		ENGLISH CHANNEL
8 AUG	*REGINA* (CORVETTE)	TORPEDOED BY *U 667*	ESCORT EBC 66	50°42N 05°03W	IRISH SEA
21 AUG	*ALBERNI* (CORVETTE)	TORPEDOED BY *U 480*	PATROL	50°18N 00°51W	ENGLISH CHANNEL
25 OCT	*SKEENA* (DESTROYER)	WRECKED IN STORM	AT ANCHOR		ICELAND
25 NOV	*SHAWINIGAN* (CORVETTE)	TORPEDOED BY *U 1228*	PATROL	47°34N 59°11W	CABOT STRAIT
24 DEC	*CLAYOQUOT*	TORPEDOED BY *U 806*	ESCORT XB 139	44°30N 63°20W	OFF HALIFAX

DATE	HMCS	CAUSE	TASK	POSITION	AREA
1945					
14 FEB	*MTB 459,MTB 461, MTB 462, MTB 465, MTB 466* (MTBS)		EXPLOSION AND FIRE IN HARBOUR		OSTEND, BELGIUM
22 FEB	*TRENTONIAN* (CORVETTE)	TORPEDOED BY *U 1004*	ESCORT BTC 76	50°06N 04°50W	ENGLISH CHANNEL
17 MAR	*GUYSBOROUGH* (MINESWEEPER)	TORPEDOED BY *U 878*	PASSAGE	46°43N 09°20W	BAY OF BISCAY
16 APR	*ESQUIMALT* (MINESWEEPER)	TORPEDOED BY *U 190*	PATROL	44°28N 63°10W	OFF HALIFAX

RCN Warships Declared Constructive
Total Losses, 1939-1945

DATE	HMCS	CAUSE	TASK	POSITION	AREA
1942					
15 NOV	*SAGUENAY** (DESTROYER)	COLLISION WITH SS *AZRA*	ESCORT		OFF CAPE RACE
1944					
4 OCT	*CHEBOGUE** (FRIGATE)	TORPEDOED BY *U 1227*	ESCORT ONS 33	49°20N 24°20W	NORTH ATLANTIC
8 OCT	*MULGRAVE*** (MINESWEEPER)	MINED	SWEEP	49°29N 00°11W	ENGLISH CHANNEL
14 OCT	*MAGOG*** (FRIGATE)	TORPEDOED BY *U 1223*	ESCORT GONS 33	49°12N 67°19W	ST LAWRENCE RIVER
1945					
29 MAR	*TEME*** (FRIGATE)	TORPEDOED BY *U 246*	ESCORT BTC 111	50°07N 05°45W	OFF LAND'S END

* Salvaged but did not return to operational service

** Declared constructive total loss

Axis Warship Losses to Canadian Forces, 1939–1945

Submarines

DATE	NAME	DESTRUCTION CREDIT	TASK	POSITION	AREA
1940					
6 NOV	*FAA DI BRUNO*	HMCS *OTTAWA*, HMS *HARVESTER*	PATROL	51°05N 17°32W	NORTH ATLANTIC
1941					
10 SEP	*U 501*	HMCS *CHAMBLY, MOOSE JAW*	ESCORT SC 42	62°50N 37°50W	NORTH ATLANTIC
1942					
24 JUL	*U 90*	HMCS *ST CROIX*	ESCORT ON 113	48°12N 40°56W	NORTH ATLANTIC
31 JUL	*U 588*	HMCS *SKEENA, WETASKIWIN*	ESCORT ON 115	49°59N 36°36W	NORTH ATLANTIC
31 JUL	*U 754*	113 SQN RCAF	AIR PATROL	43°02N 64°52W	OFF NOVA SCOTIA
6 AUG	*U 210*	HMCS *ASSINIBOINE*	ESCORT SC 94	54°25N 39°37W	NORTH ATLANTIC
28 AUG	*U 94*	HMCS *OAKVILLE*, VP 92 USN	SEA/AIR ESCO TAW 15	17°40N 74°30W	CARIBBEAN SEA
1 SEP	*U 756*	HMCS *MORDEN*	ESCORT SC 97	57°41N 31°30W	NORTH ATLANTIC
30 OCT	*U 658*	145 SQN RCAF	AIR PATROL	50°32N 46°32W	OFF NEWFOUNDLAND
30 OCT	*U 520*	10 SQN RCAF	AIR ESCORT	47°47N 49°50W	OFF NEWFOUNDLAND
27 DEC	*U 356*	HMCS *ST LAURENT, CHILLIWACK, BATTLEFORD, NAPANEE*	ESCORT ONS 154	45°30N 25°40W	NORTH ATLANTIC
1943					
13 JAN	*U 224*	HMCS *VILLE DE QUÉBEC*	ESCORT TE 13	36°28N 00°49E	MEDITERRANEAN SEA
19 JAN	*TRITONE*	HMCS *PORT ARTHUR*	ESCORT MKS 6	37°06N 05°22E	MEDITERRANEAN SEA
8 FEB	*AVORIO*	HMCS *REGINA*	ESCORT KMS 8	37°10N 06°42E	MEDITERRANEAN SEA
4 MAR	*U 87*	HMCS *SHEDIAC, ST CROIX*	ESCORT KMS 10	41°36N 13°31W	NORTH ATLANTIC
13 MAR	*U 163*	HMCS *PRESCOTT*	ESCORT MKS 9	45°05N 15°00W	NORTH ATLANTIC
7 MAY	*U 209*[1]	5 SQN RCAF	AIR ESCORT	52°N 38°W	NORTH ATLANTIC
13 MAY	*U 753*	423 SQN RCAF, HMCS *DRUMHELLER*, HMS *LAGAN*	AIR/SEA ESCO HX 237	48°37N 22°39W	NORTH ATLANTIC
4 AUG	*U 489*	423 SQN RCAF	AIR PATROL	61°11N 14°38W	WEST OF FAROES
19 SEP	*U 341*	10 SQN RCAF	AIR SUPPORT	58°34N 25°30W	NORTH ATLANTIC

---

1. The exact cause of the loss of *U 209* remains unknown, but likely came as a result of damage from air attack. Niestlé, *German U-boat losses during World War II*, 224 n18

8 OCT	*U 610*	423 SQN RCAF	AIR ESCORT	55°45N 24°33W	NORTH ATLANTIC
20 NOV	*U 536*	HMCS *CALGARY, SNOWBERRY*, HMS *NENE*	ESCORT MKS 30	43°50N 19°39W	NORTH ATLANTIC
1944					
8 JAN	*U 757*	HMCS *CAMROSE*, HMS *BAYNTUN*	ESCORT OS 64 / KMS 38	50°33N 18°03W	NORTH ATLANTIC
11 FEB	*U 283*	407 SQN RCAF	AIR ESCORT	60°45N 12°50W	NORTH ATLANTIC
24 FEB	*U 257*	HMCS *WASKESIU*, HMS *NENE*	ESCORT SC 153	47°19N 26°00W	NORTH ATLANTIC
6 MAR	*U 744*	HMCS *GATINEAU, ST CATHARINES, CHILLIWACK, FENNEL, CHAUDIÈRE*, HMS *KENILWORTH CASTLE, ICARUS*	ESCORT HX 280	52°01N 22°37W	NORTH ATLANTIC

Submarines

DATE	NAME	DESTRUCTION CREDIT	TASK	POSITION	AREA
1944					
10 MAR	*U 625*	422 SQN RCAF	AIR SUPPORT	52°35N 20°19W	WEST OF IRELAND
10 MAR	*U 845*	HMCS *SWANSEA, ST LAURENT, OWEN SOUND*, HMS *FORESTER*	ESCORT SC 154	48°20N 20°33W	NORTH ATLANTIC
13 MAR	*U 575*	HMCS *PRINCE RUPERT*, USS *HAVERFIELD, HOBSON*, AIRCRAFT FROM USS *BOGUE*, AND 172, 220 AND 206 SQNS RAF	CARRIER AIR/SEA ESCORT ON 227	46°18N 27°34W	NORTH ATLANTIC
14 APR	*U 448*	HMCS *SWANSEA*, HMS *PELICAN*	PATROL	46°22N 19°35W	NORTH ATLANTIC
17 APR ICELAND	*U 342*	NO 162 RCAF	AIR SUPPORT	60°23N 29°20W	SOUTHWEST OF
22 APR	*U 311*	HMCS *MATANE, SWANSEA*	PATROL	52°09N 19°07W	NORTH ATLANTIC
4 MAY	*U 846*	407 SQN RCAF	BAY AIR PATROL	46°04N 09°20W	BAY OF BISCAY
3 JUN	*U 477*	162 SQN RCAF	AIR PATROL	63°59N 01°37E	OFF SOUTH NORWAY
11 JUN	*U 980*	162 SQN RCAF	AIR PATROL	63°07N 00°26E	SOUTHWEST OF NORWAY
13 JUN	*U 715*	162 SQN RCAF	AIR PATROL	62°55N 02°59W	EAST OF FAROES
24 JUN	*U 971*	HMCS *HAIDA*, HMS *ESKIMO*, 311 SQN RAF	AIR/SEA PATROL	49°01N 05°35W	WEST CHANNEL
24 JUN	*U 1225*	162 SQN RCAF	AIR PATROL	63°00N 00°50W	NORTH OF SHETLAND
30 JUN	*U 478*	162 SQN RCAF, 86 SQN RAF	AIR PATROL	63°27N 00°50W	NORTH OF SHETLAND
6 JUL	*U 678*	HMCS *KOOTENAY, OTTAWA*, HMS *STATICE*	PATROL	50°32N 00°23W	ENGLISH CHANNEL
18 AUG	*U 621*	HMCS *KOOTENAY, OTTAWA, CHAUDIÈRE*	PATROL	45°52N 02°36W	BAY OF BISCAY
20 AUG	*U 984*	HMCS *KOOTENAY, OTTAWA, CHAUDIÈRE*	PATROL	48°16N 05°33W	OFF USHANT
1 SEP	*U 247*	HMCS *SAINT JOHN, SWANSEA*	PATROL	49°54N 05°49W	OFF LAND'S END
16 OCT	*U 1006*	HMCS *ANNAN*	PATROL	60°59N 04°49W	FAROES

27 DEC	U 877	HMCS ST THOMAS	ESCORT HX 327	46°25N 36°38W	NORTH ATLANTIC
30 DEC	U 772[2]	407 SQN RCAF	AIR ESCORT	50°05N 02°31W	ENGLISH CHANNEL
1945					
16 FEB	U 309	HMCS SAINT JOHN	ESCORT WN 74	58°09N 02°23W	MORAY FIRTH SCOTLAND
7 MAR	U 1302	HMCS THETFORD MINES, LA HULLOISE, AND STRATHADAM	ESCORT SC 167	52°19N 05°23W	ST GEORGE'S CHANNEL
23 MAR	U 1003	HMCS NEW GLASGOW	COLLISION	55°25N 06°53W	NORTH OF IRELAND

Canadian Units with More Than Two U-boat Kills

RCN		RCAF	
HMCS SWANSEA	4	162 SQUADRON	6
HMCS CHAUDIÈRE	3	407 SQUADRON	4
HMCS OTTAWA (II)	3	10 SQUADRON	3
HMCS KOOTENAY	3	423 SQUADRON	3
HMCS ST CROIX	2		
HMCS ST LAURENT	2		
HMCS CHILLIWACK	2		
HMCS SAINT JOHN	2		

Major Warships Destroyed by Canadian Maritime Forces

DATE	NAME	DESTRUCTION CREDIT	POSITION	AREA
27 APR	T 29	HMCS HAIDA, HURON, ATHABASKAN AND HMS ASHANTI	48°53N 03°33W	ENGLISH CHANNEL
29 APR	T 27	HMCS HAIDA	48°40N 04°23W	ENGLISH CHANNEL
24 MAY	GREIF	413 SQN RCAF	49°21N 00°19W	BAIE DE LA SEINE
9 JUN	Z 32[3]	HMCS HAIDA AND HURON	ILE DE BATZ	ENGLISH CHANNEL
24 AUG	Z 24, T 24	404 SQN RCAF, 236 SQN RAF	LE VERDON	BAY OF BISCAY

2. A recent reassessment by the Naval Historical Branch, MOD has credited HMCS *Regina* with sinking *U 772*, but Niestlé still believes it was destroyed by a Wellington from 407 Sqn RCAF.

3. After being driven aground, both *T 27* and *Z 32* were destroyed by Coastal Command strike aircraft to prevent any attempt at salvage.

APPENDIX IV

Training, Discipline, and Morale in the RCN, 1939–1945

A recurring theme in the history of RCN operations during the Second World War is the importance and often the inadequacy of training. Vital to the operational effectiveness of the fleet, training was the one essential building block on which Canada's naval establishment had to depend, if the RCN was to make a worthwhile, and identifiably Canadian, contribution to victory. It therefore deserves separate consideration from the complex story of the RCN as a whole. This appendix will deal principally with training in Canada, and will emphasise the training of escort vessels for anti-submarine warfare. Discipline and morale have a place here as well, because they are the two products of training that ensure the smooth functioning of a ship, where members of the ship's company live in close quarters for months on end.[1]

The purpose of naval training is to produce effective warships, and the single most important factor in this process is the individual, hence the first two of the seven traditional naval toasts of the day, "our ships" and "our men."[2] *King's Regulations and Admiralty Instructions* (*KR&AI*), which was the authority so far as Commonwealth navies were concerned during the Second World War, reflects this in its statements about ship organization. The officer of the watch is responsible to the captain for the safety of the ship, the safety of her company, the protection of equipment, the outward appearance of the ship, the ship's ceremonial, the orderly conduct of all on board, supervision of the ship's routine, the safe embarkation of stores of all kinds, and the instruction of men in their duties, in that order.[3]

Ships' companies in Commonwealth navies are organized into divisions, "bodies of men who normally work and mess together and who therefore know each other well." Their training, welfare and discipline are the responsibility of officers from the departments and parts of ship concerned such as engineering, supply, fo'c's'le, top, and quarterdeck, working through the hierarchy of chief petty officers, petty officers, and leading and able seamen.[4] Complementing the divisional system is the watch and quarter bill, which assigns personnel to watches and action stations. During the Second World War, depending on circumstances and the type of ship, the RCN adopted both the three-watch system (red, white and blue watches) and the watch-and-watch system (port and starboard watches). The ship's company while at sea rotated through five four-hour watches

---

1   Other aspects of naval training have been described in the chapters of this volume

2   Changed in 1999 by the Canadian Naval Board to "our ships" and "our sailors"

3   *Admiralty Manual of Seamanship* III, 189, *King's Regulations and Admiralty Instructions*, (1938, hereafter *KR&AI*), v I, article 178

4   Said to have originated with Vice-Admiral Thomas Smith, commanding the Royal Navy's Downs Squadron in 1755, this "idea like all ideas, simple, elegant, and obvious once it had been thought of," had taken on particular importance in the RN before and after the Invergordon Mutiny of 1931, when the Admiralty sought to restore relations between officers and men and to keep lower deck grievances from being aired in Parliament. N. Rodger, *The Wooden World: An Anatomy of the Georgian Navy* (London, 1986), 216-7; S. Roskill, *Naval Policy between the Wars*, II (London, 1976), 281; A. Carew, *The Lower Deck of the Royal Navy, 1900-1939: The Invergordon in Perspective*, (Manchester, 1981), 180-81; C. Bell, "The Invergordon Mutiny, 1931," in C.M. Bell and B.A. Elleman (ed) *Naval Mutinies of the Twentieth Century* (London, 2003) 170-89

beginning at 2000: the first, middle, morning, forenoon, and afternoon watches, and two two-hour stints between 1600 and 2000, the first and last dog watches.[5]

The officer of the watch, normally one of the ship's upper deck officers (although sometimes it could, in harbour, be a supply or engineering officer) was the commanding officer's representative.[6] The captain held total responsibility for the ship and everything that occurred in it. His First Lieutenant, or executive officer, was responsible for the ship's discipline and organization, and as second in command had to be capable of replacing the captain if necessary. The remainder of the ship's officers normally included the navigating, signals, gunnery, supply, and engineering officers,[7] heading up their respective departments, and one or more watchkeeping officers who were each responsible for a part of the ship and the men in the division working there.

In destroyers and smaller fighting ships there were three very important senior ratings: the Coxswain—the senior Chief Petty Officer or Petty Officer of the seaman branch on board, who not only manned the wheel at action stations but was responsible for the discipline and morale of the lower deck as a whole, (in cruisers and above, the Master-at-Arms was the lower deck's disciplinary authority)—the Chief Boatswain's Mate, or "Buffer," so called because he stood between the First Lieutenant and the crew, who implemented the First Lieutenant's instructions for employment of seamen in the ship's company, and the Chief Engine Room Artificer, responsible for men in the engineering department.[8] As often as not during the war he was in fact the "Chief," or ship's engineering officer. The Chief ERA is revealed in memoirs of the time as probably the most indispensable of the three, especially early in the war when there was little technical expertise available, but discipline and morale depended heavily on the example and leadership of all Chief Petty Officers and Petty Officers.[9]

During the Second World War the qualifications of these men varied. When as a very junior RCN officer Lieutenant L.B. Jenson found himself (during a refit period on the Clyde in Scotland) in temporary command of the corvette HMCS *Long Branch*, he "had never before even met an RCNR coxswain":

> He was very old, perhaps fortyish, and had a rum smell about him all the time. He also was not too fussy about shaving every day. I had been used to Coxswains keeping me on my toes. Within a day or two he told me that a keg of rum had vanished from stores. I fancied I could sort of see where the contents of the keg had vanished to in a number of the ship's company. I told the Coxswain to investigate this, but I could not escape the feeling that I did not have his full attention. Within a few days we were starting to look like a pirate ship. I was the only permanent force person for

---

5   *Admiralty Manual of Seamanship* I (London, 1964), 333-5

6   "Every officer or other person, under the rank of Captain, not being either the Executive Officer or the Commanding Officer of the ship, for the time being shall be subordinate to the Officer of the Watch, whatever may be his rank, in regard to the performance of the duties with which he is charged." *KR&AI* (1938) I, article 177

7   The First Lieutenant was commonly known as the "Jimmy" or "Number One," the navigating officer as "Pilot," the gunnery officer as "Guns," the supply officer as "Pay" or "the paybob," the engineering officer as "Chief"

8   Less formal arrangements obtained in such vessels as MLs, MGBs and MTBs. See e.g. C.A. Law, *White Plumes Astern* (Halifax, 1989), *passim*

9   See e.g., Alan Easton, *50 North: An Atlantic Battleground*, (Toronto, 1983) 23-31, 37-40; J.C. Littler, *Sea Fever* (Victoria, 1995), 179-80

tens of miles and I was getting the impression that all these Volunteers and Reserves considered this was a normal lifestyle in our Navy.[10]

There were of course vivid and happy contrasts. Chief Petty Officer M.L. Bernays, RCNR, for instance was coxswain of *Assiniboine* in 1942 and demonstrated great coolness under fire and ran a happy ship's company; he was still serving in the RCN twenty-five years later as the coxswain of the destroyer escort HMCS *Annapolis*, with similar effectiveness.[11] That being said, training, discipline, and morale in a ship's company only reached satisfactory standards when the ship's officers themselves provided effective leadership.

Chief Petty Officer Harry Catley, the first authentic Canadian lower deck voice in the literature, observed in 1949 that "sailors are sailors the world over. Whether they be Dutch, Irish, British, Greek, German or French. Whether they be in naval uniform or dungarees. Whether he is in command of the largest liner afloat or a coal trimmer in some dirty, greasy little tramp. Beneath the cloth, they are all pretty much the same."[12] But he also pointed out that "most sailors were civvies once." And as Frank Curry described, the transition from civilian to naval life was almost always a shocking experience :

> The wartime train to Halifax from Montreal ... revealed how quickly all the niceties of peacetime can become raw. There remains little room for human behaviour. This was a train alive with the activities of war: drunkenness, cursing, boisterousness, laughter, noise, song, and the mournful melodies of a harmonica ... At one a.m. we came to a stop. Tired, hungry and confused, I searched for a friendly face ... The crowd slowly thinned; at last I could see a sign. A check-in point for new arrivals. The petty officer glared at my travel warrant, pointed in the dark, and told me to climb aboard a truck. Transportation to ... H.M.C.S. Stadacona ... When we arrived, not a single person was there to greet us. We stood in the rain, gazing at the long, low buildings with their dim exterior lights. Welcome to the East Coast navy.[13]

For officers, the transition from civilian to naval life was seldom so abrupt, but it presented extraordinary challenges. At the beginning of the war, it should be remembered, there were in the RCN only fifty officers of the executive branch to fill all staff appointments, and all except the engineering and supply officers' billets at sea. The navy had to call on RCNR officers from the merchant service, RCNVR officers from the reserve naval divisions across the country, and officers of the supplementary reserve who by geography or workload were unable to undergo the naval training offered in peacetime.

RCNR officers were experienced seamen and were able to adapt fairly easily to seagoing appointments with a modicum of training in gunnery and other naval specialisations such as signals and torpedo, but there were only seventy-four of them in September 1939, and in a number of cases they proved too inflexible or otherwise unsuitable for naval command. There were 132 RCNVR officers

10   L.B. Jenson, *Tin Hats, Oilskins and Seaboots: A Naval Journey, 1938-1945* (Toronto, 2000) 210

11   *No Higher Purpose*, 506; Personal information from VAdm D.N. Mainguy, who commanded *Annapolis* in 1966-7.

12   Chief PO Harry Catley, GM, *Gate and Gaiters: A Book of Naval Humour and Anecdotes, Including a Glossary of Naval Language for the Uninformed* (Toronto, 1949), 28

13   F. Curry, *War at Sea: A Canadian Seaman On the North Atlantic* (Toronto, 1990), 6

with varying degrees of training and experience. Because their service was voluntary, and they had
to acquire a wide variety of uniforms at their own expense, a commission in the RCNVR before the
war had been an expensive hobby, limited to the fairly affluent. Training opportunities were scarce,
watchkeeping certificates were only available to Lieutenant-Commanders and above, and even those
did not qualify them to keep watch during manoeuvres.[14] In manoeuvres, when precise station-keeping was necessary to the safety of the ship as well as the success of the exercise, officers learned
about the movement of ships through the water. As any sailor knows, these things cannot be learned
in the classroom, but time was too short to provide adequate sea training. Moreover, the needs of a
rapidly expanding fleet militated against long training periods, ashore or afloat. Commander J.D.
Prentice, commanding the small training group at St John's in November 1941, was witness to the
consequences:

> COs have no instruction in convoy work and little chance to train watchkeepers, most
> of whom have no experience. Ships are seldom in station in low visibility and are con-
> tinually losing their convoys even on wonderful nights. In many cases ships cease
> zigzagging for fear of collision under conditions of weather and visibility which make
> it imperative that they should continue to do this for the sake of their own safety
> alone.[15]

In 1939-40 the RCN had facilities to train 360 officers and men at a time when there was a
consistent weekly intake of a hundred new recruits.[16] From 8 January to 22 June 1940 between
ninety and a hundred officers, mostly from the supplementary reserve, took training at HMCS
Stone Frigate, (see *No Higher Purpose*, Chapter 2), one of the accommodation blocks at the Royal
Military College of Canada in Kingston, Ontario.[17] After eight weeks "preliminary training in
Navigation, Pilotage, Seamanship, Gunnery, Minesweeping and the many other arts that make
up a Naval Officer's requirements," they went to Halifax for further training in "gunnery,
minesweeping and a smattering of torpedo"[18] as well as two weeks (often much less) sea training.[19] Despite the absence of antisubmarine training in this catalogue,[20] and even if "our warlike
exercises, enormously enjoyed at the time, proved to have little practical application in the curi-

---

14   William Glover, "Officer Training and the Quest for Operational Efficiency in the Royal Canadian Navy, 1939-45."
      (Unpublished doctoral dissertation, King's College, London, 1999), 30, 32, 59. This study is the only adequate treatment,
      to date, of officer training in the wartime RCN.

15   Cdr J.D. Prentice to Capt (D), 4 Nov 1941, RG 24, 11929, NS 220-3-6. See also Glover, "Officer Training," 32, where he
      points out that U-boat assessment reports repeatedly identify RCN failures to get into good position for asdic contact or
      firing their weapons, and failure to appreciate the relative motion problem.

16   In one week of August 1940, the mobilized strength of the navy increased by 569 officers and ratings, more than four
      times the total strength on 23 Sept 1939. Glover, "Officer Training," 33-4

17   This building, built during the War of 1812 as the naval stores depot for the RN on Lake Ontario, is still in use for the
      accommodation of cadets at RMC.

18   Captain L.W. Murray, DCNS to Cdr Knight, 23 Nov 1939, cited in Glover, "Officer Training," 38

19   One of these officers, James Lamb, recalled the *Stone Frigate* experience in *The Corvette Navy: True Stories from Canada's
      Atlantic War*. (Toronto, 1977), 12-14

20   "ASDIC ... got fairly short shrift" recalls Anthony Griffin. "This was because there were practically no facilities available [in
      1941], all sets going straight into new ships ... Shortly after our class graduated, an ASDIC simulator was developed, which
      was helpful." A.G.S. Griffin, *Footfalls in Memory* (Toronto, 1989), 78

ous force we were destined to join," it was a remarkably successful program.[21] By 1943 six graduates were in command of corvettes, eleven others were first lieutenants of corvettes or minesweepers, two had earned the Distinguished Service Cross, and one became Senior Officer, EG 27, in 1944.[22]

"Ninety-day wonders," the hands loved to call them. They were not always so competent. The overloaded training and accommodation facilities in Halifax, and the desperate need to man ever more ships, whether newly built or acquired, such as the eight American four-stacker destroyers (see *No Higher Purpose*, Chapter 2), led to relaxation in training standards and often to the drafting of personnel to ships before they had completed their training,[23] and constant removal of key personnel from ships already in commission to fill vacancies in newly commissioned ships just joining the fleet.[24]

The *Stone Frigate* courses had come to an end in the early summer of 1940 because the army needed the Royal Military College accommodation for its own purposes. Almost the entire weight of preliminary training for officers then fell upon Halifax, already flooded with personnel of all ranks involved in operations and training. HMCS *Stadacona* looked after both "operational" and "training" functions. An overflow of ratings, including both RN and RCN ships' companies waiting to man the former USN destroyers, went to the Halifax Exhibition Grounds, commissioned as HMCS *Stadacona II*, later called HMCS *Peregrine*.[25] In May 1941 the navy arranged to take over King's College, on the campus of Dalhousie University, for officer training. HMCS *Stadacona III*, as this establishment was first named, commissioned as HMCS *Kings* on 21 October 1941.[26] In the meantime the navy acquired Hatley Park, a property on Vancouver Island, near Esquimalt, British Columbia, for similar purposes. In November 1940 the naval minister had announced the decision to establish a naval college there, but five RCNVR officer courses went through HMCS *Royal Roads* (from late January 1941 until August 1942) before it became an education and training establishment for permanent force (RCN) naval cadets on 21 October 1942.[27]

Such measures were not nearly enough to relieve the pressure on accommodation and training facilities in Halifax. Preliminary training did take place at reserve divisions across the country,[28] but until December 1940 there was no standardization. "Some elementary evening training, morse

---

21 Lamb, *Corvette Navy*, 14

22 Glover, "Officer Training," 46-7

23 "The willingness of authorities to set aside training standards in order to meet manning commitments, to ignore the demonstrated shortcomings of individuals, is a well-documented part of RCN training inadequacies and operational efficiency." Glover, "Officer Training," 78

24 See Cmdre L.W. Murray's complaints after losing all three Leading Seamen and nine Able Seamen, including two "most reliable SD [Sound Detection] ratings" from the corvette HMCS *Collingwood* and his later complaint about the drafting of officers from *Chambly* and *Orillia*, CCNF to NSHQ, 14 Aug 1941, and 6 Nov 1941, RG 24, 11929, NS 220-3-6

25 Glover, "Officer Training," 61; Min RCN Project Committee, 23 Apr 1942, NS 95-8-1 in Stadacona (Base) 8000, DHH

26 Glover, "Officer Training," 87. The significance of the date, Trafalgar Day, may well have influenced the timing of this event, and similarly the commissioning a year later of HMCS *Royal Roads*.

27 As the naval minister had informed Parliament in his maiden speech on 19 Nov 1940, *Royal Roads* was to be part of the permanent postwar naval establishment, identified with the Royal Naval College of Canada that had closed in 1922. Glover, ibid, 82

28 By May 1942 all reserve divisions gave preliminary training to ratings only, NS 76-40-7 (82), DHH, Cornwallis (Base) 8000 v 1

code, semaphore, flag signals and theory of seamanship" occupied several months in 1940 for one officer, "wondering when the war, for me, was going to begin." On arrival in Halifax there followed "a thirteen week course covering all aspects of naval officers' duties, mainly for sea service but also for barracks ... followed by three consecutive days at sea, minesweeping off Halifax harbour ... Seamanship ... was taught by an unforgettable chief bosun's mate who looked (and smelled) as if he had risen from the sea. I learned more from that man in ten days than I ever learned in anything else in ten weeks. The *Manual of Seamanship* was a model of concision, and he took us through it down on the jetty with clarity, force and a wonderful romantic devotion: knots, lashings, rope and wire splicing, boat drill, anchor work, securing alongside or to a mooring. He made sailors out of us."[29]

Instruction of both officers and ratings took place not only in barracks but in a church gymnasium, in the basement of another church, and on the lower floor of a hotel. In January 1941 the navigation school outgrew its classroom space in the RCN Barracks in Halifax and moved to yet another church basement. The signal school occupied *Stadacona II*. That month heavy snowfalls and widespread sickness complicated the training problem. "The contacts from scarlet fever, diptheria etc. increased to such an extent that it was necessary for the Sick Bay to take over the remainder of the classroom space on the top floor of the grandstand at STADACONA II."[30] These were ingenious but piecemeal solutions to problems as they arose. Everything was being done in reaction to, rather than expectation of, crisis.[31] Thanks to the foresight of its commanding officer, Commander A.P. Musgrave, RCN, and the Staff Officer, Signals, Atlantic Coast, Commander G.A. Worth, RCN, the signals school moved to barracks at Ste Hyacinthe, about forty miles south of Sorel, Québec, lent by the army and commissioned in October 1941 as HMCS *Ste Hyacinthe*.[32] This establishment trained all the visual signalmen, wireless telegraphists, coders, radar operators and radio artificers for the navy, and from 1943 the members of the Women's Royal Canadian Naval Service (WRCNS, or popularly, "Wrens") who were to serve in these trades (See Appendix V for a separate discussion of the WRCNS).[33] Officers also took specialist courses at this establishment, and advanced training in special intelligence for the Operational Intelligence Centre took place there.[34] The signals school took a significant load off Halifax, and generally speaking ensured a

---

29   Griffin, *Footfalls in Memory*, 75-77

30   RCN Barracks ROP January 1942 NS 1000-5-13 v4, DHH, cited in Glover, "Officer Training," 85. Hospital living space was given low priority at NSHQ, "Barrack Accommodation in RCN, Mar, 1941," N/Meds to DNP 22 Mar 1941, 14-1-9, DHH, Cornwallis (Base) 8000 v 1

31   "That it was predicted that things would get worse in 1942 before they got better [points out William Glover] was merely a recognition of circumstance." Glover provides documentation for a certain lack of foresight. See esp CWC min, 14 June 1940, C.G. Powers papers, Queen's University Archives, 2150, box 38; Memorandum, DNP to CNS, 23 Aug 1940, RG 24, 5586, NS 1-24-1 v3; Memorandum ... on Manning and Training, 30 Aug 1940, RG 24, 4045, NS 1078-3-5 v1; DCNS to CNS, 25 and 27 Nov 1941, and NSec to Senior Officers in Command, Training and Manning Policy, 24 Dec 1941, RG 24, 3893, NS 1033-7-2v1; Glover, "Officer Training," 171

32   "I had five hundred signalmen under training and expected this to go to thousands in three months So Sam [Commander, later Captain G.M. Worth RCN], said 'OK, we'll find you a place.' They found two places, one in St. Hyacinthe, which was a half-battalion training barracks which they brought in before the war ... and the other place was the race track down ... in southern Québec. Sam said 'I wouldn't put a dead cat in here.' So we ... commissioned *Ste Hyacinthe*." Interview, Capt A.P. Musgrave with Hal Lawrence, DHH, biog file A.P. Musgrave; Min RCN Project Committee, 24 Apr 1942, DHH, Cornwallis (Base), 8000 v 1

33   Wrens were not trained as Radio Artificers, however. A.J. Riley, "HMCS Ste Hyacinthe," DHH, Ste Hyacinthe (Base) 8000

34   Catherine Allen, "Canadian Naval Signals Intelligence in the Second World War," unpublished narrative, DHH, 2000/5

level of competence that had been in 1940 and 1941 often conspicuous by its absence on board RCN ships.[35]

By May 1945 there were about 3000 men and women under training there. Promoted to Acting Captain, "Pappy" Musgrave was a 1916 graduate of the short-lived Royal Naval College of Canada in 1916.[36] He had left the navy in 1919, and worked between the wars in a variety of jobs, including service as a civilian schoolmaster in the RCN and running a coffee shop: he commanded *Ste Hyacinthe* with great distinction from October 1941 until February 1946.[37] By January 1942 the situation had become even worse in Halifax. The complement of HMCS *Stadacona* had risen to 5330, and in March the Chief of Naval Personnel stated a requirement to increase that number by more than 3000. It was now clear that the numbers were likely to balloon even further, to ten or twelve thousand. This was based on an estimate that the total naval establishment might reach 60,000, rather than the 90,000 or more who eventually served during the Second World War.[38] In fact the naval population in Halifax amounted to at least 17,000 by the end of the war.[39] To relieve some of the immediate pressure NSHQ authorised the commissioning of a separate training establishment, HMCS *Cornwallis*. *Stadacona* was to be responsible for fleet support and *Cornwallis* for training, but training facilities still had to be shared between the fleet and the training establishment.[40] Overcrowding was by now a crisis approaching disastrous proportions. It was another year before the new site for *Cornwallis* at Deep Brook, Nova Scotia, in the heart of the Annapolis Valley, could be selected from among several alternative sites and prepared to receive an influx of well over 3000 officers and men. By November 1943, even after *Cornwallis* had moved, there were 7,500 naval ratings on "lodge and comp" (lodging and compensation allowance) in Halifax and only 4000 in barracks. This was the last thing the navy wanted. It had a bad effect on morale, led to unhealthy conditions and poor food, and created serious problems for regulation and discipline. Moreover, almost all the additional skilled workers urgently needed in the dockyard and other war industries at Halifax were married with families, and they competed for housing. [41] There was no getting away from these problems, and under the circumstances the naval authorities took the only course of action now open to them. Clearly, however, the strategic understanding of "blue water" operations by the Canadian naval establishment in Ottawa and the generous instincts that had ensured a timely response to British pleas for help in order to meet urgent needs of the war at sea were not

---

35 For problems in signalling see e.g. Capt (D) Greenock to C-in-C WA, 10 June 1941, DO-30-1, RG 24, 11567; HMCS *Ottawa*, ROP for the period 19–28 June, 1941. Escorting H.X. 133.., 29 June 1941, Appendix III, 8280-HX 133, AC, RG 24, vol. 11311. Later examples can also be cited, e.g. Cdr A.F.C. Layard, RN, diary for June 1944, DHH, 86/130, 87/130, but they were isolated and soon corrected.

36 For a succint account of RNCC, see G. William Hines, "The Royal Naval College of Canada, 1911-1922" in Adrian Preston and Peter Dennis (ed), *Swords and Covenant: Essays in Honour of the Centennial of the Royal Military College of Canada* (London, 1976) 164-89

37 Riley, "HMCS Ste Hyacinthe," and editorial in *le Clarion* 1946, DHH, Ste Hyacinthe (Base) 8000; Interview with Capt Musgrave by Hal Lawrence

38 World War, Min RCN Project Committee, 24 Apr 1942

39 G.N. Tucker, *The Naval Service of Canada* II (Ottawa, 1952), 531

40 Ibid

41 With the closing down of the RCAF embarkation depot in Halifax 3000 naval ratings moved into that facility, ibid. J. White, "Conscripted City: Halifax and the Second World War," unpublished doctoral dissertation, McMaster University, 1994, 113, 115

matched by comparable instincts for timely organization and planning. The naval minister himself, torn between consideration for naval requirements and the real estate market in his native province, saw that building more barracks for the navy in the tight confines of Halifax—the city was surrounded by water on three sides and expansion inland presented particularly difficult problems—would mean expropriating land from the city and private owners, and demolishing existing housing. He refused to accept responsibility for the housing congestion.[42] Men continued to go on "lodge and comp." Naval training and accommodation facilities, although improving, continued to be inadequate. Halifax remained chronically overcrowded.[43] This complicated the maintenance of discipline, and led to tensions that did not make the task of operational training any easier.[44]

There is much to suggest that decisions by the Naval Board to commit resources to combined operations, coastal forces, cruisers and aircraft carriers when the RCN was hard pressed to man escort vessels in Canadian waters, reflect a preoccupation with the postwar navy. Similar concerns may have led to revival of a Canadian naval college when training facilities were stretched to the limit.[45] One British observer certainly thought so. "It is well to remember," Admiral Sir Charles Kennedy-Purvis, Commander-in Chief of the Atlantic and West Indies Squadron and a close friend of Percy Nelles, told the First Sea Lord in June 1941, "that one consideration is always in mind in all Canadian naval proposals and that is to ensure an adequate navy after the war. Every proposal is looked at from the point of view of its bearing on this in order to present post war government with a Navy of such material and moral standing that it cannot be reduced below reasonable limits."[46] The context in which this letter was written makes it clear that what was at issue was not criticism of Canadian concerns about a postwar navy, but whether it would be advisable to replace Commodore G.C. Jones, COAC in Halifax, with a flag officer from the RN. As Kennedy-Purvis pointed out, this was not acceptable: any proposals from the Admiralty to lend senior officers "might be used against the R.C.N. after the war."[47] Most British naval observers, it may be added,

---

42　Memo, "Halifax Housing," 21 Sep 1943, RG 24, v 11105, 52-3-2 v1, cited in ibid, 111-12

43　Greedy landlords, recall most naval personnel, added to the problem. Other cities were equally or more overcrowded, and in the United States the great naval base at Norfolk, Virginia, experienced and found solutions to similar problems. But Halifax did not have the strong industrial and manufacturing base that would have stimulated construction before the war, and military priorities took precedence over residential construction. Ibid, 186-93

44　In the long history of strained relations between Halifax and the navy, e.g., described in Thomas Raddall's classic history *Halifax: Warden of the North*, the anecdotal evidence during the Second World War of tensions between Haligonians and transients, service and civilian, less than half of whom were Nova Scotians, is plentiful and persuasive. Clearly, there existed a subculture feeding upon that discord. What Raddall described as "the voice of Chaos," that neither the naval establishment nor the city fathers could silence, lay close to the surface, as the VE day riots of May, 1945, demonstrated. T. Raddall, *Halifax: Warden of the North* (London, 1950), *passim*; S.R. Redman, *Open Gangway: An Account of the Halifax Riots, 1945* (Hantsport NS, 1981); and *Behind Open Gangway* (Toronto, 1999); White, "Conscripted City," 123-237

45　That the naval staff was already planning for the postwar navy is in fact doubtful. In November 1940 the Naval Council discussed the subject at its third meeting, but in May 1942 Capt H.E. Reid, then VCNS, in answer to a paper by Pay SLt J.S. Hodgson, RCNVR, of the Plans Division (a Rhodes scholar who would have a distinguished postwar career in the public service) found it "very difficult to see how we can plan a postwar navy now ... it is a big problem which should be kept in mind and the planning organization formed the moment signs of peace are in evidence." Naval Council min 22 Nov 1940; paper circulated by Dept of Planning, 10 May 1942 and VCNS to DoP, 12 May 1942, LAC, RG 24, 3844, NS 10-17-34; W.A.B. Douglas, "Conflict and Innovation in the Royal Canadian Navy, 1939-1945," in G. Jordan (ed), *Naval Warfare in the 20th Century* (London, 1977)

46　C-in-C A&WI to Adm, for 1SL, 1931Q/36 June 1941, ADM 116/4387, cited in Glover, "Officer Training," 134

47　Glover, ibid, 134

had a somewhat limited understanding of Canadian national considerations.[48] Rear-Admiral Nelles's 1941 comment to Commodore V.G. Brodeur, the Canadian naval attaché in Washington, that "we'll run our own or bust in the attempt," suggests a more immediate concern than the post-war navy.[49] Ultimately, the Canadian alliance obligations that led to diversification and "blue water" operations, all of them to help the RN solve its manpower problems, whether or not they were related to postwar planning, had no adverse effect on training. In fact, one of the results of those commitments, improved operational effectiveness, was very much on the minds of the staff officers responsible from 1943 onward for planning the "continuing RCN."

British concern about overall command in Halifax, *"not yet communicated to the Canadians,"*[50] became academic after the USN assumed command of convoy operations in the western Atlantic.[51] No matter who the commander at Halifax was, in the summer of 1941 it was impossible, under the pressure of wartime demands, to develop a visionary blueprint for the expansion of training establishments in Canada. That is what would affect the operational efficiency of Canadian ships, and the overall state of discipline and morale afloat and ashore. Heroic efforts by officers in command of ships and establishments, and their experienced Chiefs and Petty Officers, would be needed to bring the fleet up to speed as a fighting force. No one was more sensitive to this than Rear-Admiral L.W. Murray. "Remember," he wrote, in one of several long harangues he sent late in 1941 to the Vice-Chief in Ottawa, "that though the RCN has done marvels, though Brand's party has won laurels for organization of the N.C.S.O. game, and though Halifax has made a reputation for the best regulated convoys, none of these achievements will be remembered in favour of the R.C.N. if we should fall down, even once, in the active participation in the war that has been given to our charge in the Battle of the Atlantic.[52] Sea training, as explained elsewhere in this volume, took place in work-ups, during layovers in port, especially at Londonderry, and in group exercises when possible. With the dilution of ships' companies, and frequent changes in composition of groups, sea training alone seldom brought ships up to an acceptable state of efficiency. Commanding officers had to train their own officers on the job, sometimes even acting as their own First Lieutenants. When in December 1941 a report by the Assistant Director of Naval Personnel exposed the unsatisfactory ad hoc nature of training,[53] NSHQ produced a policy:

> 12. While it is unpractical in time of war to establish any hard and fast rules with regard to working up periods the Department considers it essential that newly commissioned ships should undergo not less than 8 weeks intensive training before leaving their Manning Ports. Further, such ships should not be allocated to the

48   There were of course exceptions, particularly Capt E.S. Brand, DOI and later of D of TD, to prove the rule.

49   Nelles to Brodeur, 19 May 1941, LAC RG 24, 1179/51-15, cited in W.A.B. Douglas, "Democratic Spirit and Purpose: Problems in Canadian-American Relations, 1939-1945," in J. Sokolsky and J. Jockel (ed), *Fifty Years of Canada-US Defense Co-operation: The Road from Ogdensburg* (Lewiston NY, 1992), 31-58

50   "St John's Newfoundland: Projected Base for Escorts," M.011005/41, ADM 116/4387, emphasis in the original, cited in Glover, "Officer Training," 134

51   S.W. Dziuban, *Military Relations between the United States and Canada, 1939-1945* (Washington, 1959), 122-23

52   CCNF to VCNS, personal and most secret, 15 Oct 1941, RG 24, 11979, 51-15

53   Cdr Edmund Johnstone, RCN, a most capable retired RN officer, prepared a memo along these lines, signed by Capts H.A. Grant, J.C. Hibbard, H.N. Lay and Cdr Johnstone himself. Memo to CNS, 13 Dec 1941, RG 24, 3893, 1033-7-2 v1, cited in Glover, "Officer Training," 164

Newfoundland Escort Force without at least one month's operational experience in actual Convoy Duty, such experience being obtained in escort work out of Halifax or Sydney as far as the Western Rendezvous.

13. Once HMC SHIPS have been allocated to the various Commands, maintenance of their fighting efficiency will be the responsibility of the Senior Officer of such commands.[54]

Captain (D) at Halifax was thus responsible for working up all new-construction vessels and for escort vessels coming out of a long refit. At the same time the shortage of commanding officers meant that every available experienced officer at sea, other than commanding officers, could expect an appointment away from his ship, with a regrettable but unavoidable reduction in efficiency of escort forces. To prepare such officers for command HMCS *Kings* began in January 1942 to run a specialized navigation course lasting twelve weeks. (Before this policy came into force, and when attempts to run a command course in March 1941 had proven unsuccessful, probably because of personnel shortages, some RCNVR officers without prewar experience had received commands solely on the basis of performance at sea and the judgment of officers on the spot, not an easy thing to do. This, however, was the exception rather than the rule.)[55] The "Long N," given by a team of instructors under Lieutenant-Commander B. Sivertz, RCNR, a schoolteacher before the war who had sailed before the mast in his younger years and had taught navigation at HMCS *Stone Frigate*, was rigorous and successful. Testaments to its value are abundant. "Thank God ... and you," wrote Lieutenant D.G. King, RCNVR, commanding HMCS *Arvida*, "for the Long N ... Without which we should probably still be floating around the North Atlantic."[56] The "Long N" served its purpose well, and when in February 1943 *Kings* revived command courses it was possible to extend specialized navigation training to a wider cross-section of RCNVR officers.[57]

The qualifying courses for commanding officers assumed greater significance when reduction of USN escort forces after Pearl Harbor often forced Canadian authorities to send escorts off to convoy duty before the eight-week work-ups had been completed.[58] Moreover, the need to repair weather damage during the winter months deprived ships of time for sea training. It is not surprising that Canadian escorts came in for much critical comment, especially in their failure to prosecute submarine contacts successfully. In 1941 the Admiralty offered the advice that it had met similar problems of inefficiency among its own recently commissioned antisubmarine escorts by prolonging work-ups, and ruthlessly replacing inefficient officers and antisubmarine specialists with more promising or better trained personnel. Admiral Nelles could only respond that

---

54   Manning and Training Policy, 24 Dec 1941, RG 24, 3893, 111033-7-2 v1

55   In September 1941, for instance, *Pictou*'s First Lieutenant, Anthony Griffin, who later went on to become Staff Officer (Operations) at St John's in the rank of Commander, RCNVR, received command of the corvette on the authority of Cmdre L.W. Murray, CCNF, when the ship had been in commission less than five months. *Canadian Navy List*; Griffin, *Footfalls in Memory*, 88-9

56   King to Sivertz, 29 Oct 1942, Sivertz papers in the possession of William Glover, cited in Glover, "Officer Training," 186. See also letters from Lieutenants F.A. Beck, Louis Audette, and Leslie Percy, ibid

57   Ibid, 252-53

58   From Jan to May 1942 the norm was four days of harbour work-ups and sixteen to twenty-two days of sea training. RG 24, 11501 and 11568, cited in Glover, ibid, 212

Canada had no trained personnel whatever to spare, and indeed had only recently been able to put the work-ups organization at Halifax on a firm basis with officers who had been relieved from sea duty.[59]

A long personal letter from Admiral Kennedy-Purvis, Commander-in-Chief America and West Indies, to Admiral Pound in late August 1941 confirmed much of what the Canadian naval staff was telling the Admiralty:

> During my recent visit to Halifax and Ottawa I was much impressed with the great improvement in the administration and in the keenness of training since I first came out. The work in Halifax training establishments is well carried out insofar as instructors are available. Their chief trouble is the smallness of their nucleus of trained officers and men as compared with their very great growth in numbers. They are rather inclined to think that the addition of a stripe or so is the equivalent of experience ...
>
> I am not too happy about the efficiency of their A/S escorts at the present moment. Here again they suffer from lack of experience and hurried training. Captains of Armed Merchant Cruisers have told me of the relief they experience when met at the eastern rendezvous by British escort forces with their precision of manoeuvre and obvious knowledge of what they are there for and how to do it.[60]

The staff in Ottawa admitted that things could improve only with British help. At the end of August, precisely when the British and Americans were pushing for a bigger Canadian effort, Naval Service Headquarters gratefully accepted the Admiralty offer to complete the work-ups program of newly commissioned corvettes at HMS *Western Isles*, at Tobermory in Scotland. The VCNS, Rear-Admiral H.C. Reid, was instrumental in setting up this scheme, which in part accounts for his care in warning the British and the Americans that new Canadian corvettes should not be rushed into transatlantic operations.[61]

As Reid wrote he almost certainly had to hand a recent complaint from Commodore Murray that suggested NSHQ was already making counterproductive haste in the manning and training of new construction ships.[62] So great was the shortage of trained personnel that HMCS *Stadacona* in Halifax could find qualified officers and specialist ratings only by stripping them out of ships already in service. Murray blasted this practice:

> during a recent visit to Halifax, the ship's company of H.M.C.S. "COLLINGWOOD" was reduced again to the standard of that of a newly commissioned ship by the drafting away, under orders of "STADACONA," of all three Leading Seamen and nine Able Seamen including the two most reliable S.D. [Submarine Detection] ratings.

---

59   CNS to Sec, Adm, 29 Aug 1941, LAC, RG 24, 6909, NSS 8970-330

60   C-in-C AWI to First Sea Lord, 25 Aug 1941, PRO, ADM 205/7

61   CNS to Sec, Adm, 29 Aug 1941, LAC, RG 24, 6909, NSS 8970-330. Reid had initiated arrangements for Canadian corvettes to continue to go through the Tobermory program when he visited the UK in July: CCCS to NSHQ, 1103B/19 July 1941, LAC, RG 24 (Acc 83-4/167), 218, NSS 1400-WPL-51

62   VCNS to CCNF, "Most Secret and Personal," 25 Aug 1941, LAC, RG 24 (Acc 83-4/167), 218, NSS 1400-WPL 51: "suggestions that you have recently put forward have to await the return of the C.N.S. and minister."

2. Removals from the crew of H.M.C.S. "NIAGARA" were of a similar nature …

5. It is desired, for the recreation of the ship's companies, and to reduce the congestion in St. John's Harbour, to send each group in turn to Halifax for one of their boiler cleaning periods.

6. It will be unfortunate if I cannot send H.M.C. Ships to their home port … in order to
prevent those ships' companies, who have been worked up to a state of efficiency
suitable for escort in submarine waters, from being put back into such a low state
that I hesitate to send them with a convoy.

7. It is pointed out that the ships' companies of H.M.C. Ships, (including our best
destroyers), have reached their existing state of efficiency, not through the number
of higher non-substantive ratings borne, but almost entirely through having worked
together from scratch, through being trained by their own officers whom they learn
to appreciate, and by constant work with each other. The resultant efficiency is far
above that of any one individual, but it only remains as long as that team is kept
together.[63]

The potential was there however, because when they did get the opportunity for thorough work-
ups at Tobermory, RCN corvettes showed rapid improvement. Commodore G.N. Stephenson, the
legendary "Terror of Tobermory," gave satisfactory and often high marks to all but two of twelve
Canadian corvettes he reported on between June 1941 and August 1942. He was particularly
impressed with HMCS *Pictou*:

Lieutenant Griffin is the accepted leader of as young and enthusiastic a group of officers as has ever visited Tobermory. Griffin is chock full of common sense, he is a most
likeable personality, he handles his ship and men with skill.
Sub Lieutenant Ruse, the First Lieutenant, is very young, a boy in fact, but he has
a good power of command and has applied himself whole-heartedly to learning his
work and will get on top of it …
Pictou is an efficient corvette and can be relied upon to make the most of her opportunities.[64]

The Tobermory scheme in fact went some way towards Murray's recommendation that increased
collective training of new, inexperienced crews was preferable to parachuting experienced individuals in and out of ships, but, at a pace of only three corvettes at a time at intervals of some
weeks, it was a long-term solution.

Tobermory provided better training conditions than Halifax. Captain (D) at Halifax was both a
training and an administrative authority.[65] Not until May 1942 was there a separate training commander. Commander J.C. Hibbard instituted a well thought out and innovative training program,
with a night attack teacher—installed in September 1942—which was copied by both the RN and

---

63   Murray to NSec, 14 Aug 1941, LAC, RG 24, 11929, 00-220-3-6

64   HMCS *Pictou*, Report of Working Up, 5 June 1942, LAC, RG 24, 11700, N 07-4-24 (Pictou), cited in Glover, "Officer
      Training," 194

65   A/Capt G.R. Miles and Capt H.A. Grant, RCN, held this appointment in 1942

the USN (see *No Higher Purpose*, Chapter 9) and a tactical floor along the lines of the Western Approaches Tactical Unit at Liverpool, but operational emergencies too often led to ships being detached from work-ups. Hibbard, who put a positive spin on the situation—"It has the effect of impressing upon new ships the necessity of being ready for action at all times and affords them escort experience"—generally made lukewarm assessments. For example, he said of one ship in August 1942, "The fact that the efficiency is up to the standard of the average corvette is entirely due to the C.O. and a keen coxswain and Chief Boatswain's Mate." This was faint praise indeed. "Average" could in June 1942 describe another ship in which the CO, who "usually knows what to do but is a little slow to act in an emergency,"[66] had to be relieved after putting the ship aground in August, getting only a "fair" assessment in September in the night attack teacher, and then receiving an unfavourable report in December from the captain of *Assiniboine*, escorting HX-221.[67]

Operational and training authorities in Halifax and Newfoundland identified the problem, and carried on a dialogue with Naval Service Headquarters on the subject, but the perceived need, both in Ottawa and Halifax, to meet operational requirements at the expense of training severely hampered attempts to find a solution. Murray in Newfoundland urged continuance of the Tobermory training program. Jones in Halifax wanted to suspend Tobermory training until operational commitments had been met. "Local training will continue," he argued, "and is of increasing value." Although, as Murray pointed out, WLEF and Halifax defence operations were always within range of air support, the need to escort convoys to and from Boston in addition to those in Canadian waters, as well as the tanker convoys to and from Trinidad (see *No Higher Purpose*, Chapter 7) did create a heavy burden on the six Town class destroyers and seven corvettes available to COAC for escort duty.[68] With such obstacles to single ship training, group training had little chance of success in 1942. Constant changes in group composition, as previous chapters have shown, plagued escort groups until well into the fourth year of the war. In 1942, despite a run of individual successes in July and August by some exceptionally well-trained and commanded ships (see *No Higher Purpose*, Chapter 9),[69] group instability played a significant part in several convoy battles, particularly SC 107 and ONS 154, and the reallocation of C groups to the eastern Atlantic (see *No Higher Purpose*, Chapter 10). Late in 1941 Murray, at the suggestion of Commander J.D. Prentice, had recommended group training, and proposed reorganizing the Newfoundland Escort Force, adding one additional group to permit withdrawal of one group at a time for a month of training. In May 1942 Prentice actually conducted group training at Harbour Grace, but again the need for reinforcements to escort tanker convoys to and from the Caribbean, as well as an increase in the minimum size of mid-ocean escort groups, brought the program to an end.[70]

---

66 Training reports from RG 24, vols 6909, 6910, 6911, and 11,501, cited in Glover, "Officer Training," 197-99

67 Capt (D) Halifax to FONF, 29 Jan 1943, LAC, RG 24, 6910, No. 313, 8970-331/51 cited in Glover, ibid, 200

68 FONF to NSHQ repeated COAC 1425Z, 14 Apr. 1942; NSHQ to FONF repeated COAC, 29 May 1942; FONF to NSHQ repeated COAC 2144Z, 30 May 1942; COAC to NSHQ repeated FONF, 1804Z 30 May 1942. LAC, RG 24, 11568: Capt (D) Halifax, ROPs, ibid

69 The COs concerned were LCdrs K.L. Dyer, G.S. Windeyer, and J.S. Stubbs, RCN, LCdr C.A. King, RCNR, and Lt J.J. Hodgkinson, RCNR. For a detailed analysis see R.C. Fisher, "Tactics, Training and Technology: The RCN's Summer of Success, July-September 1942," *Canadian Military History* 6/2 (1997), 7-20

70 CO HMCS *Chambly* to Capt (D) Newfoundland, 4 Nov 1941; CCNF to DCNS and CNS, 19 Nov 1941. LAC, RG 24, 3893, 1033-7-2. CCNF to NSec, 7 Dec 1941, RG 24, 11929, 00-220-00-3-6. FONF to NSec, Op Rep for May 1942, DHH, NSS 1000-5-20 v1

Canadian naval forces had no cushion to fall back on when operational commitments exceeded expectations. The Royal Navy was always stretched thin—and for that reason needed Canadian help—but that great and venerable national institution was better equipped to solve problems raised by shortages than the RCN. In May 1942, when problems in training came to a head in Britain as well as Canada, the Admiralty brought it to the attention of Winston Churchill, who took more personal interest in the conduct of operations—indeed, too much interest in the opinion of some critics—than any Canadian cabinet minister. The Canadian Naval staff sought to solve the problem without reference to Cabinet, not even to the naval minister. This proved to be a grievous error (see *No Higher Purpose,* Chapters 11 and 13), but whether or not the sailors consulted their political masters, the fact remained that there was no reserve of naval forces to call upon during a period of expansion far greater than that in any other navy. Captain H.G. DeWolf pointed this out to British and US delegates at the Washington conference on oil supplies to the United Kingdom and Africa in December 1942:

> We have never reached the 10 or 12 [trained escort ship] stage. It is a question of 5
> or 6, and then it is a little difficult. I agree that six well trained escorts are better than
> 12 untrained. But when you have only 6 untrained ones, then you hesitate to take
> one away ... We have even kept them at sea against our better judgement. [71]

It will be recalled (see *No Higher Purpose*, p. 580) that DeWolf, then Director of Plans at NSHQ, advised Nelles and Jones, who was by this time Vice-Chief of Naval Staff, to swallow their pride and allow the Admiralty to take C groups off the mid-ocean run for several months in 1943. Deficiencies in equipment as much as training may have been the cause of poor performance by Canadian escorts—as Lieutenant-Commander P.M. Bliss, RN, of the Operations Division would point out, ships companies were by late 1942 getting training during layovers in Londonderry and Liverpool[72]—the better weather and shorter run would be easier on the ships and crews, less time in harbour would be devoted to repairs, and any training would be a gain, as training on this side in the winter months is almost impossible."[73] Furthermore, Bliss observed, the real benefit of "working together abroad" would be "the inevitable contact with the fleet generally, and ... the more exciting life from the point of view of air attack, etc."[74]

In the event, as has been shown (see *No Higher Purpose*, p. 598), not all C groups left the mid-ocean run. The C groups, and the corvettes loaned to the Admiralty for Torch operations, which joined escort groups on the Gibraltar run after their rather successful operations in the Mediterranean, benefited from Tobermory work-ups, group training in the Irish Sea, and the installation of new weapons, radars and asdic sets. The training picture, given that the stability of ships' companies still left something to be desired, turned around for these groups in the spring of 1943. The situation for other ships and groups, however, remained unsatisfactory.

The excellent shore training facilities set up by Commander Hibbard in Halifax, and the appointment in December 1942 of J.D. Prentice (promoted to Acting Captain) as Captain (D), ensured a

---

71   Conference min, "Fuel Supplies to U.K. and Africa; related escort problems; Day Two, 1 January 1943," LAC RG 24, 11968, 222-1, 5

72   LCdr P.M. Bliss, memo 24 Dec 1942, RG 24, 6796, 8375-4

73   DOP to CNS and VCNS, 21 Dec 1942, ibid

74   LCdr P.M. Bliss, memo 24 Dec 1942, *ibid*.

much improved work-ups program in Nova Scotia. It was well under way when, in February 1943, the need for a "tame" submarine, and the development of Bermuda as a training base for the RN, led NSHQ to propose sending Canadian escorts to Bermuda for their work-ups instead.[75] That was an unexpected reversal of policy and it led at first to acrimonious debate between operational authorities in Halifax and the naval staff in Ottawa. In the event, delays in completion of refits and of new construction limited the number of ships that went to Bermuda under this dispensation in 1943. Work-ups in Nova Scotia waters, although they still did not bring ships up to peak efficiency, provided adequate preparation for the rapid acquisition of experience in antisubmarine warfare that occurred in the winter of 1943-4. Winter weather in Halifax did interfere with the program, and in January 1944 the Admiralty agreed to accept more Canadian escorts for training at Bermuda. In April 1944, when the RN closed its work-up base there, the RCN—with indispensable support from the RN—moved in. Commissioned in August 1944 at the harbour of St George's, Bermuda, HMCS *Somers Isles* had by the end of the war in Europe provided work-ups training for 119 Canadian escort vessels.[76] In February 1945 Prentice, who in an exhausting series of operations in command of a destroyer and an escort group in British home waters had achieved such striking success, assumed command of *Somers Isles*.[77] There could have been no more appropriate appointment for that officer. His contribution to both training and operations, at every stage of the war at sea, had been truly exceptional.

Maintaining discipline and keeping up morale in the wartime navy, given the huge influx of people with no naval or military background at all, and the ad hoc nature of training programs, made heavy demands on individual officers and senior men on the lower deck. There were, as James Lamb observed in his description of the wartime navy, some drunken captains and some mutinous crews. The disciplinary methods of "straight stripers" often did not sit well with newly minted "hostilities only" sailors. Most RCNR officers with merchant marine backgrounds adapted very well to naval service, but there were some who failed to do so and had to be relieved from their commands. A number of RCNVR officers in command also failed to measure up.[78]

In considering the impact of these problems it is important to remember that they were not unique to the RCN.[79] There were however several recorded incidents during the war of men combining to protest against some perceived injustice, and they reflect the nature of these problems in a Canadian context. The first, in December 1940, was by a largely prewar permanent force ship's company on board HMCS *Assiniboine*. Vice-Admiral R.L. Hennessey, (then a Sub-Lieutenant), who could not years later recall the details, "was struck with astonishment at the relative acceptance by the other officers of the incident, and the handling of it as an internal event."[80] In November 1942, in Sydney, Nova

75   "Working up of HMC New Construction Ships at Bermuda instead of Halifax," 20 Feb 1943, LAC, RG 24, 6909, 8970-300 v1, cited in Glover, "Officer Training," 245

76   M. Milner, "HMCS *Somers Isles*: The Royal Canadian Navy's Place in the Sun," *Canadian Defence Quarterly* 14/3, (1984), 41-47

77   Glover, "Officer Training," 300

78   Lamb, *Corvette Navy, passim*

79   See e.g. Kathryn Spurling, "Life and Unrest in the Lower Deck of the RAN in the 1930s," *Journal of the Australian Naval Institute* (Jan/Mar 1997), 41-48. Comparable data from RN and USN sources during the Second World War is not available.

80   Interview VAdm Ralph L. Hennessy, Ottawa, 25 Feb 1999 cited by R.H. Gimblett, "What The Mainguy Report Never Told Us: The Tradition of Mutiny in the Royal Canadian Navy Before 1949," *The Canadian Military Journal* 1/2 (2000), 87-94

Scotia, the hands on board the armed yacht *Reindeer*, resentful of a commanding officer who showed little concern for their welfare, refused to leave their mess deck. The coxswain persuaded the men to turn out, and a new commanding officer joined the ship at the first opportunity. Early in 1943 the corvette *Pictou*, which had so impressed Commodore Stephenson at Tobermory, had a similar incident while alongside at Greenock. A new First Lieutenant, much less easygoing than his predecessor, "came down heavily on any sign of slackness" and the men refused to turn out. On this occasion the commanding officer confronted a representative of the ship's company identified as the ringleader— "a red haired Liverpool Irishman who was combative by nature and a sea lawyer"—pointed out what punishment the regulations would hold in store for him personally if the crew persisted in their course, heard the complaint, and then successfully cleared lower deck.[81] In January 1944 on board the destroyer *Restigouche*, at sea with a convoy, some seamen new to the ship threatened to cease work because they had been unfairly accused of theft by the ship's doctor. They demanded an apology. Precisely how the captain responded is not on record, but according to Commodore G.W.G. Simpson, who was Commodore (D) at Londonderry at the time, the captain "dealt with [it] promptly, firmly and correctly, showing good powers of leadership and knowledge of his men."[82] There was another refusal to turn out in the frigate *Chebogue* in 1944: "I cannot recall the reason," Simpson wrote some years later, "except that it was not due to personalities but to routine. I also recall that the pretext was totally frivolous."[83] In March 1944 there was also a minor refusal to work and a bout of serious leave breaking in HMS *Nabob* (see Chapter 21) while alongside in Norfolk, Virginia, because of disparities between Canadian and British rates of pay and victualling scale (the RCN was better in both respects). The captain, himself dissatisfied with the substandard living conditions, was able to use these incidents to advantage in extracting concessions from both NSHQ and the Admiralty.[84] It will be recalled (see Chapter 13) that discontent in Tribal class destroyers created considerable embarrassment in 1943. *Athabaskan* experienced the very serious offence of mass leave breaking as the ship was about to sail, following a frustrating series of setbacks in the completion of the ship and a particularly rigorous work-up. In *Iroquois* the festering discontent that came to a head in July 1943, with the refusal of the ship's company to turn out and the removal of the commanding officer, became the most notorious incident in RCN ships during the war. Several men in *Athabaskan* were disrated and some petty officers relieved, and as noted above the RCN successfully resisted the Admiralty's recommendation to pay off *Iroquois* and scatter the ship's company among other ships.[85] A Canadian sailor was charged with mutiny during the Second World War, and the most serious punishments were reserved for men who were absent without leave while their ship was under sailing orders. Mass protests by

81   The term means to have the ship's company assemble on the upper deck.

82   LAC, Personnel Records Centre (PRC), D.W. Groos, Personal File, S206 [efficiency evaluation], 3 Oct 1944 [signed, Cmdre G.W.G. Simpson]; Simpson to Louis Audette, one of the Commissioners of the Mainguy Commission, which reported in postwar incidents in the *Mainguy Report* of 1949, 21 June 1950; Audette papers, Vol12-15. MG31. E18, LAC; Gimblett, "What the Mainguy Report Never Told Us"

83   Simpson to Audette, 21 June 1950

84   Lay to CNP and Minister, 15 Mar 1944, NHS 8000(1) Nabob, DHist; CWC min, 15 Mar 1944, LAC, MG 26, J4, v 425; "Report on RN-RCN Administration in HMS Nabob," 10 Apr 1944, PRO, ADM 1/16045; Adm to SNB, 31 Mar 1944, Nelles biog file, DHist; H.N. Lay, *Memoirs of a Mariner* (Stittsville, 1982), 157-59

85   Whitby, "Matelots, Martinets and Mutineers", 77-103. Subsequently of course, as shown in Chapters 15, 16, 17 and 18, *Athabaskan* and *Iroquois* both had good operational records.

men on the lower deck were of course deplored, but as in the Royal Navy they were sometimes the only way of making legitimate grievances known. A 1936 lock-in on board HMCS *Skeena* is an example.[86] Except when staged for spurious reasons—and this does not appear to have happened often—these incidents do not so much reflect indiscipline as a breakdown in communications, which is almost always a sign of leadership problems.

The style of leadership in the wartime RCN was, generally speaking, distinct. It had to be. Even before the war, and among younger "straight stripe" officers during the war, when the RN provided the model, and impressionable young men learned the fundamentals of their profession from sailors brought up in the British tradition, the men they led in Canadian ships did not tolerate the class differences that governed the British officer-man relationship. Captain F.C. Frewer, coming home after spending his obligatory two years in a sea appointment with the RN in the pre-war years, remembered "the very first trip with Saguenay" when the captain

> was seeing his defaulters the first day at sea and I think there was some leading sea-
> man who had to write up the ship's log and had been derelict in his duty ... He stood
> in front of Gus Miles, my first taste of a senior Canadian naval officer ... and gave him
> a long song and dance about the reason why he hadn't been able to write up the log
> properly. And Gus just looked him right in the eye and said "Bullshit." Having been
> reared in the RN I thought, "Hey, we're back in the Canadian Navy" [87]

Men respected and responded to professional competence. "When some Canadians got command [during the war]," observes Commander L.B. Jenson, "I think they pictured themselves as the hard, strict, unyielding captain that everybody loved. They might have been hard, strict and unyielding, but everybody did not love or, perhaps, respect them as they thought. Taking command of a body of men is a very delicate thing."[88] Joesph Schull, in *The Far Distant Ships*, sums it up thus:

> There were outlaws in the ranks; and they were tamed or broken by a system hard-
> ened to meet the iron exigencies of war. But woe to the four-flushers and the wood-
> en-heads and the brassily rank-conscious among the officers, of whom there were
> always some. They were spotted instantly by the men, tagged and talked about and
> furtively bedevilled; and their reward was a lion's share of the misery which rises like
> an acrid vapour from the messdecks of an unhappy ship. There were not many among
> them, fortunately, among the ships' companies; and for the most part there flowed
> beneath the constant griping which is part of the air breathed by every fighting for-
> mation a thoroughgoing, unsentimental harmony.[89]

Commander A.F.C. Layard, RN, commanding EG 9 in 1944-45, bore witness to this characteristic. Armed with the experience of long service—he was 44 when appointed to HMCS *Matane*—and

---

86   "It occurred alongside in Acapulco, and was precipitated when the captain delayed the expected adoption of a tropical work routine (beginning at dawn and ending by noon). Upon learning the men would refuse to resume work in the afternoon, the Executive Officer entered their barricaded mess deck and promised to intervene with the captain on their behalf, which he did, with success." Gimblett, "What the Mainguy Report Never Told Us"; Lay, *Memoirs of a Mariner,* 85-86.

87   Roger Sarty, *Canada and the Battle of the Atlantic* (Montreal, 1998), 32

88   Jenson, *Tin Hats, Oilskins and Seaboots,* 171-2

89   Schull, *Far Distant Ships,* 128

a distinguished war record (he had commanded the destroyer HMS *Broke* and earned the Distinguished Service Order during Operation Torch) his first impression was of inefficient and undisciplined ships in the group. Men were drinking to excess and going adrift in port, officers were not taking charge as they should—"I found to my disgust that the Captain was still turned in" he wrote in his diary after an unannounced visit to HMCS *Saint John*, and he had to fire his gunnery officer for incompetence—and he complained that "you can never trust a Canadian ship to do anything without being told three times." Two months later he noticed considerable improvement in efficiency, much of it undoubtedly the fruit of his efforts, and recorded in his diary: "No absentees and no drunks. Marvelous." After the glider bomb attack of 20 July (see Chapter 16) he left *Matane*. "Quite overwhelmed how much officers and men seem to have liked me in this ship," he wrote as he shifted to *Swansea*. In the following month EG 9, still under his command, sank *U 247* in a textbook operation.[90]

The behaviour of Canadian sailors in port, as Layard's diary and the complaints of shore authorities indicate, was a constant headache. "Jack Ashore," with cap flat aback and roisterous intent, is a lasting and popular image. Layard described an incident in Londonderry: "On my way home I met a Canadian sailor in a narrow part of the pavement who made no effort to move and so I stopped and said 'Who is going to get out of the way—you or I?' He said 'Well, as you are carrying a cane I guess perhaps I'd better.' Christ, there are times when I never want to see another Canadian."[91] Whether Canadians were the worst offenders or not is impossible to say. The Irish historian John de Courcy Ireland said that Londonderry people "had no good for the British soldiers here till the Canadians came and no good for them till U.S. servicemen arrived, when the Canadians seemed comparatively civilised. There is no doubt they were rather rowdy (not all), nor that thinking people, worried that the Axis might win the war, welcomed their arrival."[92] Nicholas Monsarrat's recollection confirms that rowdy behaviour was not confined to Canadians: "Northern Ireland was another place where we slackened off in a rather special way. For some reason our stay there developed into a faintly mad-house session, the effect of Ireland on a normally hard-working and routine-ridden ship's company being to induce a sort of fairy-like unreality; in fact, we all became Irish, and made the most of it."[93] In 1945 some sailors from *Riviere du Loup* attacked and severely injured members of a shore patrol in Londonderry. Commodore Simpson sailed the ship some days early and informed the captain "if there was any further nonsense the ship would not be allowed in Londonderry [again]."[94] "During my last six months," recalled Simpson, "the Boards

---

90   AFC Layard diary, DHH, 87/214. See also M. Whitby, "The Strain of the Bridge: The Second World War Diaries of Commander A.F.C. Layard, DSO, DSC, RN," in J. Reeve and D. Stevens (eds), *The Face of Naval Battle: The Human Experience of Modern War at Sea* (Crowsnest, 2003), 200-218

91   Layard diary, 7 Mar 1945

92   John de Courcy Ireland to Keith Jeffery, 27 Jan 1992, cited in Keith Jeffery, "Canadian Sailors in Londonderry: A Study in Civil-Military Relations 1942-1945," unpublished manuscript, DHH. The idea that "the Canadian *matelot* was a different breed to others, notably the British" can be too strongly emphasized. Anthony Griffin recalls that "the Canadian lad who had in many instances never glimpsed the sea had a longer way to go in submitting to discipline than his British counterpart and for the most part, he accepted the constraints of discipline remarkably well ... But there was, as always and in all navies, an unwritten conception of the responsibility for fairness in the administration of discipline and the measures available to the men in what they considered to be a violation of this principle." Griffin to Michael Whitby, 19 Apr 2000

93   *Monsarrat at Sea* (London, 1975) 45-6, cited in Jeffery, "Canadian Sailors in Londonderry"

94   Simpson to Audette, 21 June 1950

of Inquiry averaged four a week, the majority of which were to investigate a lack of discipline and recommend means to maintain it."[95]

Richard Gimblett has remarked that Simpson's recollection of only four incidents involving Canadian ships, three of them before he arrived in Londonderry, "is a sobering reflection on the possible scale of the problem in the British fleet."[96] The fact remains that even if Canadian sailors in Londonderry tended to see themselves as "nobody's baby,"[97] from late 1943 to the end of the war Canadian naval personnel formed the largest single group of sailors in that port.[98] Five Canadian escort groups, comprising 6,500 men, were using the base. As many as 3000 Canadians were liable to be ashore in the town at any one time. By 1944 there were seventy-five Canadians on Commodore Simpson's staff, but they were the minority. It was still a British base under British command. From the sailors' point of view, that did not seem to matter a great deal.

> Garden-like Loch Foyle [with] countless gardens alive with flowers and lush green grass ... was like a dream. The snow and ice of Newfoundland, the winter gales, the heavy grey seas were no more. We were surrounded on both sides with the utter beauty of green Ireland, and it was as if the fairies themselves had wafted us into a land of magic that was almost beyond belief ... It did much to restore our souls, even though we knew we would only have forty-eight hours layover. For those brief hours and days, we would become human beings again; in touch with peace and beauty and tranquility; far removed from all the ugliness of war.[99]

The preponderance of Canadian sailors in Londonderry was matched by that in St John's, Newfoundland, and modest compared to Halifax. In St John's there were hurried efforts to construct adequate accommodation for personnel of all three services, and hostels for sailors coming ashore. "Avalon II" Murray complained in October 1941, "is a pain in the neck":

> Present numbers are 426 officers and men which is a pretty tight squeeze. What is more, only very few can sleep out of the ship because the hostels are far from being ready ... At the moment we have 89 R.N. ratings all belonging to definite ships who "missed ship on sailing," or who have just been "discharged" from Hospital or "discharged from detention" and have to wait until their own ship returns. As the average length of time away from here is about 26 days we have a continual turn over of about this number just hanging on.[100]

He also complained about the shortage of detention quarters: "There is an outbreak of illicit smuggling of 'hooch' into the corvettes which has been brought about by coincidence of (1) bad weather, (2) shorter daylight and (3) this last six weeks of hell, trying to keep eight ships with each convoy which has given most of them about 28 days at sea out of 30, and as a result, I have a waiting list standing outside the detention quarters and no satisfactory method of con-

---

95 Ibid

96 Gimblett, "What the Mainguy Report Never Told Us"

97 LCdr D.W. Piers to Capt (D) Newfoundland, 1 June 1943, LAC, RG 24 3997, NS 1057-1-27

98 Jeffery, "Canadian Sailors in Londonderry," 10

99 Curry, *War at Sea*, 78

100 CCNF to VCNS, 15 Oct 1941, LAC, RG 24, 11579, 15-15

trolling the 'naughty boys' whilst they are under open arrest. Delay in dealing with offenders also reduces the number of men in the ships as we have no pool, no room to accommodate a pool, and, I gather from Halifax, no men to put in a pool if we had.[101]

As the years went by St John's adjusted to the situation, and earned the reputation of a "hospitable and storied capital where few men lacked a home to go to for a meal ... There were friendly hostels, provided, stocked and operated by Canadian service organizations: and there was a hospitality committee staffed by St. John's citizens which could receive and fill without blinking the request for an incoming ship for a hundred girls and a dance tonight."[102] The Crows Nest Club, established through the private efforts of Captain E.R. Mainguy and Leonard Outerbridge in 1942, was a haven for officers. Outerbridge also helped Mainguy establish a rest camp for men on the lower deck, some miles out of town.[103] Such safety valves did a great deal for morale in overworked ships' companies.

Halifax, however, had no effective safety valve. The overcrowding, not only by the transient shipyard workers and their families and by thousands of sailors, but by the very large and frequently disorderly numbers of seamen from merchant ships, besides the presence of generally well behaved personnel from the army and air force, created a constant state of tension in the city. From late 1942, when Rear-Admiral Murray relieved G.C. Jones as COAC, and the population of transients ballooned to proportions the RCN failed to manage, misbehaviour by naval personnel—which authorities in other ports could usually control by appropriate reprimand and punishment—became a highly visible problem, fast growing out of control. It will be recalled (see *No Higher Purpose*, Chapter 2) that Angus L. Macdonald had proposed recreational facilities for Halifax in 1940, but that the Cabinet considered this an unnecessary expenditure in time of war.[104] Whether or not this contributed to disorder in Halifax, the incidence of drunkenness and destructive vandalism outraged Haligonians, and in 1944 a number of the most influential people in town complained directly to the CNS (a Haligonian himself), bypassing Rear-Admiral Murray in Halifax. Vice-Admiral Jones evidently raised the issue with the naval minister, and Macdonald provided a letter that Jones used as authority to order his Director of Special Services, Commander J.P. Connolly, RCNVR, to look into the problem.[105] It is noteworthy that Jones never communicated directly with Rear-Admiral Murray on this matter until after the VE Day riots of 1945. Connolly, a lawyer from Halifax, had been Naval Provost Marshal there while Jones was COAC.[106] He had already opposed suggestions by Captain Edmund Johnstone RN, the Director of Organization, to establish adequate recreational facilities in Newfoundland.[107] His argument that public-funded building would take years to finish applied

101 Ibid

102 Schull, *Far Distant Ships*, 129

103 Ibid; information from VAdm D.M. Mainguy

104 Naval Council min for 24, 31 Mar and 9, 22, 29 Apr, and 5 May 1941, LAC, RG 24, 4044, NS 1078-4-3 pt 1. See also J.F.E. White, "The Ajax Affair: Citizens and Sailors in Wartime Halifax, 1939-1945," unpublished Master's thesis, Dalhousie University, 1984

105 Macdonald to CNS, 29 June 1944, Folder 17, 80/218, DHH. The correspondence is cited at length in James M. Cameron, *Murray, the Martyred Admiral* (Hantsport N.S., 1980) 317

106 Connolly, who was made an officer of the Order of the British Empire, according to a press release of the day was "widely known as the man who organized and made a success of the Navy Show during the war." J.P. Connolly biog file, DHH

107 J.P. Connolly to the Minister, Sep 1943, MG 2 C71, a briefing that revealed the rift between Cdr J.P. Connolly and Capt Edmund Johnstone on the subject of recreational facilities

equally to Halifax. Connolly's recommendations were to stiffen up the shore patrol system, and to make "a show of force ... on the streets ... to restore public confidence ... [hold] a press conference and put an end to the series of news articles ... giving out bitter criticisms."[108] Rather than relying on the Temporary Memorandum Murray had issued earlier in the year, "relying on every one to do his best to increase the efficiency of his ship and of the Navy,"[109] Connolly wanted Murray to lay down the law "in no uncertain terms ... [and ensure] Senior Officers do their duty in this regard."[110]

The day of reckoning came on 7 May 1945. Well in advance of the expected German surrender in Europe, civic and naval authorities had planned the celebrations for VE Day. In the eyes of civic authorities drunk and disorderly conduct by sailors was inevitable, and they ordered all liquor stores to close. Rear-Admiral Murray and his counterparts in the other services insisted on keeping the wet canteens in barracks open, on the theory that this would help keep men not engaged in authorized activities off the streets. Murray continued to place his trust in reasonable persuasion rather than force to keep the celebrations joyful and harmonious. There was to be a parade, a fireworks display, and a service of thanksgiving. It has to be said that neither the civic nor the service authorities, in spite of the warnings of J.P. Connolly and the fears of many citizens, realized what a powder keg lay just beneath the surface in what was by then a weary, ramshackle and desperately overcrowded old city. When news of the German surrender broke there was indeed much joyful celebration, but by nightfall on 7 May mob rule was in operation. When someone—and it appears not to have been a sailor—broke into a liquor store it apparently took no persuasion to make thousands of people, mostly sailors because there were so many of them on the streets, follow suit. An orgy of vandalism by all segments of the population, but by reason of their numbers and their distinctive dress most evident among naval personnel, ensued over the next day and a half before order could be restored. A useful interpretation of these events is offered by R.H. Caldwell:

> The sailors gave life to their own ideas about behaviour, and they moulded their behaviour to fit expectations. On 7 May, once it became apparent to the VR's that there was no attempt by their superiors to foster mutual confidence, and already knowing that their antics inside and outside *Stadacona* would be ignored and not suppressed, they escalated their drunken high jinks to include vandalism and theft. The ratings, (including WRCNS on 8 May) simply reacted in accordance with the image that they had of themselves, and at the same time delivered a final, tragic signal to authorities in Halifax. Their message was clear: their needs were those of a wartime "people's navy," which were more complex, and required more adaptation and thought—forthright leadership in other words—than the needs of RCN ratings in the 1930s.[111]

This assessment could also be applied to the response by many naval personnel to the option of volunteering for service in the Pacific theatre, as demonstrated in the case of HMCS *Uganda* (see Chapter 22). For Murray, who to the end of his days sought to justify his measures and defend the

---

108 J.P. Connolly to CNS, 3 July 44, Folder 17, DHH, 80/218

109 ACTM 1979, 29 Jan 1944, RG 24, 11657, DH 3-2-1 No. 2

110 J.P. Connolly to CNS, 3 July 44

111 R.H. Caldwell, "Morale and Discipline in the Canadian Naval Service in the Second World War," Naval team narrative, DHH, 2000/5

actions of the men and women under his command, it was the humiliating end to a distinguished career.[112]

There can be no simple explanation of this disaster, which although not the only case of riotous conduct by Canadians at the end of the Second World War was unique in its challenge to all in authority by such a wide cross-section of military and civilian people. It was not replicated in any other centre of Canadian naval activity. Murray, preoccupied with the war at sea and not on speaking terms with the CNS, may have balked at accepting the sound advice offered in 1944 by an officer so clearly Jones's protégé. He did not act on Connolly's recommendations. That Jones and the naval minister did not deal directly with its most important operational commander, and that Murray refused to cooperate with his superior officer, did enormous damage to the RCN.[113] The Halifax VE day riots, driven perhaps more by mob psychology than planned protest, represented a complete breakdown of naval discipline that might have been avoided had the navy either provided the adequate recreational facilities recommended by Captain Johnstone in 1943 or imposed the rigid punitive measures recommended by Commander Connolly in 1944.[114] From the point of view of training, morale, and discipline, this is a stark illustration of the limitations under which the RCN laboured in 1945, which the evidence suggests can be attributed to a critical absence of leadership caused by discord at the navy's most senior levels. By August 1945, taking notice of the lessons learned on VE Day, thanks to careful planning and the provision of wet canteens in barracks, sailors celebrated VJ Day without serious trouble.[115]

Clearly, the RCN was some way from solving its training problems when the war came to an end. Quite apart from shore activities, the level of efficiency in Canadian ships, escort groups, and support groups that actually engaged the enemy remained a cause for concern throughout the war. Given the rate of expansion in the RCN (not the only navy beset by such difficulties) and given the facilities available in Canada, it is scarcely surprising that the scale of the problem was greater in the RCN than in the well established navies of Britain and the United States. RN and USN authorities tended to make allowances for this, even when directing severe criticisms at Canadian escort groups and ships. Admiral Sir Peter Gretton, always a sympathetic friend to the RCN and always honest about it, recalled the familiar old saying: "The impossible can be achieved at once; the miracle takes longer," and went on to add: "The impossible was achieved but the miracles remained

---

112 Murray offered his resignation on 12 May 1945

113 At this point the Director of the Shore Patrol branch in NSHQ, LCdr V.H. Tillson, and the appointment he held, seem to have been removed from the naval establishment. According to the *Navy List* his naval service was "terminated: retired" in November 1944. Tillson, Murray's shore patrol officer in 1943 , had taken up the headquarters appointment on creation of a separate Shore Patrol branch in August 1943, even though Murray thought he was better employed in Halifax and asked that Tillson not be sent to Ottawa. What became of the Shore Patrol branch after his retirement cannot be ascertained from the *Navy List*. This series of events can be interpreted as further evidence of a serious clash between C-in-C Canadian Northwest Atlantic and the CNS. LAC, RG 24, 5638, NS 42-1-10; Caldwell, "Morale and Discipline," 94

114 Hon. Justice R.L. Kellock, Royal Commissioner, *Report on the Halifax Disorders May 7th-8th 1945* (Ottawa, 1945) assigned responsibility to RAdm Murray. Redman, *Open Gangway* and *Behind Open Gangway* elaborate on this view. Cameron in *The Martyred Admiral* directs blame at those who failed to support Murray. Caldwell, in "Morale and Discipline" offers additional documentation and discussion. See also his "The VE Day Riots in Halifax," *The Northern Mariner*.

115 Min conference, 10 Aug 1945, City Hall Halifax, chaired by Capt J.P. Connolly, DHH, 321.009 (D169); RAdm K.F. Adams, interview with Hal Lawrence, nd, biog file K.F. Adams, DHH. 1

elusive ... The RCN tried to do too much and thus the miracles were not achieved."[116] That the performance of Canadian naval forces working in close contact with their counterparts in those other navies could also (as documented in previous chapters) earn favourable comment from highly qualified observers—Cunningham in the Mediterranean in 1942 for example, and several times by Noble and Horton in Western Approaches—and that they proved effective in such a wide range of operations, demonstrates that ultimately, however flawed, the training was successful.

116 Foreword to Milner, *North Atlantic Run*

The Women's Royal Canadian Naval Service

Among the seemingly impossible tasks we have seen in these two volumes that the navy accomplished during the Second World War, the successful formation and management of the Women's Royal Canadian Naval Service (WRCNS or Wrens)[1] from 1942 to 1946 stands as a further wartime achievement.

Yet recently, Barbara Winters, a reserve naval officer and graduate history student, claimed that, while Canada was the first nation in the British Commonwealth to admit women into its naval service as integral members rather than as part of an auxiliary force, no comparative studies have been undertaken to determine what effect, if any, this had on the women, the men, and the organization of the navy. Such information would be valuable, not only in its own right, but as the historical context to another, bolder, and uniquely Canadian aspect of our present day navy—the decision to allow women to serve aboard all ships.[2]

Winters's claim is well supported. In 1952 Gilbert Tucker wrote the official administrative history of the Canadian Naval Service for the prewar and wartime periods. In the volume on the Second World War he included only a short section on the WRCNS. Neither Captain Adelaide Sinclair, the first Canadian woman appointed Director of the WRCNS, nor Commander Isabel MacNeill, CO of HMCS *Conestoga*, the Wrens Training Depot, were mentioned.[3]

Although Wrens never served at sea, any examination of their experience reveals much about Canadian women in the Second World War. The WRCNS was a wartime expedient, raised quickly without, in its early days, uniforms, suitable accommodations or infrastructure, but it sustained a reputation that belied its humble beginnings.

Close to 7000 women served as Canadian Wrens, and because their role was to save manpower, they were employed ashore in Canada and the United States, as well as overseas. Wrens were enrolled in almost forty branches, or "categories," most of which required little or no advanced training, such as messengers, cooks, messwomen, and stewards. However, several branches were highly specialized, requiring technical and operational knowledge, as well as command ability. For example, Wrens commanded a Loran radio navigation shore station, analyzed intelligence and operations in headquarters, and commanded and provided the staff at several isolated sites where they intercepted U-boat radio signals and worked out highly classified Direction Finding (D/F) data.[4] (The signals intelligence part of the Wrens experience is the subject of a later section in this appendix.)

---

1   Throughout the Second World War members of the WRNS and WRCNS were known as the "Wrens." This small industrious bird was incorporated into the WRNS badge. In Canada, the term "Wren" eventually became so strongly identified with women in the navy that in 1951 the term was authorized in all RCN publications and regulations as the official designation for "women" in naval terminology. *Handbook for Wren Officers*, nd, DHH, 92/74, File 10, 14. In 1972 a bronze statue of "Jenny Wren" was commissioned and placed in Galt, Ontario, site of the WRCNS training depot, as a tribute to all Wrens. The project was funded by ex-Wrens. Rosamond "Fiddy" Greer, *The Girls of the King's Navy* (Victoria, 1983), 6-7

2   Barbara Winters, "The Wrens of the Second World War: Their Place in the History of Canadian Servicewomen," Hadley et al (ed), *A Nation's Navy*, 296

3   Tucker, *The Naval Service of Canada* II, "Activities on Shore during the Second World War", 317-22. In a footnote Tucker cited an interview that he had completed with Capt A.H.G. Sinclair, OBE, D/WRCNS, Feb 1946, 312

4   Tucker, *Naval Service of Canada* II, 320; Greer, *Girls of the King's Navy*, 16.

From 1939 onwards Canadian women volunteered for service outside their homes in substantial numbers. Historian Ruth Roach Pierson found that "in the late 1930s and early 1940s, Canada had thousands of women eager to serve in the armed services. A host of unofficial women's paramilitary corps sprang up across Canada." One, the B.C. Women's Service Corps, affiliated groups in Edmonton, Saskatoon, Peterborough, and Halifax, and some 6700 women were believed to be enrolled by 1941. Another, the Women's Volunteer Reserve Corps of Montreal, also known as Canadian Beavers, had fifteen branches throughout eastern Canada. The Canadian Auxiliary Territorial Service (CATS) of Toronto had affiliates as far afield as Saskatoon and Vancouver. French-speaking Canada fostered the *Corps de réserve national féminin* and the *Réserve canadienne féminine*. In some cities, it should come as no surprise, two or more volunteer corps competed with one another for recruits.[5]

Furthermore, the number of women "gainfully employed," that is, working for wages outside the home or off the family farm, rose from 638,000 before Canada's declaration of war to 1,075,000 in October 1943, when employment was approximately at its peak. By war's end women serving in the Canadian armed services included 6783 in the WRCNS, 21,624 in the Canadian Women's Army Corps (CWAC), and 17,018 in the RCAF Women's Division (WD). As well, 4518 women served in the forces' medical services, most as nursing sisters.[6]

In examining the wartime Canadian forces, two considerations are essential to understanding the evolution of their women's services, particularly the WRCNS. First, as we shall see, was directing the energy of the Canadian women's volunteer movements to serve the personnel needs of the army and the RCAF in 1941. Second was the British experience, which was of no little importance, as hand-picked WRNS officers instilled their values into the Canadian women's naval service beginning in 1942.

In 1917-18 British women had responded with vigour to calls for recruits for the Women's Royal Naval Service (WRNS). Immediately after the war the Association of Wrens was formed, and in 1922 it affiliated with the Girl Guides Association, specifically the Sea Rangers, to harness "all that energy and ardent spirit." The head of the WRNS, Director Vera Laughton Mathews, remembered that "we who were missing the comradeship of Service life not only found what we were unconsciously craving, but also a great opportunity of trying to hand on to others something of what we had learned during our all too short service with the Navy ... I can testify that the Sea Ranger training was extremely useful in the W.R.N.S."[7] Director Mathews always maintained that there was a strong link between the ideals of the Girl Guide Sea Rangers and the WRNS. In February 1939, more than six months before war was declared, she was appointed Director, WRNS, a service which at the time was

---

5   Ruth Roach Pierson, *They're Still Women After All: The Second World War and Canadian Womanhood* (Toronto, 1986), 41, 97-98. The first of the volunteer women's auxiliaries, the B.C. Women's Service Corps, was modelled on the British Army's Auxiliary Territorial Service, organized in September 1938 for volunteer women in Britain.

6   Stacey, *Arms, Men and Governments*, 2, 416. Stacey's figure for enrolled Wrens was 6781. Research in the late 1990s by Donna Porter, DHH, provided a slightly higher figure of 6783

7   Vera Laughton Mathews, *Blue Tapestry* (London, 1949), 35-36. Director Mathews described the Girl Guides as a movement which "is essentially a voluntary one; it depends not on getting but on giving; its policy of training ... themselves develops leadership to an amazing degree and initiative and self-control; it has a spiritual basis without which any project will crumble to dust."

largely an unpaid volunteer organization. British women thronged to join throughout the "phoney war" period (September1939 to May 1940) and by the end of 1940 the WRNS were 10,000 strong.[8]

In early 1941 the Canadian government approved a fundamental shift in social and cultural thinking by changing federal labour legislation,[9] and this included the establishment of the Women's Volunteer Services (WVS) and the National Selective Service (NSS) branch of the Department of Labour, which allowed the Canadian Army and the RCAF to consider utilizing women to mitigate their manpower shortages. These decisions were in step with the popularity of Canadian women's volunteer auxiliaries in 1939-40, although the federal government was also responding to pressure from Britain, which had requested permission to recruit Canadian women into the RAF to support the British Commonwealth Air Training Plan (BCATP) in Canada.[10]

Operational demands therefore created a requirement for thousands of additional personnel. On 2 July 1941 the RCAF women's service (later to be renamed the Women's Division) was founded, and on 30 July 1941 the Canadian Women's Army Corps (CWAC) was formed. The aim of the two women's services was clear: women were enrolled and trained in order to increase the number of men available for battle. At this time the navy did not anticipate following suit.[11]

As we have seen in Volume II, Part 1 of this history of the Royal Canadian Navy, the naval war escalated throughout 1941. The Battle of the Atlantic demanded end-to-end transAtlantic protection of shipping, and merchant ships required escort whenever they sailed. In late 1941 the war became global, and by January 1942 U-boats were attacking off the North American coast and threatening the Gulf of St Lawrence. Throughout 1941 naval manpower demands increased in direct proportion to the overwhelming need for convoy escorts, and the complement authorized for the fiscal year 1941-42 was 4667 officers and 38,147 ratings, more than twice the naval strength in 1940-41.[12]

In early 1942 a forecast of yet another sharp increase in the numbers of naval personnel led to cautious preparations for a women's service. Much later, on 31 July 1942, an Order-in-Council authorized the WRCNS, but from as early as January plans had been underway to resolve four basic requirements: accommodations, organization, recruitment, and training.[13]

At a Naval Council Meeting of 5 January 1942 Angus L. Macdonald, the Minister for Naval Services, urged the Naval Staff to press on with the development of the WRCNS. Signals intelligence especially was a cause for concern, and the Directors of the Plans and Signals Divisions

---

8   Ibid, 54, 113

9   The clearest synthesis of government and service policies on Canadian women at war remains Stacey, *Arms Men and Governments*, 397-418. In the early 1950s J. MacKay Hitsman, a historian on Stacey's staff, prepared AHQ Report 68, "Manpower Problems of the Women's Services During the Second World War," and also AHQ Report 71, "Manpower Problems of the Royal Canadian Navy During The Second World War," which served as the background for the section on manpower in *Arms Men and Governments*. Hitsman ensured that the wartime Director WRCNS, Capt Adelaide Sinclair, "read" and "provided very helpful comments" on AHQ Report 68, published 17 June 1954. AHQ Report 71 was completed 20 July 1954. Both reports are at DHH, NDHQ, Ottawa. Hereafter cited respectively as Hitsman, Report 68, and Hitsman, Report 71

10   The British government inquired at the same time if the RCAF could "form its own women's service." Hitsman, Report 68, 3

11   Stacey, *Arms, Men and Governments*, 416. Although the evidence is slim, the navy probably benefited from the early development of these two services. One easily can imagine the highly effective Minister for Naval Services, Angus L. MacDonald, discussing the RCAF and Army experience in Ottawa offices and clubs as he carefully initiated his own women's naval service in 1942

12   Hitsman, Report 71, 3

13   Tucker, *Naval Service of Canada* II, 318

reported on the "impossibility of obtaining sufficient female clerks and typists to cope with the continually increasing volume of work." The minister, for his part, instructed that efforts be made "to obtain candidates from other parts of Canada," who might later "be given the opportunity to join the Canadian W.R.N.S." He further instructed that the Admiralty be approached for the temporary loan of two WRNS officers "and that every effort should be made to find a suitable lady to accept the position of Director [WRCNS]."[14]

Unlike the CWAC and RCAF(WD), the Canadian navy relied on British officers, six in all, to write terms of service, interview, recruit, train, and instil the highest standards in the WRCNS. On 12 May 1942 Superintendent Joan Carpenter, Chief Officer Dorothy Isherwood, and Second Officer Elizabeth Sturdee arrived in Canada.[15] WRNS Director Vera Laughton Mathews later wrote: "The Dominions all started women's naval services, and most of them wrote to us for advice. Canada went a big step further. They wrote the Admiralty asking for a loan of two senior W.R.N.S. Officers to start their service ... We sent our best to Canada and I know it was appreciated. Both Joan Carpenter and Dorothy Isherwood are great leaders of women, and they laid the foundations of a very fine Service with a wonderful spirit." According to one Canadian journalist, "there is only one opinion throughout Canada: Miss Carpenter is 'tops'."[16]

Carpenter, Isherwood, and Sturdee concentrated their talents on rapidly, but carefully, raising a Canadian Wrens service. They applied the same energy, devotion to duty and attention to high standards that Director Mathews had insisted on during the development of the WRNS in the final years of the First World War, and again in 1939-1940.[17] Although women were urgently required, the WRNS officers did not compromise their high standards to haste.

On arrival in Ottawa the three British officers were briefed by the CNS and later by the naval minister, who personally "gave us some indication of what our duties would be."[18] Chief Officer Isherwood described how she and Superintendent Carpenter "worked very closely together, discussing and debating each knotty point," and seeking advice where necessary.[19] Between May and August 1942 Carpenter drew up conditions of service, as well as organization orders and regulations, while Isherwood concentrated on recruiting, deciding "who to see and who not to see" in Ottawa and the provinces.[20] All three WRNS officers conducted interviews away from the nation's capital, concentrating at first on western Canada. Commanding officers of naval reserve units or naval bases made the interview arrangements, and Isherwood later recalled that commanding officers "made me welcome and all seemed pleased that at last the navy was about to have a women's service."[21]

---

14   Naval Council Meeting, 5 Jan 42, 44th Mtg Min, LAC, RG 24, 4044, NSS 1078-3-4 v1, 1

15   WRNS ranks compared with RN and RCN ranks as follows: Superintendent=Captain, Chief Officer=Commander, First Officer=Lieutenant-Commander, Second Officer=Lieutenant, Third Officer=Sub-Lieutenant. Vera Laughton Mathews' rank was "Director" and she wore blue braid similar to that for the Rear-Admiral's rank. Between May and August 1943 WRCNS officer ranks changed from WRNS titles to naval ranks. See *Canadian Naval List* for May and August 1943

16   Mathews, *Blue Tapestry*, 150, 151

17   Ibid, 31, 32, 119. Cdr Adelaide Sinclair, "Women's Royal Canadian Naval Service," *Canadian Geographic Journal*, 27/6, (1943), 286-91

18   Dorothy Isherwood Stubbs, "Potted History," narrative provided to Donna Porter by Isherwood Stubbs, 1999, DHH, 8

19   Ibid, 10

20   Ibid, 11

21   Ibid, 14

When the WRNS officers visited cities with naval bases, they combined recruiting duties with estimates on suitable accommodation, always a principal concern. The navy had increased its strength by 24,688 in 1942 and by 25,352 in 1943, the two largest recruiting years, and unforeseen demands for accommodations came to the fore. These collided with the need for rapid expansion of the WRCNS.[22] In June Commander Eustace A. Brock, RCNVR, Director WRCNS at NSHQ, located a vacant girls' reform school site in Galt, Ontario, for use as a basic training depot. The Ontario Training School for Girls proved to be ideal, with "accommodation, administration and lecture blocks, a sick bay, a gym and a huge courtyard for marching and Divisions" on twenty-two acres of land.[23]

The training depot was named HMCS *Bytown*, Division II, and within a year it was commissioned as HMCS *Conestoga*.[24] During these exciting summer days of 1942 the WRNS officers were confident that they were on the right course. According to Chief Officer Isherwood "between days of travel and recruiting our thoughts were always on training, basic or categorical [by trade], for the First Course in Ottawa and the permanent Depot in Galt, and the accommodation that would be required at the Naval Specialized Training Schools."[25] Later at war's end Captain Adelaide Sinclair, the Director of the WRCNS after September 1943, and her senior Wren officers would claim that the "high service standards and enthusiasm" in the WRCNS was largely thanks to the control that senior women had over the basic training of probationary Wrens from the First Course through to the training conducted at *Conestoga*.[26]

Dorothy Isherwood talked of the agonizing choices required to select applicants for the First Course, with staff having to ensure "that we found the right number, not only of the type and experience required, but from every province in the country."[27] There was no shortage of volunteers, even though at the time only seven categories were available to Wren ratings: stenographer, postal clerk, cook, steward, coder, teletype operator and motor transport driver. Women were enrolled directly for officer training in the beginning, whereas almost all future WRCNS senior ratings, chief petty officers, and officers underwent four weeks of basic training as probationary Wrens ("probies") and only then could they be considered for advancement. The exceptions were for dietitians, welfare workers and librarians, who took the training but were guaranteed commissions because of their advanced qualifications.[28]

The First Course was four weeks long and was conducted in Ottawa throughout September in a large home on Rideau Street, renamed Kingsmill House after the RCN's first director. Sixty-eight

22   Hitsman, Report 71, 3, 13

23   Isherwood Stubbs, "Potted History," 15. On 12 July 1942 NSHQ announced the new location for the WRCNS Training Depot in Galt. RCN Press Release, DHH, 72/833

24   Sub-Lt Florence Whyard, WRCNS, "His Majesty's Canadian Ship *Conestoga*," *Canadian Geographic Journal* (Apr 1945), Reprint at DHH, 92/74, 4. *Conestoga* was commissioned in Jun 1943, "the first and only ship ... a stone frigate ... of the [RCN] captained by a woman, manned by Wrens." Whyard claimed that Chief Officer Isherwood had suggested that *Bytown* II receive its own commission, 6

25   Isherwood Stubbs, "Potted History," 16. The term "categorical training" referred to trade or branch training for Wrens' categories of employment.

26   WRCNS Final Report, Dec 1945, pt IV, "Basic Training," DHH, 75/554

27   Isherwood Stubbs, "Potted History," 17

28   WRCNS Final Report, Dec 1945, pt II, "Conditions of Service," (e)

women began training, sixty-seven of them passed and agreed to serve, and twenty-three were selected for officer training.[29] Chief Officer Isherwood was in charge of the course. She was assisted by Second Officer Doris Taylor, WRCNS, a Canadian who had been educated in England as a dietitian, commissioned into the WRNS and then transferred to the Canadian service. During the course "laughter was never in short supply [said Isherwood] and we were immensely impressed by the way the older women accepted conditions that must sometimes have been intolerable. We needed so many officers and leading ratings to get the service off to a good start that women in their thirties and even early forties who had had wide experiences in civilian life were a vital necessity in a brand new service and it was for this reason that almost half the first intake had been chosen."[30]

The British Wrens were the institution's workhorses, presenting most of the lectures. Superintendent Carpenter, for one, lived up to Vera Laughton Mathews's high expectations and "had a great gift for transferring her own high principles to others and her expectations of loyalty from all who served her beloved navy were plain to see."[31] The First Course aimed to instil a high sense of devotion to duty, naval tradition, and discipline. Candidates seem to have responded well to such ideals, passing them on, formally and informally, throughout the WRCNS until the end of the war.[32]

Carpenter's ethos for the ideal Wren was very much in keeping with the mores of the age, as exemplified by excerpts from the notebook of Probationary Wren Katherine Wayling. A Wren was expected to be polite and quiet and not draw attention to herself. She was also instructed to be "well-dressed, proud of your uniform, salute smartly, hair done tidily (suitability counts), make-up unobtrusive, no bright nail polish, shoes well cleaned, and regulation stockings. Wrens must remember that they bring credit to the navy to which they belong."[33] Carpenter told the women that they were heirs to a great responsibility, and that the tradition of selfless duty was to be expressed through "an obvious and sincere interest in the W.R.C.N.S., and the creating of fine interest for the service." Wrens should show "loyalty to the Naval and W.R.C.N.S. Officers for whom they work and with whom they live." They needed to demonstrate "leadership and ability to win respect of ratings and the quality of personality." That was not all, for a Wren was expected to be imbued with "the spirit of teamwork resulting in her helping officers both practically and by example." In keeping with the social principles we have already identified, a Wren was expected to ensure "neatness and tidiness in herself" and demonstrate "capability of reacting in the right way to responsibility and authority ... knowledge of naval traditions ... conscientiousness—the realization that the navy takes all one's time. In the navy you are never off duty [and finally] impartiality and fairness."[34] All-in-all, this was a major challenge for even the most mature and balanced personality.

---

29 *Ottawa Citizen*, 28 Sept 1942, "Ottawa and District Girls Among Wrens Granted Commissions," 12. This was a photo of the twenty-three members of the first class who were granted officers' commissions. They were: Anne Innes, Helen MacDonald, Mrs James Baxter, Kathleen Robson, Phyllis Holyrode, Mrs E.A. Dobson, Mrs V. McQueen, Anne Crozier, Grace Brodie, Mrs. Sarah Aves, Mrs Evelyn Cross, M.A. Mason, Evelyn Mills, K.A. Wayling, Dorothy Ockenden, Marjorie Hazlewood, H.A. Burns, Grace Rich, E.J. McCallum, Amelia Alvey, Alexandra Graham, Isabel MacNeill, and Nora Allen.

30 Isherwood Stubbs, "Potted History," 19

31 Ibid, 18

32 The experience created strong Wrens Associations in Canadian cities in the postwar period. Most WRCNS groups—sadly much reduced in strength—are still active as this publication goes to press.

33 Katherine A. Wayling, 4 Sept 1942, "Notes taken in a lecture by Superintendent Joan Carpenter," LAC, MG 30, C 183

34 Ibid

The First Course received more advanced training than the basic course that was developed later at the Galt Training Depot. With her final report, Captain Adelaide Sinclair included a summary from an unnamed officer "who was in change of the Officer Training Course," who had emphasized that every effort was made "to give prospective Officers and senior rates an opportunity to take responsibility and to exercise their power of leadership. This was not ideal, but it was necessary to start training without further delay, and it was felt more desirable to give all personnel [an] experience of lower deck life than to select a few inexperienced civilians for commissioned rank without any training at all."[35] Chief Officer Isherwood was put in charge of the training depot, and she selected Isabel MacNeill from the First Course as Training Officer. MacNeill's philosophy was clear: "The purpose of basic training in the W.R.C.N.S. is different from that of a male training establishment. Wrens were taught to understand sufficient of the organization, traditions and customs to become an integral part of the Navy, yet were encouraged to remain feminine."[36] Presumably it was not considered necessary to encourage male colleagues to be "masculine."

December 1942 brought changes in the directing staff. Chief Officer Betty Samuel and Second Officer Lorna Kellett arrived, with Samuel taking over from Isherwood in Galt and Kellett from Sturdee in the director's office in Ottawa.[37] Two months later, in February 1943, the first of more than twenty officers' training courses was held at Hardy House in Ottawa under the direction of Chief Officer Samuel, recalled from *Conestoga*, and she was assisted by Second Officer Kellett. Captain Sinclair's final report noted that "the schedule used in training was drawn up after considerable study of the W.R.N.S. Officers' Training Course and of H.M.C.S. 'Kings,' where R.C.N.V.R. Officers were trained. Standing Orders were based as closely as possible on the latter."[38]

As for the graduates, WRCNS officers rapidly made their mark on naval staff work, as noted in the RCN report for the first quarter of 1943: "WRCNS officers are proving especially successful in Communications and Operational duties, and in some cases outshine their Naval Brethren in courses: so far the brethren have taken this in good part."[39]

By the end of April 1943 there were 1000 Wrens on active service, with about 230 at NSHQ.[40] Chief Officer Isherwood was appointed Director WRCNS on 1 March 1943, replacing Captain Eustace A. Brock, RCNVR. She was promoted Acting Captain WRCNS on 1 July 1943; she wore a WRCNS uniform although she was still serving in the Royal Navy. This was appropriate, given the British service's contribution, which had been no less than the supervision of the new service through the first critical year and a half of its wartime life.

On 29 August 1943 the Wrens celebrated their first anniversary with a birthday ball in Ottawa, as well as "parades and parties at every Wren establishment." In Halifax, "1000 Wrens took part in a march-past before Rear-Admiral Murray."[41] This new service, just over a year old, was ready for a Canadian director.

---

35   WRCNS Final Report, pt XIV, Dec 1945, "Officers," "W.R.C.N.S. Officers' Training Course," DHH, 75/554

36   WRCNS Final Report, pt VI, Dec 1945, 1946,"Basic Training," DHH, 75/554

37   Isherwood Stubbs, "Potted History," 22-23. Second Officer Sturdee returned to the UK to be married

38   WRCNS Final Report, pt XIV

39   Summary of Naval War Effort, 1 Jan to 31 Mar 1943, DHH, NSS 1000-5-8, Pt 4, 4

40   Cdr Adelaide Sinclair, "Women's Royal Canadian Naval Service," 291

41   Ibid

In 1943 Adelaide Sinclair (née MacDonald) was forty-two years old and a well-established Toronto widow who was working as a senior economist in the federal government's Wartime Prices and Trade Board, headquartered in Ottawa. In the 1930s, as a graduate student, she had been Assistant to the Dean of Women at the University of Toronto. She had studied at the London School of Economics and the University of Berlin, and eventually was appointed a professor of economics at the University of Toronto. Following her husband's death in 1938, Sinclair accepted the presidency of the 27,000 member sorority Kappa Alpha Theta, which required her to travel extensively throughout the United States and Canada.[42]

There is no record of how Sinclair was brought into the navy. The reader will recall that in January 1942 Angus L. Macdonald had urged the Naval Board "to find a suitable lady" to become Director of the WRCNS. After the war Sinclair told her friend Jean Gow that she was "escorted—all the while protesting that she had no navy connections whatsoever—by Captain Rollo Mainguy [Chief of Naval Personnel], to be interviewed by the Minister."[43] In the summer of 1943 Sinclair was sent to attend a basic WRNS Officer Training Course in the United Kingdom, and was promoted Lieutenant-Commander WRCNS on 30 July. She assumed the appointment of Director, as a Commander WRCNS, on 18 September, taking over from Captain Isherwood, following a tour in which they both visited Wrens establishments across Canada. Sinclair's proven executive abilities were a natural match for the high ideals, training, and selection standards that were already in place.

To give just one example, many years after the war, in a rare interview Sinclair described how she had opposed a father's attempt to assist his daughter who did not meet the WRCNS officer standards. "I'd never really had a battle with the navy and I didn't think I was there to have a battle [but the father's interference] was a precedent [that] would have demoralized the Wrens ... because none of the kids she was with thought she was fit to be an officer." By way of explanation she asked superiors, "Have you any idea what this will do to the Wrens if they know that one father can produce this result?" She added that she would do nothing, until she heard from the Chief of Naval Personnel, "and if I am instructed to do this, I think you should know that I shall have to see the Minister. I knew that was a bull's eye [sic]."[44]

From late 1943 through 1944 Sinclair was frequently challenged over issues of fairness in category training, pay and benefits. The WRCNS legally were integrated into the naval service, but this level of integration was not complete and did not allow women access to all trade categories.[45] Still, following the First Course, opportunities for specialized training at naval schools expanded quickly, and by 1943 over twenty categories were available, and these increased to thirty-nine by 1945. Wrens were trained and received advanced training no differently from sailors in the same

42   "Man of the Week: Commander Adelaide Sinclair Heads Wrens," 25 Sept 1943, newspaper clipping, biog file, DHH, NDHQ.

43   Jean Donald Gow, *Alongside the Navy 1910-1950: An Intimate Account* (Ottawa, 1999), 149-50. Gow described Sinclair as "a committee woman par excellance ... level-headed, even-tempered, she was adamant when fighting for her Wrens and their rights ... a modern educationalist ... She was the most absolutely private person while at the same time, fulfilling a devoted, worldwide and influential public life"

44   "Service in the WRCNS," interview with Cdr Adelaide Sinclair by Jean Gow, nd, DHH, 84/301, 17, 20 and 22

45   Tucker, *Naval Service of Canada* II, 320

trade.[46] Not surprisingly, Captain Sinclair and her officers "advocated that men and women be treated as interchangeable in those categories of employment open to women."[47]

Nevertheless, Wrens were paid only two-thirds of a comparable male salary, which was in accordance with the rules governing pay for all three women's services. This Privy Council axiom was copied from British policies, which were based on the principle, unsubstantiated by any research, that it would require three women to replace two men. Later, Canadian pay for women was increased to four-fifths of a man's salary. Barbara Winters points out, however, that "the absolute minimum salary paid by the military was clearly higher than the average wage being offered young women between the ages of fifteen and nineteen," in civilian industry. The salary of a Leading Wren was also higher than its civilian equivalent.[48] Furthermore, allowances and post-discharge benefits were almost equal to those of sailors. Allowances were also available to Wrens for transportation and travel, civilian clothing, funerals, the shipment of personal effects at public expense, $15.00 at enlistment for toiletries and necessities and $3.00 a month thereafter, as well as exemption from income tax and national defence tax. Postwar benefits included land grants, service credits, service pensions, disability pensions, university and trade school programs, and employment placement services.[49]

In her final report Captain Sinclair made recommendations for a future women's naval service in the event of a mobilization for war. Not surprisingly, she raised the contentious issue of pay and allowances. "It is hoped that equal pay for men and women may be a commonplace before the outbreak of another war. If not, it is one of the strongest recommendations of this report that it be adopted by the Navy. Apart from the obvious equity of the proposal, the women have proved in this war that they can perform the particular tasks assigned to them as well or better than their male counterparts."[50]

On the issue of whether "women who qualified should receive any trades pay or special allowances payable to the men," Captain Sinclair noted that "the Navy alone among the services refused staff pay to women officers except in a few individual cases where it was conceded only after strong arguments. If women are expected to assume responsibilities for which men require additional pay, the justification for refusing it to them is hard to see."[51]

Finally, Captain Sinclair's report listed accommodations to be a major setback in the development of the WRCNS. With hindsight we can see that the massive two-year expansion of the navy in 1942 and 1943 outstripped available housing everywhere in Canada, and particularly in Halifax. The accommodations problem in that port city was never solved, and thousands of sailors lived off-base on "lodging and compensation" in private homes. Nevertheless, WRCNS officers insisted on high quality, on-base, supervised accommodations, and "this is considered to have paid

46   Hitsman, Report 68, 7, 18

47   Winters, "Wrens of the Second World War," 284, 292-93

48   The policy change in pay to four-fifths of a man's for all Canadian servicewomen was initiated by the Minister for Air, "Chubby" Powers, in June 1943. The details of his arguments in the House of Commons were revealed in a Press Release 27 Jul 43, 181.009 (D2876), DHH. See also Winters, "Wrens," 284

49   Winters, "Wrens," 294. Winters did not cite the original documents for these financial data

50   WRCNS Final Report, Dec 1945, pt IX, "Pay and Allowances," DHH, 75/554

51   Ibid

dividends in the type of girl [*sic*] it attracted to the Service and in maintaining morale and well-being."[52]

Between 1940 and 1942 the Canadian government concentrated no small effort on signals intelligence as part of the national war effort. Such work, including HF/DF operations, was jointly conducted by the RCN and the Department of Transport.[53] With Ultra unavailable for much of 1942, HF/DF became the prime source of U-boat intelligence at a crucial time in the Battle of the Atlantic.[54] As the reader will recall, in January 1942 the minister for naval services had used signals intelligence requirements to urge the Naval Council to develop the WRCNS, and by May of that year the RCN was responsible for manning D/F equipment at seven of the nine Canadian D/F stations.[55]

Throughout 1942 HF/DF technology evolved dramatically. New developments such as the cathode ray tube display were introduced, and the RCN began to install HF/DF equipment in escorts for use at sea.[56] The navy's signal school, HMCS *Ste Hyacinthe* in Québec had to expand to keep up with these developments. Sailors trained as HF/DF operators at the D/F sites were the only source of skilled manpower; many of them were transferred to sea, leaving an operational gap in manning D/F and Y stations.

A witness to the resultant difficulties, and their eventual solution, was Captain J.M.B.P. de Marbois, RCNVR, head of RCN signals intelligence and later the first director of the Operational Intelligence Centre at NSHQ. He claimed that throughout 1942 the Director of Signals Division (DSD) had "kidnapped good Y operators and sent them to sea after a short course at *Ste Hyacinthe*. Replacements were poor. Bearings decreased in reliability ... Improvement did not come until WRCNS operators became adequate."[57] On 14 May 1942, just two days after Chief Officer Isherwood and Second Officer Sturdee arrived in Ottawa, de Marbois (then an RCNVR Commander) requested that trained Wren telegraphists be recruited because "it takes fully two months to train Y personnel who already possess a knowledge of Morse. Ratings without an elementary knowledge of Morse require a minimum of six months training plus two months of Y course."[58]

Commander de Marbois knew that skilled women telegraphists were trained and employed by the Canadian National (CN) and Canadian Pacific (CP) telegraph offices; a CN telegraphist, Irene

---

52   WRCNS Final Report, Dec 1945, pt VIII, "Quarters," DHH, 75/554

53   HF/DF was based on the triangulation of intercepted U-boat radio transmissions, which, due to atmospheric and tropospheric effects, were often received thousands of miles inland by Canadian intercept stations.

54   Catherine E. Allan, "A Minute Bletchley Park: Building a Canadian Naval Operational Intelligence Centre, 1939-1943," in Hadley et al (ed), *A Nation's Navy*, 158-69. The RCN used the British term "Y" to refer to Special Intelligence, now called Signals Intelligence or sigint.

55   Maj CE Allan, "Canadian Naval Signals Intelligence in the Second World War," Dec 1988, App 1, DHH, 223-4. Two RCN stations, Harbour Grace in Newfoundland and Gordon Head near Esquimalt, were combined D/F and "Y" intercept stations. DOT operated eight D/F stations, two of which combined "Y" intercept functions.

56   A cathode ray tube transforms electrical impulses into light. Thus the bearing of a U-boat radio signal—which was an electrical impulse —could be displayed visually on a screen. For the British development of HF/DF and cathode ray tubes during the First World War see VAdm Sir Arthur Hezlet, *The Electron and Sea Power* (New York, 1975), 177-8

57   Allan, "Canadian Naval Signals Intelligence," Dec 1988, DHH, 153

58   Excerpts of Mtg with Director of Women's Service, 14 May 1942, LAC, RG 24, NSS 1008-74-40, 3807

Carter, had confirmed this potential source of skilled operators in 1940 and again in 1941.[59] Because of the time required for security clearances, however, Commander Brock, Director WRCNS, advised that there was "not the slightest chance" that Carter's telegraphists could be enrolled for the First Course.[60] Nevertheless, Commander de Marbois and Irene Carter, who was still a civilian, kept in touch with each other throughout the summer.[61]

Almost every dimension of the naval experience increased in pace during the fall of 1942. When candidates on the first recruit course began training at Galt in October, therefore, Irene Carter was among them. The Naval Staff had secured temporary accommodations in the Guild of the Arts Hotel in Scarborough, Ontario, which provided secure space to train Wrens in HF/DF operations. Carter was quickly removed from the basic training course after less than two weeks, promoted to leading telegraphist, and sent to instruct Morse Code at the Guild. An intelligence officer later visited that facility and reported that "this class, under CPO Barrie, is making excellent progress especially in view of the fact that the class has been running for such a short period of time." Even more encouraging, "the standard of intelligence among the girls [sic] is particularly high and their interest and enthusiasm in their work must be particularly commented on."[62]

Petty Officer Telegraphist (Special Operator) Dorothy Robertson spent three months at the Guild. She described how

> we spent every weekday, earphones clamped to our heads while Chief [C. George] Barrie or one of the Leading Tels [Irene Carter and Gertrude Jardine, both CN Telegraphists] indoctrinated us into the mysteries of Morse. As a break from the buzzers, whose loud unvarying pitch could become maddening if listened to for long, we had lectures on naval wireless procedure from the Chief. Over and over he coached us in the location and call signs of the German Navy's coastal stations, and the make-up and probable meaning of various types of message; above all how to distinguish between the incessant traffic from the shore stations, in which we were really not interested, and the infrequent messages from the "units," usually U-boats, in which we were vitally interested, the prime reason for our existence being to obtain direction-finding bearings.[63]

In April 1943 most of the group at the Guild, Wrens and instructors alike, were sent to open up No. 1 Wireless Station at Gloucester, Ontario; this was a cathode ray-equipped RCN site south of Ottawa. Leading Wren Telegraphist (Special Operator) Lavinia Crane reported that "the Germans had control stations [which] used to broadcast on a certain frequency and they would carry on most of the hour sending. There'd be some silent periods, but they would carry on with routine messages. [Then, they would] allow the subs to come up ... if the sub had a routine message, say a weather report (they had weather reports, sighting reports, success reports and some other types but those were the three main ones) they would come up during that five minutes and give their messages."[64]

---

59   Lt J.R. Foster, RCNVR, 7 Nov 1941, "Women Operators for Naval Service," LAC, RG 24, NSS 1008-75-40, 3807

60   Lt C.G. Lloyd, 28 July 1942, "W.R.C.N.S. Personnel for Gloucester Development," LAC, RG 24, NSS 1008-75-40, 3807

61   Irene McLean (nee Carter) notes of interview with Donna Porter, 18 Sep 1998, DHH

62   Lt(SB) R.J. Williams, RCNVR, 19 Dec 1942, LAC, RG 24, NSS 1008-75-40, 3807

63   Dorothy Robertson, "I Go (Not) Down to the Sea in Ships: Recollections of a Canadian Wren," DHH, 95/62, 22-23

64   Leading Wren Telegraphist Lavinia Crane notes of interview with Hal Lawrence, 9 Aug 1989, DHH Biog File, 7

A year later the Navy opened its second new station, HMCS *Coverdale* near Moncton, New Brunswick. This would become the largest in a wide network of D/F and Y intercept facilities.[65] A number of experienced Wrens from Gloucester were sent to *Coverdale* along with some of the Wrens now trained at *Ste Hyacinthe*. Leading Wren Lavinia Crane reported that at Gloucester, "we'd come off at eight o'clock in the morning and there was no way you could sleep. We'd just take off on our bikes." At *Ste Hyacinthe*, she continued, "we were rather an unique group. We were not typical Navy and we had been used to being on stations of our own, more or less ruling the roost, telling our poor officers what we thought best (there were only two or three of them, and they were very good)." Apparently they had all sent home for their bicycles, and "the pusser navy was just thrown by that." Still, "we were able to keep them and use them." As for *Coverdale*, said Crane, "we had very good officers. We used to work long hours and we certainly gave our all." Their efforts did not go unrewarded, superiors ensuring that "we got things, like being able to use our bikes and sensible sort[s] of rules."[66]

By mid-1944 HF/DF had lost its position of primacy in the Battle of the Atlantic. But by then WRCNS had taken over most of the sections in the NSHQ OIC, since as Captain de Marbois pointed out, in the last six months of 1944 U-boat sighting and shadowing—and reporting—of transatlantic convoys "was practically non-existant."[67] Moreover, de Marbois noted that posting WRCNS to the establishment had proven "a success, the W.R.C.N.S. officers paying greater attention to detail and, on the whole, maintaining better discipline over an entirely female staff," which included "Wren rating loggers, plotters and discriminators and civilian T/P operators."[68]

That same year, 1944, women began to replace male signals intercept operators on the west coast of Canada. Approximately 85 Wren operators were trained in the Japanese morse code at *Ste Hyacinthe* from July 1944 until VJ Day. The first group made its way to the HF/DF and Y intercept station at Gordon Head, near Esquimalt, in October 1944. Four months after their arrival the Wrens had taken over half of the operation, and Lieutenant Dorothy M. Bruce, WRCNS, was in charge of the station.[69] The Americans insisted that Gordon Head be routinely upgraded, and in April 1945 USN signals intelligence officials "stated bluntly that they desired better output from Gordon Head." Therefore, "new aerials were erected," while Wrens were trained in groups of ten at Bainbridge, the USN signals intelligence base near Seattle, Washington. By midsummer the station was operating "on a most efficient basis."[70]

In the Atlantic, the pace of battle increased as the result of a renewed U-boat offensive. De Marbois said that "the [first] four and a half months of 1945 were more active than the second half of 1944," and in April 1945 there were a total of 488 U-boat messages, making it "the most active month since March 1944."[71]

---

65   "History and Activities of the Operational Intelligence Centre, N.H.Q., 1939-1945," 1944, OIC 1, 1440-18, DHH, 3

66   Crane, 10-12

67   "History and Activities of Operational Intelligence Centre, N.H.Q., 1939-1945," 1944, 1440-18, DHH, 1

68   Ibid, 6

69   Ibid, 3-4, 4A. Again the Wrens had freed up sailors for more arduous duty, this time to man the new isolated RCN intercept station at Masset in the Queen Charlotte Islands.

70   Ibid, 3

71   Ibid, 1

By war's end Wrens of all ranks had taken on the majority of the duties at most naval signals intelligence sites, as well as in the OIC, the Intelligence and Signals Divisions in NSHQ and in the Halifax and St. John's headquarters. Their capabilities, combined with their sense of duty and their willingness to perform hard tasks in difficult circumstances, armed them sufficiently to meet the heavy demands of operational and intelligence staff work.

By 31 August 1945, 6783 women had enlisted in the WRCNS; eleven had died as a result of illness, accidents such as drowning, or suicide. None were killed in action.[72] About one in six had served outside Canada.[73] In a recently conducted survey of wartime Wrens, most recalled that they were not aware of the differences in wages between sailors and themselves.[74] Those who remembered such inequality in remuneration, for the most part believed that the men deserved to be paid more because they had faced the possibility of being killed in battle.[75] Senior WRNS and WRCNS officers, however, although they emphasized selflessness as a value, also sought fairness and equality, particularly in pay. These officers had a longer term view, one that included the postwar future when women would be given greater responsibility and, they hoped, equality.

For many women, their service in the Wrens influenced the rest of their lives. As Petty Officer Dorothy Robertson put it, "I owe the Navy a lot, more than I could ever put on paper." What she could write was heartfelt, as "joining the Navy was the most significant step I ever took, and changed my life forever." At the time Robertson joined the colours, she needed "the compulsion provided by the Service to get me on that train to Galt; to overcome the terrible inertia, the overpowering shyness of meeting strangers, that had always held me back from breaking free" of the life she had increasingly disliked. "I *wanted* to leave so badly: home smothered me."[76] The RCN did not.

---

72   The fatality figure of 11 was calculated in 1998 by the Department of Veterans Affairs, and passed to Donna Porter, DHH

73   Tucker, *Naval Service of Canada* II, 322. Tucker's statistics included 503 "Wrens sent to Great Britain and stationed in Londonderry, H.M.C.S. *Niobe* in Scotland, and London, with a few in Plymouth." Also, 568 served in Newfoundland, and about 50 in New York and Washington.

74   Donna Porter, DHH, conducted a survey at the Wrens reunion in Toronto, 18-19 Sept 1998. Over 200 wartime Wrens responded to a comprehensive questionnaire.

75   Leading Wren Rosamond Fiddes remembered that "we were always broke ... we found our monthly pay did not begin to cover our expenses." Greer, *Girls of the King's Navy*, 86

76   Robertson, "I Go (Not) Down to the Sea," 102

RCN Coastal Forces in the Mediterranean Theatre

Although this volume cannot do justice to the hundreds of Canadian naval officers and ratings who served with the Royal Naval in the various theatres of war, some bear scrutiny because of the magnitude of their accomplishments, and the diversity of their experience. Among these are the RCNVR officers who served with RN coastal forces in the Mediterranean.

From 1940 onward, RCN personnel made an important contribution in RN coastal force flotillas. By June 1943, 110 of the 400 Canadian naval officers officers on loan to the RN were on that duty.[1] This contribution can be traced to a request from the Admiralty to the Canadian government in the spring of 1940 for experienced "yachtsmen" to join the RNVR, either as sub-lieutenants or as ratings, for training with a view to later being granted commissions. The Admiralty had already recruited coastal force personnel from the Royal Navy Supplementary Reserve, a prewar organization of 2000 "gentlemen" of nautical interest and experience, most of them yachtsmen or motorboat owners. When this source began to dry up in early 1940, the Admiralty looked further afield for manpower, and Canada was a logical source. The Canadian Chief of the Naval Staff, Rear-Admiral P.W. Nelles, regarded the Admiralty's request favourably because it would provide a nucleus of young officers "who had been trained in the school of experience, and who will still be at an age to be able to help train still younger personnel in case of further wars in the future."[2]

In order to avoid recruiting by both the RN and RCN in Canada, and because of the difference in pay scales between the two navies, NSHQ insisted that the personnel recruited for the Admiralty join through the RCNVR. A plan was worked out whereby 125 direct entry RCNVR officer candidates would be sent to the UK in groups of 25 for officer training. A further 150 select ratings, who would be considered for commissions after training and three months experience at sea, were also to be sent.[3] The first groups of 25 arrived in the UK in May 1940. Those candidates selected as officers received instruction at HMS *King Alfred* near Hove. The ratings were trained at HMS *Raleigh* (hence their nickname the "Raleighites") near Devon before serving at sea for three months, and then completing their officer training at *King Alfred*. Not all of these personnel went into Coastal Forces—for example, Lieutenant Robert Hampton Gray, who was awarded a posthumous Victoria Cross for his courage over Japan in the final days of the war, was one of many to join the Fleet Air Arm—but a large proportion did so and they formed the nucleus of the Canadian contribution into that service.[4]

---

1   Figure is from "Canadians Serving in R.N. Coastal Craft in the Mediterranean," narrative rep Lt J. George, LAC, RG 24, 11749, 4321-1. The figure for the number of RCN officers on service with the RN in 1943 is from "Statement of Officers of Canadian Naval Forces on Loan to the Royal Navy, 1 May to 30 June 1943," App A to SCNO(L) WD, June 1943, DHH, NHS 1000-5-35(1)

2   CNS memo to Min, 27 May 1940, DHH, NHS 1700-193/19

3   Ibid

4   See DHH interviews with Cornelius Burke, C.A. Burk and others, and Gordon. W. Stead, *A Leaf Upon the Sea*. (Vancouver, 1988), 7-16. For the story of the Canadians trained at HMS *Raleigh* see G.W. Stead, *The Canadian Raleighites: Ordinary Seamen and Officers at War* (Aylmer, 1988)

Many personnel of the Canadian contingent who served in light coastal forces in the Mediterranean can be roughly divided into two groups; those who served in motor launches (ML) and those in Motor Gun Boats (MGB) and Motor Torpedo Boats (MTB). The smallest group were in MLs, but they had perhaps the most interesting and varied careers. Two officers, Lieutenant-Commanders N.J. Alexander and G.W. Stead, became senior officers of British flotillas. Alexander commanded an ML out of Gibraltar from 1941 to 1943 and later became SO of the RN's 9th ML Flotilla. Stead had what is known as a "good war," which he described in his superb memoir, *A Leaf Upon the Sea*. After operating out of Gibraltar in command of *ML 126*, Lieutenant-Commander Stead took two MLs on a long, perilous voyage to Malta at the height of enemy air supremacy over the Mediterranean. Sailing under false colours and altering their silhouette to resemble Italian MTBs, Stead's force reached Malta safely, but the dangers of the voyage became apparent when two MLs that followed a short time later failed to make it, leading to the cancellation of other planned deployments. Stead thus became the senior ML officer at Malta, engaged primarily in minesweeping operations, which he had to learn from the manual. For a time when air raids made the island untenable for surface ships and submarines, Stead, albeit informally, was Senior Officer Afloat, Malta. After weathering the siege of Malta, Stead led the 3rd ML Flotilla in the assaults on Sicily and Salerno, and was ultimately awarded a Distinguished Service Cross and Bar for his service in the Mediterranean.[5] Another RCNVR officer, Lieutenant R.M. Young, also had interesting experiences in the Mediterranean. In 1942 he was awarded the DSC "for gallantry and determination" in operations off Crete in command of *ML 361*. He also participated in the evacuation of Tobruk. For the next two years, Young worked out of Alexandria and Gibraltar before going to the Adriatic, where he was primarily engaged on clandestine "false nose" jobs, landing and picking up agents, rescuing stranded airmen, and running weapons to Yugoslav resistance forces and partisans.[6]

The majority of Canadian coastal force officers in the Mediterranean served in MGBs and MTBs. A number of RCNVR officers served in the 10th and 15th MTB flotillas in 1941-42; perhaps the best known were those who served in Fairmile D Type flotillas in the Mediterranean in 1943-44. Among the most prominent of these were Lieutenant T.G. Fuller, who was awarded the DSC and three Bars, and a trio known as the "Three Musketeers": Lieutenant-Commander J.D. Maitland, Lieutenant-Commander C. Burke and Lieutenant T.E. Ladner. Their reputation for skill and audacity can be traced back to their service in British waters in 1941-42, where they learned their craft from one of the outstanding Coastal Forces officers of the war, Lieutenant P. Hitchens, RNVR. An indication of their ability to make the most of their encounters with the enemy came during their voyage from the UK to Gibraltar as part of an MTB convoy in May 1943. On the night of 3/4 May, laden with extra fuel tanks for the long passage, Maitland's *MGB 657* was attacked by *U 439*, which had been vectored onto the convoy by a Focke-Wulf Kondor. Even though the extra fuel tanks on his deck burst into flame, Maitland's determined defence forced *U 439* to

5   Adm, CFPR, var vol, DHH, 84/7. Adm, NHB, Battle Summaries No.s 35 (Op Husky) and 37 (Op Avalanche), DHH. Stead, *A Leaf Upon the Sea*, *passim*

6   Adm, CFPR, var vol. DHH, Foreign Decorations Cards. D. Pope, *Flag 4: The Battle of Coastal Forces in the Mediterranean*, (London, 1954), 97, 159-60, 213

break off its attack—with the fortuitous result that, with its watchkeepers distracted, the submarine rammed its sistership *U 659*. Both submarines sank with a heavy loss of life.[7]

Once they arrived in the Mediterranean, the MTBs under Canadian command continued to take a heavy toll on the enemy. Operating first out of Malta and then bases in Sicily, Corsica and the opulent island of Capri, they defended the Allied landings at Sicily and Salerno against E-boat attack, but their chief mission was the interdiction of enemy coastal shipping. Here—through innovative tactics, boldness that sometimes bordered on recklessness, and the determination to see missions through to their conclusion—they achieved an impressive success, which restricted the enemy's ability to transport soldiers and materiel by sea. In recognition of their leadership and skill, when Coastal Force flotillas in the Mediterranean were reorganized in early 1944, six boats commanded by RCNVR officers were formed into the "all-Canadian Commanding Officer" 56th MGB/MTB Flotilla.[8] Shortly thereafter, these boats were shifted to the Adriatic Sea, where they carried out further anti-shipping operations and supported the work of Yugoslav partisans. It was in these challenging inshore operations in particular that Lieutenant Fuller made a name for himself for initiative and tenacity.

Fuller was SO of the 61st MGB Flotilla, operating from a small island off the coast of Yugoslavia called Vis. On 2 April 1944 he was conducting a routine interdiction operation when he spotted a 30-ton schooner. According to a history of Coastal Forces operations written almost five decades later, "Normally, he would have closed on the vessel and sunk it with gunfire. But not tonight. Fuller knew the base at Vis was experiencing a supply shortage. It seemed a waste to destroy all the material the schooner, low in the water, was obviously carrying." Fuller countermanded the order to fire, and called down to some commandos and partisans who were on board. "With this, Fuller brought his gunboat alongside the schooner, crashing into its side. To the accompaniment of the Partisans' blood-curdling yells, the boarding party vaulted over the rails. There was hardly any resistance." Towed back to Vis, the schooner was handed over to the partisans for their use. Booty included explosives, a jack-hammer drill and compressor, and land mines, among less warlike goods. Nor was the operation a one-off: "Fuller repeated the operation the following night, taking two schooners with firewood, wheat, and ammunition. Two nights later it was a 400-ton schooner with food, then three nights after that two more schooners and a motorboat were taken. In April he took eight schooners, a lighter, and a motor-boat, sinking four vessels."[9] He was applying boarding and cutting-out tactics that would have been familiar to a sailor of the 18th century, and it earned him the informal moniker "The Pirate of the Adriatic." Officially, Fuller's skill, courage and resourcefulness were recognized through the award of the DSC and two Bars.

---

7   Adm, CFPR, May 1943, 18; DHH interview with LCdr J.D. Maitland, 30 May 1986, 24-28, DHH, Biog file; Gannon, *Black May*, 32-44, Blair, *Hitler's U-Boat War: The Hunted*, 295

8   Adm, CFPR, Jan–Feb 1944, 17, and Mar–Apr 1944, 14. The officers were LCdr J.D. Maitland (SO), Lt C. Burke, Lt T.E. Ladner, Lt C. McLachlan, Lt W.H. Keefer and Lt H.M. Pickard. Pope, *Flag 4*, 185. For an excellent memoir by an officer who served in the boat commanded by Lt Burke see L.C. Reynolds, *Gunboat 658* (London, 1955)

9   Brian Nolan and Brian J. Street, *Champagne Navy: Canada's Small Boat Raiders of the Second World War* (Toronto, 1991), 177-178.

Rank Equivalents

German	RCN / RN
Grossadmiral	Admiral of the Fleet
Generaladmiral	No equivalent
Admiral	Admiral
Vizeadmiral	Vice-Admiral
Konteradmiral	Rear-Admiral
Kommodore	Commodore
Kapitän zur See	Captain
Fregattenkapitän	Commander
Korvettenkapitän	Lieutenant-Commander
Kapitänleutnant	Lieutenant
Oberleutnant zur See	Sub-Lieutenant
Leutnant zur See	No equivalent
Oberfähnrich zur See	Midshipman
Fähnrich zur See	Officer candidate

Select Bibliography

HISTORICAL NARRATIVES AND SUPPORTING RESEARCH

These studies, prepared by members of the Naval History Team at DHist/DHH and other contributors, formed the intellectual basis of much of the text of *No Higher Purpose* and *A Blue Water Navy*. With the publication of this volume they are available to researchers in the DHH archives.

Allan, C.E. *RCN Communications WWII*, Part I, *State of the Art Communications 1939*. (Feb 1988).

——. *Canadian Naval Signals Intelligence in the Second World War*. (Dec 1988).

——. *Bismarck Operation May 1941* (June 1989).

——. *Building a Canadian Naval Operational Intelligence Centre, 1939–1945*. (Oct 1993).

Brunt, Lt (N), Pam. *Royal Canadian Navy messages World War II : Finding Aid RG 24 Boxes 12049–12173*. (Jan 1990).

Cafferky, Shawn. *The RCN and Operation TORCH, September 1942–March 1943*. (Mar 1991).

——. *The "Other" Theatre of Operations: RCN Escort Duties on the U.K.–Gibraltar Run, January 1943–April 1943*. (May 1991).

——. *Flying High: The Royal Canadian Naval Air Service, 1944–1946*. (May 1992)..

——. *The Organization of War: A History of the Directorate of Plans Division, 1939–1945* (Feb 1994).

——. *Québec Conference, 1943: Research Report*. (Apr 1994).

——. *Quadrant Conference, 1943: Research report, Part II (A Precis of PRO Documents)*. (May 1994).

Caldwell, R.H. *An Analysis of the Context and the Process of the Royal Canadian Navy's Achievement of Operational Autonomy 1942–43*. (Aug 1994).

——. *An Analysis of the Context and the Process of the Withdrawal of the RCN Escorts from North Atlantic Operations in 1943*. (Aug 1994).

——. *The 1943 Atlantic Convoy Conference and Canadian Command Relationships in the Battle of the Atlantic*. (Aug 1994).

——. *Admiral Murray and the ACHQ*. (Oct 1995).

——. *Change and Challenge: The Canadian Naval Staff in 1943*. (Feb 1997).

——. *The Historical Context for Canadian Pacific Policy in the Second World War*. (Feb 1997).

——. *The Golden Age of the Naval Plans Division April–December 1943*. (Feb 1997).

——. *Insights Gained by Canadian Wartime Naval Chaplains*. (July 1997).

——. *The RCN, The Battle of the Atlantic and Command Relations Oct 42–Apr 43*. (June 1998).

——. *The VE Day Riots in Halifax, 7-8 May 1945*. (July 1998).

——. *Morale and Discipline in the Canadian Naval Service in the Second World War*. (Dec 1998).

——. *A Study in Command Relations: The Allocation of Slow Convoys to the RCN, August 1941*. (Apr 1999).

Chouinard, Alain. *La Batataille du Saint-Laurent et la Presse Québécoise*. (May 1998).

Coppock, R.M. *Correspondence and Assessments on Various U-Boat Losses*. (Jan 1994).

Dillon, Lisa Y. *Naval Service Headquarters, 1939–1945: A Guide to Historical Sources and Notes on Personnel and Organization*. (Mar 1992) (Copy in DC 95/10).

Douglas, W.A.B. *Canadian Perspective of the Battle of the Atlantic*. (Aug 1993).

——. *Naval Aviation in the RCN, 1939–1945*. (Comments on naval air narratives by Graves. (May 1989), Cafferky. (May 1992), and Whitby. (Dec 1989).

——. *Closing the Greenland Air Gap, 1942–3: The Anatomy of an Anglo-American Muddle*. (Sep 1983).

Drent, Jan. *Background to Encounters with U-Boats in Eastern Atlantic, 1944–45*. (Mar 1999).

Fisher, Robert C. *Caribbean Run: The Royal Canadian Navy and the German U-Boat War against the Oil Trade in 1942*. (1990).

——. *Research Report: North Atlantic Convoys, August–December 1942*. (Nov 1990).

——. *Axis Submarine Losses to Canadian Forces*. (Sep 1995).

——. *Fog of War: The Battle of the Atlantic, Summer 1942*. (July 1991).

——. *Relative Naval Strength in 1945*. (June 1993).

——. *Canadian Merchant Ship Losses, 1939–1945*. (Apr 1994).

——. *Little to Fear? The Battle of the Atlantic, August–September 1942*. (Aug 1994).

——. *The Prelude to Torch: The Battle of the Atlantic, October-November 1942*. (Aug 1994).

——. *Canadian Escorts and the Art of Anti-Submarine Warfare, 1940–1943*. (1994).

——. *The RCN on Probation: The Battle of the Atlantic, November–December 1942*. (Aug 95).

——. *Operation "Paukenschlag": U-Boat Operations in Canadian Waters, December 1941–June 1942*. (n.d.).

Glover, William. *Assessment of RCN Officers in Staff Appointments and Major Commands at the outbreak of war*. (n.d.).

——. *Officer Training in the RCN from the Outbreak of the War to the Battle of Convoy SC 107*. (Nov 1991).

——. *The 1940 Manning Crisis and Training Consequences*. (Apr 1992).

——. *"Bricks without Straw": The Quest for Operational Efficiency in the RCN, 1940–1941*. (Aug 1995).

——. *1942: "But the Expansion of the RCN Has Created a Training Problem ..."* (Feb 1996).

——. *1943–1945: Our Escort Vessels Are Not All Trained to the Desired Pitch of Efficiency*. (Apr 1996).

Graves, D. *The RCN and Combined Operations in the Second World War*. (Apr 1988).

——. *RCN in European Waters 41–44: Liaison with Royal Navy, Combined Operation and Coastal Forces*. (Jan 1988).

——. *RN Light Coastal Forces in the Second World War and the Role of the RCN*. (June 1988).

——. *The RCN and Coastal Forces in the Second World War*. (Apr 1989).

——. *The RCN and Naval Aviation, 1942–1944*. (May 1989).

——. *Lost Opportunity: The RCN and Combined Operations in the Second World War*. (Oct 1989).

——. *"A Sweeper Fleet of Bangor Neat": RCN Minesweepers and Preparedness for Neptune, January to May, 1944*. (Feb 1990).

——. *German Navy Research Report series*. (Nov 1990-).
    G 2B Glossary of German Naval Terminology, Codenames and Abbreviations. (Rev. Nov 1991).
    G 3B German Navy Radar, 1939-1945 : Overview and Descriptive catalogue.
    G 4 German Navy Radar Detectors, Radar Foxing and IFF Equipment, 1939–1945: An Overview and Descriptive Catalogue.
    G 5 Descriptive Catalogue of German Navy Sonar and Sonar Foxers, 1939–1945.
    G 6 German Navy U-Boat Torpedoes, 1939–1945: Overview and Descriptive Catalogue.
    G 7 Researcher's Guide to U-Boat Kriegstagebuecher and other U-Boat Documents.

——. *Fear and Loathing in London: Liaison with the Royal Navy, 1939–1945*. (Apr 1993).

Gurney, Bob. *A Tale of Three U-Boats: The Gathering*. (1997).

Hennessy, M.A. *Expansion, Modernization and Maintenance of the RCN Principal ASW*. (1996).

Jeffery, Keith. *Canadian Sailors in Londonderry: A Study in Civil–Military Relations 1942–1945*. (Mar 1992).

Marker, Clayton, and David Lewis, ed. "Combined Operations," nd, 63, DHH 94/171

Mayne, LT(N) Richard. *Macdonald's Navy: The Politics of Naval Expansion*. (Sep 2001).

McEvoy, Fred. *Report on U.S. Bases in Canada*. (Feb 1995).

——. *The Wartime Port of Prince Rupert*. (Jan 1996).

——. *Report on HX, SC and ON Convoys, 1944–45*. (Mar 1998).

McKee, Fraser, "The Canadian Merchant Marine at War." (July 2000)

Mackenzie, David. *Canadian–American Naval Relations 1939–1943*. (Mar 1986).

Mackenzie, Dr. K.S. *The Preparedness of Canada`s Merchant Marine For Two World Wars, 1913–1947*. (Oct 1985).

——. *Parks, Forts, Ladies and Princes: The Canadian Merchant Marine During the Second World War*, "Backgrounder: The Modern Canadian Merchant Marine 1853–1939." (Dec 1987).

——. *Parks, Forts, Ladies and Princes: The Canadian Merchant Marine During the Second World War*. Phase I, "Bibliography and Sources." (June 1987).

——. *The Shipyard of the Freedom of the Seas*. (June 1989).

——. *Canadian Merchant Marine*. (Mar 1988).

——. *Ships for Victory Day*. (Mar 1997).

McLean, Doug. *EG 9 Monograph: A Canadian Group in British Waters: A History of Escort Group 9*. (June 1995).

——. *Escort Group 6*. (June 1995).

——. *Chronology Notes on Various Escort Groups*. (n.d.).

McNorgan, Mike. *Canada the US and Newfoundland, 1941*. (June 1995).

Milner, Dr. Marc. *The RCN and the Offensive against the U-Boats, 1939–1945*. (June 1986).

Perkins, J.D. *B.L. Johnson: Seaman, Submariner, Canadian*. (June 1985).

——. *D3's Last Patrol*. (June 1985).

——. *The Canadian Navy's First Submariner*. (June 1985).

——. *Canadian Submarines Overseas 1914–1922*. (June 1985).

——. *A World War Two Submariner from Nova Scotia: The Narrative of Keith Forbes, DSC*. (Sep 1987).

——. *A Survey of Canadians and Newfoundlanders Who Served in Royal Navy Submarines, Chariots and X-Craft during World War Two*. (Sep 1987).

——. *Activities of Operational Allied Submarines in Canadian Waters during World War Two*. (Nov 1987).

——. *Allied Training Submarines Allocated to RCN Use, 1939–1946*. (Apr 1988).

——. *Canadians in Submarines in World War II*. (1988).

Pickard, "Christmas Festival," 52, DHH 80/125, file 8

Porter, D. *The Women's Royal Canadian Naval Service during the Second World War*. (Dec 1996).

——. *The Formation and Contribution of the Women's Royal Canadian Naval Service during the Second World War*. (May 1999).

Ransom, B. *Canada, the RCN and the Defence of Newfoundland in WWII : Some Preliminary Thoughts*. (Jan 1992).

——. *Newfyjohn*. (Jan 1993).

Rawling, B. *The RCN in the Pacific*. (Mar 1994).

——. *The Shock of Modernization: Science and the RCN in the Second World War*. (Jan 1995).

——. *Inches from the Cutting Edge the RCN and the Battle of the Atlantic, 1944–45*. (Jan 1997).

——. *Taking Care of Tar: RCN Medical Practitioners of the Second World War*. (Mar 1997).

——. *Success and Disappointment: The RCN in the Western Atlantic, 1944–45*. (Dec 1997).

——. *Brief Months of Glory: The RCN in the Eastern Atlantic, 1944–45* . (Dec 1997).

——. *Only a 'Foolish Escape by Young Ratings'? A Brief Study of Mutiny in the Wartime Royal Canadian Navy*. (Dec 1997).

——. *Women in the Wartime RCN: A (Very, Very) Brief Study*. (Dec 1997).

——. *Une tâche plus que difficile: La Marine royale du Canada et la chasse aux U-boots, 1944–45*. (Dec 1997).

——. *Forging Neptune's Trident: Manufacturing Ships and Equipment for the Wartime RCN*. (Mar 1998).

Rigby, V. *HMC River Class Destroyer Operations September 1939–June 1941: A Report on the Sources*. (Sep 1987).

——. *RCN Bangor-Class Minesweepers and Operation Neptune, June–September 1944*. (Jan 1991).

——. *Operations of RCN Bangor Class Minesweepers in European Waters, October 1944–September 1945*. (Mar 1991).

Samson, J.D. *Planning for the Post-War Fleet and the Pacific War, 1939–Sept. 1943*. (Dec 1988).

——. *Planning for the Pacific War, 1943–1945*. (Aug 1993).

Sarty, R. *Canadian Naval Policy 1867–1939*. (Sep 1987).

——. *Planning, Mobilization and War November 1937–May 1940*. (Dec 1988).

Tracy, Dr. N. *Note: on the Place of the RCN in Canadian Defence Strategy before the Second World War*. (Apr 1988).

——. *Note on the Offensive and Defensive Strategic Rationale for Canadian Naval Development*. (Apr 1988).

——. Narrative General Analysis of the Wider Strategic Utility of Naval Action against Trade. (Feb 1989).

——. *Changing Motives for Naval Attack and Trade*. (n.d.).

Tremblay, Sylvie. *La marine royale canadienne, 1919–1936: Orientations, buts et activities*. (1990).

Whitby, Michael. *Crew Problems aboard Athabaskan and Iroquois*. (Aug 1988).

——. *"Little Ado about Fleets": The Acquisition of Algonquin and Sioux*. (Nov 1988).

——. *.RCN Tribal Operations: January–August 1943*. (Oct 1988).

——. *The RCN's Fleet Destroyers' Role in Operation Neptune*. (Dec 1988).

——. *RCN Destroyer Operations in Northern European Waters, 1943–1945*. (Mar 1989).

——. *RCN Training and Doctrine during the 1930s*. (July 1989).

——. *RCN Motor Torpedo Boat Operations, May 1944–May 1945*. (Oct 1989).

——. *RCN Tribal Class Destroyer Operations in the Bay of Biscay July–October 1944*. (Feb 1989).

——. *An Operational History of HMS Nabob and HMS Puncher*. (Dec 1989).

——. *RCN Corvette Operations in European Waters, May 1944–May1945*. (Apr 1990).

——. *The Development of Action Information Organization during the Second World War*. (July 1990).

——. *RCN Operations on the West Coast during the Pacific War*. (Feb 1993).

Winters, Barbara. *Canadian Servicewomen in the Second World War: A Revisionist Approach*. (May 1992).

SECONDARY WORKS

Abbazia, P. *Mr. Roosevelt's Navy: The Private War of the US Atlantic Fleet, 1939–1942*. Annapolis: Naval Institute Press, 1975.

Baker, R., ed. *Selected Papers on British Warship Design in World War II from the Transactions of the Royal Institution of Naval Architects*. Annapolis: Naval Institute Press, 1983.

Barnett, C. *Engage the Enemy More Closely*. London: Norton, 1991.

Barrie, R., and K. Macpherson. *The Ships of Canada's Naval Forces, 1910–2002*. St. Catharines, Vanwell, 2002.

Bath, A.H. *Tracking the Axis Enemy: The Triumph of Anglo-American Naval Intelligence*. Lawrence: University of Kansas Press, 1998.

Baxter, J.P. *Scientists against Time*. Boston: Little Brown, 1946.

Blair, Clay. *Hitler's U-Boat War: The Hunted, 1942-45*. New York: Random House, 1998.

Beeby, D. *Cargo of Lies: The True Story of a Nazi Double Agent in Canada*. Toronto: University of Toronto Press, 1996.

Beesly, P. *Very Special Intelligence: The Story of the Admiralty's Operational Intelligence Centre, 1939-1945*. New York: Hamilton, 1977.

——. "Operational Intelligence and the Battle of the Atlantic," in Boutilier, *The RCN in Retrospect, 1910-1968*. Vancouver: UBC Press, 1982.

Behrens, C.B. *Merchant Shipping and the Demands of War*. London: HMSO, 1955.

Bekker, Cajus. *Hitler's Naval War*. London: Macdonald, 1974.

Bell, C.M., and B.A. Elleman, eds. *Naval Mutinies of the Twentieth Century*. London: Frank Cass, 2003.

Bird, Keith W. "Erich Raeder," in S. Howarth, ed. *Men of War*, 68-71

Blair, C. *Hitler's U-Boat War*. 2 vols. New York: Random House, 1996–98.

*Blatherwick, F.J. *1000 Brave Canadians: The Canadian Gallantry Awards 1854-1989*. Toronto 1991

Bothwell, R., and W. Kilbourn. *C.D. Howe: A Biography*. Toronto: McClelland and Stewart, 1979.

Boutilier, J.A., ed. *The RCN in Retrospect, 1910–1968*. Vancouver: UBC Press, 1982.

Boyd, C., and A Yoshida. *The Japanese Submarine Force and World War II*. Annapolis: Naval Institute Press, 1996.

Brice, M. *The Tribals*. London 1971.

Brodhurst, R. *Churchill's Anchor: The Biography of Admiral of the Fleet Sir Dudley Pound*. London: Leo Cooper, 2000.

Brown, D. *Tirpitz: The Floating Fortress*. London: Arms and Armour Press, 1977.

——. *Carrier Operations in World War* II. 2 vols. London: Ian Allan, 1968.

Bryden, J. *Best-Kept Secret: Canadian Secret Intelligence in the Second World War*. Toronto: Lester, 1993.

Budiansky, S. *Battle of Wits: The Complete Story of Codebreaking in World War II*. New York: Free Press, 2000.

Buell, T.B. *Master of Sea Power: A Biography of Fleet Admiral Ernest J. King*. Boston: Little Brown, 1980.

Burn, A. *The Fighting Captain: The Story of Frederic Walker, CB, DSO***, RN and The Battle of the Atlantic*. Barnsley, UK 1993

Burrow, L., and E. Beaudoin. *Unlucky Lady: The Life and Death of HMCS Athabaskan*. Toronto: Canada's Wings, 1987.

Burton, E.F. *Canadian Naval Radar Officers: The Story of University Graduates for Whom Preliminary Training Was Given in the Department of Physics, University of Toronto*. Toronto: University of Toronto Press, 1946.

Butcher, A.D. *I Remember Haida*. Hantsport, NS: Lancelot Press, 1985.

Butler, J.R.M., ed. *Grand Strategy*. 6 vols. London: HMSO, 1956–76.

Bykofsky, J., and H. Larson. *The Transportation Corps: Operations Overseas*. Washington: Government Printing Office, 1957.

Cafferky, Shawn. *Uncharted Waters: A History of the Canadian Helicopter-Carrying Destroyer.* Halifax: Dalhousie, 2006.

Campbell, J.P. *Dieppe Revisited: A Documentary Investigation*. London: Frank Cass, 1993.

Canada, Government of. Department of External Affairs. *Documents on Relations between Canada and Newfoundland* vol I, *1935–1949*. Ottawa: Information Canada, 1974.

——. Department of External Affairs. *Documents on Canadian External Relations*. 23 vols. Ottawa : Queen's Printer and Canadian Government Publishing, 1967–2002.

——. Department of National Defence. *Report on Certain Incidents Which Occurred on Board HMC Ships Athabaskan, Cresent and Magnificent, and on Other Matters Concerning the Royal Canadian Navy*. Ottawa: King's Printer, 1949.

——. Department of the Naval Service. *Canadian Navy List*. Ottawa: King's Printer, 1939–1945.

——. Department of the Naval Service. *Royal Canadian Navy Reserve Regulations,* vol II, *Fisherman's Reserve. (West Coast)*. Ottawa: King's Printer, 1939.

——. House of Commons. *Debates*. Ottawa: King's Printer, 1939–45.

Carew, A. *The Lower Deck of the Royal Navy, 1900–39: The Invergordon Mutiny in Perspective*. Manchester: Manchester University Press, 1981.

Carter, W.R. *Beans, Bullets and Black Oil*.

Catley, H. *Gate and Gaiters: A Book of Naval Humour and Anecdotes, Including a Glossary of Naval Language for the Uninformed*. Toronto: Thorn Press, 1949.

Chalmers, W.S. *Max Horton and the Western Approaches*. London: Hodder and Stoughton, 1954.

Chandler, D., and J.L. Collins Jr, eds. *The D-Day Encyclopedia*. New York: Helicon, 1994.

Charters, D et al, eds. "Naval History: the State of the Art." *Military History and the Military Profession*. Westport: Praeger, 1992: 73-89.

Churchill, W.S. *The Second World War*. 6 vols. Boston: Houghton Mifflin, 1948–53.

Clarke, J., and R. Smith. *Riviera to the Rhine*. Washington: Government Printing Office, 1993.

A.R.A. Claasen, *Hitler's Northern War: The Luftwaffe's Ill-Fated Campaign, 1941-1945* (Lawrence, Kan 2001)

Claasen, A.R.A. *Hitler's Northern War: The Luftwaffe's Ill-Fated Campaign, 1941-1945*. Lawrence, Kan 2001.

Cohen, E.A., and J. Gooch. *Military Misfortunes: The Anatomy of Failure in War*. New York: Free Press, 1990.

Conn, S., and B. Fairchild. *The Framework of Hemisphere Defense*. Washington: Government Printing Office, 1960.

Connell, G.G. *Arctic Flotilla: The 17th Destroyer Flotilla*. London: William Kimber, 1982.

——. *Arctic Destroyers*. London: William Kimber, 1982.

Cook, O.A. *The Canadian Military Experience, 1867–1995: A Bibliography*. Ottawa: Department of National Defence, 1997.

Cremer, P. *U-Boat Commander: A Periscope View of the Battle of the Atlantic*. Annapolis: Naval Institute Press, 1984.

Crosley, M. *They Gave Me a Seafire*. Shrewsbury: Airlife, 1986.

Curry, Frank. *War at Sea: A Canadian Sailor on the North Atlantic*. Toronto: Lugus, 1990.

Danchev, A., and D. Todman, eds. *War Diaries, 1939–1945: Field Marshal Lord Alanbrooke*. London: Phoenix, 2002.

Dickens, P. *Night Action: MTB Flotilla at War*. London: William Kimber, 1974.

Dönitz, K. *Memoirs: Ten Years and Twenty Days*. Trans. by R.H. Douglas. London: Weidenfeld and Nicolson, 1959.

Douglas, W.A.B. *The Creation of a National Air Force*. Toronto: University of Toronto Press, 1986.

618

——. *The RCN in Transition*. Vancouver: UBC Press, 1988.

*——. "Conflict and Innovation in the Royal Canadian Navy, 1939-1945." In G. Jordan, ed. *Naval Warfare in the Twentieth Century*. London 1977.

*——. "How the RCN Became a Blue Water Navy." In Yves Tremblay, ed. *Canadian Military History since the 17th Century: Proceedings of the Canadian Military History Conference, 5-9 May 2000*. Ottawa 2001.

——, and B. Greenhous. *Out of the Shadows: Canada in the Second World War*. Toronto: Oxford University Press, 1977.

——, and J. Rohwer. "The 'Most Thankless Task' Revisited: Convoys, Escorts and Radio Intelligence in the Western Atlantic, 1941-43." In J.A. Boutilier, ed. *The RCN in Retrospect*. Vancouver: UBC Press, 1982.

——, Roger Sarty, and Michael Whitby, *No Higher Purpose: The Official History of the RCN in the Second World War*, Part 1. St Catharines: Vanwell Publishing, 2003.

Dziuban, S.W. *Military Relations between the United States and Canada, 1939–1945*. Washington: Government Printing Office, 1959.

Easton, A. *50 North: Canada's Atlantic Battleground*. Toronto: Ryerson Press, 1966.

Eayrs, James. *In Defence of Canada: Appeasement and Rearmament*. Toronto: University of Toronto Press, 1965.

Edwards, B. *Attack and Sink!: The Battle for Convoy SC 42*. Wimborne Minster: New Guild, 1995.

J. Ehrman, *Grand Strategy V: August 1943–S eptember 1944* (London 1956)

Edwards, K. *Seven Sailors*. London: Collins, 1945.

Ehrman, J. *Grand Strategy V: August 1943–S eptember 1944*. London 1956.

Elliot, P. *Allied Escort Ships of World War II: A Complete Survey*. London: Macdonald James, 1977.

——. *Allied Minesweepers in World War II*. Annapolis: Naval Institute Press, 1979.

Ellis, L.F. *Victory in the West*. 2 vols. London: HMSO, 1962–68.

Evans, D.C., and M.R. Peattie. *Kaigun: Strategy, Tactics and Technology in the Imperial Japanese Navy, 1887–1941*. Annapolis: Naval Institute Press, 1997.

Farrell, B. *The Basis and Making of British Grand Strategy: Was There a Plan?* Lewiston 1998.

Finlay, E.G. *RCN Beach Commando "W"*. Ottawa: Privately published, 1994.

Freeman, D. *Canadian Warship Names*. St Catharines: Vanwell, 2001.

Friedman, N. *British Carrier Aviation: The Evolution of the Ships and their Aircraft*. Annapolis: Naval Institute Press, 1988.

——. *Naval Radar*. Annapolis: Naval Institute Press, 1981

Gannon, M. *Black May: The Epic Story of the Allies' Defeat of the German U-Boats in May 1943*. New York: Harper Collins, 1998.

——. *Operation Drumbeat*. New York: Harper and Row, 1990.

Gardner, W.J.R. *Decoding History: The Battle of the Atlantic and Ultra*. Annapolis: Naval Institute Press, 1999.

——. "Admiral Sir Bertram Ramsay." In S. Howarth, (ed). *Men of War: Great Naval Leaders of World War II*. New York 1993.

Garfield, B. *The Thousand Mile War*. New York: Ballantine, 1971.

Geneja, S.C. *The Cruiser Uganda*. Corbyville: Tyendinaga Publishers, 1994.

German, A. *The Sea Is At Our Gates*. Toronto: McClelland and Stewart, 1990.

Gibson, F.W., and B. Robertson, eds. *Ottawa at War: The Grant Dexter Memoranda, 1939–1945*. Winnipeg: Manitoba Record Society, 1994.

Gilbert, M. *Finest Hour: Winston S. Churchill, 1939–41*. Toronto: Stoddart, 1983.

——. *Road to Victory: Winston S. Churchill, 1941–1945*. Toronto: Stoddart, 1986.

Golovko, A. *With the Fleet*. New York: Progress Publishers, 1988.

Goralski, R., and R. Freeburg. *Oil and War*. New York: William Morrow, 1987.

Gough, Barry. *HMCS Haida: Battle Ensign Flying*. St Catharines: Vanwell, 2001.

Gow, J.D. *Alongside the Navy, 1910–1950: An Intimate Account*. Ottawa: JDG Press, 1999.

Granatstein, J.L. *Canada's War: The Politics of the Mackenzie King Government, 1939–1945*. Toronto: Oxford University Press, 1975.

——. *A Man of Influence: Norman A. Robertson and Canadian Statecraft, 1929–68*. Toronto: Deneau, 1980.

——, and J.M. Hitsman. *Broken Promises: A History of Conscription in Canada*. Toronto: Oxford University Press, 1977.

Graves, Donald E. *In Peril on the Sea: The RCN and the Battle of the Atlantic*. Toronto: Robin Brass Studio, 2003.

——. "'Fourth Service or Problem?' The British Combined Operation Organization and the Royal Navy's Manpower Crisis, 1942-1944." In D. Bittner, ed. *Selected Papers from the 1992 (59th) Meeting of the Society for Military History Hosted by the Command and Staff College of the Marine Corps University*. np, 1994.

Greenfield, K.R., ed. *Command Decisions*. Washington: Government Printing Office, 1960.

Greenhous, B., S. Harris, W. Johnston, and W. Rawling. *The Crucible of War: The Official History of the RCAF*, vol III. Toronto: University of Toronto Press, 1994.

Gretton, P. *Crisis Convoy: The Story of HX 231*. London: P. Davis, 1974.

——. *Convoy Escort Commander*. London: Cassell, 1964.

Griffin, A.G.S. *Footfalls in Memory*. Toronto: Privately published, 1989.

Grove, E., ed. *The Defeat of the Enemy Attack on Shipping, 1939–1945: A Revised Edition of the Naval Staff History*. Aldershot: Navy Records Society, 1997.

Grove, E. "A Service Vindicated. 1939-1946." In J.R. Hill, ed. *The Oxford Illustrated History of the Royal Navy*. Oxford: Oxford University Press, 1995.

Hackmann, Willem. *Seek and Strike: Sonar, Anti-submarine Warfare and the Royal Navy, 1914–1954*. London: HMSO, 1984.

Hadley, M.L. *U-Boats against Canada: German Submarines in Canadian Waters*. Montreal: McGill-Queen's, 1985.

——, and R. Sarty. *Tin-Pots and Pirate Ships: Canadian Naval Forces and German Sea Raiders, 1880–1918*. Montreal and Kingston: McGill-Queen's University Press, 1991.

——, R.N. Huebert, and F.W. Crickard, eds. *A Nation's Navy: In Quest of Canadian Naval Identity*. Montreal and Kingston: McGill-Queen's University Press, 1996.

Hague, A. *The Allied Convoy System, 1939–1945: Its Organization, Defence and Operation*. St Catharines: Vanwell, 2000.

——. *Convoys to Russia: Allied Convoys and Naval Surface Operations in Arctic Waters, 1941–1945*. Kendal, UK: World Ship Society, 1992.

——. Hague, *Destroyers for Britain*

——. *The Towns*. Kendal, UK: World Ship Society, 1990.

Hampshire, A.C. *The Beachhead Commandos*. London: William Kimber, 1983.

Haydon, P., and A. Griffiths, eds. *Canada's Naval Pacific Presence: Purposeful or Peripheral*. Halifax: Dalhousie University Press, 1999.

Heal, S.C. *A Great Fleet of Ships: The Canadian Forts and Parks*. St Catharines: Vanwell, 1999.

Hezlet, A. *The Electron and Sea Power*. New York: Stein and Day, 1975.

Hill, J.R., ed. *The Oxford Illustrated History of the Royal Navy*. Oxford: Oxford University Press, 1995.

Hill, R. *Destroyer Captain: Memoirs of the War at Sea*. London: William Kimber, 1975.

Hilliker, J. *Canada's Department of External Affairs* I: The Early Years, 1909-1946. Montreal and Kingston: Queen's University Press, 1990

Hillmer, N., B. Kordan, and L. Luciuk, eds. *On Guard for Thee*. Ottawa: Supply and Services Canada, 1988.

Hinsley, F.H., et al. *British Intelligence in the Second World War*. 5 vols. London: HMSO, 1979–90.

Hobbs, D. *Royal Navy Escort Carriers*. Lodge Hill, UK 2003.

Holmes, J.W. *The Shaping of Peace: Canada and the Search for World Order, 1943-1957*. Toronto 1979.

Hone, T.C., N. Friedman, and M.D. Mandeles. *American and British Aircraft Carrier Development, 1919-1941*. Annapolis: Naval Institute Press, 1999.

Hooker, N.H. *The Moffat Papers: Selections from the Diplomatic Journals of Jay Pierrepont Moffat, 1919–1943*. Cambridge: Harvard University Press, 1956.

Horn, B., and S. Harris. *Warrior Chiefs: Perspectives on Senior Canadian Military Leaders*. Toronto: Dundurn, 2001.

How, D. *Night of the Caribou*. Hantsport, NS: Lancelot Press, 1988.

Howard, M. *Grand Strategy* IV: *August 1942–September 1943*. London 1972.

Howarth, S., ed. *Men of War: Naval Leaders of the Second World War*. London: St Martin's Press, 1992.

——, and D. Law, eds. *The Battle of the Atlantic, 1939–1945: The 50th Anniversary International Naval Conference*. Annapolis: Naval Institute Press, 1994.

Howse, D. *Radar at Sea: The Royal Navy in World War II*. Annapolis: Naval Institute Press, 1993.

Humble, R. *Fraser of North Cape*. London: Routledge and Paul, 1983.

Ito, R. *We Went to War*. Stittsville: S-20 and Nisei Veterans Assoc., 1984.

——. *Stories of My People: A Japanese Canadian Journal*. Hamilton: Nisei Veterans Assocation, 1994.

James, R.W. *Wartime Economic Cooperation: A Study of Relations between Canada and the United States*. Toronto: Ryerson Press, 1949.

Jenson, L.B. *Tin Hats, Oilskins and Seaboots: A Naval Journey, 1938–1945*. Toronto: Robin Brass, 2000.

Johnston, M. *Corvettes Canada: Convoy Veterans of WWII Tell Their Stories*. Toronto: McGraw-Hill Ryerson, 1994.

Jones, B. *And So to Battle: A Sailor's Story*. Battle, UK: Privately published, 1976.

Jordan, G., ed. *Naval Warfare in the Twentieth Century*. London: Croome Hall, 1977.

Kahn, D. *Seizing the Enigma: The Race to Break the German U-Boat Codes, 1939–1943*. Boston: Houghton Mifflin, 1991.

Kealy, J.D.F., and E.C. Russell. *A History of Canadian Naval Aviation*. Ottawa: Queen's Printer, 1965.

Keegan, J. *The Second World War*. New York: Viking, 1990.

Kemp, P. *U-Boat Destroyed.* Annapolis: Naval Institute Press, 1997.

——. "Admiral of the Fleet Sir Dudley Pound." In S. Howarth, ed. *Men of War: Naval Leaders of the Second World War*. London 1992.

Kennedy, J. de N. *History of the Department of Munitions and Supply*. 2 vols. Ottawa: King's Printer, 1950.

——. *The Most Unsordid Act: Lend-Lease, 1939–1941*. Baltimore: Johns Hopkins University Press, 1969.

King, Ernest J., and W.M. Whitehill. *Fleet Admiral King: A Naval Record*. New York: Norton, 1952.

King, W.L.M. *Canada and the Fight for Freedom*. Toronto: Macmillan, 1944.

Lamb, J.B. *Corvette Navy*. Toronto: Macmillan, 1977.

——. *On the Triangle Run*. Toronto: Macmillan, 1986.

Lambert, J. *The Fairmile "D" Type Motor Torpedo Boat*. London: Conway, 1985.

——, and A. Ross. *Allied Coastal Forces of World War II*. 2 vols. London: Conway, 1990-93.

Law, C.A. *White Plumes Astern: The Short, Daring Life of Canada's MTB Flotilla*. Halifax: Nimbus, 1989.

Lawrence, H. *Tales of the North Atlantic*. Toronto: McClelland and Stewart, 1985.

——. *A Bloody War: One Man's Memories of the Canadian Navy, 1939–1945*. Toronto: Macmillan, 1979.

Lay, H.N. *Memoirs of a Mariner*. Ottawa: Canada's Wings, 1982.

Leighton, R.M., and R.W. Coakley. *Global Logistics and Strategy, 1940–1943*. Washington: Government Printing Office, 1955.

Leutze, J.R. *Bargaining for Supremacy : Anglo-American Naval Collaboration, 1937–1941*. Chapel Hill: University of North Carolina Press, 1977.

Lindsey, G.R. ed. *No Day Long Enough: Canadian Science in World War II*. Toronto 1998.

Littler, J.C. *Sea Fever*. Victoria: Kiwi Publications, 1995.

Llewellyn-Jones, M. *The Royal Navy and Anti-Submarine Warfare, 1917-1949*. London: Routledge, 2006.

Loewenheim, F.L., H. D. Langley, and M. Jonas. *Roosevelt and Churchill: Their Secret Wartime Correspondence*. New York: Saturday Review Press, 1975.

Love, R.W., and J. Major. *The Year of D-Day: The 1944 Diary of Admiral Sir Bertram Ramsay*. Hull: University of Hull Press, 1994.

Lynch., J.A.M. *Orion: Mighty Warrior*. Toronto: Lugus, 1992.

MacFarlane, John M. *Canada's Admirals and Commodores*. Victoria 1992.

Macintyre, D. *U-Boat Killer*. Annapolis: Naval Institute Press, 1976.

MacKay, J., and J. Harland. *The Flower Class Corvette Agassiz*. St Catharines: Vanwell, 1993.

Macpherson, K., and R. Barrie. *Ships of Canada's Naval Forces, 1910-2002*. St. Catharines: Vanwell, 2002.

——, and M. Milner. *Corvettes of the Royal Canadian Navy, 1939–1945*. St Catharines: Vanwell, 1993.

Madgwick, Edward. *Tribal Captain*. Helston: Blue Island Books, 2003.

March, E.J. *British Destroyers, 1892–1953*. London: Seeley Service, 1966.

Marder, Arthur. *The Anatomy of British Sea Power: A History of British Naval Policy in the Pre-Dreadnought Era, 1810–1905*. New York: Knopf, 1940.

——. *Dreadnought to Scapa Flow* V

——. *Old Friends, New Enemies: The Royal Navy and the Imperial Japanese Navy–Strategic Illusions*. Oxford: Clarendon Press, 1981.

——, M. Jacobsen, and J. Horsfield. *Old Friends, New Enemies: The Royal Navy and the Imperial Japanese Navy: The Pacific War 1942-1945*. Oxford 1990.

McAndrew, W., W. Rawling, and M. Whitby. *Liberation: The Canadians in Northwest Europe*. Montreal: Art Global, 1995.

McAndrew, W., D. Graves, and M. Whitby. *Normandy 1944: The Canadian Summer*. Montreal: Art Global, 1994.

McKee, F. *The Armed Yachts of Canada*. Erin, Ont.: Boston Mills, 1983.

——. *HMCS Swansea: The Life and Times of a Frigate*. St Catharines: Vanwell, 1994

——, and R. Darlington. *The Canadian Naval Chronicle*. St Catharines: Vanwell, 1996.

McLean, D. "The US Navy and the U-Boat Inshore Offensive." In Cogar, *New Interpretations in Naval History*.

——, D.M. "Muddling Through: Canadian Antisubmarine Doctrine and Practice, 1942-45." In M. Hadley, R.N. Huebert, and F.W. Crickard, eds. *A Nation's Navy: In Quest of Canadian Naval Identity*. Kingston and Montreal: Queen's University Press, 1996.

*Meiklem, *Tartar Memoirs* (Glasgow nd)

Miller, E.S. .*War Plan Orange: The US Strategy to Defeat Japan, 1897–1945*. Annapolis: Naval Institute Press, 1991.

Milner, Marc. *Battle of the Atlantic*. St Catharines: Vanwell Publishing, 2003.

——. *Canada's Navy: The First Century*. Toronto: University of Toronto Press, 1999.

——. *North Atlantic Run: The Royal Canadian Navy and the Battle of the Convoys*. Toronto: University of Toronto Press, 1985.

——. *The U-Boat Hunters: The RCN and the Offensive against Germany's Submarines*. Toronto: University of Toronto Press, 1994.

——, "Inshore ASW: The Canadian Experience." In W.A.B. Douglas, ed. *The RCN in Transition*. Vancouver 1985.

Mitchell, W.H., and L.A. Sawyer. *The Empire Ships*. London: Lloyd's of London, 1990.

Moore, A.R. *A Careless Word ... A Needless Sinking*. Kings Point: American Merchant Marine Museum, 1984.

Morison. S.E. *Aleutians, Gilberts and Marshalls, June 1942–April 1944*. Boston: Little, Brown, 1951.

——. *History of the United States Naval Operations in World War II*. 15 vols. Boston: Little, Brown, 1947–62.

——. *The Atlantic Battle Won May 1943-May 1945. History of United States Naval Operations in World War II*, X. Boston: Little, Brown, 1956.

——. *The Two-Ocean War*. Boston: Little, Brown, 1963.

——. *Victory in the Pacific*

Mowat, F. *The Grey Seas Under*. Toronto: McClelland and Stewart, 1958.

Naval Officers Association of Canada. *Salty Dips*. 6 vols. Ottawa: NOAC, 1983–99.

Neary, P. *Newfoundland in the North Atlantic World, 1929–1949*. Montreal and Kingston: McGill-Queen's University Press, 1988.

Neary, S. *Enemy on Our Doorstep: The German Attacks at Bell Island, Newfoundland, 1942*. St John's: Jesperson Press, 1994.

Neatby, H.B. *William Lyon Mackenzie King,* vol III, *1932–1939: The Prism of Unity*. Toronto: University of Toronto Press, 1976.

Nesbit, R.C. *The Strike Wings: Special Anti-Shipping Squadrons*. London: William Kimber, 1984.

Nicholson, G.W.L. *The Canadians in Italy, 1943–1945*. Ottawa: Queen's Printer, 1956.

Niestlé, A. *German U-Boat Losses During World War II: Details of Destruction*. (Annapolis: Naval Institute Press, 1998.

Nixon, C.P. *A River in September: A Sketch of the Life and Times of HMCS Chaudière*. Montreal: J.N. Mappin, 1995.

Nolan, B., and B.J. Street. *Champagne Navy: Canada's Small Boat Raiders of the Second World War*. Toronto: Random House, 1991.

O'Brien, D. *HX 72: The First Convoy to Die: The Wolfpack Attack that Woke Up the Admiralty*. Halifax: Nimbus, 1999.

O'Neill, E.D., ed. *The Canadian Raleighites: Ordinary Seamen and Officers at War, 1940–1945*. Aylmer: Aylmer Express, 1988.

Outerbridge, L.M. *HMS Puncher, D-Day–1944 to V.E. and V.J.–1945*. Vancouver: Privately printed, nd.

Overy, R. *Why the Allies Won*. London: Jonathon Cape, 1995.

Padfield, P. *War Beneath the Sea*. New York: Wiley, 1995.

——. *Dönitz: The Last Fuhrer*. London: Gollancz, 1984.

Patterson, A.T. ed. *The Jellicoe Papers*. Shortlands, Kent: Navy Records Society, 1969.

Pawle, G. *The Secret War.* London 1959

Payton-Smith, D.J. *Oil: A Study of Wartime Policy and Administration*. London: HMSO, 1971.

Peattie, M.P. *Sunburst: The Rise of Japanese Naval Air Power, 1909-1941*. Annapolis 2001.

Peltz, S.E. *The Race to Pearl Harbor*. Cambridge: Harvard University Press, 1974.

Perkins, D. *The Canadian Submarine Service in Review*. St Catharines: Vanwell, 2000.

Perras, G. *Stepping Stones to Nowhere: The Aleutian Islands, Alaska, and American Military Strategy, 1867–1945*. Vancouver: UBC Press, 2002.

Pickersgill, J.W. *The Mackenzie King Record*. 4 vols. Toronto: University of Toronto Press, 1960–1970.

Poolman, K. *Escort Carriers, 1941–1945*. London: Ian Allan, 1972.

Pope, D. *73 North: The Defeat of Hitler's Navy*. Annapolis: Naval Institute Press,1958.

——. *Flag 4: The Battle of Coastal Forces in the Mediterranean*. London: William Kimber, 1954.

Pope, M.A. *Soldiers and Politicians: The Memoirs of Lt-Gen Maurice A. Pope*. Toronto: University of Toronto Press, 1962.

Popp, C. *The Gumboot Navy: Memories of the Men Who Served in the Fishermen's Reserve: A Special Naval Unit Formed to Patrol the Coast of British Columbia during World War II*. Lantzville, BC: Oolichan Books, 1988.

Portugal, J.E. *We Were There: A Record for Canada,* vol I, *The Navy*. Shelburne, Ont.: Royal Canadian Military Institute, 1998.

Potter, E.B. *Nimitz*. Annapolis: Naval Institute Press, 1976.

Prange, G. *At Dawn We Slept: The Untold Story of Pearl Harbor*. New York: McGraw-Hill, 1981.

——. *Miracle at Midway*. New York: McGraw-Hill, 1982.

Pratt, E.J. *Behind the Log* Toronto: University of Toronto Press, 1947.

Preston, R.A. *Canada and Imperial Defence*. Toronto: University of Toronto Press, 1967.

Pugsley, W.H. *Saints, Devils and Ordinary Seamen*. Toronto: Collins, 1945.

Raven, A., and J. Roberts. *British Cruisers of World War II*. Annapolis: Naval Institute Press, 1980.

Reid, M. *DEMS and the Battle of the Atlantic*. Ottawa: Commoner's Pub-Society, 1990.

Reynolds, C. *The Fast Carriers: The Forging of an Air Navy*. Huntington 1968

Reynolds, L.C. *Gunboat 658*. London: William Kimber, 1955.

Revely, H. *The Convoy That Nearly Died: The Story of ONS 154*. London: William Kimber, 1979.

Rodger, N.A.M., ed. *Naval Power in the Twentieth Century*. London: Macmillan, 1996.

Rohwer, J. *Axis Submarine Successes of World War Two*. Annapolis: Naval Institute Press, 1983.

——. *Critical Convoy Battles of March 1943: The Battle for HX.229/SC.122*. Annapolis: Naval Institute Press, 1977.

—— and G. Hummelchen. *Chronology of the War at Sea*. Annapolis: Naval Institute Press, 1992.

Roskill, S.W. *The War at Sea, 1939–1945*. 3 vols. London: HMSO, 1954–61.

——. *Naval Policy between the Wars*. Annapolis: Naval Institute Press, 1968 and 1976.

Rössler, Eberhard. *The U-Boat*. London: Arms and Armour Press, 1981.

Roy, P.E., and J.L. Granatstein. *Mutual Hostages: Canadians and Japanese during the Second World War*. Toronto: University of Toronto Press, 1990.

Royal Canadian Naval Association Defensively Equipped Merchant Ships Branch. *The Arming of Canadian Merchant Ships in the Second World War: Two Navies–The Same Ship*. Quyon, Que.: Chesley House, 2003.

Ruegg, B., and A. Hague. *Convoys to Russia, 1941-1945*. Kendal, UK: World Ship Society, 1992.

Ruge, F. *Sea Warfare, 1939–1945: A German Viewpoint*. London: Cassell, 1957.

Runyan, T.J., and J.M. Copes, eds. *To Die Gallantly: The Battle of the Atlantic*. Boulder: Westview Press, 1994.

Sarty, Roger. *Canada and the Battle of the Atlantic*. Montreal: Art Global, 1998.

——. *The Maritime Defence of Canada*. Toronto: Canadian Institute of Strategic Studies, 1996.

——. "The Ghosts of Fisher and Jellicoe: The RCN and the Québec Conferences." In D.B. Woolner (ed) *The Second Québec Conference Revisited, Waging War, Formulating Peace: Canada, Great Britain, and the United States in 1944-1945*. New York 1998.

Saunders, H. St George. *Royal Air Force 1939-45* III; *The Fight Is Won*. London 1957.

Schofield, B.B. *The Russian Convoys*. London: Batsford, 1984.

Schull, J. *The Far Distant Ships: An Official Account of Canadian Naval Operations in World War II*. Ottawa: Queen's Printer, 1950.

Schurman, Donald, M. *The Education of a Navy: The Development of British Naval Strategic Thought, 1867–1914*. London: Cassell, 1965.

Sclater, W. *Haida*. Toronto: Oxford University Press, 1947.

Scott, P. *The Battle of the Narrow Seas*. London 1945.

Showell, J.P. *Enigma U-Boats: Breaking the Code*. Annapolis: Naval Institute Press, 2000.

Simpson, B.M. *Admiral Harold R. Stark: Architect of Victory, 1939–1945*. Columbia, SC: University of South Carolina Press, 1989.

Smith, B.F. *The Ultra-Magic Deals and the Most Secret Special Relationship, 1940–1946*. Novato, Calif.: Presidio Press, 1993.

Smith, J.R., and A. Kay. *German Aircraft of the Second World War*. London 1972.

Smith, K. *Conflict over Convoys: Anglo-American Logistics Diplomacy in the Second World War*. Cambridge: Cambridge University Press, 1996.

Smith, P.C. *Arctic Victory: The Story of PQ 18*. London: William Kimber, 1975.

——. *Hold the Narrow Sea: Naval Warfare in the English Channel, 1939–45*. Annapolis: Naval Institute Press, 1984.

—— and J.R. Dominy. *Cruisers in Action, 1939–1945*. London: William Kimber, 1981.

Sokolsky, J., and J. Jockel, eds. *Fifty Years of Canada–US Defense Cooperation: The Road from Ogdensburg*. Lewiston: E. Mellen Press, 1992.

Soward, S. *A Formidable Hero: Lt. R.H. Gray, VC, DSC, RCNVR*. Victoria: Trafford, 2003.

Spector, R.H. *Eagle against the Sun: The American War with Japan*. New York: Free Press, 1985.

Stacey, C.P. *Arms, Men and Governments: The War Policies of Canada, 1939–1945*. Ottawa: Queen's Printer, 1970.

——. *The Victory Campaign: The Operations in Northwest Europe, 1944–1945*. Ottawa: Queen's Printer, 1960.

——. *Six Years of War: The Army in Canada, Britain and the Pacific*. Ottawa: Queen's Printer, 1955.

——. *The Canadian Army, 1939–1945: An Official Historical Summary*. Ottawa: King's Printer, 1948.

——. *The Canadians in Italy*. Ottawa: Queen's Printer, 1956.

Stead, G. *A Leaf Upon the Sea: A Small Ship in the Mediterranean*. Vancouver: UBC Press, 1988.

Stephen, M. *The Fighting Admirals*. Annapolis: Naval Institute Press, 1991.

Stephenson, U.S., ed. *British Security Coordination: The Secret History of British Intelligence in the Americas 1940–45*. London: Frank Cass, 1998.

Stevens, D. *U-Boat far from Home: The Epic Voyage of U 862 to Australia and New Zealand*. St Leonard's, Aus.: Allen and Unwin, 1997.

Stoler, M.A. *Allies and Adversaries: The Joint Chiefs of Staff, The Grand Alliance, and US Strategy in World War II*. Chapel Hill 2000.

Syrett, D. *The Defeat of the German U-Boats: The Battle of the Atlantic*. Columbia: University of South Carolina Press, 1994.Syrett , *U-Boat Situations and Trends*,

Syrett, D., ed. *The Battle of the Atlantic and Signals Intelligence: U-Boat Situations and Trends, 1941–1945*. Aldershot: Naval Records Society, 1998.

Tarrant, V.E. *The Last Year of the Kriegsmarine*. London: Arms and Armour Press, 1996.

Tennyson, B., and R. Sarty. *Guardian of the Gulf: Sydney, Cape Breton, and the Atlantic Wars*. Toronto: University of Toronto Press, 2000.

Tent, T.F. *E-Boat Alert : Defending the Normandy Invasion Fleet*. Annapolis: Naval Institute Press, 1996.

Terraine, J. *Business in Great Waters: The U-Boat Wars, 1916–1945*. London: Leo Cooper, 1989.

Thetford, O. *British Naval Aircraft Since 1912*. London: Putnam, 1971.

Thorne, C. *Allies of a Kind: The United States, Britain, and the War against Japan, 1941-1945*. New York 1978.

Thornton, J.M. *The Big U*. Unknown: J.M. Thornton, 1983.

Topp, E. *The Odyssey of a U-Boat Commander: Recollections of Erich Topp*. Westport: Praeger, 1992.

Tucker, G.N. *The Naval Service of Canada: Its Official History*. 2 vols. Ottawa: King's Printer, 1952.

United Kingdom, Government of. Admiralty. *British and Foreign Merchant Vessels Lost or Damaged by Enemy Action during the Second World War*. London: Historical Section, 1945.

——. *Naval Aircraft Attack on the "Tirpitz," 3 April 1944*. London: Historical Section, 1945.

——. *Cruiser and Destroyer Actions in English Channel and Western Approaches, 1943–1944*. London: Historical Section, 1945.

——. *Fuehrer Conferences on Naval Affairs, 1943*. London: Historical Section, 1947.

——. *Operation Neptune: Landing in Normandy*. London: Historical Section, 1947.

——. *Tirpitz: An Account of the Various Attacks Carried Out by the British Armed Forces and Their Effect upon the German Battleship*. London: Historical Section, 1947.

——. *German Mine Warfare: 1939–1945*. London: NID, 1947.

——. *Naval Operations, Okinawa*. London: Historical Section, 1950.

——. *Sinking of the Scharnhorst*. London: Historical Section, 1950.

——. *The Arctic Convoys, 1941–1945*. London: Historical Section, 1954.

——. *The Development of British Naval Aviation, 1919–1945*. 2 vols. London: Historical Section, 1954-56.

——-. *The Defeat of the Enemy Attack on Shipping, 1939–1945: A Study of Policy and Operations*. London: Historical Section, 1957.

United Kingdom, Government of. Amphibious Warfare Headquarters. *History of the Combined Operations Organization 1940–1945*. London: HMSO, 1956.

——-. Chief of Combined Operations Staff. *The Manual of Combined Operations*. London: HMSO, 1950.

——-. Ministry of Defence. *British Mining Operations*. London: HMSO, 1973.

——-. *The U-Boat War in the Atlantic,* vol I, *1939–1941*. London: HMSO, 1989.

United States, Government of. Department of Commerce. *Climatological and Oceanographic Atlas for Mariners,* vol I, *North Atlantic Ocean*. Washington: Government Printing Office, 1959.

Vian, P.L. *Action This Day*. London: Frederick Muller, 1960.

Villa, B. *Unauthorized Action*. Toronto 1989.

Warlow, B. *Shore Establishments of the Royal Navy: Being a List of Static Ships and Establishments of the Royal Navy*. Liskeard, Cornwall: Maritime Books, 1992.

Warrilow, B. *Nabob: The First Canadian-Manned Aircraft Carrier*. Owen Sound: Escort Carriers Association, 1989.

Waters, J.M. *Bloody Winter*. Princeton: Van Nostrand, 1967.

Watson, M.B. *Sea Logisitics: Keeping the Navy Ready Aye Ready.* St. Catharines: Vanwell, 2004.

Watt, F.B. *In All Respects Ready: The Merchant Navy and the Battle of the Atlantic, 1940–1945*. Scarborough: Prentice-Hall, 1985.

Webster, C., and N. Frankland. *The Strategic Air Offensive against Germany*. 4 vols. London: HMSO, 1961.

Weinberg, G. *A World at Arms: A Global History of World War II*. Cambridge: University of Cambridge Press, 1994.

Whitby, Michael (ed). *Commanding Canadians: The Second World War Diaries of A.F.C. Layard*. Vancouver: UBC Press, 2005.

Whitby, M., R.H. Gimblett, and P. Hayden (eds). *The Admirals: Canada's Senior Naval Leadership in the 20th Century.* Toronto: Dundurn Press, 2006.

Whitley, M.J. *Destroyer! German Destroyers of World War II*. Annapolis: Naval Institute Press, 1985.

——-. *Destroyers of World War II*. Annapolis: Naval Institute Press, 1988.

Wilmot, H.P. *Empires in the Balance: Japanese and Allied Pacific Strategies to April 1942*. Annapolis: Naval Institute Press, 1982.

——-. *Grave of a Dozen Schemes: British Naval Planning and the War against Japan, 1943–1945*. Annapolis: Naval Institute Press, 1995.

Wilson, T. *The First Summit: Roosevelt and Churchill at Placentia Bay, 1941*. New York: Houghton Mifflin, 1969.

Winn, Capt. R. "Anti-U-boat Results of Neptune, 28 Aug 1944." In D. Syrett, ed. *The Battle of the Atlantic and Signals Intelligence: U-boat Tracking Papers, 1941-1947*. Ashgate 2002.

Winton, J. *Death of the Scharnhorst*. New York: A. Bird, 1983.

——-. *Cunningham*. London: John Murrary, 1998.

——. *The Forgotten Fleet*. London: Michael Joseph, 1969.

——. *Sink the Haguro! The Last Destroyer Action of the Second World War*. London, 1978.

Woodman, R. *The Arctic Convoys, 1941–1945*. London: John Murray, 1994.

Woolner, D.B., ed. *The Second Québec Conference Revised. Waging War, Formulating Peace: Canada Great Britain, and the United States in 1944–1945*. New York: St Martin's Press, 1998.

Wynn, K. *U-Boat Operations in the Second World War*. 2 vols. Annapolis: Naval Institute Press, 1997.

Y'Blood, W.T. *Hunter-Killer: US Escort Carriers in the Battle of the Atlantic*. Annapolis: Naval Institute Press, 1983.

Zimmerman, D. *The Great Naval Battle of Ottawa: How Admirals, Scientists and Politicians Impeded the Development of High Technology in Canada's Wartime Navy*. Toronto: University of Toronto Press, 1989.

ARTICLES

Cafferky, S. "'A Useful Lot, These Canadian Ships': The Royal Canadian Navy and Operation Torch, 1942–1943." *Northern Mariner* 3/4 (1993): 1-18.

Caldwell, RH. "The VE Day Riots in Halifax." *Northern Mariner* 10/1 (2000): 3-20.

Chappelle, Dean. "Building a Bigger Stick: The Construction of Tribal Class Destroyers in Canada, 1940–1948." *Northern Mariner* 5/1 (1995): 1-17.

Conley, C.W. "The Great Japanese Balloon Offensive.C.W. Conley, "The Great Japanese Balloon Offensive," *Air University Review* 19/2 (1968), " *Air University Review* 19/2 (1968)

Douglas, W.A.B. "Canadian Naval Historiography." *Marnier's Mirror* 70/4 (1984): 349-362.

—— and David Syrett. "Die Wende in der Schlacht im Atlantik: Die Schliessung des Grönland-Luftlochs, 1942-1943." *Marine Rundschau*, 83/1-3 (1986)

—— "'Sink the Bastard!': Friendly Fire in the Battle of the Atlantic." *Canadian Military Journal* 2/3 (2001): 65-74.

—— "Marching to Different Drums: Canadian Military History." *Journal of Military History* 56/2 (1992): 245-60.

—— "The Prospects for Naval History." *Northern Mariner* 1/ 4 (1991):19-26.

Edwards, J. "Destruction of Convoy Faith." *Observair* (1998): 4-5.

Erskine, R. "Naval Enigma: A Missing Link." *International Journal of Intelligence and Counterintelligence* 3 (1989): 499.

——. "U-Boats, Homing Signals and HF/DF." *Intelligence and National Security* (Apr 1997): 325-6.

Fisher, R. "Tactics, Training and Technology: The RCN's Summer of Success, July–September 1942." *Canadian Military History* 6/2 (1997): 9–12.

——. "The Impact of German Technology on the Royal Canadian Navy in the Battle of the Atlantic, 1942–1943." *Northern Mariner* 7/4 (1997): 1–14.

—— "'We'll Get Our Own' : Canada and the Oil Shipping Crisis of 1942." *Northern Mariner* 3/2 (1993): 33-40.

—— "Canadian Merchant Ship Losses, 1939–1945." *Northern Mariner* 5/3 (1995): 57-73.

——- "Group Wotan and the Battle for Convoy SC 104, 11–17 October 1942." *Mariner's Mirror*. 84/1 (1998): 64-75.

Fisher, William. "The End of HMCS St. Croix." *Canadian Military History* 8/3 (1999): 63-69.

Frank, H. "E-Boats in Action Off the Coast of England, 1943–44." *Marine-Rundschau* 4/87 (1987): 8.

Gimblett, Richard. "Reassessing the Dreadnought Crisis of 1909 and the Origins of the Royal Canadian Navy." *Northern Mariner* 4/1 (1994): 35-53.

——. "What the Mainguy Report Never Told Us: The Tradition of Mutiny in the RCN before 1949." *Canadian Military Journal* 1/2 (2000): 87-94.

Gough, B., and J.A. Wood. "'One More for Luck': The Destruction of U 971 by HMCS Haida and HMS Eskimo, 24 June 1944." *Canadian Military History* 10/3 (2001): 7-22.

Graves. DE. "'Hell Boats' of the RCN: The Canadian Navy and the Motor Torpedo Boat." *Northern Mariner* 2/3 (1992): 31-45.

Henderson, T.S. "Angus L Macdonald and the Conscription Crisis of 1944." *Acadiensis* 27/1 (1997): 85–104.

Jones, B. "A Matter of Length and Breadth." *Naval Review* 38 (1950): 139.

Llewellyn-Jones, M. "Trials with HM Submarine *Seraph* and British Preparations to Defeat the Type XXI U-Boat, September–October 1944," *Mariner's Mirror* 86/4 (2000): 434-451.

Mayne R.O. "A Political Execution: Expediency and the Firing of Vice Admiral Percy W. Nelles." *Amercian Review of Canadian Studies* 29/4 (1999): 557-592.

——. "A Covert Naval Investigation: Overseas Officers, John Joseph Connolly and the Equipment Crisis of 1943." *Northern Mariner* 10/1 (2000): 37-52.

——. "Bypassing the Chain of Command: The Political Origins of the Equipment Crisis of 1943." *Canadian Military History* 9/3 (2000): 7-22.

McKee, Fraser. "Some Revisionist History in the Battle of the Atlantic." *Northern Mariner* 1/4 (1991): 27-32.

McKillip, R. "Staying on the Sleigh: Commodore Walter Hose and a Permanent Naval Policy for Canada." *Maritime Warfare Bulletin*. Special historical edition. Halifax, 1991.

McLean, Douglas. "The Battle for Convoy BX–141." *Northern Mariner* 3/4 (1993): 319-335.

——. "The Loss of HMCS Clayoquot." *Canadian Military History* 3/2 (Autumn 1994): 31-44.

——. "Confronting Technological and Tactical Change: Allied Anti-Submarine Warfare in the Last Year of the Battle of the Atlantic." *Canadian Military History* 7/3 (1998): 29-34

McLeod, M. "The Royal Canadian Navy, 1918-39." *Mariner's Mirror* 56/2 (1970): 169-86.

Milner, M. "The Battle of the Atlantic." *Journal of Strategic Studies* 13/1 (1990): 51

—— "Canada's Naval War." *Acadiensis* 12/2 (1983): 162-71.

—— "HMCS Somers Isles: The RCN's Base in the Sun." *Canadian Defence Quarterly* 14 (1984-85): 41-47.

—— "Naval Control of Shipping in the Atlantic War, 1939-45." *Mariner's Mirror* 83/2 (1997): 169-84.

—— "The Implications of Technological Backwardness: The Royal Canadian Navy 1939–1945." *Canadian Defence Quarterly* 19/3 (1989): 46-52.

——- "The Royal Canadian Navy and 1943: A Year Best Forgotten?" In Paul D. Dickson, ed. *1943: The Beginning of the End*. Waterloo: Canadian Committee for the History of the Second World War, 1995, 123–136.

Mitchell, A. "The Development of Radar in the Royal Navy, 1939–1945, Part II." *Warship* 14 (1980): 123-30.

Mitchell, RB. "Sydney Harbour: the War Years, 1939–1945." In R.J. Morgan, ed. *More Essays in Cape Breton History*. Windsor, NS: Lancelot Press, 1977.

Munton, D., and D. Page, "Planning in the East Block: The Post-Hostilities Problems Committee in Canada," *International Journal* 32/4 (1977): 687-726.

Perras, G. "Canada as a Military Partner: Alliance Politics and the Campaign to Recapture the Aleutian Island of Kiska." *Journal of Military History* 56 (1992): 423-54.

Pullen, T.C. "Convoy ON 127 and the Loss of HMCS Ottawa, 13 September 1942: A Personal Reminiscence." *Northern Mariner* 2/2 (1992): 1-27.

Rawling, W.G. "Only A Foolish Escapade by Young Ratings?" *Northern Mariner* 10/2 (2000): 59-69.

——. "The Challenge of Modernization: The Royal Canadian Navy and Antisubmarine Weapons, 1944–1945. *Journal of Military History* 63/2 (1999): 355-378.

——. "A Lonely Ambassador: HMCS *Uganda* and the War in the Pacific." *Northern Mariner* 8/1 (1998): 39-63.

——. "Paved With Good Intentions: HMCS *Uganda*, the Pacific War, and the Volunteer Issue." *Canadian Military History* 4/2 (1995): 23-33.

Reid, Escott. "An Anglo-Canadian Military Alliance?" *Canadian Forum* 17/197 (1937): 84-5.

Sarty, R. "The Limits of Ultra: The Schnorkel Boat Offensive against North America, November 1944–January 1945." *Journal of Intelligence and National Security* 12 (1997): 44-68.

Shelley, CR. "HMCS *Prince Robert*: The Career of an Armed Merchant Cruiser." *Canadian Military History* 4/1 (1995): 47-60.

Simpson, J.F., and M. Wellman. "Emotional Reactions in Survivors of HMCS Valleyfield." *Canadian Medical Association Journal*. (1944).

Syrett, D. "The Sinking of HMS *Firedrake* and the Battle for Convoy ON 153." *American Neptune* 51/2: 106-115.

——. "The Battle for Convoy ONS 154." *Northern Mariner* 8/2 (1997): 41-50.

——. "The Last Murmansk Convoys, 11 March–30 May 1945." *Northern Mariner* 4/1 (1994): 55-63.

——. "Failure at Sea: Wolf Pack Operations in the North Atlantic, 10 February–22 March 1944." *Northern Mariner* 5/1 (1995): 33-43.

——, and W.A.B. Douglas. "Die Wende in der Schlacht im Atlantik: Die Schliessung des 'Gronland-Luftochs,' 1942–43." Trans. by J. Rohwer. *Marine-Rundschau* 83/I, II, III (1986): 2–11, 70-3, 147-9.

"Walrus." "The Loss of HMCS Fraser." *Naval Review* 47/2 (1959): 174.

Watkins, J. "Actions against Elbings, April 1944." *Mariner's Mirror* 81/2 (1995): 195-206.

——. "Destroyer Action, Ile de Batz, 9 June 1944." *Mariner's Mirror* 78/3 (1992): 316-22.

Weinburg, G. "22 June 1941, The German View." *War in History* 3/2 (1966): 225-33.

Whitby, M. "The Case of the Phantom MTB and the Loss of HMCS *Athabaskan*." *Canadian Military History* 11/3 (2002): 5-14.

——. "In Defence of Home Waters: Doctrine and Training in the Canadian Navy During the 1930s." *Mariner's Mirror* 77/2 (1991): 167-77.

——. "'Foolin' around the French Coast: RCN Tribal Class Destroyers in Action, April 1944." *Canadian Defence Quarterly* 19/3 (1989): 54-61.

——. "Instruments of Security: The RCN's Procurement of the Tribal-class Destroyers, 1938–1943." *Northern Mariner* 2/3 (1992): 1–15.

——. "Masters of the Channel Night: The 10th Destroyer Flotilla's Victory off Ile de Batz, 9 June 1944." *Canadian Military History* II/1 (1993): 5-21.

——. "There Must Be No Holes in our Sweeping: The 31st Canadian Minesweeping Flotilla on D-Day." *Canadian Military History* 3/1 (1994): 64.

——. "The Seaward Defence of the British Assault Area, 6–14 June 1944." *Mariner's Mirror* 80/2 (1994): 191-207.

——. "Matelots, Martinets and Mutineers: The Mutiny in HMCS *Iroquois*, 19 July 1943." *Journal of Military History* 65/1 (2001): 77–103.

Thomas, RH. "The War in the Gulf of St. Lawrence: Its Impact on Canadian Trade." *Canadian Defence Quarterly* 21/2 (S1992): 12–17.

Zimmerman, David. "New Dimensions in Canadian Naval History." *American Neptune* 60/3: 263-275.

UNPUBLISHED THESES AND DISSERTATIONS

Cafferky, S. "Unchartered Waters: The Development of the Helicopter Carrying Destroyer in the Postwar Royal Canadian Navy, 1943-1964." Doctoral dissertation, Carleton University, 1996.

Glover, W.R. "Officer Training and the Quest for Operational Efficiency in the RCN, 1939–1945." Doctoral dissertation, University of London, 1998.

Hansen, K. "Fuel, Endurance and Replenishment at Sea in the RCN, 1935-1945." Master's thesis, Royal Military College of Canada, 2004.

Llewellyn-Jones, M. "British Responses to the U-boats, Winter 1943 to Spring 1945." Master's thesis, Kings College,1997.

Malone, Daniel P. "Breaking Down the Wall: Bombarding Force E and Naval Fire Support on JUNO BEACH." Master's thesis, University of New Brunswick, 2005.

Mayne, R.O. "Behind the Scenes at Naval Service Headquarters: Bureaucratic Politics and the Dismissal of Vice-Admiral Percy W. Nelles." Master's thesis, Wilfrid Laurier University, 1998.

McLean, D.M. "The Last Cruel Winter: RCN Support Groups and the U-boat Schnorkel Offensive." Master's Thesis, Royal Military College, 1992.

Sarty, Roger. "Silent Sentry: A Military and Political History of Canadian Coast Defence, 1860–1945." Doctoral dissertation, University of Toronto, 1982.

Whitby, M. "The 'Other' Navy at War: The RCN's Tribal Class Destroyers 1939–44." Master's thesis, Carleton University, 1988.

White, J. "Conscripted City: Halifax and the Second World War." Doctoral dissertation, McMaster University, 1994.

Index of Ships

HMC Ships

Agassiz, 96, 423, 426

Alberni, 364-365, 368, 400, 477

Algoma, 393

Algonquin, 203-205, 207-209, 231, 236, 248, 252-258, 261, 271, 288, 290, 292, 310, 453, 461-467, 470, 473-476, 479-480, 483, 489, 524, 531

Amherst, 177

Annan, 388-389

Arvida, 32, 86

Assiniboine, 175, 181, 375, 381, 387, 418, 524

Athabaskan, 151-154, 159, 161-166, 195, 197, 206, 222-229, 245, 279

Aurora, 524

Bayfield, 233, 248, 337

Beacon Hill, 374

Blairmore, 233, 248, 334, 337

Brandon, 179

Calgary, 73, 76, 103-104, 394

Canso, 233, 247, 337, 495

Caraquet, 97, 233, 247-250, 255, 337

Chambly, 35, 74, 82-83, 89-95, 383

Charlottetown, 149, 428

Chaudière, 358-360, 381

Chebogue, 376-377, 382-384, 431

Chedabucto, 96

Clayoquot, 411, 439-440, 445

Columbia, 416

Coaticook, 433, 442

Cowichan, 233, 248, 334, 337

Dawson, 497

Drumheller, 35, 82, 84, 91, 364

Dundas, 68

Dunvegan, 386, 451

Dunver, 378, 381-382, 426-427

Edmundston, 46, 49-50, 73, 103, 421-422

Ettrick, 433, 437, 442, 446

Fort William, 233, 248, 255, 334, 337, 477

Fraser, 285

Frontenac, 421-422

Gatineau, 31, 42, 82-83, 90, 181

Georgian, 233, 247, 337

Giffard, 421-422

Granby, 96

Guysborough, 233, 247, 334-337, 402

Haida, 153, 166, 191-207, 220-229, 231, 245, 276-284, 299, 302, 305-306, 317, 356, 489, 531

Halifax, 421, 478

Hamilton, 68

Hespeler, 381-382

Huntsville, 381

Huron, 153, 166, 188, 191-198, 203, 207, 222-227, 231, 245, 276-279, 283, 299-301, 306, 489, 531

Iroquois, 149, 151, 153-161, 164, 166, 191-198, 203, 222-223, 231, 283, 299, 302, 305-317, 325, 482, 489, 492-493, 531

Joliette, 374

Jonquiere, 374

Kamsack, 68

Kenora, 100, 233, 247, 291, 337

Kentville, 441

Kirkland Lake, 439

Kitchener, 73, 533

Kootenay, 30, 32, 181, 352, 355-358, 536

La Hulloise, 374, 401-402

La Salle, 433

Lethbridge, 96

Lévis, 433

Lindsay, 102, 291

Loch Achanalt, 388

Loch Alvie, 398, 482

Long Branch, 381

Lunenburg, 103

Magnificent, 493

Magog, 411, 428, 431

Mahone, 96

Malpeque, 233, 248, 334, 337

Matane, 302, 357, 384, 416, 420, 431

Meon, 368-369, 433, 442

Micmac, 152, 309, 524, 531

Milltown, 233, 248, 337

Minas, 233, 248, 255, 337

Miscou, 97

Monnow, 368-369, 472-473

Montreal, 374, 416

Morden, 35, 74, 82, 88-90, 94

Mulgrave, 233, 248, 255, 334, 419

New Glasgow, 374, 402-405, 418, 423, 530

New Westminister, 381

Niagara, 416

Nootka, 309

Ontario, 523-524, 537, 554

Orkney, 374, 428-429

Ottawa, 30, 32, 79-80, 181, 352, 355-358, 381, 521

Outremont, 286

Owen Sound, 418, 420

Port Arthur, 73

Port Colborne, 368, 370, 549

Preserver, 425, 443

Prince David, 140-141, 231, 241, 248, 251, 257, 260-263, 268, 294, 303, 317-319, 517

Prince Henry, 140-142, 231, 241, 248, 257-261, 269, 294, 303, 317-319, 517

634

Prince Robert, 76, 101, 103-104, 522, 556
Qu'Appelle, 381, 550
Rainbow, 557
Restigouche, 55, 96, 181, 205
Regina, 363-364, 368, 400
Ribble, 374
Rimouski, 96
Sackville, 74, 82, 88-89, 94-95
Saguenay, 153, 166, 387
Saint John, 366-370, 399-400, 472, 482
Sarnia, 448
Saskatchewan, 31, 181, 283-284, 381
Shawinigan, 96, 99, 411, 433-434
Sioux, 202-209, 231, 236, 248, 257-258, 261, 288, 290, 292, 310, 453, 461-467, 473, 480-489, 524, 531
Skeena, 31-32, 153, 181, 205, 284, 379, 381, 385-387, 524
Snowberry, 73-77, 103-104
Springhill, 428-429
St Croix, 74, 81-88, 90-93, 105, 482
St Francis, 30, 74, 95, 421, 521
St Laurent, 181, 352, 381, 416, 418, 420, 521
Ste Thérèse, 374
Stettler, 431
Stormont, 368-369, 416, 437
Strathadam, 401-402, 406
Summerside, 75, 549
Swansea, 416-420
Swift Current, 96
Teme, 282, 285-286, 376, 387, 404, 406
Thetford Mines, 374, 401, 405
Thorlock, 451
Thunder, 233, 247, 291, 314, 337
Toronto, 428
Transcona, 439
Trentonian, 246, 291-292, 400
Uganda, 444, 510, 519-524, 529, 532, 536-537, 540-547, 554, 556
Ungava, 96
Valleyfield, 411, 421-423

Vancouver, 497
Vegreville, 233, 247
Victoriaville, 451
Wallaceburg, 418
Warrior, 493
Wasaga, 233, 248, 337
Wetaskiwin, 32, 381
Wolfe, 508
Woodstock, 73

Shore Establishments Commissioned as HMC Ships
Cornwallis (shore base), 434, 531
Niobe (shore base), 107, 110, 119, 124, 135-136, 145-148, 154, 161, 166, 522, 557
Somers Isles (shore base), 232, 529, 531
Stadacona (shore base), 135
Ste Hyacinthe (shore base), 310

Landing Craft and Motor Vessels
LCA 856, 260
LCA 985, 260-261
LCA 1021, 260, 419
LCA 1033, 260
LCA 1372, 259
LCA 1375, 260-261
LCI 117, 248, 262
LCI 121, 262
LCI 135, 263, 292
LCI 177, 262
LCI 249, 262
LCI 255, 263
LCI 270, 263
LCI 285, 262-263
LCI 298, 262, 549
LCI 301, 262
LCI 302, 145, 263
LCI 305, 292-294
LCI 310, 264
LCI(L) 115, 263
LCI(L) 135, 263
LCS(M) 101, 260-261
LST 319, 134-135
LST 644, 363-364
ML 454, 248
MTB 460, 217, 296-297

MTB 463, 297
MTB 464, 217, 288, 328, 330-331
MTB 466, 239, 297
MTB 485, 320, 331
MTB 486, 320, 322
MTB 491, 328
MTB 726, 218
MTB 727, 218
MTB 735, 218
MTB 743, 295, 332
MTB 745, 218, 294, 323
MTB 746, 332-333
MTB 748, 294-295

HM Ships
Alnwick Castle, 488
Anson, 191-192, 207
Archer, 31, 35
Armadillo (shore base), 147
Ascension, 392
Ashanti, 222-227, 245, 276-277, 302, 305
Aylmer, 393
Bedouin, 194
Bee (shore base), 215-216
Belfast, 196-198, 200, 236, 521-523
Bellona, 223, 302, 305-306, 473-474, 483, 489
Bentinck, 393
Bermuda, 153, 191
Bickerton, 464
Biter, 31-32, 35
Black Prince, 224-226, 486, 542
Bluebell, 488
Broadway, 30, 35
Bullen, 392
Burnham, 30
Byron, 394
Calcutta, 285
Calder, 393
Campania, 470, 483, 488-489
Capel, 393, 475
Cassandra, 472
Ceylon, 520
Chanticleer, 103
Charybdis, 221-222, 479
Chelsea, 96
Churchill, 30

Conne, 394, 460

Dahlia, 394

Deane, 394

Denbigh Castle, 487

Destiny, 82

Diadem, 236

Dianthus, 30

Diomede, 524

Douglas, 154-155

Duke of York, 196, 200, 207, 453-454, 462, 465

Duncan, 33

Egret, 77, 162-163, 166

Elkins, 333

Enterprise, 207, 219, 222, 229, 275, 524

Escapade, 82-83

Eskimo, 204, 245, 276-277, 280, 284, 300-302, 356

Fencer, 207, 387

Forester, 418, 420

Formidable, 453, 462, 465, 542-543, 556

Furious, 207, 453, 462

Gentian, 417

Glasgow, 219, 222, 229, 275, 521

Goodall, 478, 493

Grenville, 161-163

Hamilcar, 134

Hargood, 421

Hillary, 295, 297

Howe, 542-543

Hurst Castle, 372

Icarus, 82, 84, 91

Implacable, 490, 545

Impulsive, 192, 196

Inconstant, 192-193

Indefatigable, 453, 461-462, 465

Indomitable, 554

Itchen, 30, 74, 82-84, 87-88, 90-92

Jamaica, 191, 196, 200, 449, 521

Javelin, 245, 276-277

Jed, 30

Kempthorne, 464

Kent, 191, 462-464, 473-474, 479, 481, 483

Keppel, 82, 84, 87-89, 93, 105

King George V, 535, 542

Kite, 467

Lagan, 30, 35, 82-83, 91, 94

Lawford, 272

Limbourne, 221

Lincoln, 99

Loyalty, 368

Malaya, 153

Manners, 393

Matchless, 197

Mauritius, 311-312, 315-316

Minotaur, 520

Montgomery, 100

Mounsey, 470

Moyola, 154-155

Musketeer, 197

Myngs, 473, 479

Nabob, 428, 454, 457-458, 461-465, 489, 493, 523

Nairana, 483, 488-489

Narcissus, 82, 87-89

Nelson, 522

Nene, 103-104, 381, 398-399

Newfoundland, 520, 545

Nigeria, 521

Norfolk, 196, 198

Nyasaland, 392

Obedient, 192

Onslaught, 192, 196

Onslow, 192, 196

Opportune, 197

Orchis, 82, 551

Orwell, 192, 196

Phoenix, 139

Pink, 33, 500

Polyanthus, 82-84, 87-88, 90, 92, 94

Premier, 491

Primrose, 30, 35

Puncher, 457, 489, 491-494

Pursuer, 207

Ramillies, 265, 318

Rathlin, 82-84, 87, 91

Redpole, 355, 485

Rodney, 298, 522

Salisbury, 482

Scourge, 196

Scylla, 267, 272, 287-288, 293, 295

Seaham, 250

Seraph, 391-392

Sheffield, 196, 198, 521

Spey, 350

Statice, 351-352, 355

Striker, 302

Superb, 520

Swift, 271, 290

Swiftsure, 542, 544

Tartar, 204, 223-224, 227, 245, 274-278, 302, 305-306, 309

Thane, 392, 465

Towy, 82, 90

Tracker, 25, 282, 285-286, 444

Trumpeter, 387, 461-464

Tweed, 73, 77, 103

Tyne, 466

Ursa, 311-312, 315-316

Valentine, 204

Valiant, 138

Vengeance, 520

Venus, 555

Verulum, 473-474

Victorious, 207, 543, 556

Vigilant, 464

Virago, 197

Vixen, 204

Warspite, 138, 265

Watchman, 406

Waveney, 141

Whitaker, 389

Witherington, 24

Wolsey, 267

Zambesi, 473

Zealous, 419, 492

Zephyr, 392

HM Tug Dexterous, 35

HMT Green Howard, 248

HMT Gunner, 248

HMT Lancer, 82-83

HMT Northern Foam, 82, 89-90, 550

HMT Northern Gem, 33, 450

HMT Vizalma, 35

Free French Warships

Georges Legues, 255

La Perle (submarine), 427

Lobelia, 82, 89

Montcalm, 255
Renoncule, 82, 90, 459
Roselys, 82, 88

German Ships
Admiral Scheer, 186, 466
Bismarck, 24
Cornouailles (freighter), 479
Falke, 243, 265, 289
Greif (freighter), 243, 479
Hipper, 186, 190
Hydra, 295
Jaguar, 243, 265, 273, 289
Kondor, 243
Lützow, 186, 190-191, 466
M 133, 289
M 4613, 295
M 4620, 300-301
M 4624, 295
M 4625, 289
Minotoure (supply ship), 295
Richtofen (aircraft tender), 312
S 167, 332
Scharnhorst, 169, 191-203, 222, 521
T 24, 225-228, 230, 243, 274-279, 312
T 27, 225, 227-228, 243
T 28, 243, 265, 273, 288
T 29, 225-227, 243
Tirpitz, 169, 186, 191, 196, 203-208, 453-454, 462-467, 556
V 208, 295
V 210, 295
V 213, 300-301
V 702, 316
V 729, 316
V 730, 316
Z 24, 243, 274-278
Z 32, 243, 271-279
Z 33, 201
ZH 1, 243, 274-278

Japanese Ships
Haguro, 555
I 25 (submarine), 503, 506
I 26 (submarine), 503, 506

Merchant Ships
Alexander Kennedy, 400
Arundel Castle, 473
Athelviking, 442
British Freedom, 442, 446
California (troopship), 154-155
Cuba, 406
Delisle, 97
Drottingholm, 473
Duchess of York (troopship), 154-155, 158
Edward H. Crockett, 470
Empire MacAlpine, (MAC) 82, 89
Empire MacCallum, (MAC) 426-427, 532
Empire MacColl (MAC), 426
Ezra Weston, 363-364
Fort Gloucester, 322
Fort Thompson, 431
Frederick Douglass, 83
Henry Bacon, 488
Jacksonville, 372
James Gordon Bennett, 91
James W. Nesmith, 406
Kelmscott, 417, 476
Lark (fishing vessel), 426, 484, 488
Leopoldville, 393, 396
Martin van Buren, 442
McKeesport, 33
Monarch, 291-292
Nieuw Amsterdam, 440
Nipiwan Park, 441
Norlys, 194
Oregon Express, 91
Penolver, 97
Polarland, 441
Port Fairy (troopship), 154-155
Port Jemseg, 91
Princess Maquinna, 507
Queen Mary, 317
Samsuva, 470
Samtucky, 439
San Francisco, 418
Silverlaurel, 393
Skjelbred, 91
Soberg, 351
Steel Voyager, 91

Theodore Dwight Weld, 83
Thomas Scott, 488
Watuka, 418
William Pepperell, 82

New Zealand Ships
Achilles, 545-546
Gambia, 542
Leander, 525

Norwegian Ships
King Haakon, VII 425
Svenner, 265

Polish Ships
Blyskawica, 245, 275-279, 302
Orkan, 100, 159-161
Piorun, 245, 276-277
Wahela, 90

United States Ships
Arkansas, 255
Asheville, 41
Bayfield, 247
Bogue, 31, 429-431, 434
Card, 426
Core, 431, 434
Doyle, 255
Duane (USCGC), 32
Emmons, 255
Lowe, 447
Missouri, 556
Natchez, 41
Plunkett, 292
Spencer (USCGC), 32
Tuscaloosa, 191

Index of U-Boats
U 107, 426
U 119, 67, 71, 95, 97
U 125, 34
U 165, 98
U 175, 32
U 189, 32
U 190, 446, 448, 451
U 192, 34
U 220, 97, 99
U 229, 105
U 233, 426
U 238, 83-84, 89-91, 103

U 246, 389, 406
U 247, 366-368, 370, 399, 482
U 248, 382
U 258, 33
U 260, 82, 88, 90
U 262, 95
U 264, 34
U 266, 34
U 270, 83, 88-89
U 275, 90
U 278, 393
U 285, 393
U 296, 392
U 297, 392
U 305, 87, 89
U 307, 193, 195
U 309, 366, 399-400
U 310, 470
U 312, 393
U 313, 393
U 315, 393
U 322, 392
U 325, 393
U 338, 83-84, 87
U 341, 83
U 344, 467
U 354, 195, 463-465, 467
U 358, 34
U 377, 34, 88-89, 95
U 378, 88
U 386, 84, 87-88
U 400, 392
U 402, 89
U 404, 32
U 406, 350
U 425, 488
U 438, 34
U 456, 35
U 459, 160
U 460, 77
U 480, 364, 368
U 482, 372, 381, 387, 392
U 483, 389, 398

U 485, 393
U 486, 393-394
U 501, 232
U 513, 98-99
U 515, 103
U 517, 98
U 518, 98-99, 448
U 531, 34
U 536, 95-96, 104
U 537, 97-100
U 539, 417
U 541, 430-431
U 543, 416
U 546, 448
U 548, 420-423, 446
U 550, 420
U 552, 34
U 571, 32
U 584, 88, 90
U 601, 196
U 618, 103
U 621, 358
U 630, 34
U 634, 34
U 636, 193
U 638, 34
U 641, 88
U 645, 83
U 666, 90
U 667, 364
U 678, 351-352, 355
U 680, 392
U 711, 488
U 731, 83-84, 90
U 753, 35
U 758, 89, 91
U 763, 356
U 764, 393
U 772, 392-394
U 775, 392
U 825, 393
U 845, 417, 420, 427
U 866, 446-447

U 880, 448
U 881, 448
U 889, 446, 451
U 89, 35
U 905, 393
U 92, 368
U 921, 470
U 952, 87-88, 90-91
U 954, 34
U 965, 462
U 968, 488, 493
U 971, 280-285, 356
U 978, 389-390
U 979, 392
U 984, 356, 358
U 992, 487
U 1003, 389, 403, 405
U 1004, 400-401
U 1006, 388-389
U 1009, 393
U 1017, 393
U 1020, 392
U 1024, 406
U 1051, 393
U 1055, 393
U 1107, 406
U 1172, 393
U 1195, 406
U 1200, 389
U 1209, 392
U 1221, 431, 435
U 1222, 426
U 1223, 431
U 1227, 382-383, 431
U 1228, 433, 435-436
U 1229, 430
U 1230, 434, 436
U 1231, 433-435, 440-441
U 1232, 395, 436, 440, 442
U 1235, 448
U 1302, 402

Index

10 Squadron (RCAF), 417, 423

10th Cruiser Squadron (RN), 302

1st Aircraft Carrier Squadron (RCN), 537

1st Canadian Army, 127, 328

1st Canadian Army Tank Brigade, 127

1st Canadian Infantry Division, 127

2nd British Army, 292, 327

2nd Canadian Infantry Division, 106, 111

3 Group (RCAF), 447-448

3rd British Division, 234

3rd Canadian Infantry Division, 141, 236, 240-241, 265

4th Light Cruiser Squadron (RN), 537, 554

4th US Division, 234

4th US Infantry Division, 265

7th British Armoured Division, 235

7th Canadian Infantry Brigade, 241, 248, 258-259

8th Canadian Infantry Brigade, 241, 248

9th Canadian Infantry Brigade, 248, 257

12 Army Camp, Hanrun, 131

19th Division, 245, 276-277

21st Panzer Division, 265

29th US Infantry Division, 234-235, 265

50th British Infantry Division, 242

50th Northumbrian Division, 147

56th British Infantry Brigade, 248, 263

82nd US Airborne Division, 265

Abbott, Hon Douglas, 557

ABC-22-Pacific (defence agreement), 507

Abwehr agent, 389

Ackermann, Oberleutnant P., 431, 435-436, 439

acoustic torpedo, Canadian (CAT); German, *see* Gnat, *Zaunk ig.* 93-94, 283-284, 296, 334-335, 337, 356, 364, 383-384, 400, 405, 414, 417

Action Information Intercom (AID), 97, 308-310

Action Information Organization (AIO), 307-308, 310-311, 325, 531

Adams, Capt K.F., 175, 309, 413-414, 489

ADR (Aircraft Direction Room), 544

Agnew, Capt R.I., 108-109, 118, 126, 134, 136

air stores, critical shortage of, 539

air strikes, *see also* Kamikaze, 208-209, 542-543

Aircraft

  Albacore, 243, 245

  Barracuda, 207

  Bristol Beaufighter, 208, 245, 274

  Canso, 33-34, 99, 422-423, 429, 434, 442, 447

  Catalina, 406

  Corsair, 207, 453, 462, 539, 549, 555-556

  Fairey Barracuda, 453-454, 461-462, 465, 477, 490-492

  Firefly, 453, 461-462, 555

  Grumman Avenger, 458, 461-464, 490-491, 539, 555

  Halifax bomber, 224

  Heinkel 177, 104, 162

  Hellcat fighter-bomber (Grumman), 207-208, 453, 461-462, 465, 539, 555-556

  Hudson, 99

  Lancaster bomber, 289, 465-466

  Liberator, 446

  Mosquito (De Havilland), fighter-bomber, 274, 465

  Mustang fighter, 241

  Seafire (Supermarine) fighter, 241, 461-462, 539

  Spitfire fighter, 111-112, 241, 259, 539

  Sunderland flying boat, 103, 426

  Swordfish, 35, 82, 89, 245, 427, 470, 487

  Wellington (Vickers) bomber, 160-161, 392, 394

  Wildcat fighter, 207, 458, 462-463, 476, 487-488, 491

aircraft (escort) carriers, Chapter 21 *passim*, 125, 133, 140, 159, 168, 170, 173-174, 184-186, 284-285, 387, 426, 428-429, 431, 434-435, 451, 455-456, 458, 465

Aircraft, German

  Ju-88 bomber, 472-473, 484, 487-488

  Kondor (Focke Wulf 200k), 155, 160, 166, 243

Alexander, Hon A.V., First Lord of the Admiralty, 395, 453, 512, 520

Algerine class minesweeper, 43, 179, 368, 418-419, 425

Allied Anti-Submarine Survey Board (AASSB), 41, 48, 50-51, 54-59, 64-65, 81

Altenfjord, 196-197, 208, 453, 462, 487

Altmeier, Oberleutnant F., 382-383

640

Amber Beach, 130

Anglo-American discussions, 168, 172, 317, 517

Anglo-Canadian disagreement on carriers, 170

Anglo-Canadian meeting, 517

anti-aircraft armament, 36, 73, 82-83, 189, 205

Anti-U-boat committee (UK), 396

Anti-U-boat Division, 232, 370, 399

Antisubmarine Command, efforts to create RCN-RCAF, 24

Antisubmarine Warfare Operational Research Group(ASWORG), 414

Area Z (Picadilly Circus , 235, 247-249

Armament Broadcast System (ABD), 308-310

Asdic
    type 123, 180
    type 127D, 180
    type 144, 179-180, 205, 232
    type 144, 144Q, 429, 530
    type 144Q/147B, 205
    type 145, 179-180

Assault forces, naval: B, G, J, L, O, S, U, 126, 231, 234

Athabaskan, loss of, 228-229

Atkinson, Lt W.H.I., 556

Atlantic (Washington) convoy conference, 498

Atlantic Convoy (Trident) Conference, 166

Atlantic Wall (German), 250, 266

Aubry, Cdr R. M., RN, 440

Audette, LCdr L. de la C., 177, 442

Auto Barrage Unit, 223

Aviation, naval. *See also* Fleet Air Arm, Naval aviation, 24-25, 29, 51, 73, 169-170

B-Dienst, Beobachtungsdienst, 31, 33-34, 36, 39, 200

Bahr, Kapitänleutnant R., 87

balanced fleet policy, RCN, 23-24, 105, 149, 184

Balfry, LCdr C.P., 388

Balmain, LS Roland, 331

Bangor class minesweeper, 43, 47, 68, 71, 97-100, 209-212, 231, 233, 247-250, 255, 290-291, 314, 334, 337, 402, 418, 425, 437-442, 495, 497-498, 503, 506-510

Barclay, SLt I.A., 121-122

Barnard, Cdr K.M., RN, 213

Barr, Mate J., 504

Bartlett, LCdr E.H., 118, 132

Battle of the Atlantic, turning point, 34

Battle of Leyte Gulf, 509, 538, 540, 542

Battle of Midway, 495

Battle of North Cape, 200

Battle of the Barents Sea, 190

Battle of the Philippine Sea, 526

Battleship Covering Force, 191

BdU, Befehlshaber der Unterseeboote. See also U-Boat Command, *Führer der U-boote.* 32-34, 73, 81, 91-92, 95, 97, 100, 103-104, 159, 283, 351, 356, 368, 372, 389, 392, 423, 426, 428, 433, 435-436, 439

Beach Commando, RCN, 133, 146, 148, 172, 231, 233-234, 270, 298

Beach Group No. 9, 299

Bechtolsheim, Kapitän zur See F. von, 276, 278-279

Beech, Cmdre W.J.R., 496-497, 505-507

Beecher, Lt, 129

Beesly, LCdr P., RNVR, 61-62

Belle Isle Force, 425

Benoît, CPO Maurice, 337

Benoit, Lt C.J., 310-311, 316

Benson, Lt J., 383

Bey, Konteradmiral E., 197-198, 200

Bidwell, Capt R.E.S., 72-73, 181, 478, 489-490, 493

Billington, AB H., 122

Birch, Cdr J.K., RNR, 104

Bishop, Lt L.C., 331

Blackett, P.M.S., 414

Bletchley Park, *see also* Enigma, Ultra. 31, 39, 221, 368

Boak, A/LCdr E.E.G., 205, 257-258, 484, 489

Boak, Lt J.E., 117

Bourke, LCdr R., 507-508

Bradley, Gen Omar, USA, 266

Bradley, Lt J.R., 369-370

Braeucker, Friedrich, 451

Brand, Capt E.S., 176, 184, 504-505

Bridgman, LCdr C.E., RNR, 30

Briggs, LCdr W.E.S., 387-388

Brind, RAdm E.D.P., RN, 537, 541-546, 554

British Admiralty Delegation (BAD), 25, 456, 511

British Assault Area, 244, 266-267, 371

British commandos, 112, 319

British Pacific Fleet, 517-518, 523, 533, 537, 539, 541, 545, 556

British Power Boat Co., 214, 320

British Steam Gun Boat, 112

British War Cabinet, 120

Brock, LCdr John, 401-402

Brodeur, RAdm V.G., 505-510

Brooke, Gen Sir Alan, CIGS, 127

Brooke, LCdr W.S., 108-109, 119, 123-125, 132, 142, 146-147, 173-174

Brown, LStoker R.W., 115-117

Browning, Capt H.W.S., RN, 492-493

Bryan, Cdr J., RNR, 418

Buckingham, Lt R.G., 260

Budge, Lt P.D., 194

Burk, Lt C.A., 273, 287-289, 297-298, 321

Burnett, Cdr P.W., RN, 31, 82-84

Burnett, VAdm R.L., 189-190, 196-198, 200-201

Burrard Drydock and Shipbuilding Co., 140, 489

Buxton, Capt R.H., RN, 171-172, 174

C groups: Allied criticism of. *See also* escort groups. 23, 29-32

C-in-C British Pacific Fleet, 529

C-in-C Canadian Northwest Atlantic (CNA), 412-413, 417, 423, 428-429, 433, 435-436, 439, 447-448, 451, 458

C-in-C Home Fleet, 467, 490, 492

C-in-C Plymouth, 158, 160, 221, 229, 245, 284, 311, 315-316, 370

C-in-C Portsmouth, 222, 267, 352

C-in-C Western Approaches, 92, 178, 245, 381, 396, 407, 410, 428, 458

Cabinet War Committee, 26, 29, 43, 133, 143, 172, 174, 455-458, 511-518, 523, 532

Campbell, AB L.G., 115-117

Campbell, Capt C.M., 134

Campbell, Sir Gerald, Br ambassador to US, 519-520

Canada House, London, 136, 153

Canadian CAT gear, *see* acoustic torpedo

Canadian government policy, 512, 514, 536-537, 557

Canadian Joint Staff mission, London, 514

Canadian Joint Staff mission, Washington, 505

Canadian Naval Mission Overseas (CNMO), 173, 294, 299, 320, 322, 371, 513, 517, 528, 531, 546

Canadian Northwest Atlantic Command, 23-24, 34, 61-62, 66, 68, 74, 105, 168, 179, 326, 354, 372, 374, 386, 411, 416

Canadian Pacific Fleet, 530, 532, 554

Canadian Scottish Regiment, 248, 259

Canadian support group (escort group), 458, 481

Canadian-American commandos, 318

Canadianization policy of RCN; hindered by British reluctance to allow Canadian evaluation and production, 182

Captain class frigate, 267, 350, 371, 421, 456, 470

Casablanca Conference, 127

Castle class corvette, 371-372, 380-381, 419, 525, 529-531

Cavanagh, OS R.A., 115-117

Chadwick, Lt E.M., 523, 547

Chadwick, Sig G., 163

Chaffey, Lt C.D., 296-297, 331

Chance, Lt P.G., 385

Chancellor, LCdr, 123

Chavasse, LCdr E.H., RN, (fn 40), 35

Chiefs of Staff, American Joint, 120, 167, 498

Chiefs of Staff, British, 107-108, 127, 170, 317, 398, 514-515, 517

Chiefs of Staff, Canadian, 166, 517

Chiefs of Staff, Combined (US-UK), 127, 167

Churchill, Rt Hon Winston S., 108, 127, 140, 150-151, 166-167, 170-172, 186, 395-396, 453, 512-518

Ciliax, Adm O., 480

Clark, Capt C.P., RN, 219

Clark, Lt A.C., 263

Claxton, Brooke, Min of Nat Defence, 410

Clayton, RAdm J.S., RN, 62

Clifford, Lt J.L., 183

Coastal Command, RAF, 155, 159, 191, 208, 223, 245, 274, 279, 284-285, 302, 317, 327, 333, 387, 391, 401, 411, 426, 461, 474, 480

Coastal Forces Command, 213-218, 267, 297-298, 310, 321, 329-330

Code-breaking; see also Bletchley Park, Decryption, Enigma, Ultra. 31, 36, 81, 229

Combined operations, Ch 14 *passim*; RCN agreement to supply personnel for, 23, 170

Combined Operations Headquarters, 108-109, 119, 123-124

Combined Operations Room, Plymouth, 221, 227

Command and control of Canadian ships, 168, 173

Commanding Officer Auxiliary Vessels, 495

Connolly, J.J., Asst to A.L. Macdonald, 175-179, 181-183

Conscription for overseas service, 171

Convoy defence, 26, 29, 216

Convoys
  BTC 10, 393
  BTC 76, 400
  BX 14, 442
  EBC 3, 291
  EBC 66, 363
  ETC 26, 356
  HHX 327, 439
  HJF 45, 448
  HX 232, 32
  HX 233, 32
  HX 234, 32
  HX 237, 35-36
  HX 256, 81-83
  HX 265, 99
  HX 286, 418
  HX 342, 447
  HX 346, 406
  HX 348, 406
  HX 350, 448
  HX-ON series, 31
  JW 51, A&B, 190, 192
  JW 54, A&B, 191-193, 196
  JW 55, A&B, 195-198, 201
  JW 58, 207
  JW 59, 454, 462-463, 467
  JW 60, 467
  JW 62, 471, 483
  JW 63, 483
  JW 64, 483-484, 486-487, 489, 491
  JW 67, 406
  JW-RA 61, 470
  JW-RA 62, 470, 473
  JW-RA 64, 489
  JW-RA series, 453
  JW/RA series, 190
  ON 137, 205
  ON 176, 32

ON 178, 32
ON 180, 34
ON 181, 35
ON 202, 82-84, 87-89, 91, 93, 100, 105
ON 225, 417
ON 300, 451
ONM 243, 426
ONS 154, 30
ONS 18, 82-84, 87-89, 91, 93, 100, 105
ONS 33, 382, 431
PQ 17, 186, 190
PQ 17 & 18, 472
PQ 18, 189-190
PQ/QP, 189-190
QP 14, 189
QP 15, 189
QS 97, 431
RA 54A & B, 191-194
RA 55A & B, 195-198, 200, 203
RA 60, 470
RA 62, 472-473
RA 63, 483
RA 64, 483, 485, 487, 489, 491
RA 65, 489
SC 107, 30, 63, 205
SC 118, 25
SC 127, 34
SC 128, 33
SC 154, 418, 420
SC-ONS series, 31, 232
SH 194 441
SL 139/MKS 30, 103-104
TBC 21, 394
UC 2, 423
UC 21, 423
WB 65, 97
WN 74, 399
XB 56, 68
XB, 139, 437, 439
Corbett, Stoker E.J., 122
Cordes, Korvettenkapitän E., 356
Corke, LCdr L., RNVR, 112
Corncobs (sunken block ships), 246
Corps: US VI, VIII, 299, 319
corvette, revised (long forecastle), 443

Cosh, LCdr D.R.B., 207
Costain, Lt C.C., 554
Creba, Lt D.G., 297, 320
Cree, Cdr C.M., 497, 507-508
Creery, Capt W.B., ACNS 150, 171, 176, 550, 556
Crescent class destroyer, 524, 554
Croil, G.M., AVM, RCAF Inspector General, 26
Cronyn, Capt St J., RN, 226, 229, 301, 479
cross-Channel invasion. See also D-Day, Normandy, Operation Overlord. 120, 143
Crothers, SLt R.J., 130
Cruiser Covering Force, 190-191, 200
cryptography. See also Bletchley Park, decryption, Enigma, Ultra. 431
Cunningham, Adm Sir Andrew, RN, 208, 234, 395-397, 514, 519
Cunningham, Adm Sir John, 134

D-Day, 141, 243, 246, 250, 255, 261-262, 272, 283, 287, 290, 292
Dalrymple-Hamilton, Vadm F.H.G., RN, 480
Danlayer, 209, 233, 235-236, 248-249
Darling, Lt T.G., 207
Davis, Capt W.W., 123, 311-312, 315-316
DD tanks (amphibious duplex drive), 241, 255
Decca (electronic navigation, previously QM), 233, 249
Declassed fleet destroyers (D to H classes), 151
Decryption, 32, 60, 78, 103, 350
Degaussing, 71
DeMarbois, Capt, 54, 57, 60-61
Department of External Affairs (DEA), 23
Department of Munitions and Supply (DMS), 41, 47, 55, 58
Department of Naval Construction, 153

DeWolf, Cdr H.G., 25-26, 56, 149, 170, 192-198, 201, 207, 222-229, 276-279, 283, 305-306, 458, 498, 503-504, 530
Dido class cruiser, 267
Diefenbaker, Rt Hon John, 536
Dieppe, 106, 110-118
Direction finding (DF); see also HF/DF. 67, 416, 418
Dobratz, Kapitän zur See K., 436, 440-446, 452
Dobson, LCdr A.H., 81, 87-88
Dogboat (Fairmile D motor launch), 244, 289, 299, 327, 329, 332
Dolphin (Heimisch) cipher key, 221
Dönitz, Grossadmiral Karl, 31, 34-36, 83, 91-93, 104-105, 190, 195-197, 243, 250, 349, 390, 406-411, 439, 445-448, 472, 487
Douty, Lt R.P.J., 448
Dover Command, 245, 321-322
Dowler, AB Charles, 90
Draeski, Lt G.L., 496
Dunn, Lt J.A., 104
Dyer, LCdr K.L., 31, 524

E-boats. See also Schnellboote. 112, 213, 215, 224, 227, 243-244, 265, 267, 274, 289, 291, 296-298, 321-322, 327, 329, 332-333
Eastbound convoys, 32-33, 81-82, 193, 418
Eastern Air Command (EAC), 99-100, 417-418, 426, 430, 441, 447
Eastern Fleet, 371, 467
Eastern Front, 195, 197
Eastern Task Force (ETF), 234, 241, 248, 250, 255, 262, 266-267, 287, 295
Easton, LCdr A.H., 284, 384, 420
Eccles, Capt J.A.S., RN, 204
echo sounder, type 761, 179
Eddy, Lt F.N., 505
Edelsten, RAdm J.H., RN, 537
Edwards, Air Cmdre H., 109
Edwards, LCdr G.C., 207

Eisenhower, Gen Dwight D., 108, 234, 246-247, 292

Elbing class destroyer, 479

Ellis, Cmdre, 132

Engineer Officers, RCN, 143-144, 153

Enigma, German code, 31-33, 35, 39, 63, 67, 77-78, 274, 417, 420, 426, 433, 436, 439

Equipment crisis, RCN, 176, 183, 204

Escort Groups

A3, 30, 32

B1, 32

B2, 32

B3, 35, 82-84, 87

B7, 33

C1 & 2, 374, 382

C4, 374, 405

C5, 86, 381-382, 406, 426

C6, 374

C7, 372, 406

C8, 372

EG1, 162, 285

EG5, 105, 388, 393, 462-463

EG6, 185, 232, 284-285, 387-388

EG7, 488

EG8, 406

EG9, 83-84, 87, 89, 94-95, 105, 185, 232, 285, 302, 357, 368- 370, 384, 398-400, 406-407, 416-418, 470-473, 482-483

EG10, 398

EG11, 52, 232, 352, 355, 357-359, 369, 381, 384, 387, 398

EG12, 232, 283-284, 356, 381

EG15, 470

EG16, 372, 374, 398, 428-431, 433-434, 440-441, 445-447

EG21, 394

EG25, 374, 381, 401

EG26, 374, 391, 402, 405

EG27, 433, 442, 444-445, 447

EG28, 398, 448

EG30, 389

EG40, 161

Canadian Support Group, 72-73, 81, 95, 103, 105, 232, 302, 350, 387

Escorts, RCN shortage of, 503

Essex Scottish Regiment, 112, 115

Exercise Gantry, 212

Exercise Tiger, 227

Exercise Trousers, 212

FAFC (Foolin' Around on the French Coast , 227

Fairmile motor launch, 425, 430, 497, 503, 508-510

Fairmile B, 214

Fairmile D (ogboat , 213-215, 289, 299, 320

Faith, troop convoy, 154-155

Fallis, Lt G.A.C., 504

Far East, RCN ships to, 153, 167, 169, 371, 395

FAT 3 pattern-running torpedo, 78, 83, 91, 463

FdS, see also Führer der Schnellboote. 327, 332-333

Fennhill, Brig, actually Brig M.S. Penhale, 138

fighting destroyer escort tactics, 186, 189-192, 195-196, 198

Fiji class cruiser, 520, 522

First Canadian Army, see also 1st Canadian Army, 123

First Special Service Force, 317-318

Fisher, RAdm D.B., 537

Fisher, Stoker William, 90

Fishermen's Reserve, 110, 496, 507-509

Flag Officer Newfoundland (FONF), 93, 97, 100, 178, 181, 414, 417, 421, 423, 425

Fleet Air Arm, 24-26, 29, 493, 539, 546, 549, 555, 556

Fleet carrier

Force 1, 462-463, 491

Force 2, 462-464

Fleet V destroyer, 524

floating coffin, nickname of HMS Puncher, 489

Forbes, Adm Sir Charles, RN, 158-160

Force 1 (Cruiser Covering Force), 191, 196-198, 200, 207

Force 2 (Battleship Covering Force), 196-197, 200-201, 207-208

Force 26, 224-225, 302, 306, 313

Force 27, 311-312, 315-316

Force G, 126, 242, 248, 257

Force J, 141, 143, 147, 234, 242, 248

Force U, 245-247

Force W, 159-160

Foreign Service Leave, 125, 141, 144-145

Förster, Oberleutnant H.J., 364, 368

Forward Observation Officer (FOO), 141

Forward Observers Bombardment (FOB), 241, 261, 546

Foxer (pipe noise-maker), 414

Franco-American forces, 319

Fraser, Adm Sir Bruce, RN, 191, 196-198, 200-201, 207-208, 529, 537-539, 554

Free French destroyers, 236

Free French submarine (La Perle), 427

French commandos, 317-318

Frigate program, Canadian, 41

Führer der Schnellboote (FDS), 296

Führer der U-boote, 463

Fusiliers Mont-Royal, 112, 115

Gamma search, 388, 391, 398, 429-430

German air force, see also Luftwaffe. 242

German Army: 352nd Infantry Division, 265

Group B, 264

German surface forces, 77, 191, 283

German torpedo boats, 161

Gilbride, SLt G.E., 412

Glassco, Lt C.S., 400

Gleason, survivor on Benoit float, 336-337

Glennie, RAdm I.G., RN, 153-154, 161

Glider bomb, 101, 104, 162, 165, 195, 222, 302, 357, 521

Gnat (German naval acoustic torpedo). *See also Zaunkönig.* 383-384, 388, 406

Gold Beach, 234, 257

Gold sector, 242, 263

Goodeve, Dr Charles, 350

Goolden, Capt M., 496-497, 505-508

Gould, Surg Lt G.A., 363-364

Gouthro, J.N., survivor on Benoit float, 335, 337

Grant, Capt H.T.W., 160-161, 207, 219, 222, 519, 524

Gray, Lt R.H., VC 549, 556

Great Marianas Turkey Shoot (Battle of the Philippine Sea), 526

Green Beach, 113, 116-117

Gretton, Cdr P., RN, 105

Griffin, Cdr A.G.S., 427

Groos, Cdr H.V.W., 489

Group U2A (Normandy convoy), 246-247

Gruppe Nord (German forces in Norway), 193, 195, 200

Gruppe West (Marinegruppe), 244, 264, 289, 302

Gruson, Sydney, 132

Gulf of St Lawrence convoys, British demand to halt, 98

Gwinner, Cdr C., RN, 285

gyroscopic compass, 46, 176, 180, 232

Hagenuk Wanze radar search receiver, 78, 91

Halifax Shipyards Ltd, 151-152, 308

Hall, Cdr G.S., 382-384

Halliday, LCdr W.C., 428

Hampson, SLt George 122

Harrison, Capt A.N., RN, 309-310

Hart, Capt F.G., 509

Headache receiver, 223-224, 276-278, 306, 310, 316

Hedgehog, 37-38, 40, 179-181, 232, 242, 350-352, 357-358, 398, 406, 420, 423, 447

Heeney, A.D.P., Sec of Privy Council, 513, 532

Hellriegel, Kapitänleutnant H., 416

Henderson, OS L., 138

HF/DF, 193, 201, 203, 382, 416-418, 421, 463-464, 471-473, 484, 487-488

Hibbard, Cdr J.C., 160-161, 192, 198, 305, 309-311, 313, 315-316, 531

Hilbig, Kapitänleutnant H., 434-436

Hill, Cdr R., RN, 162

Hitler, Adolf, 190, 196-197, 208, 250, 349, 445, 472

Hobart, SLt G.M., 330-331

Holms, Cdr W.B.L., 154-155, 157-158, 160-161

Home Fleet, Ch 16 *passim*, 151, 153, 161, 185, 236, 292, 371, 453-454, 458, 461, 465-467, 470, 489-493, 521-522

Hornbostel, Korvettenkapitän K., 435-436, 439-442, 445

Horton, Adm Sir Max, RN, 178, 284, 371-372, 381, 391, 396, 458, 473

Houghton, Capt F.L., 139, 204, 216, 322, 387, 519-520, 546-547

Housing crisis, Halifax-Dartmouth area, 49, 59

Howard-Johnstone, Capt C.D., RN, 370

Howe, Hon C.D., Min of Munitions & Supply, 59

HS 293 glider bomb, 74, 521

Hunt class destroyer, 166, 191, 221-222, 236

Hurd Deep patrol, 245

Hutton, Cmdre R.M.J., RN, 483

Hydrophone effect, 78, 88-89, 193, 291, 383, 394, 405

Hyronimus, Korvettenkapitänän Guido, 351

I class destroyers, 151, 192

IFF (Identification Friend or Foe), 223

Ile de Batz, 271, 276, 279

Ilsley, Hon J.L., Min of Finance, 26

Intermediate destroyers, 204

Italian campaign, 167

Italian fleet, 24

J class destroyer, 245

Japan, Canadian offensives against, 503, 506, 511, 515, 556

Japanese air strikes. *See also* Kamikaze. 555

Japanese offensive (silk balloons), 509

Jeffrey, LCdr D.G., 285-286

Jensen, Lt L.B., 290, 480

Jericho Beach, 497

Jermaine, LCdr D., RN, 401

Jess, LCdr R.E., 555

Johnstone, Capt E., 58

Johnstone, Dr J.H.L., 350, 414, 525

Joint Chiefs of Staff, American, 120, 167

Joint US-Canadian staffs, 508

Jones, Cdr B., RN, 224, 227, 229, 274-277, 305-306

Jones, VAdm G.C., VCNS 53, 160, 176, 178, 184, 398, 410, 514-515, 517-518, 536

Juno Beach, 141, 143, 234, 236, 241-242, 248, 258-259, 263

Kamikaze (Japanese carrier air strikes), 510, 526, 539-540, 542-544, 554-555

Kauffman, RAdm J.L., USN, 50-51, 56

Keate, SLt J.S., 132

Kekewich, Capt P.K., RN, 213

Kerwin, AB M.R., 305

Keyes, Adm of the Fleet Sir Roger, RN, 107-108

Keys, SLt John, 122

Kidd, Lt W.M., 385-386

King, Adm E.J., USN (COMINCH), 120

King, Rt Hon W.L. Mackenzie, 149-151, 166-167, 171-173, 184, 455-457, 511-518, 520, 532, 536

suspicion of RCN plans, 184

Kingsley, Capt H., 110

Kirby, A.G., 116-117

Kirk, RAdm A.G., USN 234

Kirkpatrick, LCdr J.R.H., 214-215, 289, 294-295, 329, 333

Kleinkämpferbände, 321

Kluth, Oberleutnant G., 88

Kneip, Oberleutnant A., 431, 433, 439

Knight, Lt V.M., 475, 480

Knowles, Capt K., USN, 39

Knowlton, Capt J.G., 531

Knox, Frank, Sec of USN, 175

Kohlauf, Korvettenkapitän F., 225-226

Kola Inlet, 191-194, 196, 200-201

Koyl, Lt J.E., 115, 118, 120, 131, 137-139

Krancke, Vizeadmiral T., 244, 289, 302

Kretschmer, Kapitänleutnant Otto 96

Kriegsmarine, 409, 448, 454, 466
  operations and policies of, 104, 162, 195, 197, 201, 243, 264-265, 296, 302, 317, 349-350, 357, 397, 406

Kroyer, Capt M., Royal Artillery, 261

Laidlaw, Capt D.K., 529

Landymore, LCdr W.M., 521-522, 541, 553

Lauterbach-Emden, Kapitänleutnant H., 417

Law, LCdr C.A., 214-217, 272-273, 287-288, 293-298, 320-322, 328, 331-332

Lawson, AB A.A., 523, 547, 553

Lay, Capt H.N., 161, 168, 176, 183, 213, 454-458, 460, 463-464, 490, 493

Layard, Cdr A.F.C., RN, 357, 368-370, 384, 398-399, 406-407, 417, 470-472, 481-483

Landing Craft (LC)
  LBV (Landing Barge, Vehicle), 299
  LCA (Assault), 109, 113, 118-119, 123, 126-128, 130, 132, 137, 231, 241-242, 259-260, 269, 303
  LCF (Flak), 266
  LCG (Guns), 266

LCI(L) (Infantry (Large)), 127, 133-134, 139, 142-148, 172-175, 231, 240-241, 294, 298

LCM (Mechanized), 109

LCP(L) (Personnel (Large)), 111-112, 117

LCS (Support), 130, 141

LCT (Tank), 109, 114, 127, 133, 137, 141, 143, 172-174, 241, 248, 255, 257, 260-261, 274, 293

LSI (Infantry), 111, 115, 140-141, 248, 257, 259, 261, 303, 317-319, 393

Leatham, Adm Sir Ralph, RN, 166, 221-229, 245, 276, 301, 315, 356

Lees, Capt E.V., RN, 131

Leigh light aircraft, 90, 159, 394

Leigh-Mallory, ACM Sir Trafford, RAF, 234

Lend-lease, 94, 169, 174

Leslie, Surg Lt W.L., 331

Lessing, Kapitän zur See H., 433-434, 440

Lewis, SLt D.J., 112

Liberty ship, 363, 389, 439, 442

Littler, LCdr J.C., 522

London Naval Treaty (1937), 520

Low, Lt J.H., 60

Lower Deck, concerns of, 154, 158, 210

Luftwaffe, 454, 470, 472, 483-484, 488-489, 520
  activities of. *See also* German Air Force. 77, 103-104, 155, 189, 195, 242, 264, 275, 284, 290-291, 295, 302, 327

M class minesweeper, 243, 305

M-boote (German minesweepers), 218

MAC ships (merchant aircraft carriers), 79, 426-427

MacArthur, Gen D., US Army, 540

MacDonald, AB W.G.R., 122

Macdonald, Hon Angus L., 25-27, 46, 58, 107, 110, 135, 149, 173, 175-177, 179, 181-183, 397,

410, 455-457, 513, 516-519, 536, 557

Macdonald, LCdr W.M., 147

MacFarlane, Lt H.S., 495-496

Macintyre, Capt D., RN, 463-464, 466-467

Mackenzie, Dr C.J., 413

Maclachlan, LCdr K.S., 108-111, 118-119, 123, 126-127, 144, 170

MacLachlan, Lt G.A., 412

Macmillan, Lt R.C., 448

Mader, Kapitänleutnant E., 88

Madgwick, Lt E.T.G., 158-160, 164, 524

magnetic mine, 97, 334

Mainguy, Capt E.R., 110, 213, 521, 524, 543-547, 553-554

Mair, LS, 122

Makovski, Lt H.E., 522-523, 553

manpower policy, Canadian, 532

manpower problems, British, 170-173, 175, 204, 213, 454-455, 514-515, 524

manpower problems, Canadian, 169-173, 203

Marienfeld, Oberleutnant F., 433-434

Marinegruppenkommando Nord (German forces in Norway), 463

Massey, Vincent, Cdn High Commissioner, London, 512, 518

McDiarmid, LCdr J.B., 60-62

McGrigor, RAdm R.R., RN, 464, 472-474, 478-479, 483-484, 487-488, 493

McNaughton, LGen A.G.L., senior Cdn Army officer in UK, 109-110

McTavish, AB J.R., 122

Mid-Ocean Escort Force (MOEF), 425-426

midget submarine, 466

Millard, LCdr A.T.R., 413-414

Minelaying, 67, 71, 227, 233, 273, 290, 426, 466, 473, 490-491

Minesweepers, Ch 13 *passim*; advantage of wooden over steel. *See also* Algerine, Bangor, M class, *M-boote*. 71

Mitchell, Lt J.E., 178

mobile repair base, 298

Mobilization. *See also* conscription, recruitment, volunteer. 169, 515, 532

Monrad (radar station), 267

Montgomery, Gen Sir Bernard, RAF C-in-C, 234

Moon, RAdm G.P., USN, 247

Moore, Adm Sir Henry, RN, 453-454, 462-465, 467, 473, 480, 490

Moore, VAdm H.R., RN, 192, 207-208

Morale, 110, 131, 145, 230, 505

Morice, Cdr R.A., RN, 158-160, 301

Morrow, SLt W.G., 247, 249

Motor Gun Boat (MGB), 213, 216

Motor Launch (ML), 130, 213-214, 227, 400

Motor Torpedo-boat (MTB), 467, 480, 493

Mountbatten, VAdm Lord Louis, RN, 108, 110, 170-172, 234

Möwe class German torpedo boats, 243

Mulberry Harbours, 246

Mulvey, AB J., 122

Murmansk run, 185, 223

Murray, RAdm L.W., 23, 50, 54-58, 61, 64-65, 72, 74, 96, 176, 179, 386-387, 412, 418, 425-426, 429, 435-436, 441, 447, 451

Nan White beach, 260-263

Narvik class destroyer (German), 198, 204, 466

National Resources Mobilization Act, 532

Naval Air Service, recommendation to form, 26

Naval and Merchant Ship Maintenance Committee on Manpower, 49

naval aviation. *See also* Fleet Air Arm. 454, 457, 465, 493, 511

Naval Board, 26, 47, 58, 109-110, 126, 133, 142, 146, 149, 179, 182, 386, 412, 428, 449, 455, 508, 515, 516, 520, 526, 537

Naval Council, 182

naval policy, 457, 518

Naval Policy Committee for the War Against Japan, 527

Naval Research Establishment, 414

Naval Service Headquarters, 416, 454, 557

Naval Staff, Canadian, 27-28, 53, 105-108, 170-179, 181, 204, 207, 309, 310, 413-414, 452, 456-457, 494, 498, 503, 509, 515, 526-530, 557

Naval staff, German. *See also* *Seekriegsleitung.* 195, 200

Nelles, VAdm Percy W., 25-28, 46, 51, 55, 109, 147, 150, 160, 170-178, 181-184, 203, 213-216, 288, 410, 455-457, 461, 464, 511, 513-519

Nimitz, Adm C., USN (C-in-C Pacific), 498, 538, 540

Nixon, LCdr C.P., 358, 360

Normandy, invasion of. *See also* Operation Neptune. 185, 231, 240, 244, 246, 250-251, 253-254, 287, 317, 322, 371, 423, 425-429, 452-453, 528

Norris, Capt C.F.W., RN, 223, 302, 305-306

North Sea, 221, 320, 329-330

North Shore Regiment New Brunswick, 258

Observant search, 394, 400

Octagon Conference (code name for Québec Conference, Aug 1943), 169, 175, 184, 203, 317, 515, 518, 540

OIC, Canadian Operational Intelligence Centre, 418, 425-426, 430-431, 433, 436, 439-440, 447-448

Oliver, Cmdre G.N., RN, 234

Oliver, LCdr M.F., 376, 382-384

Omaha Beach, 234, 250, 255, 265

Oneschuk, SBA W., 364

Operation
Assault, 315
Baytown, 133, 138
Begonia, 473
Cobra, 298, 357

Cork, 285

Counterblast, 473, 480-481, 493

Croquet, 209

Dracula, 517

Dragoon, 303, 317-318

Dredger, 356

Fabius, 141, 147

Fortitude, 283

Foxchase, 492

FV, 195

Goodwood, 454, 462, 465, 467

Groundsheet, 491

Hoops, 209

Husky, 72, 120, 126-127, 132-133, 136, 234

Iceberg, 537-541, 545, 555

Inmate, 545-546

Kinetic, 302, 357

Kirkwood, 139

Mascot, 453-454

Muscular, 492

Neptune, 120, 147-148, 185, 227, 231-233, 235-236, 245-247, 264, 266-267, 283-284, 286, 289-290, 363, 555

Observant, 440

Overlord, 167, 170, 175, 184, 287, 289, 292, 453, 513

Pitchbowl, 208

Salmon, 99-100

Selenium, 491

Shred, 491

SJ, 387-388

Teardrop, 447-448

Torch, 47, 120-121, 123, 126, 133, 149, 234

Tungsten, 205, 207-208, 453-454, 556

Operational Intelligence, Admiralty, 33, 39, 57, 63-65, 218, 290, 364

Operations Division, 168

Oropesa minesweeping gear, 212, 256

Oswald, Cdr G.H., 350

Otter signal, 62-63, 99, 416-417, 426, 447

Overseas Assault Force (OAF), 126

Owen, OS, 111

Oyster mine, 289-290, 295, 334

Pacific battle fleet (US), 24
Pacific Coast Command, 495-497
Pacific war, outline plan for, 168
Paravane, 93, 212, 238
Patrol Areas
    Musketry, 159-161
    Percussion, 162
    Pike, 267, 290
    Scallops, 267, 272
    Seaslug, 161
    Sword, 241, 266-267, 292
    Tunny North, 267
    Tunny South, 267, 272-273
Patton, Gen George (US), 298, 302, 317, 319
Paxton, Lt F.R., 555
Peacetime requirements (naval), 26
Peers, Cdr A.F., 94
Penhale, Brig M.S., 138
Petersen, Kapitänleutnant K., 430-431
Petrie, R.M., 451
Philippines theatre (Leyte Gulf), 509, 517, 526, 538
Phoenix breakwaters, 293
photography, as record-keeping, 118, 123, 167
photography, reconnaissance, 242, 274
PHP (Post Hostilities Planning Commmittee), 513
Pickard, Lt A.F., 83, 91
Pickford, Lt R.J., 96
Piers, LCdr D.W., 55-56, 96, 205, 257-258, 290, 466, 474, 479, 481, 483
pipe noise-maker (Foxer), 93-94
Plan Position Indicator (PPI), 223, 267, 308, 310-311, 480
Plymouth Command, 154, 159, 162, 203, 217, 222-229, 245, 276, 295, 299, 301-302, 311, 315, 317, 356-358, 368, 370, 425, 473
Polglase, Lt, RNR, 132
Portsmouth Navy Yard, 451
postwar fleet, 166, 184, 408

postwar navy, 166, 170, 455-457, 511
postwar planning, 24
Pound, Adm of the Fleet Sir Dudley, 50-51, 150, 170-172, 174, 178, 186
Prentice, Capt J.D., 51-52, 181, 232, 352, 355, 357-358, 381, 385, 418, 529-531
Pressey, Cdr A.R., 46, 54, 179
Price, Cdr F.A., 124, 132-133, 136, 170, 213
prisoners of war, 67, 95-96, 117, 216, 229, 405, 473, 551, 556
Privy Council, 513
Pugsley, Capt A.L., RN, 272, 522
Pullen, Cdr H.F., 30, 32, 360, 500, 521
Purkhold, Kapitänleutnant H., 88
Puxley, Capt W.L., RN, 96, 386-387

Q attachment (for type 144 asdic), 179, 429
QH-3 radio-navigation equipment, 223
Quadrant Conference. See also Québec Conference, Octagon Conference. 149, 167-168, 170, 184, 454, 456, 511, 516-517, 519, 532
Québec Conference. See Octagon Conference, Quadrant Conference
Queen's Own Cameron Highlanders, 112, 116-117
Quinn, LCdr H.L., 401-402

R-boats. See also Räumboote. 243, 272, 289, 297, 320, 322, 328
radar silence as Kriegsmarine doctrine, 197
Radar
    American type SL, 267
    German FuMO25, FuMO28, 275
    German Seetakt coastal, 198, 221
    RX/C, 232, 401-402, 422, 429
    SG, warning surface, 458
    SK, warning air, 458
    type SU, or 277, 530

type SW2C, 232
type 271, 271Q, 33, 44, 73, 223, 228, 232, 267, 276, 307, 383, 412, 429
type 276 search, 195, 222, 224, 267, 276, 300, 315, 480
type 277, 544
type 281, 544
type 285M, 307
type 285P gunnery, 223, 307
type 291 air warning, 155, 162, 192, 223
type 293 surface warning (centimetric), 205, 307, 310-311, 544
WS (warning surface), 194, 201
Rademacher, Kapitänleutnant E., 393
Radford, Lt J.W., 363
Raeder, Grossadmiral E., 190
Ralston, Col J.L., Min Nat'l Defence, 26, 108
Ramrod air strikes, 555
Ramsay, Admiral Sir Bertram, RN, 120, 231-236, 246, 264-266, 279, 286, 293-294
Ramsay, SLt D., 111
Rankin, LCdr A.H., 88
Ratings, 56, 107
rations, RN, 125, 321
Räumboote, 218, 272
Rayner, LCdr H.S., 188, 192, 198, 207, 300-302, 530
RCAF-RCN cooperation, 24-26, 29, 34, 59, 62, 65, 109, 350, 358
recruitment. See also conscription; volunteer. 110, 170
Red Beach, 130, 137, 255, 258
refit, crisis and problems of. See also Modernization. 46-48, 54-55, 57-59, 72, 136, 143-144, 179-180, 182
refits 458, 483, 489, 510, 519, 521, 523, 525, 529-531, 553
refuelling areas, U-boat, 77-78, 81
Regiment de la Chaudière, 248, 251, 260
Reid, Cmdre H.E., 107, 178, 207

Reith, Oberleutnant H., 448, 451

Rendtel, Kapit leutnant, 88

Rice, Lt(E) A.V., 134-135

River class destroyer, 74, 79, 107, 115, 179-180, 231, 245, 283, 310, 356, 381, 524

River class frigate, 179, 371-372, 378, 444, 525

Robertson, N.A., Under-Sec of State, DEA, 457, 513

Robinson, Cdr, RN, DC Naval Craft, 132

Roosevelt, Pres Franklin D., 120, 166-167, 186, 453, 540

Rowland, Capt J., RN, 178, 181

Royal Air Force

    15 Group, 391

    18 Group, 388

    19 Group, 191, 245, 284

    58 Squadron, 160

    120 Squadron, 32, 82, 84

    821 Squadron (RN), 477, 490-491

    852 Squadron (RN), 458

    854 Squadron (RN), 555

    881 Squadron (RN), 476, 491

    1836 Squadron (RN), 556

    1844 Squadron (RN), 556

Royal Canadian Air Force, *See also* RCAF.

    1 Group, 62

    5 Squadron, 99

    10(BR) Squadron, 82-83

    86 Squadron, 35

    160 Squadron, 447

    404 Squadron, 274

    407 Squadron, 394

    415 Squadron, 243

Royal Canadian Navy, 23

    balanced fleet policy, 409, 454-455, 511

    big ship navy, advantages of, 456, 494

    blue water navy, 452, 518, 557

    Canadian Support Group, 72-73, 81, 95, 103, 105, 232

    landing craft flotillas, formation of, 107, 123-124

    modernization of, as low priority

for RN; RN reluctance in technology transfer, 29, 46

Royal Canadian Navy Flotillas

    1st LC Flotilla, 111, 118-120, 302, 350, 387

    2nd LC Flotilla, 111, 119-120

    3rd LCI(L) Flotilla, 139

    29th MTB Flotilla, 214-217, 231, 239, 244, 265, 272-273, 287-288, 295-298, 304, 320-322, 324, 327-328, 330-332

    31st MSW Flotilla, 210, 233, 237, 247-250, 255, 334, 337

    32nd MSW Flotilla, 210

    55th LCA Flotilla, 120, 123, 126-130, 132, 141

    61st LCA Flotilla, 120, 123, 126-127, 130, 132, 141

    65th MTB Flotilla, 215-216, 218, 231, 244, 289, 294-297, 299, 320-323, 327, 329, 332-333

    80th LCM(3) Flotilla, 120, 123, 126-127, 131-132, 141

    81st LCM(1) Flotilla, 120, 123, 126-127, 132, 141

    88th Flotilla, 120

    92nd Flotilla, 120

    260th Flotilla, 241-242, 248, 257, 262

    262nd Flotilla, 248, 257, 263, 294

    264th Flotilla, 145, 242, 248, 257, 263

    528th Flotilla, 141, 259-260

    529th Flotilla, 141, 260

Royal Hamilton Light Infantry, 112, 115

Royal Marines, 236

Royal Navy Flotillas

    4th MSW Flotilla, 233, 247, 250, 255

    9th MSW Flotilla, 250

    10th Destroyer Flotilla, 225-226, 230, 243, 271, 301, 317, 473

    14th MSW Flotilla, 233, 247-250, 255

    16th MSW Flotilla, 233, 247, 255

    17th MSW Flotilla, 192

    18th MSW Flotilla, 250

    19th MSW Flotilla, 245

Royal Netherlands Navy, 427

Royal Regiment of Canada, 112, 115, 117

Royal Rifles of Canada, 556

Rundle, Lt. G.H.C., 68, 71, 97

Russell, Cmdre A.S., RN, 481

Russell, LCdr P.F.X., 385-386

Russell, Lt B.T.R., 334-335, 337

Russian convoys. *See also* Convoys, PQ-QP, JW-RA.185, 409, 428, 458, 466, 470, 472-473, 483, 487, 490, 492

Ruttan, Lt J.M., 263-264

Sakishima Gunto, 535, 541, 545, 555

Salmon signals (Operation Salmon), 416-418, 421, 423, 447

Saunders, Lt D.M., 394

Sayer, Cdr G.B., 307

Scapa Flow 151, 153, 161, 192, 203, 205, 208, 292

Schmoeckel, Kapit leutnant H., 417-418, 429-431

Schnellbooteflotille, See also E-boats, 243, 265

Schniewind, Vizeadmiral Otto, 195-197

Schnorkel boat (advanced U-boat), 243, 283, 349, 364, 372, 382, 387, 390-395, 401, 405, 428-434, 441, 472, 487, 519

Schrewe, Kapit leutnant F., 97-98, 100

Sclater, Lt W., 279, 283

SCNO(L) (Senior Canadian Naval Officer in London), 132-133, 136, 139, 142, 174, 214, 387, 519, 524

Scramble Red beach, 130-131

Second Support Group (escort), 71, 387

Secret Intelligence Service (UK), 207

Seekriegsleitung, 195

Seventh U.S. Army, 317, 319

ship repair committee, joint

Canadian, US, UK,
Newfoundland, 48
ship repair facilities, problems
with, 59
shipbuilding program, Canadian,
41, 94
ships, shortage of, 31
shipyards, British, 151, 179
shipyards, Canadian. See also
Modernization, refit, ship repair.
179
shipyards, US, 36, 47, 180
signals intelligence, 31, 35, 201,
207, 216, 221, 274, 289, 357
Simmons, Cdr E.T., 391
Simpson, Cdr (E), 144
Simpson, Cmdre G.W.G., RN, 177-
178, 183, 355, 384, 402
Sinclair, LCdr E.N., RN, 300-301
Sitka task group, 318
Skarstedt, LCdr C.W., 60
small ship navy, 490
Smiter class carrier, 458, 489
Smith, Lt R., 132, 262
Smokey Joe (minesweeper), 247
SOE (Senior Officer Escort), 30, 82,
154-155, 190, 192
Somers Isles, HMCS, Bermuda
training base, 232
South Saskatchewan Regiment, 112
Special Operations, 480, 554
Sperrbrecher (German merchant
vessel), 243
Spout, the (marked channels) 235,
267, 274, 351, 364
Spruance. Adm R.A., USN, 541,
544
Squid (antisubmarine mortar), 44,
179, 350, 381, 419
Stacey, LCdr W.R., 369-370
Stadacona, HMCS, Halifax base, 135
Stead, Lt G.W., 310-311
Stephen, Cdr G.H., 381, 418, 420,
426-427
Stephens, RAdm G.L., 179-180,
183, 381
Stephenson, Cmdre G.O.
(VAdm ret), 205
Sthamer, Oberleutnant H.J., 463-464

Stipple signals, 62
Storrs, LCdr A.G.H., 35, 84, 210,
233, 237, 249-250
Strange, LCdr H.E.W., 175-176,
178, 181
Stubbs, LCdr J.H., 195, 228-229
Support groups. *See also* Escort
groups. 31-39, 63, 72-74, 93,
105, 159
Group W10, 416, 418
Group W13, 431
Supreme Commander, Allied
Expeditionary Force (SCAEF). *See
also* Eisenhower. 234
Supreme Headquarters, Allied
Expeditionary Force (SHAEF),
246
surrender, German, 446, 448, 450,
493
surrender, Japanese, 510, 550,
555-556
Sutton, Cdr J., RN, 134
Sweeting, LS 122
Swinley, Cdr R.F., RN, 215
Sword Beach, 234, 292

Tallboy bomb, 465
Target Indicator Room, 310
Task Force J, 236
Task Groups, US
Group 111.2, 556
Group 22.14, 447
Group 22.9, 441
Group 24.14, 445, 447
Group 51.2, 541
TU 27.12, 435-436
TU 27.13, 434
Tate, Danish national captured by
MI5, 389
Taylor, Cmdre C.R.H., 184, 414,
418, 425
Teller mines, 242, 260, 263
Temple, Cdr J., RN, 210-212
Thompson, Cdr C.E., 24-25
Thorneycroft shipbuilders, 214
Timbrell, Lt R.W., 352
Tisdall, Cdr E.P., 524
Todd, LCdr G.F., 514-515

Paper on Canadian naval
development 23, 168-169
Tomlinson, AB J., 122
Tovey, Adm Sir John, RN, 186, 189-
190, 320
Town class destroyer, 30, 32, 43,
68, 94-95, 99
Trenholme, Lt H., 122, 130
Tribal class destroyer, 149-151-154,
163, 166, 168, 191-195, 198,
201-206, 220-227, 229, 275-
276, 279-280, 299-301, 308-
310, 459, 489, 492-493, 511,
517, 524, 529
Tribal class, improved destroyers,
151
Tropicalization, 527, 530-531
Trout line (patrol line), 266
Tubular signals, 62
Tunnel (offensive destroyer sweep),
221-225, 229, 479
Tyrwhitt, Cdr St J.R.J., RN, 224

U-boat, *see* U-boat Type; *also* Index
of Ships
U-boat Assessment Committee,
Admiralty, 358
U-boat Command. *See also
Befehlshaber der U-boote, Führer
der U-boote* 99-100, 103, 159,
283, 351, 355-356, 368, 387,
390, 406, 416, 426, 428, 433,
435
U-boat Groups
Adler, 32
Amsel I & II, 33-35
Drossel, 35
Eisenbart, 192-193
Elbe, 35
Fink, 33-35
Lerche, 32
Leuthen, 81, 83, 88, 95
Meise, 32
Mitte, 387, 389-390
Rasmus, 484
Rhein, 35
Schill, 103
Seewolf, 446-447
Specht, 32-33

Stern, 33
Trutz, 463
U-boat offensive, 24, 67, 91, 168
U-boat offensive, inshore, 467
U-Boat (Submarine) Tracking Room 60-62, 95, 103, 387, 416
U-boat
    Type VII, 77, 349, 372, 411
    Type IX, 349, 382, 411, 428, 430, 434, 446-447
    Type XXI, 349, 397, 407, 446-447
    Type XXIII, 349, 395, 397
    Walter or W-boat, 216, 244
U-Bootewaffe, 31, 382, 395
Ultra intelligence. See also Bletchley Park, decryption, Enigma. 32, 60-61, 65, 74, 98, 196, 207, 218, 221, 224, 227, 244, 275, 321-322, 411, 436, 458, 467, 472, 488, 493
United States Army Air Force (USAAF), 158-159, 5540
United States Third Army, 319
United States Navy
    destroyer hunter-killer groups (see also Task Groups, US), 159, 408
    failure to adopt RN methods, 51
    Tenth Fleet, 51, 59-60, 63, 159
Utah Beach, 234, 247, 250, 255, 265

V class destroyer, 202, 204, 231
VCNS (Vice Chief of Naval Staff), 54
VE-Day, 333, 371, 397-398, 448

Vest, Cdr J.P.W., USN 50-51
Vian, RAdm Sir Philip, RN, 234, 266-267, 287, 537-539, 543, 556
Vickers machine-gun, 214-215
Vickers-Armstrong shipbuilders, 151, 153
Voight, Oberleutnant zur See H., 388
Volunteer, 510, 532, 536-537, 547
Vorpostenbooteflotille (14th), 328
Vosper Co. shipbuilders, 214

Walden, PO F.A., 330-331
Walker, Capt F.J., RN, 71-72, 105, 162
Wallace, SLt C.D., 112, 117
Watson, RAdm B.C., RN, 385-386
Weber, Korvettenkapitän W., 417-418
WEF (Western Escort Force), 43, 74, 100, 179
Wehrmacht (German Army), 208, 244, 320
Welland, Cdr R.P., 489
Wenman, Lt J.G., 142-143
westbound convoys, 81-83, 417, 426
Western Approaches Command, 23, 30-31, 47, 54, 61, 65, 74, 81, 83-84, 93-94, 186, 231, 284, 355, 368, 371, 374, 381-382, 387, 390-392, 398, 401-402, 418
Western Escort Force, W 1 to W 7, 425
Western Ocean Meeting Point (WESTOMP), 425-426, 428

Western Patrol, 497-498
Western Support Force, 31, 72
Western Task Force, 233-234, 247, 255, 258, 265, 290
White Sea, 471
White, LCdr R.P., 521
Whitworth, Adm Sir William, RN, 387
Willson, Cdr W.H., 355, 536, 553
Wilson, Cdr H.M., RN, 65
Winn, Cdr R., RNVR, 78
Winnipeg Grenadiers, 556
Worth, Capt G.A., 60, 413
Wright, LCdr B.S., 554
Wrong, H.H., Asst Under-Sec of State, DEA, 512-513
Wyburd, Cdr D.B., RN, 311-312, 316

Yellow Beach, 112, 117
Young, Lt (E), 144

Zaunkönig (German naval acoustic torpedo, or Gnat), 78, 81, 83, 87-92, 100, 103, 296, 335, 383, 414, 421-422, 430-431, 433, 439, 442, 464
Zerstörerflotille, 8th , 265, 274-276, 278
Zimmerman, Kapitänleutnant E., 420-423, 425-426

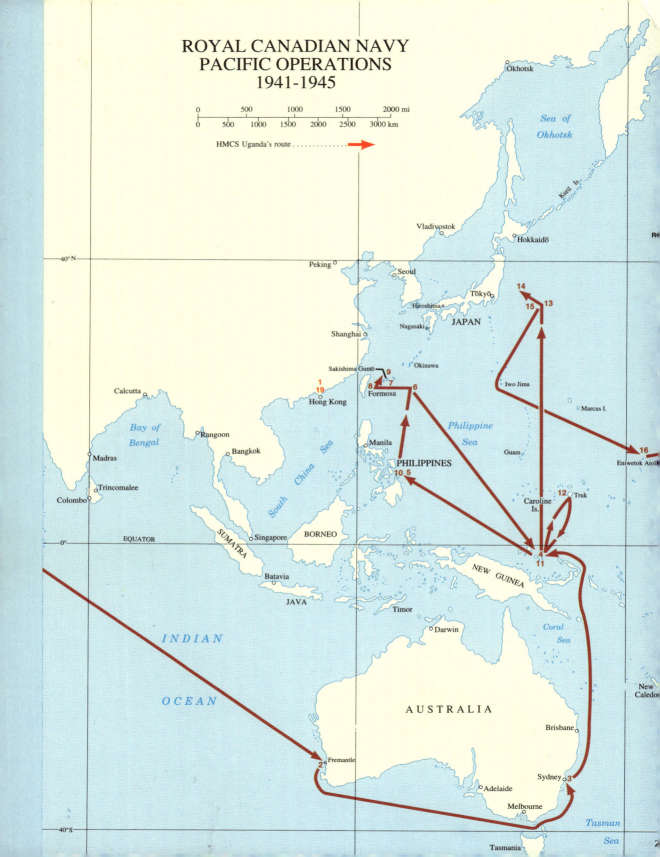

ROYAL CANADIAN NAVY
PACIFIC OPERATIONS
1941-1945

HMCS Uganda's route . . . .